THE OXFORD HANDBOOK OF

# ENGINEERING AND TECHNOLOGY IN THE CLASSICAL WORLD

THE OXFORD HANDBOOK OF

# ENGINEERING AND TECHNOLOGY IN THE CLASSICAL WORLD

*Edited by*

JOHN PETER OLESON

OXFORD
UNIVERSITY PRESS
2008

# OXFORD
### UNIVERSITY PRESS

Oxford University Press, Inc., publishes works that further
Oxford University's objective of excellence
in research, scholarship, and education.

Oxford   New York
Auckland   Cape Town   Dar es Salaam   Hong Kong   Karachi
Kuala Lumpur   Madrid   Melbourne   Mexico City   Nairobi
New Delhi   Shanghai   Taipei   Toronto

With offices in
Argentina   Austria   Brazil   Chile   Czech Republic   France   Greece
Guatemala   Hungary   Italy   Japan   Poland   Portugal   Singapore
South Korea   Switzerland   Thailand   Turkey   Ukraine   Vietnam

Published by Oxford University Press, Inc.
198 Madison Avenue, New York, New York 10016

www.oup.com

First issued as an Oxford University Press paperback, 2010

Oxford is a registered trademark of Oxford University Press

Library of Congress Cataloging-in-Publication Data
Oxford handbook of engineering and technology in the Classical world / edited by John Peter Oleson.
p. cm.
Includes bibliographical references and index.
ISBN 978-0-19-973485-6
1. Technology—Rome—History—Handbooks, manuals, etc.   2. Technology—Greece—History—
Handbooks, manuals, etc.   3. Engineering—Rome—History—Handbooks, manuals, etc.
4. Engineering—Greece—History—Handbooks, manuals, etc.   I. Oleson, John Peter.
T16.O94 2007
609.38—dc22   2007010727

Printed in the United States of America
on acid-free paper

For Martha, Olaf, and Patience

"For where your treasure is, there will your heart be also" (Luke 12:34)

# CONTENTS

...............................

# CONTRIBUTORS

Prof. David Blackman
Classics Department, Oxford
 University
Old Boys' School, George St.
Oxford OX1 2RL, UK

Prof. Willy Clarysse
Katholieke Universiteit Leuven
Afd. Geschiedenis vd Oudheid
Blijde-Inkomststraat 21
B-3000 Leuven, Belgium

Prof. Fredrick A. Cooper
Department of Art History
Heller Hall, 271 19th St. S
University of Minnesota
Minneapolis, MN 55455-0121,
 USA

Dr. Paul T. Craddock
Department of Scientific Research
The British Museum
Great Russell St.
London WC1B 3DG, UK

Dr. Serafina Cuomo
Centre for the Study of Science,
 Technology, and Medicine
Sherfield Building 447 A
Imperial College
London SW7 2AZ, UK

Prof. Robert I. Curtis
Department of Classics,
 Park Hall
University of Georgia
Athens, GA 30602-6203, USA

Dr. Gwyn Davies
Department of History
Florida International University
University Park (DM-397)
Miami, FL 33199, USA

Dr. Philip de Souza
Department of Classics
University College Dublin
Belfield, Dublin 4, Ireland

Dr. Carol van Driel-Murray
Amsterdam Archaeological Centre
Turfdraagsterpad 9
1012 XT Amsterdam, Netherlands

Prof. J. Clayton Fant
Department of Classical Studies
2376 Olin Hall
University of Akron
Akron, OH 44325-1910, USA

Dr. Kevin Greene
School of Historical Studies
The University
Newcastle upon Tyne NE1 7RU, UK

Dr. Klaus Grewe
Landschaftsverband Rheinland,
 Rheinisches Amt Für
 Bodendenkmalpflege
Endenicher Straße 133
D-53115 Bonn, Germany

Prof. Robert Hannah
Department of Classics
Box 56, University of Otago
Dunedin, New Zealand

Dr. Mark Jackson
School of Historical Studies
The University
Newcastle upon Tyne NE1 7RU,
    UK

Prof. Martin Kenneth Jones
Department of Archaeology
University of Cambridge
Downing St.
Cambridge CB2 3DZ, UK

Dr. Geoffrey Kron
Department of Greek and Roman
    Studies
Box 3045, University of Victoria
Victoria, B.C. V8W 3P4,
    Canada

Dr. Lynne Lancaster
Classics Department
Ellis Hall
Ohio University
Athens, OH 45701-2979, USA

Dr. Evi Margaritis
Department of Archaeology
University of Cambridge
Downing St.
Cambridge CB2 3DZ, UK

Prof. Carol C. Mattusch
Department of Art History
George Mason University
4400 University Drive
Fairfax, VA 22030, USA

Prof. Seán McGrail
Bridge Cottage, Chilmark
Salisbury SP3 5AU, UK

Dr. Andrew Meadows
The American Numismatic
    Society
96 Fulton St.
New York, N.Y. 10038, USA

Prof. John Peter Oleson
Department of Greek and Roman
    Studies
Box 3045, University of Victoria
Victoria, B.C. V8W 3P4, Canada

Prof. Lorenzo Quilici
Istituto di archeologia
Universitá di Bologna
Piazza S. Giovanni in Monte, 2
40124 Bologna, Italy

Prof. Georges Raepsaet
Université Libre de Bruxelles
Histoire de l'art et archéologie
Bâtiment NA, bureau NA.3.107
ULB CP175, Avenue F.D. Roosevelt 50,
1050 Bruxelles, Belgium

Prof. Michael Brian Schiffer
Department of Anthropology
University of Arizona
1009 E. South Campus Drive, Building
    30A
Tucson, AZ 85721-0030, USA

Dr. E. Marianne Stern
Willibrorduslaan 87
1216 PA Hilversum, Netherlands

Dr. Karin Tybjerg
Department of History and Philoso-
    phy of Science
University of Cambridge
Free School Lane
Cambridge CB2 3RH, UK

Dr. Roger Ulrich
Department of Classics
Dartmouth College
Hanover, NH 03755-3526, USA

Dr. Katelijn Vandorp
Katholieke Universiteit Leuven
Afd. Geschiedenis vd Oudheid
Blijde-Inkomststraat 21
B-3000 Leuven, Belgium

Prof. Charlotte Wikander
Lunds Universitet, Klassiska
  Institutionen
Sölvegatan, 2
22362 Lund, Sweden

Prof. Örjan Wikander
Lunds Universitet, Klassiska
  Institutionen
Sölvegatan, 2
22362 Lund, Sweden

Prof. John Peter Wild
Archaeology Department
The University of Manchester
Oxford Rd.
Manchester M13 9PL, UK

Prof. Andrew Wilson
Institute of Archaeology
36 Beaumont St.
Oxford OX1 ZPG, UK

# ABBREVIATIONS AND
# SPELLING NORMS

························································

AN attempt has been made throughout the book to address the perennial problem of the transliteration of Greek personal and place names, although no single solution is ideal or even workable. With the invaluable assistance of my Oxford University Press copyeditor, Mary Bellino, I have tried for uniformity among chapters, for clarity and the familiarity of the result to a nonspecialist reader. For the most part we have opted for Latinized forms. The discussion of technical processes also frequently brings up the tricky question of hyphenation, an aspect of modern English that continues to evolve. "Glassblowing," "glass-blowing," and "glass blowing" are all acceptable in English, as are "watermill" and "water-mill," and—perhaps—"water mill." Usage is tending toward, for example, "glassworking" and "metalworking." The policy of the press is to follow *Webster's Collegiate Dictionary*, 11th ed., for spelling and hyphenation, followed by *The Chicago Manual of Style*, but the result is not always completely logical.

In order to make it easier for nonspecialists to follow up on the citations of Greek and Roman literature, a particularly important source for our understanding of ancient technology, I have not abbreviated the names of classical authors (except in tables, for the sake of saving space); the titles of the individual works have, however, been abbreviated according to the system used by the *Oxford Classical Dictionary*, 3rd ed. According to this system, the titles of some single surviving works, such as Herodotus' *Histories*, are not used, while others are cited, such as Vitruvius, *De arch.* None of this, of course, has much value as a logical system, but consistency with standard systems can assist the reader, and the *Oxford Classical Dictionary* is easily available for reference. Where no abbreviations are suggested in the *OCD*, abbreviations of the works of Greek authors have been taken from the Liddell and Scott *Greek-English Lexicon* (9th ed., rev. by H. Stuart Jones; suppl. by E. A. Barber; Oxford: Oxford University Press, 1968) and of Latin authors from the *Oxford Latin Dictionary*. I have not abbreviated periodical titles. I asked contributors to avoid the use of footnotes, with the result that there are occasional clusters of references in the text. But for the most part this approach makes for a smoother presentation. Most of the translations from Greek and Latin texts not otherwise attributed have been taken from J. W. Humphrey, J. P. Oleson, and A. N. Sherwood, *Greek and Roman Technology: A Sourcebook* (New York: Routledge, 1998), with the kind permission of my co-authors.

The following abbreviations appear in the text for *corpora*, encyclopedias, and other commonly cited reference works, for papyri, and for a small number of technical terms.

| | |
|---|---|
| *AE* | *L'Année Épigraphique.* |
| *ATTA* | *Atlante tematico di topografia antica.* Rome: L'Erma di Bretschneider. |
| *CIL* | *Corpus Inscriptionum Latinarum* (1863–). |
| DarSag | C. Daremberg and E. Saglio (eds.) 1877–1919. *Dictionnaire des antiquités grecques et romaines d'après les textes et les monuments.* 9 vols. Paris: Hachette. |
| HS | *sestertius, sestertii* |
| *IG* | *Inscriptiones Graecae* (1873–). |
| *ILLRP* | E. Degrassi (ed.) 1963–1965. *Inscriptiones Latinae Liberae Rei Publicae.* Vol. $1^2$ (1965); vol. 2 (1963). Florence: La Nuova Italia. |
| *OCD* | S. Hornblower and A. Spawforth (eds.) 1996. *Oxford Classical Dictionary.* 3rd ed. Oxford: Oxford University Press. |
| *OLD* | P. G. W. Glare (ed.) 1982. *Oxford Latin Dictionary.* Oxford: Oxford University Press. |
| *P. Cairo Zeno* | C. C. Edgar 1925–1940. *Zenon Papyri: Catalogue général des antiquités égyptiennes du Musée du Caire.* 5 vols. Cairo: Imprimerie de l'Institut Français d'Archéologie Orientale. |
| *P. Lille* | P. Jouguet, P. Collart, and J. Lesquier (eds.) 1928. *Papyrus grecs. Institute papyrologique de l'Université de Lille.* Paris: Leroux. |
| *P. Petrie* | J. P. Mahaffy (ed.) 1893. *The Flinders Petrie Papyri.* Vol. 2. Dublin: Academy House. J. P. Mahaffy and J. G. Smyly 1905. *The Flinders Petrie Papyri.* Vol. 3. Dublin: Academy House. |
| *PG* | J.-P. Migne (ed.) 1857–1887. *Patrologiae Cursus Completus: Series Graeca.* Paris: P. Geuthner. |
| *RE* | A. Pauly, G. Wissowa, and W. Kroll (eds.) 1893–1978. *Real-Encyclopädie der klassischen Altertumswissenschaft.* Stuttgart: A. Druckenmüller. |
| *SEG* | *Supplementum Epigraphicum Graecum* (1923–). |
| *SIG* | W. Dittenberger 1915–24. *Sylloge inscriptionum graecarum.* 3rd ed. 4 vols. Leipzig: Hirzel. |
| *Tab. Vindol* | M. A. Speidel (ed.) 1996. *Die römischen Schreibtafeln von Vindonissa.* Veröffentlichungen der Gesellschaft Pro Vindonissa 12. Brugg: Gesellschaft Pro Vindonissa. |

THE OXFORD HANDBOOK OF

# ENGINEERING AND TECHNOLOGY IN THE CLASSICAL WORLD

# INTRODUCTION

## JOHN PETER OLESON

## THE GREEK AND ROMAN VIEW
## OF TECHNOLOGY

THIS handbook is designed to survey the role of technology in the Greek and Roman
cultures and their respective technological accomplishments, from approximately
the eighth century B.C. through the fifth century A.D. Such an approach, of course,
leaves out the remarkable technological achievements of the Bronze Age and
previous periods, but their inclusion would have required a second volume. In any
case, the Greco-Roman accomplishments in technology reveal a greater unity than
those of the earlier cultures of the Near East or the Mediterranean, reflecting the
shared attitudes and experiences of the Greek and Roman cultures themselves. The
Greeks and Romans appreciated and occasionally marveled at the structures and
artifacts that had survived from the preclassical cultures, and they understood that
human technologies had even older roots. Ancient anthropologists, like their modern counterparts, realized that human activities intentionally altering the environment to ensure survival or simply a more pleasurable lifestyle—what we call
technological activities—were inextricably bound up with the roots of human
biology. In the fifth century B.C., the philosopher Anaxagoras (Fr. 59.A.102, Diels-
Kranz) stated that "the human race is the wisest of all living creatures because it
possesses hands." A century later, Aristotle (De an. 3.8.432a) was more explicit:
"The hand is the tool that makes and uses tools." Even the stolid Roman architect
Vitruvius (De arch. 2.1.2) is almost poetic in his account of the capabilities enjoyed
by humans because of their very form and nature: "They possessed by nature a gift
beyond all other creatures: they walked not stooped downward, but erect, so they

viewed the magnificence of the world and stars. Moreover they could easily handle whatever they wished with their hands and fingers."

Lucretius (5.925–1025) attributes some of this human vigor to the survival of the fittest, while Pliny (like all the Roman authors, paraphrasing Greek philosophical commonplaces) makes a virtue of the helplessness of the infant, naked and without instinctive survival behaviors (*HN* 7, preface 1–4):

> Humans alone of all animals Nature clothes in borrowed resources...only a human on the day of birth does she cast down naked onto the bare ground, immediately to cry and wail.... All the rest of the animals know their own natural abilities, some use their agility, others swift flight, others swim; the human knows nothing unless taught: not to speak, nor to walk, nor to eat, and in short, he knows nothing by natural instinct other than to cry.

In addition to recognizing the age-old biological—perhaps even evolutionary—roots of human technologies, both Greek and Roman intellectuals appreciated that an enormous period of time must have passed as human communities formed, spread out across the known world, and mastered an increasing array of materials and technologies. Their theories of social evolution can easily be compared with nineteenth-century theories of "progress" from Paleolithic to Mesolithic to Neolithic manners of living, a neat sequence that has only recently come into question: Hesiod (*Op.* 107–78), Lucretius (5.925–1025), Vergil (*G.* 1.121–46), Vitruvius (*De arch.* 2.1.1–7), for example (cf. Cole 1967; many of the passages are collected and translated in Humphrey et al. 1998: 1–20). *Chreia* (necessity; [Aristotle], *Mech.* 10–25.847a; Diodorus 1.8.7–9) drove humans to create their *technai* (arts, technologies) and the *mechanai* (devices) to assist with them, while observation of nature provided models (Lucretius 5.1361–69; Seneca, *Ep.* 90). In metaphorical terms, the Greeks counted fire and the various technologies developed by humans as the "gifts" of the mythological figure Prometheus, whose name sounded something like "Forethought" to a Greek-speaker (Hesiod, *Theog.* 565–66, *Op.* 42–53; Aeschylus, *PV* 442–506). Plato (*Prt.* 320c–322d), however, attributes only fire and the arts in general to Prometheus, and the rest to human inventiveness, while Sophocles (*Ant.* 332–72) composed a splendid "hymn" to the independent accomplishments of humans as conscious entities (both passages are quoted in chapter 1).

Given the recent flowering of interest in an environmental basis for the great disparities in technological achievement among human communities in various parts of the world (Diamond 1997), it is striking to note that Greco-Roman culture had already hit upon an adumbration of these principles. A tribe of one-eyed giants, the Cyclopes, lived on a fertile island with a beneficent climate that provided wheat, barley, and grapes (the basis for the ancient Greek diet) spontaneously, without any need for plowing or sowing. As a result, Homer concludes (*Od.* 9.105–31), they had no need for assemblies or laws, shipwrights, or other technologies, each family living apart in caves and herding flocks of sheep in a modified hunting–gathering culture.

Greek poets and playwrights such as Hesiod, Homer, Sophocles, and Aeschylus marveled at the capacity of humans for technological advance and the techniques they had developed for managing the earth and its resources. Greek philosophers such as Plato, Aristotle, and Posidonius debated the role of technology in society, generally reflecting an intellectual posture that thought and dialectic were preferable to applied research and the arts and crafts (e.g., Plato, *Resp.* 7.530e–531a; Plutarch, *Mor.* 8.2.718e). Plato (e.g., *Resp.* 2.368e–374e, *Leg.* 8.846d–847a) proposed—more as a metaphor than as a practical suggestion—that society should segregate its thinkers, soldiers, and producers, and that the simple rhythms of an agricultural community were preferable to the "diseased" complexity of urban living. In his *Politics*, Aristotle considered in somewhat more practical fashion the role of slave labor, craftsmen, architecture, money, and trade in human society, but he reflects the same intellectual posturing as Plato (Aristotle, *Pol.* 8.2.1, 1337b):

> It is clear, therefore, that the young must be taught those of the useful arts that are absolutely necessary, but not all of them. It is obvious that the liberal arts should be kept separate from those that are not liberal, and that they must participate in such of the useful arts as will not make the participant vulgar [*banausos*]. A task or an art or a science must be considered banausic if it makes the body or soul or mind of free men useless for the practice and application of virtue. For this reason we term "banausic" those crafts that make the condition of the body worse, and the workshops where wages are earned, for they leave the mind preoccupied and debased.

The adjective *banausos*, which could also mean "vulgar" or "in bad taste," derived from *baunos*, the workman's forge or furnace. The term comes up frequently in theoretical or philosophical discussion, for example Xenophon's *Oeconomicus* (*On Household Management*, 4.2–3):

> To be sure, the so-called banausic arts are spoken against and quite rightly held in contempt in our states, for they ruin the bodies of those practicing them and those who supervise, forcing them to sit still and pass their time indoors—some even to spend the day at a fire. As their bodies are softened, so too their minds become much more sickly. In addition, the so-called banausic arts leave no leisure time for paying attention to one's friends or state, so that the persons who practice them have the reputation of treating their friends badly and being poor defenders of their homeland. In some states, particularly those with a warlike reputation, it is forbidden for any citizen to practice the banausic arts.

Roman intellectuals occasionally assumed the same attitude; for example, Cicero (*Off.* 1.42): "All craftsmen spend their time in vulgar occupations, for no workshop can have anything liberal about it." (Many of the relevant literary passages are collected in Humphrey et al. 1998: 579–97.) Although sentiments such as these have found expression to some degree in most human societies—even in those, such as nineteenth-century England, that are noted for rapid technological advance—many twentieth-century scholars hit upon this banausic prejudice as an "explanation" for a perceived blockage of technological innovation in the Greco-Roman world. The presence of slave labor was felt to be a related, concomitant factor. The historian Moses Finley was the most prominent exponent of this now discredited interpretation, and there is an extensive literature on both sides of the argument (see esp. Greene 2000, and chapters 2, 3, and 23 in this volume).

As the material in this book will make clear, the classical world was marked by remarkable technological advances in many areas, often fostered by the elite. A technological literature composed of both sophisticated compendia and workshop manuals did exist, although much of it has been lost, and both inscriptions and visual representations show that craftsmen and craftswomen were proud of their work and their products (see chapters 1 and 2). Over half of the male names on tomb inscriptions at Korykos in Rough Cilicia are accompanied by an occupation, and the number of occupations totals 110. At least 85 occupations are named in various inscriptions and graffiti at Pompeii, over 200 on tombstones in Rome, and Artemidorus, in his *Onirocritica*, refers to 264 (Hopkins 1978: 72). These numbers imply self-identification and a certain amount of pride among craftsmen and the service professions. One goal I had in editing this book was to help put an end to the myth of a "technological blockage" in the classical cultures.

## ORGANIZATION OF THE MATERIAL

This book is not intended to be a compendium of all the technological procedures, devices, and machines in use in the classical world. I have been fortunate to be able to enlist 31 expert scholars from 9 countries as contributors, and I asked each of them to look at the accomplishments of the classical cultures in their particular technology or family of technologies, or at an issue in the history of ancient technology, from primarily an analytical rather than a descriptive point of view. The objective was the creation of a critical summation of our present knowledge of the Greek and Roman accomplishments in technology and engineering, and the evolution of the technical capabilities of these cultures over the chronological period. Each chapter was designed to review the issues surrounding that topic and the recent scholarly contributions, and then to define the capacities and accomplishments of the technology in the context of the society that used it, the available "technological shelf," and the resources consumed. Since these studies are not simply descriptive in character, but introduce and synthesize the results of excavation or specialized research, the volume is not as heavily illustrated as might otherwise have been the case. Readers who want more information can easily follow up by using the full bibliographies appended to each chapter.

In working up the outline of the book, I had to make difficult decisions about the selection and organization of the topics, the relative length of the chapters and sections, and the allocation of a restricted number of illustrations. For a variety of reasons I gave particular prominence to mining and metallurgy, Roman engineering and architecture, hydraulic engineering, land and sea transport, and information technologies. The organization of the chapters into eight sections represents a first sorting of an enormously varied and complex array of data and interpretation, and I hope it will be of particular use to those first approaching the subject. The first section deals with the ancient written sources for Greek and Roman technology, the visual representations of technological activities, and the historiography of the subject. These three chapters set the stage for consideration of the individual technologies in separate chapters that assemble the evidence from archaeological remains as well as the literary evidence and visual representations. The archaeological evidence, of course, consists of raw materials, tools and equipment, workshops, by-products, and the primary products. There is a natural hierarchy of technologies, not always directly linked to the hierarchy of human needs, but generally tracking human needs closely. The primary, extractive technologies, those activities that wrest raw materials and foodstuffs or energy directly from the environment—mining, metallurgy, quarrying and stoneworking, agriculture, animal husbandry, hunting, and fishing—appear first, in the second section. Not surprisingly, many of these technologies had already reached a significant stage of development by the Middle or Late Bronze Age.

The third section includes chapters dealing with engineering and complex machines, representing dramatic human intervention to shape the physical world to human needs: Greek and Roman engineering and architecture, hydraulic engineering and water-supply systems, the engineering of tunnels and canals, and heavy machinery. The fourth section concerns secondary processing of the raw materials accounted for in the second: food processing, metalworking, woodworking, the production of textiles, leather, ceramics, and glass, and the application of the chemical substances that assisted many of these secondary technologies.

The remainder of the book deals with technologies that have a more complex relationship with their socioeconomic context and generally involve a variety of motivations and technologies beyond the extraction or processing of raw materials. The fifth section includes chapters dealing with the infrastructure for land and sea transport, and with riding, harnesses, vehicles, ships, and navigation. These technologies represent complex responses to a variety of human needs; ships, for example, were the largest machines known to the classical world. The movement of persons and goods made possible by these technologies forms the basis for the striking success of Greco-Roman urbanism and the Roman imperial system. The sixth section, which I have titled "Technologies of Death," presents warfare and fortification, the most innovative and pervasive human technology from at least the Early Bronze Age through the present day, for reasons that are all too obvious (cf. Plato, *Resp.* 2.373d–e). Ironically, until the invention of nuclear weapons this was the ultimate "labor-saving" technology: groups that excelled at making war reaped the labor and took the property of those they defeated. Despite the importance of the subject and the richness of the literary and archaeological evidence, these two chapters are relatively short, because there is already so much published literature available concerning Greek and Roman methods of warfare and fortification.

"Technologies of the Mind," the seventh section, incorporates chapters presenting technologies that have been crucial to the sophisticated development of human societies, but which deal with abstract ideas rather than making a direct impression on the physical world: recording and reading information in written form, measuring the passage of time, measuring the weight, size, or number of objects or substances, and accounting for the value and numerical relationships among these objects or substances. Another chapter presents the gadgets and scientific instruments of the Greco-Roman world, devices that represent a telling interface between the world of theoretical thought and mechanical application. A related chapter evaluates the attitude in the classical cultures toward inventors, invention, innovation, and technology.

The last chapter in the book stands on its own, but I hope it will help to stimulate a more theoretical approach to the study of technology in the classical world. For most of the twentieth century, classical archaeologists and the historians of Greek and Roman culture approached their subject matter very differently than did "prehistoric archaeologists," "historical archaeologists," "New World archaeologists," or "processual archaeologists," to use only a few of the terms applied to those outside the classical field. The reasons for this divide are numerous and complex, and mostly irrelevant to the available archaeological data; in any case the argument has now moved on to "post-processual" approaches to archaeology and history (Trigger 2006). Beginning in the 1990s, many archaeologists of the classical cultures began to make use of the theoretical tools developed by archaeologists and historians outside their own area. This shift of focus, which has naturally also affected the study of engineering and technology in the classical cultures, has lead to many important new insights. The concomitant widespread abandonment of training in the Greek and Latin languages is very unfortunate, but may reverse itself in the future.

The vocabulary and procedures of the "expanded ethnoarchaeology" presented by Michael Schiffer in chapter 33 may seem foreign to some classical archaeologists and historians of ancient technology, but in fact he simply makes explicit the methods of research that many of us have already used to one degree or another: "If ethnoarchaeology is the study of general relationships between activities and artifacts when strong evidence is available on both, then in an expanded ethnoarchaeology researchers can make use of evidence from the historical record as well." The relevance of this approach to the rich array of evidence for the technologies of the classical cultures is obvious. Schiffer's discussion of differential adoption, invention cascades, and the use of a performance matrix to evaluate the life history of complex technological systems may help to stimulate productive reevaluation of such Greco-Roman technologies as textile manufacture, glassworking, ship design, and even construction.

# THE FUTURE OF PAST TECHNOLOGIES

In addition to progress in the development of explicit theory, what does the future hold for the study of ancient technology, in particular that of the classical cultures? Archaeological excavation has become increasingly expensive and difficult, and the archaeological heritage has been badly diminished by development and illicit excavation. Nevertheless, remarkable discoveries continue to appear, in part because of better techniques of excavation and analysis. Ancient representations of technological activities or machinery continue to turn up, sometimes with very surprising new information, such as the detailed representation of a pair of water-wheel-driven saws on a sarcophagus at Pammukale—long exposed to view, but only recognized in 2006 (Ritti et al. 2007). Ancient workshops and production sites are now more readily recognized for what they are, and the animate and inanimate materials, products, or by-products can be subjected to increasingly sophisticated analytical procedures. Ceramic clay, stone, and metals can be traced to their sources; bones, phytoliths, and microscopic traces of food residue provide detailed information about diet; the analysis of ancient DNA, still in its rudimentary stage, has already provided astonishing information about the interrelationships of human groups and the domestication of plants and animals (Jones 2002). The application of three-dimensional X-ray microfocus computed tomography has extracted important new data from the corroded remains of the Antikythera Mechanism (Freeth et al. 2006). Archaeological survey, on the ground or even from space, continues to reveal important remains relevant to the history of ancient technology without excavation: the sites of previously unrecognized Roman water-mills, for example (Wikander 1985), or Roman fortifications (Kennedy and Bewley 2004). Survey in the deep Mediterranean by means of submersibles or remotely operated vehicles has revealed a rich supply of well-preserved shipwrecks of all periods (McCann and Oleson 2004).

Many technologies that were ubiquitous and important in the classical world have not received commensurate analytical attention: basketry, for example, or applied chemistry, or textile and leather production. In addition, quantitative approaches such as product life-cycle analysis should be applied to many of the ancient manufactured products. DeLaine (1997) has reached remarkable conclusions through calculation of the amount of labor and materials required for the construction of a major imperial building, and the hypothetical process and schedule of completion. This approach should be applied to other regions and periods. Experiments in the replication of ancient artifacts and materials (e.g., Lierke 1999, glass), structures (Oleson et al. 2006), and vehicles or boats (Raepsaet 2002; Morrison et al. 2000) also provide scope for further inquiry.

Finally, there is more work to be done in the analysis of ancient literary sources. Even familiar passages in Pliny the Elder's *Natural History* that concern technical processes or attitudes toward technology require further interpretation or decoding. Lewis (1997, 2001) has made remarkable discoveries by carefully mining the surviving Arabic translations of Greek technical writers whose original works are lost. The papyri from Egypt continue to require transcription and analysis, and new methods of imaging have made possible the transcription of previously illegible papyrus documents. The digitization of nearly all the works of the Greek and Latin authors now allows rapid and comprehensive searching for key words and phrases, and the enormous mass of raw data and synthetic studies on the

Internet make it possible for the historian of ancient technology to peruse a breadth of material unthinkable only five years ago.

Together, all of these resources will allow the continued reconstruction of Greek and Roman technological procedures and accomplishments, as well as ongoing analysis of the relationship between technology and the ancient economy and ancient society. Even our understanding of such an important topic as the role of women in ancient technological processes is still in its infancy (cf. Kampen 1982; Stern 1997; Glazebrook 2005). Clearly, there is a bright future for the study of ancient technology.

# REFERENCES

Cole, T. 1967. *Democritus and the sources of Greek anthropology.* Chapel Hill, NC: Press of Western Reserve University.

DeLaine, J. 1997. *The Baths of Caracalla: A study in the design, construction, and economics of large-scale building projects in Imperial Rome. Journal of Roman Archaeology* Suppl. 25. Portsmouth, RI: JRA.

Diamond, J. 1997. *Guns, germs, and steel: The fates of human societies.* New York: W. W. Norton.

Freeth, T., Y. Bitsakis, X. Moussas, J. H. Seiradakis, A. Tselikas, E. Magkou, M. Zafeir-opoulou, R. Hadland, D. Bate, A. Ramsey, M. Allen, A. Crawley, P. Hockley, T. Malzbender, D. Gelb, W. Ambrisco, and M. G. Edmunds. 2006. "Decoding the ancient Greek astronomical calculator known as the Antikythera Mechanism," *Nature* 444 (30 November 2006): 587–91.

Glazebrook, A. 2005. "Reading women: Book rolls on Attic vases," *Mouseion* 5: 1–46.

Greene, K. 2000. "Technological innovation and economic progress in the ancient world: M. I. Finley reconsidered," *Economic History Review* 53: 29–59.

Hopkins, K. 1978. "Economic growth and towns in classical antiquity," in P. Abrams and E. A. Wrigley (eds.), *Towns in society: Essays in economic history and historical sociology.* Cambridge: Cambridge University Press.

Humphrey, J. W., J. P. Oleson, and A. N. Sherwood 1998. *Greek and Roman technology: A sourcebook.* London: Routledge.

Jones, M. 2002. *The molecule hunt: Archaeology and the search for ancient DNA.* New York: Arcade Publishers.

Kampen, N. B. 1982. "Social status and gender in Roman art: The case of the saleswoman," in N. Broude and M. D. Garrard (eds.), *Feminism and art history.* New York: Harper and Row, 60–77.

Kennedy, D., and R. Bewley 2004. *Ancient Jordan from the air.* London: CBRL.

Lewis, M. J. T. 1997. *Millstone and hammer: The origins of water power.* Hull: University of Hull Press.

Lewis, M. J. T. 2001. *Surveying instruments of Greece and Rome.* Cambridge: Cambridge University Press.

Lierke, R. 1999. *Antike Glastöpferei: Ein vergessenes Kapitel der Glasgeschichte.* Mainz: Philipp von Zabern.

McCann, A. M., and J. P. Oleson 2004. *Deep-water shipwrecks off Skerki Bank: The 1997 survey. Journal of Roman Archaeology* Suppl. 58. Portsmouth, RI: JRA.

Morrison, J. S., J. E. Coates, and N. B. Rankov 2000. *The Athenian trireme: The history and reconstruction of an ancient Greek warship.* 2nd ed. Cambridge: Cambridge University Press.

Oleson, J. P., C. Brandon, L. Bottalico, R. Cucitorre, E. Gotti, and R. L. Hohlfelder 2006. "Reproducing a Roman maritime structure with Vitruvian Pozzolanic concrete," *Journal of Roman Archaeology* 19 (2006): 29–52.

Raepsaet, G. 2002. *Attelages et techniques de transport dans le monde gréco-romain.* Bruxelles: Timperman.

Ritti, T., K. Grewe, and P. Kessner 2007. "*Stridentes trahens per levia Marmora serras:* A relief of a water-powered stone saw mill on a sarcophagus at Hierapolis of Phrygia," forthcoming in *Journal of Roman Archaeology* 20.

Stern, E. M. 1997. "Neikais: A woman glassblower of the first century AD?" in G. Erath et al. (eds.), *Komos: Festschrift T. Lorenz.* Vienna: Phoibos, 129–32.

Trigger, B. G. 2006. *A history of archaeological thought.* 2nd ed. New York: Cambridge University Press.

Wikander, Ö. 1985. "Archaeological evidence for early water-mills—An interim report," *History of Technology* 10: 151–79.

# PART I

## SOURCES

# CHAPTER 1

........................................................................

# ANCIENT WRITTEN SOURCES FOR ENGINEERING AND TECHNOLOGY

........................................................................

## SERAFINA CUOMO

THERE are four types of written evidence for engineering and technology in Greek and Roman antiquity: texts dealing solely or mainly with technical knowledge and/or written by people who identify themselves as technical practitioners; nontechnical texts, that is, any other text that provides us with information about technical knowledge and its practitioners but whose main aim is not the communication of technical knowledge and whose author's primary identification is not as technical practitioner; inscriptions recording technical activities or providing information about the lives of technical practitioners; and papyri with the same content. There are several published collections of translations of ancient sources relevant to engineering and technology. The only relatively comprehensive survey is Humphrey et al. (1998), but some more specialized sourcebooks are available: Cohen and Drabkin (1948), J. B. Campbell (1994), Sage (1996), Irby-Massie and Keyser (2002). The index of 138 ancient authors and inscriptional sources quoted in Humphrey et al. (1998: 601–12) is striking evidence for the pervasive presence of technological information in Greek and Latin literature. Only about eight Greek and ten Latin authors, however, wrote works that survive (at least in part) and can be considered handbooks of a particular technology or group of technologies: Aeneas Tacticus (military), the anonymous author of *De rebus bellicis* (military) and *Periplus Maris Erythraei* (navigation), Apicius (food preparation), Biton (siege engines), Cato (agriculture), Columella (agriculture), Dioscorides (pharmacology), Frontinus (water supply), Hero (mechanics, hydraulics, surveying, siege engines), Hesiod (agriculture), Hyginus (military), Palladius (agriculture, veterinary medicine), Philo of Byzantium (mechanics, hydraulics, siege engines), Varro (agriculture), Vegetius (military), Vitruvius (architecture, machinery), and Xenophon (horsemanship, hunting, agriculture). Many fragments or short works on surveying have been collected in the *Corpus Agrimensorum* (Thulin 1913; B. Campbell 2000). The following authors wrote works that contain significant information relevant to technology but are not themselves handbooks of technology: Archimedes (mathematics and geometry), Aristotle (various sciences), Galen (medicine), Oribasius (medicine), Pappus (mathematics), Pliny the Elder (human civilization and the natural world), Ptolemy (geography), Strabo (geography), and Theophrastus (natural materials). Numerous short works and fragments of works concerning geography and navigation have survived, collected in Müller (1855–1861).

These varied textual sources present different problems for the historian. Technical and nontechnical texts have survived in the form of manuscripts, and have thus been subject to repeated selection and copying, which has often affected not only the form in which they survive, but also their content. The first phenomenon has led to the formation of technical *corpora*, "bodies" or collections of works that deal with related topics but are not necessarily related in their composition. For instance, the *Corpus Hippocraticum* consists of treatises that early on were grouped under the name of Hippocrates, but were in fact produced by different authors, writing between the fifth and second centuries B.C., and not only with very diverse views, but also perhaps different professional identities. While some Hippocratic texts were manifestly produced in a context of medical practice, some could equally well be classified as philosophy or rhetoric—above all, *On Ancient Medicine* and *On Techne* (Lloyd 1987; Schiefsky 2005). Another example is the *Corpus Agrimensorum Romanorum*, comprising a wealth of material on land-surveying, dating from possibly the first century B.C. to at least the fourth century A.D. (B. Campbell 2000; M. J. T. Lewis 2001). Finally, manuscripts concerning subjects of little interest to the literate elite could be left uncopied, and thus ultimately lost. It is no accident that most of the surviving handbooks concern agriculture and military technology.

In the second kind of transformation frequently undergone by manuscripts, the contents of a technical work can be changed in ways that range from scribal errors (especially in copying numbers) to the modification of diagrams or the addition of explanations, corollaries, or lemmas that eventually become incorporated into the main text. These issues are particularly acute in the transmission of mathematical manuscripts (Fowler 1999).

Both technical and nontechnical texts tend to offer a perspective on technical knowledge that, unsurprisingly, depends on the agenda and circumstances of individual writers. In the case of nontechnical authors, the historian ought to ask how well informed they were about the technology they present, and what attitude they had toward technology in general. In the case of technical authors, again the historian ought to wonder for whom the text was written—whether it was meant to be read by colleagues, pupils, or patrons—and what function it was meant to have: manual of instruction, celebration of the subject, or codification of knowledge that up to that point had been transmitted orally.

Inscriptions and papyri avoid some of the pitfalls of manuscript transmission, in that they come to us more or less directly from the past. We must not forget, however, that inscriptions were public documents designed to be displayed, so they again offer a particular, somewhat biased perspective. Papyri, on the other hand, coming as they do in their great majority from Egypt, do not necessarily allow generalization to other parts of the Mediterranean world.

With these words of caution in mind, in what follows I aim to give readers an idea of the range of extant ancient textual sources for engineering and technology. At the same time, I will try to sketch a broad outline of how the production of texts dealing specifically with technical matters changed in the course of antiquity (see Meißner 1999). In order to combine the two aims, I will proceed chronologically, focusing on two or three examples from each period, chosen to represent both different types of textual evidence and the technological practice of the period in question.

# CLASSICAL ATHENS

Our earliest surviving technical texts from Greek and Roman antiquity date to the fifth century B.C., and form part of the *Corpus Hippocraticum* (Nutton 2004: 60–61). We know that treatises on rhetoric, as well as on architecture, sculpture, and possibly many other forms of technical knowledge, were also written at this time, but none have survived (Lanza 1979). The emergence of a written tradition for forms of knowledge that had thus far existed only in an oral context can be linked to various phenomena that characterized the cultural and social life of Athens in the fifth and fourth centuries B.C. The increased importance of literacy is one, along with the connected significance of putting information into a form that was perceived as more stable and longer lasting than simple oral transmission (Thomas 1992). The presence of the sophists, and their claim to be able to teach pretty much anyone pretty much anything for a fee, can also be linked to the production of texts for instruction, particularly manuals of rhetoric. The existence of a widespread agonistic ideal, by which bearers of knowledge were prepared and expected to defend their ideas in public against opponents, may also have contributed to the articulation of some forms of knowledge into a written format, where arguments could be developed in a more systematic and comprehensive fashion. Several of the works in the *Corpus Hippocraticum*, for instance, have a marked polemical tone, and discussions about the status and nature of technical knowledge abound in the works of philosophers like Plato and Aristotle (Cambiano 1991).

A very different kind of text, although one equally meant for public fruition, deserves our attention, however: a marble stele inscribed on four sides with the accounts for the construction of one of the most iconic buildings of classical Athens, the Parthenon, completed around 432 B.C. after many years of work (*IG* I$^3$ 436–51). There are comparable accounts for the Erechtheum (*IG* I$^3$ 474–49; Randall 1953), also on the Acropolis, and for the temple of Asclepius at Epidaurus (*IG* IV.1$^2$ 102; Burford 1969). We know from later sources (Plutarch, *Per.* 13.9, 31.2) that financing such a massive and luxurious enterprise was fairly controversial, and that Pericles, effectively the political leader at the time, was accused, if not of embezzling funds, at least of promoting his own interests and glory, and of favoring his own friends (the sculptor Phidias, for instance) in allocating the work.

A written document such as the accounts of the Parthenon provides us with useful information about the individuals involved with the building site. For instance, we know that the works were supervised, in terms of administration, by a board of five trustworthy citizens, called *epistatai*, appointed by the assembly. The workforce consisted of people with various levels of expertise, from the architects responsible for the design (apart from Phidias, later tradition has transmitted the names of Callicrates and Ictinus) and general technical supervision, to the headmen of various teams, to the workers who specialized in tasks such as fluting the columns or quarrying the marble, to nonspecialized laborers in charge of transporting or clearing materials. The workforce was diverse also in its geographical origin: even a large city like Athens would not have been able to provide enough specialized technicians for the jobs required, and when workers are named, as in the accounts of the Erechtheum, we find several metics (resident foreigners) among them (Randall 1953; Burford 1963; Korres 1995).

Although the inscriptions do not provide us with details about how the Parthenon was built, we can reconstruct the various phases of construction by following what is recorded each year (cf. Burford 1963: 29–32). First the foundations of the temple were laid, and payments were made not only to quarrymen and builders, but also to people who carted the marble from the Mount Pentelicon to Athens, and specifically to the highest point in the city, the Acropolis. From then on, we find that for several years wood was among the materials being bought, for use in scaffolding and roof beams. One year's account specifies that work was being conducted on the columns, and later precious materials (ivory, silver, and gold) are mentioned, for decoration—including perhaps the massive cult statue of the goddess Athena. As time passed, surplus material and even equipment were sold off, perhaps to working teams producing monuments at other sites. The inscription also provided information about the costs, but great chunks of the text where the figures would have been are missing.

The stele was found in the Athenian marketplace, the agora, and was evidently meant to provide public information about exactly how the money had been spent; this tells us that the production of monuments at the time was viewed as a matter of collective concern, and that the community was expected to be directly or indirectly involved in it.

Further evidence on the status of technology in classical Athens is given by some nontechnical texts, specifically plays—as with the building inscriptions, texts meant to be presented to the public. A chorus from Sophocles' *Antigone* (332–67; ca. 440 B.C.) and a long passage from Aeschylus' *Prometheus Bound* (463–522; ca. 430 B.C.) are particularly relevant here. Sophocles presents an encomium of humans as technological beings:

> There are many wonders, but nothing more to be wondered at than humankind. This creature crosses over the grey sea in the face of the wintry south wind and ploughs his way through the roaring billows. And they vex the indestructible and inexhaustible Earth, the eldest of the gods, with their ploughs and the race of horses going up and down, turning over the earth year after year. And after snaring the race of nimble birds and the host of fierce wild beasts and the maritime creatures of the sea in the net's meshy folds, this skillful being carries them off. By his devices he masters the rustic wild animals and makes obedient to the bit the shaggy-maned, mountain-ranging horse and the unwearying mountain bull, yoking them about the neck. He has learned speech and lofty thought and public speaking, and to flee the arrows of the storm and the barbs of inhospitable frost in the open air. Always inventive, he never meets the future unprepared. Only from death he has not created an escape, but he has developed cures for unrelenting diseases; skillful beyond all hope are the devices of his art [*techne*]. And sometimes he glides toward evil, at other times toward good.

The theme of the moral ambiguity of technical knowledge is embodied by the protagonist of Aeschylus' play, the rebellious demigod Prometheus, who steals fire from Zeus to give it to humankind and is subsequently punished by being tied to a rock, his liver perpetually eaten by an eagle. In a famous monologue, the Titan remembers how his gift turned humans from a beastly existence to a life characterized by shelter, travel, metalworking, medicine, writing, numbers—in short, all the forms of technical knowledge, which were, he said, "from him":

> Their every act was without knowledge until I came. I showed them the risings and settings of the stars, hard to interpret until now. I invented for them also numbering, the supreme skill, and how to set words in writing to remember all things, the inventive mother of the Muses. I was the first to harness beasts under the yoke with a trace or saddle as a slave, to take the man's place under the heaviest burdens; I put the horse to the chariot, made him obey the rein, and be an ornament to wealth and greatness. No one before me discovered the sailor's wagon, the flax-winged craft that roam the seas. Such tools and skills I discovered for humans. . . . All arts [*technai*] possessed by mortals come from Prometheus.

Alongside a celebration of human achievements and progress in the face of an often hostile nature, these two plays recognize the potential of technology for subversion of the normal order through an empowering of the weak. It is not a coincidence that both Prometheus and Antigone are defiant rebels. That these plays were performed in front of a popular audience also tells us that technical knowledge in its various manifestations was something that the average Athenian citizen would have been familiar with, exposed to when not directly practicing it, and ready to reflect on from a historical and moral point of view.

# Hellenistic Kingdoms

The main factor that differentiates technical texts produced in the fifth and fourth centuries B.C. in classical Athens from those written from around the third century B.C. onward, and around the Hellenistic metropoleis—Alexandria, Pergamon, Rhodes—is above all the presence of patrons. The agonistic context of some of the medical treatises in the *Corpus Hippocraticum*, where the author could address a general public, real or ideal, as if he were giving a speech against an opponent, does not disappear, but it somehow loses prominence in favor of a more or less direct relationship between the technician and a powerful addressee, often a political leader. Hellenistic kings were prepared to invest heavily in culture by founding libraries, financing institutions such as the Alexandrian Museum, and supporting individual poets, philosophers, and various other "intellectuals" who often lived in relatively close contact with them at what have been called Hellenistic courts. At the same time, the practical necessities of ruling states that were much larger than the classical Greek polis called for experts in land-surveying, water-supply, architecture (including fortifications), navigation, and military engine-building.

Sometimes a strong administrative structure preexisted the formation of the Hellenistic kingdoms, and traditions, including technical traditions, merged. A good example of the intermingling of tasks, knowledge, and people in Ptolemaic Egypt is provided by a group of papyri about the *architekton* Cleon, who lived in Crocodilopolis/Arsinoe in the Fayum in the third century B.C. (*P. Petrie* II.4.1–13; N. Lewis 1986: chap. 2). As is the case for a surprising number of papyri, a good deal of Cleon's correspondence consists of complaints. For instance, a group of documents dating from 255 to 253 B.C. informed him of the problems some Egyptian men, working in a quarry, were having with one of the supervisors, Apollonius. The men, who were free and presumably on a corvée, complained through their headmen that they had not been properly and sufficiently equipped with iron tools, including wedges, and that they lacked wheat for sustenance and slaves to do some of the clearing work (*P. Petrie* II.4.1–5, 13.1; *P. Petrie* II.4.6–9 may relate to the same quarrymen). Throughout the documents, Cleon is presented as responsible for procuring materials and specialized personnel for works relating to water supply. One letter mentions a canal or conduit that was dug the year before but had now silted up; another discusses sluice-gates, bridges, and even prison walls (*P. Petrie* II.4.10–11, 13.2–5, 13.8–16, 13.18a–b; on water supply works see also *P. Lille* 1 (259–58 B.C.), with a diagram). Kleon acted through a number of delegates, at various levels of authority and presumably of expertise: we come across Greek names such as Diotimus and Clearchus, but also Egyptian ones such as Petesnites and Armas (*P. Petrie* II.11.1–2; no date is given). We also hear about Cleon's two sons, Polycrates and Philonides (Philonides at *P. Petrie* II.13.19, II.42.c, III.42.H.7; perhaps both brothers at II.16; Cleon's wife Metrodora at III.42.H.8). Polycrates wrote to him in what the papyri editor calls "a beautifully clear and correct hand," asking to be introduced to the king with a view to employment, and telling him that he was going to train as *geometres* (here probably land-surveyor). We thus learn that Cleon knew the king personally, and that technical knowledge may have run in families, although father and son were not necessarily in a master-and-apprentice relationship.

It is interesting that Cleon's main duties as they appear from these papyri seem to be administration and supervision, rather than design or even personal care of the works. Indeed, his successor, Theodorus, is called "architect" and *oikonomos* (steward/manager), and his tasks appear to have been very much the same (*P. Petrie* II.9.1–5, 15.1–3 [341–39 B.C.]; also II.42.a, III.43.2–3). No specific reference is made to Cleon's or Theodorus' specialized knowledge, but that does not mean that it did not play a crucial role in forging their identity, or that it was not determinant in procuring them jobs. Rather, we need to adjust our view of what ancient engineers were expected to do, and include administrative and management capacities alongside technical skills.

Another technician at the service of the state common in the Hellenistic period is the military expert. Kings and urban communities of the period invested heavily in city walls, weapons, ships, and the hiring of professional mercenaries, and it is not surprising that the majority of technical treatises extant from this period are war-related. We have texts dealing with what to do in the case of a siege (e.g., Aeneas Tacticus), texts teaching how to be a good general (e.g., Asclepiodotus, *Tactica*), and texts explaining how to build fortifications or machines suitable for offense and defense. A good example of the latter is the *Construction of Catapults* (*Belopoeica*) by Philo of Byzantium (ca. 240 B.C.; Marsden 1971; Garlan 1974).

Philo was a practicing technician and addressed both the *Belopoeica* and another text on fortifications to an otherwise unknown Ariston, who appears to be, rather than a fellow technician or a total layman, a member of the educated elite, whose interest in military-related technology could at the time almost be taken as a given. Biton (perhaps 241–197 B.C.) addressed his treatise on siege engines to one of the kings of Pergamon (Marsden 1971: 6, 78 n. 1; M. J. T. Lewis 1999).

Philo's treatise on catapults was part of a larger *Mechanice syntaxis* (*Synthesis of Mechanics*), and it combines engineering and geometry with epistemology and history of science. Philo begins by explaining how confusion still reigns among technicians, who often produce very different results even starting from the same principles and using the same materials. His aim is to provide a reliable method for building different kinds of catapults, and for modifying the dimension of a catapult according to the size of the projectile. This latter procedure was based on the facts that all the components of a catapult were in proportion to each other, that one of these pieces (specifically, the cylinder holding the torsion spring) was taken as a module or standard, and finally that a simple numerical relation could be established between projectile and module. In other words, in order to modify the dimension of a catapult an ancient engineer had to know how to modify the dimension of the cylinder holding the torsion spring, and he then had to increase or decrease all the other pieces accordingly. Philo and, later, Vitruvius refer to complete tables of specifications for catapults of various sizes. Philo also provides suggestions on the materials to use, and hints at the existence of accompanying diagrams.

He is quite explicit on the criteria a good catapult should satisfy: it should shoot far and be powerful, but also present an awesome appearance to the enemy, and be not too costly. Philo prizes novelty of design, and he presents himself as having improved on some of his predecessors, including Ctesibius. On the value of discovery, he says (*Belopoeica* 58.26–59.1; trans. adapted from Marsden 1971: 121):

> One must praise those who at the beginning discovered the construction of these instruments, for they were the originators of the thing and of its shape; they discovered something superior to all other artillery, I mean like the bow, javelin, and sling, in length of the shot and weight of the projectiles. To devise something at the beginning and to realize the device is of a superior nature; to bring to correction or adaptation something that exists seems rather easy. But, although very many years have passed since the putting-together [of the machine] happened to be discovered and there have been, as usual, both many machine- and artillery-makers, no one has dared to depart from the established method. We were the first to do so.

Most importantly for the historian, Philo also provides precious information on the past and the present of his discipline: he reports how former technicians experimented with their machines and through trial and error came to the realization that one piece of the catapult could be used as a module, so that all the other components could be expressed in proportion to it. Moreover, the modification of the cylinder holding the torsion spring could be carried out according to mathematical principles, because it basically amounted to a geometrical problem known as duplication of the cube. In the *Belopoeica*, Philo provides a solution to this problem, complete with proof, thus giving the stamp of ultimate mathematical stability to a result that had been arrived at empirically.

The image of technology that emerges from Philo's treatise is that of a discipline in expansion: growing through time from trial and error to a kind of mathematical certainty, accumulating knowledge, again through time, while learning from previous mistakes, and spreading geographically over the Mediterranean. Philo informs us about the existence of what we can call a network of catapult builders across Hellenistic kingdoms and cities, and he comments on the largesse and *philotechnia* (love of technical knowledge) of the Ptolemaic kings, thanks to whom particular progress had been made by the engineers in Alexandria.

On the whole, Philo may be considered representative of the Hellenistic breed of technicians: emboldened by their newly found importance in military operations, they address a public beyond their immediate circle of peers or fellow citizens. Their audience can be said to include figures of political relevance, as well as colleagues or apprentices; their perspective has widened in space (together with their travels) and in time. Philo is able to look back in order to trace the journey of his form of knowledge from a past of uncertainty to a present of mathematical reliability, and to point to a future of further innovation. He comes across as aware of the importance of what he does, and aware that he is part of a group. His work has to be understood against this background: Philo's *Belopoeica* does not simply provide information on how to build catapults. Indeed, the treatise implies much tacit knowledge, so that its actual usefulness as a manual of instruction, especially to a complete beginner, is doubtful. Rather, in an environment where, with the rise of Hellenistic scholarship and the foundation of big libraries, written sources were being collected and canonized, the text provides respectability, both for the discipline of mechanics in general and catapult-building in particular, to which it gives a history and epistemological and mathematical ratification, and also for its author, to whom it offers a platform for his claims and his designs.

It is then all the more intriguing that most of the evidence for the technological feats of possibly the most famous Hellenistic engineer of all, Archimedes of Syracuse, should be provided by nontechnical sources. Famously, and despite the survival of many of his other works, no treatise by Archimedes is extant about catapults, burning-mirrors, giant ships, or astronomical globes, all of which he is reported to have built. Plutarch later (notoriously) explained that Archimedes' all-consuming passion was mathematics, and that he engaged in machine-building only at the behest of his king, Hiero of Syracuse, and later on in order to help his city when it was besieged by the Romans. Polybius (8.3–7) and Livy (24.34), as well as later historians (Plutarch, *Marc.* 14.9–17.3), give accounts of how versatile and impressive Archimedes' catapults were, and how they managed to strike terror into the hearts of the numerically superior Roman army. When Syracuse fell, it was thanks to treason, not technical superiority (Dijksterhuis 1987).

Perhaps Plutarch's description of Archimedes is historically accurate, and he did not deem mechanical matters worthy of written treatment—a situation that would make him even more unusual among Hellenistic technical experts than he already is, thanks to his outstandingly sophisticated mathematical achievements. The circumstances of his life and even of his death, however, also mark him as typical of engineers contemporary with him: working in the service of a patron (he addressed a treatise on astronomy and arithmetic to king Gelon of Syracuse), providing for the safety and welfare of his community, and eventually being assimilated by the new world power, in the shape of the Roman troops who killed him when Syracuse was taken in 212 B.C.

# THE ROMAN EMPIRE

The rise of the Roman Empire coincides with the advent of an even bolder breed of technician, well exemplified by Vitruvius Pollio and his *De architectura*. In ten eclectic books that deal with styles of architecture, materials, and planning, but range as well from what we would call ethnography to the construction of catapults, to that of sundials, to methods for finding water, Vitruvius not only provided information useful to the specialist, but also, and especially, strengthened the claim that technical experts like himself played a fundamental part in the empire. In the opening chapter, Vitruvius famously claimed that architects were well-rounded, well-educated individuals: he said that they ought to be competent in, among other things, philosophy, law, astronomy, music, and medicine (*De arch.* 1.1–10). His treatise is scattered with anecdotes about the ethical virtues of technicians, and even contains a potted history of humankind from its brutish origins to the advent of civilization (*De arch.* 2.1.1–7). This passage, marked by stepping-stones such as the accidental discovery of fire, is essentially a tribute to technology, which, far from being contrary to nature, imitates the cosmic order and is a part of it (Romano 1987).

Vitruvius dedicated *De architectura* to the newly installed Octavian Augustus (1, preface), the man who allegedly turned Rome from a city of bricks to one of marble, and the treatise can indeed be seen as a celebration of his empire. Not coincidentally, Vitruvius explicitly drew on a wealth of earlier Greek architectural manuals, none of which survives. The Roman *De architectura* erased previous efforts in more senses than one. By comparing throughout, directly or indirectly, Roman achievements with those of the Greeks or the barbarians, Vitruvius established the former as dominant, not only in deeds, but in accumulated knowledge.

A slightly different perspective comes from the works of Hero of Alexandria. On the one hand, he writes in the mold of Philo of Byzantium and inserts himself explicitly in the Greek tradition of geometry and mechanics, to the point where some historians would tend to classify him as Hellenistic, although he lived around the mid-first century A.D. On the other hand, his treatises contain scattered clues to the fact that he lived in a world now under Roman rule. Hero's devices, with the possible exception of his catapults, have often been described as gadgets or toys, but a more correct interpretation of his contribution to technology would emphasize their capacity to produce wonder, and to engage the observers in the philosophically validated act of curiosity. For instance, he provides several designs for *automata*, that is, things that move apparently by themselves, and in particular for a device that opens the gates of a temple when someone lights a fire on an altar (*Pneum.* 1.38–39). The point of the device for Hero is that it enables him better to reflect on the properties of matter, in particular of hot air, down to the presumed characteristics of particles and void, and that it also enables him to produce a wondrous effect, which will cause amazement in the audience and by reflection empower the technician, who alone knows what is going on behind the scenes (Tybjerg 2003). This particular configuration of knowledge and power, achieved through a manipulation of reality that involved building machines, returns in the introduction to Hero's own *Belopoeica* (71–73.11; trans. adapted from Marsden 1971: 19):

> The largest and most essential part of philosophical study is the one about tranquility [*ataraxia*], about which many researches have been made and still are being made by those who pursue learning; and I think research about tranquility will never reach an end through reasoning [*logoi*]. But mechanics has surpassed teaching through reasoning on this score and taught all human beings

how to live a tranquil life by means of one of its branches, and the smallest—I mean, of course, the one concerning the so-called construction of artillery. By means of it, when in a state of peace, they will never be troubled by reason of resurgences of adversaries and enemies, nor, when war is upon them, will they ever be troubled by reason of the philosophy which it provides through its engines.

One could hardly be more explicit: pitting himself against the most prestigious form of knowledge of all, philosophy, Hero asserts the right of his own discipline and by extension of technicians as a whole to claim a crucial role in society.

As with Philo in the third century B.C., technical treatises in the Roman imperial period were not just about conveying information or instructing the novice. In fact, if we assume that the sole aim of ancient technical treatises was to enable the reader to build a house, supervise the water supply, or divide up a piece of land, we would have to come to the conclusion that many of them simply do not work. This has led some historians to say that some ancient technical writers did not know what they were doing or produced pipe dreams, detached from reality. But the incapacity of some technical treatises to enable the reader to produce a technical artifact just on the basis of the text should not be a surprise to anyone who has ever grappled with the instructions that accompany unassembled furniture kits. Technical training in antiquity relied primarily on oral teaching and on direct experience through apprenticeship. Even the simplest technical treatises often imply tacit knowledge—about how to fit pieces together, or how to choose materials, or how to turn a two-dimensional geometrical description into a working structure—that needs to be supplied independently of the text. Some scholars (e.g., Oleson 2004, 2005) propose the existence of a class of subliterary technical manuals, how-to-do-it booklets concerning metalworking, water-lifting, or agriculture that were lost as Roman imperial culture withered away. Unlike the surviving technical literature, such booklets most likely would have lacked both literary and philosophical pretensions.

We thus have to come to the conclusion that technical texts have to be seen not only as providing information, but also as constructing a certain way of knowledge, and a certain identity for their authors. In the Roman period even more than at earlier times, technical knowledge was presented as useful to the commonwealth, epistemologically solid thanks to its links with mathematics and/or philosophy, and essential to the establishment or maintenance of the political order. The technician was correspondingly represented not only as competent and able to carry out specialized tasks, but also as honest and virtuous, or even as an upright Roman citizen contributing to the welfare of the empire.

Vitruvius is but one example of this posture; another is Sextus Julius Frontinus, author of *De aquaeductu urbis Romae* (*On the Aqueducts of the City of Rome*; see now Rodgers 2004). Whereas Vitruvius seems to have been, generally speaking, an upwardly mobile member of the lower middle classes who had come up through the army, Frontinus, who also had a strong military background, was a senator and a sometime consul. He was charged in A.D. 97 with the supervision of the water supply of the empire's capital city, and *De aquaeductu* stems from that experience. It can be seen as an administrative pamphlet, written by Frontinus for his successor and possibly as a report to the Senate. It provides invaluable information on the aqueducts of Rome, their foundation and maintenance; it also provides figures on their capacity. Above all, Frontinus creates a certain image of the technically-minded high-level civil servant, who equates expertise with efficiency, good rule, and the welfare of the people of the *urbs* (DeLaine 1996; Rodgers 2004: 12–14).

A similar tone is found in many of the writers in the collection now known as the *Corpus Agrimensorum Romanorum*, which includes texts attributed to Frontinus (B. Campbell 2000; M. J. T. Lewis 2001). One author, Balbus, writes for his addressee, Celsus, a treatise titled *Description and Analysis of All Figures*, an explanation of systems of surveying and measuring. Not only does Balbus mention his apprenticeship (*tirocinium*) and his and Celsus' shared *professio*, but also the fact that he has been on a campaign to Dacia (ca. A.D. 101–6) with the emperor, here probably Trajan (B. Campbell 2000: 204). Again, we find references to training, to self-awareness as a group, and to vicinity to the top echelons of political power. The *Description* is basically a short treatise on elementary geometry, presenting roughly the same material as the beginning of the first book of Euclid's *Elements*, but in a narrative form rather than an axiomatico-deductive one. Given that Celsus, implicitly presented as more senior than Balbus, would have already known the contents of the treatise, why did Balbus write it at all? The answer is clear from the introduction: he was keen to have his name circulate among people that Celsus could indirectly introduce him to, and he wanted to show that he had some theoretical knowledge to support his technical skills (trans. B. Campbell 2000: 204–7):

> It seemed disgraceful to me that if asked how many kinds of angle there were, I should reply "many." Therefore in respect of those points relevant to our profession, as far as I could in my work, I have set out the types, characteristics, conditions, measurements, and numbers. If you, a man of considerable influence, think that this work will benefit those learning [the profession], that will be sufficient recognition of my modest talent.

It is only appropriate that a conquered province, Dacia, should be the implicit background to the exchange between Balbus and Celsus. The presence of occupied territories, non-Roman units of measurements, and pre-Roman land management traditions is very strong in the *Corpus Agrimensorum*. Surveyors inevitably had to negotiate between local realities and the demands of imperial administration. In their texts, imperial control is often equated with geometrical order, to be imposed, if only in the form of a map, on an often recalcitrant nature, full of mountains, ridges, and other obstacles to overcome.

That the Roman Empire was identified with its technical achievements is confirmed by some nontechnical sources. For instance, *Agricola*, the biography Tacitus wrote of his father-in-law around A.D. 98, describes the Roman colonization of Britain thus (21; trans. from Lewis and Reinhold 1990: 279):

> In order that people who were scattered, uncivilized, and hence prone to war might be accustomed to peace and quiet through comforts, Agricola gave personal encouragement and public assistance to the building of temples, forums and

houses. . . . He likewise provided a liberal education for the sons of the chiefs, and . . . he so encouraged them that although they had lately disdained the Roman language they now eagerly aspired to rhetoric. Hence too, our style of dress came to be esteemed, and the toga became fashionable. Step by step they turned aside to alluring vices, porticoes, baths, elegant banquets. This in their experience they called "culture," whereas it was but an aspect of their enslavement.

As well as the imposition of tribute and the institution of assize circuits and law courts, the presence of Roman power was made tangible by baths and forums, which were, ambiguously, both a means to an easier and more peaceful life and an instrument of servitude, a way through which the Britons were won over and ultimately Romanized. Similar sentiments are echoed by a passage from the *Babylonian Talmud* (*Shabbath* 33b; Lewis and Reinhold 1990: 333–34):

> Rabbi Judah began and said: "How excellent are the deeds of this nation [Rome]. They have instituted market places, they have instituted bridges, they have instituted baths." . . . Rabbi Simeon ben Yohai answered and said: "All that they have instituted they have instituted only for their own needs. They have instituted market places to place harlots in them; baths, for their own pleasure; bridges, to collect tolls."

The Roman reaction to the dissenting rabbis is appropriate to their degree of technological appreciation: Judah is praised by the authorities, whereas Simeon is condemned to death. Evidently, criticism of the Roman infrastructures is perceived as criticism of the empire. The identification of Rome with its forums, baths, and bridges appears complete, and puts a dent in interpretations that see technological achievements, ancient or modern, as "objective" or "neutral." Roman technological achievements were arguably meant, and arguably perceived, as politically charged.

## Inscriptions

Apart from the architectural monuments that represent the most visible legacy of ancient Roman technology, the empire left its mark in the form of inscriptions. We have long texts, often celebrating conquests or reminding the public of a rich individual's benefactions, and we have shorter texts, often on milestones, boundary stones, or tombstones. As was the case for classical Athens, epigraphy provides some of the most interesting written sources for the history of Roman technology, not only for the content of some inscriptions, but also for their location (when that can still be reconstructed).

For instance, a set of inscriptions recording the settlement of boundary disputes between Delphi and neighboring communities, in which a surveyor was involved, was displayed on the walls of the temple of Apollo in the sanctuary. The documents record how a Roman public officer had resolved disputes between Greek communities, and are thus appropriately bilingual, in Greek and Latin.

Their location juxtaposes them, and their indirect commemoration of superior Roman expertise, to earlier documents from the Greek past (Rousset 2002). Or, again, an inscription now found at Béjaïa (ancient Saldae) in Algeria records how the military engineer Nonius Datus, who was attacked by brigands on his way there, was sent to help the local authorities dig a water supply tunnel through a hill (*CIL* 8.2728; see chapter 12). The workforce had initially miscalculated the excavation, to the point where the two teams digging at opposite ends of the hill and hoping to meet in the middle had in fact been proceeding in divergent directions. Nonius Datus recalls how he provided not only technical expertise, but also supervising skills, in that he encouraged competition between different teams, providing them with an incentive to complete the work accurately and quickly. The inscription related Nonius' celebration at the hands of the local governor, and was accompanied by the personifications of Patience, Excellence (*Virtus*), and Hope, presumably the virtues presiding over Nonius' achievement. The inscription is also itself a pointed celebration of the triumph of Roman technical ingenuity over the North African wilderness, embodied not only by the brigands and by the hostile, possibly water-poor territory, but also by the disorganized workforce in need of guidance.

Most inscriptions from the Roman Empire, however, come from a funerary context. The particular interest of epitaphs is that they provide valuable information about how technicians chose to be remembered after their death. Many tombs are engraved with scenes of craftsmen at work, or with images of technical tools; in others, the epitaph expresses pride in technical activities. I will quote two examples. The first is the epitaph from a sarcophagus found in Arles and probably dating to the third century A.D. (*CIL* 12.722). The text is flanked by D[*is*] and M[*anibus*] (To the gods of the afterlife) and above, in small-scale relief, by an axe and carpenter's square.

> Tomb of Quintus Candidus Benignus, master builder of the Arles association.
> He had the full extent of the building art, dedication, knowledge, and discretion;
> great technicians on any occasion declared him head of the association; nobody
> was more knowledgeable than that; nobody could defeat him; he knew how to
> make instruments and direct the flow of waters, he was a cherished guest here; he
> knew how to nurture friends with ingenuity and dedication, mild and good-
> natured [*benignus*], [erected by] Candidia Quintina for her sweetest father and
> Valeria Maximina for her dearest husband.

The second epitaph was written in Greek on a tablet, originally from Hermopolis Magna in Egypt and probably dating to the early third century A.D. (Donderer 1996: A8; trans. adapted from Taylor 2003: 1; cf. Bernand 1969: no. 23, with photo).

> I am the tomb of Harpalos. Which Harpalos? Why, Harpalos most skillful in
> the Daedalian craft. This I know, O Fates: his all-inventive art has perished with
> him. What other man alive was his peer? He who laid out beetling temple walls,
> who raised columns for high-ceilinged porticoes—he would often move the very
> mountaintops, servants to his puny ropes, as easily as boys gather twigs. So Am-

phion, so Orpheus once charmed the rocks with song and led them effort-lessly away.

For all their differences—language, location—these two memorials of technicians have much in common: they both have literary pretensions (the first contains a couple of puns, the second takes the form of an epigram), and they both express not only pride in the profession, but also a certain competitive spirit (nobody could defeat Benignus, just as no man alive was Harpalos' peer). They provide an insight into the lives and values of everyday practitioners, and are the small-scale equivalent of Vitruvius' *Architecture* in celebrating the achievements made possible by technical knowledge.

## LATE ANTIQUITY

The close relationship between political power and technology changed, but was retained in late antiquity. Some of the most interesting written documents from this period come from the legal codices. In A.D. 334, 337, and 344, Constantine issued decrees according fiscal privileges to specified technical professions (*Cod. Theod.* 13.4.1; *Cod. Iust.* 10.66.1 = *Cod. Theod.* 13.4.2; *Cod. Iust.* 10.66.2 = *Cod. Theod.* 13.4.3). The last law issued prescriptions:

> With these words we compel mechanicians, geometers, and architects, who pre-serve the divisions and partitions of all pieces <of land>, and who pull together a piece of work by designing structures, and those who discover the course of water and demonstrate its size through skillful leveling, to devote themselves equally to teaching and learning. Let them enjoy their fiscal exemptions and train teach-ers, so that there are enough of them.

The usefulness of technicians for the state is recognized by the top political au-thority, to the point of turning them into privileged individuals from the point of view of fiscal obligations. As for the provisions made for teaching, there was evidently a concern about securing the future of some professions by making sure that the next generation was adequately trained.

A similar, urgent, sense of the significance of technical knowledge for the state is conveyed by an anonymous treatise, written probably around A.D. 360–68, ad-dressed to the then emperors, and commonly known as *De rebus bellicis* (Thomp-son and Flower 1952; Giardina 1989 is fully illustrated). The author presents himself as an advisor, reprising the administrative, supervisory role so many technicians appear to have played in the course of antiquity. He deplores the current state of things, with chaos reigning supreme within the empire and barbarians pressing without, and proposes technical solutions: a currency reform, codification of the laws, the fortification of the borders, and a number of military devices. These have caught the eye of historians also because three of the four main manuscripts of *De rebus bellicis* were illustrated, sometimes in lavish color; we can thus readily visualize, among others, an arrow-shooter made mobile by being installed on a cart, three types of horse-driven scythed chariots, an especially light and wearable suit of armor, and even a ship operated by oxen-driven wheels.

With *De rebus bellicis*, as with earlier and later treatises up to and including the Renaissance, historians have often asked what was the point of describing machines that were probably known to be impossible to realize, difficult to implement, or simply obsolete. The answer is different each time. Philo of Byzantium wanted to impress his audience and differentiate himself from other engineers in what can almost be described as a competitive market, with patrons likely to be impressed by new designs, and technicians traveling from place to place offering their services. The author of *De rebus bellicis* was probably not primarily an engineer, but rather a civil servant, which in the late Roman imperial sense of the term may have implied, more commonly than modern historians recognize, some specialized knowledge or expertise. He again wanted to attract the attention of a figure of authority, possibly more to his financial or administrative reforms than to the weapons he describes (Liebeschuetz 1994). We do not know how successful his bid for attention was at the time. As for the modern reader, and perhaps already the manuscript copyist, it is the weapons, the fancy feats of engineering, that catch the eye in more senses than one, and convey an attractive image of power against the odds, mechanical ingenuity triumphing over brutish enemies.

In fact, in late antiquity technical skills appear to have become widespread among the barbarians—more than one late ancient historian commented on the technical proficiency, especially with military equipment, of the tribes attacking the empire (e.g., *De rebus bellicis* 4; Procopius, *Goth.* 8.11.27–28). Another group often characterized as responsible for the decline and fall of the Roman Empire, the Christians, appear to have been equally proficient. One of the most interesting phenomena of late antiquity is the Christianization of technology, duly charted in our written sources but usually neglected by historians of ancient technology. Beginning around the fourth century A.D., the epitaphs of technicians, especially architects, not only often invoke God and the Virgin Mary, but also evaluate the activities of the deceased in relation to what they did in the service of the Church (Cuomo 2007: chap. 5). St. Augustine himself wrote a panegyric to contemporary technological accomplishments in *De Civitate Dei* (22.24), nicely bracketing the list of accomplishments Aeschylus attributed to Prometheus (*PV* 463–522, quoted earlier):

> For beside the arts of living well and gaining eternal happiness . . . , has not the human intellect discovered and put to use so many and such great technologies, in part to serve real needs, in part for the sake of pleasure . . . ? What marvelous, stupendous accomplishments human effort has achieved in the fields of construction and textile production! How far it has progressed in agriculture and navigation! What accomplishments of imagination and application in the production of all kinds of vessels, various types of statues and paintings. . . . What

great inventions for capturing, killing, taming irrational animals! And against humans themselves, how many types of poisons, weapons, devices! What medicines and remedies humans have discovered for protecting and restoring their health! How many sauces and appetizers they have found to make eating a pleasure! What a great number and variety of signs for conveying thought and for persuasion, the most important of which are words and letters! ... What skill in measuring and counting! With what sharp minds humans grasp the paths and arrangement of the heavenly bodies! How great the knowledge of this world humans have filled themselves with! Who could describe it?

The recognition and institutionalization of Christianity coincided with a massive building program to provide new places of worship, recorded by, among others, Procopius. In his treatise *Buildings*, he narrates how God himself intervened in the construction of the cathedral of Hagia Sophia in Constantinople by inspiring the emperor Justinian with the solution to several technical problems, when even his handpicked, world-famous engineers were at a loss (*Aed.* 1.1.66–78). Procopius' *Buildings* has been described as a panegyric to the emperor Justinian, or, in this case, Justinian's technical achievements, with only occasional mention of the technical experts—architects and engineers—who must have been behind them (Cuomo 2007).

It would be a mistake to consider all written sources for ancient technology as a unified group. Even the category of so-called technical treatises is less an actual, distinct genre recognized as such by the ancients than a convenient means of classification for modern historians. In the absence of official qualification standards and in the presence of an often competitive marketplace situation (including when the marketplace was extended to the whole Mediterranean region), each technical profession was stratified, with different degrees of expertise, social status, wealth, literacy, and numeracy. Thus, technical knowledge comprised many more practices than our present classifications suggest, with varying degrees of closeness to forms of knowledge that we tend to value, such as mathematics, or forms of codification that we tend to appreciate, such as the written form itself. For instance, the *techne* of the marine pilot—the art of navigation—which played a crucial role in the economy and politics of the ancient world from classical Greece onward (it is one of the arts most often mentioned by Plato), goes almost completely unrecorded, not least because of its lack of written accounts (but cf. Casson 1989). In other words, ancient technology was too motley and complicated an entity for technical treatises to be other than partial, problematic, and distorted reflections.

Texts that for their subject matter or the self-identification of their author seem to us to belong together often were written for completely different purposes and addressed to very different audiences. Each case has to be considered separately, and more finely tuned understanding is required of individual authors. In particular, the notion ought to be dispelled that technical treatises are instruction manuals in a straightforward sense, and that their tone and style are "realistic." This realization would enable us to appreciate them as literary products and, consequently, to explore the issue of their aim and audience in a more nuanced way than has so far been attempted for many of them.

Having warned against the dangers of generalization, I do think that some trends are visible in the written sources relative to ancient technology, and thus that it is possible to offer a brief overview of their shared features. Generally speaking, technicians spoke in a climate of competition, in a marketplace. Even many of the epitaphs relative to technicians reproduce a sense of comparison with others, and some of the technical treatises explicitly compare technical disciplines with other forms of knowledge, such as philosophy. The existence of competition and debate, and sometimes of open hostility, both among technicians themselves and between technicians and others, helps to make better sense of some of the evidence. Several authors throughout antiquity express, in different ways, the opinion that technical knowledge and its practitioners are or should be despised and marginalized, because their form of knowledge is questionable from an epistemological point of view, and because, as people, they exhibit unethical behavior: technicians are represented as greedy, arrogant, and base. Those authors include prestigious names such as Plato, Aristotle, Cicero, and Seneca (cf. Humphrey et al. 1998: 579–88), so that their views have often been taken to be the dominant opinion of the society in which they operated. Yet, if we consider that most of the written sources produced by technicians, including those I have focused on in this section, present a different, much more positive picture, and factor in the basically constant presence of competition and debate, we will be able to reread the statements by Plato, Aristotle, Cicero, and Seneca about technology. They will appear to be just contestants in an ongoing argument about knowledge and power that characterized Greek and Roman antiquity, and is one of its most enduring legacies.

Again generally speaking, in their written texts technicians often addressed not just other technicians, but the educated general public, and in particular people of authority—a great number of technical treatises were directed to, or implied direct familiarity with, kings and emperors. The unique selling point of technology to these people was its usefulness: the capacity, or alleged capacity, to produce results rather than mere words. Many of our written sources pair this claim with others that enable technology to stand side by side with other forms of knowledge: theoretical stability, sometimes achieved with the help of mathematics; a respectable past, including playing a role at the very dawn of civilization; religious affiliations, from the patronage of Athena or Minerva to the direct intervention of the Christian God; and the impeccable ethical credentials of its practitioners. All this was often put at the service of the established authority, with the implication that technology could help them not only achieve practical ends, but also impose and retain order at a more symbolic level.

The third, and final, overall feature of technical texts from antiquity is completely unsurprising. They generally present a very positive, even idealized, view of the discipline and of its achievements. I would go as far as to say that many technical treatises were written specifically in order to construct a positive, even idealized, view of the discipline and, by reflection, of the author himself. They celebrate as much as inform; they are monuments as much as manuals. Technical knowledge did not need to be written to be transmitted—oral tradition and apprenticeship took care of that in the majority of the cases. But writing about one's knowledge made it more visible and respectable, and created a memorial for the author. Thus, it makes perfect sense for the written sources we have discussed in this chapter to include both fully-fledged treatises and inscriptions: both Vitruvius' *Architecture* or Frontinus' *Aqueducts* and the epitaphs of Benignus and Harpalos, while celebrating technology and its achievements, preserve the unique, individual voices of their authors.

# REFERENCES

Bernand, É. 1969. *Inscriptions métriques de l'Égypte gréco-romaine. Recherches sur la poésie épigrammatique des Grecs en Égypte.* Paris: Les Belles Lettres.

Burford, A. 1963. "The builders of the Parthenon," in G. T. W. Hooker (ed.), *Parthenos and Parthenon. Greece and Rome* Suppl. 10. Oxford: Clarendon Press, 23–35.

Burford, A. 1969. *The Greek temple builders at Epidauros: A social and economic study of building in the Asklepian Sanctuary, during the fourth and early third centuries B.C.* Liverpool: Liverpool University Press.

Cambiano, G. 1991. *Platone e le tecniche.* 2nd ed. Roma/Bari: Laterza.

Campbell, B. (ed.) 2000. *The writings of the Roman land surveyors: Introduction, text, translation and commentary. Journal of Roman Studies* Monograph 9. London: Society for the Promotion of Roman Studies.

Campbell, J. B. 1994. *The Roman army, 31 BC– AD 337: A sourcebook.* London: Routledge.

Casson, L. 1989. *The Periplus Maris Erythraei.* Princeton: Princeton University Press.

Celentano, M. (ed.) 2003. *Ars/Techne: Il manuale tecnico nelle civiltà greca e romana.* Alessandria: Edizioni dell'Orso.

Cohen, M. R., and I. E. Drabkin 1948. *A source book in Greek science.* Cambridge, MA: Harvard University Press.

Cuomo, S. 2007. *Technology and culture in Greek and Roman antiquity.* Cambridge: Cambridge University Press.

DeLaine, J. 1996. "'De aquis suis'?: The 'Commentarius' of Frontinus," in C. Nicolet (ed.), *Les littératures techniques dans l'antiquité romaine: Statut, public et destination, tradition.* Genève: Vandœuvres, 117–45.

Dijksterhuis, E. J. 1987. *Archimedes.* Princeton: Princeton University Press.

Donderer, M. 1996. *Die Architekten der späten römischen Republik und der Kaiserzeit. Epigraphische Zeugnisse.* Erlangen: Universitätsbund Erlangen-Nürnberg e.V., Universitätsbibliothek Erlangen,

Fowler, D. 1999. *The mathematics of Plato's Academy: A new reconstruction.* 2nd ed. Oxford: Clarendon Press.

Garlan, Y. 1974. *Recherches de poliorcétique grecque.* Paris: Boccard.

Giardina, A. 1989. *Anonimo: Le cose della guerra.* Milano: Mondadori.

Humphrey, J. W., J. P. Oleson, and A. N. Sherwood 1998. *Greek and Roman technology: A sourcebook.* London: Routledge.

Irby-Massie, G. L., and P. T. Keyser 2002. *Greek science of the Hellenistic era: A sourcebook.* London: Routledge.

Korres, M. 1995. *From Pentelicon to the Parthenon: The ancient quarries and the story of a half-worked column capital of the first marble Parthenon.* Athens: Melissa.

Landels, J. G. 2000. *Engineering in the ancient world.* 2nd ed. Berkeley: University of California Press.

Lanza, D. 1979. *Lingua e discorso nell'Atene delle professioni.* Napoli: Liguori.

Lewis, M. J. T. 1999. "When was Biton?" *Mnemosyne* 52: 159–68.

Lewis, M. J. T. 2001. *Surveying instruments of Greece and Rome.* Cambridge: Cambridge University Press.

Lewis, N. 1986. *Greeks in Ptolemaic Egypt: Case studies in the social history of the Hellenistic world.* Oxford: Clarendon Press.

Lewis, N., and M. Reinhold (eds.) 1990. *Roman civilization: Selected readings.* Vol. 2, *The Empire.* 3rd ed. New York: Columbia University Press.

Liebeschuetz, J. H. W. G. 1994. "Realism and phantasy: The anonymous *De rebus bellicis* and its afterlife," in E. Dabrowa (ed.), *The Roman and Byzantine army in the East.* Krakow: Jagiellonian University, 119–39.

Lloyd, G. 1987. *The revolutions of wisdom: Studies in the claims and practice of ancient Greek science.* Berkeley: University of California Press.

Marsden, E. 1971. *Greek and Roman artillery: Technical treatises.* Oxford: Clarendon Press

Meißner, B. 1999. *Die technologische Fachliteratur der Antike: Struktur, Überlieferung und Wirkung technischen Wissens in der Antike (ca. 400 v. Chr.–ca. 500 n. Chr.).* Berlin: Akademie Verlag.

Müller, C. 1855–61. *Geographi graeci minores.* 3 vols. Paris: Didot.

Nutton, V. 2004. *Ancient medicine.* London: Routledge.

Oleson, J. P. 2004. "Well pumps for dummies: Was there a Roman tradition of popular, sub-literary engineering manuals?" in F. Minonzio (ed.), *Problemi di macchinismo in ambito romano.* Como: Comune di Como, Musei Civici, 65–86.

Oleson, J. P. 2005. "Design, materials, and the process of innovation for Roman force pumps," in J. Pollini (ed.), *Terra Marique: Studies in art history and marine archaeology in honor of Anna Marguerite McCann.* Oxford: Oxbow, 211–31.

Randall, R. H. 1953. "The Erechtheum workmen," *American Journal of Archaeology* 57: 199–210.

Reekmans, T. 1970. "Le salaire de Cléon," *Archiv für Papyrusforschung* 20: 17–24.

Rodgers, R. H. 2004. *Frontinus de Aquaeductu urbis Romae.* Cambridge: Cambridge University Press.

Romano, E. 1987. *La capanna e il tempio: Vitruvio o dell'architettura.* Palermo: Palumbo.

Rousset, D. 2002. *Le territoire de Delphes et la terre d'Apollon.* Paris: Boccard.

Sage, M. M. 1996. *Warfare in ancient Greece: A sourcebook.* London: Routledge.

Schiefsky, M. 2005. *Hippocrates: On Ancient Medicine, translated with introduction and commentary.* Leiden: Brill.

Taylor, R. 2003. *Roman Builders: A study in architectural process.* Cambridge MA: Harvard University Press.

Thomas, R. 1992. *Literacy and orality in ancient Greece.* Cambridge: Cambridge University Press.

Thompson, E. A., and B. Flower 1952. *A Roman reformer and inventor.* Oxford: Oxford University Press.

Thulin, C. 1913. *Corpus Agrimensorum Romanorum.* Berlin: Teubner.

Tybjerg, K. 2003. "Wonder-making and philosophical wonder in Hero of Alexandria," *Studies in History and Philosophy of Science* 34: 443–66.

CHAPTER 2

# REPRESENTATIONS OF TECHNICAL PROCESSES

## ROGER ULRICH

ANCIENT depictions that include images of technological processes offer vital evidence for the reconstruction of methods, equipment, scale of operation, labor force, and sequencing of tasks, along with a direct indication of social interest in the relevant technology. Where literary descriptions are lacking, representations offer the single most important resource for modern investigation of process. The images that survive prove unequivocally that the subject of ancient technology enjoyed a long life in a range of artistic media. Only the most durable examples are extant—bas-reliefs from Egyptian tombs, Greek images on painted pottery, and Roman-period relief sculpture constitute the lion's share of this evidence—but we must imagine that there existed a highly developed tradition of pictorial representation on less durable materials that evolved in tandem with the development of writing and literacy. In addition to the illustrations that appear within this chapter, I will naturally refer to illustrations that appear in other chapters in the book.

The importance of ancient depictions of technological processes for the general study of the subject is attested by their prominence in virtually every modern publication that addresses issues of tools, processes, engineering, and technology from the ancient Mediterranean. Both Hugo Blümner and Albert Neuburger relied on published images of relevant artifacts in their publications of 1875–1887 and 1919, respectively, although they depended on some drawn reproductions that contained errors, and on descriptions of artifacts that were lost or inaccessible at the time they compiled their evidence. Nevertheless, these early studies remain useful, written at the nascence of an industrial age that then employed many of the same techniques and tools utilized by the ancient workforce. Over the last century, new discoveries, high-quality photographic reproductions, public stewardship of artifacts, and even ease of travel have provided new opportunities to reexamine evidence long recognized as seminal for the topic and to identify new objects to add to the corpus of ancient images of ancient technologies. General studies, such as Singer's *History of Technology* (1954–1956), White's *Greek and Roman Technology* (1984), and Adam's *Roman Building* (1994) incorporate relevant illustrations of ancient devices in use (see also Forbes 1955–1964, Klemm 1964). The increasingly specialized nature of the field has resulted in focused studies that include welcome compilations of images, although few are primarily concerned with the examination of the *manner* of ancient representation per se. Included in this group are museum exhibitions that have been accompanied by important catalogs such as *Homo Faber*, a project of the Museo Nazionale of Naples (Ciarallo and De Carolis 1999) and the Fire of Hephaistos exhibit at Harvard University (Mattusch 1996), as well as monographs on subjects like Attic vase painting (Noble 1988; Schreiber 1999) or hand tools (Gaitzsch 1980; Zimmer 1985). To attempt even a brief summary of this broad range of evidence is beyond the scope of this chapter. Instead I hope to offer some general comment as to the nature of these representations, their intent, and how they may be categorized over the period of their use.

# Artistic Intent

Any modern attempt to understand an ancient artist's intent or motivation with regard to a given depicted subject is decidedly problematic. Furthermore, the context, relative chronology, and media of representations of early processes suggest that the artistic motivations or intents for reproducing such images vary significantly over the twelve centuries under consideration. Even with these caveats regarding interpretation, a review of the evidence currently available suggests strongly that there exists no single representation that includes a technical process in which the artist's primary purpose was to represent in any instructive or analytical fashion the technology portrayed. There are indeed a few representations that come close: the well-known Berlin Foundry Cup is a good example (figures 16.1–3), but here, as in virtually every example cited in this chapter, the technological process portrayed is ancillary to something else: the image serves to emphasize an activity for which divine protection is sought from a patron deity (thus we find customized votive offerings or carved altars) (figure 2.1), the image is one part of a funerary commemoration of a deceased craftsman or his patron (figures 2.2, 17.1), the image identifies the presence of a specialized guild (figure 17.3), or is simply a scene of industrial activity rendered as a charming if not humorous decorative

Figure 2.1. Corinthian pinax from Penteskouphia; mining scene, end of seventh century B.C. Height 10.4 cm. Berlin no. 871; Bildarchiv Preussischer Kulturbesitz/Art Resource. (ART180877.)

motif—this last a frequent subject of both Greek vase painting and Roman mural decoration (figure 2.3).

The representation of a building crane included in a stone relief from the Tomb of the Haterii in Rome (late first century) is illustrative in this regard (figure 2.4). The crane is carved into the left side of a marble panel that offers as its central focus the image of a monumental tomb whose construction, it appears, necessitated the use of a heavy lifting device. While other depictions of cranes exist (see Adam 1994: 44–47), the machine from the Haterii tomb provides the most detailed rendition: two workmen perched on the jib of the crane affix an inverted wicker basket, perhaps to protect the tip of the jib, or possibly a reference to a Dionysiac mystery cult (Jensen 1978; Landels 2000; Ulrich 2007). The level of detail is striking: braided ropes, heavy pulley systems, a great planked wheel turned by the shifting body weights of the laborers (five are shown), even ropes around the edge of the wheel intended for braking or applying extra force. Close examination reveals some of the wooden treenails employed to hold the rig together. Yet, despite the plethora of details, the image of the crane is incidental to the overall composition, itself conceived to place emphasis on the deceased, the adjacent monumental temple-tomb, and perhaps the family's role and wealth from its construction business. The crane serves primarily as a dramatic prop for greater pictorial themes whose exact purposes are now elusive; but certainly technical didacticism is not one or these.

No original copies of Greek or Latin technical treatises have survived; we can only speculate about the kind of graphic aids they may have included. That

Figure 2.2. Baking scenes from the Tomb of Eurysaces, Rome. Top: Baking and kneading operations; bottom: packing and weighing. Late first century B.C. (Author, composite images after Rossetto 1973.)

Figure 2.3. Frieze of *erotes* and *psychai* engaged in metalworking, House of the Vettii, Pompeii, first century. (Photograph by Michael Larvey, by permission of Michael Larvey and the Soprintendenza Archeologica di Pompeii.)

Figure 2.4. Haterii relief of a lifting crane, late first century, Museo Gregoriano Profano, Vatican Museums. Scala/Art Resource, New York. (ART85226.)

illustrations once accompanied such literary texts or how-to-do-it handbooks seems a reasonable assumption (Oleson 2004, 2005: 222–23). At least some of the intricate prose descriptions of military equipment, water-screws, or the layout of a theater we find in Vitruvius were originally accompanied by drawings (e.g., *De arch.* 3.4.5; 10.6.4). We know that Vitruvius considered Hellenistic commentaries now lost; he describes devices such as the pneumatic pump and flap-valve invented by Ctesibius in the third century B.C. (*De arch.* 10.7). Similarly, the Syracusan Archimedes' (d. 212 B.C.) lost works on elementary mechanics and the properties of mirrors must have been accompanied by diagrams, just as the mathematical formulae that computed the correct parabola for a burning-mirror used to direct the rays of the sun on enemy ships, published by Anthemius of Tralles much later in the sixth century A.D., would have required some form of illustration (Huxley 1959). Heron of Alexandria, who lived in the first century, describes numerous gadgets and mechanical devices, including devices making use of steam power. He published a monograph, now lost (titled *Baroulkos*) that described a lifting machine that operated with a combination of gears capable of hoisting great weights. Although

Heron's texts are thoroughly keyed to illustrations (now preserved only in early Arabic translations), no ancient depictions of gears or geared machinery survive in the durable media of stone or ceramic. Among the technical treatises that have survived, the topic of agriculture is paramount, but there is no reason to doubt that other handbooks on a number of practical technologies were composed and widely distributed (White 1984: 12; Oleson 2004, 2005).

The extant Greek literary corpus does not include references to drawn architectural plans or sketches; verbal specifications (*syngraphai*) might include dimensions (for example, an inscription pertaining to the fourth-century B.C. arsenal at Piraeus, *IG*² 2.1668); in addition, physical models (*paradeigmata*) of buildings similar to those found at Perachora from the eighth century B.C., or of parts of buildings, were apparently used to communicate general ideas about layout and architectural embellishment (Coulton 1977: 54–60). Roman-period architectural plans in mosaic and inscribed stone reveal that the practice of rendering buildings both as plans (sing. *ichnographia*) and elevations (sing. *orthographica*) was familiar to builders in Italy (Vitruvius, *De arch.* 1.2.2; Taylor 2003, 26–29). Full-scale elevations, inscribed on existing stone paving, were used on site (or nearly on site) for the preassembly of the entablatures or pediments of the Pantheon (Haselberger 1994). The scaled-down comprehensive plan of Rome known as the *Forma Urbis* that has survived in a fragmentary state, carved on sheets of marble in the early third century A.D. and mounted on a public wall near the Roman Forum, indicates that such renderings were in public circulation and legible to at least some of the population (Carettoni et al. 1960). Hadrian (emperor 117–38) not only exhibited a keen interest in architecture but also apparently designed buildings himself, at least on paper, and solicited the opinions of professional architects such as Apollodorus of Damascus (Dio Cassius 69.4.4). In the later first century B.C., Vitruvius urged that aspiring architects master the art of drafting (*De arch.* 1.1.3).

Representations of Greco-Roman technologies play an important role in filling gaps left even when related tools or special-purpose sites have been excavated. Particularly informative compositions include operators; the representation of the human agent can aid immensely in interpretation. Consider images of drilling in wood or stone. For boring small-diameter holes in wood, both Greek and Roman depictions indicate that a bow-and-drill could be operated by a single deft craftsman (figures 2.5–2.6). Larger diameter holes or grooves in wood or stone required the help of an assistant who could power the bit while the primary operator directed the cut. In this case, evidence includes not only a Homeric literary reference (see chapter 17), but also an unambiguous image from Rome of a sarcophagus-maker using such a tool (Gaitzsch 1980: cat. 318; Strong and Brown 1976: 200; figure 2.7). The rendering of a heavy strap (and no bow) instead of a thin thong held in tension by the bow reveals a significant variant of tool type even though the reciprocating principle of operation is identical. The recovery of isolated iron drill bits, without handles, bows, or straps, or the examination of tool marks on the surface of stone cannot by themselves lead to recognizing a significant variant of the drill that is so readily apparent via the relief in Urbino.

Figure 2.5. Vatican gold-glass vessel: detail of an operator of a bow and drill; early fourth century. Museo Biblioteca Apostolica Vaticana, inv. 60788. (Drawing by author.)

Representations of tools in use provide additional information about technical processes beyond that which artifacts or workshops can yield, such as the positioning of tools and the stances assumed by the operator, or the layout of the workshop. Painted depictions at Pompeii of fullers finishing cloth and cleaning clothing, for example, are of great interpretive value when otherwise unremarkable masonry tanks are excavated (Reg. VI.8, 20; Ciarello and De Carolis 1999: cat. 120); a stone funerary relief from Sens (Yonne, Roman *Agedincum Senonum*) provides corroborating evidence (figure 18.4). Ancient depictions can provide the appearance of components missing from excavated examples, such as wooden handles and stands, the number of operators required for a given function, or information about the age, gender, status (i.e., freeborn or slave), and ethnicity of the operators. The role of women in the workforces of Greece and Rome, for example, has been more fully understood through ancient depictions (see below).

The most apparent value of ancient depictions of technical processes is the recovery of images of tools, machines, or applications for which no physical traces or literary descriptions survive (we may know the name, and thus the existence, of a device from brief literary mention, but description is another matter). There is no extant written source, for example, that describes the process of throwing or decorating a ceramic vessel, yet the subject was well known to the Greek vase painter. We know, for example, from literary references and from the remains of turned bowls (of stone and wood) or stone columns that Greeks, Etruscans, and Romans made and operated both large and small lathes, but the appearance and operation of the machine itself is still uncertain, now only partially solved through

Figure 2.6. Attic red-figure painting by the Gallatin Painter depicting a carpenter making a chest to hold Perseus and his mother Danaë, ca. 490 B.C. Height 41.7 cm. MFA Boston inv. 13.200. (Photograph © 2007 Museum of Fine Arts, Boston.)

the examination of fragmentary depictions (see chapter 17). The appearance of large lifting cranes powered by a "great wheel" turned by the shifting weight of human operators treading within is known exclusively through carved stone depictions (figure 2.4). A schematic rendition of a water-lifting wheel is known from a fragmentary second-century A.D. mosaic from Apamea in Syria, in a region where such devices once fed irrigation and aqueduct systems (Oleson 1984: fig. 41). The use and appearance of the cylindrical water-screw (*cochlea*) invented by Archimedes, the design of which is known through Vitruvius (10.6.1–4), has been captured, somewhat improbably, in exotic depictions of Nilotic scenes on two frescoed walls from Pompeii and a terracotta relief from Roman Egypt now in the British Museum (Ciarello and De Carolis 1999: cat. 410; Oleson 1984: fig. 86, 101; BM inv. EA-37563). The Egyptian connection is fitting, since it was along the Nile that such machines were in common use, according to Diodorus, who wrote about both the Egyptian water-screws and others used in the Roman mines of Spain in the first century B.C. (1.34.2; 5.37.304).

Yet even depictions of activities that include a high degree of detail can open debate on the nature of the specific technology being depicted. The pot-decorating scene painted by the Leningrad Painter on the Caputi Hydria has been interpreted since its publication in 1876 as a scene of vase painting being undertaken by both young males and one female (figure 2.8; Richter 1923). Green (1961: 74), however, has attempted to demonstrate that the scene is one of workers decorating metal vessels (see also Venit 1988); the traditional interpretation is still defended (Kru-

Figure 2.7. Strap drill depicted on the funerary plaque of Eutropos, originally from the Via Labicana, Rome, mid fourth century. Museo Archeologico Lapidario, Urbino. (Author.)

kowski 1990). A metalworking scene from the House of the Vettii in Pompeii, discussed in more detail below, provides another example of interpretive controversy, where scholars have argued for over a century on the specific nature of the activity so carefully rendered (figure 2.3). Two terracotta reliefs from a second-century tomb (no. 29) at Isola Sacra near the Roman port town of Ostia appear to show artisans shaping or grinding tools, but the workstations vary significantly in appearance, and the exact nature of the activity portrayed is difficult to evaluate (D'Ambra 1988: 91; Zimmer 1985: pl. 4).

In the assessment of such representations of technical processes, there is no guarantee that the artisan rendering the image was himself knowledgeable about the technique he was representing or even possessed the artistic skill to reproduce the process accurately. If an anomaly is suspected in a particular representation, we must assess whether it is an artistic fault or a previously unobserved variant practice. The operator of the bow-and-drill depicted on a gilt glass vessel in the Vatican clearly holds the middle of the stock of the drill in his left hand, where the thong of the bow belongs; we expect to see him grasp the freely-rotating nave above the stock so that the drill could turn under the action of the bow (figure 2.5). Either the artist has made a mistake or an unknown variant has been depicted (the shaft of the drill bit runs entirely through the stock and is spun from above). In this case the efficacy of the drill would be greatly reduced by eliminating the downward pressure on the nave; it seems most likely that the representation is in error (Goodman 1964: 161).

Certain depictions of complicated processes or their outcomes were necessarily simplified or compressed due to the size of the rendition, the medium being used by the artist, or the limitations of his ability. A common distortion of relative scale must also be taken into account: a given tool, machine, or object being made was routinely rendered disproportionately larger or smaller in relation to the artisan depicted or the surrounding environment. For example, one may examine the

Figure 2.8. Attic red-figure hydria (Kalpis); the Caputi Hydria by the Leningrad Painter. The male artisans are about to receive crowns by Athena and two winged victories. A female artisan is at work on the far right of the scene. Ca. 475 B.C. Height 32 cm. Collezione Banca Intesa, Milan, inv. F.G. 00002A-E/BI. (Line drawing adapted from Cloché 1931: pl. 21.)

carved rendition on Trajan's Column (A.D. 113) of the great bridge that spanned the Danube to understand the principles used to construct broad, segmental arches composed from beams of wood (figure 17.6). When compared to literary accounts, such as that in Cassius Dio (13.1), or the actual site of the bridging project at Turnu-Severin, there can be no doubt that the sculptor simplified his representation of the actual structure by carving only five piers between the two riverbanks; Dio mentions that twenty were built. We may reasonably guess that the number of arced segments rendered between each span was also reduced, but by how much? Is the triangular bracing crowning each of the stone piers rendered accurately, or do the diagonal beams we see, as Richmond has pointed out (1982: 35), seem to lean in the wrong direction? How did a professional sculptor working in Rome know what the bridge in Dacia looked like? Had sketches—or drawings of a more technical nature—been brought back from the frontier? Frequently these problematic issues cannot be definitively resolved, although considering them carefully will often help to frame the correct questions when evaluating a representation of a given technical process.

Even when these limitations have been taken into account, however, one is often struck by the level of detail and accuracy achieved in the smallest of renditions. A frescoed frieze course only about 20 cm high, for example, discovered in 1895 in the House of the Vettii in Pompeii, depicts, somewhat improbably, teams of winged cupids and *psychai* engaged in a series of industrial activities: pressing grapes and making wine, fulling, wreath-making, producing scented oils or perfumes, baking, and metalworking (figure 2.3). The images were located in one of the most important rooms of the house, a formal reception and dining room (*oecus*), situated to delight the guests and presumably to celebrate the lucrative enterprises of the house's successful owners (Clarke 1991: 215; 2003: 101). In the metalworking scene we see a cupid before a furnace as he holds not only the kind of tongs seen in similar depictions but also a blowpipe to direct a stream of fresh air on the hot charcoal; in this way the heat of the furnace can be rapidly elevated for brief periods of time—useful for, among other things, soldering work. Despite the fanciful nature of the operator, the wall-painter had probably observed a craftsman working with metal at a hot furnace. To the left of the furnace scene another cupid sits on a cushioned stool while working intently with a small hammer and anvil. Before him is a box-shaped workbench that holds a set of scales and a small cabinet with partially opened drawers. This is one of the most detailed depictions of such a workstation from the Greco-Roman world, but its very uniqueness has made its precise interpretation the subject of long debate: Do we see an office where coins were minted, as some scholars have argued? Or is the scene that of a goldworker? The answer to the question, never fully resolved, depends on modern interpretation of the four principal activities and seven figures depicted. Marvin Tameanko (1990) has argued that the apparatus resting on the top of the workbench is that of a Roman *caelator*, or engraver of die-struck jewelry, and includes both scales and a unique depiction of a magnifying glass suspended over the engraver's block. The validity of this interpretation will not be explored here; the point is that an ancient wall-painter creating a decorative frieze has included carefully rendered details of a specific technique—this is no generic depiction. It is important to remember that the Pompeian wall-painter enjoyed no higher status as an "artist" than did the metalworker; presumably there were opportunities for observing each other's activities and frequent social contact (for a discussion of status see Burford 1972).

The accuracy of the depiction of a given technology can be further tested by comparing artifacts and site features with the image in question, as well as by considering variations over a range of images that show a given technique. The operation of a kiln during the archaic period in the vicinity of Greek Corinth, for example, is illustrated on at least eight painted plaques from the sanctuary of Poseidon at Penteskouphia (Noble 1988: 151; Richter 1923: 76). Each depicts a single nude male, in profile, tending to the firing process. These plaques and others like them were evidently left as votive offerings for prosperity by potters and other craftsmen. Although the images were created in the same area and are of roughly the same date, variations in the otherwise similar depictions indicate that the artists were not simply recreating an accepted "type" through mass copying. Where the details have survived (in five of the examples), the single essential tool held by the craftsman is a rod terminating in a hook, used variously to stoke the firebox or to open or close the vent hole, which itself is always shown at the very top of the beehive-shaped kiln. The door for inserting or removing the pottery is consistently depicted in the side of the kiln, and is correctly shown about halfway up the wall of the structure. In all but one example, the kiln is shown to be of modest height, perhaps slightly taller than its operator, who needs to stand on the stoking chamber to reach the vent hole. But in one example (Berlin inv. 802B), a ladder is needed to reach to the top vent, itself rendered as a broken amphora; the impression is that some establishments produced enough pots to warrant a kiln capable of firing oversized pots or larger-scale operation (figure 2.9). In the most remarkable image, unfortunately only partially preserved, the artist has provided us with a kind of

Figure 2.9. Corinthian pinax from Penteskouphia; a large kiln is depicted. The operator climbs a ladder to adjust the vent hole, which has been fashioned from the top of an amphora. Sixth century B.C. Height 10.5 cm. Berlin inv. 802B. Bildarchiv Preussischer Kulturbesitz/Art Resource. (ART317389.)

X-ray view of the kiln, which includes a depiction of the pots tightly stacked inside the chamber, the perforated floor above the stoking shaft, the vent hole, and perhaps even the test-pieces—fragments of unfired pottery—placed for easy access during the firing so that the oxidation and reducing stages of the firing could be carefully supervised (figure 2.10; Berlin inv. 893; Cook 1961; Noble 1988).

## RANGE OF DEPICTIONS

Not all technologies are represented in the extant corpus of representational art. We lack, for example, depictions of gears and timekeeping devices, even though artifacts and literary sources attest to their existence. Technologies that are portrayed are not necessarily depicted continuously over time, and for some industries only one or two visual representations may survive (e.g., mosaic manufacture and the water-powered water-lifting wheel). Since many ancient renditions are presumably lost, there may be no significance to the absence from the visual record of a certain category of technological process. A surviving scene of glassblowing on a mold-made Roman lamp, for example, suggests that multiple images might be made of a relatively esoteric practice (figure 21.7). It is clear that the most significant initial development of representation in the Greco-Roman world first took place in the sixth century B.C. with the maturation of Attic black-figure vase

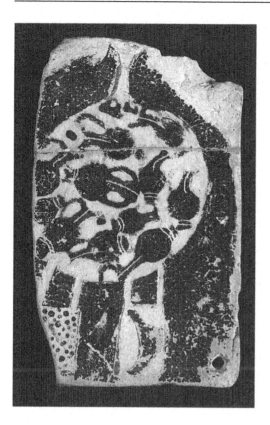

Figure 2.10. Fragment of a Corinthian pinax from Penteskouphia depicting a section of a kiln. Test pieces can be seen near the vent hole (top); sixth century B.C. Height 10.1 cm. Berlin inv. F893. Bildarchiv Preussischer Kulturbesitz/Art Resource. (ART180898.)

painting and, especially after the second half of that century, the vase painter's interest in including representations of everyday working life (table 2.1). This period of florescence lapsed by the end of the fifth century B.C., as artists moved to media (such as wall painting) that have not survived well for study. There are few depictions available from the Hellenistic world. Their absence might seem enigmatic, since this period (late fourth through second centuries B.C.) was one that fostered many technical innovations, including the experiments of Alexandrian engineers and mathematicians. These Greek scientists were apparently prolific in their inventions and their written commentaries, even though, as we have seen, only a few of their works have survived through later copies. During the Hellenistic period, however, ceramic artists turned from the representation of scenes of daily life to floral motifs or to the imitation of embossed silverware by means of molds, eliminating one of our best sources of representations of technology.

A given technology may not have been equally represented by both Greek and Roman artists, or it may even be exclusive to one alone. Images of pottery production were a well established theme for the Greek vase painter, but they are rare in Roman contexts, and unlike the Greek examples are not shown on Roman pottery itself but preserved in wall painting (e.g., Pompeii I.8.10, perhaps a shop sign; Ciarallo and De Carolis 1999: cat. 178) and relief sculpture (Dobbins 1985; Kleiner and Matheson 1996: cat. 55). Similarly, while scenes including architecture are shown on Greek artifacts, those depicting the *process* of construction are limited to the Roman sphere, although even here there are enormous gaps; there exists no depiction of the wooden centering framework for vault construction, for example. Such disparities must reflect cultural attitudes; the incomplete nature of the evidence alone does not suffice to explain the uneven pattern. The Roman's documentary approach to scenes of warfare and camp construction (Column of Trajan), or his propensity to decorate his tomb with an image of his profession, has resulted in a great number of accompanying portrayals of techniques, tools, and applications.

# CATEGORIES OF DEPICTIONS

Table 2.1 outlines the cultural range and media of surviving depictions of technical processes from the cultures of Greece, Etruria, and the greater Roman world and also offers their rough chronological distribution. Images that offer information about products of technology but nothing of *process* are not included (e.g., a wooden ship versus an image of a ship under construction). Discussion below categorizes this body of material in a more thematic and formal way. The organizing principle selected is their order of complexity, from the simplest of graphic depictions that show a single element to those that incorporate multiple graphic components within a single composition.

## Tools Depicted in Isolation

Individual tools, including adzes, calipers, tongs, miniature plows, saws, planes, and mining picks, are represented as three-dimensional miniature models or two-dimensional representations on relief sculptures, mosaics, and coins. Instruments shown in isolation or in groups (the latter commonly related by function) are generally found in specific contexts; most common is the realm of Roman funerary art from the western provinces. The Greek vase-painter generally preferred to include human agents along with depictions of tools, thus tools in isolation (unless part of a larger scene) are missing from this otherwise important medium.

Small-scale models of tools tend to be found as votive offerings; examples exist from Etruscan and Roman contexts. There may well have been similar objects made as toys for which we have no record. Minute renditions of woodworking tools are included as mint-marks on Roman republican-period silver coinage (Fava 1969). The miner's pick is depicted on the reverse of coins from the Greek city of Damastion in Epirus (fourth century B.C.; Healy 1978). One, two, or more tools carved on funerary reliefs of the Roman period served as pictograms that identified the profession of the deceased. Instead of or in addition to a tool, the sculptor may represent the product of a given technology, such as a spoked wheel, a leather shoe, a boxwood comb, the hull of a ship—although, it must be stressed, many industries are never represented (e.g., Aquileia inv. 1231: wheel; Uffizi, Florence inv. 1914: comb). In some cases these images are shown in isolation, in others the tools may be accompanied by a portrait of the deceased (see below). Isolated tools are gen-

**Table 2.1.** Depiction of technological processes (G = Greek, E = Etruscan, R = Roman).

| Technology | Sculpture | Vase Painting | Fresco | Minor Arts | Date Range (by century) |
|---|---|---|---|---|---|
| **Agriculture** | | | | | |
| Harvesting/pruning | R | G | | R | 6th B.C.–4th A.D. |
| Plowing, Digging | E, R | G | | R | 6th B.C.–4th A.D. |
| Presses | R | G | R | | 6th B.C.–4th A.D. |
| Wine-Making | R | G | R | R | 6th B.C.–4th A.D. |
| **Boatbuilding** | R, G | | | R | 2nd B.C.–4th A.D. |
| **Capstan** | R | | | | 1st A.D. |
| **Ceramics** | | | | | |
| Pottery wheel | | G | R | | 6th B.C.–1st A.D. |
| Pottery painting | R | G | | | 6th B.C.–2nd A.D. |
| Pottery firing | | G | | | 6th–5th B.C. |
| Pottery burnishing | R | G | | | 6th B.C.–2nd A.D. |
| **Construction Process** | | | | | |
| Laying Brick, Stone | R | | R | | 2nd–4th A.D. |
| Turf walls | R | | | | 2nd A.D. |
| Framing | R | | | | 2nd A.D. |
| Scaffolding | R | | R | | 2nd–4th A.D. |
| Cranes, Hoists | R | | R | | 1st A.D. |
| **Fishing, hunting, trapping** | G, R | G | E, R | R | 6th B.C.–4th A.D. |
| **Food Preparation** | | | | | |
| Butchering | R | G | E | | 6th B.C.–2nd A.D. |
| Baking & Cooking | G, E, R | | E | G | 5th B.C.–3rd A.D. |
| Furnaces/Ovens/Kilns | R | G | R | G | 6th–4th B.C. |
| **Glassblowing** | | | | R | 1st–2nd A.D. |
| **Levers** | R | G | | R | 6th B.C.–1st A.D. |
| **Leatherworking, shoes** | R | G | | | 6th B.C.–2nd A.D. |
| **Metalworking** | | | | | |
| Forge | R | G | R | | 6th B.C.–2nd A.D. |
| Bellows | G, R | G | | | 6th B.C.–1st A.D. |
| Chasing | | G | R | | 6th/5th B.C. |
| Assembly (statues) | | G | | | 6th/5th B.C. |
| Coin/Minting | R | | R? | | 1st B.C.–1st A.D. |
| Embossing | R | G | | | 6th/5th B.C.–1st A.D. |
| Gold Beating | R | | | | 1st A.D. |
| Jewelry Production | | | R | | 1st A.D. |
| **Military Machines** | R | | | | 2nd A.D. |
| **Milling** | | | | | |
| Animal power | R | | | | 1st B.C.–2nd A.D. |
| Pestles or Querns | G | G | | | 6th B.C. |
| **Water Power** | | | R | R | 3rd–5th A.D. |
| **Mining** | R | G | | G | 6th B.C.–2nd A.D. |
| **Mosaic Manufacture** | R | | | | 4th A.D. |

*(continued)*

**Table 2.1.** (*continued*)

| Technology | Sculpture | Vase Painting | Fresco | Minor Arts | Date Range (by century) |
|---|---|---|---|---|---|
| Painting and Plastering (portraits, walls) | R | G | R | R | 5th B.C.–2nd A.D. |
| Pulleys, Block and Tackle | R | | | | 1st–2nd A.D. |
| Rope Making | R | | | | 1st–2nd A.D. |
| Stone Carving | R | G | | R | 5th B.C.–4th A.D. |
| Textiles | | | | | 6th B.C.–1st A.D. |
|   Bleaching, Pressing | | | R | | 1st A.D. |
|   Fulling, Dyeing | R | | R | | 1st–3rd A.D. |
|   Rolling, Spinning | R | G | | E | 7th B.C.–2nd A.D. |
|   Looms/Weaving | R | G | R | E, R | 7th B.C.–4th A.D. |
|   Shearing/cropping | R | | | | 1st–2nd A.D. |
| Water Supply | | | | | |
|   Aqueducts | R | | | | 2nd A.D. |
|   Fountains | R | G | E, R | | 6th B.C.–2nd A.D. |
| Water-Lifting | | | | | |
|   Compartmented wheel | | | | R | 1st–2nd A.D. |
|   Archimedean Screw | R | | R | | 1st B.C.–3rd A.D. |
| Weights/Scales | R | G | R | R | 6th B.C.–3rd A.D. |
| Wheelwright | R | | | | 2nd A.D. |
| Woodworking | | | | | |
|   Tools only | R | | | R | 5th B.C.–4th A.D. |
|   Craftsman/men & tools | R | G | R | R | 6th B.C.–4th A.D. |

erally not found on public monuments of Greece and Rome, with the main exception being those carved on the faces of Roman-period altars. Of this group many depictions (e.g., a knife) were connected directly with the ritual of sacrifice performed at the altar, while others on altars made reference to the guild responsible for the donation of the altar (e.g., Capitoline Museums inv. 1909).

## Single Operators with a Tool or Machine

This group includes small models of figurines engaged in specific activities such as plowing, sawing wood, or shoemaking. Such figurines had a wide distribution, including Bronze Age sites from Egypt and the Aegean, classical Greece, and Italy. The context of such finds is generally funerary or religious in nature; the figurine may represent activity in the afterlife (here the Egyptian material seems unambiguous), or the votive is left by the petitioner to protect a given activity. Attic red-figure vase painters from the late archaic and early classical periods portrayed a single craftsman building furniture or carving stone columns (Gallatin Painter, figure 2.6; Antiphon Painter, ca. 475 B.C., Boston MFA 62.613). We do not find, however, Greek depictions of operators engaged in industrial activities on stone funerary markers from the archaic and classical periods, surely because such representation was reserved for wealthy aristocrats, who were not depicted in association with such manual skills. The situation is entirely different in Roman Italy, particularly from the period of the early empire onward and the concomitant appearance of an affluent artisan class of former slaves and their descendants (George 2006). On Roman-period funerary reliefs, depictions of single operators and their tools focus on the deceased practicing his trade. An outstanding example is that of Longidienus from Ravenna, which not only portrays a Roman boat-builder hard at work with his adze, but also provides a descriptive caption: "P. Longidienus, son of Publius, pushes on with his work" (figure 17.1; Ravenna, inv. 7; *CIL* 11.139; Ulrich 2007; Zimmer 1985: pl. 7). In other examples the operator may only pose with one of his tools in hand, identifying himself as a skilled craftsman; the presence of the handheld object identifies the primary occupation of the deceased. Such images were distributed widely in the Roman West and are indictors of affluence; the vast majority of Roman manual laborers could afford only a simple burial in a communal sepulcher, perhaps with a notebook-sized marble plaque recording his name and profession. Monuments of artisans with depictions of their trades must have been relatively rare, or clustered in cemeteries where there was an established pictorial tradition. Cemeteries connected with Roman legionary posts tend to yield such concentrations of funerary images; the site of Roman Aquileia in northern Italy provides an outstanding example.

## Depictions of Complex Operations

The portrayal of a group of individuals involved in a more or less common enterprise was a favorite topic of the Greek vase-painter, and of the Roman sculptor and fresco-painter working for private patrons. The layout tends to fall into the category of the continuous frieze, and occasionally superimposed registers, from the small scale of the figural band around a Greek pot to the larger sculpted and painted examples seen in both Roman private and, rarely, public art. Even small objects measuring only a few centimeters on a side can contain imagery that projects several stages of a single operation. The mining scene from a Corinthian pinax of the mid-sixth century B.C. provides an excellent example (figure 2.1; Berlin inv. 871). On a field measuring only 10.4 x 13.2 cm, the artist has depicted several stages of a mining operation for the extraction of ore or clay, showing four figures who swing a pickaxe, gather the raw material in baskets, and remove them from the pit, while including such details as the steps cut into the sides of the mining shaft and an amphora strung up alongside the miners, presumably to provide drinking water to relieve the hot and dirty work. More typical from the Greek world are the black- and red-figure vase paintings that depict activities such as weaving, bronze-casting, or pottery-making (figure 2.11: Amasis Painter, with eleven figures; figure 4.4: Foundry scene, with two figures; figure 16.1–3: Foundry cup, with eight figures; not illustrated: Leagros Group, with eight figures, Munich inv. 1717).

The most important Roman scenes to have survived include wall paintings and relief sculpture. From the late first century B.C., we have a continuous frieze of a large-scale bread-making operation carved on the tomb of the baker Eurysaces from Rome, which offers a unique portrayal of a large-scale industrial operation that

Figure 2.11. Attic black-figure scene of women weaving, attributed to the Amasis Painter. Metropolitan Museum of Art, New York, Inv. 31.11.10. (Photograph: Metropolitan Museum of Art, P32367.)

includes a kind of assembly-line mentality for the milling of wheat, kneading, baking, weighing, and distribution of a common and essential commodity (figure 2.2; Rossetto 1973). With this relief Eurysaces proclaimed publicly that his accumulation of wealth was due not to a highly skilled craft but to the perfection of an orchestrated process of mass production that created wealth from high volume sales of a simple product with a relatively low profit margin. Such scenes of large-scale production emphasize the success of a particular individual in organizing and managing the laborers who work below him (George 2006: 24). Eurysaces' tomb was in fact built to hold the ashes of the baker's wife, Atistia, but his full-length portrait was probably included in the decoration of the tomb, and a figure who supervises the kneading process, dressed in a toga to emphasis his elevated status, may be that of Eurysaces himself. Another first-century marble relief found in Rome, of a furniture workshop, shows six laborers, their tools—which include a large mechanized sawing machine, frame saw, calipers, and square—and furniture being assembled. The proud patron stands off to one side, in the presence of his divine patroness, Minerva (figure 17.3). A fragmentary frescoed scene of pottery production from Pompeii, perhaps intended as a shop sign, depicts at least four workers shaping vessels in one frame while in another a seated female appears to offer one of the pots for sale (see above).

Trajan's Column in Rome provides an important glimpse into large-scale building activities undertaken by a disciplined and organized military labor force. It seems unusual that more such scenes were not set up in public spaces by Hellenistic kings or later Roman dictators and emperors, particularly since both Assyrian kings of the eighth century B.C. and Egyptian pharaohs had clearly promoted art depicting monumental engineering feats involving large numbers of orchestrated workers (Barnett et al. 1998). Other canonical iconography of eastern kingship had been adopted by Greek and Roman potentates. The actions of Trajan's soldiers must of course be seen in the larger context of the Column's grand purpose, to celebrate the emperor's military victory over the Dacians, but the ultimate victory has been portrayed not only in terms of prowess on the battlefield but also of preparation and logistics: clearing forests, building camps and abutments for artillery, and crossing rivers.

# TECHNOLOGIES REPRESENTED IN MYTHOLOGICAL OR FANTASTIC SETTINGS

Certain Greek myths and their Roman adaptations, as well as Rome's own native tradition of stories, include colorful accounts of technological and engineering feats. These are reproduced primarily on extant vase painting, frescoes, and mosaics.

Some of the associated technological wonders portrayed, such as the wings worn by Icarus and his master-craftsman father Daedalus, or the wooden shell of the Trojan horse, are clearly renditions of the artist's imagination, his familiarity with a long pictorial tradition, or extrapolation from parallel and contemporary technologies (thus the planked hull of a wooden ship could form the basis for the rendition of the torso of a wooden horse). Other compositions include images of tools and devices clearly expropriated from a given artist's contemporary world.

Images related to the feats of the hero Heracles offer illustrative examples. The hero and his companion Iolaos attack the monstrous Hydria with a long sword and a toothed sickle, respectively, on an early Corinthian skyphos now in Paris (Louvre CA 3004; Kron 1988: 190). Another Attic black-figure pot from around 520 B.C. shows Heracles carrying the Cercopes suspended from either end of a straight wooden yoke balanced on his shoulders (Brommer 1984, 29). This must have been a common method of transporting heavy loads: on another pot from around 500 B.C. we see what appears to be a contemporary Greek carrying two large tuna suspended exactly as the Cercopes were carried, and in yet another scene a two-man rig bears a heavy storage vessel suspended from a pole (Hopper 1979: figs. 23, 24). The iconography associated with Hephaestus and his forge provides images of tools and procedures associated with smithing, particularly on Greek painting and sculpture. The Berlin Foundry Cup shows the god putting finishing touches on the armor of Achilles (figure 16.1); a black-figure oinochoe from the sixth century B.C., now in London, appears to show the god (or a mortal practitioner) working at his forge while associated tools seemingly "float" in the background (figure 4.4; Mattusch 1980; BM B507). In London and on the frieze of the Siphnian treasury at Delphi (ca. 525 B.C.), we can see depictions of a bellows made from an inflatable animal skin (Brommer 1978: pl. 50). The myth of Minerva and Arachne is the setting for scenes of women spinning and weaving on a marble frieze from Domitian's Forum in Rome (late first century; D'Ambra 1993).

A related category of images does not represent specific myths but uses fanciful or exotic figures in otherwise quotidian settings, including activities of a technological nature. In Greek art, examples of this genre are numerous but rather limited in scope: the Attic vase painter was fond of satyrs and winemaking scenes for decorating vessels intended for use in *symposia*. The Roman affection for "charming" scenes involving beings such as cupids or pygmies has roots in the Hellenistic artist's attraction to subjects of infants, of allegory, and of abnormal physique and ethnic physiognomy (Pollitt 1986: 127). The Nilotic scenes favored by Roman-period painters and mosaicists, often populated by caricatures of the pygmy race, likely represent a category first popularized in hellenized Alexandria in the late third or early second century B.C. (Pollitt 1986: 208). It has already been noted that this theme was imported to include renditions of the Archimedean water-screw, apparently a device that was a picturesque feature of the Nile delta. Similar is the portrayal of cupids (or *erotes*) and occasionally *psychai* (their female winged counterparts) in activities of an agricultural and even "industrial" nature; the richly-detailed frieze in the House of the Vettii (see above) is a prime example (figure 2.3).

The use of *erotes* is so widespread in a range of contexts, public and private, sacred and funerary, that their presence as agents in scenes of shoemaking, pressing grapes, or blacksmithing would not have caused much comment. Nonetheless, their employment in such scenes has the effect of elevating rather gritty tasks to a level suitable for the decoration of a wealthy artisan's reception room—or that of one who has derived his wealth through commerce. There is a playfulness and charm to such scenes that is hard to imagine in the poorly lit and often dangerous conditions we suspect characterized the ancient workshop.

# WORKFORCE

With few exceptions, images of industrial activities were made by private individuals for private commemoration. In a sense these are self-portraits of the working class made by those who shared their social station. The images place in center stage the human element that is so integral to these early machines and processes. Once again we must exercise caution in drawing conclusions from the manner in which the ancient craftsman or builder is portrayed; contemporary artistic convention accounts for much. With such caveats in mind, however, the visual record can provide information otherwise not available about the men, women, and also children engaged in ancient technologies.

One is not surprised by the dominance of women in Greek scenes of spinning and weaving, given the well-documented domestic duties of women in ancient Greek society (Barber 1992; Keuls 1983). Adolescent and adult males are predominant in industries outside the home; this is true of both the Greek and Roman workforce. Nevertheless, women and children are not excluded from activities one might predict as exclusively male domains. The Corinthian pinax from Berlin cited above (figure 2.1) clearly shows a woman—perhaps a slave—taking part in removing material from a mine, the Caputi Hydria shows a woman at work in a potter's studio (even though the scene, replete with winged Nikai, is highly idealized; cf. Venit 1988). In the Roman context, we find women involved with the distribution of food and drink on the retail level (Amedick 1991: cat. 97; Kampen 1981) and women portrait-painters, and a Roman relief in Naples shows a child alongside other laborers in a shop that manufactured metal containers (Ciarallo and De Carolis. 1999: cat. 201, 335; Veyne 1987: 54; Naples inv. 6575 and 9018).

Within both Greek and Roman scenes where multiple figures are at work, a simple gradation of status that might simply be described as manager versus laborer is often apparent. An owner or overseer, if present, watches over, but does not actively engage in, the activity shown; two examples from Rome have been discussed above (figure 17.3). The patron is inconsequential to the process being portrayed, but his presence may well account for the very existence of the depiction. The ancient viewer would have identified the patron immediately from his dress; the garment worn, usually of full length, is not suitable for a manual laborer or his class, whose "uniform," if a garment is worn at all, is utilitarian. Even so, the full drapery of the patron or overseer may well be worn by a figure who is himself of servile origin.

# Clothing and Personal Accessories

The clothing and special equipment worn by the ancient operator is not only an indicator of social status. Working conditions, as well as issues of utility and even of safety, can be surmised from the pictorial evidence. The Attic potter showed many of his subjects at work firing pottery, mining, woodworking, blacksmithing, and plowing wearing nothing at all. In some such scenes (woodworking, black-smithing, harvesting) other workers within the same composition are wearing a short strip of drapery around the waist, but are otherwise unclad. It has been recognized that Greek athletes commonly exercised while nude, but one must wonder about the comfort and safety of working without any protective clothing. Nudes and the semi-draped in industrial scenes may indicate slave and free labor, respectively, or the nudity may simply be part of the artistic convention that frequently portrayed the male as unclad. In every scene that shows a Greek work-man in front of a furnace or kiln, he is nude. Greek women at work, it should be noted, are always fully garbed, this, too, a convention for other images of women made in the archaic and classical periods. The peplos or chiton worn is the same as those worn by women in other painted scenes. Those worn in scenes of weaving or spinning might be rendered with decorative patterns, as if to emphasize the skill of the female weavers (figure 2.11). Since women of status in the Greek world spent working hours at their home-based looms, the fine garments are hardly out of place.

The Roman worker, however humble, is always garbed. The simplest covering is similar to that worn by his Greek counterpart: the short, kiltlike garment that leaves him bare-chested (milling, baking, woodworking, construction scenes, etc.). The fact that many artisans working in Italy were in fact of Greek origin, slaves and freedmen, may be reflected in this common and uncomplicated costume. The bare upper torso is common to scenes where the working environment was hot, such as around the baker's oven and the smithy's forge; I have noted above the Greek artist's treatment of analogous scenes. The most common form of artisan's cos-tume of the Roman period is the short tunic, a one-piece garment, about knee length, sleeveless or with short sleeves; it seems to have changed little over centuries of use. Clothing that can be described as protective in function can be cited from a

Figure 2.12. Sandstone relief depicting miners from Palazuelos, near Linares, Spain. Roman period, first or second century. The garments worn by the figures appear to include panniers. (Sandars 1905: pl. 69.)

small and diverse group of monuments from Roman sites: an Ostian tomb shows a man wearing a heavy apron while honing a tool (Zimmer 1985, pl. 4), as does a miller depicted on a funerary monument from Senon (Belgica). A helmet of sorts is worn by one of the men rigging the crane on the Tomb of the Haterii, while a stone relief of miners found in Spain shows the workmen wearing a heavy belt, apparently with deep pockets suitable for tools or even chunks of ore (figure 2.12; Rickard 1928; Sandars 1905). A bronze statuette of a plowman from Trier shows the field laborer protected by a hooded, heavy cape, probably made of leather (figure 2.13; Wild 1985).

A serendipitous combination of factors created the conditions under which a rich corpus of graphic material has survived from the Greco-Roman world for modern scholars of ancient technologies to study. The cultures of both Greece and Rome fostered an enduring tradition in the figural arts. No less important is the fact that representations of human activity included so-called genre scenes that documented activities associated with daily life. These everyday scenes were for the most part painted, carved, or modeled on cheap but durable media: ceramics or stone. It is ironic that other representations by famous artists on the finest of materials—precious metals, fine linens, or polished and fragile frescoes—have, in the majority of cases, not survived. By the Roman period, the rise of an affluent artisan class that tapped into this long-established figural tradition and imitated the elite's penchant

Figure 2.13. Bronze statuette of a plowman from Trier, Germany, wearing what appears to be a leather cape. Height 11.8 cm. Second–third century. Rheinisches Landesmuseum, Trier. (Photograph: Rheinisches Landesmuseum Trier.)

for commemoration produced many of the seminal pieces now so important for the reconstruction of ancient technologies.

# REFERENCES

Adam, J.-P. 1994. *Roman building: Materials and techniques.* Bloomington: Indiana University Press.

Amedick, R. 1991. *Die Sarkophage mit Darstellungen aus dem Menschenleben.* Vol. 4, *Vita Privata.* Berlin: Gebr. Mann.

Barber, E. J. W. 1992. "The Peplos of Athena," in *Goddess and polis: The Panathenaic Festival in ancient Athens.* Princeton: Princeton University Press, 103–17.

Barnett, R. D., E. Bleibtreu, and G. Turner 1998. *Sculptures from the Southwest Palace of Sennacherib at Nineveh.* 2 vols. London: British Museum Press 1998.

Blümner, H. 1875–1887. *Technologie und Terminologie der Gewerbe und Künste bei Griechen und Römern.* 4 vols. Leipzig: B. G. Teubner.

Brommer, F. 1978. *Hephaistos: Der Schmiedegott in der antiken Kunst.* Mainz: Philipp von Zabern.

Brommer, F. 1984. *Herakles II: Die unkanonischen Taten des Helden.* Darmstadt: Wissenschaftliche Buchgesellschaft.

Burford, A. 1972. *Craftsmen in Greek and Roman society.* Ithaca, NY: Cornell University Press.

Carettoni, G, A. M. Colini, L. Cozza, and G. Gatti 1960. *La Pianta Marmorea di Roma Antica.* Rome: Comune di Roma.

Ciarallo, A., and E. De Carolis. 1999. *Homo Faber: Natura, scienza e tecnica nell'antica Pompei.* Milan: Electa.

Clarke, J. 1991. *The houses of Roman Italy, 100 B.C.–A.D. 250.* Berkeley: University of California Press.

Clarke, J. 2003. *Art in the lives of ordinary Romans. Visual Representation and non-elite viewers in Italy, 100 B.C.–A.D. 315.* Berkeley: University of California Press.

Cloché, P. 1931. *Les classes, les métiers, le trafic.* Paris: Les Belles Lettres.

Cook, R. M. 1961. "The 'double-stoking Tunnel' of Greek kilns," *Annual of the British School at Athens* 56: 64–67.

Coulton, J. J. 1977. *Ancient Greek architects at work.* Ithaca, NY: Cornell University Press.

D'Ambra, E. 1988. "A myth for a smith: A Meleager sarcophagus from a tomb in Ostia," *American Journal of Archaeology* 92: 85–100.

D'Ambra, E. 1993. *Private lives, imperial virtues: The frieze of the Forum Transitorium in Rome.* Princeton: Princeton University Press.

D'Ambra, E., and G. P. R. Métraux 2006. *The art of citizens, soldiers and freedmen in the Roman world.* British Archaeological Reports, Intl. Series S1526. Oxford: Archaeopress.

Dobbins, J. J. 1985."A Roman funerary relief of a potter and his wife," *Arts in Virginia* 25: 24–33.

Fava, A. S. 1969. *I simboli nelle monete argentee republicane e la vita dei romani.* Torino: Soprintendenza alle Antichità del Piemonte e Museo Civico di Torino.

Forbes, J. 1955–1964. *Studies in ancient technology.* 9 vols. Leiden: Brill.

Gaitzsch, W. 1980. *Eiserne römische Werkzeuge: Studien zur römischen Werkzeugkunde in Italien und den nördlichen Provinzen des Imperium Romanum.* 2 vols. British Archaeological Reports, Intl. Series S78. Oxford: BAR.

George, M. 2006. "Social identity and the dignity of work in freedman's reliefs," in D'Ambra and Métraux 2006: 19–29.

Goodman, W. L. 1964. *The history of woodworking tools.* London: G. Bell and Sons.

Green, R. 1961. "The Caputi Hydria," *Journal of Hellenic Studies* 81: 73–75.

Haselberger, L. 1994. "Ein Giebelriss der Vorhalle des Pantheon: Die Werkrisse vor dem Augustusmausoleum," *Römische Mitteilungen* 101: 279–308.

Healy, J. 1978. *Mining and metallurgy in the Greek and Roman world.* London: Thames and Hudson.

Hopper, R. J. 1979. *Trade and industry in classical Greece.* London: Thames and Hudson.

Humphrey, J., J. P. Oleson, and A. Sherwood 1998. *Greek and Roman technology: A sourcebook.* New York: Routledge.

Huxley, G. 1959. *Anthemius of Tralles: A study of later Greek geometry.* Greek, Roman and Byzantine Monographs 1. Cambridge, MA: Harvard University Press.

Jensen, W. 1978. "The sculpture from the Tomb of the Haterii," 2 vols. Diss., University of Michigan.

Kampen, N. 1981. *Image and status: Roman working women in Ostia.* Berlin: Gebr. Mann.

Keuls, E. 1983. "Attic vase painting and the home textile industry," in Moon 1983: 209–30.

Kleiner, D. E., and S. B. Matheson (eds.) 1996. *I, Claudia: Women in ancient Rome.* New Haven: Yale University Art Gallery.

Klemm, F. 1964. *A history of western technology.* Cambridge, MA: MIT Press.

Kron, U. 1988. "Sickles in Greek sanctuaries: Votives and cultic instruments," in R. Hägg, *Ancient Greek cult practice from the archaeological evidence. Acta Instituti Atheniensis Regni Sueciae* 8.15: 187–216.

Krukowski, S. 1990. *Pots on pots: Images of pottery-making processes on ancient Greek vases.* http://www.cm.aces.utexas.edu/faculty/skrukowski/writings/pots.html.

Landels, J. G. 2000. *Engineering in the ancient world.* 2nd ed. Berkeley: University of California Press.

Mattusch, C. 1980. "The Berlin Foundry Cup: The casting of Greek bronze statuary in the early fifth century B.C.," *American Journal of Archaeology* 84: 435–44.

Mattusch, C. 1996. *The fire of Hephaistos: Large classical bronzes from North American collections.* Cambridge, MA: Harvard University Art Museums.

Moon, W. (ed.) 1983. *Ancient Greek art and iconography.* Madison: University of Wisconsin Press.

Neuburger, A. 1930. *The technical arts and sciences of the ancients.* Trans. H. L. Brose. New York: Macmillan. Originally published as *Die Technik des Altertums* (Leipzig: 1919).

Noble, J. V. 1988. *The techniques of painted Attic pottery.* London: Thames and Hudson.

Oleson, J. P. 1984. *Bronze Age, Greek and Roman technology: A select, annotated bibliography.* New York: Garland.

Oleson, J. P. 2004. "Well pumps for dummies: Was there a Roman tradition of popular, sub-literary engineering manuals?" in F. Minonzio (ed.), *Problemi di macchinismo in ambito romano.* Como: Comune di Como, Musei Civici, 65–86.

Oleson, J. P. 2005. "Design, materials, and the process of innovation for Roman force pumps," in J. Pollini (ed.), *Terra marique: Studies in art history and marine archaeology in honor of Anna Marguerite McCann.* Oxford: Oxbow, 211–31.

Pollitt, J. J. 1986. *Art in the Hellenistic age.* Cambridge: Cambridge University Press.

Richter, G. M. A. 1923. *The craft of Athenian pottery.* New Haven: Yale University Press.

Rickard, T. A. 1928. "The mining of the Romans in Spain," *Journal of Roman Studies* 18: 129–43.

Richmond, I. 1982. *Trajan's army on Trajan's Column.* London: British School at Rome.

Rossetto, P. C. 1973. *Il Sepolcro del Fornaio Marco Virgilio Eurisace a Porta Maggiore.* Rome: Istituto di Studi Romani Editore.

Sandars, H. 1905. "The Linares bas-relief and Roman mining operations at Baetica," *Archaeologia* 59: 311–32.

Schreiber, T. 1999. *Athenian vase construction: A potter's analysis.* Malibu, CA: J. Paul Getty Museum.

Singer, C., E. J. Holmyard, A. R. Hall, and T. Williams (eds.) 1954–1956. *A history of technology.* Vol. 1, *From early times to fall of ancient empires*; Vol. 2, *The Mediterranean civilizations and the Middle Ages.* Oxford: Oxford University Press.

Strong, D., and D. Brown (eds.) 1976. *Roman crafts.* New York: New York University Press.

Tameanko, M. 1990. "Goldsmith's, mint, or jewelry factory? A new interpretation of the wall painting from the House of the Vettii, Pompeii," *Minerva* 1: 42–46.

Taylor, R. 2003. *Roman builders: A study of architectural process.* Cambridge: Cambridge University Press.

Ulrich, R. 2007. *Roman woodworking.* New Haven: Yale University Press.

Venit, M. S., 1988. "The Caputi Hydria and working women," *Classical World* 81: 265–72.

Veyne, P. (ed.) 1987. *A history of private life.* Vol 1, *From pagan Rome to Byzantium.* Cambridge, MA: Harvard University Press.

White, K. D. 1984. *Greek and Roman technology.* Ithaca, NY: Cornell University Press.

Wild, J. P. 1985. "The clothing of Britannia, Gallia belgica and Germania inferior," in *Aufstieg und Niedergang der römischen Welt* II.12.3. Berlin: Walter de Gruyter, 362–422.

Zimmer, G. 1982. *Römische Berufsdarstellungen.* Archäologische Forschungen 12. Berlin: Gebr. Mann.

Zimmer, G. 1985. "Römische Handwerker," in *Aufstieg und Niedergang der römischen Welt* II.12.3. Berlin: Walter de Gruyter, 205–28.

# CHAPTER 3

# HISTORIOGRAPHY AND THEORETICAL APPROACHES

## KEVIN GREENE

## THE BEGINNINGS OF A "HISTORY OF ANCIENT TECHNOLOGY"

### Historiography

In *Ancient Society*, Lewis Morgan (1877) outlined the evolution of society through stages of savagery, barbarism, and civilization on anthropological rather than archaeological grounds, and he subsequently played an important part in shaping the ideas of Engels and Marx. His opening chapter concluded by looking back from the 1870s, by which time North America, along with Europe, was caught up in the Industrial Revolution. He presented an interesting list of contributions made by Greece and Rome—despite being "found deficient in great inventions and discoveries." The emphasis on social and political as well as material items conforms to modern expectations and is also reminiscent of Douglass North's institutional approach to economic history (1990).

> Passing over the mediaeval period, which gave Gothic architecture, feudal aristocracy with hereditary titles of rank, and a hierarchy under the headship of a pope, we enter the Roman and Grecian civilizations. They will be found deficient in great inventions and discoveries, but distinguished in art, in philosophy, and in

organic institutions. The principal contributions of these civilizations were imperial and kingly government; the civil law; Christianity; mixed aristocratical and
democratical government, with a senate and consuls; democratical government
with a council and popular assembly; the organization of armies into cavalry and
infantry, with military discipline; the establishment of navies, with the practice of
naval warfare; the formation of great cities, with municipal law; commerce on the
seas; the coinage of money; and the state, founded upon territory and upon
property; and among inventions, fire-baked brick, the crane, the water-wheel for
driving mills, the bridge, acqueduct and sewer; lead pipe used as a conduit with
the faucet; the arch, the balance scale; the arts and sciences of the classical period,
with their results, including the orders of architecture; the Arabic numerals, and
alphabetic writing. (Morgan 1877: 30–31)

Morgan reminds us that—unlike Neolithic farming communities, urban civilizations on the Euphrates, or early modern European states engaged in global
trade—classical civilization did not rely on new forms of settlement, technological
developments, or new sources of raw materials. Indeed, a modern consensus considers Greek and Roman culture to have been deeply conservative, disdainful of
labor, and lacking in the spirit of enterprise associated with the growth of capitalism
(Finley 1973). Much of the interest of Greek and Roman technology arises from a
contradiction between this apparent ideological devotion to the pursuit of honorable
leisure and the practical achievements of Greek city-states, Hellenistic kingdoms,
and the Roman Empire. All three states equipped their armies with plentiful weapons
and body armor, built fortifications and civic buildings designed by skilled architects, installed systems for the supply and disposal of water, and maintained de-
pendable communications to deliver agricultural and industrial goods by land, river,
or sea. Analysis of this contradiction is fundamental to understanding Greek and
Roman technology in its wider socioeconomic context, and it is not surprising
to find variations in interpretation at different stages in the history of its study. This
chapter will begin by examining work carried out on Greek and Roman technology
in recent decades, before considering how technology has come to be perceived as
an integral component of the society and economy of the classical world.

## Where Are We Now?

In 1990, I wrote an article about progress in recent publications concerning ancient technology and its interpretation. The opening sentence—"1984 was the year
in which the study of Roman technology emerged from a period of relative
obscurity"—referred to publications by K. D. White, Wikander, and Oleson that
differed in their attitude to Moses Finley's influential assessment of ancient technological stagnation (1965). Oleson (1984), having reviewed Greek and Roman
water-lifting devices, concurred with Finley that ancient technology was, in general,
a failure for social reasons (although he later changed his opinion; Oleson 2000:
287–88). Wikander made use of growing numbers of archaeological discoveries of
Roman water-mills to challenge Finley's judgment that ancient inventions were

not innovated to become technology-in-use. White's *Greek and Roman Technology* brought together a lifetime's work on archaeological evidence and classical texts—much of it summarized in more than 60 pages of appendixes and tables—whose sheer quantity invited a paradigm shift away from Finley. "The reader of these pages, having taken measure of the innovations and development of inventions reviewed in the chapters and tables, may be inclined to take a less unfavourable view of the standards reached by classical architects, builders and engineers, as well as by the farmers, the food processors and the men who built the ships that carried the products of their labours" (K. D. White 1984: 173).

These three publications were singled out because they combined technical and documentary evidence and concurred (implicitly or explicitly) with White's "less unfavourable view." More have appeared since 1984: Hill (*A History of Engineering in Classical and Medieval Times*, 1984; *Islamic Science and Engineering*, 1993) and M. J. T. Lewis (*Millstone and Hammer*, 1997; *Surveying Instruments of Greece and Rome*, 2001) have made particular use of Arabic sources, which are in some cases the only record of Greek technical treatises. Oleson, Lewis, and Wikander were all contributors to a substantial volume titled *Handbook of Ancient Water Technology* (Wikander 2000), which consolidated an enormous amount of archaeological and documentary work conducted in the later twentieth century. Meissner published a comprehensive survey of the nature and context of ancient technical literature in 1996, and specific Roman texts have been subjected to close scrutiny. Fleury's *La mécanique de Vitruve* (1993), which analyzed mechanical devices described in book 10 of *De architectura*, was followed by his study of Vitruvius' technical terms (with Callebat, 1995); a new edition of the entire work, enlivened by diagrams, has been edited by Rowland and Howe (2001). Frontinus' *De aquis urbis Romae* has also been the subject of discussion in a collection of papers edited by Blackman and Hodge (2001), a convincing analysis of its context and purpose by Peachin (2004), and comprehensive new editions by Rodgers (2004) and Del Chicca (2004). Andrew Wilson's paper "Machines, Power and the Ancient Economy" (2002) showed that scholars with expertise in ancient technology could place specialist findings in a clear social and economic setting—and communicate them to a wider audience in the influential *Journal of Roman Studies*.

Many studies of specific technologies appeared during the 1990s and the early years of this century. A good example is harnessing and traction, where analyses of artifacts and iconographic evidence have been followed up by experimental studies with animals. Raepsaet and Rommelaere (1995) Raepsaet and Lambeau (2000), and Raepsaet (2002) have helped counter the widespread condemnation of premedieval harnessing by historians of technology (cf. chapter 23). New understanding of traction methods used in transport and in farming—like Wikander's review of evidence for water-mills—has contributed to a more positive perception of Greek and Roman capabilities. Architecture can also be seen in a new light, thanks to the deduction of working practices from surviving structures in Coulton's *Ancient Greek Architects at Work* (1998), Hellmann's *L'architecture grecque* (2002), Adam's *La construction romaine* (1984; English translation 1994), and Lancaster's *Concrete*

*Vaulted Construction in Imperial Rome* (2005). The logistics of a major Roman imperial building project have been elucidated in DeLaine's *The Baths of Caracalla* (1997), while Shirley's *Building a Roman Legionary Fortress* (2001) takes a similar approach to the very different problem of marshalling building materials (mainly timber) in newly conquered territory in Scotland in the late first century A.D.

The availability of detailed technical works has fortunately been accompanied by a number of introductions to Greek and/or Roman technology. French, German, and Italian readers enjoy a range of accessible and authoritative books: *Sciences et techniques à Rome* (Chevallier 1993), *Einführung in die antike Technikgeschichte* (Schneider 1992, with expert guidance on further reading), *La tecnica in Grecia e a Roma* (Traina 1994, with a strong cultural and historiographical perspective), and *Tecnica e tecnologia nelle società antiche* (Gara 2002). In addition, a revised edition of Landels' *Engineering in the Ancient World* appeared in 2000. Access to original sources referred to in such books has been facilitated by a well-organized annotated sourcebook, *Greek and Roman Technology* (Humphrey et al. 1998). Working replicas of Greek and Roman technical devices have become a popular feature of television programs and resulted in a book (Wilkinson 2000) linked to the BBC's series *What the Romans Did for Us*, which subsequently broadened its scope to include Greece and other civilizations (Hart-Davis 2004). Conversely *The Day the World Took Off*—a sophisticated analysis of the origins of the Industrial Revolution broadcast by Channel 4 in Britain in 2000—skipped directly from the medieval period to Neolithic farming. Hellenistic automata were not even mentioned when comparable eighteenth-century devices were credited with preparing minds for mechanization (Dugan and Dugan 2000: 40–42). At the end of 2005, automata and other products of Greek science and technology were displayed in a major exhibition (unsurprisingly called *Eureka!*) at the National Archaeological Museum in Naples, accompanied by a lavishly illustrated catalogue containing scholarly essays (Lo Sardo 2005). Thus, the academic study of sources and evidence for Greek and Roman technology—and awareness among nonspecialists—has made excellent progress in recent years.

## How Did We Get Here?

The history of archaeology can only be understood in the context of wider intellectual history (Trigger 2006), and the same is true of the study of technology. A sense of awe in the face of classical art, science, technology, and literature characterized European culture from the early medieval period. Schneider (1992: 17–30) traced the history of the subject back to the Renaissance scholar Polydor Vergil (*De rerum inventoribus*, 1499), who included technology in a much wider study of inventions. From Cyriac of Ancona in the fifteenth century to Piranesi or Stuart and Revett in the eighteenth, Greek and Roman structures and works of art were recorded by artists, architects, and antiquarians, whether for their picturesque qualities or for imitation in new buildings (Greene 2002: 8–11). Although Roman authors such as Pliny the Elder and Vitruvius provided extensive information relevant to antiquarians, technical studies from Renaissance treatises to the encyclopaedias of eighteenth-century France maintained a contemporary focus even when they made use of ancient literary sources.

In 1715 a London publisher thought it worthwhile to issue *The History of Many Memorable Things Lost, Which Were in Use among the Ancients*, consisting of a series of lists of "both natural and artificial" items, originally compiled in Italian for the Duke of Savoy by Guido Pancirolli (1523–99), and translated into Latin around 1600. The lost items include manners, clothing, and forms of buildings, but few that would now be considered technological, and the compiler points out that ancient military hardware has been superseded by guns. "Lost" also meant "inaccessible," such as sources of marble under the control of the Turks. The author knew about very large quadriremes and quinqueremes unparalleled in his day, as well as the ox-powered liburnian warship described in the anonymous *De rebus bellicis* (17.1–3), and he retold Roman stories about "unbreakable" glass without skeptical comment (cf. Pliny, *HN* 36.195; Petronius, *Sat.* 50–51; Dio Cassius 57.21.6). Although he knew about the odometer from Vitruvius (*De arch.* 10.9.1–4), evidence for Roman watermills came only indirectly from Procopius and Pliny rather than Vitruvius' full description (*De arch.* 10.5.1–2). The book's contemporary focus was emphasized by a companion volume, *Many Excellent Things Found, Now in Use among the Moderns*. The novelties "now in use" begin with the New World and porcelain, but bezoar stones, rhubarb, sugar, and manna come next, long before printing, spectacles, or guns. The curious arrangement of Pancirolli's lists—and the inclusion of clothes, medicaments, food, and leisure activities—underlines the lack of a perception of technology as a distinct entity in preindustrial Europe.

Ancient technical information was taken sufficiently seriously to be included alongside current mining and metallurgical processes by Agricola in his *De re metallica*, published in Germany in 1556 (Hoover and Hoover 1912; Domergue 1989). Archimedes' water-screw appears to have been reintroduced into early modern Italy as a result of ancient documents (Drake 1976). Pioneering agricultural reformers in eighteenth-century Britain made use of the Roman agronomists, and the *vallus* described by Pliny inspired a labor-saving harvesting machine in Australia as late as the nineteenth century (Jones 1980). Roman technical achievements and organizational abilities were highly regarded, alongside the intellectual and artistic accomplishments of ancient Greece. Daniel Defoe observed the remains of a Roman road at a time when Britain's road system was very poor:

> It is true that the *Romans* being Lords of the World, had the Command of the People, their Persons and their Work, their Cattle and their Carriages; even their Armies were employ'd in these noble Undertakings. . . . But now the Case is alter'd, Labour is dear, Wages high, no Man works for Bread and Water now; our Labourers do not work in the Road, drink in the Brook; so that as rich as we are, it would exhaust the whole Nation to build the Edifices, the Causways, the Aqueducts, Lines, Castles, Fortifications, and other publick Works, which the *Romans* built with very little Expence. (Defoe 1724–1726: 520–21)

It was not until the eighteenth century that Europeans became certain that the changes being brought about by the incipient Industrial Revolution were creating a material existence that not only differed significantly from that of the ancient world but exceeded its achievements. Growing awareness of modern progress threw up a paradox: how could Greece and Rome have been so productive in literature, philosophy, art, architecture, and infrastructural engineering but so deficient in economic and technological awareness (Traina 1994: 10–13)? A comprehensive study of inventions (ancient and modern) was compiled—before the full effects of the Industrial Revolution became discernible—by Johann Beckmann, whose three-volume *Beyträgen zur Geschichte der Erfindungen* was published between 1782 and 1804; further editions and translations soon followed. His command of classical sources was thorough, and accounts of topics such as milling already include most of the references to Antipater, Vitruvius, and others familiar to us today. Other scholars based in Göttingen followed Beckmann's lead in recognizing the importance of socioeconomic factors in inventions and their diffusion, and in assigning a significant role to technology in history (Schneider 1992: 17–18).

Nineteenth-century German philologists took an interest in everyday life and laid the foundations for the history of technology. The most significant publication was Blümner's *Technologie und Terminologie der Gewerbe und Künst bei Griechen und Römern* (1875–1887 and subsequent editions), an exemplary combination of documentary, iconographic, and archaeological evidence. This work coincided with the publication of comprehensive classical dictionaries in France and Germany—Daremberg and Saglio's *Dictionnaire des antiquités grecques et romaines d'après les textes et les monuments* (1877–1919) and the first volumes of Wissowa's revision of Pauly's *Real-Encyclopädie der klassischen Altertumswissenschaft* (1893–1978)—that made occasional use of material evidence. Blümner was particularly interested in materials and production processes, from baking and textiles to stoneworking and metallurgy (Schneider 1992: 19), and the comparative neglect of transport and energy was compensated by the publication in 1899 of *Die Ingenieurtechnik im Alterthum* by his contemporary Merckel, who paid most attention to construction associated with water, roads, and bridges. Although Merckel considered the Greek and Roman periods to be a high point in engineering history, he included earlier civilizations and undertook a concise overview of developments up to his own day (1899: 12–23). In the twentieth century, further German writers (notably Neuberger and Feldhaus) extended their coverage to other ancient civilizations and to ethnographic studies of prehistoric technology, while another specific study of the classical world was provided by Diels' *Antike Technik* (1914)—highly praised by Schneider (1992: 19). Neuberger's wide-ranging *Die Technik des Altertums* (1919) appeared as *The Technological Arts and Sciences of the Ancients* in 1930. Among other early twentieth-century general writers, the American A. P. Usher was unusual in including a discussion of classical technology in his *History of Mechanical Inventions* (1929), preceded by a profound psychological consideration of the process of invention (expanded in 1954). The second of the five volumes of *A History of Technology* (C. Singer et al. 1954–1958) was devoted to the Mediterranean civilizations and the Middle Ages, but by this date expectations had risen: Finley condemned some of its contributors "who, on both external and internal evidence, have never studied, in a systematic way, the ancient world...and so we have a work by museum-keepers and technicians" (1959: 123–24).

Many twentieth-century works concentrated on specific areas of technology or spheres of production, from Drachmann's *Ancient Oil-Mills and Presses* (1932) to Davies's *Roman Mines in Europe* (1935), and combined close scrutiny of ancient sources with growing quantities of archaeological evidence. Specialization continued throughout the twentieth century, and included the remarkable series *Studies in Ancient Technology* produced by Robert Forbes from 1955 to 1964; he considered standard topics such as agriculture and hydraulic technology, alongside themes such heating and lighting, as well as energy and various raw materials. While Schneider was right to describe these volumes as "unzusammenhängende Detailuntersuchungen" (1992: 21), Forbes also wrote general works that drew conclusions about the nature of classical technology (for example, *Man the Maker*, 1950). Drachmann's *The Mechanical Technology of Greek and Roman Antiquity* (1963) improved access to key literary sources, building on his *Ktesibios, Philon and Heron* of 1948. Popular general works included Klemm's *Technik: Eine Geschichte ihrer Probleme* (1954, available in English from 1959) and de Camp's *The Ancient Engineers* in 1960. Both books made extensive use of ancient sources, and discussed Greece and Rome within a wider chronological survey of engineering. By the 1970s, monographs were becoming available on an extraordinarily wide range of specialist topics: examples from 1974 alone include *Blast-Power and Ballistics* (Lindsay), *Gears from the Greeks* (Price), *The Warpweighted Loom* (Hoffman), *Papyrus in Classical Antiquity* (N. Lewis) and *Sur la taille de la pierre antique, mediévale et moderne* (Varène). This trend continued into the 1980s and included the works discussed at the beginning of this chapter. In 1986 Oleson published an extensive, annotated bibliography of Bronze Age, Greek, and Roman technology.

# Themes in the Emergence of a "History of Technology"

## The Ancient Economy

Because economics is a relatively recent discipline, economic histories of periods earlier than the Industrial Revolution were infrequent before the twentieth century, and technology was rarely incorporated into them. Economists, however, have persistently associated innovations (whether technological or organizational) with raising productivity, usually by reducing the costs of human labor, motive power, or raw materials. Marx did much of his writing in London, capital of the world's first industrial nation, while Engels experienced the effects of the Industrial Revolution at first hand while working in Manchester in a textile company—one of the industries most dramatically affected by labor-saving technology between 1750 and 1850. In the early twentieth century, Schumpeter conceptualized economics in terms of business cycles characterized by periods during which "clusters of innovations" prompted recovery after depressions (1939; Ruttan 2001: 64–65). His contemporary Kondratieff defined economic waves of prosperity, recession, depression, and recovery (1935). After 1950, studies of innovation were situated in equilibrium or (to a much smaller extent) evolutionary economics, and the subject was given a boost after 1970 by the desire to stimulate recovery from a worldwide recession.

"Economic history" should be distinguished from sociological studies of "the ancient economy," involving polarized primitive and modern interpretations, which preoccupied German scholarship in the nineteenth and early twentieth centuries (Finley 1979; Derks 2002). A lack of technological inventiveness could be explained quite easily by categorizing Greek and Roman society in terms of primitive households whose economies lacked any capacity for growth. Campaigns against slavery in the nineteenth century highlighted the fact that Greek "democracy" and its esteemed arts and crafts were products of a slave-owning society. Thus, writers who did not share the primitive view of Greek and Roman economic activity tended to attribute a lack of technical development to slavery (a view repeated frequently in the twentieth century—Schneider 1992: 22–29).

Growing demand for economic history in the 1920s was illustrated by the launch of a *History of Civilisation*—comprising more than 50 monographs—which included translations of three French works: *Ancient Greece at Work* (Glotz 1926), *Ancient Rome at Work* (Louis 1927), and *The Economic Life of the Ancient World* (Toutain 1930). All three paid little attention to technology as a component of economic history and sought explanations for failure rather than achievements:

> Ancient industry was never governed by machines, in Alexandria, or earlier in Athens, or later in Rome. There was no inducement to adopt them, for human labour was not scarce or expensive. . . . The absence of machinery prevents the workshop from becoming a big factory, labour from concentrating in great numbers, and wholesale production from killing the work of the family. For machinery is irreconcilable with slavery. . . . The institution of slavery, inherent in the very conception of the city—that is what creates an essential difference between ancient economy and modern. (Glotz 1926: 352, 381)

A recurrent stereotype of Romans as mere imitators accompanies the diagnosis of slavery as a limit to progress:

> The warlike expeditions which led [the Roman] into contact one by one with the most diverse peoples and hewed him paths into the whole world, as it was then known, brought with them technical knowledge of all kinds besides territorial conquests, booty and slaves. . . . To be sure, the small field of knowledge and the

primitive simplicity of manufacturing processes hardly tended to engender that distribution of labour which is the basis of modern industry, but such a division was in any case incompatible with the dominant institution [slavery]. . . . Thus, long before America in the 19th century reached the same conclusion, the Roman world discovered that servile labour in spite of its apparent economic advantages was both onerous and unproductive. (Louis 1927: 5, 11)

The ideas of Louis and Glotz are constrained by a view of industrial development—shared by the contemporary economist Schumpeter—that identified innovation as the key to economic progress.

Finley's *The Ancient Economy* (1973) attributed technological stagnation not to slavery but to a mindset that could not conceptualize economic development in modern terms. This psychological disability included disdain for anything associated with work, including practical applications of technology. Finley's perception was supported not only by ancient texts (cf. Humphrey et al. 1998: 579–97) but also by substantivist economic anthropologists such as Karl Polanyi, a former colleague in the 1930s. His "primitive" stance contrasts with the "modern"/formalist Rostovtzeff, whose *Social and Economic History of the Roman Empire* (1926) made extensive use of archaeological evidence and detected signs of capitalism in the ancient world. The polarized positions of Finley and Rostovtzeff remain highly influential (Storey 2004: 106–9). In 1986 I published *The Archaeology of the Roman Economy* to assess the contribution of archaeological evidence—which had grown rapidly in recent decades—to debates between ancient historians:

> Quite simply, I believe that the level of economic activity revealed by archaeological research makes the "minimalist" approach of historians such as Finley untenable. The economy does not show signs of advance or evolution, simply an intensification of everything that had already existed in Greek and Roman republican times. . . . What is absolutely clear is that no economic history of the Roman empire can ever be written again which does not give the same detailed attention to the results and technical problems involved in archaeology as it does to the textual criticism of Roman documentary sources. (Greene 1986: 170–71)

Since I had not yet scrutinized technological evidence, convergence with the independent publications of K. D. White and others discussed at the beginning of this chapter was encouraging.

## Revolutions and Determinism

As Finley and Schneider's critical comments about the *Oxford History of Technology* and Forbes' *Studies in Ancient Technology* demonstrate, twentieth-century publications were increasingly expected to engage with the historical and cultural context of technology. The 1930s saw the appearance of influential works with a monocausal determinist outlook, notably two by Lefèbvre des Noëttes: *L'attelage, le cheval de selle à travers les âges* (1931) and *De la marine antique à la marine moderne: La révolution du gouvernail* (1935). Ancient harnessing and steering oars were implicitly condemned as inefficient by associating the medieval horse collar and the sternpost rudder with the word "revolution"—an opinion echoed in 1935 by Bloch's claims for the medieval "advent and triumph" of the water-mill, published in the new socioeconomic periodical *Annales*. It was sustained over the next fifty years by Lynn White, Jr. (e.g., *Medieval Technology and Social Change*, 1962) and Jean Gimpel (*La révolution industrielle du Moyen Age*, 1975). Powerful narratives of this kind require the accumulation of overwhelming contrary evidence before a paradigm shift takes place. Wikander and Wilson's documentary and archaeological investigations of water-mills have not yet changed accounts of medieval technology (e.g., Gies and Gies 1994; Landers 2003).

It is hardly surprising that technological determinism became a feature of the period between the two world wars of the twentieth century. Nineteenth-century Scandinavian archaeologists had organized the past on the basis of raw materials into Stone, Bronze, and Iron Ages. Anthropologists had reinforced theories of social evolution with ethnographic descriptions of social structure and material culture. Engels and Marx combined production and social structure to give technical change a dynamic revolutionary role. World War I provided a frightening mirror image of the Industrial Revolution and mass production as enormous numbers of soldiers faced new technical methods for killing them. After the Russian Revolution, competition with the capitalist powers increased Soviet demands for the transformation of industrial and agricultural production by technology. The Marxist archaeologist V. Gordon Childe, who visited the Soviet Union in 1935, had a particularly enduring impact on the interpretation of the past (Greene 1999; Gathercole 1994). Childe's Neolithic and Urban revolutions defined in *Man Makes Himself* (1936) and *What Happened In History* (1942) gave Marxist social evolution a longer pedigree by identifying prehistoric revolutions—unknown to Marx—on the basis of archaeological evidence.

Unsurprisingly, the technology of Greece and Rome appeared insignificant to general commentators who considered that the most important revolutions in technology and economics had taken place in the prehistoric Near East and/or eighteenth-century England. Destrée's *Histoire des techniques* (1980: 41) identified "deux révolutions essentielles: l'une à partir de 7000 ACN, la révolution agricole; l'autre entre 1750 et 1850, la révolution industrielle," a view shared by two Italian surveys (Forti 1963, Mondini 1973). Destrée and other writers emphasize energy and materials; like the Scandinavian Three Age System (anticipated by Greek philosophers), such categorizations bypass the classical world. Lewis Mumford's *Technics and Civilization* described pseudo-archaeological "eotechnic," "paleotechnic," and "neotechnic" phases of technology based on water and wood, coal and iron, and electricity and alloys, respectively (1934: 109–51). For Morgan, the production of iron was "the event of events in human experience, without a parallel, and without an equal, beside which all other inventions and discoveries were inconsiderable" (1877: 43), while Buchanan saw direct production of cast iron around A.D. 1500 as the critical division between the Old Iron Age and the New Iron Age (1992: 16). Merckel, who knew more about Greek and Roman technology than any of these writers, identified an even more precise turning point—6 October 1829—when the success of Stephenson's *Rocket* at the Rainhill trials ushered in the railway age (1899: 4).

## Relevance and Continuity

By the late 1940s, it seemed timely to reconnect technology with humanity, and at the same time to emphasize its continuity and benign aspects, since World War II had risen out of the unstable politics of radical regimes of the Right and Left. The war had been brought to an end by atomic weapons of unparalleled power, developed by a well-organized program of scientific and technical research. By the 1950s, a new conflict was growing between capitalism and communism, which would be fought as much through technology and economics as through military might. Charles Singer, a prominent British historian of science and medicine, was commissioned to prepare *A History of Technology* for Oxford University Press (in five volumes, with the help of an endowment from Imperial Chemical Industries) in the late 1940s:

> The main object of this work is to provide students of technology and applied science with some humane and historical background for their studies. They may thus be helped to realize that the subjects of their special training are parts of a very ancient process and are rooted in many civilizations. . . . [The editors] are convinced of the human value, in our technological civilization, of an under-standing of the methods and skills by which man has attained a gradual easing of his earthly lot through mastery of his natural environment. (C. Singer et al. 1954–1958:1: v)

Singer's emphasis on "a gradual easing" of human conditions by means of technology differs from the inevitable revolutions associated with Marxism. Never-theless, Childe still employed revolutionary vocabulary in his contributions to Singer's first volume—at a time when an avowed Marxist would have lost his job in the United States.

In response to reviews, Derry and Williams produced a single-volume sequel to Singer's five volumes in 1960. It aimed to be "as much a technological history as a history of technology," following an "important modern trend," because techno-logical factors were still "far too little recognized" (v–vi). In common with most general overviews it had a western (primarily European) focus and a tapered chro-nological range with a large modern section (434 pages on the period from 1750 to 1900) and a small prehistoric "tail" (27 pages); early civilizations occupied 40 pages, Greece and Rome 61, and the Middle Ages 71. Other books followed Beckmann by adopting a thematic approach; the Routledge *Encyclopaedia of the History of Technology* (McNeil 1990) was divided into sections, each beginning with a brief summary of its prehistoric or early historical origins. McNeil (1990: 1) echoed the feeling of neglect voiced 30 years earlier by Derry and Williams: "It is strange that, in the study and teaching of history, so little attention is paid to the history of technology.... Technology is all around us: we live in a world in which everything that exists can be classified as either a work of nature or a work of man. There is nothing else." *Technology in Western Civilisation* (Kranzberg and Pursell 1967), which included such distinguished contributors as Forbes, Usher, and Lynn White, Jr., was designed for teaching in the U.S. Armed Forces Institute because "technology has been one of the major determinants in the development of Western civilization; yet only recently has there been a recognition of this fact.... No single available text stressed sufficiently the cultural, economic, and social implications of technology and history" (v). In France, Daumas' five-volume *Histoire générale des techniques* was more metaphysical about continuity: "Si les civilisations sont mortelles, chacune d'elles, avant de succomber à son destin, a préparé un héritage qui n'a jamais été ignoré de celles qui lui ont succédé" (1962: v, repeated on the cover of a low-priced paperback edition in 1996).

## Ethnography and Material Culture

Advances in Greek and Roman archaeology in the nineteenth century were founded on sociological or ethnographic descriptions of everyday life based on ancient written sources but enlarged by material evidence (e.g., Blümner 1911; Marquardt 1879). Ethnography, or more specifically ethnoarchaeology, is now a well-established approach to ancient technologies (e.g., Peacock 1982; cf. chapter 33 here). Scientific analyses of materials and experimental simulations of processes are integrated into mainstream archaeological theory and practice, although confidence in the ability of ethnoarchaeology and experiment to generate direct analogies and explanations has waned since processual approaches have been modified or replaced by symbolic/contextual interpretations (Shennan 1996). The dangers of collecting data in an ethnographic manner and embedding it in explanations derived from ancient documentary sources were highlighted by Bradley (2002) in a study of evidence for Roman fulling (although his use of empirical data was criticized by Wilson 2003). Bradley challenged the "fantasy reconstruction" of a single standardized narrative from scattered and fragmentary material evidence:

> A classical dictionary's "Fulling" presents a bold advertisement of Roman technical ingenuity and aggressive cleanliness. There is no single account in Roman literature of the process of fulling. What we have is a handful of isolated texts and images collected and fused together, as if each bit of evidence were a piece of a jigsaw, just one fraction of a long and rigorous washing-machine programme.... What, archaeologically speaking, counts as a *fullonica* is usually represented by the presence of features which might conceivably have reproduced some or all of the functions described in the dictionary synopsis. (Bradley 2002: 24–25)

Ethnography has enhanced the significance of the material world and artifacts in both anthropology and archaeology: *How Things Tell the Stories of People's Lives* was the subtitle of Janet Hoskins' influential book *Biographical Objects*, which concluded that "an object can thus become more than simply a 'metaphor for the self.' It becomes a pivot for reflexivity and introspection, a tool of autobiographical self-discovery, a way of knowing oneself through things" (1998: 198). Anthropologists adopt a far broader definition of technology than most historians, probably because of the influence of philosophers such as Heidegger, whose definition has been summarized as "the various ways in which I-as-body interact with my environment by means of technologies" (Ihde 1990: 72). Broad definitions are frequently indicated by the plural form "technologies," exemplified in an archaeological context by Crummy and Eckardt's description of sets of Roman cosmetic tools (for nail-cleaning, etc.) as "technologies of the self" (2003).

For several centuries archaeologists have approached material culture through the classification of collections. Classification was accompanied by typology from the early nineteenth century, and typological sequences or stylistic attributions were reinforced by whatever chronological evidence could be obtained from documents or from archaeological excavations (Greene 2002: 140–51). Devices—such as the wood-block force-pump—that were not described in ancient sources still necessitate this kind of approach (Oleson 2004; Stein 2004). Since most of the evidence, however, comes from accidental survivals of pumps in the bottom of wells, emphasis is placed primarily on their construction and performance rather than their invention and innovation.

## Evolution and Progress

Alongside ethnographic and contextual studies of technology, reflection about the nature of change—whether or not it is considered to have been "progress"—has stimulated the exploration of evolutionary ideas. Nineteenth-century ideas about "survival of the fittest" have been refined in the twentieth century into investigations of the selective mechanisms that determine whether businesses and economies succeed or fail, for example in the evolutionary or institutional approaches of modern economists Nelson and Winter (1982; on technology, Nelson 1987) and North (1990). Much thought has also been given to establishing the limits of using biological evolutionary theory to explain technological innovation and change, from pioneers such as George Basalla and Joel Mokyr in the late 1980s and early 1990s to a volume edited by Ziman in 2000. Evolutionary studies are at particular risk from "futurism," whereby the choice of technologies and institutions for study is determined by their contribution to the present, rather than their relevance to the past (Edgerton 1999: 123).

A capacity for adaptation is highly regarded by those who have a teleological perception of human evolution. Some general overviews present technological change in linear, social-evolutionary terms and regard developments before around A.D. 1500 as necessary steps toward the modern world, rather than significant components of their own time. Indeed, Buchanan's *The Power of the Machine* (1992) and Williams' *The Triumph of Invention: A History of Man's Technological Genius* (1987) embody this progressive narrative in their titles. Studies of twenty-first-century global consumerism place considerable emphasis on the origins of the modern world economy, which are generally seen to lie in the early modern period between the Voyages of Discovery and the Industrial Revolution (Berg 2004). Inventions and innovations are plentiful in this period, from infrastructural concerns (such as ship design or banking systems) to patterns of consumption (such as tea drinking and polite table behavior involving fine ceramics). Technological innovations are even more visible with the growth of modern industrial production, when the names of engineers and inventors become well known—Arkwright, Stephenson, Parsons and others.

Rostovtzeff's *Social and Economic History of the Roman Empire* (1926), written by a Russian émigré who had witnessed the 1917 revolution, made many references to social revolution, but had little to say about technology. Negative assessments of Greek and Roman stagnation, rather than progress, in technology were consolidated by Finley in the widely-read periodical *Economic History Review* in 1959 and 1965. The frequency with which his views have been repeated by general historians of technology since the 1960s led me to publish in the same periodical a review of Finley's position in the light of new archaeological evidence (Greene 2000).

## Alternative Technology

In 1992, I published a short paper (Greene 1992) about technology transfer in the Roman Empire that explored the vocabulary of modern development economics and drew attention to useful concepts such as the "technology shelf" (the range of known solutions to technical problems that might be drawn on in differing circumstances: H. Singer 1977). This concept was helpful in explaining why technology did not advance on a single front, and why less "efficient" devices such as hand-mills could coexist with water-powered mechanisms of the kind described by Vitruvius in the first century B.C. A key element in this concept, however, was knowledge: the metaphorical technology shelf only existed in the minds of people aware of the range of products laid out on it. There is a growing consensus that Greek and Roman technical treatises, and perhaps a range of simpler instruction and maintenance manuals, played a major role in promoting awareness of technical solutions to practical problems (e.g., Oleson 2004). In the context of Hellenistic kingdoms and especially in the expanding Roman Empire, the combination of literacy and reference works produced a result observable from archaeological remains: similar devices for water-lifting really were deployed from Egypt to Britain.

Development economics in the second half of the twentieth century was increasingly concerned with mechanisms of technology transfer, and failures led to increased awareness of the importance of contextual factors (as well as tacit knowledge) in people's willingness to entertain change. This awareness paralleled the growth of institutional economics, which related economic progress (measured in essentially free-market capitalist terms) to the existence of appropriate legal and administrative frameworks for businesses to risk investment (North 1990). An opposite effect was the emergence of the appropriate technology movement, inspired by Schumacher's *Small Is Beautiful* (1973), which anticipated the devastating effects of globalization on local social systems, and favored the introduction of technology that would allow a slower form of endogenous growth that benefited internal participants rather than external investors.

In the early twenty-first century, concern has deepened about the conflict between people's addiction to the material benefits of First World industrialization and its unsustainability in the face of global warming and competition for resources. The difficulties involved in bringing about change underline the role of psychological factors, and illustrate how the conceptualization of knowledge is based on belief (Winder 2005: 154). Widely shared beliefs become institutionalized and difficult to change without a phase of major disruption that clears the ground for the acceptance of new beliefs. Winder has described these events as "epiphanies" and the process as the "Phoenix Cycle" (2005: 10–14). Political fear that a Dark Age is a necessary precursor to a Renaissance has led the European Union to invest in research into the nature of innovation in the hope of finding a less disruptive manner of transition (TiGrESS: Time-Geographical approaches to Emergence and Sustainable Societies: Winder 2005).

# THEORY: THE LOSS OF INNOCENCE

By the late twentieth century, the history of technology had become a subject of central importance that could no longer be neglected. Meanwhile, specialized studies of both modern technology and prehistoric material culture had witnessed a rapid growth in sociological and anthropological approaches, frequently combined with postmodern deconstruction (Greene 2004: 157–60). Publications of such work were unlikely to be read by classical archaeologists or ancient historians, and met with resistance from some technological historians (Buchanan 1991). In advocating the practical study of industrial archaeology, Gordon and Malone claimed that the material record is independent and lacks inherent bias (1997: 13–14). Rejection of this stance is central to postprocessual archaeology (e.g., Hodder 1999), for reasons explored in David Clarke's elegant essay "Archaeology: The Loss of Innocence": "Theory exists, in however unsatisfactory a form, in everything that an archaeologist does regardless of region, material, period and culture.... It is this pervasive, central and international aspect of archaeological theory, multiplied by its current weakness, which makes the whole issue of major importance in the further development of the discipline" (Clarke 1973: 17–18).

The very act of compiling a handbook of Greek and Roman technology involves theoretical choices both in its subject matter and its period of study. Division of the past relies on a consensus that a specific period has a coherence that allows it to be considered as an entity—Finley has been criticized for treating the Greek and Roman period as an amorphous whole that allowed him to make generalizations based on evidence and examples plucked from different parts of it. It is difficult to avoid social-evolutionary judgments: Are Greece and Rome direct antecedents of Western civilization, and therefore of special significance in understanding the globalization of European culture after A.D. 1500? And why focus on engineering and technology? Has the rhetoric of Singer or Williams persuaded us that because science and technology are the most significant components of modern industrial civilization, they will provide the key to understanding the classical world? Since explicit terminology is a basic requirement in theoretical discussion, key terms such as discovery, invention, and innovation will be discussed before further approaches to technology are examined.

## Discovery and Invention

*Discovery* suggests the revealing of something that already existed but had not been recognized or conceptualized. In the simplest terms, a technical discovery is most likely to take place in the context of science or as a by-product of a practical process such as smelting metal ores. *Invention* implies originality, and a conscious act of implementing an idea in a new device or process that may well rely on a prior discovery. Invention is an action (although it may require sustained effort) while *innovation* is the process whereby an invention is brought into use: "Nylon . . . was first invented in 1928, but not innovated until 1939" (*Shorter Oxford English Dictionary*, 5th ed.). The meanings of "invention" and "inventor"—from the Latin *invenire* (to come upon, to discover)—have changed little over recent centuries and have never been restricted to technical rather than general intellectual endeavors. The Greek verb *heurisko* is not as specific as the English term "invent," and can mean "found" or "observed." "Innovation"—from *innovare* (to renew, to alter)— has long-established political and economic associations, but its force has been diminished by hyperbolic use of the adjective "innovative" for "new" since the later twentieth century.

Usher included Greek and Roman technology in his pioneering *History of Mechanical Inventions* (1929). Vernon Ruttan (2001: 66) follows Usher (1955) in dismissing both the *transcendentalist concept* (flashes of brilliance from remarkable individuals) and the *mechanistic* view (inventions arising in response to perceived needs), and finds Usher's *cumulative synthesis* approach most attractive. The definition of four steps involved in invention—perception of the problem; setting the stage; the act of insight; and critical revision—provides "a unified theory of the social processes by which 'new things' come into existence, a theory broad enough to encompass the whole range of activities characterized by the terms science, invention, and innovation" (Ruttan 2001: 67–68).

## Technology

"Invention" and "technology" tend to be considered as givens in modern studies; attention is focused on the circumstances that will prompt them and favor their implementation. The focal points are commercial institutions, which are fully conscious of innovation as a key to competitiveness, operating in market economies. Institutions may include research and development (R&D) facilities designed to generate inventions and innovations that might reduce production costs or introduce profitable new products; such activities are encouraged by systems of copyrights and patent laws unknown in ancient Greece or Rome (May 2002). Archaeological and anthropological approaches to technology understandably focus on material objects (Greene 2004; Sigaut 1994), but in the case of innovation theory "the macro-oriented part . . . will rarely relate to the specific form of technology" (Sundbo 1998: 23). Rogers employs modern computing terminology to broaden his definition: "A technology is a design for instrumental action that reduces the uncertainty in the cause–effect relationships involved in achieving a desired outcome. Most technologies have two components: (1) hardware, consisting of the tool that embodies the technology as a material or physical object, and (2) software, consisting of the knowledge base for the tool" (Rogers 1995: 35).

## Innovation

While studies of discovery and invention are concerned with the history of science and/or technology, modern studies of innovation only begin once a new element has been devised. It is important to remember that—in economic thinking—innovation does not require inventions of a technical kind; any new ways of doing things in organizations are significant if their implementation leads to economic growth.

> "Innovation" will here mean the work of developing an invented element for practical and commercial use and of ensuring that the introduction of the element is accepted. In other words, it does not involve the actual invention, or the subsequent introduction of the element by other companies. (Sundbo 1998: 19–20)

> The innovations can also have different characters: 1. Technological (objects). 2. Intellectual, e.g. consultancy. 3. Physical movements (which are not technology), e.g. a new transport (but without a change in technology). 4. Behavioural, e.g. a new strategy for the company's market behaviour or a new organizational structure. (Sundbo 1998: 21)

Concepts of this kind were not articulated in the ancient world (Finley 1973). Furthermore, most artifacts and monuments studied by archaeologists are the results of a complete trajectory of invention, innovation, and diffusion. Classical Greek intellectual innovations in philosophy and science certainly assisted the development of Hellenistic astronomical and mechanical technology, and Roman imperialism involved major changes in behavior, organizational structure, physical movement, and transport. Modern studies of innovation reinforce the view that the *context* of Greek and Roman technology was as important as its content (Greene 1994). As an economic activity, innovation is clearly a social phenomenon requiring a "renewal of social behaviour" on the macro scale as well as individual activities at the micro scale (Sundbo 1998: 1; Winder 2005).

Invention has greater significance if innovation is *path-dependent*, in that the original form of an invention (technological or organizational) exerts a strong controlling influence over all subsequent developments or patterns of innovation. In practice, few ancient technologies were sufficiently complex to exclude alternative inventions. An *evolutionary* approach to the success of innovations incorporates the Darwinian concept of selection, but questions arise over precisely what undergoes selective processes—machines? organizations? working routines? (Ziman 2002). Nevertheless, analyses of invention and innovation that are aware of path dependence and selection are more likely to acknowledge social and behavioral factors and to avoid judgments based on cost factors alone (Ruttan 2001: 117).

## Diffusion and Technology Transfer

> Diffusion is the process by which an innovation is communicated through certain channels over time among the members of a social system. Diffusion is a special type of communication concerned with the spread of messages that are perceived as new ideas. Communication is a process in which participants create and share information with one another in order to reach a mutual understanding. (Rogers 1995: 35)

Rogers emphasizes the two-way nature of communication and describes the creation and sharing of information as *convergence* (1995: xvi–xvii). The implications lead directly into a social rather than technological perception of the diffusion of innovations, which are "gradually worked out through a process of social construction" (Rogers 1995: xvii). "Technology transfer" has become associated with the process of diffusing material equipment and intellectual knowledge from developed economies to the Third World in the later twentieth century (e.g., H. Singer 1977; Greene 1992).

Ruttan has drawn attention to the fact that "the tacit character of much technical knowledge can represent a major obstacle to the rapid interregional or international transfer of technical capability" (2001: 168). The preclassical civilizations of Mesopotamia and Egypt were characterized by a considerable amount of tacit knowledge encoded in written form, accessible to a literate minority, which became available to early Greece only through interactions with its eastern neighbors. The Hellenistic eastern Mediterranean region (and successor Roman provinces and the Byzantine Empire in that area) inherited much technical and scientific literature written in Greek that was not translated into Latin, and reached western Europe only during the Renaissance. Thus, innovation is inextricably connected to technology transfer, given that an invention or discovery cannot be innovated without the communication of knowledge between receptive practitioners (Winder 2005). That communication must include essential tacit knowledge, of course, for example the industrial processes involved in making molded *terra sigillata* understood by skilled slaves who were established in branch workshops in Lyon by their Italian owners (Desbat et al. 1997).

## Technological Theory: Social Construction

> By its nature contextual history is a vulnerable process in which the historian is deeply affected by the humanity of the subject matter. To reject as ahistorical the ideology of autonomous progress is to recognize that technological designs are intimately woven into the human tapestry and that all of the actors in the drama, including the storyteller, are affected by tensions between design and ambience. (Staudenmaier 1985, 201)

Like Foucault's general history of discourses (1970, 1972), Bradley's specific study of fulling underlined the way that interpretations have been constructed according to a changing consensus about the constitution of knowledge. This concept is a commonplace in anthropological approaches to modern technology (e.g., Latour's *Science in Action: How to Follow Scientists and Engineers through Society*, 1987; Grint and Woolgar's *The Machine at Work*, 1997). These writers are particularly interested in the sociocultural or infrastructural side of technology, notably where it impacts on technology transfer or innovation (e.g., Tann 1995, or Hughes 1992). Such works rarely look beyond modern industrial societies, although Schürmann's specialized study of Hellenistic mechanical devices (1991) did organize them according to their social or ritual functions.

If much theoretical writing about the history of technology has little time depth, how can it assist in the study of Greece and Rome? The approach most compatible with the thinking of archaeologists and ancient historians is the Social Construction of Technology (conveniently abbreviated to SCOT) or Social Shaping of Technology (SST) (Fox 1996; Greene 2004). SCOT is associated with a collection of "classic" papers edited by Bijker, Hughes, and Pinch in 1987, and its agenda is encapsulated in the title of one chapter: "The Social Construction of Facts and Artifacts: Or How the Sociology of Science and the Sociology of Technology Might Benefit Each Other" (Pinch and Bijker 1987). It requires acceptance of the view that technology is not an independent force that shapes society (i.e., technological determinism: Smith and Marx 1994); the focus of interest is the social shaping *of* technology.

A shift from determinism to social production reflects wider intellectual changes. Critical Theory, hermeneutics, and phenomenology undermined positivism throughout the social sciences and humanities in the second half of the twentieth century. In archaeology, a division opened up between New Archaeology (processualism) and a diffuse range of approaches described as interpretive or postprocessual between 1970 and 1980 (Greene 2002: 243–66). The focus on humans shifted from groups, caught up in ecological systems that determined the form of their social and economic organization, to "knowledgeable actors" engaged in a dynamic interaction whereby they shaped the world in addition to being shaped by it (Johnson 2004; Bintliff 2004). A collection of studies edited by Lemonnier (1993) conveyed this active role in its title, *Technological Choices*:

> Because technical actions under construction as well as changes in technology are in part determined or encompassed by social representations or phenomena that go far beyond mere action on matter, societies seize, adopt or develop certain technological features (principles of action, artefacts, gestures) and dismiss others. It is as though societies *chose* from a whole range of possible technological avenues that their environment, their own traditions and contacts with foreigners lay open to their means of action on the material world. (Lemonnier 1993: 6)

While the concept of individuals as actors might seem far removed from Greco-Roman technology, M. J. T. Lewis's observations about the products of the Museum at Alexandria indicate considerable complexities in the relationships between royal patrons and scientists/engineers (2000). Engineering simultaneously involved prestige, gained from working on military equipment and automata for court displays, and the negative associations of utility and work. Although the primary purpose of the devices associated with Hellenistic Alexandria was to entertain diners and to impress worshippers in temples (Schürmann 1991), Lewis emphasized their importance in demonstrating important scientific principles. Thus, Greek "fine engineering" was not only concerned with "respectable" pursuits such as the design of instruments for astronomy; interactions took place between practical work and theoretical science, and between peasant labor and royal leisure.

Oleson (2004, 2005) explored the relationship between Ctesibian force-pumps made from metal tubes (which are well documented in ancient sources and known from a small number of archaeological finds) and force-pumps created by drilling chambers in a solid block of oak (known from a larger number of archaeological finds but undocumented in antiquity). The latter display considerably greater uniformity in design and dimensions than bronze pumps, leading Oleson to posit the existence of "subliterary" technical manuals that have not survived alongside the treatises of Heron and others. This genre presumably circulated among the large numbers of literate military and civilian architects, engineers, and craft workers who moved around the Roman Empire, leaving ample signs of literacy at relatively humble social levels (Harris 1989, 1993). Thus, the variability and complexity of the social embeddedness of science, technology, and craft activities in the Greek and Roman periods make it difficult to study technology from any perspective *other* than "social construction."

## "Technology-in-Use"

> The histories of innovation and of technology-in-use are remarkably different, in terms of geography, chronology, and sociology. (Edgerton 1999: 115)

Although it is clearly essential to have achieved a proper understanding of the significance of the terms *invention* and *innovation*, even more is to be gained from exploring *use*. David Edgerton, whose work has an entirely twentieth-century focus, first published "From Innovation to Use: Ten Eclectic Theses on the Historiography of Technology" in French in *Annales* in 1998; it subsequently appeared in English (1999) and several other languages. He believes that "most (Anglo-Saxon) historiography of technique is concerned with innovation rather than technology, which, because of a failure to differentiate the two, leads to very unfortunate results" (111).

Edgerton's Thesis I provides considerable encouragement to the archaeological study of technology:

> The study of the relations of technology and society must necessarily deal with technology which is in widespread use. However, most writing on the history of technology and on the relations of technology and society is concerned with innovation, with the emergence of new technologies. It fails to distinguish this from the study of technology in widespread use, which is necessarily old, and is often seen as out-of-date, obsolete, and merely persisting. (Edgerton 1999: 112)

Archaeological discoveries of technology-in-use have given us indications of the geographical diffusion of devices described in treatises originating in (or inspired by) the Museum at Alexandria. Thus, we know that large compartmented wheels were employed to drain deep mines in Spain and Wales, bucket-chains lifted water at Cosa in Italy and London in Britain, and geared water-mills ground wheat at Roman villas in Provence and near forts on Hadrian's Wall. The study of technology-in-use rather than innovation "also involves a massive shift in social class, social status, gender and race of people involved with technology" (Edgerton 1999: 116). The apparent paradox that most "Greek" technology is found in the Roman period is elucidated by Edgerton's observation that "rapid innovation need not correspond to periods of rapid productivity growth; innovations will have the greatest impact on productivity growth at the time of the fastest diffusion, which typically takes place long after innovation" (1999: 115).

On a broader cultural scale, Thesis III—"The conflation of innovation and technology is especially apparent in national histories" (Edgerton 1999: 117)—helps to release historians from narratives contrasting Greek inventiveness with Roman practicality. The contribution of Mesopotamian and Egyptian water technology to the work of individuals such as Archimedes or Philon is undisputed, but Hellenistic Greece is never criticized for benefiting from technology transfer. The fact that Hellenistic technology was innovated and diffused much later in a Roman imperial context should be seen in a positive light. The use of automata invented in Alexandria for courtly entertainments and as "temple toys" merely illustrates the time lag between the development of new technology and its impact on economic growth. The diffusion of Hellenistic inventions and innovations took place in the context of Roman political institutions, and was facilitated by the long-distance communication of know-how by the movement of people, literacy, and technical manuals in the context of an expanding empire. The disjointed trajectory of technology transfer, invention, innovation, and diffusion tells us nothing about the relative quality of thought in Greece and Rome, especially when it is measured by modern historians of technology who put priority on novelty and sophistication over established functionality.

Archaeologists are constantly involved in the study of "processes of maintenance, repair, remodeling, re-use, and re-cycling [that] have been fundamental to material culture, but are obliterated by the emphasis on initial creation" (Edgerton 1999: 120). Technical changes brought about as a result of everyday use and experience rather than abstract thought may explain the development of lewis holes for lifting heavy blocks of stone, force-pumps made from wooden blocks rather than bronze tubes, parchment codices rather than papyrus rolls, or hollow glass vessels blown from molten blobs rather than molded or formed around a core. Thus, archaeological studies of long-term change accord well with Edgerton's Thesis VIII: "Invention and innovation rarely lead to use, but use often leads to invention and innovation" (1999: 123). Studies of use rather than invention also avoid the pitfall of "technological futurism" because they avoid being "systematically biased by the future in that we study innovations which succeed later." Futurist studies place unreasonable expectations on the ancient world by scrutinizing Greek and Roman inventions for signs of progress or stagnation (Greene 1993, 2000).

As noted above, judgments about inventiveness also lead to ideas about technological determinism, which Edgerton's Thesis VI usefully dismisses as "primarily a theory of society, not a theory of technology." He notes, however, that "refuting innovation-determinism is much simpler. First, only a small minority of innovations are widely used; second, the extent of use surely determines the extent of the effect, not the act of innovation" (Edgerton 1999: 121). Andrew Wilson's clear exposition of the importance of machinery in supporting the political structure of the Roman Empire by guaranteeing supplies of bullion for coinage is good example of a study of effect—and therefore use—rather than innovation (Wilson 2002: 29):

> The corollary is that, by contrast, the economic performance of the first and second century, and to a certain degree the high level of imperial or state spending—on the army, construction works, the annona, etc.—was partly dependent on the use of advanced technology and industrial-scale operation in the mines. The importance of technology to the ancient economy, and to wider historical processes, can be measured by what happened when the larger-scale hydraulic mining operations were no longer active.

The lesson to be learned from these brief intimations of theoretical complexity is that it is important for researchers, writers, and readers to have an awareness of their own ways of understanding history—starting with an appreciation of the subtleties of terms such as "innovation." Does natural selection govern cultural as well as biological processes? Is progress inherent in the activities of humans? Do political systems move from one equilibrium state to another, or does chaotic collapse normally occur? Does economic change take place in a smooth linear manner, proceed by steps, undergo revolutionary jumps, or pass through repeating cycles of growth, flowering and decline? Abstract questions of this kind should be considered as part of any investigation of evidence for Greek and Roman technology.

# REFERENCES

Adam, J.-P. 1984. *La construction romaine.* Paris: Picard.

Adam, J.-P. 1994. *Roman building: Materials and techniques.* Trans. A. Mathews. London: Routledge.

Basalla, G. 1988. *The evolution of technology.* Cambridge: Cambridge University Press.

Beckmann, J. 1782–1804. *Beyträge zur Geschichte der Erfindungen.* 3 vols. Leipzig: Kummer.

Berg, M. 2004. "In pursuit of luxury: Global history and British consumer goods in the eighteenth century," *Past and Present* 182: 85–142.

Bijker, W., T. P. Hughes, and T. Pinch (eds.) 1987. *The social construction of technological systems: New directions in the sociology and history of technology.* Cambridge, MA: MIT Press.

Bintliff, J. 2004. "Time, structure, and agency: The Annales, emergent complexity, and archaeology," in J. Bintliff (ed.), *A companion to archaeology.* Oxford: Blackwell, 174–94.

Blackman, D. R., and A. T. Hodge (eds.) 2001. *Frontinus' legacy: Essays on Frontinus' 'De aquis urbis Romae.'* Ann Arbor: University of Michigan Press.

Bloch, M. 1935. "Avènement et conquêtes du moulin à eau," *Annales* 7: 538–63.

Blümner, H. 1875–1887. *Technologie und Terminologie der Gewerbe und Künst bei Griechen und Römern.* 4 vols. Leipzig: Teubner.

Blümner, H. 1911. *Die römischen Privataltertümer.* Munich: Beck.

Bradley, M. 2002. " 'It all comes out in the wash': Looking harder at the Roman fullonica," *Journal of Roman Archaeology* 15: 20–44.

Buchanan, R. A. 1991. "Theory and narrative in the history of technology," *Technology and Culture* 32: 365–76.

Buchanan, R. A. 1992. *The power of the machine: The impact of technology from 1700 to the present.* London: Viking.

Callebat, L., and P. Fleury 1995. *Dictionaire des termes techniques du 'De architectura' de Vitruve.* Hildesheim: Olms-Weidmann.

Chevallier, R. 1993. *Sciences et techniques à Rome.* Paris: Presses Universitaires de France.

Childe, V. G. 1936. *Man makes himself.* London: Watts Library of Science and Culture.

Childe, V. G. 1942. *What happened in history.* Harmondsworth: Penguin.

Clarke, D. L. 1973. "Archaeology: The loss of innocence," *Antiquity* 47: 6–18.

Coulton, J. J. 1988. *Ancient Greek architects at work.* Oxford: Oxbow.

Crummy, N., and H. Eckardt 2003. "Regional identities and technologies of the self: Nail-cleaners in Roman Britain," *Archaeological Journal* 160: 44–69.

Daumas, M. (ed.) 1962. *Histoire générale des techniques*. Vol. 1, *Des origines au XVe siècle*. Paris: Presses Universitaires de France.

Davies, O. 1935. *Roman mines in Europe*. Oxford: Clarendon Press.

de Camp, L. Sprague. 1960. *The ancient engineers*. New York: Doubleday.

Defoe, D. 1724–1726. *A tour through the whole island of Great Britain*. London. Edited by G. D. H. Cole. London: Davies, 1927. 2 vols.

DeLaine, J. 1997. *The Baths of Caracalla: A study in the design, construction, and economics of large-scale building projects in imperial Rome. Journal of Roman Archaeology* Suppl. 25. Ann Arbor, MI: JRA.

Del Chicca, F. 2004. *Frontino, De aquae ductu Urbis Romae: Introduzione, testo critico, traduzione e commento*. Rome: Herder.

Derks, H. 2002. " 'The ancient economy': The problem and the fraud," *The European Legacy* 7.5: 597–620.

Derry, T. K., and T. I. Williams 1960. *A short history of technology from the earliest times to AD 1900*. Oxford: Oxford University Press.

Desbat, A., M. Génin, and J. Lasfargues (eds.) 1997. *Les productions des ateliers de potiers antiques de Lyon, 1ère partie: Les ateliers précoces. Gallia* 53. Paris: CNRS.

Destrée, A. (ed.) 1980. *Histoire des techniques*. Brussels: Medders.

Diels, H. 1914. *Antike Technik*. Leipzig/Berlin: Teubner.

Domergue, C. 1989. "Les techniques minières antiques et la *De re metallica* d'Agricola," in C. Domergue (ed.), *Minería y metalurgia en las antiguas civilizaciones mediterraneas y europeas*. Madrid: Ministerio de Cultura, 2:76–95.

Drachmann, A. G. 1932. *Ancient oil-mills and presses*. Copenhagen: E. Munksgaard.

Drachmann, A. G. 1948. *Ktesibios, Philon and Heron: A study in ancient pneumatics*. Copenhagen: E. Munksgaard.

Drachmann, A. G. 1963. *The mechanical technology of Greek and Roman antiquity: A study of the literary sources*. Copenhagen: E. Munksgaard.

Drake, S. 1976. "An agricultural economist of the late Renaissance," in L. T. White, B. S. Hall, and D. C. West (eds.), *On pre-modern technology and science: A volume of studies in honor of Lynn White Jr.* Malibu, CA: Undena.

Dugan, S., and D. Dugan 2000. *The day the world took off: The roots of the Industrial Revolution*. London: Channel 4 Books.

Edgerton, D. 1999. "From innovation to use: Ten eclectic theses on the historiography of technology," *History and Technology* 16.2: 111–36.

Finley, M. I. 1959. "Technology in the ancient world," *Economic History Review* 12: 120–25.

Finley, M. I. 1965. "Technical innovation and economic progress in the ancient world," *Economic History Review* 18: 29–45.

Finley, M. I. 1973. *The ancient economy*. London: Chatto and Windus.

Finley, M. I. 1979. *The Bücher-Meyer controversy*. New York: Arno Press.

Fleury, P. 1993. *La mécanique de Vitruve*. Caen: Centre d'Études et de Recherche sur l'Antiquité, Université de Caen.

Forbes, R. J. 1950. *Man the maker: A history of technology and engineering*. London: Constable.

Forbes, R. J. 1955–1964. *Studies in ancient technology*. 9 vols. Leiden: Brill.

Forti, U. 1963. *Tecnica e progresso umano*. Vol. 1, *La tecnica nelle preistoria e nell'antichita*. Milan: Fratelli Fabbri Editori.

Foucault, M. 1970. *The order of things: An archaeology of the human sciences*. London: Tavistock Publications.

Foucault, M. 1972. *The archaeology of knowledge.* London: Tavistock Publications.

Fox, R. 1996. "Introduction: Methods and themes in the history of technology," in R. Fox (ed.), *Technological change: Methods and themes in the history of technology.* Amsterdam: Harwood Academic, 1–15.

Gara, A. 2002. *Tecnica e tecnologia nelle società antiche.* Milan: CUEM.

Gathercole, P. 1994. "Childe in history" (Sixth Gordon Childe Memorial Lecture), *Bulletin of the Institute of Archaeology, University of London* 31: 25–52.

Gies, R., and J. Gies 1994. *Cathedral, forge, and waterwheel: Technology and invention in the Middle Ages.* New York: Harper Collins.

Gimpel, J. 1975. *La révolution industrielle du Moyen Age.* Paris: Éditions de Seuil.

Glotz, G. 1926. *Ancient Greece at work: An economic history of Greece from the Homeric period to the Roman conquest.* London: Kegan Paul, Trench, Trubner and Co.

Gordon, R. B., and P. M. Malone 1997. *The texture of industry: An archaeological view of the industrialization of North America.* New York: Oxford University Press.

Greene, K. 1986. *The archaeology of the Roman economy.* London: Batsford.

Greene, K. 1990. "Perspectives on Roman technology," *Oxford Journal of Archaeology* 9: 209–19.

Greene, K. 1992. "How was technology transferred in the Roman empire?" in M. Wood and F. Queiroga (eds.), *Current research on the Romanization of the western provinces.* British Archaeological Reports, Intl. Series S575. Oxford: BAR, 101–5.

Greene, K. 1993. "The study of Roman technology: Some theoretical constraints," in E. Scott (ed.), *Theoretical Roman archaeology: First conference proceedings.* Aldershot: Avebury, 39–47.

Greene, K. 1994. "Technology and innovation in context: The Roman background to mediaeval and later developments," *Journal of Roman Archaeology* 7: 22–33.

Greene, K. 1999. "V. Gordon Childe and the vocabulary of revolutionary change," *Antiquity* 73: 97–109.

Greene, K. 2000. "Technological innovation and economic progress in the ancient world: M. I. Finley reconsidered," *Economic History Review* 53: 29–59.

Greene, K. 2002. *Archaeology: An introduction.* 4th ed. London: Routledge.

Greene, K. 2004. "Archaeology and technology," in J. Bintliff (ed.), *Blackwell companion to archaeology.* Oxford: Blackwell, 155–73.

Grint, K., and S. Woolgar 1997. *The machine at work: Technology, work and organisation.* Cambridge: Polity Press.

Harris, W. V. 1989. *Ancient literacy.* Cambridge, MA: Harvard University Press.

Harris, W. V. (ed.) 1993. *The inscribed economy: Production and distribution in the Roman empire in the light of instrumentum domesticum. Journal of Roman Archaeology* Suppl. 6. Ann Arbor, MI: JRA.

Hart-Davis, A. 2004. *What the ancients did for us: A brief history of ancient inventions.* London: BBC Books.

Hellmann, M.-C. 2002. *L'Architecture grecque.* Vol. 1, *Les principes de la construction.* Paris: Picard.

Hill, D. R. 1984. *A history of engineering in classical and medieval times.* London: Routledge.

Hill, D. R. 1993. *Islamic science and engineering.* Edinburgh: Edinburgh University Press.

Hodder, I. 1999. *The archaeological process: An introduction.* Oxford: Blackwell.

Hoffman, M. 1974. *The warpweighted loom: Studies in the history and technology of an ancient implement.* Oslo: Robin and Russ Handweavers.

Hoover, H. C., and L. H. Hoover 1912. *Agricola's De re metallica, translated from the first Latin edition of 1556.* London: The Mining Magazine.

Hoskins, J. 1998. *Biographical objects: How things tell the story of people's lives*. New York: Routledge.

Hughes, T. P. 1992. "The dynamics of technological change: Salients, critical problems and industrial revolutions," in G. Dosi, R. Giannetti, and P. Toninelli (eds.), *Technology and enterprise in a historical perspective*. Oxford: Clarendon, 97–118.

Humphrey, J. W., J. P. Oleson, and A. N. Sherwood 1998. *Greek and Roman technology: A sourcebook*. London: Routledge.

Ihde, D. 1990. *Technology and the life world: From garden to earth*. Bloomington: Indiana University Press.

Johnson, M. 2004. "Archaeology and social theory," in J. Bintliff (ed.), *Blackwell companion to archaeology*. Oxford: Blackwell, 92–109.

Jones, L. J. 1980. "John Ridley and the south Australian 'stripper,' " *History of Technology* 5: 55–101.

Klemm, F. 1954. *Technik: Eine Geschichte ihrer Probleme*. Freiburg: K. Alber.

Klemm, F. 1959. *A history of western technology*. London: George Allen and Unwin.

Kondratieff, N. D. 1935. "The long waves in economic life," *Revue of Economic Statistics* 17.6: 105–15.

Kranzberg, M., and C. W. Pursell (eds.) 1967. *Technology in western civilization*. Vol. 1, *The emergence of modern industrial society, earliest times to AD 1900*. New York: Oxford University Press.

Lancaster, L. 2005. *Concrete Vaulted Construction in Imperial Rome: Innovations in Context*. Cambridge: Cambridge University Press.

Landels, J. G. 2000. *Engineering in the Ancient World*. 2nd ed. Berkeley: University of California Press.

Landers, J. 2003. *The field and the forge: Population, production, and power in the pre-industrial west*. Oxford: Oxford University Press.

Latour, B. 1987. *Science in action: How to follow scientists and engineers through society*. Cambridge, MA: Harvard University Press.

Lefebvre des Noëttes, Ct. 1931. *L'attelage, le cheval de selle a travers les ages*. 2 vols. Paris: Picard.

Lefebvre des Noëttes, Ct. 1935. *De la marine antique a la marine moderne: La revolution du gouvernail*. Paris: Masson.

Lemonnier, P. (ed.) 1993. *Technological choices: Transformations in material cultures since the Neolithic*. London: Routledge.

Lewis, M. J. T. 1997. *Millstone and hammer: The origins of water power*. Hull: Hull University Press.

Lewis, M. J. T. 2000. "The Hellenistic period," in Wikander 2000: 631–48.

Lewis, M. J. T. 2001. *Surveying instruments of Greece and Rome*. Cambridge: Cambridge University Press.

Lewis, N. 1974. *Papyrus in classical antiquity*. Oxford: Clarendon

Lindsay, J. 1974. *Blast-power and ballistics: Concepts of force and energy in the ancient world*. London: Frederick Muller.

Lo Sardo, E. (ed.) 2005. *Eureka! Il genio degli antichi*. Naples: Electa.

Louis, P. 1927. *Ancient Rome at work: An economic history of Rome from the origins to the Empire*. London: Kegan Paul, Trench, Trubner and Co.

Marquardt, J. 1879. *Das Privatleben der Römer*. Leipzig: S. Hirzel.

May, C. 2002. "Antecedents to intellectual property: The European pre-history of the 'ownership' of knowledge," *History of Technology* 24: 1–20.

McNeil, I. (ed.) 1990. *An encyclopaedia of the history of technology*. London: Routledge.

Meissner, B. 1996. *Die technologische Fachliteratur der Antike*. Berlin: Akademie Verlag.

Merckel, C. 1899. *Die Ingenieurtechnik im Alterthum*. Berlin: Julius Springer.

Mokyr, J. 1990. *The lever of riches: Technological creativity and economic progress*. Oxford: Oxford University Press.

Mondini, A. 1973. *Storia della tecnica*. Vol. 1, *Dalla preistoria all'anno mille*. Turin: Editrice Torinese.

Morgan, L. H. 1877. *Ancient society; or, Researches in the lines of human progress from savagery through barbarism to civilization*. New York: Henry Holt.

Mumford, L. 1934. *Technics and civilization*. London: Routledge and Kegan Paul.

Nelson, R. R. 1987. *Understanding technical change as an evolutionary process*. Amsterdam: New Holland.

Nelson, R. R., and S. Winter 1982. *An evolutionary theory of economic change*. Cambridge, MA: Harvard University Press.

Neuberger, A. 1919. *Die Technik des Altertums*. Leipzig: Voigtlander.

Neuberger, A. 1930. *The technological arts and sciences of the ancients*. Trans. H. L. Brose. London: Methuen.

North, D. C. 1990. *Institutions, institutional change and economic performance*. Cambridge: Cambridge University Press.

Oleson, J. P. 1984. *Greek and Roman mechanical water-lifting devices: The history of a technology*. Toronto: University of Toronto Press.

Oleson, J. P. 1986. *Bronze Age, Greek and Roman technology: A select, annotated bibliography*. New York: Garland.

Oleson, J. P. 2000. "Water lifting," in Wikander 2000, 217–302.

Oleson, J. P. 2004. "Well-pumps for dummies: Was there a Roman tradition of popular sub-literary engineering manuals?" in F. Minonzio (ed.), *Problemi di macchinismo in ambito romano*. Archaeologia dell'Italia Settentrionale 8. Como: Comune di Como, 65–86.

Oleson, J. P. 2005. "Design, materials, and the process of innovation in Roman force pumps," in J. Pollini (ed.), *Terra marique: Studies in art history and marine archaeology in honor of Anna Marguerite McCann*. Oxford: Oxbow Press, 211–31.

Pancirolli, G., and H. Salmuth 1715. *The history of many memorable things lost, which were in use among the ancients, and an account of many excellent things found, now in use among the moderns, both natural and artificial*. 2 vols. London: John Morphew.

Peachin, M. 2004. *Frontinus and the curae of the curator aquarum*. Stuttgart: Steiner.

Peacock, D. P. S. 1982. *Pottery in the Roman world: An ethnoarchaeological approach*. London: Longman.

Pinch, T. J., and W. E. Bijker 1987. "The social construction of facts and artifacts: Or how the sociology of science and the sociology of technology might benefit each other," in W. Bijker, T. P. Hughes, and T. Pinch (eds.), *The social construction of technological systems*. Cambridge, MA: MIT Press, 17–31.

Price, D. J. de Solla. 1974. *Gears from the Greeks: the Antikythera Mechanism—A calendar computer from c 80 BC*. Transactions of the American Philosophical Society, n.s. 64.7. Philadelphia: American Philosophical Society.

Raepsaet, G. 2002. *Attelages et techniques de transport dans le monde gréco-romaine*. Brussels: Le Livre Timperman.

Raepsaet, G., and F. Lambeau (eds.) 2000. *La moissonneuse gallo-romaine*. Bruxelles: Université Libre de Bruxelles.

Raepsaet, G., and C. Rommelaere (eds.) 1995. *Brancards et transport attelé entre Seine et Rhin de l'Antiquité au Moyen Age: Aspects archéologiques, économiques et techniques*. Treignes: Ecomusée de Treignes.

Rodgers, R. H. 2004. *Frontinus De aquaeductu urbis Romae*. Cambridge Classical Texts and Commentaries 42. Cambridge: Cambridge University Press.

Rogers, E. M. 1995. *Diffusion of innovations*. 4th ed. New York: Free Press.

Rostovtzeff, M. 1926. *Social and economic history of the Roman empire*. Oxford: Oxford University Press.

Rowland, I. D., and T. Noble Howe (eds.) 2001. *Vitruvius: Ten Books on Architecture*. Cambridge: Cambridge University Press.

Ruttan, V. W. 2001. *Technology, growth, and development: an induced innovation perspective*. New York: Oxford University Press.

Schneider, H. 1992. *Einführung in die antike Technikgeschichte*. Darmstadt: Wissenschaftliche Buchgesellschaft.

Schumacher, E. F. 1973. *Small is beautiful: A study of economics as if people mattered*. London: Blond and Briggs.

Schumpeter, J. A. 1939. *Business cycles: A theoretical, historical and statistical analysis of the capitalist process*. 2 vols. New York: McGraw-Hill.

Schürmann, A. 1991. *Griechische Mechanik und antike Gesellschaft: Studien zur staatlichen Förderung einer technischen Wissenschaft*. Boëthius 27. Stuttgart: Franz Steiner.

Shennan, S. (ed.) 1996. *Symbolic aspects of early technologies*. Special issue, *World Archaeology* 27.1. London: Routledge.

Shirley, E. 2001. *Building a Roman legionary fortress*. Stroud: Tempus.

Sigaut, F. 1994. "Technology," in T. Ingold (ed.), *Companion encyclopedia of anthropology*. London: Routledge, 420–59.

Singer, C., E. J. Holmyard, A. R. Hall, and T. I. Williams (eds.) 1954–1958. *A history of technology*. 5 vols. Oxford: Clarendon.

Singer, H. 1977. *Technologies for basic needs*. Geneva: UN International Labour Office.

Smith, M. Roe, and L. Marx (eds.) 1994. *Does technology drive history? The dilemma of technological determinism*. Cambridge, MA: MIT Press.

Staudenmaier, J. M. 1985. *Technology's storytellers: Reweaving the human fabric*. Cambridge, MA: Society for the History of Technology and MIT Press.

Stein, R. 2004. "Roman wooden force pumps: A case-study in innovation," *Journal of Roman Archaeology* 17: 221–50.

Storey, G. R. 2004. "Roman economies: A paradigm of their own," in G. M. Feinman and L. M. Nicholas (eds.), *Archaeological perspectives on political economies*. Salt Lake City: Utah University Press, 105–28.

Sundbo, J. 1998. *The theory of innovation: Entrepreneurs, technology and strategy*. Cheltenham: Edward Elgar.

Tann, J. 1995. "Space, time and innovation characteristics: The contribution of diffusion process theory to the history of technology," *History of Technology* 17: 143–63.

Toutain, J. 1930. *The economic life of the ancient world*. London: Kegan Paul.

Traina, G. 1994. *La tecnica in Grecia e a Roma*. Roma: Laterza.

Trigger, B. G.2006. *A history of archaeological thought*. 2nd ed. Cambridge: Cambridge University Press.

Usher, A. P. 1929. *A history of mechanical inventions*. Cambridge, MA: Harvard University Press.

Usher, A. P. 1954. *A history of mechanical inventions*. 2nd ed. Cambridge, MA: Harvard University Press.

Usher, A. P. 1955. "Technical change and capital formation," in Universities National Bureau Committee for Economic Growth, *Capital formation and economic growth*. Princeton: Princeton University Press, 423–550.

Varène, P. 1974. *Sur la taille de la pierre antique, mediévale et moderne.* Dijon: Université de Dijon.

White, K. D. 1984. *Greek and Roman technology.* London: Thames and Hudson.

White, L. T. 1962. *Medieval technology and social change.* Oxford: Clarendon Press.

Wikander, Ö. 1984. *Exploitation of water-power or technological stagnation? A reappraisal of the productive forces in the Roman empire.* Scripta Minora 111. Lund: C. W. K. Gleerup.

Wikander, Ö. (ed.) 2000. *Handbook of ancient water technology.* Leiden: Brill.

Wilkinson, P. 2000. *What the Romans did for us.* London: Boxtree.

Williams, T. I. 1987. *The triumph of invention: A history of man's technological genius.* London: Macdonald.

Wilson, A. I. 2002. "Machines, power and the ancient economy," *Journal of Roman Studies* 92: 1–32.

Wilson, A. I. 2003. "The archaeology of the Roman *fullonica*," *Journal of Roman Archaeology* 16: 442–46.

Winder, N. 2005. *Breaking the Phoenix cycle: An integrative approach to innovation and cultural ecodynamics.* University of Newcastle upon Tyne: School of Historical Studies.

Ziman, J. (ed.) 2000. *Technological innovation as an evolutionary process.* Cambridge: Cambridge University Press.

Ziman, J. 2002. "Introduction: Selectionist reasoning as a tool of thought," in M. Wheeler, J. Ziman, and M. Boden (eds.), *The evolution of cultural entities.* London: British Academy, 1–8.

# PART II

# PRIMARY, EXTRACTIVE TECHNOLOGIES

CHAPTER 4

..................................................................................................

# MINING AND
# METALLURGY

..................................................................................................

## PAUL T. CRADDOCK

## TRADITION AND INNOVATION

..................................................................................................

The first millennium B.C. saw great developments in all aspects of metal production, resulting from changing patterns of demand brought about by the spread of iron usage and the introduction of coinage. The tremendous increase in the production of metals across the Old World, particularly in the Roman, Mauryean-Gupta, and Han Empires, is recorded in the heavy metal content of the cores taken through the Greenland ice sheet (Hong et al. 1996). The established economic foundations of the Bronze Age cultures of the Mediterranean, based on long-distance trade in copper and even more on tin, were disrupted forever by the emergence of iron. By the beginning of the period covered by this book, iron had supplanted bronze, extending metal usage well beyond what had previously been feasible. Iron above all else was available; most regions had some ore deposits.

The introduction of coinage in the mid-first millennium B.C. created an enormous demand for precious metals: gold and, above all, silver. The great mines of the Bronze Age had been worked for copper, but in the succeeding millennium they were worked for silver. Rio Tinto, Laurion, and others to the east through to the mines of northwest India flourished in the first millennium B.C. and were primarily producing silver destined for coinage (Craddock et al. 1989). This new demand for deep-mined ore encouraged developments in mining technology aided by new developments in knowledge.

The first millennium saw the rise of the study of secular knowledge, or philosophy, and its application to the world, with theories to cover the nature and origins of matter and the material world. This was an obvious area where observations made during mining could help the formulation of theory, and conversely where a real understanding of geological matters could have helped with mine strategy. Although theories on the origin of rocks, and in particular on the origins of metals, were developed, there is very little mention of phenomena observed during mining. This lack of oversight is reflected in the mines, where there is very little evidence of an understanding of the nature and extent of the ore bodies (see below).

It is in the developing knowledge of mathematics and all aspects of mechanics to move large quantities of air, water, and other materials in difficult conditions that the application of the new knowledge is most evident. There was probably a synergy between the problems posed by winning ore from ever deeper and more difficult deposits, and the possible solutions offered by the new knowledge. The familiar adage of the Industrial Revolution, "Science owes more to the steam engine than the steam engine owes to science," could well be expressed in the classical world as "Science owes more to mining than mining owes to science."

# SOURCES OF METAL ORES

## Northern and Western Europe

On the peninsula of Italy, the main source of metals seems to have been in Tuscany, with many mines in the Colline Metallifere (the ancient *Massa Metallorum*) inland from Piombino (Badii 1931; Davies 1935: 63–75; Cambi 1959; Minto 1955). On Sardinia there are many copper and silver/lead deposits where, although activity is now mainly associated with the Bronze Age, there was certainly Punic and probably Roman production (Tylecote et al. 1983).

Rather surprisingly, with the exception of gold, there does not seem to have been much Roman activity in the mineral deposits of the Alps compared to that in the prehistoric and medieval periods. The Romans exploited copper in southern France (Davies 1935: 76–92). In the Central Massif region of central France there were important gold-workings in the first millennium B.C. (Cauuet 1995, 1999), and there were also tin workings (Penhallurick 1986: 85–94). Further north, it seems likely that the lead/zinc deposits at Stolberg near Aachen in Germany were worked from the beginning of the Roman occupation for zinc ore to make brass (see below). Together with the deposits just over the border in Belgium at La Vieux Montainge, these provided the zinc minerals for the major early medieval and medieval *dinanderie*, or brass industry (Dejonghe et al. 1993). The distant province of Britannia certainly produced some iron and copper, and large quantities of lead (noted by Pliny, *HN* 34.164), although the silver content was probably disappointing. The gold mines at Dolaucothi in central Wales are well known, and recent work has supported their probable Iron Age origins and emphasized their scale and importance in Roman times (Lewis and Jones 1969; Burnham and Burnham 2004).

Iberia was probably the greatest source of mineral wealth through the first millennium B.C., certainly in the western Mediterranean (J. C. Allan 1970; Davies 1935: 94–139; Domerque 1990). Silver was the metal that generated the first outside interest, attested by the Phoenicians in the south from the end of the second millennium B.C., and it continued to be the most important metal produced through the first millennium B.C., but gold, lead, copper, and to a lesser extent tin and mercury were also produced. The silver occurred in the form of both jarosite and argentiferous lead ores, especially in the south. Gold was mined principally in the northwest (J. C. Allan 1970: 29–33; Lewis and Jones 1970; Domerque and Hérail 1999), and tin (J. C. Allan 1970: 23–29; Penhallurick 1986: 95–104) and mercury were worked in northern and central Iberia. Copper and lead were mined all over the peninsula (Davies 1935; Domerque 1990).

The silver and copper mines at Rio Tinto were first operated on a substantial scale by the Phoenicians and their successors, the Carthaginians (Blanco and Luzon 1969; Kassianidou et al. 1995). The famous mine of Baebelo described by Pliny (*HN* 33.97) is almost certainly to be identified with Rio Tinto. This was one of the most important mines of the early Roman Empire (J. C. Allan 1970: 3–9; Rothenberg et al. 1989). The underground workings explored so far probably date from the end of the first millennium B.C., but were of considerably earlier origin (Willies 1997).

## The Balkans and Greece

Although base metals were produced, the region was more famed overall for precious metals. In the mid-first millennium B.C., silver from the mines at Laurion in Attica and gold and silver from Siphnos and Thasos (Wagner and Weisgerber 1988) in the Aegean were of great importance, but thereafter declined. Latterly the Balkans supplied much of the gold used in the Roman and Byzantine Empires. The gold mines of Illyria, at Urbas in Dalmatia, operated until about the second century A.D., and thereafter Dacia, supplying gold from the *Aurariae Dacicae*, must have been one of the most advanced and productive mining regions of late antiquity (Wollmann 1976).

## Cyprus and Anatolia

Cyprus, whose very name is derived from "copper," was one of the great sources of that metal through the Bronze Age and classical antiquity (Muhly et al. 1982). Comments by Galen (Walsh 1929) suggest it may also have been an early source of zinc minerals for the brass industry. Anatolia was another important source of metals (de Jesus 1980; Pernicka et al. 1984). In the first part of the first millennium B.C., there was clearly a major gold strike in the alluvial deposits of the Pactolus

River in the immediate vicinity of Sardis. Geophysical surveys carried out in the early 2000s (as yet unpublished) have revealed major buried trenches in the gravels of the Pactolus just to the north of the city. These have been interpreted as docks, but it seems more likely that they are the old gold workings. By the first century B.C., Strabo described these gold mines as exhausted (13.1.23). While they lasted, they were the source of the fabled Lydian wealth and the gold for the new innovation of coinage (Ramage and Craddock 2000; Craddock et al. 2005).

Copper is relatively abundant at many places, with evidence of major early mining along the Black Sea hinterland from Küre to Rize, and also at Ergani in the southeast (Wagner and Öztunali 2000). Silver/lead/zinc ores are also found in the Black Sea region as well as further west, as is exemplified by the Bayla Madan mine (see below).

## Syria and Palestine

The principal mines on both sides of the Wadi Arabah exploited copper. These are the mines in the Wadi Feinan, now in Jordan, which include the well-preserved Roman mining system at Umm el Amad (Hauptmann and Weisgerber 1992), and further south on the other side, the mines in Beer Ora and the Wadi Amran (Rothenberg 1972: 208–23; Willies 1991). The deposits are somewhat unusual in that they are either of malachite (copper carbonate hydroxide) or of chrysocolla (hydrated copper silicate), rather than the more common sulphidic deposits.

## Egypt

The mines of the eastern deserts of Egypt were a major source of gold from Pharonic times through classical antiquity, as is attested by the writings of Agatharchides (Burstein 1989) and their physical remains (Klemm and Klemm 1989).

# MINING TECHNOLOGY

The first millennium B.C. saw developments in mining technology from Spain to China that were radical in both scale and concept. Mining had previously been constrained by problems of ventilation and drainage, which meant that a mine could not penetrate far below the water table and a gallery could not extend far from the shaft into the deposit. Thus a major Bronze Age mine such as Timna, in the Negev Desert of southern Israel, was no more than a large collection of very small mines, with thousands of shafts often only a few meters apart (Conrad and Rothenberg 1980). In the first millennium B.C., much of this changed. At just the time when mathematics and mechanics were beginning to receive serious study through the Greek world, major mines were being systematically laid out for the first time (Craddock 1995: 69–92; Healey 1978). Deep shafts were now sunk that penetrated far below the water table, with galleries stretching out for many hundreds of meters. The sciences of hydrostatics, pneumatics, and mechanics were being applied, if only empirically. (For a collection of relevant Greek and Latin literary sources, see Humphrey et al. 1998: 173–92.)

Where the deposits lay in mountainous country, there was always the possibility of driving a passage (known in English as an adit) into the hillside up from the valley bottom to link with the workings inside. This would drain the workings above the adit. Rio Tinto provides good examples of a variety of drainage systems (Palmer 1926–1927; Salkield 1987: 10, 40; Willies 1997; Guerrero Quintero 2006). An adit was driven for over 3 km through barren rock just to meet up with and drain the mine workings. When the mines were reopened in the nineteenth century, this adit was cleared and for the next century continued to drain the modern workings.

Where the workings were below the level of the adit, the water had to be raised up to it. In antiquity this could be achieved in several different ways (Oleson 1984). A series of small reservoirs could be built up an incline and water bailed from a lower to the next higher reservoir and so on until the drainage adit was reached. Such systems were still in use in Japan in the nineteenth century (Gowland 1899). Pliny (*HN* 33.97) seems to describe something similar: "The Baebelo mine . . . now dug 1,500 paces (2,200 m) into the mountain. Along this distance watermen are positioned day and night, pumping out the water in shifts measured by lamps, and making a stream." There is probably some conflation here. It is more likely that the watermen bailed the water up to a long adit, which, if it was anything like the existing adit at Rio Tinto, sloped down, allowing the water to flow away out of the mine.

A variety of mechanical devices for the raising of water seem to have been developed in the Hellenistic world from about the third century B.C. (Oleson 1984, 2000; Wilson 2002; see chapter 11). Water-wheels were another method of raising water used in the mines of the south of Spain and elsewhere (Palmer 1926–1927; Weisgerber 1979). The series of wheels at Rio Tinto raised water through about 30 m. They were operated by slaves treading the rim, and it is estimated that one person could raise about 80 liters of water per minute through about 4 m. Another method of raising water at this period employed the Archimedean screw, examples of which have been found in ancient mines in France and Spain. A force pump with moveable nozzle was found in the Roman mine at Sotiel Coronoda (figure 13.5).

The movement of air through the mine workings was probably achieved mainly by the use of carefully placed fires at the bottom of shafts in conjunction with shuttering and doors within the mines. Air could be drawn up one shaft by the fire at its base, pulling air through the workings drawn in from another shaft. This result could be achieved with a single shaft with a partition down the middle, sucking the air in one side, through the workings, and up the other side (Healy 1978: 83). Pliny (*HN* 31.49) also describes the use of linen sheets, shaken in the manner of an Indian *punka*.

The usual method of breaking up hard rock since the inception of mining had been fire-setting, and this continued long after the introduction of gunpowder for blasting in seventeenth-century Europe (Craddock 1992, 1995: 33–37; Willies 1994; Weisgerber and Willies 2000). The traditional perception has been that it was necessary to extinguish the fire suddenly with water, but more recent experimental work suggested that this was unnecessary and often impracticable. However, some classical sources, including Pliny (*HN* 23.57, 33.71), not only describe dousing but also suggest it should be done with vinegar. This seems inherently unlikely, but experiments on limestone showed it worked remarkably well (Shepherd 1992). Pliny (*HN* 33.72–73) also describes a method of exposing mineral deposits by undermining them with tunnels allowed intentionally to collapse (*arrugiae*).

The main innovation in mining technology in the first millennium B.C. was the introduction of iron and steel tools, completely replacing the stone mining hammers and array of bone, antler, and bronze tools that had been used previously. By the end of the first millennium, the complete premodern kit of mining tools was in use: picks, hammers, wedges, chisels, hoes, and rakes (figure 4.1). Metallographic examination of a selection of Roman tools from Rio Tinto has shown that many are of heat-treated steel, with properties comparable to their modern counterparts (Maddin et al. 1996). Pliny (*HN* 33.72) described the use of machines with hammerheads of iron weighing 150 Roman pounds (49 kg) for breaking the *silices* (quartz, not flint, in these instances). He could be referring to the iron-shod stamps for crushing the ore (see below), but the passage implies that they were used underground against the rock face, so possibly large battering rams are meant, such as have been found in the Indian mines of the same period. The mined material was removed in small baskets or trays. The broad straight galleries in some of the larger mines would be suitable for wheeled transport, and at Três Minas parallel grooves in the floor seem to indicate some form of controlled trackway (Wahl 1998: fig. 3). The wheelbarrow was unknown to the Roman world.

In addition to the deep mines, open cast pits were also worked, especially for gold. Good examples survive in Spain (Lewis and Jones 1970; Domerque and Hérail 1999; Bird 2004). The overburden was washed from these workings by the sudden release of millions of liters of water stored in reservoirs above the workings, known in English as hushing. Pliny (*HN* 33.74–76) provides a dramatic description of the Spanish operations. This method of mining is apparently a Roman innovation, relying on their practiced ability to collect, store, and control the release of huge volumes of water.

In contrast to the application of the mathematical and engineering sciences, there seems to have been but little appreciation of the geology of the deposits. From the post-medieval period on, miners attempted to define the extent of a deposit, then to sink a shaft or to drive an adit beneath it. They then excavated upward (known as overhand stoping), bringing down the material to the base of the shaft or adit from where it could be conveniently raised to surface. In antiquity an ore body, once located, was dug out directly (known as underhand stoping), the ore and waste being brought to surface through the worked-out deposit. Very often deposits are faulted, which means that the deposit has slipped and continues some distance away. Sometimes there clearly was an understanding that the vein was likely to continue somewhere in the vicinity and efforts were made to try and

Figure 4.1. Selection of Roman iron and steel tools from Rio Tinto mine, including wedges or gads (bottom left), picks (bottom right) and hoes (top). Huelva Museum. (Photograph by P. Craddock.)

relocate it. At the Roman mines in the Wadi Amran (Israel), a series of exploratory holes each several meters in length had been cut in several directions at the end of gallery where the deposit terminated at a fault (Willies 1991).

# MINE ORGANIZATION

The organization and administration of mining in classical antiquity have been much discussed but are still imperfectly understood (Davies 1935: 1–16; Healy 1978: 103–32; Hopper 1979: 164–89). The evidence is derived from a large number of disparate sources, chance references, and inferences that are now difficult to interpret and from which it is difficult to obtain an overall coherent picture, if such a concept is even realistic. Contemporary accounts that do survive often seem to be in serious error, or seriously prejudiced. Hagiographers, for example, recorded the apparently appalling working conditions suffered within the mines by the Christian martyrs. Few direct records of real legislation and administration exist, the famous bronze tablets from a mine of the second century A.D. at Aljustrel in Portugal being an important exception (Elkington 2001), from which a very different picture of a more organized and workable management regime emerges.

In most societies, the ruling authority lays claim to all valuable mineral deposits in the ground, and in classical antiquity the state took an active interest in getting the maximum yield, especially from the deposits of precious metals. It seems that the state sometimes operated the mines directly, at least in their developmental stages in newly won territories, as exemplified by the apparent military involvement in both the lead and gold mines in Britain (cf. Tacitus, *An.* 11.20; Aristotle, *Ath. pol.* 47.2).

From some surviving descriptions and contracts, particularly from Greece and Spain, it appears that the mines were often leased to private concerns, although they were still answerable to the state mining department. At Laurion, for example, several different concessions operated within one mine (Crosby 1941, 1950). This system could explain why the mining operations seem to have been confined to digging in the ore. There would be little incentive to develop the infrastructure of the mine if a concession of only a few years was in operation. It is clear, however, from the large-scale drainage works in the mines at Rio Tinto and elsewhere that long-term development work away from the immediate ore body was carried out, and it does seem that state involvement went far beyond just collecting the dues, ensuring that the deposits were worked to the best overall advantage. The second-century A.D. Aljustrel tablets from Spain are important because they list all sorts of detailed regulations regarding the maintenance of drainage systems, support timbers, and ore dumps (Mommsen et al. 1909: 293–95, no. 113). This was not done out of any altruistic concern for the welfare of the miners, but pragmatically to ensure maximum efficiency. In the major silver and gold mines, the state monitored the operations quite carefully and probably sometimes ran the mines directly. Pliny, who had been a fiscal procurator in Hispania Tarraconensis, wrote what are clearly detailed firsthand descriptions of the gold mining operations, and his comprehensive and technically accurate descriptions of the silver smelting processes show that state officials could be fully conversant with the processes involved.

Much of the labor force seems to have been made up of slaves, and criminals could be sentenced to the mines as a form of essentially capital punishment (Xenophon, *Vect.* 4.14–18; Plutarch, *Nic.* 1.1–2; Diodorus 3.12–3.14.4). As a result, there are very few representations of miners (figure 2.12; cf. figure 2.1). In remote areas, the local population could be conscripted to work in the mines on a corvée system. As well as this enforced labor, there were clearly also specialist technical staff who would be necessary to operate the mine and who, even if not free, were living a more tolerable life than is popularly perceived (Mrozek 1989).

# BENEFICIATION OF ORES

This is an important stage in the production of metal, as Merkel (1985, 1990) and Maréchal (1985) have stressed. The ores of most metals needed to be reduced to between the size of a pea and a walnut for smelting and would usually have been broken up manually with hammers. Trip hammers were possibly in use by the Roman period, as the distinctive stone anvils (figure 4.2) survive at a number of mines in Iberia and elsewhere (Wahl 1993, 1998; Sánchez-Palencia 1989), and they may have been water-powered (M. J. T. Lewis 1997, and below). Gold ores needed to be finely ground to release the tiny particles of metal, and for this grinding mills were used, based on the mills used for grinding food grains but with harder grinding stones (Diodorus 3.13.2–14.4; Wilson 2002). For other metals, where the ore had to be smelted, fine powders would probably have been mixed with animal dung to make discrete lumps to charge into the furnace. This was the practice in the Middle East and India until the nineteenth century (Craddock 1995: 152, 161).

The crushed ores could be concentrated by washing and allowing the lighter dross to wash away. This process could be effected by shoveling the ore against a controlled flow of water, but more elaborate arrangements are also known, most famously the washeries from the mines at Laurion in Attica (Conophagos 1980; Jones 1984; Photos-Jones and Ellis Jones 1994). These are very sophisticated and well-preserved systems, but their true function is still not fully understood, and they are unique to Laurion. At Rio Tinto, more simple washing floors for concentrating the jarosite silver ore prior to smelting have been excavated (figure 4.3); in these, water was introduced from the left, washing dross down the large drain on the right.

Figure 4.2. Anvil of an ore-crushing stamp battery from the Roman gold mines at Três Miñas. Deutsches Bergbau Museum, Bochum. (Photograph by P. Craddock.)

Figure 4.3. Roman washing floor at Rio Tinto. (Photograph by P. Craddock.)

# SMELTING

In contrast to mining, the smelting methods that had evolved in the eastern Mediterranean and Middle East during the third and second millennia B.C. remained largely unchanged in the classical cultures (for a collection of Greek and Latin literary sources, see Humphrey et al. 1998: 205–33). The typical smelting furnace through antiquity was a cylindrical shaft of clay and stone (Craddock 1995: 169–74). The dimensions were quite small, typically about 30 to 60 cm internal diameter, and 1–2 m tall. Taller and presumably broader furnaces are recorded by Strabo (3.2.8) for the smelting of silver ores. Based on Strabo and the evidence from Laurion, Conophagos believed some of the furnaces could have been between three and four meters in height (see below).

Early furnaces were very impermanent structures; archaeologists usually have to reconstruct their form from little more than their bases. Furnaces are represented on some Greek vases depicting scenes of metalworking, but there are problems with interpretation. The furnaces usually appear to have a pot set on the top, sometimes complete with lid (Oddy and Swaddling 1985). In this type of furnace, however, the objective is to ensure an unimpeded flow of air through the chimneylike system to remove spent gases up the shaft, and a pot set on top would prevent this (figures 4.4, 16.2). Possibly these representations all illustrate furnaces used specifically for annealing purposes, but a simple hearth would seem better suited for that purpose. The illustrations remind us that there is still much to learn about early metallurgical processes.

One of the few real improvements to take place in smelting technology was the introduction of more efficient bellows. Early bellows, in use from about the third

Figure 4.4. Shaft furnace on a Greek oenochoe, 525 B.C. BM inv. B507. (From Oddy and Swaddling 1985; by permission of Swaddling.)

millennium B.C., were either bag-bellows or pot-bellows that could deliver no more than about 200 liters a minute of air (Tylecote 1981; Merkel 1990). The well known carving of the workshop of Hephaestus on the north frieze of the Siphnian Treasury at Delphi depicts bag-bellows (Lullies and Hirmer 1960: fig. 48). In the first millennium B.C., the familiar hinged concertina bellows were introduced into the Mediterranean area (Weisgerber and Roden 1985, 1986), but they seem not to have spread beyond Europe. Although still manually operated, they were capable of delivering about 500 liters of air/minute (Merkel 1990). The inability to deliver air at sufficient pressure using manually operated bellows was the major constraint on furnace size. Only in the medieval period did powerful water-driven bellows allow much larger furnaces to evolve in Europe, initially in large part for the smelting of iron.

There are no detailed contemporary descriptions of the smelting processes, but replication experiments, such as those carried out by Merkel (1990), coupled with scientific examination of the surviving smelting debris, have gone a long way toward reconstructing the operations. First, the furnace was brought up to a temperature of about 1,000°C by burning charcoal alone for about an hour, after which roasted ore and more charcoal were added. In the smelting process, the metal minerals in the ore were reduced to droplets of molten metal, and the waste minerals formed a molten slag. Much of the success of the operation depended on the slag (Bachmann 1982). Even the richest ore after beneficiation would still be made up of about 60 to 80 percent of waste material, typically silica and/or iron oxides. By themselves, these minerals have very high melting temperatures and would rapidly choke the furnace. Silica and iron oxides, however, react to form iron silicates, which have a much lower melting temperature, enabling them to be run out of the furnace as a liquid, known in English as tap slag. Occasionally, the ore had just the right proportions of silica and iron minerals to remove all of the waste material without intervention, but usually there was an imbalance. If there was too much silica, then a little iron oxide would be added; conversely if there was too much iron then a little silica would be added (known as the flux) to create a free-flowing slag. The slag was periodically drained from furnace, and the process continued with the addition of more ore and fuel. The metal would drain through the slag to form an irregular mass at the base of the furnace. Typically a smelt lasted for about six to ten hours, allowing some tens of kilograms of metal to accumulate in the base of the furnace. This activity would usually take place at night, both to take advantage of the cooler conditions and to enable those in charge of the smelt to be better able to judge the color of the flames at the top of the furnace, which was the best indicator of the conditions within.

The smelting of silver was somewhat more complicated, because by the first millennium B.C. even the richest remaining silver ores in the Mediterranean region contained no more than traces of silver, which would certainly have been lost in the conventional process outlined above. Much silver was obtained from the traces contained in lead ores (Bachmann 1991; Conophagos 1980, 1982). The lead was smelted in the usual manner, and the silver went into the lead. The argentiferous lead was then heated to about 1,000°C and exposed to a blast of air, causing it to oxidize to lead oxide, in the process known as cupellation (Conophagos 1980, 1989; Craddock 1995: 221–31). The molten silver, however, did not oxidize, but floated on the molten lead oxide "like oil on water," according to Pliny (*HN* 33.95, 34.159). After cooling, the litharge was broken and a lump of silver released.

Ancient silver regularly contains from several hundred ppm to a few percent of gold, leading Meyers (2004) to suggest that the usual sources exploited in antiquity were oxidized ores such as cerussite (hydrated lead carbonate) or jarosite (a mixed sulphatic ore), both ores that have enhanced gold contents. It has long been debated whether the main ore smelted at Laurion was cerussite or galena. Photos-Jones and Jones (1994) stated the ore found in the washeries was cerussite, but Rehren et al. (2002) claim that it had been galena originally. With ores such as the jarosites from Rio Tinto, which contained little or no lead, it was necessary to add lead to the smelting charge (Craddock et al. 1985; Craddock 1995: 216–21; Dutrizac et al. 1983).

Gold usually occurs as metal, so it could be separated by finely crushing the rock in which the tiny particles were embedded and then washing the result to separate the heavier metal. There is some evidence that the Romans were smelting auriferous iron pyrites, in which the gold is very finely distributed almost at the molecular level. Silica was added to the roasted iron pyrite to form a slag allowing the gold to separate and coalesce. Pliny mentions gold smelting (*HN* 33.69, possibly 33.79), and slag heaps from the process have been found at the Roman mines at Três Miñas in northern Portugal (Bachmann 1993).

# Metallurgy and the Environment

A new area of archaeometallurgical research concerns the effects of mining and smelting on the environment and on the health of those involved in the work. The fuel used in antiquity was invariably charcoal, and the major smelting establishments required enormous quantities, necessitating the establishment of large areas of managed woodland to supply the timber (Craddock 1995: 193–95; J. C. Allan 1970: 9–11; Fulford and Allen 1992). In desert areas, such as Palestine, it is possible that smelting operations had to be curtailed periodically because the charcoal sources in the vicinity had become exhausted. Strabo (14.6.5) mentions deforestation on Cyprus resulting from copper refining. The conclusion of the studies of Mighall and Chambers (1993) on smaller, prehistoric iron and copper mining and smelting operations in temperate Europe was that they did not bring about long-term degradation.

Another potential source of environmental pollution was noxious fumes. Most of the nonferrous ores smelted in classical antiquity were sulphidic, and the roasting and smelting operations produced sulphur dioxide in quantity. In the absence of tall chimneys, these fumes were not dissipated but remained in the vicinity of the mines. Xenophon (*Mem.* 3.6.12) and Strabo (3.2.8) both allude to the problem of fumes and consequent environmental devastation. This aspect of ancient metal refining is difficult to study now, but sulphur dioxide pollution certainly was a major problem in many nineteenth-century mining areas, such as Rio Tinto (Salkield 1987: 43–44). The highly acidic groundwaters that resulted effectively controlled the mosquito population, keeping the area free of malaria. Yet another environmental concern is the poisoning of the surrounding land with heavy metals, particularly with lead and cadmium from silver production by means of the cupellation of argentiferous lead, and to a lesser extent from copper production. This very persistent pollution has been studied by Mighall (2003) for prehistoric copper mining sites and by Pyatt et al. (2000) for the much larger Roman operations at Feinan. At the latter site there are enhanced levels of heavy metals in the soil that must inevitably have entered the local plants, including those grown for food. The ores are near surface, however, and in places are cut by the streams; thus the local alluvial fans would have enhanced levels of heavy metals anyway. Similarly, attempts to study how this pollution affected the local population by analyzing bones from the cemeteries are compromised by the propensity of bone to absorb heavy metals from the soil.

# Refining

Copper and the other base metals were refined by remelting in an open crucible and allowing impurities such as iron, sulphur, arsenic or antimony to oxidize. Some elements, such as the arsenic and sulphur, evaporated from the molten metal;

others, notably iron oxide, could be removed by skimming the surface, possibly aided by adding a little silica to form a slag. Fire-refining remained the usual method of refining until the twentieth century.

One of the major technical developments in classical antiquity was the introduction of gold refining in response to the introduction of gold coinage by the Lydians. The remains of a gold refinery of the sixth century B.C. have been excavated at their capital, Sardis (Ramage and Craddock 2000; Craddock et al. 2005). The study of the refinery at Sardis, coupled with Agatharchides' description of gold refining as practiced in Ptolemaic Egypt in the second century B.C. (Diodorus 3.13.2–14.4; Burstein 1989), has illuminated the ancient gold refining process (known in English as parting). Native gold typically contains between 5 and 30 percent silver. The gold granules and dust were mixed with salt and possibly alum in an earthenware vessel. This was placed in a furnace and heated at a carefully controlled moderate heat to between 600° and 800°C for many hours or even days. The astringent vapors generated by the hot salt penetrated the gold and removed the silver as a vapor of silver chloride, leaving behind pure gold. The silver could be recovered from the clay parting vessels and furnace walls by cupellation.

The necessity of producing metal of uniform weight and purity required a change in the perception of the very nature of metals and introduced the concept of elements. Our idea of gold as an element with precisely defined properties is based on relatively modern scientific concepts, in particular on the Law of Constant Composition, which states that each element has precise and invariant properties. To us this seems no more than stating the obvious, but the ancients did not have such a concept of materials as elements. The widely held belief, as set down by Empedocles, was that metals "grew" in the ground. Thus it would seem logical to expect the properties of the metal to depend on their environment; metals such as gold, coming from various sources, could have widely differing properties but still be gold. For example, a light-colored gold from a given locality would be regarded as the intrinsic gold of that place, rather than as a naturally occurring alloy of gold with a rather high silver content.

Coinage introduced the concept of an invariant standard of purity (usually expressed by the metal refiners in antiquity in practical terms when repeated refining failed to reduce the weight any further). It was also noted that natural gold could be recreated by adding silver to the refined gold, and conversely that silver could be recovered from the refining waste. Thus, although natural gold was still "growing" and still contained silver that would in time turn into gold, there was an ultimate gold, and through refining the gold could attain that state.

This new perception, brought about by the need to refine precious metals for coinage, was already extending to other metals by Roman times. For example, Pliny (HN 34.94) stated that the Cypriot mines produced ductile "bar" copper that could be hammered without breaking, unlike other mines that produced "fused" copper, which was too brittle to be hammered. But he continued, "in the other mines, this difference of bar copper from fused copper is produced by treatment; for all copper after impurities have been rather carefully removed by fire and melted out of it become bar copper." That is, the difference was not just an intrinsic property of Cypriote copper but was also associated with the degree of refining.

# IRON AND STEEL

In the first centuries of the first millennium B.C., the use of iron spread very rapidly throughout the Old World, supplanting bronze as the usual material for tools and weapons, as is exemplified by the tools used in mining (see above). Through most of its history iron has been used in a variety of states: wrought iron, phosphoric iron, cast iron, steel, and crucible steel (Craddock 2003).

In Europe, the Mediterranean world, and the Middle East, iron was always smelted by the bloomery process (Tylecote 1987; Craddock 1995). The furnaces and smelting conditions were not dissimilar to those used to smelt other metals, although some of the furnaces were of considerable size by the Roman period (Crew 1998). The iron was produced as a solid pasty mass, called the bloom, invariably containing some slag. This was removed while still white-hot and vigorously hammered to squeeze out as much of the slag as possible, and also to consolidate it (Diodorus 5.13.1–2). The wrought iron so produced could also contain small quantities of carbon, sometimes sufficient to be classified as steel.

If the iron ore contained phosphorus, as most bog ores do, then this could enter the iron. Small quantities of phosphorus have much the same effect as carbon in iron, but can lead to serious brittleness. For this reason phosphorus is now regarded as a harmful impurity, but in Iron Age Europe phosphoric iron was deliberately selected for blades such as sickles and knives, since they kept their edge, even if they occasionally broke (Craddock 1995: 238; Ehrenrich 1985). The smith can have had no notion of the presence of phosphorus but knew that certain ores, when smelted in a particular way, resulted in an iron suitable for blades.

If the temperature of the furnace was increased and the conditions made more reducing, then carbon could dissolve in the iron as it formed, reducing the melting temperature down to about 1,200°C. Thus, instead of a solid bloom, liquid iron could be run from the furnace containing about 3.5 to 4.5 percent of carbon (called "cast iron"). Cast iron is not a very useful material, and it seems not to have been used in the classical world; the use of cast iron was a great achievement of Chinese metallurgy. Iron with a small amount of carbon (typically between about 0.2 and 1 percent) is known as steel, and when correctly heat-treated it has properties much superior to wrought iron (see below); getting a regular amount of carbon into the solid iron, however, was very difficult.

The ideal material would be iron with about 1 percent of uniformly distributed carbon and containing no slag. This result could be produced by reacting wrought iron with charcoal and wood in small sealed crucibles at very high temperatures (1,500°C) to produce crucible steel. This technology was in widespread use through central and southern Asia over 2,000 years ago, and it seems that the classical world had some inkling of the process and possibly imported sword blades made from it (see below). Crucible steel was always forged to shape, never cast.

Wrought iron could be shaped by hammering at red heat (hot forging) using methods and tools not dissimilar to those used by traditional blacksmiths to this day (Tylecote 1987; Sim and Ridge 2002). The iron could not be cast, but good metallurgical joins could be made by hammering pieces together at red heat (hammer welding) or by hot riveting. The archaeological record shows that iron was a very familiar low-cost material. Estimates have been made for iron production of 2,250 tons per annum in Roman Britain, and 82,500 tones per annum through the rest of the Empire (Sim and Ridge 2002: 23; cf. Cleere and Crossley 1985: 57–86).

Iron was used on such a scale that technologists such as David Sim have speculated whether some more advanced production techniques might have already been in use. For example, it is usually held that the production of wire through a draw plate is a post-Roman technique, and that iron wire would have had to be laboriously made by hammering a thin rod. Even a simple tunic of chain mail (the *lorica hamata*), however, contained hundreds of meters of wire that it would not have been feasible to make except by drawing. Draw plates have now been recognized, appropriately enough in the floor of armorers' workshops inside Roman frontier forts (Sim 1997, 1998).

Wrought iron could be turned into steel by heating it for many hours in close contact with a variety of organic materials and charcoal dust (carburizing). There were two techniques: small pieces of iron could be totally carburized and then welded to the wrought iron of the remainder of the tool (the tip of a chisel, for example), or the entire artifact could be forged and then the surface carburized all over (case hardening).

The famous Noricum iron praised by Pliny (*HN* 34.145) and others was a natural steel (Davies 1935: 173; Tylecote 1987: 168). The iron ores in the vicinity of Magdelensburg in Austria are rich in manganese, and thus the slag had a great deal of manganese oxide. Ordinary iron slag contains iron oxide, which reacts with any carbon dissolved in the iron in the furnace. Manganese oxide does not react in this way, and thus there is a better chance of any carbon in the iron surviving; in the Noricum iron sufficient carbon remained for it to be classified as a steel. Steel can be greatly improved by heat treatments, as the Greeks knew as early as the eighth century B.C. The steel was heated to a cherry-red heat and held at that temperature for some time before being plunged into water. The resulting steel was very hard, suitable for files but too brittle for other uses. To produce a steel more suitable for chisels or saw blades, for example, the quenched steel was gently heated (tempered). The smith judged the degree of tempering by the color of the oxidized layer on the steel.

With so many imponderables in the production of good steel, it is not surprising that things often went wrong, and the proportion of tools and weapons that
had been correctly heat-treated is low. Studies of prestige blades, however, have
shown that they are regularly of good-quality, correctly tempered steel (Lang 1995).
Swords could be made by hot-forging and folding the iron. The folding could be
repeated several times, resulting in a blade made up of many thin layers of iron
(Lang 1988), a process known as piling; it was probably done to homogenize the
iron. From the end of the first millennium B.C. in Europe the practice began of
twisting the iron sheets or rods into decorative patterns during the forging, sometimes alternating iron and steel. Pattern welding, as this is called, is usually associated
with the post-Roman barbarians, but the technique was certainly practiced in the
late Roman Empire.

Studies of Roman armor have shown that steel and iron were intelligently and
deliberately combined to produce a superior product (Williams 1977). For example,
the *lorica segmenta* plates of Roman armor were fabricated from wrought-iron sheet
to which steel sheet had been welded (Sim and Ridge 2002: 96). The outer hard steel
layer would stop penetration, and the inner tough iron layer would prevent the
*lorica* from breaking and absorb the energy of the blow.

As early as the first millennium B.C., the Chinese were producing iron castings
on a prodigious scale, and crucible steel was being produced in central and southern
Asia (Craddock 2003). What knowledge the Romans had of these materials, or what
access they had to them, is uncertain. Tylecote (1987: 325–27), for example, listed
finds of iron castings from Roman sites and suggested that they could have been
imports from China. Ongoing work in southern Germany has shown that the blast
furnace process developed from about the eighth century A.D., much earlier than
previously believed, although the liquid iron so produced was not used for castings
but instead was treated (fined) to produce solid wrought iron (Craddock 2003). The
ancestry of the process in Europe is not known, but excavations of Iron Age and
Roman iron-smelting sites have shown a hitherto unappreciated variety of processes
(Crew and Crew 1997). At the major iron-smelting site at Oulche (France), there is
evidence that granules of high carbon iron may have been separately collected from
the ordinary iron and forged to produce high carbon steel (Dieudonné-Glad 1997).

It has been claimed that various passages in classical literature refer to liquid
iron or steel, but these can be discounted (Craddock 2003), with the exception of
the writings of the Alexandrian alchemist Zosimos, who lived in the third century
A.D. (Berthelot 1893: 332). He gave a detailed and accurate description of how the
Indians produced crucible steel, and he indicated that this material was used by the
Persians to make high-quality swords that were then traded to the Romans. Blades
from central Asia dating from the third century A.D. (Feurerbach 2001), and from
Sassanian Persia (Lang et al. 1998), have been identified as crucible steel, but so far
no crucible steel blades have been reported from the Roman or Byzantine Empires.
Since literary evidence suggests that crucible steel was already known in the late
Roman and Byzantine world, it is very likely that continuing research will uncover
more evidence of sophisticated processes and products.

# BRASS: THE NEW METAL

Bronze—the alloy of copper and tin—appeared in the fourth millennium B.C. and was in universal use by the first millennium B.C. Throughout the classical period, lead was added in ever greater quantities to bronze intended for castings (Craddock 1976, 1977, 1986). The major change in copper alloys in the ancient world, however, was the introduction of brass—an alloy of copper and zinc—sometime within the first millennium B.C. By the late Roman and Byzantine periods, once the technology for its preparation had been developed, brass had largely replaced bronze as the usual copper alloy (Caley 1964; Bayley 1998; Craddock 1978; 1995: 292–302; 1998; Craddock and Eckstein 2003). Zinc ores are abundant compared to those of tin. The reason for the relatively late introduction of brass as an alloy is the volatility of zinc. At the temperatures necessary to smelt it, zinc is a very reactive gas. As a result, the pure metal was not produced commercially until about A.D. 1000, in India (Craddock et al. 1998a).

Almost from the inception of metallurgy, some copper artifacts from all over the world have been found to contain varying quantities of zinc (Welter 2003). They always seem to be isolated examples among items that otherwise consist of copper and bronze, and they are probably the unintentional result of smelting zinc-rich copper ores. From the end of the second millennium B.C. in Anatolia and the Middle East, copper artifacts containing between about 5 and 15 percent of zinc become more common, contemporary with references to a special copper known as "copper of the mountain" in Assyrian and other documents. From the mid-first millennium B.C. there were also references in Greek literature to *oreichalkos*, "copper of the mountain," as a distinct metal, and by the first century B.C. this term, and its Latin form *aurichalcum*, certainly referred to brass (Halleux 1973). Early production seems to have been centered in western Anatolia, although production in Persia and east as far as India is a distinct possibility. The first series of artifacts regularly made of brass that have been identified so far are the base metal coins of Mithradates VI, who ruled western Anatolia during the early first century B.C. (Craddock et al. 1980). These issues include both copper and brass coins and are directly ancestral to the Roman reformed coinage of 27 and 23 B.C., which saw the introduction of brass *dupondii* and *sestertii* (Burnett et al. 1982) (figures 4.5, 30.1). It seems likely that through the first century B.C. brass rapidly gained in popularity and was extensively used by the military. Istenic and Šmit (2008) have shown that the Alesia type of brooches, associated with the military, are of brass from about 60 B.C., and by the first century A.D. military brooches, trappings, and fittings were regularly made of brass (Jackson and Craddock 1995; Ponting and Segal 1998). These brasses and the contemporary brass coins (Calliari et al. 1998) are usually an alloy of copper with about 20 to 25 percent of zinc and minor amounts of lead derived from the zinc ore. The contemporary civilian metalwork is often of an alloy containing less zinc but more lead along with some tin, suggesting the indiscriminate mixing of scrap bronze and brass.

Figure 4.5. Early brass coins. Top: Early first century B.C., Pergamum (BMC 130, 144). Middle: Roman SC coin of the reformed eastern coinage of 27 B.C. Bottom: *dupondius* and *sestertius* of the general reform of 23 B.C. (After Craddock 1995.)

The ancient written sources do not state how brass was made. The only physical evidence is a number of distinctive small, lidded crucibles, heavily vitrified and massively impregnated with zinc (figure 4.6) (Bayley 1998). It has always been assumed that the alloy was made by cementation, the process that was used in post-medieval Europe up to the nineteenth century (Rehren 1999). In this process the calcined zinc ore together with charcoal was added to finely divided solid copper in a closed crucible and heated to temperatures of about 900°C, whereupon the zinc oxide was reduced to zinc gas that dissolved into the copper. The first mention of cementation, however, is by Biringuccio in the 1540s (Smith and Gnudi 1942: 70–76), and the only medieval accounts—those of Theophilus, dating from the twelfth century (Hawthorne and Smith 1963), and those of al-Hamdānī and al-Kāshānī, dating from the tenth and twelfth centuries, respectively (J. W. Allan 1979; Craddock et al. 1998b)—all make it clear that the zinc ore and charcoal were added to molten copper in the crucible, rather than to solid shavings. This process was much simpler and quicker, but less zinc entered the copper (Craddock and Eckstein 2003). That this was the process used in classical antiquity is supported by the composition of the ancient brasses. Roman and medieval brasses contain up to a maximum of 28 percent of zinc, but after the sixteenth century this proportion rises to a maximum of 33 percent.

There was a further complication to the production of brass. The ore added to the copper must contain no sulphur. The zinc deposits of western Europe that were very probably worked by the Romans (at Stolberg in Germany, Vieux Montaigne in Belgium and the Mendip Hills in Britain) are carbonates and could have been used directly, but the zinc ores of Anatolia and the Middle East are sulphides. The sulphidic ores first had to be roasted to produce zinc oxide. As zinc oxide had

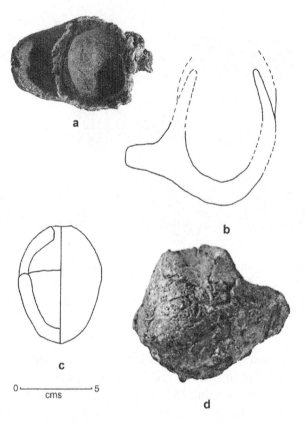

Figure 4.6. Small Roman lidded crucibles probably used to make brass; a-b from Culver, St. Colchester; c from Palace St. Canterbury; d from extramural settlement at Ribchester. (After Bayley 1998; copyright English Heritage, by permission.)

medicinal uses—the familiar zinc ointment or calamine lotion (Lehmann 2000)—there are detailed descriptions of its preparation in contemporary pharmaceutical texts, especially that of Dioscorides (Gunther 1934; Riddle 1985). The sulphidic ore was roughly roasted to convert most of it to the oxide, and then smelted in an ordinary shaft furnace. The zinc vapor ascended the furnace flue where it met oxygen and promptly reoxidized. Complex arrangements of iron bars suspended in the flue, or even of whole chambers above the flues, were set up to catch and condense the fumes of zinc oxide. Debris of this process has been excavated at Zawar in India, dating from the last centuries B.C. (Craddock and Eckstein 2003). The process continued in use in the Middle East at least until the thirteenth century, when it was observed by Marco Polo at Kerman in Persia.

The zinc content of the *dupondii* and of the *sestertii* declined during the first century, leading Caley (1964) to believe that brassmaking had already become a lost art. It is true that coins of the central mint cease to be made of brass, but analyses of other classes of metalwork show that it continued in production (Craddock 1978;

Dungworth 1996). More interestingly, the major analytical study of thousands of brooches from Roman Britain (Bayley and Butcher 2004) has shown that different types of brooch used different and very specific alloys, some of brass and others of leaded bronze. Similarly, local issues of copper-base coins in the eastern empire were often struck in brass, whereas the corresponding issues from the central mints were of bronze (Cowell et al. 2000). After the collapse of the western empire, with the attendant loss of the tin producing provinces of Iberia and Britannia and easy access to the tin fields of the Erzgebirge in central Europe, brass became the usual alloy (Hook and Craddock 1996; Schweizer 1994). The earliest Islamic metalwork reverted to bronze (Schweizer and Bujard 1994; Ponting 1999), presumably until the capture of the brass-making sources in Anatolia, after which brass replaced bronze almost completely (Craddock et al. 1998b).

## Survival and Development

The production of metals survived the collapse of the Roman Empire in the west, with every indication, for example, that tin production in Britain and brass production in Flanders continued. The Byzantine successors of the Roman Empire in the East seem to have maintained production, and this in turn was continued by the Islamic regimes. These later mines and smelters have been poorly investigated, and so comparison with earlier classical practice is difficult. Not until the sixteenth century do detailed descriptions appear for comparison, especially those of Biringuccio (Smith and Gnudi 1942) and Agricola (Hoover and Hoover 1912). It is clear that Agricola (a pseudonym for Georg Bauer) was familiar with Strabo's *Geography* and Pliny's *Natural History*, and in some ways his *De re metallica* contains striking parallels (Domerque 1989b). There are also striking and significant differences, not least between the authors and their intended audiences. Strabo and Pliny wrote as interested and educated observers, and their work was intended for gentlemanly diversion, not for practical instruction. Agricola was trained as a doctor with strong interests in geology and metallurgy, and he wrote his works with official encouragement as real working manuals.

Clearly, both the classical and Renaissance mining ventures could be on a considerable scale. Investigations at Rio Tinto, Três Mìnas, and other sites have shown that sophisticated drainage methods were employed. The major difference seems to have been the prevalence of water-powered, and to a lesser extent animal-powered, machinery (M. J. T. Lewis 1997). Water power certainly was harnessed in the classical world, but how widespread was its use? This has been a major issue in the history of technology for many years (see chapters 6 and 13); some scholars, such as Wilson (2002), believe that water-powered devices were quite common even in mining operations. A thousand years after Rome, the pages of *De re metallica* are full of descriptions and illustrations of drainage pumps, crushing machinery, and bellows all powered by water wheels. These do seem to be generally absent in Roman mines, although it is dangerous to assume their absence. In the few years since the stamps at Très Miñas were announced, several more have been recognized, including one at Dolaucothi in Wales adjacent to a Roman water mill and surrounded by heaps of crushed debris (Burnham and Burnham 2004). Thus water power might have been more prevalent than believed at present, although it does seem that earlier mining relied far more on large labor forces.

There are more clearcut differences between classical and medieval smelting practices because of the application of water power. As noted above, the early furnaces were necessarily small because of the limitations of manually operated bellows to produce a blast of sufficient volume and power to penetrate a larger furnace charge. With the introduction of water power the bellows grew to enormous dimensions, and the furnaces expanded to over a meter in internal diameter and several meters in height. Especially in iron smelting, a single operation could last for weeks, producing many tons of metal with just a few highly skilled operators, totally different from the small-scale, labor-intensive operations of the classical world.

# REFERENCES

Allan, J. W. 1979. *Persian metal technology, 700–1300 AD*. London: Ithaca Press.

Allan, J. C. 1970. *Considerations on the antiquity of mining in the Iberian peninsula*. London: Royal Anthropological Institute.

Bachmann, H-G. 1982. *The identification of slags from archaeological sites*. London: Institute of Archaeology.

Bachmann, H-G. 1991. "Archäometallurgie des Silbers." *Die Geowissenschaften* 9.1: 12–16.

Bachmann, H-G. 1993. "Zur metallurgie der römischen Goldgewinnung in Treês Miñas und Campo de Jales in Nordportugal," in H. Steuer and U. Zimmermann (eds.), *Montanarchäologie in Europa*. Sigmaringen: Jan Torbecke, 53–60.

Badii, G. 1931. "Le antiche miniere del Massetano," *Studi Etruschi* 5: 455–73.

Bayley, J. 1998. "The production of brass in antiquity with particular reference to Roman Britain," in Craddock 1998: 7–25.

Bayley, J., and S. Butcher 2004. *Roman brooches in Britain*. London: Society of Antiquaries of London.

Berthelot, M. P. E. 1893. *La Chemie au Moyen Âge*. Paris: Georges Stenheil.

Bird, D. 2004. "Water power in Roman gold mining," *Mining History: Bulletin of the Peak District Mines Historical Society* 15.4/5: 58–63.

Blanco, A., and J. M. Luzon 1969. "Pre-Roman silver mining at Rio Tinto," *Antiquity* 43: 14–31.

Burnett, A. M., P. T. Craddock, and K. Preston 1982. "New light on the origins of *orichalcum*," in T. Hackens and R. Weiller (eds.), *Proceedings of the 9th International Congress of Numismatists*. Louvain-la-Neuve: Association internationale des numismates professionnels, 263–68.

Burnham, B., and H. Burnham 2004. *Dolaucothi-Pumsaint: Survey and excavations at a Roman gold-mining complex 1987–1999.* Oxford: Oxbow.

Burstein, S. M. (trans. and ed.) 1989. *Agatharchides of Cnidus: On the Erythraean Sea.* London: The Hakulyt Society.

Caley, E. R. 1964. *Orichalcum and related ancient alloys.* Numismatic Notes and Monographs 151. New York: American Numismatic Society.

Calliari, I., M. Magrini, and R. Martini 1998. "Characterization of Republican and Imperial Roman coins," *Science and Technology for Cultural Heritage* 7.2: 81–89.

Cambi, L. 1959. "Problemi della metallurgia," *Studi Etruschi* 27: 415-32.

Cauuet, B. 1995. *Les mines d'or gauloises du Limosin.* Limoges: Association Culture et Patriomoine en Limoussin.

Cauuet, B. 1999. "L'exploitation de l'or en gaulle á l'Age du Fer," in B. Canuuet (ed.), *L'or dans l'antiquité.* Toulouse: Aquitania, 31-86.

Cleere, H., and D. Crossley 1985. *The iron industry of the weald.* Leicester: The University Press.

Conophagos, C. E. 1980. *Le laurion antique et la technique grecque de la production del'argent.* Athens: Ekdotike Hellados.

Conophagos, C. E. 1982. "Smelting practice at Laurion," in T. A. Wertime and S. F. Wertime (eds.), *Early pyrotechnology.* Washington, DC: Smithsonian Institution Press, 181–91.

Conophagos, C. E. 1989. "La technique de la coupellation des Grecs anciens au Laurium," in Y. Maniatis (ed.), *Archaeometry.* Amsterdam: Elsevier, 271–89.

Conrad, H-G., and B. Rothenberg 1980. *Antikes Kupfer im Timna Tal. Der Anschnitt* Monograph 1. Bochum: Bergbau Museum.

Cowell, M. R., P. T. Craddock, A. W. G. Pike, and A. M. Burnett 2000. "An analytical survey of Roman provincial copper-alloy coins and the continuity of brass production in Asia Minor," in B. Kluge and B. Weisser (eds.), *XII. Internationaler Numismatischer Kongress Berlin 1997.* Berlin: Association Internationale des Numismates Professionnels, 70–77.

Craddock, P. T. 1976. "The composition of the copper alloys used by the Greek, Etruscan and Roman civilisations, 1: The Greeks before the archaic period," *Journal of Archaeological Science* 3.2: 93–113

Craddock, P. T. 1977. "The composition of the copper alloys used by the Greek, Etruscan and Roman civilisations, 2: The archaic, classical and Hellenistic Greeks," *Journal of Archaeological Science* 4.2: 103–24.

Craddock, P. T. 1978. "The composition of the copper alloys used by the Greek, Etruscan and Roman civilisations, 3: The origins and early use of Brass," *Journal of Archaeological Science* 5.1: 1–16.

Craddock, P. T. 1986. "The metallurgy and composition of Etruscan bronze," *Studi Etruschi* 52: 211–71.

Craddock, P. T. 1992. "A short history of firesetting," *Endeavour* 16.3: 145–50.

Craddock, P. T. 1995. *Early metal mining and production.* Edinburgh: Edinburgh University Press.

Craddock, P. T. (ed.) 1998. *2000 years of zinc and brass.* 2nd ed. British Museum Occasional Paper 50. London: British Museum.

Craddock, P. T. 2003. "Cast iron, fined iron, crucible steel: Liquid iron in the ancient world," in Craddock and Lang 2003: 231–57.

Craddock, P. T., A. M. Burnett, and K. Preston 1980. "Hellenistic copper-base coinage and the origins of brass," in W. A. Oddy (ed.), *Scientific Studies in Numismatics.* British Museum Occasional Paper 18. London: British Museum, 53–64.

Craddock, P. T., and M. J. Hughes (eds.) 1985. *Furnaces and smelting technology in antiquity*. British Museum Occasional Paper 48. London: British Museum.

Craddock, P. T., I. C. Freestone, N. H. Gale, N. D. Meeks, B. Rothenberg, and M. S. Tite 1985. "The investigation of a small heap of silver smelting debris from Rio Tinto, Huelva, Spain," in Craddock and Hughes 1985, 199–218.

Craddock, P. T., I. C. Freestone, L. K. Gurjar, A. Middleton, and L. Willies 1989. "The production of lead, silver and zinc in ancient India," in Hauptmann, Pernicka, and Wagner 1989: 51–70.

Craddock, P. T., I. C. Freestone, L. K. Gurjar, A. P. Middleton, and L. Willies, L. 1998a. "Zinc in India," in Craddock 1998: 27–72.

Craddock, P. T., S. C. La Niece, and D. R. Hook 1998b. "Brass in the medieval Islamic world," in Craddock 1998: 73–114.

Craddock, P. T., and K. Eckstein 2003. "Production of brass in antiquity by direct reduction," in Craddock and Lang 2003: 216–30.

Craddock, P. T., and J. Lang (eds.) 2003. *Mining and metal production through the ages*. London: British Museum Press.

Craddock, P. T., M. R. Cowell, and M.-F. Guerra 2005. "Controlling the composition of gold and the invention of gold refining in Lydian Anatolia," in Ü. Yalçin (ed.), *Anatolian metal, III.Der Anschnitt* Monograph 11. Bochum: Bergbau Museum, 67–77.

Crew, P. 1998. "Laxton revisited," *Journal of the Historical Metallurgy Society* 32.2: 49–53.

Crew, P., and S. Crew (eds.) 1997. *Abstracts: Early ironworking in Europe*. Maentwrog: Snowdonia National Park.

Crosby, M. 1941. "Greek inscriptions: A *poletai* record of the year 367/6 B.C.," *Hesperia* 10: 14–30.

Crosby, M. 1950. "The leases of the Laureion mines," *Hesperia* 19: 189–312.

Davies, O. 1935. *Roman mines in Europe*. Oxford: Oxford University Press.

Dejonghe, L., E. Ladeuze, and D. Jans 1993. *Atlas des gisements plombo-zinciferes synclinorium de Veviers (Est de la Belgique)*. Brussels: Service Géologique de Belgique.

Dieudonné-Glad, N. 1997. "Oulches, a late Roman iron smelting and smithing workshop," in Crew and Crew 1997: 17–20.

Domerque, C. (ed.) 1989a. *Mineria y metalurgia en las antiquas civilizaciones mediterraneas y Europas I & II*. Madrid: Institutio de Conservaciones y Restauracion de Benes Culturales.

Domerque, C. 1989b. "Les techniques minières antiques et le *De re metallica* d'Agricola," in Domerque 1989a: II, 76–95.

Domerque, C. 1990. *Les mines de la Péninsule Ibérique dans l'Antiquité romaine*. Bibliothèque de l'Ecole française de Rome 127. Rome: Ecole française de Rome

Domerque, C., and G. Hérail 1999. "Conditions de gisement et exploitation antique á Las Médulas (Léon, Espagne)," in B. Cauuet (ed.), *L'or dans l'antiquité*. Toulouse: Aquitania, 93–116.

Dungworth, D. 1996. "Caley's 'zinc decline' reconsidered," *The Numismatic Chronicle* 156: 228–34.

Dutrizac, J. E., J. L. Jambor, and J. B. O'Reilly 1983. "Man's first use of jarosite: The pre-Roman mining and metallurgical operations at Rio Tinto, Spain," *Bulletin of the Canadian Institute of Mining and Metallurgy* 76.859:78–82.

Ehrenreich, R. M., 1985. *Trade, technology and the ironworking community in the iron age in southern Britain*. British Archaeological Reports 144. Oxford: BAR.

Elkington, D. 2001. "Roman mining law," *Mining History: Bulletin of the Peak District Mines Historical Society* 14.6: 61–65.

Feurerbach, A. M. 2001. *Crucible steel in central Asia*. PhD Thesis, Institute of Archaeology, University College, London.

Fulford, M. G., and J. R. L. Allen 1992. "Iron-making at the Chesters Villa, Woolaston, Gloucestershire: Survey and excavations 1987–91," *Britannia* 23: 188–91.

Gowland, W. 1899. "The early metallurgy of copper, tin and iron in Europe, as illustrated by ancient remains, and the primitive processes surviving in Japan," *Archaeologia* 56. 2: 267–322.

Guerrero Quintero, C. (ed.) 2006. *La rueda elevadora de aqua romana de Rio Tinto en el Museo de Huelva*. Seville: Junta de Andalucia, Consejeria de Cultura.

Gunther, R. T. (ed.) 1934. *The Greek Herbal of Dioscorides: John Goodyer's translation of 1655*. Oxford: Oxford University Press.

Halleux, R. 1973. "L'orichalque et le laiton," *Antiquite Classique* 42: 64–81.

Hauptmann, A., E. Pernicka, and G. A. Wagner (eds.) 1989. *Old world archaeometallurgy. Der Anschnitt* Monograph 8. Bochum: Bergbau Museum.

Hauptmann, A., and G. Weisgerber 1992. "Periods of ore exploitation and metal production in the area of Feinan, Wadi Araba, Jordan," in M. Zaghoul et al. (eds.), *Studies in the history and archaeology of Jordan*, vol. 4. Amman: Department of Antiquities, 61–66.

Hawthorne, J. G., and C. S. Smith (eds.) 1963. *On divers arts: The treatise of Theophilus*. Chicago: Basic Books.

Healy, J. F. 1978. *Mining and metallurgy in the Greek and Roman world*. London: Thames and Hudson.

Hong, S., J.-P. Candelone, C. C. Patterson, and C. F. Boutron 1996. "History of ancient copper smelting pollution during Roman and medieval times recorded in Greenland ice," *Science* 272: 199–206.

Hook, D. R., and P. T. Craddock 1996. "The scientific analysis of the copper-alloy lamps: Aspects of classical alloying practices," in D. M. Bailey, *A catalogue of the lamps in the British Museum: IV. Lamps of metal and stone and lampstands*. London: British Museum Press, 144–63.

Hoover, H. C., and L. H. Hoover (trans. and eds.) 1912. *Agricola: De re metallica*. London: The Mining Magazine.

Hopper, R. J. 1979. *Trade and industry in classical Greece*. London: Thames and Hudson.

Humphrey, J. W., J. P. Oleson, and A. N. Sherwood 1998. *Greek and Roman technology: A sourcebook*. London: Routledge.

Istenic, J., and Z. Šmit 2008. "The beginning of the use of brass in Europe with particular reference to the south-eastern Alpine region," in S. La Niece, D. R. Hook, and P. T. Craddock (eds.), *Metals and mines: studies in archaeometallurgy*. London: Archetype.

Jackson, R. P., and P. T. Craddock 1995. "The Ribchester Hoard: A descriptive and technical study," in Raftery et al. 1995: 75–102.

de Jesus, P. S. 1980. *The development of prehistoric mining and metallurgy in Anatolia*. British Archaeological Reports, Intl. Series S74. Oxford: BAR.

Jones, J. E. 1984. "Ancient Athenian silver mines, dressing floors and smelting sites," *Journal of the Historical Metallurgy Society* 18.2: 65–81.

Kassianidou, V., B. Rothenberg, and P. Andrews 1995. "Silver production in the Tartessian period: The evidence from Monte Romero," *ARX: World Journal of Prehistoric and Ancient Studies* 1: 17–34.

Klemm, D. D., and R. Klemm 1989. "Antike Goldgewinnung in der Ostwüste Ägyptens," in Hauptmann, Pernicka, and Wagner 1989: 227–34.

Lang, J. 1988. "Study of the metallography of some Roman swords," *Britannia* 19: 199–216.

Lang, J. 1995. "A metallographic examination of eight Roman daggers from Britain," in Raftery et al. 1995: 119–32.

Lang, J., P. T. Craddock, and St. J. Simpson 1998. "New evidence for early crucible steel," *Journal of the Historical Metallurgy Society* 32.1: 7–14.

Lehmann, J. 2000. "Seit wann wird mit zincweiô gemalt? Chemische Untersuchungen, mittelalterliche Quellenschriften," *Restauro* 106.5: 356–60.

Lewis, M. J. T. 1997. *Millstone and hammer: The origins of water power.* Hull: Hull University Press.

Lewis, P. R., and G. D. B. Jones 1969. "The Dolaucothi gold mines I," *Antiquaries Journal* 49.2: 244–72.

Lewis, P. R., and G. D. B. Jones 1970. "Roman gold-mining in North West Spain," *Journal of Roman Studies* 60: 169–85.

Lullies, R., and M. Hirmer 1960. *Greek sculpture.* New York: Abrams.

Maddin, R., A. Hauptmann, and G. Weisgerber 1996. "Metallographische Untersuchungen an römischen Gezähe Rio Tinto, Spanien," *Metalla* 3.1: 27–44.

Maréchal, J. 1985. "Methods of ore roasting and the furnaces used," in Craddock and Hughes 1985: 29–42.

Merkel, J. 1985. "Ore beneficiation during the Late Bronze Age/Early Iron Age at Timna, Israel," *MASCA Journal* 3.5: 164–69.

Merkel, J. F. 1990. "Experimental reconstruction of Bronze Age copper smelting based on archaeological evidence from Timna," in B. Rotherberg (ed.), *The ancient metallurgy of copper.* London: Institute for Archaeo-metallurgical Studies, 78–122.

Meyers, P. 2004. "Production of silver in antiquity: Ore types identified based upon elemental compositions of ancient silver artifacts," in L. van Zelst (ed.), *Patterns and process.* Suitland: Smithsonian Center for Materials Research and Education, 271–88.

Mighall, T. 2003. "Geochemical monitoring of heavy metal pollution and prehistoric mining," in Craddock and Lang 2003: 43–51.

Mighall, T., and F. M. Chambers 1993. "Early mining and metalworking: Its impact on the environment," *Journal of the Historical Metallurgy Society* 27.2: 71–83.

Minto, A. 1955. "L'antica industria mineraria in Etruria ed il porto di Populonia," *Studi Etruschi* 23: 317–23.

Mommsen, T., O. Gradenwitz, and C. G. Bruns 1909. *Fontes iuris Romani antiqui.* 7th ed. Tubingen: Mohr.

Mrozek, S., 1989. "Le travail des hommes libres dans les mines romaines," in Domerque 1989: 163–71.

Muhly, J. D., R. Maddin, and V. Karageorghis (eds.) 1982. *Early metallurgy in Cyprus, 4000–500 B.C.* Nicosia: Peirides Foundation.

Oddy, W. A., and J. Swaddling 1985. "Illustrations of metalworking furnaces on Greek vases," in Craddock and Hughes 1985: 43–58.

Oleson, J. P. 1984 *Greek and Roman water-lifting devices: The history of a technology.* Toronto: University of Toronto Press.

Oleson, J. P. 2000. "Water Lifting," in Ö. Wikander (ed.), *Handbook of ancient water technology.* Leiden: Brill, 217–302.

Palmer, R. E. 1926–1927. "Notes on some ancient mine equipments and systems," *Transactions of the Institute of Mining and Metallurgy* 36: 299–336.

Penhallurick, R. D. 1986. *Tin in antiquity.* London: The Institute of Metals.

Pernicka, E., T. C. Seeliger, G. A. Wagner, F. Begemann, S. Schmitt-Strecker, C. Eibner, O. Öztunali, and I. Baranyi 1984. "Archaömetallurgische Untersuchungen in Nord-westanatolien," *Jahrbuch der Römisch-Germanischen Zentralmuseum Mainz* 31: 553–600.

Photos-Jones, E., and J. Ellis Jones 1994. "The building and industrial remains at Agrileza, Laurion, and their contribution to the working of the site," *Annual of the British School at Athens* 89: 307–58.

Ponting, M. J. 1999. "East meets West in post-classical Bet Se'an: The archaeometallurgy of culture change," *Journal of Archaeological Science* 26.11: 1311–21.

Ponting, M. J., and I. Segal 1998. "Inductively coupled plasma-atomic emission spectroscopy analyses of Roman military copper-alloy artefacts from the excavations at Masada, Israel," *Archaeometry* 40.1: 109–22.

Pyatt, F. B., G. Gilmore, J. P. Grattan, C. O. Hunt, and S. McLaren 2000. "An Imperial legacy? An exploration of the environmental impact of ancient mining and smelting in southern Jordan," *Journal of Archaeological Science* 27: 771–78.

Raftery, M. B., J. V. S. Megaw, and V. Rigby (eds.) 1995. *Sites and sights of the iron age: Essays on fieldwork and museum research presented to Ian Mathieson Stead.* Oxford: Oxbow.

Ramage, A., and P. T. Craddock 2000. *King Croesus' gold.* London: British Museum Press.

Rehren, T. 1999. "Small size, large scale: Roman brass production in Germania Inferior," *Journal of Archaeological Science* 26.8: 1083–87.

Rehren, T., D. Vanhove, and H. Mussche 2002. "Ores from the washeries in the Lavriotiki," *Metalla* 9.1: 27–46.

Riddle, J. M. 1985. *Dioscorides on pharmacy and medicine.* Austin: University of Texas.

Rothenberg, B. 1972. *Timna.* London: Thames and Hudson.

Rothenberg, B., F. G. Palomero, and H.-G. Bachmann 1989. "The Rio Tinto Enigma," in Domergue 1989a: 57–70.

Rinuy, A., and F. Schwiezer (eds.) 1994. *L'Oeuvre d'art sous le regard des sciences.* Geneva: Musée d'art histoire and Editions Slatkine.

Salkield, L. U. 1987. *A technical history of the Rio Tinto Mines: Some notes on exploitation from pre-Phoenician times to the 1950s.* London: The Institution of Mining and Metallurgy.

Sánchez-Palencia, J.-F. 1989. "La explotacion del oro en la Hispania Romana: Sus inicios y precedents," In Domergue 1989a: II, 35–49.

Schweizer, F. 1994. "Etudes techniques de laitons byzantins," in Rinuy and Schwiezer 1994: 175–86.

Schweizer, F., and J. Bujard 1994. "Aspect Metallurgie de quelques objets byzantins et omeyyades decouverts recemment en Jordanie," in Rinuy and Schwiezer 1994: 191–203.

Shepherd, R. 1992. "Hannibal the rock breaker," *Minerals Industry International* 1992: 39–47.

Sim, D. 1997. "Roman chain mail: Experiments to reproduce the techniques of manufacture," *Britannia* 28: 359–71.

Sim, D., 1998. *Beyond the bloom.* British Archaeological Reports, Intl. Series S725. Oxford: BAR.

Sim, D., and I. Ridge 2002. *Iron for the eagles.* Stroud: Tempus.

Smith, C. S., and M. T. Gnudi (trans. and eds.) 1942. *The Pyrotechnia of Vannoccio Biringuccio.* Chicago: Chicago University Press.

Tylecote, R. F. 1981. "From pot bellows to tuyeres," *Levant* 13: 107–18.

Tylecote, R. F. 1987 *The early history of metallurgy in Europe.* London: Longman.

Tylecote, R. F., M. S. Balmuth, and R. Massoli-Novelli 1983. "Copper and bronze metallurgy in Sardinia," *Journal of the Historical Metallurgy Society* 17.1: 63–78.

Wagner, G. A., and G. Weisgerber (eds.) 1988. *Antike Edel- und Buntmetallgewinnung auf Thasos. Der Anschnitt* Monograph 6. Bochum: Bergbau Museum.

Wagner, G., and Ö. Öztunali 2000. "Prehistoric copper sources in Turkey," in Ü. Yalçin (ed.), *Anatolian Meta*Vol. 1. *Der Anschnitt* Monograph 11. Bochum: Bergbau Museum, 31–66.

Wahl, J. 1993. "Trés Miñas-Vorbericht über die archäologischen Ausgragungen in Bereich des Römischen Goldwerks 1986–7," in H. Steuer and U. Zimmermann (eds.), *Montanarchäologie in Europa*. Sigmaringen: Jan Torbecke, 123–52.

Wahl, J. 1998. "Aspectos technológicos da indústria minera e metalúrgica Romana de Três Miñas e Campo de Jales," *Actas do Seminário Arquelogia E Museologia Minerias*. Lisboa: Museu Geológico, 57–68.

Walsh, R. 1929. "Galen visits the Dead Sea and the copper mines of Cyprus (166 AD)," *Bulletin of the Geographical Society of Philadelphia* 25: 92–110.

Weisgerber, G. 1979. "Das römisch Wasserheberad aus Rio Tinto in Spanien im British Museum London," *Der Anschnitt* 2–3: 52–79.

Weisgerber, G., and C. Roden 1985. "Römische Schmiedeszenen und ihre Gebläse," *Der Anschnitt* 37.1: 2–21.

Weisgerber, G., and C. Roden, C. 1986. "Griechische Metallhandwerker und ihre Gebläse," *Der Anschnitt* 38.1: 2–26.

Weisgerber, G., and L. Willies 2000. "The use of fire in prehistoric and ancient mining: Firesetting," *Paléorient* 26.2: 131–49.

Welter, J-M. 2003. "The zinc content of brass," *Techne* 18: 27–36.

Williams, A., 1977. "Roman arms and armour: A technical note," *Journal of Archaeological Science* 1.4: 77–87.

Willies, L. 1991. "Ancient copper mining at Wadi Amran, Israel," *Mining History*, special issue of *Bulletin of the Peak District Mines Historical Society* 11.3: 109–38.

Willies, L. 1994. "Firesetting technology," in T. D. Ford and L. Willies (eds.), *Mining before powder*, special issue of *Bulletin of the Peak District Mines Historical Society* 12.3: 1–8.

Willies, L. 1997. "Roman mining at Rio Tinto, Huelva, Spain, and appendix: The 1981 archaeological survey," *Mining history: Bulletin of the Peak District Mines Historical Society* 13.3: 1–30.

Wilson, A. I. 2002. "Machines, power and the ancient economy," *Journal of Roman Studies* 92: 1–32.

Wollmann, V. 1976. "Römischer Goldbergbau in Alburnus Major (Roşia Montănă) in Drakien, *Der Anschnitt* 6: 182–91.

# CHAPTER 5

# QUARRYING AND STONEWORKING

## J. CLAYTON FANT

THE impulse toward monumental religious architecture in Greece during the archaic period and the consequent shift from building in wood to stone construction made quarrying and stoneworking activities central to communal identity. Nevertheless, down to the Hellenistic period quarrying remained relatively small in scale, static in technology, and local in reach. The notable exceptions, such as Mt. Pentelicon near Athens, and the quarries of fine statuary marble on the island of Paros, also flag the growing preference in this period for marble over the abundant supplies of local limestone (conventionally called *poros*). These centers of activity foreshadow the larger quarrying ventures of the Hellenistic period and the enormous quarries and empire-wide distribution of the Roman epoch.

## GREEK QUARRYING AND STONEWORKING

The origins of Greek quarrying are not entirely clear, but by 500 B.C. the techniques were already well established. There seems to have been no carryover from the Bronze Age across two centuries of deep cultural discontinuity. The common assumption has been that the source was Egypt (Ward-Perkins 1971a: 143, 1971b: 528; Boardman 1976: 19, 77), where quarrying goes back into the third millennium B.C.

Although the basic technique of freeing a block by trenching around it does seem to have been pioneered in Egypt, the absence of iron wedges and quarry picks before about 600 B.C. calls this assumption into question (Waelkens 1992; Klemm and Klemm 1981: 36). In fact, iron wedges are first documented in Egypt in the fourth century B.C., but they may have been introduced even earlier from the Greek colony at Naukratis in the Delta (Herrell 2002: 241). Important new work points to connections with the Middle East (Waelkens et al. 1988, 1990), particularly the Hittite and neo-Hittite tradition of the Levant. This suggestion gains support from a modern sculptor's observation that early Greek carving techniques owe more to Hittite work than to their presumed Egyptian models (Rockwell 1993: 198–99). In fact, quarrying practices were so refined by the end of the sixth century B.C. that there was little subsequent change, at least down to the early Roman Empire. The result is that quarry faces can rarely be dated without related evidence, such as ceramics, graffiti, or obvious association with a datable building. Roman innovations were few and subtle, so ancient quarrying retained its character virtually from beginning to end, and evolved with few obvious changes into medieval quarrying.

## Trenching Technique

The basic method of separating a block of limestone or marble from the parent rock was common to all quarrying areas and all periods of ancient extractive technology. Variations in the means of freeing a block once it was isolated above and on four sides were considerable, creating the appearance of greater divergence in fundamental practice than was actually the case. Moreover, there was no basic difference in technique between marble and limestone (some varieties of which are as hard as marble), or for that matter other relatively soft stones. Distinct techniques, however, were necessitated by the harder igneous stones, of which there were few in the Greek world.

To free a block, a column drum (basically a block), or a monolithic column (in the Roman period), the quarryman used a quarry pick, shaped like a modern sledgehammer but with a longer handle and with a lighter iron head. One or both ends of the iron implement were brought to a dull point. The motion of the quarryman was to raise the pick above his head and bring it down to a point of impact between his legs, so the worker faces forward and the movement of his body is an easy bend at the waist. Twisting motions such as are seen today when using an axe, scythe, or leaf rake, were avoided, reducing stress on the back and making it more feasible to work long hours without injury. The picks used for most of the Greco-Roman period had long handles and sharp points on the iron head. The impact crushed the crystals in a small area, allowing precise work with a minimum of waste. Because the point of the pick did not penetrate very deeply at each stroke, the quarryman had to edge back constantly. The effect, in skilled hands, was to create a very shallow trench in a straight line, leaving a tool mark on the quarry wall resembling that created by a point chisel driven across a flat surface. The quarryman then moved laterally to widen the trench, until finally a separation trench about 40–80 cm wide was created to the desired depth (figure 5.1). Since the iron pick head was narrow, it was possible to create a vertical face with little deviation. Quarry surfaces

Figure 5.1. Quarry trenches at Docimium. (Photograph by J. C. Fant.)

show traces of this light pick as early as the late sixth century, as graffiti at Belevi near Ephesus reveal, in the extensive quarries opened for construction of the Artemisium (figure 5.2).

Once a block was isolated, it was separated by splitting it free from the bedrock base. From the beginning of Greek quarrying, the standard tool was the iron wedge, but there is greater variation in this specific technique than in trenching around blocks. Wooden wedges, which are recognizable by the large dimensions of the holes cut for them (up to 60 x 60 cm) and their wide spacing, are very rare and perhaps restricted to deposits of stone that could be easily split (e.g., Doliana: Waelkens et al. 1990: 65). Holes chiseled for iron wedges were much smaller and somewhat more closely spaced. Sometimes they were connected by a more irregular cavity that permitted hammering directly on the wedges in place. This system is evident already at the quarry for the colossus at Apollonas on Naxos, the archaic-period quarry at Phanari on Thasos, and the sixth-century quarry for the tumulus at Belevi near Ephesus. Splitting the block off was one of the riskiest moments in quarrying, and several means were devised to provide better control of the direction and angle of the break. Runs of heavy chisel lines connecting the wedge holes in a *pointillé* technique, as in the Roman quarries of Aliki on Thasos, can be seen as early as the sixth century at Apollonas on Naxos (Waelkens et al. 1990: 62–65). Another method was to place the wedge holes within a continuous chisel-cut groove, which would weaken the stone along the intended break line prior to hammering on the wedges themselves. Highly fissile stone such as the marble of Carystus in southern Euboea was sometimes split free simply by the pressure of a pry bar, underlining the fact that the key factor was the nature of the stone deposits, rather than a chronological development of technique documented by, for instance, size or shape of wedge holes (Roeder 1965: 518–34; Nylander 1968: 6–10).

Figure 5.2. Quarry face with marks of the light pick, sixth century B.C. Belevi, near Ephesus. (Photograph by J. C. Fant.)

Most Greek quarrying, being tied to specific construction projects, was episodic and small. Quarrymen sought deposits easily accessible without extensive preliminary work, an investment that would be repaid only over a long periods of production. Many Greek quarries thus give the appearance of small-scale and shallow workings, where only one or two layers of trenches were cut. Larger projects producing greater quantities of debris would quickly choke such flat quarry beds, and so quarry schemes cutting into slopes, which facilitated removal both of debris and finished blocks, were often preferred. The great vein of fine marble on the western side of Mt. Pentelicon, which provided material for the Periclean Acropolis and a variety of structures down to the stadium of Herodes Atticus in the mid-second century A.D., is a spectacular example (Korres 1995). Few early quarries were as large as Belevi, with its 35 m vertical faces, since few architectural projects were on the scale of the Artemisium. Nor was all quarrying purely for local uses. As early as the late sixth century B.C., quarries on Paros were in a position to export substantial quantities of marble to help Cleisthenes win over the Delphians (Herodotus 5.62.3).

## Transport

Once a block was freed, the next challenge was transport; this obvious and difficult requirement explains why most quarries in the premodern era served very local needs. Since quarries were often sited on ridgelines—because prospecting was easy and removal of the overburden greatly simplified—gravity, used with caution, provided an advantage. Runways, often bordered with heavy bollards to control the paying out of lines attached to sledges or directly to the blocks, were probably developed as early as quarrying itself. Mt. Pentelicon near Athens provides early examples. Probably the most spectacular of these *lizza* paths (the common term comes from Carrara), however, date to the Roman period, as at Mons Porphyrites in the eastern desert of Egypt. Intra-quarry transport was by ox or mule cart; extended overland carriage was obviously avoided, but evidence from Egypt shows that carts with very wide axles (2.22 m and 2.66 m), possibly drawn by camels, carried the products of the numerous quarries of the Eastern Desert down to the Nile (Peacock and Maxfield 1997: 261) (cf. figure 23.10). More desirable was a seaside location, such as the quarries of Vathy, Phanari, and Aliki on the island of Thasos, or proximity to a harbor like that of Saraylar, which served the ancient quarries of Proconnesus. It was no accident that these two sources of white marble were among the earliest to export; Proconnesian marble was used for the Mausoleum at Hali-carnassus (Pliny, *HN* 36.47). Cranes using a fixed mast and mobile boom studded harbors and waterfronts (Vitruvius, *De arch.* 10.2.10; Sodini et al. 1980). Seaborne transport of stone, blocks, and monolithic columns was a significant proportion of trade in the Mediterranean during the Roman Empire, judging by the represen-tation of such cargoes among recorded shipwrecks (Parker 1992). In the late Hel-lenistic period, finished sculptural and architectural objects predominate (for ex-ample, the cargo of the Mahdia wreck: Hellenkemper Salies 1994); during the early empire, however, cargoes consist of blocks and monolithic columns, and in the later empire prefabricated church kits appear (Kapitän 1961).

Shaping of quarry products, whether for sculpture, architecture, or the fabri-cation of objects such as basins or sarcophagi, followed a common procedure in which tools of tempered iron were essential. Preliminary shaping could still be done with the quarry pick or with a chisel with a heavy point. The point chisel was the chief tool for all rough shaping work in architecture as well as sculpture. With the chisel held at about 70 degrees, large volumes of stone can be removed quickly. At 45 degrees, strokes producing splits with less propagation are used to approach the final surface (Rockwell 1993: 39). Fine dressing, however, was the task of the flat chisel; a flat chisel with teeth, essentially a row of very small flat chisels, was apparently a Roman innovation. Very fine shaping was done with abrasive tools, rasps, files, and at the end, emery and pumice if a reflective surface was wanted (rare until Antonine times). The last category of tool was the drill, of no great significance until horizontal motion was introduced; then the deep continuous channels of the running drill become characteristic of the chiaroscuro effects of Roman sculpture from the second century A.D. on (figure 2.7; Strong and Claridge 1976; Rockwell 1993: 37–38).

# ROMAN QUARRYING

During the Roman period the principal development was the growth of a central organization for fine stone supplies. This led in turn to some technical innovations, but more important was the exponential rise in scale of stone quarrying and stone use. Under the emperors, new lithic resources from Egypt were explored and exploited more extensively than they had been even during the Middle Kingdom. A new taste for colored stone spurred the opening of new quarries, and the volume of building projects in Rome from Augustus (31 B.C.–A.D. 14) onward, mirrored over time by prosperity in the provinces, made marble the dominant material for building and decoration.

Whereas research on Greek quarrying has generally been piecemeal, with studies often linked to investigation of entire sites, research on the Roman marble trade has become a subject in its own right since its launch in the essays of John Ward-Perkins and the quarry surveys of Josef Roeder in the 1960s and 1970s. Roeder directed our attention to the neglected sources of well-known Roman lithic materials, while Ward-Perkins sketched a picture of an empire-wide system with particular units finding specialized niches, a process he repeatedly characterized in the language of capitalism.

Using criteria like workshop identification in architectural carving and sarcophagus production, Ward-Perkins formulated a list of factors that he highlighted as fundamental to the marble trade under the empire. Rationalization, standardization of practices—including dimensions of quarry products, use of prefabrication, especially in sarcophagus production, stockpiling rather than production for individual projects, and centralization under imperial ownership and administration. Although the mercantile mentality this model assumes must be modified, Ward-Perkins' work stimulated a generation of new research and, most valuably, it challenged art historians to look beyond the hand of individual artists to the nature of the raw material and the production processes.

# CENTRALIZED MARBLE TRADE
# IN THE ROMAN EMPIRE

By the second century A.D., the Roman emperors owned most of the major sources of fine stone. But the idea of a centralized trade embraces more than the actual imperial organization, about whose nature there are still areas of doubt. The prestige of imperial buildings as tastemakers, and the scale of imperial production of marble caused the rest of the marble trade—other than the purely local—to orbit around it.

Both the idea of using marble and the material itself were imports to Rome in the second century B.C. Proconsuls returning from victorious and lucrative campaigns in the eastern Mediterranean found that a dramatic way to celebrate their success was to build a pious monument with imported marble. In 190 B.C., Scipio Africanus and his brother built an arch (Livy 37.3.7) that may have been in marble. The phenomenon expanded in the second half of the century with manubial temples (built from spoils of war), most of them designed and built by Hermodorus of Salamis (Gros 1976). Where we know it, the source of the marble, and certainly of the masons schooled in working it, was Mt. Pentelicon in Attica. The reference to Athens suited the programmatic aspect of these dedications well. One of their purposes was to advertise the culture as well as the wealth of the donors, and ever since the treaty with the Aetolians of 212 B.C. the Romans had deferred to Athens as the cultural center of Greece. Marble was also imported as columns for the temporary wooden theaters that aediles (junior magistrates eager to gain public approval) constructed for public festivals; these had the additional advantage that it could be resold when the sets were broken down, or even moved into the private house of one of the sponsors (Pliny, *HN* 17.6, 36.7). Polychrome marble began to appear in Rome in the next century, associated in anecdote with leading political figures—orange Numidian used as a house threshold by M. Aemilius Lepidus, consul in 78 (Pliny, *HN* 36.49), red and black Lucullan imported by its namesake, M. Licinius Lucullus—while others became familiar at first in Italy as carved legs for atrium tables or wall cladding. During their propaganda war in the 50s B.C., Caesar responded to Pompey's construction of the spectacular Theatrum Pompeii by preparing for his own building campaign, opening Italy's first white marble quarries, near Luna in Liguria, near modern Cararra (Strabo 5.2.5; Fant 1989). Although Caesar did not live to see the result of his investment in infrastructure, his political heir took full advantage of it and demonstrated that he understood the value of marble displays as a weapon in political campaigning.

One component of the regime that Augustus set about establishing after a century of intermittent civil wars was a massive building campaign. Infrastructure projects and smaller public buildings were delegated to Agrippa or other members of the Augustan circle, but Augustus himself took responsibility for the most conspicuous and emblematic projects. The Forum of Augustus used both colored marbles already well known and those imported only recently. Later evidence labels all of them imperial property, and the clear inference is that the emperor's agents both gathered up the famous stones of the late Republic and searched out a number of new ones. Surveys in the 1990s have produced evidence of an extensive campaign of prospecting and development at Mons Porphyrites in the Eastern Desert of Egypt, where one Cominius Leugas, position not named but beyond doubt an imperial agent, congratulated himself in A.D. 18 on having discovered porphyry, black porphyry (*knekites*), and other colored stones. Given the logistical difficulty of working in the Eastern Desert and the number of finds he had made, the inference is inescapable that the effort had begun well before the demise of Augustus in A.D. 14 (Peacock and Maxfield 1997: 23; Fant 1999: 279–80).

Thus was created the imperial institution that, in the second century A.D., was probably called the *ratio marmorum*, or marble bureau (*CIL* 6.8631, 301, 8482, 33790; 11.3199; Fant 1993: note 3). A provisional list of stone sources owned and exploited by the Bureau includes the following (the traditional Italian name follows the Latin) (Fant 1993: 163–67):

*Colored marbles (and other stones)*

*marmor Numidicum, giallo antico*: Numidian, from Chemtou in western Tunisia.

*marmor Luculleum, africano*: Lucullan, from Teos, near Smyrna/Izmir.

*marmor Synnadicum* or *Phrygium, pavonazzetto*: Phrygian, from Docimium.

*marmor Lacedaemonium* (or *lapis Lacedaemonius*), *serpentino* or *porfido verde*: green porphyry, from Laconia.

*marmor Carystium, cipollino*: Carystian, from southern Euboea.

*marmor Chium, portasanta*: Chian.

*marmor Troadense, granito violetto*: Troad granite, from Kozak Dag in the Troad.

All exported Egyptian stones, most notably *lapis Thebaicus* or *pyrropoikilos* (Aswan granite), *marmor Claudianum* (*granito del Foro*, Mons Claudianus granite), *marmor Porphyrites* (purple and black porphyry), *lapis basanites* (*bekhen* stone from Wadi Hammamat), alabasters, and many igneous stones quarried in limited quantities.

*White marbles*

*marmor Lunense, marmo di Carrara*: Luna, Carrara in northwestern Italy.

*marmor Parium, lychnites* and lesser qualities: island of Paros.

*marmor Proconnesium, Proconnesian*: Sea of Marmara.

*Likely imperial, but poorly documented*

*marmor Thasium*: white marble from Thasos.

*marmor Scyrium, breccia di Settebassi*: colored marble from Scyros.

*cipollino rosso, rosso brecciato* or *africanone*: polychrome marble of Iasos.

*marmor Heracleioticum*: Heraclea sub Latmus.

(no known Latin name): a coarse white marble from St. Beat in the Pyrenees.

Such well-known quarries of white marbles as Mt. Pentelicon and Hymettus, Aphrodisias, and Belevi, and other quarries near Ephesus seem to have remained in the hands of their cities. Stones with clear imperial associations were the most desirable, and within that group the most prestigious were Numidian and Phrygian, the dominant colors in the interior of the Pantheon, then Lucullan, Chian, Carystian, and the breccia of Scyros, in about that order. The Egyptian granites were also highly prestigious but in such short supply that few individuals outside the court could expect to obtain them. A partial exception was Aswan granite, the quarries of which were accessible by water (the first cataract of the Nile is a dike of this granite), and thin slabs of the purple and green porphyries for floor compositions (*opus sectile*) were also available to the well connected (Jongste et al. 1992). Since these stones were not widely obtainable, other similar examples entered the market as substitutes (*marmi sostituivi*): granite from Sardinia in place of Aswan granite; granite from Kozak Dag near Pergamon for Mons Claudianus granite; *breccia corallina* from Bithynia for *breccia di Settebassi*, and so forth. In this way, the imperial marble trade indirectly controlled private as well as public markets.

Quarries in Egypt deserve special mention. New research in the Eastern Desert has provided the most dramatic advance in quarry studies in the last two decades. We now have a picture of an immense effort, starting with the prospecting campaign mentioned above, continuing with the development of an extensive system of roads and forts (Maxfield 1996) apparently centered at first on Mons Porphyrites, where a large infrastructure had to be built in very difficult terrain, to an eventual network of dozens of small quarries and several large ones like Mons Claudianus, which was staffed (as we know from more than 7,000 ostraka recovered; Bingen et al. 1992 and 1997) by a force of about one thousand workers and guards (Peacock and Maxfield 1997).

Like many institutions of the Roman Empire, the imperial marble bureau reached its height in the second century A.D., both in scope and bureaucratic organization. But in terms of technology, both in quarrying and transport, innovation was modest and elicited directly by the needs of scale and of adaptation to the uses for which Roman quarry products were intended. And it never became a modern entity, in the terms that Ward-Perkins used to describe it.

## Innovation in the Roman Period

One technological change, first noticed by Waelkens, was the introduction of a heavier quarry pick at the end of the first or beginning of the second century A.D. The thicker iron point of this pick could penetrate farther at each blow; consequently the quarryman could execute many blows before having to move his feet, and this speeded trenching. The cost was greater waste and, to some extent, less precise work. The characteristic tool marks left by this pick are tracks forming segments of circles, rather than the nearly horizontal lines of the light pick. To counteract the tendency of the heavy pick to stray to the outside as it cuts downward, the workmen often reversed direction, leaving alternating bands of marks resembling festoons (hence the Italian description *a festoni*). The heavy pick also contributed to the typical visual impression of a Roman quarry with its huge hills of debris (figure 5.3). The major Roman quarries were active on a large scale for two centuries or more, so it was crucial to plan exploitation so that crews would not block each other, and that debris would not choke the working faces. In fact, at Docimium dated blocks in the debris show that the piles were moved around from time to time in order to build up a working platform to attack a face at a higher level or to expose a new working area (Fant 1989: 42–47). Central organization at the

Figure 5.3. Quarry face with debris. Bacakale, Docimium. (Photograph by J. C. Fant.)

quarries is visible also in the practice of inscribing blocks at the moment of extraction; it was standard at most polychrome marble quarries, but products at white marble quarries were usually anepigraphic (Fant 1993: 157–62). These inscriptions record the date, crews responsible for the work, and the site within the quarry. In the first third of the second century A.D., blocks on hand were marked and perhaps graded at irregular intervals, probably in response to requests for details on inventory. Blocks were shipped from the quarries and to imperial stockpiles, first at the Marmorata in Rome and later (when the Marmorata became overcrowded) along the south bank of the canal connecting Trajan's harbor at Portus with the Tiber (Maischberger 1997; Fant 2001).

Another Roman innovation was the taste for monolithic columns, which developed during the first century A.D. This technique may simply have been seen as a better way to display the colors and patterning of the new imperial polychrome marbles, although both gray and white marble columns were rendered as monoliths just as early. One may even suspect that the popularity of the monolithic column lay at least in part in the utterly unnecessary additional effort involved in production and transport. This effect was redoubled in the case of the spectacular 40-Roman-foot monoliths of Mons Claudianus and Aswan granite supporting the porch of the Pantheon, since any citizen of Rome could estimate the distance and terrain over which they had been safely transported—especially since Agrippa's map of the world could be consulted in the Porticus Vipsania nearby (Pliny, *HN* 3.16–17). The imperial stockyard and workshop at Portus has produced some columns with elaborate patching, which demonstrates the astonishing effort expended to salvage monolithic columns of very expensive stone (figure 5.4).

Column drums were simply blocks that could be quarried like any other, and then rounded. But monolithic shafts had to be isolated as such in the quarry beds

Figure 5.4. Column of Lucullan marble at Portus with numerous patches to correct or enhance surface coloration. (Photograph by J. C. Fant.)

before being broken free, a much more chancy process. Columns in the making and still attached to bedrock show that the quarrymen did as much rounding as possible even before separation, and a set of unfinished columns at Proconnesus has permitted the entire process to be reconstructed (Asgari 1992; for finishing on site see Pensabene 1992; Wilson Jones 2000: 130–32). Other architectural elements, (capitals and bases), as well as sarcophagus blanks, were also roughed out in the quarries. Ward-Perkins saw in this an industrial process of prefabrication in which continuous production to standardized modules was stockpiled as an inventory against which architects all over the Mediterranean could confidently draw without having to place special orders and wait for them. He pointed to the number of columns at quarries and in finished buildings in standard lengths, especially 40 Roman feet, as evidence for this, but it has always seemed unlikely that quarry practices would constrain an architect's choices. Subsequently Wilson Jones provided a better explanation based on the developing canon of the Roman Corinthian order during the Augustan age, in which a proportion of shaft length to total column length of 5:6 tended to favor easily computed lengths in whole numbers of Roman feet (Wilson Jones 2000: 155).

The Roman emphasis on veneer as opposed to structural blocks had both technical and artistic results. Since Roman marble use was never structural—apart from columns and architraves—marble was needed only as sheathing. Architects continued to use traditional materials such as native tuff and travertine even alongside concrete. As colored stones became available in the first century A.D., cut stone floors (*opus sectile*) became popular as inserts within floors of limestone or slate tesserae, or, when possible, as the entire paving material. Both these uses required accurately sliced panels. The stone saw, a long iron blade with flat edges, was mounted in a heavy frame allowing it to travel back and forth in a level plane while a worker trickled in a slurry of sand and water to provide the cutting agent. Pliny (*HN* 36.47) attributes the invention of sawn veneer to Mausolus of Caria in the fourth century B.C., but he focuses his discussion not on the tool but on the sand: coarse sand produces rough cuts and leaves more work for the polishers in the next stage. If the stone saw did originate with Mausolus, it was likely a freehand saw; the addition of a frame to direct the motion should be a Roman refinement. Roman saw-cuts in fact produce surfaces that seem polished, and this had to be an important advantage. Saws were set up at construction sites so that veneer could be cut from blocks and fitted directly to the building in progress. A dramatic example is at the Temple of Venus at Pompeii, where blocks of Proconnesian marble were being sawn when work was interrupted (Bruno et al. 2002). Stocks of veneer prepared for a renovation project were found in the Villa of the Sulpicii near Pompeii (de Simone and Ciro Nappo 2000: 190). Saws were not a common quarrying tool, but there is one case of a sawn quarry face at Docimium (Roeder 1971). Ausonius (*Mosella* 359–64) mentions water-powered marble saws near quarries in the fourth-century A.D. Rhineland. The discovery of water-wheel-driven saws for sawing stone veneer at the site of Jerash in Jordan, at the other side of the empire, now vindicates this text (figure 6.5; Seigne 2002; Wilson 2002), along with a very clear representation of a water-wheel-driven stone saw identified on a Roman sarcophagus at Pammukale (Ritti et al. 2007). Another innovation of uncertain date is the lathe for turning stone columns, tabletops, and vessels. Large columns or column drums may have been given a final finish on a slow lathe, smaller elements on a fast lathe. Pliny (*HN* 36.90) mentions the production of large column drums on a lathe (probably for the Temple of Hera on Samos): "The drums for which [150 columns] were so well balanced in the workshop that they were turned with a boy supplying the force" (*quarum in officina turbines ita librati pependerunt ut puero circumagente tornarentur*). Both Theophrastus (*De lap.* 5, 41) and Pliny (*HN* 44.159) also allude to the finishing of stone vessels with a lathe on the island of Siphnos. The marks of lathe turning have been noticed on a variety of objects in Italy (Blanc and Monthel 2006; Metz 1989: 171–81).

# Diocletian's Price Edict: The Twilight of Roman Quarrying

A chapter of the emperor Diocletian's Edict on Maximum Prices lists some famous stones, but this does not necessarily mean that they were still being quarried in the same manner or at the same rate as earlier in the high empire. Since most of the quarries and stones were under state control, their original price could be set without recourse to decree. It is, however, likely that actual new supplies were earmarked for imperial projects. The inference should be that prices were being set for *reused* quantities of these stones, and a persuasive argument that the unit of this chapter of the Edict was the linear square foot, not a cubic measure (Corcoran and DeLaine 1994), points strongly to veneer, an easily portable and reusable format of stone. Veneer was not a product rough-cut at the quarry (thin slabs were simply too breakable) but one of secondary workshops. Thus the marble trade of the fourth century was already foreshadowing that of the medieval period, when most quarries had become inaccessible and crumbling Roman structures became the chief source of supply.

# REFERENCES

Asgari, N. 1992. "Observations on two types of quarry-items from Proconnesus: Column-shafts and column-bases," in Waelkens et al. 1992: 73–80.

Bingen, J., A. Bülow-Jacobsen, W. E. H. Cockle, H. Cuvigny, L. Rubinstein, and W. Van Rengen 1992. *Mons Claudianus, Ostraca Graeca et Latina I (O.Claud.1–190)*. Cairo: Institut francais d'archéologie orientale.

Bingen, J., A. Bülow-Jacobsen, W. E. H. Cockle, H. Cuvigny, L. Rubinstein, F. Kayser, and W. Van Rengen 1997. *Mons Claudianus, Ostraca Graeca et Latina II (O.Claud. 191–414)*. Cairo: Institut francais d'archéologie orientale.

Blanc, N., and G. Monthel 2006. "Le tournage des elements porteurs en Pierre dans l'Antiquité." Conference abstract. *La Pierre dans tous ses etats*, Colloque International, Association for the Study of Marble and Other Stones in Antiquity, Aix-en-Provence, June 12–18, 2006.

Boardman, J. 1976. *Greek sculpture: The archaic period*. New York: Oxford University Press.

Bruno, M. et al. 2002. "Pompeii after the A.D. 62 earthquake: Historical, isotopic, and petrographic studies of quarry blocks in the Temple of Venus," in J. J. Herrmann, N. Herz, and R. Newman (eds.), *Association for the Study of Marble and Other Stones in Antiquity, V:. Interdisciplinary studies on ancient stone*. London: Archetype Publications, 282–88.

Corcoran, S., and J. DeLaine 1994. "The unit measurement of marble in Diocletian's Prices Edict," *Journal of Roman Archaeology* 7: 263–73.

de Simone, A., and S. Ciro Nappo (eds.) 2000. *Mitis Sarni Opes*. Naples: Denaro.

Fant, J. C. (ed.) 1989. *Cavum antrum Phrygiae: The organization and operations of the Roman imperial marble quarries in Phrygia*. British Archaeological Reports, Intl. Series S482. Oxford: BAR.

Fant, J. C. 1993. "Ideology, gift and trade: A distribution model for the Roman imperial marbles," in W. V. Harris (ed.), *The inscribed economy: Production and distribution in the Roman Empire in the light of instrumentum domesticum.Journal of Roman Archaeology* Suppl. 6. Ann Arbor. MI: JRA, 145–70.

Fant, J. C. 1999. "Augustus and the city of marble," in M. Schvoerer (ed.), *Archeomateriaux, marbres et autres roches. Association for the Study of Marble and Other Stones in*

*Antiquity, IV: Actes de la iv^{éme} conférence internationale, Bordeaux France, 9–13 octobre 1995.* Talence: CRPAA, 277–80.

Fant, J. C. 2001. "Rome's marble yards," *Journal of Roman Archaeology* 14: 167–98.

Gros, P. 1976. *Aurea Templa: Recherches sur l'architecture religieuse de Rome à l'époque d'Auguste.* Rome: École française de Rome.

Harrell, J. A. 2002. "Pharaonic Stone Quarries in the Egyptian Deserts," pp. 232–43 in R. Friedman (ed.), *Egypt and Nubia: Gifts of the Egyptian Deserts.* London: British Museum.

Hellenkemper Salies, G. (ed.) 1994. *Die Antike Schiffsfund von Mahdia.* Köln: Rheinland Verlag.

Jongste, P. F. B., J. B. Jansen, L. Moens, P. De Paepe, and M. Waelkens 1992. "The use of marble in Latium between 70 and 150 A.D. IPCAES for determination of the provenance of white marbles," in Waelkens et al. 1992: 263–67.

Kapitän, G. 1961. "Schiffsfrachten antiker Baugesteine und Architekturteile vor den Küsten Ostsiziliens," *Klio* 39: 276–318.

Klemm, R., and D. Klemm 1981. *Die Steine der Pharaonen.* Munich: Staatliche Museen Aegyptischer Kunst.

Korres, M. 1995. *From Pentelicon to the Parthenon.* Athens: Melissa.

Maischberger, M. 1997. *Marmor in Rom: Anlieferung, Lager- und Werkplätze in der Kaiserzeit.* Wiesbaden: Reichert.

Maxfield, V. A. 1996. "The Eastern Desert forts and the army in Egypt during the principate," in D. M. Bailey (ed.), *Archaeological research in Roman Egypt. Journal of Roman Archaeology* Suppl. 19. Portsmouth, RI: JRA.

Maxfield, V., and D. Peacock 2001. *The Roman Imperial Quarries: Survey and Excavation at Mons Porphyrites. 1994–1998.* Vol. 1, *Topography and Quarries.* London: Egyptian Exploration Society.

Metz, A. 1989. "Ein gedrehter Sandsteintisch aus Augst," *Jahresberichte aus Augst und Kaiseraugst* 6: 171–81.

Nylander, C. 1968. "Bemerkungen zur Steinbrüchgeschichte von Assuan," *Archäologischer Anzeiger* 1968: 6–10.

Parker, A. J. 1992. *Ancient shipwrecks of the Mediterranean and the Roman provinces.* Oxford: Tempus Reparatum.

Peacock, D. P. S., and V. A. Maxfield 1997. *Survey and excavation Mons Claudianus.* Vol. I, *Topography and quarries.* FIFAO 37. Cairo: Institut francais d'archeologie orientale.

Pensabene, P. 1992. "On the method used for dressing the columns of the Colosseum portico," in Waelkens et al. 1992: 81–89.

Ritti, T., K. Grewe, and P. Kessner 2007. "A relief of a water-powered stone saw mill on a sarcophagus at Hierapolis and its implications," *Journal of Roman Archaeology* 20: 138–63.

Rockwell, P. 1993. *The art of stoneworking.* Cambridge: Cambridge University Press. 1993.

Roeder, J. 1965. "Zur Steinbrüchgeschichte des Rosengranits von Assuan," *Archäologischer Anzeiger* 1965: 467–552.

Roeder, J. 1971. "Marmor phrygium: Die antiken Marmorbrüche von Iscehisar in Westanatolien," *Jahrbuch des deutschen archäologischen Insituts* 86: 253–312.

Seigne, J. 2002. "A sixth-century water-powered sawmill at Jarash," *Annual of the Department of Antiquities of Jordan* 46: 205–13.

Sodini, J.-P., A. Lambraki, and T. Kozelj 1980. *Aliki: Les carrieres de marbre a l'epoque paleocretienne.* Études thasiennes 9. Paris: École française d'Athèns.

Strong, D, and A. Claridge 1976. "Marble Sculpture," in D. Strong and D. Brown (eds.), *Roman Crafts*. New York: New York University Press, 195–207.

Waelkens, M. 1992. "Bronze Age quarries and quarrying techniques in the Eastern Mediterranean," in Waelkens et al. 1992: 5–20.

Waelkens, M., P. de Paepe, and L. Moens 1988. "Patterns of extraction and production in the white marble quarries of the Mediterranean: History, present problems and prospects," in Fant 1989: 81–116.

Waelkens, M., P. de Paepe, and L. Moens 1990. "The quarrying techniques of the Greek world," in M. True and J. Podany (eds.), *Marble: Art historical and scientific perspectives on ancient sculpture*. Malibu, CA: J. Paul Getty Museum, 47–72.

Waelkens, M., N. Herz, and L. Moens (eds.) 1992. *Ancient stones: Quarrying, trade and provenance. Acta Archaeologica Lovaniensia* monographia 4. Leuven: Leuven University Press.

Ward-Perkins, J. B. 1971a. "Quarrying in antiquity: Technology, tradition and social change," *Proceedings of the British Academy* 57: 137–58.

Ward-Perkins, J. B. 1971b. "Quarries and stone-working in the early Middle Ages: The heritage of the ancient world." *Settimane di Studio del Centro Italiano di Studi sull' Alto Medievo XVIII Spoleto 2–8 Aprile 1970*. Spoleto: Centro Italiano di Studi sull'Alto Medievo, 525–44.

Wilson, A. I. 2002. "Machines, power and the ancient economy," *Journal of Roman Studies* 92: 1–32

Wilson Jones, M. 2000. *Principles of Roman architecture*. New Haven, CT: Yale University Press.

## CHAPTER 6

# SOURCES OF ENERGY AND EXPLOITATION OF POWER

### ÖRJAN WIKANDER

HUMAN history is directly related to the sources of available energy, since human muscular strength is extremely restricted. The "degree of efficiency" of a working man or woman amounts to less than 25 percent; that is, more than three-quarters of the power input (food) is needed to keep the individual alive. In consequence, during most of human history, humans have been compelled—like most animal species—to use a considerable part of their time just to stay alive. No essential change in this situation occurred until the Neolithic period, when the domestication of several animal species made available for exploitation the muscular power of animals. From that time onward, the growth in available energy sources made it possible for humans to divert a greater portion of their energy to activities other than the gathering or production of food. There have been two periods of particularly major change: the centuries around the birth of Christ, when water power was harnessed, and the last three centuries, when steam power, internal combustion engines, and nuclear power were exploited and new scientific advances made it possible to use earlier sources of energy more efficiently.

Prior to the twentieth century, almost all useful energy sources were ultimately dependent on solar energy. The Greco-Roman cultures were well aware of the electromagnetic energy manifested by magnetism (Radl 1988) and electricity (Pernot 1983; Keyser 1993), but neither played any real part in the energy supply. The use of geothermal energy was realized in limited areas, for example in providing hot water to Roman baths in volcanic regions, particularly at the Bay of Naples (Strabo 5.4.5; Dio Cassius 48.51.1–2). In practice, however, derivatives from solar energy dominated completely. Solar radiation is converted into the combustible hydrocarbons stored in wood (and, in the longer run, in coal, bitumen, and petroleum). In addition, solar radiation nurtures human and animal musculature indirectly through their consumption of vegetation. The evaporation of water by the sun creates the potential energy necessary for the exploitation of water power, and, by changes in the atmosphere, the air flow necessary for wind power.

Human muscle power is virtually negligible compared to most other forms of available energy. According to usual calculations (e.g., Forbes 1955b: 83), a mule can provide about five times as much energy as a working man, an ox seven, and a horse ten (see also chapter 23). Compared to a water-mill, however, even the power of a horse remains insignificant. These figures are, of course, approximate, but they do show the impact the harnessing of draft animals and water power had on human society. The common assertion that the classical cultures did not need water power because of their abundant supply of slaves has now been decisively repudiated. Even the most ruthless exploitation of enslaved humans would not have increased the amount of available energy more than marginally. Slaves represent a considerable economic investment and must be nourished even when sick and old, and the true gain of energy remains limited. In fact, slavery is a zero-sum game that transfers surplus human energy from one group (the slaves) to another (their owners) but in no way alters the total amount of energy available. Furthermore, an average modern household consumes more energy than did a Roman upper-class home employing hundreds of slaves. In consequence, this survey will concentrate on five groups of nonhuman energy sources: direct solar radiation, chemical energy, animal power, water power, and wind power.

# DIRECT SOLAR RADIATION

The importance of sunlight for achieving a pleasant indoor climate must have been obvious as early as the Palaeolithic period. The Roman architect Vitruvius devotes an entire chapter to the varying influence of climate on men and architecture depending on their position on the earth, and therefore the angle of the sun (*De arch.* 6.1; cf. Xenophon, *Mem.* 3.8.8–10; Pliny, *Ep.* 2.17.23). In the classical world, several authors recommend the building of private houses with deep, south-facing porches, so that they would admit the heat of the sun in winter but be bathed in shade in the summer (Xenophon, *Mem.* 3.8.8–10). By observing these simple rules, two aims were attained: cooler temperatures in summer and more effective heating in winter (Butti and Perlin 1980). Other buildings were also designed to make good use of the sun, particularly the Roman baths; parts of which had to be heated to high temperatures, requiring great amounts of fuel. Vitruvius comments on the need for solar heating in baths (*De arch.* 5.10.1; Ring 1996): "First of all, one must choose the warmest possible place, that is, turned away from the north and northeast. The hot and tepid rooms should get their light from the southwest, but if the nature of the place prevents this, at least from the south, as the time for bathing is mostly set from noon to evening."

Sunlight has been important from time immemorial for drying various materials, for instance, washed clothes. The intentional drying of foodstuffs such as meat, fish, or fruit was probably customary from pre-Neolithic times onward, making it possible to save food for longer periods by preventing putrefaction. In littoral areas, salt was produced by allowing evaporation of seawater in artificial pools.

The concentration of solar radiation in order to create very high temperatures was known by at least the classical period. Curved glass vessels or lenses and mirrors were used to focus sunlight to kindle fire (Aristophanes, *Nub.* 771–73; Theophrastus, *De igne* 73; Pliny, *HN* 2.239, 36.199, 37.28). Nevertheless, the report found in some late sources that Archimedes set enemy ships on fire at a distance with the help of burning-mirrors seems impossible, given the relatively poor quality of the available reflective surfaces (Simms 1977).

# CHEMICAL ENERGY

The exploitation of chemical energy began with the taming of fire by humans about half a million years ago (Rehder 2000). Through combustion (an oxidation process), hydrocarbons are converted into heat and light, while emitting carbon dioxide and water. Cooking makes both vegetable and animal food more digestible, wholesome, and nourishing and allowed humans a greater selection of foodstuffs. Fire also made it possible for humans to live in temperate and subarctic climate zones. For heating dwellings, not only did wood prove useful but also various vegetable fibers, reeds, straw, and dried cow dung. Moreover, fire provided artificial lighting, first by the use of burning sticks and torches, and later of lamps with animal or, more commonly, vegetable oils. With artificial light, the dark hours of night could be used for other productive activities (Forbes 1958: 119–93).

In the Greek and Roman world, the growing need for higher temperatures for the production of metals, pottery, terracotta, and glass necessitated the use of more efficient fuels. The most important of these was charcoal, created from wood by dry distillation (*pyrolysis*), which liberates the wood from water through heating in a reducing atmosphere. Charcoal is documented in Egypt at least from the early third millennium B.C. In the classical world, it is first mentioned by Homer (*Il.* 9.213). The technical procedure for transforming wood into charcoal is described in detail by Theophrastus (*Hist. pl.* 4.8.5, 5.9.1–6; *De igne* 37.75), who also recommends charcoal from various tree species for particular uses (cf. Pliny, *HN* 16.23). The benefits of using charcoal rather than wood are not restricted to the more efficient combustion with higher temperatures but also involve the fact that its weight is considerably less, which makes it much easier to transport. Considering the wealth of written and archaeological information at our disposal, it is obvious that enormous amounts of charcoal were produced in the ancient world.

Heating, the firing of terracotta and pottery, and the metal industry required increasing amounts of fuel in antiquity, a fact that inspired contemporary comment. For instance, Strabo (14.6.5) attributes deforestation in Cyprus to the production of copper and silver and notes that, during the Empire, iron ore from Elba had to be transported over the sea to Populonia, where there were still large enough forests to supply wood for the smelting (5.2.6). Pliny (*HN* 34.20.96) comments on the similar situations causing the shortage of fuel in Campania and Gaul. Moreover, since the 1970s, growing interest in the technology of Roman iron-making has pointed out the far-reaching destruction of vegetation that resulted from the production of charcoal (e.g., Cleere 1976; Horne 1982).

Even though this established view of the environmental effect of wood harvesting has been questioned, there is little doubt that both Greece and Italy were subjected to serious deforestation during the last half-millennium B.C. Import from well wooded areas in the north may have lessened the shortage, but some argue that the eventual moving of pottery and glass production first to Gaul and later to Britain and the Germanic provinces in the first centuries A.D. was at least partly the result of the shortage of fuel in the Mediterranean area.

There were other fuels available to the classical cultures, but neither petroleum and bitumen nor coal were exploited more than marginally. Bitumen was found in several parts of the Middle East but was used primarily to provide a waterproof coating for wood and the like (Forbes 1955a: 1–120; Séguin 1938). The rich potential of petrochemicals for heating remained almost unexploited, although a late Byzantine author states that Septimius Severus constructed a bath in Byzantium (later Constantinople) fueled with bitumen or petroleum (Humphrey et al. 1998: 43). Coal was known in many parts of Europe, but in Mediterranean areas mostly in the form of lignite, which is of much inferior quality. Nevertheless, it was used for metalworking in Hellenistic Greece and Liguria (Theophrastus, *Lap.* 16; Forbes 1958: 25–26). Mineral coal of a higher quality was extracted and used with some frequency in Britain, where it is known from a great number of archaeological sites. The finds are particularly rich at military forts along the Hadrianic and Antonine Walls, but coal was used extensively also in villas and towns in central and western England (Webster 1955). The exploitation of British coal started as early as the first century A.D. and was spread over large parts of Britain in the second. It was mostly used for domestic heating, particularly in hypocaust furnaces, and in iron forges, both military and civil (Dearne and Branigan 1994).

# ANIMAL POWER

Although human muscular power is very limited in potential compared to most other available energy sources, human energy nevertheless provided two essential advantages over the others. First of all, mobility, particularly the flexibility of our hands, made it possible for humans to carry out actions that required a complex series of movements; second, humans could be trained by oral or written instruction to execute complex tasks independently.

In their natural form, animal, water, and wind power can be used only to perform horizontal, linear work, while most human activities are much more complicated. Today, industrial robots can imitate almost any human movement, but it was not until the third century B.C. that the first important steps were taken in this direction. The invention, on the one hand, of devices that could convert a movement from horizontal to vertical and from linear to rotary (or the other way around), and, on the other hand, of machines that could adapt these movements to various activities, created entirely new potentials for harnessing other sources of energy than human muscles (see chapter 13).

It seems natural that this development first took place to provide for the needs of agricultural production. The intense urbanization process discernible in areas around the eastern Mediterranean from the mid-fourth century B.C. onward, with great numbers of newly-founded cities and rapidly expanding old ones, made heavy demands on the agricultural sector. Above all, the search for new power sources involved the two most energy-consuming agricultural activities: the lifting of water to irrigate otherwise uncultivable land and the grinding of flour.

In the technology of water-lifting, an earlier invention had made it possible to transfer at least some work to animals: the so-called *cerd*, in which a draft animal pulls a rope running over a vertical pulley wheel mounted over a well. By walking away from the well, the animal lifts a bucket with water. But since the animal has to return to the starting point in order to repeat its effort, the operation is rather inefficient and requires human supervision; in consequence it did not offer a sufficient solution to the problem. The *cerd* is known in Persia from at least the early fourth century B.C., but it is nowhere attested in the classical world (Oleson 1984: 39–41, 387–88). The technological boom in the third century B.C. gave rise to far better solutions: more efficient use of human power with the water-screw and of animal power with the *saqiya*, and above all the transmission of effort to water power with the *noria*. Even the grinding of grain could now be effected with the help of animals by means of the hourglass-shaped Pompeian mill, or by water power.

# WATER POWER

At a very early stage, humans must have become aware of the possibilities offered by the potential energy of water. Throwing a wooden stick into running water clearly indicates that even bigger and heavier pieces of wood may be moved downstream with no more than a minimum muscular effort. In fact, the driving of timber is known from various parts of the earth from very early times—in eighth-century B.C. Assyria, for example, this activity is attested in a great number of documents (e.g., Lanfranchi and Parpola 1990: nos. 4, 6, 25, 33, 111, 127, fig. 2). By replacing the wooden logs with rafts, barges, or boats that could drift downstream and be rowed, sailed, or pulled upstream, even stone and other heavy goods could easily be conveyed on navigable streams. An early example is the transport of granite from Upper Egypt, documented from at least the time of the Old Kingdom in the third millennium B.C. Later examples are the conveyance of enormous amounts of brick and tile to the rapidly expanding city of Rome in the beginning of the empire from brickworks located far up the Tiber (Lancaster 2005: 17) and the importation of vast quantities of marble from the eastern Mediterranean to Rome during the high empire (cf. chapter 5).

Exploitation of water power for more diversified purposes than transport needed a particular device: the paddle-driven water-lifting wheels, first mentioned in the late third century B.C. by Philo of Byzantium (*Pneum.* 61, 65), but probably invented in Egypt almost a century earlier (see chapter 13). The next step in the utilization of water power, the vertical-wheeled water-mill, deserves a special place in the history of technology. As a true prime mover, it contributed much to the late Roman economy and later constituted the basis of the industrial breakthrough of the Middle Ages and, thus, of the modern, economic development in general.

It has never been seriously questioned that the water-mill was invented in classical antiquity. Historians of technology from Beckmann (1788: 1–68) to Blümner (1912: 45–49) took it as confirmation of the advanced technological standard of that period. From 1935 to about 1975, however, research was hampered by a group of scholars who forcibly pursued the thesis that water-powered mills did not play any important part until the fifth or even sixth century A.D. (esp. Bloch 1935, Finley 1965). Since the 1980s, however, the pace of water-mill studies has been fast. More archaeological finds of pre-medieval water-mills have been published than the total number known before, and our appreciation of the importance of water power in the Roman empire has steadily deepened. Various summaries of the ancient development have appeared during this period, but they have all soon come into conflict with new consensus (see particularly Wikander 1979; Smith 1983–1984; Oleson 1984: 370–80; Wikander 1985, 2000; Wilson 1995; Lewis 1997; for a critical review of the research, see Wikander 2004; Lucas 2006). The presentation that follows here may be better founded than its forerunners, but it, too, should be taken for what it is: a working hypothesis.

The invention of the water-powered mill has, for a long time, been dated somewhere between the invention of the right-angle gear (now generally dated about 270 B.C.) on the one hand, and the first three unambiguous literary mentions of the device (all to be dated around the end of the first century B.C.) on the other. Considering the fact that the three authors describe the water-mill as brand new, uncommon, and more or less unique, respectively, it is only natural that most scholars have placed the invention in the last century B.C., or possibly slightly earlier. It is also worthy of note that all three texts seem to locate the mills in the eastern Mediterranean world, that is, in Greece or Asia Minor (Antipater of Thessalonica, *Anth. Pal.* 9.418; Vitruvius, *De arch.* 10.5.2; Strabo 12.3.30; Wikander 1992: 10–11).

In 1997, however, a totally new theory was presented, assigning the invention of the vertical-wheeled mill to Alexandria in the 240s B.C. and that of the horizontal-wheeled mill to Byzantium ten or twenty years earlier (Lewis 1997: 13–73, esp. 56–61). The argument is based on close scrutiny of various technical treatises originating from the third century B.C. Some dubious points notwithstanding, the new date has been accepted by a number of scholars, particularly because it locates the invention in the dynamic, scientific environment of the third century B.C., where it logically belongs.

If we accept the new, early date of invention, we must also recognize that it is more than two hundred years earlier than the next evidence we find of the existence of water-mills, in the three Augustan authors referred to above. This time gap, together with the mentions of the machine as new after it, needs an explanation. It is easiest to blame the gap on the problems necessarily involved in transforming an elegant, scientific model to a full-scale operating machine with a wooden right-angle gear. There are, in fact, various dubious points in the three Augustan texts that may indicate initial problems in adapting the invention to real life (Wikander 1992: 12–13; Wikander 2004: 109–11).

After the reign of Augustus, reliable literary testimonia for water-mills are mysteriously absent for three hundred years, but some inscriptions and a growing number of archaeological finds conveniently fill out the record. It should be noted that even the earliest two mills attested by archaeological remains, the Augustan mill at St. Doulchard "Les Avrillages" (Cher) in France and at Avenches in Switzerland (the latter dated by dendrochronology to A.D. 57/58; Castella et al. 1994; Champagne et al. 1997), had a mill-channel, millstones of ordinary shape, and presumably a right-angle gear that increased the velocity of the stones. In other words, they did not differ markedly from vertical-wheeled mills from early modern times. The alleged early-first-century A.D. mill at S. Giovanni di Ruoti is apparently not a water-mill at all (Greene 1999; Wilson 2002: 11 n. 56.)

During the second and third centuries, the number of archaeologically known water-mills increases, and the epigraphical evidence for *collegia* of water-millers at such disparate localities as Hierapolis in Phrygia (Pleket 1988: 27–28) and Günzburg in Bavaria (*CIL* 3.5866) proves beyond doubt that the water-mill had already begun to play so central a part in the Roman economy that the empire would have met with serious problems without it.

In the Price Edict of Diocletian (A.D. 301), significantly, the water-mill is mentioned beside the other main mill types: the horse-, donkey- and hand-mill (15.54; cf. Lauffer 1971: 257). In the fourth and fifth centuries, water-mills are in evidence over most of the Roman Empire, from Britain in the northwest to Palestine in the east and Tunisia in the south. But, as far as we know today, the device did not pass beyond the imperial frontiers until the sixth century A.D. India may be an exception, if the story in Cedrenus' *Historiarum Compendium* (516, p. 295 Bekker), of a certain Metrodorus, who constructed baths and water-mills in India after A.D. 325, is based, as is generally believed, on Ammianus Marcellinus.

The water-mill needs running water, but in practice this is not enough: it needs a more or less constant water supply to make the water-wheel efficient, and it must be feasible to turn off the water completely for inspection and repairs. In other words, it is not enough just to immerse the wheel into a natural stream in the way actually suggested by Vitruvius (see below). The difficulties of solving this problem may have contributed to the apparent delay in the breakthrough of the water-powered mill. The most simple solution is leading a mill-channel from a nearby stream; if this is accomplished at a fall or rapids, it also offers the possibility of creating a substantial water-head. In some cases, channels have been dug for several kilometers in order to transfer the potential energy to the preferred location; for instance, at Martres-de-Veyre, France (late second century A.D.), the water was probably derived from a river about 2.5 km away (Romeuf 2001: 25).

After this realization, it was a natural step to power the mills with water from ordinary aqueducts as, for instance, the Janiculum mills in Rome (third century A.D.; Bell 1994; Wilson 2000; Wikander 2002), or from aqueducts constructed for this very purpose as, for instance, at Barbegal in southern France (early second century A.D.; Benoit 1940; Leveau 1996). Wikander (1991) provides a general introduction to the relationship between water-mills and aqueducts. By means of sluice-gates, the amount of water admitted to the wheel could be varied, and when necessary completely cut off.

When the slope of a natural stream was too shallow, the construction of a weir across it could raise the water level of the millrace enough to power the wheel. Such a weir was constructed as early as the third century A.D. at the Haltwhistle Burn mill in northern England (Simpson and Wilson 1976: 33–35, pl. I), and a detailed description of the construction of a weir around A.D. 450 is preserved in the *Vita S. Romani abbatis* (18 Krusch = 57 Martine). The ultimate solution, the building of a dam creating a true millpond, is not known with certainty until the sixth century, but the technique was probably in use even earlier. The millpond had a double function: not only did it create a substantial water-head, but it also made it possible to save the potential energy of the water for periods when the water supply became scarce.

Two more peculiar methods of securing the necessary amount of running water may also belong to the early medieval period rather than classical antiquity: floating mills, in which the machinery was placed on small boats anchored in rivers that turned their paddles, and tide-mills using inflowing tidewater along the Atlantic coasts. The former is first attested in Rome in A.D. 537 (Procopius, *Goth.* 1.19.19–22; Wikander 1979: 29–32; Lohrmann 1992), the latter at Strangford Lough and Little Island in Ireland, around A.D. 620 and 630, respectively (Rynne 1992).

During the Roman Empire, a series of water-mill types evolved suited for different volumes of water supply and different water-heads. All water-powered mills may be divided into two main types: the vertical-wheeled ("Vitruvian") mill and the horizontal-wheeled ("Greek" or "Norse") mill. Both use a water-wheel to convert the linear power of the running (or falling) water to a circular movement. In the horizontal-wheeled mill, this movement is transferred directly (by means of a vertical shaft or spindle) to the rotating, upper millstone (the runner), while, in the vertical-wheeled mill, the vertical, circular movement must be converted (by a right-angle gear) to a horizontal one.

There are three functional variants of the vertical-wheeled mill (figure 6.1). The simplest (and certainly earliest) is the undershot mill, described in detail by Vitruvius between 30 and 10 B.C. (*De arch.* 10.4.1, 5.1–2):

> (5.1) Even in rivers, there are wheels of the same construction as described above. Wings [i.e., paddles] are attached around the periphery which, when they are hit by the impact of the river, force the wheels to rotate by their forward movement.

> (4.1) The shaft, manufactured on a lathe or with compasses, its ends shod with sheet-iron . . . is placed on wooden blocks that have iron sheets on them beneath the ends of the shaft.

> (5.2) Water-grinders, too, are turned in the same manner. In them everything is the same, except that a toothed drum is fixed to one end of the shaft. This drum, set vertically on its edge, is turned together with the water-wheel. Next to this drum, there is a larger, horizontal one, also toothed, with which it meshes. Thus, the teeth of the wheel fixed to the shaft, by driving the teeth of the horizontal drum, necessarily bring about the revolution of the millstones. A hopper hanging in this machine supplies grain to the millstones.

This is also the type of mill used in the earliest archaeological finds, those at St. Doulchard "Les Avrillages" and Avenches (both constructed before A.D. 60; Castella et al. 1994).

The overshot mill needs a water-head higher than the wheel, so that the water can be led above it on a wooden chute and move the wheel by both weight and impulse. Mills of this subtype were apparently less common in antiquity than the undershot ones, but they are in evidence just as early, in an epigram by Antipater of Thessalonica dated to between 20 B.C. and A.D. 10 (*Anth. Pal.* 9.418.4–6). The breastshot mill represents a middle course, being powered by water that hits the back of the wheel. This variation was never common, and I know of only one obvious example from antiquity, at Martres-de-Veyre, France, from the second century A.D. (Romeuf 2001: 25, pls. 5–7).

The horizontal-wheeled mill, too, has functional variants (figure 6.2). The simplest one, in which the water falls through a steep chute on the oblique vanes of the wheel, is not known with certainty until the early seventh century A.D., in

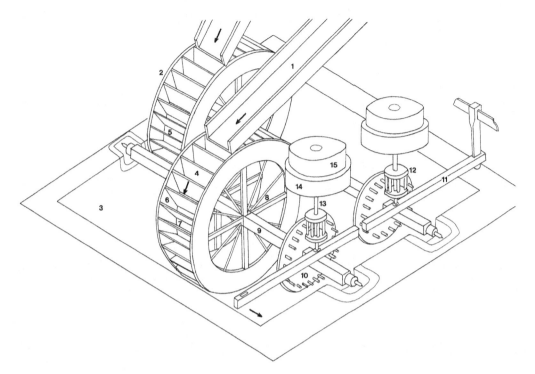

Figure 6.1. Reconstruction of the double vertical-wheeled mill in the Baths of Caracalla, Rome. 1. Wooden chute. 2. Overshot water-wheel. 3. Wheel-pit. 4. Paddles (vanes). 5. Buckets. 6. Shroud. 7. Sole. 8. Spokes. 9. Wheel-shaft. 10. Vertical cog-wheel (pit-wheel). 11. Bridge-tree. 12. Lantern pinion 13. Vertical shaft (iron spindle). 14. Lower stone (bed-stone). 15. Upper stone (runner). (Drawing: Ö. Wikander, after Schiøler and Wikander 1983: fig. 15.)

Ireland (Rynne 1992: 58–66, figs. 3, 6). A similar mill, combined with a tower filled with water (functioning more or less as a millpond), has been used from an early period in Algeria, Palestine, Jordan, Arabia, Iraq, and Iran. A number of these "drop-tower" mills (or *arubah* penstock mills, as they were called by Avitsur [1960: 39–44]) have been dated to the third to sixth centuries A.D. (Wikander 1985: 161–63; Wilson 1995: 507–9), but only one of them can be shown with reasonable certainty to be earlier than the Arab conquest (a mill at the Crocodilion River, Palestine, dated by carbon-14 analysis to A.D. 345/380, see Schiøler 1989: 133–36, figs. 1–3).

A third variant of the horizontal-wheeled mill is attested by two triple-helix turbines at Chemtou and Testour in Tunisia (Rakob 1993; Röder and Röder 1993; Wilson 1995: 500–506). This design is evidence of a highly advanced technology, otherwise not known until the sixteenth century, but the installations are dated without reservation by the excavators to the late third or early fourth century A.D. They resemble the drop-tower mills in using a cylindrical pit filled with water, but here the horizontal wheel was placed in the bottom of this pit. The rotating water column makes this mill a true turbine.

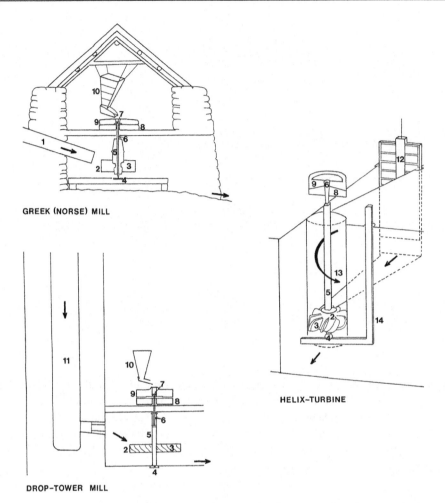

GREEK (NORSE) MILL

DROP–TOWER MILL

HELIX–TURBINE

Figure 6.2. The three variants of horizontal-wheeled mills. 1. Wooden chute. 2. Horizontal water-wheel. 3. Paddles (vanes). 4. Bearing stone. 5. Wheel-hub/vertical shaft. 6. Iron spindle. 7. Rynd. 8. Lower stone (bedstone). 9. Upper stone (runner). 10. Hopper. 11. *Arubah* penstock shaft. 12. Sluice-gate. 13. Rotating water column. 14. Bridge-tree. (Drawing: Ö. Wikander, after Curwen 1944: fig. 5; Avitsur 1960: fig. 2; Rakob 1993: fig. 1.)

In sum, of the ancient water-mills whose type can be ascertained, almost two-thirds were undershot and one-third overshot, while only a few examples were breastshot or with horizontal wheels.

In vertical-wheeled mills, the millrace continued into the wheel-pit, which, for undershot mills, was narrow and conforming as closely as possible to the shape and size of the wheel, in order to use the water more efficiently. In overshot wheels, on the other hand, this is not necessary, and the wheels are often found in larger, rectangular wheel-pits with lengths varying from 4.20 to 6.40 m and widths from 0.80 to 2.20 m.

The shape of the wheels themselves is fairly well known from representations and archaeological finds—in some cases including preserved parts of the wood. Overshot wheels differ from the undershot inasmuch as they must have soles and shrouds (i.e., bases and side walls) that converted the compartment between two paddles into a true bucket. Otherwise, overshot and undershot wheels apparently differed little, at least as far as their dimensions were concerned. Obviously, ancient mill wheels diverged in one fundamental aspect from their modern counterparts: the wheels were constructed with real spokes (between 12 and 28 in preserved wheels and representations) joining the periphery with the wooden hub. Most diameters (10 out of 13) are estimated at between 1.60 and 2.56 m; two exceed 3 m, and one allegedly attains 6 m. The widths of the water-wheels vary significantly, from 0.22 to 1.65 m, without any apparent system—typological, chronological, or other (for details and references, see Wikander 2000: 384–89).

The traces left by the wheel-shafts indicate that these were normally constructed more or less according to the description given by Vitruvius (quoted above). Their lengths were mostly between 2.90 and 3.60 m, their thickness less than 30 cm, tapering to between 18.5 and 21 cm at the iron-shod ends (Wikander 2000: 289–90).

The most complicated part of the power transmission was the right-angle gear consisting of a vertical cogwheel (the "toothed drum" of Vitruvius) and a horizontal one, described as "larger" by Vitruvius, but in later mills always replaced by a small, lantern pinion. The text of Vitruvius has been questioned, but nowadays most scholars tend to believe that it is correct. Some ancient mills have actually been reconstructed with a larger horizontal cogwheel, although in the case of the well-known Agora II mill at Athens (fifth century A.D.), this is probably wrong (Parsons 1936: 83; cf. critical comments by Spain 1987: 341–42, 348–51), but for the most recently published Crocodilion River mill, the idea is at least worth considering: the unique hourglass-shaped millstones found there may well have justified a gearing down of the speed (see below).

The size of the pit-wheel can be estimated at four mills (all diameters being between 0.95 and 1.11 m), that of the lantern pinion in one only: it was apparently in use already in the third-century mill in the Baths of Caracalla in Rome, where its width was less than 35 cm (Schiøler and Wikander 1983: 54, fig. 11).

The vertical shaft or spindle connecting the horizontal cogwheel with the runner stone is not mentioned by any written source until Gregory of Tours (*Vitae patrum* 18.2) around A.D. 500, but three finds of late Imperial iron spindles in England and Germany (between 53 and 92 cm long) show that they were of the same appearance as their medieval and later counterparts. The spindle rotated on a bearing stone protecting the bridge-tree, and its upper end passed through the bedstone to be fixed to the runner by an iron rynd.

The millstones are the best known part of ancient water-mills. Apart from the many stones discovered in excavations of early mill sites, hundreds of un-provenanced stones are found in museums all over the former Roman Empire. Some probably derive from horse or mule-powered mills, which used a machinery almost identical to that of the water-mills, but the majority were certainly water-powered. Ancient millstones were much smaller than their modern successors. Their diameter varies from 48 to 109 cm, the great majority being between 55 and 85 cm. There is a clear tendency for mills dating to the first two centuries A.D. to have conical bedstones, while those from late antiquity are almost flat (as later stones invariably are), perhaps because the speed of the early mills was not high enough to make the grain pass between the stones by centrifugal force alone.

It is worthy of note that Antipater of Thessalonica wrote about the "hollow weights of the millstones," a fact that has led some scholars to believe that he described hourglass-shaped stones, similar to the "Pompeian" donkey-mills (Wikander 1992: 12–13). This hypothesis would also help to explain why Vitruvius wrote that the horizontal cogwheel should be larger than the pit-wheel: hourglass-shaped stones would run a greater risk of cracking if the speed was high. But the finds of "ordinary" stones at the early mill at Avenches made the hypothesis less attractive.

Subsequently, however, the publication of some further water-mills at the Crocodilion River gave reason to reconsider the question (Ad et al. 2005: 162, 169, figs. 6–11). There, two mills powered by one common, vertical wheel obviously used stones lower but strikingly reminiscent of hourglass mills (figure 6.3). The date of the mills is quite late (between the fourth and the mid-seventh century), but the excavators point out that similar stones, presumably deriving from water-powered mills, have been found in another site in the Hula Valley, at Kibbutz Ma'ayan Barukh. They suggest that these hourglass-stones are, in fact, "a local survival from

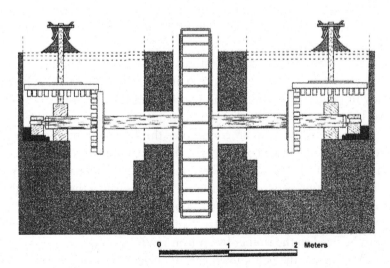

Figure 6.3. Reconstruction of the twin, vertical-wheeled mill at the Crocodilion River (Nahal Tanninim), Israel. (Ad et al. 2005: fig. 6; courtesy of R. Frankel, University of Haifa.)

earlier times." If so, it could very well be that the text of Antipater presents a correct description of the very earliest, eastern water-mill stones.

Today, we may state with confidence that the breakthrough of the water-powered mill did not take place, as maintained by Bloch (1935: esp. 545) and his followers, in the early middle ages, but rather half a millennium earlier, in the first century A.D., or perhaps even slightly earlier. The large numbers of water-mills that happen to be attested in sixth and seventh-century Merovingian charters and hagiography do not indicate a sudden rise in the actual number of mills, but are just the first documentation of a situation already established in the Roman Empire. Water-mills were constructed wherever the necessary conditions were at hand: a suitable stream and a large enough concentration of people, possibly between 200 and 400, to justify the expense (cf. Wikander 1985: 26–32). Where the concentration of population was even greater, clusters of mills or even multi-unit mill establishments were built to supply them with ground flour.

Two such establishments have long been known, the Janiculum mills in Rome and the mill building at Barbegal, near Arles in southern France. At Barbegal (figure 6.4), an aqueduct supplied water to a large establishment with 16 overshot

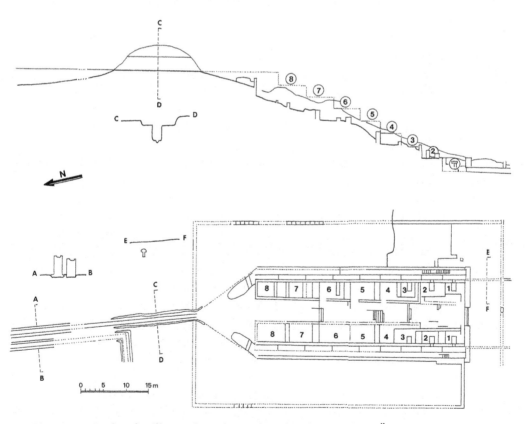

Figure 6.4. Barbegal mill complex, plan and section (Drawing: by Ö. Wikander, after Benoît 1940: fig. 3.)

wheels, constructed in the early second century A.D. (Benoit 1940; Leveau 1996: 138–49). On the slope of the Janiculum hill in Rome, large numbers of mills used aqueduct water to provide flour to the city from the third century up to A.D. 537 (Wikander 1979: 15–29; Bell 1994; Wilson 2001; Wikander 2002).

For long, the Barbegal and Janiculum mills remained isolated exceptions, but today there is reason to believe that such large-scale milling establishments were not uncommon. The existence of collegia of water-millers in Hierapolis and Günzburg (above) and of large numbers of water-mills in Promona (Dalmatia, *CIL* 3.14969.2), and Orkistos (Phrygia, Chastagnol 1981: 406–9), during the third and fourth centuries show convincingly that great efforts were made in towns with enough running water to exploit this asset. Moreover "a multiple mill complex akin to the great Barbegal mill is suspected at Colossae . . . in Phrygia" (Lewis 1997: 71, with a reference to the London *Times*, 15 August 1991), and a passage in Ammianus Marcellinus (18.8.11; A.D. 359) has been shown to refer to another mill cluster at Amida in eastern Turkey (Wilson 2001).

The economic consequences of this development are difficult to evaluate, but, considering the enormous amounts of muscular work that could be saved by the breakthrough of the water-powered mill, it must necessarily have been of utmost importance for the Roman economy, particularly from the third century onward, when the supply of labor started to grow short. This is true even though the "breakthrough" was in no way complete: mills powered by animals or men remained important up to the twentieth century. Wikander (2004: 111) provides a discussion of the meaning of the word "breakthrough" in this context. The economic importance of the ancient water-mill is obvious. The next question to be answered is whether we may actually talk of a "power revolution" in the classical world, comparable to the one earlier alleged for the Middle Ages. But here our evidence still remains ambiguous.

Besides water-lifting and milling, ancient sources mention both marble-saws and grain-processing pestles powered by water. The evidence of sawmills in a tributary of the Moselle (Ausonius, *Mos.* 362–64) and in Cappadocia (Gregory of Nyssa, *In Ecclesiasten* 3, 656A Migne), as well as the mention of a *serratoria machina* (sawing machine) by Ammianus Marcellinus (23.4.4) are all to be dated around A.D. 370–390 (Moselle: Ludwig 1981; Simms 1983; Wikander 1985. Cappadocia: Wikander 1981: 99. Sawing machine: Rosumek 1982: 135). These testimonies in literature have all been questioned, but the literary evidence for this labor-saving machine is now supplemented by archaeological finds at Jerash/Gerasa, Jordan, from the sixth century (Seigne 2002a, 2002b) and Ephesus from the seventh (Vetters 1984: 225). In addition, a second- or third-century relief found at Pammukale provides a clear representation of a water-wheel powered stone saw (Ritti et al. 2007).

The written sources are of little assistance when trying to ascertain the technical design of the saws. Various suggested reconstructions have been rejected, but a careful study of the remains at Jerash indicates a possible solution (figure 6.5):

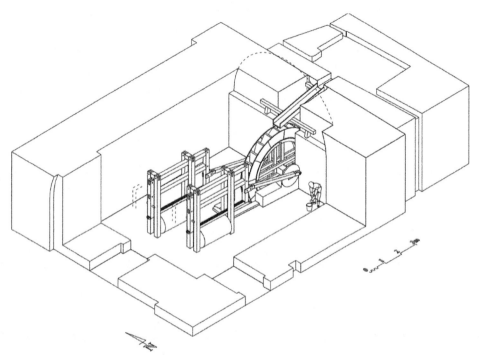

Figure 6.5. Reconstruction of the water-powered saw-mill at Jarash (Gerasa), Jordan. (Courtesy of Prof. Jacques Seigne, CNRS-Université de Tours.)

> Each saw assembly would have had four blades mounted in parallel on a stout wooden frame at least 2.5 m long and 2.0m wide, and weighing about 300 kg. These saws must have cut vertically down through the stone, with the blades moving back and forth horizontally, so as to take advantage of their weight.... The evenness of the saw-cut channels shows that the saw frame would have been mounted within a fixed structure. (Seigne 2002a: 15)

Our knowledge of ancient water-powered pestles rests entirely on two ancient texts: Pliny (*HN* 18.23.97, ca. A.D. 70) and the *Vita S. Romani abbatis* (17 Krusch = 52 Martine, ca. A.D. 520). Both texts involve uncertainties, but the most probable readings favor the use of water-powered pestles—as argued convincingly by Lewis (1997: 101–2). So far, no archaeological evidence supports the identification, but there is little reason for doubt, as the existence of cam-operated tilt-hammers in small-scale gadgets from Hellenistic times onward is generally acknowledged (Lewis 1997: 84–115; cf. chapter 31). In the Middle Ages, the tilt-hammer appears in a whole series of water-powered machines, none of which, however, has so far been attested with certainty in the classical world. In the field of metallurgy, a number of excavations in Britain have yielded finds that may be connected with water-powered trip-hammers (Lewis 1997: 106–11). At Marseille, the excavators suggest that a water-wheel discovered in close vicinity to a pile of iron slag powered the bellows of an iron furnace (Guéry and Hallier 1987: 274, fig. 4).

Other industrial applications of water power in antiquity remain qualified guesses—as, for instance, the attempts at detecting fulling-mills in first-century A.D. Antioch on the Orontes (Lewis 1997: 95–99). Moreover, Vitruvius (*De arch.* 10.5.2) mentions water-powered dough-kneading machines, but it is very doubtful whether the idea was ever transferred into practical use (Wikander 1981: 95–96). Nevertheless, a mule-powered dough-kneading machine illustrated on the tomb of Eurysaces in Rome might well have been adapted to water power (late first century B.C.; chapter 14; figure 2.2).

In consequence, for the time being we must be cautious when speaking of an ancient power revolution. However, the slow, but constant, growth of evidence for exploitation of water power for varying industrial purposes in the Roman empire is justification enough for not abandoning the thought altogether. It may well be that we have still no idea of the true economic importance of water power in antiquity.

# WIND POWER

The most important use of wind power dates back to the fourth millennium B.C., when sails were adopted for driving ships. The art of sailing was gradually refined, particularly during classical antiquity, when advances in sail rigs and ship design made it possible to exploit wind power even when the wind came from an unfavorable direction (see chapter 24). A probably much earlier use of the wind was a necessary part of the process of threshing. Well into the twentieth century, the wheat was sifted from the chaff by throwing the threshed grain in the air to allow the wind carry the light chaff away.

Apart from these two areas of use, absolutely basic for ancient populations, we have only one written document that mentions possible further uses of this source of energy: Hero of Alexandria's description of the wind-powered organ (*Pneum.* 1.43). The text is a direct continuation of his preceding chapter, where Hero describes the water-organ, showing how the air pressure necessary for the organ might instead by created by a wind-wheel which, by way of cams on the wheel-shaft, drives a piston up and down a cylinder. It goes without saying that an organ that needs favorable wind to be played would be of little practical use, and Hero's device is generally dismissed as a toy or as sheer nonsense. This attitude, however, leaves two important circumstances out of account. First, the wind-organ was admittedly hardly meant for use, but Hero's intention was certainly not to construct a toy but to illustrate the potentials of a physical principle. Second, the text includes a comment that has mostly been overlooked: the wind-wheel should, according to

Hero, be provided with vanes "like the so-called *anemouria.*" The last word is found only here in Greek literature. It has often been translated as "windmill," but this is hardly what Hero meant. If windmills had been known in antiquity, we would perhaps not find much trace of the buildings and the machinery but—as windmills power the stones from above—we should have found runners with a central hole and bedstones without, a fact that would clearly distinguish them from stones from horse or water-powered mills. The word *anemourion* is apparently a compound of *anemos* and *ourion,* both of which mean "wind." The precise meaning remains obscure, but a reasonable guess would be "windwhirl" or the like. Nor is it obvious what this "windwhirl" would be: a toy for children or, perhaps, a useful machine? In the latter case, one would rather think of a water-raising plant of the simple kind still common in the Italian countryside. Wind power remains a dark horse in the field of ancient energy exploitation (Drachmann 1961; Lewis 1993).

The economy of the Roman Empire declined markedly from the end of the second century A.D. onward. Many factors in combination brought about this decline, and this is not the place to enter deeply into the process in general—only into the question to what extent the available energy sources may have affected the development. On the one hand, we have good reason to believe that the central parts of the empire suffered from a serious lack of fuel, but on the other hand, the diffusion and breakthrough of water power must have played an important, positive role.

As I have already pointed out, deforestation in Mediterranean countries may have been of consequence for the moving of various industries northward to Gaul, Britain, and Germany, where the supply of wood (charcoal) and mineral coal was far better. This migration of industries, however, provided no definite solution to the problem, perhaps because the exploitation of energy depended not only on the amounts available but on other factors, too, particularly the potentials for the storage, transport, and conversion of energy. Storage did not constitute a major problem as far as chemical and animal energy is concerned. Water power could initially be hampered by low water levels (and even total desiccation) during summer and autumn, but as soon as the construction of millponds became common this problem could be minimized

Transport of energy was more complicated. Draft animals could walk themselves to the desired locality, fuel could be transported both on sea and land, particularly charcoal, which has a notably small weight compared to its energy content. Here, too, water power constituted a greater problem. Water could be led to a mill through long channels or aqueducts but, on the whole, the exploitation remained restricted to the sites offered by nature.

The main problem was the conversion of energy and, particularly, the conversion of chemical energy in wood and coal to power. True, there was less access to fuel in the center of the empire, but if a practicable solution to the conversion problem had appeared, large parts of the central and western European forests and coal deposits would have been at the empire's disposal. But these resources were never utilized in an intensive fashion.

Several of Hero's automata include the conversion of chemical energy to power via the heating of water and pressure of hot air or steam. Most interesting is the aeolipile, a kind of simple reaction turbine, which in theory should be able to act as a prime mover (*Pneum.* 2.11). This device proves that ancient scientists understood the principles behind this kind of energy conversion, but it also reveals their inability to transfer the theory to practical use. The steamball rotates when water is heated, but it is unable to drive anything else (Landels 1978: 28–31; Keyser 1994). Only through the steam engines of Newcomen and Watt in the eighteenth century were the possibilities created for the conversion of fuel to power that became the basis for the Industrial Revolution in Europe.

# REFERENCES

Ad, U., 'A. Sa'id, and R. Frankel 2005. "Water-mills with Pompeian-type millstones at Nahal Tanninim," *Israel Exploration Journal* 55: 156–71.

Avitsur, S. 1960. "On the history of the exploitation of water power in Eretz-Israel," *Israel Exploration Journal* 10: 37–45.

Beckmann, J. 1788. *Beiträge zur Geschichte der Erfindungen.* 2 vols. Leipzig: Kummer.

Bell, M. 1994, "An Imperial flour mill on the Janiculum," in *Le ravitaillement en blé de Rome et des centres urbains dès débuts de la République jusqu'au Haut Empire.* Collections Centre Jean Berard 11. Naples and Rome: Centre Jean Berard, 73–89.

Benoit, F. 1940. "L'usine de meunerie hydraulique de Barbegal (Arles)," *Revue archeologique* 15: 19–80.

Bloch, M. 1935. "Avènement et conquêtes du moulin à eau," *Annales d'histoire économique et sociale* 7: 538–63.

Blümner, H. 1912. *Technologie und Terminologie der Gewerke und Künste bei Griechen und Römern.* 2nd ed. Vol. 1. Leipzig and Berlin: Teubner.

Butti, K., and J. Perlin 1980. *A golden thread: 2500 years of solar architecture and technology.* New York: Van Nostrand Reinhold.

Castella, D., et al. 1994. *Aventicum VI. Le moulin hydraulique gallo-romain d'Avenches "En Chaplix," Fouilles 1990–1991.* Cahiers d'Archéologie Romande 62. Lausanne: Cahiers d'archéologie romande.

Champagne, F., A. Ferdière, and Y. Rialland 1997. "Re-découverte d'un moulin à eau augustéen sur l'Yèrre (Cher)," *Revue archéologique du Centre de la France* 36: 157–60.

Chastagnol, A. 1981. "L'inscription Constantinienne d'Orcistus," *Melanges de l'École française de Rome et de Athènes* 93: 381–416.

Cleere, H. F. 1976. "Some operating parameters for Roman iron-works," *Bulletin of the Institute of Archaeology of the University of London* 13: 233–46.

Curwen, E. C. 1944. "The problem of early water-mills," *Antiquity* 18: 130–46.

Dearne, M., and K. Branigan 1994. "The use of coal in Roman Britain," *Antiquaries Journal* 74: 71–105.

Drachmann, A. G. 1961. "Heron' s windmill," *Centaurus* 7: 145–51.

Finley, M. I. 1965. "Technical innovation and economic progress in the ancient world," *Economic History Review* 18: 29–45.

Forbes, R. J. 1955a. *Studies in ancient technology.* Vol. 1. Leiden: Brill.

Forbes, R. J. 1955b. *Studies in ancient technology.* Vol. 2. Leiden: Brill.

Forbes, R. J. 1958. *Studies in ancient technology*. Vol. 6. Leiden: Brill.

Greene, K. 1999. "Review of A. M. Small and R. J. Buck, *The excavations at San Giovanni di Ruoti*. Vol. 1, *The villas and their environment*," *American Journal of Archaeology* 103: 577–79

Guéry, R., and G. Hallier 1987. "Réflexions sur les ouvrages hydrauliques de Marseille antique retrouvés sur le chautier de la Bourse," in *L'eau et les hommes en Méditerranée*, 4. Paris: CNRS, 265–82.

Horne, L. 1982. "Fuel for the metal worker: The role of charcoal and charcoal production in ancient metallurgy," *Expedition* 25:1: 6–13.

Keyser, P. T. 1993. "The purpose of the Parthian galvanic cells: A first-century A.D. electric battery used for analgesia," *Journal of Near Eastern Studies* 52: 81–98.

Keyser P. T. 1994. "Classics and technology: A re-evaluation of Heron's first century A.D. steam engine," in S. Wisseman and W. Williams (eds.), *Ancient technologies and archaeological materials*. London: Gordon and Breach, 71–86.

Lancaster, L. 2005. *Concrete vaulted construction in imperial Rome: Innovations in context*. Cambridge: Cambridge University Press.

Landels, G. 1978. *Engineering in the ancient world*. London: Chatto and Windus.

Lanfranchi, G. B., and S. Parpola 1990. *State archives of Assyria*. Vol. 5, *The correspondence of Sargon II*, Part 2: *Letters from the northern and northeastern provinces*. Helsinki: Helsinki University Press.

Lauffer, S. 1971. *Diokletians Preisedikt: Texte und Kommentare*. Berlin: de Gruyter.

Leveau, P. 1996. "The Barbegal water mill in its environment: Archaeology and the economic and social history of antiquity," *Journal of Roman Archaeology* 9: 137–53.

Lewis, M. J. T. 1993. "The Greeks and the early windmill," *History of Technology* 15: 141–89.

Lewis, M. J. T. 1997. *Millstone and hammer: The origins of water power*. Hull: University of Hull Press.

Lohrmann, D. 1992. "Schiffmühlen in spätantiken und mittelalterlichen Städten," in *Medieval Europe: A conference on medieval archaeology in Europe, 21st–24th September at the University of York. Pre-printed papers*, Vol. 3: *Technology and innovation*. York: Society for Medieval Archaeology, 27–29.

Lucas, A. 2006. *Wind, water, work: Ancient and medieval milling technology*. Leiden: Brill.

Ludwig, K.-H. 1981. "Die technikgeschichtlichen Zweifel an der 'Mosella' des Ausonius sind unbegründet," *Technikgeschichte* 48: 131–34.

Oleson, J. P. 1984. *Greek and Roman mechanical water-lifting devices: The history of a technology*. Toronto: University of Toronto Press.

Parsons, A. W. 1936. "A Roman water-mill in the Athenian agora," *Hesperia* 5: 70–90.

Pernot, L. 1983. "Pour une préhistoire de l'électricité: la Grèce antique et l'ambre jaune," *Bulletin d'histoire d'électricité* 2: 19–30.

Pleket, H. W. 1988. "Greek epigraphy and comparative ancient history: Two case studies," *Epigraphica Anatolica* 12: 25–37.

Radl, A. 1988. *Die Magnetstein in der Antike: Quellen und Zusammenhänge*. Stuttgart: Steiner Verlag.

Rakob, F. L. 1993. "Der Neufund einer römischen Turbinenmühle in Tunesien," *Antike Welt* 24: 286–87.

Rehder, J. E. 2000. *Mastery and uses of fire in antiquity*. Montreal: McGill-Queens Press.

Ring, J. W. 1996. "Windows, baths and solar energy in the Roman empire," *American Journal of Archaeology* 100: 717–24.

Ritti, T., K. Grewe, and P. Kessner 2007. "A relief of a water-powered stone saw mill on a sarcophagus at Hierapolis and its implications," *Journal of Roman Archaeology* 20: 139–63.

Röder, J., and G. Röder 1993. "Die antike Turbinenmühle in Chemtou," in F. Rakob (ed.), *Simitthus*. Vol. 1, *Die Steinbrücke und die antike Stadt*. Mainz: von Zabern, 95–102.

Romeuf, A. M. 2001. *Le quartier artisanal gallo-romain des Martres-de-Veyre (Puy-de-Dôme)*. Cahier du Centre Achéologique de Lezoux 2. Lezoux: Revue Archéologique Sites.

Rosumek, P. 1982. *Technischer Fortschritt und Rationalisierung im antiken Bergbau*. Bonn: Habelt.

Rynne, C. 1992. "Early medieval horizontal-wheeled mill penstocks from Co. Cork," *Journal of the Cork Historical and Archaeological Society* 97: 54–68.

Schiøler, T. 1989. "The watermills at the Crocodile River: A turbine mill dated to 345–380 A.D," *Palestine Exploration Quarterly* 121: 133–43.

Schiøler, T., and Ö. Wikander 1983. "A Roman water-mill in the Baths of Caracalla," *Opuscula Romana* 14: 47–64.

Séguin, A. 1938. "Étude sur le pétrol dans l'antiquité grecque et latine: Gisements de pétrole connus des Latins et des Grecs," *Revue des Questions Historiques* 261: 36–70.

Seigne, J. 2002a. "A sixth-century waterpowered sawmill," *International Molinology* 64: 14–16.

Seigne, J. 2002b. "A sixth-century water-powered sawmill at Jarash," *Annual of the Department of Antiquities of Jordan* 46: 205–13.

Simms, D. L. 1977. "Archimedes and the burning mirrors of Syracuse," *Technology and Culture* 18: 1–24.

Simms, D. L. 1983. "Water-driven saws, Ausonius and the authenticity of the *Mosella*," *Technology and Culture* 24: 635–43.

Simpson, F. G., and Lord Wilson of High Wray 1976. *Watermills and military works on Hadrian's Wall: Excavations in Northumberland, 1907–1913*. Edited by G. Simpson. Kendal: T. Wilson.

Smith, N. A. F. 1983–1984. "The origins of water-power: A problem of evidence and expectations," *Transactions of the Newcomen Society* 55: 67–84.

Spain, R. J. 1987. "The Roman watermill in the Athenian agora: A new view of the evidence," *Hesperia* 56: 335–53.

Vetters, H. 1984. "Ephesos: Vorläufiger Grabungsbericht 1983," *Anzeiger der Österreichischen Akademie der Wissenschaften in Wien, Philologisch-historische Klasse* 121: 209–32.

Webster, G. 1955. "A note on the use of coal in Roman Britain," *Antiquaries Journal* 35: 199–216.

Wikander, Ö. 1979. "Water-mills in ancient Rome," *Opuscula Romana* 12: 13–36.

Wikander, Ö. 1981. "The use of water-power in classical antiquity," *Opuscula Romana* 13: 91–104.

Wikander, Ö. 1985. "Archaeological evidence for early water-mills—An interim report," *History of Technology* 10: 151–79.

Wikander, Ö. 1991. "Water-mills and aqueducts," in A. T. Hodge (ed.), *Future currents in aqueduct studies*. Leeds: Francis Cairns, 141–48.

Wikander, Ö. 1992. "Water-mills in Europe: Their early frequence and diffusion," in *Medieval Europe: A conference on medieval archaeology in Europe, 21st–24th September at the University of York. Pre-printed papers*, Vol. 3: *Technology and innovation*. York: Society for Medieval Archaeology, 9–14.

Wikander, Ö. 2000. "The water-mill," in Ö. Wikander (ed.), *Handbook of ancient water technology*. Leiden: Brill, 371–400.

Wikander, Ö. 2002. " 'Where of old all the mills of the city have been constructed': The capacity of the Janiculum mills in Rome," in *Ancient history matters: Studies presented* to J. E. Skydsgaard on his seventieth birthday. *Analecta Romana Instituti Danici* Suppl. 30. Rome: Danish Institute, 127–33.

Wikander, Ö. 2004. "Invention, technology transfer, breakthrough—The ancient water-mill as an example," in F. Minonzio (ed.), *Problemi di macchinismo in ambito romano*. Archeologia dell'Italia Settentrionale 8. Como: Commune di Como, 107–12.

Wilson, A. I. 1995. "Water-power in North Africa and the development of the horizontal water-wheel," *Journal of Roman Archaeology* 8: 499–510.

Wilson, A. I. 2000. "The water-mills on the Janiculum," *Memoirs of the American Academy in Rome* 45: 219–46.

Wilson, A. I. 2001. "Water-mills at Amida: Ammianus Marcellinus 18.8.11," *Classical Quarterly* 51: 231–36.

Wilson, A. I. 2002. "Machines, power and the ancient economy," *Journal of Roman Studies* 92: 1–32.

CHAPTER 7

# GREEK AND ROMAN AGRICULTURE

EVI MARGARITIS

MARTIN K. JONES

IN the period for which we have written records, much of the agricultural technology of those parts of the world that came under European influence finds its roots in the classical world. This legacy includes the usage of a range of heavy metal implements, in particular the moldboard plow, long sickle, and scythe, as well as the management of drainage schemes, meadows, water-driven mills, and grinding equipment. These important technological legacies, however, were not typical of farms in the classical world itself. Several of the more enduring technologies developed quite late in the classical epoch, and moreover around the boundaries of the Roman world, where classical and local traditions came together and jointly contributed to agrarian development.

A far more typical form of classical agriculture has its roots instead in a long-standing harmonization between Mediterranean farmers and the particular challenges of their environment. It entailed the implementation of simpler and more ancient technologies, based in wood and with much sparser use of metal, powered either by human energy or by a single cow, donkey, or mule. Throughout the course of the classical epoch, the great majority of farmers were engaged in these smaller-scale agrarian technologies rather than in the capital-intensive technologies associated with the later Roman world. In this chapter, we explore the nature of agriculture in the Mediterranean epicenter, paying special attention to the combination of arboriculture and arable agriculture typical of the region. In the context of that account, we also follow developments on the periphery of that world that led to a range of enduring innovations in agricultural technology. Our evidence comes from two principal sources, texts and archaeology, and the interpretation of that evidence draws repeatedly on ethnographic observation of more recent small-scale Mediterranean agriculture.

A great deal of the debate on the roots of the ancient economy has been drawn from incidental references in Athenian legal speeches and philosophical dialogues. Sources that directly describe Greek agriculture and farming practices are extremely scarce, which is paradoxical considering the multitude of sources referring to the importance of agriculture on a theoretical, idealistic basis. Thus, the methods of cultivating and processing various crops, their different uses, their individual economic and social value and status, and the character of the rural landscape are barely mentioned (cf. Isager and Skydsgaard 1992: 4). Sources such as the Athenian legal speeches and philosophical dialogues are in any case likely to reflect cultural ideals as much as historical realities (Cahill 2001: 223). The literary sources generally concern the upper strata of society, those involved in legal cases, mortgages of land, and similar situations (Cahill 2001: 224). In addition, most of the available information concerns the large urban centers, especially Athens, and therefore the paucity of written sources from the rural, farming areas of Greece, does not allow for a closer investigation of agricultural systems and patterns in the agricultural countryside.

The textual evidence is more direct during the Roman period, with a much richer body of works specifically on agricultural matters, by such authors as Cato, Varro, and Columella. These, however, must also be read in the context of both the regions of the Roman world and the strata of Roman society (again, the upper stratum of estate-owning society) about which they were writing. A complementary picture, with different regional and social emphases, is coming from a growing body of archaeological evidence from throughout the classical world and beyond, and particularly the direct bio-archaeological evidence of the remains of crops, livestock, and implements. Visual representations of ancient farmers at work constitute another invaluable source (e.g., figure 2.13).

# THE MEDITERRANEAN EPICENTER

Mediterranean ecosystems are characterized by abrupt topography and marked seasonality, features that have the effect of fragmenting the accessibility of natural resources and partitioning them across space and time (Horden and Purcell 2000). Much of classical agrarian practice was aimed at containing and controlling this spatial and temporal fragmentation. It began with the choice of combinations of plant and animal species that were themselves well adapted to coping with such fragmentation in space and time. These species were contained and nurtured within modestly sized plots to which the supply of water was often managed and moderated. Distinct altitudinal zones of this rugged landscape were used in complementary manners for crop growth, animal feed, and woodland resources (figure 7.1).

Figure 7.1. Mediterranean polyculture: olives in the forefront, vines in the middle distance, arable fields and hillside grazing in the distance. (Photograph by Graeme Barker.)

There were some broad differences in the manner in which Greek and Roman societies adapted to the Mediterranean ecosystem (Foxhall et al. 2007). Agriculture on Roman estates was geared toward a control and mastery of nature. Through interaction with neighboring communities, technologies were developed that could be taken beyond the Mediterranean, to cooler and wetter environments in the north and hotter, more arid environments in the south and east. By contrast, Greek agriculture was more a process of harmonization with, rather than a mastery of, the Mediterranean ecosystem. The Greek world remained more closely tied to that particular region, as can be seen from the correlation between the distribution of Greek settlements and that of the olive tree (Foxhall et al. 2007).

Two models have been proposed for this harmonizing interpretation of Greek agriculture. Hodkinson described them as "models of symbiosis and divorce" (1988: 38). The first, "traditional" model uses records of Mediterranean agriculture and animal husbandry from recent centuries as analogues for the more distant classical past (Semple 1932: 386; Finley 1973: 108; Duncan-Jones 1982: 49). According to this model, agriculture was practiced in a biennial cycle in which cereal crops alternated with bare fallow. Bare fallow involves the plowing of weeds before they set seed, and therefore this method would have limited weed growth and resulted in the accumulation of two years' moisture in the field for the succeeding cereal crop (Semple 1932: 386). This conservation is important, considering the limiting factor of the availability of water in the arid environment of Greece (Halstead 1987: 78, 81). Following the ramifications of this model, the maintenance of soil fertility was dependant neither on manuring nor on pulse rotation; in some cases these were even considered disadvantageous (Semple 1932: 411). As agricultural experiments have shown, however, manured annual cropping is far more productive than a bare fallow–cereal rotation, provided, of course, that sufficient manure is available (Littlejohn 1946).

The cereal-to-bare-fallow rotation would have resulted in the scarcity of lowland grazing sources, in turn forcing the livestock to move to other areas for sustenance. This model envisages the seasonal transhumance of sheep and goats, migrating from the arid environment of the lowlands, to the cooler and more lush highlands (Semple 1932: 297; Michell 1963). The removal of the livestock from the lowlands would also have deprived the arable fields of manure from the grazing animals. Consequently, this model envisages a separation between arable farming and pastoralism, a separation that could be seen in traditional economies of Greece and other Mediterranean countries, and a feature that has also been taken to distinguish traditional farming in the Mediterranean and temperate European regions (Halstead 1987: 79). Reinders and Prummel (1998: 82) have inferred specialized pastoralism and transhumance in Hellenistic Thessaly and the site of New Halos on the basis of faunal remains, two literary sources attesting to the use of summer pastures in the Orthis Mountains during the Hellenistic period, and contemporary ethnographic observations. The same variety of faunal remains (sheep, goats, cattle, pigs, equids, and dogs) found at New Halos (Reinders and Prummel 1998: 82) were also found at Cassope in western Greece from the fourth to first century B.C. (Boessneck 1986), and they have been interpreted as compatible with mixed farming (Halstead 1990: 71).

An alternative model to the one described above questions the uncritical use of contemporary traditional practices as analogies for antiquity. Drawing instead on direct bio-archaeological evidence for crop harvests and livestock, it posits a closer connection between animal husbandry and arable agriculture (Halstead 1981, 1987; Gallant 1982; Garnsey 1988: 93–94). In this model, agriculture and animal husbandry are seen as integrated components in an intensive farming system involving the raising of fodder crops, manuring, and crop rotation. The rotation of cereals and pulses is emphasized, resulting in the availability of fodder in the lowlands during summer. This availability of fodder would in turn obviate the need for the seasonal movement of the animals, who would consume weeds and produce manure, enhancing at the same time the fertility and productivity of the land (White 1970: 119; Halstead 1981: 328).

# WATER MANAGEMENT
# AND IRRIGATION

The alternative model described here presupposes some degree of water management, and there remain doubts about the intensity and extent of water management on Greek farms (Isager and Skydsgaard 1992). The role of irrigation in ancient Greek agriculture has been debated extensively, and many researchers have argued against complex water management in classical Greece (Gallant 1991: 56–57). On the other hand, it has been posited that classical farmhouses had developed private rather than communal sources of water, such as wells, which suggests an intensification of agriculture (Hanson 1999: 60). Others have advocated for the use of intensive watering and irrigation systems only at the gardens located near the city houses and the independent farmhouses (Krasilnikoff 2002). The extent of irrigation and water control in classical Greece remains a matter for debate (Oleson 2000a: 205–8), but many Greek authors allude to the problem (e.g., Plato, *Leg.* 6.761a–b), and Aristotle uses garden irrigation as an analogy for the human circulatory system (*Part. an.* 3.5.668a).

The situation in the Roman world is clearer, and it seems that the expansion of Roman influence to the east and the south facilitated the flow of technological ideas from western Asia and the Nile corridor to various arid regions around the Mediterranean. A number of Roman authors refer to the irrigation of some arable fields, orchards, vineyards, pastures, and gardens (Butzer et al. 1985). Water management was also applied to large-scale schemes involving drainage reclamation, flood control, and navigation (White 1970).

A series of devices for lifting and moving water were adopted from the eastern and southern boundaries of the Roman world (see chapters 11 and 13). In Andalucia during the first century B.C., the geographer Strabo (3.2.9) recorded the use of a water-lifting device that Archimedes had invented two centuries earlier in Egypt (Dalley and Oleson 2003). The Archimedean screw or "water snail" was a hand-turned helical device, originally used to lift water out of irrigation ditches and subsequently adapted for a variety of purposes (Oleson 2000b: 242–51). A similar trajectory can be followed for other water-lifting devices first recorded in Egypt. The *shaduf*, a device involving a bucket on a counterweighted beam, appears in the Near East by the seventeenth century B.C. and remained common throughout the Mediterranean nearly up to the present. Pliny (*HN* 19.60) mentions its use in Italy in the first century A.D., and it had become common in Spain by at least the late Roman period (Butzer et al. 1985). Animal-propelled water-lifting wheels worked through an angle gear (*saqiya*), known in Egypt from the third century B.C., probably formed the basis for the undershot water-mills familiar to Vitruvius (*De arch.* 10.5.1) and Pliny (*HN* 19.4), and subsequently the basis for water-powered milling (Oleson 1984: 371–80; see also chapter 6). Elaborate irrigation systems based on underground tunnels (the *qanat*) are first recorded in ancient Persia then subsequently in Roman Tunisia (Hodge 1992: 20–24). While the *shaduf* and *qanat* are products of the arid Near East, the mechanical water-lifting devices were all invented in Hellenistic Alexandria (Oleson 1984, 2000b), and the most intensive use of a number of these irrigation technologies clearly follows the arid perimeters of the Roman world in North Africa and Spain rather than the central regions of Greece and Italy.

# ARBORICULTURE

Perennial woody crops have continuously constituted a central element of Mediterranean agriculture. A wide variety of species may be involved, sometimes interplanted with other crops or pasture, at other times grown alone in orchards, and utilized for food, fodder, fuel, or construction materials. Their ecological advantage is that by their perennial habit and extensive root systems, their long-term growth in itself ameliorates the sharp climatic seasonality and its effects on soil and water. Alongside almonds, figs, carobs, oak, pistacia, pine, and many others, the two perennial crops that became most closely associated with the classical Mediterranean world are the olive and grape (cf. chapter 14).

Models for the technology of classical oil and wine production have often drawn on analogues from contemporary ethnography (Loukopoulos 1938; Aschenbrenner 1972; Forbes 1982, 1992; Gavrielides 1976; Zivas 2000). Much information can be extracted from ancient literature and archaeological data, but many factors related to these commodities are still uncertain, such as the area of land planted, the labor expended in their production, and the scheduling of agricultural activities. Although modern data requires critical evaluation, ethnographic studies offer some basis for estimating labor as well as yield and production rates in ancient agricultural communities.

## The Grapevine

For the classical and postclassical periods, both Greek and Roman ancient writers provide information about the winemaking procedures and the cultivation of the vine. In the texts, numerous instructions are given on how to make good wine and how to add the right flavorings (Humphrey et al. 1998: 154–59). They specified the optimal way to store products and classify different wines in relation to their place of production, variety of grapes, color, taste, and ways of being processed. Drawing from written sources, Kissopoulos (1947, 1948, 1949) provided details about tools, pottery, and other equipment used during and after vintage and wine making. Both pictorial representations and written sources, however, can be biased, and critical evaluation is fundamental (Isager and Skydsgaard 1992).

Among Greek writers, Theophrastus remains the main source of our knowledge of Greek viticulture through two major works: *Historia plantarum* and *De causis plantarum* (Isager and Skydsgaard 1992: 29). As a botanist, Theophrastus took a natural interest in the growing requirements and cultivation of plants and therefore provided general information about the vine. Only in rare cases did he provide a more thorough account of viticulture and give detailed descriptions of planting or pruning, or information about suitable soils. Theophrastus took it for granted that the reader was fully familiar with the meaning of terms, and we therefore have no explanation or definition of the words employed (Isager and Skydsgaard 1992: 28). Despite these difficulties, it is evident from his presentation that viticulture required a great degree of care and tending. Theophrastus gives us the first consistent description of the continuous process from pruning until the concluding work prior to the ripening of the grapes. Only Homer and Hesiod mention the actual vintage, although it was frequently shown in art together with the treading of the grapes (Isager and Skydsgaard 1992: 33). In his *Works and Days*, Hesiod deals also with the agrarian calendar and the pruning of vine, while Xenophon in his *Oeconomicus* (19) describes the planting process in detail. In the

*Deipnosophistae* (11.10), Athenaeus explains how wine should be mixed and how to produce vessels suitable for wine; many names for the vessels used in viticulture are preserved in this work. Roman viticulture is discussed by a number of authors, principally Cato, Varro, Columella, and Pliny. Their various discussions of the many ways of training the vine, planting, cultivation, and pruning are summarized in White (1970: 229–46; see also Humphrey et al. 1998: 114–20).

As with many crops, an important and laborious task in viticulture was digging. This took place in the winter while the vine was still dormant. Deep digging was carried out around the trunk of each vine to allow rain, air, and manure to break through to the roots. In this way, greater nourishment could reach new, fruit-bearing growth. If digging was not done, or was not done in the correct way, the new roots would not develop properly and the yield of the vine would be greatly reduced (Pliny, *HN* 15.188; Columella, *Rust.* 4.28.2; Palmer 1994: 14). Repeated digging also reduced the weed growth, which could otherwise compete with trees or vines for moisture and soil nutrients (Foxhall 1990: 107). During summer, when grapes and other fruits expand and ripen, they depend entirely on the moisture retained in the subsoil by the layer of broken soil at the surface. In comparisons made by Forbes (1976: 9) on two variously managed contemporary vineyards, the one that was carefully and repeatedly dug yielded almost twice the amount of grapes. It is common practice to manure the vineyard while digging. Manuring usually involved animal dung, although various components such as bones, scraps of leather and other domestic waste, charred grape pips, ash, and charred wood could also be used. The spread of potsherds over ancient agricultural fields is usually the incidental result of the dumping of household debris as fertilizer. Even the addition of (dry) soil, transported from elsewhere, is mentioned in the ancient literature (Palaiologos 1838: 19–20). Tilling the soil is another major task in the vineyard, and Theophrastus (*Hist. pl.* 3.9.5, 3.10) is conscious of the importance of aerating the soil and controlling weeds by tilling.

Vines require a greater degree of attendance and control of the environment than any other ancient crop. They require skilled labor to plant, prune, and tend throughout their growing period, and perhaps to guard when the grapes are ripening, as appears to have been the case in ancient Athens (Morris and Papadopoulos 2005: 179). Extra labor is required during harvesting and processing for the production of either raisins or wine. Archaeobotanical methods applied to the site of Komboloi in southern Macedonia have charted the harvesting and processing of grapes at a first-millennium B.C. farmstead (Margaritis and Jones 2006).

## The Olive Tree

As olives produce a full crop in alternate years, Columella proposed that farmers should divide olive groves into two parts that would give an equal return each year (*Rust.* 5.99, 2.7). At present, many farmers gather their olives green and immature in an attempt to make the trees produce the following year as well, as it is believed that when olives are gathered mature (black) the tree does not have enough re-sources and strength to produce olives for two successive years.

The maintenance and cultivation of olive groves involves digging, weeding, pruning, harvesting, fertilizing, and maintaining terraces, if necessary (Pansiot and Rebour 1961). As with viticulture, the most laborious and time-consuming part of tree cultivation was digging. This activity is best done during late autumn, although many farmers do it in springtime. The purpose of the digging is to assist surface water reaching the roots. Many farmers merely dig a ditch around the trees to the same diameter as the spread of the branches, so that the rainwater can accumulate there (Gavrielides 1976: 83). Repeated digging destroys roots close to the surface, thus encouraging the development of roots at lower levels where more moisture is available and they are less likely to suffer from sun-scorch or exposure, hence allowing trees to utilize available water more efficiently. This procedure is partic-ularly important for olives, which naturally have wide-spreading roots close to the surface (Foxhall 1990: 106–7). Repeated digging also reduces the growth of weeds that would otherwise compete with trees or vines for moisture and soil nutrients.

Pruning is also a very important task for olive cultivation, as it encourages the growth of new shoots and helps in the concentration of the juices of the tree (Isager and Skydsgaard 1992: 32). If the yield is not abundant, pruning is done at the same time as harvesting. When the yield is average or good, pruning begins after the harvest and continues during the months of December and January. Weeding begins in early September and lasts all month. During this period, the trees are loaded with fruit ready to be harvested. Weeding is done in order to clear the land under the trees from weeds and thorns in order to facilitate harvesting the portion of the crop that happens to fall on the ground.

A further aspect of olive grove maintenance is the repair of any existing terrace walls. The amount of time expended depends on the number of terraces in a given orchard and the time available. It is hard, time-consuming work and provides no immediate tangible returns (Foxhall 1990: 90). The culmination of the agricultural year is the time of the harvest. Harvesting could be carried out by several methods, such as hand-stripping, beating the branches, or gathering from the ground (Brun 1986: 36–38).

# ARABLE CULTIVATION

The principal cereal of the Greek world was barley, a crop that was well adapted to the Mediterranean environment. Its relative tolerance of drought and salinity suited it well to the typical hydrological conditions. The only cereals that can tolerate a shorter growing season are the millets, which were grown in irrigated fields, as their water demands during that growing season are higher. Legumes are also well attested in the archaeobotanical record, as well as a range of oilseeds such as sesame and flax. Wheat grew steadily in prominence during the classical epoch. A number of the key wheat species are more demanding than barley and require a more careful management of the Mediterranean ecology. The impetus behind the expanded use of wheat may well have been more cultural than ecological, and there is much textual evidence for the status of different types of bread in Greek and Roman society, for example in Athenaeus' *Deipnosophistae* (3.108–16; cf. Pliny, *HN* 18.105–6). Pliny (*HN* 18.86–92) discusses the relationship between types of wheat and varieties of bread.

Before planting, the ground could be prepared with a range of manual sod-breaking tools, including wooden mallets and mattocks. These were particularly important in the cultivation of small plots. In larger fields, the majority of Greek and Roman farmers throughout the classical period cultivated their soils with the same implement that had been in use since the Neolithic period: the scratch plow, or ard, with a single, simple share, light enough to be pulled by a single cow, donkey, or mule (figure 7.2). In *Georgics* (1.169–75), Vergil provides a detailed description of what is probably a bow-ard, constructed from elm, linden, and beech wood, with *aures* or "ears" attached to the share (figure 7.3; Varro, *Rust.* 1.29.2 terms them *tabellae*, "boards"; Aitken 1956; Manning 1964). Like moldboards, these "ears" probably helped turn the soil. Bronze models of such ards with turning boards are known from Britain and Germany, and complete wooden ards have been recovered from the peat deposits of Northern Europe, though generally lacking the *aures,* which appear to have been more common in the south.

Pliny (*HN* 18.48) refers to an invention that was recent at the time he wrote (the mid-first century A.D.), the addition of two small wheels, implying that the plow was becoming heavier. From the late third century A.D., we find archaeological evidence for the development of an implement that went on to become the principal tool of arable cultivation, first in Europe, and then accompanying the expansion of European influence around the world. The moldboard plow, with a heavy cutting blade at its front, followed by an asymmetrical share and sod-turning moldboard, and assisted by a variety of wheels, makes its appearance during the later stages of the Roman epoch (figure 7.4; Jones 1981, 1991).

Little, if any, metal was used in the construction of an ard—in line with the wood-based technology of farmers in general. Metal was scarce and conserved, used only where a durable cutting edge was absolutely necessary. Even then, obsidian flakes often provided a more accessible material for a sharp edge in areas with the appropriate geology, blades of obsidian being inserted both in threshing sleds and sickle mounts. The heavy investment in metal seen in the later plow was simply not within the resources of the great majority of classical-period farmers. Indeed, the need for it only arose beyond the limits of the Mediterranean region, where the soils were heavier.

North of the Alps, within temperate Europe, the environmental challenges faced by farmers were significantly different from those faced in the Mediterranean. While the annual level of sunshine is lower in more northerly latitudes, peaks of

**Figure 7.2.** Modern cross-cultivation with an ard. (Photograph by M. Jones.)

sunshine and rainfall are no longer segregated to separate seasons. In fact, neither water nor the unevenness of its supply are factors limiting biological productivity. The different conditions had significant implications for animal husbandry, particularly for animals with large water requirements, such as horses and cattle. There is much archaeological evidence for prehistoric traditions of cattle husbandry on a variety of scales in Europe north of the Alps, sometimes indicating large herd sizes. There is, furthermore, growing evidence for long traditions for the production of secondary bovine products such as milk and butter (chapter 8).

Temperate Europe is characterized by much larger expanses of plains and gently rolling topographies than the Mediterranean. Rather than gardens and terraces (cf. Van der Veen 2005), the emphasis was on extensive fields growing a diverse range of cereal and legume crops. While small enclosures and paddocks are widespread, we know of no clear evidence of what might be described as a "garden" in prehistoric temperate Europe. As we move north and east across Europe, the limiting factors to growth in these fields were depressed sunlight hours and constraints on both ends of the growing season by late spring frosts and late summer storms. The winter and spring frosts in particular were ameliorated on the Atlantic face of Europe by the Gulf Stream, and, significantly, it was along the Atlantic face of Europe, in Spain, France, and Britain, that the Roman Empire proved ecologically able to extend furthest beyond the Mediterranean (Cunliffe 2001: 365–421). There is now clear evidence that mixed farming with cattle and cereal agriculture is attested in many parts of prehistoric temperate Europe.

However, the imperial *limes* only stabilized where cereals were not simply *grown*, but were already being *mobilized* as surplus on at least a local scale. Rather than being attached to a particular set of farming practices and environmental

Figure 7.3. A traditional "eared" plow similar to that described by Vergil. (Photograph by Martin Millett.)

resources, the ecology of Roman farming was instead attached to a style of living and of agrarian management, and, critically, an exchange network to which these were attached. In Germany, the Netherlands, and northern Britain that ecological pattern fluctuated around the limits of its sustainability, ultimately settling along the Rhine valley on the east and the line of Hadrian's Wall on the north (Van der Veen 1992, Zacchariasse 2003).

Archaeobotanical evidence from this period of temperate Europe suggests a continuity of traditional agrarian practice, of extensive field agriculture using the same crops that had been grown in the region for centuries, and the same farming techniques. Roman imperial expansion northward was clearly manifest in styles of consumption, networks of exchange, military appropriation, and rural villa architecture, but the agrarian base initially remained the same, and quite distinct from Mediterranean practice. With time, however, these styles of ecological engagement were themselves transformed.

The first discernible transformation was in the use of metal. Iron production was greatly stimulated by the imperial process, and unprecedented quantities of this hitherto scarce resource were distributed around the imperial network. Some was used to fashion a new generation of harvesting tools, which have been interpreted as hay scythes (Rees 1979). The harvesting equipment attested in prehistory would have been poorly suited to gathering herbaceous hay, which can only be effectively harvested with a much longer blade than was available to prehistoric farmers. There is scattered evidence that the branches of leafy fodder that can be harvested with more modest blades was the prevailing winter-feed of livestock (Jones 1991). The long iron blades that appear in the early Roman Empire allowed the plant community we know as hay meadows to proliferate. This technological innovation may even have led to their original genesis as distinct plant commu-

Figure 7.4. A contemporary moldboard plow with wheel and coulter before the share. (Photograph by M. Jones.)

nities (Jones 1991). Although the first appearance of hay meadows seems linked to Roman expansion, the Roman favorites of pork, chicken, and oysters are little augmented by the maintenance of hay meadows. This novel ecological product of metal technology, the hay meadow, was of more relevance in the sustenance (and especially the winter survival) of those essentially northern symbols of prestige and wealth, horses and cattle.

Otherwise, the clearest indications of change in food have to do with handling and mobilization on an unprecedented scale. The *limes* forts along Hadrian's Wall contain a series of vast granaries storing cereals in unprecedented quantities, and the traces of mechanical mills that transformed their contents into flour. More valuable and transportable foods such as wine and olive oil were traveling across the Empire and beyond (Bakels and Jacomet 2003). The peppercorns that have been recovered from a number of sites in Roman Britain may well have traveled from the Malibar coast in southern India, entering the imperial network at the African port of Berenice (Cappers 1999).

# MEADOWS, GARDENS, AND MOLDBOARD PLOWS

Ornamental gardens had appeared in conjunction with the earliest villas and "palaces" within the northern *limes*, notably attested at Fishbourne in Sussex (Cunliffe 1971). We are not sure to what extent, if at all, they had a strictly economic dimension, just as we are unclear whether the hay meadows attested by hay scythes and fragments of the hay itself were of widespread ecological significance or something specifically for raising prestigious animals. From the late third century A.D. onward, however, there is recurrent evidence from villa plans, planting pits, "dark earths," and the diversification of subsidiary food plants that an economic garden was becoming a recurrent feature of the northwest provinces (Jones 1989). This was also a period in which the balance of investment between the town and the countryside was shifting, and the imperial margins, in both the north and the south, were witnessing a surge in conspicuous rural wealth. In the northwest provinces, this provided the context for a highly significant ecological shift. This shift was the consequence of a fusion between the core elements of temperate European agriculture—adequate water, gentle topography, deep soils, and a long tradition of cattle management—and the core elements of Roman agrarian ecology, particularly the ease of mobilization and exchange of goods, materials, and investment. Just as with the earlier hay scythes, a crucial material that was mobilized was iron.

Three iron implements that recur on Romano-British sites of the late third and fourth centuries A.D. are the long harvesting scythe, the coulter, and the asymmetrical plowshare (Rees 1979). All three can be linked to the intensification of cereal production, and the latter two to the moldboard plow, designed to cut deep into the soil and invert the furrow (figure 7.4; Jones 1981). Contemporary inverted furrows have also been found with a buried soil at the north German site of Feddersen Wierde (Körber-Grohne 1967). Like some of the metalwork finds, this latter site lies beyond the boundary of the Empire itself. In a manner that mirrors the development of irrigation techniques in the south and east, these find spots beyond the *limes* in the north and west suggest that moldboard plowing arose from a fusion between ecological traditions rather than as a simple introduction. Furthermore, the moldboard plow was developed to deal with environmental conditions specific to European landscapes north of the Alps—the simple ard, which did not invert the soil and was associated with shallow tillage, continued as the cultivation implement of preference in much of the Mediterranean until the twentieth century A.D. (figure 7.2). Interestingly, Körber-Grohne (1967) has interpreted some of the economic plant remains from Feddersen Wierde as deriving from what were essentially managed "gardens" within the settlement. The crop repertoire also shifts with the spread of deep moldboard plowing, with a particular emphasis on bread wheat in the western regions of temperate Europe, and rye in the East, both crops favored by deep cultivation.

Although the full impact of deep plowing and bread-wheat cultivation came after the end of the classical period, a key element of the late classical world, Christianity, took bread wheat and the plow first across Europe, and then across the world, as hallmarks of the new faith. In the process it raised bread wheat to the status of the primary food source of the human species (figure 7.5). The early roots of that process lie in a particular style of Roman ecology that emphasized control, management, and distribution, rather than overstamping or eradicating any existing agrarian practice.

**Figure 7.5. Raised stone-built military granary at Corbridge fort, Northern England. (Photograph by Martin Millett.)**

The technology of classical agriculture owed much to its roots in adaptation to the seasonal fluctuations of the Mediterranean ecosystem and its effect on water availability and soil stability. Conversely, the dynamics of change through time owed much to the economic structures of the classical world. These in particular related to the extensive nature of trade and exchange, whereby both biological resources, such as seed stock, and technological resources, crucially metal, as well as expertise in oral and written forms, reached a wide range of farms in many regions. These structures also related to the potential of land ownership and long-term arboriculture. Some of the most enduring legacies of classical agriculture, however, particularly extensive water management and the heavy plow, owe much to the interaction between agricultural technologies in the Mediterranean heartland of the classical world and long-standing practices in the geographical regions to which classical influence subsequently spread.

# REFERENCES

Aitken R. 1956. "Virgil's plough," *Journal of Roman Studies* 46: 97–106.
Alcock, S., J. Cherry, and J. Davis 1994. "Intensive survey, agricultural practice and classical landscape of Greece," in I. Morris (ed.), *Classical Greece: Ancient histories and modern archaeologies*. 2nd ed. Cambridge: Cambridge University Press, 137–70.

Aschenbrenner, S. E. 1972. "Contemporary community," in W. A. McDonald and G. R. Rapp Jr. (eds.), *The Minnesota Messenia expedition: Reconstructing a Bronze Age regional environment*. Minneapolis: University of Minnesota Press, 47–63.

Bakels, C., and S. Jacomet 2003. "Access to luxury goods in central Europe during the Roman period: The archaeobotanical evidence," *World Archaeology* 34: 542–57.

Boessneck, J. 1986. "Zooarchaologische Ergebnisse an den Tierknochen- und Molluskenfunden," in W. Hoepfer and E.-L. Schwandner (eds.), *Haus und Stadt im Klassischen Griechenland*. Munich: Deutscher Kunstverlag, 136–40.

Brun, J. P. 1986. *L'Oleiculture antique en province: Les huileries du departement du Var*. Paris: CNRS.

Butzer, K. W., J. F. Mateu, E. Butzer, and P. Kraus 1985. "Irrigation agrosystems in eastern Spain: Roman or Islamic origins?" *Annals of the Association of American Geographers* 75: 479–509.

Cahill, N. 2001. *Household and organization at Olynthus*. New Haven: Yale University Press.

Cappers, R, 1999. "Trade and subsistence at the Roman port of Berenike, Red Sea coast, Egypt," in: Van der Veen (ed.), *The exploitation of plant resources in ancient Africa*. New York: Kluwer, 185–97.

Cunliffe B. W. 1971. *Fishbourne: A Roman palace and its garden*. London: Thames and Hudson.

Cuniffe, B. W. 2001. *Facing the ocean: The Atlantic and its peoples*. Oxford: Oxford University Press.

Dalley, S., and J. P. Oleson 2003. "Sennacherib, Archimedes, and the water screw: The context of invention in the ancient world." *Technology and Culture* 44: 1–26.

Duncan-Jones, R. 1982. *The economy of the Roman Empire*. Cambridge: Cambridge University Press.

Finley, M. I. 1973. *The ancient economy*. Berkeley: University of California Press.

Forbes, H. A. 1976. "The 'thrice-ploughed field': Cultivation techniques in ancient and modern Greece," *Expedition* 19.1: 5–11.

Forbes, H. A. 1982. "Strategies and soils: Technology, production and environment in the peninsula of Methana, Greece." PhD diss., University of Pennsylvania.

Forbes, H. A. 1992. "The ethnoarchaeological approach to ancient Greek agriculture," in B. Wells (ed.), *Agriculture in ancient Greece. Proceedings of the Seventh International Symposium at the Swedish Institute at Athens, 16–17 May 1990. Acta Instituti Atheniensis regni Sueciae 42*. Stockholm: Paul Åstroms Förlag, 87–101.

Foxhall, L. 1990. "Olive cultivation within Greek and Roman agriculture: The ancient economy revisited." PhD diss., University of Liverpool.

Foxhall L., M. K. Jones, and H. Forbes 2007. "Human ecology and the classical landscape," in S. Alcock and R. Osborne (eds.), *Blackwell guide to classical archaeology*. Oxford: Blackwell.

Gallant, T. W. 1982. "Agricultural systems, land tenure, and the reforms of Solon," *Annual of the British School at Athens* 77: 111–24.

Gallant, T. W. 1991. *Risk and survival in ancient Greece: Reconstructing the rural domestic economy*. Stanford: Stanford University Press.

Garnsey, P. 1988. *Famine and food supply in the Graeco-Roman world: Responses to risk and crisis*. Cambridge: Cambridge University Press.

Gavrielides, N. E. 1976. "A study in the cultural ecology of an olive-growing community: The southern Argolid, Greece." PhD diss., Indiana University.

Halstead, P. 1981. "Counting sheep in Neolithic and Bronze Age Greece," in I. Hodder, G. Isaac, and N. Hammond (eds.), *Pattern of the past: Studies in honour of David Clarke*. Cambridge: Cambridge University Press, 307–39.

Halstead, P. 1987. "Traditional and ancient rural economy in Mediterranean Europe: *Plus ça change?*" *Journal of Hellenic Studies* 107: 77–87.

Halstead, P. 1990. "Present to past in the Pindos: Diversification and specialisation in mountain economies," *Rivista di Studi Liguri* 56: 61–80.

Hanson, V. D. 1999. *The other Greeks: The family farm and the agrarian roots of Western civilization*. 2nd ed. Berkeley: University of California Press.

Hodge, A. T. 1992. *Roman aqueducts and water supply*. London: Duckworth.

Hodkinson, S. 1988. "Animal husbandry in the Greek *polis*," in C. R. Whittaker (ed.), *Pastoral economies in classical antiquity*. Cambridge Philological Society Suppl. 14. Cambridge: Cambridge Philological Society, 35–74.

Horden, P., and N. Purcell 2000. *The corrupting sea: A study of Mediterranean history*. Oxford: Blackwell.

Humphrey, J., J. P. Oleson, and A. N. Sherwood 1998. *Greek and Roman technology: A sourcebook*. London: Routledge.

Isager, S., and J. E. Skydsgaard 1992. *Ancient Greek agriculture: An introduction*. London: Routledge.

Jones, M. K. 1981. "The development of crop husbandry," in M. K. Jones and G. W. Dimbleby (eds.), *The environment of man: The Iron Age to the Anglo-Saxon period*. British Archaeological Reports 87. Oxford: BAR, 95–127.

Jones, M. K. 1989. Agriculture in Roman Britain: The dynamics of change," in M. Todd (ed.), *Research on Roman Britain, 1960–1989*. London: Society for the Promotion of Roman Studies, 127–34.

Jones, M. K. 1991. "Agricultural productivity in the pre-documentary past," in B. Campbell and M. Overton (eds.), *Land, labour and livestock: Historical studies in European agricultural productivity*. Manchester: Manchester University Press, 78–93.

Kissopoulos, D. 1947. "Greek and Roman wine making," *Chemistry Journal* 12A: 22–28.

Kissopoulos, D. 1948. "Wine making of the classical, Roman and Byzantine periods," *Chemistry Journal* 13A: 24–30.

Kissopoulos, D. 1949. "Wine making of the classical, Roman and Byzantine periods," *Chemistry Journal* 14A: 13–17.

Körber-Grohne, U. 1967. *Geobotanische Untersuchungen auf der Feddersen Wierde*. Wiesbaden: Steiner.

Krasilnikoff, J. A. 2002. "Water and farming in classical Greece: Evidence, method and perspectives," in K. Ascani, V. Gabrielsen, K. Kvist, and A. H. Rasmussen (eds.), *Ancient history matters: Studies presented to Jens Erik Skydsaggard on his seventieth birthday*. Analecta Romana Instituti Danici Romae Suppl. 30. Rome: L'Erma di Bretschneider, 47–61.

Littlejohn, L. 1946. "Some aspects of soil fertility in Cyprus," *Journal of Experimental Agriculture* 14: 123–34.

Loukopoulos, D. 1938. *Agricultural practices in central Greece*. Athens: Folklore Library, Sideris Editions.

Margaritis, E. E., and M. K. Jones 2006. "Beyond cereals: Crop-processing and *Vitis vinifera* L: Ethnography, experiment and charred grape remains from Hellenistic Greece," *Journal of Archaeological Science* 33.6: 784–805.

Manning, W. H. 1964. "The plough in Roman Britain," *Journal of Roman Studies* 54: 54–65.

Michell, H. 1963. *Economics of Ancient Greece.* 2nd ed. Cambridge: Cambridge University Press.

Morris, S., and J. Papadopoulos 2005. "Greek towers and slaves: An archaeology of exploitation," *American Journal of Archaeology* 109: 155–225.

Oleson, J. P. 1984. *Greek and Roman mechanical water-lifting devices: The history of a technology.* Toronto: University of Toronto Press.

Oleson, J. P. 2000a. "Irrigation," in Wikander 2000, 183–215.

Oleson, J. P. 2000b. "Water-lifting," in Wikander 2000, 217–302.

Palaiologos 1838. *Vine cultivation and wine making.* Athens: Royal Editions.

Palmer, R. 1994. *Wine in the Mycenaean palace economy.* Liège: Université de Liège.

Pansiot, F. P., and H. Rebour 1961. *Improvement in olive cultivation.* Rome: F.A.O.

Rees, S. 1979. *Agricultural implements in prehistoric and Roman Britain.* British Archaeological Reports 69. Oxford: BAR.

Reinders, H. R., and W. Prummel 1998. "Transhumance in Hellenistic Thessaly," *Environmental Archaeology* 3: 81–95.

Semple, E. C. 1932. *The geography of the Mediterranean region: Its relation to ancient history.* London: Constable.

Van der Veen, M. 1992. *Crop husbandry regimes: An archaeobotanical study of farming in northern England, 1000 BC–AD 500.* Sheffield Archaeological Monographs 3. Sheffield: J. R. Collis.

Van der Veen, M. (ed.) 2005. *Garden agriculture.* Special issue, *World Archaeology* 37.2.

Wikander, Ö. (ed.) 2000. *Handbook of ancient water technology.* Leiden: Brill

White, K. D. 1970. *Roman farming.* London: Thames and Hudson.

Zachariasse, F. 2003 "Lowland farming: A comparative study of agricultural variation and change in the Netherlands during the 1st millennium A.D." PhD diss., Cambridge University.

Zivas, D. A. 2000 *Pre-industrial agricultural buildings at the island of Zakynthos.* Athens: ETBA Publications.

# CHAPTER 8

## ANIMAL HUSBANDRY, HUNTING, FISHING, AND FISH PRODUCTION

### GEOFFREY KRON

ARCHAEOZOOLOGICAL research offers impressive, long-neglected evidence for the technical sophistication and productivity of Greco-Roman animal husbandry. Historians once portrayed ancient livestock farming as crippled by summer drought and a chronic shortage of fodder (White 1970: 272; Frayn 1984), with farmers forced to raise a limited number of animals predominantly for their wool or for work rather than for meat (White 1970: 276–77). In fact, Greek and Roman farmers, graziers, and shepherds supplied large urban populations with meat from an impressive range of livestock, game, domestic fowl, birds, fish, and shellfish. Animal bones reveal a significant increase in the size of most Greco-Roman domestic animal species over those found on Bronze Age, Iron Age, or medieval sites (Peters 1998; Kron 2002; MacKinnon 2004), often reaching levels that were consistently found again only in nineteenth-century Europe (Kron 2002: 63; cf. Moriceau 1999: 47). The writings of the Roman agronomists consistently reflect sound and intelligent principles of management, differing little from contemporary organic animal husbandry. Moreover, evaluations of the writings of Greek and Roman veterinarians by their modern counterparts show knowledge of most of the surgical procedures used on livestock as late as the mid-twentieth century and of the properties of medicinal herbs appropriate for many veterinary ailments.

A case can be made that the classical and Hellenistic Greeks should be credited for many of the critical innovations in animal husbandry (Kron 2002: 65–68), game-farming, and both fishing and fish-farming (Trotta 1996: 242–43; Colin-Bouffier

1999). The Greek origin of many of the most highly prized livestock breeds is well known (Magerstedt 1859: 20–22, 94–98, 100–101; Ryder 1983: 147–50), and the Roman agronomists made no secret of their reliance on methods pioneered by the Greeks and Carthaginians (Varro, *Rust.* 3.3.6–7, 3.10.1; Columella, *Rust.* 8.1.3–4, 8.2.4, 8.2.13), citing a long list of lost works (Varro, *Rust.* 1.1.8–10; Columella, *Rust.* 1.1.7–12; Georgoudi 1990: 65–72). The scattered references to animal husbandry in Greek literary sources and inscriptions (Osborne 1987; Hodkinson 1988; Chandezon 2003) likewise suggest that many of the methods of animal husbandry described by Columella and Varro date back to the fifth and fourth centuries B.C., if not earlier. This hypothesis is supported by the archaeozoological evidence of the increased size of classical and Hellenistic Greek livestock (Benecke 1994a: 304; Kron 2002: 65–68), but definitive proof will remain elusive until more studies can be carried out on post-Bronze Age Greek sites (Payne 1985; Reese 1994; Kotjabopoulou et al. 2003). Improved Greco-Roman livestock did not entirely supplant smaller breeds, some of which were still prized, presumably for their adaptation to the climate, hardiness, good wool, or high milk production (e.g., *cevae* from Altinum; cf. Columella, *Rust.* 6.24.5). The transition to more intensive methods was likely less complete in regions that were only gradually hellenized or romanized, and increases in size varied by species.

The Greeks and Romans also developed sophisticated new techniques to improve the capture, farming, or fattening of a large range of game, wild birds, and fish. The farming of game and fish for sale in urban markets was particularly sophisticated and intensive. Efficient commercial game farming of the sort described by the Greeks and Romans and attested by archaeozoological studies would not be revived in Europe or North America until the late twentieth century (Fletcher 1989: 325; Binder 1971). Roman aquaculture of the late Republic and early Principate was even more impressive. Fish farmers invested large amounts of capital into building elaborate fish-tank complexes for mariculture and experimented with some of the most important techniques of modern fish farming.

# ANIMAL HUSBANDRY

Greek and Roman farmers kept a wide variety of domesticated animals: cattle, sheep, goats, pigs (figure 8.1), horses, donkeys, and mules, as well as dogs and cats, chicken, ducks, geese, rock doves, and even camels (table 8.1). The best methods of Greco-Roman animal husbandry were highly intensive, often matching the relatively modern methods of improved husbandry introduced in Holland and Brabant in the sixteenth and seventeenth centuries (de Vries 1974; Moriceau 1999: 47) and England in the eighteenth and nineteenth (Trow-Smith 1959; Davis 1997). Less intensive traditional methods continued, of course, and were attractive for farmers

Figure 8.1. Roman livestock. Bull (not to scale), sheep, and pig from relief showing Tiberius carrying out the Suovetaurilia sacrifice, ca. A.D. 14, Rome. Louvre Museum. (Alinari photo: 22685.)

who did not have access to large urban markets and needed to keep costs low. As historians of technology, however, our primary interest is in state-of-the-art techniques, and limitations of space make it impossible to describe the full spectrum of approaches in detail.

The innovations in Greco-Roman animal husbandry can be broken down into four main areas: breeding, nutrition, housing, and health and veterinary care. In each field, the classical agronomists strongly emphasize intensification of production—e.g., the battery farming of poultry in dark confined cages (Varro, *Rust.* 3.9.19–20; Columella, *Rust.* 8.7.1–3; Martial 13.62), so similar to modern factory farming (Peters 1998: 201; cf. Fox 1984: 14–18, 21–24)—and close observation of the normal behavior of the livestock being raised (Columella, *Rust.* 8.8.4–5, 10.5, 14.4–5; Varro, *Rust.* 3.7.6, 10.7).

## Breeding

Although some have downplayed the use of selective breeding by Roman farmers (e.g., White 1970: 272–75), the references in the agronomists show that they had considerable expertise (Vigneron 1968: 30–31; Ryder 1983: 164; Bökönyi 1984: 21–22). They were not aware of the science of genetics, but neither were legendary eighteenth-century English cattle breeders such as Bakewell or many of his successors, who were responsible for setting many of the principal livestock breeds of today (Pawson 1957). Even modern breeders of thoroughbred racehorses rely largely on intuition and experience rather than genetics to make their decisions (Wynmalen

**Table 8.1.** The principal Greco-Roman domestic animal species.

| Common name | Scientific name | References |
|---|---|---|
| Cattle | *Bos taurus* | Keller 1909: 329–71; Toynbee 1973: 149–62; Flach 1990: 290–96; Benecke 1994a: 260–88; Peters 1998: 25–71; MacKinnon 2004: 76–99; King 2002: 408–10 |
| Pig | *Sus scrofa domesticus* | Keller 1909: 388–404; Toynbee 1973: 131–36; Flach 1990: 311–15; Benecke 1994a: 248–60; Peters 1998: 107–34; MacKinnon 2001: 138–62 |
| Sheep | *Ovis aries* | Keller 1909: 309–28; Toynbee 1973: 163–64; Ryder 1983: 117–81; Flach 1990: 301–9; Benecke 1994a: 228–38; Peters 1998: 71–106; MacKinnon 2001: 100–37 |
| Goat | *Capra hircus* | Keller 1909: 296–308; Toynbee 1973: 164–66; Flach 1990: 309–11; Benecke 1994a: 239–48; Peters 1998: 71–106; MacKinnon 2001: 100–137; King 2002: 415–16 |
| Horse | *Equus caballus* | Keller 1909: 218–58; Toynbee 1973: 167–85; Flach 1990: 297–99; Benecke 1994a: 288–310; Peters 1998: 135–65; King 2002: 423–26 |
| Ass | *Equus asinus* | Keller 1909: 259–70; Toynbee 1973: 192–97; Flach 1990: 296–97; Benecke 1994a: 310–18; Peters 1998: 135–65; King 2002: 421–22 |
| Mule | *Equus caballus X asinus* | Keller 1909: 259–70; Toynbee 1973: 185–92; Flach 1990: 299–300; Benecke 1994a: 318–23; Peters 1998: 135–65; King 2002: 422–23 |
| Camel | *Camelus dromedarius; Camelus bactrianus* | Keller 1909: 275–76; Toynbee 1973: 141–42; Benecke 1994a: 323–32; Peters 1998: 189–90; Gilbert 2002: 18–21 |
| Dog | *Canis familiaris* | Keller 1909: 91–151; Benecke 1994a: 208–28; Peters 1998: 167–87; King 2002: 410–14 |
| Cat | *Felis catus* | Keller 1909: 64–80; Benecke 1994a: 344–52; Peters 1998: 187–88; King 2002: 426–27 |
| Chicken | *Gallus gallus domesticus* | Keller 1913: 131–45; Thompson 1936: 33–44; André 1967: 130–32; Zeuner 1963: 449–55; Toynbee 1973: 256–57; Flach 1990: 315–20; Benecke 1994a: 362–73; Watson 2002: 380–81; Benecke et al. 2003: 78–79 |
| Greylag goose | *Anser anser domesticus* | Keller 1913: 220–26; Thompson 1936: 325–30; André 1967: 132–33; Zeuner 1963: 466–70; Toynbee 1973: 261–64; Salza Prina Ricotti 1987: 95–96; Flach 1990: 322–23; Benecke 1994a: 373–79; Olson and Sens 2000: 213–14; Watson 2002: 365–66; Benecke et al. 2003: 79 |
| Mallard duck | *Anas platyrhynchos domesticus* | Keller 1913: 226–35; Thompson 1936: 205–6; André 1967: 133; Zeuner 1963: 470–71; Toynbee 1973: 264–73; Salza Prina Ricotti 1987: 95; Benecke 1994: 379–83; Watson 2002: 364–65 |
| Rock dove | *Columba livia* | Keller 1913: 122–31; Thompson 1936: 238–46; André 1967: 124; Zeuner 1963: 460–62; Toynbee 1973: 258–59; Pollard 1977: 104; Salza Prina Ricotti 1987: 96; Flach 1990: 320–22; Benecke 1994: 383–90; Watson 2002: 372–74; Benecke 2003: 79–80 |

1950: 88, 99). Like their Greek and Roman predecessors (White 1970: 328–29; Columella, *Rust.* 6.29.2–3, 36.1–5; 7.2.5–3.2; Varro, *Rust.* 2.2.3–5, 7.5), they still rely heavily on points (Wynmalen 1950: 96–107), and their advice often broadly corroborates the recommendations of the ancients (White 1970: 185–86; Peters 1998: 28–29, 77–78, 199). Modern historians of horse breeding often single out Xenophon's explanation of the points of the horse (*Eq.* 1.9–10), like much of his advice, as exemplary (Vigneron 1968: 5–9; Goodall 1977: 117).

As Vigneron points out (1968: 35–38), the ancient agronomists had ably resolved all the technical problems involved in breeding and raising the young of that most delicate of domestic animals, the horse, and the same care was given to breeding the other major domestic animals. For example, Columella advised farmers not only to use the best breeding stock, but also to use only sexually mature animals in their prime (*Rust.* 7.3.6, 6.3, 6.8, 9.2); to control the breeding process (*Rust.* 6.37.1–2, 8–10; 7.3.11–16, 6.6–8); to provide prompt veterinary help in cases of difficult births (*Rust.* 7.3.16); and to show great care for the newborn young (*Rust.* 7.3.16–19; cf. Ryder 1983: 685–87). Unfortunately, the agronomists only occasionally allude to the more sophisticated methods used by breeders to consciously manipulate and improve their livestock. They allude to crossbreeding with new breeds and even wild species (Columella, *Rust.* 6.37.3ff; 7.2.4–5) and show an awareness of recessive traits that had to be guarded against (Columella, *Rust.* 7.3.1–2; Vergil, *G.* 3.355; cf. Ryder 1983: 143, 164), but the skill of Greek and Roman breeders must be inferred primarily from their results. They were very successful, for example, in breeding sheep with a wide range of fleece types. These included several distinct breeds with fine wool, comparable to some of the finest modern merino wool (Ryder and Hedges 1973; Ryder 1983: 154–55); as well as true medium wool (long wool) and short wool, both of which had long been credited to medieval breeders (Ryder 1983: 177–80).

An important stimulus to classical animal breeding came from its vigorous commercial development (Rinkewitz 1984: 21–23). There is circumstantial evidence of a significant market not only in breeding stock, but also presumably in stud services, as pioneered in eighteenth-century England by Bakewell (Pawson 1957: 70), whose breeding bulls (worth only about £8 as beef) could command stud fees of £152 for a four-month season. Certainly, the extremely high prices obtained by certain Roman breeding animals imply a hierarchy of breeders, some public knowledge of pedigrees and performance, and the potential to recoup one's investment through fees as well as sales of one's own livestock. To cite just one example, a pair of fine-quality pedigree pigeons, presumably a monogamous pair proven to be compatible and to perform well as breeders (Naether 1964: 155–56), could command 1,000 HS or even 1,600 HS (Varro, *Rust.* 3.7.10; cf. Columella, *Rust.* 8.8.9–10). The vigorous trade and broad contacts of the Greeks and Romans were also instrumental in spreading new breeds of livestock and innovative methods throughout the Mediterranean and, with the Roman conquest, western Europe (Columella, *Rust.* 6.1.1–2, 7.2.3–4, 8.2.4–8; Benecke 1994a: 304–5; Anderson 1961: 15–39). Fine-wooled sheep breeds from Attica and Asia Minor spawned new fine-wooled breeds in Tarentum, Apulia, Parma, Pollentia, and Mutina (Columella, *Rust.* 7.2.3–4; Magerstedt 1859: 2:

95–98), and large long-horned cattle from Italy were crossed with small short-horned Celtic breeds in Pannonia, Germany, and France (Bökönyi 1984: 21–24; but cf. Kokabi 1988: 475). The larger and more diverse flocks and herds of the Greeks and Romans are reflected in the improved genetic health of livestock, as is indicated, for example, by far fewer teeth abnormalities in Roman-era cattle than in the Celts' herds (Peters 1998: 70).

## Nutrition

Although improved breeding most likely played a significant part in increasing the size of Greco-Roman livestock, any gains would prove transient without continued improved nutrition, as the marked decline in the size of Roman cattle breeds over the course of the Middle Ages shows (Riedel 1994; Forest and Rodet-Belarbi 2000). Improved Greek or Roman cattle typically showed gains of as much as 20 percent in height at the withers over Bronze and Iron Age as well as medieval cattle (Kron 2002; MacKinnon 2004: 85, table 24; Sternberg 2005b), and significant increases in bone thickness, indicative of sharply increased weight (Forest and Rodet-Belarbi 2002). Studies show increases in withers heights of 10 or even 20 percent in some improved sheep breeds (Lepetz 1996: 100; Peters 1998: 94–98; MacKinnon 2004: 104–5), and large sheep appear in Greece from at least the fifth century B.C. (Leguilloux 1999). Although the remains of horses are much less common (Peters 1998: 148–49, 164–65), and likely exclude the "noble" breed of race-horses (Columella, *Rust.* 6.27.1–2), they too show a consistent increase in withers heights, one that was already well advanced in classical Greece (Peters 1998: 149–52; de Grossi Mazzorin et al. 1998; Chiliardi 2000). The increases in withers heights of improved Greek or Roman pigs are often more modest (Peters 1998: 124–25; MacKinnon 2004: 148, table 44), but there is a more marked increase in bone thickness, indicative of greater weight (Peters 1998: 126; cf. 125, tables 24–25). We also see the appearance of a short-snouted, white, smooth, quick-fattening breed (Peters 1998: 124, 126; MacKinnon 2001, 2004: 150) similar to the Chinese breeds introduced by eighteenth-century European pig breeders (Zeuner 1963: 268–69) alongside the more bristly and feral, slow-fattening pig phenotype (Peters 1998: 110). The Romans, presumably adapting the methods of the renowned Greek breeders (Columella, *Rust.* 8.2.4), raised chickens in significant numbers (Lauwerier 1983; Benecke 1994b: 114–16; Lauwerier 1993) and to a high standard (Peters 1998: 197–213). Archaeozoological studies demonstrate good health (Brothwell 1997) and a dramatic improvement in size, with Roman hens clustering in the middle range of modern breeds at about 2 kg, significantly heavier than the hens of 1 to 1.5 kg occasionally found on Celtic sites (Bökönyi 1984: 93–94; Brothwell 1997; Peters 1998: 222–26).

Improved nutrition is not only critical in optimizing the growth and health of livestock but also in maintaining a high level of reproduction (Lemming 1969), and evidence from both Greek and Roman sources, as well as from animal bones, suggests that ancient domestic animals were extremely fecund and thus must have been well fed. Aristotle claims that Greek domestic sheep often bore twins and sometimes had as many as three or four lambs (*Hist. an.* 593b 19–20). This is a very high reproductive rate (Ryder 1983: 145), significantly superior to most medieval and many early modern sheep, of which only the best fed, improved breeds regularly bore twins, and many failed to lamb altogether (Ryder 1983: 448, 496). Greco-Roman pigs were equally prolific (Aristotle, *Hist. an.* 573a 30; Columella, *Rust.* 7.9.13; Peters 1998: 114), and Columella makes it clear that Roman intensive pig farmers induced their sows to farrow twice a year (Columella, *Rust.* 7.9.4; MacKinnon 2004: 150–51), as has been confirmed archaeozoologically (Ervynck and Dobney 2002). Roman villas specializing in pig production will therefore have produced a great deal of pork. Bökönyi estimates the yield on one of the less productive sites at over 330 percent of the breeding stock, even on the conservative assumption of just one farrowing (Bökönyi 1988: 174). Like modern livestock farmers, the ancient agronomists were very conscious of the value of high-protein feed for breeding and nursing animals (Columella, *Rust.* 8.5.1–2; cf. Farrington 1913: 56). While they did not have access to some of the industrial processed feeds or the additives and antibiotics used today, such artificial feeds can cause serious behavioral and health complications from lack of roughage (Fox 1984: 161–63; Houpt 2005: 98–100), and antibiotics are generally unnecessary if management methods are sound (Fox 1984: 76–77).

The Greeks and Romans improved animal nutrition partly through new fodder sources and improved fodder management, but mostly through greater integration of livestock into arable farming. The most intensive system of animal husbandry, and the dominant method of mixed farming today, is convertible husbandry—ley farming—in which part of the land is seeded with artificial grass, generally for several years, and used as pasture or meadow, while the rest is cropped continuously with a rotation of cereals and leguminous fodder crops. Agrarian historians have plausibly identified this system as the single most important factor in the agricultural revolution in modern western Europe (Kerridge 1967). Regarding the ancient world, several historians, most notably Hodkinson (Hodkinson 1988), have acknowledged the importance of mixed livestock farming and crop rotations in Greek and Roman animal husbandry, while denying that the ancients used convertible husbandry (Hodkinson 1988: 50–51; Pleket 1993: 324 n. 8, citing Sallares 1991). A careful reading of the Roman agronomists, however, seems to prove that they fully understood and applied the principles (Kron 2000; cf. Carandini 1984).

Convertible husbandry offers two key advantages. The incorporation of legumes in the continuous crop rotation ensures a large quantity of highly nutritious fodder for livestock, supplementing the pasture during winter dormancy or summer drought, and the artificial leys provide much better grazing or hay production than permanent pasture. One can therefore feed more livestock better, while producing more manure and achieving higher yields for cereals, as well as (often) a surplus of quality fodder (Kron 2004b: 312). The classical Greeks had already identified many of the best leguminous fodder crops for arable cultivation (Hodkinson 1988: 44–45). With Varro's and Columella's careful attention to Hellenistic (and

Carthaginian) agronomy, the inventory of Roman fodder crops expanded to include most of the species native to western Europe that were used during the past century (White 1970: 213–19; Kron 2004b: 276–77). Planting artificial leys demands awareness of the best forage plants, and the Roman literary sources (Kron 2004b: 276–81) and studies of the remains of carbonized hay (Kron 2004b: 281–307) suggest that an impressive array of excellent forage legumes were exploited by Greek and Roman farmers and graziers. Some of the most notable included alfalfa (*Medicago sativa*)—considered the best forage by ancient and contemporary experts alike— first imported into Greece from Persia in the fifth century B.C. (Georgoudi 1990: 171; Kron 2004b: 278–79), tree medick (*Medicago arborea*), a highly nutritious shrub ideally suited for sheep and milk production, publicized by the fourth-century B.C. Athenian agronomist Amphilochus (Pliny, *HN* 13.130; Hodkinson 1988: 45; Kron 2004b: 279–80), subterranean clover, one of the best drought-resistant forage legumes for seeding in pasture (Kron 2004b: 297–98), and a significant number of the best clover and medic species (Kron 2004b: 298–300), as well as such proven fodder species as vetch, yellow serradella, vetchling, and lupines.

There was clearly a strong preference on the part of the agronomists in favor of labor-intensive mixed farming, but mountainous terrain, *macchia*, and marginal rangelands covered a great deal of Italy and Greece, and many livestock were certainly pastured extensively. While there is little scholarly consensus, it is likely that sedentary and transhumant pastoralism, often integrated with arable agriculture (Rosada 2000: 107–11), played a significant role in Greco-Roman animal husbandry (Pasquinucci 2004), albeit a much more modest one than in the medieval Mezzogiorno (Brun 1996; Chandezon 2003: 391–97; Kron 2004a). The technical expertise that the Greeks and Romans developed from mixed farming also helped to increase the productivity of permanent pasture and rangelands. With effective management, ranching can be ecologically sound and highly productive (Heady and Childs 1994).

The Roman agronomists give excellent advice for the management of rangelands, very much in accord with modern research (Kron 2004b: 311–17). They recommend the most effective technique for entirely renewing and improving worn out rangeland: to plow it up, carry out a brief arable rotation, and then reseed the land with leguminous forage plants (Kron 2004b: 315; cf. Pawson 1957: 79–80). Such methods have proven highly effective in modern studies, increasing forage yield from two to five times, and we have evidence that *saltus* were indeed plowed for the sake of improving the pasture or cultivated periodically (Lirb 1993: 272 n. 10; Festus p. 392, 33 Lindsay). The most effective, albeit expensive, way of boosting forage production is to irrigate meadows (Heath et al. 1973: 627–93; Columella, *Rust.* 2.17.1; Pliny, *HN* 18.258–63). Although such water meadows typically were created on arable farms as a source of extra hay, the Romans made very effective use of aqueducts for irrigation (White 1970: 146–72), and some very large tracts were irrigated, as has been confirmed archaeologically (Quilici-Gigli 1989). Other valuable Roman recommendations for improving the productivity of pasture (Kron 2004b: 311–17) included protecting the range from overgrazing and physical damage through controlled grazing (cf. Heady and Childs 1994: 248–50); seeding it with forage legumes; fertilizing it, particularly with potash or lime; and periodic burning (Corbier 1999; cf. Heady and Childs 1994: 333–35).

## Housing

The Roman agronomists show considerable care in providing appropriate housing for their livestock, reflecting once again their capital- and labor-intensive approach to animal husbandry. Modern research suggests that the provision of shelter generally improves the health of livestock and their reproductive and growth performance (Fox 1984: 58–70, 86–87, 91–92, 106, 108), provided they are not confined in overcrowded conditions, where lack of exercise and stress cause many behavioral and health problems (Fox 1984: 75–77, 151–61). Few excavators have shown interest in investigating purely utilitarian farm buildings, but we can glean enough information from the agronomists and archaeological evidence to get some idea of the design of many shelters (Rinkewitz 1984: 27–29; Carandini 1984: 160–62; Flach 1990: 227–45). The discovery and exemplary study (Badan et al. 1996) of approximately 130 Roman sheepfolds on the famous sheep pastures of the Crau (Pliny, *HN* 21.57; Congès 1997; Leveau and Segard 2003; Leveau 2004) in southern France show the large investments made by Roman sheep farmers or perhaps landowners (Corbier 1999) eager to maximize the productivity of even transhumant sheep raising. Extremely large—one example at Négreiron-Négrès covers 288 square meters, and most are capable of holding from 700 to 900 sheep—they are remarkably similar in their design and construction to the sheepfolds first built on the Crau in the twentieth century (figure 8.2; Badan et al. 1996: 290–95, figs. 21–23).

While housing for sheep and cattle is generally relatively simple (Fox 1984: 88; Ryder 1983: 682–85), the success of intensive pig and chicken farming depends more on the design of their sties and coops. The recommendations of the Roman authorities for pigsties (Columella, *Rust.* 7.9.9–10; Varro, *Rust.* 2.4.13–15), several examples of which have been excavated (Morris 1979: 52; Carandini 1984: 182–84), represent a good illustration of the sophistication of their methods. The size of the stalls; the inclusion of hay or litter; the clever design to keep nursing piglets segregated while permitting the sows to leave; the attention to cleanliness; the provision of clean food and water and the care taken to prevent sows from crushing their young—all correspond closely to modern recommendations for making pig farming more productive and minimizing the stress and high mortality common in many modern confinement systems (Fox 1984: 58–60, 65–70, 75).

## Health and Veterinary Care

We can see further evidence of the intensive nature of Greco-Roman animal husbandry in the high level of veterinary care available. Studies of animal bones not only suggest good nutrition, as we have seen, but also show low levels of disease and generally good health (Peters 1998: 69–71, 86–87, 133–34; MacKinnon 2004:

Figure 8.2. Roman sheepfold at Négeirion-Négrès, La Crau plain, Provence, reconstruction. Dimensions: 46.3 x 9.55 m. (From Badan et al. 1996: 294, fig. 25.)

96–97, 148–49, 159) and even reveal direct evidence of veterinary intervention (Udrescu and Van Neer 2005). The agronomists paid careful attention to the behavioral and hygienic needs of livestock (Columella, *Rust.* 6.23.1–3; 7.3.8, 9.14; Varro, *Rust.* 2.2.7; cf. Senet 1953: 26, 80–81). They also gave detailed, generally sound, prophylactic and veterinary advice (Peters 1998: 36–38, 85–89, 365–68), which was widely disseminated for the use of farmers and their slaves, shepherds, or tenants (Varro, *Rust.* 2.2.20, 5.18; Georgoudi 1990: 80–81; Adams 1995: 72–79). Good nutrition and management as well as simple prophylactic measures helped to prevent disease. For example, as in the recent past (Ryder 1983: 708, 781), farmers controlled scab by dipping sheep using medicinal ingredients of proven effectiveness against insects and parasites (Peters 1998: 87–88; Frizell 2004; cf. Ryder 1983: 708–9). Varro also gave sound advice to protect sheep from possible sunstroke and to avoid pasturing them on dewy grass, a possible cause of foot rot (Varro, *Rust.* 2.2.7; cf. MacKinnon 2004: 114) and a breeding ground of the larvae of *Haemonchus contortus* or the barber pole worm, a dangerous parasite (Peters 1998: 79, 85–86).

Farmers in classical and Hellenistic Greece and the late Republic could also call on skilled professional veterinarians (Adams 1995: 51–65, 72–102), provided, of course, such treatment was cost-effective. Several extant treatises on veterinary medicine (see Moulé 1891: 9–50; Georgoudi 1990: 60–63; Peters 1998: 135) give a good idea of their expertise, although they arguably underrepresent the treatment of the other domestic animals in favor of horses (Senet 1953: 78–79; cf. Columella, *Rust.* 7.3.5–6). The study of anatomy was very sophisticated (Adams 1995: 362–63), based on dissection and even the performance of post-mortem analysis (Adams 1995: 48 n. 155). The Greek veterinary writers formulated a large technical vocabulary that covered both anatomical features and many of the diseases identified by modern veterinarians (Adams 1995: 239–331), and the symptoms of these diseases were accurately described (Leclainche 1936: 9–96; Adams 1995: 49–50).

The most impressive achievements of the practitioners of classical veterinary medicine lay in their surgical expertise. The ancient manuals describe a remarkable number of the most common surgical procedures performed by twentieth-century veterinary surgeons, including virtually all of the standard obstetrical operations and even eye surgery (Moulé 1891: 147–66; Senet 1953: 43, 83–86; Bourdy 1995; Peters 1998: 209–10). Veterinarians used many different specialized surgical instruments, most remarkably similar to modern instruments, and even a special machine designed to restrain animals during surgery (Moulé 1891: 147–50; Senet 1953: 83–84, 86). Medicines prescribed for veterinary use were largely herbal or mineral (Moulé 1891: 174–77), and frequently demonstrate an accurate understanding of a number of tannins and anti-inflammatory, antipyretic, diuretic, or analgesic plants (Bourdy 1995: 207–8; Peters 1998: 209–10). Although Greco-Roman veterinarians are often criticized for their ignorance of effective treatments of bacterial and viral infections (Senet 1953: 25–26), the scientific knowledge necessary to achieve workable cures was unknown to modern veterinary science prior to the revolutionary discoveries of Koch and Pasteur in the late 1870s and 1880s (Pattison 1984: 77–78, 87–89). The ancient veterinarians recommended the quarantine or slaughter of infected livestock (Columella, *Rust.* 6.5.1), which was the most rational approach in the circumstances. Modern veterinarians ultimately gave the same advice, despite popular resistance (Pattison 1984: 60–61).

# Hunting, Fowling, and Game Farming

Ancient hunting has generated many studies, including a number of substantial monographs (Aymard 1951; Hull 1964; Anderson 1985), but we will focus here primarily on its economic function as a source of meat and secondary products. In Europe during the Middle Ages and the ancien régime, only the nobility and large landowners enjoyed hunting rights, and poachers were subject to draconian punishments including castration, blinding, mutilation, and death (Trench 1967: 26;

114–21, 128–29; E. P. Thompson 1975)—although these did not prevent poaching or the virtual extinction of the red deer in England (Trench 1967: 130; Grant 1988: 139). Greco-Roman hunting, on the other hand, was not restricted to a social elite. Roman law granted ownership of game and wild birds to the hunters who captured them, regardless of their social status or the ownership of the land on which they hunted (*Dig.* 41.1.pr–4), although Roman law did acknowledge the ownership of wild animals raised on game farms (*Dig.* 41.1.3.2, 1.5–6). Most Greek and Roman hunters therefore practiced the "petit bourgeois" method of hunting on foot (Aymard 1951: 373), employing the relatively inexpensive and efficient methods employed by professional hunters who captured game for sale (Arrian, *Cyn.* 3.1; Rinkewitz 1984: 103–4; Bortuzzo 1990: 100).

This traditional Greco-Roman hunt employed nets (Aymard 1951: 207–18; Hull 1964: 10–18), foot snares (Hull 1964: 18–19), and the *formido* or scare (Aymard 1951: 218–28; Hull 1964: 19), along with highly trained foxhounds and tracking dogs (table 8.2) to trap the quarry. Hunters on foot would then dispatch the game, using spears (Hull 1964: 5–6), javelins (Hull 1964: 6), longbows (Hull 1964: 7–8), crossbows (Baatz 1991), swords (Hull 1964: 6; Aymard 1951: 316–17), or the specialized boar spears (Aymard 1951: 5–6) in the highly hazardous but prestigious boar hunt (Aymard 1951: 310–16, 323–30; Hull 1964: 103–5). As illustrated in the classic account in Xenophon's *Cynegetica*, classical Greek hunting techniques were already very highly refined, based on the selection and training of appropriate hunting dog breeds (Aymard 1951: 246–54, 369–71; Hull 1964: 39–58) and close scientific observation of the behavior of the game (Aymard 1951: 366; Hull 1964: 60–75).

The most important Greco-Roman innovation increasing the supply of game was surely game farming, which reached a level of sophistication not matched until the late twentieth century. Carthaginian and Hellenistic agronomists were already adept at raising wild fowl and game (Varro, *Rust.* 3.2.13; Peters 1998: 197), coining the term *theriotropheion* to describe these farms (Hudson 1989: 22–23), and Columeau's analysis of the age and sex distribution of bones from Kassope (2000: 155) reveals that the Greeks farmed red deer in the classical and Hellenistic periods. Other sites identified as supplying game to urban markets include the Roman villa at Neftebach in Switzerland (Olive and Deschler-Erb 1999). Here again, many deer were slaughtered as subadults, which is consistent with game farming (Columella, *Rust.* 9.1.7; cf. Fletcher 1989: 331) rather than hunting.

By the first century B.C., game farming had become a very profitable business in Italy (Rinkewitz 1984, 21–23 and passim; Bortuzzo 1990). Such prominent Roman aristocrats as L. Licinius Lucullus (Rinkewitz 1984: 81–82, no. 17) and Q. Hortensius (Rinkewitz 1984: 80, no. 14) participated enthusiastically, and the most up-to-date techniques were widely disseminated in agronomic treatises (Varro, *Rust.* 3.2.13 and passim; Columella, *Rust.* 9.1.1–9). There was a healthy market among Romans eager to incorporate new game species into their diet (table 8.3). Large game were raised in a forest habitat, enclosed with walls of rough stone and mortar or mud brick, or wooden post fences, which represented one of the greatest expenses (Columella, *Rust.* 9.1.2–5), as in modern game farming (Hudson 1989: 17; Fletcher 1989: 327). The

**Table 8.2. Greco-Roman hunting dog breeds.**

| Hunting Dog Breed | Ancient sources | Modern authorities |
| --- | --- | --- |
| Iberian | Opp., *Cyn.* 1.371; Poll. 5.37; Nemes., *Cyn.* 228 | Hull 1964: 23 |
| Indian | Arist., *Hist. an.* 8.23; Xen., *Cyn.* 9.1; Hdt. 1.192; Diod. Sic. 17.92; Poll. 5.37–38; Ael., *NA.* 4.19; 8.1 | Keller 1909: 109–10; Aymard 1951: 244–45; Toynbee 1973: 103; Peters 1998: 171 |
| Molossian (Epirus) | Arist., *Hist. an.* 9.3; Mart. 12.1; Nemes., *Cyn.* 107ff.; Ael., *NA* 3.2, 10.1; Lucan, *Phars.* 4.402; Lucr. 5.1076; Verg., *G* 3.404–5; Ath. 201 B; Opp., *Cyn.* 1.375; Grat., *Cyn.* 181, 197; Hor., *Epod.* 6.5, *Sat.* 2.6.19; Poll. 5.37, 39 | Keller 1909: 103–7; 111–13; Aymard 1951: 251–54; Hull 1964: 29–30; Toynbee 1973: 103; Peters 1998: 171, Abb. 63 |
| Cretan | Xen., *Cyn.* 10.1; Grat., *Cyn.* 212; Arr., *Cyn.* 2.5, 3.4; Claud., *Cons. Hon. Cons. Stil.* 3.300; Poll. 5.40f.; Philostr., *VA* 8.30.2 | Keller 1909: 117–18; Aymard 1951: 246–51; Hull 1964: 34; Toynbee 1973: 103; Peters 1998: 172 |
| Vertragus (Gaul) | Arr., *Cyn.* 3.6, 5.7f.; Grat., *Cyn.* 203 | Keller 1909: 101–3; Aymard 1951: 265–66; Hull 1964: 24–26; Toynbee 1973: 104; Peters 1998: 172 |
| Sicilian | | Keller 1909: 125–26; Peters 1998: 171 |
| Laconian | Xen., *Cyn.* 3.1, 4.1; 10.1; Varro, *Rust.* 2.5.5; Grat., *Cyn.* 212; Oppian, *Cyn.* 1.372; Arist., *Hist. an.* 6.20, 8.28, 9.1; Ael. 8.2; Verg., *G* 3.403; Pl., *Prm.* 128 B; Soph., *Aj.* 5 | Keller 1909: 120–24; Aymard 1951: 2354–57; Hull 1964: 31–33; Toynbee 1973: 103–4; Peters 1998: 171 |
| Molossian-Epirote sheepdog | Arist., *Hist. an.* 9.3 | Keller 1909: 103 |
| Tuscan | Opp., *Cyn.* 1.396; Nemes., *Cyn.* 231–37 | Aymard 1951: 261–62; Hull 1964: 24 |
| Umbrian | Verg., *Aen.* 12.753; Seneca, *Thy.* 497ff.; Grat., *Cyn.* 171–73; 194 | Keller 1909: 124–25; Aymard 1951: 263–64; Hull 1964: 24; Toynbee 1973: 104; Peters 1998: 172–73 |
| Segusius | Grat., *Cyn.* 171; Catull. 42.9 | Keller 1909: 102–3; Aymard 1951: 267–68; Hull 1964: 24; Peters 1998: 173 |
| Scottish (Britain) | Strabo 4.5.2; Nemes., *Cyn.* 225 | Aymard 1951: 268–70; Toynbee 1973: 104–5; Peters 1998: 173 |
| Agassaeans (Britain) | Strabo 4.5.2; Opp., *Cyn.* 1.468–78; Claud., *Cons. Hons. Cons. Stil* 3.301 | Aymard 1951: 268–70; Hull 1964: 26; Toynbee 1973: 104–5; Peters 1998: 173 and Abb. 57c |
| Tibetan | Grat., *Cyn.* 159 | Keller 1909: 108–9; Hull 1964: 27 |
| Carian | Ael., *NA* 7.38, *VH* 14.46; Arr., *Cyn.* 3.1ff.; Dio Chrys. 1.371, 373, 396; Poll. 5.37, 47 | Hull 1964: 28; Peters 1998: 171 |

natural sources of food in the forest could generally cover most of the nutritional needs of the game, but supplemental feeding, often by hand, was used in winter, when mast was scarce, as well as when the animals were breeding or rearing young (Columella, *Rust.* 9.1.6–8), as in modern practice (Fletcher 1989: 326–27, 329). The performance of modern game farming shows the dramatic improvements in productivity that Greco-Roman game farming could have achieved. For example, 100 wild Scottish red deer hinds will generally produce 40 to 46 calves, only 30 of which will live to a year, but with good management a similar number of farmed deer can generally raise up to 90 calves to weaning. Likewise, shelter and adequate feeding can increase the live weight of wild red deer stags from 120 kg to more than 185 kg (Fletcher 1989: 328–29).

Like poultry and pork, game was a prestigious food and appears to have been most popular among the well off and those who adopted Roman cultural food habits (Lehman and Breuer 1997: 490–92; Olive and Deschler-Erb 1999), but its consumption was by no means restricted to an elite. Ordinary Greeks and Romans were free to hunt, of course, but they could also take advantage of the ample supply of farmed game meat sold in many local markets, where it was not much more expensive than many ordinary domestic animals. Note, for example, that red deer and roe deer sold for 12 denarii per Roman pound according to Diocletian's price edict (4.44–5), only 50 percent more than beef or mutton and equal to pork. Moreover, while game did not often exceed 5 to 10 percent of the meat consumed on Italian sites, game meat was common and rarely fell below about 1 to 3 percent of total meat consumption on sites where it was found (McKinnon 2004: 228–29, App. 13). Game was also widely consumed in the transalpine Roman provinces (Lepetz 1996: 225–26, 228; Peters 1998: 241, 246–48), particularly on Roman military sites, as one would expect (Aymard 1951: 469–81; Davies 1971; King 1984; Epplett 2001), and in luxury villas, *vici*, and civil settlements. With the exception of western European countries such as France and Italy (Ministry of Agriculture and Forestry, New Zealand 1994; cf. Binder 1971), game consumption today is generally much lower, constituting only about 0.5 percent of total meat consumption worldwide in 1978, falling to barely half as much in 1984 (Hudson 1989: 46).

The art of fowling was very highly developed by the Greeks and Romans, and the fattening of birds captured in the wild—or raised from eggs gathered from the nests of wild birds (Lindner 1973: 96)—was a significant feature of Roman *pastio villatica*. Our literary sources often allude to the practice and methods of fowling (Lindner 1973: 15–28), and a number of mosaics, frescoes, sculptures, lamps, and gems illustrate it in detail (Lindner 1973: 29–77, figs. 1, 15). Nets (Capponi 1959: 729; Lindner 1973: 92–93; Cox 1686: 104–6) and snares, particularly for birds such as the plover or woodcock (Cox 1686: 111–13), were effective tools, widely used by professional fowlers. But most ancient literary and artistic depictions emphasize the capture of birds using specially made reeds topped by twigs coated with birdlime, a viscous substance manufactured from myrtle berries and oil (Pliny, *HN* 9.248; Lindner 1973: 95). Capponi gives a particularly lucid analysis of the method, based

**Table 8.3. Principal Greco-Roman game species with references to ancient and modern consumption (ranked by their prominence in archaeozoological excavations).**

| Common name | Scientific name | Ancient References | References | Modern References |
|---|---|---|---|---|
| Red deer | *Cervus elaphus* | Apicius 8.2.1, 3–8; Varro, *Rust.* 3.13.3; Columella, *Rust.* 9.1.1; Celsus, *Med.* 2.18.2; Galen, *Vict. Att.* 4.664; Plin., *HN* 8.115, 119; 10.182; Verg., *G.* 1.307; Mart. 1.49, 13.94; Justin., *Dig.* 9.2.28.pr; 41.1.5.5; SHA, *Heliogab.* 8.3 | Keller 1909: 277–79; Aymard 1951: 16–17, 331–69; Toynbee 1973: 143–45; André 1981: 120; Hull 1964: 76–81; King 2002: 417–19 | Montagné 1961: 344; Bonnet and Klein 1991; Hansen-Catta 2002: 66–72 |
| Roe deer | *Capreolus capreolus* | Apicius 8.3.1–3; Columella, *Rust.* 9.1.1; Varro, *Rust.* 3.3.3; 13.3; Celsus, *Med.* 2.18.2; Juv. 11.142; Auson. 18; Verg., *G.* 2.374 | Keller 1909: 277–79; Aymard 1951: 17–18; 331–50; André 1981: 120; Hull 1964: 82–83; Toynbee 1973: 143–45; King 2002: 416–17 | Montagné 1961: 812–14; Hansen-Catta 2002: 72–81 |
| Hare | *Lepus europaeus* | Verg., *G.* 1.308; Mart. 1.49.25; 3.27; 13.92; Varro, *Rust.* 3.3.2; 3.12.1–6; Columella, *Rust.* 9.1.8; Mart. 13.92; Hor., *Sat.* 2.4.44, 8.89; *Epod.* 2.35; Apicius 8.8.1–3; Juv. 11.139; Petr., *Satyr.* 56.9; Ar., *Ach.* 1110; *Eq.* 1192–93; 1199; *Vesp.* 709; *Pax* 1150, 1196; *Ec.* 843; Telecl., fr. 34; Antiph., fr. 131; Alex., fr. 168 | Keller 1909: 210–17; Aymard 1951: 364–76; Hull 1964: 59–67; Toynbee 1973: 200–202; André 1981: 118–19; Benecke 1994b: 356–62; Olson and Sens 2000, 207–8; King 2002: 430–32 | Montagné 1961: 485–88; Hansen-Catta 2002: 178–83 |
| Wild boar | *Sus scrofa scrofa* | Apicius 1.8.1–9; Columella, *Rust.* 9.1.1; Hor., *Sat.* 2.2.89; Pliny, *HN* 8.210; 10.182; Juv. 1.140–41; Mart. 14.221.2; Plin., *Ep.* 1.6.1; Mart. 1.43, 49, 3.77, 7.27.1, 10.45.3–4; Hor., *Sat.* 2.4.40, 42, 2.8.6; *Carm.* 1.1.28; Stat., *Silv.* 4.6.1; Petron., *Sat.* 40.3 | Keller 1909: 389–93; Aymard 1951: 13–17; 299–316; Toynbee 1973: 131–36; André 1981: 118–19; King 2002: 443–45 | Montagné 1961: 1009–10; Hansen-Catta 2002: 60–65 |

*(continued)*

**Table 8.3. (continued)**

| Common name | Scientific name | Ancient References | References | Modern References |
|---|---|---|---|---|
| Red fox | *Vulpes vulpes* | Plut., *Quaest. Nat.* 22; Tert. *Apol.* 9.11; Petron., *Sat.* 66.5; Justin., *Dig.* 9.2.28.pr | Keller 1909: 88; Hull 1964: 96–97; Toynbee 1973: 102; King 2002: 446 | Montagné 1961: 428 |
| Brown bear | *Ursus arctos* | Plin., *HN* 8.38; Sen., *Phaed.* 64 | Keller 1909: 175–81; Aymard 1951: 12–13; Hull 1964: 94–95; Toynbee 1973: 93–100; King 2002: 445–46 | Montagné 1961: 115 |
| Aurochs | *Bos primigenius* | Caes., *B Gal* 6.27.1; Plin. 8.39 | Keller 1909: 342–43; Hull 1964: 85–86, 89; Toynbee 1973: 148–49 | Montagné 1961: 73 |
| Elk | *Alces alces* | Catull. 37. 18; Plin., *HN* 8.217; 226; Strabo 3.2.6, 5.2; Ael., *NA* 13.15; Polyb. 12.3; Varro, *Rust.* 3.12.6–7; Apicius 2.2.6; Mart. 13.60 | Keller 1909: 281–83; Zeuner 1963: 425–29; Toynbee 1973: 145; King 2002: 408 | Montagné 1961: 399; Ferlin 1989: 3 no. 6 |
| Rabbit | *Oryctolagus cuniculus* | | Keller 1909: 217–18; Zeuner 1963: 409–15; Hull 1964: 59–67; Toynbee 1973: 202–3; King 2002: 436–37 | Montagné 1961: 799–800; Hansen-Catta 2002: 172–77 |
| Ibex | *Capra ibex* | Columella, *Rust.* 7.12.8, 9.1.1; Mart. 1.49, 3.58, 4.74, 13.94; Juv. 11.121; Plin., *HN* 8.214; Verg., *G* 1.308, 3.410 | Keller 1909: 299–301; Aymard 1951: 19–20; Toynbee 1973: 147 | Montagné 1961: 531; Hansen-Catta 2002: 92–95 |
| Fallow deer | *Dama dama* | Apicius 9.1.1; Mart. 3.58; Amm. Marc. 28.4.13; Varro, *Rust.* 3.15; Plin. *HN* 8.209, 211, 224, 16.18; Petron., *Sat.* 31.10 | Keller 1909: 277–79; Aymard 1951: 18–19; André 1981: 120; Zeuner 1963: 429–33; Hull 1964: 81–82; Toynbee 1973: 143–45; King 2002: 417 | Montagné 1961: 408; Ferlin 1989: 3 no. 5; Boisaubert and Boutin 1988: 202–5 |
| Dormouse | *Myoxus glis* | | Keller 1909: 191–93; Zeuner 1963: 415–16; Hull 1964: 92; Toynbee 1973: 204; André 1981, 119–20; Colonnelli et al. 2000; King 2002: 428–29 | Montagné 1961: 350 |

| Common name | Scientific name | Ancient sources | Modern references | |
|---|---|---|---|---|
| European Bison | *Bison bonasus* | Plin., *HN* 8.38; Sen., *Phaed.* 64 | Keller 1909: 341–42; Toynbee 1973: 148 | Montagné 1961: 148 |
| Wild goat, chamois | *Capra aegagrus, Rupicapra rupicapra* | Varro, *Rust.* 2.3.3; 2.1.5; Columella, *Rust.* 9.pr.1; Celsus, *Med.* 2.18.2 | Keller 1909: 296–99; Aymard 1951: 19–20; Hull 1964: 84–85; Toynbee 1973: 147 | Hansen-Catta 2002: 82–86 |
| Gazelle | *Gazella dama Gazella dorcas* | Juv. 11.138; Hdt. 4.192; Plin., *HN* 8.214; Ael., *NA* 7.19 | Keller 1909: 286–88; André 1981: 121; Zeuner 1963: 434; Hull 1964: 83; Toynbee 1973: 147; Gilbert 2002, 23–24; King 2002: 437 | Montagné 1961: 459 |
| Arabian Oryx | *Oryx leucoryx* | Columella, *Rust.* 9.1.1, 1.7; Juv. 11.140 | Keller 1909: 292–93; André 1981: 120–21; Hull 1964: 83–84; Toynbee 1973: 146; Gilbert 2002: 21–23; King 2002: 437 | Montagné 1961: 684 |
| Oryx dammah | *Oryx beisa beisa* | | Keller 1909: 191–92; Hull 1964: 83–84 | |
| Mouflon | *Ovis orientalis* | Varro, *Rust.* 2.1.5; Apicius 8.4.1, 3; Polyb. 12.3; Plin., *HN* 8.199, 28.151; 30.146; Strabo, 5.2.7 | Youatt 1837: 133–34; Keller 1909: 317–18; Aymard 1951: 19–20; André 1981: 121; Hull 1964: 84–85; Toynbee 1973: 163 | Montagné 1961: 629; Hansen-Catta 2002: 88–91 |
| Wild ass | *Equus africanus* | Verg., *G* 3.410; Celsus, *Med.* 2.18.2; Plin., *HN* 8.69; Xen., *An.* 1.5.1–3 | Ridgeway 1905: 46–54; Keller 1909: 271–74; Toynbee 1973: 192–93; André 1967: 121; King 2002: 420–21 | Ferlin 1989: 7 |

on the ancient sources and his own experience of fowling using birdlime in twentieth-century Italy (Capponi 1959).

Although fowling was a popular sport, most birds were likely captured by professional fowlers for sale in markets (Aristophanes, *Aves* 526–38; Plato, *Leg.* 824a; Pollard 1977; Longo 1989: 62–72). The impressive scale of Greco-Roman fowling and the astonishing range of birds offered for sale in Greek or Roman markets is illustrated in many mosaics (Tammisto 1997; Watson 2002), wall paintings (De Caro and Boriello 2001; Watson 2002), and references in the literary sources (Pollard 1977; Watson 2002), and can be confirmed through archaeozoological research. For Italy and the northern provinces of the Roman Empire we can document the capture and exploitation of dozens of bird species. More than 70 of these species are attested by ancient or modern sources as being game birds of some interest for human consumption (table 8.4; Parker 1988).

The farming and fattening of game birds greatly enhanced the stock available in Greek and Roman markets and became a very profitable business (Columella, *Rust.* 8.1.2; Varro, *Rust.* 3.2.13–4; Rinkewitz 1984: 21–23, 111–30). Varro himself claimed a revenue of 60,000 HS per year, more than a typical 200-*iugera* farm, from his aviary stocked with 5,000 thrushes (Varro, *Rust.* 3.2.15), and such profits were by no means atypical (Varro, *Rust.* 3.6.1, 6.6; Pliny, *HN* 10.45). Varro (*Rust.* 3.7.11) claimed that some dove breeders had invested as much as 100,000 HS in equipment and physical plant alone, yet still managed to achieve good returns on their investment. Archaeologists have studied towers furnished with small niches matching ancient descriptions of dovecotes (Varro, *Rust.* 3.7.1–4, Plato, *Tht.* 197c–d) in Etruria (Carandini 1984: 125; Chamoux and Hillier 1996: 56 n. 5), at Apollonia in Libya (Chamoux and Hillier 1996), and at Thysdrus in Tunisia (Leveau et al. 1993: 103), as well as several locations in Israel and Egypt (Zissu 1995). Many are extremely large, more than 9 m in diameter and several stories tall, and capable of holding more than a thousand niches for pairs of breeding pigeons (figure 8.3). Columella's recommendations for habitats for the breeding of wild ducks are no less elaborate. The pond is paved in part with pebbles or concrete to keep some clear water for the ducks to swim, furnished with appropriate aquatic vegetation and plastered breeding enclosures, and surrounded with 20 feet of grassy banks. It is even fitted with special channels for flushing fresh water and the ducks' favorite foods including crayfish, pickled river fish, and small aquatic animals (Columella, *Rust.* 8.15.1–7; cf. Varro, *Rust.* 3.11.1–4; Rinkewitz 1984: 35–37). Modern experts offer remarkably similar, if less elaborate, recommendations (Coles 1971: 237–42, 263–64, 268–92).

The Roman agronomists hand down detailed instructions for raising a number of wild species (Rinkewitz 1984: 29–73): doves, geese, mallard ducks, teal, pochards and coots, turtle-doves, song thrushes, peafowl, pheasants, quail, blackbirds, and buntings. The Greeks and Romans also fattened other species in captivity for later sale: partridges (Varro, *Rust.* 3.11.4), cranes (Varro, *Rust.* 3.2.14), and ortolans (Varro, *Rust.* 3.5.2) certainly, and presumably many others. The technical quality of the agronomists' advice is impressive. The enclosures and the breeding and feeding regimen recommended for peafowl (Columella, *Rust.* 8.11.3–17; Varro, *Rust.* 3.6.3–5)

**Table 8.4.** Evidence for the consumption of Greco-Roman gamebird species (ranked according to number of archaeological sites with remains).

| Common Name | Scientific Name | References—Ancient Sources | References—Modern Scholarship | References—Modern Use |
|---|---|---|---|---|
| Greylag goose | *Anser anser* | Col., *Rust.* 8.13–4; Pall. 1.30; Varro, *Rust.* 3.10.6; *Gp.* 14.22; Apic. 6.8; Juv. 5.114; Plin., *HN* 10.56; foie gras: Ath. 384b; *Gp.* 14.13; 22; Plin., *HN* 10.52; Hor., *Sat.* 2.8.88; Juv. 5.114; Mart. 13.58; Apic. 6.5; 8.87; Pers. 6.71; Archestr. fr. 58; Ar., *Pax* 1004; Anaxandr. fr. 42.64; Antiph. fr. 295; Cratin. fr. 49 | Keller 1913: 220–26; Thompson 1936: 325–30; André 1981: 132–33; Zeuner 1963: 466–70; Toynbee 1973: 261–64; Salza Prina Ricotti 1987: 95–96; Flach 1990: 322–23; Benecke 1994b: 373–79; Olson & Sens 2000: 213–14; Watson 2002: 365–66; Benecke et al. 2003: 79 | Montagné 1961: 467–70; Escoffier 1984: 478–79; Martin 1993: 24–29; Aksakov 1998: 99–105 |
| Mallard duck | *Anas platyrhynchos* | Hdt. 2.77; Col., *Rust.* 8.15; *Gp.* 14.23; Apic. 6.f2.1–6; Petr., *Satyr.* 93; Mart. 13.52; Varro, *Rust.* 3.11; Auson., *Epist.* 3.12 | Keller 1913: 226–35; Thompson 1936: 205–6; André 1981: 133; Zeuner 1963: 470–71; Toynbee 1973: 264–73; Salza Prina Ricotti 1987: 95; Benecke 1994b: 379–83; Watson 2002: 364–65 | Montagné 1961: 363–64; Escoffier 1984: 480–90; Martin 1993: 72–76; Aksakov 1998: 108–19 |
| Woodcock | *Scolopax rusticola* | Mart. 13.76; *Anth. Lat.* 2.884; Nemes., *Cyn.* 2.1–10; Plin., *HN* 10.56, 111 | Keller 1913: 181; Thompson 1936: 261–62; Prummel 1987: 194–95; Salza Prina Ricotti 1987: 98 | Montagné 1961: 1022–27; Escoffier 1984: 530–33; Aksakov 1998: 266–77 |
| European teal | *Anas crecca* | Ar., *Av.* 880, 1300; Col., *Rust.* 8.15.1; Varro, *Rust.* 3.3.3, 3.11.4; Macrob., *Sat.* 3.13.12 | Keller 1913: 233; Thompson 1936: 205–6; André 1981: 126; Toynbee 1973: 264–73; Salza Prina Ricotti 1987: 95 | Montagné 1961: 363–64, 956; Aksakov 1998: 127–29 |
| Jackdaw | *Corvus monedula* | Ath. 65c–e, 393b; *Gp.* 14.24 | Keller 1913: 92, 110; André 1981: 129; Pollard 1977: 105; Bökönyi 1984: 99 | Ferlin 1989: *HN.* 974 |

*(continued)*

**Table 8.4.** (*continued*)

| Common Name | Scientific Name | References—Ancient Sources | References—Modern Scholarship | References—Modern Use |
|---|---|---|---|---|
| Common crane | *Grus grus* | Ath. 131f; Dionys., *Av.* 3.11; Plut., Mor. 997a; Varro, *Rust.* 3.2.14; Hor., *Sat.* 2.8.86–87; *Epod.* 2.35; Verg., *G.* 1.307; Stat., *Silv.* 4.6.9; Gell. 6.16.5; Plin., *HN* 10.60; Apic. 6.2.1–6; Cels. 2.18.2 | Keller 1913: 184–93; Thompson 1936: 74–75; Zeuner 1963: 474; Toynbee 1973: 243–44; Pollard 1977: 105–6; Rinkewitz 1984: 73; Salza Prina Ricotti 1987: 99–100 | Montagné 1984: 316; Aksakov 1998: 157–62 |
| Rock dove | *Columba livia* | Varro, *Rust.* 3.7; Col., *Rust.* 8.11.1–7; Gp. 14.1–6; Mart. 2.37.6, 13.66; Apic. 6.4.1–4; Pall. 1.24; Hor., *Sat.* 2.8.91; Philumen. 2.126 | Keller 1913: 122–31; Thompson 1936: 238–46; André 1981: 124; Zeuner 1963: 460–62; Toynbee 1973: 258–59; Pollard 1977: 104; Salza Prina Ricotti 1987: 96; Flach 1990, 320–22; Benecke 1994b: 383–90; Watson 2002: 372–74; Benecke et al. 2003: 79–80 | Montagné 1961: 733–34; Naether 1964, 153–68; Escoffier 1984: 500–505 |
| Stock dove | *Columba oenas* | | | Montagné 1961: 733–34; Naether 1964, 153–68; Escoffier 1984: 500–505 |
| Carrion crow | *Corvus corone* | Zacharias, *Epist.* 13 | Keller 1913: 92; Thompson 1936: 168–72; André 1981: 128; Watson 2002: 375–76 | Montagné 1961: 329; Coles 1971: 27–36 |
| Wood pigeon | *Columba palumbus* | Apic. 6.4.1–4; Ar, *Ach.* 1105, 1107; Varro, *Rust.* 3.9; Cato, *Agr.* 90.1; Cels. 2.30; Mart. 3.58, 13.67; Petr. *Satyr.* 70.2; Plaut., *Poen.* 676 | Keller 1913: 122–31; Thompson 1936: 300–302; André 1981: 133; Zeuner 1963: 460–62; Toynbee 1973: 258–59; Pollard 1977: 104; Salza Prina Ricotti 1987: 96; Flach 1990, 320–22; Benecke 1994b: 383–90; Watson 2002: 374–75 | Montagné 1961: 733–34; Rocher 1979, 362–65; Escoffier 1984: 500–505; Aksakov 1998: 252–55 |

| Grey partridge | *Perdix perdix* | Ath. 390b; Dionys., *Av.* 3.7; Hor., *Epod.* 2.53–54; Mart. 3.58.15, 13.61, 65, 76; Varro, *Rust.* 3.11.4; *Gp.* 14.19–21; *SHA* 41.7; Apic. 6.3.1–3; Plin., *HN* 10.101–2; Philumen. 1.112; 2.126 | Keller 1913: 156–60; Thompson 1936: 234–38; Toynbee 1973: 255–56; Pollard 1977: 104; Rinkewitz 1984: 55; Salza Prina Ricotti 1987: 98–99 | Montagné 1961: 700–704; Coles 1971: 177–95; Escoffier 1984: 513–17; Aksakov 1998: 181–88 |
| Widgeon | *Anas penelope* | | Keller 1913: 226–35; Thompson 1936: 205–6; Toynbee 1973: 264–73; Salza Prina Ricotti 1987: 95; Watson 2002: 364 | Montagné 1961: 363–64; Martin 1993: 77–81; Aksakov 1998: 123–25 |
| Rook | *Corvus frugilegus* | | Keller 1913: 91; Thompson 1936: 168–69; Bökönyi 1984, 99 | Montagné 1984: 814–15; Coles 1971: 27–36 |
| Starling | *Sturnus vulgaris* | Diocletian, *Price Edict* 4.42; Ath. 65e; Plin., *HN* 28.110; Mart. 9.5; Philumen. 2.126 | Keller 1913: 90–91; Thompson 1936: 334–35; Toynbee 1973: 276; Salza Prina Ricotti 1987: 100; Watson 2002: 395 | Montagné 1961: 933; Aksakov 1998: 290 |
| Golden plover | *Pluvialis apricaria* | Ar., *Av.* 265; Plt., *Grg.* 494b | Thompson 1936: 311–14; Prummel 1987: 194–95 | Montagné 1961: 744; Escoffier 1984: 536; Aksakov 1998: 189–92 |
| Blackbird | *Turdus merula* | Dionys., *Av.* 3.13; Arist. *Av.* 1080; Hor., *Sat.* 2.8.91; *Ars Poetica* 458–59; Varro, *Rust.* 3.5.6–7; Philumen. 1.112, 2.126; Ath. 65d; Plin., *HN* 10.141–42 | Keller 1913: 75–76; Thompson 1936: 174–76; Toynbee 1973: 277; Pollard 1977: 104; Prummel 1987: 195; Watson 2002: 397–98 | Montagné 1961: 149, 957–58; Escoffier 1984: 527 |

*(continued)*

Table 8.4. (*continued*)

| Common Name | Scientific Name | References—Ancient Sources | References—Modern Scholarship | References—Modern Use |
|---|---|---|---|---|
| Song thrush | *Turdus philomelus* | Ath. 64f-65b; Ar., *Av.* 1080; *Ach.* 961, 1007; *Nub.* 339; Apic. 5.3.1, 8.7.14; Col., *Rust.* 8.10; Varro, *Rust.* 3.3.3; Hor., *Ep.* 1.15; 41; *Sat.* 1.5.72, 2.5.10; Ov. *Ars. am.* 2.269; Plin., *Ep.* 5.2.1; Pall. 1.26; Petr. *Satyr.* 40; Mart. 3.47.10; 13.51, 92; *Gp.* 14.24, 15.1.19; schol. Pers. 6.24; Macr. 2.4.22; Philumen. 1.112 | Keller 1913: 76–79; Thompson 1936: 149; André 1981: 125; Toynbee 1973: 277–78; Salza Prina Ricotti 1987: 100; Watson 2002: 398–99 | Montagné 1961: 957–58; Escoffier 1984: 525–27 |
| Sparrow | *Passer sp.* | Diocletian, *Price Edict* 4.37 | Keller 1913: 88–90; Thompson 1936: 268–70; Salza Prina Ricotti 1987: 100 | |
| Quail | *Coturnix coturnix* | Dionys., *Av.* 1.60, 3.9; Ath. 393a; Varro, *Rust.* 3.5.2; Pliny, *HN.* 10.69; Diocletian, *Price Edict* 4.41; *Gp.* 14.24; Ar., *Pax* 789; Juv. 12.97; Plaut., *Asin.* 666; Lucr. 4.640 | Keller 1913: 161–64; Thompson 1936: 215–19; André 1981: 125–26; Zeuner 1963: 458; Toynbee 1973: 256–57; Pollard 1977: 105; Rinkewitz 1984: 67–68; Salza Prina Ricotti 1987: 100; Watson 2002: 376–77 | Montagné 1961: 792–96; Escoffier 1984: 517–27; Aksakov 1998: 202–12 |
| Gerganey | *Anas querquedula* | | Keller 1913: 233; Thompson 1936: 205–6; Toynbee 1973: 264–73; Salza Prina Ricotti 1987: 95; Watson 2002: 365 | Montagné 1961: 363–64; Martin 1993: 94–98; Aksakov 1998: 127–29 |
| Curlew | *Numenius arquata* | | Keller 1913: 183; Thompson 1936: 207; Prummel 1987: 194–95 | Montagné 1961: 336; Aksakov 1998: 170–78 |
| Finch | *Carduelis or ringilla sp.* | Diocletian, *Price Edict* 4.34; Ath. 65c-d | Keller 1913: 86–87; Thompson 1936: 266; André 1981: 128; Pollard 1977: 107 | |

| Common name | Scientific name | | | |
|---|---|---|---|---|
| Jay | *Garrulus glandarius* | Ath. 65e; Zacharias, *Epist.* 13 | Keller 1913: 112–14; André 1981: 128 | Coles 1971: 27–36 |
| Peacock | *Pavo cristatus* | Varro, *Rust.* 3.6.1–6; Col., *Rust.* 8.11.1–7; Pall. 1.28; *Gp.* 14.18; Plin., *HN* 10.45; Ael., *NA* 3.42; Diocletian, *Price Edict* 4.39–40; Hor., *Serm.* 1.2.115, 2.2.23–31; Apic. 2.2.6; *SHA, Alex. Sev.* 41.6; Ael., *NA* 5.4; *Heliogabalus* 20.7; Cic., *Fam.* 9.18.3; Suet., *Vit.* 13.2; *Tib.* 60.1; *Calig.* 22.3; Juv. 1.143, 7.32; Mart. 3.58, 70; 14.67, 85; Varro, *Sat. Men.* 13.18; Gell. 6.16.5; Ath. 58b; Curt. Ruf. 9.1.13; Petr. *Satyr.* 33.5 | Keller 1913: 148–54; Thompson 1936: 277–81; Zeuner 1963: 456–57; Toynbee 1973: 250–53; Salza Prina Ricotti 1987: 96; Watson 2002: 388–89 | Montagné 1961: 719 |
| Magpie | *Pica pica* | Mart. 3.60.8 | Keller 1913: 112–14; André 1981: 128 | Coles 1971: 27–36 |
| Turtle dove | *Streptopelia turtur* | Varro, *Rust.* 3.8.3; Col., *Rust.*8.9; Apic. 6.2.1, 3.3; Pall. 1.25; *Gp.* 14.24; Juv. 6.39; Mart. 3.60.7, 82.21; 13.53; Ael., *NA* 13.25; Plaut., *Most.* 46; Philumen. 1.112, 2.126 | Keller 1913: 125, 127; Thompson 1936: 290–92; André 1981: 124; Zeuner 1963: 460–62; Pollard 1977: 104; Salza Prina Ricotti 1987: 98; Watson 2002: 394–95 | Montagné 1961: 733–34; Rocher 1979, 15–16, 303–16, 365–66; Escoffier 1984: 500–505; Aksakov 1998: 257–60 |
| Whooper swan | *Cygnus cygnus* | Ath. 393c–d; Plut., *De esu carn.* 997a; Hor., *Sat.* 2.2.49; Plin., *HN* 10.60, 30.30, 30.69; Orib. 4.77; Zacharias, *Epist.* 13 | Keller 1913: 213–20; Thompson 1936: 179–86; André 1981: 127; Toynbee 1973: 259–61; Pollard 1977: 106–7; Rinkewitz 1984: 71; Watson 2002: 377 | Montagné 1961: 945; André 1981: 127 note 166; Aksakov 1998: 96–98 |
| Mute swan | *Cygnus olor* | Ath. 393c–d; Plut., *De esu carn.* 997A; Hor., *Sat.* 2.2.49; Plin., *HN* 10.60, 30.30, 30.69; Orib. 4.77 | Keller 1913: 213–20; Thompson 1936: 179–86; Toynbee 1973: 259–61; Pollard 1977: 106–7; Rinkewitz 1984: 71 | Montagné 1961: 945; Martin 1993: 9–16; MacGregor 1996; Aksakov 1998: 96–98 |
| Goosander | *Mergus merganser* | | Keller 1913: 244 | Martin 1993: 168–72; Aksakov 1998: 136–39 |

(*continued*)

**Table 8.4. (continued)**

| Common Name | Scientific Name | References—Ancient Sources | References—Modern Scholarship | References—Modern Use |
|---|---|---|---|---|
| Coot | *Fulica atra* | Ath. 65e; 393c; Varro, *Rust.* 3.3.3, 11.4; Col., *Rust.* 8.15.1; Ar., *Av.* 565; Macr. 3.13.12; Plin., *HN* 10.67 | Keller 1913: 235–37; Thompson 1936: 298; André 1981: 126; Watson 2002: 379 | Montagné 1961: 305; Aksakov 1998: 140–42 |
| White-fronted goose | *Anser albifrons* | | Keller 1913: 224 | Montagné 1961: 467–70; Martin 1993: 38–43 |
| Stork | *Ciconia ciconia* | Hor., *Serm.* 2.2.49–50 and *schol. ad loc.*; Gell. 6.16.3; Mart. 13.75; Plin., *HN* 10.60–61, 68; Petr. *Satyr.* 55.6 | Keller 1913: 193–202; Thompson 1936: 221–25; Toynbee 1973: 244–45; Watson 2002: 371–72 | Ferlin 1989: 64 HN. 818 |
| Pochard | *Aythya ferina* | | Keller 1913: 226–35; Thompson 1936: 205–6; Toynbee 1973: 264–73; Salza Prina Ricotti 1987: 95 | Montagné 1961: 745; Martin 1993: 110–14 |
| Goldeneye duck | *Bucephala clangula* | | Keller 1913: 226–35; Thompson 1936: 205–6; Toynbee 1973: 264–73; Salza Prina Ricotti 1987: 95 | Montagné 1961: 363–64; Martin 1993: 152–57; Aksakov 1998: 130–32 |
| Cormorant | *Phalacrocorax carbo* | | Keller 1913: 239; Thompson 1936: 164; André 1981 | Ferlin 1989: 824 |
| Ring-neck pheasant | *Phasianus colchicus* | Apic. 2.2.1, 2.6; Ar., *Nub.* 108; Ath. 386c, 387b; Mart. 3.58.16, 3.77; 13.72; Plin., *HN* 10.132; Juv. 11.139; Pall. 1.29; Gp. 14.19; Silv. 1.1.77–78; Ammian. Marc. 16.5.3; Paul, *Dig.* 32.1.66; SHA, *Alex. Sev.* 41.6; SHA, *Pert.* 12.6 | Keller 1913: 145–46; Thompson 1936: 298–300; Zeuner 1963: 458; Toynbee 1973: 254–55; Rinkewitz 1984: 54–55: 67; 96; Salza Prina Ricotti 1987: 98–99; Watson 2002: 389–90 | Montagné 1961: 726–30; Coles 1971: 60–72, 107–76; Escoffier 1984: 506–12; Hansen-Catta 2002: 208–13 |

| Snipe | *Gallinago gallinago* | | Prummel 1987: 194–95; Watson 2002: 379–80 | Montagné 1961: 883–84; Coles 1971: 293–96; Escoffier 1984: 530; Aksakov 1998: 24–30, 39–41 |
|---|---|---|---|---|
| Capercaillie | *Tetrao urogallus* | Plin., *HN* 10.56; Suet, *Calig.* 22.3; Nemes., *Cyn.* 1.1–15; Nemes., *De Aucupio* fr. 1 | Keller 1913: 165–66; Thompson 1936: 283; Toynbee 1973: 256; Rinkewitz 1984: 29; Watson 2002: 396 | Montagné 1961: 475–76; Aksakov 1998: 222–26; Hansen-Catta 2002: 226–31 |
| Black grouse | *Tetrao tetrix* | | Keller 1913: 156–60 | Montagné 1961: 475–76; Aksakov 1998: 227–44; Hansen-Catta 2002: 232–37 |
| Tufted duck | *Aythya fuligula* | | Keller 1913: 226–35; Thompson 1936: 205–6; Toynbee 1973: 264–73; Salza Prina Ricotti 1987: 95 | Martin 1993: 115–19; Aksakov 1998: 132–34 |
| Gadwall duck | *Anas streptera* | | Keller 1913: 226–35; Thompson 1936: 205–6; Toynbee 1973: 264–73; Salza Prina Ricotti 1987: 95 | Montagné 1961: 363–64; Martin 1993: 90–94; Aksakov 1998: 122–23 |
| Black-tailed godwit | *Limosa limosa* | | | Montagné 1961: 467; Coles 1971: 296–98; Aksakov 1998: 42–47 |
| Redwing | *Turdus iliacus* | Ath. 65a | Keller 1913: 76; Thompson 1936: 121 | Montagné 1961: 804, 957–58 |
| Bustard | *Otis tarda; Otis* | Xen. Anab. 1.5.1–3; Ael., *HA.* 4.24; Ath. 393d; Gal., *Vict. Att.* 3 = Med. Gr. 6.703.9; Plin., *HN* 10.57, 30.61; Synesius, *Epist.* 4.165 | Keller 1913: 175–77; Thompson 1936: 338–39; André 1981: 126–27; Pollard 1977: 106; Anderson 1985: 61–62 | Montagné 1961: 188; Escoffier 1984: 535; Aksakov 1998: 153–56, 163–69 |
| Fieldfare | *Turdus pilaris* | Arist., *Hist. an.* 6.1.6 | Keller 1913: 76; Toynbee 1973: 277–78; Prummel 1987: 195 | Montagné 1961: 957–58 |
| Black grouse | *Lyrurus tetrix* | | Keller 1913: 156–60 | Montagné 1961: 475–76; Ferlin 1989: 62 HN. 752 |

*(continued)*

**Table 8.4.** (*continued*)

| Common Name | Scientific Name | References—Ancient Sources | References—Modern Scholarship | References—Modern Use |
|---|---|---|---|---|
| Buntings | *Emberiza sp.* | Ath. 65e; Varro, *Rust.* 3.5; 5.11; Varro, *Ling.* 5.76 | Keller 1913: 72; Thompson 1936: 136; André 1981: 127 | Montagné 1961: 184, 689–70; Aksakov 1998: 291 |
| Barnacle goose | *Branta leucopsis* | Plin., *HN* 10.54 | Martin 1993: 57–61 | Martin 1993: 57–61 |
| Northern pintail duck | *Anas acuta* | | Keller 1913: 226–35; Thompson 1936: 205–6; Toynbee 1973: 264–73; Salza Prina Ricotti 1987: 95 | Montagné 1961: 740; Martin 1993: 86–90; Aksakov 1998: 119–21 |
| Shoveler duck | *Anas clypeata* | | Keller 1913: 226–35; Thompson 1936: 205–6; Toynbee 1973: 264–73; Salza Prina Ricotti 1987: 95 | Montagné 1961: 363–64, 877; Martin 1993: 99–103; Aksakov 1998: 125–27 |
| Red-legged partridge | *Alectoris rufa* | | Keller 1913: 156–60 | Montagné 1961: 700–704; Coles 1971: 55–59; Hansen-Catta 2002: 202–7 |
| Skylark | *Alauda arvensis* | Dionys., *Av.* 3.15; Arist. *HA.* 617 B | Keller 1913: 86; Pollard 1977: 104 | Montagné 1961: 581 |
| Grey plover | *Pluvialis squatarola* | Ar., *Av.* 266; Enn. *Heduph.* 48 | Keller 1913: 179–80; Thompson 1936: 311–14 | Montagné 1961: 744; Escoffier 1984: 536 |
| Hazel grouse Francolin | *Tetrastes bonasia* | Mart. 13.61; Apic. 6.3.3; Ath. 398c-f; Ar., *Av.* 885 | Thompson 1936: 282–83; Salza Prina Ricotti 1987: 99 | Montagné 1961: 490–91; Escoffier 1984: 534; Aksakov 1998: 245–48; Hansen-Catta 2002: 238–39 |
| Corncrake | *Crecex* | Ath. 393a | Keller 1913: 208; Thompson 1936: 214–15 | Aksakov 1998: 196–201 |
| Pink footed goose | *Anser rachyrhynchos* | | Keller 1913: 220–26; Thompson 1936: 325–30; Toynbee 1973: 261–64; Salza Prina Ricotti 1987: 95–96 | Montagné 1961: 467–70; Martin 1993: 34–7 |

| Common name | Scientific name | Classical sources | References | Modern references |
|---|---|---|---|---|
| Willow grouse | *Lagopus lagopus* | | Keller 1913: 156 | Montagné 1961: 700–704; Coles 1971: 299–323; Aksakov 1998: 249–50; Hansen-Catta 2002: 240–41 |
| Rock ptarmigan | *Lagopus mutus* | Hor., *Sat.* 2.2.22; Plin., *HN* 10.133 | Keller 1913: 156; Thompson 1936: 190; Rinkewitz 1984: 55 | Montagné 1961: 700–704; Hansen-Catta 2002: 240–41 |
| Cuckoo | *Cuculus canorus* | Plin., *HN* 10.27; Arist., *HA* 564a 3–4 | Keller 1913: 63–67; Thompson 1936: 151–53; André 1981: 128; Watson 2002: 377 | Montagné 1961: 330; Aksakov 1998: 290 |
| Shelduck | *Tadorna tadorna* | Plin., *HN* 10.29.56; Ath. 58b | Keller 1913: 235; Thompson 1936: 205–6; Toynbee 1973: 264–73; Pollard 1977: 65; Salza Prina Ricotti 1987: 95; Watson 2002: 396 | Montagné 1961: 363–64; Martin 1993: 65–71 |
| Spoonbill duck | *Platalea leucorodia* | | Keller 1913: 203; Thompson 1936: 193; Toynbee 1973: 264–73; Salza Prina Ricotti 1987: 95 | Ferlin 1989: 64 HN. 816 |
| Guinea fowl | *Numida meleagris* | Apic. 6.4.1–4; Col., *Rust.*8.2.2–3; Varro, *Rust.* 3.9.18; 8.12; Ath. 655b–e; Hor., *Ep.* 2.53; Juv. 11.142–43; Petr. *Satyr.* 93; Mart. 3.77.3, 13.45.1, 13.73; Plin., *HN* 8.223, 10.74; *Gp.*14.19; Suet., *Calig.* 22.3 | Keller 1913: 154–56; Thompson 1936: 197–200; André 1981: 133–34; Zeuner 1963: 457; Toynbee 1973: 253–54; Lamblard 1975; Rinkewitz 1984: 53; Watson 2002: 384–85 | Montagné 1961: 476; Escoffier 1984: 512 |
| Ruff | *Philomachus pugnax* | Plin., *HN* 10.74 | Keller 1913: 181; Thompson 1936: 200–1; Prummel 1987: 194–95 | Aksakov 1998: 71–74 |
| Wild turkey | *Meleagris gallopavo* | | | Montagné 1961: 976–78 |
| Nightingale | *Luscinia egarhynchos* | Hor., *Sat.* 2.3.235; SHA, *Heliogab.* 20.5 | Keller 1913: 73–75; Thompson 1936: 16–22; Toynbee 1973: 276–77; Watson 2002: 383–84 | |

*(continued)*

**Table 8.4.** (continued)

| Common Name | Scientific Name | References—Ancient Sources | References—Modern Scholarship | References—Modern Use |
|---|---|---|---|---|
| Golden Oriole | *Oriolus oriolus* | Mart. 13.68 | Keller 1913: 120; Thompson 1936: 332–23; André 1981: 128; Watson 2002: 386–87 | Montagné 1961: 467 |
| Ostrich | *Struthio camelus* | Apic. 6.1.1–2; SHA, *Heliogab.* 22.1, 28.4, 30.2; SHA, *Firmus* 4.2; Ath. 145d | Keller 1913: 166–75; Thompson 1936: 270–73; Zeuner 1963: 476–77; Toynbee 1973: 237–40; Pollard 1977: 106; Salza Prina Ricotti 1987: 100 | Montagné 1961: 690 |
| Flamingo | *Phoenicopterus ruber* | Mart. 3.58.14; 13.71; Apic. 6.6.1–2; Juv. 11.139; Seneca, *Epist.* 110.12; Suet., *Vit.* 13; *Calig.* 22; Ar., *Av.* 273; Cels. 2.18.3 | Keller 1913: 209–13; Thompson 1936: 304–6; André 1981: 128; Toynbee 1973: 246; Salza Prina Ricotti 1987: 99; Watson 2002: 390 | Ferlin 1989: 54 |
| Figpecker | *Sylviaatricapilla/ borin* | Ath. 64b–c; Mart. 13.49; Gell. 15.8.2; Juv. 14.9; Petr. *Satyr.* 33.8; Suet., *Tib.* 42.2; Macr. *Sat.* 3.13.12; Diocletian, *Price Edict* 2.5 | Keller 1913: 118–20; Thompson 1936: 274–75; Rinkewitz 1984: 72; Salza Prina Ricotti 1987: 98; Watson 2002: 396 | |
| Green Parrot | *Psittacus Krameri manillensis* | Apic. 6.6.1; SHA, *Heliogab.* 20.6; Claud. in *Eutrop.* 2.329 | Keller 1913: 45–49; Thompson 1936: 336–38; Toynbee 1973: 247–49 | |
| Black francolin | *Francolinus francolinus* | Apic. 6.3.3; Ath. 387f, 388b; Ar., *Ach.* 875; Mart. 2.37, 13.61; Ov. *Fast.* 6.175; Plin., *HN* 8.83, 10.68, 10.133; Aul. Gell. 6.16.5; Hor., *Ep.* 2.54; Mart. 2.37; 13.61; *Gp.* 14.19 | Keller 1913: 158; Thompson 1936: 61; André 1981: 126; Rinkewitz 1984: 56 | |
| Purple swamphen | *Porphyrio porphyrio* | Plin., *HN* 10.129, 135; Mart. 13.78; Ath. 388d | André 1981: 135 | Ferlin 1989: 63 HN. 803 |

| Moorhen | *Gallinula chloropus* | | Aksakov 1998: 75–78 |
| Lapwing | *Vanellus vanellus* | Keller 1913: 178 | Montagné 1961: 580; Aksakov 1998: 81–83 |
| Bean Goose | *Anser fabalis* | | Martin 1993: 30–34 |

203

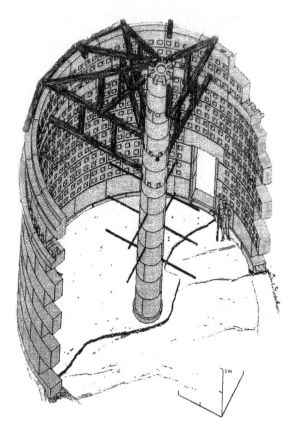

Figure 8.3. Roman columbarium at Apollonia in Cyrenaica, reconstruction. (From Chamoux and Hallier 1996: fig. 9.)

and pheasant (Palladius 1.29.4; Rinkewitz 1984: 54, 67), for example, find many parallels with methods used today (Delacour 1964: 29–39; Coles 1971: 96–100). The precautions against aggression (Columella, *Rust.* 8.11.7; cf. Delacour 1964: 32), and the use of broody hens of the domestic chicken to incubate the eggs of these and many other wild species (Columella, *Rust.* 8.11.10–14, 15.7), thereby encouraging further egg production, are especially important and very much in accord with modern practice (Farrington 1913: 119, 122; Coles 1971: 75–80).

## FISHING AND FISH FARMING

Research has begun to document in increasing detail the impressive scale and sophistication of the fishing industry in classical and Hellenistic Greece and late Republican Rome (Salza Prina Ricotti 1999; Sahrhage 2002; Bekker-Nielsen 2005b). The remains of fish processing plants (chapter 14; Trakadas 2005) reflect fishing on an industrial scale for mackerel, anchovies, sardines and other gregarious migratory pelagic fish in the eastern Mediterranean and along the coasts of Spain, North Africa, and Sicily (Sahrhage 2002: 76–79; Højte 2005). Greek and Roman tuna fishing was equally impressive (Sternberg 1998: 98–103; Sahrhage 2002: 58–69; Shepherd and Dallai 2003). The vivid interest in fishing on the part of the Greco-Roman public is evident from Aristotle's superb work on ichthyology (Mair 1928: xxvi–xxviii, citing Cuvier and Valenciennes 1828–1848), the popularity of representations of fish and fishing in the decorative arts (Reese 2002a, b; Bekker-Nielsen 2002), and the many accounts of fishing—both lost technical manuals like that of Leonidas of Tarentum, and popularizing works such as those of Oppian, Aelian, Archestratus, and Ovid (Mair 1928: xxxvii–xxxviii; Bekker-Nielsen 2005b). Finally, a significant proportion of the *demos* of several Greek cities, most notably Byzantium, Tarentum, and Syracuse, made their living from fishing (Trotta 1996: 234–43), and fishermen often enjoyed the same social status and pride in their craft as many other skilled artisans (Lubtchansky 1998).

As in the other Greco-Roman skilled trades, one can observe a great deal of innovation and creativity in the development of new methods and technologies. Del Rosso, a leading expert on contemporary Italian fisheries and on Roman fishing, argued forcefully at the beginning of the twentieth century that there had still been few meaningful advances in Italian fishing methods over those already known in Roman times (Del Rosso 1905: 26–27, 32–36, 61–70). Dietrich Sahrhage's brief account of fishing techniques (Sahrhage 2002: 41–56), informed by his own expertise in modern fisheries, shows just how many important modern fishing techniques can be attested in Greek or Roman use.

Ancient references for these techniques, along with comparative evidence from the contemporary Mediterranean, are listed in table 8.5. Although it is sometimes claimed (Gallant 1985: 25) that Greco-Roman net fishing was a predominantly shore-based activity, literary sources and mosaics make it absolutely clear that fishing nets were used from a range of small seacraft (Bekker-Nielsen 2002), as well as from ships of significant size (Bekker-Nielsen 2002: no. 9; Sahrhage 2002: 92 pl. 4, top; Bekker-Nielsen 2005b: 88). Likewise, despite claims that deep sea fish were not exploited (*pace* Gallant 1985: 27), archaeozoological studies of fish landed at Greek and Roman sites in southern France clearly show a marked increase in the number of benthic and pelagic species (Sternberg 1995, 1998, 2005a: 247). One effective method for catching large numbers of fish simultaneously at almost any depth is longline fishing (Gabriel et al. 2005: 114–35) referred to clearly several times by our sources (Oppian, *Hal.* 3.78, 3.468–81; Aristotle, *Hist. an.* 532b25; 621a15; Aelian, *NA* 12.53; 15.10). Fishermen fix a large number of shorter branch lines called snoods, each with up to a hundred hooks, to a single main line, thereby permitting hundreds or thousands of hooks to be set. The labor of baiting so many hooks is the main limitation on the size of the catch, but the markedly improved design, manufacture, and standardization of Roman fish hooks, including small streamlined ones similar to those now used in longlining (Cleyet-Merle 1990: 166–70), confirms the importance of this method in Roman fishing.

The most significant limitation on Greco-Roman fishing technology was presumably the absence of steam or internal combustion power for trawling (Gabriel et al. 2005: 402–5) or winching (Gabriel et al. 2005: 9). Nevertheless, given that there were only four steam-powered fishing boats in the whole of the Mediterranean as late as 1905 (Del Rosso 1905: 34), we should not exaggerate the significance of this factor. Moreover, while modern industrial trawling produces large catches, these often cannot be sustained over the long term, but soon lead to a reduction in the size of fish and, eventually, a severe depletion of fish-stocks. While they fished on a very large scale, particularly for the *garum* and salt-fish industry, and did so over centuries, Greco-Roman fishermen seem generally to have avoided the destructive overfishing typical of modern trawling. Several studies have shown that fish captured by Greco-Roman fishermen were often significantly larger than are typically caught today (Desse-Berset 1993). Moreover, the highly prized sturgeon (Martial 13.91; Pliny, *HN* 9.60) still represented about half of the total number of fish caught by Hellenistic and Roman fishermen in the Black Sea in some surveys, compared to barely 3 to 4 percent of the fish caught in the same waters today (Ivanova 1994: 280).

## Fish Farming

The Greeks and Romans did not rely solely on fishing to supply their great demand for seafood, but also put great efforts into improving existing fish stocks and into fish farming. Gallant's use of modern fisheries' statistics to place limits on possible Greco-Roman fish production (Gallant 1985) has been criticized on a number of grounds (Jacobsen 2005), as have a number of the claims in his book (Purcell 1995; Sahrhage 2002: 5 n. 1; Bekker-Nielsen 2005b: 84–86). Perhaps the most critical objection, however, comes from his neglect of the significance of fish farming. Modern fish farmers, using techniques which were widely applied by the Romans, produce quantities of a number of popular Mediterranean sea fish far in excess of those that can be harvested from natural fish stocks (Kron forthcoming). For example, according to Food and Agricultural Organization statistics (FAO 2002) Mediterranean fishing of gilthead seabream, gray mullet, and European sea bass provides barely one-tenth to one-fifth as many fish as aquaculture.

The Greeks and Romans put considerable effort into enhancing and even managing their fish stocks. They introduced eggs, fingerlings, and adult fish, including new fish species, into fresh water lakes and the Tyrrhenian Sea to enhance fish stocks (Pliny, *HN* 9.62–63; Lafon 2001: 162). Moreover, in addition to intensive aquaculture, they practiced a more extensive system of exploiting and enhancing stocks of fish in brackish lagoons, first alluded to by Greek sources (Aristotle, *Hist. an.* 504b33). Similar techniques were widely used in Italy since the late medieval period under the title of *vallicoltura* (Del Rosso 1905: 59; De Angelis 1959; Bevilacqua 1987), and equally widely in modern Greece (Apostolides 1883; Guest-Papamanoli 1986). McCann's study of the massive Tagliata canal at Cosa and the associated fish processing plant and fish farming tanks offers the best

**Table 8.5. Greco-Roman fish-catching methods.**

| Method | Ancient Sources | Modern Scholarship | Comparative Evidence |
|---|---|---|---|
| gathering by hand | | Sahrhage 2002: 40–41 | Gabriel et al. 2005: 12–20 |
| wounding gear in general | | Sahrhage 2002: 43–44 | Gabriel et al. 2005: 53–82 |
| spearing swordfish from boats | Opp., *H* 3.543–67; Polyb. 34.3.1–8; Str. 1.24–25; Poll., *Onom.*10.133; Pl., *Soph.* 220c; Ath. 7.314e-f. | D'Arrigo 1956; Gallant 1985: 13; Longo 1989: 27–30; Trotta 1996: 242; Olson and Sens 2000: 171; Bekker-Nielsen 2002: nos. 2, 8; Sahrhage 2002: 43–44, fig. 17, 18a-b; Bekker-Nielsen 2005b: 89; Højte 2005: 135–36 | Apostolides 1883: 49; D'Arrigo 1956; Sisci 1992: 139–45; Romdhane 1998: 65; Gabriel et al. 2005: 53–57, 60, 68–69 |
| poison | Opp., *H* 4.640–84; Pliny, *HN* 25.98, 120; Arist., *Hist. an.* 602b31 | Mair 1928: 452–53, notes a–c; Gianfrotta 1999: 10; Sahrhage 2002: 41–2 | Gabriel et al. 2005: 44–47 |
| hook and line | | Cleyet-Merle 1990: 166–70; Rossi 1990: 114, no. 255; Gianfrotta 1999: 26–27, fig. 17; Sahrhage 2002: 45, fig. 18c–d; Højte 2005: 135–36 | Gabriel et al. 2005: 89–96 |
| hand line | Opp., *H* 1.72 f.; 3.76–77; Hom., *Il.* 16.406 | Mair 1928: xxxix; 350–51, note f | Gabriel et al. 2005: 105–8 |
| pole and line | Opp., *H* 3.74–75 | Mair 1928: xxxix; Gallant 1985: 14–15, pl. 3, 4, 6; Sahrhage 2002: 17 fig. 3, 46 fig. 19, 47 fig. 21, 92 pl. 4, bottom; Bekker-Nielsen 2002: notes 9, 12; Bekker-Nielsen 2005b: 89–90 | Gabriel et al. 2005: 108–12 |
| weighted line | Opp., *H* 3.77 | Mair 1928: xxxix 351 note g; Cleyet-Merle 1990: 169; Sahrhage 2002: 45 fig. 18e–g | |

(*continued*)

**Table 8.5.** (continued)

| Method | Ancient Sources | Modern Scholarship | Comparative Evidence |
|---|---|---|---|
| troll line | Opp., H 4.78–125 | Gallant 1985: 15; Sahrhage 2002: 49 | Gabriel et al. 2005: 121–26 |
| longlines | Opp., H 3.78, 468–81; Arist., Hist. an. 532b25, 621a15 | Mair 1928: xxxix-xl; Gallant 1985: 15–66; Sternberg 1998: 96–8 tab. 5–6; Bekker-Nielsen 2005b: 89–90 | Gabriel et al. 2005: 114–26 |
| rip hooks | Opp., H 4.439–49; Opp., H 3.529–41 (swordfish); Ael., NA 14.26 (S. Russia sturgeon) | Rossi 1990: 114–15, no. 254; Purpura 1992: 92; Gianfrotta 1999: 26–27, fig. 17; Sahrhage 2002: 49–51 | Gabriel et al. 2005: 167–80 |
| baiting for specific species | Opp., H 3.176–93, 443–528ff., 4.308f. | Sahrhage 2002: 47–48 | Gabriel et al. 2005: 146–47 |
| fly fishing | Ael., NA 15.1 | Sahrhage 2002 50–51 | Romdhane 1998: 70; Gabriel et al. 2005: 220–21 |
| trapping barriers made of fences | Opp., H 3.73–90, 342, 401; Ael., NA 12.43 | Gallant 1985: 13; McCann et al. 1987 | Apostolides 1883: 51; Romdhane 1998: 67; Gabriel et al. 2005: 221–26 |
| wooden fish pots, fyke nets | Opp., H 3.85–7 (generic); Arist., Hist. an. 534a11; b10; Opp., H 3.338ff; Sil., Pun. 4.47; Pliny, HN 9.132; Pl., Leg. 823e, Ti. 79d; Theocr. 21.11; Poll., Onom. 10.132; Anth. Pal. 6.23 | Mair 1928: xlvi, 352 notes a, b; Gallant 1985: 13; Sahrhage 2002: 56–57; Bekker-Nielsen 2002: nos. 1–5 | Romdhane 1998: 70–72; Gabriel et al. 2005: 207–13 |
| watched catching chambers | Aesch. Pers. 424–26; Opp., H 3.623–27; 3.637–46; Ael. NA 13.16f.; 15.5–6; Philost. Imag. 1.13 | Dumont 1976–77; Gallant 1985: 21–23; Trotta 1996: 231–33; Sternberg 1998: 98–103; Mastromarco 1998; Sahrhage 2002: 58–69; Shepherd and Dallai 2003; Bekker-Nielsen 2005b: 93 | |
| terracotta pots | Opp., H 4.64–71 | Gianfrotta 1999: 21–22, figs. 11–3 | Rendini 1997; Romdhane 1998: 66–67; Gabriel et al. 2005: 195–96 |

| | | | |
|---|---|---|---|
| verandah net | Opp., *H* 3.98–116 | | Apostolides 1883: 34; Romdhane 1998: 73–74; Gabriel et al. 2005: 257–61 |
| scoop, dip nets | Opp., *H* 4.251 | Gallant 1985: 18–19; Bekker-Nielsen 2002: no. 9; Sahrhage 2002: 54, pl. 4 bottom | Gabriel et al. 2005: 352–59 |
| dredge nets | Opp., *H* 3.83; Hom. *Il.* 5.487 | Mair 1928 xliii–liv; Trotta 1990: 36–46; 1996: 231; Sternberg 1998: 96–98, tab. 5–6 | Gabriel et al. 2005: 377–89 |
| trawl | | Trotta 1990: 36–46; 1996: 231 | Gabriel et al. 2005: 392–430 |
| seines | Opp., *H* 3.79–84, 4.468 ff. (sardines), 4.491–96; Alciphr. 1.13; 20; 21; Plut. *Mor.* 977f | Mair 1928: xliii–xlv; Trotta 1996, 231–32; Sternberg 1998: 96–98, tab. 5–6; Sahrhage 2002: 52–54; Bekker-Nielsen 2005b: 92 | Gabriel et al. 2005: 431–37 |
| seining below ice | Ael., *NA* 14.26; Str. 7.3.18 | Sahrhage 2002: 55–56 | Gabriel et al. 2005: 437–39 |
| beach seine | Opp., *H* 3.124; 4.490–503; Plut., *Mor.* 977 f. | Mair 1928: xliv–xlv; Gallant 1985: 19; Bekker-Nielsen 2002; Sahrhage 2002: 53, pl. 5 top | Romdhane 1998: 74; Gabriel et al. 2005: 439–40 |
| boat seine | | Mair 1928: xliv–xlv; Bekker-Nielsen 2002: fig. 4, nos. 20–29; Sahrhage 2002: 53–54, pl. 4 bottom, fig. 26 | Romdhane 1998: 75; Gabriel et al. 2005: 441–44 |
| frightening fish into seine or barrier net | Opp., *H* 4.566–76 | Bekker-Nielsen 2002: no. 6 | Gabriel et al. 2005: 160–61 |
| dip nets, lift nets | Ael., *NA* 1.39 | Gallant 1985: 19–20; Sahrhage 2002: 54, abb. 29 | Gabriel et al. 2005: 329–36; Romdhane 1998: 72–73 |
| falling nets | Opp., *H* 3.82; Aesch., *Ch.* 494 | Mair 1928: xlv | Apostolides 1883: 41 |

(*continued*)

**Table 8.5.** (*continued*)

| Method | Ancient Sources | Modern Scholarship | Comparative Evidence |
|---|---|---|---|
| cast nets | Opp., *H* 3.80 | Mair 1928: xli–xlii; Gallant 1985: 18–19; Trotta 1990: 36–46; 1996, 231; Sahrhage 2002: 54–55, figs. 3, 20, 29; Bekker-Nielsen 2002: no. 7; Bekker-Nielsen 2005b: 91 | Apostolides 1883: 32 f.; Romdhane 1998: 72; Bekker-Nielsen 2005b: 91 fig. 3b |
| gillnets | Opp., *H* 3.577–95 | Gallant 1985: 20–21; Sahrhage 2002: 54 | Gabriel et al. 2005: 275–83 |
| attracting fish with sexual lures | Opp., *H* 4.127–46; Arist., *Hist. an.* 541a19 | Mair 1928: 412 note d, 414 note a; Sahrhage 2002: 49 | Apostolides 1883: 45, 51; Romdhane 1998: 65–66; Gabriel et al. 2005: 154 |
| attracting fish with chum or chemical lures | Opp., *H* 4.404–36 | Sahrhage 2002: 47–48 | Gabriel et al. 2005: 153–54 |
| attracting fish with light | Pl., *Soph.* 220d; Poll., *Onom.* 7.138; Opp., *H* 4.640–46; Quint. Smyrn. 7.569–76; Plin., *HN* 9.33; Ael. *NA* 2.8 | Mair 1928: xlvii; Gianfrotta 1999: 21; Sahrhage 2002: 48 | Apostolides 1883: 40 (night fishing for gar-fish (*Belone belone*) in Sporades); Mair 1928: 450–1 note b ("burning the waters" in Scotland); Gabriel et al. 2005: 151–53 |
| attracting fish with sound (acoustic bait) | | Sahrhage 2002: 56 | Sahrhage 2002: 56; Gabriel et al. 2005: 155–57 |
| attracting fish with artificial shade | Opp., *H* 4.404–36 | | Romdhane 1998: 75–76; Gabriel et al. 2005: 190–92 |
| use of cattle to exhaust large catfish | Ael., *NA* 14.25 | Cleyet-Merle 1990: 161–62; Sahrhage 2002: 48–49, pl. 5 | Sahrhage 2002: 49 (same method used in Danube in recent past) |

archaeological evidence and analysis, with extensive attention to the many parallels with modern practice (McCann et al. 1987: 35–43, 137–59). The creation by the Roman state of a massive mole to control the flow of seawater, and the ingress and egress of fish, between the Tyrrhenian Sea and the Lago Lucrino (Servius, *ad. Verg. G.* 2.161; Pagano 1983–1984: 127–29) shows the economic importance of fishing in brackish lakes and lagoons. Finally, the so-called Emissario Romano connecting the Lago di Paola with the sea between Monte Circeo and the modern Sabaudia was likely motivated (at least in part) by similar considerations (Lugli 1928: 31–34, no. 32; figs. 37–38).

The Greco-Roman fish-farmers soon developed more intensive methods to increase production even further, spawning fish in artificial ponds or tanks and feeding them to maximize stocking density and growth. They raised many different species. Higginbotham lists the common eel, conger eel, moray eel, several species of gray mullet, sea bass, gilthead seabream, red mullet, and the *rhombus*, most likely either sole or turbot (Higginbotham 1997: 41–53). In addition to increasing supply, the Roman practice of fish farming helped bring about some significant changes in the way Romans marketed and ate fish. Higginbotham has identified more than 70 small pools in the gardens or peristyle courts of houses in Pompeii and Herculaneum alone that show evidence of being used as fishponds (Higginbotham 1997: 198 n. 257), and several sources (Martial 10.30; cf. Lafon 2001: 310) imply that it was fashionable to catch live fish from one's own fishpond to ensure their freshness.

The impressive remains of fish farms all along the Tyrrhenian coast (figure 8.4), from Faleria in the north to Briatico in the south (catalogued in depth in several syntheses: Giacopini et al. 1994; Higginbotham 1997; Lafon 2001) reveal the lavish capital investment and technological innovation of Roman fish farming. Although many literary sources allude to the popular fascination with fish-farming (Conta 1972; Kajava 1998–1999), the high productivity of Greco-Roman aquaculture can be illustrated most clearly through an analysis of the fish farms themselves in the light of modern fish farming practice. Research still makes limited use of comparative evidence (Higginbotham 1997: 9–40; Giacopini et al. 1994: passim), but a few tentative observations are in order. In order to maximize overall production, artificial feeding is generally critical (Huet 1986: 334–85; Shepherd and Bromage 1988: 78–83), and it is clear from the ancient sources that this practice was very common (Varro, *Rust.* 3.17.2–3, 6–7; Columella, *Rust.* 8.17.12–13, 15; Pliny, *HN* 37.2). Some fish tanks were equipped with gangways (Higginbotham 1997: 133), allowing one to feed the fish by hand and observe their behavior (Shepherd and Bromage 1988: 79). A critical limiting factor on the stocking rate of fish tanks is oxygen, which requires constant water exchange (Shepherd and Bromage 1988: 69–71, 317; Huet 1986: 8–9) or artificial aeration (Boyd and Tucker 1998: 306–53). The Romans recognized the problem (Pliny, *HN* 9.56) and had practical means to address it (Varro, *Rust.* 3.17.8–9; Columella, *Rust.* 8.17.1–6), and many excavated fish tanks show careful design to maximize water flow (e.g., Higginbotham 1997: 152–57, fig. 62–65; Gianfrotta 2002: 77, figs. 11–12). A number of tanks used fountains and inflow canals well above water level (e.g., Higginbotham 1997: 125–28, fig. 44, 45; Cunliffe 1971: 131) that would have

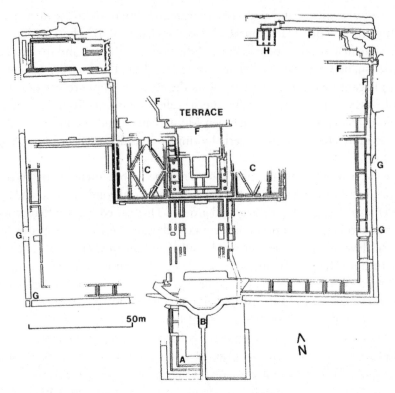

Figure 8.4. Roman concrete *piscina* at Torre Astura. B: main seawater inlet; F: freshwater canal; G: breaches in perimeter mole to admit seawater; H: cistern for fresh water. (Higginbotham 1997: 145, fig. 57.)

served very effectively to aerate the water and further enhance the oxygen level (Boyd and Tucker 1998: 372 with table 7.3). Other features that seem to correspond closely with modern practice include the creation of smaller tanks for spawning and as nursery ponds for the growth of fingerlings (figure 8.4; Higginbotham 1997: 140–51, figs. 55–61, 153–54, figs. 162–63; cf. Huet 1986: 6–7), and measures to recreate the fish's natural habitat (Columella, *Rust.* 8.16.6–9.).

The artificial cultivation of oysters, mussels, and other shellfish was highly developed, using techniques very similar to those used today (Higginbotham 1997: 125–28, figs. 44–45, 202–4, figs. 94–95, 210–13; Cunliffe 1971: 131). Aristotle is aware of the scientific background (Aristotle, *Gen. an.* 763b), and the cultivation of shellfish may well have been underway when he wrote (Del Rosso 1905: 147). Pliny credits the invention of oyster cultivation to the enterprising Roman fish farmer C. Sergius Orata, who created artificial oyster beds or *ostriaria* at Baiae and in the Lago Lucrino (Lafon 2001: 177–79). A series of glass souvenir flasks (Kolendo 1977: fig. 1a–c; Ostrow 1979: 129, figs. 6–8) illustrates the famous Roman *ostriaria* along the sea coast of Baiae. They illustrate a technology remarkably similar in form to modern bouchot culture, or even more so to modern oyster culture at Taranto (Kolendo 1977: 120–22, fig. 8), or to Spanish rope culture (Hurlburt and Hurlburt 1980: 79–85). Kolendo (1977: 122) and Pagano (1983–1984: 126) make the attractive suggestion that these flasks show canals channeling fresh water into the *ostriaria*, as is done by some contemporary French oyster farmers (Pagano 1983–1984: 126) to enhance the growth and taste of the shellfish. Orata also cultured oysters on terracotta *tegulae* (Valerius Maximus 9.1.1; Cicero, *Hortensius* fr. 69 Müller), as is still done today in Médoc (Pagano 1983–1984: 124 n. 49). The discovery of an oyster still fused to a small piece of potsherd, identified in this case as part of an amphora, was likely the result of this practice (Pinto-Guillaume 2001). Innovative methods of preserving shellfish were also developed, similar to the practice of keeping harvested oysters alive in shallow freshwater pools (*parcs à huitres*) (Del Rosso 1905: 152–53; Abad 2002: 522–24), which revolutionized the consumption of shellfish in France in the late eighteenth century (Abad 2002: 519–64, especially 549–61). Excavations near Aquileia have revealed large numbers of oysters laid out carefully in pits irrigated with fresh water from a nearby canal (Balista and Sainati 2003).

It is not surprising, therefore, that shellfish figured prominently in the Greco-Roman diet. Oyster shells have been found on more than a hundred sites, mostly associated with Roman villas or military encampments, in Germany, Switzerland, and Austria alone (Thüry 1990), and a single deposit of more than a million oysters was found at Silchester (Sahrhage 2002: 101–3). Although no similar survey yet exists for Italy, dozens of sites provide evidence for the consumption of oysters and shellfish, occasionally in considerable quantity (Balista and Sainati 2003). One of the few detailed regional studies, of southern Provence, shows a dramatic increase in the consumption of shellfish, primarily the most popular cultivated species—oysters, mussels, and scallops—following the Roman conquest, penetrating even into very modest villages (Brien-Poitevin 1996).

# REFERENCES

Abad, R. 2002. *Le grand marché: L'approvisionnement alimentaire de Paris sous l'Ancien Régime*. Paris: Fayard.

Adams, J. N. 1995. *Pelagonius and Latin veterinary terminology in the Roman Empire*. Leiden: Brill.

Aksakov, S. T. 1998. *Notes of a provincial wildfowler*. Evanston, IL: Northwestern University Press.

Anderson, J. K. 1961. *Ancient Greek horsemanship*. Berkeley: University of California Press.

Anderson, J. K. 1985. *Hunting in the ancient world*. Berkeley: University of California Press.

André, J. 1967. *Les noms d'oiseaux en latin*. Paris: C. Klincksieck.

André, J. 1981. *L'alimentation et la cuisine à Rome*. 2nd ed. Paris: C. Klincksieck.

Apostolides, N. C. 1883. *La pêche en Grèce: Ichthyologie, migrations, engins et manières de pêche, produits, statistique et législation*. Athens.

Aymard, A. 1951. *Essai sur les chasses romaines des origines à la fin du siècle des Antonins*. Paris: École Française de Rome.

Baatz, D. 1991. "Die römische Jagdarmbrust," *Archäologisches Korrespondenzblatt* 21: 283–90.

Badan, O., J.-P. Brun, and G. Congès 1996. "Les bergeries romaines de la Crau d'Arles," *Gallia* 52: 263–310.

Balista, C., and C. Sainati 2003. "Ostrea non pectines ad Altino: Le evidenze archeologiche," in G. C. Marrone and M. Tirelli (eds.), *Produzioni, merci e commerci in Altino preromana e romana: Atti del convegno, Venezia 12–14 dicembre 2001*. Rome: Qasar, 331–46

Bekker-Nielsen, T. 2002. "Nets, boats and fishing in the Roman world," *Classica et Medievalia* 53: 215–33.

Bekker-Nielsen, T. (ed.) 2005a. *Ancient fishing and fish processing in the Black Sea region*. Aarhus: Aarhus University Press.

Bekker-Nielsen, T. 2005b. "The technology and productivity of ancient sea fishing," in Bekker-Nielsen 2005a: 83–96.

Benecke, N. 1994a. *Der Mensch und seine Haustiere: Die Geschichte einer jahrtausendealten Beziehung*. Stuttgart: Theiss.

Benecke, N. 1994b. *Archäozoologische Studien zur Entwicklung der Haustierhaltung: In Mitteleuropa und Südskandinavien von den Anfängen bis zum ausgehenden Mittelalter*. Berlin: Akademie Verlag.

Benecke, N., P. Donat et al. (eds.) 2003. *Frühgeschichte der Landwirtschaft in Deutschland*. Langenweißbach: Beier and Baran.

Bevilacqua, E. 1987. "Diffusion des techniques de l'eau du monde antique au monde contemporain: Les 'valli da pesca' dans la Lagune de Venise," in A. de Réparaz (ed.), *L'eau et des hommes en Méditérranée*. Paris: CNRS, 67–76.

Binder, F. 1971. *Organisation, production et controle de l'élevage du gibier en France*. Diss. École Nationale Vétérinaire d'Alfort. Paris: Copedith.

Boisaubert, B., and J.-M. Boutin 1988. *Le Chevreuil*. Paris: Hatier.

Bökönyi, S. 1984. *Animal husbandry and hunting in Tác-Gorsium—The vertebrate fauna of a Roman town in Pannonia*. Budapest: Akadémiai Kiadó.

Bökönyi, S. 1988. "Animal breeding on the Danube," in C. R. Whitakker (ed.), *Pastoral economies in classical antiquity*. Cambridge: Cambridge Philological Society, 171–76.

Bonnet, G., and F. Klein 1991. *Le Cerf*. Paris: Hatier.

Bortuzzo, N. 1990. "Il leporarium: Un esempio di pastio villatica nella Gallia Cisalpina di tarda età repubblicana-prima età imperiale? Alcune ipotesi sulla Transpadana orientale," *Aquileia Nostra* 66: 85–112.

Bourdy, F. 1995. "L'ophthalmologie équine dans l'antiquité tardive d'après Végèce," in R. Chevallier and F. Bourdy (eds.), in *Homme et animal dans l'antiquité romaine*. Tours: Centre de récherches André Piganiol, 205–15.

Boyd, C. E., and C. S. Tucker 1998. *Pond aquaculture water quality management*. Boston: Kluwer.

Brien-Poitevin, F. 1996. "Consommation des coquillages marins en Provence dans l'époque romaine," *Revue Archéologique de la Narbonnaise* 29: 313–20.

Brothwell, D. 1997. "Interpreting the immature chicken bones from the Romano-British ritual complex on West Hill, Uley," *International Journal of Osteoarchaeology* 7.4: 330–32.

Brun, J.-P. 1996. "La grande transhumance à l'époque Romaine à propos des recherches sur la Crau d'Arles," *Anthropozoologica* 24: 31–44.

Capponi, F. 1959. "Le rôle de l'arundo dans l'oisellerie," *Latomus* 18: 724–41.

Carandini, A. 1984. *Settefinestre: Una villa schiavistica nell'Etruria meridionale.*Vol. 1, *La villa nel suo insieme*. Modena: Panini.

Chamoux, F., and G. Hallier 1996. "Le colombier d'Apollonias," in *Scritti di antichità in onore di Sandro Stucchi*. Vol. 1, *La Cirenaica: La Grecia e l'Oriente mediterraneo*. Rome: L'Erma di Bretschneider, 51–60.

Chandezon, C. 2003. *L'élevage en Grèce, fin Ve – fin Ier siècle a.C. L'apport des sources épigraphiques*. Bordeaux: Ausonius.

Chiliardi, S. 2000. "I cavalli siracusani in età ellenistica," in *Atti del 2 Convegno Nazionale di Archeozoologia, Asti, 14–16 Novembre 1997*. Forli: Abaco, 285–92.

Cleyet-Merle, J.-J. 1990. *La préhistoire de la pêche*. Paris: Errance.

Coles, C. L. (ed.) 1971. *The complete book of game conservation*. London: Barrie and Jenkins.

Collin-Bouffier, S. 1999. "La pisciculture dans le monde grec: État de la question," *Mélanges de l'École Française de Rome* 111: 37–50.

Colonnelli, G., G. M. Carpaneto, and M. Cristaldi 2000. "Uso alimentare e allevamento del ghiro (*Myoxus glis*) presso gli antichi romani: Materiale e documenti," in *Atti del 2 Convegno Nazionale di Archeozoologia, Asti, 14–16 Novembre 1997*. Forli: Abaco, 315–25.

Columeau, P. 2000. "Sacrifice et viande dans les sanctuaires grecs et chypriotes (VIIe siècle–Ier siècle av. J.C.) et l'apport de l'habitat de Kassopè," *Pallas* 52: 147–66.

Congès, G. 1997. "Bergeries et transhumance dans la Crau antique: Innovation et adaptation," in D. Garcia and D. Meeks (eds.), *Techniques et économie antiques et médévales: Le temps de l'innovation. Actes du colloque d'Aix-en-Provence, mai 1996*. Paris: Errance, 149–52.

Conta, G. D. 1972. "Note sulle pescherie marittime nel mondo romano," in G. Schmiedt (ed.), *Il livello antico del Mar Tirreno: Testimonianze dei resti archeologici*. Florence: Olschki, 215–36.

Corbier, M. 1999. "La transhumance: Aperçus historiographiques et acquis récents," in E. Hermon (ed.), *La question agraire à Rome: Droit romain et société: Perceptions historiques et historiographiques*. Como: Edizioni New Press, 37–57.

Cox, N. 1686. *The gentleman's recreation in four parts, viz. hunting, hawking, fowling, fishing*. London: Freeman Collins.

Cunliffe, B. 1971. *Excavations at Fishbourne, 1961–69*. London: Society of Antiquaries.

Cuvier, G., and M. A. Valenciennes 1828–1848. *Histoire naturelle des poissons*. 22 vols. Paris: F. G. Levrault.

D'Arrigo, A. 1956. "La pesca del pescespada in Calabria dal secondo sec. av. Cr. ai nostri tempi," *Archivio Storico di Calabria e la Lucania* 25 (1956) 101–21.

Davies, R. W. 1971. "The Roman military diet," *Britannia* 2: 122–42.

Davis, S. J. M. 1997. "The agricultural revolution in England: Some zoo-archaeological evidence," *Anthropozoologica* 25–26: 413–28.

de Vries, J. 1974. *The Dutch rural economy in the golden age, 1500–1700*. New Haven: Yale University Press.

De Angelis, R. 1959. *Fishing installations in brackish lagoons, General Fisheries Council for the Mediterranean*. Rome: FAO.

De Caro, S., and M. Boriello (eds.) 2001. *La natura morta nelle pitture e nei mosaici delle città vesuviane*. Naples: Electa Napoli.

de Grossi Mazzorin, J., A. Tagliacozzo, and A. Riedel 1998. "Horse remains in Italy from the Eneolithic to the Roman period," *Proceedings of the XIII International Congress of Prehistoric and Protohistoric Sciences, Forlì (Italia) 8–14 september 1996*. Forli: Abaco, 87–92.

Del Rosso, R. 1905. *Pesche e peschiere antiche e moderne nell'Etruria Marittima.* 2 vols. Firenze: Osvaldo Paggi.

Delacour, J. 1964. *The pheasants of the world.* London: Country Life.

Desse-Berset, N. 1993. "Contenus d'amphores et surpêche; l'exemple du Sud-Perduto," in J. Desse and F. Audoin-Rouzeau (eds.), *Exploitation des animaux sauvages à travers le temps: XIIIe Rencontres internationales d'archéologie et d'histoire d'Antibes, IVe colloque international de l'homme et l'animal, 15–17 octobre 1992.* Juan-les-Pins: Editions APDCA, 341–46.

Dumont, J. 1976–1977. "La pêche du thon à Byzance à l'époque hellénistique," *Revue des Études Anciennes* 78–79: 96–116.

Epplett, C. 2001. "The capture of animals by the Roman military," *Greece and Rome* 48: 210–22.

Escoffier, G.-A. 1984. *Ma cuisine.* New York: Random House.

Everynck, A., and K. Dobney 2002. "A pig for all seasons? Approaches to the assessment of second farrowing in archaeological pig populations," *Archaeofauna* 11: 7–22.

Farrington, E. I. 1913. *The home poultry book.* Toronto: McClelland and Goodchild.

Ferlin, G. R. 1989. *Elsevier's dictionary of the world's game and wildlife.* Amsterdam: Elsevier.

Flach, D. 1990. *Römische Agrargeschichte.* Munich: Beck.

Fletcher, T. J. 1989. "Deer farming in Europe," in R. J. Hudson et al. (eds.), *Wildlife production systems: Economic utilisation of wild ungulates.* Cambridge: Cambridge University Press, 323–33.

Food and Agricultural Organization 2002. *FISHSTAT Plus: Universal Software for Fishery Statistics Time Series, Version 2.3.* Rome: FAO.

Forest, V., and I. Rodet-Belarbi. 2000. "Ostéometrie et morphologie des bovins médiévaux et modernes en France méridionale," in M.-C. Marandet (ed.), *L'homme et l'animal dans les sociétés méditéranéennes: 4e journée d'études du Centre de Recherches Historiques sur les Sociétés Méditerranéennes et du Pôle Universitaire Européen de Montpellier et du Languedoc-Roussillon.* Perpignan: Presses Universitaires, 27–92.

Forest, V., and I. Rodet-Belarbi 2002. "À propos de la corpulence des bovins en France durant les périodes historiques," *Gallia* 59: 273–99.

Fox, M. W. 1984. *Farm animals: Husbandry, behaviour, and veterinary practice (Viewpoints of a critic).* Baltimore: University Park Press.

Frayn, J. M. 1984. *Sheep-rearing and the wool trade in Italy during the Roman period.* Liverpool: Cairns.

Frizell, B. S. 2004. "Curing the flock: The use of healing waters in Roman pastoral economy," in B. S. Frizell (ed.), *Pecus: Man and animal in antiquity. Proceedings of the conference of the Swedish Institute in Rome, September 9–12, 2002.* Rome: Swedish Institute in Rome, 84–97.

Gabriel, O., K. Lange, E. Dahm, and T. Wendt (eds.) 2005. *Von Brandt's fish catching methods of the world.* 4th ed. Oxford: Blackwell.

Gallant, T. W. 1985. *A fisherman's tale.* Gent: Peeters.

Georgoudi, S. 1990. *Des chevaux et des boeufs dans le monde grec: Réalités et représentations animalières à partir des livres XVI et XVII des "Géoponiques."* Paris and Athens: Daedalus.

Giacopini, L., B. B. Marchesini, and L. Rustico 1994. *L'itticoltura nell'antichità.* Rome: Istituto Grafico Editoriale Romano.

Gianfrotta, P. A. 1999. "Archeologia subacquea e testimonianze di pesca," *Mélanges de l'École française de Rome* 111: 9–36.

Gianfrotta, P. A. 2002. "Ponza (puntalizzazioni marittime)," *Archeologia Subacqea* 3: 67–90.

Gilbert, A. S. 2002. "The native fauna of the ancient Near East," in B. J. Collins, *A history of the animal world in the ancient Near East*. Leiden: Brill, 3–78.

Goodall, D. M. 1977. *A history of the domestic horse*. London: R. Hale.

Grant, A. 1988. "Food status and religion in England in the Middle Ages: An archae-ozoological perspective," in L. Bodson (ed.), *L'animal dans l'alimentation humaine – les critères du choix*. Paris: Anthropozoologica Numero Special, 139–46.

Guest-Papamanoli, A. 1986. "Ethnographie ou Ethnoarchéologie des ressources marines de sites cotiers: Le cas de la pêche aux muges dans les lagunes de la Grèce Occidentale," in *L'exploitation de la mer de l'antiquité à nos jours, I: La mer, lieu de production: V Rencontres internationales d'archéologie et d'histoire d'Antibes, 24, 25, 26 octobre 1984*. Juan-les-Pins: Éditions APDCA, 381–403.

Hansen-Catta, P.-H. 2002. *Larousse de la chasse d'aujourd'hui*. Paris: Larousse.

Heady, H. F., and R. D. Childs 1994. *Rangeland ecology and management*. Boulder, CO: Westview Press.

Heath, M., D. S. Metcalfe, and R. F. Barnes 1973. *Forages: The science of grassland agriculture*. Ames: Iowa State University Press.

Higginbotham, J. 1997. *Piscinae: Artificial fishponds in Roman Italy*. Chapel Hill: University of North Carolina Press.

Hodkinson, S. 1988. "Animal husbandry in the Greek polis," in C. R. Whitakker (ed.), *Pastoral economies in classical antiquity*. Cambridge: Cambridge Philological Society, 35–74.

Højte, J. M. 2005. "The archaeological evidence for fish processing in the Black Sea region," in Bekker-Nielsen 2005a: 133–60.

Houpt, K. A. 2005. "Maintenance behaviours," in D. S. Mills and S. M. McDonnell (eds.), *The domestic horse: The origins, development and management of its behaviour*. Cambridge: Cambridge University Press, 94–109.

Hudson, R. J. 1989. "History and technology," in R. J. Hudson et al. (eds.), *Wildlife production systems: Economic utilisation of wild ungulates*. Cambridge: Cambridge University Press, 11–27.

Huet, M. 1986. *Textbook of fish culture: Breeding and cultivation of fish*. 2nd ed. Farnham: Fishing News Books.

Hull, D. B. 1964. *Hounds and hunting in ancient Greece*. Chicago: University of Chicago Press.

Hurlburt, C. G., and S. W. Hurlburt 1980. "European mussel culture technology and its adaptability to North American waters," in R. A. Lutz (ed.), *Mussel culture and harvest: A North American perspective*. Amsterdam: Elsevier, 69–98.

Ivanova, N. V. 1994. "Fish remains from archaeological sites of the northern part of the Black Sea region (Olvia, Berezan)," *Offa* 51: 278–83.

Jacobsen, A. L. L. 2005. "The reliability of fishing statistics as a source for fish stocks and catches in antiquity," in Bekker-Nielsen 2005a: 97–104.

Jashemski, W. F., and F. G. Meyer (eds.) 2002. *The natural history of Pompeii*. Cambridge: Cambridge University Press.

Kajava, M. 1998–1999. "Murenae, oysters and gilt-heads. Fish for name, table, and show in ancient Rome," *Acta Classica Debrecensis* 34–35: 253–68.

Keller, O. 1909–1913. *Die antike Tierwelt*. 2 vols. Leipzig: Engelmann.

Kerridge, E. 1967. *The agricultural revolution*. London: Allen and Unwin.

King, A. C. 1984. "Animal bones and the dietary identity of military and civilian groups in Roman Britain, Germany and Gaul," in T. F. C. Blagg (ed.), *Military and civilian in Roman Britain*. Oxford: BAR, 187–217.

King, A. C. 2002. "Mammals: Evidence from wall paintings, sculpture, mosaics, faunal remains, and ancient literary sources," in Jashemski and Meyer 2002: 401–50.

Kokabi, M. 1988. "Viehhaltung und Jagd in römischen Rottweil," in *Arae Flaviae IV*. Stuttgart: Müller and Gräff, 105–234.

Kolendo, J. 1977. "Parcs à huîtres à Baiae sur un flacon en verre du Musée National de Varsovie," *Puteoli: Studi in storia antica* 1: 108–12.

Kotjabopoulou, E., Y. Hamilakis, P. Halstead, et al. (eds.) 2003. *Zooarchaeology in Greece: Recent advances*. British School at Athens Studies 9. Oxford: Oxbow.

Kron, G. 2000. "Roman ley-farming," *Journal of Roman Archaeology* 13: 277–97.

Kron, G. 2002. "Archaeozoology and the productivity of Roman livestock farming," *Münstersche Beiträge zur antike Handelsgeschichte* 21.2: 53–73.

Kron, G. 2004a. "Roman live-stock farming in southern Italy: The case against environmental determinism," in M. Clavel-Léveque and E. Hermon (eds.), *Espaces intégrés et gestion des ressources naturelles dans l'Empire romain*. Franche-Comté: Presses Universitaires de Franche-Comté, 119–34.

Kron, G. 2004b. "A deposit of carbonized hay from Oplontis and Roman fodder quality," *Mouseion* 4: 275–331.

Kron, G. forthcoming. "L'importance du poisson dans l'alimentation romaine et son effet sur le développement de la pisciculture à Rome," *Revue en Ligne, Points de vue*, Chaire de recherche du Canada en interactions société-environment dans l'empire romain (http://www.chaire-rome.hst.ulaval.ca/revue.htm).

Lafon, X. 2001. *Villa maritima: Recherches sur les villas littorales de l'Italie romaine, IIIe siècle av. J.C. – IIIe siècle ap. J.C.* Paris: Bibliothèque des Ecoles françaises d'Athènes et de Rome.

Lamblard, J.-M. 1975. "Les étapes de la domestication de la Pintade *Numida meleagris* Linné," in *L'homme et l'animal: 1er colloque d'Ethnozoologie*. Paris: Institut International d'Ethnosciences, 421–30.

Lauwerier, R. G. C. M. 1983. "Bird remains in Roman graves," *Archaeofauna* 2: 75–82.

Lauwerier, R. G. C. M. 1993. "Twenty-eight bird briskets in a pot: Roman preserved food from Nijmegen," *Archaeofauna* 2: 101–13.

Leclainche, E. 1936. *Histoire de la médecine vétérinaire*. Paris: Office du Livre.

Leguilloux, M. 1999. "Sacrifices et repas publics dans le sanctuaire de Poséidon à Ténos: Les analyses archéozoologiques," *Bulletin de Correspondance Hellénique* 123: 423–55.

Leguilloux, M. 2000. "L'alimentation carnée au Ier millénaire avant J.C. en Grèce continentale et dans les Cyclades: Premiers résultats archéozoologiques," *Pallas* 52: 69–95.

Lehman, P., and G. Breuer 1997. "The use-specific and social-topographical differences found in the composition of animal species found in the Roman city of Augusta Raurica (Switzerland)," *Anthropozoologica* 25–26: 487–94.

Lemming, G. E. 1969. "Nutrition and reproduction," in D. P. Cuthbertson (ed.), *Nutrition of animals of agricultural importance*. Vol. 1, *The science of nutrition of farm livestock*. Oxford: Pergamon Press, 411–53.

Lepetz, S. 1996. *L'animal dans la société gallo-romaine de la France du Nord*. Amiens: Révue Archéologique de Picardie.

Leveau, P. 2004. "L'herbe et la pierre dans les textes anciens sur la Crau: Relire les sources écrites," *Ecologia Mediterranea* 30: 25–33.

Leveau, P., and M. Segard 2003. "Le pastoralisme en Gaule du Sud entre plaine et montagne: De la Crau aux Alpes du Sud," *Pallas* 55: 93–113.

Leveau, P., P. Sillières, and J.-P. Vallat 1993. *Campagnes de la Méditerranée Romaine: Occident*. Paris: Hachette.

Lindner K. 1973. *Beiträge zu Vogelfang und Falknerei im Altertum*. Berlin: de Gruyter.

Lirb, H. J. 1993. "Partners in Agriculture: The pooling of resources in rural *societates* in Roman Italy," in H. Sancisi-Weerdenburg (ed.), *De Agricultura: In memoriam Pieter Willem de Neeve (1945–1990)*. Amsterdam: J. C. Gieben, 263–95.

Longo, O. 1989. *Le forme della predazione: Cacciatori e pescatori nella Grecia antica*. Naples: Liguori Editore.

Lubtchansky, N. 1998. "Le pêcheur et la mètis: Pêche et statut social en Italie centrale à l'époque archaïque," *Mélanges de l'École Française de Rome* 110: 111–46.

Lugli, G. 1928. *Forma Italiae* Vol. 1, part 2, *Ager Pomptinus, Circeii*. Rome: Danesi.

MacGregor, A. 1996. "Swan rolls and beak markings: Husbandry, exploitation and regulation of *Cygnus olor* in England, c. 1100–1900," *Anthropozoologica* 25–26: 39–68.

MacKinnon, M. R. 2001. "High on the hog: Linking zooarchaeological, literary and artistic data for pig breeds in Roman Italy," *American Journal of Archaeology* 105: 649–73.

MacKinnon, M. R. 2004. *Production and consumption of animals in Roman Italy: Integrating the zooarchaeological and textual evidence. Journal of Roman Archaeology* Suppl. 54. Portsmouth, RI: JRA.

Magerstedt, A. F. 1859. *Die Viehzucht der Römer für Archäologen und wissenschaftliche gebildete Landwirthe*. Walluf: Sändig.

Mair, A. W. 1928. *Oppian, Colluthus, Tryphiodorus, with an English translation*. Cambridge, MA: Harvard University Press.

Martin, B. P. 1993. *Wildfowl of the British Isles and north-west Europe*. Devon: Newton Abbot.

Mastromarco, Giuseppe 1998. "La pesca del tonno nella Grecia antica: Dalla realtà quotidiana alla metafora poetica," *Rivista di Cultura Classica e Medioevale* 40: 229–36.

McCann, A. M., J. Bourgeois, E. K. Gazda, J. P. Oleson, and E. L. Will 1987. *The Roman port and fishery of Cosa: A center of ancient trade*. Princeton: Princeton University Press.

Ministry of Agriculture and Forestry, New Zealand 1994. "Market dynamics for venison," http://www.maf.gov.nz/mafnet/rural-nz/profitability-and-economics/structural-change/market-dynamics-for-venison/conf4-03.htm.

Montagné, P. 1961. *Larousse Gastronomique*. New York: Crown Publishers.

Moriceau, J.-M. 1999. *L'élevage sous l'Ancien Régime: Les fondements agraires de la France moderne, XVIe–XVIIIe siècles*. Paris: SEDES.

Morris, P. 1979. *Agricultural buildings in Roman Britain*. British Archaeological Reports 70. Oxford: BAR.

Moulé, L. 1891. *Histoire de la médecine vétérinaire. Première periode: Histoire de la médecine vétérinaire dans l'antiquité*. Paris: Bulletin de la Société Centrale de Médecine Vétérinaire.

Naether, C. A. 1964. *The Book of the pigeon and of wild foreign doves*. 5th ed. New York: D. McKay.

Olive, C., and S. Deschler-Erb 1999. "Poulets de grain et rôtis du cerf: Produits de luxe pour les villes Romaines," *Archäologie der Schweiz* 22: 35–38.

Olson, S. D., and A. Sens 2000. *Archestratos of Gela: Greek culture and cuisine in the fourth century BCE*. Oxford: Oxford University Press.

Osborne, R. 1987. *Classical landscape with figures: Ancient Greek city-states and their countryside*. London: Sheridan House.

Ostrow, S. 1979. "The topography of Puteoli and Baiae on the eight glass flasks," *Puteoli: Studi di Storia Antica* 3: 77–140.

Pagano, M. 1983–1984. "Il lago Lucrino: Ricerche storiche e archeologiche," *Puteoli: Studi di Storia Antica* 7–8: 113–226.

Parker, A. J. 1988. "The birds of Roman Britain," *Oxford Journal of Archaeology* 7: 197–226.

Pasquinucci, M. 2004. "Montagna e pianura: transumanza e allevamento," in M. Clavel-Léveque and E. Hermon (eds.), *Espaces intégrés et gestion des ressources naturelles dans l'Empire romain*. Franche-Comté: Presses Universitaires de Franche-Comté, 165–78.

Pattison, I. 1984. *The British veterinary profession, 1791–1948*. London: Allen.

Pawson, H. C. 1957. *Robert Bakewell: Pioneer livestock breeder*. London: Lockwood.

Payne, S. 1985. "Zoo-archaeology in Greece: A reader's guide," in N. C. Wilkie and W. D. E. Coulson (eds.), *Contributions to Aegean archaeology: Studies in honor of William A. McDonald*. Dubuque, IA: Kendall/Hunt Publishing, 211–44.

Peters, J. 1998. *Römische Tierhaltung und Tierzucht: Eine Synthese aus archäozoologischer Untersuchung und schriftlich-bildlicher Überlieferung*. Rahden: Leidorf.

Pinto-Guillaume, E. M. 2001. "Observations on a very singular oyster," in G. Missineo (ed.), *Ad Gallinas Albas: Villa di Livia*. Rome: L'Erma di Bretschneider, 209–11.

Pleket, H. W. 1993. "Agriculture in the Roman Empire in comparative perspective," in H. Sancisi-Weerdenburg (ed.), *De Agricultura: In memoriam Pieter Willem de Neeve (1945–1990)*. Amsterdam: Gieben, 214–37.

Pollard, J. 1977. *Birds in Greek life and myth*. London: Thames and Hudson.

Prummel, W. 1987. "Poultry and fowling at the Roman era *castellum*," *Palaeohistoria* 29: 183–201.

Purcell, N. 1995. "Eating fish: The paradoxes of seafood," in J. Wilkins, D. Harvey, and M. Dobson (eds.), *Food in antiquity*. Exeter: Exeter University Press, 132–49.

Purpura, G. 1992. "Pesca e stabilimenti antichi per la lavorazione di pesce nella Sicilia occidentale: IV un bilancio," in *V Rassegna di archeologia subacquea, Atti (Giardini Naxos 19–21 ottobre 1990)*. Messina: Edizioni P&M Associati, 87–101.

Quilici-Gigli, S. 1989. "Paesaggi storici dell'agro falisco: I prata di Corchiano," *Opuscula Romana* 17: 123–35.

Reese, D. S. 1994. "Recent work in Greek zooarchaeology," in P. N. Kardoulias (ed.), *Beyond the site: Regional studies in the Aegean area*. Lanham, MD: University Presses of America, 191–221.

Reese, D. S. 2002a. "Fish: Evidence from specimens, mosaics, wall paintings, and Roman authors," in Jashemski and Meyer 2002: 274–91.

Reese, D. S. 2002b. "Marine invertebrates, freshwater shells, and land snails: Evidence from specimens, mosaics, wall paintings, sculpture, jewelry, and Roman authors," in Jashemski and Meyer 2002: 292–314.

Rendini, P. 1997. "Vasi per la pesca del polpo?" in *Atti del convegno nazionale di archeologia subacquea, Anzio 30–31 maggio e 1° giugno 1996*. Bari: Edipuglia, 75–78.

Ridgeway, W. 1905. *Origin and influence of the thoroughbred horse*. Cambridge: Cambridge University Press.

Riedel, A. 1994. "Archaeozoological investigations in north-eastern Italy: The exploitation of animals since the Neolithic," *Preistoria Alpina* 30: 43–94.

Rinkewitz, W. 1984. *Pastio Villatica: Untersuchungen zur intensiven Hoftierhaltung in der römischen Landwirtschaft*. Frankfurt am Main: Lang.

Rocher, C. 1979. *Les chasses des palombes et des tourterelles*. Bordeaux: Editions de l'Orée.

Romdhane, M. S. 1998. "La pêche artisanale en Tunisie: Évolution des techniques ancestrales," *Mélanges de l'École Française d'Athènes* 110: 61–80.

Rosada, G. 2000. "La centuriazione di Padova nord (Cittadella–Bassano) come assetto territoriale e sfruttamento delle risorse: Una riflessione dallo studio di Plinio Fraccaro," *Aquileia Nostra* 71: 85–122.

Rossi, R. 1990. "Gli atrezzi di pesca," in F. Berti (ed.), *Fortuna maris: La nave romana di Comacchio*. Bologna: Nuova Alfa Editoriale, 114–15.

Ryder, M. L. 1983. *Sheep and man*. London: Duckworth.

Ryder, M. L., and J. W. Hedges 1973. "Ancient Scythian wool from the Crimea," *Nature* 242: 480.

Sahrhage, D. 2002. *Die Schätze Neptuns: Eine Kulturgeschichte der Fischerei im römischen Reich*. Frankfurt am Main: Lang.

Sallares, R. M. 1991. *The ecology of the ancient Greek world*. London: Duckworth.

Salza Prina Ricotti, E. 1987. "Alimentazione, cibi, tavola e cucine nell'età imperiale," in *L'alimentazione nel mondo antico*. Rome: Istituto poligrafico e Zecca dello Stato, 71–130.

Salza Prina Ricotti, E. 1999. "L'importanza del pesce nella vita, nel costume e nell'industria del mondo antico," *Rendiconti: Atti della Pontificia Accademia Romana di Archeologia* 71: 111–65.

Schmiedt, G. 1972. *Il livello antico del Mar Tirreno: Testimonianze dei resti archeologici*. Florence: Olschki.

Senet, A. 1953. *Histoire de la médecine vétérinaire*. Paris: PUF.

Shepherd, C. J., and N. R. Bromage 1988. *Intensive fish farming*. Oxford: Blackwell.

Shepherd, E. J., and L. Dallai 2003. "Attività di pesca al promontorio di Piombino (I sec.a.C.–XI sec.d.C.)," in *Atti del II Convegno di Archeologia Subacquea, Castiglioncello 7–9 settembre 2001*. Bari: Edipuglia, 189–207.

Sicsi, R. 1992. "La pesca nell'area dello Stretto di Messina nell'antichità: Continuità fra presente e passato," in *V Rassegna di archeologia subacquea. V Premio Franco Papò. Atti. Giardini Naxos 19–21 ottobre 1990*. Messina: P&M Associati, 127–46.

Sternberg, M. 1995. *La pêche à Lattes dans l'antiquité à travers l'analyse du ichtyofaune*. Lattes: Lattara.

Sternberg, M. 1998. "Les produits de la pêche et la modification des structures halieutiques en Gaule Narbonnaise du IIIe siècle av. J.-C. au Ier siècle ap. J.-C. Les données de Lattes (Hérault), Marseille (Bouches-du-Rhone) et Olbia-de-Provence (Var)," *Mélanges de l'École Française de Rome et d'Athènes* 110: 81–109.

Sternberg, M. 2005a. "La pêche," in M.-P. Rothé and H. Tréziny (eds.), *Marseille et ses alentours. Carte Archéologique de la Gaule 13/3*. Paris: Belles Lettres, 245–47.

Sternberg, M. 2005b. "L'élevage," in M.-P. Rothé and H. Tréziny (eds.), *Marseille et ses alentours. Carte Archéologique de la Gaule 13/3*. Paris: Belles Lettres, 247–49.

Tammisto, A. 1997. *Birds in mosaics: A study on the representation of birds in Hellenistic and Romano-Campanian tessellated mosaics to the early Augustan age*. Rome: Gummerus Kirjapano Oy.

Thompson, E. P. 1975. *Whigs and hunters: The origin of the Black Act*. London: Lane Allen.

Thompson, D. W. 1936. *A glossary of Greek birds*, 2nd ed. London: Oxford University Press.

Thüry, G. E. 1990. "Römische Austerfunde in der Schweiz, im rechtsrheinischen Süddeutschland und in Österreich," in *Festschrift für Hans R. Stampfli – Beiträge zur Archäozoologie, Archäologie, Anthropologie, Geologie und Paläontologie*. Basel: Helbing and Lichtenhahn, 285–301.

Toynbee, J. M. C. 1973. *Animals in Roman life and art*. Ithaca, NY: Cornell University Press.

Trakadas, A. 2005. "The archaeological evidence for fish processing in the western Mediterranean," in Bekker-Nielsen 2005a: 47–82.

Trench, C. C. 1967. *The poacher and the squire: A history of poaching and game preservation in England*. London: Longmans.

Trotta, F. 1990. "Le reti di pesca nell'antichità classica," in *Quel filo azzuro tra l'uomo e il lago*. Bergamo: Gruppo Editoriale Walk Over, 34–46.

Trotta, F. 1996. "La pesca nel mare di Magna Grecia e Sicilia," in F. Prontera (ed.), *La Magna Grecia e il mare: Studi di storia marittima*. Taranto: Istituto per la Storia e L'Archeologia della Magna Grecia, 227–50.

Trow-Smith, R. 1959. *A history of British livestock husbandry, 1700–1900*. London: Routledge and Kegan Paul.

Udrescu, M., and W. Van Neer 2005. "Looking for human therapeutic intervention in the healing of fractures of domestic animals," in J. Davies et al. (eds.), *Diet and health in past animal populations: Current research and future directions*. Oxford: Oxbow, 24–33.

Vigneron, P. 1968. *Le cheval dans l'antiquité gréco-romaine: Des guerres médiques aux grandes invasions. Contribution à l'histoire des techniques*. Nancy: Faculté des lettres et des sciences humaines de l'Université.

Watson, G. E. 2002. "Birds: Evidence from wall paintings, mosaics, sculpture, skeletal remains and ancient authors," in Jashemski and Meyer 2002: 357–400.

White, K. D. 1970. *Roman farming*. New York: Thames and Hudson.

Wynmalen, H. 1950. *Horse breeding and stud management*. London: Country Life.

Youatt, William. 1837. *Sheep: Their breeds, management, and diseases*. London: Baldwin and Craddock.

Zeuner, F. E. 1963. *A history of domesticated animals*. London: Hutchinson.

Zissu, B. 1995. "Two Herodian dovecotes: Horvat Abu Haf and Horvat 'Aleq," in *The Roman and Byzantine Near East: Some recent archaeological research. Journal of Roman Archaeology* Suppl. 14. Ann Arbor, MI: JRA, 57–69.

# PART III

# ENGINEERING AND COMPLEX MACHINES

.....................................................................................................

# CHAPTER 9

# GREEK ENGINEERING AND CONSTRUCTION

.....................................................................................................

## FREDERICK A. COOPER

THIS discussion for the most part deals with public structures, in particular temple architecture. This bias results from the emphasis the Greeks themselves placed on public structures at the expense of private homes and commercial establishments, a focus which resulted in structures that pushed the boundaries of the materials and the procedures for design and construction. Only in the mid-Hellenistic period did this pattern begin to change. The best temples, stoas, and theaters represent vividly what the Greek architect and engineer could accomplish, making them paradigms for a study of Greek engineering technology. Many of the modern handbooks cited in this chapter provide further information on domestic and utilitarian architecture, and several chapters in this book will provide further information on the considerable Greek expertise in hydraulic engineering (chapter 11), tunnel and canal construction (chapter 12), construction cranes (chapter 13), and harbor design (chapter 25). Since ancient Greek architects based their designs on engineering and structural theory and practice, the organization of this chapter intentionally follows the section topics typical of a modern engineering and construction handbook (e.g., Merritt and Rickets 2000; cf. Merritt 1975, 1976).

As early as Theodorus of Samos (ca. 575 B.C.; Vitruvius, *De arch.* 7, preface 12), architects wrote books on architecture, presumably treatises setting forth their ideas on the facts and theory of construction. The handbook *De architectura* by the Roman architect Vitruvius (late first century B.C.) cites earlier texts, but his own approach emphasizes architectural design, especially the history and use of the canons, the application of proportions and modular dimensions, designs dictated by function, architectural refinements, and the advantages of siting buildings for exploitation of sun, wind, and natural resources. Vitruvius devotes shorter sections to building materials, construction machinery, foundations, and surveying. The former topics are not customarily included in a builder's engineering handbook, but the latter certainly are. From the time of the renaissance scholarship on Greek architecture, the study of Greek architecture has been wedded to Vitruvian precepts on appearance and proportion and the spatial planning of buildings as a point of departure to a study of the topic. But while Vitruvius touches on topics that extend from mathematics to medicine, the fact is that he provides little insight for an understanding of the architectural engineering that went into ancient Greek building practice.

I propose that the engineering observed in ancient building practice expresses a coherent set of rules and procedures founded in experience and preserved and passed along in an oral tradition, or better, by written handbooks. The works of Theophrastus (ca. 370–288/5 B.C.), pupil and successor to Aristotle, especially his *Inquiry into Plants* (*Peri phyton,* or *Historia plantarum*) and *On Stones* (*Peri lithon,* or *De lapidibus*), provide clear evidence for a body of scientific theory and engineering practice behind the applications of scientific technology to building. The distinction between engineering and construction technology should be emphasized. Certainly the theories embodied in engineering lead to the technology, but the reverse process does not always follow. Empirical applications of a technology, even a sophisticated technology, can happen in the absence of engineering theory and computation.

The invaluable surveys of Martin (1965), Orlandos (1966–1968), White (1984), Coulton (1977), and Hellmann (2002) provide a wealth of evidence for the technologies behind the practice of architecture in ancient Greece. Landels (2000: 210) omits architecture but compliments Vitruvius for his "common sense and guesswork." Published abstracts by the occasional symposium on ancient Greek technology recognize the breadth and range of ancient Greek technology in all its aspects; few, however, address whether or not this technology comes at the front end of an underlying scientific, engineering practice (e.g., Tassios and Palyvou 2006). This chapter rests on the proposition that construction theory, especially the mechanics of building materials—principally wood and stone, but others as well— and aseismic design constituted the starting point for Greek architectural design. Proportions, siting, propriety of architectural decoration, and use of the orders certainly played a part in the design process, but the genius lay in the engineering, not in the tweaking of style. My aim is to show the existence of an ancient scientific approach through juxtaposition of the evidence for Greek practice with pertinent excerpts from contemporary engineering construction handbooks.

For example, Theophrastus' *Inquiry into Plants*, especially book 5, contains all the earmarks of a modern-day handbook on wood construction. He has collected testimonia from lumbermen: lumberjacks, sawyers, jobbers, carpenters, wholesalers, and *architektones*, specialists working with species of wood indigenous to their home regions. Theophrastus understood that various grades of the same wood, or the same timber cut in different ways, can have different strengths and characteristics when used as a building material. He set out clear guidelines as to appropriate use of species of oak—kermes, cork, holm, and turkey—noting that some oaks are hard, some easily worked, while others are only good for firewood (cf. also chapters 10 and 17).

# BACKGROUND: THE ARCHAEOLOGICAL EVIDENCE

My involvement in the inventory and recovery of demolished ancient Greek buildings has led in all cases to reconstructions on paper and to actual reconstruction or anastylosis for some (F. A. Cooper 1992–1996). This process has afforded many opportunities to observe the ancient architect's understanding of foundations and aseismic design, strength of materials, paving, ceiling and roof systems—a set of topics far closer to what is found in a modern building engineering and construction handbook than to what Vitruvius presents (F. A. Cooper 1983, 1999). Another modern-day experience is relevant. With the AutoCAD software application it is possible to program scripts in AutoLISP. In using this system, my purpose was to generate plan and elevation drawings of not only the standard *corpus* of Greek temples, but also the lesser known and the newly discovered. The AutoLISP program prompts for basic dimensions of the kind found in the tables in Dinsmoor (1950: fold-out chart) and Robertson (1964: 322–46): length and width of stylobate, facade, and flank; bottom column diameters; height of colonnade and entablature. Missing measurements can be supplied by secondary information, such as proportions indexed by approximate date. The program computes a Drawing Unit and generates a plan and an elevation. A plan of the cella and other details are added to the AutoCAD drawing. This computer generation of a plan and elevation simply automates what the ancient Greek architect must have done routinely: manipulation of proportions and modules, alteration and improvement of details such as the glyph design or an extra triglyph over the intercolumniation. This was the humdrum part of architectural practice; the real expertise lay in the engineering that underlay the design of structurally successful Greek architecture.

The scholarship on architectural construction in ancient Greece frequently reflects the widely held but erroneous assumption that architects adhered to a pan-Hellenic standard of measurement or an absolute length (or lengths), such as a Doric or Ionic foot or an Ionian ell. These measurements, however, varied from town to town and from project to project, but were usually a value between 0.27 m and 0.36 m (Pakkanen 2004, 2006: 227; cf. chapter 30, part 1).

# Design Stage

Vitruvius (*De arch.* 3.4.5) writes of stylobate curves in temples, achieved by the use of *scamilli impares*, and other kinds of subtle deflections from the true: the tilting and curving of verticals and horizontal lines and planes, called refinements (Haselberger 1999). These deflections began to appear in the sixth century B.C. as exaggerations visible to the naked eye; over time the refinements became increasingly subtle, and not perceptible except by careful measurement with modern instruments. Such refinements required the utmost control in surveying. On the one hand, there is no apparent structural or visual necessity; on the other hand, the slightest amount of settlement in any of a building's components renders useless the optimal effort and care to achieve one or more of the refinements. In other words, a stable foundation construction permitted successful, in the sense of long-lasting, architectural refinements. There is a standing assumption that earthquakes felled many buildings across the Greek mainland. In fact, in most cases, human demolition, not natural forces, leveled Greek architecture.

## Structural Design

Coulton (1977: 140) provides a sweeping judgment of Greek architectural design: "Structural conservatism is inherent in the Greek conception of architecture as concerned primarily with external form rather than internal space.... Changes in structure could not make it cheaper." Coulton qualifies this statement by brief references to quality control of stone and to the evolution of clamp design. At the same time, he and others overlook the impressive accomplishments of the Greek architect as engineer: the loading of a colonnade on a continuous base on fill under a foundation requires an understanding of the engineering problems of differential loading-stress. This is just one aspect of engineering in which the Greek architect continuously made improvements over time. It should also be stressed that, with a few exceptions, successful engineering applications did not come and go. The simple truss system, for example, seems to appear in structures only during the Roman Empire (cf. chapters 10 and 17).

## Business, Art, and the Profession of Greek Architecture

The financial practice of an ancient Greek architect differed little from that of a successful architectural practice today: a professional who manages his personal finances and the budget of his project. Some ancient contracts contained provisions to award the architect for a project coming under budget, while specifying a penalty and personal assessment for projects more than a quarter over estimate. The reasons for a client's choice of an architect in ancient Greece are as unfathomable as a client's motivations now. Reputation counted a great deal, but there may have been a preference for a local professional—such as Libon of Elis, "a local man" according to Pausanias (5.10.3), for the design of the temple of Zeus at Olympia (ca. 457 B.C.). More broadly, reconstruction of the venerable temple of Apollo at Delphi, destroyed by a landslide in 373 B.C., was undertaken by the Amphictyonic League, an alliance of Greek states, which raised funds from public and private sources. The league appointed Spintharus of Corinth as architect (Pausanias 10.5.13). Construction lingered for 40 years, and successor architects included Xenodorus and Agathon.

Among the several hundred ancient Greek architectural projects known by name, many were collaborations; for example, Antistates, Callaeschrus, Antimachides, and Porinus for the design of the giant temple of Zeus Olympius at Athens (ca. 525 B.C.; Vitruvius, *De arch. 7*, preface 15). These architects were members of the intellectual circle of the Pisistratids, which included philosophers. A bias toward teams of intellectuals certainly persisted to the age of Pericles, who engaged the likes of Phidias, Ictinus, Callicrates, and other artists and architects in the building programs in Athens in the third quarter of the fifth century B.C. (Plutarch, *Per.* 12.1–13.8). There are instances in which slaves were appointed architects for a major temple. Examples include Demetrias of Ephesus (ca. 350 B.C.; Vitruvius, *De arch. 7*, preface 16) and, quite possibly, Ictinus, architect of the Parthenon, a phase of the Telesterion at Eleusis, and the temple of Apollo at Bassae (ca. 450–410 B.C.; F. A. Cooper 1992–1996: I, 377). In antiquity, as today, the term *architektones* (architect) could indicate any number of roles: master designer, principal contractor, overseer, master craftsman, architect-builder, or builder-architect. "Architect" is here taken to mean the professional who contributed to all aspects of the building project from concept and design through execution (Coulton 1977: 15; McCredie 1979).

The ancient architect-designer often produced a model or drawing for public discussion and approval (Coulton 1977: 51–73; Petronotis 1972; Haselberger 1997). A few inscribed decrees survive in which the architect is directed to draw up specifications for construction: temple of Athena Nike (*IG* $1^3$ 35), the arsenal of Philo (*IG* $2^2$ 1668), and a temple at Lebadia (*IG* 7 3073; Martin 1965: 189–90). Equally common, inscribed accounts of a building project were put on public display, the most famous being those for the Parthenon (*IG* $I^3$ 436–51; Pollitt 1990: 185–205).

# GEOTECHNICAL ENGINEERING

The built structures of mainland Greece are in various conditions of preservation. It is widely assumed that the natural phenomenon of earthquakes was responsible for leveling the many buildings of ancient Greece, but this is not the case. High winds toppled more columns than did earthquakes, and those buildings in the worst shape were demolished in the late antique period to recover the metal clamps and dowels. Had human destruction not intervened, much ancient Greek architecture would still be standing today, as do the temple at Bassae, the Hephaisteion in Athens, and a number of Greek temples in Italy and Turkey. Along with the Parthenon, these structures were engineered far beyond what any contemporary engineer or architect would call the test of time, putting them into a special class "of the best final design and construction" (Ambrayses 1971: 379).

The ancient Greeks held the sanctity of site, prominence on the skyline, and situation within a sanctuary to be of greater importance than the quality of soil and rock on which a temple or building was constructed. Unavoidable and unpredictable soil conditions at building locations led to geotechnical engineering, sophisticated even by modern standards. The fifth-century B.C. architect did not have at his disposal tests for rock mechanics, formulae for load distributions, or tables of presumptive standards for soil types. In fact, until the 1950s, architects and engineers could only hope that rock conditions would not cause trouble, and "most foundation designs were based on assumed properties deduced from surface observation" (Harvey 1982: I).

## Foundation Design

The accumulated evidence at most Greek sites points to architectural components designed or laid to maximize the geotechnical properties of the stone: foundations that double the bearing capacity of the poor bedrock underneath. The design represents as well the highly successful drainage of water off the foundations. Frequently, limestones were selected that had nearly the same appearance as the local limestone, but double the bearing strength. There was also systematic quarrying and coursing of ashlars and drums, keeping the planar structure of the stone horizontal when in compression, and vertical for suspension in unsupported spans. The list is impressive and consistent: the architect knew and grasped geotechnical engineering and the mechanics of his materials.

The archaeological evidence for a survey of ancient Greek engineering practice in sub-foundation preparation is limited by the failure of early excavators to excavate properly ancient backfills against the perimeters of buildings, a difficult undertaking. Nonetheless, in those cases where excavation reports are sufficiently detailed, there is evidence for a mat foundation, consisting of large rock fragments and boulders contained by cribbing walls for lateral stabilization, which isolates the platform from bedrock. Often there was a bed of silty clay or soil, alone or in conjunction with the stone layer. A mat foundation with a spread footing placed within it represents an excellent solution to the problem of a low bearing capacity of the terrain, but its function goes far beyond this single purpose. This type of foundation also incorporates an aseismic design called "base isolation," an alternative to "conventional methods [that] seek to protect buildings against earthquake attack by increasing the strength of structures and their capacity to dissipate energy. Seismic regulations require that the earthquake attack be absorbed by inelastic action of the structural system" (Merritt 1976: arts. 6-99, 6-116; cf. Merritt 1975: arts. 3-84). Kelly (1982: 17) sets forth the principles of this alternative system, aseismic base isolation, in which the "base reduces the transmission of horizontal acceleration into the structure."

In the mid-sixth century B.C., the sculptor and all-around inventor Theodorus of Samos acquired additional fame for his substructure beneath the temple of Artemis at Ephesus. Pliny (*HN* 36.95–97) gives credit to Theodorus' expertise: "[The temple of Ephesus] was constructed on marshy ground so that it would be neither subject to earthquakes nor in danger of earth-slips; on the other hand in order that such massive work would not be placed on shifting and unstable foundations, they were underlain with a layer of packed charcoal, and after that with a layer of sheepskins with the fleece." Diogenes Laertius (2.103) gives an abbreviated account in which Theodorus "advised the placing of a layer of ashes beneath the foundations of the temple in Ephesus."

In 1870, John T. Wood sank four trenches at the temple of Artemis, three in the cella and one in the northern peristyle, where he found a four-inch-thick (ca. 0.10 m) layer of "putty" (a form of mortar?) underneath a layer of charcoal, and beneath that another layer of "putty" (Hogarth 1908: 10–11). The layers have not been detected in subsequent excavations, nor have the wooly sheepskins mentioned by Pliny, but the deposits of charcoal alternating with other materials, including marble chips, appear in cross-sections and hint at an engineering solution of "base isolation" (cf. Bammer 1984: figs. 78, 79, 82, 113). Bammer's so-called *Hekatempedos*

Figure 9.1. Delphi, massive settlement of walls. (Photograph by F. Cooper.)

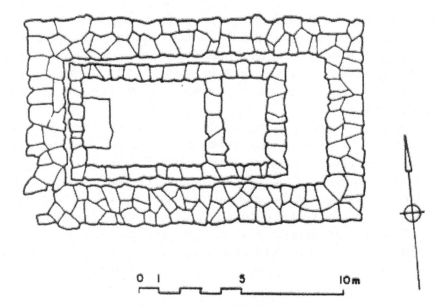

Figure 9.2. Polygonal foundation stonework, Demetrias temple. (F. Cooper, adapted from Bequignon 1937: pl. 3.)

looks more like a layer of packed stone fill (Bammer 1984–85: 13–28, figs. 1, 17, 20; cf. Vetters 1986: 78–79, figs. 1–4).

The terrace that supported the temple of Apollo at Delphi quite likely retained large unhewn stones and reused building blocks in a mat foundation comparable to that at Bassae and elsewhere. A mass of large stones still lies behind the southeast inside corner of the polygonal wall at Delphi (Algren-Ussing and Bramnaes 1975: N180–N190; W130–W170); the area, however, had been used as a dump for miscellaneous excavated material (Amandry 1981: 679). A gap or an interlayer of earth between the Acropolis bedrock and the foundation course of the Parthenon also indicates a possible design of base isolation, as do photographs and drawings of the sub-foundations along the south side. Here thick layers of huge stones, both unhewn blocks and discarded building material, were interlayered with earth (Kawerau et al. 1974: figs. 38, 59–62, 82; Tschira 1972: pls. 1–2; Korres 1983: 11–12, 667; Orlandos 1977: vol. 2, fig. 75). A mat foundation similar to those just described underlies the temple of Nemesis at Rhamnus. "Temporary" or cribbing walls inside the outer retaining walls stabilized the large rock fill. Petrakos (1983: 10) exposed the fabric of "an artificially made terrace, supported on the north and east by strong isodomic retaining walls erected in the fifth century B.C. before the large temple was built."

Merritt's engineering handbook (1976: art. 7-7) states that "A successful design distributes concentrated loads in order to inhibit differential settlements." A spread footing, running underneath the peristyle and common nearly to all Greek designs, achieves this very end with the additional advantage of transmitting the concentrated loads at the intercolumniations over as wide an area as possible. This design reduces the weight-to-area ratio appreciably and ensures that the maximum loads do not exceed the bearing capacity of a usually unstable rock terrain (Herubin and

a.

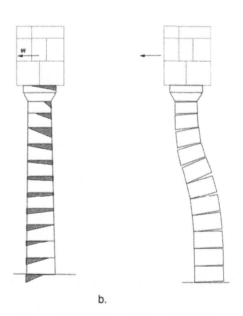

b.

Figure 9.3. a. Shifted column drums, Hephaisteion, Athens; b. Resistance of Doric columns to seismic stress. (F. Cooper, adapted from Ambraseys 1985.)

Marotta 1987: 43–7). Sometime in the fourth century B.C., soft, brown conglomerate or a red breccia became a standard material for sub-foundation construction, especially in Attica. Where the conglomerate was not placed underground, it was encased by a durable limestone facing, often of Peireus *poros*. A crumbly volcanic rock also became a common foundation material (Thompson and Wycherly 1972: 37, 80, 104, 129, 160–61, 167; Kousell and Dimou 2006: 29). The conglomerate or breccia consists of a coarse, reddish material, tending to degrade when exposed to the weather, but, like a rubble stone core, absorbing stresses from settlement or seismic waves by means of shifts brought about by micro-fracturing. The conglomerate base served the same engineering design principle as the aseismic mat foundation mentioned earlier.

The skewed and unclamped jointing of blocks in basement courses (biased jointing) retards differential settlement in the area where settlement is most likely to happen (F. A. Cooper 1992–1996: vol. 3, pl. 39.b–d; vol. 4, pl. 9). Polygonal jointing was not uncommon in the construction of foundations. It was used, for instance, in the later temple of Aphaea on Aegina and in the Tholos at Delphi. In all cases, the joint work in the substructure does not mesh with the jointing in the platform, thus distributing subsidence evenly over a wide area rather than through a seam of vertical joints. All too often, this polygonal stonework in foundation courses has been associated with archaic masonry technique (Shear 1971: 243–55), but this design was structural, not stylistic. The technique was used for foundation jointing into the Hellenistic period (Stählin et al. 1934: pls. 47–48), e.g., for the foundations to the temple of Artemis Agoria at Demetrias (Bequignon 1937: pl. 3) for the temple of Zeus at Pherae, and for the temple at Hermione (figures 9.1–2).

## Hydraulics and Building Construction

Drainage is crucial to foundation stabilization procedures because the strength of soil generally decreases with an increase in water content. Retention of ground water produces several adverse effects: pore water reduces the cohesiveness of soil particles, increases plasticity, and thereby increases the potential for slippage (Merritt 1975: art. 4-11; 1976: art. 7-15). When loaded, soil consolidation takes place through the voiding of water, often resulting in unpredictable settlement and deformation. Moreover, saturation of certain rocks, such as limestones, can reduce compressive strengths (Vutukuri 1974: 50–57). Tests have demonstrated that the temple podia at Bassae and Messene were constructed so as to dissipate all ground water rapidly and completely. At both sites and elsewhere the subfoundation consists of alternating layers of earthy clay and small cobblestones. Tests consisted of pumping water under pressure into borings and a systematic observation of the effects. The mat foundation design of other structures provided this benefit as well.

Comparison of an ancient solution with contemporary geotechnical procedures suggests a remarkable sophistication in ancient engineering knowledge, despite the absence of most formulas in the fifth century B.C. The juxtaposition highlights the formidable feats of engineering on the part of a temple's architect, who gained insight into the problems of good foundation design through empirical observation and experiment. These observations make it clear that the ancient builder had a practical, scientific knowledge of geotechnical engineering. Empirical experience over time was the guide, rather than mathematical proof.

# PERISTYLE AND CELLA AS
# INDEPENDENT UNITS

Segmented drums form an elastic design of tightly fitted, undowelled drums and capitals that makes the Doric shaft intrinsically responsive to tremors and thereby especially stable (figure 9.3; Ambraseys 1985). Engineering research into the dynamics of seismic forces on Doric columns, in general, proves the remarkable stability of the peristyle. Forces that overcome the shear strength of columns sitting on their stylobates must be greater than those that will set the column rocking. That is, severe storms with high gusts can subject columns to greater stresses than can high-velocity earthquakes. "We find that the [earthquake] 'intensity' required to overturn a column is so high that before a column is overturned most other man-made structures around it should have collapsed" (Ambraseys 1985: 214).

The Greek architect's treatment of peristyle and *sekos* (the cella, or central building containing the cult statue) as two separate entities follows a logic consistent with the overall aseismic design of a building. Nowhere throughout the lower levels of construction does a block or wall bind peristyle to *sekos*. Paving in the *pteromata* (circumferential corridor) was never bonded to the stylobate (platform on which the columns stand) and toichobate (series of blocks at the base of a wall) in Greek temple architecture, because exposed clamps were considered unsightly. Less usual are detached sleepers embedded on earth fill that brace the paving stones. Only at ceiling level with coffer spans did the physical bond between peristyle and *sekos* begin. Clamps were not all dispersed at this level; sometimes an infrequent dowel had the single purpose of being a temporary prop while intermediary coffers were slipped into place (F. A. Cooper 1992–1996: vol. 3, pl. 32.c).

# BUILDING MATERIALS: LIME-BASED
# SUBSTANCES

## Masonry

The Greeks developed a variety of limes and cements appropriate to a number of applications: grouting, waterproofing, a matrix for pebble flooring, and different types of wall plastering. Through the Hellenistic period there was an increasing use of grouting, using slaked lime mixed with earth, for the stabilization of foundation fill. Conspicuously absent is the use of the mortars to bond masonry and the mixture of an aggregate with cement to form concrete—the latter a building technique that arrives in the Roman period (chapter 10). Glues were applied in wood construction (Theophrastus, *Hist. pl.* 5.6.2, 5.7.2; see chapter 17). But Theophrastus (*Hist. pl.* 5.7.2) emphasizes the fact that glue will not bind woods of different fibers—whether mismatched grains or dissimilar wood species—or altogether different materials. He goes on to assert that "one piece should be of similar character, and not of opposite character, like wood and stone." Vitruvius (*De arch.* 7.3.9, 7.6.1) alludes to a plaster admixture, a substance added to plaster to alter its properties, which may date to the classical period: "[A plaster of] sand mortar and of marble, thinly and completely applied, [is] brilliant after being subjected to repeated polishing," This is comparable to modern Keene's cement, a dead-burned gypsum product that yields a hard, high-strength plaster (Merritt and Rickets 2000: sec. 24).

## Plaster and Stucco Wall Surfacing

A water-resistant hydraulic cement was used to line the interior of cisterns from the sixth century B.C. onward (Thompson and Wycherly 1972; Camp 1984). Water basins at fountain houses were treated in much the same manner, but with the additional precaution of cutting the vertical joints of the orthostate slabs into a V shape and sealing them with poured hydraulic cement or lead. Otherwise, the ashlar or dressed masonry was treated with a layer of plaster. The concern was an engineering problem: the permeability of stone. Stone fabric can suffer from disintegration due to thermal variation and the passage of water and water vapor, due to both the porosity of the stones and the interstices between blocks. The application of plaster to some surfaces shows an engineering awareness of this property of stone, that is, a knowledge of rock mechanics.

The use of a plaster coating for the protection of adobe walls against weathering can be seen as early as the Neolithic period. This simple type of protection against weathering was universal and continues today. Monumental Greek architecture in stone starts in the late eighth to early seventh centuries B.C. in the Corinthia. It begins a long tradition of finely dressed ashlar masonry construction, especially for sacred and public buildings meant to be beautiful and imposing. One of the earliest examples of an ashlar temple is that of Isthmian Poseidon (ca. 700–670 B.C.). A block preserves a patch of stucco with traces of a painted design, making it probable that frescoes decorated the entire exterior walls. The procedure, both as protection and decoration, most likely was inherited from earlier mud-brick design.

The practice of coating finely-dressed and jointed masonry walls continued to evolve. Much of the architecture at Olympia throughout its building history was constructed of the local shelly limestone, a friable material that easily weathers. Typically, it was protected by a thin coat of stucco, nearly all of which has weathered away, subjecting the exposed stone surfaces to further erosion. The marl limestone used for the fourth-century B.C. temple of Zeus at Nemea likewise was given a thin coat of stucco, a variety of dead-burned gypsum, a hard, high-strength plaster with an admixture of marble dust. The plaster was painted in Egyptian blue and red across appropriate areas of the frieze (triglyphs) and entablature (guttae). The remaining plaster was polished to a gleaming finish in imitation of marble, as prescribed by Vitruvius (*De arch.* 7.3.9). One obvious reason for the plaster was its brilliant appearance, but the protection afforded by the stucco was another, a sign of a developed engineering practice for the preservation of stone.

The unusual treatment of vertical joints in the Hephaisteion in Athens might be explained in this regard. The ashlar joint faces have the same sort of vertical, slotted groove described above. In all probability, the purpose of the grooved joint faces in the Hephaisteion was the same as found in water basins, namely, a form of waterproofing to reduce the sweating of the walls during atmospheric condition of high humidity coupled with the sometimes radical daily thermal changes. Not only does this procedure keep the interior dry, it also retards the disintegration of the stone. By contrast, the temples of the Parthenon and Zeus at Olympia had shallow pools of water in slight recesses in their interior paving to provide the opposite effect (Pausanias 5.11.11); the Phidian chryselephantine statues needed the heightened humidity for preservation of the ivory fabric.

Rubbing stone or a stuccoed surface with a chamois helps seal the porosity of the material and increases, sometimes appreciably, the resistance to water and hence to weathering. Decorated frescoes of the Bronze Age, Hellenistic, and Roman periods show signs of polishing. The marble-compound plaster over porous stone architecture noted above also shows traces of polishing, indicating this preservation technique was widespread (cf. Vitruvius, *De arch.* 7.3.9–10). Evidence that marble architectural surfaces were polished in the same manner and for the same purpose comes from marble sculpture. The subject of polishing Greek marble sculpture is controversial but deserves closer study than it has been afforded to date (Haynes 1975). It is widely held that Roman marble statuary was commonly polished, but not Greek. Cult statues and other works displayed within a building were not subject to any degree of weathering. I have, however, observed a few cases of well-preserved marble pedimental statuary where the outside portions have a matte or weathered surface, but there are patches of polished surface on the backside of the same pieces, where the marble had been sheltered by the corona of the geison and the tympanum wall. This appraisal of the scant evidence leads to a conclusion that the resilience of the exterior of marble buildings was improved by an understanding of the long-term benefit of increased water-resistance attained through the chamois polishing of both plaster and stone surfaces.

## House Flooring and Plastered Walls

The earliest Greek temples (late eighth century B.C.) had tamped, earthen floors, as did the contemporary houses. Temples acquired stone flooring very quickly, while house floors continued as earthen; that is, the floors of temples and houses came to be treated in quite different ways. In the earliest temple examples, stone paving often was laid as decorative, crazy-quilt flagging. In the sixth century B.C. and onward, temple floors consisted of unclamped rectangular pavers laid on top of a grillage of free-floating slippers. This design reduced heaving from frost and settlement and reduced cracking of the stonework. Not until the late fourth century B.C. and the Hellenistic period did house floors acquire a more durable surface. A layer of terracotta chips, usually fragments of roof tiles, were embedded in the earth base. Increasingly, colored river pebbles, set in a matrix of cement or grout, became the norm (Thompson and Wycherly 1972: 46, 77, 179, 197). In the Hellenistic period, decorative pebble mosaics appear in finely finished residences and public buildings (Dunbabin 1999: 5–17).

Prior to the late fifth and fourth centuries B.C., the Greek house was a crude affair, for the most part adobe on top of a rubble or roughly coursed stone wall socle, with packed earth floors. House architecture became increasingly sumptuous during the late classical and Hellenistic periods. Walls increasingly were built of field stones or even masonry, although not always coursed. There are examples at Eretria and classical Thira and in Ionia that also preserve surfaces of painted plaster shaped like drafted ashlar masonry, a forerunner of the Pompeian First Style of wall painting. Fashion may have been in play, but the engineering technology of stucco insulation also made the interior spaces more comfortable and the walls more durable.

# Building Materials: Baked Clay Architectural Units

Architectural terracottas—roof tiles and decorated revetments—appear early, with the rise of the first monumental Greek temples at Isthmia and Corinth in the later seventh century B.C. (Coulton 1977: 34–35; Hellmann 2002: 298–326; Rhodes forthcoming). Coinciding with the technical developments of stone carving, the firing of very large roof tiles made a permanent impact on subsequent building practice and design. Chronologically, roof tiles undergo a cycle of technological development, starting with complicated design and high-quality clay and firing in the archaic period, then moving to a less fastidious production in the late classical and Hellenistic periods. The proto-Corinthian roof tiles were handmade, but the late archaic and classical period Corinthian and Laconian tiles were molded. In the Hellenistic period, tiles were mass-produced by fabricants, and the quality became indifferent to poor. By Roman times terracotta roof tiles were mass-produced, but the quality could be quite high.

The earliest proto-Corinthian tiles were fashioned for double-sided hipped roofs. By the second generation, the proto-Corinthian tile was made into a combination pan and cover tile, a very complicated design, so much so that modern scholars struggle to identify the fragments and how they work together (Rhodes 1984, forthcoming). In the first half of the sixth century B.C., the Laconian type of

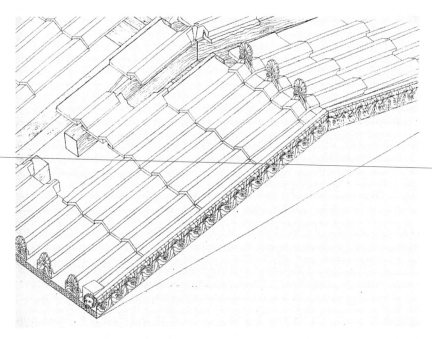

Figure 9.4. Typical Corinthian style tiled roof, reconstruction. (F. Cooper.)

tile was introduced, along with an akroterion disk that adorned a single gabled facade. At the heart of the development of the Greek terracotta roof tile (in the classical period imitated in marble, see below) is a realization that the roof "costs 10% of the building program but causes 90% of the problems" (Merritt and Rickets 2000). The pan and cover tile appear to be simple in design but, in fact, are a complex of interlocking lips and overlaps, sized to fit a two-foot building module, laid bottom to top from ends of building to the center. Ridge cover tiles, antefixes, and spouts often were adorned with finials, but at the same time were fashioned so that the hundreds of pieces for any given roof worked together for a watertight covering (figure 9.4; N. K. Cooper 1989).

Clay preparation for roof tiles, even firing in the kiln, and application of protective slips in red and black continued to develop in pace with the sophisticated pottery-making technology of the sixth to fourth century B.C. The earliest roof tiles sometimes were given alternating red and black slips for a bright checkerboard pattern. In the fourth century B.C. the color slips seem to disappear; instead, the top sides of pan tiles and sometimes cover tiles have finger-impressed swirls. The patterns may be decorative; more likely, the technique served to slow the force of water runoff during heavy storms.

Roof tiles were always popular for practical secondhand use; for example, as drain walls and grave covers. When broken into small pieces they were packed as flooring, sometimes in a cement matrix. Flat ceramic tiles were produced only for use in suspended hypocaust floors in baths.

# Roof Slope

Greek roof pitch varied little after the early archaic period; it became one of adjustment rather than experimentation. The earliest Greek temple roofs can only be reconstructed through interpretation of the interior arrangement of stone plinths for columns, along with their building plans. These sources give rise to their restoration as a gabled facade with pitched apsidal rear or the alternative rear gable as well. Confirming this, terracotta models of houses and shrines of this period have the same styles of roofs as temples and also show that the roofs were steeply pitched. A single- or double-hipped roof comes with the advent of terracotta tiles for the proto-Corinthian roof design. These were low-pitched and maybe crooked at the eaves to make a "Chinese roof" (Hellmann 2002: fig. 405). The low-pitched, hipped roof was given up shortly thereafter, and by the sixth century B.C. the double-gabled roof had become the standard. This linear development follows that of the roof tile, the engineering design of the one affecting the other. Some surviving early- and mid-sixth century pediments on the Athenian Acropolis have a relatively steep pitch, 3:1 (horizontal to vertical at peak height). By the early fifth century B.C., the roof pitch normalized at 4:1, or about a 15 degree rise in the angle at the horizontal vertexes. This pitch is optimal for water runoff (Merritt 1976: art. 11-27; Merritt and Rickets 2000: art. 3-4), and allows for a roof covering of unattached tiles to stay in place rather than sliding down the slope or tearing away under high winds. These roof tiles were not fastened to the underpinning rafter; a pierced hole to accommodate a hook or nail attachment in the plate of the pan tile or a slot at the edge is rarely found in terracotta or in stone tiles.

Flat roofs may have existed but cannot be proved either way. Flat roofs are given to failure from the ponding of water (American Institute of Timber Construction 1974: arts. 4-165 and 4-166). Shed roofs covered buildings that demanded unusual design, such as the Stoa of the Athenians at Delphi (ca. 470 B.C.).

# Building Materials: Metal

## Iron

The Greek blacksmith rendered a variety of grades of iron, from pig iron, which is "weak brittle but very hard" (Herubin and Marotta 1987: 209) to wrought iron (very low in carbon and slag; see chapter 4). Wrought iron was the principle material for architectural hardware, as "it is highly resistant to corrosion, highly ductile, and readily machined. It is easily worked" (Herubin and Marotta 1987: 209). Iron was used invariably for clamps and dowels; the former secured blocks across the tops of joints and the latter the bottoms of blocks to the course below. Iron pins stationed vertical struts underneath the ridge beam and purlins to the wooden members below (Arsenal of Philo, *IG* $2^2$ 1668; Pollitt 1990: 199–202; Meiggs 1982: 213). In classical Athens, Thucydides (1.93.5) boasts of "stones of large size hewn square, closely laid together, bound to one another on the outside by iron clamps and lead." Iron nails, however, were not commonly used for the joinery of wood members in Greek architecture. This is indicated in part by the rarity with which they are found in archaeological contexts, with the exception of libraries, where they may have been used for the attachment of cabinets to a wall. Protective grates and grills over window and door openings were made of iron bar. Hinges were also rare, but used for folding doors on several West Greek temples. Doors swung on pivots, made of wood (see below). A few preserved locks and keys also were wrought in iron. Nails and certain tools may have been smithed from carburized iron, whereas wrought iron went into the clamps and dowels.

Theophrastus tried to come to terms with the paradox of "hardness" in different types of iron, stone, and wood; poorer grades of iron cut some grades of wood but not others (*Hist. pl.* 5.5.1, 5.6.2–4). The same paradox applied to iron on stone and stone on stone. "It was not until the time of Mohs (1773–1839) and other modern mineralogists that differences in hardness became important criteria for classifying and identifying minerals" (Caley and Richards 1956: 147). Iron clamp and dowel design evolved over time, responding to an optimization of the ductile and strength properties of the materials (Dinsmoor 1950: fig. 64).

## Experiments in Structural Iron

There are two instances where a Greek designer/engineer experimented with a structural use of iron bars. The examples are separated by geography and by time: the temple of Zeus at Agrigento, Sicily (ca. 490 B.C.), and the Propylaea at Athens (ca. 438 B.C.). In both cases, a linear cavity was cut along the axis of a horizontal stone architrave for the insertion of iron bars (figure 9.5). In 1823, traces of iron were found inside the slot at Agrigento (Broucke 1996: 115), a cutting 0.31 m deep and 0.10 m wide that runs along the longitudinal center line of the soffits to pairs of adjoining exterior architrave blocks. Both ends of the architrave pairs are supported above interaxial and engaged piers, while the vertical joint is unsupported.

The slot at the Propylaea at Athens differs in several details: it runs along the tops of girders that support the ceiling beams. Some distance from either end of the block the slot terminates; also the cutting deepens along the middle portion of its length. Dinsmoor (1922: 148–58; 1950: 102) and Coulton (1977: 83) interpret the slot and iron bar feature in both buildings as "a direct support" between the intercolumniation spans. Heyman (1972) correctly understands the purpose and value of the iron bar at Agrigento: a temporary brace that "only had a function during construction." The iron bar inserted across the top of the girder in the Propylaea served the same function. In this case the bar was cambered upward, rising above

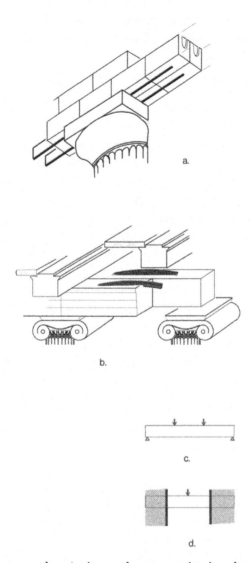

Figure 9.5. a. Iron support bar, Agrigento; b. compression iron bar, Propylaia; c. simple beam; d. fixed end beam. (F. Cooper.)

the top of the bedding surface and opposite the anticipated deflection movement. When loaded by the weight of the ceiling beams, the iron bar pressed horizontally outward, while the countersunk portion of the slot received the flattened iron bar. This stress along the upper portion of the marble girder increased its tensile strength (i.e., the load-bearing capacity of the beam; Merritt and Rickets 2000: art. 5-99; American Institute of Timber Construction 1974: art. 4-65) by improving the stone's bending moment and thereby reducing the amount of deformation and possible failure as the superimposed block settled into place (see figure 9.5).

Figure 9.6. Delphi, ductile iron clamp and setting. (Photograph by J. P. Oleson.)

## Lead

Iron clamps and dowels were embedded in cuttings below the surface of stone blocks and sealed into place by lead, for the most part poured in a molten state but sometimes pounded around the iron fastening. Although inevitably tight, such clamp and dowel assemblies were never left exposed, but were sealed in by adjoining blocks. The lead inhibited water penetration and consequent corrosion of the iron, but that was not the primary reason for use of the softer material. The lead added to the flexibility of the overall clamp or dowel fastening. The ductile properties of the iron fasteners encased in lead allowed for a fractional and organic movement of the structure during times of stress, particularly that caused by earthquakes (figure 9.6; see also below). In the Hellenistic period, "blind dowels," those embedded within the bottom side of a block rather than at the end, were rammed into position without lead. The vertical, protruding dowel head slipped into a rectangular cutting in the block underneath. The slot was large enough to allow for maneuvering the block into exact position; lead then was poured around the insertion. Now and then, sheets of lead served as pliable shims for a final leveling of a block or capital.

## Bronze

The properties of bronze are more appropriate to sculpture than to architecture: a low enough melting point to allow casting, relatively low tensile strength, capacity for decoration by coloring, chasing, and inlay (see chapter 16). The material was more resistant to weathering than iron, but it was far more expensive. In buildings, bronze bosses and medallions decorated faces of wooden doors and disguised the seams between wooden panels. Bronze plates have been found in pivot sockets in sills, as a simple device to ease the rotation of the door.

# Building Materials: Stone

## Wall Construction

Generally, walls in temples were made of solid stone ashlars that passed through the thickness of the wall, while house walls were built of adobe, a sun-dried brick. Fabrication of adobe goes back to Neolithic times in Greece and the Near East and represents a continuous technology, summarized by Vitruvius (*De arch.* 2.3.2). Stone or rubble wall socles about 0.35 m wide supported single-story domestic buildings; socles double that width suggest two-story construction. All home-building depended on vernacular technology. Wall engineering came into play in the seventh-century B.C. generation of temples called *hekatompeda* ("one-hundred-footers" in length, ca. 30 m), where an adobe wall had to be reinforced by engaged stone or wooden piers. These strengthened the flank wall as a structural precaution for the load of the new type of permanent roof incorporating painted terracotta tiles. The temple of Hera at Olympia, built around 600 B.C., is the best known and studied example of a design where engaged columns reinforced an adobe superstructure above stone orthostates. With the advent of all-stone architecture, the interior, engaged supports moved toward the center of the cella, positioned as a pair of free-standing colonnades. They supported not only the longitudinal purlins directly above, but also crossbeams that carried the struts in support of the ridge beam.

The cella flank wall and the outer peristyle provided two additional supports for the untrussed roof system. In the late fifth and fourth centuries B.C., interior design changed, and interior colonnades pushed back against the cella wall (Norman 1980, 1984). The interior colonnade all but disappeared in the Hellenistic period, most likely due to a greater confidence in materials engineering, namely that of wood spans.

## Rock Mechanics

Merritt's analyses of the forces acting within stone blocks are relevant to ancient Greek architecture (1976: art. 6-23): "The unbalanced moment of the external forces. About a vertical section through a beam in equilibrium, there is an unbalanced moment due to external forces. It is called the bending moment. Thus, when the bending moment is positive, the bottom of the beam is in tension and the top is in compression." At both Agrigento and the Propylaea, the ambitious spans

Figure 9.7. Fissures along stone bedding planes, Bassae Temple. (F. Cooper).

were engineering achievements, though the success never entered into standard Greek architectural practice. Greek engineering expertise in rock mechanics embraced building stone and extended to the geochemical engineering of foundation preparation. From my studies at Bassae, Nemea, and Messene, and from published research by others (e.g., Germann 1988), it is clear that the ancient architect, perhaps in consultation with a quarryman, selected outcrops of stone having the highest tensile and compressive strength, values available through simple analysis at a given source. Preferential judgments were based on assessments of the evenness and minimal frequency of bedding planes and the related question of concentrations of impurities such as iron oxides contained in the rock.

In numerous visits to Greek (and Roman) building sites over the years, I have observed a consistent feature of building stone: blocks were extracted from quarries with bedding planes running horizontally in cases of wall blocks (maximizing compressive strength) and vertically in cases of spans (beams and epistylia) to maximize tensile strength (figure 9.7). This geotechnical selectivity did not happen by chance; most outcrops in Greece are thrusted rock formations, and thus bedding planes rarely run horizontally. Marble deposits contain bedding planes that also dip from the horizontal; but the crystal fabric of marble, for the most part, is more homogeneous and structurally uniform than limestone. It is also obvious that thick seams of rock were reserved for the larger blocks laid across wide spans, while thinner bedded stone blocks went toward orthostate and wall blocks.

Today's geotechnical engineer uses a classification of rock type by strength. The greater the homogeneity and cohesiveness of stone fabric, the greater the strength and suitability for architectural and sculptural purposes. Building stone in ancient Greece was limited to limestone (mainly) and marbles, and occasionally serpentines and gneiss. Quality limestone has a toughness and modulus of rupture greater than that of marble, while the toughness and resistance of granite is about two to six times greater than that of marble. Granite, however, appears not to have been used for building material in the classical Greek world. Had it been available, it would have been uneconomic to shape it into blocks.

The ancient Greek architect's sense of building materials extended to the selection of superior grades of limestone or marble in quarry faces (Theophrastus, *Lap.* 5–7). Other signs indicate the Greek architect possessed a knowledge of the mechanical properties of stone: he invariable placed blocks within the temple so as to use the bedding planes of the rock to optimal advantage. Preferential selection of stone does not require a background in geotechnology, which, after all, is a young science. A first-rate sculptor, ancient or modern, predicts certain physical properties of stone by inspection and thereby makes qualitative selections based on judgments of personal and accumulative experience. Personal experience, however, cannot account for the awareness that one stone has a compressive and tensile strength that a stone of similar appearance does not have. Perhaps engineering experience led to a realization that concentrations of iron oxides not only reduced the load-bearing capacity, but also caused detrimental weathering. Only routine geochemical testing will show how extensive this knowledge of stone properties was in antiquity, but a few comparable analyses of stone from other sites indicate that this ancient awareness existed. "Analysis of frequency distribution of iron contents in Thessalian marbles reveals a distinct shift of the distribution curves for stelae marbles toward lower values as compared to marble samples taken from ancient quarries. This means that the ancient quarrymen selectively mined marbles of high quality and purity which today cannot be sampled adequately, a fact which should be considered carefully not only in geochemical analysis" (Germann et al. 1980: 103–4). Elsewhere, Peschlow-Bindokat and Germann (1981: fig. 96) publish a variation diagram of iron/magnesium ratios of southwest Anatolian marbles, again showing concentrations of iron content in quarry samples as being higher than concentrations in samples from ancient buildings.

# DESIGN BENDING MOMENT

The colonnade, whether as a peristyle around a temple or as a row of columns along a stoa, depended on the fixed-end beam system. On occasion, the Greek architect experimented with a shaped profile of a stone member as a means to counteract stress when a stone member was put into suspension. The ceiling coffers of the Bassae temple were shaped with cambered backs; their profile follows the convex curve of bending moments, rising in a direction opposite to the deflection of the stone put into suspension. Engineers today draw up a bending moment diagram determined from mathematical calculations. These graphs assume a curvature of a beam subjected to loading. A predicted moment of rupture increases when the deflection is decreased by means of a design reinforcement; on the Propylaea on the Acropolis this involved the thickening of the back side of the coffer panel or the placement of the tension bar in the ceiling girder. This economical solution increased the strength of the coffer; it did not, however, increase the stiffness, as is sometimes supposed. The ceiling above the porch of the temple at Sangri, Naxos, also carried cambered beams (F. A. Cooper 1992–1996: vol. 4, pl. 38.b 4; Coulton 1977: 143–47, figs. 63–64), a situation that continues the engineering experiment of the girder tension rod in the Propylaia design noted above.

# STONE ROOF TILES

Beginning with the Periclean building program at Athens in the mid-fifth century B.C., major temples and public buildings were outfitted with an all-stone roof, usually of marble: on the Acropolis, the Parthenon, Propylaea, Nike temple; in the agora, the temple of Hephaestus, and the third-century B.C. Stoa of Attalus. Other stone roofs may have existed, but, as today, roof coverings were the first to be lost as the ancients hauled the stone and terracotta tiles away as building material and for a variety of other purposes. Marble and limestone stone roofing almost disappears, but there are surviving examples; for example, the original limestone roof of the heroon at Messene (ca. 170 B.C.). In this later period, replacement and new roof covering were increasingly made by commercial and often indifferent manufacturers.

For both early and classical stone roofs, an ingenious interlocking system for the tile joints is indicative of an engineering design to eliminate leakage. The early, proto-Corinthian terracotta roofs at Isthmia and Corinth (late eighth to early seventh centuries B.C.) have covers attached to pans. As Rhodes (forthcoming) shows in his experimental recreations of these tiles, the laborious manufacturing process proved successful in the reduction of the number of open joints between rows of tiles. The combination tile went out of fashion, but then returned by the time of the Periclean Acropolis program. The Parthenon sports a marble, double-pan tile with a fake cover running down midway. An attached cover tile at one edge further reduced the open jointing for a watertight roof, a necessity given the ivory statue of Athena Parthenon underneath. The marble roof over the temple at Bassae reflects the Parthenon design, but elaborate, tightly-fitted marble roofs were too expensive for routine use. As mentioned above, repairs at Bassae and the heroon at Messene and elsewhere were made in terracotta. The earlier translucent marble gave these roofs a secondary purpose: a diffused illumination of the interior space. Bassae had an all-marble interior ceiling, and it could be that the Parthenon had no woodwork between the cross-beams at ceiling level, exposing the interior of the marble roof.

# Building Materials: Wood

Evidence of the exploitation of timber for building purposes in ancient Greece depends almost entirely on written testimonia rather than surviving physical and archaeological evidence—in contrast to the other engineering techniques and practices. Hodge (1960), Hellmann (1986: 237–47; 2002), and Liebhart (1988) have interpreted the sockets for beams, rafters, and doors in extant buildings in combination with citations from epigraphical evidence. Meiggs (1982) presents the overall picture, including a particularly acute overview of the written sources.

Wood played a prominent role in the engineering of the rooftree of temples and other large structures. Rafters lodged in cuttings spaced along the top and back sides of the horizontal *geison* (crowning molding above entablature) and were underpinned by a pair of purlins (longitudinal roof beams), which divide the slope into two nearly equal parts. Ordinarily, rafters were spaced two building feet apart and carried the edges of two-foot-long roof tiles on top. A set of three longitudinal beams, a ridge, and a pair of intermediate purlins, one on either side of the pitched roof, supported each rafter at three positions. The purlins ran above the flank wall, while the bottom end of the rafter was slotted into a sloping cutting along the horizontal geison course or into a substitute rafter rail resting on the *geison*. The structural design was that of a horizontal beam supported at three positions (*geison*, purlin, and ridge), and having minimal force of a lateral thrust.

There are no examples in which horizontal beams tie directly into the rafters, for example by a pivot connector or gusset plate, devices that allow movement within the joints of a simple truss design (Salvadori and Heller 1986: 112). Furthermore, in Greek building design, cross beams supporting roof struts always have an interval greater than the two-foot interval of the rafters. Even in those cases where the interval between the rafters coincides with that between the cross beams, the members are quite different in thickness. In other words, the simple truss had not been devised for Greek architecture, although the argument against it is too complex to summarize here (White 1984: 74, n. 111; cf. chapter 17). The cross section of rafters usually measured 0.16 m–0.32 m, and they were usually square or nearly square in section. Purlins were larger (ca. 0.60 m sq.), but they are also trapezoidal to coincide with the slope of the rafters. Ridge beams were quite a bit stouter and ranged around 0.60 m ± 0.10 m in width and 0.80 ± 0.10 m in height. The cross section sizes of rafters, purlins, and ridge beams are standard and do not vary a great deal between large temples and small.

## Wood Mechanics and Theophrastus

The topic of ancient Greek engineering in wood deserves a far more expansive treatment than can be provided here. Indeed, Theophrastus' overriding thesis—that wood is a valuable commodity which serves a variety of building applications—was based on a quasi-scientific understanding of particular properties such as knots and direction of grain and has the same commercial purpose as the tables in modern handbooks (e.g., Forest Products Laboratory, U.S. Department of Agriculture 1990). As late as 1975, Rhude (in Merritt 1975: art. 8-0) could declare that "practice, not engineering design, has been the criterion in home building. As a result, the strength of wood often was not fully utilized." This analysis does not apply to the situation in Theophrastus' time, since book 5 of Theophrastus' *Historia plantarum* contains statements comparable to those in a contemporary engineering handbooks such as Herubin and Marotta 1987 and Merritt and Rickets 2000. The section headings in Merritt and Rickets 2000 are closely comparable with those in Theophrastus: "Mechanical Properties of Wood" (4-33; *Hist. pl.* 5.1.5–4.1), "Effects of Hygroscopic Properties of Wood" (4-34; *Hist. pl.* 5.4.2–4.8), "Commercial Grades of Wood" (4-35; *Hist. pl.* 5.5.1–7.8), "Destroyers and Preservatives" (4-36; *Hist. pl.* 5.4.2–4.8), "Glues and Adhesives for Wood" (4-50; *Hist. pl.* 5.7.2, 4). Issues presented in Merritt and Rickets supplement this list: for example, the seasons for felling timber (*Hist. pl.* 5.1.1–1.4). In other words, the topics considered by Theophrastus, and often their ordering, resemble the organization of the modern engineering handbook: the proper season to fell a particular tree, the need to season the timber, the deficiencies of certain woods, the mechanical properties of the different species, the paradoxes observed between strength, hardness, and bending, the rules of wood production, and the effect of growth locality on these properties.

Theophrastus, followed by Vitruvius (*De arch.* 2.9.13–10.2) and Pliny (*HN* 12–17 passim), envisioned boundaries, sometimes corresponding to geographical and political ones, demarcating land where one species of tree would grow and where another would not. In other words, the pine tree was rare in Arcadia, but common in Elis (Theophrastus, *Hist. pl.* 3.9.4), whereas the Holm oak was abundant in Arcadia, but did not grow anywhere in Elis and Sparta (Pliny, *HN* 16.34). To these ancient authors, many individual species of trees could be found only in particular sections of the world. The Old Oligarch (*Ath. pol.* 2.12) states the same notion: "But no other town possesses two of these commodities; for instance, the same town has not both timber and flax." In building contracts and commercial agreements at major Greek sanctuaries, inscriptions give the source of wood as Macedonia, perhaps because it was subject to politically-based price fluctuation (Eleusis, 329/8

B.C., *IG* 2² 1672.66; Delphi, Bourguet 1932: 3.5.41, line 7; Delos, *IG* 2² 199A.57). In a treaty of 389/83 B.C. between Amyntas III (King of the Macedonians) and the Chalcidians, silver-fir was the single material for ship-building and house-building materials permitted for export by the Chalcidian League (Tod 1946–48: no. 111). Theophrastus (*Char.* 23) also seems to refer to the restrictive policies of the Macedonians regarding the exportation of timber from their country.

## Wood Mechanics in the Fifth Century B.C.

This scientific approach to the mechanics of wood can be documented more than a century earlier, during the Periclean building program on the Acropolis at Athens, by three fragmentary inscriptions. An Athenian decree (*IG* I³ 1454, ca. 430 B.C.) bestows honor on an Eteocarpathian for a dedication and contribution of a tall and venerated cypress tree for the temple of Athena. The donation's recipient Athena is ambiguous; it has been argued both that it was meant to serve as the wooden mast for the chryselephantine statue of Athena Parthenos by Phidias, and that it constituted some part of the entrance to the *opisthodomos* (rear, treasury room) of the Parthenon. An ordinary, mature cypress tree would have fit the needs for the wooden mast of the Phidian statue, which can be estimated as about 13.4 m tall, including a sinking of 1.8 m into a socket 0.75 m x 0.45 m in the Parthenon floor (Stevens 1955: 244–46). An even shorter cypress tree could yield the planks for the pieced panels of a door. Yet the cypress was used for neither the mast nor the door panels. Instead, the probable purpose for the Carpathus cypress was the ridge beam of the Erechtheum. This roof member can be restored as having measured about 75 feet (ca. 23 m), the height of a very tall cypress. A table giving an economical span range for main wood-framing members lists 10–25 feet for a solid-sawn, continuous span, a value that increases to 10–50 feet for a laminated beam (Merritt 1975: table 10.2). According to these figures, the ridge beam for the Erechtheum was a successful experiment, testing the bearing limits of the cypress timber.

The second inscription, *IG* I³ 461, is attributed to the accounts of the construction of the Parthenon. The fragmentary text specifies elm and cypress, but the context is lost. This combination of woods, as Meiggs (1982: 200) rightly notes, suggests they were destined for the east entrance of the Parthenon. A third inscription from the Parthenon account, *IG* I³ 439.107, dated to 442/441 B.C., specifies pine, but the quantity, price, and purpose do not survive. A logical assumption is that, five years into construction, the pine was destined for scaffolding to build walls and/or to start the roof. Theophrastus suggests that elm and cypress were coveted woods. This is reflected in the high value attached to doors, windows, and framing of elm and cypress in the inscribed accounts from 414 B.C. of the confiscated properties of those convicted of the mutilation of the Herms. In *IG* I³ 421–39, the prices are much above those given to other types of household goods and property (Pritchett 1956).

Timber is likewise a specified commodity in inscriptions. What these inscriptions tell us, in connection with Theophrastus, is that the designer, Ictinus in the case of the Parthenon, specified species of wood optimally appropriate to structural function and placement. In other words, there already existed by the mid-fifth century B.C. an engineering basis for the mechanics of wood as well as stone.

# FIRE PROTECTION ENGINEERING

Greek architecture follows a linear development from adobe to thatch and wood, and finally to stone construction. Literary references to catastrophic fires in temples include Delphi, Argos, and Ephesus, along with many others. For the most part, sacrifice burning took place at outdoor altars, not in the temple. This arrangement may be in part due to tradition, but it was also a means to reduce the hazard of conflagration within the temple. The danger of fire came from roof timbers, textiles, and inflammable dedications inside the temple. The stone rafters of the temple at Naxos were perhaps intended to avert the danger of fire (Gruben 1982). Modern building code requires ventilation in attics and enclosed areas, especially in hot climates where temperatures can reach the combustion point. In antiquity, a common solution was ventilation of the attic by an *opaion* roof tile; this piece has an oculus at the center ringed by a raised lip. *Opaion* roof tiles along with interior staircases and open pedimental frames to attic fronts were some of the engineering solutions employed by the ancient Greek architect. The latter two designs are found typically in West Greek architecture, for instance in Temple F at Agrigento. Examples are known at the Parthenon and Bassae.

During his travels in Greece in 1911, Le Corbusier realized that ancient Greek architectural engineering was practiced in classical times as an interdisciplinary profession. Coulton (1977: 16) expresses a more usual view: "Until the development of theoretical mechanics in the late fourth and early third centuries, there was no distinct concept of engineer as opposed to architect." My use of the term for engineer derives from *mechana*, a term Herodotus uses to mean both "contrivance" (3.83; 3.152; 8.57) and "a lifting machine" (2.125), the latter in his description of the erection of pyramids. Had Aristotle's treatise *Mechanica* survived, it could have led to a much clearer appreciation today of the role of architectural engineering in the history of Greek architecture. Aristotle and Theophrastus wrote at a time when siege warfare and elaborate theatrical productions came of age and a *mechanikos* designed both war and theater machines, as in modern day mechanical engineering. Yet, Le Corbusier recognized the genius of the Greek architect-engineer. In his *Towards a New Architecture* (1987: 11) he not only interweaves

Greek architecture, especially monuments on the Acropolis, with automobiles and American grain elevators, but also explicitly states his comprehension in his introduction: "The engineer's aesthetic and architecture—two things that march together and follow one from the other."

Although often portrayed as an impractical, idealistic artist, the Greek architect in fact was well aware of the demands and opportunities of the available materials, and prepared to confront the challenges of constructing very demanding designs in a seismic environment. The focus of classical Greek society on the communal temple or sanctuary, which helped to define the city state identity, and the innate conservatism of the Doric and Ionic orders limited the scope of design innovation. At the same time, this intense concentration of talent and funding fostered the development of exquisitely appropriate refinements in detail, and lasting solutions to the problems of stability and endurance.

# REFERENCES

Algren-Ussing, G., and A. Bramnaes 1975. *Fouilles de Delphes.* Vol. 2, *Atlas.* Paris: De Boccard.

Amandry P. 1981. "Chronique delphique (1970–1981)," *Bulletin de Correspondence Hellénique* 105: 673–769.

Ambrayses, N. 1971. "The value of the historical records of earthquakes," *Nature* 232: 375–79.

Ambraseys, N. 1985. "On the protection of monuments and sites in seismic areas," in *Restoration of the Acropolis monuments.* Athens: Ministry of Culture and Sciences, Committee for the Preservation of the Acropolis Monuments, 207–28.

American Institute of Timber Construction 1974. *Timber construction manual.* 2nd ed. New York: Wiley.

Bammer, A. 1984. *Das Heiligtum der Artemis von Ephesos.* Graz: Akademische Druck- und Verlaganstalt.

Bammer, A. 1984–85. "Plinius und der Kroisostempel," *Österreichisches Jahrbuch* 55: 13–28.

Bequignon, Y. 1937. "Recherches archéologiques à Phères de Thessalie." Diss., Université de Strasbourg.

Bourguet, E. 1932. *Fouilles de Delphes.* Vol 3.5, *Les comptes du ive siècle.* Paris: E. de Boccard.

Broucke, P. 1996. "The temple of Olympian Zeus at Agrigento." Ph.D. diss., Yale University.

Caley, E. R., and J. F. C. Richards 1956. *Theophrastus: On stones.* Columbus: Ohio State University Press.

Camp, J. McK. II, and W. B. Dinsmoor Jr. 1984. *Ancient Athenian building methods.* Princeton: American School of Classical Studies at Athens.

Cooper, F. A. 1983. *The temple of Zeus at Nemea: The reconstruction project.* Athens: Benaki Museum.

Cooper, F. A. (ed.) 1992–1996. *The temple of Apollo Bassitas.* 4 vols. Princeton: American School of Classical Studies.

Cooper, F. A. 1999. "Curvature and other architectural refinements in a Hellenistic heroon at Merrene," in Haselberger 1999: 185–97.

Cooper, N. K. 1989. *The development of roof revetment in the Peloponnese.* Studies in Mediterranean Archaeology, Pocketbook. Partille: Paul Åströms Forlag.

Coulton, J. J. 1977. *Ancient Greek architects at work: Problems of structure and design.* Ithaca, NY: Cornell University Press.

Dinsmoor, W. B. 1922. "Structural iron in Greek architecture," *American Journal of Archaeology* 26: 148–58.

Dinsmoor, W. B. 1950. *The architecture of ancient Greece.* 3rd ed. New York: Batsford.

Dunbabin, K. M. D. 1999. *Mosaics of the Greek and Roman world.* Cambridge: Cambridge University Press.

Forest Products Laboratory, U.S. Department of Agriculture 1990. *Wood engineering handbook.* Englewood Cliffs, NJ: Prentice Hall.

Germann, K., et al. 1988. "Provenance characteristics of Cycladic (Paros and Naxos) marbles, a multivariate geological approach," in N. Herz and M. Waelkens (eds.), *Classical marble: Geochemistry, technology, trade.* Dordrecht: Kluwer, 251–62.

Germann, K., G. Holzmann, and F. J. Winkler 1980. "Determination of marble limits of isotope analysis," *Archaeometry* 22: 99–106.

Gruben, G. 1982. "Der Burgtempel A von Paros. Naxos-Paros, Vierter Vorläufiger Bericht," *Archäologischer Anzeiger* 1982: 197–229.

Harvey, J. C. 1982. *Geology for geotechnical engineers.* Cambridge: Cambridge University Press.

Haselberger, L. 1997. "Architectural likenesses: Models and plans of architecture in classical antiquity," *Journal of Roman Archaeology* 10: 77–94.

Haselberger, L. (ed.) 1999. *Appearance and essence: Refinements of classical architecture—curvature.* Philadelphia: University Museum.

Haynes, D. E. L. 1975. "A question of polish," in *Festschrift Ernst Homann-Wedeking.* Waldsassen: Stiftland-Verlag, 131.

Hellmann, M.-C. 1986. "A propos du vocabulaire architectural dans les inscriptions deliennes: Les parties portes," *Bulletin de Correspondence Hellenique* 110: 237–47.

Hellmann, M.-C. 2002. *L'Architecture grecque.* Vol. 1, *Les principes de la construction.* Paris: Picard.

Herubin, C. A., and T. W. Marotta 1987. *Basic construction materials: Methods and testing.* 3rd ed. Englewood Cliffs, NJ: Prentice-Hall.

Heyman, J. 1972. "'Gothic' construction in ancient Greece," *Journal of the Society of Architectural Historians* 31: 3–9.

Hodge, A. T. 1960. *The woodwork of Greek roofs.* Cambridge: Cambridge University Press.

Hogarth, D. G. 1908. *Excavations at Ephesus: The archaic Artemisia.* London: The British Museum.

Kawerau, G., J A Bundgaard, and W. Dörpfeld 1974. *The excavation of the Athenian Acropolis, 1882–1890: The original drawings,* 2 vols. Copenhagen: Gyldendal.

Kelly, J. M. 1982. "Aseismic base isolation," *Shock and Vibration Digest* 14.5 May: 17–25.

Korres, M. 1983. *Melete apokatastaseos tou Parthenonos* [Study for the restoration of the Parthenon]. Athens: Upourgeio politismou kai epistemon. Epitrope suntereseos mnemeion Akropoleos.

Korres, M. 1999. "Refinements of refinements," in Haselberger 1999: 79–104.

Kousell, K., and E. Dimou 2006. "Building materials (except for Pentelic marble) used in ancient Athens," ASMOSIA, 8éme Colloque International, Aix-en-Provençe, France, 12–18 June 2006. Abstracts: 29.

Landels, J. G. 2000. *Engineering in the ancient world.* 2nd ed. Berkeley: University of California Press.

Le Corbusier 1987. *Towards a new architecture.* Trans. F. Etchells. London: The Architecture Press.

Liebhart, R. F. 1988. "Timber roofing spans in Greek and Near Eastern monumental architecture during the early Iron Age." Diss., University of North Carolina at Chapel Hill.

Martin, R. 1965. *Manuel d'architecture grecque, I: Matériaux et techniques.* Paris: Picard.

McCredie, J. R. 1979. "The architects of the Parthenon," in G. Kopcke and M. B. Moore (eds.), *Studies in classical art and archaeology: A tribute to Peter Heinrich von Blanckenhagen.* Locust Valley, NY: Augustin, 69–73.

Meiggs, R. 1982. *Trees and timber in the ancient Mediterranean world.* Oxford: Oxford University Press.

Merritt, F. S. (ed.) 1975. *Building construction handbook.* 3rd ed. New York: McGraw-Hill.

Merritt, F. S. (ed.) 1976. *Standard handbook for civil engineers.* 2nd ed. New York: McGraw-Hill.

Merritt, F. S., and J. T. Rickets (eds.) 2000. *Building design and construction handbook.* 6th ed. New York: McGraw-Hill.

Norman, N. J. 1980. "The 'Ionic' cella: A preliminary study of fourth-century B.C. temple architecture." Diss., University of Michigan.

Norman, N. J. 1984. "The temple of Athena Alea at Tegea," *American Journal of Archaeology* 88: 169–94.

Orlandos, A. 1966–1968. *Les matériaux de construction et la technique architecturale des anciens grecs.* 2 vols. Paris: De Boccard.

Orlandos, A. 1976–1978. *He architektonike tes Parthenonos.* 3 vols. Athens: Athens Archaeological Society.

Pakkanen, J. 2004. "The Temple of Zeus at Stratos: New observations on the building design," *Arctos* 38: 95–121.

Pakkanen, J. 2006. "The Erechtheion construction work inventory (*IG* $1^3$ 474) and the Dörpfeld temple," *American Journal of Archaeology* 110: 275–82.

Peschlow-Bindokat, A., and K. von Germann 1981. "Die Steinbrüche von Milet und Herakleia am Latmos, mit einem Beitrag, Lagerstätteneigenschaften und herkunftstypische Merkmalsmuster von Marmoren am Südwestrand des Menderes-Massivs (Südwestanatolien)," *Jahrbuch des deutschen archäologischen Instituts* 96: 157–235.

Petrakos, B. 1983. *A concise guide to Rhamnous.* Athens: Archaeological Society of Greece.

Petronotis, A. 1972. *Zum Problem der Bauzeichnungen bei den Griechen.* Athens: Dodona-Verlag.

Pollitt, J. J. 1990. *The art of ancient Greece: Sources and documents.* 2nd ed. Cambridge: Cambridge University Press.

Pritchett, W. K. 1956. "The Attic *Stelai*, Part II," *Hesperia* 25: 178–317.

Rhodes, R. F. 1984. "The Beginnings of monumental architecture in the Corinthia." Diss., University of North Carolina.

Rhodes, R. F. forthcoming. "The Manufacture of early Corinthian rooftiles," forthcoming in *Symposium on Issues of Architectural Reconstruction, Notre Dame University, 20–23 January 2006.*

Robertson, D. S. 1964. *Handbook of Greek and Roman architecture.* 2nd ed. Cambridge: Cambridge University Press.

Salvadori, M. G., and R. A. Heller 1986. *Structure in architecture: The building of buildings.* 3rd ed. Englewood Cliffs, NJ: Prentice-Hall.

Shear, T. L. 1971. "The Athenian agora: Excavations of 1970," *Hesperia* 40: 243–55.

Stählin, F., E. Meyer, and A. Heidner 1934. *Pagasai und Demetrias: Beschreibung der Reste und Stadtgeschichte.* Berlin/Leipzig: de Gruyter.

Stevens, G. P. 1955. "Remarks upon the colossal chryselephantine statue of Athena in the Parthenon," *Hesperia* 24: 240–76.

Tassios, T. P., and C. Palyvou (eds.) 2006. *Ancient Greek technology: Proceedings of the 2nd International Congress.* Athens: Technical Chamber of Greece.

Thompson, H. A., and R. E. Wycherley 1972. *The agora of Athens: The history, shape, and uses of an ancient city center.* Excavations in the Athenian Agora 14. Princeton: American School of Classical Studies at Athens.

Tod, M. N. 1946–1948. *Greek Historical Inscriptions.* 2 vols. Oxford: Clarendon Press.

Tschira, A. 1972. "Untersuchungen im Süden des Parthenon," ed. S. Sinos, *Jahrbuch des deutschen archäologischen Instituts* 87: 158–231.

Vetters, H. 1986. "Ephesos: Vorläufiger Grabungsbericht für die Jahre 1984 und 1985," *Anzeiger der Österreichischen Akademie des Wissenschaften in Wien, Philosophische-Historische Klasse* 123: 75–110.

Vutukuri, V. S., R. D. Lama, and S. S. Saluja 1974. *Handbook on mechanical properties of rocks.* Vol 1. Bay Village, OH: Trans Tech Publications.

White, K. D. 1984. *Greek and Roman technology.* Ithaca, NY: Cornell University Press.

# CHAPTER 10

# ROMAN ENGINEERING AND CONSTRUCTION

## LYNNE LANCASTER

## THE ROMAN-BUILT ENVIRONMENT

Strabo (5.3.8), writing in the Augustan period, notes that the Greeks were adept at founding beautiful and strategically located cities that took advantage of natural harbors and productive soils, whereas the Romans focused on practicality with the construction of roads, aqueducts, sewers, tunnels, and viaducts. With the benefit of hindsight we can also add man-made harbors to his list. Each of these is treated in other chapters of this volume. This chapter, however, presents developments that affected actual buildings, many of which occurred after Strabo wrote. The study of building technology involves two main issues: the available materials and the methods of putting them in place so that they stay put, which in modern parlance translates to "materials technology" and "structural engineering" (White 1984: 73). However, advances were also affected by the reorganization of work practices and the combination of existing technologies (Greene 1992: 101), a skill at which the Romans were most adept. The Romans drew on many technological innovations made in the Greek world, so with this in mind, I focus here on the aspects of Roman building technology that go beyond what had been accomplished earlier and thus provide insight into broader trends in the Roman world.

## LABOR SUPPLY AND CONTRACTS

The acquisition of manpower for large projects, the legal framework in which it occurred, and the social institutions involved all played a role in the development of building technology. During the Republic, public projects were let out to private contractors (*redemptores*), usually by the censors or aediles using a contract called *locatio conductio*, which stipulated certain obligations for each party (Martin 1989: 29–40). A similar use of contractors for major public works continued during the imperial period, as attested by Frontinus (*Aq.* 2.119) and the funerary inscriptions of the *redemptores* who worked on such projects (Anderson 1997: 108–13). The use of multiple contractors within the same project may go some way in explaining the differences in building techniques found within a single project, such as at the Colosseum, Trajan's Markets, and the Baths of Caracalla (Rea et al. 2002: 370–74; Lancaster 1998: 305–8; DeLaine 1985: 196). Both architects and builders used measured drawings to communicate ideas, as indicated by Vitruvius (*De arch.* 1.2.2, 3.5.8) and demonstrated by examples preserved on papyrus, carved on walls and pavements, and depicted in mosaics and stone reliefs (Wilson Jones 2000: 49–58 with bibliography), but the differences in details within single projects suggest that there was a greater degree of flexibility in executing the instructions than one would expect today. Unfortunately, evidence for how large projects were overseen is scant. An inscription from Tunisia notes the use of an *exactor* to oversee four *redemptores* on a project in Thuburbo Maius (*AE* 1940.16), but for large imperial projects presumably an architect was involved. Social institutions, such as *clientela*, whereby persons of different social strata were bound by certain obligations for each other's welfare (especially in the case of freed slaves), also played a vital role in the way labor was acquired. DeLaine (2003: 723–32) has traced such connections between freedmen and former masters in the building industry at Ostia. This type of interaction was often financially beneficial for both parties and could provide incentives for technological innovations.

## THE ARCH, VAULT, AND TRABEATED ARCHITECTURE

The Romans were known for their creative exploitation of the arch, and research has shown that it appeared in Rome by the sixth century B.C. (Cifani 1994: 194). The success of the arch relies on the radiating joints between the wedge-shaped voussoirs to direct the load toward the sides and away from the opening underneath. It is the optimal form for stone construction because the material is subjected to compressive rather than tensile stresses. Stone is very strong in compression but weak in tension, so a stone arch can span a larger distance than a flat stone beam, which undergoes both compressive and tensile stresses. Moreover, builders in Rome were relying on the local volcanic tuff, which has much less tensile strength than marble. The arch became a basic element for Roman architectural types such as the freestanding theater and amphitheater. It was translated into concrete construction, and the resulting curvilinear forms transformed the architectural vocabulary in the Mediterranean.

Once travertine and marble became available in Rome in the late second and early first centuries B.C., the builders were also faced with lifting heavier stones of much larger dimensions than earlier. Lifting technology using cranes, ropes, pulleys and capstans came from the Greek world (Coulton 1974; see also chapter 13), but the Roman contribution was to use these elements on a scale far beyond what had occurred earlier (figures 2.4, 13.1). For example, the appearance of multiple lewis holes on single blocks, such as the 58-ton architrave of the Temple of Jupiter at Baalbek (first century A.D.), suggests that multiple lifting devices were coordinated and used together (Wiegand 1921: 66–67). From a much later period, the base of the obelisk of Theodosius at Constantinople (A.D. 390) depicts the use of multiple capstans to move the obelisk itself. No doubt similar techniques were used in the early second century in Rome to lift the blocks (25–77 tons) of Trajan's Column (Lancaster 1999). This procedure contrasts sharply with Pliny the Elder's (*HN* 35.96) description of the use of ramps to lift the massive architrave of the Temple of Artemis at Ephesus in the fourth century B.C.

A significant difference between Greek and Roman stone architecture was in the construction of columns: the Greeks using stacked drums and the Romans preferring monolithic shafts. The Roman preference for monoliths had a great effect on the technological requirements of supplying the stone, and it also demonstrates the importance of reorganized work practices mentioned above. The period from the late first century B.C. to the early second century A.D. was one in which the imperial administration increasingly took control of quarries supplying marble for imperial projects (chapter 5). Wilson Jones (2000: 147–56) notes that this was also the period when a new type of standardized design procedure developed: what he calls the 6:5 rule, whereby column shafts were typically five-sixths the total height of the column (i.e., base + shaft + capital). This phenomenon appears from the Augustan period and is related to the production in imperial quarries of standard-sized roughed-out Corinthian capitals and of monolithic column shafts in lengths of multiples of either 4 Roman feet or 5 Roman feet (= RF). This rule of thumb resulted in a 50-RF column with a 40-RF shaft, a 48-RF column with a 40-RF shaft, a 36-RF column with a 30-RF shaft, and so on. Such standardization was only possible once the technology existed for the quarrying, transporting, and lifting of large monolithic shafts.

An analysis of the Pantheon porch facade illustrates the types of issues that arose when building with the largest of these monolithic shafts. Wilson Jones (2000: 199–212) has suggested that the Pantheon porch, which is supported on 40-RF shafts of Mons Claudianus and Aswan granite, was originally intended to be taller and to be supported on 50-RF shafts. The argument is based on various constructional anomalies in the building as well as an analysis of the relationship of the facade to the rotunda, which shows that the taller version would have yielded a more proportionally pleasing porch. One explanation for why the change occurred is that the 50-RF shafts (ca. 100 tons) were twice as heavy as the 40-RF ones (ca. 50 tons) and would have been much more difficult to quarry and transport. Two other tantalizing pieces of evidence regarding this problem have come to light. Carved onto the pavement in front of the Mausoleum of Augustus have been found full-scale working drawings, one of which matches the pediment of the Pantheon and was likely used by the workers to lay out the blocks (Haselberger 1994). Another of the drawings depicts a capital for a 50-RF column shaft; Wilson Jones therefore suggests that these were designs for the original, taller porch that was ultimately lowered. Moreover, a papyrus (A.D. 118–119) records an urgent request for more barley to feed the large number of draft animals transporting a 50-RF shaft (almost certainly from Mons Claudianus) to the Nile, thus highlighting the complexity of the logistics of transporting a 100-ton stone (Peña 1989). Given the date and the rarity of such large columns, the column mentioned in the document was likely destined for either the Pantheon or the Temple of Divine Trajan. The true sequence of events leading to the ultimate porch design at the Pantheon may never be known, but the issues raised above demonstrate the technological and logistical problems that could be encountered in transporting and lifting such large stone elements.

   With the continual development of larger structures, the establishment of a secure base on which to build became critical, especially in areas of inherent instability. One method was simply to build very deep foundations, reaching to bedrock when possible. At Sardis, which was completely destroyed by an earthquake in A.D. 17, one of the characteristics of the post-earthquake reconstructions is that they have very deep (8 m) mortared rubble foundations (Hanfmann 1983: 142). The enormous Temple of Jupiter at Baalbek, also in an earthquake zone, has stone foundations that extend to a depth of up to 17 m in places (Ragette 1980: 105). The geological nature of the terrain also affected the stability of structures. At the Basilica of Maxentius in Rome, the depth of the foundations (up to 8 m) was regulated according to the nature of the subsoil and the degree of stress to which they were subjected (Calabresi and Fattorini 2005: 77–79). The builders of the Colosseum also took special precautions to avoid settling by building a 6-m deep solid concrete foundation ring that spanned soils of different densities (Funiciello et al. 2002: 161–67; Lancaster 2005b: 57–59). In marshy areas, a common technique was to drive wooden piles (often iron-tipped) into the soil to create a stable platform on which to build (figure 10.1A), as at the Theater of Marcellus in Rome (Ciancio Rossetto 1995: 99) and the Circus at Arles (Sintès and Arcelin 1996: 78). Another method to stabilize the soil and to facilitate drainage was to bury amphoras underneath the foundations (figure 10.1B; Pesavento Mattioli 1998). On sites where a new building was constructed over the remnants of an older one, the builders often included relieving arches in the new walls to channel the loads to particular points in order to avoid different settling patterns within the building

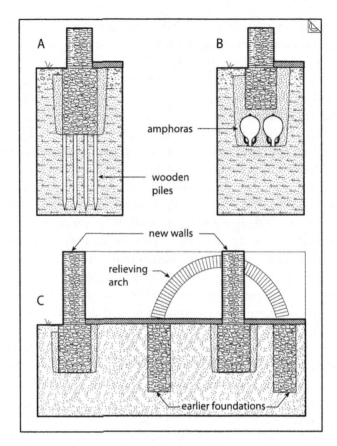

Figure 10.1. Methods of stabilizing foundations. A: wood piles; B: amphoras; C: relieving arches. (L. Lancaster.)

(figure 10.1C) as in the Domitianic walls built over Neronian foundations along the Clivus Palatinus (Tomei and Morganti 1986: 521).

## CONCRETE AND ITS FACINGS

One of the most renowned of the Roman contributions to building technology was the development of concrete, which affected not only vaulted roofing schemes but also bridge and harbor construction. By the late third century B.C., the builders were beginning to experiment with a type of mortared rubble construction, *opus caementicium*, which consisted of fist-sized pieces of stone, or *caementa*, set in mortar to create a solid mass. The main differences between *opus caementicium* and modern concrete are the size of the stones used and the method of putting the mixture in place. Modern concrete typically consists of a mix of cement-based mortar and an aggregate of small stones that is poured into place, whereas Roman concrete uses larger stones that are hand laid in the mortar and tamped into place. This type of construction belongs to what might be called a "wet technology," in that it requires great quantities of water to mix the mortar, and in fact the earliest examples occurred only after aqueducts began supplying a continuous flow of water into Rome, the earliest of which was the Appia (312 B.C.).

Roman concrete was different from earlier attempts at mortared rubble construction in that it contained a volcanic ash called pozzolana, which both increased the strength of the mortar and gave it hydraulic properties so that it could set under water. A simple lime mortar made of quartz sand, slaked lime, and water hardens and gains strength through its contact with carbon dioxide in the air, so the mortar at the center does not develop the same degree of strength as that closer to the outer surface. In contrast, when pozzolana is added, it plays an active role in the chemical transformation of the mortar throughout the mass. It contains both silica and alumina, which through the heat of the eruptive process are converted into soluble forms. The resulting chemical reaction creates internal formations that bind the elements together and strengthen the cohesiveness of the mortar (Lechtman and Hobbs 1987: 96–99; Oleson et al. 2006); studies show that the resistance to compression of pozzolana-lime mortar is five to eight times that of lime mortar (Ferretti 1997: 70). Roman builders also recognized that adding crushed terracotta to mortar would create a strong hydraulic mortar (Vitruvius, *De arch.* 2.5.7; Pliny, *HN* 36.175). This mixture (often referred to as *opus signinum* or, in Italian, *cocciopesto*) was used mainly as a waterproofing material for cisterns and elements exposed to the weather and as a setting bed for stone revetment, but in nonvolcanic areas outside of central Italy, crushed terracotta came to be added to the mortar of structural elements as a strengthening agent; the best known, although late, example is Hagia Sophia in Constantinople (Mainstone 1988: 70).

Pozzolana was produced by a number of different volcanic systems in central Italy from Rome to the Bay of Naples, and over time Roman builders learned that most varieties produced strong hydraulic mortar. The most famous sources of pozzolana are near Pozzuoli (ancient Puteoli), from which the modern term takes it name. The Colli Albani volcanic system south of Rome, however, produced vast quantities of pozzolana, which was used by builders in Rome. Scientific methods of analysis are being used to identify the constituent elements within Roman mortar, and future results should help clarify the patterns of use of the different types of pozzolana throughout the empire (Jackson and Marra 2006, Oleson et al. 2004, 2006; Saturno 2001; Chiari et al. 1996; Lamprecht 1987: 41–69).

Walls built of *opus caementicium* were faced with stone or brick, and the changes in the facing methods provide some insight into the relationships among building technology, society, and the economy. The facing elements of concrete walls formed a smooth outer surface, while the inner core consisted of *caementa* laid in abundant mortar. Both the facing and the core were laid and rose together as a single unit, usually with two masons working on opposite sides of the wall, as shown in a painting from the tomb of Trebius Justus outside Rome (Rea 2004: figs. 82–83). Vitruvius (*De arch.* 2.8.1) mentions two types of facing, *opus incertum* and *opus reticulatum*. The earlier of the two, *opus incertum*, appeared by the late third century B.C. and consisted of small blocks of stone placed in a random pattern (figure 10.2A). In Rome, the blocks were of soft volcanic tuff, whereas outside the volcanic zone around Rome, limestone was used. By the late second century B.C., the facing had become more regularized, so that it eventually consisted of square, pyramid shaped blocks of tuff set in a diagonal grid pattern, *opus reticulatum* (figure 10.2B). Two other modern terms, *opus quasi reticulatum* and *opus mixtum*, have been coined to describe different types of *opus reticulatum*. *Opus quasi reticulatum* refers to a rough type of *reticulatum* that does not form a regular grid, but it is a subjective term that should be used with caution. *Opus mixtum* refers to the technique that became common in the first and second centuries A.D. in which panels of *reticulatum* were separated by bands of brick facing (figure 10.2D).

The origins of *opus reticulatum* are inherently connected to Rome and its environs by both the building materials used and the social institutions involved. The earliest examples of the technique (Lacus Iuturnae, 116 B.C., and Temple of Magna Mater, 110–100 B.C.) employ pieces of the local, easily carved volcanic tuff. Vitruvius (*De arch.* 2.8.1, 2.8.5) makes clear that soft stones were used, and the availability of the tuff was no doubt a factor in the development of the technique. In spite of the decorative potential of *opus reticulatum*, one of the early polychrome examples, the Capitolium in Terracina (mid-first century B.C.), was apparently covered with plaster (Kammerer-Grothaus 1974: 229). Thus, aesthetics was unlikely to have been a major impetus for the initial development of the technique, although it was used later for decorative purposes (A. Wilson 2003). Structural superiority also can be eliminated as a reason for its development, as Vitruvius (*De arch.* 2.8.7) specifically states that it was inferior to *opus incertum* because of the tendency to develop cracks along the diagonal joints. He also stresses, however, that the mortared techniques were developed as a means of building more quickly than was possible with cut-stone construction, which he considered more stable and long lasting. Some scholars have argued that the development of *opus reticulatum* was part of a move toward more efficient work practices that took advantage of the increased slave pool after military conquests during the mid-second century B.C. (Coarelli 1977; Torelli 1980). The separation of the fashioning of the stone from the laying of the wall would have created a division of labor that allowed for newly acquired slave labor to be employed in the tasks requiring less training, and for the highly skilled labor (slave or free) to be used exclusively for putting the preformed blocks into place more efficiently. So the initial development of *opus reticulatum* was likely influenced by the availability of the easily shaped volcanic tuff of central Italy coupled with the military conquests that provided an increased labor force.

The use of *opus reticulatum* in the provinces is not common and often held special significance. The earliest datable example occurs in the retaining wall for the monument celebrating Octavian's victory over Mark Anthony at Actium in 31 B.C.

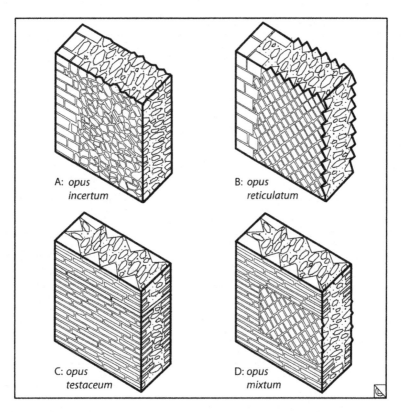

Figure 10.2. Wall facings used at Rome. A: *opus incertum*; B: *opus reticulatum*; C: *opus testaceum*; D: *opus mixtum*. (L. Lancaster.)

In this case, the choice probably carried a political message of Rome's dominance (Malacrino 2004: 119). Another Augustan example with possible imperial connections appears in the winter palace of Herod the Great at Jericho, where the workers may have been provided by Agrippa in 15 B.C. (Netzer 1990: 45). Sometimes the use of the technique can be directly related to a military presence, as in the Flavian city walls at Samosata in Syria, or to imperial intervention, as in the aqueduct at Antioch on the Orontes funded by Caligula after an earthquake in A.D. 37. At other times, the choice to use *opus reticulatum* stems from a desire to express a connection with the power base of Rome itself, as at Emesa (Syria) in the tomb of a prominent citizen, C. Julius Samsigeramos (A.D. 78–79) (Dodge 1990: 112; Spanu 1996: 923–39). Medri (2001) provides the most recent methodical examination of *opus reticulatum* in the provinces and concludes that it was often used to convey meaning but that the meaning changed according to the context. It is a building technique that provides an instructive example of the role played by technology in the transmission of messages of power, pride, and central authority.

During the first century A.D., *opus testaceum* (figure 10.2C), or brick-faced concrete, superseded *opus reticulatum* in Rome, although the two continued to be used together in *opus mixtum* until the late second century A.D. Fired brick is a latecomer to the building technology of ancient Rome—not for lack of knowledge but rather for lack of incentive. Fired terracotta was well known from the seventh century B.C., as is shown by roof tiles and decoration the Romans borrowed from the Etruscans (Cifani 2004: 220). The intensive production of flat bricks, however, developed only after the Augustan period. The earliest examples of brick/tile facing on concrete walls in Rome (first century B.C.) consist almost exclusively of roof tiles, usually with the flanges knocked off. Facing made with a mix of bricks and tiles then appears in the walls of the Castra Praetoria (A.D. 21–23) under Tiberius. Only under Claudius in the mid-first century A.D. were the walls faced predominantly with small bricks (*bessales* = ⅔ Roman foot square) cut or sawed into triangles (Lugli 1957: 588–90). One advantage of creating bricks specifically for walling rather than for roofs is that fuel costs could be reduced, because bricks for walling can be fired at a lower temperature than roof tiles, which require higher temperatures to ensure impermeability (Lugli 1957: 545; Olcese 1993: 124). The most critical change in brick production was the introduction of large bricks, *sesquipedales* (1½ Roman feet square) and especially *bipedales* (2 Roman feet square). Significantly, the increased use of brick coincides with the period after the fire under Nero in A.D. 64 that destroyed much of Rome and left in its wake a great concern for building fireproof structures in the city (Tacitus, *Ann.* 15.42). Within half a century, the brick industry had grown significantly and was providing income both to the wealthy who owned property with clay beds and to the workers who fashioned the bricks (Steinby 1993: 139–43).

The production of bricks in imperial Rome is a prime example of technological advance that resulted from increased organization rather than innovation. Bricks (as opposed to roof tiles) were produced in both southern and northern Italy at the sites Velia and Aquileia by the third and second centuries B.C., long before they became common in Rome (Righini 1970; Johannowski 1982: 23–26). The significant change in the first century A.D. in Rome is that brick manufacture reached an industrial scale never before achieved (cf. chapter 15). The appearance of bricks in Republican Rome was delayed largely because the abundance of tuff left little incentive to use them; only once the scale of building grew during the early imperial period was there sufficient demand to warrant dramatically increased production. Once it occurred, evidence shows that the bricks were often made in the same production units as other coarse wares such as dolia, mortaria, and terracotta sarcophagi (Gasperoni 2003: 39, 145, 176–80); thus the brick industry grew from a previously existing infrastructure.

The large-scale adoption of brick in Rome during the first century A.D. was certainly a factor behind its increased use in the provinces by the second century A.D.; nevertheless, brick was often used in the provinces in a different manner and for different reasons than in Rome. In the Greek east, brick tended to be used in bands of a few courses that extended the full thickness of the wall or as the main structural material composing the wall, whereas in Rome it was used only as a facing for concrete walls (Dodge 1987: 106–16). For example, compare the brick bands of facing in *opus mixtum* at Rome (figure 10.2D) and the solid brick bands in

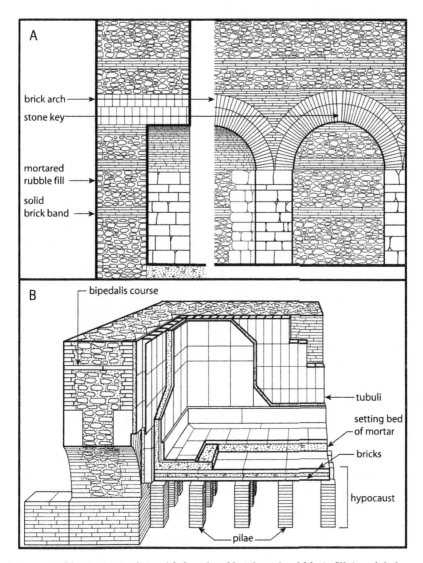

**Figure 10.3.** A: Pier construction with bands of brick and rubble infill (modeled on Gymnasium Complex at Sardis); B: Typical hypocaust construction in imperial Rome (adapted from Yegül 1992: fig. 442). (L. Lancaster.)

mortared rubble walls in Asia Minor (figure 10.3A). Yegül (1986: 124) suggests that the solid brick bands would have served to solidify the mortared rubble walls by compartmentalizing them so that uneven settlement and cracks could be better controlled. He points to a method still used by local builders in the earthquake-prone zone around Sardis, in which timbers are built into the fabric of the mortared walls to arrest vertical cracks. In Rome the builders sometimes used courses of *bipedales* that ran through the entire thickness of the wall (figure 10.3B), but these seem to have served more as a constructional aid by providing flat surfaces at critical points in the structure (top of foundations, spring of arches, stages of scaffolding), by aiding in keeping the wall true as it rose, and by marking critical levels within the building process, to name a few uses (DeLaine 1997: 143–45; Lancaster 1998: 285–99).

# LARGE-SCALE VAULTED STRUCTURES

The development of large-scale vaulted structures is one of the most significant Roman contributions to the history of building technology and engineering. One issue debated since the nineteenth century is whether large concrete vaults acted monolithically without exerting lateral thrusts on the walls. Some scholars have asserted that the pozzolana mortar created a concrete strong enough to resist internal tensile stresses so that it did indeed act monolithically (Blake 1959: 163; Ward-Perkins 1981: 101). Structural analyses have shown, however, that this claim is not true except for very small vaults where stresses remain low enough so that cracks do not develop (Mainstone 1975: 118; Mark et al. 1992: 120–31). For large concrete vaults, including the dome of the Pantheon, the existing cracks demonstrate that the material was not strong enough to remain monolithic. Moreover, the various building methods developed by the Roman builders to counter these lateral thrusts indicate that by the imperial period they understood that the outward thrusts had to be controlled.

The mastery of large and complex wooden centering was an important factor in building the most imposing concrete vaulted structures, and the use of the triangular truss was critical in this development. A truss has the advantage over a simple beam of spanning great distances using a number of smaller timbers that employ the principle of diagonal bracing. That trusses were in use by the time of Augustus is suggested by comments by Vitruvius (*De arch.* 4.2.1, 5.1.9; figure 17.8) and as implied by large spans achieved in structures like the Odeum of Agrippa at Athens (24.5 m span). The earliest graphic representation of the principle occurs on a relief found under the Palazzo della Cancelleria in Rome that depicts a wooden amphitheater with triangular trusses, dating from either the first (Coarelli 2001: fig. 3) or second century A.D. (Rodriguez-Almeida 1994: 215–17). Diagonal bracing was probably used much earlier in the Hellenistic siege towers of the fourth and third centuries B.C., as implied later on by Apollodorus's second-century A.D. treatise that describes the construction of such towers (Lendle 1983: 77–107). In fact, similar structures may well have been used to form the central towers for the centering of large domes like that of the Pantheon (Rasch 1991: 365, 369–70; Lancaster 2005a: 45), although some scholars maintain that large domes were built without the aid of a central tower (Adam 1994: 175–76; Taylor 2003: 195–208).

Studies using photogrammetry on domes have shed light on the development of wooden centering structures. Rakob's (1988) photogrammetric documentation

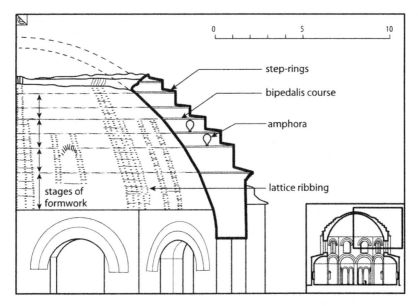

Figure 10.4. Section through dome of "Temple of Minerva Medica" in Rome (first half of fourth century A.D.). (L. Lancaster.)

of the dome of the "Temple of Mercury" at Baiae (21.6 m span) revealed that the dome has significant deformations in profile from one part to another suggesting that the technology used to build the wooden structure was not yet perfected. A complementary study is included in Rasch's (1991: 370–79) documentation of a series of fourth-century A.D. domes around Rome, including the Tor de'Schiavi (13.2 m span), the "Temple of Minerva Medica" (24.0 m span), and the Mausoleum of Helena (20.2 m span). These domes show no sign of deformation, and the details of construction, such as the use of courses of *bipedales* that coincide both with the ends of the formwork board imprints and with the tops of the step-rings surrounding the extrados of the dome (figure 10.4) show that the construction process had become much more systematic and regularized.

Along with the ability to build large wooden centering structures came a greater understanding of the behavior of vaults once the centering was removed. An advantage of concrete is that the weight of the material in different parts of the building can be controlled by regulating the type of *caementa* used. This proved to be a critical factor in the success of the largest and most daring vaults. The local volcanic geology of central Italy provided a variety of different types of stones from leucititic lava, or *selce*, (2,800 kg/m$^3$) to pumice (600–700 kg/m$^3$), which were used to regulate the weight of the concrete with lighter stones at the top and heavier stones lower down. The move toward using lighter stones in vaults had already begun in the second half of the first century B.C., but the technique was used systematically only from the latter part of the first century A.D. It was later used outside of central Italy in isolated areas with access to lightweight volcanic stones, such as in the volcanic region of the Hauran in Syria in the baths at Bostra and Philippolis of the late second and third centuries (Ward-Perkins 1958: 343–46) and near a volcanic zone in southeast Turkey in baths at Hieropolis Kastabala, Anazarbus, and Tarsos (Spanu 2003: 25).

The most advanced use of lightweight *caementa* began to appear in Rome in the early second century A.D. under Trajan, when Vesuvian scoria from the Bay of Naples was imported specifically for the purpose of use in vaults at the Baths of Trajan and the Basilica Ulpia. It was then used later in the dome of the Pantheon and various other imperial structures through the third century A.D. The scoria is somewhat heavier (750–850 kg/m$^3$) but more durable than the pumice (600–700 kg/m$^3$) that was available closer to Rome. Structural analyses of the Pantheon have shown that its use at the crown of the dome significantly reduced the tensile stresses within the material and the outward thrust on the walls (Mark and Hutchinson 1986: 24–34; Lancaster 2005a: 158–61). The scoria appears almost exclusively in imperially sponsored buildings in Rome, suggesting that the builders were well enough aware of its advantages to cause the imperial administration to import it for the most daring vaulted structures. It was one of the only nondecorative construction stones imported from outside the immediate environs of Rome.

The Pantheon dome also illustrates another method of controlling the mass of vaults: the use of step-rings. The finite element structural analysis by Mark and Hutchinson (1986: 24–34) revealed that the addition of the step-rings along the haunch of the vault played a critical role in reducing the tensile stresses in the dome once it cracked. The combination of lightweight *caementa* together with the step-rings suggests that the builders understood that simply making the dome lighter was not sufficient; the critical issue was to make the crown of the dome as light as possible while adding weight, or surcharge, to its haunch. Thrust-line analyses show that if the entire dome had been made as light as the crown, the lateral thrust actually would have increased (Lancaster 2005a: 158–61).

One of the basic methods of countering the lateral thrusts in vaults was to juxtapose the vaults so that they balanced each other. This technique was used in the earliest concrete vaulted structures in Italy from the second century B.C., such as the Sanctuary of Fortuna Primigenia at Palestrina, the vaulted structure in Rome traditionally associated with the Porticus Aemilia (Tucci 2006), and the Stabian Baths at Pompeii. Later, this technique was honed and used as a way of providing buttressing for very large vaults. A particularly impressive example was the "Serapeum" (second/third century A.D.) at Ephesus (17 m span), where the cut stone vault of the central room was buttressed by narrow vaulted passages on either side (Walters 1995: 295–304).

From the principle of juxtaposing vaults grew the idea of the buttressing arch, which was developed in the context of the imperial thermae. The control of the outward thrusts of vaults became critical once bath buildings grew in size, because the central cross-vaulted frigidarium had to be elevated above the surrounding rooms to allow for natural light. In fact, Seneca (*Ep.* 86.8, 90.25) notes that the lighting of the new baths of his day (mid-first century A.D.) was one of the major

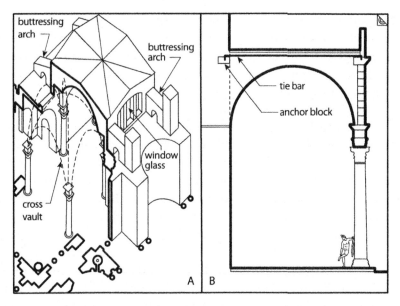

Figure 10.5. Methods of countering lateral thrusts in vaults. A: Buttressing arches at Baths of Diocletian; B: Typical tie bar construction found in palaestra vaults of imperial bath buildings in Rome. (L. Lancaster.)

differences from the old-fashioned baths, and he relates this phenomenon directly to the recent introduction of window glass. Once the cross vaults of the frigidarium were elevated, the lateral thrusts were contained and directed down to the lower walls by placing buttressing arches along the sides of the elevated cross vault (figure 10.5A). The buttressing elements are isolated at the corners of the cross vaults, thereby allowing for light to enter the lunettes through the glass panes that filled them. These buttressing arches represent the first step toward the development of the flying buttresses of such medieval masterpieces as Chartres Cathedral.

# THE STRUCTURAL REINFORCEMENT OF VAULTS AND ARCHES

Another means of controlling the lateral thrusts of vaults was the iron tie bar, which was used in conjunction with vaults supported on colonnades, usually made up of monolithic shafts of foreign colored stones. The growing taste for colored stones during the first century A.D. occurred together with the development of advanced vault forms, so that a natural progression occurred toward the integration of two building methods: the post and lintel system, which showed off the colored stone columns, with the concrete vaulted system, which allowed for curvilinear forms with flat terraces above. There were probably early attempts at the use of tie bars under Augustus, but the fully developed form appeared in the early second century A.D. in the Baths of Trajan and possibly the Basilica Ulpia. The technological conundrum encountered by the builders was how to stabilize a row of columns that supported a concrete vault, which could produce lateral thrusts both during and after construction. At the palaestrae of the Baths of Trajan, and later the palaestrae of the Baths of Caracalla (DeLaine 1985: 198–202) and of Diocletian, they solved it by embedding a stone anchor block into the concrete wall for the attachment of an iron tie bar that extended through the crown of the vault to one of the entablature blocks above the colonnade (figure 10.5B). In this way, they were able to stabilize the colonnades and also to provide a flat concrete terrace from which to watch the activities in the palaestra. This use of the tie bar is different from that in later Byzantine and Renaissance architecture because the tie bar was concealed in the crown of the vault rather than exposed at the springing of the vault. Presumably this was an aesthetic decision by the designers, who did not want the tie bars to intrude on the space created by the curving form of the vaults (Lancaster 2005a: 113–25 with bibliography).

The shift toward the use of exposed tie bars can ultimately be related to the decline of the marble trade and with it a transformation of aesthetic values. During the fourth century, flat architraves were often replaced by arcuated lintels, which were typically created with brick arches supported on columns taken from earlier structures, as in Santa Costanza (Guidobaldi 1995: 419–41). The new style became popular, at least in part, because it eliminated the necessity for marble architraves, which were no longer easily available unless taken from earlier structures (Pensabene 2001: 122–23). By the time arcades became the preferred style in fourth-century Rome (they had been popular in the east for some time), concrete vaults were not as common as they had once been, and therefore, the tie bars were not so necessary. However, once the imperial court moved to Constantinople in A.D. 330 and the resources were concentrated in the Byzantine world, vaulted architecture combined with arcades became the dominant style, and metal tie bars and wooden tie beams became exposed design elements (Ousterhout 1999: 210–16). The transition to the use of exposed ties ultimately represents the different aesthetic values of a culture that no longer had access to the same material resources that the imperial capital had once commanded; therefore, new styles were adopted that incorporated the former technology but in a different form.

The Roman interest in controlling the forces within their vaulted structures is demonstrated by the development of vaulting ribs. The earliest concrete vaults were built with the stone *caementa* set radially in imitation of the voussoirs of an arch, but by the imperial period in Rome the *caementa* were set in horizontal courses, thus indicating an increased understanding of the strength of pozzolana mortar. In places of extraordinary loads, however, the builders continued to reinforce the concrete vault with radially-set stones or bricks that acted as ribs. Sig-

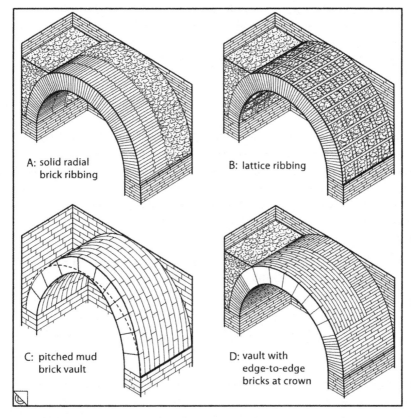

Figure 10.6. Types of brick vault construction. A: Solid radial brick ribbing; B: Lattice ribbing; C: Pitched mud brick vaulting; D: Vaulting with edge-to-edge bricks at crown. (L. Lancaster.)

nificantly, the earliest example occurs at the Sanctuary of Hercules Victor at Tivoli (mid-first century B.C.), where the reinforcement consists of arches of the locally quarried travertine. The earliest and only example of the use of such travertine vaulting ribs in Rome occurs over a century later in the substructures at the Colosseum, to reinforce concrete vaults that supported walls above. All other ribs in subsequent buildings in imperial Rome employ large bricks, *bipedales*, in one form or another (figure 10.6A; Lancaster 2005a: 86–112). The idea of reinforcing the vault developed in cut-stone construction and was then translated into brick during the first century A.D. The concept of reinforcing the vault at particular points grew from a need to create larger and more complicated structures in which walls did not necessarily align from one level to the next, so the use of concrete reinforced with ribs ultimately allowed for a greater freedom of design.

The subsequent development of the vaulting rib in Rome followed the vicissitudes of the brick industry and demonstrates the way in which technological development goes hand in hand with economic fluctuations. From the late first century A.D., brick stamps often give the name of the landowner of the clay bed as well as the brick maker, so we have an indication of the number and types of people involved in the brick industry and how they changed over time. Indeed the brick industry in Rome involved the gamut of social classes including slaves, freedmen, and members of the senatorial class (both men and women), who all benefited financially from the production of bricks. The period during the late first and early second centuries when the greatest number of people was involved is the period when the *bipedalis* ribs were most common. During the second half of the second century, imperial building in Rome declined and with it so did the production of bricks. The brick ribs then changed in both form and function. The *bipedalis* ribs were eventually superseded by ribs built of a latticework of *bipedales* separated by smaller bricks, so that fewer large bricks were used (figure 10.6B). Whereas the solid *bipedalis* ribs had once been carefully placed in specific load-bearing situations, the lattice ribs commonly extend the entire length of a barrel vault. In some cases they appear to be intended to reinforce the vaults against the loads of walls above, as in the Baths of Maxentius on the Palatine (Lancaster 2005a: 104–5), but in others, such as the Basilica of Maxentius, the lattice ribbing was used to help evenly distribute the loads within the enormous (25 m span) barrel vaults (Amici 2005: 134–36). The change in the form and use of brick ribbing is one example of the effect that the local economy had on building technology.

The use of radially-laid brick ribbing in Rome can be contrasted with the brick vaulting in the provinces, where the material and technique were applied in a different manner and for different reasons. Outside of Rome, radially-laid brick vaults had different roots and were not used primarily as reinforcement. Early examples occur in a mid-first-century B.C. tomb (ca. 1.0 m span) at Sarsina, Italy (Ortalli 1987: 166, pl. 23a) and in Asia Minor at a first-century A.D. tomb (2.2 m span) at Sardis (Hanfmann and Waldbaum 1975: 59–60), but they both covered very small spaces that were built into the ground so that lateral thrusts were not an issue. Later examples of brick barrel vaults in large standing structures, which began to appear in the late first or early second century A.D. in Asia Minor (Hume-i Tepe Baths at Miletus), differ from the typical brick ribbing in Rome in that the entire intrados of the vault was built of radially-laid brick with an infill of mortared rubble at the haunches. Barrel vaults built entirely of radially-laid brick occur in Rome, but they are not common and usually relate to special structural circumstances (Lancaster 2005a: 91–98). Bricks offered the advantage of acting as substitutes for stone voussoirs, thus avoiding the meticulous carving of the wedge-shaped blocks, and in doing so avoiding the need for high quality pozzolana mortar. Moreover, bricks ($1{,}350$–$1{,}600$ kg/m$^3$) were much lighter than the typically available stones, often limestone ($2{,}600$ kg/m$^3$). Bath buildings, which were particularly well suited to vaulted construction for reasons of fireproofing and resistance to the moist environment, tended to be the harbingers of new vaulting techniques outside of Rome. Examples of large-scale radial brick barrel vaulting (12–18 m spans) can be seen from the second century A.D. at Ephesus in the Harbor Baths, East Baths, and Theater Baths, and at Sardis in the Bath-Gymnasium Complex (Yegül 1986: 127–28; 1992: 258).

The large bath complexes at Ephesus and Sardis also provide instructive examples of the way the provincial builders, working within a tradition of cut stone masonry, were thinking about transferring loads in large structures. The vaults of radially-laid brick (or mortared rubble) were often supported on stone piers connected by brick or stone arches, whereas the partition walls between the piers typically consisted of less solid mortared rubble or brick (figure 10.3A). The system implies a desire to channel the load to the stone piers, which were perceived as more stable but took greater effort to build, while the mortared rubble walls were left largely non–load bearing (Yegül 1992: 266–70). Similarly, in Republican architecture in Rome the builders had been careful to use the stones with the greatest resistance (typically travertine) at points of greatest stress, such as under columns and at the springing of arches. The reinforcing ribs in imperial vaults reflect a developed form of the same principle.

# HEATING SYSTEMS

The spread of the bathing habit and consequent desire for bath buildings led to technological advances in heating methods, such as the invention of the hypocaust for heating the floors (figure 10.3B) and later the related innovations for heating the walls and vaults. The fundamental idea for a raised heated floor was probably already developed in the Greek world, as is shown by the third-century B.C. baths at Gortys in Arcadia, but the systematic exploitation seems to have occurred in Campania in the late second century B.C., where there was a thriving tradition of fired architectural terracottas (DeLaine 1989: 124). Terracotta was advantageous because it was fireproof and bricks made of it were produced in modular sizes so that the four corners would fit onto the regularly spaced *pilae* that supported them (Webster 1979: 287). The next step, to heat the walls, seems to have occurred in the first century B.C., when one finds *tegulae mammatae*, bricks with bosses at the corners of one side, used to create a space for hot air along the walls at Pompeii in the Forum Baths and Stabian Baths (Yegül 1992: 363). The most advanced form of wall heating came with the introduction of *tubuli*, rectangular hollow tubes that lined the walls (figure 10.3B). The combination of the hypocausts with the *tubuli* created a much higher percentage of warm surfaces in a single room so that larger rooms could be adequately heated. Only after such innovations had occurred could bath buildings reach the scale of the imperial thermae and maintain the appropriate temperature while also allowing glass-filled openings for light.

# PROVINCIAL CONTRIBUTIONS TO CONSTRUCTION TECHNIQUES

New building techniques were often added to the Roman repertoire by builders in the provinces. An example is pitched brick vaulting, a technique that had developed as early as the third millennium B.C. in Egypt and Mesopotamia. Such vaults were constructed by placing mud bricks edge-to-edge so that they formed the curve of the vault (figure 10.6C). The bricks were leaned at an angle against the wall so that each ring of brick could be "glued" onto the preceding ring by means of a fast-drying gypsum mortar. Slanting the bricks helped ensure that the succeeding rings did not slip off before the mortar dried, so that the vault could be built with minimal, if any, wooden centering, which was a critical issue in areas where wood was scarce. In Roman Egypt this traditional building method continued into the Roman period, as is shown by the pitched mud brick vaulting in the first-century A.D. grain warehouses at Karanis (Ward-Perkins 1958: 91–93).

A variation on pitched brick vaulting appeared in the second century A.D. in Greece at Argos (Aupert and Ginouvès 1989), Eleusis (Durm 1905: fig. 275), and Isthmia where fired bricks were set edge-to-edge, albeit upright (not pitched). The examples at Eleusis and Isthmia are small drain vaults that could have been built without centering, but the largest of the Greek examples, the Theater Baths at Argos, has a span of almost 11 meters. Given the size of this vault, the fact that the bricks are not pitched, and the use of lime-based rather than gypsum-based mortar, the motive for using the technique is not likely to have been to eliminate the need for centering. A somewhat different variation appears in barrel vaults in Asia Minor from the mid-second century A.D. where radial brick vaulting at the haunch is combined with edge-to-edge brick vaulting in the crown (figure 10.6D) Examples can be seen in Slope House 2 at Ephesus and the late second to early third-century substructures of the basilicas at Aspendos and at Izmir (Dodge 1987). These barrel vaults with vertically set, edge-to-edge bricks are typically listed among examples of "pitched" brick vaulting, but the bricks are not actually pitched. They may well be influenced by military contact at this time with Parthia, where the bricks were already set in similar fashion in the first-century A.D. palace at Assur (Reuther 1938: fig. 100).

True pitched brick vaulting occurs particularly in shapes of double curvature, such as the dome, semidome, and sail vault (domical vault set on a square base). Small sail vaults can be seen at Ephesus in the third-century A.D. Slope House 2, EM6 (ca. 2 m span), and by the early fourth century the technique was used at a larger scale in the dome (ca. 13.5 m span) of the mausoleum of Diocletian at Split (Hebrard and Zeiller 1912: 89–90, 93–94). That this type of construction was intended to reduce the amount of centering needed is implied by a fourth-century letter of Gregory of Nyssa (*PG* XLVI, 1097) to the Bishop of Iconium requesting workmen skilled in constructing vaults without centering because of a dearth of wood in the area. Earlier large domes had been built of radially-laid brick, as can be seen in the two rotundas to either side of the mid-second-century A.D. "Serapeum" at Pergamon (12 m span). Fragments of radially-laid brick found in the excavation of the Temple of Aesclepius at Pergamon suggest that it too had a massive dome (23.9 m span) of radially-laid brick (Ziegenaus 1981: 46). The technique of using pitched brick does not appear in Rome until the early fifth century in the restoration of some of the towers of the Aurelian walls under Honorius. It was likely brought to Rome by eastern craftsmen, if not by military personnel directly (Cozza 1987: 42, fig. 4).

Other terracotta vaulting techniques were also developed in the provinces. At the legionary baths at Chester (third century) in Britain, the barrel vaults were built with hollow terracotta voussoirs placed end to end (figure 10.7A). These elements have been found at numerous nonmilitary sites in southeast England as well, usually in bath buildings (Brodribb 1987: 80–81; Johnston 1978: 82). Some (but not all) of the hollow voussoirs have holes cut in the sides indicating that they were intended to have hot air circulating within them (Brodribb 1987: 79–83). The most notable examples, however, occur at the Great Baths at Bath (second half of second century A.D.), in two large barrel vaults (13.5 m and 10.5 m spans), and there they did not have holes in the sides and were clearly not used to form a heated ceiling (Cunliffe 1969: 98, pl. 20.b and 1). In this case, hollow tiles would have provided a means of reducing the weight of such large vaults in a region with no access to lightweight volcanic stones. This technique was probably introduced into Britain by the military. The legions had their own terracotta manufacturing units that would have facilitated technological experimentation. Both the bathing habit and the technology that accompanied it then spread to civilian contexts.

Another innovative means of constructing vaults, also connected to bath buildings, is the so-called armchair voussoir, which is a voussoir (typically of terracotta but occasionally of stone) that has notches to support flat bricks that form hollow channels between each arched rib (figure 10.7B). The earliest example (terracotta) of the concept has been found in excavations at Fregellae in a bath building dating to the early second century B.C., but there the voussoirs supported only one layer of bricks such that there were no hollow channels between the ribs (Tsiolis 2001: 106–8, figs. 6–7; Coarelli 1998: 61). This example represents an early attempt at creating a vault without having to carve the individual voussoirs at a time before concrete vaulting had been fully developed. The more advanced form with hollow channels appeared during the second and third centuries A.D. in various parts of the western Mediterranean, including Britain (Brodribb 1987: 46), France, southern Spain, Portugal, and northern Morocco (Torrecilla Aznar 1999; Finker 1986 both with bibliography).

A third vaulting technique employing terracotta is the use of vaulting tubes, or *tubi fittili* (figure 10.7C). Vaults using this system consist of a series of interlocking terracotta tubes often connected by quick-setting gypsum mortar that held them in place to form the curved intrados. The earliest examples occur in a third-century B.C. bath building at Morgantina, Sicily (Allen 1974: 376–79) in both a domed and

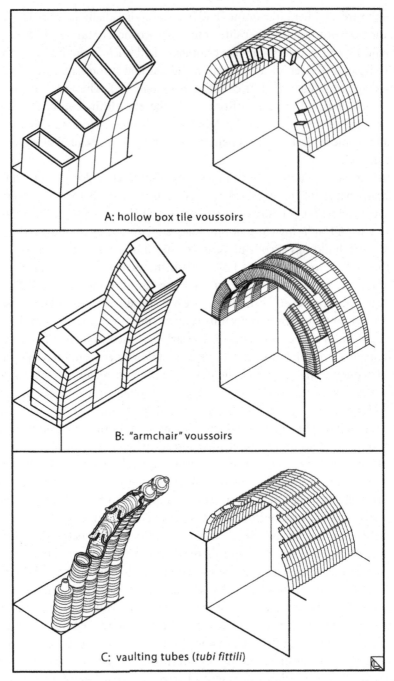

Figure 10.7. Methods of terracotta vault construction. A: Hollow terracotta voussoirs; B: Armchair voussoirs; C: Vaulting tubes (*tubi fittili*). (L. Lancaster.)

a barrel vaulted room (spans ca. 6 m). The tubes are about three times larger (60–70 cm long) than the tubes that became common four centuries later in North Africa (12–20 cm) and are clearly in an experimental phase. Another early example has been found in a second-century B.C. bath at Cabrera del Mar in southern Spain (Martín 2000: 160). R. J. A. Wilson (1992: 107–8) cites later examples of a method of kiln construction in which pots were interlocked mouth to foot to create the vaulted superstructure of the firing chamber and suggests that the original idea for the vaulting tubes may be an adaptation of this type of kiln construction. The vaulting tubes at Morgantina are quite similar in size and manufacture to the drainage tubes found throughout the site. The existing infrastructure for creating the drainage tubes probably provided the impetus for this creative adaptation. As with the early example of the armchair voussoirs at Fregellae, the creation of these vaulting tubes was likely a response to the functional needs of a bath structure at a time before concrete vaulting had developed.

The greatest proliferation of the *tubi fittili* occurs in Tunisia in the late second century A.D., once concrete vaulting was well established. As with pitched brick vaulting, a motive for their use may have been to avoid the use of wooden centering (Storz 1994: 67). Tunisia was the center of various terracotta industries, including transport amphoras for agricultural products, especially olive oil. Finds of Africana 1 Tunisian oil amphoras suggest that oil production in this area had begun to increase in the late second century A.D. (Mattingly 1988: 51, 6), precisely when the vaulting tubes began to appear. The proliferation of the technique in North Africa at this time must have been in part inspired by the existing terracotta infrastructure (Rakob 1982: 114). The initial spread of the technique outside of North Africa during the early third century tends to be focused on military sites. Examples include Bath F3 at Dura Europus and baths at British legionary forts at Caerleon (Zienkiewicz 1986: 336), Chester (Mason 1990: 215–22), and York (Whitwell 1976: 45). The date of Bath F3 at Dura Europos, which contains the vaulting tubes, was originally considered to be the first century A.D., but more recent reevaluations put it in the latter part of the second century A.D. (Deichmann 1979: 483–85; Storz 1994: 83 n. 56; Downey 2000: 165). The use of vaulting tubes offered a variety of advantages, but it is also a technique that was intimately connected to the wider terracotta industry that in turn was related to both agricultural production and military production.

A method of vault construction often confused with the vaulting tubes is the technique of embedding amphoras into concrete vaults (figure 10.4), but the two techniques are quite different in origins and application. The placing of amphoras within concrete vaults has typically been seen as an independent phenomenon, but it is best viewed as part of a long history of the reuse of amphoras for land reclamation projects going back to at least to the fourth century B.C. (see above, figure 10.1B). Embedding the amphoras into concrete seems to have been modeled on this practice, and the earliest examples at Aosta and Pompeii occur in foundations and walls rather than vaults. The earliest examples in vaults occur during the Hadrianic period outside of Rome proper and usually consist of the globular Dressel 20 oil amphoras from Spain (at the Villa alla Vignaccia in the suburbs of Rome, at a horrea building at Ostia, and in the Casa de la Exedra at Italica, Spain). Another second-century example has been found in a barrel vault at the Harbor Baths at Elaeussa Sebaste on the southern coast of Turkey, employing Anemurium A type amphoras (Borgia and Spanu 2003: 308, fig. 260). After these early sporadic occurrences, the technique reappears within the city of Rome in the late third to early fourth century A.D., with a concentration during the reign of Maxentius (A.D. 306–12), when as many as 6,000 or more were used in the vaults of the circus at his villa on the Via Appia. The common explanation for the use of the amphoras in vaults is that they were intended to lessen the weight and therefore the lateral thrusts of the vaults, but a calculation of the weight reduction shows that it was negligible and often occurred in the wrong part of the structure to have been effective (Lancaster 2005a: 68–85, 160–64 with bibliography). The examples in fourth-century Rome coincide with a period of decline in Italy after the economic crisis of the mid-third century when building materials were not as easily attainable as earlier. The initial use of the amphoras was probably an attempt to save on materials and labor following the practice of using them for land reclamation.

Both the amphoras and the vaulting tubes became common in early Christian architecture in Italy and in the Byzantine east (Ousterhout 1999: 229), but both were used in a different manner than they had been earlier. The vaulting tubes, which in the second and third centuries were used as permanent centering for concrete vaults, were later used in early Christian architecture as a type of lightweight vaulting in its own right, often without significant fill on top (Storz 1994: 68). The lightweight vaults exerted less horizontal thrust than a solid concrete vault, so thinner, more economical walls could be used while also reducing the amount of wooden formwork needed. The use of amphoras in Byzantine vaults also reveals changing motives. In some cases, rather than embedding the amphoras into the concrete, the builders simply stacked them up above the haunches of the vault as a means of providing a lightweight filler to support a wooden roof structure or to create a level surface above (Ousterhout 1999: fig. 194). By the early medieval period the vessels were not limited to transport amphoras as earlier but often included kiln clinkers and household pots (Mazzucato 1970: 339–41), a situation that reflects the changing economic conditions of the times.

Technological prowess, today as in antiquity, is equated with cultural superiority, and the Romans certainly promoted it as such. The ability to amass the resources to fund and to provide the materials, expertise, and manpower for large construction projects was a major display of power that became evident throughout the Empire. Technological innovation occurs in response to a number of conditions including *accumulated knowledge*, *evident need*, *economic possibility*, and *social/cultural acceptability* (White 1984: 21), and a brief summary of the conditions that influenced Roman innovation provides some additional insight into the motivating forces within Roman culture. For the builders in Rome during the Republic, the *accumulated knowledge* was partially inherited from the Greek world and partially a result of their own experience with the wide variety of materials available in the volcanic region of central Italy. Later, during the imperial period, technological knowledge was transferred back and forth throughout the Roman world with extended trading patterns and military movements as the primary agents. The unification of Roman territories during the imperial period was a critical factor in providing financing as well as establishing various production infrastructures that paved the way for technological change. The terracotta industry in particular provided the *economic possibility* for new materials and methods such as hypocausts, hollow terracotta voussoirs, vaulting tubes, and even the advanced uses of fired bricks for vaulting ribs. The *evident need* for advances in previously existing building technologies both in Rome and in the provinces most often accompanied the desire for public amenities, namely places of entertainment such as theaters and amphitheaters and, most importantly, bath buildings. Theaters and baths, which provided a place to display the latest materials and architectural forms, were at the forefront of building technology in every part of the Roman world. Moreover, the natural resources and traditions of particular regions within the empire often resulted in creative modifications of techniques developed in Rome or in entirely new solutions better suited to the local materials. *Social/cultural acceptability* also played a role in the development of new techniques. The sporadic use of *opus reticulatum* in the provinces provides an example of the way in which technology could be used as used as a means of expressing Roman identity. The marble trade and the availability of colored stones from conquered territories was an expression of power that resulted in changing aesthetic preferences, which in turn led to technological developments such as the use of hidden metal tie bars in vaulted colonnades. The various industries that supplied large building projects throughout the empire relied on the social institution of slavery and with it manumission of slaves into freedmen; these saw the building industry as a means of social and economic advancement, which provided impetus for innovation in building techniques and in the manufacturing, production, and supply processes on which they were dependent. With the rise of Christianity in the fourth century, the situation changed with the redirection of funds and resources toward the building of ecclesiastical structures, the most impressive of which were no longer centered in Rome itself. So, by the sixth century, the advanced building techniques of the day, such as exposed tie bars/ beams, pitched brick vaults, and thin and lightweight vaults of *tubi fittili,* were more often found further east in Byzantine centers such as Constantinople.

# REFERENCES

Adam, J.-P. 1994. *Roman building: Materials and techniques.* Translated by Anthony Mathews. London: Batsford.

Allen, H. L. 1974. "Excavations at Morgantina (Serra Orlando)," *American Journal of Archaeology* 78: 361–83.

Amici, C. M. 2005. "Construction techniques and processes," in Giavarini and Amici 2005, 125–60.

Anderson, J. C. 1997. *Roman architecture and society.* Baltimore: Johns Hopkins University Press.

Aupert, P., and R. Ginouvès 1989. "Une toiture revolutionnaire a Argos," in S. Walker and A. Cameron (eds.), *The Greek renaissance in the Roman Empire.* Papers from the 10th British Museum Classical Colloquium. London: University of London, Institute of Classical Studies, 151–55.

Blake, M. E. 1959. *Roman construction in Italy from Tiberius through the Flavians.* Washington, D.C.: Carnegie Institution of Washington.

Borgia, E., and M. Spanu 2003. "Le terme del porto," in E. Equini Schneider (ed.), *Elaiussa Sebaste II. Un ponte tra Oriente e Occidente.* Rome: L'Erma di Bretschneider, 247–335.

Brodribb, G. 1987. *Roman brick and tile.* Gloucester: Alan Sutton Publishing.

Calabresi, G., and M. Fattorini 2005. "Subsoil and foundations," in Giavarini and Amici 2005, 75–91.

Chiari, G., L. Cimitàn, G. della Ventura, M. G. Filetici, M. L. Santarelli, and G. Torraca 1996. "Le malte pozzolaniche del mausoleo di Sant'Elena e le pozzolane di Torpignattara," *Materiali e Strutture* 4.1: 1–36.

Ciancio Rossetto, P. 1995. "Indagini e restauri nel Campo Marzio meridionale: Teatro di Marcello, Portico d'Ottavia, Circo Flaminio, Porto Tiberino," *Archeologia Laziale* 12.1: 93–101.

Cifani, G. 1994. "Aspetti dell'edilizia romana arcaica," *Studi Etruschi* 60: 185–226.

Cifani, G. 2004. "Recenti approcci e metodi per lo studio dell'edilizia antica: Il caso della Roma arcaica," in E. De Sena and H. Dessales (eds.), *Metodi e approci archeologici: L'industria e il commercio nell'Italia antica.* Oxford: Archaeopress, 219–25.

Coarelli, F. 1977. "Public building in Rome between the Second Punic War and Sulla," *Papers of the British School in Rome* 45: 1–23.

Coarelli, F. 1998. *Fregellae.* Vol. 1, *Le fonti, la storia, il territorio.* Rome: Quasar.

Coarelli, F. 2001. "Gli anfiteatri a Roma prima del Colosseo," in A. La Regina (ed.), *Sangue e arena.* Milan: Electa, 43–77.

Coulton, J. J. 1974. "Lifting in early Greek architecture," *Journal of Hellenic Studies* 94: 1–19.

Cozza, L. 1987. "Osservazioni sulle mura aureliane a Roma," *Analecta Romana* 16: 25–52.

Cunliffe, B. W. 1969. *Roman Bath.* Oxford: Society of Antiquaries.

Deichmann, F. W. 1979. "Westliche Bautechnik im römischen und rhomaischen Osten," *Römische Mitteilungen* 86: 473–527.

DeLaine, J. 1985. "An engineering approach to Roman Building techniques: The Baths of Caracalla in Rome," in C. Malone and S. Stoddart (eds.), *Papers in Italian archaeology IV, Part iv: Classical and medieval archaeology.* Oxford: British Archaeological Reports, Intl. Series S246. Oxford: BAR, 195–206.

DeLaine, J. 1989. "Some observations on the transition from Greek to Roman baths in Hellenistic Italy," *Mediterranean Archaeology* 2: 111–25.

DeLaine, J. 1997. *The Baths of Caracalla: A study in the design, construction, and economics of large-scale building projects in Imperial Rome. Journal of Roman Archaeology* Suppl. 25. Portsmouth, RI: JRA.

DeLaine, J. 2003. "The builders of Roman Ostia: Organization, status and society," in S. Huerta (ed.), *Proceedings of the First International Congress on Construction History,* Vol. 2. Madrid: Instituto Juan de Herrera, Escuela Técnica Superior de Arquitectura, 723–32.

Dodge, H. 1987. "Brick construction in Roman Greece and Asia Minor," in S. Macready and F. H. Thompson (eds.), *Roman architecture in the Greek world*. London: Society of Antiquaries of London/Thames and Hudson, 106–16.

Dodge, H. 1990. "The architectural impact of Rome in the East," in M. Henig (ed.), *Architecture and architectural sculpture in the Roman Empire*. Oxford: Oxbow, 108–20.

Downey, S. 2000. "The transformation of Seleucid Dura-Europos," in E. Fentress (ed.), *Romanization and the City: Proceedings of a conference held at the AAR to celebrate the 50th anniversary of the excavations at Cosa 14–16 May 1998*. Journal of Roman Archaeology Suppl. 38. Portsmouth, RI: JRA, 155–72.

Durm, J. 1905. *Handbuch der Architektur: Die Baukunst der Etrusker und der Römer*. Stuttgart: A. Kröner.

Ferretti, A. S. 1997. "Proposte per lo studio teoritico-sperimentale della statica dei monumenti in *opus caementicium*," *Materiali e strutture* 7.2–3: 63–84.

Finker, M. 1986. "Les briques claveaux: Un matériau de construction spécifique des thermes romains," *Aquitania* 4: 143–50.

Funiciello, R., L. Lombardi, and F. Marra 2002. "La geologia della Valle dell'Anfiteatro," in R. Rea (ed.), *Rota Colisei: La valle del Colosseo attraverso i secoli*. Milan: Electa, 161–67.

Gasperoni, T. 2003. *Le fornaci dei Domitii: Ricerche topografiche a Mugnano in Teverina*. Viterbo: Diadalos.

Giavarini, C., and C. M. Amici (eds.) 2005. *The Basilica of Maxentius: The monument, its materials, construction and stability*. Rome: L'Erma di Bretschneider.

Greene, K. 1992. "How was technology transferred in the eastern provinces?" in M. Wood and F. Queiroga (eds.), *Current research on the Romanization of the western provinces*. Oxford: Tempus Reparatum, 101–5.

Guidobaldi, F. 1995. "Sull'originalità dell'architettura di età costantiniana," *Corsi di Cultura sull'arte ravennate e bizantina* 42: 419–41.

Hanfmann, G. M. A. 1983. *Sardis from prehistoric to Roman times*. Cambridge, MA: Harvard University Press.

Hanfmann, G. M. A., and J. C. Waldbaum 1975. *A survey of Sardis and the major monuments outside the city walls*. Cambridge, MA: Harvard University Press.

Haselberger, L. 1994. "Ein Giebelriss der Vorhalle des Pantheon: Die Werkrisse vor dem Augustusmausoleum," *Römische Mitteilungen* 101: 279–308.

Hebrard, E., and J. Zeiller 1912. *Spalato: Le palais de Diocletian*. Paris: Ch. Massin.

Jackson, M., and F. Marra 2006. "Roman stone masonry: Volcanic foundations of the ancient city," *American Journal of Archaeology* 110: 403–36.

Johannowski, W. 1982. "Considerazioni sullo sviluppo urbano alla cultura materiale di Velia," *La Parola del Passato* 37: 225–46.

Johnston, D. E. 1978. "Villas of Hampshire and the Isle of Wight," in M. Todd (ed.), *Studies in the Romano British villa*. Leicester: Leicester University Press, 71–92.

Kammerer-Grothaus, H. 1974. "Der Deus Rediculus im Triopion des Herodes Atticus: Untersuchungen am Bau und zu polychromer Ziegelarchitektur des 2. Jahrhunderts n. Chr. in Latium," *Römische Mitteilungen* 81: 130–252.

Lamprecht, H.-O. 1987. *Opus caementicium: Bautechnik der Römer*. Düsseldorf: Beton-Verlag.

Lancaster, L. C. 1998. "Building Trajan's Markets," *American Journal of Archaeology* 102: 283–308.

Lancaster, L. C. 1999. "Building Trajan's Column," *American Journal of Archaeology* 103: 419–39.

Lancaster, L. C. 2005a. *Concrete vaulted construction in Imperial Rome: Innovations in context*. New York: Cambridge University Press.

Lancaster, L. C. 2005b. "The process of building the Colosseum: The site, materials, and construction techniques," *Journal of Roman Archaeology* 18: 57–82.

Lechtman, H. N., and L. W. Hobbs 1987. "Roman concrete and the Roman architectural revolution," *Ceramics and Civilization* 3: 81–128.

Lendle, O. 1983. *Texte und Untersuchungen zum technischen Bereich der Antiken Poliorketik*. Wiesbasden: F. Steiner.

Lugli, G. 1957. *La tecnica edilizia romana con particolare riguardo a Roma e Lazio*. Rome: G. Bardi.

Mainstone, R. J. 1975. *Developments in structural form*. Cambridge, MA: M.I.T. Press.

Mainstone, R. J. 1988. *Hagia Sophia—Architecture, structure and liturgy of Justinian's Great church*. London: Thames and Hudson.

Malacrino, C. G. 2004. "L'approvvigionamento idrico di Nicopoli e l'acquedotto presso Haghios Georghios: Una nuova attestazione di opus reticulatum in Grecia," *Rivista di Archeologia* 28: 107–24.

Mark, R., A. S. Çakmak, and M. Erdik 1992. "Preliminary report on an integrated study of the structure of Hagia Sophia: Past, present, and future," in R. Mark and A. S. Çakmak (eds.), *Hagia Sophia: From the age of Justinian to the present*. New York: Cambridge University Press, 120–31.

Mark, R., and P. Hutchinson 1986. "On the structure of the Pantheon," *Art Bulletin* 68: 24–34.

Martín, A. 2000. "Las termas republicanas de Cabrera del Mar (Maresme, Barcelona)," in C. Fernández Ochoa and V. García Entero (eds.), *Termas romanas en el occidente del Imperio II* (Gijón): 157–62.

Martin, S. D. 1989. *The Roman jurists and the organization of private building in the late Republic and early Empire*. Brussels: Latomus.

Mason, D. J. P. 1990. "The use of earthenware tubes in Roman vault construction: An example from Chester," *Britannia* 21: 215–22.

Mattingly, D. J. 1988. "Oil for export? A Comparison of Libyan, Spanish, and Tunisian olive oil production in the Roman Empire," *Journal of Roman Archaeology* 1: 33–56.

Mazzucato, O. 1970. "Ceramica medievali nell'edilizia laziale," in *Atti del Convegno Internazionale della Ceramica* (Albisole): 339–70.

Medri, M. 2001. "La diffusione dell'opera reticolata: Considerazioni a partire dal caso di Olimpia," in J.-Y. Marc and J.-C. Moretti (eds.), *Constructions publiques et programmes édilitaires en Grèce entre le IIe siècle av. J.-C. et le Ier siècle ap. J.-C.: Actes du colloque organisé par l'École Française d'Athènes et le CNRS, Athènes 14–17 mai 1995*. Paris: CNRS, 15–40.

Netzer, E. 1990. "Architecture in Palestina prior to and during the days of Herod the Great," in *Akten des XIII Internationalen Kongresses für Klassische Archäologie*. Mainz: von Zabern, 37–50.

Olcese, G. 1993. "Archaeologia e archeometria dei laterizi bollati urbani: primi resultati e prospettive di ricerca," in W. V. Harris (ed.), *The inscribed economy*. *Journal of Roman Archaeology* Suppl. 6. Ann Arbor, MI: JRA, 121–27.

Oleson, J. P., C. Brandon, S. M. Cramer, R. Cucitore, E. Gotti, and R. L. Hohlfelder 2004. "The ROMACONS Project: A contribution to the historical and engineering analysis of hydraulic concrete in Roman maritime structures," *International Journal of Nautical Archaeology* 33.2: 199–229.

Oleson, J.P., C. Brandon, L. Bottalico, R. Cucitorre, E. Gotti, and R. L. Hohlfelder 2006. "Reproducing a Roman maritime structure with Vitruvian pozzolanic concrete," *Journal of Roman Archaeology* 19 (2006) 29–52.

Ortalli, J. 1987. "La via dei sepolcri di Sarsina: Aspetti funzionali, formali e sociali," in H. von Hesberg and P. Zanker (eds.), *Römische Gräberstrassen: Selbstdarstellung-Status-Standard*. Munich: Verlag der Bayerischen Akademie der Wissenschaften, 55–82.

Ousterhout, R. 1999. *Master builders of Byzantium*. Princeton, NJ: Princeton University Press.

Peña, J. T. 1989. "*P. Giss*. 69: Evidence for the supplying of stone transport operations in Roman Egypt and the production of 50 foot monolithic column shafts," *Journal of Roman Archaeology* 2: 126–32.

Pensabene, P. 2001. "Criteri di reimpiego e nuovo mode architettoniche nella basilica paleocristiana di Roma," in M. Cecchelli (ed.), *Materiali e techniche dell'edilizia paleocristiana a Roma*. Rome: De Luca, 103–26.

Pesavento Mattioli, S. (ed.), 1998. *Bonifiche e drenaggi con anfore in epoca romana: Aspetti tecnici e topografici*. Modena: Franco Cosimo Panaini Editore.

Ragette, F. 1980. *Baalbek*. Park Ridge, NJ: Noyes Press.

Rakob, F. 1982. "Römische Architektur in Nordafrika, Bautechnik und Bautradition," *150-Jahr-Feier, Deutsches Archäologisches Institut Rom. Römische Mitteilungen* Supp. 25. Mainz: von Zabern, 107–115.

Rakob, F. 1988. "Römische Kuppelbauten in Baiae," *Römische Mitteilungen* 95: 257–301.

Rasch, J. J. 1991. "Zur Konstruktion spätantiker Kuppeln vom 3. bis 6. Jahrhundert," *Jahrbuch des deutsches Archäologischen Instituts* 106: 311–83.

Rea, R. 2004. *L'ipogeo di Trebio Giusto sulla Via Latina*. Vatican City: Pontificia commissione di archeologia sacra.

Rea, R., H.-J. Beste, and L. C. Lancaster 2002. "Il cantiere del Colosseo," *Römische Mitteilungen* 109: 341–75.

Reuther, O. 1938. "Parthian architecture. History," in A. U. Pope (ed.), *A Survey of Parthian art from prehistoric times to the present*. Oxford: Oxford University Press, 411–44.

Righini, V. 1970. *Lineamenti di storia economica della Gallia Cisalpina: La produttività fittile in età repubblicana*. Brussels: Latomus.

Rodriguez-Almeida, E. 1994. "Marziale in marmo," *Mélanges de l'École française de Rome et d'Athènes* 106.1: 197–217.

Saturno, P. 2001. "Analisi minero-petrografiche di alcune malte antiche (IV–VII secolo d.C.) da edifici romani," in M. Cecchelli (ed.), *Materiali e techniche dell'edilizia paleocristiana a Roma*. Rome: De Luca, 159–79.

Sintès, C., and P. Arcelin 1996. *Musée de l'Arles antique*. Arles: Actes sud.

Spanu, M. 1996. "L'opus reticulatum e mixtum nelle province asiatiche," in M. Khanoussi, P. Ruggeri, and C. Vismara (eds.), *L'Africa romana 11.2. Atti dell'XI Convegno di studio, Carthage 15–18 december 1994*. Ozieri: Il Torchietto, 923–39.

Spanu, M. 2003. "Roman influence in Cilicia through architecture," *Olba* 8: 1–38.

Steinby, E. M. 1993. "L'organizzazione produttiva dei lateri: Un modello interpretivo per l'instrumentum in genere?" in W. V. Harris (ed.), *The inscribed economy. Journal of Roman Archaeology* Suppl. 6. Ann Arbor: JRA, 139–43.

Storz, S. 1994. *Tonröhren im antiken Gewölbebau*. Mainz: Philipp von Zabern.

Taylor, R. 2003. *Roman builders: A study in architectural process*. New York: Cambridge University Press.

Tomei, M. A., and G. Morganti 1986. "Ambienti lungo il Clivo Palatino," *Bollettino Comunale* 91.2: 514–22.

Torelli, M. 1980. "Innovazioni nelle techniche edilizie romane tra il I sec. a.C. e il I sec. d.C.," in *Technologia, Economia, e Società' nel Mondo Romano*. Como: Banca Popolare, 139–61.

Torrecilla Aznar, A. 1999. "Materiales de construcción en las termas de la Hispania romana: A propósito de los materiales hallados en la villa de El Saucedo (Talavera la Nueva, Toledo)," in *Actas del XXIV Congreso Nacional de Arqueología 1997*, vol. 4. Murcia: Instituto de Patrimonio Histórico, 397–416.

Tsiolis, V. 2001. "Las termas de Fregellae. Arquitectura, tecnologia y cultura balnear en el Lacio durante los siglos III y II a.C," *Cuadernos de prehistoria y arqueología Universidad autónoma de Madrid* 27: 85–114.

Tucci, P. L. 2006. "*Navalia*," *Archeologia Classica* 57: 175–201.

Walters, J. C. 1995. "Egyptian religions in Ephesos," in H. Koester (ed.), *Ephesos metropolis of Asia: An interdisciplinary approach to its archaeology, religion and culture*. Vally Forge, PA: 281–310.

Ward-Perkins, J. B. 1958. "Notes on the structure and building methods of early Byzantine architecture," in D. Talbott Rice (ed.), *The Great Palace of the Byzantine emperors, 2nd Report*. Edinburgh: Edinburgh University Press, 52–104.

Ward-Perkins, J. B. 1981. *Roman imperial architecture*. 2nd ed. Harmondsworth: Penguin.

Webster, G. 1979. "Tiles as a structural component in buildings," in A. McWhirr (ed.), *Roman brick and tile*. British Archaeological Reports, Intl. Series S68. Oxford: BAR, 285–93.

White, K. D. 1984. *Greek and Roman technology*. London: Thames and Hudson.

Whitwell, J. B. 1976. *The Church Street sewer and an adjacent building. The archaeology of York: The legionary fortress*. London: Council for British Archaeology.

Wiegand, T. 1921. *Baalbek: Ergebnisse der Ausgrabungen und Untersuchungen in den Jahren 1898 bis 1905*. Berlin/Leipzig: Walter de Gruyter.

Wilson, A. 2003. "*Opus Reticulatum* panels in the Severan Basilica at Leptis Magna," *Quaderni di archeologia della Libia* 18: 369–79.

Wilson, R. J. A. 1992. "Terracotta vaulting tubes (*tubi fittili*): On their origin and distribution," *Journal of Roman Archaeology* 5: 97–129.

Wilson Jones, M. 2000. *Principles of Roman architecture*. New Haven: Yale University Press.

Yegül, F. K. 1986. *The bath-gymnasium complex at Sardis*. Cambridge, MA: Harvard University Press.

Yegül, F. K. 1992. *Baths and bathing in classical antiquity*. Cambridge, MA: MIT Press.

Ziegenaus, O. 1981. *Altertumer von Pergamon 11.3. Das Asklepieon. Die Kultbauten aus romischer Zeit and der Ostseite des Heiligen Bezirks*. Berlin: Walter De Gruyter.

Zienkiewicz, J. D. 1986. *The legionary fortress baths at Caerleon*. Vol. 1. *The buildings*. Cardiff: C.A.D.W., Welsh Historic Monuments.

# CHAPTER 11

# HYDRAULIC ENGINEERING AND WATER SUPPLY

## ANDREW I. WILSON

SINCE the beginnings of agriculture and urbanization, the control and management of water has been vital to all societies. Natural rivers and springs were exploited wherever possible, but where they were lacking, alternative means of water supply were needed. In the highly urbanized Greco-Roman world, artificial techniques of water supply not only supported large city populations but also shaped the amenities that defined urban living. Many of the achievements of Greek and Roman civilization would not have been possible without the infrastructure based on skills in hydraulic engineering.

## WELLS

Wells were the earliest and simplest form of artificial water supply, consisting in their most basic form of a simple hole dug down to the water table. Neolithic wells are known from Cyprus (ninth and eighth millennia B.C.), Crete (Peltenburg et al. 2001; Manteli 1992), and Israel (Garfinkel et al. 2006), and until the invention of rainwater-collection cisterns, wells remained the sole artificial technique of water supply; later, they continued to be important alongside other technologies. Wells were nearly ubiquitous throughout the ancient world, wherever groundwater could be reached at moderate depth by sinking a shaft (Jardé 1907; Hodge 1992: 51–58; 2000).

Most domestic wells, and many public wells, were either circular or square, just large enough for the digger—about 0.80–1.0 m across. Where the geology was sufficiently stable, the shaft would simply be cut into the rock, but in unstable sands, earth or gravels the sides would need lining (called "steining"); this was frequently the case in the upper part of the shaft above bedrock. In the Athenian agora from the fourth century B.C. onward, some wells were lined with terracotta rings made of three curved sections, each with a handle that served as a foothold when put in place (Lang 1968: 6–7). More often, however, the well was stabilized with a lining of mud bricks or steined with masonry. In northern Europe during the Roman period, wooden barrels with their ends knocked out were sometimes used to line wells dug in clay or soft earth, as at Roman Silchester or numerous sites along the Rhine *limes* (Marlière 2002: 40–89). Alternatively, wooden shoring or framework was used.

Depths varied considerably; wells up to 15 m deep are not uncommon, and although wells of more than 25–30 m are rare, examples are known of Roman wells about 60 m deep in the Aurès region of Algeria, and even 80 m in the case of a Roman well near Poitiers in Gaul. For really deep wells, perhaps the biggest disadvantage was the sheer effort required to haul the water up (Hodge 2000: 30). To prevent people falling in accidentally, the top of a well was usually surrounded with a wellhead or *puteal*—either of terracotta or stone; the latter in some cases elaborately decorated. Some stone well-surrounds show deep scoring marks from the friction of ropes where the jars were pulled up by hand. A stone or wooden framework might support a pulley to ease the task of hauling up the water jars. Cuttings in stone well-surrounds sometimes indicate that the well could be covered with a metal or wooden cover (e.g., on the Odeon Hill at Carthage).

Larger wells are occasionally encountered. In some cases they might take the form of a deep and wide excavation with a staircase leading down to the water table, to enable people to descend into the well and draw water. More often, an exceptionally wide well indicates the use of some kind of mechanical water lifting device (chapter 13). Rectangular wells with an opening about 3 m long and 1 m wide seem designed to house a chain of pots strung over a wheel and moved by draft animals through an angle gear drive (*saqiya*). A Roman example was found in the center of the Square of the Cisterns at Ptolemais (over 11 m deep), and probable Byzantine examples are known from Andarin and Qasr Ibn Wardan in Syria (A. I. Wilson 2004: 120–21). In London, a well 2.6 m square and some 5 m deep housed a mechanical water-lifting device with a series of wooden containers connected by iron chain links, and probably driven through a *saqiya* gear (now lost); it may have served a set of public baths (Blair and Hall 2003). The well itself was lined with wood and cross-braced with timbers that could also have served as a kind of ladder to enable descent for maintenance or cleaning.

Domestic wells were usually located centrally in the house, often in peristyle courtyards; sometimes a well shaft placed between two rooms might have an arched opening within the wall to allow access from both sides. The quality of well water depended on the local geology, and also on population density and the drainage technologies in use. Urban wells were at risk of contamination if sewage or refuse was discharged back into the aquifer via cesspits; this potential problem did not deter their use, and the consequent risk of disease may have been little appreciated in antiquity. It was understood, however, that overextraction from a well could have an effect on neighboring wells. One of Solon's laws decreed that if there was an existing public well within 4 *stadia* (720 m) one had to use it rather than dig another; otherwise people could dig their own wells. But if water was not found after digging to a depth of 60 ft, the party could draw water from a neighbor's well twice a day (Plutarch, *Sol.* 23.5-6).

# CISTERNS

Cisterns were developed as an alternative to wells, storing rainwater collected from the roofs, courtyards, or other paved areas of buildings. Domestic cisterns were widespread around the Mediterranean in the Greek and Roman worlds, although less common in the wetter regions of northern Europe.

Among the earliest rainwater-collection cisterns are examples from the MM III period at Zakro, and from the LM III period at Tylissos. Both are open and circular, with steps for access; the Tylissos example had a rectangular settling tank (Biernacka-Lubanska 1977: 27–28). Later cisterns were usually covered, to reduce contamination and evaporation; a common form in the Greek and Roman worlds was the bottle- or carafe-shaped cistern (depending on proportions), with a narrow neck or shaft at the top and a wider body below. Depths commonly range between 3 m and 7 m, and volume was achieved by widening the body of the cistern as far as the solidity of the rock into which it was cut would allow. In Athens, bottle cisterns make an appearance perhaps in the early fourth century B.C., and from the middle of that century onward increasingly came to replace wells in the agora (Camp 1982: 12). In the Hellenistic period a different form of cistern became common in North Africa and the western Mediterranean—long and narrow, often with rounded ends, its width was limited by the constraints of roofing with cover slabs either laid flat or pitched against each other in pairs. Depth compensated for the narrow width to achieve sufficient storage capacity. Examples are found in Hellenistic Cyrenaica (Berenice) from the second century B.C. onward, in the Punic world (e.g., Carthage and Ampurias), Cosa in the third century B.C. (Capitolium cistern), and even in southern Gaul (Ensérune, first century B.C.). Rectangular cisterns roofed with slabs carried on a series of arches first make their appearance in the Hellenistic period (Delos), and later spread to the Nabataean kingdom and other parts of the Near East (Oleson 1991: 57–58; 1995).

The introduction of cisterns was made possible by the invention of waterproof lining mortars, allowing the cistern to retain water even where the rock it was cut into was permeable. With the exception of the large, open circular cisterns associated with the fourth-century B.C. ore washeries in the mining region of Laurion, where the mortars have been shown to contain high proportions of lead litharge, a by-product from the silver extraction process (Conophagos 1980, 1982), very little analysis has been done on ancient Greek waterproof mortars. Better understood are the Punic hydraulic linings—often a bluish-gray mortar derived from marl clays, mixed with ash, and bulked out with a gravel aggregate. The Carthaginians used a pinkish cement, containing crushed terracotta, for cement floors, and although this material was later to become standard Roman cement for waterproof linings (often referred to in modern archaeological literature as *cocciopesto* or *opus signinum*), the Carthaginians themselves seem to have preferred the ash and gravel mortars as waterproof linings.

At Carthage in the third century B.C., many domestic wells were replaced by cisterns, at considerable effort and expense, and disused wells were reused as soakaways for cistern overflow (A. I. Wilson 1998: 65–67). This change may have been the result of either climatic change (lowering of the water table) or increasing population pressure (leading to greater abstraction, or to contamination of the water table). A similar switch from wells to cisterns in the Athenian agora in the fourth century B.C. has been attributed to drought (Camp 1982), but this hypothesis encounters the objection that increased reliance on rainfall collection seems a poor response to drought. In the case of Carthage, at least, increasing population pressure on groundwater resources seems a more likely explanation.

Other forms of cistern include tunnel cisterns, where a well-like shaft leads down to two (or occasionally more) rock-cut tunnel chambers branching off the base. The depth of such cisterns depends on what depth a sufficiently solid rock stratum could be reached in which to excavate the lateral chambers. An early Hellenistic cistern at Euesperides (Benghazi, Libya) with four arms was barely over 2 m deep. Tunnel cisterns are common in late Republican and early Imperial Italy, especially in Latium where they could be dug into the soft volcanic bedrock, and in Campania, as at Pompeii; they are also found at Roman sites in North Africa such as Lepcis Magna (Walda 1996: 126). These tunnel cisterns, like the other types described above, stored collected rainwater; but in Italy a variant type might be dug down into the aquifer, collecting groundwater seeping through the sides of the chambers. The greater the surface area of the walls, the greater the collecting ability of such a cistern; consequently, some were developed as networks of parallel or intersecting tunnels, particularly in Latium and Campania (Devoti 1978; Döring 2002a).

The Roman period saw an important technological advance in cistern construction, with the introduction of mortared rubble building techniques and vaulting, which allowed much larger covered cisterns to be constructed. The volume of earlier cisterns had been constrained by the limitations of roofing methods or rock-cut techniques, but now barrel and cross vaults allowed much greater widths to be spanned, and multiplying the number of chambers could increase volume further. The strength and durability of mortared rubble construction meant that, with thick walls and external buttresses to counter the lateral pressure exerted by the water inside, cisterns could now be built partly or wholly above ground, rather than necessarily being sunk underground. This not only allowed their construction in areas where groundwater was close to the surface, but also meant that water could be run out by gravity flow from large aboveground cisterns, allowing irrigation of gardens or orchards, rather than having to be lifted out arduously by hand.

The most common type of Roman cistern is, therefore, rectangular and barrel-vaulted, with one or more chambers, and a draw-hole about 0.50 m square in the center of the vault. Terracotta supply pipes or cement-lined built channels from the roof or courtyard enter above the spring of the vault; tide marks on the lining mortar suggest that most cisterns were rarely filled above the spring of the vault. Like wells, cistern mouths were usually protected by a surround or *puteal*, and a frame with a pulley was often set over them.

Cisterns of all kinds were waterproofed by the application of mortar linings; the most widespread type used in the Roman world was the pinkish *opus signinum* containing crushed terracotta, but in parts of North Africa the Punic ash-based bluish-gray mortars remained in use alongside this formula. The joints between wall and floor were sealed with a quarter-round molding, and the corners were rounded internally to assist cleaning; sometimes a circular sump was provided in the floor to assist removal of sludge.

Domestic cisterns collected water from the roof and courtyard of the house in which they were located; the amount of water they collected was therefore determined by the local rainfall combined with the roof area or *impluvium* available for rainwater collection. Rural cisterns might have specially constructed paved or plastered areas acting as collection *impluvia*, as for example in Hellenistic and Byzantine cisterns on Yeronisos Island, Cyprus (Connelly and Wilson 2002).

The so-called *astynomoi* inscription from Pergamon in Asia Minor (a Trajanic regulation repeating a Hellenistic decree) illustrates the importance of domestic cisterns to the overall water supply of a town; among other duties the town magistrates were required to keep a register of all private cisterns in the town and check annually that they were kept in good order (Klaffenbach 1954). The importance of rainwater collection as a complementary water supply technique alongside wells, springs, and aqueducts is highlighted not only by the virtual ubiquity of domestic cisterns in the Mediterranean region, but also by the fact that many public buildings with a large footprint were equipped with large rainwater-collection cisterns. In Delos, the Hellenistic theater supplied runoff water to a large cistern roofed with slabs carried on cross arches (Oleson 1995: 716–17). In Roman North Africa, theaters and odea at Bararus, Thugga, and Carthage were provided with cisterns under the stage, fed by runoff from the cavea and orchestra, while the third-century A.D. amphitheater at Thysdrus in Tunisia acted as an *impluvium* for cisterns some 100 m to the north. Large paved public spaces, such as the forum at Pompeii, the precincts of the Temple of Saturn at Thugga, or the South Forum Temple at Sabratha, also collected water for large cisterns (A. I. Wilson 1997: 59).

The quality of water stored in rainwater collection cisterns was acknowledged to be inferior to that from wells or sources of running water (Pliny, *HN* 31.21.34; Oleson 1992: 887–88). Standing water became stagnant and less aerated, and although the underground placement of most cisterns helped to keep the water cool and away from sunlight, inhibiting somewhat the growth of algae and insects, ancient authors often recommended boiling cistern water before drinking it, or adding salt. The water collected in large cisterns fed from public spaces must have been nonpotable, and indeed it is likely that, where other sources were available, cistern water was used primarily for purposes other than drinking, such as washing floors or watering gardens. Basic methods of water purification were employed, such as metal grilles on the inlets of feed pipes, and settling tanks, and large quantities of charcoal found in domestic cisterns in Thysdrus and Leptiminus in North Africa may suggest the addition of charcoal to cistern water to remove odors by the absorption of colloids, a practice still current in the nineteenth century (A. I. Wilson 1997: 81). Vitruvius (*De arch.* 8.6.15) recommends adding salt to cistern water to purify it.

# Aqueducts and Long-Distance Supply

## The Near Eastern Background

The Assyrian empire saw the development of ambitious water supply schemes involving long-distance artificial canals, usually derived from perennial rivers, and led through intervening ridges by means of tunnels several hundred meters, or even several kilometers, long. The longer tunnels were dug between pairs of vertical shafts, which enabled the overall course of the tunnel to be surveyed on the surface. This shafts-and-gallery tunneling technique broke up the problem of underground surveying into short, manageable sections, and the shafts were set at sufficiently close intervals that the tunneling gangs could find each other underground. They served also for the removal of spoil, and to assist ventilation (cf. chapter 12).

The Assyrian king Assurnasipal II (884–859 B.C.) dug a canal 19.5 km long from the Upper Zab river to supply Nimrud; it passed under a rock ridge at Negoub via a tunnel 7 km long dug between pairs of vertical shafts. The system both supplied the city of Nimrud and irrigated the fields around it. Two later tunnels in the region seem to be repairs or additions to this scheme: one was cut by Tiglath-Pileser III (744–727 B.C.), but later blocked, and the other by Esarhaddon (680–669 B.C.), whose construction inscription records that the earlier tunnel of Assurnasipal II had silted up. Renovation and maintenance are constant themes in both ancient and modern water-supply systems.

Similar techniques were used for the water supply for Arbela in eastern Iraq. This tapped water from three rivers at Bastura and included a tunnel dug between vertical shafts; an inscription on the entrance of the tunnel records construction by Sennacherib (704–681 B.C.). Traces of what may be a comparable system were recorded at Babylon by Rassam in the late nineteenth century; he mentions four wells lined with rings of red granite, in a straight line, which communicated with a subterranean aqueduct. The source of the aqueduct was not established with certainty, but it was thought to have come either from the Euphrates or from a canal northeast of the main mound at Babylon. Suggested dates for the system range from the late eighth to the mid-fifth century B.C. (Dalley 2001–2002).

Sennacherib's aqueduct to Nineveh, completed in 690 B.C., was a long and wide canal used for both irrigation and (probably) urban supply, tapping the waters of the Gomel River at Bavian. It crossed a wadi at Jerwan on a bridge over 280 m long and 22 m wide, built in ashlar masonry with five corbelled arches (Jacobsen and Lloyd 1935). Hezekiah's approximately contemporary tunnel (715–696 B.C.) that brought water into the city of Jerusalem from an underground spring is a 537-m winding spring-capture tunnel (chapter 12).

The Assyrian water supply schemes involving tunnels dug between sets of vertical shafts have a bearing on the vexed question of the origin of *qanats*. *Qanats* are one of the most important developments in the history of water engineering; they have enabled human habitation and agriculture in some of the most inhospitable, arid areas on earth. A *qanat* is an underground gallery that collects groundwater and leads it by gravity flow to emerge where the ground surface level is lower, hundreds of meters or even many kilometers from the source (figure 11.1). The long underground tunnels were dug in relatively short sections between pairs of vertical shafts, again using the shafts-and-gallery tunneling technique, just as in the tunnels on the large Assyrian aqueducts. The difference lies in the water source, which is not a flowing river or spring, but groundwater, usually tapped at a considerable depth in a piedmont zone in an arid region. *Qanats* are found from China to the Sahara and North Africa; they were even introduced to the New World by the Spanish, and, despite the increasing use of motorized pumped wells, they are still used today in many arid regions.

It was long held that the *qanat* must have originated in Persia, largely because that is where the largest numbers of *qanats* are found; and their origin has frequently been attributed to the Achaemenids. More recently, several archaeologists working in the Arabian Peninsula have argued that *qanats* (*aflaj*) originated there, claiming to have discovered pre-Achaemenid *qanats* of the early first millennium B.C. (Magee 2005). To date the arguments are inconclusive; some *qanats* in southeastern Arabia seem to be spatially associated with sites dated by pottery to the Iron Age II period, but that period extends from about 1000 to 600 B.C., and there is no conclusive proof that the *qanats* in question were created at the beginning rather than the end of it. A late date within this bracket would still allow the possibility of Achaemenid introduction to the region. It is true, however, that no *qanat* in Iran has yet been shown to be of Achaemenid date—although the significance of this

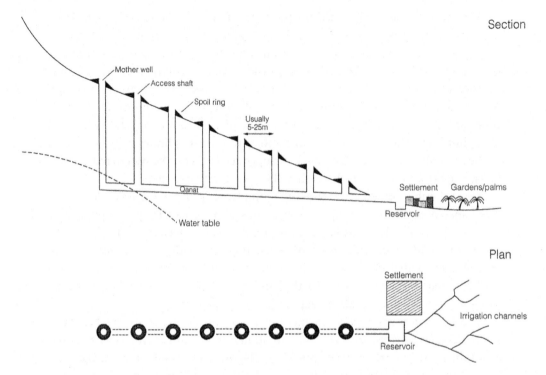

Figure 11.1. Diagram of a *qanat* or *foggara*. (Drawing by Alison Wilkins, reproduced by permission.)

observation diminishes when one remembers that almost no *qanats* in Iran have been investigated archaeologically.

The earliest securely dated *qanats* belong to the Achaemenid period at Ayn-Manawir in the Kharga Oasis in Egypt, where remains of 22 ancient *qanats* are known. They are dated both by stratigraphic finds and by associated *ostraka* recording the sale of water rights from 443 B.C. onward (Wuttman 2001). Polybius (10.28), describing campaigns in Media in 210/209 B.C. between the Seleucid king Antiochos III and the Parthian king Arsaces II, clearly refers to *qanats*, whose construction he says was encouraged by the Achaemenid kings by tax concessions on the land thus brought under cultivation.

In his fundamental study of *qanats*, Goblot (1979) proposed that the technique was spread to regions around the Mediterranean by invading peoples or refugee groups; thus the Romans would have introduced *qanats* to North Africa, while refugees from Persia introduced them to the Sahara in the early Middle Ages. More recent work provides a very different model. The spread of the technique to Africa was due not to transfer through the Mediterranean, but to diffusion along Saharan trade routes. In the late first millennium B.C., *qanats* (*foggaras*) formed the agricultural basis of the emergent Garamantian state in Fazzan (Libyan Sahara); the technology had probably been introduced from the oases in the western desert of Egypt, where, as we have seen, it was already in use in the Achaemenid period. From

Fazzan it later spread to the Algerian Sahara, and diffused northward to Roman North Africa (A. I. Wilson 2005, 2006a), where some Roman aqueducts display a blend of traditional *qanat* technology with Roman techniques of reinforcement of the water channel. Very similar *qanat*-aqueducts are found in the region around Trier and Luxembourg and may have been introduced there from North Africa (Luxembourg: Kohl and Faber 1990; Kohl et al. 1995; Faber 1992; Schoellen 1997; Germany: Kremer 2005; Grewe 1988: 93). Elsewhere in the Roman world, however, the use of the *qanat* was largely limited to Syria, Judaea, and Egypt. Further east, its spread from Iran to Afghanistan at an unknown but probably early date may also have been facilitated by trade contacts along the Silk Road.

The development and spread of *qanats* is important because—as the Achaemenid examples at Ayn Manawir show—it demonstrates the availability and use at an early date of complex and difficult engineering water schemes in communities outside the main civic centers. In many parts of the ancient world the *qanat* was the only long-distance water supply technology available prior to the Hellenistic or Roman periods.

As we have seen, already in the early ninth century B.C. Assyrian water engineers were able to dig tunnels several kilometers long using the same principle as for the tunnels of *qanats*. The evidence currently available suggests two possibilities. Either the Assyrians developed the shafts-and-gallery tunneling technique, which was later applied to the realization that groundwater found at depth in one place may nevertheless lie above the ground surface elsewhere and could be led out to the surface via a tunnel that could be dug only by the shafts-and-gallery technique; or the *qanat* was invented as a package both of the shafts-and-gallery technique and the realization that groundwater found at depth could be transported elsewhere. Until further early *qanats* have been reliably dated, certainty is impossible, but a priori the first of these two possibilities seems easier to believe. Furthermore, if the Assyrians invented the shafts-and-gallery technique and it was only later applied to the *qanat*, the separate diffusion trajectories of the *qanat* and the shafts-and-gallery tunneling technique become easier to understand: the shafts-and-gallery tunneling technique spread to the Greek and Etruscan worlds while the *qanat* did not.

# GREEK WATER SUPPLY SYSTEMS

The archaic period saw the first public water projects of the Greek world, with the development of springs with fountain houses at Megara by the tyrant Theagenes (ca. 640–620 B.C.; Pausanias 1.40.1), and perhaps the monumentalization of the spring of Lower Peirene at Corinth, although this is not closely dated (Hill 1964). For Samos and Athens, long-distance aqueducts were constructed. The projects at Megara, Samos, and Athens were all initiated by tyrants wanting to secure popular favor by public works engineering schemes that were both grandiose and useful. The aqueduct at Samos, 2.5 km long and built by the tyrant Polycrates (ca. 550–522 B.C.), is best known for the famous tunnel named after its designer, Eupalinus of Megara (Herodotus 3.60), a 1-km-long gallery just before the aqueduct enters the city (Kienast 1995). The height of the overlying hill prevented construction by the shafts-and-gallery technique, so the tunnel was surveyed from opposite ends, meeting near the middle (chapter 12). The aqueduct itself tapped water from a spring, and apart from the tunnel of Eupalinus it largely runs along the contours; significantly, for considerable stretches immediately up- and downstream from the tunnel of Eupalinus the structure takes the form of an underground tunnel dug in the shafts-and-gallery technique. Given the cultural and technological contacts between the Persian Empire and eastern Greek states at the time, it seems that this must represent an adoption of shafts-and-gallery tunneling methods from the Achaemenid practitioners of this Assyrian technique.

The Enneakrounos seems to have been a monumental fountain house for the local Callirhoe spring, sponsored by Pisistratus (Thucydides 2.15.2–3; Pausanias 1.14.1); its location is disputed. In the late sixth century the Pisistratids also built a long-distance aqueduct, bringing water from over 8 km away in the Ilissus valley in a conduit made of ceramic pipes laid, for much of its length, in a tunnel. Calcareous deposits extending only halfway up the pipe walls show that the pipeline did not run full or under pressure. In any case, the openings in the top of each pipe section, which allowed the workmen to insert a hand to plaster the inside of the joints, and were closed by ceramic covers that were not watertight, made that impossible (Tölle-Kastenbein 1994, 1996).

The archaic-period aqueducts seem to have fed only public fountain houses, but already in the fifth century B.C. it seems that people had begun to tap them illegally for private uses; Themistocles as *hydaton epistates* at Athens in 490 B.C. fined those who diverted water from the public system (Plutarch, *Them.* 31.1). How quickly, and when, aqueduct networks developed to serve uses other than public fountains remains unclear, since accurately dated Greek aqueducts are rare between the archaic and Hellenistic periods, and relatively few residential areas in Greek cities have been systematically investigated. The aqueduct of Priene in Asia Minor may be contemporary with the refoundation of that city on its present site in the late fourth century B.C.; the aqueduct consisted of a terracotta pipeline laid in a ditch covered with stone slabs. It fed a reservoir inside the walls in the upper part of the city, which in turn supplied public fountains and numerous private houses through a network of terracotta pipes. At Syracuse, the three earliest aqueducts probably belong to the reign of Hieron II (270–215 B.C.); all take the form of rock-cut tunnels with access shafts, although curiously with a second gallery excavated just above the one carrying water (R. J. A. Wilson 2000: 12–14).

Although Greek architects occasionally employed the arch (Boyd 1978; Hellmann 2002: 266–77), they did not use it to create arcades to carry aqueducts across natural depressions in the terrain. Greek aqueducts, therefore, largely followed the contours of the landscape, either in rock-cut channels or, more commonly, terracotta pipelines, which were not primarily intended to run full under pressure

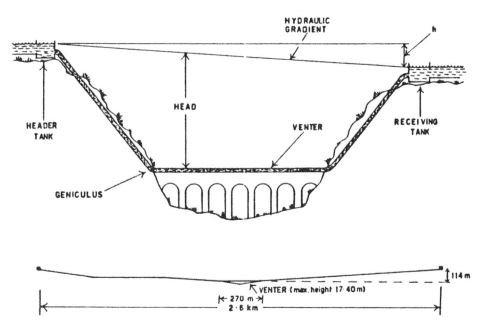

Figure 11.2. Diagram of an inverted siphon (h: loss of head). (After Hodge 1992: 148, fig. 102, by permission of A. T. Hodge.)

but nevertheless allowed a greater latitude in surveying accuracy than did an open channel. Large-gauge pipelines of about 15 to 25 cm internal diameter were used for main long-distance conduits; a double or triple line allowed for greater capacity. Greek aqueducts were, however, of relatively limited scale. The development of more ambitious, long-distance projects with complex engineering works was pioneered by the twin centers of Rome and Pergamon. Republican Rome (discussed below) led the way with the channel aqueducts of the Aqua Appia (312 B.C.) and the Anio Vetus (272–269 B.C.), while Hellenistic Pergamon developed large-scale and long-distance pipeline systems, although there was probably mutual influence between the two centers (Lewis 1999).

A key development that helped liberate aqueducts from the tyranny of the contours by enabling the crossing of deep valleys was the invention of the inverted siphon. Some of the earliest known large-scale examples are at Pergamon, although there is a small inverted siphon 10 m deep on the 8 km pipeline supplying Olynthus, dating between the sixth and fourth centuries B.C. (Lewis 1999: 157. n. 49). This structure employed the principle that water could be conveyed across a depression in a closed pipe and would rise at the other end to nearly the same level at which it entered the pipe (figure 11.2). Five Hellenistic pipelines are known at Pergamon, all later than the two earliest aqueducts at Rome. The first two Pergamene systems supplied the lower city: the Attalus line (before 200 B.C.; a single clay pipeline ca. 20 km long); the Demophon (early second century B.C.; a double pipeline also ca. 20 km long), both with inverted siphons of between 20 and 25 m depth. To bring water to the royal palace on the citadel, the engineers working for Eumenes II (197–158 B.C.) constructed an aqueduct from a spring on the Magra Dağ hill that ran for 42 km, initially in a single pipeline, but then in a double pipe and after 15 km in three parallel terracotta pipes (16–19 cm internal diameter)—perhaps as a result of adding tributary branches. The system had to cross a depression 3.5 km long and approximately 200 m deep just before it reached the citadel. The considerable pressure that the siphon had to withstand precluded the use of terracotta pipes, so it was built instead of lead pipes held in place by pierced stone framing blocks set at close intervals. Broadly contemporary with the Madra Dağ aqueduct was Pergamon's Apollonius line, followed in the later Hellenistic period by the Selinous West pipeline, both without siphons. The Madra Dağ aqueduct may well have inspired the 150 m deep inverted siphon on the Karapinar aqueduct at Smyrna, which probably belongs to the second century B.C. (Lewis 1999).

# Roman Aqueducts

Although aqueducts are often considered a quintessentially Roman engineering accomplishment, we have seen that they have a long tradition in the ancient Near East and in the Greek world, including gravity flow conduits, tunnels, pipelines and inverted siphons. The Roman contribution consisted of innovations that together enabled a much wider and more effective uptake of the basic technology: the use of arcades to carry channels over valleys and low-lying terrain; the availability of concrete as a cheap and adaptable building material; the adoption of waterproof cement linings from the Punic world or Hellenistic Sicily; the expanded use of lead piping and of bronze stopcocks on distribution systems; and the introduction of settling tanks and storage and regulation reservoirs on the network. Increasing levels of state and personal wealth helped fund the construction of numerous aqueducts, for which increasing urbanization generated demand. Aqueducts also fostered the growth of a culture of public bathing, doubtless with a feedback effect whereby the increased popularity of public baths in turn generated a need for more copious urban water supplies; by the early Principate, aqueducts and public baths had become linked features of Roman urbanism. The ornamental use of water in public fountains and *nymphaea* also became a striking feature of Roman civic architecture—coexisting with the practical function of these structures.

Bathing and ostentatious display were certainly not the driving forces, however, behind the three earliest Roman aqueducts, which were constructed long before public baths or display fountains. Rome's first aqueduct, the Aqua Appia, was built in 312 B.C.; it ran for about 16 km from springs east of Rome, and seems to have run entirely underground in a vaulted conduit until it reached the city. We do not know what structures it fed; presumably a few public fountains, and it provides indirect but suggestive evidence for the growing needs of the city. It was followed by the Anio Vetus (272–269 B.C.), a vastly more ambitious project, running originally for 81 km from the Anio River along the contours of the landscape, although later modifications, with tunnels and arcades, shortened its course considerably by cutting across valleys. The next aqueduct, the Aqua Marcia (144–140 B.C.), was funded with the booty obtained from Rome's defeat of Corinth and Carthage in 146 B.C. and ran for about 91 km, mostly underground, but with the final approach into Rome for some 10 km on substructures and arcades. In all, some 1.5 km were on substructures and 9.5 km on arcades (Aicher 1995: 36–37). For the Anio Vetus and the Marcia, the irrigation of suburban *horti* may have been a subsidiary motive, but this can hardly apply to the Aqua Appia, which ran underground and, in the time of Frontinus, distributed very little of its water outside the city.

In the later second century B.C. (126–125 B.C.), the Aqua Tepula was added, drawing water from warm springs in the Alban hills; for much of its course it piggybacked on the arcade of the Marcia. Three further aqueducts were added by Octavian/Augustus—the Julia (33 B.C.), again superimposed on the Marcia/Tepula arcade; the Virgo (22–19 B.C.) and the Alsietina (2 B.C.). The latter brought poor quality lake water from the Lacus Alsietinus northwest of Rome, which was used for irrigation and Augustus' *naumachia*. The continued development of Rome, with growth in population and an increase in the public bathing habit, prompted the construction of four more aqueducts: the Aqua Claudia and the Anio Novus (both begun by Caligula and finished by Claudius in A.D. 52), the Aqua Traiana in 109, and the Aqua Alexandrina in 226. The network not only became larger, but increasingly complex, with cross-links between aqueducts within Rome, to enable continued delivery of water if one aqueduct was under repair.

Rome's political and economic dominance of Italy enabled her to lead the way in developing ambitious water-supply schemes on a scale unmatched in the Greek east except by Pergamon. But in the second half of the second century B.C., other towns were beginning to follow suit. The censor L. Betilienus Varus was honored around 130/120 B.C. by his home town of Alatri for various gifts, including an aqueduct, whose final stretch carried water to the hilly citadel in an inverted siphon of lead pipes, 3 km long and 100 m deep. It has similarities with the Hellenistic inverted siphons of Madra Dağ at Pergamon and Karapinar at Smyrna, in that it follows rises in the intervening depression to reduce the length run at maximum pressure, and Lewis has suggested a Pergamene link. But at Alatri the two deepest points along the course of the inverted siphon were crossed by arcades, and the channel leading to the inverted siphon was a built conduit (Lewis 1999: 153–54, 161–62).

By the first century B.C., the use of aqueducts was spreading, perhaps slowly, throughout Italy. Research on the Pompeii aqueduct suggests that its initial phase dates from the colony founded by Sulla around 80 B.C. (Ohlig 2001)—it ran almost entirely underground from the vicinity of Avella to the north of Pompeii, feeding some public fountains and, presumably, public baths. In a further four towns of central Italy, allegedly Republican inscriptions (but not closely dated) refer to aqueducts or water supply systems built by local magistrates or decurions: Firmum

Picenum (fermo, Marche), Interamna Nahars (Terni, Umbria), Praeneste (Palestrina), and Superaequum (*ILLRP* 594, 615, 659, 671).

We begin to see Roman aqueduct construction outside Italy with Caesar's aqueduct at Antioch on the Orontes (Lassus 1983: 211; Downey 1961: 153), but the real proliferation of the technology began in the Augustan period. This development might be attributable to a concatenation of factors: increased prosperity after the cessation of civil war, the spread of the public bathing habit, and perhaps most importantly, the foundation of numerous veteran colonies which exported the Roman urban model, with its bathing and amenities, to the provinces—although not all Augustan colonies built aqueducts immediately. Augustan aqueducts at new colonial foundations within Italy include Venafro (*CIL* X.4842 = *ILS* 5743), Lucus Feroniae, Minturnae, Bononia, and Brixia (Keppie 1983: 114–16; Potter 1987: 144–45). The largest was the Serino aqueduct, a complex network running for 96 km, drawing water from sources at Serino and Avella and delivering it to several towns, including Naples, Puteoli, Nola, Cumae, Pompeii, Atella, Acerrae, Baia, and Misenum (Sgobbo 1938; Döring 2002a; 2002b), a striking example of regional planning. Augustan water-supply schemes overseas include the Cornalvo aqueduct at Mérida (Grewe 1993) and possibly the vast, doubtless aqueduct-fed La Malga cisterns at Carthage. Other projects of the Augustan period include Sextilius Pollio's aqueduct at Ephesus and the pipeline "Aqueduct C" at Berenice in Cyrenaica, probably privately funded (Alzinger 1987; Lloyd 1977: 199). The technical aid given by Rome to client kings to assist in developing showpiece Roman-style towns seems also to have included the services of water engineers: the aqueduct at Iol Caesarea (Cherchel, Algeria) was probably built by Juba II (Leveau and Paillet 1976: 151–53; Leveau 1984: 61–62), while Herod's building projects in Judaea included aqueducts at Jerusalem (also using Roman military labor) and possibly Caesarea, and his own palace/fortresses at Jericho and Herodion (Amit 2002; Porath 2002; Patrich and Amit 2002). During the first century A.D. numerous aqueducts were built in Italy, and increasingly in the provinces, but the bulk of dated provincial aqueducts date from the late first through second centuries. New aqueducts were still being built in the Severan period, but very few new constructions postdate A.D. 230, although existing aqueducts were repaired. There was some resurgence in aqueduct construction in the Byzantine period, especially under Justinian and especially in the east. In the west, the maintenance even of existing aqueducts seems increasingly to have been beyond the resources of most cities from the fifth century onward. In Rome, only four of the city's eleven aqueducts were repaired after they had been cut and blocked in the Gothic siege of 537, and their restoration and (intermittent) maintenance was a burden assumed by the popes.

The interaction between Hellenistic and Roman aqueduct traditions is shown by the fact that book 8 (on water) of Vitruvius' *De architectura* is largely derived from Greek sources, probably in particular a source from Hellenistic Pergamon. But for this reason Vitruvius' text is a poor reflection of current aqueduct technology in Roman Italy at the time he wrote. Although he has added some of his own material on water distribution, his account of conduit design omits all mention of arcades, the most distinctive feature of Roman aqueducts for a century before he wrote (Lewis 1999).

For most of their course Roman aqueducts usually took the form of built masonry or concrete channels, vaulted or roofed with flat slabs or gabled slabs or tiles (figure 11.3) (Hodge 1992; Bodon et al. 1994; R. J. A. Wilson 1996; A. I. Wilson. 1997, 2000a). As far as possible, the course would follow the contours of the terrain, running just below the surface in a back-filled trench. This was the simplest and cheapest method of construction, while at the same time minimizing obstacles to movement at surface level. Legal regulations protected its course from planting, to avoid the channel being fissured by roots or damaged by agricultural activity. Where the land surface rose significantly above the level of the channel, the channel had to be tunneled, using techniques described in chapter 12. In other places the aqueduct might cross lower-lying terrain, out of necessity or because this afforded a shortcut, instead of winding along the contour up one side of a valley and back down along the other. In these cases, the channel would run on a low wall or substructure, up to a height of about 2 m; beyond this height, an arcade was used, since it required less material and allowed movement through the structure. These aqueduct arcades—the modern image of the Roman aqueduct—were frequently ambitious affairs, either in their length (Aqua Claudia from Romavecchia to the city, 10 km; Carthage at Oued Miliane, 2 km; figure 11.4), or their height, achieved either through bracing arches between piers (Mérida, Los Milagros, 28 m; Cherchel; Dougga) or by stacking arcades at two or even three levels (Tarraco, 26 m; Segovia, 28 m; Pont du Gard, 49 m). The Pont du Gard on the Nîmes aqueduct is the tallest surviving aqueduct arcade, made of three levels of different sized arches; it approaches the limits of stability for an arcaded structure. As Roman engineers grew more confident in the use of the audacious arcade, in the later first or during the second century A.D., some aqueducts were shortened by replacing a section that ran upstream along one side of a valley and back down the other with an arcade straight across (e.g., at Chabet Ilelouine on the Cherchel aqueduct, and the Hadrianic Ponte S. Gregorio on the Anio Novus). Such shortening of a route reduced maintenance costs.

For reasons of both stability and cost, Roman engineers employed inverted siphons to cross valleys deeper than 50 m, or a combination of inverted siphon and arcade bridge (possibly termed *venter*), as at Aspendos and Lyon. The inverted siphons usually employed lead pipes, frequently in a battery of multiple pipes laid side by side to achieve the same capacity as the open channel and to achieve redundancy in case of pipe failure. The transition between open channel flow and the pipeline was usually achieved by means of header and receiving tanks, of which good a example can be seen near Soucieu on the Gier aqueduct at Lyon. On the aqueduct of Termini Imerese (Sicily) the siphon seems to have started as a large-diameter concrete tube dropping vertically from the base of the channel (Belvedere 1987: 61–62). In the eastern Mediterranean region, inverted siphons were frequently

Figure 11.3. Channel of the Aqua Traiana in Rome. (Photograph by A. I. Wilson.)

built as stone pipelines, constructed of squared blocks with a hole bored through and fitted together with male–female joints. These were once thought to be Hellenistic; they are now nearly all recognized as Roman in date. Many of the blocks have small holes bored through their walls, stoppered by small plugs set in mortar, probably to facilitate cleaning. Examples have been reported from other parts of the Roman world, too: Dalmatia, Italy, Gaul, North Africa (figure 11.5), and Spain (Stenton and Coulton 1986: 45–53; Hodge 1992: 33–41; A. I. Wilson 2000a: 599). The reasons for the preponderant use of lead pipes in the west as opposed to stone pipe blocks in the east remain unclear but may be related to the greater availability of lead in the western Mediterranean (chapter 4).

Small-scale aqueducts, especially those serving rural estates, might consist entirely of terracotta pipes. In the provinces of northwest Europe, some aqueducts consisted of timber pipes made from hollowed out tree-trunks and jointed together with iron rings (R. J. A. Wilson 1996: 21–23; A. I. Wilson 2000a: 602).

Ideally, aqueducts maintained a fairly consistent gradient along their course, although in practice gradients varied considerably along the course of a single aqueduct. Recorded extremes vary between falls of 0.07 m and 16.4 m per km. Where an aqueduct needed to lose height rapidly, a series of cascades or drop-shafts was used to dissipate energy (Grewe 1985; Hodge 1992: 171–97; Chanson 2000).

Figure 11.4. Arcade of the second-century A.D. Zaghouan-Carthage aqueduct, crossing the valley of the Oued Miliane. (Photograph by A. I. Wilson.)

Roman aqueducts often tapped sources of water with high levels of dissolved calcium carbonate and other minerals. These precipitated out of solution in the aqueduct, leaving calcium carbonate deposits (sinter) on channel walls and floor; turbulence and heat increased the rate of precipitation. As Frontinus mentions (*Aq.* 122), such deposits needed to be cleared if flow was not to be reduced and ultimately blocked, and piles of sinter fragments around shaft openings of the aqueducts in the Roman Campagna (Ashby 1935: 44) and along the course of the Nîmes aqueduct testify to such maintenance. But equally, the massive thickness of the sinter deposits elsewhere on the Nîmes aqueduct (at the Pont du Gard) and on numerous other systems, suggests that such maintenance was neither universal nor perfect.

Efforts to improve or protect water quality were made, but they took the form of mechanical rather than chemical purification. Settling tanks were sometimes provided along the course of an aqueduct, where sediment could settle out (e.g., on the Aqua Virgo and the Anio Novus; Hodge 1992: 123–24), or small basins were provided in the floor of the channel (on the Zaghouan-Carthage aqueduct), or as an afterthought added to the aqueduct (as at Siga in Algeria; Grewe 1998). Mesh filters might also be provided on distribution tanks (see below), or on the outlet pipes of reservoir cisterns (e.g., Carthage, Bordj Djedid, and Dar Saniat; A. I. Wilson 1997: 81–82) and there are occasional instances of water being filtered through sandbags (at Cirta) or through a bank of potsherds and shells (Dar Saniat, Carthage). Some improvement in the taste and odor of water could also be achieved by aerating it, for example by running it over a stepped cascade as it entered a storage or distribution cistern (A. I. Wilson 1997: 81–82).

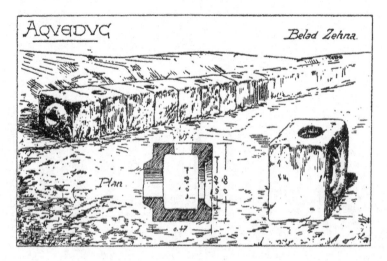

**Figure 11.5.** Stone pipeline aqueduct at Bled Zehna, near Dougga in Tunisia, possibly part of an inverted siphon. (After L. Carton, "Études sur les travaux hydrauliques des romains en Tunisie," *Revue Tunisienne* 312 [October 1896]: 544, fig. 17.)

## THE URBAN DISTRIBUTION NETWORK

Distribution to the end user almost always occurred through closed pipes. In some larger cities areas of the town were served by branch channels, but ultimately water was delivered to most fountains and all houses through pipes (Last 1975; Eschebach 1983; Lassus 1983; Hodge 1992; A. I. Wilson 1998, 2001; Jansen 2000). The transition from main channel to a multiplicity of pipes was often made by means of distribution tanks or basins (*castella divisoria*). The earliest known such *castellum* is at Pompeii, consisting in its first phase (ca. 80 B.C.?) of an open circular basin into which the aqueduct discharged, and from which three lead mains led to different parts of the town. In its second, Augustan phase, the basin was enclosed within a roofed building and arrangements were added to allow manual regulation of flow into the different pipes; screen filters were also provided to trap debris (Ohlig 2001). At Nîmes, a circular distribution basin with five pairs of pipes leading off, presumably to different quarters of town, was also equipped with filter grilles. At Rome, the only terminal distribution tank whose form is known seems to be the elevated terminal basin of the Aqua Claudia, drawn by Piranesi before its destruction by fire; numerous lead pipes departed from a rectangular tank, elevated on tall vaulted substructures, into which the main aqueduct discharged. Smaller circular distribution chambers on the Aqua Marcia near Porta Viminalis and on the Aqua Traiana seem to belong to subsidiary branches or to have been placed upstream of the main terminus of the aqueduct (Ashby 1935: 149; Lanciani 1881: 459–61). In none of the archaeologically known *castella* is there any support for Vitruvius' principle of delivery to different classes of user being handled differently, and his proposed arrangements for distribution of water from a *castellum* (*De arch.* 8.6.1–2) must be treated as idiosyncratic suggestions that may never have been realized in practice (Ohlig 2001).

At Pompeii, the city whose distribution network is best understood, the pipes from the main *castellum* led to a series of 12 subsidiary distribution points, which took the form of small lead tanks (now lost) of about 1 m$^3$ capacity, elevated on brick towers. Pompeii is on a sloping site, the lowest parts of the town some 20 m below the *castellum*, and if the piping system had gone straight from the *castellum* to the houses in the lowest part of the city the head of pressure would have been 20 m, inconvenient for users and making operation of stopcock taps difficult. The use of intermediate open tanks, elevated on towers about 5 m high, broke the system up into segments where the head on the section to the final user was no more than 5 m, reducing the problem of excess pressure while retaining enough pressure to supply the upper stories of houses in the vicinity of each tower. Herculaneum had a similar system, but such a systematic use of intermediate pressure towers is not paralleled elsewhere. One suspects, however, that the dendritic schema of this distribution system, with a primary *castellum* from which a few pipes led to subsidiary distribution centers, from which connections led to multiple end-users, was found at other sites. This was not, however, the only model. Some aqueduct networks, such as the second-century A.D. Zaghouan aqueduct at Carthage, had distribution networks which—in their primary divisions—consisted of a binary division or bifurcation of a subsidiary channel off the main channel, with a small chamber in which sluice gates could regulate the flow into one or the other channel (A. I. Wilson 1998). Despite Frontinus' insistence that all connections to an aqueduct had to be made from a *castellum* (*Aq.* 103.4, 106.1; Rodgers 2004: 135–36, 289; cf. Vitruvius, *De arch.* 8.6.1–2), this is an administrator's ideal and did not always happen in practice. At Carthage, Volubilis, Pompeii, and elsewhere, numerous piped connections were made directly from the main channel, either inside or outside the city (A. I. Wilson 1998, 2006b).

In the eastern Mediterranean, the Greek tradition of ceramic pipe distribution networks persisted in the Roman period, and ceramic pipes were normal for urban distribution systems. By contrast, in the Roman central and western Mediterranean the use of lead pipes for distribution systems was much more prevalent. Although lead pipes on extramural lines had been used in the east at Ephesus in the archaic period (Alzinger 1987: 180) and in the inverted siphon of the Madra Dağ line at Pergamon, it is unclear when their use became common, especially for intramural distribution. The use of lead piping in the west was doubtless facilitated by the opening of large silver and lead mines in Spain in the late Republic, although lead sources are not lacking in the east. Lead piping was probably a feature of the Pompeian distribution system even in the original phase, around 80 B.C.

As with lead-pipe networks, the date of invention of stopcocks or taps, and the process and rate at which their use spread, remains unknown. The stopcock may be either a Hellenistic or a Republican invention (Hodge 1992: 322–26). Roman taps consisted of a bronze cylinder set vertically across the pipeline, in which sat a

Figure 11.6. Bronze stopcock on a lead pipe supplying an ornamental fountain in the peristyle of the House of the Vettii, Pompeii. (Photograph by: A. I. Wilson.)

bronze plug pierced by a hole (figure 11.6). When the hole was aligned with the pipe, water could flow; a quarter-turn either way would shut the flow off; the action is easy, precise, and can handle fairly high pressure. Such taps are found both as stopcocks along the course of a pipe and as discharge taps to turn a fountain or spout on and off at the point of use. The widespread use of taps on urban distribution systems in the western Mediterranean seems to be a feature of the first centuries B.C. and A.D. Taps were common at Pompeii by A.D. 79, one house having as many as 33 (Hodge 1992: 322–26; Fabio and Fassitelli 1992[?]; Jansen 2002: 50–53).

Piped water was distributed to a minority of elite private houses—at Pompeii, some 10 percent of households—and was evidently a sign of status, as well as—or even more than—utility. Where domestic piping systems are traceable, there seems to be more emphasis on feeding ornamental fountains or pools rather than supplying water to kitchens (A. I. Wilson 1995; Jansen 2002; Jones and Robinson 2005).

# RESERVOIR CISTERNS

Very large cistern complexes are sometimes found on aqueduct networks, which served as reservoirs. These reservoir cisterns are found in the Mediterranean region, and not in northern Europe, because of patterns of use and of precipitation. They fall into two categories: terminal reservoirs, into which the entire aqueduct discharges, and which therefore govern the entire distribution system downstream from them; and reservoirs on branches or subdivisions of the urban distribution network, which regulate supply only to their particular branch. These latter are frequently connected with large bath complexes.

Terminal reservoir cisterns are found in North Africa and very occasionally in other arid regions (Aptera, Crete; Sepphoris, Israel; Resafa, Syria), where seasonal fluctuations in aqueduct delivery affected the whole distribution network. They usually consisted either of multiple parallel, barrel-vaulted chambers communicating through arches pierced in the division walls so that they formed a single hydraulic space, or of a large cross-vaulted chamber with the arches supported on piers (figure 11.7). At the outlet, one or more lead pipes passed from the main reservoir through the wall into a chamber where the outflow could be controlled by means of stopcocks on the pipes (e.g., Hippo Regius; Rusicade; A. I. Wilson 1998, 2001). Terminal reservoir cisterns in North Africa could have a capacity of up to 50,000 m$^3$ (Carthage, La Malga), although most fell in the range of 3,500–13,500 m$^3$ (A. I. Wilson 1997: 79–80). The large reservoir cistern at the end of the Serino aqueduct, at Bacoli on the Bay of Naples, held some 12,600 m$^3$ and probably supplied the fleet stationed at Misenum (Hodge 1992: 276, 279). Because of rainfall on the karst aquifer from which they drew their water, the delivery of the Byzantine aqueducts of Constantinople was subject to such considerable seasonal fluctuations that several large reservoirs, so vast they could not be roofed over, were constructed within the Theodosian walls to provide a seasonal reserve capable of supplying much of the city; the reservoirs were named for Aëtius (A.D. 421; 270,000 m$^3$), Aspar (pre-471; 230,000 m$^3$), and St. Mocius (A.D. 419–518; 250,000 m$^3$). In the reign of Justinian, these were supplemented by several very large, covered reservoir cisterns, closer to the imperial palace, with brick roofs supported on numerous columns reused from classical buildings. The most famous is the Yerebatan Saray (A.D. 532; 83,500 m$^3$) and the Binbirdirek cisterns (57,800 m$^3$) (Procopius, *Aed.* I.11.10–15; Freely and Çakmak 2004: 55–56, 146–51).

Large reservoir cisterns specifically associated with large bath complexes are found throughout a wider area, and illustrate a solution to supplying these water-thirsty complexes while minimizing the impact on the rest of the distribution network. If these cisterns were filled overnight, the baths could run on the stored reserve during the following day, meaning that the full delivery of the aqueduct was available for distribution to fountains and private users during the day. Reservoir cisterns for baths are particularly common in North Africa and Italy, where they are associated with baths of the imperial *thermae* type: the Sette Sale, for Trajan's Baths (7,000 m$^3$); the cisterns of the Baths of Caracalla (11,500 m$^3$); the Botte di Termini, serving the Baths of Diocletian in Rome; the Bordj Djedid cisterns for the Antonine Baths at Carthage (20,000 m$^3$). Large supply cisterns are found elsewhere in Italy, at Chieti, and in Crete at Aptera. Aqueduct-fed cisterns on a smaller scale, 100–400 m$^3$ capacity, are commonly found associated with medium-sized baths (e.g., the Baths of Julia Memmia at Bulla Regia, Tunisia).

Figure 11.7. One of seven parallel vaulted chambers in the large reservoir cisterns at Oudhna (ancient Uthina) in Tunisia. (Photograph by A. I. Wilson.)

## Fountains and Nymphaea

The most important destination within the urban water network was public fountains. For many people, perhaps the majority of urban dwellers, these represented their main source of drinking water. We have seen that fountains were the major destination of the Greek and Hellenistic aqueducts, and of the earliest aqueducts at Rome. Many of the street fountains at Pompeii probably belong to the early phase of that system (ca. 80 B.C.); simple and functional, they consist of a stone basin with a spout, often emerging from a decorative plaque or head. Over the course of the first century A.D., however, first in Rome and then in the provinces, fountains grew more elaborate and decorative, and they were increasingly ornamented with statues, sculpted motifs, and colonnades. Nero's colossal *nymphaeum* along the east side of the base of the Temple of Divus Claudius, whose overflow fed the lake of the Domus Aurea on the site of the later Colosseum, was a precocious example of the trend. By the early second century, *nymphaea* with elaborate facades were appearing in provincial cities, initially in coastal Asia Minor and later in North Africa. These often incorporated basins in front of a curved, colonnaded backdrop with statues of deities, the imperial family, and local dignitaries who had paid or helped to pay for the aqueduct. There was every conceivable gradation along a range from functional to ostentatious, ranging from the simple street fountains of Pompeii, Herculaneum, and Saepinum to the elaborate *nymphaea* of Lepcis, Perge, or Olympia. But we should not allow the lavish architecture of the largest *nymphaea* to blind us to their utility. An inscription from Cirta (Constantine, Algeria) makes the point. Part of an inventory of the city's wealth, it lists in the *nymphaeum* 40 gilded letters and 10 punctuation points (doubtless from the inscriptions honoring the emperor or private person who paid for the aqueduct), six chained goblets with gold inlay, a fountain basin inlaid with gold, six bronze statues and a Cupid, six marble statues, six bronze Silenus-head water spouts, and six hand towels (*CIL* 8.6982 = *ILS* 4921b). This account reflects a level of wealth and display (the gold inlay and other metal ornaments) lacking in the surviving archaeology. While the lavish use of colored marbles is attested by surviving remains, precious metals have invariably been looted. The inscription also hints at the ways in which the fountain was used on a daily basis: people went to drink from the chained goblets, splashed their faces and hands from the basin, and then dried themselves on the towels, doubtless handed out and retrieved by a public slave, in whose absence they would rapidly have disappeared. Doubtless, the fountain was also a place of gossip and social exchange. At Pompeii, the importance of the unostentatious public fountains to the city's life is indicated by the fact that most houses are within 50 m of a street fountain. By the late first century A.D., Rome had 39 display fountains (*munera*) and 591 street fountains (*lacus*) (Frontinus, *Aq.* 78), and the fourth-century Regionary Catalogues list between 1,216 and 1,352 fountains (*lacus*) and 15 nymphaea. (Jordan 1871–1907: 539–74).

# Baths

From the late Republic onward, public baths were among the most demanding consumers of water on an urban aqueduct network. Greek public baths had consisted of many individual hip-baths in the same room, in which bathers would have water that had been drawn from a well poured over them by attendants. Roman baths differed in that the bathers shared large pools, and the water could be heated in large lead boilers mounted over furnaces, whose exhaust gases also heated rooms and pools by means of the hypocaust. In this arrangement, pools and floors were supported on a series of (usually) brick piers, allowing hot air from the furnace to circulate beneath before escaping up flues in the walls. The temperature of the water in hot or warm pools could be maintained by a device called a *testudo*, a bronze half-cylinder open at one end, which communicated with the pool near its base, so that it was full of water. The other end of the *testudo* was mounted over the furnace, heating the water within it; the heated water escaped upward into the pool, being replaced by cooler water so that circulation was achieved by convection. To the *frigidaria*, *tepidaria*, and *caldaria* (cold, warm, and hot rooms) of early baths, later baths sometimes added sweating rooms and indeed suites of exercise areas, lecture halls, and libraries to form veritable leisure centers. While smaller public baths were sometimes supplied from wells, usually with the aid of water-lifting machinery (chapter 13), the larger ones had to be fed by aqueducts, and the largest elaborately decorated imperial *thermae* of Rome and other major cities could accommodate hundreds or even thousands of bathers, and demanded special arrangements, such as large reservoir cisterns to minimize their impact on the rest of the network (DeLaine 1988; Nielsen 1990; Yegül 1992; Fagan 1999). The cutting of Rome's aqueducts by the Goths in the siege of A.D. 537 put the city's baths out of action, and although four of the aqueducts were subsequently repaired, public bathing never regained its former importance in the early Middle Ages. Elsewhere, public bathing also declined as the aqueducts fell out of use.

# THE PURPOSE OF ROMAN AQUEDUCTS

Were aqueducts necessary to Roman cities, or were they a luxury? Early aqueduct studies assumed that these elaborate systems were primarily useful, and a marker by which Rome's civilization could be judged. From the 1970s onward, the tide of scholarly opinion began turning in favor of a view that saw them as useless luxuries, built primarily to advertise Rome's control over natural resources, to use water as an ostentatious symbol of conspicuous consumption, and to support an urban lifestyle in which public bathing played a major role—in other words, aqueducts were ideological symbols of empire (Leveau and Paillet 1976: 167, 181; 1983; Leveau 1987; Shaw 1984, 1991; Corbier 1991: 222). But today, with more attention paid to the role of public fountains in the overall pattern of water supply and to the regulation of delivery using terminal reservoirs and bath-related reservoir cisterns, this binary opposition between utility and luxury appears too stark (A. I. Wilson 1997, 1998: 89–93; 1999, 2001). The priorities of early aqueduct systems were not baths and display. Even as civic and social ostentation became important (with private display developing before civic display), the very utility of aqueducts increased their ideological impact. Much more detailed research is needed on the chronology of the spread of aqueducts throughout the Roman world, and on the chronology of the spread and development of cities in the western provinces of the empire, but at least for Rome, Pompeii, and North Africa it appears that urban growth and the building of aqueducts went hand in hand. Cause and effect cannot be completely disentangled, but we have no reason to reject the idea that aqueducts enabled cities to grow to larger sizes and support more people than would have been possible with reliance solely on water from wells, rainwater cisterns, and local springs.

# IRRIGATION SYSTEMS

Although the major riverine civilizations of the ancient Near East had relied on complex state-controlled systems of irrigation from major rivers, most irrigation in the Greco-Roman world took other forms (Hodge 1992: 246–53; Oleson 2000). The exception was Egypt, where the Nile flood was the main source of water for agriculture, and irrigation canals derived from the river. *Shadufs* (tip-beams with buckets lifted by a counterweight) were used to raise water out of the river or its canals, and they were joined in the Ptolemaic period by other, more effective forms of water-lifting machine (see also chapter 13 on water-lifting devices).

One of the most common forms of passive irrigation was agricultural terracing, which inhibited erosion and retained water in the soil. In arid zones such as the Negev desert or the Tripolitanian pre-desert, stone and earth walls built on the *hamada* or rock-desert plateaus concentrated on a small area runoff water from a catchment zone many times the size, thus increasing the effective rainfall equivalent on the cultivated plot. Small check dams built across the wadi floors retained water and soil from flash floods, creating fertile parcels of soil in the wadi beds that could be farmed; excess water was directed into cisterns and stored (Barker 1996; Glueck 1959; Evenari et al. 1982; Avner 2001–2002). Such systems supported a considerable expansion of settlement into these pre-desert or desert areas in the Roman and late Roman periods. On the more arid fringes of the Greco-Roman world—in the oases of the Egyptian western desert, on the southern flank of the Aurès range in Numidia, and in the Garamantian lands of the Sahara—*qanats* or *foggaras* provided water for both settlements and irrigation.

Much irrigation, everywhere, was small-scale and has left little archaeological record. The exceptions we can trace are the large-scale schemes, often representing massive investments of time, labor, and money. In the Roman period, large irrigation systems shared much with aqueduct technology. The main differences were conditioned by the requirement for larger quantities of water than for urban supply, but with less concern for quality; hence there was a greater propensity to take irrigation water by diversion from rivers, as in the Ebro valley (Spain) or the Safsaf plain (Algeria). Diversion dams are found both on permanent water courses and, in northern Tunisia, in wadis which run for only part of the year, or in spate after occasional rainfall (du Coudray de la Blanchère 1895). Other, larger dams, as at Kasserine in Tunisia, may have retained water for irrigation purposes; large concrete dams in Tripolitania may have served a similar purpose, or, as at Lepcis Magna, protected sites downstream from the erosive force of spate floods.

Irrigation channels frequently were not covered over, and they were often wider than urban aqueducts—the Alcanadre channel in the Ebro valley is 2.5 m wide with a water depth of 1.1 m (Dupré 1997: 726–29). Indeed, the Ebro valley was home to a number of large irrigation schemes; the first-century B.C. *Tabula Contrebiensis* is a bronze table recording the settlement of a dispute between two communities about building an irrigation canal over land purchased from a third (Richardson 1983; Birks et al. 1984), and a bronze inscription from Agón, northwest of Zaragoza, discovered in 1993, is a Hadrianic law regulating the use of a large irrigation system (Beltrán Lloris 2006). The Agón system drew water from the river Ebro and was evidently a large-scale irrigation system involving several communities (of which two, Agón and Gallur, were between 5 and 10 km apart) that contributed to its upkeep. The central organization and planning of this system, with legal regulations and a local court, anticipates the much better known hydraulic communities of Islamic Spain. While this inscription describes the general legal framework for the use and upkeep of the system, another (stone) inscription from Lamasba (Algeria) records the specific irrigation schedule for a local community, in the reign of Elagabalus, with details of which estates were to receive water between which hours (*CIL* 8.18584; De Pachtère 1908; Shaw 1982; Meuret 1996).

One of the underground aqueducts of Carthage, from La Soukra in the Ariana plain, was equipped with large wells or shafts (3 m x 1 m) at intervals along the channel. These shafts are much larger than normal access shafts on Roman aqueducts, and the most likely explanation is that water-lifting machinery was installed over the shafts to raise water from the aqueduct to irrigate the intensively cultivated, centuriated land northwest of Carthage. The size, shape, and chronology of the shafts suggest the use of bucket-chains, coupled with the animal-driven angle-gear (*saqiya*; chapter 13). In the early twentieth century, French colonists mounted wind-pumps over these shafts and used them once again for irrigation (Renault 1912: 471–75; Fornacciari 1928–1929). The archaeological evidence, while not closely dateable within the Roman period, confirms Tertullian's evidence for the pre-Islamic use of the *saqiya* in North Africa (*de Anima* 33.7; mules and donkeys driving *aquilegas rotas*).

While some systems were constructed specifically for irrigation, urban aqueducts were also sometimes tapped for the irrigation of estates along their course. The evidence for this practice is clearest for the network of aqueducts serving Rome (Frontinus, *Aq.* 76, 92, 97; A. I. Wilson 1999). Two inscriptions from Rome or its suburbs record the scheduling of rights to draw water to particular estates (*CIL* 6.1261; 14.3676), but the practice was more widespread. The aqueduct serving Amiternum seems to have provided off-take *castella* for several estates through which it ran, and scattered evidence indicates the use of aqueduct water by rural villas and estates in other provinces (A. I. Wilson 1999). Some villa estates in Italy, Spain, and North Africa constructed their own small-scale aqueducts to supply water for drinking, bathing, and the irrigation of vegetable plots—the latter often regulated from aqueduct-fed cisterns of 100–1,000 m$^3$ capacity (Thomas and Wilson 1994; A. I. Wilson forthcoming).

# Sewers and Drainage

The emergent city-states of archaic Greece made use of much the same range of drainage elements as the urban civilizations of the ancient Near East—soakaway drains for foul water, and terracotta pipes for overflow water from fountains. Until the classical period, street drains were rare in Greek cities. Athens' "Great Drain" began as a storm-drain for the agora in the fifth century B.C., but even in the fourth century B.C. much domestic waste water was discharged straight into the streets (Aristotle, *Ath.Pol.* 50.1). Although many cities (e.g., Smyrna, Euesperides) did without street drains well into the Hellenistic period, the classical era saw the adoption at some sites of integrated drainage networks, in which domestic drains fed into street drains that united in main collector drains under the principal streets, eventually discharging outside the city. In the Roman world, the foundation of numerous new colonies often allowed a more systematic adoption of planned, integrated drainage networks, with under-street drains often built of masonry. Rainwater entered the drains through gratings, either functional or with holes in a decorative petal design. Overflow from aqueduct-fed fountains helped flush the sewers, but the gradient was usually insufficient to prevent accumulation of solid wastes, and street drains periodically had to be cleared manually by public slaves or contractors. The need for access and maintenance determined a relationship between the size of drains and the manner in which they were roofed. Drains large enough to walk through might be vaulted, while smaller ones were covered with flat slabs that could be removed. Yet despite the relative sophistication of Roman hydraulic engineering, some cities still continued to have open drains until the second century A.D. Ancient drainage systems are related to increasing urban complexity, but drainage follows urban development with a considerable time lag, due to the need for strong political control, a developed legal framework of property law, and access rights prior to implementation of integrated drainage networks (A. I. Wilson 2000b).

Large land-drainage schemes in the Mediterranean region predate the archaic period; the Bronze Age drainage of the Kopais basin in Boeotia channeled surface waters to natural swallow-holes in the limestone. By the reign of Alexander the Great (336–323 B.C.) this system had failed, and an engineer, Crates, was engaged to drain the area again, a project left unfinished because of strife among the Boeotians (Strabo 9.2.18). His scheme has been identified with a partially completed outlet tunnel, with 16 vertical shafts descending to stretches of an unfinished horizontal gallery. The same kind of shaft-and-gallery tunneling technique, already familiar from Assyrian aqueducts and the aqueduct of Samos, is implied in a contract between the city of Eretria and the engineer Chaerephanes for a scheme to drain the marshes of Ptechae (*IG* 9.9.191.1; Argoud 1987). Chaerephanes was to drain the marsh by means of surface channels discharging into a collecting reservoir; this could then be drained to the sea by means of an outlet tunnel, controlled by a sluice gate that enabled the water in the reservoir to be used for irrigation in the spring. The contract stipulates what land Chaerephanes can and cannot use; he must purchase the land necessary for the access shafts to the outlet tunnel.

The same kind of shaft-and-gallery tunneling technique was used for the Etruscan *cuniculi*, underground drainage galleries that either diverted one stream under a ridge into an adjacent valley, or drained the marshy bottoms of valleys in the easily-eroded tufa landscape of South Etruria, where natural surface drainage was poor (chapter 12; cf. Judson and Kahane 1963; Bergamini 1991). The large Roman lake drainage schemes, which relied on tunneling an outlet channel (*emissarium*) through a ridge, are dealt with in chapter 12.

Extensive Roman land drainage and wetland reclamation schemes have been identified in numerous areas of Roman centuriation (in the Ager Falernus, the Campania, and the Po Valley), and also in Britain, with wetland reclamation in the Severn estuary and the partial drainage of the East Anglian fens. Here, a large drain, the Car Dyke, acted as a collector for smaller land drains from the high ground to the west, and discharged the water through a series of canalized natural streams into a roughly parallel system, the Midfendic, several miles further east. The Midfendic, protected from the sea by a sea bank, stored the water until it could be released into the sea at low tide. The backflow of water into the Car Dyke at high tide could be prevented by sluice-gates on the cross-streams. The whole system anticipates the *ringvart* systems of the medieval and later Netherlands; it was probably connected with the establishment of salt workings on imperial estates in the Fenland under Hadrian (Simmons 1979).

Notable advances were made in hydraulic engineering during the last six centuries B.C., involving not only new inventions—waterproof cement compounds, the inverted siphon, lead piping, taps, and means of conserving and distributing water—but also their increasingly widespread uptake. In the sixth century B.C. major hydraulic engineering works were exceptional projects undertaken by a handful of rulers with the necessary resources, but under the Roman Empire long-distance water supply lines and public water distribution networks became very common, so that many Roman cities had a water-supply system that was not equaled again until the nineteenth century. Ancient concepts of hygiene and public health were deficient, but the spread of organized water supply enabled a level of urban growth and development that could hardly have been achieved or sustained without reliance on long-distance aqueducts that tapped remote sources. The level of hydraulic development achieved in the ancient world is one of the key reasons why the regions making up the Roman Empire saw a greater degree of urban settlement at that period than at any subsequent time before the eighteenth century.

# REFERENCES

Aicher, P. J. 1995. *Guide to the aqueducts of ancient Rome.* Wauconda: Bolchazy-Carducchi.

Alzinger, W. 1987. "Ephesos," in G. Garbrecht (ed.), *Die Wasserversorgung antiker Städte,* vol. 2. Mainz: von Zabern, 180–84.

Amit, D. 2002. "New data for dating the high-level aqueduct and the Wadi el Biyar aqueduct, and the Herodion aqueduct," in D. Amrit, J. Patrich, and Y. Hirschfeld (eds.), *The aqueducts of Israel,* 253–66. *Journal of Roman Archeology* Suppl. 46. Portsmouth, RI: JRA, 253–66.

Argoud, G. 1987. "Eau et agriculture en Grèce," in P. Louis, F. Métral, and J. Métral (eds.), *L'homme et l'eau en Méditerranée et au Proche Orient.* Travaux de la Maison de l'Orient 14. vol. 4, *L'eau dans l'agriculture: seminaire de recherche 1982–1983 et journées des 22 et 23 octobre 1983.* Lyon: Maison de l'Orient, Presses Universitaires de Lyon, 25–42.

Ashby, T. 1935. *The aqueducts of ancient Rome,* ed. I. A. Richmond Oxford: Clarendon Press.

Avner, Uzi. 2001–2. "Ancient water management in the Southern Negev," *Aram* 13–14: 403–21.

Barker, G. W. W. (ed.) 1996. *Farming the desert: The UNESCO Libyan Valleys Archaeological Survey.* vol. 1. Paris, Tripoli, and London: UNESCO Publishing, Department of Antiquities (Tripoli) and the Society for Libyan Studies.

Beltrán Lloris, F. 2006. "An irrigation decree from Roman Spain: The *Lex Rivi Hiberiensis,*" *Journal of Roman Studies* 96:147–97.

Belvedere, O (ed.) 1987. *Aquae Corneliae Ductus: L'approvvigionamento idrico di Termini Imerese in età romana.* Palermo: Università di Palermo.

Bergamini, M. (ed.) 1991. *Gli Etruschi maestri di idraulica.* Perugia: Electa Editori Umbri.

Biernacka-Lubanska, M. 1977. "A preliminary classification of Greek rainwater intakes," *Archeologia (Warszawa)* 28: 26–36.

Birks, P., A. Rodger, and J. S. Richardson. 1984. "Further aspects of the Tabula Contrebiensis," *Journal of Roman Studies* 74: 45–73.

Blair, I., and J. Hall. 2003. *Working water: Roman technology in action.* London: Museum of London.

Bodon, G., I. Riera, and P. Zanovello (eds.) 1994. *Utilitas necessaria: Sistemi idraulichi nell' Italia romana.* Milano: Progetto Quarta Dimensione.

Boyd, T. D. 1978. "The arch and the vault in Greek architecture," *American Journal of Archaeology.* 82: 83–100.

Camp, J. M. 1982. "Drought and famine in the 4th century B.C," in *Studies in Athenian architecture, sculpture and topography presented to Homer A. Thompson.* Hesperia Suppl. 20. Princeton, NJ: American School of Classical Studies at Athens, 9–17.

Chanson, H. 2000. "Hydraulics of Roman Aqueducts: Steep chutes, cascades and dropshafts," *American Journal of Archaeology* 104: 47–72.

Connelly, J. B., and A. I. Wilson. 2002. "Hellenistic and Byzantine cisterns on Geronisos Island," *Report of the Department of Antiquities, Cyprus:* 269–92.

Conophagos, C. E. 1980. *Le Laurium antique, et la technique grecque de la production de l'argent.* Athènes: Ekdotike Hellados s.a.

Conophagos, C. E. 1982. "Concrete and special plaster waterproofing in ancient Laurion (Greece)," in T. A. Wertime and S. F. Wertime (eds.), *Early pyrotechnology: The evolution of the first fire-using industries.* Washington, D.C.: Smithsonian Institution Press, 117–23.

Corbier, M. 1991. "City, territory and taxation," in J. Rich and A. Wallace-Hadrill (eds.), *City and country in the ancient world*. Leicester-Nottingham Studies in Ancient Society. London and New York: Routledge, 211–39.

Dalley, S. 2001–2. "Water management in Assyria from the ninth to the seventh centuries B.C," *Aram* 13–14: 443–60.

DeLaine, J. 1988. "Recent research on Roman baths," *Journal of Roman Archaeology* 1: 11–32.

De Pachtère, F.-G. 1908. "Le règlement d'irrigation de Lamasba," *Mélanges de l'École française de Rome* 28: 373–400.

Devoti, L. 1978. *Cisterne del periodo romano nel Tuscolano*. Frascati: Associazione Tuscolana "Amici di Frascati."

Döring, M. 2002a. "Wasser für den Sinus Baianus: Römische Ingenieur- und Wasserbauten der Phlegraeischen Felder," *Antike Welt* 33: 305–19.

Döring, M. 2002b. "Die römische Wasserversorgung von Pozzuoli, Baia und Miseno (Italien)," in C. Ohlig, Y. Peleg, and T. Tsuk (eds.), *Cura Aquarum in Israel*. Siegburg: Deutsches Wasserhistorisches Gesellschaft, 253–65.

Downey, G. 1961. *A history of Antioch in Syria from Seleucus to the Arab conquest*. Princeton: Princeton University Press.

du Coudray la Blanchère, René M. 1895. *L'aménagement de l'eau et l'installation rurale dans l'Afrique ancienne*. Paris: Imprimerie Nationale.

Dupré, N. 1997. "Eau, ville et campagne dans l'Hispanie romaine: À propos des aqueducs du bassin de l'Ebre," in R. Bedon (ed.), *Les aqueducs de la Gaule romaine et des regions voisines*. Caesarodunum 31. Limoges: Presses Universitaires de Limoges, 715–43.

Eschebach, H. 1983. "Die innerstädtische Gebrauchswasserversorgung dargestellt am Beispiel Pompejis," in J.-P. Boucher (ed.), *Journées d'études sur les aqueducs romains: Tagung über römische Wasserversorgungsanlagen. Lyon 26–28 mai, 1977*. Paris: Les Belles Lettres, 81–132.

Evenari, M., L. Shanan, and N. H. Tadmor. 1982. *The Negev: The challenge of a desert*. 2nd ed. Cambridge, MA: Harvard University Press.

Faber, G. 1992. "Der Römische Qanat von Helmsingen (le Qanat romain de Helmsange)," *Vie Souterraine* 2: 13–15.

Fabio, E., and L. Fassitelli n.d. [1992?]. *Roma: tubi e valvole*. 13th ed. Milan: Petrolieri d'Italia.

Fagan, G. G. 1999. *Bathing in public in the Roman world*. Ann Arbor: University of Michigan Press.

Freely, J., and A. Çakmak. 2004. *Byzantine monuments of Istanbul*. Cambridge: Cambridge University Press.

Fornacciari, C. 1928–1929. "Note sur le drain romain de la Soukra [communication à la séance de la Commission de l'Afrique du Nord, 10 décembre 1929]," *Bulletin archéologique du Comité des travaux historiques et scientifiques*: 413–15.

Garfinkel, Y., A. Vered, and O. Bar-Yosef 2006. "The Domestication of water: the Neolithic well at Sha'ar Hagolan, Jordan Valley, Israel," *Antiquity* 309: 686–96.

Glueck, N. 1959. *Rivers in the desert: The exploration of the Negev. An adventure in archaeology*. London: Weidenfeld and Nicolson.

Goblot, H. 1979. *Les qanats: Une technique d'acquisition de l'eau*. Industrie et artisanat 9. Paris and New York: Éditions Mouton/École des Hautes Études en Sciences Sociales.

Grewe, K. 1985. *Planung und Trassierung römischer Wasserleitungen*. Schriftenreihe der Frontinus-Gesellschaft, Supplementband 1. Wiesbaden: Verlag Chmielorz.

Grewe, K. 1988. "Römische Wasserleitungen nördlich der Alpen," in G. Garbrecht (ed.), *Die Wasserversorgung antiker Städte*, vol. 3. Mainz: von Zabern, 43–97.

Grewe, K. 1993. "Antike Welt der Technik V: *Augusta Emerita*/Mérida—Eine Stadt römischer Technikgeschichte," *Antike Welt* 24: 244–55.

Grewe, K. 1998. "Antike Welt der Technik IX: Der Aquädukt von Siga (Algerien)," *Antike
Welt*. 29: 409–20.

Hellmann, M.-C. 2002. *L'architecture grecque*. vol. 1,: *Les principes de la construction*. Paris:
Picard.

Hill, B. H. 1964. *Corinth* vol. 1.6, *The springs: Peirene, Sacred spring, Glauke*. Princeton:
American School of Classical Studies at Athens.

Hodge, A. T. (ed.) 1991. *Future currents in aqueduct studies*. Leeds: Francis Cairns

Hodge, A. T. 1992. *Roman aqueducts and water supply*. London: Duckworth.

Hodge, A. T. 2000. "Wells," in Wikander 2000: 29–33.

Jacobsen, T., and S. Lloyd 1935. *Sennacherib's aqueduct at Jerwan*. Chicago: University of
Chicago Press.

Jansen, G. C. M. 2000. "Urban water transport and distribution," in Wikander 2000:
103–25.

Jansen, G. C. M. 2002. *Water in de Romeinse stad. Pompeji—Herculaneum—Ostia*. Leuven:
Peeters.

Jardé, A. 1907. "Puteus," DarSag, vol. 4.1, 779–81.

Jones, R., and D. Robinson 2005. "Water, wealth and social status at Pompeii: The House
of the Vestals in the first century," *American Journal of Archaeology* 109: 695–710.

Jordan, H. 1871–1907. *Die Topographie der Stadt Rom im Altertum*. 2 vols. in 4. Berlin:
Weidmannsche buchhandlung.

Judson, S., and A. Kahane. 1963. "Underground drainageways in Southern Etruria and
Northern Latium," *Papers of the British School at Rome* 31: 74–99.

Keppie, L. 1983. *Colonisation and veteran settlement in Italy, 47–14 B.C.* Rome: British School
at Rome.

Kienast, H. J. 1995. *Die Wasserleitung des Eupalinos auf Samos*. Samos 19. Bonn: Deutsches
Archäologisches Institut.

Klaffenbach, G. 1954. *Die Astynomeninschrift von Pergamon*. Abhandlungen der deutschen
Akademie der Wissenschaften zu Berlin, Klasse für Sprachen, Literatur und Kunst,
Jahrgang 1953, 6. Berlin: Akademie-Verlag.

Kohl, N., and G. Faber 1990. *25 Jahre Raschpëtzer Forschung, 1965–1990*. Walferdange.

Kohl, N., G. Waringo, and G. Faber 1995. *Raschpëtzer: Die Ausgrabungschronik der Jahre
1991–1995*. Walferdange.

Kremer, B. 2005. "Antike Wassergewinnung an der Mosel. Der römische Qanat von Pö-
lich," *Schriftenreihe der Frontinus-Gesellschaft* 26: 127–55.

Lanciani, R. 1881. "Topografia di Roma antica: I comentarii di Frontino intorno le
acque e gli acquedotti. Silloge epigrafica aquaria," *Memorie della Reale Accademia dei
Lincei*, Serie 3, no. 4: 215–616.

Lang, M. 1968. *Waterworks in the Athenian agora*. Excavations of the Athenian Agora,
Picture Books 11. Princeton, New Jersey: American School of Classical Studies at
Athens.

Lassus, J. 1983. "L'eau courante à Antioch," in J.-P. Boucher (ed.), *Journées d'études sur les
aqueducs romains: Tagung über römische Wasserversorgungsanlagen, Lyons, 26–28
mai, 1977*. Paris: Les Belles Lettres, 207–29.

Last, J. S. 1975. "Kourion: The ancient water supply," *Proceedings of the American Philosophical Society* 119: 39–72.

Leveau, P. 1984. *Caesarea de Maurétanie: Une ville romaine et ses campagnes*. Collection de
l'École Française de Rome 70. Rome: École Française de Rome.

Leveau, P. 1987. "A quoi servaient les aqueducts romains?" *L'Histoire* 105 (Nov.): 96–104.

Leveau, P., and J.-L. Paillet 1976. *L'alimentation en eau de Caesarea de Maurétanie et l'aqueduc de Cherchell.* Paris: Éditions l'Harmattan.

Leveau, P., and J.-L. Paillet 1983. "Alimentation en eau et développement urbain à Caesarea de Maurétanie," in J.-P. Boucher (ed.), *Journées d'études sur les aqueducs romains: Tagung über römische Wasserversorgungsanlagen, Lyons, 26–28 mai, 1977.* Paris: Les Belles Lettres, 231–34.

Lewis, M. J. T. 1999. "Vitruvius and Greek aqueducts," *Papers of the British School at Rome* 67: 145–72.

Lloyd, J. A. 1977. "Water supply and storage systems," in J. A. Lloyd (ed.), *Excavations at Sidi Khrebish, Benghazi (Berenice). Libya Antiqua*, suppl. 5. Tripoli: Department of Antiquities, vol. 1, 199–209.

Magee, P. 2005. "The chronology and environmental background of Iron Age settlement in southeastern Iran and the question of the origin of the qanat irrigation system," *Iranica Antiqua* 40: 217–31.

Manteli, K. 1992. "The Neolithic well at Kastelli Phournis in eastern Crete," *Annual of the British School at Athens* 87: 103–20, pls.1–2.

Marlière, É. 2002. *L'outre et le tonneau dans l'Occident romain.* Monographies Instrumentum 22. Montagnac: Éditions Monique Mergoil.

Meuret, C. 1996. "Le règlement de *Lamasba*: Des tables de conversion appliquées à l'irrigation," *Antiquités africaines* 32: 87–112.

Nielsen, I. 1990. *Thermae et Balnea: The architecture and cultural history of Roman public baths.* 2 vols. Aarhus: Aarhus University Press.

Ohlig, C. P. J. 2001. *De aquis Pompeiorum. Das Castellum Aquae in Pompeji: Herkunft, Zuleitung und Verteilung des Wassers.* Circumvesuviana 4. Nijmegen: Books on Demand Norderstedt.

Oleson, J. P. 1991. "Aqueducts, cisterns, and the strategy of water supply at Nabataean and Roman Auara (Jordan)," in Hodge 1991, 45–62.

Oleson, J. P. 1992. "Water works," in D. N. Freedman (ed.), *Anchor Bible dictionary*, vol. 6. New York: Doubleday, 883–93.

Oleson, J. P. 1995. "The origins and design of Nabataean water-supply systems," in *Studies in the history and archaeology of Jordan*, 5. Amman: Department of Antiquities, 707–19.

Oleson, J. P. 2000. "Irrigation," in Wikander 2000: 183–215.

Patrich, J., and D. Amit 2002. "The aqueducts of Israel: An introduction," in D. Amit, J. Patrich, and Y. Hirschfeld (eds.), *The aqueducts of Israel. Journal of Roman Archaeology* Suppl. 46. Portsmouth, RI: JRA, 9–20.

Peltenburg, E., P. Croft, A. Jackson, C. McCartney, and M. A. Murray 2001. "Well-established colonists: *Mylouthkia* I and the Cypro-Pre-Pottery Neolithic B," in S. Swiny (ed.), *The earliest prehistory of Cyprus: From colonization to exploitation.* Cyprus American Archaeological Research Institute Monograph Series 2. Boston: American Schools of Oriental Research, 61–93.

Porath, E. 2002. "The water-supply to Caesarea: A re-assessment," in D. Amit, J. Patrich, and Y. Hirschfeld (eds.), *The aqueducts of Israel. Journal of Roman Archaeology* Suppl. 46. Portsmouth, RI: JRA, 104–29.

Potter, T. W. 1987. *Roman Italy.* London: British Museum Press.

Renault, J. 1912. "Les bassins du trik Dar-Saniat à Carthage," *Revue Tunisienne* 19.95: 471–98.

Richardson, J. S. 1983. "The Tabula Contrebiensis, Roman law in Spain in the early first century B.C," *Journal of Roman Studies* 73: 33–41.

Rodgers, R. H. 2004. *Frontinus* De aquaeductu urbis Romae, *edited with introduction and commentary.* Cambridge: Cambridge University Press.

Schoellen, A. 1997. "Des surprenants ouvrages hydrauliques romains," *Archeologia Paris* 332: 62–66.

Sgobbo, I. 1938. "Serino—L'acquedotto romano della Campania: 'Fontis Augustei Aquaeductus,'" *Notizie degli scavi di antichità:* 75–97.

Shaw, B. D. 1982. "Lamasba: An ancient irrigation community," *Antiquités africaines* 18: 61–103.

Shaw, B. D. 1984. "Water and society in the ancient Mahgrib: Technology, property and development," *Antiquités africaines* 20: 121–73.

Shaw, B. D. 1991. "The noblest monuments and the smallest things: Wells, walls and aqueducts in the making of Roman Africa," in Hodge 1991, 63–91.

Simmons, B. B. 1979. "The Lincolnshire Car Dyke: Navigation or drainage?" *Britannia* 10: 183–96.

Stenton, E. C., and J. J. Coulton. 1986. "Oinoanda: The water supply and aqueduct," *Anatolian Studies* 36: 15–59.

Thomas, R. G., and A. I. Wilson 1994. "Water supply for Roman farms in Latium and South Etruria," *Papers of the British School at Rome* 62: 139–96.

Tölle-Kastenbein, R. 1994. *Das archaische Wasserleitungsnetz für Athen und seine späteren Bauphasen.* Mainz: Philipp von Zabern.

Tölle-Kastenbein, R. 1996. "Das archaische Wasserleitungsnetz für Athen," in N. de Haan and G. C. M. Jansen (eds.), *Cura Aquarum in Campania.* BABESCH Suppl. 4. Leiden: BABESCH, 129–36.

Walda, H. M. 1996. "Lepcis Magna excavations Autumn 1995: Report on surveying, archaeology and pottery," *Libyan Studies* 27: 125–27.

Wikander, Ö. (ed.) 2000. *Handbook of ancient water technology.* Leiden: Brill.

Wilson, A. I. 1995. "Running water and social status in North Africa," in M. Horton and T. Weidemann (eds.), *North Africa from antiquity to Islam.* Bristol: Centre for Mediterranean Studies (University of Bristol), 52–56.

Wilson, A. I. 1997. "Water management and usage in Roman North Africa: A social and technological study." D. Phil. Thesis, University of Oxford.

Wilson, A. I. 1998. "Water supply in ancient Carthage," in *Carthage papers: The early colony's economy, water supply, a private bath, and the mobilization of state olive oil. Journal of Roman Archaeology* Suppl. 28. Portsmouth, RI: JRA, 65–102.

Wilson, A. I. 1999. "Deliveries *extra urbem*: Aqueducts and the countryside," *Journal of Roman Archaeology* 12: 314–31.

Wilson, A. I. 2000a "The aqueducts of Italy and Gaul," *Journal of Roman Archaeology* 13: 597–604.

Wilson, A. I. 2000b. "Drainage and sanitation," in Wikander 2000: 151–79.

Wilson, A. I. 2001. "Urban water storage, distribution and usage in Roman North Africa," in A. O. Koloski-Ostrow (ed.), *Water use and hydraulics in the Roman city.* Boston: Kendall Hunt, 83–96.

Wilson, A. I. 2004. "Classical water technology in the early Islamic world," in C. Bruun and A. Saastamoinen (eds.), *Technology, ideology, water: From Frontinus to the Renaissance and beyond.* Acta Instituti Romani Finlandiae 31:115–41.

Wilson, A. I. 2005. "Foggara irrigation, early state formation and Saharan trade: The Garamantes of Fazzan," *Schriftenreihe der Frontinus-Gesellschaft* 26: 223–34.

Wilson, A. I. 2006a. "The spread of foggara-based irrigation in the ancient Sahara," in D. J. Mattingly, S. McLaren, E. Savage, Y. Fasatwi, and K. Gadgood (eds.), *Natural resources and cultural heritage of the Libyan desert.* London: Society for Libyan Studies, 205–16.

Wilson, A. I. 2006b. "Water for the Pompeians," *Journal of Roman Archaeology* 19: 501–8.

Wilson, A. I. forthcoming. "Villas, horticulture and irrigation infrastructure in the Tiber Valley," in F. Coarelli and H. Patterson (eds.), *The Tiber Valley in antiquity.* Rome: British School at Rome.

Wilson, R. J. A. 1996. "*Tot aquarum tam multis necessariis molibus . . . :* Recent studies on aqueducts and water supply," *Journal of Roman Archaeology* 9: 5–29.

Wilson, R. J. A. 2000. "Aqueducts and water supply in Greek and Roman Sicily: The present *status quaestionis,*" in G. C. M. Jansen (ed.), *Cura Aquarum in Sicilia.* BABESCH Suppl. 6. Leuven: Peeters, 5–36.

Wuttmann, M. 2001. "Les qanats de 'Ayn-Manâwîr," in P. Briant (ed.), *Irrigation et drainage dans l'antiquité: Qanâts et canalisations souterraines en Iran, en Egypte et en Grèce.* Paris: Éditions Thotm, 109–35.

Yegül, F. 1992. *Baths and bathing in classical antiquity.* Cambridge, MA: MIT Press.

CHAPTER 12

# TUNNELS AND CANALS

## KLAUS GREWE

## TUNNEL AND CANAL ENGINEERING

Even in the early period of human cultural development, it was impossible to build streets and roads, or aqueducts and canals, without planning the route ahead. Roads, aqueducts, and canals have in common that they extend across the landscape in a long linear course, and in the process they often have to negotiate topographical obstacles and resort to structural solutions. Among the buildings that are included in these structures, valley crossings are conspicuous and often even spectacular. Bridges 50 m high, such as the road bridge across the Tajo near Alcántara in Spain and the aqueduct bridge Pont du Gard near Nîmes in France, are testaments to the flourishing state of civil engineering in Roman times. If, instead of a valley, a mountainous obstacle was in the way of the planned structure, a tunnel was often the only possibility for providing passage. Since tunnels are naturally less conspicuous than bridges, they have remained somewhat in the background of the study of history of technology. The great technological achievement inherent in the tunnels realized in classical antiquity, from the Eupalinus tunnel on Samos to the tunnel Nonius Datus supervised in Saldae, has never been denied, but the accomplishment deserves discussion. Grewe (1998) provides a comprehensive treatment (table 12.1).

It would be ideal to be able to compare a surviving tunnel with its original plan, allowing reproduction of the ancient thought processes during the planning stage and the work procedures. The directional accuracy achieved below ground could be easily evaluated if any ancient plans or diagrams had survived, but we are deprived of this evidence. Contemporary descriptions of the tunnels give little information about the amount of technological know-how that went into them. Rather, these

Table 12.1. Selection of important tunnels in the classical world.

| Name | Place | Country | Purpose | Length | Building Technique | Patron (Director, if known) | Period of Construction |
|---|---|---|---|---|---|---|---|
| Hezekiah Tunnel | Jerusalem | Israel | Water supply | 533 m | Counter-excavation | King Hezekiah | 705–701 B.C. |
| Eupalinus Tunnel | Island of Samos | Greece | Water supply | 1,036 m | Counter-excavation | Polycrates (Eupalinos) | 2nd half 6th c. B.C. |
| Ponte Terra | Tivoli | Italy | River diversion for road construction | ca. 60 m | Counter-excavation | Etruscans | 6th/5th c. B.C. |
| Ponte Sodo | Veii | Italy | River diversion | ca. 70 m | Counter-excavation | Etruscans | 6th/5th c. B.C. |
| Ariccia Tunnel | Ariccia | Italy | Lake drainage | ca. 650 m | Qanat | Etruscans | 6th c. B.C. |
| Lake Nemi Tunnel | Nemi | Italy | Lake drainage | 1,600 m | Counter-excavation | Etruscans | 6th/5th c. B.C. |
| Alban Lake Tunnel | Castel Gandolfo | Italy | Lake drainage | 1,400 m | Counter-excavation with shafts | Etruscans/Romans | 398/397 B.C. |
| Cocceius Tunnel | Cumae | Italy | Road traffic | ca. 1,000 m | Counter-excavation with shafts | Agrippa (L.Cocceius Auctus) | 1st c. B.C. |
| Cripta Neapolitana | Naples / Pozzuoli | Italy | Road traffic | 705 m | Counter-excavation | (L.Cocceius Auctus ?) | 1st c. B.C. |
| Grotta di Seiano | Naples / Pozzuoli | Italy | Road traffic | 780 m | Counter-excavation with side shafts | (L. Cocceius Auctus ?) | 1st c. B.C. |

| Name | Location | Country | Purpose | Length | Method | Builder | Date |
|---|---|---|---|---|---|---|---|
| Galerie de la Perrotte | Sernhac / Nîmes | France | Water supply | 65 m | *Qanat* | Claudius | A.D. 41–52 |
| Galerie des Cantarelles | Sernhac / Nîmes | France | Water supply | 60 m | *Qanat* | Claudius | A.D. 41–52 |
| Claudius Tunnel | Avezzano | Italy | Lake drainage | 5,642 m | *Qanat* | Claudius (Narcissus) | A.D. 41–52 |
| Passo del Furlo Tunnel | Furlo-Pass | Italy | Road traffic | 37 m | Counter-excavation | Vespasian | A.D. 69–79 |
| Titus Tunnel | Çevlik / Antakya | Turkey | River diversion for flood control | 185 m (86 m and 31m) | Counter-excavation with rock-cut shafts | Vespasian and Titus | ca. A.D. 79 |
| Petra Tunnel | Petra | Jordan | River diversion for flood control | 90 m | Counter-excavation | (Nabateans) | Nabatean/Roman period |
| Rio Sil Tunnel | Montefurado | Spain | River diversion with gold trap | | Counter-excavation | Romans | Roman period |
| Briord Tunnel | Briord | France | Water supply | 197 m | *Qanat* | Romans | Roman period |
| Reno-Valley Tunnel | Bologna | Italy | Water supply | ca. 20 km | *Qanat* with vertical and side shafts | Romans | Roman period |
| Cave du Curé | Chagnon / Lyon | France | Water supply | 80 m | Counter-excavation | Romans | Mid-1st c. A.D. |
| Nonius Datus Tunnel | Saldae / Bejaia | Algeria | Water supply | 428 m | Counter-excavation | City of Saldae (Nonius Datus) | A.D. 147/148–151 |
| Raschpëtzer Tunnel | Walferdange | Luxemburg | Water supply | ca. 600 m | *Qanat* | Romans | Mid-2nd c. A.D. |
| Drover Berg Tunnel | Düren | Germany | Water supply | 1,660 m | *Qanat* | Romans | Mid-2nd c. A.D. |

sources relate to the circumstances that led to the construction of a tunnel, and to its patrons and their motivation for the commissioning and finally the financing of the structure.

Even the inscription of Nonius Datus regarding a tunnel built in the second century A.D. (see below), while giving an insight into the organization of an ancient tunnel building site, leaves many open questions about the actual route planning. Hence Mommsen (1871: 9), one of the first scholars to work on the Nonius Datus inscription, hoped that "perhaps a competent engineer of our period will be able to solve from the structure itself what is incomprehensible to us from the report of his Roman predecessor." As early as the late nineteenth century, then, Mommsen touched on one of the basic problems of research in the history of ancient engineering. In the absence of authentic technical reports, or design plans, the information about the technology that lies within a structure can often be read only from the structure itself—an interesting task, of course, but not always without peril in terms of interpretation and conclusion.

# EARLY TUNNELS AND THE QANAT

With the emergence of ironworking around 1000 B.C., humans had at their disposal a new material for the manufacturing of tools. As a result it was possible to revolutionize building construction, since now there were new possibilities for working stone. It is generally assumed that the small tunnels of the Israelite royal cities owe their appearance to the introduction of iron tools. In the cities that are sited on *tels*, access was provided to springs gushing from the outer slope by means of stairs and underground walkways built from the occupation level to the original level of the spring (Grewe 1998: 41–44).

The history of tunnel construction in the circum-Mediterranean region begins with the development of a special type of water catchment from underground resources, the *qanat*, an early masterful engineering accomplishment that exerts its influence even in our time as a particular method of tunnel construction (chapter 11). In order to supply oases in arid and semiarid zones with water, underground aqueducts were built into water-bearing strata, which were usually located at the foot of the slopes of distant mountains. After the presence of water was ascertained by means of a trial shaft, known as the mother shaft, the planned line to the oasis was staked out. A chain of shafts was dug in close proximity, and underground tunnels were excavated between them, finally forming the *qanat*. Surviving examples conducted water over distances of up to 70 km. Al-Karaji (1973; cf. Grewe 1998: 33–40), an Arabian mathematician from the eleventh century A.D., wrote a handbook on *qanat* building that presents this ancient technique with great clarity. He explains the tools, the building methods, and also the method of line layout. His description gives a complete picture of the process and is therefore a unique resource for the history of this technology, most likely reflecting his ancient sources. In the *qanat* technique of tunnel construction (also called the manhole technique because of the regular pattern of vertical shafts), the entire line is subdivided into many individual units to keep the distances to be excavated underground short and the consequent directional error small. For that reason it is necessary to sink a number of shafts. The planned route of the tunnel is laid across any intervening elevations in a line that allows the shafts to be as shallow as possible; therefore they are found mostly in saddles, shifted to the side by a few meters to prevent the shafts from flooding if it rained during construction. In most cases, the line surveyed across the mountain curved to follow the topography. Next the shafts were staked out and sunk. After reaching a precisely calculated depth below ground, a straight connection was driven between the central shaft and the two adjoining shafts. The excavated spoil was transported to the surface in leather bags or baskets lifted by winches. Seen as a plan, the line of the tunnel consists of many short, straight sections. This *qanat* technique was later applied in numerous situations by the Etruscans and the Romans.

But by the sixth century B.C., a second method had appeared, the counter-excavation technique. In this procedure the tunnel is driven from two sides in an attempt to meet in the middle of the mountain to be perforated. This method required the builder to have a much greater knowledge of the basics of surveying and geometry. The projected meeting point could be reached only by constantly controlling and correcting the direction of advance. As a result, thorough planning and layout work were necessary for such a tunneling project, and the excavation generally was carried out towards a central point, in two separate sections on the same alignment, or occasionally side-by-side and parallel. The line staked out across the mountain on the surface was transferred underground to provide the proper orientation. Once the excavation had made some progress, the builder could get his bearings by looking back at the light that penetrated through the tunnel mouth in order to verify if his course was straight. In counter-excavation, deviations from the planned course could be discovered and subsequently corrected only through continuous control measurements. Geological problems might necessitate a departure from the projected line; necessary deviations within the mountain would require additional control measurements. On top of all these difficulties related to surveying, tunnel construction by counter-excavation over long stretches was rendered even more difficult by problems of water drainage and ventilation.

The decision by an ancient builder whether to construct a tunnel by the *qanat* method or by counter-excavation depended, on the one hand, on his experience with these respective techniques; on the other hand, the height of the mountain to be tunneled would have been important, as the effort required to sink the shafts was dependent on the extent of overburden above the tunnel. Another important factor was that application of the *qanat* technique could shorten construction time significantly, since the mountain could be excavated not only from the tunnel mouths but also from shafts. The average rate of advance through solid rock, derived from construction marks on a tunnel in Bologna, was 30 cm per day (Giorgetti 1988: 180–85; Grewe 1998: 139–41), although of course the rate would depend on local geological conditions. Suetonius (*Claud.* 20) gives a construction time of 11 years for the almost 6 km long tunnel Claudius built to drain the Fucine Lake, with shafts up to 120 m deep. These dimensions set it apart from all other ancient tunnels, but given the use of the *qanat* method with multiple work faces, the statistics from Bologna are within the realm of possibility.

# SPECIAL ACHIEVEMENTS IN ANCIENT TUNNEL CONSTRUCTION

Both the Hezekiah Tunnel in Jerusalem (705–701 B.C.) and the Eupalinus Tunnel on Samos (end of the sixth century B.C.) were built by counter-excavation. The plans of the Hezekiah tunnel as well as the Eupalinus tunnel show the difficulties in transferring directions from the surface to the excavation below ground. Completion of the Hezekiah tunnel in Jerusalem in 701 B.C. was possible only after many corrections in the advancing counter shafts. This event caused great rejoicing, since not only did it assure the water supply of Jerusalem at a time of threat from the Assyrians, but it also prevented the enemy's access to the water. The Old Testament enthusiastically acknowledges Hezekiah's achievement (2 Chron. 31), and an inscription describes the tunnel breakthrough (Grewe 1998: 45–52). The hypothesis that the Hezekiah tunnel was not a planned structure, but that the builders were simply following crevices in the mountain during construction, cannot be sustained after examination of the tunnel plan. Several corrections in direction that are evident can only be the results of controlled measurements, which presuppose that the tunnel was built according to a plan.

The Eupalinus tunnel on the Greek island of Samos can be considered the first large-scale tunnel that was planned as an engineering structure in the modern sense, since a strategy of planning and layout is evident in the execution (Grewe 1998: 58–69). The tunnel, which was built by Eupalinus during the reign of Polycrates (535–522 B.C.), was planned as a counter-excavation tunnel with a meeting point in the middle (figures 12.1–2). The hypothesis that the meeting point of the two sections was planned by Eupalinus to occur not in the middle of the line but rather underneath the ridgeline of the mountain it perforates cannot be sustained (Kienast 1995). Eupalinus succeeded in making the two sections meet despite an undetected error in direction in one of the two galleries, and despite changes in plan that were possibly necessary because of geological problems. For that purpose he used a grid that he laid over his plan, which allowed him to control the tunnels in real time. It was possible for him to calculate a deviation within the mountain through a change in the angle of advance in the order of magnitude of tangent 1:3. This can be

Figure 12.1. Tunnel of Eupalinus, Samos. Access tunnel and trench for pipeline. (Photograph by K. Grewe.)

ascertained from the existing line of the tunnel. Eupalinus' strategy for the final stage of advance before the breakthrough was ingenious. He halted excavation in one section and determined through measurements the exact position of its end point. Then, to ensure success, he directed that a curve be excavated in the opposing tunnel, a bend that would eliminate all detected and undetected errors (figure 12.2). The tunnel proper Served for excavation and later access to the terracotta pipeline, which was laid in a narrow, more easily leveled trench beside the walkway (figure 12.1). The achievement of Eupalinus is unique in antiquity, and not without reason did Herodotus (3.60) count the tunnel among the greatest structures in the entire Greek world. In the case of these first two historically large-scale tunnels, we know King Hezekiah to be the patron in one instance, and Eupalinus to be the builder in the other. But we still know nothing about the methods of planning and laying out the structures. It is a challenge for a modern engineer to work out these methods, since in neither case do we have plans or survey sketches transmitted from antiquity.

Historians of technology have paid little attention to the fact that almost simultaneously with the great achievements in Jerusalem and Samos, significant tunnels were being built in central Italy by the Etruscans, the cultural and technological teachers of the Roman Republic. Countless *cuniculi*—drainage and water-supply tunnels designed like *qanats*—were built in the area northeast of Rome (Grewe 1998: 70–77). Large tunnels in the Alban Mountains, all serving to drain lakes, are either Etruscan structures or, if they were built under the Romans, at least structures influenced by Etruscan technology. The tunnels at Ariccia, at Lago Albano, and at

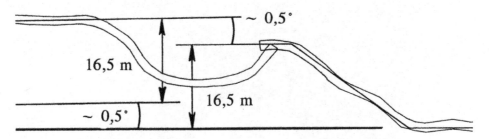

Figure 12.2. Tunnel of Eupalinus, Samos. Plan of breakthrough point, showing error correction gallery. (Drawing by K. Grewe.)

Lago di Nemi must also be counted among the large-scale tunnels. The last two were built by counter-excavation. Two Etruscan structures at Veii and Ponte Terra, built to divert rivers, could be termed large-capacity tunnels. The achievements in Roman tunnel construction cannot be evaluated without including the prior achievements and models of the Etruscans in the study. The technology of tunnel construction spread with the Romans over those parts of Europe, North Africa, and Asia Minor that they controlled (Grewe 1998: 78–192). Tunnels were cut for roads, for river diversion, for lake drainage, and even for gold extraction. Most often, however, tunnels were built in connection with aqueducts. The preferred method was the *qanat* technique, since short allotments at the construction site reduce the risk of two excavations missing each another.

One tunnel built by counter-excavation almost resulted in the failure of the entire aqueduct project, because the opposing galleries missed each other underground. As we will see, an inscription left behind by Nonius Datus, the engineer in charge of the project at Saldae in North Africa, tells us a great deal about the planning and organization of an ancient large-scale construction site. The status of a Roman engineer is clarified as well, since Nonius Datus was a legionary officer, and was assigned to the construction of the aqueduct. The workmen, too, were detailed from their military units to build this civilian structure. Nonius Datus even quotes the correspondence that was exchanged during his employment as the engineer in charge of the project. This commission must have been the greatest challenge in the professional life of this engineer, but presumably that was not the only reason he set up his report in a public inscription; it is very likely that he was responding to attempts to blame him for the mistakes made during construction.

Tunnel construction was a type of engineering accomplishment very well suited for demonstrating both the benevolence and the sheer power of a ruler. Therefore it is not surprising that an inscription seems to have been placed at every substantial tunnel, as at the river diversion at Çevlik near Antakya in Turkey, where the names of the patrons, in this case the emperors Vespasian and Titus, appear (figure 12.3). This was a substantial diversion tunnel designed to carry floodwater around the basin of the harbor of Seleucia Pieria, near Antioch on the Orontes. It is conse-

Figure 12.3. Tunnel of Titus, near Çevlik (Antakya, Turkey). (Photograph by K. Grewe.)

quently understandable that the greatest tunnel executed in the ancient world—the tunnel cut through Monte Salviano by the emperor Claudius to drain the Fucine Lake, 80 km east of Rome—attracted great attention even while it was still in the construction stage. Pliny the Elder (*HN* 36.124), who seems to have been an eye-witness, describes the construction in significant detail and terms it one of "the most memorable achievements" of that active emperor: "The expense was in-describable and the workers numberless over so many years because, where the mountain was earthy in character, the spoil from the channel had to be cleared out through vertical shafts by means of winches, and elsewhere the bedrock had to be cut away. All of this great effort...took place in darkness." Even contemporary court gossip is recorded, as several ancient authors suggest that Claudius' wife, Agrippina, was scheming against the palace bureaucrat Narcissus, who was in charge of the financial administration of the project (Tacitus, *Ann.* 12.57; Cassius Dio 60.11; Suetonius, *Claud.* 20). Inaugurated in A.D. 52, the tunnel allegedly took 30,000 workmen 11 years to complete. With a length of 5,595 m, and shaft depths of up to 122 m, it was supposed to drain the bed of the Fucine Lake for agriculture and keep the water level constant. Despite the careful planning and execution, the tunnel was only partially successful, and proper drainage of the lake was managed only in the nineteenth century.

Figure 12.4. Drover Berg Tunnel near Düren, Germany. Covered water channel and clay fill. (Photograph by K. Grewe.)

In the German Rhineland and neighboring Luxemburg, a large number of aqueduct tunnels were built, presumably from the second century A.D. on (Grewe 1998: 176–92; Frontinus-Gesellschaft 2003). Here only the *qanat* technique was applied. It is striking that exclusively small settlements, generally affluent *villae rusticae*, were supplied in this manner, rather than the big cities. A particularly impressive example is the Roman Raschpëtzer-Tunnel in Walferdange (Luxemburg), since more extensive archaeological investigation has revealed several of the ancient shafts.

The longest Roman tunnel north of the Alps was driven under the Drover Berg near Düren (Germany). Surprisingly, this structure, with a length of 1,660 m, seems to have supplied only one single *villa rustica* with water (figure 12.4). The water channel, covered with roof tiles, turned from a sloping course and entered the tunnel. After construction was completed, the tunnel and its more than 100 construction shafts were filled with clay. Archaeological investigation of this tunnel provided valuable clues about building techniques, including determining that the individual shafts were as far apart as they were deep. The only likely explanation of this detail is that the surveyor could not always be present at the site, or could make only a single visit, and he therefore had to find an easy way to give the builders a guideline for the depth of the shafts. He simply surveyed and staked out locations for the shafts as far apart as they had to be deep. The builders merely had to measure this distance by means of a string and then transfer it to the vertical shaft. Once the weighted string was taut in each shaft, the required depth had been reached and the tunneling linking the foot of each shaft could start. As a consequence of this method the distance between shafts at the Drover-Berg tunnel increases sequentially from 6 to 8 m at the slopes at each end of the tunnel to 26 m toward the middle.

# NONIUS DATUS AND THE AQUEDUCT TUNNEL AT SALDAE

Ancient Saldae (today Bejaïa, Algeria) was a coastal town whose origins reach back to the Carthaginian period. Under Augustus a settlement was founded there for the veterans of the seventh legion, but the town was not supplied with drinking water by means of an aqueduct until the first half of the second century. The aqueduct was designed to bring water from abundant, clear springs 17 km west of the city at the foot of Djebel Arbalou, the westernmost peak of the great Kabylei; at present the springs discharge 10,000 m³/day. The line chosen for the course of the aqueduct, 21 km in total, contained two major obstacles that could be overcome with the technological means of the period. In its upper stretch the line followed an east–west ridge with a slight gradient but a deep saddle at one point. Since the aqueduct could not traverse this depression at ground level without losing the head of water that was needed for coping with subsequent topographical obstacles, the dip had to be crossed by means of an aqueduct bridge 300 m long. The central pillars of this massive bridge were up to 15 m high. Further on, the line met a second obstacle in the form of a mountain range that crossed its path obliquely from northwest to southeast and could be overcome only by building a tunnel (Grewe 1998: 135–39).

Considered as a whole, the Saldae aqueduct system therefore corresponds to the common image of the water supply system of a Roman city. A 300 m bridge and a 428 m long tunnel hardly made this aqueduct stand out from significantly more technologically challenging aqueducts built elsewhere. What makes it interesting to the modern observer is an inscription that came to light as an isolated find in the nearby Roman city of Lambaesis in 1866 (*CIL* 8.2728, *ILS* 5795). The inscription had been cut on a three-sided semicolumn 1.7 m high, with a matching hexagonal base; both pieces had been built as spoils into a wall and had suffered some damage (figure 12.5). Fortunately, the inscription has remained largely legible, but the three heads at the upper part of the inscribed areas—personifications of virtues—were destroyed. Mommsen (1871) pointed out that the inscription is incomplete and that

Figure 12.5. Inscription of Nonius Datus (CIL 8.2728), in Lambaesis, Algeria. (Photograph by K. Grewe.)

the stone that was found may have belonged to a group of several columns that stood side by side.

The surviving portion of the inscription is of outstanding importance for the history of ancient engineering, since it not only provides technical details about the construction of the tunnel at Saldae, but also provides details about the background to the project. This contemporary report informs us who carried out the planning and who created the technical basis for the construction of the tunnel. By means of this practical information, we learn that the technical staff necessary for the execution of such construction works was available only in the army. Following a request by the governor of the province of Mauretania Caesarensis to the legate of Numidia, Nonius Datus, a military *librator* (surveyor) of the Legio III Augusta, was assigned to the project. It was apparently this engineer who set up the inscribed monument, which includes both background documents and personal narration of the progress of the project. Nonius Datus explains the main problems involved with tunnel construction by counter-excavation, as well as his solution. He also describes how the two teams of builders missed each other in the mountain, and how he remedied the earlier mistakes in his successful attempt to complete the tunnel. This report, therefore, goes well beyond the usual contents of a building inscription, even including drama and personal emotion. Since the very person in charge of the construction of the tunnel composed the text, we have a nearly unique primary source for the history of technology (translation adapted from Grewe 1998: 136–37, Lewis 2001: 345–46) (*CIL* 8.2728, *ILS* 5795):

PATIENCE, VIRTUE, HOPE
(*or* PATIENCE, ENERGY, CONFIDENCE)

[A.D. 153 Varius Clemens to M. Valerius] Etruscus. Saldae is a most splendid city, and I, together with the citizens of Saldae, ask you, Sir, to request Nonius Datus, retired surveyor of the Legio III Augusta, to complete the remainder of his work.

I set out and on the way was attacked by bandits; my staff and I were stripped and injured, but escaped. I came to Saldae and met Clemens the [then] procurator, who took me to the hill where they were bemoaning the poor quality of workmanship on the tunnel. It seemed that they were considering abandoning it, because the length of tunnel that had been driven was longer than the width of the hill. Their bearings had evidently diverged from the straight line, so that the bearing on the upper side had deviated to the right, the south, while that of the lower side had likewise deviated to the right, toward the north, and thus the two sections both deviated from the straight line. But the straight line had been staked out across the hill from east to west. To save the reader from confusion about the headings which are called "upper" and "lower," the "upper" is understood to be the part of the tunnel where water is admitted, the "lower" that where it is discharged. When I allocated the labor, I organized a competition between the marines and the Alpine auxiliaries, so that they could learn each other's methods of tunneling; and so they began driving through the hill. Therefore, since it was I who had first taken the levels, marked out the aqueduct, and had a second copy of the plans made which I gave to Petronius Celer the procurator [around A.D. 137], [I completed] the task. When it was done and the water admitted, Varius Clemens the procurator dedicated it.

[The capacity of the aqueduct is?] 5 *modii*.

To clarify my work on this aqueduct at Saldae, I append a few letters.

[A.D. 147/149] Porcius Vetustinus to [L. Novius] Crispinus. Sir, you acted most generously and from your humanity and kindness in sending my Nonius Datus, retired, so that I could use him on the works whose supervision he undertook. So, though pressed for time and hurrying to Caesarea, yet I dashed to Saldae and saw that the aqueduct was well begun, though of great magnitude, and that it could not be completed without the superintendence of Nonius Datus, who handled the job both diligently and faithfully. For this reason I would have asked you to second him to us, so that he could stay for a few months dealing with the matter, had he not succumbed to an illness contracted [ . . . ]

The course of events around the construction of this tunnel, as they are related in this text, can be reconstructed as follows: In the first half of the second century A.D., the inhabitants of Saldae planned the building of an aqueduct from Djebel Toujda to increase the water supply to the city. They turned to the responsible official in Mauretania, the procurator Petronius Celer, with the request to help them find a capable engineer. The procurator in turn asked his colleague, the legate of Numidia, to provide an expert for technical problems from the headquarters of the Third Legion Augusta to evaluate the scheme. The surveyor Nonius Datus was chosen. He traveled to the area, did some surveying, and subsequently gave his plans for the building of the aqueduct to the procurator Petronius Celer. All of this must have taken place by the year A.D. 138, since Celer was procurator of Mauretania only until the end of Hadrian's rule.

Work on the project, however, did not commence until ten years later, when Porcius Vetustinus was procurator (A.D. 147–150). The long delay is very interesting in itself. Crispinus was governor of Numidia at the time, and he instructed Nonius Datus to contact the procurator Vetustinus to discuss the project once again. Crispinus was in office in the years 147 and 148, so the start of the aqueduct's construction has to be dated to this time. Nonius Datus got in touch with the builders who had taken over the execution of the construction, organized the work, and for some time directed the operation. He would have stayed in Saldae for several months had illness not forced him to return to Lambaesis. The work crew was composed of military personnel.

Even during the engineer's absence work progressed well, and the project probably would have been finished in time had there not suddenly been problems at the tunnel site. Nonius Datus had staked out the line of the tunnel for the builders across the mountain, and it was planned to excavate the tunnel from two sides. In his absence, however, the builders had difficulty transferring the directions underground, and each of the tunnel sections drifted off the planned bearing. Since the length of the allotments was known from the prepared plans, at some point it was noticed that the work had advanced far beyond the intended meeting point. The realization that the teams had missed each other brought the builders to despair, and they were about to abandon the project.

The procurator of Mauretania, now Varius Clemens (A.D. 151 or 153), turned once again to the current legate of Numidia, M. Valerius Etruscus, asking him to dispatch Nonius Datus a second time. Nonius Datus, by now a discharged veteran, set off to Saldae but was waylaid by bandits. He and his escort managed to escape and reached Saldae. From there, he was immediately taken to the mountain and confronted with the tunneling problems. By taking measurements, he determined the consequences of the erroneous advance and had a lateral link established between the two allotments. The aqueduct was completed and ready when the breakthrough succeeded shortly after, and the procurator Varius Clemens inaugurated it. When the French authorities cleared the tunnel to use it for a water pipe in the later nineteenth century, its length was measured as 428 m, and the maximum depth beneath the mountain summit as 86 m.

Nonius Datus used the construction of the Saldae aqueduct and its problem-plagued tunnel to present himself on his tombstone as an engineer to whom an outstanding building project had been entrusted. In the inscription he emphasized his achievement in the construction and successful completion of the aqueduct tunnel. The recording of the correspondence between the procurators of Mauretania and the legates of Numidia put the project on the highest official level and removed any doubt with respect to his report. As an ancient technical source, the inscription of Nonius Datus is unique.

Nonius Datus placed his report under three key words, *Patientia*, *Virtus*, and *Spes*, each virtue personified by a female head. Presumably he was not so much calling on three deities but rather stressing the three virtues required of the engineer entrusted with the difficult task of constructing such a tunnel. The literal translation would be "Patience, Courage, and Hope," but given the context, there might be a better rendering. Mommsen replaced "Courage" with "Valor," but one might go even further. The degree of difficulty in the task of tunnel construction requires not courage or valor, but rather energy. Hope would be better interpreted as the confidence of the expert who trusts on the basis of his know-how that the difficult job will be accomplished. Perhaps Nonius Datus was commemorating his own virtues of "Patience, Energy, and Confidence."

While quite a respectable number of tunnels were completed in the Greco-Roman period, the medieval accomplishment is much more modest. In the period from the fifth century A.D. to the beginning of the modern era, only a handful of tunnels were built north of the Alps, for example. In the modern era, tunnel construction flourished once again, particularly as a result of the spread of railway networks in the nineteenth century. These systems required numerous tunnels due to the special problems of low gradient and gradual turns. It is astonishing, however, that the nineteenth-century methods of tunnel construction had hardly changed from those of Roman times. The first two railway tunnels in Germany, for example, were built like *qanats*.

# CANALS

Even today, water transport is the most economical method for the exchange of goods between two places. This of course was especially true in antiquity, when the overland routes were often relatively badly developed and maintained. For heavy goods, such as building materials for cities, no other means of transport was viable. The preferred waterways were navigable rivers. If there were no such rivers immediately nearby, the loads were transported on the shortest land route, or an artificial waterway was built to ease the transport. One reason for building canals was therefore to link a production site or a destination to an existing navigable waterway. But it was much more important to link different bodies of water with one another in order to open up large regions with respect to water traffic. Many canals in the ancient world were intended primarily for irrigation or drainage (Oleson 2000; Wilson 2000), but these on the whole were technically less impressive than the navigational canals.

The history of the construction of canals for shipping reaches back to the Bronze Age (C. Wikander 2000). The earliest canals can be found in Egypt,

Mesopotamia, and China. They are important testimony to the cultural importance of these countries: the canal from the Nile to the Red Sea, built around 600
B.C. by the Pharaoh Necho, was renovated repeatedly, by Darius I, the Ptolemies,
and Trajan, among others (Redmount 1995). The canal was wide enough to allow
two ships to pass each other. Herodotus (2.158; cf. Diodorus 1.33.9–12) reported
that the entire journey took four days.

Another early canal, cut by the Persian king Xerxes through the narrow strip of
land at the north end of Mount Athos between 483 and 480 B.C. (Isserlin 1996), is
described by Herodotus (7.23–24) as an undertaking intended more for prestige
than practical use. Herodotus gives a partial account of the methods of construction of this canal, which was wide enough to allow two warships to pass each other.
Xerxes had the structure subdivided into several allotments and apportioned the
work to the various nations and ethnic groups that formed his empire and his army.
All but one of the allotments experienced difficulty:

> The foreigners, dividing up the ground by ethnic origin, dug in the following way.
> They made a straight line by the town of Sane, and when the trench became deep,
> some took positions at the bottom and dug, while others handed over the earth
> that was constantly being excavated to another group positioned higher up on
> the stepped construction face. The latter, in turn, as they received it, handed the
> earth on to yet another group, until they came to those at the top, who carried
> it away and dumped it. Everyone except the Phoenicians had double the work
> when the steep sides of their excavations collapsed. Since they made the trench the
> same width at the top and bottom, this was bound to happen. But the Phoenicians
> showed their skill in this, as in so many other matters. Taking in hand the por-
> tion that was allotted to them, they excavated the upper portion of the canal to
> double the width that the channel itself was supposed to have, and narrowed it
> as the work proceeded. At the bottom their excavation was equal in width to that
> of the others.

Herodotus' attention to the details of the canal cross-section and dimensions is
atypical of ancient descriptions of canals, and it hints at the enormous physical
effort involved.

The Isthmus of Corinth, another narrow (6 km) and low (75–80 m high) obstacle separating two important shipping lanes, early on attracted solutions to
allow the passage of ships. By the sixth century B.C. the *diolkos* (the word means
"haul across") had been constructed, a paved overland track over which smaller
ships were dragged (see chapter 23). Serious attempts to build a canal began with
Nero, whose project finally failed (Suetonius, *Ner.* 19; Dio Cassius 63.16). The extensive traces of his attempt were obliterated by the construction of the modern
canal (1881–93) and are no longer visible.

In Europe, the first shipping canals were built under the Romans, but not all of
these projects were successful. A project to build a canal linking the Saône and
Moselle rivers, and thus allow passage by ship from the mouth of the *Rhône* to the
mouth of the Rhine, is mentioned by Tacitus (*Ann.* 13.53), who alludes to the intent
to link the two seas. Although this canal was presumably conceived as a diversion

canal without locks, the project proved not to be feasible with the technology available. The connection was completed only in 1882, as the Canal de l'Est.

No visible traces remain of a canal built by Drusus on the Lower Rhine, but two ancient passages refer to the structure (Suetonius, *Claud.* 1; Tacitus, *Ann.* 2.8). Suetonius praises it: "the Drusus Canal, as they still call it, a remarkable engineering work which connects the Rhine with the Ijssel." This shipping route was probably only 3 km long, but it saved the Romans the perilous passage of the North Sea off the mouth of the Rhine. A similar purpose was served by a second canal that created a 35 km link on the other side of the Rhine between the Rhine and the river Maas, although Tacitus (*Ann.* 11.20) refers as well to a need to keep the soldiers busy. This may have been a partial motive for many of these extremely labor-intensive engineering projects. The construction of the Fossa Mariana (Marius Canal) between Arles (France) and the Mediterranean Sea east of the Rhone satisfied the need for an alternative shipping route to the Rhone delta, which was subject to continuous silting (Strabo 4.1.8; Pliny, *HN* 3.34), and it made Arles an easily accessible harbor town. This canal undoubtedly featured in the abortive scheme to connect the Mediterranean Sea with the North Sea via the planned Moselle-Saône canal. Both Horace (*Sat.* 1.5.9–23) and Strabo describe the famous canal that crossed the Pontine marsh (*Geography* 5.3.6; cf. chapter 22): "Near Terracina, as you go toward Rome, a canal runs alongside the Appian Way, fed at numerous points by the flow from marshes and rivers. People navigate it mostly at night, so that embarking in the evening they can disembark at dawn and continue the rest of the way by the road—but it is also navigated by day. A mule tows the boat."

The feasibility of large-scale engineering projects was at all times dependent on a number of essential prerequisites: in addition to availability of appropriate materials and labor, and the technical knowledge to complete the project, funding was essential, and the power to conceive the project and see that it was brought to completion. As the example of Nonius Datus shows, experts had to be borrowed from the military for the most difficult part of the works in Roman tunnel construction. It will have been no different for the construction of canals, since these works, too, were difficult and required a high level of technological skill. The correspondence between Pliny the Younger, at the time governor of the province of Bithynia in Asia Minor, and the emperor Trajan amply confirms the need for imported expertise (Pliny, *Tra.* 10.41–42). Pliny had been persuaded of the commercial value of a canal linking a lake near Nicomedia with the sea (Moraux 1961), and he asked Trajan for a *librator*, that is, an expert in planning and surveying, such as Nonius Datus. In his reply, Trajan advised Pliny to contact the governor of Lower Moesia, "since in the provinces there is no lack of such experts." He furthermore suggested that the engineer ought to make certain through measurement that the lake would not be completely drained by the planned canal.

Despite the lack of explosives and machine-operated earth-moving equipment, all the great states and empires in the ancient Mediterranean world managed to create tunnels and navigational canals. The major prerequisites were the availability of large quantities of cheap manpower, along with a certain level of surveying skill. The difficulties involved meant that such projects were generally undertaken only for purposes of enormous importance to the state, such as urban water supply, flood control, or the facilitation of trade.

# REFERENCES

al-Karaji, M. 1973. *La civilisation des eaux cachées*. Trans. A. Mazaheri. Nice: Université de Nice.

Frontinus-Gesellschaft e.V. 2003. *Wasserversorgung aus Qanaten: Qanate als Vorbilder im Tunnelbau; Symposiumsberichte*. Bonn: Frontinus-Gesellschaft.

Giorgetti, D. 1988. "Die antike Wasserversorgung von Bologna," in *Die Wasserversorgung antiker Städte*. Frontinus-Gesellschaft Geschichte der Wasserversorgung 3. Mainz: von Zabern, 180–85.

Grewe, K. 1998. *Licht am Ende des Tunnels: Planung und Trassierung im antiken Tunnelbau*. Mainz: von Zabern.

Isserlin, B. S. J. 1996. "The Canal of Xerxes," *Annual of the British School of Archaeology at Athens* 91: 329–40.

Kienast, H. J. 1995. *Die Wasserleitung des Eupalinos auf Samos*. Samos XIX. Bonn: Habelt.

Lewis, M. J. T. 2001. *Surveying instruments of Greece and Rome*. Cambridge: Cambridge University Press.

Mommsen, T. 1871. "Tunnelbau unter Antoninus Pius," *Archäologische Zeitung* n.s. 3: 5–9.

Moraux, P. 1961. "Die Pläne Plinius des Jüngeren für einen Kanal in Bithynien," in G. Radke (ed.), *Aparchai: Untersuchungen zur klassischen Philologie und Geschichte des Altertums*, vol. 4. Tübingen: Niemeyer, 181–214.

Oleson, J. P. 2000. "Irrigation," in Ö. Wikander 2000, 183–215.

Redmount, C. 1995. "The Wadi Tumilat and the 'Canal of the Pharaohs,'" *Journal of Near Eastern Archaeology* 54: 127–35.

Wikander, C. 2000. "Canals," in Ö. Wikander 2000, 321–30.

Wikander, Ö. (ed.) 2000. *Handbook of ancient water technology*. Leiden: Brill.

Wilson, A. 2000. "Land drainage," in Ö. Wikander 2000, 303–17.

# CHAPTER 13

......................................................................................................................

# MACHINES IN GREEK
# AND ROMAN
# TECHNOLOGY

......................................................................................................................

## ANDREW I. WILSON

A MACHINE is a device in which a combination of fixed and moving parts are used to perform work either by multiplying an effort to exert greater force than can human or animal muscle power alone, or by changing the direction of a force, or by automating simple or complex repetitive operations. Hero of Alexandria lists as simple machines (or mechanical powers) the wheel and axle, lever, pulley, winch, wedge, and screw (*Mechanica* 2.1–5; cf. Pappus 8.52); one should also add the inclined plane and the gear wheel (which Hero considered as belonging to the winch). All these, except the gear wheel and the screw, which are Hellenistic inventions, were known before the archaic period. Complex machines combine and multiply simple machines, with additional improvements or variations like the cam, crank, or rack-and-pinion. Sources of power in the ancient world included human muscle power, animal traction, heat, wind power, and water power (chapter 6). On ancient mechanics, the mechanical writers, and machines, see especially Drachmann (1948 and 1963), and Lewis (1997). Gille (1980) is an accessible introduction but unreliable in some details, notably chronology. General accounts such as Hodges (1970: 209–41) and Landels (2000) are outdated on, for example, the introduction of the water-mill and the question of technological stagnation. Hill (1984) is useful on the relation between Greek and Islamic automata (but cf. Lewis 1985).

Greek and Roman machines were used primarily in construction, water-lifting, mining, the processing of agricultural produce, and warfare. The use of machines in manufacture was relatively limited, although the loom mechanized complex weaving procedures (chapter 18), and in the Roman and late Roman periods we find some evidence for the diversification of water-power for productive ends. Other uses included medical implements and entertainment devices.

Sources of evidence are not straightforward. Representations of known devices are often lacking, and where they do survive may be inaccurate. Because machines tend to be composed of materials of varying survivability (e.g., wood, metal, sinews, rope), only fragments may survive; more usually, only those machines requiring durable fixing or infrastructure in masonry leave traces (presses, mills). Many devices are not described in surviving texts or are mentioned only in passing. Our main sources are several writers on mechanics, but many treatises are now lost, and even some of those that survive do so only in medieval Arabic translations.

The earliest writings on mechanics dealt largely with engines of warfare. The creation around 305 B.C. of the Museum at Alexandria, a scholastic research center under the patronage of the Ptolemies, brought about major advances through the concentration of scholars working on many different aspects of science. Several of these wrote on machines or mechanical problems. Although in the Peripatetic tradition, the pseudo-Aristotelian *Mechanical Problems*, concerning levers and circular motion, was probably written at Alexandria between about 280 and 260 B.C. Around the same time Ctesibius (fl. 270 B.C.) invented the force-pump and hydraulic organ; his writings are lost, but some of their content may be deduced from surviving works of Philo of Byzantium, Vitruvius, and Hero. Archimedes (287–212 B.C.) visited Alexandria around the mid-third century B.C.; his work *Equilibriums of Planes* is important for mechanics.

In the later third century B.C. Philo of Byzantium spent time at Alexandria, although his partially surviving *Mechanice syntaxis* dates from after his visit. Of its nine original books we have books 4 (*Belopoeica*, "Artillery"), 8 (*Poliorcetica*, "Siege Techniques"), and parts of 7 (*Parasceuastica*, "Preparation for Sieges") in Greek, and book 5 (*Pneumatica*, "Pneumatics," or the "Interaction of Air and Water") in Arabic translation and partial Latin translation. The lost books included works on levers and mechanics, harbor construction, automata, and water supply (Lewis 1997: 20). A slightly younger contemporary was Apollonius of Perge (fl. ca. 200 B.C.), who besides writing on conic sections produced a now lost work on a flute-player driven by compressed air released by valves controlled by the operation of a water wheel (see Gille 1980: 79; Lewis 1997: 49–57).

Apart from some works on engines of war, we have no further surviving works on mechanics until Vitruvius (ca. 25 B.C.): book 10 of his *De Architectura* is devoted to machines (cranes, water-lifting devices, the water-mill, force pump, and water organ, and siege engines). Hero of Alexandria, one of our most important sources, wrote during the later first century A.D. (his *Dioptra* mentions an eclipse datable to A.D. 62). His *Pneumatica* and *Automatopoieca* ("On Automata-making") survive in Greek, and three books of his *Mechanics* in Arabic translation, along with excerpts preserved in Pappus of Alexandria's *Mathematical Collection* 8 (ca. A.D. 362). The Arabic translation is prefaced by the *Baroulkos*, "On the Lifting of Heavy Objects," originally a separate work that became incorporated also into his *Dioptra*. Fragments survive of other treatises relevant to mechanics, for example, one of four books of his *Water Clocks*, quoted by Proclus and referred to by Pappus. Pappus provides a useful source for and control on the parts of Hero's work that do not survive in Greek, but adds little new.

The surviving literature shows that while the lever, winch, inclined plane, and wedge were known in the Greek world during the classical period, considerable advances in mechanical technology occurred in the early Hellenistic period under the stimulus of Ptolemaic royal patronage at Alexandria. Philo of Byzantium explicitly refers to the discovery of formulae governing the power and range of artillery discovered by repeated experiments financed by the Ptolemies (*Belopoeica* 50.3); but the Alexandrian school seems also to have been responsible for the invention of gearing, and the multiple combinations of several mechanical powers to produce a variety of complex machines and automata.

# Simple Machines or Mechanical Powers

The mechanical advantage (MA) of a machine is the factor by which it multiplies the input force or effort into an output force. A lower input force must be applied over a greater distance than the greater output force travels; the ratio of the distances is the velocity ratio (VR). Theoretically, MA = VR, so that in a machine with a mechanical advantage of 2, the input force is half the output force but must be exerted over twice the distance. In practice, friction reduces the ideal mechanical advantage of a machine. A machine can be used to convert an input force into a greater output force applied more slowly, or into a smaller output force that operates more quickly; in this case a mechanical disadvantage is converted to speed advantage.

The simplest mechanical power is the inclined plane. To raise a weight a certain distance it is easier to drag or roll it up a slope than to lift it vertically (MA = length/ height of the slope). Before the invention of cranes, dragging or rolling architectural elements up temporary earthen ramps was almost the only way to place large blocks in elevated positions on a structure. The lever was also used at a very early date, although the theory behind its operation was not fully understood until Archimedes, who described it in *Equilibriums of Planes* 1. The MA of a lever is the distance between the fulcrum and the point where the force is applied divided by the distance between the fulcrum and the weight to be lifted. Crowbars were used in construction from very early times for levering large blocks into place. Levers were also used in balances: the equal arm balance was known to the Egyptians (Skinner 1954: 779–84), and the unequal arm balance (steelyard) is referred to in the third-century

B.C. pseudo-Aristotelian *Mechanical Problems*, which also uses the nutcracker and dental forceps as illustrations of the lever. It was used in Roman dental and surgical forceps and in anal specula (Jackson 1990: figs. 3, 5–6).

The simple pulley was known to the Assyrians and was used from at least the ninth century B.C. for drawing water from wells. It confers no mechanical advantage in itself but changes the direction of pull; it is easier to pull down than up. The triple pulley, however, with two pulleys attached to the crane and a free pulley suspended from them, has a mechanical advantage of 3; for compound pulleys of *n* pulleys in a similar arrangement, MA = *n*, although because of friction ancient pulley systems were probably limited in practice to five sheaves (Vitruvius' *pentaspaston*; see below on cranes). The surviving ancient pulley blocks—for the most part found on shipwrecks—include a single-sheaved pulley from the first-century A.D. Lake Nemi barge, and remains of third- and fourth- or fifth-century A.D. double-sheaved pulley blocks from London and Cenchreae, respectively, presumably the upper blocks of triple-pulley systems (Shaw 1967; Oleson 1983).

The windlass/winch and capstan (the winch has a horizontal axle and the capstan a vertical one) use handspikes or levers inserted into slots on a drum to gain a mechanical advantage in circular rotation, given by the radius of the handspike to the radius of the drum or axle. The winch was known by the fifth century B.C., used by surgeons for traction when setting limbs (Drachmann 1963: 184, and below). Simple windlasses were used for horizontal haulage, for example the overland haulage of boats (and on occasion light warships) along parts of the *diolkos* or trackway across the Isthmus of Corinth, built by Periander (625–585 B.C.). Boats were dragged on large trolleys running, in places, in guide ruts, and rope-wear marks and sockets cut in a guide wall on a long incline suggest that capstans may have been used to haul trolleys up the slope (Lewis 2001b; cf. chapter 23). Windlasses are discussed further in combination with other powers in the sections on cranes and presses below.

Gearing allows the multiplication of force or speed, or changing the direction of rotation, by a number of different means. Mechanical advantage can be gained by using a smaller wheel to drive a larger one, which will rotate more slowly and in the opposite direction. Alternatively, a speed advantage can be gained by making the driven wheel smaller than the driver. Gears meshing in the same plane will rotate in opposite directions and can thus reverse rotation; but direction can also be changed from vertical to horizontal rotation with right-angle gearing. Gearing was probably developed in the early third century B.C. at Alexandria. Ctesibius' anaphoric water clock, developed around 270 B.C., used a rack-and-pinion driven by a descending float as water flowed out of the clock. The contemporary *Mechanical Problems* refers to the opposite rotation of adjacent wheels, but it does not explicitly mention gearing and may refer to effects produced by friction of touching, untoothed wheels. This detail may hint that the principles of gearing were just beginning to be explored at this date, but subsequent development was evidently rapid. Archimedes invented the worm drive around 250 B.C., which presupposes the prior existence of simpler cogwheel gearing. Indeed, Apollonius of Perge's treatise *On the Fluteplayer* and other evidence implying the invention of the vertically-wheeled water-mill and the *saqiya* drive between 270 and 240 B.C. also indicate the existence of right-angled gearing at this date (Drachmann 1963: 200–205; de Solla Price 1974: 53–54; Lewis 1993, 1997: 49–57).

Gears used in practical machines had wooden teeth projecting radially as spokes from the disc, or at right angles as in a lantern pinion. These were adequate for applying force, but a different shape of tooth was used in precision instruments such as planetaria, and preserved in the Antikythera Mechanism (figure 29.1). These devices used gears cut from bronze discs, with small teeth filed into the shape of equilateral triangles. Rack-and-pinion gearing was used in Hero's self-trimming lamp to adjust the length of the wick as the oil level fell (*Pneumatica* 33).

Very few ancient gears survive. A lantern pinion of six iron bars between two oak disks on a mill-spindle was found at the Saalburg Roman fort (before A.D. 270; Jacobi 1912: 89–90; Moritz 1958: 123–28). For fine gearing, apart from the Anti-kythera Mechanism, there are finds from Bolsena and possibly Timgad, as well as several devices of unknown origin. At Bolsena, a screw and cogwheel were found in a hoard of metalwork in the villa of Laberius Gallus (Oleson 1984: 193). The Timgad finds come from a bronzeworker's shop destroyed by fire in the fourth or fifth century A.D. They are described briefly (but not illustrated) as fragments of a gear wheel ("de roue de machine"), one of which had a diameter of 52 cm, and a fragment of what the excavator describes as a circular saw ("scie circulaire") (Ballu 1911: 23, 169). Since these objects are all of bronze, not iron, the alleged circular saw (internal diameter 32 cm) may in fact be part of a toothed wheel. Perhaps they were intended for a planetarium or the jack-work of an anaphoric clock (chapters 29 and 31), but without further details this can only be speculation. A Byzantine geared sundial calendar without provenance is now in London (figure 31.3; Field and Wright 1985).

The screw works like an inclined plane applied in a rotary sense, either to exert pressure, or in combination with gearing as a worm drive. Although high levels of friction reduce its efficiency, it has a considerable mechanical advantage. The worm drive first appears between 241 and 239 B.C. as part of Archimedes' device for launching Hieron's ship; it was then used in two medical stretching racks of the later third century (Lewis 1997: 54–56). Early screws had a male thread with a square cross-section. Initially, this groove simply engaged with a peg thrust through the side of the hole into which the screw was inserted. In the first century A.D. Hero of Alexandria described a screw-cutting machine that allowed the cutting of female screws (*Mechanica* 3.21), enabling the wooden screw to be used in presses, both for drawing down the arm of a lever press and in a direct screw press (below). A thread with a lenticular cross-section produced less friction and was less prone to jam-ming, and was consequently used in bronze precision gearing and in wooden screws with a female nut rather than a peg (Drachmann 1936, 1963).

Bronze screw gearing was incorporated into devices in Hero's *Dioptra* to im-prove existing models of the instrument by using the velocity ratio, rather than mechanical advantage, to allow fine adjustment. One turn of the handle connected to the screw produced only a small rotation of the geared sighting disc in the horizontal or vertical plane, allowing precise setting. A groove along the length of the screw acted as a release mechanism; if aligned with the geared disc, it could be rotated rapidly by hand (Hero, *Dioptra* 3; cf. Lewis 2001b: 83). Gynecological specula (also called *dioptra*) used the screw's mechanical advantage and high velocity ratio, coupled with precision adjustment, for vaginal dilation. Made of bronze (sometimes with a brass screw), they had three or sometimes four vanes adjusted by a handle attached to a screw (Jackson 1990: 9, 21, figs. 8–9; Longfield-Jones 1986).

Power sources applied to large machines might include animals or flowing water (chapter 6); in both cases this usually involved a wheel or gearing producing a rotary motion. From the third century B.C., however, the principle was understood of converting rotary to reciprocating linear motion by means of the cam on an axle (chapter 31), and it seems that this device was applied not only in automata but probably also in larger machines by the first century A.D.

# CRANES AND TRACTION

The earliest complex machines were cranes that employed pulleys in combination with a windlass (figure 13.1b). Power output could be increased by compound pulleys and geared windlasses, driven by men in a treadmill (figures 2.4, 13.1c and d; Vitruvius, *De arch.* 10.2.5; Hero, *Mechanica* 2.3, 23, 3.1–5; Drachmann 1956; Cotterell and Kamminga 1990: 89–93). There is no evidence for the use of cranes or hoists in architecture before the late sixth century B.C., and until then heavy blocks must have been raised by pulling them up earth ramps, as the Egyptians had done. The introduction of cranes eliminated the labor-intensive building and progressive heightening of such ramps during construction and their subsequent removal on completion, and enabled the more widespread lifting of heavier blocks than had previously been possible. One immediate effect however, was a reduction in the size of the very largest blocks used. The first cranes are implied by the use of lifting tongs and of lewis irons, the characteristic holes for which appear in Greek structures in the late sixth century B.C. (Coulton 1974). Cranes using pulleys or a block and tackle might consist of one pole held in position by stays, with the pulley attached at the top; this arrangement was unstable but allowed the load to be swung in an arc by adjusting the angle of the pole using the stays. A more stable version used two poles fixed together in an inverted V, allowing the load to be moved back and forth by raising or lowering the frame (figure 13.1). More secure frames with three or four uprights only allowed the weight to be lifted vertically (Vitruvius, *De arch.* 10.2.1–10; Hero, *Mechanica* 3.2).

(a)  (b)

(c)  (d)

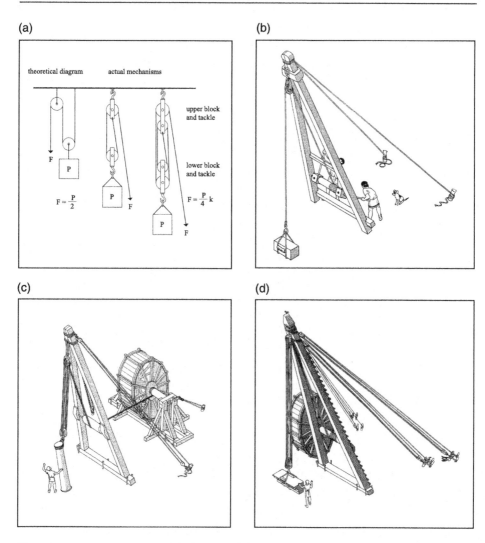

Figure 13.1. Ancient cranes: (a) theoretical diagram and mechanism of pulley block and tackle; (b) reconstruction of a crane shown on a wall-painting from Stabiae (Villa of S. Marco); (c) reconstruction of a crane with separate tread-wheel drive shown on a relief from Capua; (d) crane with multiple pulleys and axle-mounted tread-wheel, based on the Haterii relief. (J. P. Adam, *La Construction Romaine*, figs. 91, 89, 93, and 95.)

Before the invention of the compound pulley, early cranes must have used a rope passed over a simple pulley and wound around a windlass or capstan to provide mechanical advantage. Capstans winding ropes running over pulleys are shown on the first- or second-century A.D. relief found near the drainage outlet of the Fucine Lake, and representing the extraction of spoil from the underground drainage tunnel via vertical shafts (Faccenna 2003; Giuliani 2003). Extra mechanical advantage could be achieved using a capstan in series with the axle of the crane (Vitruvius, *De arch.* 10.2.5).

The invention of triple and compound pulleys (*trispaston* and *polyspaston*) was a major advance in the design and mechanics of cranes. This has been ascribed, probably erroneously, to Archimedes, as a result of ancient authors' usage of *trispastos* and *polyspastos* to mean both three (or multiple) pulleys and three (or multiple) winches. Some clues, in fact, point to a date before Archimedes for this invention. An inscription of 329/328 B.C. (*IG* 1672.156) mentions multiple pulleys, although the situation might involve simple pulleys in parallel (Coulton 1974: 1). The earliest secure mention of the compound pulley appears in the pseudo-Aristotelian *Mechanics* 18 (ca. 270 B.C.). Coulton (1974) argues on the basis of weights lifted in archaic and classical-period architecture that the compound pulley may have been known from the late sixth century B.C., although it should be observed that the required mechanical advantage might have been produced from multiple ropes each attached to simple pulleys and a windlass.

Several ancient sources report that Archimedes invented a method of dragging enormous weights, and that he demonstrated this to Hiero II of Syracuse, allegedly by singlehandedly launching a large ship laden with passengers. The details are confused by uncertainty over whether our sources are using *trispaston* and *polyspaston* to mean pulleys or winches. Vitruvius clearly uses them to mean pulleys when he is describing cranes; Hero, in his *Baroulkos*, uses them to mean a geared winch, with three or multiple axles.

Plutarch (*Marcellus* 14.8) says Archimedes used a *polyspaston* to move Hieron's ship, with his left hand only and while sitting down. John Tzetzes (ca. A.D. 1150) refers to a *trispaston* (*Chil.* 2.107–8). Oribasios (*Coll. Med.* 49.6, 23), following Galen (A.D. 129–99), ascribes the invention of the *polyspaston* to Archimedes and says that Archimedes invented the *trispastos* for hauling ships. The machine he goes on to describe as the doctors' reduction of this instrument has no pulleys, but rather multiple winches (Drachmann 1963: 178–80), and it bears a generic resemblance to Hero's *baroulkos* (below). Since Athenaeus (*Deipnosophistae* 5.207a–b), in what seems to be a version of the same tradition, says Archimedes used a *helix* (screw or worm drive) to launch Hieron's vast grain freighter, we may conclude that Archimedes' device involved geared winches driven by a screw. Drachmann (1973: 50–51) considered that Plutarch's description of singlehanded operation implies a crank handle. This mode of operation sounds like Hero's *Baroulkos* and may be implied by Pappus: "The same theory applies to the work of moving a given weight by a given power; this was found out by Archimedes, who is said thereupon to have exclaimed: 'Give me somewhere to stand, and I shall move the earth.' Heron of Alexandria has shown quite clearly in his so-called *Baroulkos* how this may be contrived . . . " (*Mathematical Collection* 8.19; trans. Drachmann 1963: 28). Indeed, Tzetzes implies that Hero's *Baroulkos* was derived from one of Archimedes' writings (*Chil.* 12.964–71; cf. Lewis 2000: 332).

Hero's *Baroulkos* survives in Greek (*Dioptra* 37), and in Arabic as the opening of his *Mechanics,* where it evidently does not belong, since another version exists within the *Mechanics* proper as chapter 2.21 (Drachmann 1963: 22–32). The passage describes how to use a windlass with a series of gears to multiply the power input to a crane or winch. The first gear is turned by a screw with a *cheirolabe* (apparently a cross-handle or windlass handle rather than a crank—Drachmann 1973: 43–44). Drachmann (1963) thinks the *baroulkos* was a theoretical device only. But it is very similar to some medical benches for surgical traction (below); could it be Hero's practical revival of Archimedes' *polyspaston*? Who was the engineer who proposed to Vespasian (reigned A.D. 69–79) a method for hauling columns up to the Capitol (Suetonius, *Vesp.* 18)? It is tempting to wonder whether this was either Hero or someone who had read his description of the *baroulkos*, which must date from around this time—the *Dioptra*, in which it appears, was written after A.D. 62.

A variation on the crane was the pile driver, which raised a heavy weight with pulleys and then suddenly dropped it onto a pile to drive it into wet ground. Pile drivers are mentioned by Vitruvius (*De arch.* 3.4.2) and Caesar (*BG* 4.17), but not described. The framework must have consisted of three or four timbers joined near the top. Usually the weight was dropped vertically onto the head of the pile, but for the sloping support piles used in Caesar's bridge over the Rhine it must have slid down an inclined ramp to drive them in at an angle. Caesar may also have used pile drivers mounted on tethered rafts (Frau 1987: fig. 69). How the weight was released suddenly is unclear, but may have involved some kind of trigger mechanism like those of catapults, onagers, or perhaps the starting gates in a circus.

# SURGICAL TRACTION

Oribasius, writing around A.D. 362, describes several surgical traction machines for resetting broken limbs, some of which go back to the fifth century B.C. (Oribasius 49; Drachmann 1963: 171–84; cf. 1973). These machines spawned a progeny of later torture implements, notably the rack. The original was the bench of Hippocrates (ca. 420 B.C.), a rack with simple winches at each end, winding ropes that stretched the patient. The bench of Neileus was essentially a winch with handspikes that could be attached either to a bench, or, if carried to treat the patient away from the doctor's surgery, to a ladder. The bench of Andreas (court doctor at Alexandria, murdered 217 B.C.) used a screw thread instead of a winch. The chest of Nymphodorus (fl. ca.250–200 B.C. at Alexandria) was more compact and powerful, turned by a screw engaging a gear wheel on the winch (Lewis 1997: 55). Later improvements to Hippocrates' bench used either pulleys or geared winches to gain a mechanical advantage. In the mechanical chest of Galen, ropes attached to one end of the patient's limb were wound around two pulleys and taken back to each end of a windlass axle, while another rope attached to the other end of the limb was wound around the center of the axle (Oreibasios 49.7, from Galen, *On Engines*;

Drachmann 1963: 173). Other machines, including the *trispaston* of Apellis or Archimedes, and its modifications by Pasicrates, Heliodorus, and Aristion, used multiple axles with ropes wound around them for mechanical advantage, like the geared winches in Heron's *Baroulkos* (Oreibasios 49.23; Drachmann 1963: 178–84).

# ENGINES OF WAR

Constraints on the bow's effectiveness and range were the power that could be applied to draw it, limited by human strength to about 45 lb, and the length through which it could be drawn, limited by the length of an archer's arms. For the construction of larger artillery, one needed to create a bow or springs with considerable power and apply sufficient traction to pull back the arms of the machine. In all artillery pieces except the *gastraphetes*, traction for spanning the bow was achieved by variants on the means already described for cranes and surgical traction benches. Marsden 1969 and 1971 remain fundamental for this topic, although written before the identification of much of the archaeological material; a number of his ideas are now challenged. An accessible overview including the archaeological finds is Campbell 2003; more specialized accounts appear in Baatz 1978, 1994, 1999.

In 399 B.C., Dionysius of Syracuse offered high rates of pay to craftsmen from around the central Mediterranean to come to Syracuse and produce for him numerous weapons, in preparation for war against Carthage. According to Diodorus Siculus, "The catapult was invented at that time in Syracuse, since the most skillful craftsmen from everywhere had been gathered in one place" (14.42.1). Artillery was first used in anger at Dionysius' siege of Motya in 397 B.C. This first artillery weapon was probably the *gastraphetes* or belly shooter (Marsden 1969: 48–49). Like a large crossbow, it had a large bow attached to a stock, in which ran a slider carrying the bolt; the back of the slider engaged with the bowstring, so that before the bow was spanned the slider projected well forward beyond the end of the stock. A curved crosspiece at the end of the stock fitted the archer's stomach, allowing him to span the weapon by leaning the end of the slider against the ground or a wall, and pushing against the stock with his body. Ratchets on the stock and a pawl on the slider prevented the slider moving forward again. The trigger consisted of an iron bar with a claw at one end hooked over the bowstring, fired by pulling a hinged bar from underneath the back end of the trigger, so that the claw tilted up and released the bowstring. During the fourth century B.C., larger versions were developed, mounted on a base and spanned by a windlass. One version shot two bolts at once (Marsden 1969: 5–16; Campbell 2003: 3–7).

The *gastraphetes* was more powerful than an ordinary bow, but further development was limited by the size of composite bow that could be made from horn, wood, and sinew. In the catapult, therefore, the single bow was replaced with two separate arms, each thrust though a twisted skein of sinews or hair held in a frame. Metal levers placed over circular metal washers at the top and bottom of the spring frames allowed the skeins to be tightened. The bowstring was strung between the free ends of the arms, and the slider was pulled back by a windlass, or, in more powerful catapults, by a windlass and multiple pulley system as in the larger cranes or medical benches. The catapult was mounted on a tilt-and-swivel base so that it could be rotated and elevated or—in the case of arrow-shooters—depressed to fire from city walls (Marsden 1969; Campbell 2003).

Torsion machines of this kind, in which the spring frame formed a straight line, were called *euthytonoi* (straight spring) and were used for shooting bolts. More powerful variants, in which the springs were turned away from each other so that the arms could be bent back through a greater arc, were called *palintonoi* (back-spring devices). These could shoot heavy bolts but were more commonly used for stone shot, using a wider slider and a sling rather than a bowstring. An inscription of 306/5 B.C. from Athens mentions a catapult that could shoot either bolts or stones, presumably by changing the slider (Marsden 1969: 70).

Philo (*Belopoeica* 50) says that a program of systematic research under the Ptolemies developed formulae for the optimal proportions for the different parts of euthytone and palintone machines in relation to the missiles they were intended to fire. These took as a module the spring diameter, which in the arrow-shooter was to be one-ninth of the arrow's length. In the palintone stone-shooter the formula was more complicated, based on the weight of shot:

$$\text{Diameter of spring in dactyls} = 1.1 \sqrt[3]{(100 \times \text{weight in minae})}$$

Dimensions of all the parts of the machines are expressed as multiples of the spring diameter (Marsden 1969: 24–41).

Philo (*Belopoeica* 73–78) describes a repeater catapult built by Dionysius of Alexandria, in which bolts were fed one at a time from a hopper into a groove on a cylinder revolving inside a case, which dropped them into the firing groove on the stock. The machine was spanned by a chain of wooden pallets and iron links fitted around a pentagonal cogwheel turned by the winch. This cog also rotated the magazine in a synchronized fashion so that each bolt dropped into the groove after the arms were pulled back, and released the trigger; and then drew back the arms and cocked the machine for the next shot. Reconstructions have proved the device fast and accurate, but Philon criticized it for firing all of its shots at the same target and thus wasting ammunition when one shot would do: "The missiles will not have a spread, since the aperture has been laid on a single target and produces a trajectory more or less along one segment of a circle, nor will they have a very elongated dropping zone" (*Belopoeica* 76).

Philo presents several alternative catapults: a wedge catapult, whose torsion springs are tightened by wedges; a catapult in which twisted sinews are replaced by bronze springs (*Bel.* 59–73), and the pneumatic catapult of Ctesibius in which, as the machine is spanned, pistons are driven into tight-fitting cylinders; the air thus compressed provides the motive power for the arms when the trigger is released

(*Bel.* 77–78). These machines may have been built as experimental prototypes, but were never adopted in general production (Marsden 1969: 41–42).

Some subsequent design improvements can be traced (Marsden 1969: 42, 174–98). The catapult on a second-century B.C. balustrade relief from the sanctuary of Athena at Pergamon has curved arms, allowing a greater arc of travel than in straight-armed *euthytonoi* or *palintonoi*, and hence a more powerful shot. By around 25 B.C., when Vitruvius wrote, more efficient oval washers had been developed, allowing more sinew to be put in the springs. Philo's dimensional formulae probably no longer held good: the improvements allowed smaller, lighter machines to be constructed with the same firepower, facilitating their use by field armies. Indeed, Trajan's Column and the column of Marcus Aurelius show catapults mounted on small carts, which must be the *carroballistae* mentioned by Vegetius (*Mil.* 2.25, 3.14, 24). Heron's *Cheiroballistra* (possibly not by Heron of Alexandria) describes parts of a handheld ballista. There is controversy over its reconstruction (Wilkins 1995, 2000; Iriarte 2000), but the term *cheiroballistra* (hand-ballista) and its Latin equivalent, *manuballista*, surely imply a handheld, portable weapon (figure 13.2).

Further debate rages around the design of late Roman catapults. In 1972 the bronze frame of a stone-throwing catapult of the mid third century A.D. was excavated at Hatra in Iraq (Baatz 1978: 3–9). Its exceptional width (2.40 m) and two notches on the inside of the spring frames suggested to several scholars that the arms at rest projected forward and were drawn inward through the frame when the weapon was spanned. This would allow a travel of some 120 degrees as opposed to about 67 degrees achievable in a *palintone* machine with outward-swinging arms, giving a performance increase of about 50 percent. The inward-swinging design seems to have been introduced in the late first century A.D., and despite some disagreement (Wilkins 2000), inward-swinging arms were probably also used in the *cheiroballista* (figure 13.2) (Anstee 1998; Iriarte 2003; Anon. 2004).

Torsion machines were capable of considerable range. Agesistratus, in the first-century B.C., built an arrow-shooter that could fire a three-span arrow 700 yards, and a larger *palintone* engine that shot a four-cubit bolt 800 yards. Effective ranges would have been shorter. Modern reconstructions have not achieved such ranges, but most use hair or nylon rope for the springs instead of the much more elastic sinew preferred in antiquity. Stone catapult balls from Carthage, Pergamon, Rhodes, and Tel Dor range in weight between 3 minae (1.3 kg) and 180 minae (78.6 kg). Josephus says that at the siege of Jerusalem (A.D. 69) the Roman stone-throwers shot stone balls of one talent some 400 yards; but this may have been against personnel, and Marsden thinks the effective range against a wall might have been less than half that.

Trajan's architect Apollodorus of Damascus mentions "one-armed stone-throwers" in his *Poliorcetica*, possibly the machines referred to by Vegetius as *onagri*. Ammianus Marcellinus (23.4.4–7) attempted a technical description of the *onager* (wild ass, so called perhaps because of its back-kicking recoil), a one-armed ballista for hurling stones from a sling. Most authors (e.g., Marsden 1969; Campbell

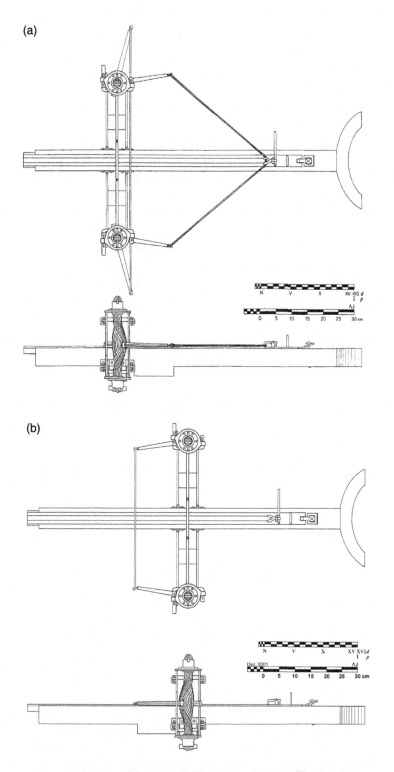

Figure 13.2. Reconstructions of the *cheiroballistra* (hand-held ballista) as (a) an outswinger and (b) an inswinger. (Reconstruction by Aitor Iriarte, reproduced by permission.)

2003: 42–43) reconstruct this as similar to the medieval mangonel. An arm with a sling is inserted in a torsion bundle stretched horizontally across the frame of the machine, and the arm is drawn back to the horizontal by a windlass. A trigger mechanism releases the arm, which swings upward, hurling a stone from the sling, and a padded buffer in front of the machine absorbs the impact of the arm. A completely different reconstruction has been proposed (Cherretté 2001–2002), but has yet to be tested as a full-size working model.

Archaeological finds, representations, and especially the design of fortifications, in which provision for stationing torsion artillery is common in the Hellenistic and Roman periods, suggest that between the fourth century B.C. and the fourth century A.D. Greek and Roman armies made frequent and widespread use of powerful artillery in both offensive and defensive roles in siege warfare. They made more use of artillery, apparently, than did medieval western European armies. Moreover, the Roman army deployed massive firepower in the field, with each legion possessing some 55 mobile ballistae, and the in-swinging design allowed for the construction of lighter and more powerful engines and even hand-held weapons. This ballistic technology, although available also to some of Rome's enemies, particularly those in the East, gave the Roman army a key technological edge and must have been one of the factors in Rome's ability to withstand for so long repeated attacks on the frontiers with a comparatively small army. In the eastern Mediterranean, arrow-shooting catapults (including the *carroballista* and *cheiroballista*) survived in use into Byzantine times (Wilkins 2000). The *onager* seems to have become more popular in late antiquity and to have survived into the Middle Ages. Although it was less maneuverable and probably less accurate than other devices, it was simpler to build and maintain than the two-armed Greco-Roman *palintone* stone throwers.

# WATER-LIFTING DEVICES

An important early class of machines was for lifting water, to supply places above where it naturally occurred or to drain underground workings (Schiøler 1973; Oleson 1984, 2000). The earliest water-lifting machine was the *shaduf*, in which a horizontal lever arm that pivoted on a vertical support had a bucket on one end and a counterweight on the other. The operator pulled the bucket down into the water and the counterweight lifted it up so the water could be emptied into a channel or container. The *shaduf* conferred no mechanical advantage, but enabled the operator to pull downward, a more efficient and less tiring motion using stronger muscles than lifting a weight up. It is shown in an Egyptian wall painting from Thebes of about 1300 B.C. (Hodges 1970: fig. 112) and mentioned by several classical authors (White 1975: 45–47; Oleson 2000: 225–29). Lifts are low, but discharge volume is

Figure 13.3.  Water-powered water-lifting wheel (*noria*) at Hama, Syria. (Photograph by A. Wilson.)

relatively high. The well windlass or pulley also allows a conversion of direction of force for ease of operation; both systems were common in the Greco-Roman world. Lifts can be high (limited only by the tensile strength of the rope) but discharge volume is low, limited by the size of container and the time taken to pull the rope up.

More complicated machines appear in the Hellenistic period, using rotary motion for continuous operation. The wheel with compartmented body (*tympanum*) was powered by men treading the outside of the wheel; it had a high discharge but relatively low lift, as the water discharged through a hole near the axle. The compartmented rim wheel had a higher lift—closer to the diameter of the wheel— and might also be powered by men treading the rim, or by animals yoked to a capstan driving the wheel by right-angled gearing (*saqiya*), or by water turning paddles on the exterior of the rim (*noria*) (figure 13.3). The traditional water-lifting wheel shown here is very similar to one represented on a fourth-century A.D. mosaic from nearby Apamea. For higher lifts, a chain of buckets or (later) pots could be looped over a wheel, powered either by men in a treadmill or by animals via a geared *saqiya* drive. An interesting, early example was discovered in London in 2001 (figure 13.4). A cogwheel on the vertical shaft of a capstan engages a drive wheel on one end of an axle; on the other end of the axle is a wheel over which is looped a set of wooden containers held together by cranked iron links. As the containers come over the top of the wheel, they discharge their contents forward into one of eight compartments on the outside of the wheel, from which the water then discharges into a trough or launder through side-ports in the compartments. The original device was probably driven by an animal yoked to a bar on the vertical axle.

Philo of Byzantium's *Pneumatics* indicates that many of these new machines were invented in the mid-third century B.C. This work survives only in Arabic, but

Figure 13.4. Working reconstruction of the first-century A.D. water-lifting device discovered at Gresham St, London, on display at the Museum of London. (Photograph by A. Wilson.)

Lewis (1997: 26–36) shows that letter sequences referring to details on the illustrations demonstrate that the chapters on the bucket chain and overshot wheel certainly, and the *noria* and the *saqiya* drive possibly, are in fact translations of the original Greek. Furthermore, in another clearly genuine section Philo refers to animal-powered and water-powered lifting machines among the devices with which one might expect engineers to be familiar, and opposed to which his description of a siphon system is a novelty (*Pneumatics* 5; Lewis 1997: 32). More generally, Philo's *Parasceuastica* (91.43–44) which survives in Greek, refers to "wheels driven around" for raising water to flood siege mines. Lewis also gives strong reasons for seeing Philo as the source for Vitruvius' descriptions of the hodometer, screw, *tympanum*, *rota*, bucket chain, *noria*, and water-mill (1997: 46).

These water-lifting devices and other machines were therefore already known when Philo wrote in the later third century B.C. While his *Hydragogia* and *Mechanics* may not have been written at Alexandria, the subsequent importance of rotary water-lifting devices in Egypt strongly suggests that these machines, at least, were known at Alexandria around the mid-third century B.C., and may have been invented there.

Water-lifting devices like the *saqiya* and the *noria* were widely used in later Hellenistic and Roman Egypt, and although they are usually associated with the east, there is growing evidence for their use in the western provinces, including North Africa and probably Spain (Wilson 2003), Italy, Dalmatia, Gaul, and Britain (Bouet 2005). A *saqiya*-type bucket-chain was used at Cosa in Italy in the later second century B.C., and another, using wooden buckets, in the later first century B.C. (Oleson 1984: 201–2). The earliest of four bucket chains from London, built in A.D. 63 and used for about 10 years, shows that this technology reached Britain within 20 years of the Roman conquest (Blair and Hall 2003; Blair 2004; Blair et al. 2005). The London devices used wooden box-buckets linked by a double iron chain, which must have turned over a facetted axle (figure 13.4). In the use of a double iron chain the device is similar to Vitruvius' description (*De arch.* 10.4.4), with the difference that the buckets were of wood and not bronze; the facetted axle recalls Philo's bucket-chain (*Pneumatica* 65) or the repeater catapult (above). The Cosa and London devices may have been powered by men in a treadmill or by animals via a *saqiya* drive. At some point, perhaps between the first and third centuries A.D., terracotta pots replaced wooden buckets on the *saqiya*, making the machines more affordable in regions like Egypt, where wood was scarce and expensive. Such pots form the most durable and recognizable archaeological evidence for the use of the *saqiya*, and document its use in Israel from the late second or early third century A.D. onward (Ayalon 2000). Papyri and finds of *saqiya* pots in Egypt and elsewhere suggest that the use of the *saqiya* increased during the early fourth century A.D., possibly as a result of Diocletian's decree of tax relief on irrigated land (Oleson 1984: 379–80). It seems therefore that uptake of the technology was first encouraged by design modifications using cheaper materials, and then by state incentives for investment in irrigation technology with the goal of increasing agricultural output.

Two other devices are attributed to named individuals—the force pump to Ctesibius, and the water-lifting screw to Archimedes, although a more recent theory argues (controversially) that this was an invention of the ancient Near East which Archimedes merely refined and popularized (Dalley 1994; Dalley and Oleson 2003). The water screw's discharge is high, but the height lifted is low—a fraction of the length of the barrel. The device was used in irrigation, particularly in Egypt, and in mine drainage, where batteries of them in series have been found to achieve the requisite lift (Oleson 1984: 291–301; 2000: 242–51).

The force pump is the most complex ancient lifting device. In its original (bronze) form, pistons working in a pair of cylinders connected by transverse pipes pushed water up a central delivery pipe; the water was prevented from returning under the force of gravity by one-way bronze flap valves at the entrance to a chamber at the base of the delivery pipe (figure 13.5). The pistons could be connected by a rocker at the top, and worked reciprocally. The main uses attested in literary sources were firefighting and spraying perfumed water in theaters and amphitheaters and during banquets; the bronze pumps found at several archaeological sites, often portable and of fairly small capacity, may have been suited to these purposes. The firefighting version had a nozzle that could swivel and be raised for directing against a blaze (Hero, *Pneumatics* 27), and may have been mounted on a cart. Several bronze pumps from mines may have been used in fire-setting—spraying cold water on a rock face heated by fire, to make it crack. In the first century A.D., the force pump was re-engineered in wood, making it more affordable and easier to produce or repair. It begins to appear at rural villas and farms, for raising water from wells, and this is the most commonly attested archaeological use, followed by bilge pumps in wrecks (Oleson 1984; Stein 2004; cf.

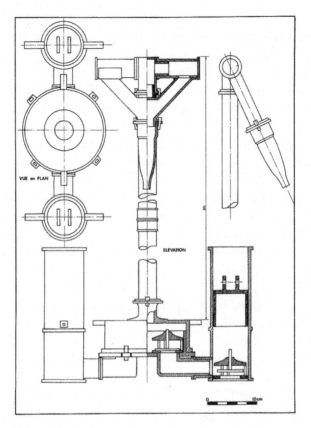

VUE en PLAN

ELEVATION

0        10 cm

Figure 13.5. Drawing of Roman bronze force pump from the copper mine at Sotiel Coronada (Domergue 1990: fig. 35, by permission of C. Domergue.)

Fleury 2005, whose list of pumps is incomplete). At least 32 Roman force pumps are known: 11 bronze, 1 lead, and 20 wood (Stein 2004, plus the imprint of the wooden pump recorded by Jones 1980: 95; Oleson 2000: 272–85). At Alet (St. Malo) a late-first-century A.D. pumping installation included a block with eight cylinders, worked by two or three men, to pump spring water from just above the shore to a basin higher up (Langouet and Meury 1976; Oleson 1984: 261–63).

The chain pump was used mainly or exclusively for bilge-pumping in ships, from at least the start of the first century B.C. and probably earlier. A series of wooden disks strung on a chain or rope was looped round an upper slotted drive wheel, and passed over a roller in the bilge (Oleson 2000: 263–67). The upward-moving disks entered a wooden tube mounted inside of the ship, whose lower end was immersed in the bilge water. Water entered the tube between disks and was pulled up the tube after each disk entered, discharging through the gunwales at the top of the tube. This machine could handle silty water, was self-cleansing, and could operate in a pitching and rolling ship in a way that other devices could not. Uncertainty remains, however, over the drive mechanism; a crank-handle on the upper drive wheel would be the obvious solution, but this has been doubted given the rarity of evidence for the use of cranks in antiquity. The best evidence for a possible Roman crank handle, however, is a slotted disk from one of the Nemi barges (ca. A.D. 40), which also produced evidence consistent with a wooden chain pump (incorrectly reconstructed as a bucket chain at the time), and the crank handle therefore seems the most likely solution (Drachmann 1973: 37–38; cf. Oleson 1984: 230–33; 2000: 263–67).

The new Hellenistic water-lifting devices revolutionized opportunities for irrigating land that lay above running water courses. Roman and Byzantine papyri from Egypt commonly record the hire, construction, or repair of irrigation devices—although frequently the type is unspecified—and such machines, which could be expensive to construct, were often an indispensable part of an estate (Rathbone 1991: 223–24). Although much of the evidence for *saqiyas* comes from Egypt, treadmill-driven wheels with compartmented rims have long been known from bath buildings in Pompeii and Ostia. As a result of recent publications, more examples are increasingly being recognized and reported by excavators, and the body of available evidence is growing rapidly (cf. Bouet 2005: 21–26; Bedello Tata and Fogagnolo 2005; Coadic and Bouet 2005; Conche et al. 2005; Morvillez et al. 2005). The ancient chain pump, previously thought to be a Renaissance invention, was only recognized during the 1980s, and took a decade or so to become accepted in the literature on water-lifting devices. Generalized statements about uptake of water-lifting technology must therefore remain provisional, but already it is clear that such devices were widely used earlier than previously thought.

# WATER-MILLS

The rotary hand quern is an early application of the crank principle to facilitate rotary or oscillating motion. The rotary mill allowed animals to be yoked to the mill and to turn it using a lever. The water-mill capitalizes on the automation of rotary motion by using a flowing stream, and it represents one of the earliest successful attempts to use natural forces for productive mechanical work. Since the mid-1980s our understanding of the origins and spread of water-milling has been transformed by a growing body of archaeological evidence from across the Roman Empire (Wikander 1985, 2000c; Brun and Borréani 1998; Wilson 2001a: 234–36, 2001b, 2002: 9–15.). It now seems that the water-mill was invented in the mid-third century B.C., with vertical and horizontal versions appearing almost simultaneously (Lewis 1997). By the first century A.D. water-mills had spread widely through the Roman world, with the full variety of vertical wheel types—undershot, overshot, and breastshot—in use by the late second century A.D. (chapter 6). Vertical mills require right-angled gearing to convert the vertical rotation about the water-wheel axle into the horizontal rotation of the spindle passing through the lower millstone, which supported and turned the upper millstone.

Horizontal mills, by contrast, require no gearing. Water delivered down a chute or via a nozzle from a tall reservoir (called a drop-tower) struck the inclined blades of the horizontal wheel almost tangentially and turning it with its spindle, which supported the upper millstone. This design is suited to channels or streams with a small or slow flow, as it utilizes the pressure of water in the reservoir rather than the speed or gradient of a stream. Horizontal mills are attested in third-century B.C. works of Philo of Byzantium (Lewis 1997), but archaeological evidence is lacking before the fourth century A.D. Curiously, the earliest identified surviving remains of horizontal mills, at Chemtou and Testour in Tunisia, indicate the most complex type of mill, in which water in a tapering wheel race entered a circular wheel shaft tangentially at the top and exited at the base; a horizontal wheel with angled blades ran fully submerged at the base of the shaft in a rotating column of water. As a true turbine wheel, this design was relatively efficient, avoiding dissipation of energy around the sides of the wheel. The Chemtou and Testour mills were relatively large, with three wheels each (Röder and Röder 1993; Rakob 1993; Wilson 1995). Together with the developed design, this sophistication suggests a previous period of development for which no archaeological evidence remains. This heritage probably included the so-called *arubah* or drop-tower mill, common in the Near East from the late Roman period onward, and also used probably in the Roman or late Roman period in North Africa. Water stored in a cylindrical reservoir (drop-tower) several meters high emerges under pressure through a nozzle at the base, spraying onto the spokes of a horizontal wheel.

Whatever the drive arrangement, the millstones required careful adjustment. To control the fineness of the meal produced, and to compensate for wear, the clearance between the millstones could be adjusted by a tentering mechanism. The lower end of the spindle was supported on a horizontal beam (bridge tree), pivoted at one end; a vertical rod attached to the other end allowed the bridge tree to be raised or lowered slightly, raising or lowering the spindle and thus also the upper millstone. Archaeological evidence for this arrangement has been found at Chemtou (Röder and Röder 1993). Grain was delivered to the millstones from a hopper suspended over them (Vitruvius, *De arch.* 10.5.2), and by analogy with later milling practice it is usually assumed that delivery from the hopper was regulated by a device attached to the upper millstone, which vibrated the hopper as the millstone rotated, ensuring a continuous and even flow of grain and preventing blockage.

The physical evidence for ancient water-mills usually consists of a millrace (rock-cut, stone-, or timber-lined), a wheel-pit and a gear-pit; sometimes wooden elements of the wheel or the wheelrace survive. Nearly all Roman water-mill structures recognized to date in the Mediterranean are of stone or brick-faced concrete. North of the Alps, timber construction is more common, with evidence from Britain, Germany, Switzerland, and northern Italy indicating a developed tradition of engineering headraces and tailraces, with timber linings and revetments, between the first and fourth centuries A.D. (Castella et al. 1994; Volpert 1997).

Two mill spindles from ironwork hoards at Silchester and Great Chesterford may suggest the presence of water-mills nearby. But the largest body of evidence is stray finds of large, power-driven millstones. In Britain alone large millstones of Roman or probably Roman date have been found on at least 57 different sites (including seven different locations in London, but excluding the Blackfriars wreck), and were probably water-powered.

The boat mill or floating mill, in which the machinery is mounted on a boat, allowing the wheel mounted on the side of the boat to rise and fall with the river level, was a solution to the problem of operating undershot wheels on large rivers whose levels fluctuate. According to Procopius (*Goth.* 5.19.18), Belisarius invented the floating mill during the siege of Rome in A.D. 537, after the Goths cut the aqueducts on which Rome's water-mills depended. Whatever the truth of this account, the invention spread rapidly, and river mills at bridges, probably floating mills, were operating in Paris, Geneva and Dijon from the 550s to the 570s (Wikander 2000c: 384).

# OTHER APPLICATIONS
# OF WATER POWER

Besides the water-mill and water-powered *noria*, water power was also used for other purposes: dough-mixing, sawmills (figure 6.5), pestles for pounding grain, and recumbent trip-hammers or vertical ore stamps for crushing ore in mining regions (figure 4.2; chapter 6; cf. Wikander 1981, 1989, 2000b; Lewis 1997). A relief discovered at Pammukale in Turkey provides a clear representation of a pair of stone-cutting saws powered by a water-wheel by means of a crank and connecting rod (Ritti et al. 2007). Other evidence for the early diversification of water power is more circumstantial. Lewis (1997: 95–99) argues that the fullers' canal at Antioch, dated to A.D. 73/74 and known only from inscriptions, could only have been intended to drive water-powered fulling stocks; and the use of water-powered bellows has been proposed at Marseille in the fifth century (Guéry and Hallier 1987, 273 fig. 5, 274–75; Varoqueaux and Gassend 2001).

Pliny mentions a *fractaria machina* (breaking machine) incorporating 150 lb weights, used for attacking outcrops of hard flint in the adits of gold mines in Spain (*HN* 33.21.72). It is difficult to see how this could have operated in underground adits, or how it might have been powered, and it would be tempting to believe that Pliny has confused this with ore-stamps, were it not for the fact that it is firmly embedded in his description of workings at the face of the adit. What form the device took is unknown.

## Dough-Kneaders

Roman dough-kneading machines consisted of a cylindrical stone tub with a metal spindle rotating in a socket in the base; paddles or "arms" projecting from the spindle passed between rods stuck horizontally through holes in the side of the tub. The spindle was rotated by a man or a yoked animal pushing a lever, kneading the dough as it was caught between the paddles and the rods (Mau 1886; Besnier 1877–1919: 496; Curtis 2001: 363–65). Dough-mixers are common in bakeries at Pompeii and Ostia, and are found from Volubilis in Morocco (Luquet 1966) to Tomis (Constanta) in Romania on the Black Sea; none is yet known north of the Alps, although wooden versions may perhaps have been used there. Their origin remains uncertain, although a depiction on the Augustan Tomb of Eurysaces gives a rough terminus ante quem (figure 2.2). Broadly contemporary is Vitruvius' reference to water-powered dough mixing in the context of a water-mill (*De arch.* 10.5.2). Systematic collation of published examples might help to refine the date of the dough-mixer's introduction, although frequently they remain unpublished despite their common occurrence on many Mediterranean sites.

# TRANSPORT AND PADDLEWHEELS

Vitruvius and Hero describe a hodometer in which gears attached to the axle of a wagon are arranged to drop a stone ball into a receptacle every mile (figure 31.4); its invention perhaps by Archimedes in the third century B.C. may have been connected with the Roman road-building program in Italy at this period (Lewis 2000: 332; see chapter 31). Both Vitruvius (*De arch.* 10.9) and Hero (*Dioptra* 38) also describe a hodometer for ships, driven by a paddle wheel rotating as the ship goes through the water; this may have been another of Archimedes' inventions (Tzetzes, *Chil.* 12.967–71; Lewis 2000: 332). Drachmann (1963: 159, 165–68) considers this an armchair invention, but it may be this device that, via a reversal of principles like that linking the *saqiya* and the water-mill, inspired one of the most extraordinary inventions of the Roman world. The anonymous fourth-century author of *De rebus bellicis* proposes a ship propelled by three pairs of paddle wheels driven by oxen via a geared capstan (chapter 17). This proposal is usually dismissed as impractical, and certainly there is no evidence for its having been used in the Roman world. Intriguingly, though, from probably the fifth century A.D., and certainly from the eighth century onward, the Chinese had boats driven by treadmill-powered paddlewheels. Their practical efficacy is shown by their importance in twelfth-century warfare, when a kind of naval arms race between government forces and southern rebels led to the construction of boats with between 8 and 24 paddle wheels (Needham and Ling 1965: 414–35). Needham and Ling consider the transmission of the ideas of the anonymous author of *De rebus bellicis* to China as unlikely, and prefer to see the Chinese paddleboats as independent inventions of about 50 years later. Similar horse-driven boats were in common use as ferry boats on Lake Champlain in the eighteenth and nineteenth century A.D. (Crisman 2005), underlining the practicality of the concept.

# OIL AND WINE PRESSES

To produce olive oil or wine, olives or grapes had to be pressed—in the case of olives, after a preliminary crushing in *trapetum* or edge-runner mills (chapter 14). Although for small quantities this could be done by piling weights directly on the basket of fruit, usually a mechanical press was used. Ancient oil and wine presses were based on different simple machines (lever, screw, and wedge), combined in some cases with the winch or compound pulleys. The lever press was the earliest, and in its simplest form consisted of a long wooden beam fixed at one end, resting on the stack of baskets of fruit—either olives that had previously been pulped in a mill or the grapes and skins that remained after the initial treading. Stone weights were hung off the free end (an Attic black-figure vase shows a man swinging on the end of the beam instead). Greater force could be exerted with the lever and windlass press, using a windlass fixed to the floor of the press-room to winch down the free end of the beam. Variations had the windlass attached to the beam, or to a large stone weight; operating the windlass drew the beam down until the resistance of the fruit stopped it and the weight began to rise off the floor; once the weight had been winched fully up its weight compressed the stack of fruit further and it began to settle to the floor.

The lever and screw press was in many respects an improvement using the mechanical advantage of the screw to apply greater pressure. Pliny the Elder (*HN* 18.317), writing in the A.D. 70s, mentions this as a Greek invention of the last 100 years (i.e., late first century B.C.); it probably operated with a male screw, but the female element was probably a simple hole in the press beam with a peg pushed through the side to engage the male screw. Variants existed in which the screw was attached to the floor, or was attached to the counterweight to raise it off the floor as in the lever-and-windlass press. Pliny also says that the direct screw press for grapes, which is much smaller and lacks the lever, had been invented in the last 22 years, that is, since A.D. 55. This sounds like the small olive-press with one screw described in Hero's *Mechanics* 3, whose construction seems to have been made possible by the invention (by Hero ?) of the screw-cutter to cut female screws (*Mechanics* 3.21; Drachmann 1936, 1963). The direct screw press was particularly favored in urban environments, where space was at a premium, and was also used by fullers to press clothes. Its drawback was that its operation was more labor-intensive than the lever-and-windlass press, which once the counterweight had been raised could run unattended until the stack was fully compressed.

The wedge press was another compact press suited to urban use; it seems to have been used particularly by perfume makers, who needed high-grade oil as the base for their scents. Boards held between a pair of uprights over the fruit to be pressed were forced apart by knocking in wedges between them, compressing the stack (Mattingly 1990). Besides Philo's wedge catapult, this is one of the few instances of the use of the wedge in ancient complex machines, although the Chinese had wedge presses too (Cotterell and Kamminga 1990: 100).

# ENTERTAINMENT

The water organ (*hydraulis*) is the first keyboard instrument; invented by Ctesibius, it is clearly related to his force-pump. Two cylinders worked by levers forced air into an inverted funnel in a chamber partly filled with water, forcing some of the water out of the funnel. Because of the constant force of ambient air pressure, the surrounding water maintained a fairly constant pressure within the air space of the funnel. From the top of the funnel, air was distributed to the organ pipes via a number of channels, each of which could be opened or closed by valves attached to a keyboard (Vitruvius, *De arch.* 10.8; Hero, *Pneumatics* 76; Drachmann 1948: 7–21). The *hydraulis* is represented in Roman terracotta models, mosaics, and reliefs, and surviving parts have been found at Aquincum, from where there is also a tombstone of a female singer and *hydraulis* player (*CIL* 3.10501), and at Dion. Mosaics from Nennig (Germany) and Zliten (Libya) show the water organ providing accompanying music at gladiatorial shows and executions of prisoners or criminals by wild animals. A wind-driven version used cams on a wind-driven wheel to pump a cylinder up and down (Hero, *Pneumatica* 77). Apollonius' Fluteplayer (ca. 240 B.C.; Lewis 1997: 49–57), adapts the principle of water maintaining air pressure but uses a water-powered wheel to operate valves controlling the water flow into the air chamber, and tipping spoons to operate the valves that release the air into the flute's pipe. This device may have been inspired partly by Ctesibius' *hydraulis*, but it is a more complex development.

Besides musical instruments, a variety of mechanical devices was used in public entertainment, especially in Greek and Roman theaters, and Roman amphitheaters and circuses. The Greek theater machines, which from the fifth century B.C. allowed actors to appear suddenly high up as a *deus ex machina* (and which are parodied by implication in Aristophanes' *Thesmaphoriazusae*, 1009–15), probably involved little more than a winch and crane. More complex was the mechanism used in circuses, hippodromes, and stadia to open the starting gates (*carceres*) simultaneously. Each stall had two gates held closed by a bar, and when this was removed the gates flew open instantaneously. The speed with which the gates opened suggests that they were sprung; the word *hysplex*, used in an inscription of 280–272 B.C. from Pergamon but referring to the hippodrome of Olympia, and by Dionysius of Halicarnassus (3.68.3) referring to the Circus Maximus, seems to imply the use of twisted rope or sinew for the hinges, as in the torsion catapult. Humphrey reconstructs the arrangement in Roman circuses such as Lepcis Magna, with ropes running down from a gallery over the *carceres* to each gate and attached to a latch to draw the bolt that held the gates closed, and suggests that the ropes to pull the latches of all 12 gates were released simultaneously by attaching them to a small catapult (Humphrey et al. 1972–1973: 82–87; Humphrey 1986: 133, 157–70).

In amphitheaters, lifts operated from below by capstans and ropes over pulleys were used to hoist animal cages up from cells below the arena to near the arena level, so the animals could emerge through trapdoors. Numerous square shafts in the arenas of the Colosseum and the amphitheaters at Capua and Pozzuoli illustrate this arrangement; these and several other amphitheaters also have longer slots in the arena floor that may have been used for raising scenery by similar mechanisms.

Elements of revolving circular wooden platforms were discovered during the excavation of Caligula's barges on Lake Nemi. One, nearly a meter in diameter, revolved on eight small bronze spheres each fitted with an axle; the other was smaller and turned on wedge-shaped conical wooden rollers (Ucelli 1950: 186–90). Their function is unknown; bases for cranes or revolving statues have been suggested, but it is also tempting to wonder if they might have been for rotating seats such as those described in Pertinax' auction of Commodus' property: "There were also carriages of an unusual technique of construction with meshing and branching gear trains and seats accurately designed to rotate, sometimes to face away from the sun, sometimes to take advantage of the breeze, and hodometers, and clocks, and other items appropriate to his vices." (*HA, Pertinax* 8.6–7; translation Lewis 2001b: 331).

The role of machines in the social and economic development of antiquity has perhaps been excessively downplayed in the past. The idea that slavery made machines unnecessary, or that animism discouraged the exploitation of water power, is now rejected. Mechanical automata (discussed in chapter 31) were not mere toys: they elaborated, developed and illustrated mechanical principles, of which the most significant include early instances of feedback control (Ctesibius' float regulator for the water-clock and Philo's lamp for constant level: Mayr 1970a, 1970b); programming (Hero's theatrical automata), and auto-propulsion (Hero's stages, whose wheels were driven by a descending weight). Their development was closely related to the jack-work of clocks and planetaria (Drachmann 1948: 70–71).

In a world without patents, some of the biggest mechanical advances occurred under royal patronage—the invention of artillery at Syracuse under Dionysius in 399 B.C., the Ptolemaic experiments on ballistae, and also of course the development of gearing, pneumatics, and mechanics at the Museum of Alexandria. For the Roman world, both the anecdote of the engineer and Vespasian (Suetonius, *Vesp.*

19) and the dedication of *De rebus bellicis* to the emperor suggest that there was an expectation that the emperor might reward invention, even if that was not always realized.

How widespread was the use of machines? For cranes, at least, we can attempt an answer: from their beginnings in the late sixth century B.C. they had become common in the Greek world by the late fifth century, and were ubiquitous in the Hellenistic and Roman worlds. Every public building with monolithic columns or large blocks with lifting lugs or Lewis holes is indirect but certain testimony to the use of cranes. In this regard, the use of cranes to lift material in construction appears more common in the Roman world, where nearly every city possessed several buildings whose construction and repair required them, than in medieval Europe, where in many towns the cathedral and the castle might be the only structures needing them. There is the impression that oil and wine presses dating from the Roman and late Roman periods are much more frequent than those of subsequent times until the early modern period; the archaeological (as opposed to documentary) evidence for water-mills and millstones also appears scarcely less abundant for the Roman than for the high medieval period.

Arguably, the use of machines was in fact more widespread in ancient Greece and Rome, together with ancient China, than in any other civilization until certainly the twelfth or perhaps even the fourteenth century A.D. in western Europe. While most of the simple machines were known to ancient Near Eastern civilizations, it was the Classical and Hellenistic Greek and the Roman worlds that produced a variety of complex machines and spread their use both outward geographically and downward through levels of society, sometimes by re-engineering a complex design in cheaper materials. There is still much work to do on the question of the relationship between the early appearance of mechanical technology in Greece and Rome and in China: independent invention or technology transfer; and if so, in which direction? Our understanding of many classical machines has advanced considerably since Needham and Ling addressed the question of the priority of Chinese and classical mechanical inventions (1965: 366–70, 405–8). Much evidence now points, especially for water-powered machines, to diffusion from the classical Mediterranean to China, presumably along the Silk Road. The first device that can be shown to have come from China to the Mediterranean world is the traction trebuchet, introduced by the Avars, who used it at the siege of Thessaloniki in A.D. 597 (Nicolle 2003: 10–11).

Older notions of Greek and Roman technological stagnation contrasting with the technological vibrancy of the early Middle Ages, which saw a kind of "medieval industrial revolution," must now be rethought. Not only does it appear that, for example, in the Roman world water power was more widespread, earlier, and used for more varied purposes than was believed even in the 1970s, but reassessment of the medieval evidence now suggests that the diversification of water power for uses other than grain-milling and fulling was a relatively late (fourteenth- or fifteenth-century) phenomenon (Lucas 2005). The technological gap between the Roman Empire and the early Middle Ages looks smaller than it did before. Indeed, there are areas (pressing, artillery), where Roman machine use may have been in advance of early medieval use. The implications for our views of progress and of the relationship between technology and economic development are profound.

# REFERENCES

Anonymous 2004. "Trajan's artillery: The archaeology of a Roman technological revolution," *Current World Archaeology* 3: 41–48.

Anstee, J. 1998. "'Tours de force': An experimental catapult/ballista," *Studia Danubiana* 1998: 131–39.

Ayalon, E. 2000. "Typology and chronology of water-wheel (*saqiya*) pottery pots from Israel," *Israel Exploration Journal* 50: 216–26.

Baatz, D. 1978. "Recent finds of ancient artillery," *Britannia* 9: 1–17.

Baatz, D. 1994. *Bauten und Katapulte des römischen Heeres.* Mavors Roman Army Researches 11. Stuttgart: F. Steiner.

Baatz, D. 1999. "Katapulte und mechanische Handwaffen des spätrömischen Heeres," *Journal of Roman Military Equipment Studies* 10: 5–19.

Ballu, A. 1911. *Les ruines de Timgad: Sept années de découvertes, 1903–1910.* Paris: Neurdein Frères.

Bedello Tata, M., and S. Fogagnolo 2005. "Una ruota idraulica da Ostia," in Bouet 2005: 115–38.

Besnier, M. 1877–1919. "Pistor, pistrina," in *DarSag* 4.1: 494–502.

Blair, I. 2004. "The water supply and the mechanical water-lifting devices of Roman Londinium—'New evidence from three archaeological sites in the City of London,'" in F. Minonzio (ed.), *Problemi di macchinismo in ambito romano: Macchine idrauliche nella lettatura tecnica, nelle fonti storiografiche, e nelle evidenze archeologiche di età imperiale.* Como: Commune di Como, 113–24.

Blair, I., and J. Hall 2003. *Working water: Roman technology in action.* London: Museum of London.

Blair, I., R. Spain, and T. Taylor 2005. "The technology of the 1st- and 2nd-century Roman bucket chains from London: From excavation to reconstruction," in Bouet 2005: 85–114.

Bouet, A. (ed.) 2005. *Aquam in altum exprimere: Les machines élévatrices d'eau dans l'Antiquité.* Scripta Antiqua 12. Pessac: Ausonius.

Brun, J.-P., and M. Borréani 1998. "Deux moulins hydrauliques du Haut Empire romain en Narbonnaise: *Villae* des Mesclans à La Crau et de Saint-Pierre/Les Laurons aux Arcs (Var)," *Gallia* 55: 279–326.

Campbell, D. B. 2003. *Greek and Roman artillery, 399 BC–AD 363.* Oxford: Osprey Publishing.

Castella, D., E. Beza, and P.-A. Bezat 1994. *Le moulin hydraulique gallo-romain d'Avenche en Chaplix.* Aventicum 6. Lausanne: Cahiers d'archéologie romande.

Cherretté, M. 2001–2002. "The *onager* according to Ammianus Marcellinus," *Journal of Roman Military Equipment Studies* 12–13: 117–33.

Coadic, S., and A. Bouet 2005. "La chaine à godets des thermes de Barzan (Charente-Maritime): Une première approche," in Bouet 2005: 31–44.

Conche, F., É. Plassot, and C. Pellecuer 2005. "Puiser, élever et distribuer l'eau dans la *villa de Careiron et Pesquier à Milhaud (Gard)*: Premiers commentaries," in Bouet 2005: 69–84.

Cotterell, B., and J. Kamminga 1990. *Mechanics of pre-industrial technology.* Cambridge: Cambridge University Press.

Coulton, J. J. 1974. "Lifting in early Greek architecture," *Journal of Hellenic Studies* 94: 1–19.

Crisman, K. 2005. "A horse-powered ferry: Burlington Bay, Lake Champlain," in G. F. Bass (ed.), *Beneath the seven seas.* New York: Thames and Hudson, 218–19.

Curtis, R. I. 2001, *Ancient food technology.* Leiden: Brill.

Dalley, S. 1994, "Nineveh, Babylon and the hanging gardens: Cuneiform and classical sources reconciled," *Iraq* 56: 45–58.

Dalley, S., and J. P. Oleson 2003. "Sennacherib, Archimedes, and the water screw: The context of invention in the ancient world." *Technology and Culture* 44: 1–26.

de Solla Price, D. 1974. "Gears from the Greeks: The Antikythera Mechanism, a calendar computer from ca. 80 B.C.," *Transactions of the American Philosophical Society* 64: 1–70.

Drachmann, A. G. 1936. "Heron's screwcutter," *Journal of Hellenic Studies* 56: 72–77.

Drachmann, A. G. 1948. *Ktesibios, Philon and Heron: A study in ancient pneumatics.* Copenhagen: Munksgaard.

Drachmann, A. G. 1956. "A note on ancient cranes," in C. Singer, E. J. Holmyard, A. R. Hall, and T. I. Williams (eds.), *A history of technology,* vol. 2. Oxford: Oxford University Press, 658–62.

Drachmann, A. G. 1963. *The mechanical technology of Greek and Roman antiquity: A study of the literary sources.* Copenhagen: Munksgaard.

Drachmann, A. G. 1973. "The crank in Graeco-Roman antiquity," in M. Teich and R. Young (eds.), *Changing perspectives in the history of science.* London: Heinemann, 33–51.

Faccenna, D. 2003. "I rilievi," in A. Campanelli and S. Agostini (eds.), *La Collezione Torlonia di antichità del Fucino.* Pescara: Carsa, 69–79.

Field, J. V., and M. T. Wright 1985. *Early gearing: Geared mechanisms in the ancient and medieval world.* London: Science Museum.

Fleury, P. 2005. "La pompe à pistons dans l'antiquité," in Bouet 2005: 139–51.

Frau, B. 1987. *Tecnologia greca e romana.* Pubblicazioni dei gruppi archeologici d'Italia Monografie 29). Rome: Gruppo archeologico romano.

Gille, B. 1980. *Les mécaniciens grecs: La naissance de la technologie.* Paris: Seuil.

Giuliani, C. F. 2003. "La rappresentazione degli argani," in A. Campanelli and S. Agostini (eds.), *La Collezione Torlonia di antichità del Fucino.* Pescara: Carsa, 81–82.

Guéry, R., and G. Hallier 1987. "Réflexions sur les ouvrages hydrauliques de Marseille antique retouvés sur le chantier de la Bourse," in A. De Réparaz (ed.), *L'eau et les hommes en Méditerranée.* Paris: CNRS, 265–82.

Hill, D. 1984. *A history of engineering in classical and medieval times.* London: Croom Helm.

Hodges, H. W. M. 1970. *Technology in the ancient world.* New York: Alfred A. Knopf.

Humphrey, J. H. 1986. *Roman circuses: Arenas for chariot racing.* Berkeley: University of California Press.

Humphrey, J. H., F. B. Sear, and M. Vickers 1972–1973. "Aspects of the circus at Lepcis Magna," *Libya antiqua* 9–10: 25–97.

Iriarte, A. 2000. "Pseudo-Heron's *Cheiroballistra,* a(nother) reconstruction: I. Theoretics," *Journal of Roman Military Equipment Studies* 11: 47–75.

Iriarte, A. 2003. "The inswinging theory," *Gladius* 23: 111–40.

Jackson, R. 1990. "Roman doctors and their instruments: Recent research into ancient practice," *Journal of Roman Archaeology* 3: 5–27.

Jacobi, H. 1912. "Römische Getriedemühlen," *Saalburg-Jahrbuch* 3: 75–95.

Jones, G. D. B. 1980. "Il Tavoliere romano: L'agricoltura romana attraverso l'aerofotografia e lo scavo," *Archeologia classica* 32: 85–100.

Landels, J. G. 2000. *Engineering in the ancient world.* Rev. ed. Berkeley: University of California Press.

Langouet, L., and J.-L. Meury 1976. "Les éléments de la machinerie gallo-romain d'Alet," *Les Dossiers du Centre régional archéologique d'Alet* 4: 113–25.

Lewis, M. J. T. 1985. "Review of D. Hill, *A history of engineering in classical and medieval times*," *Journal of Roman Studies* 75: 260–62.

Lewis, M. J. T. 1993. "Gearing in the ancient world," *Endeavour* 3: 110–15.

Lewis, M. J. T. 1997. *Millstone and hammer: The origins of water power.* Hull: University of Hull.

Lewis, M. J. T. 2000. "Theoretical hydraulics, automata and water clocks," in Wikander 2000a: 343–69.

Lewis, M. J. T. 2001a, "Railways in the Greek and Roman world," in A. Guy and J. Rees (eds.), *Early railways: A selection of papers from the First International Early Railways Conference.* London: Newcomen Society, 8–19.

Lewis, M. J. T. 2001b. *Surveying instruments of Greece and Rome.* Cambridge: Cambridge University Press.

Longfield-Jones, G. M. 1986. "A Graeco-Roman speculum in the Wellcome Museum," *Medical History* 30: 81–89.

Lucas, A. R. 2005. "Industrial milling in the ancient and medieval worlds: A survey of the evidence for an industrial revolution in Medieval Europe," *Technology and Culture* 46: 1–30.

Luquet, A. 1966. "Blé et meunerie à Volubilis," *Bulletin d'archéologie marocaine* 6: 301–16.

Marsden, E. W. 1969. *Greek and Roman artillery: Historical development.* Oxford: Oxford University Press.

Marsden, E. W. 1971. *Greek and Roman artillery: Technical treatises.* Oxford: Oxford University Press.

Mattingly, D. J. 1990. "Paintings, presses and perfume production at Pompeii," *Oxford Journal of Archaeology* 9.1: 71–90.

Mau, A. 1886. "Su certi apparecchi nei pistrini di Pompei," *Mitteilungen des Deutschen Archäologischen Instituts, Römische Abteilung* 1: 45–48.

Mayr, O. 1970a. *The origins of feedback control.* Cambridge, MA: MIT. Press.

Mayr, O. 1970b. "The origins of feedback control," *Scientific American* 223: 110–18.

Moritz, L. A. 1958. *Grain mills and flour in classical antiquity.* Oxford: Oxford University Press.

Morvillez, É., P. Chevalier, J. Mardesic, B. Pender, M. Topic, and M. Causevic 2005. "La noria découverte à proximité de 'L'oratoire A,' dans le quartier épiscopal de Salone (mission archéologique franco-croate de Salone)," in Bouet 2005: 153–69.

Needham, J., and W. Ling 1965. *Science and civilisation in China.* Vol. 4. Cambridge: Cambridge University Press.

Nicolle, D. 2003. *Medieval siege weapons (2): Byzantium, the Islamic World and India, AD 476–1526.* Oxford: Osprey Publishing.

Oleson, J. P. 1983. "A Roman sheave block from the harbour of Caesarea Maritima, Israel," *International Journal of Nautical Archaeology* 12: 155–70.

Oleson, J. P. 1984. *Greek and Roman mechanical water-lifting devices: The history of a technology.* Toronto: University of Toronto Press.

Oleson, J. P. 2000. "Water-lifting," in Wikander 2000a: 217–302.

Rakob, F. 1993. "Der Neufund einer römischen Turbinenmühle in Tunesien," *Antike Welt* 24.4: 286–87.

Rathbone, D. W. 1991. *Economic rationalism and rural society in third-century AD Egypt: The Heroninos Archive and the Appianus Estate*, Cambridge: Cambridge University Press.

Ritti, T., K. Grewe, and P. Kessner 2007. "A relief of a water-powered stone saw mill on a sarcophagus at Hierapolis and its implications," *Journal of Roman Archaeology* 20: 138–63.

Röder, J., and G. Röder 1993. "Die antike Turbinenmühle in Chemtou," in F. Rakob (ed.), *Simitthus*, vol. 1. Mainz: von Zabern, 95–102.

Schiøler, T. 1973. *Roman and Islamic water-lifting wheels*. Odense: Odense University Press.

Shaw, J. W. 1967. "A double-sheaved pulley block from Kenchreai," *Hesperia* 36: 389–401.

Skinner, F. G. 1954. "Measures and weights," in C. Singer, E. J. Holmyard, and A. R. Hall (eds.), *A history of technology*, vol. 1. Oxford: Oxford University Press, 774–84.

Stein, R. 2004. "Roman wooden force pumps: A case study in innovation," *Journal of Roman Archaeology* 17: 221–50.

Ucelli, G. 1950. *Le navi di Nemi*. Rome: Libreria dello Stato.

Varoqueaux, C., and J.-M. Gassend 2001. "La roue à aubes du grand bassin de la Bourse à Marseille," in J.-P. Brun, P. Jockey, M.-C. Amouretti (eds.), *Techniques et sociétés en Méditerranée*. Paris: Maison méditerranéenne des sciences de l'homme, 529–49.

Volpert, H.-P. 1997. "Die römischer Wassermühle einer villa rustica in München-Perlach," *Bayerische Vorgeschichtsblatter* 62: 243–78.

White, K. D. 1975. *Farm equipment of the Roman world*. Cambridge: Cambridge University Press.

Wikander, Ö. 1981. "The use of water-power in classical antiquity," *Opuscula romana* 13: 91–104.

Wikander, Ö. 1985. "Archaeological evidence for early water-mills—an interim report," *History of Technology* 10: 151–79.

Wikander, Ö. 1989. "Ausonius' saw-mills—once more," *Opuscula romana* 17: 185–90.

Wikander, Ö. (ed.) 2000a. *Handbook of ancient water technology*. Leiden: Brill.

Wikander, Ö. 2000b. "Industrial applications of water-power," in Wikander 2000a: 401–10.

Wikander, Ö. 2000c. "The water-mill," in Wikander 2000a: 371–400.

Wilkins, A. 1995. "Reconstructing the cheiroballistra," *Journal of Roman Military Equipment Studies* 6: 5–59.

Wilkins, A. 2000. "*Scorpio* and *cheiroballistra*," *Journal of Roman Military Equipment Studies* 11: 77–101.

Wilson, A. I. 1995. "Water-power in North Africa and the development of the horizontal water-wheel," *Journal of Roman Archaeology* 8: 499–510.

Wilson, A. I. 2001a. "Water-mills at Amida: Ammianus Marcellinus 18.8.11," *Classical Quarterly* 51.1: 231–36.

Wilson, A. I. 2001b. "The water-mills on the Janiculum," *Memoirs of the American Academy in Rome* 45: 219–46.

Wilson, A. I. 2002. "Machines, power and the ancient economy," *Journal of Roman Studies* 92: 1–32.

Wilson, A. I. 2003. "Classical water technology in the early Islamic world," in C. Bruun and A. Saastamoinen (eds.), *Technology, ideology, water: From Frontinus to the Renaissance and beyond*. Acta Instituti Romani Finlandiae 31: 115–41. Rome: Institutum Romanum Finlandiae.

# PART IV

# SECONDARY PROCESSES AND MANUFACTURING

# CHAPTER 14

## FOOD PROCESSING AND PREPARATION

### ROBERT I. CURTIS

THE Mediterranean Sea and surrounding lands provided the Greeks and Romans with a wide variety of foods, both plant and animal. Ancient agricultural writers, satirists, physicians, and "food specialists" record the types of foods consumed (André 1981; Humphrey et al. 1998: 147–71). Archaeological evidence of food resources, increasingly supported by their scientific examination, augments much of what ancient literary sources tell us. Also informative are modern studies that look at Greco-Roman food from different perspectives, such as food and politics and food in daily life. Food technology, however, apart from a few specialist studies, has rarely formed the object of serious investigation, usually receiving attention only as part of broader studies of agriculture or of ancient technology generally (e.g., Forbes 1955–1964; Moritz 1958; White 1984; Curtis 1991; Isager and Skydsgaard 1992). Not until 2001 did a comprehensive study of the subject appear (Curtis 2001), now complemented by Thurmond (2006).

Food technology, as the term applies today, is the practical application of the principles of science and technology to the preparation, processing, preservation, storage, packaging, and transportation of food. Although agriculture is closely allied to food processing, they are distinct activities. All actions associated with growing, tending, and harvesting produce fall clearly under agriculture. Some foods, such as grapes and olives, often receive further treatment after harvesting, and cereals are only selected for their various uses after they have been separated from the stalk through threshing. Food technology, therefore, begins at the point when these plant foods undergo specific processes to change their form in some way (such as milling grain into flour) or to so alter them as to create a different food product altogether (for instance, transforming the grape into wine). In other words, for the grape and olive the division between agriculture and food technology lies in the press room; for grain, it is on the threshing room floor. The care and feeding of animals belong to animal husbandry, as does the milking of cows, sheep, and goats. Producing butter, cheese, or yogurt from milk, however, falls into the realm of food processing. So also does butchery of animals preparatory to preservation of their meat. And, finally, methods and tools for catching fish are not part of food processing, but what one does to preserve the fish for later consumption clearly qualifies.

In antiquity, as today, foods fell broadly into two categories. First were those that could be eaten fresh as they came to hand. These included both wild and cultivated plants, such as fruits, nuts, and certain vegetables, and animal by-products, including milk and honey. Certain of these foods might, as necessary, require some preparation, such as washing, cutting, and cooking—be it roasting, boiling, baking, frying, and so forth—before consumption. The second group required more sophisticated processing to make them edible, processes so extensive as to result in significant changes in physical appearance or chemical composition from its original state. So, for instance, cereals, especially wheat and barley, in some places, like northern Europe, underwent extensive processing to convert the grain into a fermented beverage (beer), but Greeks and Romans more often ground them into flour to make porridge and, especially, to produce bread (figure 14.1). Neither the Greeks nor the Romans liked or produced beer, considering it much inferior to wine and the drinking of it a characteristic of barbarians, such as Thracians and the Celtic populations of Spain, northern Europe, and Britain. In the imperial period, Roman soldiers, especially those of Celtic background, stationed in northern Europe and Britain consumed it as part of their rations, and beer was apparently a major product traded in the northern provinces (Curtis 2001: 131–34, 370–71; Nelson 2001: 95–178; 2005: 9–65).

In a few instances, certain foods fell into both broad groups; that is, consumers had the choice of eating the item raw or cooked or of processing it to create a distinctly different product. These include the grape, which could be eaten fresh or dried (as raisins) or, after treading and pressing, consumed as a drink either directly in nonalcoholic form or fermented into wine. The olive could be eaten only after undergoing curing with salt water to remove its bitter taste but often underwent crushing and pressing to extract its oil (figure 14.2). These three agricultural products—cereals, grape, and olive—all requiring extensive processing before being consumed in their most popular form, were the most important staple foods in the classical diet and formed what is commonly called the Mediterranean Triad (Sarpaki 1992b; Isager and Skydsgaard 1992: 19–40). Certain animals or animal by-products also required processing before being eaten. This included butchery to reduce complete animals, such as pigs, cattle, and fish, into smaller pieces of meat that could be cooked or processed further in some fashion for later consumption and the processing of dairy products to produce butter and cheese.

Plants and animals underwent processing for several reasons. First, some foods in their natural state, such as olives, some legumes, and certain tubers, are inedible,

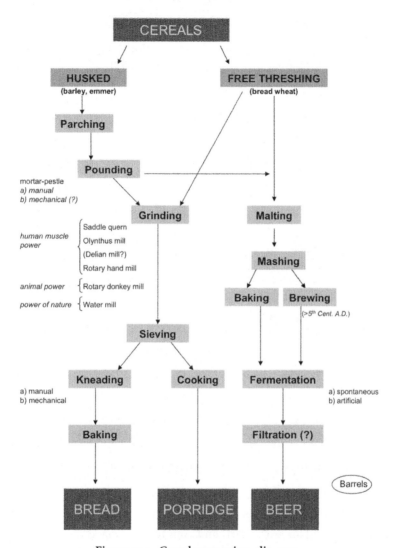

Figure 14.1.  Cereal processing, diagram.

indigestible, or even unsafe for human consumption. Second, some foods, although capable of being eaten in their natural state, were more popular in a completely different form. Bread from grain and wine from grapes have already received mention. Third, many foods in their primary state have a short shelf life and must be preserved in some fashion to extend their keeping potential. Such is the case with raisins from grapes, cheese from milk, and cured olives. And, finally, many foods received processing for social, economic, and political reasons. Not every level of Greco-Roman society had equal access to every kind of food. Furthermore, not all foods were available at all times of the year, nor were all foods available in every market throughout the Mediterranean basin. Additionally, recurrent food crises characterized life in classical antiquity. Farmers grew crops and raised livestock,

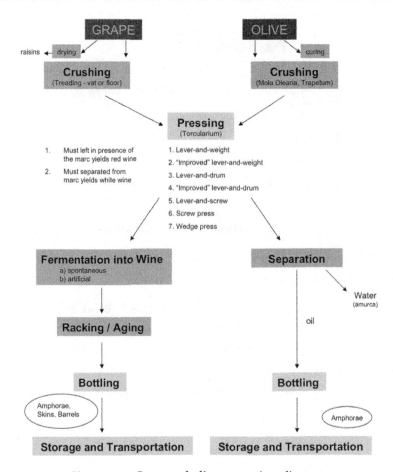

Figure 14.2. Grape and olive processing, diagram.

consuming some products, preserving others, and sending the surplus to local markets. The potential for both short- and long-term storage, therefore, was critical to ensure that some foods were available during periods of the year when others were not, and that a reserve was on hand to offset crop failures. On a larger scale, political motivations of the state and economic incentives of individuals or corporate entities also contributed to the decision to process food. Natural foods could travel short distances, but long-distance transportation, whether for reasons of state or private enterprise, required food in stable form.

Through the 1970s, a rather pessimistic picture of ancient technological advancement, best articulated by M. I. Finley, carried the day among historians (Finley 1959, 1965; cf. Reece 1969, Pleket 1973). This vision attributed factors inhibiting progress to the effects of slavery, a general contempt for labor, especially among the elite, a natural propensity to conservatism, and lack of adequate energy, raw materials, financial resources, and technical curiosity (Oleson 1984: 398–403; A. Wilson 2002: 2). Since the 1980s, however, this view has undergone significant revision. Innovation has replaced invention as a more important indicator of technological progress; the absence of an "ancient industrial revolution" no longer implies stagnation; and gradual improvements to machines and application of new technology create over time a range of choices, arrayed, as it were, on a "technological shelf" available for use depending on the economic resources of the user and the type and scale of the task envisioned (White 1984; Houston 1989; Greene 1990, 1993, 2000; A. Wilson 2002). This change in approach is seen particularly clearly in the area of ancient food processing, a field that even Finley recognized, at least in regard to bread-making, was an exception to his otherwise negative view of ancient technology (Finley 1959: 120; 1965). More recent studies of archaeological material, much of it available only since Finley's day, have shown this to be the case in other areas of food technology as well.

Ancient food technology does not lend itself well to discussion of its separate principles, since several technological applications are often relevant to a single product. So, for instance, grain milling could involve four distinctly different processes: parching or roasting, pounding, grinding, and sieving (figure 14.1). Wine production entails not only treading and pressing of grapes but also fermentation of the grape juice (figure 14.2). To concentrate on each activity or principle separately would, I believe, result in a loss of understanding of the whole, thereby giving a false impression of the technology itself. Consequently, a better approach is to focus on foods that required processing to distinguish what tools and machines Greeks and Romans used to process them, to determine what principles these tools reflect, and to evaluate their successes and failures.

# CEREAL PROCESSING

Cereals, principally barley and wheat, provided an estimated 70 to 75 percent of the calories in the classical diet (Foxhall and Forbes 1982: 74). Both required processing before consumption, but the degree varied according to the species. Husked cereals, such as barley and the glume wheats, emmer and einkorn, require special preparation beyond threshing before they yield their grain. This includes either pounding in a stone mortar with a wooden pestle or roasting or parching to render it brittle before pounding to release the kernel. This extra work explains the popularity, especially among Romans, of free-threshing cereals, such as durum and bread wheat, that release their grain with threshing alone. For these, once threshed and sieved, grinding proceeded directly. Regardless of the advantage of wheat, barley remained an important cereal for Greeks and Romans, since it grows more easily and has a higher yield under adverse conditions of decreased rainfall and increased heat. Consequently, the mortar and pestle, the basic pounding tools, served their purpose so well that they remained in use almost unchanged throughout antiquity, even while grinding methods underwent significant development (Moritz 1958:

xx–xxv; Foxhall and Forbes 1982: 75–81; Isager and Skydsgaard 1992: 21–23). The assertion that Pliny (*HN* 18.97) refers to a water-powered pestle acting in the manner of a trip hammer remains debatable (Lewis 1997: 101–5; Curtis 2001: 280).

Operation of the Neolithic saddle quern to grind grain involved moving a hand stone over a lower stone in a somewhat circular motion to separate off the chaff and to crush the endosperm. Exceedingly labor intensive, this method produces a meal that, once sieved, yields flour to make porridge or bread. Like the mortar and pestle, the saddle quern remained a basic home processing tool well into the Hellenistic period, undergoing only slight alteration. A thinner, flatter lower stone with striations cut into the grinding surface made it more portable and efficient, while a larger hand stone altered the grinding motion to a more back-and-forth, or reciprocal, pattern (Curtis 2001: 264, 280–81).

The first significant innovation in milling was the introduction of the hopper or Olynthus mill. Known in the Greek world by the late fifth century B.C., it spread rapidly into the western Mediterranean, especially Sicily and southern France (Curtis 2001: 282–87; Frankel 2003: 7–8) Developed from the saddle quern, the Olynthus mill consisted of rectangular-shaped lower and upper stones placed on an elevated platform. The upper stone had cut into it a hollow cavity, or hopper, at the bottom of which was a narrow slot through which the miller fed the grain. The miller crushed the grains falling between the upper and lower stones by moving the top stone in a reciprocal motion from side to side. He did this with a long handle attached in a groove on the upper stone and anchored at its short end either by a pivot or by insertion into a slot in a wall. The Olynthus mill, with moveable parts, was the first milling machine, although its motive power remained human (Moritz 1958: 42–52; Amouretti 1986: 140–42) Its operation approached that of modern mills in that it controlled its own feeding by means of the hopper and automatically discharged the processed meal by way of grooves cut into the milling surfaces of both stones.

Advantages of the hopper mill were twofold. First was its labor-saving benefit. The mill, placed on a flat, raised surface and operated by a fixed handle moved from side to side in wide sweeps, was ergonomically easier to operate by one person or two individuals working in unison. Second, the hopper mill increased production per unit of time expended and did so more efficiently. The handle not only increased the mechanical advantage and reduced the effort needed to grind the grain, but also allowed for use of a larger, heavier upper stone with wider grinding area, resulting in greater output of milled grain. Feeding kernels through the hopper meant that the miller did not have to stop as often to add more kernels. Overall, the result was greater output more rapidly achieved with less energy expended than could be done with the saddle quern. Increasing output through mechanical innovation (addition of handle and hopper) constituted a significant departure from the approach characteristic of the Near East, Egypt, and Bronze Age Greece that had sought higher output through increasing the number of workers using traditional technology (Sarpaki 1992a; Curtis 2001: 131, 201–2, 265) The hopper mill, however, had its limitations. It was less mobile than the saddle quern and lacked provisions for adjusting the gap between the stones and so for varying the fineness of the meal produced.

The application of rotary motion to milling was a landmark innovation in food processing technology. Although its use in olive processing almost certainly predated its employment in grain milling, rotary motion saw its greatest extension in cereal processing. How the idea developed is unknown, but it may have had its origins in observation of the potter's wheel and the development of iron tools that significantly increased the ability of stoneworkers to fashion round millstones (Moritz 1958: 103–21; Alonso Martinez 1997; Curtis 2001: 287–88, 336–41). Perhaps applied first to hand mills in Spain in the fifth century B.C., rotary milling spread from there into other parts of the western Mediterranean and northern Europe, probably by Roman soldiers, reaching Greece only in the first century B.C. (Runnels 1990). A fragmentary stone discovered in Carthage and identified as part of a round hand mill, however, may imply a specifically Carthaginian origin for hand-powered rotary mills, dating perhaps to the sixth century B.C. (Morel 2001). The earliest rotary grain mill in Greece was possibly the rather large third-century B.C. Delian mill whose operational design looked more to the *trapetum*, used to crush olives, than to other known rotary grain mills, human or animal powered. It seems to have been an evolutionary dead end, lacking both predecessors and descendants (Brunet 1997; Curtis 2001 288–89).

In its most developed form, the hand mill had a lower stone (*meta*) of slightly convex shape with a socket in its center to accommodate a wooden or iron spindle. On top of this sat the upper stone (*catillus*) whose bottom was slightly concave. This stone had a hole through its center and a rynd to accommodate the spindle of the *meta*, a shallow, flat-bottomed hopper at top center, and a hole, or metal band, at or near the periphery for placement of a vertically inserted wooden handle. The miller fed grain through the hopper and turned the handle of the *catillus* to grind the kernels as they fell between the two stones (cf. "Vergil," *Moretum* 16–29).

The advantages of the rotary hand mill over previous mills are fourfold. Smaller, portable like the saddle quern that it replaced, and probably cheaper than the hopper mill, the rotary hand mill was no doubt more readily available to people of all social and economic classes. Second, operation of the rotary hand mill from a sitting or standing position by grasping the handle with extended arm proved easier and more efficient than the equivalent operations for either the saddle quern or hopper mill. Third, the rynd-and-spindle arrangement permitted the miller to adjust the distance between the *meta* and *catillus*, thereby allowing production of meal of varying fineness, which, after one or more sievings, produced flour of varying grades. The advantages of the rotary hand mill probably account for the lack of spread of the Olynthus mill into Spain and northern Europe, and the rapid replacement of the latter by the former throughout the western Mediterranean generally. Finally, rotary motion, unlike reciprocal motion, allows for continuous action and ultimately permits the development of animal and water-driven devices.

It is not known what precipitated a shift in milling from the simple rotary hand mill with small stones to a mill of much larger size and capacity incorporated into a wooden frame and operated by animals, but a relationship with rotary mills used in Spanish lead and silver mines has been suggested (Domergue et al. 1997). Although perhaps ultimately of fourth-century B.C. Punic origin, the animal-driven rotary mill, termed "Pompeian mill" from the location of the best known examples, appeared in Italy a little over a century later. Its adoption in Italy may be associated with the rise of commercial bakeries at about the same time (Moritz 1958: 74–96; Curtis 2001: 341–48)

The Pompeian mill (figure 14.3), driven by two donkeys harnessed to a wooden frame attached to the mill, comprised the usual two parts, *meta* and *catillus*, both made of rough vesicular basalt. The former, with a rounded top cut to accommodate a spindle at its apex, was embedded in a rubble foundation. The monolithic *catillus* had the form of two cones stacked apex to apex, creating an hourglass shape. The interior of each cone was hollow, and a hole ran through the part where the apexes met to accommodate the spindle affixed in the top of the *meta*. The upper cone of the *catillus* served as a hopper while the lower cone fit over the *meta*. When rotated by animals, the exterior surface of the *meta* and the interior surface of the cone fitting over it ground the grain between them. After a period of operation, the grinding surfaces would rub smooth. At that point the *catillus* could be reversed to make the upper cone the grinding surface, thereby doubling its working life (Moritz 1958: 77).

The major advantage of the animal-driven rotary grain mill was that it released humans almost completely from the drudgery of the milling process. Since the animal performed the heavy work, the miller had only to feed grain into the hopper as necessary and collect, then sieve, the meal to produce the flour. In addition, since donkeys, with their greater stamina, could drive the mill for longer periods of time than a human, flour output increased significantly over what previous mills produced. Given the scale and expense of the Pompeian donkey mill, it is not surprising that most of them are found in the context of commercial bakeries (figures 14.3, 15.1). Nevertheless, in addition to the health and condition of the donkey, technological limitations restricted output. Inadequate harnessing of the animals may have not only shortened the amount of time the animal could work but also curbed the speed of the *catillus* in grinding the grain, thereby reducing the flour output from what would otherwise have been possible. The second-century novelist Apuleius provides a vivid picture of the poor conditions in milling establishments (*Met.* 7.15, 9.10–13).

The most dramatic advance in milling came with the application of water power, an event that even Finley called "radical." Seeing no evidence that its use was anything more than sporadic, however, he dismissed it as ultimately an opportunity lost (Finley 1965: 29). More recent studies on ancient water technology, however, have shown that in both scale and quantity water-powered grain mills played a much more important role in ancient cereal processing than previously thought (Leveau 1996; R. J. A. Wilson 1996; Wikander 2000: 371–410; Curtis 2001: 348–58; cf.

Figure 14.3. Pompeian donkey mills and oven (*furnus*) in bakery at Reg. VII.2.22. (Photograph: Sommer 1224).

chapters 6 and 13). Although the water mill may have arisen in the East, the earliest clear evidence of it comes from first-century A.D. Aventicum in Switzerland, where carbonized grains of barley, wheat, and other cereals found in the vicinity of a mill site indicate its use to process grain (Castella 1994; Lewis 1997: 58–61; Wikander 2000: 394–97, 644–45). The best preserved examples include the early-second-century A.D. vertical overshot water-mill complex at Barbegal in southern France and the undershot mills constructed during the following century in Rome on the Janiculum Hill (Moritz 1958: 122–39; A. Wilson 1995; Leveau 1996; Wikander 2000: 373–78). Vitruvius (*De arch.* 10.5.2) provides the only ancient technical description of a water-mill, in his case undershot. The number of identifiable water-mills dating between the first and third centuries A.D. clearly argues for its early integration into the Roman economy (figures 6.1–6.3). As of 2002, more than 60 water-mills had been identified from archaeological remains, and epigraphic sources record others that operated in the eastern Mediterranean (Leveau 1996; A. Wilson 2000, 2002: 9–15; Wikander 2000: 397–98). For a full discussion of water-mill design, see chapters 6 and 13.

The major breakthrough in milling technology derives from the use of water, a natural force, to operate the mill; the actual grinding continued to be accomplished through rotary motion applied to the upper millstone. The force of the water striking the paddle of the wheel either directly operated the spindle to drive the *catillus* (horizontal water-mill) or indirectly transferred that power "geared up" through a system of shafts and cogwheels to the spindle that turned the *catillus* at a faster speed (vertical water-mill). The advantages were immediately clear. First, water not only applied a stronger force than could be achieved by human or animal power and so allowed for use of much larger millstones, but also the "gearing-up" arrangement of vertical water-mills attained a higher rate of milling. Large millstones moving more rapidly significantly increased product output over that possible with either hopper mill or donkey mill. Second, although most mill buildings were small and utilized a single water wheel, the use of a stream, river, or aqueduct allowed for the placement of a series of mills along the water course, such as was done on the Janiculum Hill and at Barbegal. On one level, this method of increasing product output constitutes a reversal in conceptual thinking, as it parallels the eastern practice of merely increasing the number of saddle querns within a single location. What is different is the huge scale of production made possible through use of water power. And, third, as long as water flowed continuously and the mechanical parts of the mill did not break down, the miller could theoretically grind cereal indefinitely, although in practical terms this was impossible. Nevertheless, subject to wear on moving parts, time lost due to breakdowns and repairs, and interruptions of water or grain supply, the potential for labor savings and increased product output offered by water-mills greatly exceeded what was possible with human and animal-powered grain mills.

Water-mills were expensive to build and to operate and were subject to practical limitations on location. Nevertheless, the large number of water-mills now shown to have been operating between the first and seventh centuries A.D. in the western Mediterranean indicates that Romans recognized the economic potential of water-driven grain mills. It remains unclear who owned and financed their construction and operation, whether as small individual mills or mill complexes. Individuals or small corporations may have operated small mills, while large complexes, such as the 16-mill installation at Barbegal driven by water diverted from an aqueduct, may have had municipal or imperial ownership. So, for example, the Janiculum mills in Rome probably served the imperial *annona*.

Once milling was complete, the baker moved directly to produce bread, a process involving three steps: sieving the meal to obtain flour, kneading the flour with water to produce dough, and baking in an oven. Technological innovation attending these steps is important but less impressive than for milling. Sieving, for example, advanced little beyond improvement in quality of the mesh and so ability to improve the fineness of the flour (Moritz 1958: 151–94; Curtis 2001: 361–62). The major contribution to the technology of kneading was the Roman application of rotary motion to the development of a mechanical kneading machine for use in commercial establishments. Nowhere clearly described in literary sources (cf. Vitruvius. *De arch.* 10.5.2), a mechanical kneading machine may be represented in the sculpted relief of a bakery on the first-century B.C. tomb of Eurysaces, a professional baker and government contractor, in Rome, and archaeological remains have been discovered in Italy and Tripolitania (figure 2.2; Bakker 1999: 78; Drine 2001; Curtis 2001: 362–65). The one major innovation in baking was the development by Romans of large beehive ovens (figures 2.2, 14.3) for use in commercial bakeries that utilized animal-driven mills to process substantial amounts of flour to bake bread for sale or distribution to urban populations (Curtis 2001: 366–70). Animal and water-driven mills, the mechanical kneading machine, and large ovens allowed for a significant increase in the capacity to produce bread on a large scale.

# GRAPE AND OLIVE PROCESSING

Before the classical period, wine produced from grapes was an alcoholic beverage reserved for the wealthy, while oil from olives was used less as a food item than for producing expensive perfumes. By the fifth century B.C. wine became the basic drink for Greeks of all social levels, and oil served a number of purposes, including as a food. Although wine assumed a central place in Greek social life and played an important role in commerce in the classical and Hellenistic periods, oil, although produced abundantly in many local areas and perhaps exported regionally, was generally not the object of long-distance trade (Ault 1999; Jameson 2001; Lund 2004). During the Roman period, however, many areas, particularly Spain and North Africa, produced wine and oil on a large scale and actively engaged in long-distance trade to make these products available to markets throughout the Mediterranean (Chic Garcia 2000).

Although grapes are edible whether fresh or dried as raisins, the olive can only be eaten after curing the pulp through fermentation in salt water to remove the bitter taste caused by phenolic compounds. The primary form of consumption for both fruits, however, was a processed product, wine from the grape and oil from the olive. In each case, the fruit had to be crushed and then pressed. Following these two procedures, grapes underwent fermentation into wine, while workers separated oil from the liquid expressed from the olive pulp. Although the manner of crushing differed, the same kind of apparatus served to press both fruits. For this reason, distinguishing a winemaking installation from an olive oil–extraction emplacement can be difficult. Consequently, building on Drachmann's technical treatise on ancient oil mills and presses, many studies have focused on recognizing wine and oil installations, classifying the types of equipment utilized, tracing the development of the production apparatus, and determining the technological principles involved in their processing (Drachmann 1932; Amouretti 1986; Mattingly 1988; Frankel 1999; Brun 2003, 2004a, 2004b).

Crushing grapes, a simple and easy process requiring only human feet, remained unchanged throughout antiquity. Paintings, mosaics, and sculpted reliefs frequently represented scenes of individuals treading grapes in large containers such as terracotta *pithoi* or masonry vats. One sixth-century B.C. Attic black-figure amphora shows a satyr treading grapes in a basket sitting in a spouted trough placed on an incline, so the expressed must flowed into a nearby collecting vat (Curtis 2001: pl. 22). This scene may represent a method to keep the marc separate from the must in order to produce white wine. If so, it is the earliest clear evidence for the process used to make a white as opposed to a red wine, types clearly distinguished in Greco-Roman literary sources (Sparkes 1976).

Recognizing archaeological evidence for treading is difficult, since portable apparatuses are not likely to have survived, and permanent masonry treading vats can be difficult to identify as such. The fifth-century A. D. agricultural writer Palladius, in his description of a treading floor with a system of channels for conducting the must to tanks (*Agr.* 1.18), does not mention mechanical presses. It is unknown how common completely manual processing was, since most excavated wineries had a press room (*torcularium*). Those who could not afford a press no doubt availed themselves either of portable treading vats or, like Palladius, permanent treading floors, either cut in the rock or made of masonry. Such installations are difficult to connect with wine without some corroborating evidence. Although some wineries may have had a separate, portable treading apparatus, no longer extant, in most cases the press room, if the floor had a waterproof covering (*opus signinum*) that sloped toward a channel that led to a collection vessel, probably doubled as a place both to tread and to press grapes. Cato (*Agr.* 112.3) mentions this practice, and there is physical evidence for it at the second-century B.C. winery at Mirmekion in the Strait of Kerch on the Black Sea, as well as the first-century A.D. Roman press room in the Villa of the Mysteries at Pompeii (Curtis 2001: 302, 385–88; Brun 2003: 53–58; 2004a: 122–23). Workers could transfer the marc directly from the floor into the "frail" (pressing basket) for use with the press. The must from treading and from pressing ran directly into vats or similar containers.

The first step in the production of olive oil is crushing to reduce the fruit to a pulp. The earliest methods used a pestle to pound them in a rock-cut or free-standing stone mortar, a stone roller to mash them in a shallow basin, or wooden sandals worn on the feet to tread them (Curtis 2001: 381; Brun 2003: 146–49). For small-scale production, these techniques sufficed. When growing economic activity during the Hellenistic period, and particularly later during the Roman period, gave rise to large-scale production and long-distance trade, however, a radically new method was developed, the mechanical olive crusher. It remains unclear whether the rotary olive crusher originated in the Levant or Anatolia as early as the mid-eighth century B.C. and spread west (Frankel 1999: 75), or arose somewhat later on mainland Greece, the Greek islands, or Macedonia (Sagiv and Kloner 1996; Brun 1997). The Roman *trapetum*, the best known rotary olive crusher (figure 14.4), consisted of a stone receptacle (*mortarium*) having a concave inner surface and a central post (*miliarium*) at the top of which was fixed an iron pivot (*columella*). The pivot secured a horizontal wooden beam (*cupa*) that on each end penetrated through an upright crushing stone (*orbis*), a truncated sphere with the convex side facing out. Olives placed in the *mortarium* were crushed between its inner, concave surface and the outer, convex surface of the *orbes* when two workers pushed the horizontal beam, causing the stones to revolve on the pivot around the central post.

Figure 14.4.  Roman olive crusher (*trapetum*) from Boscoreale. (Photograph by R. Curtis.)

Although its operation is clear, many questions of detail remain unanswered. For instance, what distinguished the *trapetum*, described by Cato (*Agr.* 20–22), from the *mola olearia*, according to Varro (*Rust.* 1.55.5) virtually the same device but mentioned as a separate apparatus by Columella (*Rust.* 12.52.6–7)? Only three sculpted relief representations are known. Since Columella (*Rust.* 12.55.6) asserts that crushing the pit imparted a bitter taste to the oil, olive crushers must have been adjustable, but how was this accomplished (White 1975: 226–29; Frankel 1993; Tyree and Stefanoudaki 1996; Curtis 2001: 381–82; Brun 2004a: 8–9)?

Grapes and olives, although differing in many respects, share an essential step in their processing, pressing (figure 14.2). The scene of a lever-and-weight press painted on a sixth-century B.C. Attic black-figure skyphos provides a terminus ante quem for the earliest Greek use of a mechanical press (figure 14.5). One end of the beam was usually fixed into a wall that served as a fulcrum. The free end of the beam, when pulled down, crushed the fruit gathered up in a frail or wrapped in cloth and placed at the point below the beam that allowed the most pressure to be exerted. The use of a beam significantly increases the mechanical advantage in applying force to the fruit over that possible by treading alone. This increased efficiency and achieved greater output, while reducing the labor required (Foxhall 1993; Curtis 2001: 227–33).

The principle of the lever remained a constant in press construction until the invention of the direct screw press in the first century A. D. Technological innovation in beam presses followed two lines of development: improvements in the method of pulling the beam down to crush the fruit and in the mode of anchoring the rear end of the beam. As shown in the vase painting cited above (figure 14.5), use of a large stone or bag of stones was the simplest method. The difficulty in manipulating a single large stone may have made a bag more common for small

Figure 14.5. Lever-and-weight press. Attic black-figure skyphos, ca. 520–510 B.C. Museum of Fine Arts, Boston, Henry Lillie Pierce Fund, inv. No. 99-525. (Courtesy of the Museum of Fine Arts.)

enterprises. The amount of force applied by the beam was directly related to the weight of the attached stones. To increase the pressure, as engagingly shown on the skyphos, humans could also apply additional force to the beam. Later, stones shaped and cut to permit easy attachment of a rope allowed for increased weight. The first development to the lever-and-weight press was the addition of a winch, operated with a rope attached to the beam and wrapped around a drum that could be turned by means of handspikes. As the drum rotated, the rope wrapped more tightly around it and, so, pulled the beam down. This obviated the need for direct muscle power to assist the weights. It is a short step from this to the lever-and-drum press without weights. The drum was secured beneath the free end of the beam by two wooden uprights (*stipites*) anchored in the ground. The second development to the lever press altered the manner by which the rear end of the beam was fixed. Rather than anchoring the rear of the beam (*prelum*) in a wall, such as is found in Halieis in the Argolid and Praesos on Crete, of the late fourth and third centuries B. C., respectively, by the second century B. C. it was inserted into a single wooden upright (*arbor*), or slotted pier, or between two wooden uprights firmly seated in the ground, in a manner not entirely clear, so as to offset any upward thrust caused by the winch drawing the beam down onto the fruit. This arrangement, typified by the lever-and-drum press described by Cato (*Agr.* 18–19), may have had an origin in the Hellenistic Levant (Frankel 2001). North African versions of this development utilized large, heavy upright stone *arbores* with a drum attached to a counterweight operating the beam. In both cases, the beam could be adjusted in the *arbores* to allow for the compression of the frail containing the fruit (Drachmann 1932: 50–55; Mattingly 1988; Sagiv and Kloner 1996; Curtis 2001: 307–11, 382–90; Jameson 2001: 283–84; Brun 2003: 58–60).

The second major innovation in pressing technology was the application of the screw. This improvement was made possible by the invention of the screw and screw nut, or female screw, by Hellenistic scientists in the third century B.C. (Kiechele 1967; Drachmann 1968). It appeared in practical use in Greece by the first century B. C., either as an assist to the drum of the lever-and-drum press or as the principal method of drawing down the beam. By the mid-first century A.D., the beam was being discarded altogether in favor of the screw alone (Pliny, *HN* 18.317). The purpose of the screw was to extract even more juice from the grape or olive, even if that meant increasing the bitter liquid from the skins that lowered its quality (Drachmann 1932: 55–59, 69–82, 96–99; White 1975: 230–32; Curtis 2001: 390–93; Lawton 2004: 15–21; Brun 2003: 60–63; 2004b: 48–49).

Pressed oil flowed out of the frail onto a circular stone press bed etched with a groove that conducted the liquid to a spout where it emptied into a vat or other container. In the absence of evidence for an oil crusher, this spouted stone bed constitutes the clearest indication of an oil installation. One other construction that can serve to identify an oil installation leads us to the final step in olive oil production, separation. Since oil and water do not mix, the usual way to separate the two is to skim the oil off the top of an oil/water mix with a ladle and to transfer it to another vessel. Workers at Hellenistic Praesos apparently used a more efficient two-handled jar with a spout at the bottom, not unlike Bronze-Age terracotta tubs found on Crete. The purpose of this Minoan artifact remains uncertain. Suggestions include oil separation, grape treading, or even activities not connected with food preparation (Curtis 2001: 269–70). Once filled, the worker unplugged the spout, drained the water, and then plugged it again to retain the oil. Romans also used ladles, a labor-intensive and time consuming method when working with large amounts of liquid obtained with the mechanical press (Cato, *Agr.* 66; Columella, *Rust.* 12.52.8–12). Although archaeologists in Italy, Sicily, North Africa, and elsewhere have uncovered sites at which a series of vats was used to separate oil from water and other waste material (*amurca*), either by the principle of overflow or of underflow (the principle at work in the spouted jars at Praesos) or a combination of both, in classical antiquity skimming remained the most widespread method of oil separation (Frankel 1999: 174–76; Curtis 2001: 269–72, 393–94; Brun 2003: 156–58; Brun 2004a: 114–15; Brun 2004b: 38–42). Wine and oil installations used similar presses, although not the same press, as one product would taint the other and, for wine production, necessitate the additional step of separation.

Following pressing, grape must (*mustum*) was set aside for various uses, including processing into different nonalcoholic beverages, but the greatest portion underwent fermentation into wine (Brun 2003: 63–83). No significant advancement can be discerned in the fermentation or aging processes over methods used in earlier periods, nor is there any evidence that Greeks or Romans knew distilled spirits as a drink distinct from wine. Aristotle (*Mete.* 2.3) discusses distillation, but does so in the context of experimentation in the evaporation of wine and the condensation of what he viewed only as water with a specific taste. Finally, although Greeks and Romans employed ice or snow to cool wine, and the Romans even had shops reserved specifically for storing snow (Seneca, *Ep.* 78.23), neither society developed the use of ice or snow into a method of long-term food preservation (Curtis 2001: 254–55, 419)

# VEGETABLES, FRUITS, AND NUTS

Greeks and Romans consumed many vegetables, fruits, and nuts, and, in the case of the first two, preserved them by various methods for short- and long-term storage. Legumes, and certain fruits such as apples, figs, dates, cherries, and grapes, were dried. Fruits, olives, herbs, onions, and leafy vegetables were often pickled in brine or vinegar, while other plant foods, such as apples, peaches, quinces, and roots, were preserved in a variety of liquids, such as wine, grape juice (*defrutum*), and honey. Dehydration, fermentation, pickling, and preservation in various liquids were conservation methods practiced well before the classical period and show little or no technological improvement; they are mentioned as routine procedures by ancient authors (e.g., Apicius 1.12.1–11; Cato, *Agr.* 116; Varro, *Rust.* 1.58–59; Columella, *Rust.* 12; Pliny, *HN* 15.59–67, 102–4; see also André 1981: 45–48, 86–91; Thurmond 2006: 165–87). The techniques of food processing could affect the dietary quality of plant foods for better or worse (Stahl 1989).

# ANIMAL BY-PRODUCTS

The classical diet included fish and various wild and domesticated fowl and meat animals, including cattle, pigs, sheep, and goats. Butchery is a basic process requiring a variety of simple tools, some that are heavy and sturdy for breaking bones, and others that are sharp for cutting through muscle and tendons. Little is known of butchery tools in the Greek Bronze Age, and much of what we know of butchery in the classical and Hellenistic periods centers on butchery for ritual purposes. For the Roman period, archaeological material and sculpted reliefs, such as the tomb relief showing a butcher holding a cleaver and standing next to a rack of meat in a butcher shop, or the funerary altar of Atimetus that shows a cabinet filled with variously shaped knives and cleavers offered for sale (Zimmer 1982: 93–106, 180–84), illustrate the types of instruments used to butcher animals. A quick comparison of butchery tools used during the Greco-Roman period with those from earlier periods, however, shows no marked improvement beyond changes in the material making up the tool and in the variety of shapes and sizes. Indeed, butchers today use almost identical tools to cut up meat as did the Greeks and Romans—with the exception of electric saws (Isager and Skydsgaard 1992: 66; Curtis 2001: 313–14, 395–99).

Once butchered, meat, particularly from cattle and pigs, underwent preservation by various methods: drying, smoking, pickling, preserving in honey, or a combination of these methods. Most meat, however, was preserved with salt. Literary sources frequently refer to salted pork, probably the most popular meat, preserved as sausages or specific cuts, either deboned and filleted or with the bone, particularly hams and the head (*sinciput*) (e.g., Cato, *Agr.* 162; Columella, *Rust.* 12.55.1–4). A first-century B.C. shipwreck off Provençe yielded bones of a boar's head apparently bisected and possibly salted for long-distance transport, and ham bones are frequently found on Roman wrecks in conditions favoring the preservation of organic remains (Tchernia et al. 1986: 231–56; Frost 1999: 241–52; Leguilloux 2001: 411–14; Curtis 2001: 396–99; MacKinnon 2004: 173–75, 184–86.).

Animals maintained on farms and villas provided various food by-products, such as milk from cattle, sheep, and goats. Milk, because it spoils quickly, often underwent processing to produce cheese, a longer-lasting food item. Finds of bronze cheese graters in Lefkandi in Euboea indirectly affirm the knowledge of hard cheeses as early as the ninth century B.C. Greek literary sources of the classical period mention many types of local and imported cheeses, including fresh and cream cheeses and hard cheeses that could be crushed, grated, and sliced. None, however, describes the production in more detail than the comment by Aristotle (*Hist. an.* 522a22–b6) that milk could be curdled by fig juice or rennet. Roman agricultural writers, on the other hand, provide specific detail on cheese production. The three-stage process they describe no doubt paralleled the Greek method and differs little in its essentials from cheesemaking today: curdling by warming and the addition of rennet, separating the liquid whey from the curds, which were pressed and salted, and ripening. The value of cheese, especially hard cheese, was its extended shelf life and consequent marketability as an item of long-distance trade (Curtis 2001: 315–16, 400–2).

Two other animal by-products received attention from the Greeks and Romans, but their production required little or no processing. Butter, produced by shaking warm milk, was considered primarily a fatty substance similar to oil and was used more as an additive for medicine than as a food. Columella (*Rust.* 9.15.12–13) explains the procedure for gathering and pressing honeycombs to extract the honey, the most important sweetener available to the classical cultures (Curtis 2001: 399–400, 417–19).

Although Greeks and Romans consumed fresh fish when and where available, they most often processed fish meat into dried, smoked, or salted form (*salsamentum*). Fish innards and small whole fish went into producing fish sauces, especially *garum*, used as a condiment. Columella (*Rust.* 12.55.4) indicates that processing salt fish paralleled the method used to salt pork. Indeed, sheep and cattle bones excavated from fish-salting vats in Kerobestin and Telgruc on the Atlantic coast of Gaul imply that salting of meat in the off season kept fish-salting installations active year round. Fish preservation involved placing alternate layers of fish meat and salt in a container until reaching the top. Added weights applied pressure on the mass and facilitated the expression of the moisture from the fish meat and its replacement through osmosis with salt. The species of fish used and time allowed for the process determined the shelf life of the final product. In the second century Athenaeus, in his *Deipnosophistae* ("Sophists at the Dinner Table"), records names for varieties of salted fish products that betray specific details of the production process. So, for example, certain terms indicate that salt-fish were cut into various shapes and preserved fully or partially salted with or without scales. Certain parts of the fish, such as the dorsal part or stomach, were particularly selected for preservation (Curtis 1991: 6–15; 2001: 397). Although numerous variables came into play in producing fish sauce, the basic process involved mixing salt in a container of small fish or fish innards in a specified ratio. This mixture, covered and allowed to sit in the sun for a period of time up to three months with occasional stirring, underwent autolysis, during which most of the fish material dissolved, creating a top layer of liquid (*garum*) and a bottom layer of undissolved fish matter (*allec*). This production method parallels almost exactly the process for producing modern fish sauces, such as Vietnamese *nuoc-mam* (Curtis 1991: 15–26, 191–94).

Recognizing ancient drying and smoking facilities today is nearly impossible, but large-scale salting establishments have left considerable remains (figure 14.6). Greeks imported salt-fish products from the Black Sea and from the western Mediterranean, particularly Punic areas of Sicily and Spain, a source confirmed by salt-fish pieces adhering to Punic amphoras found in the fifth-century B.C. "Punic Amphora Building" at Corinth (Curtis 1991: 115). Archaeologists have uncovered Punic salteries that operated at the same time or a little later in the area of Cadiz. The best evidence for processed fish, however, comes from excavations of Roman salteries in the western Mediterranean in Spain, Portugal, North Africa, and the Atlantic coast of France, and in the eastern Mediterranean in the northern Black Sea areas of the Strait of Kerch and Chersonese, all of which date primarily between the first century B. C. and the fourth century A. D. (Ponsich 1988; Curtis 1991; Étienne et al. 1994; Étienne and Mayet 2002; Højte 2005; Trakadas 2005). A comparison of salting apparatuses at all of these Roman sites with earlier Punic installations indicates that methods of salting fish remained practically unchanged over this time period. There was, however, a significant increase in the volume of production and trade in these products. Studies of salt-fish amphoras found in shipwrecks or at inland sites are yielding a clearer picture of the importance of this processed food to specific areas and to the Roman economy generally (Curtis 1991; Chic Garcia 2000; Martin-Kilcher 2003).

Food technology during the Greco-Roman period achieved significant advances in some areas, small incremental improvements in others, and remained stagnant in a few. Milling of cereals saw the greatest strides. The first mechanical application to milling, the Greek hopper mill, permitted automatic feeding of grain between millstones, an innovation that characterized all subsequent mills. Most important was the employment of rotary motion to drive the millstones. Knowledge of this

Figure 14.6. Roman fish-salting vats from Baelo, Spain. (Photograph by B. Lowe.)

principle brought new inventions, such as the rotary hand mill, the animal-driven mill, and, most impressive, the water-mill. Additionally, knowledge of rotary motion led to the invention of the mechanical kneading machine and the *trapetum* to crush olives. Except in one instance, advances in grain storage during the Greco-Roman period differed from earlier periods primarily in quantity and scale rather than in principles applied. The one exception is the employment of subfloor ventilation for large, aboveground buildings, providing cool, dry, dark storage for "clean" grain awaiting milling (Curtis 2001: 276–79, 325–35; figure 7.5). Incremental improvements appeared in pressing technology as new ways were developed to increase efficiency of the press beam, first by weights, then with a winch, and finally through use of screw technology. Other aspects of food technology, however, saw little or no improvement over earlier periods. In this category must be listed butchery, fermentation and distillation of alcoholic beverages, and refrigeration.

Innovation and invention in Greco-Roman food processing tended in two directions. The first trend led to more efficient, labor-saving machines requiring fewer operators per unit of output. Unlike earlier cultures where augmented capacity came from iteration of basic tools, Greeks and Romans turned to larger size and improved functional efficiency. Most new or improved apparatuses were directed toward commercial production and consequently tended toward machines bigger, more technically sophisticated, and costlier than the simpler forms prevailing beforehand. Chief among innovations illustrating this theme was the development of four distinct types of grain mill (hopper mill, rotary hand mill, animal mill, and water-mill), and of four basic olive and grape presses (wedge, lever-and-drum, lever-and-screw, and direct screw presses) with intermediary forms. Because of its low production output, the wedge press, possibly used in perfumeries in Hellenistic Delos and first-century A.D. Paestum and illustrated in four paintings found in Pompeii and Herculaneum, was probably used only to press olives for particularly refined oil used for making perfume. It most likely represents a dead-end technology in that the faulty structural design of its wooden frame inadequately controlled the thrusts caused by pounding in the wedges (White 1975: 232; Mattingly 1990; Brun 2000: 282–302). Although the concept of improved workplace comfort may have played no role in labor savings, it often was an unintended consequence of innovation in both milling and pressing technology.

The second trend in Greco-Roman food processing brought increased availability of food to a larger number of consumers and contributed to economic growth. Increasing populations, growing foreign markets, and heightened governmental concerns for food shortages and the political and social unrest potentially arising from them, particularly during the Roman period, constituted primary incentives to increase production capacity and long-distance trade. The presence of animal-driven mills, water-mills, olive and grape presses, and large-scale fish-salting installations implies significant capital investment to increase surplus so as to satisfy immediate needs, to establish a reserve, and to maximize profits (A. Wilson 2002). Consequently, new technologies led to enlarged food resources for consumers and to fresh employment opportunities for workers involved at various stages along the route from point of processing, to loading and offloading conveyances, to transportation by land and sea, and to sale in the market.

Yet, with all this innovation, the Greco-Roman period displayed a persistent conservatism. The implements for butchery showed no marked improvement, nor did the processing of husked cereals improve beyond mortar and pestle. This apparent stagnation most likely resulted not from any lack of imagination but from recognition that the technology had already achieved a level of efficiency sufficient for its purpose. Most revealing in this respect, however, is the contemporaneous availability of simple tools for food processing alongside new, more efficient apparatuses. In the early fourth century A.D., for example, the Edict of Diocletian simultaneously listed maximum prices for hand mills, animal mills, and water-mills in a veritable "technology shelf" from which to choose (*Edictum Diocletianum* 15.54). The consumer had the option to select which technology best suited his needs and available resources.

Invention and innovation in food technology brought significant benefits to inhabitants of the Greco-Roman world. First, increased production, larger storage capacity, and longer shelf life augmented food supply and provided greater access to foods year round, especially in times of want. Second, transportability of food preserved in a form more stable than in its natural state provided better access to food in greater variety to a larger number of people over a wider geographic area. Finally, in addition to providing more food at a higher quality and in greater variety than was necessary for survival, food processing, particularly in the form of alcoholic beverages such as wine and beer, increased the enjoyment of life. Although the

Greco-Roman period may not have seen an industrial revolution, the technology necessary to create machines operated first by human power, then by animals, and finally by water power to achieve greater output more efficiently with fewer workers cannot be called stagnant.

# REFERENCES

Alonso Martínez, N. 1997. "Origen y expansion molino rotativo bajo en el Mediterráneo occidental," in Meeks and Garcia 1997: 15–19.

Amouretti, M.-C. 1986. *Le pain et l'huile dans la Grèce antique.* Paris: Les Belles lettres.

Amouretti, M.-C., and J.-P. Brun (eds.) 1993. *La production du vin et de l'huile en Méditerranée. Bulletin de Correspondance Hellénique* Suppl. 26. Paris: École Française d'Athénes.

André, J. 1981. *L'alimentation et la cuisine à Rome,* 2nd ed. Paris: Les Belles Lettres.

Ault, B. A. 1999. "*Koprones* and oil presses at Halieis: Interactions of town and country and the integration of domestic and regional economies," *Hesperia* 68: 549–73.

Bakker, J. T. 1999. *The mills-bakeries of Ostia: Description and interpretation.* Amsterdam: J. C. Gieben.

Bekker-Nielsen, T. (ed.) 2005. *Ancient fishing and fish processing in the Black Sea region.* Aarhus: University of Aarhus,

Brun, J.-P. 1997. "L'introduction des moulins dans les huileries antiques," in Meeks and Garcia 1997: 69–78.

Brun, J-P. 2000. "The production of perfumes in antiquity: The cases of Delos and Paestum," *American Journal of Archaeology* 104: 277–308.

Brun, J.-P. 2003. *Le vin et l'huile dans la méditerranée antique: Viticulture, oléiculture et procédés de transformation.* Paris: Editions Errance.

Brun, J.-P. 2004a. *Archéologie du vin et de l'huile de la préhistoire à l'époque hellénistique.* Paris: Editions Errance.

Brun, J.-P. 2004b. *Archéologie du vin et de l'huile dans l'Empire romain.* Paris: Editions Errance.

Brun, J.-P., and P. Jockey (eds.) 2001. *Technai: Techniques et sociétés en Méditerranée.* Paris: Maisonneuve et Larose.

Brunet, M. 1997. "Le Moulin Délien," in Meeks and Garcia 1997: 29–38.

Castella, D. 1994. *Le moulin hydraulique gallo-romain d'Avenche "en Chaplix."* Aventicum VI. Lausanne: Cahiers d'archéologia romande.

Chic Garcia, G. (ed.). 2000. *Congreso Internacional Ex Baetica Amphorae: Conservas, aceite y vino de la Bética en el Imperio Romano.* Sevilla-Ecija, 17 al 20 diciembre de 1998. 4 vols. Ecija: Editorial Graficas Sol.

Curtis, R. I. 1991. *Garum and salsamenta: Production and commerce in materia medica.* Leiden: Brill.

Curtis, R. I. 2001. *Ancient food technology.* Leiden: Brill.

Domergue, C., D. Béziat, B. Cauuet, C. Jarrier, C. Landes, J.-G. Morasz, P. Oliva, R. Pulou, and F. Tollon 1997. "Les moulins rotatifs dans les mines et les centres métallurgiques antiques," in Meeks and Garcia 1997: 48–61.

Drachmann, A. G. 1932. *Ancient oil mills and presses.* Copenhagen: Levin and Munksgaard.

Drachmann, A. G. 1968. "The screw of Archimedes," in *Actes du VIIIe Congrès International d'Histoire des Sciences, Florence-Milan 1956.* Florence/Paris: 1968, 3:940–43.

Drine, A. 2001. "Meules à grain et pétrins autour du lac El Bibèn et à Gigthi," in Brun and Jockey 2001: 251–60.

Étienne, R., M. Yasmine, and F. Mayet 1994. *Un grand complexe industriel à Tróia (Portugal).* Paris: de Boccard.

Étienne, R., and F. Mayet 2002. *Salaisons et sauces de poisson hispaniques.* Paris: de Boccard.

Finley, M. I. 1959. "Technology in the ancient world," *Economic History Review* 12: 120–25.

Finley, M. I. 1965. "Technical innovation and economic progress in the ancient world," *Economic History Review* 18: 29–45.

Forbes, R. J. 1955–1964. *Studies in ancient technology.* 9 vols. Leiden: Brill.

Foxhall, L. 1993. "Oil extraction and processing equipment in classical Greece," in Amouretti and Brun 1993: 183–200.

Foxhall, L., and H. A. Forbes 1982. "*Sitometreia*: The role of grain as a staple food in classical antiquity," *Chiron* 12: 41–90.

Frankel, R. 1993. "The *Trapetum* and the *Mola Olearia*," in Amouretti and Brun 1993: 477–80.

Frankel, R. 1999. *Wine and oil production in antiquity in Israel and other Mediterranean countries.* Sheffield: Sheffield Academic Press.

Frankel, R. 2001. "Cato's Press a Reapraisal [*sic*]," in Brun and Jockey 2001: 313–25.

Frankel, R. 2003. "The Olynthus mill, its origin, and diffusion: Typology and distribution," *American Journal of Archaeology* 107: 1–21.

Frost, F. 1999. "Sausage and meat preservation in antiquity," *Greek, Roman and Byzantine Studies* 40: 241–52.

Greene, K. 1990. "Perspectives on Roman technology," *Oxford Journal of Archaeology* 9: 209–19.

Greene, K. 1993. "The study of Roman technology: Some theoretical constraints," in *Theoretical Roman Archaeology: First Conference Proceedings.* Aldershot: Avebury, 39–47.

Greene, K. 2000. "Technological innovation and economic progress in the ancient world: M. I. Finley re-considered," *Economic History Review* 53: 29–59.

Højte, J. M. 2005. "The archaeological evidence for fish processing in the Black Sea region," in Bekker-Nielsen 2005: 133–60.

Houston, G. W. 1989. "The state of the art: Current work in the technology of ancient Rome," *Classical Journal* 85: 63–80.

Humphrey, J. W., J. P. Oleson, and A. N. Sherwood 1998. *Greek and Roman technology: A sourcebook.* London: Routledge.

Isager, S., and J. E. Skydsgaard 1992. *Ancient Greek agriculture: An introduction.* London: Routledge.

Jameson, M. H. 2001. "Oil presses of the late classical/Hellenistic period," in Brun and Jockey 2001: 281–99.

Kiechle, F. 1967. "Zur Verwendung der Schraube in der Antike," *Technikgeschichte* 34: 14–22.

Lawton, B. 2004. *The early history of mechanical engineering.* 2 vols. Leiden: Brill.

Leguilloux, M. 2001. "La boucherie et l'artisanat de sous-produits animaux en Gaule romaine," in Brun and Jockey 2001: 411–21.

Leveau, P. 1996. "The Barbegal water mill in its environment: Archaeology and the economic and social history of antiquity," *Journal of Roman Archaeology* 9: 137–53.

Lewis, M. J. T. 1997. *Millstone and hammer: The origins of water power.* Hull: University of Hull.

Lund, J. 2004. "Oil on the waters? Reflections on the contents of Hellenistic transport amphorae from the Aegean," in J. Eiring and J. Lund (eds.), *Transport amphorae and trade in the eastern Mediterranean*. Acts of the International Colloquium at the Danish Institute at Athens, September 26–29, 2002. Athens: Aarhus Universitetsforlag, 211–16.

MacKinnon, M. 2004. *Production and consumption of animals in Roman Italy: Integrating the zooarchaeological and textual evidence. Journal of Roman Archaeology* Suppl. 54. Portsmouth, RI: JRA.

Martin-Kilcher, S. 2003. "Fish-sauce amphorae from the Iberian peninsula: The forms and observations on trade with the north-west provinces," *Journal of Roman Pottery Studies*. 10: 69–84.

Mattingly, D. J. 1988. "Megalithic madness and measurement—Or, how many olives could an olive press press?" *Oxford Journal of Archaeology* 7: 177–95.

Mattingly, D. J. 1990. "Paintings, presses and perfume production at Pompeii," *Oxford Journal of Archaeology* 9: 71–90.

Meeks, D., and D. Garcia (eds.) 1997. *Techniques et économie antiques et médiévales: Le temps de l'innovation*. Colloque international (C.N.R.S.) Aix-en-Provence 21–23 mai 1996. Paris: Editions Errance.

Morel, J.-P. 2001. "Aux origines du moulin rotatif? Une meule circulaire de la fin du VIe siècle avant notre ére à Carthage," in Brun and Jockey 2001: 241–50.

Moritz, L. A. 1958. *Grain-mills and flour in classical antiquity*. Oxford: the Clarendon Press.

Nelson, M. 2001. "Beer in Greco-Roman antiquity." Ph.D. diss., University of British Columbia.

Nelson, M. 2005. *The barbarian's beverage: A history of beer in ancient Europe*. London: Routledge.

Oleson, J. P. 1984. *Greek and Roman mechanical water-lifting devices: The history of a technology*. Toronto: University of Toronto Press.

Pleket, H. W. 1973. "Technology in the Greco-Roman world: A general report," *Talanta* 5: 6–47.

Ponsich, M. 1988. *Aceite de oliva y salazones de pescado: Factores geo-economicos de Betica y Tingitania*. Madrid: Universidad Complutense.

Reece, D. W. 1969. "The technical weakness of the ancient world," *Greece andRome* 16.1: 32–47.

Runnels, C. 1990. "Rotary querns in Greece," *Journal of Roman Archaeology* 3: 147–54.

Sagiv, N., and A. Kloner 1996. "Maresha: Underground olive oil production in the Hellenistic period," in D. Eitam and M. Heltzer (eds.), *Olive oil in antiquity*. Padua: Sargon, 255–92.

Sarpaki, A. 1992a. "A palaeoethnobotanical study of the West House, Akrotiri, Thera," *Annual of the British School at Athens* 87: 219–30.

Sarpaki, A. 1992b. "The palaeoethnobotanical approach: The Mediterranean triad or is it a quartet?" in B. Wells (ed.), *Agriculture in ancient Greece*. Proceedings of the Seventh International Symposium at the Swedish Institute at Athens, 16–17 May 1990. Stockholm: Aströms, 61–76.

Sparkes, B. A. 1976. "Treading the grapes," *Bulletin Antieke Beschaving* 51: 47–56.

Stahl, A. B. 1989. "Plant-food processing: Implications for dietary quality," in D. R. Harris and G. C. Hillman (eds.), *Foraging and farming: The evolution of plant exploitation*. London: Unwin Hyman, 171–94.

Tchernia, A., M. Girard, and F. Poplin, 1986. "Pollens et ossements animaux de l'épave romaine 3 de Planier (Provence)," in *La mer comme lieu d'échanges et de communication*. Vol. 2 of *L'exploitation de la mer de l'antiquité a nos jours*. VIémes rencontres internationales d'archéologie et d'histoire d'Antibes. Valbonne: Association pour la Promotion et la Diffusion des Connaissances Archéologiques, 231–56.

Thurmond, D. L. 2006. *A Handbook of food processing in classical Rome: For her bounty no winter*. Leiden: Brill.

Trakadas, A. 2005. "The archaeological evidence for fish processing in the western Mediterranean," in Bekker-Nielsen 2005: 47–82.

Tyree, E. L., and E. Stefanoudaki 1996. "The olive pit and Roman oil making," *Biblical Archaeologist* 59: 171–78.

White, K. D. 1975. *Farm equipment of the Roman world*. Cambridge: Cambridge University Press.

White, K. D. 1984. *Greek and Roman technology*. Ithaca, NY: Cornell University Press.

Wikander, Ö. 2000. *Handbook of ancient water technology*. Leiden: Brill.

Wilson, A. 1995. "Water-power in North Africa and the development of the horizontal water-wheel," *Journal of Roman Archaeology* 8: 499–510.

Wilson, A. 2000. "The water-mills on the Janiculum," *Memoirs of the American Academy in Rome* 45: 219–46.

Wilson, A. 2002. "Machines, power and the ancient economy," *Journal of Roman Studies* 92: 1–32.

Wilson, R. J. A. 1996. "*Tot aquarum tam multis necessariis molibus*...: Recent studies on aqueducts and water supply," *Journal of Roman Archaeology* 9: 5–29.

Zimmer, G. 1982. *Römische Berufdarstellungen*. Berlin: Mann Verlag.

CHAPTER 15

# LARGE-SCALE MANUFACTURING, STANDARDIZATION, AND TRADE

ANDREW I. WILSON

## PRINCIPLES

"Industry," in the sense of large-scale mechanized production of nonagricultural products, is a term rarely applicable to the ancient world, although there are occasional instances where it might be used. Nevertheless, the material culture of Roman world, perhaps more than any other society until the Industrial Revolution, was characterized by the widespread availability of mass-produced artifacts. Pottery, glassware, bricks, coins, plate, and humble metal objects such as nails were produced in enormous quantities to standard shapes and sizes, and widely traded around the Roman Mediterranean and northern Europe and even beyond the frontiers of the empire, reaching India and the Sahara. The apparent sameness of Roman statuary and sarcophagus sculpture, long contrasted unfavorably by art historians with the artistic creativity of the Greeks, may now be recognized not only as a significant facet of a culture in which replication was ideologically important, but also as an economic phenomenon, a response by a finite body of artisans and sculptors to booming market demand. Most of the phenomena discussed in this chapter relate to the Roman period, but some of the elements of Roman mass production are traceable as far back as the Hellenistic world, if not before. This chapter examines the chief features and limitations of mass production in the ancient world, and attempts to explore what the phenomenon might imply about the nature and performance of the ancient economy. It will examine technologies not only of large-scale manufacturing, but also technologies of organization.

By "mass production," I mean the production of very large quantities of the same artifact, or of essentially similar artifacts, by the same production means. "Large-scale production" extends the concept to include also the creation of large quantities of bulk produce (olive oil, salted fish) as well as replicated individual artifacts. Mass production usually, and large-scale production frequently, involves one or more of the following factors: division of labor, standardization of sizes and forms, and sometimes the creation of standardized, interchangeable parts.

Adam Smith began his *Inquiry into the Nature and Causes of the Wealth of Nations* (1776) with the observation that the key to economic growth lies in the division of labor. This is true both for the differentiation of trades, which is found in any complex society (in which farmers, blacksmiths, spinners, weavers are all different individuals), and for the division of labor within a single trade or profession. The latter is simply an extension of the former principle, but it is our main concern here. If a complex task within a single trade is split into a series of smaller and simpler operations, each performed by one worker, per capita productivity is greatly increased. Each worker, repetitively performing the same limited sequence of actions, acquires a dexterity and speed that a worker performing a wider range of tasks could not achieve; furthermore, time is not lost by switching between the different parts of a job. The greater the number of separate steps a manufacturing process is broken into and divided among different workers, the more people must be employed, but their per capita production increases. The downside is that division of labor leads to deskilling of the workforce, since the greater the division of labor, the more limited is the job each worker does.

Division of labor is one of three main factors enabling per capita economic growth, the others being improved techniques for doing the same things, and mechanization, which is a logical progression of division of labor when a manufacturing process has been split into tasks so simple that individual steps can be performed by a machine. The identification of evidence for the increased division of labor in a particular economic sector over time therefore may reflect per capita economic growth in that sector, and may be brought to bear on larger arguments over the possibility and achievement of per capita economic growth in antiquity.

Two ancient texts explicitly address the division of labor. The first is Xenophon's *Cyropaedia* (8.2.5), which anticipates Adam Smith's observation that division of labor is limited by the size of the market. Writing in the fourth century B.C., Xenophon accounts for the excellence of the cuisine at the Persian court by the multitude of specialized chefs employed:

> Nor should it surprise us; for if we remember to what a pitch of perfection the other crafts are brought in great communities, we ought to expect the royal dishes to be wonders of finished art. In a small city the same man must make beds and

chairs and ploughs and tables, and often build houses as well; and indeed he will be only too glad if he can find enough employers in all trades to keep him. Now it is impossible that a single man working at a dozen crafts can do them all well; but in the great cities, owing to the wide demand for each particular thing, a single craft will suffice for a means of livelihood, and often enough even a single department of that; there are shoemakers who will only make sandals for men and others only for women. Or one artisan will get his living merely by stitching shoes, another by cutting them out, a third by shaping the upper leathers, and a fourth will do nothing but fit the parts together. Necessarily the man who spends all his time and trouble on the smallest task will do that task the best.

The second relevant text appeared some 800 years later. In the fifth century A.D., St. Augustine mocked pagan polytheism, with different gods having different spheres of influence, in terms that draw on the division of labor in silversmithing (*De civ. D.* 7.4).

Indeed we laugh when we see them [the pagan gods] distributed by the fancies of human opinions to particular works, like contractors for tiny portions of the public revenue, or like workmen in the street of the silversmiths, where one vessel, so that it may go out perfect, passes through many craftsmen, when it might have been finished by one perfect craftsman. But the reason why a multitude of workmen was thought necessary was so that individual workers could learn individual parts of an art quickly and easily, rather than that they should all be compelled to be perfect in one entire art, which they could only attain slowly and with difficulty.

Both authors stress the increased quality brought about by division of labor, rather than the efficiency gains and lowered costs, although in both passages this emphasis is based on their function as an analogy. Interestingly, Augustine does comment on the reduced cost and effort of training, picking up on the fact that, as we have noted, division of labor leads to deskilling. Classical authors, who were not trying to write Smithian economics, can only take us so far. To proceed any further in the study of large-scale production, we need to turn to the evidence of archaeology.

# PRODUCTION SITES

Study of the layout of production sites can sometimes shed light on the scale of labor employed and the division of labor achieved, while the built structure of the premises in which a group of workers were gathered under the same roof, any water supply or other production infrastructure, or even the provision of machinery such as presses or mills, can sometimes hint at the nature or degree of investment made for the production of particular goods.

In his study of Roman pottery production, Peacock distinguished several types of production (Peacock 1982: 9–10), which are relevant also to the production of goods other than pottery. In studying the technologies of organization for mass production, we are here concerned with his categories of workshops, nucleated workshops, manufactories, and factories. His other categories, of household production, household industry, estate production, and military production, are not discussed here, the first two because they operate on too small a scale to be relevant to mass production, and the latter two because they are simply variants of the other types, in one case located on a villa estate and in the other under military control, but not necessarily showing any different physical or technical characteristics. A *workshop* is a building or part of a building in which an artisan, perhaps with several assistants, makes products. The *nucleated workshop* is a cluster of several individual workshops forming a production complex with shared access to raw materials, labor, or markets. A *manufactory* is a dedicated production facility in which numerous artisans "co-operate in producing a single and often highly specialized product. . . . Archaeologically the manufactory will be distinguished by the size of premises, the degree of specialization in the products, by the scale of output, and by evidence of worker specialization" (Peacock 1982: 10). For the pottery industry, Peacock made a largely arbitrary distinction, based on ethnographic parallels from twentieth-century Tunisian pottery production, between workshops, with up to twelve workers, and manufactories, with more than twelve. The manufactory is not usually equipped with machinery powered by other than human or animal means, but it does employ division of labor. True *factories*, by contrast, operate on a large scale, employ division of labor, and utilize powered machinery.

# MASS-PRODUCED ARTIFACTS

The component elements of mass production began to appear in the sixth century B.C., with the use of molds and separately made parts in the production of Corinthian "plastic vases," in which mold-made heads of different kinds of animals might be applied to essentially similar wheel-thrown bodies (Biers 1994), although the relatively small quantities in which these were made hardly merit the term "mass production." During the fifth to third centuries B.C., Corinthian mortaria were made in molds and widely exported, and from the Hellenistic period onward mold-made wares become increasingly common for relief-decorated bowls, enabling elaborate but standardized vessels to be turned out quickly and relatively cheaply. This tradition carried through into the tradition of red-slipped Italian *terra sigillata* (ITS), and its later Gaulish derivative, "Samian ware." Roman lamps were also usually mold-made in two parts (upper and lower) that were then fitted together.

Mass-produced high-quality tablewares, whether decorated and mold-made, or wheel-thrown and plain, are ubiquitous in the Roman world, even reaching Britain and India; mass-produced and standardized cooking wares are also common (figure 20.4; chapter 20). Their distribution implies an integrated pan-Mediterranean trading network, in which the aggregate size of the market stimulated producers with access to export distribution networks to enormous quantities of production. Many ITS and Samian vessels are stamped with the potter's name on the underside of the base, often understood as relating to the organization of production or for identifying batches during firing in shared kilns. Fülle (1997) has argued that these stamps mark the products of *officinatores* or workshop managers, who may have been renting potteries or space in a pottery from a landowner under a contract of *locatio conductio rei*. Such contracts are known from third-century A.D. Egypt; a potter leasing a pottery or a part of a pottery and undertaking to produce a certain quantity of amphoras (in one case, 15,000) in return for cash payment in staged installments (Cockle 1981). The landowner provided the facilities and materials, while the potter provided the labor (including assistants). Presumably the potter could sell any excess production above the stipulated amount at his own profit.

The mass production of Roman tablewares has led many scholars to see the organization of Arretine production in terms of manufactories, from the numbers of personnel recorded on stamps in relation to particular individuals, and a set of large tanks, interpreted as being for clay levigation, found at Arezzo in association with numerous shards bearing the stamp of C. Perennius and dependent workers. Neither piece of evidence, however, is sufficient: not all people appearing on stamps as dependants of the same individual need have been active simultaneously, and the large vats might equally be clay preparation tanks, or evaporation tanks to produce fine red slip by slow evaporation from fine mud, neither of which need imply exceptionally large operations (Fülle 1997: 134–35; Pasqui 1896; cf. Peacock 1982: 54). Fülle therefore argues that Arretine production is that of nucleated workshops rather than manufactories.

But if stamps cannot be used to estimate the numbers of people simultaneously active in the same workshop, neither can they be used to estimate the maximum sizes of such workforces—we do not know what fraction of the total number of people who originally stamped their products have been recovered. Furthermore, if the people recorded on stamps are *officinatores*, they could each have had several people working for them whose names are not recorded. Moreover, this approach relies on the epigraphic evidence from stamped products. But the production of African Red Slip ware surpasses Arretine and Gaulish Samian production both in chronological range and in extent of distribution, and very few of these products are stamped. If the stamps on Arretine and Samian ware reflect *locatio–conductio* contracts between potters and the owners of production facilities, then the implication is that a different system may have operated in Africa—perhaps one in which the landowner directly employed or owned the potters. Classic manufactory production would be easier to envisage in these circumstances, but would be epigraphically invisible.

The physical evidence for the number and scale of production facilities, and for possible division of labor, helps us here. While the African production centers have not been excavated—the center whose products we know best, El Mahrine, has been investigated only by surface collection (Mackensen 1993)—there is other evidence for large-scale production in Italy and Gaul.

The derivative Gaulish productions involving potters attested at Arezzo, which appear at Lyons from 10 B.C. and then at La Graufesenque in Southern Gaul, are now thought to reflect migration of expert potters rather than the establishment of branch workshops (Fülle 1997: 141–44; cf. Oxé et al. 2000: 49–50). Some specialization and division of labor can be seen in the case of the South Gaulish potteries at and near La Graufesenque. The separately prepared foot ring of molded bowls of form Dragendorff 37, produced from the 60s to about 120, would have facilitated a basic division of labor in the preparation of these vessels (Mees 1994: 19). A labor account from La Graufesenque mentions *pueri* (slaves, or perhaps apprentices) preparing the clay, fetching fuel, and assigned to the task *ad samiandum*, probably applying the glossy slip most characteristic of Samian ware (Marichal 1988: 226–27, no. 169; Bulmer 1980: 29). Clearly, these slaves were not the actual potters but were assigned to a variety of ancillary tasks. Most importantly, firing was in the hands of specialist kiln-masters operating massive kilns used by groups of potters. Bilingual graffiti in Gaulish and Latin on broken or rejected dishes list vessels loaded into kilns for firing; each charging-list gives the names of several potters with hundreds or thousands of vessels in that firing—up to 12 potters and over 30,000 vessels in a single firing (Hermet 1923, 1934: 291–355; Albenque 1951; Aymard 1952, 1953; Duval and Marichal 1966; Marichal 1988; Vernhet and Bémont 1991). The largest number of vessels recorded in a firing is 33,845 (with a ready-reckoning total of 33,500; Hermet 1934: 309; on the language of these documents, see Adams 2003: 687–724). One kiln excavated in 1980 confirms the capacities given by the charging lists: it measured about 4 m square internally, and about 4 to 5 m high, giving a volume approaching 80 m$^3$ (Bémont 1996: 125).

The charging lists from La Graufesenque also seem to provide evidence for the simultaneous use of up to ten large kilns there. The tally lists are headed either with the Gaulish word *tuθos* followed by a Gaulish ordinal number up to ten (e.g., *tuθos decametos*, "tenth *tuθos*") or with the Latin word *furnus* ("kiln") followed by a Latin ordinal (e.g., *furnus secundus*). It has been argued that the Gaulish *tuθos* means a kiln-load rather than the kiln itself, and that the documents therefore refer to a firing cycle throughout the year and not to the number of physical kilns (Marichal 1988: 97; Flobert 1992: 105; Vernhet and Bémont 1991, 1993; Fülle 2000: 72–76). However, Marichal 83, which starts "[ . . . ]bres incepit furnus pri[mus]," must refer to a month ending in *–bres* (Duval and Marichal 1966: 1349), and even September would be far too late in the year for the firing season to start. This detail appears to exclude the use of ordinal numbers to denote a particular firing in an annual cycle; they must instead refer to the number of the kiln. The uniform structure of the lists and the consecutive numbering of the kilns suggest that the kilns were under single ownership or operation. As each firing might take perhaps three weeks, it is likely that the ten or more kilns were fired in rotation – perhaps loading and commencing the firing of a different kiln every couple of days. This would indicate considerable investment in plant, so that the whole operation could be managed with a small firing crew and the potters could continue to produce vessels without having to wait long for another kiln to become available.

The La Graufesenque documents thus give a picture of nucleated workshops operating with communal firings in massive shared kilns; the size of the operation and the nature of the tally lists imply that the kiln-masters were separate from the potters. This practice operated for a considerable time—one series of tally lists is dated A.D. 40–60, and another to between the reigns of Trajan and Antoninus Pius (Albenque 1951: 80). Communal firings are also known from other large pottery production centers: Arezzo, Les-Martres-de-Veyre, and Rheinzabern, for example (*CIL* 11.6702, nos. 2, 5, 23a; Duval and Marichal 1966: 1341, n. 3).

Important evidence for the actual layout of pottery workshops comes from two sites: Le Rozier, about 20 km from La Graufesenque, and Scoppieto in the upper Tiber valley. At Le Rozier, part of a workshop has been excavated, a building at least 22 m long, with a store for prepared clay at the east end, and a workroom to the west (Thuault and Vernhet 1986; Thuault 1996). The workroom was at least 17 m long by 7 m wide, with eleven surviving clay storage tubs about 1.1 to 1.2 m square in a row along the south wall, and a water channel between the tubs and the wall. Although no potters' wheels were found in situ, the arrangement of the channel and the tubs excludes these being elutriation or decantation tanks, and parallels from Scoppieto confirm that these are tubs to hold the clay used by the potters while working. The arrangement thus provides evidence for a common workroom with at least eleven potters working side by side. The west end of the room had been eroded by the river, so the original number may have been more. The Le Rozier workshop was active between A.D. 50 and 80, during which period 21 potters are attested by stamps on the pottery, of whom 18 are also known at La Graufesenque.

Scoppieto is a rural site in the upper Tiber valley watershed, much better placed than Arezzo for supplying the market of Rome. Excavations have revealed a large workroom with a row of working places for 27 potters, evident from the emplacements of the potters' wheels and clay bins similar to those at Le Rozier (Bergamini 2003, 2004; Nicoletta 2003; cf. also Moscara 2003). More than 50 different potters are attested over the life of the establishment (Augustan period to early second century A.D.); some may have worked there only for a limited time (Nicoletta 2002: 213–15). Here it is not the stamps but the operational arrangement that gives us the number of potters working simultaneously: 27.

At Scoppieto, mass production was achieved by the replication of similar work units, but each worker carried out many of the stages of production of the vessel. Economies of scale would have been produced, though, in the organization and supply of raw materials to several craftsmen all working in the same location, in the sharing of common facilities and services, notably the kilns but also probably clay preparation and levigation tanks, and in the marketing and distribution of the products. Although each potter probably made an entire vessel from the forming of the wet clay to air-drying ready for firing, it is likely that the initial preparation and levigation of the clay, and the slipping and firing of the vessels, were carried out by other workers (as at La Graufesenque), thus implying a basic division of labor.

At both Le Rozier and Scoppieto, we cannot be sure whether the potters were all the employees of a single owner or independent potters renting space and facilities in the workshop. If the stamping of Arretine and Samian pottery reflects leasing of production facilities under contracts of *locatio–conductio*, then this implies a more complex and cooperative model of production than is usually associated with the concept of manufactory, where the workers are normally employees of the owner. Le Rozier and Scoppieto, therefore, do not fall neatly into Peacock's categories. On the one hand, they display the physical characteristics and layouts of basic manufactories, with replication of identical work units in the same place, and some very elementary division of labor; they qualify for the term "manufactory" chiefly on grounds of scale. Yet the organization, the relationship between owner and workers, is very different from the manufactories of immediately preindustrial eighteenth-century Europe. This would suggest that the categories we commonly use to classify production units with an implied sense of progression—from household production to household industry to individual workshops to nucleated workshops to manufactories and finally to factories—do not represent the full available range. Put another way, this is a teleological perspective assuming that all development builds in a similar manner toward an industrial revolution culminating in factories. The production facilities of Le Rozier and Scoppieto may have stood somewhat to one side of the linear trajectory of workshop development that, retrojecting from the late medieval and early modern periods, we like to see as paradigmatic. In the Roman world, some landowners appear to have invested heavily in the infrastructure for large-scale pottery manufacture, building facilities that could accommodate numerous workers with economies of scale through shared access to raw materials, resources, clay preparation and firing facilities, and marketing and distribution structures. Yet rather than employing the potters who used the facilities, they may have preferred to engage them via relatively short-term contracts. This could have worked in one of two ways. The landowners could have subcontracted to the potters the production of a certain number of vessels, for which the landowner would pay the potter and then sell himself. Here the landowner assumes the final risk in terms of market demand and price. Alternatively, the potters might have rented the facilities from the landowner—who was thus assured of a fixed income—and the potter would retain ownership of the vessels until sale. This latter strategy would limit the landowner's risk, so long as there was sufficient demand by itinerant or mobile potters to use well-organized facilities.

While pottery is one of the most obvious categories of mass-produced artifact in the ancient world, others are also very common. Roman sites produce extraordinarily large quantities of blown-glass vessels as well, and glass output did not reach similar levels again until Venice began large-scale exports in the fifteenth century. Coins were struck in enormous issues, and quotidian metal objects were also produced in vast numbers. When the partially completed fortress at Inchtuthil in Scotland was abandoned as the Romans withdrew, over a million iron nails (weighing nearly ten tons) were buried at the site to prevent them falling into enemy hands (Manning 1985: 289). Imperial arms factories existed in the late Roman empire, but we know nothing of their layout or detailed operation. Nevertheless, the production of arms and armor is one obvious area where the large-scale demand may have stimulated methods of mass production, and some preliminary indications hint in that direction. The design of spearheads, arrowheads and ballista bolts enabled their batch production from strips of iron, cut into triangular blanks and forged into shape by hammering in a curved "bottom swage." The iron strips for these blanks, and also for scale armor, may have been produced using rollers, which would have enabled a division of labor between semiskilled artisans who forged and rolled the sheets and cut the blanks, and a skilled smith who shaped the projectile heads (Sim 1995). The scale of iron smelting and smithing sites on Exmoor suggests mass production of iron tools and weapons (Juleff 2003).

Many different types of object were stamped—ceramic vessels, bricks, lead pipes, barrels, loaves of bread—in what sometimes looks like a frenzy of bureaucratic control but often relates to production contracts, water rights, or food entitlement, depending on the object concerned (Harris 1993). Among these stamped objects, bricks are worth examining in more detail. The large imperial building projects erected in the city of Rome, coupled with the demand for private accommodation, required many millions of bricks. Mass production of fired bricks started in the reign of Augustus and lasted throughout the empire; it was particularly intense in Italy, especially around Rome. Many bricks were stamped with the names of estate owners or workshop managers, and numerous prosopographic studies have used these brick stamps to examine the scale and organization of the industry (Bloch 1938–1939, 1947; Helen 1975, 1976; Setälä 1977; Steinby and Helen 1978; Steinby 1974–1975, 1977, 1993). Such was the scale of the Roman building industry, and of the brick manufacture that supplied it, that the term "industry" becomes justified here. The demands of the building industry at Rome, Ostia, and Portus, and in the suburbs of Rome, were met by the brick industry of the Tiber valley, which was dominated initially by senatorial families. Through intermarriage and the confiscation of senatorial estates, the emperor or the imperial family increasingly came to control it. As with large-scale pottery production, these are not standard capitalist industries; exploitation was carried out principally by landowners letting *locatio–conductio* contracts for brickmaking to individuals who carried out the work via dependants; these individuals are the *officinatores* or workshop managers named on the stamps (Helen 1975).

Bricks were made in standard sizes, thus allowing builders to mix bricks from different suppliers in the same building without changing working patterns. This removed a supply bottleneck inherent in masonry construction, where an important factor controlling building rates is the output capacity of the quarry supplying the stone (Wilson 2005). The use of brick facing also allowed concrete walls to be constructed without formwork, which speeded up the process of construction and lowered costs (chapter 10). These two factors enabled an enormous project such as the Baths of Caracalla, which used approximately 6.9 million bricks (DeLaine 1997: 124, table 10, 126, table 11), to be finished in five years. The brick producers produced to stock, for an indefinite market, rather than to order. While the massive demand generated by imperial building projects and private construction meant that most of the bricks made in the Tiber valley were destined for Rome or its ports at Ostia and Portus, some were exported, and Italian bricks are present at most of the major North African ports from Caesarea Mauretaniae (Cherchel) to Lepcis Magna, arriving perhaps as salable ballast (Tomber 1987; Wilson 2001b). Bricks from the region of Aquileia were also exported to Dalmatia. The standardization of bricks, as part of the technology of concrete construction, represents one of the most impressive indicators of the scale of the Roman building industry.

# MARBLE TRADE

While brick-faced concrete was increasingly used in many areas for the structural core of a building, quarried stone, and particularly marble, remained necessary for architectural ornament and also for structural elements, especially columns, in trabeated architecture. Accordingly, the marble trade evolved over the first to third centuries A.D. in response to increasing demand. Architectural marbles, such as column shafts, capitals, bases and entablatures, begin to be produced to standard shapes and perhaps also lengths, and shipped in near-final form, for finishing and polishing on arrival at the importing site; columns in particular were left with rough collars at the end to protect against damage in transport (Asgari 1978, 1990; Dodge and Ward-Perkins 1992; Waelkens et al. 1988: 110; Waelkens 1990: 64–70). Such prefabricated marble architectural elements from Proconnessus and Docimium have been found in several shipwrecks off Sicily (Pensabene 2003), and also in one at Sile in the Black Sea alongside roughed-out sculptural marbles. By the second century, the major marble quarries had moved from a quarry-to-order to a quarry-to-stock regime, a sign that the aggregate market had become so large that a whole range of different architectural elements was virtually guaranteed to find a buyer—or to be needed by an imperially-funded building program (chapter 5). This procedure also enabled the quarries to fulfill orders more quickly. Systems of quarry marks carved on blocks and columns, both at the quarries and at major delivery yards at Ostia and Rome, facilitated accounting and stock-taking (Dodge and Ward-Perkins 1992; Fant 1989; Hirt 2004).

Concurrently with the standardization of architectural marbles, we can also observe high levels of standardization in the sarcophagus trade. The white marble quarries of Proconnesus, Ephesus, Aphrodisias, and an as yet unidentified site in Caria roughed out garland sarcophagi to a basic shape before export, as is shown by unfinished sarcophagi both in the quarries themselves and in shipwrecks. Each quarry had its own roughed-out design, with garlands, roundels, and other blocked-out motifs—pendants or plaques for an inscription—that could be refined later into a variety of decorative shapes. Hollowing and roughing out minimized the weight and added value, but was not carried to the point where detailed carving might be damaged in transit. The sarcophagi were finished by workshops in the city to which they were shipped, where the same basic rough design might be turned into swags between bukrania, or Nikai or putti holding garlands, while the blocked-out roundels might become rosettes, busts, or lion heads. Sometimes sides were left unfinished if they would not be seen because of the sarcophagus's position in the tomb; or the entire sarcophagus might even be used in its roughed-out, quarry-state form, for reasons that remain uncertain.

This standardized production of sarcophagi probably began in the late first century A.D., and lasted into the third century. By the late second century, the practice of shipping and even using quarry-state garland sarcophagi had become so common that the red granite quarries of Assos in the Troad actually produced sarcophagi in a form imitating the quarry state of the white marble quarries, but designed to be used without further finishing. They were decorated with a basic swag motif and a panel for an inscription but, apart from the occasional addition of an inscription to the central panel, were never further finished at the importing centers. Assos sarcophagi are found mainly in the eastern Mediterranean in Syria, Palestine and especially Alexandria; but also at Thessalonica, Dyrrhachium, Nicopolis, Ravenna, and some western sites, and in a wreck off Methone. Their main production runs from the late second century into the early third century (Koch 1993: 172–73).

Also standardized were strigillated sarcophagi from the Saliari quarries on Thasos, whose products were exported to Italy and the central Mediterranean, and several types produced at the quarries of Docimium in Asia Minor. These included columnar sarcophagi exported finished in every respect except for the portrait details of the deceased, added by workshops where the products were imported (Waelkens 1982). Simpler funerary monuments, fashioned as an aedicula with a false door, are found throughout Asia Minor and were roughed out at several quarries including Docimium and finished in urban workshops elsewhere (Waelkens 1982; 1986: 20 and index s.v. "Halbfabrikat"). Even the most luxury end of the market shows an extension of the same phenomenon: sarcophagus lids with reclining couples, in Thessalonica and in Cyrene, are finished in every respect (including drapery and patterns on the mattress), except their heads, which are left rough. This clearly shows manufacture of common types to stock, with the intention that client-specific portrait details would be added later (or not at all!)— apparently confirmed by quarry-state rough-outs of such sarcophagus lids in the quarries at Docimium (Thessalonica: Koch and Sichtermann 1982: ill. 421; Cyrene Museum: personal observation; Docimium: Waelkens 1990: 69, figs. 35–36).

Sarcophagi and the false-door funerary monuments share, of course, a large potential market. But the vast building activity of the first to early third centuries A.D. also created in its wake a huge demand for marble statuary—not only to adorn niches of nymphaea or the halls of public baths, but also for the reciprocal gestures by which towns honored benefactors with statues. One might expect that the combination of this considerable demand, from several hundred or even thousand cities around the Mediterranean, coupled with the limited number of quarries able to supply statuary-grade white marble, would have led to more efficient ways of producing statues. Indeed, there is evidence to show that precisely the systems of standardization identified for architectural marbles, sarcophagi, and—crucially—the full-length reclining portrait figures on some sarcophagus lids, were extended also to freestanding portrait sculpture during the second and early third centuries A.D. The evidence may be grouped into three categories: roughed-out statues found abandoned in the quarries; rough-outs found in wrecks; and pieces found elsewhere that show signs of standardized basic working and but with certain details left unfinished.

The numerous statues of Dacian prisoners in Trajan's Forum were roughed out in the quarries at Docimium, as a rejected piece left there shows (Waelkens 1990: 69–70, fig. 39). A group of roughed-out statues found in a quarry near Xylophagon on Cyprus (in hard white limestone rather than marble) included a cuirassed emperor, a draped female figure, and a nude male, all over life-size, and a less than life-size statue said to be the Small Herculaneum Woman type (Karageorghis 1969: 494–99). A late imperial, cuirassed emperor statue has been found in quarry state on Proconnesus (Asgari 1978: 480, pl. 142; 1990: 125–26); roughed-out statues are reported from the Saliari quarries on Thasos (Kozelj et al. 1985: 75), and the practice has also been suggested in the case of the Thasos white marble quarries at Cape Vathy, in particular for a type, common in the second and early third centuries, of a figure of Eros sleeping on a torch (Herrmann and Newman 1995: 79–80; 1999: 296; Tykot et al. 2002: 189).

While it could be argued that rough-outs abandoned in the quarry might have been intended to be finished completely before export, but some flaw prevented their completion, rough-outs from wrecks prove that some sculptures were exported partially finished. A wreck excavated at Sile (Black Sea) had been carrying a cargo of Proconnesian marble including capitals, a sarcophagus lid, a female bust, and an imperial cuirassed statue, all roughed out in quarry state to be finished at the final destination (Asgari 1978, 1990). The quarry and wreck evidence suggests that the export of roughed-out, or even nearly finished, statues, whose portrait details would be added at the importing centers in consultation with the clients, may have been common. This hypothesis is supported both by the general likeness of common stances and poses in full-length Roman portraits, both male and female, and by specific examples from Cyrene, in which the accomplished details and finishing of the portrait heads contrasts with the schematic rendering of the drapery (e.g., Alföldi-Rosenbaum 1960: nos. 43, 95; personal observation in Cyrene Museum, 2006; Ben Russell oral communication). In these cases, it seems, the statues have been exported from the quarries nearly finished, with the drapery schematically rendered as a guide for the receiving workshop, but not taken to the point where damage in transit could not be rectified, and the heads either left for finishing or indeed separately worked. The heads have been finished by portrait sculptors who have ignored the other details; indeed, the schematized drapery quickly became an accepted style in its own right.

Cumulatively, the evidence suggests increasing specialization, with the quarries in the second and early third centuries A.D. producing increasingly finished statues rather than exporting raw blocks of marble to be worked elsewhere. The advantage of doing as much as possible of the carving at the quarry was twofold: first, it reduced the weight of the item to be shipped; and secondly, craftsmen used to working only on the marble from a particular quarry, familiar with its grain, could work it faster than generalists who might have to work with a variety of different marbles. The disadvantage was that finely finished fluted drapery or other details might be chipped in transit; rough-finishing the statue, with the head left for portrait details to be added, was therefore a good compromise. The Roman practice of replication in sculpture, originally developed in part for cultural reasons, naturally lent itself to standardization and shipping of quarry-state statues. Trimble (2000) presents a study of the social and political context of the standardized representation of two female statue types, the so-called Large and Small Herculaneum Women. Indeed, the shipping of quarry-state rough-outs in the second century A.D. goes some way toward explaining the widespread diffusion of common poses in which details of drapery vary somewhat. There was, however, no single uniform system; some sculptures were clearly exported after simple roughing out of the pose, others with the drapery schematically worked, and others, like the reclining couple sarcophagi, even with the drapery finished. In addition, and particularly for statues that did not conform to the common types, raw blocks were shipped for working from scratch at the receiving workshop. Practice probably varied by quarry, and over time. The important point is that by the early second century the market for honorific and portrait statuary (both of private citizens and the imperial family), had grown to such a size that it could support standardized production to stock of common types, and an articulation of production between, on the one hand, the quarries producing standardized poses and drapery treatment, and, on the other, the importing work-shops where the portrait details and final finishing were carried out.

# DIVISION OF LABOR

The marble trade as discussed above shows a basic division of labor, spatially separated between quarries and final workshops. But the staged division of labor in a single workshop, described by Augustine in his analogy of the silver vessel passing through the hands of numerous silversmiths, can in fact be detected in the layout of certain production facilities. Two examples will be examined here: the production of bread, and the manufacture of decorative marble objects.

## Baking and Milling

Increasing subdivision of labor over time can be traced in the baking trade, a mundane and therefore important example. Improvements in the technology or organization of bread production would have far-reaching effects on activities affecting every household. The baking trade also illustrates the introduction of rudimentary mechanization.

Bakeries as a specialized workshop are known from the sixth century B.C., but the introduction of animal-driven grain mills in the second century B.C. boosted the specialization of the miller-cum-baker as a separate trade, progressively replacing laborious domestic bread production using hand querns (chapter 14; Curtis 2001: 280–93, 358–69; Moritz 1958: 62–74). Animal-driven mills required capital investment, but had a much larger output, allowing centralized grain grinding and bread production by miller-bakers. Such mills became particularly common in urban contexts where large market demand existed. By A.D. 79, Pompeii had about 35 bakeries, indicating near-universal consumption of shop-bought bread by town-dwellers.

By the Augustan period if not earlier, Roman bakers were also using mechanical dough-mixers (chapter 13). The layout of two very large bakeries at Ostia also hints at a basic specialization of labor. In the purpose-built bakery in Insula I.XIII.4 (ca. A.D. 100–125), grain was brought into a long rectangular courtyard, and processed in an aisled hall to the north, with seven animal mills in the southern aisle and five kneading machines in the northern aisle (Meijlink 1999). The basalt paving of the hall (to withstand the wear of the animals continually walking in circles) indicates that both the mills and the kneading machines were animal-powered. Although the layout is tidy, it is not optimal. The only available space for sieving the flour after milling is in the south range; the sieved flour must then have been carried back across to the north aisle for kneading in the machines, and the dough must then have been transferred back again across the courtyard to room 10, on which it was shaped into loaves on tables, and then baked in the oven at the end of the room.

In the Via dei Mulini, a large bakery was installed in a commercial building apparently in the Severan period, and functioned, with modifications, until around 280 (Heres 1999; Bakker 1999b: esp. 57–60.). Here the plan is more efficient, showing a clear division of the stages of grinding grain, kneading dough, and baking the bread (figure 15.1). A large vaulted hall housed at least ten animal-driven mills paved with basalt slabs; the flour was probably sieved in the northern part of this hall. In the adjacent room are five dough-mixing machines, also animal-powered on the evidence of the basalt-paved floor. Beyond the dough-mixing

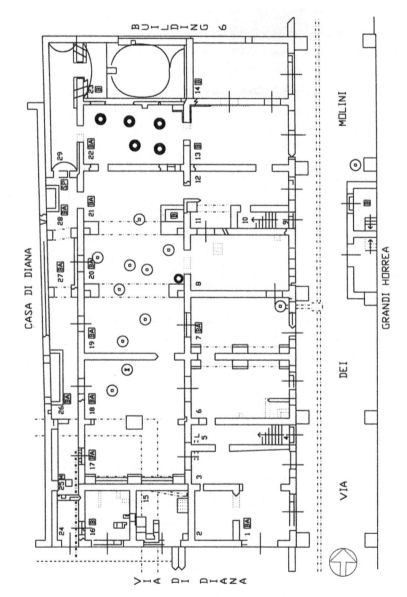

Figure 15.1. Plan of the second-century A.D. bakery at Casseggiato dei Molini, Ostia. (Courtesy of Jan Theo Bakker.)

room, two vast, domed bread ovens were sited at the end of the building in the first phase of the bakery (one was later removed). Overall this bakery displays a degree of rational planning, with the different stages of production separated into different rooms and laid out in a rudimentary production line.

The large bakeries at Ostia may reflect arrangements at Rome, where much less is known about bakeries since few have been excavated or published. The iconography of the tomb of the baker Eurysaces at Porta Maggiore seems to imply operations on a similar or even larger scale. This travertine monument (dated stylistically between 40 B.C. and A.D. 5) is decorated in its lower zone with sets of cylinders stacked three deep, surmounted by the funerary inscription naming Eurysaces as a contractor (*redemptor*), and above this is a zone with three layers of circular holes. Around the top, a frieze shows scenes of bread production (figure 2.2). The curious circular holes which form the most characteristic and striking element of the monument are in fact dough-mixing machines laid on their sides (the spindle sockets are visible at the end of each void), and the stacked cylinders below them represent the same dough-mixers seen from the side (Ciancio Rossetto 1973: 33–34; Brandt 1993).

The frieze shows the different stages of bread production (Ciancio Rossetto 1973: 41–61; cf. Zimmer 1982: 106–8). On the south face, from right to left, is shown the delivery of grain, with the state officials who had contracted out large baking orders to Eurysaces recording their receipts; grain being milled in two donkey-driven mills, and the flour being sieved by two men at a table; finally an official in a toga is sampling it for quality. On the north face dough is kneaded in an animal-powered mixing machine, with a man scooping out the dough; two groups of four men roll out dough into loaves at two tables under the eye of an overseer; on the left-hand side a man loads an oven with a long bread shovel. The frieze is broken to the left, but part of a leg may indicate another man loading or unloading an oven in the missing part. On the west face, reading from left to right, loaves are carried to be weighed under the supervision of officials whom Eurysaces, as a contractor to the state, is supplying; they make records in tablet-books, and the loaves are taken away in baskets.

The frieze illustrates exactly the sort of production-line operation implied by the physical layout of the larger bakeries at Ostia a century and a half later. The different numbers of men engaged in the different operations show that this is not the same worker or set of workers performing all the operations in sequence; the action is simultaneous and we focus on different steps. The exactitude of such representations cannot be insisted upon, but the ratio of eight men rolling out dough to one operating the animal-driven dough mixer, and one (or two) loading the oven is at least suggestive of the scale of manpower required to keep pace with the mechanized stages of production and with the large-batch baking. The number of workers shown also conveys the idea that this is a large-scale operation; similarly, the repeated motifs of stacked dough-mixers stress the size of Eurysaces' business and its command of mechanical technology. The production-line narrative of the frieze and the dough-mixers convey the message of a large and rationally organized, partially mechanized bread manufactory.

## The Chemtou Marble Workshops

The imperial quarries at Chemtou (Simitthus) in Tunisia, which produced the pinkish-yellow *marmor Numidicum,* seem to have been given over to private exploitation in the early third century A.D. Large-scale quarrying of architectural marble ceased and activity concentrated on the production of small but often decorated marble objects—bowls, plates, and statuettes, often reworked from unused blocks extracted under imperial ownership. The six parallel halls, originally a secure barracks for the quarry workers condemned *ad metallas,* were converted into workshops. The spatial distribution of production waste and rejected artifacts in various stages of production when the workshops were abandoned suggests a production-line process, with the products moving through different operations, each carried out at a different place in the halls (figure 15.2) (Rakob 1994: 66–89, 107–31; 1995: 42–43; 1997: 10–17; Mackensen 2000: 493; Ruger 1997). Excavations of an area to the east of the six-halled building have also shown that the seriated production of marble cups and statuettes extended well beyond the limits of the former barracks building (Mackensen 2000: 500–502).

Two phases were identified. In the first, blocks were sawed in the westernmost hall and then rough- and fine-dressed before polishing on marble benches in the central halls. The final polishing, with river cobbles or small marble polishing stones and wet sand, happened at the north end of the halls, over the drain of what had been the barracks latrine. Relief-decorated bowls and statuettes, many of Venus, were produced to a limited number of standardized patterns.

The second phase, from the mid-third century until the 280s, followed the collapse of part of the vaulted roof. Production continued on a reduced scale, but although the spatial layout changed, the production-line principle did not. Sawing took place along the south and west sides of the workshops, with rough- and fine-dressing close by. Products then moved through the central halls for polishing, with final polishing again being carried out in two of the former latrine bays at the north. In both phases, the scale and the production-line nature of the operation allow us to consider this a manufactory.

## Large-Scale Production in the Food Sector

The urban populations of the Roman world, particularly those distributed around the Mediterranean, but also some towns in northwest Europe, and army garrisons stationed on the imperial frontiers, were usually too large to be fed entirely from local resources and depended considerably on long-distance trade. Together with a more distributed rural population, they provided a vast aggregate market for various foodstuffs. The size of this market, coupled with particular production factors in some regions, facilitated the development of some installations producing certain foodstuffs on a remarkable scale—principally salted fish and derivative products, olive oil and wine, and milled flour.

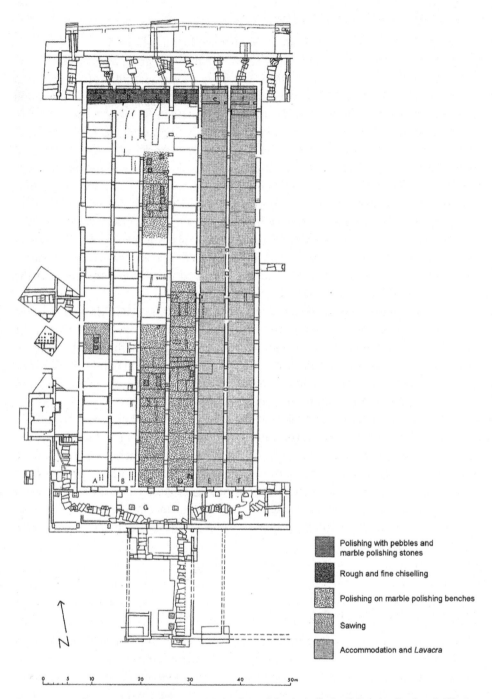

Figure 15.2. Chemtou (Simitthus, Tunisia), plan of the *Fabrika* building in the first half of the third century A.D., with distribution of waste from different stages of the production of small stone objects. (After Rakob 1994; reproduced by permission.)

In the western Mediterranean, especially around the Straits of Gibraltar, but also along the modern Tunisian coast and, to a lesser extent, the coasts of Sicily and southern France, the seasonal migrations of fish led to the potential for enormous catches at particular times of the year. These far outstripped the demands of local populations, but needed to be preserved by gutting and salting before they could be shipped to more distant markets packed in amphoras. The guts and small fry could be processed to make various kinds of fish sauces—*garum* or *liquamen*, used widely in cooking and appreciated as a delicacy (chapter 14). Roman fish sauces have captured the modern imagination, but they should be seen as merely epiphenomenal to a much larger trade in salted fish that provided a substantial protein source for both coastal and inland communities. From the second half of the first century B.C. onward, we see the emergence of large salting factories, with concrete salting vats lined with waterproof mortar arranged around a courtyard, and areas for gutting and fish preparation. A particularly clear example is at Cotta in Morocco, with a long fish-gutting hall and 16 vats around a courtyard, with a total capacity of 258 m$^3$; an area with hypocaust heating was probably designed for producing the necessary salt by lixiviation from beach sand, rather than for producing *garum* (Ponsich 1988, 150–59; Hesnard 1998). The Cotta factory, apparently an isolated coastal establishment, though possibly linked to an undiscovered villa, was by no means the largest. One of the estimated 50 factories at Troía (Portugal) had a total capacity in excess of 606 m$^3$, while another at Iulia Traducta (Algeciras Bay) had a capacity of 150 m$^3$. While these larger units were usually outside urban centers, substantial factories were also sometimes located within towns, as at Baelo Claudia in Spain, Lixus in Morocco, and Tipasa in Algeria (Wilson 2006).

In the western Mediterranean region, the majority of fish-salting factories were built between 50 B.C. and A.D. 100, and operated until the fifth century, although usually on a reduced scale after around 200 or 250. Fish were salted and exported both before and after these dates, but in lesser quantities that could be accommodated in smaller salting containers (*pithoi* and *dolia*); but from the first century B.C. to the fifth century A.D. the economic conditions of Mediterranean trade were such that the considerable investment in salting plant could be justified by the colossal market one could reach. In the first century A.D., similar factories were also built in Amorica (northwest Brittany), another area with marked seasonal shoaling patterns. These included the second largest single installation in the Roman world, at Plomarc'h in the Bay of Douarnenez, with a total salting capacity of over 466 m$^3$. Epigraphic evidence suggests that these factories were built by investors from the Mediterranean, presumably in response to the emergence of new markets in northwest Europe, as increasing numbers of troops were stationed along the Rhine frontier and in Britain, and the inhabitants of the newly conquered province of Britain began to acquire Roman dietary habits, including a taste for salted fish. Salting factories are also found from the first to third centuries A.D. in several towns of the Crimea, especially on the Kerch peninsula at Tiritace and Chersonesus, taking advantage of migration routes through the Cimmerian Bosphorus (Curtis 1991; Højte 2005; Wilson 2006).

In North Africa, the combination of the universal demand for olive oil as a food source, lamp fuel, massage oil, and multipurpose lubricant, with the availability of cheap seasonal labor from transhumant tribes who came north to summer pasture around the olive harvest, encouraged the development of cash-crop olive growing. Numerous rural press sites are found throughout parts of Numidia, Africa Proconsularis, and Tripolitania, and some are very large, well-built functional establishments with multiple presses. Sites with four presses are common, and some have six, eight, or even more—the largest are Henchir Sidi Hamdan (nine presses) and Senam Semana (17 presses). These veritable factories must have processed the olives from enormous orchards, and imply massive landowning wealth, as well as the resources to set up such batteries of press machinery. Yet these functional buildings lack any decoration (mosaics, wall paintings, elaborate residential architecture) commensurate with such wealth, and were probably administered by a slave bailiff (*vilicus*) on behalf of an owner residing elsewhere. The scale of olive oil production suggested by some of these estate centers is unparalleled in later societies before the nineteenth century. It is frequently difficult to distinguish between presses for olive oil and for wine, especially on unexcavated sites, and some of these sites may in fact have been for wine. This is certainly the case for the massive factory at Kherbet el-Agoub, a site in inland Numidia with ten pairs of presses and treading vats, arranged around three sides of a courtyard with a storage room on the fourth (Meunier 1941; Brun 2004: 233–38). But whether for wine or oil, these huge factory sites with multiple presses represent major investments by landowners in the processing plants necessary for cash-crop production for export. Large multiple press sites are also found in some other Mediterranean provinces outside North Africa—up to four presses in Spain, six in southern Gaul, and ten double presses at Barbariga in Istria at the head of the Adriatic.

Large investments in processing machinery are also shown by the construction of water-powered grain milling factories with multiple wheels (chapter 13). The earliest example is the early second-century A.D. complex at Barbegal in southern France near Arles, with 16 wheels; in the third century, if not before, a series of large water-powered mills was built along the course of two branches of the Aqua Traiana, and possibly also the Aqua Alsietina, on the slopes of the Janiculum hill in Rome (Wilson 2001a).

The early Hellenistic period saw the beginnings of mass ceramic production for export in both the Greek and Punic worlds. But it is the Roman period that is remarkable for the spread of mass production in a variety of sectors, and for the scale of some operations. Large-scale production is particularly apparent in certain kinds of food production and the processing of agricultural produce—fish-salting, oil and wine production, and bread-making; in some of these, the scale of production was achieved by limited use of machines (presses, mills, and dough-mixers). For manufactured goods, mass production largely took the form of replication of individual items (ceramics, statues); in some cases simple production-line technologies were employed. In certain areas, this mass production reached levels unparalleled until probably seventeenth-century Britain in the half century leading up to the Industrial Revolution. This is an impressive achievement. At the same time it is important also to recognize the limits of Roman mass production: there is no hard evidence of the mass production of complex items using standardized interchangeable parts, in a manner foreshadowing the so-called American System that evolved out of eighteenth-century French small arms production. It is not impossible that interchangeable parts were used, for example in vehicles or siege engines, but there is as yet no evidence for them. Nevertheless, there is much more research to be done, particularly on the mass production of arms and armor, and we are only just beginning to see how to read clues about organization and division of labor from the archaeology of production sites. Strikingly, most of the sectors in which we can detect mass production relate to the manufacture of goods or produce from raw materials (clay, iron, marble) or agriculture, and represent either modes by which landowners (including the state) could maximize return on their properties, exploiting resources either by agents or through contracting out. Either way, the arrangement ensured that a large share of the profits flowed to the landowner, thus limiting the ability of those directly involved in the manufacturing to emerge as a separate entrepreneurial class.

# REFERENCES

Adams, J. N. 2003. *Bilingualism and the Latin language.* Cambridge: Cambridge University Press.

Albenque, A. 1951. "Nouveaux graffites de La Graufesenque," *Revue des études anciennes* 53: 71–81.

Alföldi-Rosenbaum, E. 1960. *A catalogue of Cyrenaican portrait sculpture.* London: British Academy.

Asgari, N. 1978. "Roman and early Byzantine marble quarries of Proconnesus," in E. Akurgal (ed.), *The proceedings of the Xth International Congress of Classical Archaeology.* Ankara: Türk Tarih Kurumu, 467–80.

Asgari, N. 1990. "Objets de marbre finis, semi-finis et inachevé du Proconnese," in M. Waelkens (ed.), *Pierre éternelle: Du Nil au Rhin: Carrières et préfabrication.* Brussels: Crédit Communal, 106–26.

Aymard, A. 1952. "Nouveaux graffites de La Graufesenque II," *Revue des études anciennes* 54: 93–101.

Bakker, J. T. (ed.) 1999a. *The mills-bakeries of Ostia: Description and interpretation.* Dutch Monographs in Ancient History and Archaeology 21. Amsterdam: J. C. Gieben

Bakker, J.-T. 1999b. "The Caseggiato dei Molini, Part III: Interpretation," in Bakker 1999a, 39–60.

Bémont, C. 1996. "Les comptes de potiers," *Dossiers d'Archéologie* 215: 122–27.

Bergamini, M. 2003. "Una produzione firmata da Marcus Perennius Crescens a Scoppieto," *Rei Cretariae Romanae Fautorum Acta* 38: 133–44.

Bergamini, M. 2004. "Scoppieto e il commercio sul Tevere," paper delivered at the conference "Mercator Placidissimus: The Tiber Valley in Antiquity," British School at Rome, February 28, 2004.

Biers, W R. 1994. "Mass-production, standardized parts, and the Corinthian plastic vase," *Hesperia* 63: 509–16.

Bloch, H. 1938–1939. *I bolli laterizi e la storia edilizia romana: Contributi all'archeologia e alla storia romana.* Rome: C. Colombo.

Bloch, H. 1947. *I bolli laterizi e la storia edilizia romana: Contributi all'archeologia e alla storia romana. Indici analitici.* Rome: Comune di Roma, Ripartizione antichità e belle arti.

Brandt, O. 1993. "Recent research on the Tomb of Eurysaces," *Opuscula romana* 19: 13–17.

Brun, J.-P. 2004. *Archéologie du vin et de l'huile dans l'Empire romain.* Paris: Éditions Errance.

Bulmer, M. 1980. *An introduction to Roman Samian ware, with special reference to collections in Chester and the North West.* Chester: Chester Archaeological Society.

Ciancio Rossetto, P. 1973. *Il sepolcro del fornaio Marco Virgilio Eurisace a Porta Maggiore.* I monumenti romani. Rome: Istituto di studi romani.

Cockle, H. 1981. "Pottery manufacture in Roman Egypt: A new papyrus," *Journal of Roman Studies* 71: 87–95.

Curtis, R. I. 1991. *Garum and salsamenta: Production and commerce in materia medica.* Leiden: Brill.

Curtis, R. I. 2001. *Ancient food technology.* Leiden: Brill.

DeLaine, J. 1997. *The Baths of Caracalla: A study in the design, construction and economics of large-scale building projects in imperial Rome. Journal of Roman Archaeology* Suppl. 25. Portsmouth, RI: JRA.

Dodge, H., and B. Ward-Perkins (eds.) 1992. *Marble in antiquity.* London: British School at Rome.

Duval, P.-M., and R. Marichal 1966. "Un 'compte d'enfournement' inédit de La Graufesenque," in R. Chevallier (ed.), *Mélanges d'archéologie et d'histoire offerts à André Piganiol.* Paris: SEVPEN, 1341–52.

Fant, J. C. 1989. *Cavum antrum Phrygiae: The organization and operations of the Roman imperial marble quarries in Phrygia.* British Archaeological Reports, Intl. Series S482. Oxford: BAR.

Flobert, P. 1992. "Les graffites de la Graufesenque: Un témoignage sur le gallo-latin sous Néron, III," in M. Iliescu and W. Marxgut (eds.), *Latin vulgaire—latin tardif: Actes du IIIème colloque international sur le latin vulgaire et tardif (Innsbruck, 2–5 septembre 1991).* Tübingen: Niemeyer, 103–14.

Fülle, G. 1997. "The internal organization of the Arretine terra-sigillata industry: Problems of evidence and interpretation," *Journal of Roman Studies* 87: 111–55.

Fülle, G. 2000. "Die Organisation der Terra sigillata-Herstellung in La Graufesenque: Die Töpfergraffiti," *Münsterische Beiträge zur antiken Handelsgeschichte* 19.2: 62–98.

Harris, W. V. (ed.) 1993. *The inscribed economy: Production and distribution in the Roman empire in the light of instrumentum domesticum. Journal of Roman Archaeology* Suppl. 6. Ann Arbor, MI: JRA.

Helen, T. 1975. *Organization of Roman brick production in the first and second centuries A.D.: An interpretation of Roman brick stamps.* Acta Instituti romani Finlandiae 9. Helsinki: Academia Scientiarum Fennica.

Helen, T. 1976. "A problem in Roman brick stamps: Who were Lucilla n(ostra) and Aurel(ius) Caes(ar) n(oster), the owners of the figlinae Fulvianae?" *Arctos* 10: 27–36.

Heres, T. 1999. "The Caseggiato dei Molini, Part I: The building history," in Bakker 1999a, 16–33.

Hermet, F. 1923. *Les graffites de La Graufesenque près Millau (Aveyron)*. Rodez: Imprimerie Carrère.

Hermet, F. 1934. *La Graufesenque (Condatomago)*. 2 vols. Paris: Ernest Leroux.

Herrmann, J. J., Jr., and R. Newman 1995. "The exportation of dolomitic sculptural marble from Thasos: Evidence from Mediterranean and other collections," in Y. Maniatis, N. Herz, and Y. Basiakos (eds.), *The study of marble and other stones used in antiquity*. London: Archetype, 73–86.

Herrmann, J. J., Jr., and R. Newman 1999. "Dolomitic marble from Thasos near and far: Macedonia, Ephesos and the Rhone," in M. Schvoerer (ed.), *Archéomatériaux: Marbres et autres roches*. Bordeaux: CRPAA, 293–303.

Hesnard, A. 1998. "Le sel des plages (Cotta et Tahadart, Maroc)," *Mélanges de l'École française de Rome* 110.1: 167–92.

Hirt, A. M. 2004. "Mines and quarries in the Roman Empire: Organizational aspects, 27 BC–AD 235." D.Phil. thesis, University of Oxford.

Højte, J. M. 2005. "Archaeological evidence for fish processing in the Black Sea region," in T. Bekker-Nielsen (ed.), *Ancient fishing and fish processing in the Black Sea region*. Aarhus: Aarhus University Press, 133–60.

Juleff, G. 2003. "Mass iron production on Roman Exmoor, England," *Minerva* 14: 4–5

Karageorghis, V. 1969. "Chronique des fouilles à Chypre en 1968," *Bulletin de Correspondance Hellénique* 93: 431–569.

Koch, G. 1993. *Sarkophage der römischen Kaiserzeit*. Darmstadt: Wissenschaftliche Buchgesellschaft.

Koch, G., and H. Sichtermann 1982. *Römische Sarkophage*. Munich: Beck.

Kozelj, G., A. Lambraki, A. Muller, and J.-P. Sodini 1985. "Sarcophages découverts dans les carrières de Saliari (Thasos)," in P. Pensabene (ed.), *Marmi antichi: Problemi d'impiego, di restauro e d'identificazione*. Rome: L'Erma di Bretschneider, 75–81.

Mackensen, M. 1993. *Die spätantiken Sigillata- und Lamptöpfereien von El Mahrine (Nord Tunesien). Studien zur nordafrikanischen Feinkeramik des 4. bis 7. Jahrhunderts*. Vol. 1. Munich: Beck.

Mackensen, M. 2000. "Erster Bericht über neue archäologische Untersuchungen im sog: Arbeits- und Steinbruchlager von *Simitthus*/Chemtou (Nordwesttunesien)," *Römische Mitteilungen* 107: 487–503.

Manning, W. H. 1985. "The iron objects," in L. F. Pitts and J. K. St Joseph (eds.), *Inchtuthil, the Roman legionary fortress: Excavations 1952–65*. London: Society for the Promotion of Roman Studies, 289–99.

Marichal, R. 1988. *Les graffites de La Graufesenque*. Paris: Éditions du CNRS.

Mees, A. 1994. "Potiers et moulistes: Observations sur la chronologie, les structures et la commercialisation des ateliers de terre sigillée décorée," in L. Rivet (ed.), *Actes du Congrès de Millau, 12–15 mai 1994*. Marseille: Société française d'étude de la céramique antique en Gaule, 19–41.

Meijlink, B. 1999. "Molino I.XIII.4," in Bakker 1999a, 61–79.

Meunier, J. 1941. "L'huilerie romaine de Kherbet-Agoub (Périgotville)," *Bulletin de la Société historique et géographique de Sétif* 2 (1941): 35–55.

Moritz, L. A. 1958. *Grain mills and flour in classical antiquity*. Oxford: Oxford University Press.

Moscara, S. 2003. "I motivi iconografici sulle lucerne prodotte a Scoppieto," *Rei Cretariae Romanae Fautorum Acta* 38: 153–60.

Nicoletta, N. 2002. "Un vano di lavorazione del complesso produttivo di Scoppieto," *Rivista di studi liguri* 67–68: 209–303.

Nicoletta, N. 2003. "I produttori di terra sigillata di Scoppieto," *Rei Cretariae Romanae Fautorum Acta* 38: 145–52.

Oxé, A., H. Comfort, and P. Kenrick 2000. *Corpus Vasorum Arretinorum: A catalogue of the signatures, shapes and chronology of Italian Sigillata*. 2nd ed. Bonn: Habelt.

Pasqui, U. 1896. "Nuove scoperte di antiche figuline della fornace di M. Perennio," *Notizie degli scavi di antichità*: 453–66.

Peacock, D. P. S. 1982. *Pottery in the Roman world: An ethnoarchaeological approach.* London: Longman.

Pensabene, P. 2003. "Sul commercio dei marmi in età imperiale: Il contributo dei carichi naufragati di Capo Granitola (Mazara)," in G. Fiorentini, M. Caltabiano, and A. Calderone (eds.), *Archeologia del Mediterraneo: Studi in onore di Ernesto de Miro*. Rome: L'Erma di Bretschneider, 533–43.

Ponsich, M. 1988. *Aceite de oliva y salazones de pescado: Factores geo-económicos de Bética y Tingitania*. Madrid: Editorial de la Universidad Complutense.

Rakob, F. 1994. "Das römische Steinbruchlager (*Praesidium*) in *Simitthus*," in F. Rakob (ed.), *Simitthus*, vol. 2, *Der Tempelberg und das römische Lager*. Mainz: Philipp von Zabern, 51–139.

Rakob, F. 1995. "Chemtou/Simitthus: The world of labour in ancient Rome," in M. Horton and T. Weidemann (eds.), *North Africa from antiquity to Islam*. Bristol: Centre for Mediterranean Studies, 39–44.

Rakob, F. 1997. "Chemtou: Aus der römischen Arbeitswelt," *Antike Welt* 28.1: 1–20.

Ruger, C. B. 1997. "Zu Marmorschalen in Chemtou," *Römische Mitteilungen* 104: 379–85.

Setälä, P. 1977. *Private domini in Roman brick stamps of the Empire: A historical and prosopographical study of landowners in the district of Rome*. Acta Instituti Romani Finlandiae 9.2. Helsinki: Suomalainen Tiedeakatemia.

Sim, D. 1995. "Weapons and mass production," *Journal of Roman Military Equipment Studies* 6: 1–3.

Steinby, E. M. 1974–1975. "La cronologia delle figlinae doliari urbane della fine dell'età repubblicana fino all'inizio del III secolo," *Bullettino della Commissione archaeologica communale di Roma* 84: 7–132.

Steinby, E. M. 1977. *Lateres Signati Ostienses*. Vol. 2, *Tavole*. Acta Instituti Romani Finlandiae 7. Rome: Bardi.

Steinby, E. M. 1993. "L'organizzazione produttiva dei laterizi: Un modello interpretivo per l'*instrumentum* in genere?," in Harris 1993: 139–43.

Steinby, E. M., and T. Helen. 1978. *Lateres Signati Ostienses*. Vol. 1, *Testo*. Acta Instituti Romani Finlandiae 7. Rome: Bardi.

Thuault, M. 1996. "Un atelier campagnard: Le Rozier," *Dossiers d'Archéologie* 215: 18–19.

Thuault, M., and A. Vernhet. 1986. "Le Rozier," in C. Bémont and J.-P. Jacob (eds.), *La terre sigillée gallo-romaine: Lieux de production du Haut Empire: Implantations, produits, relations*. Paris: Éditions de la Maison des Sciences de l'Homme, 110–13.

Tomber, R. 1987. "Evidence for long-distance commerce: Imported bricks and tiles at Carthage," *Rei Cretariae Romanae Fautorum Acta* 25–26: 161–74.

Trimble, J. 2000. "Replicating the body politic: The Herculaneum Women statue types in early Imperial Italy," *Journal of Roman Archaeology* 13: 41–68.

Tykot, R. H., J. J. Herrmann Jr., N. J. van der Merwe, R. Newman, and K. O. Allegretto 2002. "Thasian marble sculptures in European and American collections: Isotopic and other analyses," in J. J. Herrmann Jr., N. Herz, and R. Newman (eds.), *Interdisciplinary studies on ancient stone*. London: Archetype, 188–95.

Vernhet, A., and C. Bémont 1991. "Un nouveau compte de potiers de La Graufesenque portant mention des flamines," *Annales de Pegasus* 1: 12–14.

Vernhet, A., and C. Bémont 1993. "Le graffite des nones d'octobre," *Annales de Pegasus* 2: 19–21.

Waelkens, M. 1982. "Carrières de marbre en Phrygie (Turquie)," *Bulletin des Musées royaux d'art et d'histoire, Bruxelles* 53: 33–55.

Waelkens, M. 1986. *Die kleinasiatischen Türsteine: Typologische und epigraphische Untersuchungen der kleinasiatische Grabreliefs mit Scheintur.* Mainz: Philipp von Zabern.

Waelkens, M. 1990. "Technique de carrière, préfaçonnage et ateliers dans les civilisations classiques (mondes grec et romain)," in M. Waelkens (ed.), *Pierre éternelle: Du Nil au Rhin: Carrières et préfabrication.* Bruxelles: Crédit Communal, 53–72.

Waelkens, M., P. de Paepe, and L. Moens 1988. "Patterns of extraction and production in the white marble quarries of the Mediterranean: History, present problems and prospects," in J. Clayton Fant, *Ancient marble quarrying and trade.* British Archaeological Reports, Intl. Series S453. Oxford: BAR, 81–116.

Wilson, A. I. 2001a. "The water-mills on the Janiculum," *Memoirs of the American Academy at Rome* 45: 219–46.

Wilson, A. I. 2001b. "Ti. Cl. Felix and the date of the second phase of the East Baths," in L. M. Stirling, D. J. Mattingly, and N. Ben Lazreg (eds.), *Leptiminus (Lamta): A Roman port city in Tunisia. Report no. 2. Journal of Roman Archaeology* Suppl. 41. Ann Arbor, MI: JRA, 25–28.

Wilson, A. I. 2005. "The economic impact of technological advances in the Roman construction industry," in Elio Lo Cascio (ed.), *Innovazione tecnica e progresso economico nel mondo romano. Pragmateiai. Atti degli Incontri capresi di storia dell'economia antica (Capri 13–16 aprile 2003).* Bari: Edipuglia.

Wilson, A. I. 2006. "Fishy business: Roman exploitation of marine resources," *Journal of Roman Archaeology* 19: 525–37.

Zimmer, G. 1982. *Römische Berufsdarstellungen.* Deutsches Archäologisches Institut. Berlin: Mann Verlag.

# CHAPTER 16

---

# METALWORKING
# AND TOOLS

---

## CAROL MATTUSCH

WHAT we know about metalworking in the ancient Mediterranean world derives primarily from literary testimonia and from depictions of bronze- and ironworkers on Greek vases and Roman grave monuments (Zimmer 1982: 37–40, 179–96). The authors and artists were probably not practitioners of these arts, and as a consequence they were only superficially familiar with the industry. Today's classicists and archaeologists also tend to suffer from a lack of direct experience with the technologies. Furthermore, the major sources of our information have been literary and pictorial testimonia, because so little archaeological evidence for ancient workshops has been excavated—none, in fact, until the mid-twentieth century. Such workshops were not usually located in a city center or a sanctuary, where excavations have focused, but on the periphery, and so relatively few ancient metalworking establishments have been excavated to date. For example, no signs of production have been found during the lengthy excavations of the sanctuary at Delphi, a site that has yielded hundreds of metal dedications of all kinds, whereas about 25 workshops and dumps have been identified around the Acropolis, the agora, and the Ceramicus of ancient Athens (Mattusch 1977a; Zimmer 1990). Such sites are found unexpectedly, and they may not be correctly identified, since the finds consist of dumped debris that may have been shifted several times. Today, we consider both the evidence of surviving workshop materials and the metal finds from ancient cities and sanctuaries. Learning to read the surfaces of a bronze for information about its production has become part of the process as well. But we still rely heavily on the secondary evidence of literary testimonia and artistic representations in piecing together the practices associated with ancient metalworking establishments. This discussion focuses for the most part on the production of bronze sculpture, since that field of metalworking, with its expensive, complex, and often very large products made use of nearly all the techniques applied to the production of more practical, everyday objects and the use of other metals and alloys.

# HEPHAESTUS AND ANCIENT METALWORKERS

According to Homer, the workshop of Hephaestus, god of fire and of metalworking, was equipped with an anvil set on a block, as well as with crucible, bellows, hammer, and tongs (*Il.* 18). Similarly, hammers and anvils are the most common accessories in vase paintings depicting armorers. The tondo of the early fifth-century B.C. Berlin Foundry Cup (figure 16.1) shows Hephaestus presenting armor for Achilles to Thetis, the hero's mother. Hephaestus sits beside his anvil, a double-headed hammer in hand. Gems are also engraved with similar images depicting an armorer wielding a hammer over a helmet, a shield, or a metal vase. The scene is a familiar one, and it appears both on vases, and—later on—in Pompeian wall paintings (cf. figure 2.3). The scene may include the god's tools—tongs, a bowed saw, and a file. On one vase, Hephaestus polishes a shield with pumice (Boston, Museum of Fine Arts: red-figure vase painting no. 13.188), examples of which have been found in ancient workshops, stained green by corroded bronze. Human smiths are shown with various rasps, scrapers, files (as on a red-figure kylix in Oxford: Ashmolean G 267), perhaps a punch or a drill, and hammers, which they use to fashion helmets, shields, greaves, and knives. Ironworkers are represented holding tongs and thrusting blooms of iron toward a fire (as on London, British Museum: black-figure amphora B 507), hammers and anvils nearby. Tall crucible-furnaces and bellows appear in many such scenes.

Clearly, Greek metalworkers, like their patron deity, were skilled in extracting gold, silver, copper, tin, lead, and iron, and in forging, hammering, and casting a wide variety of objects in these metals. Gold and silver were used primarily to make jewelry, coins, and vessels. Objects were cast, hammered, cut, and soldered. Forms of decoration included repoussé, stamping, filigree, granulation, engraving, niello, and inlaying. Lead was used to make various utilitarian objects that had to be shaped by casting, resistant to corrosion, and inexpensive, such as architectural clamps, water pipes, cooking utensils, and occasional votive plaques and statuettes. The Greeks and Romans also continued the ancient Near Eastern practice of inscribing curses on lead tablets (*defixiones*).

Ironworking was introduced to Greece from Anatolia sometime around 1000 B.C. There were major sources of iron ore in Macedonia, Euboea, Attica, the Peloponnese, the Aegean islands, and Crete. Objects such as tools, spearheads and

Figure 16.1. Berlin Foundry Cup, interior, early fifth century B.C. Berlin, Antikensammlung F 2294. (Courtesy of Isolde Luckert, Antikensammlung, Staatliche Museen zu Berlin, Preussischer Kulturbesitz.)

arrowheads, daggers, knives, axes, architectural clamps, pins, and vessels were produced by smelting and hot-forging. In some places, there is evidence that iron was worked together with bronze by the same craftsmen in the same workshops (Mattusch 1991a: 389).

# EVIDENCE FROM VASE PAINTINGS

Representations of ironworkers in Greek vase painting show that the tools used for working hot iron were anvil, hammer, and tongs, as on an Attic kylix of around 500 B.C. (Berlin Antikenmuseum no. 1980.7). As for bronze workers, the illustrations on the Berlin Foundry Cup (figures 16.1–3) provide the best ancient description of

Figure 16.2. Berlin Foundry Cup, exterior, early fifth century B.C. Berlin, Antiken-sammlung F 2294. (Courtesy of Antikensammlung, Staatliche Museen zu Berlin, Preussischer Kulturbesitz.)

Greek metalworking activities in both smithy and foundry (Mattusch 1982), and they show the close link between the two. The scenes on this cup also make specific reference to hierarchies within the foundry, and to two artistic styles that were available on the market during the early fifth century B.C. In the tondo, Hephaestus works alone, whereas on the exterior of the cup, foundry workers are engaged in joining the pieces of one statue and cleaning the surface of another one. Clearly metalworking activities of all kinds could be carried out in a single shop.

On one side of the cup, a tall metallurgical furnace is being heated, and the sections of a naturalistic bronze statue of an athlete are being joined. On the other side, workmen wielding curved rasps are polishing a large archaic bronze statue of a warrior. Tools and equipment illustrated on the vase include models for body-parts, hammers, rasps, a two-handled saw, an anvil, and a poker and bellows for the furnace. The bearded senior metalworkers wear either skullcaps or waistcloths, the equivalent of aprons, whereas their junior assistants are nude, beardless, and hatless. To judge from the two statues represented in different styles on the cup, the archaic style continued to be in demand even after a more naturalistic style had been introduced. There are numerous other representations of metalworkers on Greek vases, most notably helmet makers, depicted as squatting naked and shaping a helmet by hammering it over a small anvil (Thaliarchos Painter, 480 B.C.; Paris, Petit Palais no. 381; Beazley 1963: 81.1, 1610), or finishing the surface with a file (Antiphon Painter, 485 B.C.; Ashmolean Museum, Inv.G.267/V.518; Beazley 1963: 336.22, 1646).

Figure 16.3. Berlin Foundry Cup, exterior, early fifth century B.C. Berlin, Anti-kensammlung F 2294. (Courtesy of Antikensammlung, Staatliche Museen zu Berlin, Preussischer Kulturbesitz.)

# EARLY GREEK METALLURGY

Bronze, in the classical world an alloy of copper with about 10 percent tin, was known in the Mediterranean region from approximately 3000 B.C. onward. The Greek word for both bronze and copper was *chalkos*; in Latin it was *aes*. With bronze, the Greeks and Romans made jewelry, mirrors, pins and needles, tripods, lamps, vessels, tools, nails and other hardware, medical instruments, candelabra, dinnerware, official weights and ballots, coins, weapons and armor, furniture parts, architectural ornaments, inscriptions, figurines, and large-scale statuary. They shaped it by casting, beating and annealing, or repoussé (beating from behind, over a bed of pitch) and assembled sections by soldering or riveting. Decoration involved chasing, inlay, patination, differential alloying, and gilding.

Solid bronze statuettes and other household objects were being cast by the lost-wax process from the time of their first appearance in ninth-century Greece. Wax was cut, rolled, pinched, and carved; the wax body parts were stuck together; the wax model was invested with a clay mold; the mold was baked to burn out the wax; and bronze was poured into the mold to replace the wax. The base was often cast along with the figurine, occupying the space used as a funnel during the pour. Each work produced in such a manner was, of course, unique.

Olympia has yielded the largest number of these early offerings, but the Heraion at Argos has also produced many of these generic figurines, including large numbers of birds, cows, deer, horses, and humans. There is much repetition, particularly among those bronzes that come from a single site, both because the demand for them depended on their adherence to the particular types that suited their votive function, and because they were produced in quantity. Groups of like figures no doubt come from a single workshop. Various idiosyncratic ways were found by which to produce an item in demand quickly, again and again, and serially produced bronzes soon became the norm (Mattusch 1996: 18–23).

# EGYPTIAN INFLUENCE ON GREEK METALWORKING

The sophisticated metalworking industry in Greece owed much to Egypt, where the Greeks not only learned about metallurgical materials and techniques, but also about the design and production of monumental stone architecture and sculpture. Greeks settled at Naucratis in the Nile delta during the seventh century B.C. By that time, the Egyptians had been using the same basic formulas for representing human figures, as well as the same techniques for carving and casting them, for more than 2,500 years. Metal objects of all kinds were being cast and hammered in large numbers, many of them richly inlaid, others sheathed with gold or silver (Ziegler 1987: 85–101; Bianchi 1990: 61–84).

During the Twenty-Sixth Dynasty, Psammetichus I (664–610 B.C.) encouraged intercourse between the Greek colonists and the Egyptians (Herodotus 2.154). The Greeks must have marveled at the technological virtuosity and the richness that they saw in Egyptian buildings, images, materials, and technology (Bianchi 1990). The legendary Daedalus was said to have made statues that looked Egyptian (Diodorus 1.97.6); Pausanias thought that his works were "rather odd . . . but inspired" (2.4.5). Diodorus (4.76.3) said that he was the first to bring a degree of naturalism to statues, "for which men naturally admired him." Diodorus also reports (1.98) that "the most renowned of the ancient sculptors—Telecles and Theodorus, the sons of Rhoecus—visited with [the Egyptians]." He also explains that they worked according to the Egyptian system, the proportions of a figure's parts being determined by formula. It is no accident that Daedalus should be associated with Crete, which lay on the crossroads of Mediterranean trade, and where resources and ideas were introduced directly from Egypt and the Near East. Daedalus made a lifelike bronze cow for Queen Pasiphaë and the labyrinth for King Minos, before falling out of favor and having to fly to Athens on wings that he designed and made from feathers glued together with wax.

Like Crete, the island of Samos in the eastern Aegean was a trading center and as such also a focal point for the introduction of new ideas. Although ancient authors tend to confuse the lineage of Rhoecus, Theodorus, and Telecles, they are unanimous in associating them with Samos and with a wide range of achievements in the arts, design, and engineering. Egypt is mentioned as well. The innovations attributed to them were not limited to a single medium. The chief authority for the introduction of large-scale bronze casting to Greece in the sixth century B.C. is Pausanias, writing in the second century A.D. He says that the first to melt bronze and cast statues were the Samians, Rhoecus the son of Philaeus and Theodorus the son of Telecles (8.14.8, 9.41.1), but he admits that he has not seen any of their work (10.38.6). Pliny the Elder's assignment of the introduction of clay modeling to these two artists, though tentative (*HN* 35.152), is appropriate to work conducted in a foundry. Pliny (*HN* 34.83) refers to a statue that Theodorus cast of himself holding a file, thereby implying that Theodorus was seen as both an artisan and an artist. Pliny attributes production of the labyrinth on Samos to Theodorus (*HN* 34.83), and Herodotus (3.41) mentions a seal ring made by Theodorus, adding that Rhoecus worked on the construction of the Heraion on Samos (3.60). Rhoecus and Theodorus may or may not be actual historical figures, but these passages clearly suggest that sixth-century Samos was responsible for a good measure of innovation by metalworkers, with the obvious link to artistic activity. Like the renowned sixth-century Samians, the great artists of the Classical period are credited with working in more than one medium. The fifth-century B.C. artist Phidias, for example, made bronze statues, chryselephantine (gold-and-ivory) statues, and even a gilded wooden statue with marble face, hands, and feet (Pausanias 9.4.1). It is likely that most Greek and Roman metalworkers were similarly adaptable.

In statuary, the market was driven by a demand for new types and styles, which was followed by the development of the necessary technology. The tensile strength of bronze and the lighter weight of hollow-cast forms, which might seem to encourage the casting of statues in active poses, were not immediately exploited. Instead, the earliest Greek freestanding sculptures in both bronze and stone were frontal standing figures with their arms close to their sides, very much like the self-contained sculptures that the Greeks had seen in Egypt. The poses soon became looser, but the tensile strength of bronze never seems to have driven stylistic change in Greece. Rather it seems to have been the introduction of athletic victors' statues in the sixth century that eventually led to more varied and active poses (Mattusch 1988: 99–100, 128–29, 212–13).

# Technical Practices

The lost-wax process of casting (described below) was used throughout the ancient world for both utilitarian objects and statuary. The advantages are obvious: a model can be re-used in case of casting failure, or applied to the production of multiple copies, and production costs are generally lower than with unique objects. Large, thin-walled objects such as armor and vessels were produced by a combination of casting and hammering. Production of armor was a major Athenian industry, and even well-known artists participated, such as Phidias, who was said to have once also painted a shield (Pliny, *HN* 35.54). Helmets were first cast in rough form, then hammered into their final shapes and finished with rasps.

Bronze, which could be cast into complicated shapes and was resistant to corrosion, was particularly suitable for cosmetic instruments, serving vessels, and furniture fittings. Both standing mirrors and hand mirrors were being cast in Greece during the sixth century B.C. By the fourth century B.C., both types had been largely replaced by the round box mirror, consisting of a cast disc, polished on the front, that was hinged to a hammered or cast lid, to which a repoussé decoration might be soldered with lead.

When the Greeks first made bronze vessels, during the Geometric period, they used them for dedications and for funerary offerings; later, bronze vessels were the prizes for athletic victories. These vessels could be very large, technically sophisticated products. A bronze tripod cauldron made on Samos during the seventh century cost six talents, a tenth of the profit from a merchant trading expedition to Spain (Herodotus 4.152). The cauldron was decorated with griffin protomes, and it was supported by a tripod that consisted of three kneeling bronze figures seven cubits in height (ca. 3.5 m). It is not known whether the cauldron was cast or hammered, but the griffins and the kneeling figures were no doubt cast as multiples, which was the norm by the seventh century. Herodotus describes several cauldrons that would have been supported by three or more similar figures. He mentions two other huge cauldrons with figures around the rim, one made by the Lacedaemonians for King Croesus of Lydia that held 12,275 litres, and one made for Ariantes of Scythia that held twice as much (Herodotus 1.70, 4.81). Metalwork on this scale, undoubtedly weighing hundreds of kilograms, represents a remarkable repertory of skills, even if elements of the monument were cast and worked separately.

Physical evidence from the Orientalizing period suggests that dedications of colossal tripod cauldrons were not unusual. During the seventh century, the groups of protomes that were used to decorate these cauldrons might be produced in a series, or, one might say, in editions—for speed as well as to ensure that they all looked alike (Mattusch 1990). Griffins' heads were particularly common attachments, first hammered from sheet-bronze, and then hollow-cast. Some particularly large cast heads were fitted onto metal necks hammered over cores.

Three large seventh-century B.C. griffins' heads from Olympia, all produced by the same unusual method (Mattusch 1990), illustrate the sophisticated nature of the early founder's craft. They were formed from nearly identical groups of wax slabs, to each of which were added wax ears, tongue, and knob. Finally, scales were punched in the surfaces of all three heads with a single set of tools, further proving that these protomes were produced simultaneously. Each wax head was then invested and cast, after which it was fitted to a neck, probably made of hammered sheet metal over a core. The proportions of the griffins show that the tripod cauldron that they adorned stood between 4.5 and 5.5 m in height. Part of another remarkably large dedication is preserved in the form of a hollow-cast column consisting of entwined snakes, now in the hippodrome in Istanbul. This column originally supported a tripod cauldron in Delphi that approached 6 m in height, set up to honor the Greek cities that had defeated the Persians at Plataea in 479 B.C. (Herodotus 9.81; Thucydides 1.132; Pausanias 10.13.9). By the Classical period, Greek bronze vessels of a more manageable size were being sold throughout the Mediterranean world as luxury items. Examples have been found in Greece, southern Italy and Sicily, Asia Minor, northern Europe, North Africa, and at sites along the coast of the Black Sea.

Bronze vessels were usually made by hammering discs of sheet-bronze into hollow shapes that might then be turned on a lathe for further shaping and detailing. Occasionally the bodies were cast. Handles, very often feet, and sometimes the rims of vessels were separately cast, and were mass-produced. Feet and handles were soldered or riveted to the body of the vessel, which might be decorated by the addition of other cast features. Sometimes the walls of bronze vessels were elaborated by embossing (repoussé), engraving, inlay, or gilding. Certain types of vessels were particularly well suited to manufacture in bronze, such as tripod cauldrons, double-handled buckets (*situlae*), and bowls with human- and animal-figured handles (*paterae*). Other bronze vessels parallel the forms of contemporary pottery, including craters, hydrias, amphoras, oenochoes, and the like. The range of plastic decoration that can be realized in bronze is vast and is usually more fully exploited than in pottery. During the Hellenistic and Roman periods, tastes tended toward expensive and elaborately decorated elegant vessels, whether in bronze or in silver or gold. Major centers for the production of later metal vessels were apparently located in Macedonia, Thessaly, Asia Minor, South Italy, and, of course, Rome. During the first century A.D., the lathe was used to produce elaborate rim and base shapes both by folding and shaping the sheet metal with tools as it turned at high speed ("spinning"), and by trimming and cutting thicker rim or base castings with a chisel (Mutz 1972; Haüser and Mutz 1973; Cave 1977). The small, elaborate containers prepared in this manner resemble contemporary blown glassware vessels, and the metalworking technique probably was developed under the stimulus of the new glassworking technique—an interesting example of imitation, competition, and innovation across materials and workshops. The uniformity of the vessels suggests either the activity of a small number of workshops or the free exchange of technical information among them.

# Techniques of Statuary Production

As large, expensive, usually public monuments, Greek and Roman statues provide a glimpse at the most sophisticated techniques and accomplishments of metalworking. Freestanding statues made of metal were being produced in the Greek world as early as the eighth century B.C., and their technical evolution was not unlike that of utilitarian objects. According to Pausanias (3.17.6), the earliest technique involved hammering metal sheets into the shape of a figure and riveting them together; Daedalus, the legendary master to whom important discoveries and early works in various media were often attributed, made such a statue. Ancient authors refer to this method as *sphyrelaton*. Three such statues, called *sphyrelata*, were found in a small late-eighth- or early-seventh-century B.C sanctuary at Dreros in Crete (Romano 2000). They were made of cylindrical forms of hammered sheet metal, riveted at the seams, just as Pausanias describes them.

Pausanias (9.10.2) also mentions a sixth-century B.C. image of which there are two versions, one in bronze, presumably cast, and one carved in wood. "The statue [of Apollo Ismenius in Thebes] is the same size as the one in Branchidae [Didyma], and the form is no different; whoever has seen one of these statues and learned its sculptor does not need much skill to see that the other one is also a work by Canachus. They differ in that the one in Branchidae is bronze, whereas the one in Thebes is cedar-wood." If we think of ancient statuary as being produced in editions, what Pausanias says about sculptures by the archaic-period sculptor Canachus is perfectly clear. He also implies that buyers choose the medium. Canachus could have taken molds from the wooden statue to use in making a bronze version of the same thing, or the production staff could have used molds taken from the artist's model to produce a working-model for a bronze and a plaster model for a wooden statue. In the same vein, a passage about a wooden statue that was made in two halves, one by Theodorus working in Ephesus, and the other by Telecles working in Samos, also reflects the use of a single original model (Diodorus Siculus 1.98).

Surviving mold fragments, as well as finger marks, brush marks, and tool marks on the inside surfaces of surviving bronze statues, show that the indirect process, in which the original artist's model is not destroyed in the production process, is the form of lost-wax casting that was the most widely used during classical antiquity. Large sculptures, even some statuettes, were cast hollow and in pieces, which were then joined by flow welding (Mattusch 2005). The original design for a statue could be made of almost anything: it could, in fact, have been no more than a drawing by the artist. Usually, however, the artist's model was made in clay or plaster so as to allow for addition and subtraction. After the design had been modeled on a large scale, skilled artisans took piece casts from it in clay. These molds were lined with a thin layer of wax that could be removed and assembled with others to produce a hollow wax working-model. The finished wax working-model was cut up, and the statue was cast in pieces inside clay molds by means of the lost-wax method. The working-model could be cast in bronze just as it came from the molds, or it could be reworked before casting, which might involve adjusting limbs or adding or embellishing particular features, such as ears, free-hanging locks of hair, or a beard. Should a buyer request a unique piece, a wax working-model made from the molds could be altered extensively by the artist before casting. After casting, the separately cast parts of the statue were put together. The original model, like the molds taken from it, could be re-used to make as many copies as were required by the artist. As is the case today, each phase of the process—molding, making the wax, pouring the bronze, cleaning, joining, and patinating—was handled by different individuals. Horace (*Ars P.* 32–35) describes a craftsman who can model fingernails and make wavy locks but is unhappy because he cannot make the whole statue.

Because of the extraordinary difficulty and risk of casting large, complex forms, statues were cast in pieces. A vivid picture of the problems and dangers involved in casting a large statue in one piece can be found in Benvenuto Cellini's account of the casting of his *Perseus* in 1554 (*Autobiography* 2.73–78). In antiquity, human nudes were usually cast in six or seven major pieces, their fabricators taking advantage of natural anatomical divisions to conceal flow-welded joins (Mattusch 2005: 133–35, 189–337), while draped statues might be cast in fifteen or twenty pieces, the joins concealed by garments. The joints are often marked by a row of ovals, sometimes reinforced by inserted rectangular patches. The rectangular pins or chaplets that stabilized the core within the investment while the bronze was being poured sometimes remain in place. The division of statues at mid-neck is characteristic of archaic and classical-period bronzes from the Greek world, while Roman bronze workers tended to place the seams along the hairline or jawline so as to conceal the joins more easily. During the archaic and classical periods, the heads of Greek statues are often thick and irregular castings, indicating that they were modeled directly and/or worked over in the wax, making them unique works. Thin regular walls throughout a statue are the norm in the Roman period, along with evidence on the inner surface of the bronze for application of the wax to piece molds. Both features are clear indications that a work was cast by the indirect lost-wax method, with minimal reworking of the wax working-model before it was invested with clay for the pour.

An artist's direct work on the wax working-model was often what distinguished one statue from another. The classical-period Riace Bronzes (figures 16.4–5) illustrate the advantages of using the indirect lost wax practice (Mattusch 1996: 62–67). The two statues have almost exactly the same contours and dimensions, and their profiles, poses, and gestures are nearly identical. In other words, both statues are likely to have come from the same model. The wax working-models made from the molds were differentiated by pulling one statue's feet farther apart than the other's, and by adding individualized wax hair and beards to the two figures. Inscriptions providing specific identities would have completed the production of two very different editions of one original model. Statue-types were standardized, making them easily recognizable as generals, philosophers, or the like. Such statues were even sometimes re-used, as was the case with one that Pausanias saw in Argos (2.17.3), which had been cast in Greek times to represent the mythical Orestes but was renamed in Roman times so that it could serve as the emperor Augustus.

Two epigrams allegedly written in the fifth century B.C. reflect the use of the indirect lost wax process of casting. "Perhaps Myron himself would say this: I did not form this heifer, but of her I modeled the statue" (*Anth. Pal.* 2.9.718). "Myron feigned a cow with his own hands that was not formed in molds, but that turned to

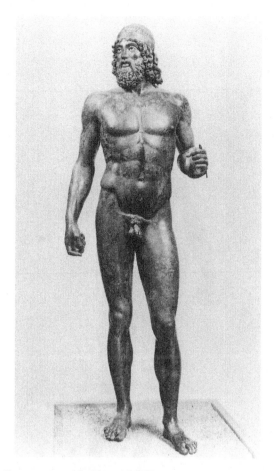

Figure 16.4. Riace Bronze A, probably mid-fifth century B.C. H 2.05 m. (Courtesy Soprintendenza Archeologica della Calabria.)

bronze through old age" (*Anth. Pal.* 2.9.716). The implication of the first epigram is that Myron took molds from a cow and used them to cast his statue. Both epigrams, however, may mean simply that Myron's cow looks so realistic that it is hard to believe it could have been made by man. Had Myron actually developed a system of molding from life he would no doubt have received the kind of recognition accorded to Lysistratus a century later for using or, more likely, streamlining the indirect lost wax process.

A passage written by Plutarch (*Quaest. conv.* 2.3.2, 636C; *De prof. virt.* 17.86A) about the mid-fifth century B.C. sculptor Polyclitus has generated much debate, but it indicates that the artist's model for a bronze was generally modeled in clay: "As for the arts, first they model the unformed and shapeless (material), and later they articulate all the details; whence Polyclitus the sculptor said that the work is the most difficult when the clay is on the nail." This passage probably refers to the finishing of the artist's model. Molds were then taken from the clay model and

Figure 16.5. Riace Bronze B, probably mid-fifth century B.C. H 1.96 m. (Courtesy Soprintendenza Archeologica della Calabria.)

lined with wax to make a working-model, which could be customized or not, and from which a bronze would be cast.

Lysippus of Sicyon was said to have produced an astounding total of 1,500 statues during his career in the fourth century B.C. (Pliny, *HN* 34.37). He was said to have used nature as his model (Pliny, *HN* 34.61). Lysippus differed from most artists in that he came from a family of bronze workers, and he was obviously familiar with the technology involved in producing statuary. His brother Lysistratus is said to have been the first Greek to produce portraits by pouring wax into plaster molds taken from living models, and to have developed a similar means of taking casts from statues (Pliny, *HN* 35.153). It is logical to conclude from this information that Lysippus and Lysistratus either used human beings as their models or used finished models which, when molded, produced waxes that needed no additional work, but were ready to invest and cast. This would mean that the artist did not need to finish the waxes, and that the production of a statue could be left entirely to technicians. The savings in time, effort, and money would have resulted in increased production, and might explain how Lysippus could have produced so many statues during his career.

There are other references to use of the indirect process in the fourth century B.C., one by Plutarch (*Mor., De soll. an.* 984a) about two men dispatched to Sinope by Ptolemy Soter (ca. 367–282 B.C.) in order to bring him back a statue: "Of the two statues, they thought that they could take with them the one of Pluto, but that they should take a mold of the Kore and leave behind the actual statue." This is perhaps more interesting as an example of transporting molds of large-scale statuary for the purpose of reproduction.

## Alloys and Color

So few Greek or Roman bronzes have been systematically analyzed that questions about the value of alloys in determining the origins of bronzes cannot be adequately addressed. Quantitative analyses of alloys, however, have given an important new dimension to the study of ancient statuary (Mattusch 2005: 136–40, 333–34). Copper, tin, and lead are the principal intentional ingredients of bronze. Statuary bronzes tend to contain between 70 and 90 percent of copper and less than 10 percent of tin, but lead content ranges widely, from less than 1 percent to nearly 30 percent. Lead lowers the melting point of the alloy and increases the fluidity of molten bronze during casting, facilitating the casting of large bronzes. A sufficient percentage of lead also promotes fusion during the joining of cast sections by flow welding. Trace elements are elements that appear by chance and in very small quantities in an alloy, because they were present in the ores from which the major elements were smelted. Unlike the principal elements, they can provide reliable matches between alloys and can be used to identify objects cast from a single batch of metal, particularly when the bronzes also match in design, style, and subject matter.

The eyes of Greek and Roman statues were usually inset with bone (or ivory) and stone (Mattusch 1996: 24, pl. 1), though occasionally they were simply marked in the wax and reproduced in the bronze. Bronze plates cut with fringed edges sometimes served as eyelashes, while holding the eyes in their sockets. Eyebrows, lips, nipples, fingernails, toenails, wreaths, and bracelets could be inset or added in copper, tin, and even gold or silver (Hellenkemper Salies et al. 1994).

Apart from a number of ancient bronzes that are known to have been gilded, such as the equestrian statue of Marcus Aurelius on the Capitoline Hill in Rome, little is known about the patination of ancient bronze statuary beyond what the ancient authors tell us—and they were not experts in the field. Interest in this subject is growing, however, and the widespread use of mechanical methods for cleaning ancient metals has reduced the damage to the metal caused in the past by invasive chemical cleansing. As a result, it now appears that the Riace Bronzes (figures

16.4–5) originally had black skin (Formigli 1985), and other bronzes are showing signs of having once been patinated. This evidence lends some credence to remarks by ancient authors that bronzes had different colors, though they tend to ascribe the color to alloy rather than to patination. Pliny advises us that Delian bronze differs in color from Aeginetan bronze (*HN* 34.10), and an alloy that was preferred for portrait statues was "liver-colored" (*HN* 34.8). Plutarch (*Quaest. conv.* 5.1.2) mentions a statue whose face was a different color from the body, as is often seen today in sculptural bronzes by such artists as J. Seward Johnson. Corinthian bronze was said to be whitish because of having some gold or silver in the alloy.

## Evidence from Workshops

### Olympia

The surviving physical evidence for metalworking in the ancient Mediterranean world consists primarily of workshop debris, which may be more reliable than what nonspecialists reveal about the industry in literary testimonia and in ancient illustrations. The excavations at Olympia have uncovered workshops and workshop debris from the production of statuettes that were dedicated in the Sanctuary of Zeus (Heilmeyer 1969). The workshops lay outside the sanctuary in a sand-filled ravine that had once been a streambed. They were temporary installations, consisting of simple furnaces made of stone, mudbrick, and baked clay, from which canals led to molds that were packed in the sand. Debris tossed back into the casting area after use and scattered around the edges of the Sanctuary of Zeus consists of charcoal, bricks with vitrified inner surfaces, lumps of bronze, clay mold fragments, bellows nozzles, and clay stoppers. There are bronze funnels cut from the pour, gates that are both round and rectangular in section, and clay crucibles and molds, as well as failed castings of statuettes. Some of the foundries date from as early as the Geometric period. Theophrastus (*Lap.* 16) refers to the fuel used at Olympia: "Among the materials that are dug because they are useful, those known as coals are made of earth, and, once set on fire, they burn like charcoal. They are found in Liguria . . . and in Elis as one approaches Olympia by the mountain road; and they are used by those who work in metals."

### Athens

Metalworking shops were located in and around the agora of Athens from the sixth century B.C. to the sixth century A.D. (Mattusch 1977a). Their centrality suggests the importance of the metalworking industry in ancient Athens. Some work areas had hearths, others had casting pits, and they all left behind their debris. The finds excavated in these establishments and in the dumps associated with them include broken clay molds, vitrified bricks from furnaces, scraps of waste metal, and slag. Some of the deposits contained debris associated specifically with bronzeworking or ironworking, while some deposits yielded iron, bronze, and even lead debris.

The industrial area around the Temple of Hephaestus, overlooking the agora, has produced many of these installations and artifacts. An inscription of around 421–415 B.C. even records the purchase of copper, tin, lead, wood, and charcoal for the completion of the (bronze) cult statues and for the pedestal for the Temple of Hephaestus (*IG* I$^2$, 370–71). A curse directed at two bronze-smiths and a woman was inscribed on a lead tablet (Athens: Agora Excavations no. IL 997) and hidden beneath the floor of the smithy in the fourth century B.C.

Although the traces of ironworking from the area of the Athenian agora are substantial, only one actual iron smithy has been excavated. The same holds true for the single bronze smithy, which contained only a hearth, some slag, and the hidden curse tablet. The trash from bronze foundries provides far more revealing information about processes. All were temporary establishments, some for statuary and others for small utilitarian objects. Clay molds from the earlier Greek period are thick and heavy, with inclusions such as sand, straw, hair, and shells, whereas molds from foundries of the Roman period are thinner and more lightweight. Molds were propped up for baking in the pit that would later serve for casting. No traces of actual furnaces have been found, although curved vitrified bricks can be identified as having come from the furnace lining.

A fragmentary inscription from the Acropolis of Athens contains the records of the overseers who were in charge of producing the colossal bronze Athena Promachus designed by Phidias and erected on the Acropolis between 460 and 450 B.C. The inscription lists the wages paid and the materials purchased at various points in the project. In one year, the large sum of 78,110 drachmas seems to have been available for the project. Charcoal and firewood for the furnace are mentioned repeatedly, as are clay and hair, for which 26 drachmas were spent in one year. The clay would have been for core or mold material, and the hair was probably mixed with the clay to reduce shrinkage and/or strengthen the molds. Wax is listed only once in the text, if the word *kerós* is correctly restored (Mattusch 1988: 166–69). Copper, tin, and silver are purchased, the latter for the decoration of the statue. The cost of a talent of copper was only 35 drachmas and one or two obols, but the average price of tin was 232$\frac{2}{6}$ drachmas per talent. Wages were paid by the day, by the prytany (administrative period slightly longer than a month), and by the job. In one year, 6,600$\frac{2}{6}$ drachmas were paid in wages; in another year, 10,100 drachmas were paid. This single large statue was a very expensive undertaking, nearly on the scale of an architectural project.

## Corinth

Corinthian bronze was highly prized for its color, and the Corinthian metalworking industry was highly respected. Pausanias (2.3.3) wrote that Corinthian bronzes were quenched in the spring of Peirene, perhaps implying that this was one reason for its special character. Pliny the Elder asserted that Corinthian bronze was the most highly praised bronze known from earlier times, and he cited famous individuals who coveted objects made of it (*HN* 34.1, 6–8; 34.48). Petronius (*Sat.* 15.31.50) reports that the nouveau-riche Trimalchio had a collection of "Corinthian" bronzes. Athenaeus (5.199e) refers to two famous Corinthian bowls with capacities of more than 360 liters, each with seated figures on the rim and relief figures on the neck and body. Pliny listed three special Corinthian alloys that were used specifically for utensils or vessels (*HN* 34.8): one was silvery white, and he thought that it contained silver; the second was tawny like gold, supposedly from the addition of that metal; and the third alloy contained equal parts of gold and silver. Whatever we make of Pliny's passage, it is clear that craftsmen deliberately chose and produced their alloys to obtain particular effects (Mattusch 1991b).

Bronzeworking and ironworking were carried out in the Forum Area at Corinth from the sixth century B.C. to as late as the twelfth century A.D. (Mattusch 1977b). Casting pits sometimes were no more than small holes in the floor with vents at the sides for flues or for attaching bellows nozzles. An iron smithy is attested by corroded lumps of iron and by magnetic, silvery flakes of iron. Bronze and iron slag and clay crucibles and molds were found, as well as bivalve molds for such items as belt buckles, spearheads, handles, and furniture legs. The join between the halves of bivalve clay molds was secured by an outer investment of clay, which could also have been used to form the funnel. A bronze fulcrum panel with damascened copper, silver, and niello acanthus-and-flower motif provides a tantalizing introduction to the sophisticated production techniques that were standard fare in the workshops of one of Corinth's major industries (Mattusch 1991b).

Numerous small fragments broken from bronze statues were found in the Forum area, apparently to be melted down for re-use. Only one large-scale foundry has so far been identified at Corinth, and it lies well outside the heart of the city near the gymnasium (Mattusch 1991a). It consists of a casting pit and a furnace pit. The installation, which had been filled with foundry debris after its final use, contained wood charcoal, a few bronze statue fragments, bronze slag, bronze drips, pumice, iron nails, investment mold fragments, mold bases, and props to support the molds during baking, a vivid testimony to the complexity of the process. Visual representations assist our understanding (figures 4.4, 16.1–16.3). The uniformity and quantity of the material dumped into the workshop suggest that this was a temporary installation, constructed for a single large commission and then closed down, in keeping with the usual practice in ancient foundries.

# GREEK AND ROMAN STATUARY
## IN CONTEXT

Today, ancient bronzes have an aura about them that marbles do not, because there are far fewer surviving bronze statues than there are marbles, mainly because bronze could be melted down and reused. No more than a few hundred Greek and

Roman bronzes are left today, even if we count all the surviving heads without bodies and bodies without heads. But this statistic is not representative of the numbers of bronze statues that were produced during antiquity. Mummius filled Rome with the statues that he brought home after defeating Greece in 146 B.C. (Strabo 6.381; Pliny *HN* 34.36). In 179 B.C., statues had to be removed from the Forum of Rome, and the Capitoline Hill cleared of statues that were obstructing the view of the Temple of Jupiter (Livy 40.51.3). Cicero was one of many homeowners in the first century B.C. who had antique sculptures shipped to him from Greece. In the first century A.D., Pliny (*HN* 34.36) reports that there were still about 12,000 bronze statues standing in Athens, Olympia, Delphi, and Rhodes. He also lists 160 bronze sculptors who worked between the fifth and the first centuries B.C. (*HN* 34.49–93). Pausanias singles out for description unusual statues he saw in the course of his journey around Greece—a dozen or more bronzes in Delphi, about 60 in Athens, and more than 40 in the Sanctuary of Zeus at Olympia, besides mentioning hundreds of victors' statues, although not all of these may have been made of bronze.

In contrast to this abundance, surviving bronze statues are usually found one at a time, prompting scholars to consider them as unique objects. It is also rare that more than a single example of a particular type survives, although there was, of course, a great deal of repetition among classical bronze statues, so many of which represented athletes, statesmen, and heroes. These were not individualized portraits for the most part, but standardized public monuments that celebrated the familiar. Anyone walking through a Greek or Roman city or sanctuary would have been looking at statues whose meaning was easily recognizable by the body, the gesture, and the attributes, as well as the inscription.

# THE ROLE OF COPIES

Taking molds from statues to produce copies was a common practice in antiquity, perhaps even more so than it is today, to judge from a remark by Lucian (*Iupp. trag.* 33): "It is your brother, the Hermes of the Agora, the one beside the Stoa Poecile: he is covered with pitch from being molded every day by statue-makers." The copying industry was particularly active during the Late Republic and the Imperial period. A Roman sculpture shop at Baiae on the Bay of Naples yielded many fragments of plaster casts that had been used to produce marble copies of Greek bronze statues, including the Athenian Tyrant-Slayers by Critius and Nesiotes, three types of Amazons, and, most famous of all, the Doryphorus by Polyclitus (Landwehr 1985). Theophrastus (*Lap.* 67) remarks that "For (taking) impressions, (plaster) seems to surpass greatly the other materials, and it is used for this especially in Greece, owing to its stickiness and smoothness." Pliny the Elder also mentions plaster models (*HN* 35.156).

Copies of the Doryphorus in both stone and bronze from the area around the Bay of Naples indicate that, as we should expect, the buyer could choose whatever medium he or she preferred for the reproduction. He could also choose the format, buying, for example, a bronze herm reproducing only the head of the Doryphorus (Naples, National Museum, herm: no. 4885). A measure of the immense popularity of this particular statue can be seen in the fact that the bronze herm is inscribed, not with the name of Polyclitus, but with the name of the copyist, Apollonius, who also noted his Athenian heritage, a circumstance that would have enhanced his credentials and increased the marketability of the bronzes he produced (Mattusch 2005: 276–82).

# The Market for Bronze Statuary

The practice of making more than one copy of a bronze statue—in fact, of making whole editions of statues—applied in antiquity as it does today. By the sixth century B.C., duplicates and mirror images were being produced for erection in sanctuaries. In the classical period, public statues of leaders and heroes were produced according to standard types so as to be easily recognizable, and by the Hellenistic period statues were being produced for a growing private market. Workshops had specialties, works that were of one particular type, or of a certain style, or possessing some standardized features. A buyer might want a pair of sculptures—identical or mirror images—or variations on a theme. The buyer might choose a bronze or a marble version of a particular work. In looking at the many marble examples of, for example, the Discus-Thrower by Myron, one might wonder how many bronzes were produced of that type. Was there only one bronze "original" that Myron claimed as his own, or did he authorize the production of more than one? Did Myron make changes to his original model after seeing the first bronze statue(s), thereby creating more than one edition of the Discus-Thrower? As a successful artist, Myron would surely have sold more than one example of each sculpture that he designed. He might have had a few bronzes produced, perhaps varying the patina, then a marble or two, and perhaps a few reduced versions of the Discus-Thrower. After all, works in all media are reproducible, and they can be repeated if the market demands it, in whatever medium the buyer wants.

The physical evidence for alloys, workshops, and techniques used in the production of ancient bronzes reveals that the complete repertoire of mechanical and chemical techniques was applied to the production of a wide variety of political and religious monuments as well as everyday objects. Lost-wax casting, in particular, was a highly sophisticated process in the ancient Mediterranean world, from the time of its beginnings in the ninth century B.C. Lost-wax casting was essentially an indirect process with innumerable variations, and it was used for the production of multiples, of editions, and of unique works.

# REFERENCES

Beazley, J. D. 1963. *Attic red-figure vase-painters*. 2nd ed. Oxford: Oxford University Press.

Bianchi, R. 1990. Egyptian metal statuary of the Third Intermediate period (ca. 1070–656 B.C.), from its Egyptian antecedents to its Samian examples," in M. True and J. Podany (eds.), *Small bronze sculpture from the ancient world*. Malibu, CA: J. Paul Getty Museum, 61–84.

Cave, J. F. 1977. "A note on Roman metal-turning," *History of Technology* 2: 78–94.

Formigli, E. 1985. "Die Restaurierung einer griechischen Grossbronze aus dem Meer von Riace/Italien," in H. Born (ed.), *Archäologische Bronzen: Antike Kunst, Moderne Technik*. Berlin: Reimer, 168–74.

Haüser, K., and A. Mutz 1973. "Wie spannten die römischen vascularii (Dreher) ihre Werkstücke." *Technikgeschichte* 40: 251–69.

Heilmeyer, W.-D. 1969. "Giessereibetriebe in Olympia," *Archäologische Anzeiger* 84: 1–28.

Hellenkemper Salies, G., H.-H. von Prittwitz, and G. Bauchhenss (eds.) 1994. *Das Wrack: Der antike Schiffsfund von Mahdia*. Cologne: Rheinland-Verlag.

Landwehr, C. 1985. *Die antiken Gipsabgüsse aus Baiae: Griechische Bronzestatuen in Abgüssen römischer Zeit*. Berlin: Gebr. Mann.

Mattusch, C. 1977a. "Bronze- and ironworking in the area of the Athenian agora," *Hesperia* 46: 340–79.

Mattusch, C. 1977b. "Corinthian metalworking: The Forum area," *Hesperia* 46: 380–89.

Mattusch, C. 1982. "The Berlin Foundry Cup: The casting of Greek bronze statuary in the early fifth century B.C.," *American Journal of Archaeology* 84: 435–44.

Mattusch, C. 1988. *Greek bronze statuary: From the beginnings through the fifth century B.C.* Ithaca, NY: Cornell University Press.

Mattusch, C. 1990. "A trio of griffins from Olympia," *Hesperia* 59: 549–60.

Mattusch, C. 1991a. "Corinthian metalworking: The Gymnasium bronze foundry," *Hesperia* 60: 383–96.

Mattusch, C. 1991b. "Corinthian metalworking: An inlaid fulcrum panel," *Hesperia* 60: 525–28.

Mattusch, C. 1996. *Classical bronzes: The art and craft of Greek and Roman statuary*. Ithaca, NY: Cornell University Press.

Mattusch, C. 2005. *The Villa dei Papiri at Herculaneum: Life and afterlife of a sculpture collection*. Los Angeles: J. Paul Getty Museum.

Mutz, A. 1972. *Die Kunst des Metalldrehens bei den Römern: Interpretationen antiken Arbeitsverfahren auf Grund von Werkspuren*. Basel and Stuttgart: Birkhäuser.

Romano, I. B. 2000. "The Dreros sphyrelata: A re-examination of their date and function," in C. C. Mattusch, A. Brauer, and S. E. Knudsen (eds.), *From the parts to the whole: Acts of the 13th International Bronze Congress*, vol. 1. *Journal of Roman Studies* Suppl 39.1: 40–50.

Ziegler, C. 1987. "Les arts du metal à la Troisième Période Intermédiataire," in *Tanis: L'or des pharaons*. Paris: Association française d'action artistique, 85–101.

Zimmer, G. 1982. *Römische Berufsdarstellungen*. Berlin: Gebr. Mann.

Zimmer, G. 1990. *Griechische Bronzegusswerkstätten: Zur Technologieentwicklung eines antiken Kunsthandwerkes*. Mainz: von Zabern.

Zimmer, G. 2003. "Hellenistische Bronzegusswerkstätten in Demetrias," in *Demetrias: Die deutschen archäologischen Forschungen in Thessalien*, vol. 6. Bonn: Deutsches archäologisches Institut, 9–82.

# CHAPTER 17

........................................................................................................

# WOODWORKING

........................................................................................................

## ROGER B. ULRICH

Iron Age inhabitants of the Mediterranean inherited and practiced a tradition of working with wood that was already thousands of years old. With the exception of a few arid regions, wood had been a readily available resource with a seemingly limitless array of applications. Exploitation was universal, and the scale and complexity of technical processes increased dramatically with the introduction of metal tools. Virtually every part of the harvested tree could be put to good use. Even the leaves of many species were valued for feeding livestock, and bark, always useful as a fuel, could serve as sheathing for roofing or, in some cases, provide the raw material for twines and ropes. The discovery in 1991 of many wooden artifacts—tool handles, arrow shafts, cylindrical containers, and the frame of a backpack—with the frozen body of the now famous "Iceman" of the Italian alps has demonstrated that at the end of the Neolithic period in central Europe, 5,000 years ago, the properties of diverse species of wood for specific applications were already understood at a sophisticated level. The yew used for the Iceman's bow, for example, is still favored by the makers of traditional longbows today (Fowler 2000).

There is virtually no aspect of ancient life that was not affected by those who handled and shaped wood. Transportation on land and sea depended on wooden materials and joinery. Wooden elements, first left in their natural "roundwood" state and later formed into squared beams and planks, played a dominant, if not exclusive, role in the first built structures and never lost prominence; most stone and brick structures of later Greek and Roman cities were covered with wooden roofs and sometimes even rested on wooden post or pile foundations. Roman vaults could not have been built without wooden centering (Taylor 2003; Lancaster 2005a). Woodworkers shaped agricultural tools and household objects for every function. Although coal played a minor role as a fuel source in the Mediterranean world (Theophrastus, *Lap.* 16), and was known in Roman Britain (Dearne and

Branigan 1995), wood and charcoal provided the sole significant source of energy for heating and industrial processes that included fired pottery, roof tiles, bricks, metal tools, and weapons. Given the ubiquity of wood as a building material, it is no accident that the Latin word *materia* can mean wood as a building material, wood forming a tree, or "any substance of which a physical object is made or composed" (*OLD* s.v. "materia").

# EVIDENCE

Despite the absence of actual wooden artifacts in many archaeological contexts (although sophisticated techniques in recovery and analysis have indicated that finds of worked wooden objects are not as rare as might be assumed), the evidence for the technology of woodworking is abundant. This evidence can be summarized under four broad categories: 1) ancient written sources, including inscriptions; 2) artistic representations of tools, craftsmen at work, and wooden objects; 3) artifacts connected with the technology of woodworking (e.g., tools), actual wooden objects, and objects of which wood formed an important component. The fourth and final category is the important role of ethnographic analogy and experimental archaeology. Many ancient woodworking practices and tools exhibit a striking continuity that exists virtually unbroken up to the time of the modern Industrial Revolution.

## Ancient Accounts

The Homeric descriptions of Odysseus blinding the Cyclops Polyphemus or making his marriage bed in his palace on Ithaca provide us with some of the earliest passages in western literature (ca. eighth century B.C.) of the carpenter at his trade (Richter 1966). The mutilation of the Cyclops's single eye with a stake of olivewood is compared to the bidirectional rotation of a strap drill: "just as a man bores a ship's timber with a drill while those below him twirl it with a strap they hold at either end, so the bit spins continuously" (*Od.* 9: 384–86). In a quieter passage the poet describes Odysseus as a talented craftsman; to make his bed the hero

> cut away the foliage of the long-leaved olive,
> and trimmed the trunk from the roots up, planing it with a brazen
> adze, well and expertly, and trued it straight with a chalkline,
> making a bed post of it, and bored all holes with an auger.
> —*Od.* 23: 195–98; trans. Lattimore (1965), by permission

These early passages attest to the existence and use of relatively complicated tools, such as the strap drill, at the dawn of historical Greek civilization, and they reveal that the art of woodcraft in legend was seen as an appropriate skill for a king. Here and elsewhere, extant written sources provide vital information about methods of woodworking and reveal some of the technical parlance used by Greek and Roman craftsmen (Mark 2005).

Inscriptions, including building contracts and accounts as well as funerary epitaphs that mention specialties within the woodworker's trade, have proven to be important sources for information. The contract for the wooden gallery constructed on the fortification walls of Athens, for example, and another for the arsenal, include technical names of roofing components ($IG^2$ 2.463; $IG^2$ 2.1668; Caskey 1910; Hodge 1960). Another inscription dating to the mid-first century B.C. from Puteoli in Italy records a contract for an ornamental doorway to a sanctuary (*CIL* 1.577, 10.1781; *ILS* 5317). The inscription includes the technical terms used for the framing of a door and protecting porch and lists the species of wood to be used for the individual components of the project.

Between the third century B.C. and the first century A.D., Theophrastus, Cato, Varro, and Pliny the Elder wrote extensively about silviculture and the uses of various species of trees. Julius Caesar's vivid account of a wooden pile bridge constructed over the Rhine in 55 B.C. (Caesar, *B Gall.* 4.17; Saatmann et al. 1938–1939) includes an important vocabulary associated with large timber-framed projects: the description includes details about piles (*tigna, sublicae*) and their installation, the bracing of wooden trestles (*derecta*), and the use of wattle-work (*cratis*) to form a roadbed. The only surviving architectural treatise from the ancient world, written by Vitruvius around 25 B.C., is a compendium of both Greek and Roman building practices that offers a rich array of terms used for the wooden structural elements of buildings and military equipment, including the roofing elements of a basilica at Fanum designed by the author himself.

## Representations of Woodcraft, Tools, and Wooden Objects

Most ancient depictions of woodworkers and their craft have survived in the form of painting and relief sculpture, but the media and contexts of these images can differ widely. For Greece, Attic vase painting from the archaic and early classical periods (sixth to early fifth centuries B.C.) is the dominant form of evidence. In both Greece and Rome, artwork associated with private individuals (as opposed to state-funded commissions) is the most informative and varied, as is exemplified by a Roman funerary relief from Ravenna (first century A.D.) depicting Publius Longidienus swinging his adze; the dedicatory inscription identifies him as a *faber navalis*, or shipwright (figure 17.1; Clarke 2003; Kampen 1981; Zimmer 1985).

Examples less obviously referential to woodcraft per se, but no less important for understanding technique, include the Athenian funerary relief of Hegeso sitting on a bentwood wooden chair (*klismos*, fifth century B.C.; Richter 1966: 33–37, fig. 175), or a carved bed-leg in the eponymous seventh-century B.C. Etruscan tomb at Populonia that imitates a wooden element that in reality would have been turned

Figure 17.1. Relief of P. Longidienus, first century A.D., Ravenna. Total height: 2.66 m. Museo Nazionale, Ravenna inv. 7. (Photograph courtesy of the National Museum, Ravenna.)

on a lathe (Steingräber 1979: 340–41, pl. 44). A depiction of Daedalus, the ur-craftsman of Greek myth, still *in situ* at the House of the Vettii at Pompeii, features a detail of the master's son Icarus cutting mortises in a plank with a tanged chisel and mallet (Gaitzsch 1980: vol. 2, 154). A bow and drill lie on the floor; a simple plane leans against one leg of the workbench. The Pompeian wall-painter surely had contemporary models in mind when he created the mythological scene (figure 17.2).

The Roman penchant for recording historical events with a documentary eye occasionally yields a rich dividend of information regarding ancient technologies. For woodcraft the premier example is the Column of Trajan (dedicated A.D. 113) in Rome, of which the sculpted frieze features the exploits of the emperor's legionary forces in two campaigns against the Dacians. Here is a prominent example of public art that included depictions of tools in use, wooden buildings, timbered bridges, wheeled vehicles, and the felling and hauling of trees, from which one

Figure 17.2. Daedalus and Icarus presenting the decoy heifer to Pasiphäe, House of the Vettii, first century A.D., Pompeii. (Photograph by Michael Larvey, by permission of Michael Larvey and the Soprintendenza Archeologica di Pompeii.)

can compile a broad spectrum of the carpenter's craft. Specific examples are considered below. The reliefs also underline the ubiquity of wood as a construction material.

Dedications of altars by pious guilds (*collegia*) of woodworkers to gods associated with woodcraft, while few in number, can include scenes of workshops in operation and, invariably, tools. We find again the Roman evidence most striking. A relief from an altar dedicated to Minerva in Rome, probably from the late first century, offers the most complete picture of a busy furniture shop in operation: handtools, including a carpenter's square (*norma*), large calipers (*circinus*), and a bucksaw (*serra*) hang from the walls; a three-legged table nears completion on a workbench, and two larger machines, perhaps for ripping and turning wooden blanks, stand in the foreground. A lathe may be depicted on the stand in the center left of the relief, or before the seated figure to the right (figure 17.3; Colini 1947).

A final category of representational evidence includes miniature renditions of tools associated with woodworking. For reasons not fully understood, tiny images of planes and saw blades were used as mint marks on Roman Republican silver coinage of the first century B.C. (Fava 1969). The British Museum holds a collection of miniature bronzes from a tomb in Sussex that depict, among other objects, adzes, axes, and saws (Goodman 1964: 24; Manning 1966).

Figure 17.3. Marble relief of a furniture shop, Rome. Late first century A.D.? Length 1.38 m. Capitoline Museums (Montemartini), inv. 2743. (Photograph by R. B. Ulrich.)

## Wooden Objects

Wooden artifacts ranging from grains of sawdust to heavy squared timbers have been reported from sites throughout the littoral Mediterranean, the Black Sea, mainland Europe, Asia Minor, and North Africa. Conservation techniques adopted from the mid-twentieth century have saved increasing numbers of wooden artifacts and ecofacts (Mols 1999; Tampone 1989). Wood is preserved under conditions of extreme dry, wet, or cold. The recovery of structural timbers from ancient shipwrecks has permitted a highly detailed picture of how Egyptian, Greek, and Roman boats were constructed; many still reveal tool marks left from the day they were fashioned (see chapter 24). Notable assemblages of recovered wooden artifacts include timbered tomb chambers containing finely-crafted wooden furniture from the "Royal Tombs" of Gordion (eighth century B.C.; Simpson et al. 1992), a group of wooden sarcophagi with carved wooden moldings from the cemetery of Kertch on the Black Sea dating from Hellenistic and Roman times (Wasowicz and Vaulina 1974; Watzinger 1905), a large number of tables, benches, beds and other wooden household furnishings from Herculaneum (prior to A.D. 79; Mols 1999), and wooden floors, walls, shingles, and pipes from the Roman legionary camp at Vindolanda in Scotland (Birley 1977). The first-century B.C. wooden ship and its cargo found at Comacchio, and those at Pisa still under excavation, have yielded finds of wooden objects in near-pristine condition (Berti 1990; Bruni 2000). Wooden artifacts preserved in Egyptian tombs provide important comparative data.

## Tools

Modern scholars have exhibited a keen interest in the use and appearance of ancient tools. For woodworking, prominent studies include those of Gaitzsche, Goodman, Greber, Manning, Matthäus, Mercer, Petrie, and Zimmer (see bibliography).

Woodworking tools can be divided into two broad categories: those that were employed to cut, trim, or bore wood, and those used for marking and measuring. The latter group, including rulers, calipers, framing squares, and levels, will not be described here. They were used by all manner of artisans and builders. Variants of many of the cutting tools associated with woodworking, such as the chisel, were also used for stone and metalwork. Identification of function in such cases is based on physical attributes. The thin flaring blade of a paring chisel, for example, would not have been found in the toolbox of the stonecutter.

The first woodworking tools were the axe and the adze, originally handheld instruments of stone but better utilized when paired with a wooden handle. Copper, bronze, and iron blades were successively introduced in step with advances in metallurgy. The earliest cast copper and bronze blades (from ca. 5,000 years ago) lacked sockets and were sometimes hafted to wooden handles with the aid of attached flanges (Arnold 1982; Petrie 1917). Axe and adze blades could be fashioned by bending a sheet of metal around a dowel to form a socket for a handle (a method used by European artisans well into the nineteenth century) or by casting the blade in a mold; the latter produced a stronger tool but required a more specialized workshop for production. By the Roman Imperial period the most common form of axe was characterized by a long, flaring blade opposed by a squarish, heavy poll (Manning and Saunders 1972). Examples of the double-bladed axe and the broadhead axe also have been found at both Greek and Roman sites (Ciarallo and De Carolis 1999).

The mortise (see below) was efficiently cut with the drill and the chisel, the former to remove the core of the mortise and the latter to square up its sides. Iron drill bits and chisel blades have been found throughout the Mediterranean world. With few exceptions ancient drill bits exhibit a flat diamond-shaped point at the terminus of an iron rod that was inserted into a cylindrical wooden handle. When held at the top by a cupped "nave," the handle could be spun bidirectionally by the reciprocal motion of a thong and bow. The wooden elements of the drill rarely survive, although an example from a Roman-period tomb from Hawara, Egypt, is preserved intact (Petrie 1917). This and representations on Attic vase paintings (Boston, MFA 13.200; figure 2.6), Roman frescoes (figure 17.2), grave reliefs, and minor arts (figure 2.5) leave little doubt about the ancient appearance of the drill (Ulrich 2007: 30). The diameter of the bore was limited to the effectiveness of a tool operated by one man and the friction generated by the thong; a more powerful strap drill, which worked on the same basic principle, was operated by at least two workmen (Gaitzsch 1980: no. 318; figure 2.7). Pugsley (2003: 186) has proposed and reconstructed a simple fixed drill held in a stand for the boring of small objects.

The hand-operated bow could also power simple lathes of the Greco-Roman period, at least those machines that were called on to turn workpieces of a relatively small diameter. The existence and wide distribution of the lathe (Grk. *tornos*, Lat. *tornus*) is known best by the wooden artifacts and their representations in painting and sculpture that could only have been made by turning. Lathes were used extensively for furniture (see below) and for small containers such as pyxides, bowls and goblets, and for the handles of agricultural implements and tools (Pugsley 2003; Rieth 1940). A third-century B.C. relief from a tomb of Petosiris, Egypt, shows a workman turning a slender dowel; the workpiece is rotating on a vertical axis (Grodde 1989; Rieth 1940). A sarcophagus from Roman-period Greece depicts an incomplete rendition of a bow-driven machine in a more familiar horizontal configuration (Rieth 1940). Greater power may have been achieved by the use of a flywheel; a damaged depiction on the furniture-makers relief from Rome (figure 17.3) may offer a unique glimpse of such a machine.

The carpenter's plane may have evolved from the hand-adze; Gaitzsch has identified a hybrid type (*ascia-hobel*) from depictions on Roman funerary reliefs: a short, broad blade is attached to one or two curved handles. The tool is visible leaning against one leg of the carpenter's bench depicted in the Pompeian fresco of Daedalus (figure 17.2; Gaitzsch 1980; Gaitzsch and Matthäus 1981). Unknown in Pharaonic Egypt, the plane appears to be a Greek invention, but no actual specimens have been reported. The Latin *runcina* is clearly derived from the Greek *rhykane*, and Greek cabinetry work, including paneled doors, attests to the use of this essential woodworking tool. The earliest Roman-period representations appear as mint marks on silver coinage (above); the oldest actual planes have been found at Pompeii, and therefore must date to before A.D. 79. Since the carriage, or stock, that formed the main body of the plane was most easily cut from a solid block of wood, and thus generally lost from the archaeological record, plane blades (called "irons") are found in isolation at many Roman sites (Mutz 1980). The nearly two dozen surviving examples of planes fitted with an iron baseplate (the sole) are all medium-sized smoothing planes ranging from 21 to 44 cm in length, with a relatively steep rake (the cutting angle of the blade) of 50 to 66 degrees (Gaitzsch 1980: 113; Gaitzsch and Matthäus 1981; Greber 1956). Depictions indicate that the common smoothing plane was held by oval handles cut into or through the stock in front of and behind the blade. The width and profile of the cutting edge indicate usage: convex or toothed cutting edges could remove wood quickly or provide a rough surface for gluing veneers. Straight, broad edges were for smoothing operations, narrow irons were used for cutting rabbets, while others were shaped to produce ogee and bead moldings.

Saws included two-man crosscut tools, bow saws, large and small frame-saws with tensioning devices (some strikingly similar to the modern buck saw), and smaller handsaws similar to modern keyhole and backed saws. The ripping of a large bole or beam into boards took place in a saw pit. The saw consisted of a long blade held in tension within a rectangular wooden frame operated by one man positioned on top of the log while his partner stood below. There is an excellent illustration in a first-century fresco from a workshop at Pompeii (VI.7.8–9) depicting a procession of carpenters (figure 17.4). The decorated float depicts, from the left, Minerva (only her shield is visible), a man pushing a long bench plane, two men ripping a plank with a frame-saw, and a rendition of Daedalus, patron of carpenters, standing over the body of his son Icarus (or nephew, Perdix). Saw-teeth were often "set" (splayed alternately to one side and the other) and "sloped," or

Figure 17.4. Roman-period fresco depicting a procession of carpenters carrying a deco-rated float with depictions of Minerva, a man pushing a long bench plane, two men ripping a plank with a frame-saw, and Daedalus, patron of carpenters. Pompeii, first century, now in the Naples Museum, inv. 8991. Height 66 cm; width 75 cm. (Photograph: Rossa, DAI Rome, Inst. Neg. 75.1536, by permission.)

slanted, to create a primary cutting stroke (Manning in Frere 1972; Theophrastus, *Hist. pl.* 5.6.3, Pliny, *HN* 16.227 ).

The best chisels and gouges were of iron; cutting edges were hardened by tempering (Tylecote in Zienkiewicz 1986: 195). The metal blade was tanged or socketed to accommodate a handle. The socket was more difficult to form, but its handle less likely to split when struck by a mallet. A tanged paring chisel from Aquileia was found intact with a wooden handle ending in a mushroom-shaped butt that fit perfectly in the palm of the hand for delicate shaving operations (Gaitzsch 1980: vol. 2, no. 181). The most common form is the mortising chisel, with a thick shank and a sharply beveled cutting edge designed for deep penetration in the hardest of woods.

## Evidence from Extant Architecture

At sites where no wood survives it is nevertheless possible to recover significant information of usage. Most Greek and Roman buildings of the historical period were constructed with a combination of stone, concrete, and wood. Roofing and upper flooring framed with wooden beams can be substantially reconstructed by examining the cavities into which the ends of beams were fitted (Hodge 1960; Klein 1998; Ulrich 1996). Extant terracotta revetments that protected the otherwise exposed wooden beams of Etruscan temple roofs reveal the dimensions of ridgepoles, main rafters, and architraves (Andrén 1940; Colonna 1985). Vanished wooden wall decorations can be restored by examining the cuttings in adjacent masonry; examples from the Greek mainland (Olympia) and Sicily (Selinunte) are notable (Martin 1965). The layout of door and window casings can be understood by observing scars in surviving wall plaster. The dimensions and arrangement of wooden planks for the formwork of foundations (shuttering) or for framing domes and vaults (centering) can still be directly studied by examination of the imprints left by boards in the concrete as it set (Lancaster 2005a, 2005b; Rasch 1991). Rock-cut chamber tombs built by the Etruscans in central Italy at sites such as Cerveteri, Tuscania, and San Giuliano feature full-scale carvings of ceiling beams, coffering, architectural moldings, and even furniture that imitate wooden components employed in the homes of the living; the best examples date to the sixth century B.C. (Oleson 1978; Steingräber 1979).

# Theophrastus and Pliny on Raw Materials: Species and Uses

Theophrastus (ca. 370–287 B.C.) composed two extant major studies on trees and other plants: *Historia Plantarum* and *De Causis Plantarum*. Three centuries later, Pliny (A.D. 23–79) devoted six books (12–17) of his *Natural History* to commentary on the typology and uses of trees and woody plants; much is derived directly from Theophrastus. Even with such treatises, in the absence of canonical and universal methods of illustrating and describing plants the transmission of botanical knowledge was severely hampered (Baker 1978: 20). The modern scholar is commonly frustrated when trying to identify a specific tree when confronted with an ancient reference (Rackham in Salmon and Shipley 1996: 38; Meiggs 1982: 410) (cf. table 17.1).

The trees most favored by Greek and Roman woodworkers grew in the wild. With the exception of the north coast of Africa, supplies were plentiful. Fertile, low-lying land was first cleared of timber for agricultural use, in higher elevations woodcutters exhausted stands of mature trees and then moved on to new sources of wood. Trees were cut at different times of year depending on intended use, but most timber was harvested during the cooler months, when the sap content was at its lowest (Cato, *Rust.* 31.1–2; Vitruvius 2.9.1–2). Some woodcutters would girdle the bark from a tree some time before cutting, allowing the tree to die and begin the drying process while still standing (Pliny, *HN* 16.192; Vitruvius, *De arch.* 2.9.3).

Table 17.1. Mediterranean wood species and their primary ancient uses.

| Latin name | Botanical Family | English name | Use |
|---|---|---|---|
| abies | Pinaceae | fir | general use, roofing |
| acer | Aceraceae | maple | furniture |
| alnus | Betulaceae | alder | pilings, pipes |
| betula | Betulaceae | birch | furniture, tableware |
| buxus | Buxaceae | box | combs, inlay |
| carpinus | Corylaceae | hornbeam | yokes, olive-presses |
| castanea | Fagaceae | chestnut | general use |
| cedrus | Pinaceae | cedar | roofing, shipbuilding |
| citrus | Cupressaceae | thuja/sanderac | furniture, veneer |
| cornus | Cornaceae | cornel/dogwood | dowels, spokes, spears |
| corylus | Corylaceae | hazel | torches, small implements |
| cupressus | Cupressaceae | cypress | doors, statuary |
| fagus | Fagaceae | beech | furniture, general use |
| ficus | Moraceae | fig | inferior-grade applications |
| fraxinus | Oleaceae | ash | spears, wheels |
| hebenus | Ebenaceae | ebony | furniture, inlay |
| ilex | Fagaceae | holm-oak | architraves, tools |
| iuglans | Juglandaceae | walnut | general use, furniture |
| iuniperus | Cupressaceae | juniper | furniture |
| larix | Pinaceae | larch | heavy structural applications |
| olea | Oleaceae | olive | utensils, wooden hinges |
| palma | Palmae | palm | veneer |
| pinus | Pinaceae | pine | general use |
| populus | Salicaceae | poplar | general use, veneer |
| quercus | Fagaceae | oak | general use |
| salix | Salicaceae | willow | baskets, bentwood, trellises |
| taxus | Taxaceae | yew | bows |
| terebinthus | Anacardiaceae | terebinth | tableware |
| tilia | Tiliaceae | linden, lime | furniture |
| ulmus | Ulmaceae | elm | wheel hubs |

The delimbing of the tree was achieved rapidly by the woodcutter's axe; the transportation of the heavy and bulky trunk was no small feat, especially if long beams were required. Soldiers on Trajan's Column are shown dragging logs from the forest on rope slings (Scene XV). Logs were conveyed with the greatest ease by water; Strabo reports that the Tiber afforded Rome a steady supply of timber and other building materials (Strabo 5.3.7; Meiggs 1982). Overland transport was inevitable; Seneca writes of roads "trembling" under the weight of wagons carrying logs (Seneca, *Ep.* 90.9).

In both Greece and Italy, the most highly prized timbers for large construction projects were the mountain pines (*Pinus nigra*) and high-altitude silver firs (*Abies alba*). Those slopes that fell to substantial waterways were certainly exploited first of all. Less accessible areas were bypassed; mature stands of trees in terrain difficult to access were always part of most cities' greater environment. Other fine forests near towns and cities were protected as sacred groves, including the large tracts of beech and oak growing on the Alban Hills near Rome and the Altis of Greece's Olympia.

Species exhibiting coveted properties were traded across the Mediterranean. Among the cargoes of the oldest shipwrecks discovered to date, such as that from Uluburun (1325 B.C.), are logs of boxwood (*Buxus sempervirens*), the dense grain of which was highly prized for the manufacture of combs and other small luxury objects (Pulak 1993). Twelve centuries later boxwood logs formed the cargo of another ship wrecked off the Adriatic coast of Italy near present day Comacchio (Berti 1990). Fragrant Lebanese cedar (*Cedrus libani*) seemed to last forever and was widely used along the coast of the Levant and in Egypt. Julius Caesar's army witnessed firsthand the resistance of larchwood (*Larix decidua*) to fire (Vitruvius 2.9.15–16); the tall straight trunks that grew in the Alps were later transported to Rome for some of the empire's most ambitious building projects. The most coveted of furniture woods, called *citrus*, was evidently cut from the burls or roots of the Sanderac tree (*Thuja articulata, Callitris quadrivalvis*, or *Tetraclinis articulata*, all of which refer to the same tree) of North Africa, particularly from the region of Mauritania. *Citrus*, with its delightful grain (compared by Pliny to the leaves of parsley), honey color, and high polish, was used for small, round tables that fetched astronomical prices (Pliny, *HN* 13.96–7). The high value of these exotic woods spawned a class of woodworkers (*citrarii*) expert in the art of veneering.

Oak, beech, elm, chestnut, maple, and alder, the more common hardwoods in the lands of Greece and Italy, were used in a wide range of applications. Literary and physical evidence indicates that woodworkers were keenly aware of their intrinsic properties and best applications. From the commentaries of Theophrastus, Pliny, and Vitruvius emerges a theory of the composition of wood based on the four elements of air, earth, fire, and water. It is the relative presence of these constituents assigned to a given species that provided the ancient mind with a rationale for describing observable properties such as resistance to water, hardness, or flammability. The apprentice learned that the wood of the alder, for example, was highly suitable for piling because of its resistance to rot, or that the wood of the elm, nearly impossible to split, made it perfect for the hub of a wheel, while the springiness of ash was widely exploited for the rims (felloes) of wheels. Oaken strakes protected the hull of a merchant ship from the pounding of waves, but oak's tendency to warp made it less suitable for flooring. Beech did not impart an unpleasant flavor to food when turned to fashion cups and plates; tall pines from Corsica made strong roofing timbers (table 17.1).

# JOINERY

Objects both large and small were shaped from single pieces of wood: tableware, tool handles, stakes, pilings, spars, rafters, and water pipes. The first wheels, often with an attached hub or "nave," were carved from single thick planks of wood

(Piggott 1983). Woodworking techniques, however, usually involved joining two or more pieces of wood to create a composite object. The type of joint employed is a product of several related factors including aesthetic appeal, species of wood, available tools, and a given artisan's skill level. But the single most important factor is the nature of the anticipated stress placed on the wooden joint. A scarf joint used to connect two timbers end to end for the keel of a ship is not an appropriate solution for two similar beams employed vertically to support a heavy load. In the latter the fibers of the wooden are submitted to constant forces of compression, while the former may undergo equally intense forces of tension (when, for example, a heavy hull was dragged up a beach). Some joins were planned to be fixed but flexible (pivots and hinges) others firm but with a certain degree of give. Thus shipwrights are known to have sewn the planking of ships together even when more unyielding (and conventional) methods of joinery were the norm (McGrail 1985; Mark 2005). In addition to factors of stress, the craftsman must consider the nature of the wooden piece to be joined. A tenon, for example, can only be cut so that the fibers of the wood (generally referred to as the grain) run parallel to its long axis, otherwise the tenon itself will quickly break in half. But the cavity, or mortise, into which the tenon fits can be cut either with or across the grain. Finally, aesthetics play an important role. The miter joint, used to form corners, hides the end-grain of wood and is thus indispensable for jointing decorative moldings at right angles, but without reinforcement the mitre provides little strength (figure 17.5).

Today makers of fine furniture and cabinetry take pride in creating wooden chairs, tables, and boxes without the use of any metal fasteners; whether this sense of superior craftsmanship was shared by the ancient woodworker is difficult to know. Certainly nails of all sizes were available, each made by hand from bronze or iron. But nails were expensive and required the services of a blacksmith. For projects requiring the assembly of small wooden pieces, such as chairs or small tables, nails tend to split wood and loosen over time. Heavier beams, such as those used for roofing projects, might employ spikes and iron straps. Plaques of terracotta that covered the wooden structural elements of early Italic temples were held in place by bronze nails. Floorboards were fastened to joists by nails. Iron rivets connected wooden handles to iron tools. Although the principle of the screw was well known to Greeks and Romans—large-diameter versions were used for agricultural presses and small metal bolts were used by metalworkers for jewelry and parade armor (Kiechle 1967; Klumbach 1973; Deppert-Lippitz et al. 1995)—there was no ancient equivalent of the wood-screw or the carriage bolt. Only in the eighteenth century was it possible to manufacture threaded screws on any scale.

The repertoire of joints used by ancient woodworkers will be familiar to anyone practicing the traditional (based on hand tools) craft today (Milne 1982). The single most versatile of wooden joints is the mortise-and-tenon. The tenon may take the form of a cylindrical dowel, or a fan (or swallowtail), also known in Latin as a *sericula* (little hatchet), or a rectangular, tongue-shaped piece of wood. The tenon may be formed by shaping the end of the workpiece to be joined, or it

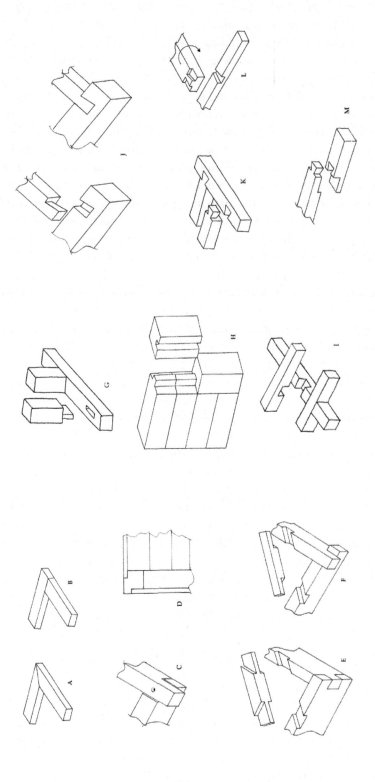

Figure 17.5. Woodworking joints (Roman contexts): A–F: corner joints: A. simple mitre; B. butt-joint; C: half-lap; D: rebate in a corner post for attachment to side planks; E–F: corner braces with half-lap and saddle joints. G: mortise and tenon; H: tongue and groove joint hides end grain of parallel glued boards; I: half-lap (saddle). Dovetail joints: J: asymmetrical ("half") dovetail; K: dovetail or dovetail halving joint; M: edge-halved scarf with one dovetail butt.

may be carved from an independent wooden element. The "shell-first" planking system used by both Greek and Roman shipwrights employed thousands of mortises and tenons in every hull (figure 24.3). Individual strakes were joined at the edges to one another with a tenon that was held in place by a dowel (Ucelli 1950; see also chapter 24). Scarfs were used for the longitudinal joins, perhaps reinforced by iron nails or treenails. The mortise and tenon joint was used for joining heavy beams in architectural applications and was essential for assembling wooden furniture, particularly the rails and legs of tables, chairs, benches, and beds. The felloes of a wheel rim were attached to one another with tenons, wooden spokes were tenoned into the hubs (called "naves").

Overlapping pieces of wood were frequently jointed by half-lap or saddle joints, which involved the use of the saw and chisel to create opposing notches so that the two pieces could join while maintaining the thickness of one. Such joints were used to build lattices or grids of wooden slats. These assemblies might be used to support the mattress of a bed or couch or to protect a window or the upper panel of a door (Mols 1999). Finds of small boxes and larger chests reveal that corners were jointed with mitres and box (or "finger") joints, the latter either of a consistent rectilinear configuration, or of the more elegant pins and tails of the dovetailed joint (Keepax and Robson 1978: 38; Desantis in Berti 1990: 266).

Strong and durable glue has always been essential to most small-to-medium-size projects, including household utensils, furniture, and cabinetry. Glue can be used alone as a binding agent, most often for edge-to-edge connections such as those that might be used for the boards of a broad tabletop. Without glue the highly developed arts of veneering and parquetry would not have been possible. Even with finely-cut wooden joints, glue was employed to strengthen and tighten the final bond. That the Greeks and Romans credited the mythological craftsman Daedalus with the invention of glue indicates the antiquity and importance of the process (Pliny, *HN* 7.198). Natural glues were made from the cartilaginous parts of cattle and fish; Pliny considers a type made from the genitalia of bulls especially efficacious (*HN* 28.236).

# Wood Technology in Large Building Projects

Wood was used in all phases of ancient building projects, in both temporary and permanent installations. Its use can be documented for below-grade foundation work, the framing of walls, doors, and windows, the installation of floors, and the construction of roofs (Adam 1994). Large masonry structures regularly employed all-wooden upper stories or galleries (DeLaine 1996; Ulrich 1996). In frontier military camps of the Roman period wood was the predominant building material and was even used for the defensive walls and towers of a legionary encampment (Shirley 2000). On military campaigns siege machines and artillery were largely constructed of wooden elements. The first theaters of Rome were built entirely of wood.

Waterlogged wood can survive even in temperate zones for thousands of years. Wooden piling was considered suitable for foundation work from prehistoric times. Vitruvius (*De arch.* 2.9.11) tells us that in his day most of the buildings of coastal Ravenna were supported on piles. The practice of constructing houses on piling in northern Italy and the adjacent Alpine regions had been common since at least the second millennium B.C. (Arnold 1982). Piling was a staple for bridge construction. Vertical or splayed supports could be driven directly into waterways without the construction of cofferdams (Caesar, *B Gall.* 4.17). Rome's earliest bridge over the Tiber River was always known as the Pile Bridge (*Pons Sublicius*; cf. Plutarch, *Num.* 9.2–3; Dion. 3.45.2). Arched stone bridges of the Roman Imperial period were seated on grids of tightly-packed piles, many of which have been recovered from excavations in the northern provinces, their tips sharpened and reinforced with iron plates to aid the process of ramming them into place (Cüppers 1969; Marchetti 1891).

On dry land, wooden posts buried in pits formed the structural uprights of Greece and Rome's earliest structures; the post-holes of the well known Heroon from the site of Lefkandi on Euboia (ca. 950 B.C.) or the "Hut of Romulus" on the Palatine in Rome (eighth century B.C.) provide complementary examples (Popham et al. 1982; Puglisi 1951). The use of sleeper beams—horizontal wooden footings into which timber uprights were mortised, was a northern European tradition of great antiquity later enthusiastically adopted by Roman military builders (Birley 1977; Rickman 1971).

With the Roman introduction and rapid adoption of concrete as a foundation material for land and maritime applications in the late second century B.C., wooden planks and beams played an important role in shaping and stabilizing the wet concrete as it cured (figure 25.2). For the building of harbors, wooden caissons, some large enough to be considered "single-mission barges," reinforced with transverse interior beams, were sunk into place and filled with concrete that was capable of curing underwater; examples from Caesarea in Palestine have been described in detail (Brandon 1999; Oleson in Raban 1989). On dry land, temporary formworks of beams and planks were erected; the planked shuttering could be removed for reuse (Taylor 2003). Similar arrangements of beams and planks or walls formed of squared timbers placed either horizontally or vertically were used as retaining walls or to form quays; the waterfront of Roman London has revealed well preserved examples of such timberwork (Marsden 1994).

Vitruvius (*De arch.* 2.1.4) writes about a rustic cabin made from interlocking notched logs that was built by the indigenous peoples of the timber-rich lands around the Black Sea; the simple technique was used by Roman military engineers to built abutments for field artillery. A vertical, planar grid formed by roundwood or squared beams filled in with panels of another material such as wattle-and-daub

Figure 17.6. Trajan's bridge over the Danube as depicted on the Column of Trajan (cast in Museo della Civiltà Romana), ca. A.D. 113, Rome. (Photograph by R. B. Ulrich.)

or mud-brick was widely employed for domestic architecture during the Mediterranean Iron age. The practice was probably well known from Neolithic times and never fell out of use. Vitruvius (*De arch.* 2.8.20) refers to the flammability of walls built from *opus craticium*, a closely-related method involving an open timber frame filled with panels of concrete and rubble. While the technique is usually associated as a cheaper alternative to solid (and thicker) walls of concrete, its lightness makes it especially suitable for upper floors with minimal support. Furthermore, the combination of a wooden framework and masonry may have been recognized as being particularly resilient to the frequent tremors that shook the towns along the mountainous spines of Italy and Sicily (Papaccio 1993). It is notable in this regard that at both Herculaneum and Pompeii walls of *opus craticium* were still standing after the ground tremors and volcanic eruption of A.D. 79. In mainland Europe, small buildings were apparently commonly built with sawed planks nailed to a beam frame; these structures feature prominently on depictions of Dacian villages shown under attack by Roman soldiers on Trajan's Column in Rome.

Among the largest of all timber-framed buildings constructed in the Roman period were the timbered theaters, amphitheaters, and large bridges known primarily through references in ancient literature and the occasional artistic rendition (Dio Cassius 68.13.1; Tacitus, *Ann.* 4.62). In the Greek world the largest wooden constructions were the warships of the late third century; these super-galleys were up to 120 m long (Casson 1991). Masonry theaters, amphitheaters, and bridges were all built around open wooden frameworks designed to bear tremendous loads; Lancaster (2005a: 34) has identified buildings in Rome where the wooden centering may have distorted under the immense load of partially-built concrete vaults. Wooden bridges were either supported by some form of wooden trestle spanned by horizontal timbers, perhaps cantilevered for larger spans, or stone piers were set in place across the river and carried a wooden carriageway (Milne 1985). Perhaps the greatest of Roman wooden bridges, despite its short life, was the one constructed by Trajan's gifted engineer, Apollodorus, which spanned the Danube on 20 piers for a total length in excess of 3,500 Roman feet (O'Connor 1993). A simplified representation of the Danube bridgework on Trajan's Column reveals a solution realized by building a wooden segmental arch reinforced by an arrangement of radial struts (Lepper and Frere 1988). The use of multiple shorter timbers would have aided the process of construction over the long spans of open water and allowed the procurement teams to cut local trees of modest dimensions (figure 17.6).

While the Greek theater was characteristically built against a natural slope that directly supported wooden bleachers (*ikria*) or stone blocks, Roman theaters and amphitheaters often stood on level ground; the inwardly sloping seating areas needed to be supported in a way that provided access to the interior of the structure and was sufficiently stable to support the weight of thousands of spectators. The simple trestle, each consisting of a pair of uprights spanned by a horizontal beam, would have formed the essential component of each bay. Knee braces placed to reinforce the architraves would have created a unit that approximates the form of the bays found in the superimposed arcades of stone and concrete arenas. Unfortunately, there are no detailed literary descriptions of what these structures looked like or how they were assembled. A rare notation of structural collapse from an ancient source records the failure of a timber-framed amphitheater in A.D. 27 at Fidenae in Italy; Tacitus (*Ann.* 4.62) tells us specifically that both the footings and the joinery of the project were inadequate. The date of the event also proves that these colossal wooden places for public spectacle were still being built long after permanent and fire-resistant masonry versions had been erected in central Italy (the Pompeian amphitheater of ca. 80 B.C.; Pompey's Theater in Rome, ca. 55 B.C.). Nero constructed an amphitheater of "interwoven beams" in A.D. 57, the last such structure to be built in Rome before the construction of the Colosseum a dozen years later (Calpurnius Siculus, *Ec.* 7.23–4). A hybrid stone and timbered amphitheater is represented on Trajan's Column (Lepper and Frere 1988: 151, pl. 73).

Floors and flat roofs were constructed by building a deck of joists and planking; by the late first century planked floors in multistoried structures were routinely covered with a thick layer of concrete that supported a paving of tiles or stone mosaic. Vitruvius (*De arch.* 7.1) offers specific recommendations; actual finds indicate that his strictures were only loosely followed. Abundant evidence in the form of joist-holes left in the standing walls of houses, shops, and public buildings at Pompeii and Herculaneum indicate that wooden joists, rectangular in section, were more closely spaced than necessary to support the concrete subfloor (Ulrich 1996). By the high imperial period evidence from buildings in the Roman port town of Ostia indicate that the framers of upper floors may have preferred em-

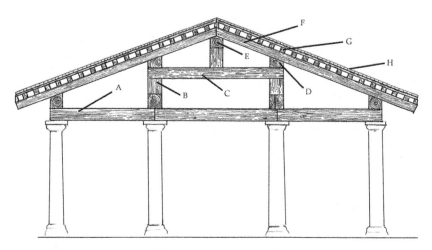

Figure 17.7. Prop-and-lintel roofing system: A: architrave; B: prop; C: lintel; D: purlin; E: ridgepole; F: primary rafters; G: secondary purlins; H: sheathing.

ploying two or three heavy crossbeams that supported a set of lighter joists, which in turn carried the planking and masonry floor.

In terms of framing and joinery, wooden roof construction posed the greatest challenge to the framing carpenter. Large structures in the west were not covered with masonry vaults until the second-century B.C., and even from that point all-wooden roofing was preferred for traditional buildings like temples and large covered public spaces, including the Greek stoa, the Roman basilica, or the meeting places for Greek and Roman councils (e.g., the *bouleuterion* and *curia*, respectively). In the historical period, most wooden roofs were pitched in order to shed precipitation (Cicero, *Orat.* 3.180). Pitched roofs also provided basic insulation from heat and cold by virtue of an enclosed attic that was integral to their design.

The double-pitched, or gabled, roof, oriented to the long axis of a rectangular ground plan, characterizes the most "classical" of monumental buildings from the Greco-Roman world. Depending on how the roof was framed, the gabled roof could cover spaces up to about 30 meters (just over 100 Roman feet) with a free-span (Gibson et al. 1994). The double-pitched wooden roof was generally framed in one of two ways: the prop-and-lintel method or the tie-beam truss (Klein 1998; Hodge 1960; Meiggs 1982). The former involved supporting the ridgepole and purlins (if used) with a series of vertical supports that were themselves carried by crossbeams, interior columns or walls. The rafters of the prop-and-lintel system were not physically connected to the crossbeams (generally defining the ceiling). The prop-and-lintel system was widely used in classical Greece and in Italy even though the principle of the truss may have been understood from archaic times (contra, see chapter 9). By the mid-second century B.C., the tie-beam truss was adopted with enthusiasm by Roman builders (cf. chapter 10).

The basic tie-beam truss is composed of three timbers: two diagonal rafters and a horizontal tie-beam that form a fixed triangle with jointed corners (Lancaster

Figure 17.8. Timber-truss, hypothetical arrangement in Vitruvius's basilica at Fanum.
(After Warren in Morgan 1914: 135.)

2005a: 22; Ulrich 2007: 138). The apex of the triangle either supports or is integrated
with the ridge-beam. The tie-beam truss was capable of sustaining great loads and
spanned the broadest of open spaces (up to 30 m), surpassing those covered by
concrete barrel or cross vaults (generally no more than 26 m across) (Lancaster
2005a: 138). Only the dome was capable of a broader clear span. The horizontal tie-
beam, kept under tension by the rafters and their load, could support the dead
weight of a heavy coffered ceiling. For larger spans the interior of the truss could be
reinforced with a kingpost, queenposts, collar beams, or diagonal braces (Giuliani
2006).

To hypothesize the appearance and to reconstruct the language of framed
wooden roofs one must turn to the abundant evidence of cuttings in stone architectural elements and revetments, to literary references, and to artistic representations. In both Greek and Etruscan applications, prop-and-lintel roofs tended to
employ a heavy ridge beam. The socket for the ridge beam at the archaic Temple of
Hera I at Paestum was a full 91 cm high by 67 cm wide, perhaps 20 cm higher than
that of the Parthenon (Hodge 1960: 46). In Etruria, the ridge beams of temples may
have been even larger. The terracotta plaques that covered the exposed ends of the
beams have survived in a good enough state to offer an idea of dimensions; at Pyrgi
and Tarquinia the crowning beams may have measured as much as 1.25 m high by
1.80 m wide. Beams of this size running the length of a monumental temple (the Ara
della Regina of Tarquinia was nearly 40 m long) were most likely made up of
composites of smaller timbers, a practice that was certainly used for wooden architraves, for Vitruvius writes about the use of such "composite beams" (*De arch.*

4.7.4: *trabes conpactiles*) for epistyles. The emphasis on width over height on these early ridge beams is probably due to the requirement of creating a broad bedding for the principle rafters, themselves of hefty dimensions, which in turn supported the purlins and a series of lighter rafters and sheathing (figure 17.7).

The viability of the timber truss depended in large part on the strength of the critical join at the outer corners of the triangular frame, where rafters, under the immense force of compression, met the tie-beam, itself under great tension (figure 17.8). It appears unlikely that builders employed composite or scarfed beams for the constituent members of the truss, thus the greatest attempted spans were probably limited to available timber of sufficient dimension. The broadest spans identified were achieved in the covered music halls and the palatial audience halls of the late Roman Republic and early Empire (first century B.C. through first century A.D.); beyond this point it seems that the tallest procurable firs and larches had been felled (Cassius Dio 55.8.4; 66.24.2).

# Furniture: Carving, Bending, and Veneering Wood

Wooden furniture fashioned by Greek and Roman craftsmen provides evidence of additional woodworking practices. These specialized skills included the ability to shape and apply moldings, to carve three-dimensional figural images in relief and in the round, to bend wood and to apply veneers, such as parquetry, to objects of high value. These arts were not limited to the makers of furniture. In both Greek and Roman temples, for example, sculptors created images of deities in wood (cf. Pliny, *HN* 16.216), and decorative architectural moldings required carving ability. But it was in the manufacture of common household furniture that the skills listed above were routinely applied.

The most common of wooden moldings, such as the unadorned bead or the cyma (the latter known today as a Roman ogee) were rendered with relative ease using customized molding planes (above). Foliate friezes, the egg-and-dart, or similar decorative bands known so well from carved stone examples have been observed on the carbonized wooden chests and upright cabinets from Hercula-neum and on the Greek and Roman period wooden sarcophagi recovered from the Kertch region of the Black Sea (Mols 1999; Watzinger 1905).

The lathe played a special role in the furniture-maker's shop. The legs of couches and beds, for example, were commonly turned, as were those of heavy, backed chairs. By the Roman period the aggressive turning of legs produced ele-ments incapable of supporting heavy loads. Such turned "wooden" legs were in fact composite structures of vertical iron bars on which deeply-turned wooden elements were separately "strung" (Mols 1999). Yet other popular furniture types, such as the elegant Greek *klismos* or round serving tables, were built without any significant use of the lathe.

Carving in high relief, to the point of being rendered in the round, abounded on Greco-Roman furniture. Every household had at least one three-legged table with a round top (*mensa delphica*) invariably decorated with a carved animal head, such as a lion or griffin, on the "knee" of each leg, and a "foot" rendered as a claw or hoof. The universal application of such elements indicates that the rank-and-file furniture maker was skilled at least in producing these stock figural images.

There exists no ancient literary passage that describes the process of bending wood by the use of hot water or steam, but there can be little doubt that the practice existed. Pliny identifies a number of species considered good for bending, but the use of moist heat is not explicit (*HN* 16.227). The curved back and flaring legs of the Greek *klismos* would have been fashioned best from bending the components with steam. The same can be said about the light frame of a chariot, the rim of a shield, the yoke for a draft animal, the bent frame of a wicker chair, or the thin-walled, cylindrical box (*capsa*). The outer rims of wooden wheels could be made from single pieces of wood bent into a circle (Curle 1911).

Veneering was a highly developed skill among Greek and Roman craftsman. Thin sheets or strips of valuable woods were glued over the surfaces of less valuable species. In addition to wood veneers, craftsman applied plaques of ivory, bone, and tortoiseshell to furnishings. Actual examples of veneer-work, including parquetry, have been documented over a broad chronological and geographical spectrum, from the furniture found in eighth-century B.C. Gordion to the carbonized furniture of first-century Herculaneum.

The full range of woodworking techniques employed by woodworkers of the ancient Mediterranean throughout the historical period and the practical knowledge concerning species and their most suitable applications attest to the importance of wood technologies for agriculture and hunting, domestic life, trade, warfare, and leisure activities. The tools and techniques employed by the end of the Roman period would show little change until the appearance of the Industrial Revolution fifteen centuries later. Given twentieth-century developments in preservation and the science of analysis, the recovery and restoration of ancient wooden artifacts has enabled modern scholars to document with increasing detail this vital component of ancient life.

# REFERENCES

Adam, J.-P. 1994. *Roman building*. Bloomington: Indiana University Press.
Andrén, A. 1940. *Architectural terracottas from Etrusco-Italic temples*. Lund and Leipzig: Gleerup.

Arnold, B. 1982. "The architectural woodwork of the Late Bronze Age village Auvernier-Nord," in McGrail 1982: 111–28.

Baker, H. 1978. *Plants and civilization.* Belmont, CA: Wadsworth.

Berti, F. 1990. *Fortuna Maris, la Nave Romana di Comacchio.* Bologna: Nuova Alfa.

Birley, R. 1977. *Vindolanda:A Roman frontier post on Hadrian's Wall.* London: Thames and Hudson.

Brandon, C. 1999. "Pozzolana, lime, and single-mission barges (Area K)," in K. Holum, A. Raban, and J. Patrich (eds.), *Caesarea papers,* vol. 2. *Journal of Roman Archaeology* Suppl. 35. Portsmouth, RI: JRA, 169–78.

Bruni, S. (ed.) 2000. *Le nave antiche di Pisa: The ancient ships of Pisa.* Florence: Edizioni Polistampa.

Carver, M. O. H., S. Donaghey, and A. B. Sumpter 1978. *Riverside structures and a well in Skeldergate and buildings in Bishophill.* The Archaeology of York 4.1. York: Council for British Archaeology.

Caskey, L. D. 1910. "The roofed gallery on the walls of Athens," *American Journal of Archaeology* 14: 298–309.

Casson, L. 1991. *The ancient mariners.* Princeton: Princeton University Press.

Ciarallo, A., and E. De Carolis 1999. *Homo Faber: Natura, scienza e tecnica nell'antica Pompei.* Milan: Electa.

Clarke, J. 2003. *Art in the lives of ordinary Romans.* Berkeley: University of California Press.

Colini, A. M. 1947. "Officina di Fabri Tignarii nei Frammenti di un Ara Monumentale Rinvenuti fra il Campidoglio e il Tevere," *Capitolium:* 21–28

Colonna, G. (ed.) 1985. *Santuari d'Etruria.* Milan: Electa, Regione Toscana.

Cüppers, H. 1969. *Die Trierer Römerbrücken.* Mainz: von Zabern.

Curle, J. 1911. *A Roman frontier post and its people: The fort of Newstead in the parish of Melrose.* Glasgow: Maclehose.

Dearne, M. J., and K. Branigan 1995. "The use of coal in Roman Britain," *Antiquaries Journal* 75: 71–105.

DeLaine, J. 1996. "The Insula of the Paintings: A model for the economics of construction in Hadrianic Ostia," in A. G. Zevi and A. Claridge (eds.), *"Roman Ostia" revisited.* London: The British School at Rome: 165–84.

Deppert-Lippitz, B., et al. 1995. *Die Schraube zwischen Macht und Pracht: Das Gewinde in der Antike.* Sigmaringen: Jan Thorbecke.

Fava, A. S. 1969. *I simboli nelle monete argentee republicane e la vita dei romani.* Turin: Soprintendenza alle Antichità del Piemonte e Museo Civico di Torino.

Fowler, B. 2000. *Iceman: Uncovering the life and times of a prehistoric man found in an Alpine glacier.* New York: Random House.

Franchi dell'Orto, L. (ed.) 1993. *Ercolano 1738–1988: 250 anni di ricerca archeologica. Atti del Convegno Internazionale Ravello-Ercolano-Napoli-Pompeii 1988.* Roma: L'Erma di Bretschneider.

Frere, S. 1972. *Verulamium Excavations.* Vol. 1. Society of Antiquaries of London Research Committee Reports 28. London: Thames and Hudson.

Gaitzsch, W. 1980. *Eiserne römische Werkzeuge: Studien zur römischen Werkzeugkunde in Italien und den nördlichen Provinzen des Imperium Romanum.* 2 vols. British Archaeological Reports, Intl. Series S78. Oxford: BAR.

Gaitzsch, W., and H. Matthäus 1981. "*Runcinae*—römische Hobel," *Bonner Jahrbücher* 181: 205–47.

Gibson, S., J. DeLaine, and A. Claridge 1994. "The Triclinium of the Domus Flavia: A new reconstruction," *Papers of the British School at Rome* 62: 67–97.

Giuliani, C. 2006. *L'edilizia nell'antichitá*. Rome: Carocci.

Goodburn, D. 1991. "A Roman timber framed building tradition," *Archaeological Journal* 148: 182–204

Goodman, W. L. 1964. *The history of woodworking tools*. London: Bell.

Greber, J. M. 1956. *Die Geschichte des Hobels*. Zürich: VSSM-Verlag.

Grodde, B. 1989. *Hölzernes Mobiliar im vor- und frühgeschichtlichen Mittel- und Nordeuropa*. Frankfurt am Main: P. Lang.

Hodge, A. T. 1960. *The woodwork of Greek roofs*. Cambridge: Cambridge University Press.

Kampen, N. 1981. *Image and status: Roman working women in Ostia*. Berlin: Mann.

Keepax, C., and M. Robson 1978. "Conservation and associated examination of a Roman chest," *The Conservator* 2: 35–40.

Kiechle, F. 1967. "Zur Verwendung der Schraube in der Antike," *Technikgeschichte* 34: 14–22.

Klein, N. L. 1998. "Evidence for West Greek influence on mainland Greek roof construction and the creation of the truss in the archaic period," *Hesperia* 67: 335–74.

Klumbach, H. (ed.) 1973. *Spatrömische Gardehelme*. Münchner Beiträge zur Vor- und Frühgeschichte 15. Munich: Beck.

Lancaster, L. 2005a. *Concrete vaulted construction in imperial Rome*. Cambridge: Cambridge University Press.

Lancaster, L. 2005b. "The process of building the Colosseum: The site, materials and construction techniques," *Journal of Roman Archaeology* 18: 57–82.

Lattimore, R. (trans.) 1965. *The Odyssey of Homer*. New York: Harper and Row.

Lepper, F., and S. Frere 1988. *Trajan's Column: A new edition of the Cichorius plates*. Gloucester: Alan Sutton.

Manning, W. H. 1966. "A group of bronze models from Sussex in the British Museum," *Antiquaries Journal* 46: 50–59.

Manning, W. H., and C. Saunders 1972. "A socketed iron axe from Maids Moreton, Buckinghamshire, with a note on the type," *Antiquaries Journal* 52: 276–92.

Marchetti, D. 1891. "Di un antico molo per lo sbarco dei marmi reconosciuto sulla riva sinistra del Tevere," *Bullettino della Commissione archeologica Comunale di Roma* ser. 4: 45–60.

Mark, S. 2005. *Homeric seafaring*. College Station: Texas A&M University Press.

Marsden, P. 1994. *The ships of the Port of London: First to eleventh Centuries AD*. English Heritage Archaeological Report 3. London: English Heritage.

Martin, R. 1965. *Manuel d'architecture grecque*. Vol. 1, *Matériaux et techniques*. Paris: Picard.

McGrail, S. (ed.) 1982. *Woodworking techniques before A.D. 1500*. British Archaeological Reports, Intl. Series S129. Oxford: BAR.

McGrail, S. (ed.) 1985. *Sewn plank boats: Archaeological and ethnographic papers based on those presented to a conference at Greenwich in November, 1984*. British Archaeological Reports, Int. Series S276. Oxford: BAR.

Meiggs, R. 1982. *Trees and timber in the ancient Mediterranean world*. Oxford: Oxford University Press.

Mercer, H. C. 1960. *Ancient carpenters' tools*. Doyleston: Bucks County Historical Society.

Milne, G. 1982. "Recording timberwork on the London waterfront," in McGrail 1982: 7–23.

Milne, G. 1985. *The port of Roman London*. London: Batsford.

Mols, S. T. 1999. *Wooden furniture in Herculaneum*. Amsterdam: Gieben.

Morgan, M. H. 1914. *Vitruvius: The Ten Books on Architecture*. Cambridge, MA: Harvard University Press.

Mutz, A. 1980. "Ein fund von Holzbearbeitungs-Werkzeugen aus Augst Insula 31," *Jahresberichte aus Augst und Kaiseraugst*. Liestal: Amt für Museen und Archäologie des Kantons Basel-Landschaft.

O'Connor, C. 1993. *Roman bridges*. Cambridge: Cambridge University Press.

Oleson, J. P. 1978. "Technical aspects of Etruscan rock-cut tomb architecture," *Römische Mitteilungen* 85: 283–314.

Papaccio, V. 1993. "Il telaio ligneo (*opus craticium*) ercolanese: Considerazioni e ricerche sui requisiti antisismici," in Franchi dell'Orto 1993: 609–16.

Petrie, W. M. F. 1917. *Tools and weapons illustrated by the Egyptian Collection in University College, London*. London: British School of Archaeology in Egypt.

Piggott, S. 1983. *The earliest wheeled transport*. Ithaca, NY: Cornell University Press.

Popham, M., E. Touloupa, and L. Sackett 1982. "The Hero of Lefkandi," *Antiquity* 56: 169–74.

Pugsley, P. 2003. *Roman domestic wood*. British Archaeological Reports, Intl. SeriesS1118. Oxford: BAR.

Puglisi, S. M. 1951. "Gli abitatori primitivi del Palatino attraverso le testimonianze archeologiche e le nuove stratigrafiche sul Germalo," *Monumenti Antichi* 41: 1–98.

Pulak, C. 1993. "The shipwreck at Ulu Burun, Turkey: 1992 excavation campaign," *INA Quarterly* 20: 4–12.

Raban, A., 1989. *The harbours of Caesarea Maritima*, vol. 1. J. P. Oleson (ed.). British Archaeological Reports, Intl. Series S491. Oxford: BAR.

Rasch, J. 1991. "Zur Konstruktion spätantiker Kuppeln vom 3. bis 6. Jahrhundert," *Jahrbuch des Deutschen Archäologischen Instituts* 106: 311–83.

Richter, G. M. A. 1966. *The furniture of the Greeks, Etruscans, and Romans*. London: Phaidon.

Rickman, G. 1971. *Roman granaries and store buildings*. Cambridge: Cambridge University Press.

Rieth, A. 1940. "Das Holzdrechseln." *Ipek: Jahrbuch für prähistorischer und ethnographische Kunst* 13: 85–107.

Rowland, I., and T. N. Howe 1999. *Vitruvius: Ten Books on Architecture*. Cambridge: Cambridge University Press.

Salmon, J., and G. Shipley 1996. *Human landscapes in classical antiquity*. London: Routledge.

Simpson, E., K. Spirydowicz, and V. Dorge 1992. *Gordion wooden furniture*. Ankara: Museum of Anatolian Civilization.

Saatmann, K., E. Jüngst, and P. Thielscher 1938–39. "Caesars Rheinbrücke," *Bonner Jahrbücher* 143–44: 83–208.

Shirley, E. A. M. 2000. *The construction of the Roman legionary fortress at Inchtuthil*. British Archaeological Reports, Intl. Series S298. Oxford: BAR.

Steingräber, S. 1979. *Etruskische Möbel*. Rome: Giorgio Bretschneider.

Tampone, G. 1989. *Il Restauro del Legno*. Atti del 2°Congresso Nazionale Restauro del Legno. Florence: Nardini.

Taylor, R. 2003. *Roman builders: A study in architectural process*. Cambridge: Cambridge University Press.

Ucelli, G. 1950. *Le Navi di Nemi*. Roma: La Libreria dello Stato.

Ulrich, R. B. 1996. "*Contignatio*, Vitruvius, and the Campanian Builder," *American Journal of Archaeology* 100: 137.

Ulrich, R.B. 2007. *Roman woodworking*. New Haven: Yale University Press.

Wasowicz, A., and M. Vaulina 1974. *Bois grecs et romains de l'Ermitage*. Warsaw: Narodowy.

Watzinger, C. 1905. *Griechische Holzsarkophage aus der Zeit Alexanders des Grossen*. Leipzig: Hinrichs.

Weeks, J. 1982. "Roman carpentry joints: Adoption and adaptation," in McGrail 1982, 157–68.

Zienkiewicz, J. D. 1986. *The legionary fortress baths at Caerleon*, vol. 2: *The finds*. Cardiff: National Museum of Wales.

Zimmer, G. 1985. "Römische Handwerker," in *Aufstieg und Niedergang der römischen Welt* 2.12.3. Berlin: de Gruyter, 205–28.

CHAPTER 18

.......................................................................................................

# TEXTILE PRODUCTION

.......................................................................................................

## JOHN P. WILD

THE metaphorical use of textile terminology is a characteristic of the classical languages that reflects the ubiquity of textile crafts in contemporary life (Scheid and Svenbro 2003). To us, however, such textile concepts may seem obscure. Moreover, textiles and textile implements were mostly of organic origin and hence survive infrequently in the archaeological record; it is hard to appreciate what is not tangible. Nevertheless, an array of sources can be tapped in the study of Greco-Roman textile technology. At first glance they may appear complementary; but rarely can they be fitted together neatly (Wild 2000, 2004). Written evidence offers detailed poetic descriptions of weaving contests on the one hand, humdrum lists of commodities and prices in private documents on the other. Earlier commentators looked no further (Yates 1843), but over the past seventy years textile fragments recovered during scientifically conducted archaeological excavations where specific microclimatic conditions have facilitated preservation, provide a new and more immediate perspective. Nonetheless, the problem of matching an artifact or craft skill to a putative account of it in a Greek or Roman source is considerable; the precise meaning of many ancient terms remains ill defined, and they changed over time.

Representations in art—weaving scenes on Greek pottery, for example—are a valuable, but sometimes coded, resource. The craftsmen and women themselves, however, did not communicate their experience or skills in any of the above media (Bender-Jørgensen 2003). They are best approached through the study of still existing "primitive" practice, a facet of the ethnographic record that has also been the inspiration behind much modern experimentation in the reconstruction of lost techniques (Fansa 1990).

Four basic processes characterize ancient textile production: growing and harvesting the raw fibers, converting them into yarn, weaving or interlacing the yarns to make a fabric, and, possibly, fabric finishing. In a developed industrial context further techniques can be identified within and between these basic stages. My account will consider the processes in that order, but it will draw somewhat arbitrary lines between them for clarity's sake. Dyeing, however, does not fit into the sequence neatly and has been treated at the end of the chapter, where it would belong today.

# FIBERS: HARVESTING AND PREPARATION

The textile industry was rurally embedded (Wild 1999; Erdkamp 1999). Some aspects became urbanized through increasing division of labor, but its dependence on domestic plants and animals, and hence the farming community, is undeniable. There was little bulk transport of raw fibers over long distances (in contrast to medieval and modern practice), and the most famous textile centers, like that of the Po Valley, developed where ample quantities of high-quality raw materials were at hand.

## Animal Fibers

Sheep yielded the most varied and versatile textile fiber: wool. Present-day relict populations, such as the Orkney sheep of North Ronaldsay, indicate the general character of Greco-Roman sheep: small bodied, long necked, with a fleece rarely weighing more than 1.5 kg (Maltby 1981; Wild 1982: 110–12; Melena 1987: 397–99). While wool was historically a secondary product after meat and milk (Sherratt 1983), it is clear that Mycenaean flock-masters with their large numbers of wethers were already concentrating on wool production (Killen 1964). The mountainous terrain of Greece and Italy saw flocks in seasonal transhumance from lowland to highland grazing (Whittaker 1988; Small et al. 2003: 189–93), and in Asia Minor the hinterland of Miletus was noted for its fine-woolled sheep (Carter 1969; Morel 1978). Traditionally, fine-woolled flocks were protected against dirt and damage by jackets of skin, a classical Greek practice later familiar in the Roman world (Xenophon, *Mem.* 2, 757; Kraemer 1928; Frayn 1984: 35, 164).

Both rich and poor—even the emperors (Frayn 1984: 176–79)—kept sheep (King 1999). In Egypt, Apollonius, chief finance officer to Ptolemy II, upgraded the quality of his wool by importing animals from Miletus (*P.Cair.Zen.* 59195; Loftus 2000: 175). Roman agriculturalists such as Columella were familiar with the principles of selective breeding for wool quality (Columella, *Rust.* 7.2.4–5), as were Iron-Age farmers in central Europe (Ryder 2001). Fiber diameter measurement of wool yarns in ancient textiles indicates the existence (often in the same flock) of fleece-types ranging from hairy medium wool (typical of the earliest domesticated sheep) through generalized medium, to medium, semifine and true fine wool, arguably achieved through selective breeding (Ryder 1983: 45–49; Wild 2002: 2). Since the gene for white is dominant, selection led to pure white wool, although the "primitive" pigmented light-, dark-, and reddish-brown and gray (mixed white and brown) wools were still in evidence (Ryder 1990), and were used for decorative effect without overdyeing.

The presence of white, fine-woolled sheep in the Greek world is confirmed by surviving yarns (Ryder 1988). Textiles in the Roman west reflect a preponderance of generalized medium-woolled fleeces (Ryder 1969: 509, table 5; Ryder 1981); in the eastern provinces more fine wools have been identified, but in Egypt sheep with unpigmented, hairy medium wool seem to have been the norm (Wild 1994: 34–35, table 1; Walton Rogers 1994).

Sheep were usually shorn with a pair of sprung iron shears, in spring or early summer (Varro, *Rust.* 2.11.6–9; Wild 1982: 116). The older practice of plucking the wool at the time of the molt persisted into the Roman period (Pliny, *HN* 8.191); this method had the advantage of leaving behind most of the coarser outer hair. On Apollonius' estate in Egypt, the fine-woolled, jacketed sheep were plucked, while the coarser-woolled Arabian animals were shorn (*P.Cair.Zen.* 59430). Surprisingly, we hear nothing about wool sorting or grading (Ryder 1995). Fleeces were beaten to remove foreign bodies (Aristophanes, *Lys.* 574–78; Wipszycka 1965: 33–34). The extent to which they were washed to remove suint (dried perspiration) and excess lanolin, especially before dyeing, is hard to estimate. At Pompeii a fixed wool-washing installation consisted of a cauldron over a boiler, flanked by draining surfaces (Borgard and Puybaret 2004: 49–52; Frayn 1984: 148–49), and in Verecundus' workshop portable draining boards are depicted (Wild 1970: 171, fig. 52). Where sales of fleeces are recorded, as at Dura-Europos (Baur et al. 1933, nos. 247, 252, 272), the wool had probably not yet been degreased. Washed (and sorted) wool was sold by weight (Wild 2002: 5), since cleaning a fleece reduces its weight by 30 percent or more.

Wool was often—but not always and not of necessity—combed to align fibers for spinning and to separate short from long fibers. Wool-combing, a low-status craft, is encountered everywhere in the Greco-Roman world (Wipszycka 1965: 34–35; Frayn 1984: 150; Wild 2000: 210–11). Roman wool combs were flat rectangles of iron with teeth cut or welded on both short ends (only one end in eastern Britain); they were mounted on a post behind which the operative sat (Wild 1982: 118). On a second-century relief from Ostia (figure 18.1) the wool is seen being drawn through the teeth with a flat wooden implement and formed into carefully weighed rovings (Holliday 1993: 96, fig. 7).

Goat hair was of minor commercial value, except in arid environments where it served for tentage and sacking (Ryder 1993; Wild 2003a: 38). The yarns were usually plied to improve tensile strength (Batcheller 2001). Whether the fine underwool of the "cashmere" goat of central and southern Asia was ever imported (as is claimed by Moulherat and Vial 2000; Schmidt-Colinet et al. 2000: 11) is debatable.

Figure 18.1.  Woolcomber T. Aelius Evangelus seated at his combing-post, Ostia. In the Medelhavsmuseet, Stockholm. (Drawing by Priscilla Wild.)

## Vegetable Fibers

Flax (*linum usitatissimum* L.), the principal ancient plant fiber, is hardy, but flourished best in well-watered, fertile soils (Körber-Grohne 1987: 366–79). It was grown in the Peloponnese in classical Greek and earlier times (forbes 1956: 36–38; Robkin 1979). Egypt's well documented linen industry flourished under Ptolemaic and Roman control (Wipszycka 1965), but there were other minor centers of repute in the Roman Empire (Gleba 2004; Forbes 1956: 35–43). Paleobotanical sampling indicates that flax was a regular component of mixed farming regimes (Gleba 2004: 31–32; Wild 2002: 6–7).

The bast fibers of flax have to be separated from the woody core and bark between which they lie, in a series of traditional operations that involved all members of a peasant family (Wild 1970: 27–29). The stalks (ca. 1 m high) were uprooted, dried, and then retted, allowing bacterial action stimulated by moisture to loosen the fibers. Retting could be undertaken in ponds or tanks—or simply by long exposure in the fields (dew retting; Freckmann et al. 1979: 91–102). The stalks were dried, then "broken" with a wooden mallet and "scutched" with a wooden blade to remove any remaining bark and core. Finally, bundles of fiber were drawn across the multiple teeth of a fixed comb (hackle) to free them from residual cellulosic matter (tow) and isolate the individual fibers (Wild 1968). Sacking and cordage were made from the tow.

Hemp (*cannabis sativa* L.) also contains bast fiber, tougher and coarser than flax but similar in character. Well established in late prehistoric Europe (Körber-Grohne 1987: 379–89; Godwin 1967), it was converted in classical antiquity into cordage, netting, and sailcloth (Wild 1970: 16–17). The harvested stems (ca. 1.5 m high or more) were processed like flax (Wild 1970: 29–30).

The annual form of cotton (*gossypium herbaceum* L.) grown in India and the Persian Gulf region was known to Herodotus (3.47, 106; 7.65) and Theophrastus (*Hist. pl.* 4.4.8; 4.7.7–8) and through occasional imports of cotton cloth into Greece. In the oases of Roman Egypt it became an increasingly popular crop and was planted under irrigation in the Fezzan and the Jordan valley. Lower Nubia and India were alternative external sources of cotton textiles (Wild 1997; Wild et al. forthcoming). How the short fibers (lint) were detached from the seeds on which they formed in the boll is uncertain—possibly just with the fingers.

## Insect Fibers

In a famous passage Aristotle accurately describes how the filament extruded by the silk worm of Cos in the Aegean to build its cocoon was unwound, reeled up, and woven into garments prized for their sheen (*Hist. an.* 5.19.551b; Wild 1984). The wild silk moth in question was probably *Pachypasa otus*, now virtually extinct (Good 1995: 965, fig. 3; Panagiotakopulu et al. 1997). Cultivated silk from the *Bombyx mori* was available only in China until the sixth century A.D.; its importation as yarn and woven cloth may not have begun before the Augustan period. Despite its cost, it was a powerful and enduring status symbol, the basis of some of the most complex decorative textiles of antiquity.

## Miscellaneous Fibers

A group of fibers with special properties were exploited in the Roman period. Rabbits, reared in enclosed warrens, provided soft hair for expensive clothing (*Edictum Diocletiani* 19.73a–73c; Varro, *Rust.* 3.3.1–3, 8–10). The earliest archaeological evidence for this fiber dates to the seventh century (Amrein et al. 1999: 93). The *Pinna nobilis*, a large Mediterranean mollusk, anchored itself to the seabed with filaments that could be converted into a smooth, shiny cloth (Wild 1970: 20; Maeder et al. 2004). Table napkins spun and woven from asbestos were a dinner-party amusement, since they could be burnt clean (Wild 1970: 21).

# SPINNING

Spinning was not just an essential stage in the conversion of processed raw fibers into yarn for weaving or interlacing, but a social and economic obligation falling on all female members of a household, whatever their status, from the Homeric Iron

Age to late antiquity (Homer, *Od.* 4.125–35; St. Jerome, *Ep.* 130.15; Wild 1970: 31–40; Larsson-Lovén 1998). The technique was learned at an early age, and it is rare to find anything but the highest-quality yarn, sometimes unbelievably fine, in archaeological textiles. Two implements were required: the distaff, a short rod to the upper section of which wool rovings or hackled flax bundles were attached, and the spindle, a carefully profiled rod with a swelling somewhere along its length on which the spindle whorl was wedged (Wild 2003c: 25–29). The whorl, a disc of wood or terracotta or a shaped, recycled potsherd with a central perforation, provided the necessary momentum. In Greece the rovings were prepared on an *epinetron*, a ceramic sheath laid on the upper leg while seated (Jenkins 2003: 72–73). The act of spinning involved drawing out fibers from the distaff (held in the left hand) and inserting twist into them with rotating spindle, manipulated by the right hand.

Deeply conservative cultural norms governed the precise ways in which the spinning operation was performed. The spindle might be rotated in the hand, rolled down the thigh, supported on a dish, or suspended to spin free on the end of the drafted yarn, the mode most commonly depicted in classical art (Crowfoot 1931). In Europe the whorl was usually mounted at the lower end of the spindle, but in Egypt and some adjacent regions at the upper end. The direction of spin—generally clockwise (Z-direction) in the western Roman world, anticlockwise (S-direction) in the eastern—also reflected cultural predilections (Wild 2003b: 82, 108). "Z" and "S" refer to the resulting direction of the slant in the fibers of the thread. Spindles loaded with yarn were traditionally stored in a basket (Wild 2003b: 83). The second-century Roman grave of a young girl at Les Martres-de-Veyre (Clermont-Ferrand) contained a distaff loaded with wool rovings (held in place by colored ribbons), a spindle, and remains of a basket (Audollent 1923: 305, no. 31, pl. VI.12).

Two twist-inserting crafts were entrusted to men: rope-making with flax, hemp, or another coarse vegetable fiber (Pliny, *HN* 19.18; Gaitzsch 1986: Abb. 34) and making "gold thread." For the latter, narrow ribbons of gold (less than 0.5 mm wide), cut from thin foil sheets, were wound around a silk or flax core (Bedini et al. 2004; Rinuy 2000).

# Looms and Weave Structure

Weaving was the center of gravity in the textile industry, but there was a potential risk of a production bottleneck, for it took some ten spinners in continuous employment to keep one loom supplied with yarn. In practice, however, much textile work was part-time and seasonal, and in highly industrial milieus like Roman Egypt much yarn was bought and sold. The ancient weaver set out to create on the loom a textile item of predetermined form and function, ensuring minimal wastage of yarn and minimal cutting and sewing (Granger-Taylor 1982). The tailor's main preoccupation was with recycling old clothing. Except for sailcloth sold as yardage, the marketing of bolts of cloth in a medieval and modern sense was unknown.

While the horizontal loom of dynastic Egypt, spanned between two beams, was still used by nomadic groups, it cannot be identified in the Greco-Roman world, where the principal looms were vertical (Kemp and Vogelsang-Eastwood 2001: 310–12). The warp-weighted loom dominated weaving in classical Greece and most of the Roman Empire until at least the first century A.D. (figure 2.11; Hoffmann 1964; Staermose Nielsen 1999: 63–78: Wild 2002: 10–11). The loom was large (up to 2.50 m wide) with two timber uprights, a cloth beam across the top, and a fixed shed rod below (figure 18.2). It inclined at a slight angle to facilitate the natural shed between the two warp sheets, which were tensioned by two rows of fired (sometimes un-fired) clay loom-weights—which are the sole archaeological remains that survive. The front warp sheet with its weights hung over the fixed shed rod, while the rear warp sheet hung vertically from the cloth beam. The shed was changed by means of heddles attached to a heddle rod that was supported in the forward position for the artificial shed on two brackets. The weavers beat weft upward using a wooden sword-beater inserted into the shed. Warp was kept in due order by passing a pin-beater (*kerkis, radius*) across it so that it "sang" (Wild 1967a; Guðjónsson 1990: 173–74).

The warp was secured to the cloth beam by means of a flat-woven or tablet-woven starting-border prepared in a preliminary operation (Hoffmann 1964: 151–83). It characterizes textiles woven on the warp-weighted loom, which range from plain weaves (1/1 tabby) of varying weight to complex diamond twills. In classical Greece, decorative figured bands in tapestry weave (for which the design was built up from individual lengths of colored weft) were inserted into the web (Wace 1948), although on a warp-weighted loom this was not straightforward (Granger-Taylor 1992: 20–21, fig. 3; Staermose Nielsen 1999: 95, fig. 53).

In the Nordic world, where weaving on the warp-weighted loom is a living tradition, considerable diversity can be documented in the techniques of the weavers (Guðjónsson 1990; Hoffmann 1964: 188). In the Greco-Roman world the variety in shape and weight of loom-weights recorded even on a single site points to similar diversity. Pyramidal, fired clay loom-weights perforated at the apex are the most widely distributed; conical weights are common, while discoidal weights (some-times mold-made) are typically Hellenistic (Davidson 1952: 146–57; Staermose Nielsen 1999: 41–48). Compared to those from prehistoric Europe, Greek and Roman loom-weights were light (70–250 g), with up to 70 in a set for one loom (Tébar Megiás and Wilson forthcoming).

The two-beam vertical loom, on which a second, lower, horizontal beam replaced the warp-weights, began to displace the warp-weighted loom in the first century A.D.; the latter survived, however, in a few contexts (Servius, *Ad Aen.* 7.14; Hope and Bowen 2002: 67, 165). The new loom's advantage lay in being readily adaptable to the devices and techniques required for the patterned fabrics in-creasingly popular in the eastern Mediterranean. Weavers beat the weft downward with a wooden comb rather than a sword beater (Thomas 2001: 15, figs. 15, 17, 23)

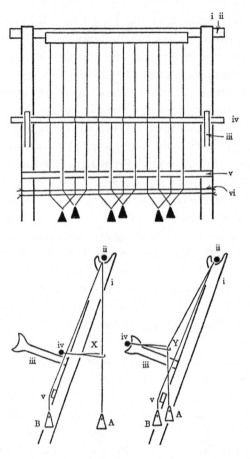

Figure 18.2.   Structure of the warp-weighted loom. (After Wild 1970: fig. 53, by permission of the Faculty of Classics, Cambridge University.)

and could sit at the loom; starting-borders are often of twined cords, variously constructed (Verhecken-Lammens 1992).

A range of decorative techniques can be seen in the surviving ancient textiles, some of them with a regional or chronological bias. The simplest was a check, based on bands of yarn in contrasting colors (or contrasting spin-directions) set up in the warp and repeated in the weft by the weaver (Wild 1964). The so-called shaded bands with rainbow color-effects were even simpler to weave, for their progressively changing colors had already been blended by the spinner (Schmidt-Colinet et al. 2000: 133). The two-beam loom was particularly associated with the insertion of monochrome or figured tapestry bands or panels into otherwise plain textiles. For this purpose specific warp-threads could be controlled by extra shed rods or heddles, and either temporarily eliminated or crossed to allow tighter beating up of the weft and hence a stronger color effect (Granger-Taylor 1992). Tapestry patterns could also be highlighted in the "flying needle" technique, whereby obliquely floating (usually linen) yarns were introduced with separate spools on the loom itself (easily mistaken for embroidery; De Jonghe 1988: 27, pl. 130). Designs brocaded with floating weft-threads are also found (De Jonghe 1978).

Surface enhancement—for warmth as well as decoration—by means of rows of loops added in the weft direction was widely practiced in the Mediterranean region on wool, linen, and even silk garments and furnishings (van 'T Hooft et al. 1994: 145, fig. 9). Cut-loop pile and classic "carpet knots" are found on eastern Roman textiles, where they reflect the textile culture of western and central Asia (Fujii 1980).

It has long been recognized that the complex nature of damask, compound tabby, and compound twill weaves called for correspondingly complex devices to open multiple sheds, set up and manipulated by exceptionally capable weavers. A horizontal loom, it has been argued, would best facilitate such arrangements, perhaps the forerunner of the medieval and modern draw-loom (Wild 1987). There is, however, no solid evidence for it. Rather, the *zilu* loom still in use today in Iran for compound weaves suggests that the Roman loom for advanced weaves remained a vertical one (Thompson and Granger-Taylor 1995–1996; Ciszuk 2004).

Damask twill carries an overall geometric pattern based on juxtaposed areas of warp-and weft-faced fabric. Weaving faults in Roman examples indicate that the design was achieved by raising in a planned order pairs of heddle rods from a set of as many as 20 rods (De Jonghe and Tavernier 1978: pls. II, V). The most striking pieces are late Roman silk tunics incorporating tapestry-woven features in purple wool and gold thread (Bédat et al. 2005); but simpler 2/1 and 3/1 twill damasks in wool from early Roman Egypt hint that the weave may be a Hellenistic invention (Schrenk 2001; Cardon 1999a).

Weft-faced, compound tabby can be claimed as another Hellenistic development (Pliny, *HN* 8.196). Its structure allows the interplay of two or more colors of weft in a near-reversible pattern: weft threads can be raised to the surface of the cloth or concealed beneath neighboring wefts (De Jonghe 1988: figs 140–45; Desrosiers 2004: 14–23, figs. 1–2: Ciszuk 2000). On the *zilu* loom a set of heddle rods governs the basic underlying weave, while the numerous sheds for the design are opened by drawing on combinations of individual heddles (Thompson and Granger-Taylor 1995–1996). Both work at a right angle to the vertical warp. Assuming that the Roman loom was similarly equipped, the Roman master weaver must have had the mental agility of a modern computer programmer, along with a prodigious memory. Tuck (2006) has proposed that chants and songs assisted the ancient weaver in the accurate reproduction of complex textile patterns. Most compound tabbies were furnishing fabrics in wool, a few in silk; but the development by the fourth century A.D. of compound twill (see figure 18.3) and the increasing use of fine silk led to some of the most spectacular textiles of antiquity (Schrenk 2004: 180–92).

The weaving of bands and narrow fabrics did not necessarily depend on a framed loom, but on warp spanned between the weaver and a distant fixed point. For simple 1/1 tabby, the two sheds could be opened by a single heddle-frame of bone, wood, or bronze (Wild 1970: 72–75). Tablet-weaving, a method of warp-cord patterning, involved a pack of slim square or triangular tablets with a hole in each

Figure 18.3. Fourth-century A.D. silk tunic in weft-faced compound twill weave showing erotes in medallions, now in the Abegg-Stiftung, Riggisberg. (Photograph by C. von Viràg, by permission of the Abegg-Stiftung.)

corner for the passage of a warp-thread (Hansen 1990a). There is either direct evidence or a strong presumption that such bands were familiar in Greece and Rome (Giroire 1997).

# INTERLACED AND NON-WOVEN
# FABRICS

*Naalebinding*, a technique of openwork construction with a single needle, was popular in antiquity for three-dimensional textiles, particularly socks, of which many examples have come to light in Roman Egypt (Hansen 1990b; Burnham 1972). For bag-shaped headdresses, fashionable in the Mediterranean world, the technique of sprang was employed, whereby threads spanned on a frame in a single sheet were twisted around one another to create a netlike structure (Jenkins and Williams

1985). Ply-split braiding and simpler braiding forms were used for girth-straps and webbing (Collingwood 1998). The propensity of wool fibers to interlock and shrink under pressure and with moisture was exploited to make felt, sometimes for clothing, often for helmet or shield linings (Gervers 1973).

Small-scale textile manufacture with the techniques just described was probably based in the home, even if it had a commercial aspect. Work on larger looms was carried out by a team of men and/or women and children in environments ranging from a cramped sweatshop in Roman Egypt (McGing 1990), an airy courtyard in Pompeii (Jongman 1991: 162–65), or a well lit villa workshop as designed by Vitruvius (*De arch.* 6.4.2). The respective skills of wool and linen weavers, who took due note of the physical properties of their materials, are reflected in the differing structures (e.g., selvedge types) of their products.

# Finishing and Fulling

Clothing and items of soft furnishing were—or could be—ready to wear or use virtually as soon as they had been cut from the loom. Texture, surface appearance, and handle, however, could be greatly improved by "finishing," a task entrusted in urban contexts to specialists with their own workshops and staff, supplies of cleansing agents, and ample water. Wool and linen fabrics were treated in different ways that took note of their respective properties.

The fuller, who handled principally wool textiles, was a well known figure from the Mycenaean period onward (Chadwick 1976: 43, 71; Pliny, *HN* 7.57). He treated items straight from the loom and also acted as laundryman for soiled clothing (Wild 1970: 82–86; Wilson 2003). The focal point of a fuller, exemplified by some well preserved establishments in Pompeii (Moeller 1976: 41–51; Jongman 1991: 170–79) and Ostia (Pietrogrande 1976), was an array of large ceramic vessels with pointed bases set in a masonry bench against a wall. Elsewhere, slightly different dispositions have been recorded (Wilson 2001: 274–77), and wooden tubs employed (Wild 1970: 82, fig. 73). The fulling vessels contained a solution of water and a cleansing agent, commonly (and most cheaply) stale human urine, the ammonia component of which reacted with grease in the wool to form a soapy compound (Bradley 2002: 30–32). Fuller's earth (calcium montmorillonite) was a more expensive alternative (Robertson 1986: 42–81). The fuller trod the cloth vigorously in the solution; the result, for loom-state cloth particularly, was to shrink and compact it. This "waulked" cloth was then rinsed in tanks, and dried. Some towns made special provision for fullers' water supplies (*SEG* 35.1483). Optional extras included having the nap raised to a soft finish with a board set with spines (*aena*) (Wild 1968) and then trimmed with shears (see figure 18.4). Provision for this soft finish could be made at the yarn-spinning stage (Wild 1967b).

Figure 18.4. Fuller's tombstone from Sens (Yonne), showing one operative treading textiles in a tub and another shearing raised nap. (After Wild 1970: fig. 73, by permission of the Faculty of Classics, Cambridge University.)

Pure white garments, which might be achieved by bleaching them over a pot of smoldering sulphur, were a social desideratum (Wild 1970: 83). In the late fourth century B.C., Theophrastus, whose father was a fuller, lists types of kaolin and chalk that could be applied to cloth surfaces to enhance the bright effect (*Lap.* 63, 67–68). Romans were also impressed by carefully pressed clothes, for which a screw press and auxiliary devices might be employed (Granger-Taylor 1987). Linen could be bleached by boiling it with natron (sodium carbonate and sodium bicarbonate), where this was available, notably in Egypt (Wipszycka 1965: 23–24; Lucas 1932). The surface of a linen textile, including in particular any seams, might be smoothed and polished with a glass "slick-stone" (Wild 1970: 85, pl. XII.d; Walton Rogers 1997: 1775–79).

# DYEING

The topic of dyeing is a branch of applied chemistry. It is worth emphasizing, however, that, given the rich palette of colors the ancient dyer had to offer, his or her work was integral to that of the spinner and weaver, with whom there was cooperation at several levels in the textile production sequence.

Wool was most commonly dyed in the fleece to ensure maximum uptake of dyestuff (Halleux 1981: 44, 151; Edict of Diocletian 24). Flax, on the other hand, was dyed in the hank, as cross-sections of yarns sometimes reveal (Sheffer and Granger-Taylor 1994: 161). Piece-dyeing seems to have been comparatively rare, except for the redyeing of faded monochrome textiles. Resist-dyeing of woven cloth was an art of Roman Egypt: the design was drawn out in a resist-medium, often hot wax, applied with a brush, so that in the vat only the background took up the dye (Schrenk 2004: 82–93; Cardon 1998). Some textiles were simply painted (Gerziger 1975).

Dyers' workshops in Pompeii, some associated with probable wool-washing facilities, housed various types of heated vats, variously disposed. The larger lead-lined vats were arguably for mordanting wool prior to dyeing in smaller vats nearby. Others may have been for fermentation dyes like woad (Borgard and Puybaret 2004: 52–56).

Advances in the analysis of dyestuff traces in archaeological textiles have shed new light on the dyestuff sources tapped by Greek and Roman dyers (Cardon 1999b; Cardon et al. 2004; Wouters 1995); to understand how they achieved their colors has been the objective of experimentation (Edmonds 2000; Cardon 1999b: 46–57).

The fact that only an expert can spot the difference between a Greek or Roman textile and its modern equivalent is testimony to the consistently high level of skills deployed by ancient textile operatives. Gender divisions are blurred: spinners tend to be female, professional weavers male, but there are exceptions. The role of children in the (relatively safe) industry has been vastly underestimated. Technological advances, arguably driven by change in clothing fashion, are hard to identify; but the innovative spirit of Hellenistic Alexandria seems to have made itself felt in the textile industry, as in so many other technologies.

# REFERENCES

Alfaro, C., J. P. Wild, and B. Costa (eds.) 2004. *Purpureae vestes: Textiles y tintes del Mediterráneo en época romana; Actas del 1 symposium internacional sobre textiles y tintes del Mediterráneo en época romana (Ibiza 8 al 10 de noviembre 2002)*. Valencia: University of Valencia.

Amrein, H., A. Rast-Eicher, and R. Windler 1999. "Neue Untersuchungen zum Frauengrab des 7. Jahrhunderts in der reformierten Kirche von Bülach (Kanton Zürich)," *Zeitschrift für schweizerische Archäologie und Kunstgeschichte* 56: 73–114.

Audollent, A. 1923. *Les tombes gallo-romaines à inhumation des Martres-de-Veyre*. Mémoires présentés à l'Académie des sciences et belles-lettres 13. Paris: Académie des Sciences et Belles-Lettres.

Batcheller, J. 2001. "Goat-hair textiles from Karanis, Egypt," in P. W. Rogers, J. B. Jørgensen, and A. Rast-Eicher (eds.), *The Roman textile industry and its influence: A birthday tribute to John Peter Wild*. Oxford: Oxbow, 38–47.

Baur, P. V. C., M. I. Rostovtzeff, and A. R. Bellinger (eds.) 1933. *The excavations at Dura-Europos conducted by Yale University and the French Academy of Inscriptions and*

*Letters: Preliminary report of fourth season of work, October 1930–March 1931.* New Haven: Yale University Press.

Bédat, I., S. Desrosiers, C. Moulherat, and C. Relier 2005. "Two Gallo-Roman graves recently found in Nantré (Vienne, France)," in F. Pritchard and J. P. Wild (eds.), *Northern archaeological textiles.* North European Symposium for Archaeological Textiles 7. Oxford: Oxbow, 5–11.

Bedini, A., I. A. Rapinesi, and D. Ferro 2004. "Testimonianze di filato e ornamenti in oro nell'abigliamento di età romana," in Alfaro et al. 2004: 77–88.

Bender-Jørgensen, L. 2003. "The epistemology of craftsmanship," in L. Bender-Jørgensen, J. Banck-Burgess, A. Rast-Eicher (eds.), *Textilien aus Archäologie und Geschichte: Festschrift für Klaus Tidow.* Neumünster: Wachholtz, 30–36.

Bender-Jørgensen, L. forthcoming. "Archaeological textiles between the arts, crafts and sciences," in A. Rast-Eicher (ed.), North European Symposium for Archaeological Textiles 9.

Borgard, P., and M.-P. Puybaret 2004. "Le travail de la laine au debut de l'Empire: L'apport du modèle pompeien. Quels artisans? Quels équipements? Quelles techniques?" in Alfaro et al. 2004: 47–59.

Bradley, M. 2002. " 'It all comes out in the wash': Looking harder at the Roman fullonica," *Journal of Roman Archaeology* 15: 21–44.

Burnham, D. K. 1972. "Coptic knitting: An ancient technique," *Textile History* 3: 116–24.

Cardon, D. 1998. "Textiles archéologiques de Maximianon-Al Zarqa et Didymoi: Exemples précoces de teinture par réserve sur laine," *Bulletin de Liaison du Centre International d'Étude des Textiles Anciens* 75: 15–20.

Cardon, D. 1999a. "Les damassés de laine de Krokodilô (100–120 apr. J.-C.)," *Bulletin de Liaison du Centre International d'Étude des Textiles Anciens* 76: 6–21.

Cardon, D. 1999b. *Teintures précieuses de la Méditerranée: Pourpre—kérmes—pastel.* Carcassonne: Musée des Beaux-Arts de Carcassonne.

Cardon, D., and M. Feugère (eds.) 2000. *Archéologie des textiles des origines au Ve siècle: Actes du colloque de Lattes, oct. 1999.* Montagnac: Monique Mergoil.

Cardon, D., J. Wouters, I. Vanden Berghe, G. Richard, and R. Bréniaux 2004. "Dye analyses of selected textiles from Maximianon, Krokodilô and Didymoi (Egypt)," in Alfaro et al. 2004: 145–54.

Carter, H. B. 1969. "The historical geography of the fine-woolled sheep (1)," *Textile Institute and Industry* 7: 15–18, 45–48.

Chadwick, J. 1976. *The Mycenaean world.* Cambridge: Cambridge University Press.

Ciszuk, M. 2000. "Taquetés from Mons Claudianus: Analyses and reconstruction," in Cardon and Feugère 2000: 265–82.

Ciszuk, M. 2004. "Taqueté and damask from Mons Claudianus: A discussion of Roman looms for patterned textiles," in Alfaro et al. 2004: 107–13.

Collingwood, P. 1998. *The techniques of ply-split braiding.* London: Bellew.

Crowfoot, G. M. 1931. *Methods of handspinning in Egypt and the Sudan.* Halifax: Bankfield Museum.

Davidson, G. R. 1952. *Corinth XII: The minor objects.* Princeton: Princeton University Press, 3–189.

Desrosiers, S. 2004. *Soieries et autres textiles de l'antiquité au XVIe siècle.* Paris: Réunion des Musées Nationaux.

Edmonds, J. 2000. *The mystery of imperial purple dye.* Little Chalfont: Privately printed.

Erdkamp, P. 1999. "Agricultural underemployment and the cost of rural labour in the Roman world," *Classical Quarterly* 44: 556–72.

Fansa, M. 1990. *Experimentelle Archäologie in Deutschland*. Archäologische Mitteilungen aus Nordwest-Deutschland Beiheft 4. Oldenburg: Isensee.

Forbes, R. J. 1956. *Studies in ancient technology*. Vol. 4. Leiden: Brill.

Frayn, J. M. 1984. *Sheep-rearing and the wool trade in Italy during the Roman period*. Liverpool: Cairns.

Freckmann, K., G. Simons, and K. Grunsky-Peter 1979. *Flachs im Rheinland: Anbau und Verarbeitung*. Köln: Rheinland-Verlag.

Fujii, H. 1980. *Al-Rafidan I: Special edition on the studies of textiles and leather objects from Al-Tar caves, Iraq*. Tokyo: Kokushikan University.

Gaitzsch, W. 1986. *Antike Korb- und Seilerwaren*. Schriften des Limesmuseums Aalen 38. Aalen: Limesmuseum Aalen.

Gervers, V. 1973. "Methods of traditional felt-making in Anatolia and Iran," *Bulletin de Liaison du Centre International d'Étude des Textiles Anciens* 38: 152–63.

Gerziger, D. 1975. "Eine Decke aus dem sechsten Grab der 'Sieben Brüder,' " *Antike Kunst* 18: 51–55.

Giroire, C. 1997. "Tissage aux cartons à Antinoë," *Bulletin de Liaison du Centre International d'Étude des Textiles Anciens* 74: 6–17.

Gleba, M. 2004. "Linen production in pre-Roman and Roman Italy," in Alfaro et al. 2004: 29–38.

Godwin, H. 1967. "The cultivation of hemp," *Antiquity* 41: 42–46, 137–40.

Good, I. 1995. "On the question of silk in pre-Han Eurasia," *Antiquity* 69: 959–68.

Granger-Taylor, H. 1982. "Weaving clothes to shape in the ancient world: The tunic and toga of the Arringatore," *Textile History* 13: 3–25.

Granger-Taylor, H. 1987. "The emperor's clothes: The fold lines," *Bulletin of the Cleveland Museum of Art* 74: 114–23.

Granger-Taylor, H. 1992. "The grouping of warp threads for areas of weft-faced decoration in textiles of the Roman period: A means of distinguishing looms?" *Vlaamse Vereniging voor Oud- en Hedendaags Textiel Bulletin* 1992: 19–28.

Guðjónsson, E. 1990. "Some aspects of the Icelandic warp-weighted loom, *vefstaður*," *Textile History* 21: 165–79.

Halleux, R. 1981. *Les alchimistes grecs*. Vol. 1. Paris: Société d'Édition 'Les Belles Lettres'.

Hansen, E. H. 1990a. *Tablet weaving: History, techniques, colours, patterns*. Højbjerg: Hovedland.

Hansen, E. H. 1990b. "Nålebinding: Definition and description," in P. Walton and J. P. Wild (eds.), *Textiles in northern archaeology*. North European Symposium for Archaeological Textiles 3. London: Archetype, 21–27.

Hoffmann, M. 1964. *The warp-weighted loom*. Oslo: Universitetsforlaget.

Holliday, P. J. 1993. "The sarcophagus of Titus Aelius Evangelus and Gaudenia Nicene," *J. Paul Getty Museum Journal* 21: 85–100.

van 'T Hooft, P. P. M., M. J. Raven, E. H. C. van Rooij, and G. M. Vogelsang-Eastwood 1994. *Pharaonic and early medieval Egyptian textiles*. Leiden: Rijksmuseum van Oudheden.

Hope, C. A., and G. E. Bowen 2002. *Dakhleh Oasis project: Preliminary reports on the 1994–1995 to 1998–1999 field seasons*. Oxford: Oxbow.

Jenkins, I. 2003. "The Greeks," in D. Jenkins (ed.), *The Cambridge history of western textiles*. Cambridge: Cambridge University Press, 71–76.

Jenkins, I., and D. Williams 1985. "Sprang hair-nets: Their manufacture and use in ancient Greece," *American Journal of Archaeology* 39: 411–18.

De Jonghe, D. 1978. "Met selectieroeden geweven Koptische weefsels," *Bulletin van de Koninklijke Musea voor Kunst en Geschiedenis* 50: 75–106.

De Jonghe, D. 1988. "Aspects technologiques," in J. Lafontaine-Desogne, *Textiles coptes des Musées royaux d'Art et d'Histoire*. Brussels: Musées royaux d'Art et d'Histoire, 22–33.

De Jonghe, D., and M.Tavernier 1978. "Les damassées de la proche-antiquité," *Bulletin de Liaison du Centre International d'Étude des Textiles Anciens* 47/48: 14–42.

Jongman, W. 1991. *The economy and society of Pompeii*. Amsterdam: Gieben.

Kemp, B., and G. M. Vogelsang-Eastwood 2001. *The ancient textile industry of Amarna*. London: Egypt Exploration Society.

Killen, J. T. 1964. "The wool industry of Crete in the late Bronze Age," *Annual of the British School at Athens* 59: 1–15.

King, A. C. 1999. "Diet in the Roman world: A regional intersite comparison of mammal bones," *Journal of Roman Archaeology* 12: 168–202.

Körber-Grohne, U. 1987. *Nutzpflanzen in Deutschland: Kulturgeschichte und Biologie*. Stuttgart: Theiss.

Kraemer, C. J. 1928. "On the skin-clad sheep of antiquity," *Classical Weekly* 21: 33–35.

Larsson-Lovén, L. 1998. "Lanam fecit: Woolworking and female virtue," in L. Larsson-Lovén and A. Strömberg (eds.), *Aspects of Women in Antiquity: Proceedings of the first Nordic Symposium on womens' lives in antiquity*. Sövedalen: Aström, 85–95.

Loftus, A. 2000. "A textile factory in the third century BC Memphis: Labor, capital and private enterprise in the Zeno archive," in Cardon and Feugère 2000: 173–86.

Lucas, A. 1932. "The occurrence of natron in ancient Egypt," *Journal of Egyptian Archaeology* 18: 62–66.

McGing, Brian C. 1990. "Lease of a linen-weaving workshop in Panopolis," *Zeitschrift fürPapyrologie und Epigraphik* 89: 115–21.

Maeder, F., A. Hänggi, D. Wunderlin, and G. Carta Martiglia 2004. *Bisso marino: Fili d'oro del fondo del mare*. Basel: Naturhistorisches Museum.

Maltby, J. M. 1981. "Iron-Age, Romano-British and Anglo-Saxon animal husbandry," in M. Jones, G. Dimbleby (eds.), *The environment of man: The Iron Age to Anglo-Saxon period*. British Archaeological Report 87. Oxford: BAR: 155–203.

Melena, J. L. 1987. "On the Linear B ideogrammatic syllogram *ZE*," in J. T. Killen, J. L. Melena, and J.-P. Oliver (eds.), *Studies in Mycenaean and classical Greek presented to John Chadwick. Minos* 20–22: 389–457.

Moeller, W. O. 1976. *The wool trade of ancient Pompeii*. Leiden: Brill.

Morel, J.-P. 1978. "La laine de Tarente (de l'usage des textes anciens en histoire économique)," *Ktema* 3: 93–110.

Moulherat, C., and G. Vial. 2000. "Première attestation d'un tissu en laine de chèvre cachemire en Gaule," in Cardon and Feugère 2000: 107–13.

Panagiotakopulu, E., P. C. Buckland, P. M. Day, C. Doumas, A. Sarpaki, and P. Skidmore 1997. "A lepidopterous cocoon from Thera and the evidence for silk in the Aegean Bronze Age," *Antiquity* 71: 420–29.

Pietrogrande, A. L. 1976. *Le fulloniche*. Scavi di Ostia 8. Rome: Libreria dello Stato.

Rinuy, A. 2000. "Analyse der Goldfäden," in A. Schmidt-Colinet, A. Stauffer, and K. al-As'ad (eds.), *Die Textilien aus Palmyra*. Mainz: von Zabern, 16–19.

Robertson, R. H. S. 1986. *Fuller's earth: A history*. Hythe: Volturna.

Robkin, A.-L. 1979. "The agricultural year, the commodity SA and the linen industry of Mycenaean Pylos," *American Journal of Archaeology* 83: 469–74.

Ryder, M. L. 1969. "Changes in the fleece of sheep following domestication (with a note on the coat of cattle)," in P. J. Ucko and G. E. Dimbleby (eds.), *The domestication and exploitation of plants and animals*. London: Duckworth, 495–521.

Ryder, M. L. 1981. "Wools from Vindolanda," *Journal of Archaeological Science* 8: 99–103.

Ryder, M. L. 1983. *Sheep and man*. London: Duckworth.

Ryder, M. L. 1988. "Report on the wool," in V. Tatton-Brown (ed.), *Cyprus and the eastern Mediterranean in the Iron Age: Proceedings of the seventh British Museum Classical Colloquium, April 1988*. London: British Museum, 154–55.

Ryder, M. L. 1990. "The natural pigmentation of animal textile fibres," *Textile History* 21: 135–48.

Ryder, M. L. 1993. "The use of goat hair: An introductory historical review," *Anthropozoologica* 17: 37–46.

Ryder, M. L. 1995. "Fleece grading and wool sorting: The historical perspective," *Textile History* 26: 3–22.

Ryder, M. L. 2001. "The fibres in textile remains from the Iron-Age salt-mines at Hallstatt, Austria," *Annalen des Naturhistorischen Museums Wien* 102A: 223–44.

Scheid, J., and J. Svenbro 2003. *Le métier de Zeus: Mythe du tissage et du tissu dans le monde gréco-romain*. Paris: Errance.

Schmidt-Colinet, A., A. Stauffer, and K. al-As'ad 2000. *Die Textilien aus Palmyra*. Mainz: von Zabern.

Schrenk, S. 2001. "Die spätantiken Seiden in der Schatzkammer des Kölner Domes," *Kölner Domblatt* 66: 83–118.

Schrenk, S. 2004. *Textilien des Mittelmeerraumes aus spätantiker bis frühislamischer Zeit*. Riggisberg: Abegg-Stiftung.

Sheffer, A., and H. Granger-Taylor 1994. "Textiles from Masada: A preliminary selection," in E. Netzer (ed.), *Masada IV: The Yigael Yadin excavations, 1963–1965: Final reports*. Jerusalem: Israel Exploration Society, 151–255.

Sherratt, A. 1983. "The secondary exploitation of animals in the Old World," *World Archaeology* 15: 90–104.

Small, A., V. Volterra, and R. G. V. Hancock. 2003. "New evidence from tile-stamps for imperial properties near Gravina and the topography of imperial estates in SE Italy," *Journal of Roman Archaeology* 16: 179–99.

Staermose Nielsen, K.-H. 1999. *Kirkes Vaev: Opstadvaevens historie og nutidige brug*. Lejre: Historisk-Arkaeologisk Forsøgscenter.

Tébar Megías, E., and A. Wilson forthcoming. "Classical and Hellenistic textile production at Euhesperides (Benghazi, Libya): Preliminary results," in C. Alfaro Giner (ed.), *Textiles and dyes in the ancient Mediterranean world: 2nd international symposium, Athens, 24–26 November 2005*.

Thomas, T. K. 2001. *Textiles from Karanis, Egypt, in the Kelsey Museum of Archaeology: Artifacts of everyday life*. Ann Arbor: Kelsey Museum.

Thompson, J., and H. Granger-Taylor 1995–1996. "The Persian *zilu* loom of Meybod," *Bulletin de Liaison du Centre International d'Étude des Textiles Anciens* 73: 27–53.

Tuck, A. 2006. "Singing the rug: Patterned textiles and the origins of Indo-European metrical poetry," *American Journal of Archaeology* 110: 539–50.

Verhecken-Lammens, C. 1992. "Opzetboorden bij Koptische weefsels," *Vlaamse Vereniging voor Oud- en Hedendaags Textiel Bulletin* 1992: 29–36.

Wace, A. J. B. 1948. "Weaving or embroidery?" *American Journal of Archaeology* 52: 51–55.

Walton Rogers, P. 1994. "Types of wool in a Roman damask tunic Abegg-Stiftung no. 4219," *Riggesberger Berichte* 2: 37–40.

Walton Rogers, P. 1997. *Textile production at 16–22 Coppergate: The archaeology of York: The small finds 17/11*. York: York Archaeological Trust.

Whittaker, C. R. 1988. *Pastoral economies in classical antiquity*. Cambridge Philological Society Suppl. 14. Cambridge: Cambridge Philological Society.

Wild, J. P. 1964. "The textile term *scutulatus*," *Classical Quarterly* 14: 263–66.

Wild, J. P. 1967a. "Two technical terms used by Roman tapestry-weavers," *Philologus* 111: 151–55.

Wild, J. P. 1967b. "Soft-finished textiles in Roman Britain," *Classical Quarterly* 17: 133–35.

Wild, J. P. 1968. "The Roman flax hackle (*aena*)," *Museum Helveticum* 25: 139–42.

Wild, J. P. 1970. *Textile manufacture in the northern Roman provinces*. Cambridge: Cambridge University Press.

Wild, J. P. 1982. "Wool production in Roman Britain," in D. Miles (ed.). *The Romano-British countryside: Studies in rural settlement and economy*. British Archaeological Report 103. Oxford: BAR, 109–22.

Wild, J. P. 1984. "Some early silk finds in northwest Europe," *Journal of the Textile Museum* 23: 17–23.

Wild, J. P. 1987. "The Roman horizontal loom," *American Journal of Archaeology* 91: 459–71.

Wild, J. P. 1994. "Tunic no. 4219: An archaeological and historical perspective," *Riggisberger Berichte* 2: 9–36.

Wild, J. P. 1997. "Cotton in Roman Egypt: Some problems of origin," *Al-Rafidan* 18: 287–98.

Wild, J. P. 1999. "Textile manufacture: A rural craft?" in M. Polfer (ed.), *Artisanat et productions artisanales en milieu rural dans les provinces du Nord-Ouest de l'empire romain*. Monographies Instrumentum 9. Montagnac: Monique Mergoil, 29–37.

Wild, J. P. 2000. "Textile production and trade in Roman literature and written sources," in Cardon and Feugère 2000: 209–13.

Wild, J. P. 2002. "The textile industries of Roman Britain," *Britannia* 33: 1–42.

Wild, J. P. 2003a. "Facts, figures and guesswork in the Roman textile industry," in L. Bender-Jørgensen, J. Banck-Burgess, and A. Rast-Eicher (eds.), *Textilien aus Archäologie und Geschichte: Festschrift für Klaus Tidow*. Neumünster: Wachholtz, 37–45.

Wild, J. P. 2003b. "The Romans in the West," in D. Jenkins (ed.), *The Cambridge history of Western textiles*. Cambridge: Cambridge University Press, 77–93.

Wild, J. P. 2003c. *Textiles in archaeology*. Aylesbury: Shire.

Wild, J. P. 2004. "The Roman textile industry: Problems but progress," in Alfaro et al. 2004: 23–28.

Wild, J. P. 2005. "Methodological introduction," in M.-L. Nosch and C. Gilles (eds.), *Ancient textiles: Production, crafts and society*. Oxford: Oxbow.

Wild, J. P, F. C. Wild, and A. J. Clapham forthcoming. "Roman cotton revisited," in C. Alfaro Giner (ed.), *Textiles and dyes in the ancient Mediterranean world: 2nd international symposium, Athens, 24–26 November 2005*.

Wilson, A. 2001. "Timgad and textile production," in D. J. Mattingly and J. Salmon (eds.), *Economies beyond agriculture in the classical world*. London: Taylor and Francis, 271–96.

Wilson, A. 2003. "The archaeology of the Roman *fullonica*," *Journal of Roman Archaeology* 16: 442–46.

Wipszycka, E. 1965. *L'industrie textile dans l'Égypte romaine*. Warsaw: Polskiej Akademii Nauk.

Wouters, J. 1995. "Dye analysis in a broad perspective: A study of 3rd- to 10th-century Coptic textiles from Belgian private collections," *Dyes in History and Archaeology* 13: 38–45.

Yates, J. 1843. *Textrinum antiquorum: An account of the art of weaving among the ancients*. Part 1. London: Taylor and Walton.

..........................................................................................................

# CHAPTER 19

# TANNING
# AND LEATHER

..........................................................................................................

## CAROL VAN DRIEL-MURRAY

LEATHER is antiquity's plastic, supplying a versatile, supple, hardwearing, and waterproof material. It is also one of the few organic materials to survive intact in any quantity, providing a wealth of both direct and indirect evidence for the form and construction of essential military equipment such as saddles and tents, along with military and domestic footwear and clothing. This class of artifact can also be a source of social and economic information (van Driel-Murray 1987, 1998a, 1998b, 1999). In function, leather complements textiles and may have provided a cheaper and longer-lasting alternative to woven cloth, particularly when employed for wrappings, awnings, and tents. This contribution draws extensively on previous studies, where further literature can be found (van Driel-Murray 2000, 2001a, 2002b, 2003).

Leather is simply the resilient portion (collagen) of animal tissue preserved by means of drying (resulting in rawhide), or by curing with smoke, fat (chamoising), or soaking in a mineral bath (tawing), or by tanning with vegetable extracts. Tanning is often regarded as an industrial process of immense antiquity, with techniques virtually unchanged until modern times. Archaeological research has shown, however, that true tanning involving the use of vegetable extracts cannot be traced back much further than the fifth century B.C., and in many regions it was only introduced after the Roman conquest. Indeed, in northern Europe outside the Roman Empire, tanning remained unknown until about the seventh century A.D. Even in Egypt, artifacts of vegetable-tanned leather only become common under Roman rule: here, as in Europe, the Romans stimulated major technological developments in leatherworking. But these developments were not necessarily permanent, and some

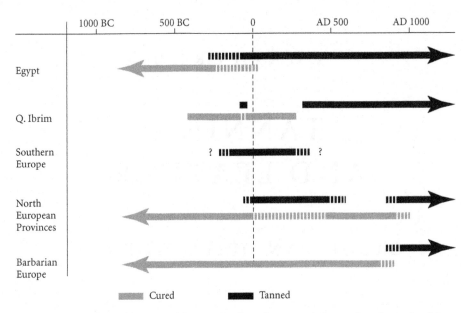

Figure 19.1. The spread of vegetable tanning based on surviving archaeological evidence.

regions lost all knowledge of tanning following the Roman withdrawal in the fourth century A.D. and reverted to simpler methods (figure 19.1).

Although the role played by tanners and shoemakers in classical literature is interesting in itself, references are mainly anecdotal and are rarely helpful in assessing the nature of leatherworking or its scale, particularly as interpretations of terminology are inevitably colored by modern preconceptions concerning the technology used (Forbes 1966; Lau 1967; Leguilloux 2004: 60–65). Although the use of preserved hairy skins and fur is attested outside the Roman frontier, there is little evidence for the use of furs by the Mediterranean elites before the eighth century A.D. (Howard-Johnston 1998). This cultural antipathy toward fur-clad barbarians, as opposed to civilized wearers of processed clothing (Pausanias 10.38.3), extended to all those concerned with leather working, imparting a subtext of physical and moral pollution which was gratefully exploited by satirists such as Aristophanes (*Eq.* 315–21; cf. Artemidorus 1.51, 2.20).

Archaeological finds have brought new perspectives to the subject, the most detailed information coming from the large amount of military and civilian leatherwork preserved in waterlogged deposits in the northwestern provinces of the Roman Empire. In the Mediterranean region organic materials do not survive as well, and although the dry conditions of Egypt have preserved a wide variety of leather artifacts, their dating is often problematical.

# SKIN PROCESSING

The processes involved in transforming animal skins into their more permanent form as leather are well understood (Table 19.1; Forbes 1966; Leguilloux 2004). Contrary to general assumption, the techniques were not necessarily similar to medieval and more recent practices; indeed, certain procedures such as liming and bating are not attested before the fourteenth century or even later. Two basic forms of skin processing are archaeologically recognizable: curing and tanning. Curing includes relatively simple methods of delaying the onset of decay, by means of smoking or applications of fat or mineral earth. These processes are chemically unstable and reversible, limiting survival. Tanning is a complex process involving infusions of tannins extracted from tree bark or oak galls. The tannins combine permanently with the skin collagen, resulting in a chemically stable product that is water resistant and not susceptible to bacterial decay. Vegetable tanned leather survives well in waterlogged conditions.

## Curing

The earliest methods of preserving skin seem to be smoking and/or rubbing in oils or fats, followed by vigorous stretching to ensure pliability. In ancient Egypt and Mesopotamia, sesame oil was the standard dressing, and the importance of *camelina sativa* (Gold-of-Pleasure) to Iron Age communities may also be linked to the use of its thin oil in skin processing. The earliest Greek references are also consistent with curing by means of such methods (Homer, *Il.* 17.389–93). Dressing with oil to produce light-colored leather continued in parallel with vegetable tanning, and its widespread use for footwear may explain the poor survival of shoe uppers as opposed to soles in Roman find complexes. The red, purple, and white leathers of classical literature imply the use of cured leather, which is easier to dye.

In ancient Mesopotamia and Egypt, alum occurs solely as a mordant in combination with madder used to stain leather red. The utility of alum in producing soft white leather was certainly known to the Romans, even if the term *aluta* seems to refer rather to the color of the leather and not to the substance used to produce it. Pliny (*HN* 35.183–91) only mentions alum in passing as "giving a finish to skins and textiles," that is, as a mordant. Since leather tawed with alum is not moisture resistant, the leather sails of the Veneti, which Caesar describes as *aluta* (*B Gall.* 3.13), must actually have been oil-drenched. The Richborough Type 527 amphoras have been linked to the trade in alum from the Lipari Islands to Britain, but the relevance to tanneries is uncertain, since alum has numerous other applications (Borgard et al. 2002; Leguilloux 2004: 31–32).

Cured leathers survive mainly in dry conditions, such as in Egypt, where research on Roman sites is beginning to reveal the extent of the use of untanned

**Table 19.1. Procedures associated with tanning.**

| Process | Procedure | Residue | Tools or Structures | Time Required | Byproduct |
|---|---|---|---|---|---|
| Flaying | Cut and strip hide from carcass | None | Knives; frame or table | A few hours | Carcass to butcher |
| Trimming | Trim with knives | Horns, hoofs | Knives | A few hours | Horn, sinew, bone to craft workers |
| De-hairing | Soaking to loosen hairs in lye or biological agents (fermenting bran) | Ash deposits, mashed grains | Pits, vats, wood, bone tools | 1–5 days (repeated) | Hair, wool to craft workers |
| De-hairing (medieval) | Alkaline soak | Lime | Pits, vats | 2–6 days | Hair, wool to craft workers |
| Bating or drenching (post-medieval) | Soaking in acid or alkaline bath | Dung, bran mash | Pits, vats | A few hours to 10 days | None |
| Rinsing, fleshing | Washing, scraping | Reuse of de-hairing agents | Wood, bone tools, water-supply | A few hours | Fleshing residue to tallow and glue renderers |
| Tanning | Immersion in tannins | Deposits of finely ground vegetable matter | Permanent vats, pits, water channels | Successive baths of increasing strength; 9–12 months for hide | Fertilizer |
| Drying | Air drying | None | Covered sheds and frames | Weeks to months | None |
| Currying | Smoothing and feeding leather | Oil, fat | Tables, rubbers, pounders, clamps | A few hours to a few days | Finished product to leatherworkers and shoemakers |

leathers for water bags and other equipment (Leguilloux 2004: 142; Winterbottom 1990; Volken 2008). Cato (*Agr.* 135.3–5) describes how fresh hides, dressed with fat, are dried and twisted into cables for wine presses. In Dura Europos, untanned skins were used for shield surfaces: the moistened rawhide contracts as it dries, clamping the shield boards together, and providing a good surface for painted decoration (James 2004: 163, 186–87). No such artifacts would survive in north European contexts. Although the presence of vegetable tannins in ancient desiccated leather can be established by analysis, distinguishing among the various methods of curing is not yet feasible (van Driel-Murray 2002a).

## Vegetable Tanning

The sudden visibility of leather items in the archaeological record of northwestern Europe following the Roman conquest is the result of the introduction of vegetable tanning into regions previously unfamiliar with this technology. For the Mediterranean region there is no such archaeological evidence, and literary references are ambiguous, as the substances later used for tanning first appear independently as dyestuffs or astringents (Aristotle, *[Pr.]* 32.18; Dioscorides 1.106–11). By the time of Theophrastus (*Hist. pl.* 3.8.6, 4.2.8; cf. Pliny *HN* 16.26, 24.91), however, the properties of different trees with regard to tanning seem to be thoroughly familiar, suggesting that the method was already well established by the close of the fifth century B.C. Iron hobnails in the so-called House of Simon the Shoemaker in the Athenian agora imply sturdy soles perhaps more likely to be made of tanned hide (Thompson 1960, dated to ca. 450–410 B.C.; Theophrastus, *Char.* 4.15), but there is no further datable evidence for nailed footwear before the mid-first century B.C., nor is it depicted in Greek or Etruscan art. The sandals and apparently soft, pliable shoes attested by Greek shoe-vases and depicted on Etruscan frescoes could all have been made of cured leather, although when shoes with separate soles are colored black, tanned leather may be intended. The shoe blacking described by Pliny is the basis for a modern tanning test (*HN* 34.123–24; van Driel-Murray 2002a).

Tanning is a complex and time-consuming process, requiring significant investment in installations and raw material. Its introduction into northern Europe following the Roman conquest profoundly changed the nature of native crafts in Gaul and Britain, affecting not only procurement of raw materials but also the organization of labor. In many nonurban societies leather working is the task of women, but as hides and skins become a commercial commodity, there is a shift from domestic production to a male controlled, centralized, fulltime industry, altering women's economic roles in the household economy (van Driel-Murray 2001a: 58). Some indication of the amount of capital which might be tied up during tanning is given by markups of 25% and more between the price of raw and finished hides listed in Diocletian's Edict (Lauffer 1971: VIII.9–14). The relatively simple procedures involved in curing leather could have been accommodated in nondescript structures; tanning, however, required distinctive and dedicated complexes.

## Tanneries

In ancient Athens, a tanning quarter lay well away from the center, and in Rome it was apparently situated on the right bank of the Tiber, although there is no supporting archaeological evidence for the nature of the installations. Vegetable tanning involves immersion in successive vats of tan liquor of increasing strength, making a series of interlinked vats a basic requirement, together with drying rooms, good access to water, and provision for waste disposal. The only tannery identified in Pompeii (Reg. I.5) contains 15 closely-set vats and various other built-in features. The contrast with the number of fulleries is striking, although—if the fulleries were in fact primarily laundries (Bradley 2002)—the disparity only emphasizes the distinction between servicing and manufacturing trades within the urban fabric. Leguilloux (2002: 44–50) reconstructs the route of operations through the building, revealing a logical and well thought out enterprise, which, considering the inadequate water supply, probably specialized in luxurious alum- and oil-cured leathers or in finishing skins cleaned and depilated elsewhere. A small tannery in the civilian settlement of Vitudurum (Switzerland) contains six interconnected vats surrounded by drying rooms (figure 19.2; Janke and Ebnöther 2001: fig. 4). Most other sites mentioned in this context can be rejected on grounds of structural unsuitability or incorrect interpretation of the finds assemblage, with the result that—despite the importance of the leather trade—evidence for tanneries in urban situations remains remarkably rare. It is a common misconception that dumps of worn-out leather goods are indicative of tanneries and workshop remains. Vindolanda, for example, was regarded as a tannery in the 1970s, but the leather deposits have since been recognized as fill in abandoned structures. The deposits at Catterick and Walbrook (and many other similar sites) are simply leather-rich rubbish dumps (Hooley 2002; van Driel-Murray 2003: 110). Only isolated tanks were found at Liberchies (Belgium), and the bone refuse indicates glue boiling (Dewert-Brulet and Vilvorder 2001: 401–5).

In the Roman context, tanning is but one element in the systematic and highly efficient processing of animal carcasses, in which the waste from one craft activity forms the raw material of the next (Vanderhoeven and Ervynck 2007). The composition of waste products is culturally determined by the demand (or lack of it) for particular products, and in the Roman period bone refuse—which characterizes medieval tannery locations—should probably be regarded as an indicator of bone working rather than a by-product of leather production. Associations of pits with horn cores identify horn working rather than tanneries, although the two may be intimately connected, as at Tongeren (Vanderhoeven and Ervynck 2007). Collections of foot bones attest to the enormous demand for sinew, the uses of which range from cobbler's sewing thread to heavy cables for artillery pieces (Rodet-Belarbi et al. 2002: 323). A text from Vindolanda mentions delivery of no less than 100 pounds of sinew in one consignment (Bowman and Thomas 1994: no. 343.2; Lewis 2004: 48; James 2004: 209). Waste from the tanneries themselves stimulated

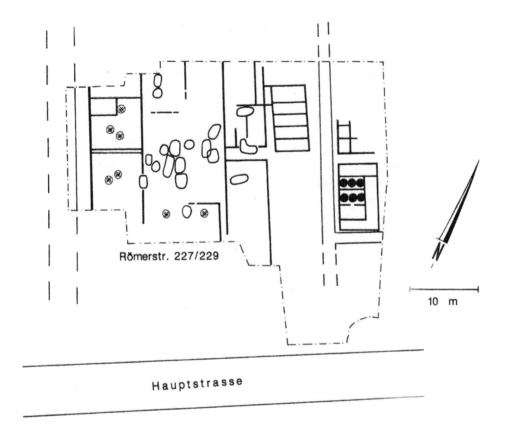

Figure 19.2. Plan of the tannery at Vitudurum. (After Janke and Ebnöther 2001: fig. 4.)

further industries around them (cf. table 19.1), while spent tan could be used as a fertilizer (Pliny, *HN* 17.46, 258). The analysis of organic deposits and insect remains is important in differentiating these interdependent and noisome trades (Hall and Kenward 2003: 122–23).

Reliance on inappropriate models drawn from more recent practices may also hamper the identification of tannery structures. Instead of the small, family-run backyard businesses of medieval times, constrained by guild restrictions and urban toll barriers, we should perhaps be looking for large complexes at the edges of settlements or further afield, with access to water the main factor. Conditions in the Roman Empire seem to have stimulated rural industries, and although rural potteries are well known, tanneries are less likely to be recognized and excavated. It is worth noting that in Britain, improvements in transport and the relaxation of guild restrictions led to the establishment of rural tanneries in the eighteenth century, and it is perhaps significant that in the second century A.D. Artemidorus envisages tanners banished to the countryside (1.51, 2.20).

# SCALE OF PRODUCTION

Only anecdotal evidence is available for the nature of Greek tanneries, but for the Roman Empire the massive scale of operations and the high degree of organization is attested in the size and variety of leatherwork complexes from northern Europe. Experimental research gives some insight into both the scale of Roman military demands and the highly efficient methods of production (Bishop and Coulston 2006: 247–48; Himmler forthcoming; Volken forthcoming). A legion required a minimum of 68,000 goatskins to make tents, and more than 3,000 cattle hides annually for boots alone. What with bags, equipment covers, and animal harnesses, equipping the army was a formidable task requiring time and forward planning. Judging from the quality of surviving military leatherwork, Roman commanders already had highly successful supply systems in place by the first century B.C. A fragment of a leather tent from Caesar's siege at Alesia employs the same complex, waterproof construction as the tents used in Britain 150 years later, while military footwear found in Qasr Ibrim (Egypt) is virtually identical in construction to that from northern forts. Techniques perfected in Republican times went virtually unchanged until the army began to devolve supply into civilian hands as expansion ceased (van Driel-Murray 1985; 1999; 2001b: 362–64; 2001d).

Efficient tanning is a continuous process dependent on a regular supply of hides and skins. Despite the prominence of exotic skins in Diocletian's Edict, the vast majority of leather artifacts recovered were made of bovine hide (footwear) or goatskin, with doeskin occasionally used for luxury items. Urban and military slaughterhouses were best placed to meet this demand, but imports of salted skins feature regularly in accounts of trade with foreign lands and on Roman tariff lists (Leguilloux 2004: pl. IIb). Wholesalers, like those of the *corpus pellionum* at Ostia (*CIL* 14. supp. 1, no. 4549[2]) form another indication of the scale of the industry. The army also drew on local sources of tribute: an unreasonable exaction of hides imposed on the Frisians caused the revolt that ended Roman aspirations north of the Rhine delta (Tacitus, *Ann.* 4.72). Tariff differentiation on the second-century Zarai list from Numidia (*CIL* 8.4508) suggest that the trade in raw (presumably salted) skins was welcomed to serve the needs of the Roman industry, while that of processed leather was discouraged.

# LEATHERWORKERS AND TANNERS

Cleon of Athens (425 B.C.) seems to be an early representative of a class of wealthy entrepreneurs investing in tanneries. Since this period coincides with the emergence of distinct words for tanners (*bursodepses, skulodepses*) and for shoemakers (*skutotomos, neurorraphos, skuteus*) in Greece, it may mark the point at which vegetable tanning, with its complex organizational structure, emerges as a distinct trade in the classical world (Lau 1967: 56). Despite their wealth, few certain tombstones of tanners are known, even though what seem to be individual shoemakers appear regularly on monuments in Rome and the provinces, as well as on the much earlier Greek vases (cf. Zimmer 1982: nos. 47–55; Leguilloux 2004; Dé Spagnolis 2000: 64–72). An elaborate tomb belonging to a supposed shoemaker at Pizzone, with its unexpected link to other inscriptions at Ostia, suggest profits from manufactories on a much larger scale than one might guess from the depictions of lone shoemakers working modestly at their bench (Dé Spagnolis 2000: 53–55, 71–72). The discrepancy raises the suspicion that such tombstones might belong to entrepreneurs, illustrating the source of their wealth by means of a single representative vignette, and are not intended to show the deceased in his actual daily work (cf. chapter 2). Men like C. Iulius Alcimus, a *comparator mercis sutoriae* from Ravenna, and C. Iulius Helius, *sutor* (the *caliga* on his exceptionally fine tombstone hinting at military contracts), were controllers of labor, not workmen, even if shoemaking was the most presentable of their economic activities (*CIL* 5.5927, 6.33914). The craftsmen themselves are perhaps attested by control stamps on footwear that suggest they banded together in corporations, not only in Rome but also in small, lackluster towns such as Noviomagus Batavorum (Nijmegen) (van Driel-Murray 2001b: 338–39).

Other forms of organization can also be distinguished. In military workplaces and large establishments such as the Egyptian estates, work was streamlined and highly controlled. An unpublished text from Oxyrhynchus dealing with the manufacture of harnesses specifies the leftovers, down to a few narrow strips and a couple of small offcuts (Dominic Montserrat, personal communication). Such meticulous accounting explains the careful bundles of offcuts of both new and old leather that are such a feature of excavated military complexes such as Castleford (van Driel-Murray, 1998b).

# Technological Change

In the northern provinces of the Roman Empire tanning belongs to a package of innovations encompassing all aspects of leatherworking, including the sewing and construction of articles, the range of finished products, and the introduction of composite, nailed footwear. Civilian footwear was not usually nailed in the Mediterranean region, and the popularity of hobnailed shoes in the provinces is probably due to the role of the military in the spread of technical knowledge. A similar association between the military, hobnailed *caligae* and vegetable tanned leather marks the short-lived Roman occupation of Qasr Ibrim in

Figure 19.3. Fourth-century off-cut with clamp marks, from Cuijk, Netherlands. (Photograph by A. Dekker, Amsterdam University.)

southern Egypt, a region with strong traditions of fine leatherwork employing cured skins.

Desirable Roman products such as footwear drew rural communities into marketing networks, giving all levels of society access to the rapidly changing fashions. Stylistic dating of footwear, refined for Greece by Morrow (1985), has an even greater potential in the Roman period, since archaeological contexts provide securely dated sequences of shoes actually in use (van Driel-Murray 2001b, 2001c). Despite its initial popularity, by the 330s A.D. nailed footwear was in sharp decline in the Rhineland, although in southern Gaul it may continue into the fifth century. Other changes in tanning practice are also discernable, in part to meet the needs of different shoemaking methods, but also to reduce processing time. More attention is paid to finishing, and marks of clamps to hold the leather during currying appear on late Roman offcuts in the Netherlands (figure 19.3; Mould 2003). More profound changes in organization were evidently taking place at the same time, for by the end of the fourth century leather disappears entirely from the archaeological record of northwestern Europe. In contrast, tanning continued in Egypt, and the technology was, indeed, reintroduced into Qasr Ibrim in the so-called Christian levels. Regional differences suggest that the loss of tanning technology is somehow linked to the weakening of the urban economy and the breakdown of the system of supply.

Assessment of the archaeological contribution reveals the limitations of the static view of ancient technology based on literary sources. In reality, the technology of skin processing underwent considerable development in scale and technology, linked to the expansion of the Hellenistic and Roman economic areas. In the absence of detailed work on the subject in the Mediterranean area, the loss of technological knowledge after the fourth century A.D. in western Europe cannot be verified elsewhere, though the development serves as a reminder that technology is intimately linked to social and economic factors governing its implementation.

# REFERENCES

Audoin-Rouzeau, F., and S. Beyries 2002. *Le travail du cuir de la préhistoire à nos jours.* Antibes: Editions APDCA.

Bishop, M. C., and J. C. N. Coulston 2006. *Roman military equipment.* 2nd ed. Oxford: Oxbow.

Borgard, P., V. Forest, C. Bioul-Pelletier, and L. Pelletier 2002. "Passer les peaux en blanc: Une practique gallo-romaine? L'apport du site de Sainte-Anne à Dijon (Côte-d'Or)," in Audoin-Rouzeau and Beyries 2002, 231–49.

Bowman, A. K., and J. D. Thomas 1994. *The Vindolanda writing tablets. (Tabulae Vindolandenses II).* London: British Museum Press, 217–26.

Bradley, M. 2002. "'It all comes out in the wash': Looking harder at the Roman *fullonica,*" *Journal of Roman Archaeology* 15: 21–44.

Dewert-Brulet, R. J.-P., and F. Vilvorder 2001. *Liberchies IV Travail de Rivère.* Louvain-la-Neuve: Departement d'archéologie et d'histoire de l'art.

Dé Spagnolis, M. 2000. *La Tomba del Calzolaio: Dalla necropolis monumentale romana di Nocera Superiore.* Rome: Bretschneider.

Forbes, R. J. 1966. *Studies in ancient technology.* Vol. 5, *Leather in antiquity.* Leiden: Brill.

Hall, A., and H. Kenward 2003. "Can we identify biological indicator groups for craft, industry and other activities?" in P. Murphy and P. E. J. Wiltshire (eds.), *The environmental archaeology of industry.* Oxford: Oxbow, 114–30.

Himmler, F. forthcoming. "Testing the 'Ramshaw' boot on a long march," *Journal of Roman Military Equipment Studies.*

Hooley, A. D. 2002. "Leather from the 1958–9 by-pass excavations (Site 433)," in P. R. Wilson, *Cataractonium: Roman Catterick and its hinterland: Excavations and research, 1958–97 Part II.* CBA Research Report 129: 318–80.

Howard-Johnston, J. 1998. "Trading in fur, from classical antiquity to the early Middle Ages," in E. Cameron (ed.), *Leather and fur: Aspects of early medieval trade and technology.* London: Archetype, 65–79.

James, S. 2004. *The excavations at Dura Europos conducted by Yale University and the French Academy of Inscriptions and Letters 1928 to 1937. Final Report VII: The arms and armour and other military equipment.* London: British Museum Press.

Janke, R., and C. Ebnöther 2001. "Struktur und Entwicklung des Vicus Vitudurum im 1. Jahrhundert n. Chr," in G. Precht (ed.), *Genese, Struktur und Entwicklung römischer Städte im 1. Jahrhundert n. Chr. in Nieder- und Obergermanien.* Mainz: von Zabern, 217–26.

Lau, O. 1967. *Schuster und Schusterhandwerk in de griechisch-römischen Literatur und Kunst.* Inaugral-Dissertation Rheinischen Friedrich-Wilhems-Universität, Bonn.

Lauffer, S. 1971. *Diokletians Preisedikt.* Berlin: de Gruyter.

Leguilloux, M. 2002. "Techniques et équipements de la tannerie romaine: L'example de l'*officina coriaria* de Pompéi," in Audoin-Rouzeau and Beyries 2002: 267–81.

Leguilloux, M. 2004. *Le cuir et la pelleterie à l'époque romaine.* Paris: Éditions Errance.

Lewis, M. 2004. "Reconstruction of Heron's *cheiroballistra,*" *Current World Archaeology* 3: 46–48.

Morrow, K. D. 1985. *Greek footwear and the dating of sculpture.* Madison: University of Wisconsin Press.

Mould, Q. 2003. "Man pinches leather?" *Archaeological Leather Group Newsletter* 18: 1.

Rodet-Belarbi, I., C. Olive, and V. Forest 2002." Dépôts archéologiques de pieds de mouton et de chèvre: S'agit-il toujurs d'un artisanat de la peau?" in Audoin-Rouzeau and Beyries 2002: 345–49.

Thompson, D. B. 1960. "The house of Simon the shoemaker," *Archaeology* 13: 234–41.

Vanderhoeven, A., and A. Ervynck 2007. "Not in my backyard! The industry of secondary animal products within the Roman civitas capital of Tongeren (Belgium)," in R. Hingley and S. Willis (eds.), *Roman finds: Context and theory. Proceedings of a conference held at the University of Durham, 2002.* Oxford: Oxbow, 156–75.

van Driel-Murray, C. 1985. "The production and supply of military leatherwork in the first and second centuries AD: A review of the archaeological evidence," in M. C. Bishop (ed.), *The production and distribution of Roman military equipment.* British Archaeological Reports, Intl. Series S275. Oxford: BAR, 43–81.

van Driel-Murray, C. 1987. "Roman footwear: A mirror of fashion and society," in D. E. Friendship-Taylor, J. M. Swann, and S. Thomas (eds.), *Recent research in archaeological footwear.* Association of Archaeological Illustrators and Surveyors Technical Paper no. 8. London [?]: 32–42.

van Driel-Murray, C. 1998a. "Women in forts?" *Gesellschaft Pro Vindonissa, Jahresbericht 1997.* Brugg: Vindonissa Museum, 55–61.

van Driel-Murray, C. 1998b. "The leatherwork from the fort," in H. E. M. Cool and C. Philo (eds.), *Roman Castleford*, vol. 1, *The small finds.* Wakefield: West Yorkshire Archaeology Service, 285–334.

van Driel-Murray, C. 1999. "Dead men's shoes," in W. Schlüter and R. Wiegels (eds.), *Rom, Germanien und die Ausgrabungen von Kalkriese.* Osnabrücker Forschungen zu Altertum und Antike-Rezeption 1. Osnabrück: Universitätsverlag Rasch, 169–89.

van Driel-Murray, C. 2000. "Leatherwork and skin products," in R. T. Nicholson and I. Shaw (eds.), *Ancient Egyptian materials and technology.* Cambridge: Cambridge University Press, 299–319.

van Driel-Murray, C. 2001a. "Technology transfer: The introduction and loss of tanning technology during the Roman period," in M. Polfer (ed.), *L'artisanat romain: Evolutions, continuités et ruptures (Italie et provinces occidentales).* Montagnac: Éditions Monique Mergoil, 55–68.

van Driel-Murray, C. 2001b. "Footwear in the north-western provinces of the Roman Empire," in O. W. Goubitz, G. van Waateringe, and C. van Driel-Murray (eds.), *Stepping through time: Archaeological footwear from prehistoric times until 1800.* Zwolle: Stichting Promotie Archeologie, 337–75.

van Driel-Murray, C. 2001c. "Vindolanda and the dating of Roman footwear," *Britannia* 32: 185–97.

van Driel-Murray, C. 2001d. "Les restes d'une tente Césarienne en cuir," in M. Reddé and S. von Schnurbein (eds.), *Alésia: Fouilles et recherches Franco-Allemandes sur les travaux militaires Romains autour du Mont Auxois (1991–1997).* Mémoires de l'Académie des Inscriptions et Belles-Lettres 22. Paris: de Boccard, 363–68.

van Driel-Murray, C. 2002a. "Practical evaluation of a field test for the identification of ancient vegetable tanned leathers," *Journal of Archaeological Science* 29: 17–21.

van Driel-Murray, C. 2002b. "Ancient skin processing and the impact of Rome on tanning technology," in Audoin-Rouzeau and Beyries 2002: 251–65.

van Driel-Murray, C. 2003. "The leather trades in Roman Yorkshire and beyond," in P. R. Wilson and J. Price (eds.), *Aspects of industry in Roman Yorkshire and the North.* Oxford: Oxbow, 109–23.

Volken, M. 2008. "The water bag of Roman soldiers," *Journal of Roman Archaeology* 21: 264–74.

Volken, M. forthcoming. "Making the Ramshaw boot: An exercise in experimental archaeology," *Journal of Roman Military Equipment Studies*.

Winterbottom, S. 1990. "The leather objects," in J. Bingen, "Quatrième campagne de fouilles au Mons Claudianus," *Bulletin d'Institut Français Archéologie Orientale* 90: 78–81.

Zimmer, G. 1982. *Römische Berufsdarstellungen*. Berlin: Gebr. Mann Verlag.

# CHAPTER 20

# CERAMIC PRODUCTION

## MARK JACKSON
## KEVIN GREENE

## HISTORICAL, GEOGRAPHICAL, AND CULTURAL PERSPECTIVES

Applying the labels "Greek" and "Roman" to the study of ceramic technology from 700 B.C. to A.D. 500 involves profound problems of cultural labeling. All areas brought within Greek and Roman cultural and political hegemony already possessed distinctive methods of making, decorating, and using pottery—many of them stretching far back into prehistory. Furthermore, no fundamental technical changes took place during this 1,200-year period. Thus, what we are studying is less a question of technology per se than the intersection of diverse political cultures, artistic styles, trading systems, and forms of consumption.

Greek influence extended to the Mediterranean coasts of Spain and France, and it rivaled the economic power of the Carthaginians of North Africa long before Roman expansion absorbed all of these areas. Thus, Italy (including early Rome itself) was heavily influenced by Greek material culture, while Greek colonies in France and Spain engaged in trade with "barbarians" to the extent that Greek pottery is regularly found on Iron Age sites on the Iberian peninsula and north well into France and Germany (Osborne 1996; Cunliffe 1998: 345). This pattern of trade, in which amphoras containing wine and oil were accompanied by vessels (metal, glass, and ceramic) suitable for their consumption, continued into the Roman period. In the first few centuries A.D., Roman pottery exports can be found beyond the borders of the empire from the Scottish Highlands to Scandinavia, from the Sahara desert to the upper Nile valley, and even across the Indian Ocean in Bengal. Return cargoes presumably consisted of luxuries, raw materials, and slaves, forming a pattern repeated in many post-Roman episodes of colonization and imperial expansion. Parallels of this kind make it interesting to compare Greek and Roman ceramics with their medieval and post-medieval counterparts.

In addition to cultural complexity, the study of Greek and Roman ceramics carries a major historiographical burden. Whereas the technical and aesthetic accomplishments of classical architecture and art were closely copied from medieval and Renaissance times onward, Greek and Roman pottery had no direct successors. When its forms and finishes *were* copied in the eighteenth century, potters employed completely different techniques (e.g., Sèvres or Wedgwood "Etruscan" red-figure kraters in porcelain and stoneware—Charleston 1968: 243, fig. 689, 272, fig. 776). European potters from the medieval period onward were acutely aware of technically superior products imported from East Asia—notably Chinese porcelain, with its high-fired impermeable fabric, which could not be matched in the West until the early eighteenth century (Freestone and Gaimster 1997: 194–99). The sixteenth-century Italian writer Pancirolli ranked porcelain second only to the the New World in his list of discoveries unknown to the ancients (*Many Excellent Things Found, Now in Use among the Moderns*; 1715). Early Chinese imports were frequently mounted in precious metals, as if they were rock crystal (e.g., Snodin and Styles 2001: 27, fig. 36). Even more influential was the Islamic decorated and glazed pottery made as far west as Spain (Freestone and Gaimster 1997: 110–15). Although classical motifs and mythological scenes were commonplace on European pottery from the Renaissance onward (Freestone and Gaimster 1997: 116–21), they were achieved by imitating the appearance of Islamic or Chinese imports, many of which used colorful motifs on a white background (e.g., Cohen and Hess 1993: 48 [Iznik ware], 59 [Ming porcelain]).

European products—such as Italian majolica and North European delftware—that copied these elaborately decorated oriental imports retained relatively soft and permeable earthenware fabrics until the eighteenth century. The only truly impermeable pottery made in Europe was stoneware, made from clay that could be fired at a sufficiently high temperature to fuse the fabric without it melting and collapsing (Freestone and Gaimster 1997: 122–27). German and Dutch salt-glazed mugs and bottles were successfully imitated in stoneware in England in the late seventeenth century as a result of careful experimentation (Snodin and Styles 2001: 128–29). Something very similar had already been achieved by potters making "purple-gloss" beakers in the New Forest industry of later Roman Britain (Fulford's fabric 1a, Fulford 1975: 24–25; Cook and Charleston 1979: pl. 122), but in common with most Greek and Roman pottery the surface bore a slip, not a glaze. Like some of its oriental counterparts (e.g., Ding ware; Freestone and Gaimster 1997: 182–87), the earliest porcelain manufactured in Europe in the early eighteenth century came from state-sponsored workshops. Royal control guaranteed prestigious use in aristocratic households, and elaborately decorated Meissen or Sèvres porcelain joined glass and silverware for serving and eating meals (Charleston 1968: 216–24,

236–45). In contrast, British entrepreneurs such as Wedgwood produced robust and well-glazed earthenware or stoneware for a wider market in the later eighteenth century. The prestige of British porcelain was maintained at centers such as Chelsea or Worcester by making ornate hand-painted vases (Snodin and Styles 2001: 294) and exclusive table services, emblazoned with coats of arms, for fashionable individuals such as Lord Nelson.

Many aristocrats took part in the Grand Tour in the eighteenth century and visited Italy, where extensive excavations of ancient cemeteries and other sites were underway. It became fashionable to buy Greek red- or black-figured pottery to display in neoclassical houses (Greene 2002: 19, fig. 1.6), although much of it was actually thought to be Etruscan at the time (Sparkes 1996: 34–63). Thus, by a historical coincidence, Greek vases first became widely known at a time when contemporary ceramic products were used by royalty and the aristocracy. This gave rise to a perception of Greek painted pottery as the artistic and economic equivalent of expensive porcelain (Vickers and Gill 1994: 19–27).

# Pottery in Greek and Roman Society

A high regard for Greek vases was sustained by admiration of the comparative purity of Greek, rather than Roman, artistic and architectural models for Greek Revival architecture and interior design in the late eighteenth and nineteenth centuries. Such tastes also embodied respect for ancient Greek democracy (and its associated philosophy and science), rather than Roman imperialism—a sentiment heightened by the liberation of Greece from Turkish rule in 1830. By the nineteenth century it was common to use Greek and Roman pottery as evidence for the decline of ancient civilization (Greene 2005: 37–39) in a manner epitomized by an expert at the British Museum:

> We have traced the development of painted decoration from monochrome to polychrome, from simple patterns to elaborate pictorial compositions, and so to its gradual decay and disappearance under the luxurious and artificial tendencies of the Hellenistic Age, when men were ever seeking for new artistic departures, and a new system of technique arose which finally substituted various forms of decoration in relief for painting. And lastly, we have seen how this new system established itself firmly in the domain of Roman art, until with the gradual decay of artistic taste and under the encroachments of barbarism, it sank into neglect and oblivion. (Walters 1905: 2: 554–55)

An additional negative perception of Roman pottery arose from the influence of the Arts and Crafts movement, which associated industrial production with poor craft skills:

Roman vases, in a word, require only the skill of the potter for their completion, and the processes employed are largely mechanical, whereas Greek vases
called in the aid of a higher branch of industry, and one which gave scope for great
artistic achievements—namely, that of painting.... The Romans, who used
metal vases to a far greater extent than the Greeks—at least under the late Republic and Empire—did not hold the art of pottery in very high estimation, and
their vases, like their tiles and lamps, were produced by slaves and freedmen,
whereas at Athens the potter usually held at least the position of a resident alien.
(Walters 1905: 2:430, 433–34)

The final element in the elevated perception of Greek pottery was the growth of
connoisseurship in the twentieth century, pioneered by Beazley and modeled on
studies of early Renaissance artists and their workshops (Beazley 1951; Boardman
2001: 128–38). This approach has been challenged since the 1970s, notably by
Vickers, who has questioned the status of individual "artists" who painted vases,
and the monetary (and social) value of pottery in the Greek world. Vickers' position
is that pottery was never anything more than a cheap substitute for metalwork, and
that the art-historical model is inappropriate (Vickers and Gill 1994). Neer has
summarized the strength of the conventional position, using documentary evidence to conclude, "Given that ceramic fine ware was made for an elitist pastime,
adorned with elitist pictures, and described in elitist literature, it seems reasonable
to conclude that it was used by elites" (Neer 2002: 215). Support has come from
archaeological fieldwork in Greece, where more fine pottery associated with formal
dining has been recovered from Greek than from Roman settlement sites (Bintliff
2002: 31). Boardman (2001: 122–27)—like Walters in the passage quoted above—
acknowledges the greater role of metal vessels after the demise of painted vases.

This debate underlines the importance of taking modern preconceptions into
account, for it is impossible to assess the technology of Greek and Roman pottery if
we do not know its social and economic status. Modern consumerism maintains a
contradictory cultural attitude to mass production and individuality; the latter may
be achieved either through making things by hand or by manufacturing them
exclusively according to the ideas of a named designer. A visitor to the ceramic
displays of a museum may see a Roman "Arretine" *terra sigillata* bowl with relief-
molded decoration and the name-stamp of an Italian workshop (Hayes 1997: pl.
18.2). This is likely to create an impression of lower status and sophistication than
an Athenian red-figure calyx-krater signed by an artist, Euphronius—especially if
the viewer knows that the Metropolitan Museum of New York paid $1 million for it
in the early 1970s (Sparkes 1996: 35, fig. II.1).

A hard-nosed economist might take a very different view. Who were the customers for Greek vases? What were the rival products? How large was the scale of
production? How effectively were the products distributed through a mass market?
Did classical Athens have a small and inelastic distribution of wealth, and did the
very rich display their status by means of exquisite gold and silver tableware,
accompanied perhaps by rock crystal and glass vessels (Vickers and Gill 1994: 33–
54)? Whatever the answer, since the work of skilled artisans was relatively cheap,

modest households would have benefited from the expansion of Greek colonization and trade, and could buy hand-painted pottery like that of their social superiors. Potters' workshops could also sell their wares to merchants trading wine into less sophisticated markets around the Black Sea and the western Mediterranean (Osborne 1996). As economic development continued, customers who had previously bought fine ceramics moved up to metal and glass, while a new (and larger) number could now afford mass-produced molded pottery and tablewares with simpler decorative schemes.

While Hellenistic molded pottery and plainer fine wares circulated in some quantity around the Mediterranean, their distribution was modest compared to Roman *terra sigillata* and other red-slipped wares, first from Italy, and then from centers in northwestern Europe, North Africa, and Asia Minor, which provided basic and serviceable table vessels in astonishing quantities (Johns 1971; Hayes 1972). The scale of manufacture and extent of distribution of *terra sigillata* and red-slip wares to modest households recalls Staffordshire earthenware or stoneware rather than porcelain (Charleston 1968: 259–70). They also reveal a high degree of cultural conformity throughout the Roman world to ideas about the appropriate color and form of tablewares. Our economist might well suspect the existence of a mass market, and deduce from the simplicity of decorative styles and techniques that pottery was aimed at a still lower social level than before. Further economic growth apparently now allowed even the modestly rich to use blown glass and metal vessels to a far greater extent than had been possible in classical Greece. A switch to tablewares with red surfaces that mimicked the coppery sheen of ancient gold may indicate that the elite had become accustomed to using gold vessels at meals, and had left behind "black-glazed" pottery that imitated the dark lustrous finish favored by users of silver (Vickers and Gill 1994: 174–78). Thus, while art historians may regard long-term changes in the quality and manufacturing technique of ceramics as symptoms of cultural decline, our fictional economist might interpret them as indicators of expanding wealth.

Discussion of differing social and economic perceptions of Greek and Roman ceramics is not an abstract exercise. Broken pottery is rarely useful for secondary purposes, because conversion of the raw materials to fired clay makes it difficult to recycle. Thus, it survives in enormous quantities to be excavated in good condition by archaeologists. Metal and glass vessels only survive when put beyond recovery or reuse in graves or other ritual deposits; gold and silver vessels are found even less frequently, usually in ancient hoards that were not recovered after being concealed in times of trouble. Even finds from Pompeii and Herculaneum are not fully representative, because many of the inhabitants had time to remove their most precious possessions. Archaeologists probably underestimate the use of precious metals, despite the occasional discovery of extraordinary treasures such as the 165 fourth-century B.C. silver and silver-gilt table vessels found at Rogozen in Bulgaria in 1985 and 1986 (Cook 1989; Vickers and Gill 1994: 52–53). If the Mildenhall treasure found in Suffolk in the 1940s is a reliable indicator of the kinds of vessels used in late Romano-British households for serving, eating and drinking (Kent and Painter

1977: 33–39), it is not hard to envisage much greater wealth among the aristocratic landowners of early Roman Italy. Vickers, Impey, and Allan (1986) illustrated the consistent way in which pottery followed the forms and surface finishes of metal and glass in many different periods and areas in the Old World. This kind of perspective is essential if ceramic technology is to be evaluated meaningfully.

Furthermore, because Greek figured vases have been the subject of art-historical study, less attention has been paid to the everyday undecorated pottery. Few excavators of Greek sites have quantified the pottery recovered in the manner that has become commonplace among students of Roman pottery (e.g., Slane 2003). It cannot be stressed too highly that it is the artistic quality of painted decoration, especially realistic human figures in narrative scenes, which is the distinctive feature of Greek pottery from the sixth to the fourth centuries B.C., not its production technology. Furthermore, although figured vessels have dominated the academic study of Greek pottery for more than 200 years, excavations on occupation sites rather than cemeteries show that most pottery in everyday use either had a plain slip or—more frequently—none at all (Sparkes and Talcott 1970). These important points govern what is said here about Greek and Roman ceramics, for, unlike glass production, which was transformed by the invention of blowing in the first century B.C., there were no major technical changes from archaic Greece to the Byzantine Empire. Thus, methods of forming and decorating pottery can be described thematically rather than chronologically.

# Production Technology

## Clay Preparation and Pottery Forming

Production technology is governed by the physical properties and firing behavior of clays (Rice 1987: 31–112). In particular the size and shape of its constituent particles, which vary markedly according to depositional environments, determine a clay's relationship with water and therefore its plasticity and susceptibility to shrinkage (Rice 1987: 58). Potters routinely manipulate these properties by mixing different clays or by including other matter as temper: "Potters assess a clay's plasticity according to its 'working range,' 'workability,' or 'plastic limits,' characteristics that can be determined adequately, though non-quantitatively, by a skilled potter through 'feel' and experience" (Rice 1987: 61). Broken pottery is sometimes crushed and reincorporated into clay as temper (Britain: Freestone and Gaimster 1997: 59; Turkey: Poblome 2000). The preparation and modification of clays begins with the drying of excavated clay, which is then broken down into small lumps before the re-addition of water, kneading or treading, and the mixing in of temper. Such clay can be used to make utilitarian pottery, which is often made by hand from coils or on a slow turntable. No Roman turntables survive, but this forming method can be deduced from examination of vessels such as black burnished ware cooking pots that continue Iron Age traditions throughout Roman-period Britain (Peacock 1982: 55; Greene 1992: 49, fig. 21). Ethnographic observations reveal a variety of tools used in this process, including heavy bent sticks, used to beat the dry clay, and turntables made from wood (Greene 1992: 54, fig. 26; Ionas 2000: 138). This kind of processing has been observed in modern communities in a mode of production categorized by Peacock as "household production" or more typically "household industry" (1982: 13–17). Peacock's attempt "to impose a conceptual framework upon a situation that in practice may be almost infinitely variable" (1982: 8) was designed to define "modes of production" (Greene 2005: 40–42). Analogies suggest that for many Greek and Roman utilitarian wares, this relatively local scale of production would either be the main source of subsistence or supplement other work such as seasonal farming (Peacock 1982: 9).

Once pounded into smaller fragments, dry clay will absorb water readily and can be mixed to form a slurry that may be sieved or allowed to settle in levigation tanks. The heaviest particles sink first, leaving lighter particles to settle into fine clay above them. Once the water has evaporated, clay of different consistencies can be extracted according to the potter's needs. Levigation tanks facilitate the production of fine-grained fabrics and tend to be found at higher levels of production, for example at nucleated workshop sites, together with heavy turntables or wheels and kilns (Peacock 1982: 9, 25, 54). Examples were found on a fifth-century B.C. production site at Phari, on the Greek island of Thasos (Blondé et al. 1992: 17) and at the Roman *terra sigillata* production site at Rheinzabern in Germany (Reutti 1991; Peacock 1982: 54, fig. 20*). Terra sigillata* and other fine wares, including Late Roman red-slip wares, are well levigated and were produced on a large scale on sites of this kind. Greek potters' wheels are depicted on painted vases (Boardman 2001: 143, fig. 167), and Peacock has collated evidence for wheels (including possible socket stones) from Oxford, Rheinzabern, and Argonne, and flywheels made from wood and stone from Speicher and Rheinzabern (1982: 55–57).

Ethnoarchaeological research uses analyses of modern potters to find analogies for processes used in the past, to identify variables in manufacturing technology, and to explore the dynamics of production (Stark 2003: 203; Rice 1987: 114). Such studies help us to evaluate technological decisions made by potters when selecting and preparing clays (Stark 2003: 211–12). Technology is only one of many topics addressed by ethnoarchaeologists; others include taxonomy, vessel function, longevity, recycling and disposal, division of labor, learning, style, ethnicity, distribution, and technological and stylistic change (Rice 1987: 202). A related approach "involves the experimental manipulation of raw materials and tools of a particular archaeological context to try to replicate the conditions of their use or production or both" (Rice 1987: 114; Coles 1973). Ancient visual representations of workshops, of which there are many, provide invaluable information (figures 2.8–2.10).

Scientific investigation of the production of ceramics has concentrated on provenance studies, which aim to identify sources of production by comparing vessel fabrics with clays from sources near their suspected place of manufacture (Rice 1987: 413–26). Positive geoarchaeological matching is complicated by mixing and modification of clay by potters during processing and manufacture (Rice 1987: 421–24). The comparison of source clays with final products, however, helps us to understand these technological processes and to recognize the considerable technological expertise that potters used in manipulating clay properties to produce wares with desired characteristics. Whitbread's studies at Corinth have demonstrated the complex processes used by potters in that city and are a model for approaches elsewhere. He stresses the need for well-excavated deposits and the careful collection of samples during excavation (2003: 1):

> Ceramic technology, in its own right, should be an integral component of pottery production studies at centers such as Corinth. For example, variety in ceramic compositions may reflect workshop distribution, restricted access to raw materials, or different materials preferences for specific types of ceramics, such as tablewares, storage vessels, tiles, waterjars, or cooking pots. All aspects of pottery manufacture, from selection and processing of clays and temper, through forming and drying, to firing, are intimately dependent upon the nature of the raw materials. As a result, few conclusions about ceramic technology can be reliably established without information concerning the raw materials that were used.

Compositional analysis of pottery fabrics can also increase our understanding of the ancient economy by examining patterns of continuity and change in the trading of ancient ceramics (Rautman et al. 1999: 377; Rautman 1995: 331; Blondé and Picon 2000).

# Firing

Firing methods were closely related to choices of raw materials so that vessels could survive changes in their physical properties, including loss of volatiles, weight loss, and changes in chemical and mineral structure (Rice 1987: 86–94). The most common inclusions in clay—whether occurring naturally or added by the potter—are quartz, feldspars, and lime, and they are "important during firing in modifying the expansion, shrinkage, and microstructure of a clay body" (Rice 1987: 93). Firing technology varied across the Greek and Roman world, with all types being used from archaic Greece to Late Roman times. In Britain the processes included bonfires used to fire black burnished wares in Dorset (Hearne and Smith 1992), simple updraft kilns (Swan 1984), and more complex structures used for firing tiles (e.g., at the legionary pottery works at Holt: Grimes 1930: fig. 19). Cuomo di Caprio (1992) has outlined a broad typology of kiln types, but regional variations are common (e.g., Gaul: Peacock 1982: 68). A number of Greek votive plaques represent kilns (e.g., 2.9–2.10).

Vessels were stacked carefully in kilns to make efficient use of space and fuel during firing. Occasionally vertical piles of open plates or bowls became fused together if the firing temperature became too high (Johns 1977); normally, grains of sand on their foot rings prevented one pot from adhering to the vessel below.

Differences in the external and internal coloring of fired closed vessels also show that they were stacked closely together, affecting the oxygen content of the atmosphere that reached the pot. Skilled clay preparation and kiln control allowed Greek workshops to produce the glossy surface of plain black-glazed vessels and the color contrasts of black- and red-figured vases:

> In an initial oxidising atmosphere, body and slip fired red, due to the formation of hematite, ferric oxide. A reducing atmosphere was then induced by closing the vents of the kiln and adding wood to the fire, which converted the iron oxide of the slip to magnetite, which is black. At the peak of the firing, in the range 850–1000°C, the potash content of the slip, coupled with its very fine grain size, caused it to fuse into a dense black glossy layer which was essentially impervious to oxygen. As the wood burnt down, the vents were opened and the kiln atmosphere became oxidising once more. Due to its dense, fused condition, the slip remained black. However, the coarse clay of the body retained an open, porous structure throughout the firing, which allowed oxygen to diffuse in, converting the reduced iron oxide to the oxidised form, hematite. Depending upon the precise composition of the clay and the firing temperature, the body then gave a red or buff background to the black slip. (D. Williams 1997: 89; cf. Noble 1988)

Numerous pottery manufacturing sites have been excavated. The Greek kiln at Phari (on the west coast of Thasos), dated to the archaic period by vessels datable between 525–480 B.C., is one example (Blondé et al. 1992), and it has the same basic form as Romano-British kilns (Swan 1984). The rural potter's workshop at Phari was ideally located in terms of raw materials in a wooded coastal region, on a rich clay source, with its own water supply and near a safe harbor. Different clays were extracted and processed for making specific wares (Blondé et al. 1992: 19). The site included clay preparation areas with two settling tanks, for preparing and refining the clay, and two kilns. The rectangular updraft kilns were well constructed in large undressed stones with pear-shaped internal chambers and a central pillar to support a raised floor. Complex *terra sigillata* kilns separated the smoke from the pottery by sending it through ceramic flues (figures 20.1, 20.2), an arrangement that allowed the atmosphere of the kiln to be controlled independently of the fire to ensure that vessels were fired with an even oxidized red slip. The figures show the Roman pottery kiln excavated at the east Gaulish *terra sigillata* manufacturing center at Rheinzabern, Germany. The fire was lit in an arched flue more than 3 m long. The firing chamber, almost 3 m in diameter, contains pipes to protect *terra sigillata* vessels from direct heat and smoke from the fire; kilns for ordinary pottery dispensed with this feature. Broadly similar kilns can be found throughout the Greek and Roman periods.

## The Range of Ceramic Products

Most of the Greek and Roman world and its neighboring areas had long histories of ceramic production stretching back into prehistory, and few areas lacked pottery made on the wheel and fired in kilns. In the first century, Pliny (*HN* 35.160) states

Figure 20.1. Roman pottery kiln for *terra sigillata*, Rheinzabern (Germany). (Photograph courtesy of F. Reutti.)

that "The greater part of the human race uses pottery vessels." Parts of the lower Rhineland and Britain had not adopted the potter's wheel before the Roman conquest, but in both cases its introduction came through an expansion of nearby indigenous wheel-thrown pottery production rather than through the establishment of Mediterranean industries (Greene 1993). Roman military potters did introduce essential new forms such as flagons and mortaria (large bowls with gritted interior surfaces used in food preparation), but traditional pottery making was not displaced. The most widely distributed cooking pottery in Roman Britain came from a region on the southern coast where vessels had been made by hand and fired in bonfires since the Iron Age (black burnished ware: Tyers 1996: 192–96). Simpler handmade pottery coexisted with "Roman" wares in northern Gaul for centuries (De Clerq 2005). Even the peripheral Roman province of Britain provided sufficient markets, consumers, and transport to allow local production to be expanded out of all recognition without changing the technology of manufacture. The distinctive handmade cooking pots from Dorset, whose form extended back into prehistory, were so successful that potters around the Thames estuary imitated them using wheel-throwing and kiln technology (Tyers 1996: 182, 186–87).

Archaeologists typically classify ceramics on functional rather than technological grounds. Vessels may be considered to belong to the same class if they are of the same general form and are used for the same purpose "irrespective of date, fabric, and details of form" (Webster 1976: 6). Specific fabrics, forms, methods of decoration, and technology vary in time and space, but products throughout the Greek and Roman world employed the full spectrum of technological processes.

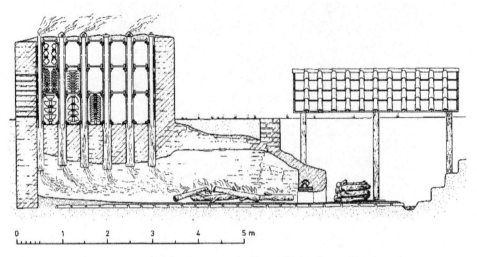

Figure 20.2. Roman pottery kiln for *terra sigillata*, Rheinzabern (Germany), reconstruction. (Reutti 1991: 23.)

The range includes wheel-made, handmade, and mold-made vessels, as well as other objects made from clay.

Vessels were produced in both open and closed forms, and those found in household contexts include thin-walled and slipped wares for the table. Tablewares such as black glazed ware and *terra sigillata* were wheel-made and traded over long distances, as were some plain and painted wares; plain wheel-made vessels were also used for food storage and preparation. Pots with coarser fabrics—both wheel-made and handmade—were used in the kitchen for cooking, and some traveled a considerable distance from their place of manufacture. Other clay products included utilitarian items from lamps to beehives.

A greater volume of clay probably went into the production of bricks, tiles, pipes, and other products than into pottery vessels (DeLaine 1995; Freestone and Gaimster 1997: 158–63; see also chapters 9 and 10). Pliny commented on the ubiquity of ceramic products in first-century Rome (*HN* 35.159): "Nor are we sated by the presence everywhere of pottery products, with jars devised to hold wine, pipes for water, flue ducts for baths, tiles for roofs, fired bricks for walls and foundations. . . ." The conventional image of classical architecture is one of stone buildings, especially Greek temples made from marble. By the Roman imperial period, however, even prestigious public building projects such as baths or palaces were constructed substantially from brick and concrete, which suited their enormous size and elaborate architectural form (DeLaine 1997; see also chapter 10). The combination of brick and concrete allowed the construction of huge vaults for the first time, and some incorporated ceramic pipes and even amphoras to make them lighter (Störtz 1993; Lancaster 2005: 68–85). Brick walls could easily be covered with a thin decorative cladding of stone, mosaic, or painted plaster. Even when buildings were constructed in masonry, roofs were made from clay tiles unless a convenient source of stone slates was available.

A system of ceramic roofing elements developed in the seventh century B.C. in Greece—notably at Corinth—and was rapidly taken up in Italy and continued into the Late Roman period (Winter 1993). Roofing systems comprised rectangular pan tiles with raised edges on their longer sides, and narrow cover tiles with a semicircular cross-section, which fitted neatly over the raised edges of two adjacent pan tiles. Cutout notches and tapered forms allowed the construction of roofs with overlaps that provided effective weatherproofing (Winter 1993: frontispiece). Greek buildings had additional tiles to project rainwater away from their walls, while the visible edges of roofs were decorated with elaborate panels and antefixes that were sometimes painted as well as molded in relief (Winter 1993: 28, fig. 4); simpler versions were still made in Roman times. These *tegulae* were formed in wooden frames, and careful control over dimensions was necessary to ensure a good fit. The extensive use of manufacturers' stamps and other control marks (Adam 1994: 64) would have assisted the selection of tiles of the right form and size for use on an individual roof. In the Roman period, brickyards around Rome produced thousands of stamped rectangular bricks which give insights into the organization of the industry (Helen 1975; Steinby 1993). Tiles of more specialized shapes, as well as pipes, were required in the construction of bathhouses and water supply systems (Bouet 1999). Large-scale building projects continued to require enormous numbers of bricks with makers' stamps well into the Byzantine Empire (Bardill 2004).

Fired earthenware (terracotta) was also a major medium for the production of sculpture, especially in Greek and Etruscan contexts (Higgins 1954; Merker 2003). At Corinth, 24,000 fragments of figurines were recovered by excavations in the sanctuary of Demeter and Kore (Merker 2000: 1):

> This number encompasses a great range in scale, from miniatures to statuettes originally measuring more than ca. 50 cm in height; a corresponding range of different types; and a surprising differential in technique and concept, from plaques stamped out in large numbers, which are pale reflections of their original models, to pieces that, although moldmade, nevertheless preserve something of the freshness of new creations and probably are close to their archetypes. Such diversity is a key element in the Corinthian coroplastic industry as a whole.

The makers of terracotta figurines may have worked alongside sculptors casting bronze statues, since this craft also required knowledge of the working properties of clay used in the creation of molds and cores (see chapter 16). Figures, antefixes, or plaques made from plastic or molded clay could of course be decorated with painted slips and even gilding to produce finished works that might be difficult to distinguish from stone or wooden sculptures in a dimly lit temple. Although less common than in Greek times, the production of figurines remained part of the Roman repertoire—for example, molded white pipe-clay representations of deities made in central France, probably for display in household shrines or for making dedications at temples (Bémont et al. 1993; Rouvier-Jeanlin 1972).

While wheel-thrown open oil-lamps had a long history before classical times, closed lamps with a projecting nozzle made in two-piece molds were an increasingly common product of Hellenistic and Roman pottery workshops (Bailey 1979, 1980; Bailey et al. 1988; Freestone and Gaimster 1997: 164–69). They shared many of the decorative features of tablewares, such as relief-molded decoration and glossy slips; indeed, many were made in the same workshops as tablewares. A workshop was found within the walls of Pompeii containing two-piece molds, matrices for making molds, and kilns for firing finished lamps (Cerulli Irelli 1977). Like pottery fine wares, clay lamps clearly imitated metal prototypes that only survive in small numbers; metal lamps could even be used as matrices for making molds. Lamps frequently bear a name under the base, perhaps that of the manufacturer of the mold or the owner of the workshop in which they were made (Harris 1980). In addition to providing lighting, lamps commonly bore religious ornament that suggests ritual functions: Late Roman lamps with Christian crosses, for example, were produced in enormous quantities. Small containers such as unguentaria and pilgrim flasks used for carrying perfume or oil also had ritual functions.

Agricultural production of wine and oil not only created long-distance trade networks but also generated an enormous demand for large ceramic containers; estates with good clay could organize ceramic production directly or lease its exploitation to tile makers and potters (Cockle 1981). Enormous spherical dolia (frequently set into the ground) were used in the storage or fermentation of wine, which would then be decanted into amphoras for transport and distribution. Amphoras had been adopted in Greece from the eastern Mediterranean seaboard in the eighth century B.C. (Whitbread 1995: 3–4), and retained the same basic form (narrow neck with two handles, globular or cylindrical body, narrow or pointed base) right through to the Byzantine period (Peacock and Williams 1986). Dolia and amphoras were wheel-thrown in stages, with intermittent periods of drying to allow completed sections to support the weight of further additions, and then fired in large kilns; identical techniques have been documented by ethnographers on Crete (Hampe and Winter 1962: pls. 36–41). Amphoras were made for transporting both liquid and dry foodstuffs. The scale of amphora production is reflected in the Monte Testaccio beside the Tiber in Rome—an artificial hill of amphora shards, mostly of Spanish origin, representing as many as 53 million amphoras (Blázquez Martínez et al. 1994: 13). Heavy mortaria, with internally gritted surfaces, thick flanges, and a pouring spout, were used for grinding and mixing foodstuffs in the kitchen (Hayes 1997: 80–82). They were distributed over particularly wide areas, and they frequently have makers' names stamped on the rim that indicate production in specialist workshops (like bricks and amphoras). Neither amphoras nor mortaria show significant technical differences over time. The lack of standard amphoras of optimum form is consistent with the diversity of their geographical sources and variety of contents. A merchant observing a ship arriving at Marseille in the first century A.D. could see at a glance whether the cargo included Spanish olive oil in the globular Dressel 20 or Italian wine in the cylindrical Dressel 2–4 (Peacock and Williams 1986: 105, fig. 39, 139, fig. 67). A large sample of amphoras from the

Byzantine shipwreck at Yassi Ada, Turkey (early seventh century A.D.), shows that their sizes related to Byzantine *litra*, and that their volumes were more precisely standardized than those of Roman and Hellenistic amphoras (Van Alfen 1996: 189).

Name-stamps or distinctive regional pottery forms occasionally allow us to detect the establishment of branch workshops or the movement of potters (Hartley 1977), but such activity is of greater significance to economics than to technology. "Technology transfer" only took place when a new form or manufacturing method was introduced into a peripheral area, such as the occasional establishment of Greek potters in Italy in the seventh to fifth centuries B.C. (Boardman 2001: 74–78) or the opening of a *terra sigillata* workshop in Colchester in the second century A.D. (Hull 1963). There is no parallel to the westward diffusion of new glassblowing technology from the East Mediterranean after 50 B.C, although it may have stimulated the production of "thin-walled" cups and beakers, which proliferated in the first century A.D. (Hayes 1997: 67–71; Carandini 1977; Greene 1979)—presumably in response to the new popularity of glass drinking vessels.

## Surface Finishes and Decoration

While no new techniques were invented in the Greek or Roman periods, styles and methods of finishing and decorating pottery varied in their popularity over time. Throughout this period of study most forms of pottery were made simply in undecorated hand-finished clay, frequently in quite coarse fabrics. Much could be done to produce a smooth surface by burnishing the unfired "leather-hard" pot, and decorative effects could be achieved by burnishing linear designs onto matt zones (e.g., black burnished cooking pots from Dorset: Tyers 1996: 183, fig. 227) or by spiral-burnishing African Red Slip Ware Form 109 (Hayes 1972: 172). While still soft, pots could be decorated by hand or with simple tools—incising designs, impressing the surface with decorative stamps (found especially in the Late Roman period on African and Phocaean red slip wares—Hayes 1972: 217 ff., 346 ff.) or cutting or gouging to imitate cut glass (Charleston 1955: pls. 14–15). Surfaces of vessels could be intentionally roughened by the addition of coarse particles to produce a finish known as roughcasting that made them easier to grip when wet (Greene 1979: 33–34, figs. 13–14). Ridges are frequently found on the exterior surface of vessels, made by the potter's fingers or with a tool; such decoration is common on Late Roman cooking pots, plain wares and on amphoras (Hayes 1997: pl. 1).

The next level of complexity involved the addition of further clay to produce relief decoration. Liquid clay could be trailed or dropped onto the surface by hand (Hayes 1997: pl. 4; Greene 1979: 69, fig. 30), or handmade or molded motifs could be stuck onto the surface (Hayes 1997: 13, pl. I; for molds from a production site, see Bergamini 2005: 75–76, figs. 2–3). Relief decoration could be formed by pinching and impressing bands of clay, whether part of the vessel or applied to the surface, to create images such as faces (Charleston 1955: pl. 92). "Pie-crust" or "rope" decoration is common on pithoi, and also occurs on Late Roman storage vessels

(C. Williams 1989: 53–56). Decoration in relief could be produced more reliably and rapidly by forming vessels in a single stage in molds rather than decorating them afterward.

Molding became more common in Greek ceramics in the late third century B.C., when so-called Megarian bowls were made in hemispherical relief molds that would have been almost identical to those used in the manufacture of similar vessels in metal or glass (Hayes 1997: 40, pl. 13; Rotroff 1982, 2006). Relief-molding in wheel-mounted molds remained standard in the production of decorated *terra sigillata* tableware into Late Roman times. Wheel-made clay molds were decorated by impressing stamps (poinçons) into their interior surfaces to form repeating designs. Bowls could then be thrown inside the wheel-mounted molds, and their rims finished by hand. As the bowl dried and shrank, it could be withdrawn from the mold, which would then be used again to produce another vessel with identical decoration (Johns 1971: pls. 14b, 15).

Derivatives of *terra sigillata* made in North Africa and elsewhere around the Mediterranean from the late first century A.D. (Red Slipped Ware) were no longer made in relief molds. They were decorated by means of impressed stamps, roller-stamping (or "rouletting"—rolling a small wheel bearing motifs around a vessel to impress repeated decoration into the clay) or applied molded motifs (Hayes 1997: 62–63, pls. 21–22; Mackensen 1993). This was not a technical departure—stamps and applied reliefs had always been used on the plainer Greek and Roman forms manufactured alongside figure-painted and molded vessels (Hayes 1997: 38, pl. 11; Sparkes and Talcott 1970: 23). Some large rectangular plates (Form 56) were press-molded in the African Red Slip Ware industry in Tunisia (Hayes 1972: 293).

Many of the decorative techniques described above were combined with a slip—a liquid suspension of fine clay particles which can be added to an unfired pot by painting it onto all or part of the surface or by dipping the pot into it. The complex technology of slips has been investigated through a combination of experimental and scientific research for many decades (Peacock 1982: 63). Particularly fine slips containing suitable minerals (notably illite) can be fired so that the clay particles fuse to produce very glossy surfaces of the best Greek black glazed ware and Roman *terra sigillata*, usefully reducing the permeability of these tablewares. Slips could be thin and easily worn, and might simply be used to disguise the actual fabric color of a vessel. Slips containing minerals different from those of the body fabric were often used as decoration on otherwise plain vessels, while the use of more than one kind of slip allowed polychrome effects (Hayes 1997: pls. 3–4). In the early Roman period, delicate painted decoration was found on Nabataean thin-walled tablewares from Jordan (Schmid 2003), and painting—frequently using more than one color—continued as a technique into Late Roman times across the empire as far afield as fourth-century Britain and Coptic North Africa (Bourriau 1981: 92–94).

Greek pottery vessels suitable for use in formal dining (the *symposion*) usually displayed a characteristically glossy black slip; Athenian painted pottery produced from the sixth to the fourth centuries B.C. had a particularly high reputation (Figure 20.3; Athenaeus, *Deip.* 1.28c). The column krater (figure 20.3, back right) has

Figure 20.3. Selection of sixth- to fourth-century B.C. Attic pottery vessels. (Photograph courtesy of Shefton Museum, University of Newcastle upon Tyne.)

black-figure decoration with incised details, while the large cup (front, second from left) has a red-figured central panel. All were wheel-thrown in fine earthenware, with handles formed separately and added after the vessels had dried. The small jug (front left) has a molded face and applied dots of clay forming a textured area representing hair. One cup (front right) represents the much larger quantity of Greek tableware that did *not* bear additional painted decoration. Its black "glaze" is technically identical to the slips of Roman *terra sigillata* tableware fired in an oxidising kiln atmosphere to produce a red rather than black finish.

Roman ceramics also made use of a wide variety of methods of decoration and surface finish (figure 20.4). The techniques include colored slips (figure 20.4, back center and right), painted slip decoration (front left), molding (bottom center and right) and modeling by hand (flagon with face mask). The lamp (front center) was made by pressing leather-hard clay sheets into a two-piece mold. The four beakers are typical of Roman fine wares, and their decoration illustrates "barbotine" trailed liquid slip (right), "roughcast" clay particles (center), indentation (back center), and "rouletting" (left).

The greatest variety of decorative effects achievable using slips and painting can be observed on Greek red- and black-figured pottery. It developed from earlier styles traceable back through Corinthian and Geometric painting to Mycenaean and Minoan pottery of the second millennium B.C., which drew on a longer ancestry of pottery decoration in Egypt and other Near Eastern civilizations (Boardman 2001: 13, figs. 1–3; Freestone and Gaimster 1997: 41, fig. 4). Fine details of

Figure 20.4. Vessels and sherds from the Roman fort and town at Corbridge, Northumberland. (Photograph courtesy of Corbridge Museum and English Heritage.)

figures and draperies on Greek black-figure vases could be incised into areas of dark slip to reveal the contrasting paler clay beneath the surface (Boardman 2001: 44–78). The transition to the red-figure style allowed greater delicacy, as details could be added in painted lines of dark slip over a red background; painting with a fine brush obviously permitted greater subtlety than incision (Boardman 2001: 79–106). Additional effects enriched painted decoration even further:

> White was used extensively for details of costume like wreaths and especially for the flesh of female figures and Erotes. Details within these large white fields were added in a golden brown tone created with dilute glaze. The wings of Erotes were frequently gilded. Inlays in metal vessels were suggested by beads or lines of clay that were painted white to evoke silver or tinted yellow with dilute glaze or gilded to represent gold inlays. Contemporary Attic white-ground vases, on the other hand, may have imitated wall-paintings; figures were outlined in thin black glaze, and yellows and browns were created with diluted glaze. Reds, yellows, blues, and greens were also produced with added earth and vegetable colors. (Padgett et al. 1993: 18)

White slip motifs contrasted attractively with the surface of Greek and Hellenistic black-glazed pottery. Similar decoration can be found in the Roman period on a number of categories of table and drinking vessels. Wheel-thrown drinking vessels made at Trier in Germany in the second to third centuries A.D. were decorated with white, yellow, and red painted designs over a black lustrous slip (Kunzl 1997). They are technically identical to Hellenistic West Slope pottery from Athens or Gnathia ware from southern Italy (Rotroff 1991; Green 1976).

A clear contrast between Greek and Roman ceramics and those of later centuries is the rarity of fully impermeable glazed finishes rather than fused slips (Greene 2007). Vitreous glazes had been known in Egypt and Mesopotamia for many centuries (Freestone and Gaimster 1997: 74–89, 104–9). Lead glazes were used sporadically on Hellenistic Greek and Roman pottery (Hayes 1997: pl. V; Hochuli-Gysel 1977), including provincial products made as far away as the Danube and Rhine provinces and in Britain (Cvjetićanin 2001; Höpken 2003; Arthur 1978). A distinction must be drawn between the alkaline glazes of western Asia and the lead glazes used in Hellenistic and Roman Asia Minor and the western provinces of the Roman Empire (Römer-Strehl et al. 2005: 216; Peacock 1982: 65). Glazed vessels were often fired in "saggars" to protect their surfaces in the kiln (Peacock 1982: 64, fig. 27). Glazed pottery became increasingly common in Late Roman to early medieval times (Paroli 1992) and dominated Byzantine ceramics (and their early Islamic equivalent) by the eleventh century (Vroom 2003: 58).

# CONSUMPTION

The intertwining of history, culture, economics, production, and consumption is particularly clearly demonstrated by Greek and Roman pottery. State building programs demanded enormous quantities of ceramic tiles and other architectural fittings, and the industries that produced them also supplied building materials to individuals constructing town houses or country villas (Martins 2005). Transport infrastructure and security allowed producers to risk sending goods over long distances, while coins—invented to perform high-value state functions—rapidly became a medium for exchange when base metal denominations proliferated. Flows of heavy goods, whether agricultural or industrial, provided transport opportunities for items such as pottery whose low value would not have justified trade on their own (Greene 1986: 162–64). Pliny (*HN* 35.159–63) comments on the import and export of particularly valued ceramic wares around the Mediterranean.

The expansion of Greek city states and the city of Rome into territorial empires spread styles of living and consuming—and the material wherewithal for cooking, eating, and drinking—from their original urban centers to the fringes of political control and beyond (Bats 1988). Greek and Roman cuisine and dining conventions extended the range of vessel forms imported into, and subsequently manufactured in, newly Hellenized and Romanized regions. In a similar manner, the popularity of drinking coffee and chocolate—and especially tea—in early modern Europe required specialized drinking and serving vessels that were increasingly supplied by local industries rather than being imported (Snodin and Styles 2001: 129, fig. 18, 252–53). Diffusion of the use, and subsequently the production, of decorated tablewares was closely related to trade in slaves, wine, oil, and grain.

One vessel form that epitomizes the importance of the diffusion of consumption practices is the plate. In Britain, plates make their first appearance in the late Iron Age, when examples were imported along with Italian and Gaulish wine in the first century B.C. (Freestone and Gaimster 1997: 57–59, figs. 2 and 4). After having been a consistent part of the British potters' output for more than 400 years, plates disappeared in the fifth century A.D., when Roman rule ended and the monetized economy collapsed. The only exceptions were rare imports into aristocratic and Christian centers around the Irish Sea that maintained connections with the Mediterranean. Wheel-thrown pottery was not made in Britain again until the late Saxon period, and plates did not become a regular feature of either imports or British production until the Tudor period, when the diversity of trade and a monetary economy—combined with Renaissance eating habits—regained a level of complexity approaching that of the Roman period. Even then, plates did not become common until fundamental changes in ceramic production technology occurred in the eighteenth century, when earthenware and porcelain approaching the quality of Islamic and Chinese imports began to be manufactured.

The mass production, diversity, and wide diffusion of Greek and Roman ceramics coexisted with technological stability (cf. chapter 32). It took a world economy, a consumer society, and an Enlightenment approach to the implementation of scientific techniques in industrial production to move ceramics into a different orbit (Berg 2004; Snodin and Styles 2001: 281–307).

# REFERENCES

Adam, J.-P. 1994. *Roman building: Materials and techniques.* London: Routledge.

Annecchino, M., et al. (eds.) 1977. *L'instrumentum domesticum di Ercolano e Pompei nella prima età imperiale.* Rome: Giorgio Bretschneider.

Arthur, P. R. 1978. "The lead-glazed wares of Roman Britain," in P. R. Arthur and G. D. Marsh (eds.), *Early fine wares in Roman Britain.* British Archaeological Reports 57. Oxford: BAR, 293–356.

Bailey, D. M. 1979. *A catalogue of the lamps in the British Museum 1: Greek, Hellenistic and early Roman pottery lamps.* London: British Museum.

Bailey, D. M. 1980. *A catalogue of the lamps in the British Museum 2: Roman lamps made in Italy.* London: British Museum.

Bailey, D. M., S. Bird, M. J. Hughes 1988. *A catalogue of the lamps in the British Museum 3: Roman provincial lamps.* London: British Museum.

Bardill, J. 2004. *Brickstamps of Constantinople.* 2 vols. Oxford: Oxford University Press.

Bats, M. 1988. *Vaisselle et alimentation à Olbia de Provence (v 350-v 50 av J-C): Modèles culturels et catégories céramiques. Revue Archéologique de Narbonnaise* Suppl. 18. Paris: CNRS.

Beazley, J. 1951. *The development of Attic black-figure.* Berkeley: University of California Press.

Bémont, C., et al. (eds.) 1993. *Les figurines en terre cuite galloromaines.* Documents d'Archéologie Française 38. Paris: Maison des Sciences de l'Homme.

Berg, M. 2004. "In pursuit of luxury: Global history and British consumer goods in the eighteenth century," *Past and Present* 182: 85–142.

Bergamini, M. 2005. "Matrici per terra sigillata da Scoppieto: Studio preliminare dei motivi iconografici," *Acta Rei Cretariae Romanae Fautorum* 39: 71–79.

Bintliff, J. 2002. "Settlement pattern analysis and demographic modeling," in P. Attema et al. (eds.), *New developments in Italian landscape archaeology.* British Archaeological Reports, Intl. Series S109. Oxford: BAR, 28–35.

Blázquez Martínez, J. M., J. Remesal Rodríguez, and E. Rodríguez Almeida 1994. *Excavaciones arqueológicas en el monte Testaccio (Roma).* Madrid: Ministerio de Cultura.

Blondé, F., and J. Y. Perreault (eds.) 1992. *Les ateliers de potiers dans le monde Grec aux époques Géometrique, Archaïque et Classique. Bulletin de Correspondance Hellénique* Suppl. 23. Athens: École Française d'Athènes.

Blondé, F., J. Y. Perreault, and C. Péristéri 1992. "Un atelier de potier archaïque à Phari (Thasos)," in Blondé and Perreault 1992: 11–40.

Blondé, F., and M. Picon 2000. "Artisanat et histoire des techniques: le cas des céramiques," in F. Blondé and A. Muller (eds.), *L'artisanat en Grèce ancienne: Les productions, les diffusions: Actes du colloque de Lyon, 10–11 décembre 1998.* Lille: Université Charles-de-Gaulle, 1–26.

Boardman, J. 2001. *The history of Greek vases: Potters, painters and pictures.* London: Thames and Hudson.

Bouet, A. 1999. *Les matériaux de construction en terre cuite dans les thermes de la Gaule Narbonnaise.* Paris: De Boccard.

Bourriau, J. 1981. *Umm El-Ga'ab pottery from the Nile Valley before the Arab Conquest.* Cambridge: Cambridge University Press.

Carandini, A. 1977. "La ceramica a pareti sottili di Pompei e del Museo Nazionale di Napoli," in M. Annechino et al. 1977: 25–31; pls. VIII–XIX.

Cerulli Irelli, G. 1977. "Una officina di lucerne fittili a Pompei," in M. Annechino et al. 1977: 53–72.

Charleston, R. J. 1955. *Roman pottery.* London: Faber.

Charleston, R. J. (ed.) 1968. *World ceramics: An illustrated history.* Feltham: Hamlyn.

Cockle, H. 1981. "Pottery manufacture in Roman Egypt: A new papyrus," *Journal of Roman Studies* 71: 87–97.

Cohen, D. H., and C. Hess 1993. *Looking at European ceramics: A guide to technical terms.* Malibu, CA: J. Paul Getty Museum.

Coles, J. 1973. *Archaeology by experiment.* London: Hutchinson.

Cook, B. F. (ed.) 1989. *The Rogozen treasure.* London: British Museum.

Cook, R. M., and R. J. Charleston 1979. *Masterpieces of Western and Near Eastern ceramics.* Vol. 2, *Greek and Roman pottery.* Tokyo: Kodansha.

Cunliffe, B. W. (ed.) 1998. *The Oxford illustrated prehistory of Europe.* Oxford: Oxford University Press.

Cuomo di Caprio, N. 1992. "Les ateliers de potiers en Grande Grèce: Quelques aspects techniques," in Blondé and Perreault 1992: 69–88.

Cvjetićanin, T. 2001 *Glazed pottery from Upper Moesia.* Beograd: Narodni Muzej.

De Clerq, W. 2005. "Shaped by tradition: On the persistence of hand-made pottery traditions in northern Gaul, c. 100 B.C.–300 A.D.," *Acta Rei Cretariae Romanae Fautorum* 39: 201–8.

DeLaine, J. 1995. "The supply of building materials to the city of Rome," in N. Christie (ed.), *Settlement and economy in Italy, 1500 B.C. to A.D. 1500.* Oxford: Oxbow, 555–62.

DeLaine, J. 1997. *The Baths of Caracalla: A study in the design, construction, and economics of large-scale building projects in imperial Rome. Journal of Roman Archaeology* Suppl. 25. Portsmouth, RI: JRA.

Dore, J., and K. Greene, (eds.) 1977. *Roman pottery studies in Britain and beyond.* British Archaeological Reports, Intl. Series S30. Oxford: BAR.

Freestone, I., and D. Gaimster, (eds.) 1997. *Pottery in the making: World ceramic traditions.* London: British Museum Press.

Fulford, M. G. 1975. *New Forest Roman pottery manufacture and distribution, with a corpus of the pottery types.* British Archaeological Reports. 17. Oxford: BAR.

Green, J. R. 1976. *Gnathia pottery in the Akademisches Kunstmuseum Bonn.* Mainz: von Zabern.

Greene, K. 1979. *Report on the excavations at Usk, 1965–1976: The pre-Flavian fine wares.* Cardiff: University of Wales Press.

Greene, K. 1986. *The archaeology of the Roman economy.* Berkeley: University of California Press.

Greene, K. 1992. *Roman pottery.* London: British Museum Press.

Greene, K. 1993. "Part 1; the fortress coarse ware," in W. H. Manning (ed.), *Report on the excavations at Usk, 1965–1976: The Roman pottery.* Cardiff: University of Wales Press, 1–124.

Greene, K. 2002. *Archaeology: An introduction.* 4th ed., London: Routledge.

Greene, K. 2005. "Roman pottery: Models, proxies and economic interpretation," *Journal of Roman Archaeology* 18: 34–56.

Greene, K. 2007. "Late Hellenistic and early Roman invention and innovation: The case study of lead-glazed pottery, *American Journal of Archaeology* 111: 653–72.

Grimes, W. F. 1930. *Holt, Denbighshire: The works-depot of the Twentieth Legion at Castle Lyons.* London: Society of Cymmrodorion.

Hampe, R., and A. Winter 1962. *Bei Töpfern und Töpferinnen in Kreta, Messenien und Zypern.* Mainz: von Zabern.

Harris, W. V. 1980. "Roman terracotta lamps: The organization of an industry," *Journal of Roman Studies* 70: 126–45.

Hartley, B. R. 1977. "Some wandering potters," in Dore and Greene 1977: 251–61.

Hayes, J. W. 1972. *Late Roman pottery.* London: British School at Rome.

Hayes, J. W. 1997. *Handbook of Mediterranean Roman pottery.* London: British Museum.

Hearne, C. M., and R. J. C. Smith 1992. "A late Iron Age settlement and Black Burnished ware (BB1) production site at Worgret, near Wareham, Dorset (1986–7)," *Proceedings of the Dorset Natural History and Archaeology Society* 113: 55–105.

Helen, T. 1975. *Organisation of Roman brick production in the first and second centuries AD.* Helsinki: Suomalainen Tiedeakatemia.

Higgins, R. A. 1954. *Catalogue of the terracottas in the Department of Greek and Roman Antiquities, British Museum 1: Greek, 730–330 B.C.* 2 vols. London: British Museum.

Hochuli-Gysel, A. 1977. *Kleinasiatische glasierter Reliefkeramik (50 v. Chr. bis 50 n. Chr.) und ihre oberitalischen Nachamungen.* Acta Bernensia 7. Bern: Stämpfli.

Höpken, C. 2003. "Die Produktion glasierter Keramik in römischen Köln," *Acta Rei Cretariae Romanae Fautorum* 38: 365–66.

Hull, M. R. 1963. *The Roman potters' kilns of Colchester.* Society of Antiquaries of London Research Report 21. Oxford: Society of Antiquaries of London.

Ionas, I. 2000. *Traditional pottery and potters in Cyprus: The disappearance of an ancient craft industry in the 19th and 20th centuries.* Aldershot: Ashgate.

Johns, C. M. 1971. *Arretine and Samian pottery.* London: British Museum.

Johns, C. M. 1977. "A group of Samian wasters from Les-Martres-de-Veyre," in Dore and Greene 1977: 235–46.

Kent, J. P. C., and K. S. Painter (eds.) 1977. *Wealth of the Roman world.* London: British Museum.

Kunzl, S. 1997. *Die Trierer Spruchbecherkeramik.* Trier: Rheinisches Landesmuseum.

Lancaster, L. 2005. *Concrete vaulted construction in imperial Rome: Innovations in context.* Cambridge: Cambridge University Press.

Mackensen, M. 1993. *Die spätantiken Sigillata- und Lampentöpfereien von El Mahrine (Nord-Tunisiens): Studien zur nordafrikanischen Feinkeramik des 4. bis 7. Jahrhunderts.* Münchner Beiträge zur Vor- und Frühgeschichte 50. Munich: Beck.

Martins, C. B. 2005. *Becoming consumers: Looking beyond wealth as an explanation for villa variability.* British Archaeological Reports 403. Oxford: Hadrian Books.

Merker, G. S. 2000. *The sanctuary of Demeter and Kore: Terracotta figurines of the classical, Hellenistic, and Roman periods.* Corinth vol. 28, pt. IV. Princeton: The American School of Classical Studies at Athens.

Merker, G. S. 2003. "Corinthian terracotta figurines: The development of an industry," in Williams and Bookidis 2003: 233–45.

Meyza, H., and J. Mlynarczyk (eds.) 1995. *Hellenistic and Roman pottery in the Eastern Mediterranean—Advances in scientific studies.* Warsaw: Research Centre for Mediterranean Archaeology, Polish Academy of Sciences.

Neer, R. T. 2002. *Style and politics in Athenian vase-painting: The craft of democracy, ca. 530–460 B.C.E.* New York: Cambridge University Press.

Noble, J. V. 1988. *The techniques of painted Attic pottery.* London: Thames and Hudson.

Osborne, R. 1996. "Pots, trade and the archaic Greek economy," *Antiquity* 70: 31–44.

Padgett, J. M., et al. 1993. *Vase-painting in Italy: Red-figure and related works in the Museum of Fine Arts, Boston.* Boston: Museum of Fine Arts.

Pancirolli, G., and H. Salmuth 1715. *The history of many memorable things lost, which were in use among the ancients, and an account of many excellent things found, now in use among the moderns, both natural and artificial.* 2 vols, London: John Morphew.

Paroli, L. (ed.) 1992. *La ceramica invetriata tardo-antica et altomedievale in Italia.* Florence: Edizioni all'Insegna del Giglio.

Peacock, D. P. S. 1982. *Pottery in the Roman world: An ethnoarchaeological approach.* London: Longman.

Peacock, D. P. S., and D. F. Williams. 1986. *Amphorae and the Roman economy: An introductory guide.* London: Longman.

Poblome, J. 2000. *Sagalassos red slip ware: Typology and chronology.* Turnhout: Brepols.

Rautman, M. 1995. "Neutron activation analysis of Cypriot and related ceramics at the University of Missouri," in Meyza and Mlynarczyk 1995: 331–51.

Rautman, M., H. Neff, B. Gomez, S. Vaughan, and M. D. Glascock 1999. "Amphoras and roof-tiles from Late Roman Cyprus: A compositional study of calacareous ceramics from Kalavasos-Kopetra," *Journal of Roman Archaeology* 12: 377–91.

Reutti, F. 1991. *Neue archäologische Forschungen im römischen Rheinzabern.* Rheinzabern: Terra Sigillata-Museum.

Rice, P. M. 1987. *Pottery analysis: A sourcebook.* Chicago: University of Chicago Press.

Römer-Strehl, C., A. Gebeland, and G. Frischat. 2005. "Bleiglasurtechnologie in Mitteleuropa (1–12 Jh.n.Chr.): Eine Untersuchung zur Glasurtechnik und –rezeptur," *Acta Rei Cretariae Romanae Fautorum* 39: 209–16.

Rotroff, S. I. 1982. *The Athenian Agora.* Vol. 22, *Hellenistic pottery: Athenian and imported moldmade bowls.* Athens: American School of Classical Studies at Athens.

Rotroff, S. I. 1991. "Attic West Slope vase painting," *Hesperia* 60: 59–102, pls. 14–46.

Rotroff, S. I. 2006. "The Introduction of the moldmade bowl revisited: Tracking a Hellenistic innovation," *Hesperia* 75: 357-78.

Rouvier-Jeanlin, M. 1972. *Les figurines gallo-romaines en terre cuite au Musée des Antiquités Nationale.* Paris: Maison des Sciences de l'Homme.

Schmid, S. G. 2003. "Nabataean Pottery," in G. Markoe (ed.), *Petra rediscovered: Lost city of the Nabataeans.* New York: Abrams, 75–81.

Slane, K. W. 2003. "Corinth's Roman pottery: Quantification and meaning," in Williams and Bookidis 2003: 321–35.

Snodin, M., and J. Styles 2001. *Design and the decorative arts: Britain, 1500–1900.* London: Victoria and Albert Museum.

Sparkes, B. A. 1996. *The red and the black.* London: Routledge.

Sparkes, B. A., and L. Talcott. 1970. *The Athenian Agora.* Vol. 12, *Black and plain pottery of the 6th, 5th, and 4th centuries B.C.* 2 vols. Princeton: American School of Classical Studies at Athens.

Stark, M. 2003. "Current issues in ceramic ethnoarchaeology," *Journal of Archaeological Research* 11.3: 193–242.

Steinby, M. 1993. "L'organizzazione produttiva dei laterizi: un modello interpretativo per l'instrumentum in genere?" in W. V. Harris (ed.), *The inscribed economy. Journal of Roman Archaeology* Suppl. 6. Ann Arbor, MI: JRA, 139–44.

Störtz, S. 1993. *Tonröhren im antiken Gewölbebau.* Deutsches Archäologisches Institut Rom Sonderschriften 10. Mainz: von Zabern.

Swan, V. G. 1984. *The pottery kilns of Roman Britain.* London: H.M.S.O.

Tyers, P. 1996. *Roman pottery in Britain.* London: Batsford.

Van Alfen, P. G. 1996. "New light on the 7th-c. Yassi Ada shipwreck: Capacities and standard sizes of LRA1 amphoras," *Journal of Roman Archaeology* 9: 189–213.

Vickers, M., and D. Gill. 1994. *Artful crafts: Ancient Greek silverware and pottery.* Oxford: Clarendon Press.

Vickers, M., O. Impey, and J. Allan. 1986. *From silver to ceramic: The potter's debt to metalwork in the Graeco-Roman, oriental and Islamic worlds.* Oxford: Ashmolean Museum.

Vroom, J. 2003. *After antiquity: Ceramics in the Aegean from the 7th to the 20th century AC: A case study from Boeotia, Central Greece.* Leiden: University of Leiden.

Walters, H. B. 1905. *History of ancient pottery: Greek, Etruscan and Roman.* 2 vols. London: John Murray.

Webster, P. 1976. *Romano-British coarse pottery: A student's guide.* London: Council for British Archaeology Research Report 6. London: Council for British Archaeology.

Whitbread, I. K. 1995. *Greek transport amphorae.* Fitch Laboratory Occasional Paper 4. Athens: British School at Athens.

Whitbread, I. K. 2003. "The study of a basic resource for ceramic production," in Williams and Bookidis 2003: 1–14.

Williams, C. 1989. *Anemurium: The Roman and early Byzantine pottery.* Toronto: Pontifical Institute of Mediaeval Studies.

Williams, C. K., and N. Bookidis. 2003. *Corinth: The centenary, 1896–1996.* Princeton: American School of Classical Studies at Athens.

Williams, D. 1997. "Ancient Greek pottery," in Freestone and Gaimster 1997: 86–91.

Winter, N. A. 1993. *Greek architectural terracottas: From the prehistoric to the end of the archaic period.* Oxford: Clarendon.

# CHAPTER 21

# GLASS PRODUCTION

## E. MARIANNE STERN

## PRIMARY AND SECONDARY WORKSHOPS

Throughout antiquity, glassmaking and glassworking were two separate crafts. Glassworkers imported raw glass which they turned into finished products, just as metalsmiths and other metalworkers imported refined material to be worked into the final product. Women and men glassblowers are known from the first century A.D. (Stern 1999b: 456–57; 2004: 115–17), but there is no evidence regarding gender before this time.

Before the invention of glassblowing in the first century B.C., raw glass was made in just a few specialized centers, from which it was exported throughout the ancient world. Glass continued to be made in few primary workshops in the Roman period. The amazing uniformity of the composition of Roman glass from different areas and periods has been ascribed to the use of just one source of sand, located in the eastern Mediterranean (Picon and Vichy 2003: 17–31), but ancient literary sources of the first century A.D. mention five glassmaking areas that made use of local sands (Stern 2004: 96–97; Freestone forthcoming). Seen against this background, the excavation of materials possibly indicative of primary glassmaking at Rhodes in the Hellenistic period is exciting (Triantaphyllides 2000: 193–94; Rehren et al. 2003).

Glassmaking took place in the Roman province of Germania in the second half of the fourth century A.D. (Gaitzsch et al. 2003), but numerous remains of glass furnaces elsewhere in western Europe and Britain have been identified almost without exception as secondary workshops (Foy and Sennequier 1991; Foy and Nenna 2001: 47–60).

Very little is known about how the trade was organized to keep a steady supply of raw glass for glassworkers and other artisans, but it must have been quite complex, since arrangements involved provisions for transport over land and over water. (On the structure of the Roman glass industry, commerce and trade, and the usage of glass in a social context, see Stern 1999b and Nenna 2000.)

The division into primary workshops for making the glass and secondary workshops for working and shaping it affected not only the structure of the glass industry; it also influenced early theories about the nature of glass. Plato (*Ti.* 61b) expressed the opinion that glass belonged to the class of bodies that are compounds of earth and water: "And of these substances, those which contain less water than earth form the whole kind known as 'glass' and all the species of stone called 'pourable.'" Aristotle associated glass with metals: "gold, silver, bronze, tin, lead, glass, and many kinds of stone which have no name, for all of these are produced by heat" (*Mete.* 4.389a; cf. Theophrastus, *Lap.* 49). These theories fit traditional explanations of the natural world as a product of transformation of the four elements, air, water, earth, and fire. Greek philosophers did not recognize that glass was created by a true transmutation of materials (Beretta 2004b: 10–14, 17). The confusion can be explained, probably, by the fact that, although glass objects were common in classical and early Hellenistic Greece, the raw glass was imported. The difference between a metal ingot made by refining and a glass ingot made by transmutation went unrecognized.

# GLASSMAKING

Glass is the earliest man-made, artificial material. The basic raw materials of ancient glass—soda, lime, and silica—are the same as those used in other areas of ceramic technology, such as faience and glazes, but the materials are mixed in different proportions and processed differently. Melted silica (sand, crushed quartz, or crushed flint) would make the ideal glass, but this material requires such high temperatures that it has only become possible in modern times. Adding alkali (soda, natron, or potash), which acts as a flux, lowers the melting temperature but has the disadvantage of making the mixture soluble in water. Lime counteracts the solubility and acts as a stabilizer, making the glass durable.

In antiquity, the lime needed for durability was not always recognized as a separate component. We can only guess how many glass objects have completely disintegrated, leaving only those that happened to contain sufficient lime. The absence of this stabilizer may in part explain the dearth of glass objects from the late second to early first millennia B.C. (Reade et al. 2003). Ancient glassmaking recipes indicate that the lime came either with the alkali, because some plant ashes contain lime, or with the silica, for example in the form of crushed shells mixed with sea sands (Brill 1988: 264–69; Newton and Davison 1989: 54). Most Mesopotamian glassmakers made glass from a pure silica, in the form of river pebbles, mixed with plant ashes, which contained lime, while most Mediterranean and later most Roman glassmakers used sands containing lime with a relatively pure form of mineral soda called natron that formed naturally, for example in the Wadi Natrun between Cairo and Alexandria (Pliny, *HN* 31.46; Shortland 2004). There were numerous recipes for glass. Silica is the main ingredient, constituting more than half the total amount. Most Roman glass probably contained about 15 to 20 percent $Na_2O$ and about 10 percent $CaO$.

Pliny (*HN* 36.190–92) mentions the occasional addition of shells to the batch, which would have been a source of lime, but he does not recognize its importance. When he describes the "new method of making glass" he names only two ingredients: sand and soda. The stabilizing lime content explains the renown of particular sands for glassmaking, such as those from the Belus River in ancient Phoenicia and from the Volturnus River in Campania.

In antiquity, the process of making glass from basic ingredients involved two or more stages, each requiring a different furnace (Newton 1980; Newton and Davison 1989: 61–62). Clay tablets with cuneiform texts found at Nineveh in the library of king Assurbanipal (668–627 B.C.) preserve recipes for making and coloring a vitreous material that was probably glass (Brill 1970; Oppenheim 1970; Moorey 1994: 210–14). The recipes show that Mesopotamian glassmakers made a basic glass in a two-step heating process: first the production of frit and then transforming the frit into raw glass.

At least three types of installations for preparing raw glass existed. Small round cakes of colored glass, as found on the Late Bronze Age shipwreck at Ulu Burun, were made individually in cylindrical pots (Nicholson et al. 1997; Rehren 2005). Roman-period shipwrecks have produced large chunks of natural bluish green glass (e.g., Foy and Nenna 2001: 108, fig. 132); these came probably from large tank furnaces of the type excavated at Hadera and elsewhere in Israel (Gorin-Rosen 2000; Freestone et al. 2000). Chunks with rounded edges, as retrieved from the late third-century B.C. Sanguinaires A Shipwreck (Foy and Nenna 2001: 25, fig. 3), were made by a third method, recognized at Beirut (Foy 2005b: 12) and in the Wadi Natrun area (Nenna et al. 2000; Thirion Merle et al. 2003). The raw glass flowed from a tank into a shallow basin with curved walls in which it cooled and stiffened (cf. Nenna 2003: 54). The surviving installations probably date from the first or second century A.D. (M.-D. Nenna, personal communication 2005).

# THE WORKING PROPERTIES OF GLASS

The properties of glass were recognized sporadically, over a long period of time. The earliest glass objects (first half of second millennium B.C.) were beads and small ornaments. After the discovery of glass as a material, it took about 500 years before

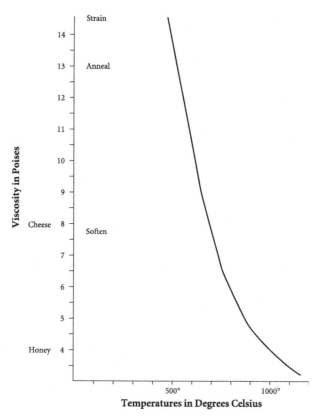

Figure 21.1. Viscosities and temperatures of soda-lime-silica glass. (After Stern 1995: 34, fig. 16.)

the first vessels were produced, and an additional 1,500 years before a glassworker realized that glass could be inflated, or blown. The most important property of glass is the fact that the transformation from a solid to a fluid state takes place gradually. Unlike ice, which melts to water at one specific temperature, glass softens very slowly. The hotter the glass, the lower its viscosity (resistance to flow). The degree of viscosity depends not only on temperature, but also on the composition of the glass. Modern soda-lime-silica glass has the consistency of a hard cheese at approximately 700°C; it is called molten when it is as drippy as honey at approximately 1,050°C. The graph in figure 21.1 (based on Brill 1988: 270–80) demonstrates the relationship between temperature and viscosity. The horizontal line of the graph shows temperatures in degrees Celsius, the vertical shows the viscosity. Viscosity is measured in units known as Poises. The value is so high that these are noted as logarithms: (log) 7.6 is equivalent to $10^7.6$ Poise (about the consistency of hard cheese). Ancient glass probably softened and melted at lower temperatures (R. Lierke, personal communication 2005).

The difference between the softening point ($10^7.6$ Poise) and the temperature for removing molten glass from a furnace or crucible ("gathering") is the working

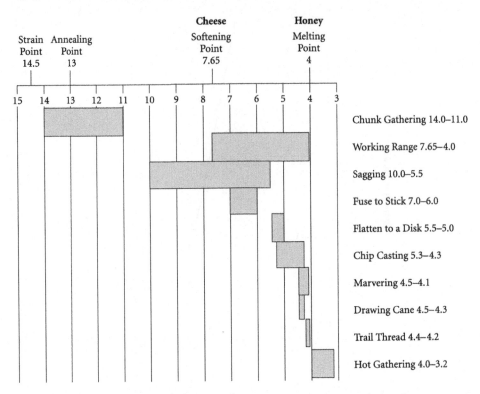

Figure 21.2. Viscosities required for various glassworking operations. (After Stern 1995: 35, fig. 17A.)

range. The time during which different glasses can be worked can vary considerably because the temperatures needed to reach a specific viscosity depend on the composition of the glass. In addition, the heating time required to reach a specific temperature varies per composition. The working range of most soda-lime-silica glasses runs from approximately 700°C to 1000°C. Ancient glassworkers gauged the temperature and viscosity of the glass by its color and feel (its movement on the tool), just as glassblowers do today. Color is an accurate indicator of temperature. The cuneiform texts from Nineveh describe a three-stage sequence of colors: "to glow red," "to glow green/yellow" (perhaps orange yellow is meant?), and "to glow golden yellow," the highest temperature they could reach (Oppenheim 1970: 73). Each glassworking operation requires a specific viscosity (figure 21.2). The graph in figure 21.3 shows the approximate temperatures required for most soda-lime-silica glasses (Stern and Schlick-Nolte 1994: 21–24).

Glass shrinks during cooling. To relieve stress and tension between the surface, which cools first, and the interior, which retains heat for a much longer time, glass needs to be cooled slowly so that all areas shrink at the same rate: the thicker the glass, the longer the annealing period. Annealing cracks in many ancient glasses suggest they were not annealed sufficiently. Ancient glassblowers may have let their

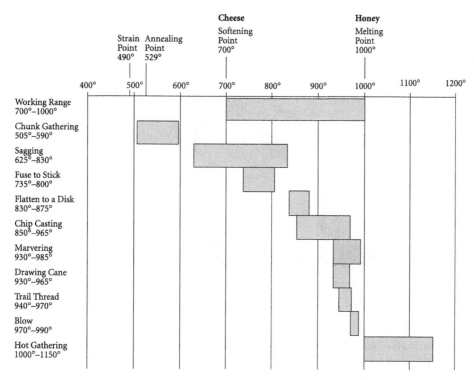

Figure 21.3. Temperatures required for various glassworking operations. (After Stern 1995: 35, fig. 17B.)

pieces cool in trays or baskets of ashes, olive pits, or the like. It is thought that "two black ash heaps on either side of the (glassblowing) furnace, containing olive pits, and several vessels, some of them distorted" excavated in a glassblower's shop at Bet Shean, Israel, served for annealing; the olive pits "were probably used for their heat-conserving properties" (Gorin-Rosen 2000: 59–60).

Glass adheres to other materials when both materials are hot. This creates a problem for artisans working with molds. Greek clay molds of the late fifth to early fourth century B.C. preserve on their surface traces of corundum, thought to have served as a separator (Schiering 1991: 19–21). An experiment at the Toledo Museum of Art revealed accidentally that bone ash, a substance readily available in antiquity, can act as a separator (Stern and Schlick-Nolte 1994: 23–24).

A salient difference between ancient and modern glassworking is the limited use of molten glass in antiquity. The reasons were probably twofold: insufficient pyrotechnology (the glassblowing furnace, invented in the first century A.D., changed this) and unawareness that glass can be melted entirely (Stern 1991; 1999b: 450–54). Crushed glass and individually heated small chunks sufficed for the production of most early artifacts. Artisans took care not to overheat, because a piece was lost if the glass got too hot and melted.

Figure 21.4. Beehive-shaped core-forming furnace. (Drawing by D. F. Giberson, after-Lierke 1999: 30, fig. 53.)

Before glassblowing, glassworkers probably made do with small mobile fire pots similar to those used by metalsmiths in Pharaonic Egypt (Stern and Schlick-Nolte 1994: 24–25, 82, fig. 153). Open at the top, the beehive-shaped firepot allowed the artisan to work above the heat and control the temperature in the piece (figure 21.4; Giberson 1995, 1996). Similarly-shaped clay bread ovens are still produced near Antakya (personal observation, 2005). Glassworkers resorted to potter's kilns for firing glass in molds and preparing flat glass.

Consequently, it should be no surprise that glassworking furnaces predating the invention of blowing have not been found. The materials from a Hellenistic workshop at Rhodes are illuminating. No traces of furnaces were observed, although the finds include thousands of glass beads made by a variety of techniques, mono-chrome and polychrome overlay canes, small chunks of raw glass, and waste from bead and vessel-glass production as well as objects of bone and clay which might have been tools for shaping the glass and "shallow clay receptacles . . . covered with a thin, uneven layer of glass, either all one color or streaked with several colors . . ." (Weinberg 1969: 149, pls. 85–86; Triantaphyllides 1998: 31–32 adds new finds).

# COLORED GLASSES

Due to impurities in the ingredients (Verità 1995), the natural color of glass is usually a pale bluish green, often yellowish green in late Roman times (Cool and Price 1995: 11–12; Foy 1995a: 198–200). Depending on the amount of oxygen in the atmosphere of the furnace, a wide range of yellowish and bluish greens can be achieved without the addition of colorants. In a reducing atmosphere, the iron impurities, combined with sulphur, can produce yellowish and greenish browns, often called amber (Brill 1988: 269–76). Beginning in the sixteenth century B.C., when the first glass vessels were made, glassmakers produced a wide range of bright colors by adding small amounts of metallic oxides to the frit. Copper produced blues, greens, and reds; manganese produced pinks and purplish reds; and cobalt produced deep blues (Newton and Davison 1989: 42–45; Fiori and Vandini 2004: 185–90). Much depended on the amount added, the combination of elements in the glass, temperature and length of heating, and—last but not least—the atmosphere in the furnace (oxidizing or reducing).

The opacity or limited translucency of most early glasses resulted from low melting temperatures that allowed microscopic air bubbles to remain in the glass as it cooled. Sometimes antimony was added deliberately. Lead and antimony produced a yellow glass, calcium and antimony opaque white. The addition of a copper oxide produced opaque red and orange glasses; these were difficult to make because the glass had to be heated for a long time under reducing conditions (Brill 1970: 119–21). For black glass, ancient artisans employed strongly colored translucent and transparent glasses, because these appear black when no light is transmitted. Ptolemaic and Romano-Egyptian inlays often use manganese pinks and purples, but dark blues and dark greens also occur (Stern and Schlick-Nolte 1994: 21). In Roman glass of western Europe, black glass was made with ambers and greens.

In Pharaonic Egypt, coloring took place in primary workshops (Rehren et al. 1998; Rehren 2005); the trade in ingots attests to this practice. The Ulu Burun shipwreck produced ingots of two tones of blue, purple, and orange (Pulak 2005: 68–71); opaque red ingots come from Nimrud (Barag 1985a: 108–9, nos. 166–67; Bimson and Freestone 1985: 119–22). The cuneiform tablets from Nineveh provide recipes for adding colorants in a third heating process (Oppenheim 1970: 79). In Pliny's time, however, coloring appears to have been done also in secondary workshops (*HN* 36.193; cf. Stern 1995: 67; 2004: 99).

The change in practice would have reduced problems of compatibility, because glasses with different compositions often have different rates of shrinkage, and these can cause the glass to crack when it cools. A secondary workshop at Jerusalem, active in the first half of the first century B.C., produced transparent colors by adding manganese and/or cobalt (Israeli 2003: 57). Raw glass was colored on the spot, probably, also at Rhodes (Triantaphyllides 2000: 194).

Pliny mentions several gemstones counterfeited in glass: amethyst (*HN* 12.72, 37.51), opal (*HN* 37.83), *carbunculi* (*HN* 37.98), *callainae* (*HN* 37.112), jasper (*HN* 37.117), and a saffron-yellow stone (*HN* 37.128); he also discusses the detection of fakes (*HN* 37.199–200). Most glass gems, however, were not deliberate fakes (Krug 1995: 182–83; Stern 2001: 358–60). Counterfeits were traditionally the domain of alchemists, who studied the transmutation of substances and counterfeited precious stones. Several collections of ancient alchemists' recipes exist for creating counterfeits in stone and glass (Halleux 1981; Beretta 2004b: 21–30; Tolaini 2004:

211–19). The earliest recipes probably were written down in the fourth century A.D., but they call to mind Theophrastus' comments (*Lap.* 48) on artificial stones made by melting earth, softening it, and hardening it again.

Many ancient glasses have lost their original colors because moisture and chemicals in the soil attack the surface of the glass, leach away the alkali, and alter the composition of the glass in a process called weathering. Weathering can produce a variety of effects, from a thick creamy white or dull black layer, beneath which the original color is often preserved, to a metallic or oily sheen known as iridescence.

# Colorless Glass

Pliny (*NH* 36.194) and Strabo (16.2.5) report technical improvements for making crystal clear (decolorized) glass. If they refer to the same improvements, these must have been developed before Strabo's death in 24/25 A.D. The exact nature of the improvements is not clear. They may have resulted from a new furnace technology that allowed for higher temperatures during melting (Stern 1995: 23–25), or they may have been associated with an intermediate stage in the production of raw glass when a material Pliny calls *hammonitrum*, "sandsoda," was formed (Stern 2004: 80–82).

Ancient artisans decolorized glass with manganese or antimony, of which the latter was more effective (Verità 1995: 292). Colorless glass was not a new invention of the Roman period, since cast glass vessels of the eighth to seventh century B.C., decolorized by the inclusion of antimony in the batch, have been excavated at Gordion (Saldern 1959). In the fifth to fourth centuries B.C., glass bowls almost as clear as rock crystal, the so-called Achaemenid vessels, were produced in some quantity (Oliver 1970; Triantaphyllides 2001; Ignatiadou 2004a). High quality, colorless glass vessels continued to be produced throughout the Hellenistic and Roman periods.

In Greece, the optic qualities of colorless glass were a source of fascination from the moment the material became available. Aristophanes (*Nub.* 768) joked about a glass lens that could be used to burn away a record of debt, but the archaeological evidence for such lenses is scant (Sines and Sakellarakis 1987; Plantzos 1997). Gorgias (483–376 B.C.) and Theophrastus (*Ig.* 73) mention glass "burning-mirrors," but there is no archaeological evidence for mirrors in this period. Pliny (*HN* 36.193) attributes the invention to Sidon. Small convex glass mirrors, coated with lead on the interior, were made from the first century A.D. (Amrein 2001: 41–48; Lazar 2004: 78, no. 93).

In addition to its magnifying, reducing, and reflecting powers, the transparency of glass was a major attraction. A famous painting by Pausias (ca. 350 B.C.)

depicted "both the glass cup (from which she was drinking) and the woman's face showing through it" (Pausanias 2.27.3). Transparent glass appeared in the construction of mechanical devices and gadgets, many of which are described by Hero of Alexandria (Di Pasquale 2004). Ancient medicine and anatomy, in particular research on the working of the human eye, benefited in a variety of ways from increased understanding of the properties of clear glass (Beretta 2004c).

The experiments of Claudius Ptolemy, who was active in Alexandria in the second century A.D., are of interest from the point of view of glass technology. Ptolemy describes two sets of experiments requiring pure transparent glass (*Optics* 5.14–20, 67–86). He measures the refraction of the visual ray when it passes between and through transparent substances of diverse density (air, water, and glass) with a solid piece of decolorized glass, and he uses thin-walled transparent colorless vessels to measure the distortions in form and dimension of objects seen through surfaces of various curvatures (Strano 2004). Previously, Seneca had noted that "fruits are much larger when seen through glass" (*Q Nat* 1.3.9; cf. 1.6.5), a phenomenon that must already have been familiar in the second half of the first century B.C., as is shown by numerous frescoes in Rome and Campania depicting glass bowls filled with fruit (Naumann-Steckner 1991; Sabrié and Sabrié 1992). Ptolemy's *Optics* (ca. 160–170 A.D.; Smith 1996: 3) is our earliest evidence for the decolorized glass that would eventually make "Alexandrian" glass the generic name for clear glass (cf. Diocletian's *Price Edict* 16.1,3: Giacchero 1974; Barag 1985b: 113–16; 2005; Stern 1999b: 460–62).

With regard to optics, we may probably credit glass cutters with two discoveries (Stern 1997: 202–4; 2004: 119–20): first, that the close-set, slightly concave facets with which they began to decorate tableware in the early 70s A.D. created an optical illusion of countless reflections on the surface, improving, as it were, the natural shimmer of rock crystal; second, that facets hollowed out on the underside of a piece of transparent glass appeared as convex bosses when seen from above. Artisans exploited this optical illusion to create a new line of cast and cut colorless glass tableware that "improved" upon the effect of embossed silver. (Grose 1991: 12–18).

# GLASSWORKING IN CLASSICAL GREECE

The most authoritative study of ancient glass in Greece stresses the curious discrepancy between the silence of ancient writers on the subject of glassworking in Greece and the archaeological evidence which shows clearly that Greece played a significant role in the development of the craft (Weinberg 1992: 9). More recent research now allows us to suggest that several important discoveries regarding the properties of glass and the development of new glassworking techniques originated in Greece.

The largest numbers of glass vessels produced in the Mediterranean area in the seventh to first centuries B.C. were small polychrome scent bottles shaped around a core (or just a rod) that was removed after completion of the vessel. Core-formed vessels were made in Greece from the late sixth century B.C. to the early first century A.D., when they were supplanted by blown vessels (Harden 1981; Grose 1989). Dating back to about 1500 B.C., the curious technique is one of the earliest known for making glass vessels. The artisan prepared a core of clay and sand, mounted the core on a metal working rod (mandrel), coated the core with glass, and scraped out the core after the vessel was completed. It required the barest minimum of pyrotechnology to pack crushed glass against a wetted core. Water made the glass stick like wet sand. Careful heating caused the glass to glaze over, and subsequent layers could be added by rolling the core through more crushed glass (Stern 1998: 186–88, 200–203, figs. 1–19; 2002b, 356–59, figs. 8–17). Coils observed near the bottoms of Greek core-formed vessels (Stern and Schlick-Nolte 1994: 39–41, fig. 22) suggest these were made by coiling a thick trail of glass around the core, a procedure that would have speeded up production. The colorful decoration was trailed on either with prefabricated, thin, monochrome canes or with hot bits of colored glass on other mandrels. Dragging the threads up and/or down with a pointed tool or hook created zigzag patterns, festoons, feather patterns, and the like.

While core-forming was suitable for the production of narrow-necked, closed vessel forms, casting was more appropriate for open vessels. The artisan probably filled the mold and/or the mold's sprue with one or more chunks of glass at room temperature and "fired" it in a potter's kiln. Unlike bronze, glass is not a good conductor of heat. Crucible pouring (called hot-pour casting) would have been difficult, because it requires temperatures of approximately 1150° C or more to prevent the glass from cooling and stiffening before filling the mold completely.

Casting was primarily a means of making a hollow object, not of making multiples. Early cast vessels are precious, individual pieces, made often of transparent, colorless glass imitating rock crystal (Saldern 2004: 53–62). Both the wax model and the mold were destroyed in the process: the wax model when the artisan burned it out of the mold in preparation for casting and the mold after the piece was fired. Made of plaster that was soluble in water, the mold was broken away to extract the piece. In the fourth century B.C. casting was largely supplanted by glass pottery (see below).

In Greece, transparent colorless glass seems to have been reserved at first for temples and conspicuous private luxury in the form of jewelry and dedications to the gods. In the fourth century B.C., colorless glasswares began to grace the tables of the wealthy. The evidence from excavations on Rhodes (Triantaphyllides 2000: 195–201) and in Macedonia (Ignatiadou 2002) indicates that clear glass vessels were produced in Greece in the second half of the fourth century B.C. Literary evidence and records in the Athenian Inventory Lists suggest vessel production may have begun already in the first half of the fourth century B.C., with casting in the Achaemenid tradition (Stern 1999a).

Excavations in Phidias' workshop at Olympia added an unexpected dimension to our knowledge of glassworking in fifth-century B.C. Greece (Schiering 1991). Solid ornaments, cast in open clay molds, decorated the throne and/or some other part of the statue of Zeus. This technique was then already centuries old (Stern and Schlick-Nolte 1994: 49–50). The most exciting finds were thin, curved scraps of colorless glass, thought to be waste from glass drapery for a female statue, perhaps the figure of Nike perched on Zeus' outstretched hand (Schiering 1999). The curved fragments were not cast, but sagged.

Sagging required flat glass. Preparing large slabs of flat glass with a consistent thickness and building sturdy molds for sagging them were technical feats in themselves. The slabs could not be made by crucible pouring. Their production was based, probably, on a newly discovered property of glass: if a sizable chunk of glass is heated sufficiently, it will flatten out into a round disk, about 0.7 cm thick; the diameter depends on the size of the original chunk (Stern and Schlick-Nolte 1994: 66–67; Stern 2002b: 362–63). Multiple slabs could be prepared in a potter's kiln. The fragments from Phidias' workshop are the earliest examples of sagging known today (Stern and Schlick-Nolte 1994: 68; Stern 2002b: 361–63), and it is tempting to credit Phidias with the invention. Sagging was to become one of the most important techniques for shaping vessels in the Hellenistic period.

Even if Phidias' original goal may have been protection of the statue's gold leaf decoration, he would have soon discovered the magnifying effect of the glass and exploited its artistic qualities (on similar modern experiments see Schiering 1999). The concept of covering gold leaf with clear colorless glass was to become a major element in the artistic repertoire of Greek artisans. It inspired the great Greek tradition of gold-glass, which flourished, and possibly originated, at the Macedonian court (Stern 1999a: 40–41; Ignatiadou 2001, 2002).

Closely related to the preparation of large disks of flat glass is the production of small roundels with one convex surface. Any small piece of glass will do (Lierke 1999: 22, figs. 34–36). The colored glass inlays in the capitals of the Erechtheion and the base of the Nemesis statue at Rhamnous were probably made this way (Stern 1985; 1989), as were numerous "buttons" and gaming pieces.

# GLASS POTTERY

Casting was a time-consuming process. Rotary mold-pressing could achieve the same result more quickly. The technique is familiar from the production of mold-made Hellenistic pottery (Rotroff 1982), thought to have been invented in Athens in the last quarter of the third century B.C. (S. Rotroff, personal communication 2005). The main difference was that potters employed molds for mass production, while glassworkers could not reuse molds with decoration in (high) relief because they had to be broken away from the finished product. There are indications that the basics of the technique were explored by Greek glassworkers. The earliest evidence comes from Macedonia in the second half of fourth century B.C. (Ignatiadou 1998, 2004b), although it can not be excluded that some Achaemenid vessels were mold-pressed (Lierke 1993b: 324–25; 1999: 36; for cast Achaemenid vessels, see Stern and Schlick-Nolte 1994: 166–67; Ignatiadou 2004a.). The role of faience production in the development of mold-pressing needs to be researched.

The potter's wheel is unknown in modern glass production. Lierke (1991) broke new ground when she discovered that it provided the solution to the riddle of Hellenistic spiral reticella bowls, which are made from bicolored trails coiled spiral-fashion as in a basket. Subsequently, she identified several other groups of wheel-made glass vessels. These include shapes that previously had not been satisfactorily explained, as well as vessels previously thought to have been made by other methods, such as casting, kiln-sagging, blowing, and grinding from a blank. Characteristic tool marks of glass pottery are rotary scratches (Lierke and Lindig 1997) and indents in the external rim area (Stern and Schlick-Nolte 1994: 78, figs. 134–36).

There are two main groups of glass pottery. Mold-pressing and its variants required concave molds, which were usually made of plaster because they had to be removed after completion of the piece. The other techniques could be executed with reusable ceramic molds. As a result, most mold-pressed vessels were individual pieces, while sagging and tooling were used frequently for mass production. Some of Lierke's proposals are under dispute, such as those concerning the production of cameo glass vessels and cage-cups (*diatreta*). Closer attention to tool marks, more research, and more experiments are needed. Nevertheless, the creativity of ancient glassworkers in adapting the potter's wheel to their needs is astonishing, and a striking example of the close relationship between glassmaking and ceramic production. The following selection gives an impression of the wide range of application of the wheel in ancient glass production.

## Mold-Pressing

A concave mold is mounted on a wheel (figure 21.5). The artisan inserts a gob of hot glass into the mold, which shapes the future vessel's exterior, and uses a moist wooden plunger to press the glass against the mold's wall and shape the vessel's interior. In theory, mold-pressing could have been done with a stationary mold, but the rotary movement of the wheel helped to distribute the glass evenly throughout the mold. The combination of two forces—vertical pressing and rotary rubbing— required lower temperatures than modern mold-pressing. After the invention of blowing, this technique remained popular for luxury wares such as vessels with ceramic profiles (Lierke 1993b; 1998; 1999: 55–58), cameo glass (Lierke 1995b; 1999: 67–96), and vessels decorated with high relief (Lierke 1999: 100–107).

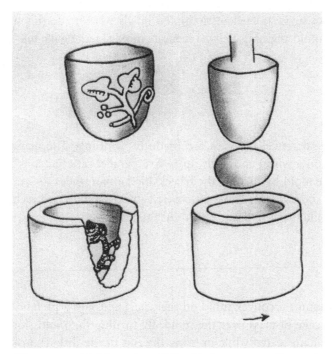

Figure 21.5. Moldpressing. (After Lierke 1999: 82, fig. 210.)

## Double Mold-Pressing

Lierke's proposal that cage cups (*diatreta*) were cut from mold-pressed, double walled blanks (Lierke 1995a: 60–61; 1999: 116–29) has evoked strong reactions from scholars who believe the entire vessel was made by cutting (Saldern 2004: 386–87). Nevertheless, her arguments against cutting the entire vessel, including all the struts from a thick-walled blank, are convincing (Lierke 2001; 2004). The artisan first made a solid cup (the future cage) with a mold and a moist wooden plunger. Then a smaller, perforated mold was placed inside the cup and a second gob of hot glass was pressed into this mold to form the inside cup. The plunger forced part of the glass outwards through the perforations until it touched the outer cup and formed struts joining the two cups. The walls of the outer cup were then cut away between the struts, the perforated plaster mold soaked and scraped away, and all the edges (and often the struts) were ground and polished to create a lacelike openwork cage.

## Rotary Pressing

This technique, a variant of mold-pressing not yet verified by experiments, combined elements of mold-pressing with elements of sagging. A convex mold resembling an upside down bowl is mounted on a wheel. The artisan presses down the glass flowing over the convex mold with a concave mold applied from above. The convex mold shapes the vessel's interior, the concave mold the vessel's exterior. Lierke suggests Hellenistic footed bowls were made this way. The foot was added by mold-pressing, using a separate mold (Lierke 1998: 198–200; 1999: 49, fig. 110).

## Winding

Hellenistic spiral reticella vessels are made by winding. The artisan mounts a convex mold on a wheel and pulls up to five parallel reticella coils from the hot bit(s) onto the mold by turning the wheel (Lierke 1991; 1999: 39–43; cf. Stern and Schlick-Nolte 1994: 71–72). The multicolored strands making up each reticella coil are twisted while they are being pulled off the bit.

## Sagging

The artisan mounts a convex mold on the wheel and sags a prefabricated, heated disk or a hot cake of glass over the mold. By turning the mold slowly the glass-worker can remain seated while pressing the rim of the disk against the mold to stem the flow of the glass (Stern and Schlick-Nolte 1994: 70–71). This technique was used for mass-producing Hellenistic grooved bowls and for early imperial luxury wares such as mosaic glass. It is closely related to tooling.

## Tooling

The glass disk or hot cake is tooled while it sags or flows down over the turning convex mold. (figure 21.6) The ubiquitous ribbed bowls, whose production began in the first century B.C., were tooled. Lierke identified the technique with Pliny's term *torno terere* "tooling on a potter's wheel" (*HN* 36.193), one of three glass production methods for which Sidon had been famous "once upon a time" (Lierke 1993a; 1999: 51–55; cf. Stern and Schlick-Nolte 1994: 72–79).

## Free Shaping

This curious technique, apparently invented in Crete in the early second century B.C. and used exclusively for a small group of vessels known as Cretan pyxides (Weinberg 1959), consisted of "throwing" the glass and raising the wall by pressing the glass with a moist wooden paddle against a plunger sunk in the middle of the glass (Lierke 1999: 37–39; Stern and Schlick-Nolte 1994: 79–81). Plunger and paddle replaced the potter's hands for manipulating the hot glass while the wheel turned. The influence of ceramic technology seems obvious.

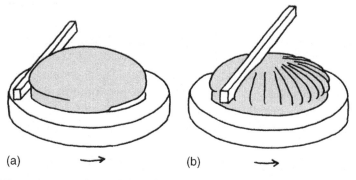

Figure 21.6. Tooling of ribbed bowls. (After Lierke 1999: 54, fig. 124.)

# GLASSBLOWING

The Roman Empire is renowned for many inventions and institutions that shaped the cultures of the West; among the most lasting is the art of glassblowing. The almost unlimited possibilities of transforming the shape of glass on blowpipe or punty are still a source of fascination for glassblower and spectator alike: the glass-blower gathers a gob of molten glass on a metal blowpipe about 1.0 to 1.5 m long, blows and shapes the vessel, affixes a solid metal rod, also known as a punty or pontil, about 0.80 to 1.25 m long, with a wad of glass to the bottom of the vessel, separates the vessel from the blowpipe, and holds it on the punty while he or she finishes the mouth of the vessel. During blowing, glass seems to defy the laws of nature. Even if a piece falls on the ground, it will not shatter. If the blower reattaches it quickly and reheats, he or she can restore the shape and complete the piece as planned. Such a workshop accident may be at the root of ancient stories about an unbreakable glass cup that was dropped on the floor, was dented like a metal vase, and was hammered back to shape in front of the emperor (Petronius, *Sat.* 51; Pliny 36.195; Dio Cassius 57.21.6; cf. Stern 1999b: 441–42).

Pliny (*HN* 36.193) says that *flatu figurare* "shaping by breath," was another of the three production techniques for which Sidon had been famous in the past. The discovery that glass can be blown revolutionized the entire glass industry. The invention of the blowpipe meant that hollow objects and vessels that previously required labor intensive operations could be made in a fraction of the time, and that less glass was needed per object. Moreover, blowing permitted the production of new classes of items. Blown glass tableware played an important role in bringing Roman culture to the provinces of the empire.

Our earliest evidence for inflation comes from Jerusalem, where numerous glass tubes, some of them inflated at one end, were found in the waste of a workshop active in the first half of the first century B.C. (Israeli 1991; 2003: 56). It is revealing that glassblowing began with tube-blowing. Similar tubes were found in a Hellenistic bead-making shop at Rhodes (Weinberg 1969). The thread hole of a glass bead was made either by cutting a prefabricated tube into small sections (drawn bead) or by winding a trail of softened glass around a mandrel (wound bead).

Like other major discoveries that have shaped the course of history, the discovery that hot air will expand softened glass was accidental. Similar accidents must have happened previously, but it took an observant artisan to notice what went wrong and why, and—most importantly—to be curious enough to try to duplicate the event (Stern 2004: 87–88). If the accident took place during bead-making, this would explain in part why it took so long before inflation was discovered. Ancient glassworkers were often specialized; they produced either vessel glass, or beads and jewelry (Spaer 2001), or window glass (Stern 1999b: 462, 464–66; Dell'Acqua 2004; Foy 2005a). Beads and vessels usually were not made by the same artisan, with the possible exception of rod- and core-formed vessels, the techniques of which had much in common with wound beads. The techniques for producing glass vessels— casting, core-forming, and glass pottery—afforded little opportunity for discovering that glass can be inflated, and bead-makers had little use for inflation.

While the initial discovery took place somewhere along the Syro-Palestinian coast, where glassworking and glassmaking boasted a centuries-old tradition, glassblowing was perfected in Italy (Stern 1999b: 442–50). Over a century of experiments, inventions, and improvements separate the first trial inflation of a heat-softened glass tube from full-fledged Roman glassblowing in the second half of the first century A.D. Most of the tools and techniques now taken for granted as integral to the craft were invented during this period: the glassblowing furnace with a closed heat-chamber, the iron blowpipe, the introduction of molten glass for gathering, and the pontil technique for fire-finishing the vessel's rim.

Working with molten glass prepared the way for recycling (Stern 1999b: 450– 54), but it was not universal in Roman glassblowing. Many glassblowers began their piece by picking up a preheated chunk of glass at the tip of the blowpipe instead of gathering molten glass. Both techniques had advantages and disadvantages (Stern 1995: 36–37; 1999b: 452–54).

## Glassblowing Tools and Equipment

Unlike the chance discovery that hot air will expand softened glass, most of the tools and equipment needed for blowing resulted from purposeful research in antiquity. The Roman glassblowing furnace has a closed heat-chamber that allows for evenly heating the glass on the pipe, necessary in order to expand the glass evenly (Stern 1999b: 446–47). The glassblower shown on a first-century A.D. lamp found in Slovenia (figure 21.7) sits on a stool in front of the marver, the flat working surface for shaping and cooling the glass, depicted here as a small ledge sticking out from the furnace on the right (Lazar 2005). The man squatting on the left is probably working the bellows. The lamp dates from around A.D. 70, when iron blowpipes existed (Stern 1999b: 447–48) but probably were not yet used universally. The

Figure 21.7. Glass worker at furnace, Roman lamp from Školarice, Slovenia, ca. A.D. 70. Koper, Regional Museum. (after Lazar 2004: 27, fig. 15, with permission).

depicted pipe is too short to be of iron, since it would have become too hot to handle. A curious narrow strip tied to the underside suggests reinforcement of a fragile ceramic (?) blowpipe for blowing a large, heavy tall-necked bottle. Prime reasons for the persistence (and invention) of ceramic blowpipes would have been the ease and low cost of their production (Stern and Schlick-Nolte 1994: 81–85; Stern 1995: 39–42; 2001: 88–89; 2005).

Very few iron blowpipes have been excavated (Sternini 1995: 83–85; Foy and Nenna 2001: 41, 77, no. 59). It has not yet been established beyond doubt whether a thin length of clay stuck into a glob of glass excavated in Turkey is hollow or solid (Lauwers et al. 2005: 27–28, fig. 4). If it is hollow, it may be a small blowpipe; if solid, it is perhaps a mandrel for adding small handles or decorative threads.

In addition to blowpipe and punty, the most commonly used tools in any glass shop today are various types of shears. Of these, only the U-shaped iron shears with parallel blades, also known as jacks, were used in antiquity (Stern 2002a: 162–64; 2004: 109–12). Originally a Celtic invention, the U-shaped shears (Greek, *psalis*; Latin, *forfex*) were the universal cutting tool of the Greco-Roman world, but one cannot cut semi-viscous glass with them. For that one needs shears with two cross mounted blades moving on a pivot, like a pair of scissors. There are dubious indications that this tool had been invented in the Roman empire, but finds are extremely scarce, difficult to date, and all come from Europe, north of the Alps. Several characteristics of ancient glass vessels can be explained by the lack of pivoted shears. Roman glassblowers usually began the handle of a vessel at the shoulder, pulled the glass up, and attached it at the top where they drew the extra glass out thin and snapped it off. Many glassblowers exploited the fact that they could not cut the glass: they folded it back and forth to create interesting folds and spurs at the upper end of the handle.

Today, many glassblowers shape and cool the glass in moist wooden block molds, shaped like a cup or bowl, while seated at the bench. Although the tool itself is simple, there was no need for it in antiquity. This tool was invented after the introduction of the glassblower's bench in the seventeenth century, when glassblowers moved away from their traditional seat in front of the furnace with its marvering ledge (cf. figure 221.7) and created a new workstation at a distance from the heat (Stern 2002a: 161–62; 2004: 86).

## Mold-Blowing

While free or "offhand" blowing was being perfected in Italy, glassblowers on the Syro-Palestinian coast explored the intricacies of the multipart mold, also known as piece mold (Stern 1995). Free blown vessels imitated first polychrome and later colorless precious stones; mold-blowing concentrated on recreating the chiseled and chased relief of contemporaneous silver vessels. According to Pliny (*HN* 36.193) *argenti modo caelare* ("chasing like silver") was the third glass forming technique for which Sidon had been famous in the past. Since glass cannot be chased or chiseled, and vessels decorated with engraving or wheel cutting postdate Pliny, he probably meant mold-blown glass since mold-blown vessels "look embossed as well on the outside as on the inside" (Isings 1957: 45; cf. Stern 1995: 67; 2000: 166–67). Apparently, Pliny did not understand how mold-blown vessels were made and reasoned that they were produced by the same techniques as their metal counterparts. An ancient glassblower queried on the subject may well have left Pliny in the dark or even misled him on purpose. The same misconception reappears in Martial (*Epigr.* 14.94): *audacis plebeia toreumata vitri* ("plebeian chased cups of dreadnought glass").

The ancient glassblower who presented the emperor with an unbreakable glass cup (above) had no luck with his gift. After learning that no one else knew the secret, the emperor had the artisan put to death and his workshop destroyed because unbreakable glass "might cause a devaluation of metals such as copper, silver, and gold" (Pliny, *HN* 36.195). If Pliny associated the invention of *vitrum flexile* "flexible, malleable glass" correctly with the emperor Tiberius, mold-blowing may have experienced an early setback in Italy under Tiberius' rule (Stern 1999b: 441–42). After his death, workshops in the west began producing a formidable quantity of mold-blown tableware and other vessels (Price 1991). In the eastern Mediterranean, commercial mold-blowing began earlier. The earliest mold-blown glass currently known was excavated in an Augustan context at Magdalensberg, Austria, but it was blown by an eastern Mediterranean glassblower, perhaps by Ennion, the most famous glassblower of antiquity (Stern 2000: 165–67).

The first glassblowing molds were piece-molds that included the base of the vessel. Mold seams in preserved vessels show how complex the molds were, consisting often of three or four parts (Stern 1995: 29–30, fig. 15). As time went on construction became simpler, and by the second half of the first century many molds in Italy and the west had just two parts. The glassblower did not necessarily create the archetype, which could be a silver vessel or even another glass vessel. Successful designs were sometimes pirated, with the result that distant workshops produced seemingly identical vessels.

The production of mold-blown glass decorated with relief fell out of favor just around the time that Mount Vesuvius erupted in A.D. 79. The reason was probably the increased use of molds for utility wares (Stern 2001: 41–42). Large storage bottles, blown in smooth-walled molds, began to flood the market in the third quarter of the first century A.D. (Cool and Price 1995). Their prismatic shape facilitated packing in wooden boxes, and the base moldings promoted brand recognition. The realization that mold-blown vessels could be mass produced caused their value to drop. In the eastern Mediterranean, particularly Asia Minor, where mold-blowing did not become a means of mass production, elegant mold-blown beakers featuring mythological imagery remained in use well into the second century A.D. (Weinberg 1972; Wight 1988).

Decorative mold-blowing experienced a revival in the fourth century A.D., when glassblowers discovered a new way of using patterned molds. By expanding and shaping the vessel after it exited the mold, a wide range of shapes could be blown with just one mold. The technique appears to have been developed by Syrian glassblowers who began to expand geometric patterns made in full-size piece molds (Stern 2001: 133–34). Although this particular technique remained a regional curiosity, it pointed the way to a novel use of the one-piece mold that would dominate mold-blowing for all times to come: pattern-blowing. Using one-piece molds, also known as dip molds, Syro-Palestinian glassblowers produced a distinct group of vessels decorated with barely expanded geometric patterns, known collectively as Honeycomb Bowls. The real success story was to be the straight-walled, tapered mold with ribbing or fluting on the interior. Easy to make and easy to use, the mold enabled glassblowers to create a large variety of expanded vertical and spiral ribs. Immediately popular throughout the Roman Empire, pattern-blowing with expanded ribs was destined to become a lasting success that returned to mold-blowing some of its original appeal. Delicately ribbed glass vessels evoked the luxury of fine fluted silverware, but without the odium of mass production, because the glassblower shaped each piece individually.

# OTHER DECORATIVE TECHNIQUES

Around 200 B.C., polychrome glass objects imitating precious stones became fashionable and remained in vogue until about A.D. 70. The modern names given to various types of luxury glass of this period are self-explanatory: variously patterned mosaic glass vessels, reticella or network vessels, and gold band vessels. They were made with prefabricated polychrome elements, such as mosaic glass bars, twisted reticella trails, or strips of gold foil encased between two layers of transparent colorless glass. The most sophisticated objects were so-called sandwich gold glass vessels: two glass vessels fitted one into the other, with a pattern cut out of gold foil attached to the outside of the interior vessel (Stern and Schlick-Nolte 1994: 54–66). When commercial glassblowing began in the last quarter of the first century B.C., glassblowers tried to emulate the effect of polychrome luxury wares.

Decorative techniques are classified as "hot" or "cold," depending on whether the artisan decorates the glass while it is hot—threads, flecks, ribs, indents—or cold, in which case the artisan need not be the glassblower in person—painting, wheel-cutting, wheel-abrading, freehand scratching, and facet cutting. Sophisticated cold decoration, such as painting and figural cutting, probably was executed by specialized artisans. Simple wheel-cutting in the form of horizontal grooves took place in the glassblower's shop, as at Jalame in Israel (Weinberg 1988: 87–98).

Winding a colored glass trail around a vessel was one of the oldest techniques for beautifying glass (cf. the early core-formed vessels). Applying the trail before inflating the vessel to its full size could create a marbled pattern imitating precious stone; threads in relief were applied after fully inflating the vessel. Pinching ribs in the wall of a vessel likewise took place at an early stage. One particularly attractive group of early blown vessels, the so-called *zarte Rippenschalen*, combines wound trails with pinched ribs (Stern 2001: 82–83).

Many new shapes and decorative techniques imitated contemporary pottery, stone, and metal, indicating the remarkable adaptability of this technology. Glassblowers in Campania and northern Italy copied the colored sand decoration of thin-walled Augustan pottery by rolling the inflated vessel through crushed glass laid out on the marver, but they abandoned this technique after discovering they could do something potters could not. By applying the crushed glass before fully inflating the vessel, glassblowers created colored flecks that expanded and flattened out during blowing, imitating the more expensive mosaic glass (Stern 2004: 119, pls. 9–12). A variant technique made use of failed glass vessels. Broken into small pieces, the colorful shards were applied individually to the walls of a new vessel (Stern 2001: 68).

# The Ancient Glassblower's
# Output

A survey of the archaeological vestiges of workshops has shown that in comparison with other fire-based crafts the total number of workshops producing any kind of glass was much lower. In Switzerland, remains were found of just 23 workshops (6%) producing glass objects, as compared to 87 (23%) workshops for copper alloys, 143 (39%) for iron working, and 116 (32%) for pottery. These percentages are in agreement with those found elsewhere north of the Alps (Amrein 2006).

In view of the particular exigencies of the métier, modern assumptions that Roman glassblowing was a large-scale industry comparable to the pottery industry—with hundreds of employees or even slaves laboring in one establishment—are unrealistic. Every glassblower needs his or her own working port at the furnace, and ancient pyrotechnology did not permit expanding the glassblowing furnace with a second working port. Our earliest evidence for a furnace accommodating more than one glassblower is a late fifteenth-century drawing in the Vatican Library (Stern 2002a: 160, fig. 3). The only way to boost production was by building a series of small furnaces, as may have been the case in the Hambacher Forst (Gaitzsch et al. 2000) and elsewhere north of the Alps, where series of round and rectangular furnaces have been excavated at single sites.

The Roman glassblowing furnace was small (cf. figure 21.7). The interior diameter was approximately 0.45–0.65 m, a measurement confirmed by excavated remains at Avenches, Switzerland, and elsewhere (Amrein 2001; Foy and Nenna 2001: 62–63). Where the remains of more than one furnace are excavated in close proximity, it is not always clear to what extent they operated simultaneously. Multiple furnaces may have been required for blowing on a daily basis. In the mid-twentieth century, a primitive glassblowing furnace at Herat, in Afghanistan, operated only every other day because the furnace took 24 hours to cool down after a day's work. When demand suddenly increased, the owner built a second furnace. Other impediments to expanding into large-scale operations were the size of the crucible containing molten glass and the amount of space available for annealing.

To gain a sense of the ancient glassblower's output, it is useful to look at the output of contemporary low-technology workshops (Stern 1999b: 454–56). Based on examples from Herat and Cairo, an ancient glassblower probably averaged 100 vessels per day, or 11,000 per year. This works out to 330,000 vessels in 30 years! Such a long period of activity may not have been common, but it was not impossible, given the witness of the tombstone of the opifex artis vitriae ("glass artist") Julius Alexander who died in Lyon at age 75.

The physical restrictions imposed by size and design of the ancient glassblowing furnace on the number of persons who could blow simultaneously in one shop affected many aspects of the industry, from the number of people blowing in one shop and their relationships with each other to external transactions such as buying raw glass and the marketing and selling of the finished product.

While glassmaking benefited from the achievements of metal and faience production, glassworkers were closely related to potters. The development of recipes for coloring and decolorizing glass contributed to ancient chemistry; the ancient glassblower's need for a new furnace advanced pyrotechnology. The discovery and exploitation of the properties of glass was an ongoing process that began in the late third millennium B.C., but the story is not straightforward, as is exemplified by the rediscovery of glass pottery in the twentieth century. Discovery of a new property often lead to the development of a new tool or piece of equipment. It usually took many decades before the full potentialities of a property were realized. As in all crafts, tools determined what was feasible.

Unlike other fire-based industries, such as pottery, bronze, and metalworking, glassblowing did not develop into a large-scale enterprise in antiquity. This was probably due entirely to physical restraints. The division into primary and secondary glass production affected not only the structure of the industry but also ancient thought about the nature of glass. Advances in glass technology and the discovery of the properties of glass were the exclusive domain of artisans. Unlike philosophers who attempted to explain natural phenomena in a systematic way, glassworkers were (and still are) primarily practical. They built on experience, did things "on the spur of the moment," and learned from unforeseen events and accidents, which they might—at first for fun—try to duplicate.

# REFERENCES

Amrein, H. 2001. *L'atelier de verriers d'Avenches: L'artisanat du verre au milieu du 1er siècle après J.-C.* Cahiers d'archéologie romande 87 = Aventicum 11.

Amrein, H. 2006. "Quelques reflexions sur l'implantation et l'organisation des ateliers de verriers dans les provinces romaines au Nord des Alpes," in G. Creemers, B. Demarsin, and P. Cosyns (eds.), *Roman glass in Germania Inferior.* Atuatuca 1.Tongeren: Provinciaal Gallo-Romeins Museum, 58–63.

Barag, D. 1985a. *Catalogue of western Asiatic glass in the British Museum.* Vol. 1. London: British Museum.

Barag, D. 1985b. "Recent important epigraphic discoveries related to the history of glassmaking in the Roman period," *Annales de l'Association Internationale pour l'Histoire du Verre* 10: 109–16.

Barag, D. 2005. "Alexandrian and Judaean glass in the Price Edict of Diocletian," *Journal of Glass Studies* 47: 184–86.

Beretta, M. (ed.) 2004a. *When glass matters: Studies in the history of science and art from Graeco-Roman antiquity to early modern era.* Florence: Olschki.

Beretta, M. 2004b. "Between nature and technology: Glass in ancient chemical philosophy," in Beretta 2004a: 1–30.

Beretta, M. 2004c. "From the eye to the eye-glass: A pre-history of spectacles," in Beretta 2004a: 249–82.

Bimson, M., and I. C. Freestone 1985. "Scientific examination of opaque red glass of the second and first millennia B.C.," in Barag 1985a: 119–22.

Brill, R. H. 1970. "The chemical interpretation of the texts," in Oppenheim et al. 1970: 105–28.

Brill, R. H. 1988. "Scientific investigations of the Jalame glass and related finds," in Weinberg 1988: 257–94.

Cool, H. E. M., and J. Price. 1995. *Roman vessel glass from excavations in Colchester, 1971–85*. Colchester Archaeological Report 8. Colchester: Colchester Archaeological Trust.

Dell' Acqua, F. 2004. "Le finestre invetriate nell'antichità romana," in M. Beretta and G. Di Pasquale (eds.), *Vitrum: Il vetro fra arte e scienza nel mondo romano*. Florence: Giunti: 109–19.

Di Pasquale, G. 2004. "Scientific and technological use of glass in Graeco-Roman antiquity," in Beretta 2004a: 31–76.

Fiori, C., and M. Vandini 2004. "Chemical composition of glass and its raw materials: Chronological and geographical development in the first millennium A.D.," in Beretta 2004a: 151–94.

Foy, D. 1995a. "Le verre de la fin du IVe au VIIIe siècle en France Méditerranéenne: Premier essai de typo-chronologie," in Foy 1995b: 187–242.

Foy, D. (ed.). 1995b. *Le verre de l'antiquité tardive et du haut moyen-âge: Typologie-chronologie-diffusion*. Association française pour l'archéologie du verre, 8e rencontre. Guiry en Vexin: Musée archéologique du Val d'Oise.

Foy, D. (ed.) 2005a. *De transparentes spéculations: Vitres de l'antiquité et du haut moyen-âge (Occident-Orient)*. Bavay: Musée/Site d'Archéologie Bavay-Bagacum.

Foy, D. 2005b. "Une production de bols moulés à Beyrouth à la fin de l'époque hellénistique et le commerce de ces verres en Méditerranée occidentale," *Journal of Glass Studies* 47: 11–35.

Foy, D. and M.-D. Nenna. 2001. *Tout feu tout sable: Mille ans de verre antique dans le Midi de la France*. Marseille: Edisud.

Foy, D., and G. Sennequier (eds.) 1991. *Ateliers de verreries de l'antiquité à la période pré-industrielle*. Association française pour l'archéologie du verre, 4e rencontre. Rouen: Musée départemental des Antiquités.

Freestone, I. C. et al. 2000. "Primary glass from Israel and the production of glass in late antiquity and the early Islamic period," in Nenna 2000: 65–83.

Freestone, I. C. forthcoming. "Pliny on Roman glassmaking," in M. Martinón-Torres and T. Rehren (eds.), *Archaeology and texts*.

Gaitzsch, W. et al. 2000. "Spätrömische Glashütten im Hambacher Forst—Produktionsort der ECVA-Fasskrüge: Archäologische und naturwissenschaftliche Untersuchungen," *Bonner Jahrbücher* 200: 83–241.

Giacchero, M. 1974. *Edictum Diocletiani et collegarum de pretiis rerum venalium*. Pubblicazioni dell'Istituto di storia antica e scienze ausiliarie dell' Università di Genova 8. Genoa: Istituto di storia antica e scienze ausiliarie.

Giberson, D. F. 1995. "The volcano dream," *The Glass Art Society Journal*: 77–84.

Giberson, D. F. 1996. "Ancient glassmaking: Its efficiency and economy," *Ornament* (Summer): 76–79.

Gorin-Rosen, Y. 2000. "The ancient glass industry in Israel: Summary of the finds and new discoveries," in Nenna 2000: 49–63

Grose, D. F. 1989. *Early ancient glass: The Toledo Museum of Art*. New York: Hudson Hills.

Grose, D. F. 1991. "Early Imperial Roman cast glass: The translucent coloured and colourless fine wares," in Newby and Painter 1991: 1–18.

Halleux, R. 1981. *Les alchimistes grecs*. Vol. 1. Paris: Les Belles Lettres.

Harden, D. B. 1981. *Catalogue of Greek and Roman glass in the British Museum*. Vol. 1, *Core- and rod-formed vessels and pendants and Mycenaean cast objects*. London: British Museum Publications.

Ignatiadou, D. 1998. "Three cast-glass vessels from a Macedonian tomb in Pydna," *Annales de l'Association Internationale pour l'Histoire du Verre* 14: 35–38.

Ignatiadou, D. 2001. "Glass and gold on Macedonian funerary couches," *Annales de l'Association Internationale pour l'Histoire du Verre* 15: 4–7.

Ignatiadou, D. 2002. "Macedonian glass-working in the 4th c. B.C.," in Kordas 2002: 63–70.

Ignatiadou, D. 2004a. "Glass vessels," in J. Zahle and K. Kjeldsen, *The Maussolleion at Halikarnassos*, Vol. 6: *Subterranean and pre-Maussollan structures on the site of the Maussolleion: The finds from the tomb chamber of Maussollos*. Jutland Archaeological Society Publications XV.6. Aarhus: Aarhus University Press, 181–201.

Ignatiadou, D. 2004b. "Keramikê kai ualourgia stên prôimê ellênistikê Makedonia," in *St' epistêmonikê sunantêsê gia tên ellênistikê keramikê, Volos 2000*. Athens, 693–702.

Isings, C. 1957. *Roman glass from dated finds*. Archaeologica Traiectina 2. Groningen: Wolters.

Israeli, Y. 1991. "The invention of blowing," in Newby and Painter (eds.) 1991: 46–55.

Israeli, Y. 2003. "What did Jerusalem's first cent. BCE glass workshop produce?" *Annales de l'Association Internationale pour l'Histoire du Verre* 16: 54–57.

Kordas, G. (ed.) 2002. *Hyalos vitrum glass: History, technology and conservation of glass and vitreous materials in the Hellenic world*. Athens: Glasnet.

Krug. A. 1995. "Römische Gemmen im Rheinischen Landesmuseum Trier," *Bericht der Römisch-Germanischen Kommission* 76: 159–218.

Lauwers, V. et al. 2005. "Le verre de Sagalassos: De nouvelles preuves d'une production locale de verre," *Bulletin de l'association française pour l'archéologie du verre*: 26–29.

Lazar, I. 2004. *Rimljani: Steklo, Glina, Kamen*. Celje: Pokrajinski Muzej.

Lazar, I. 2005. "An oil lamp depicting a Roman glass furnace: A new find from Slovenia," *Instrumentum* 22: 17–19.

Lierke, R. 1991. "Glass bowls made on a potter's wheel," *Glastechnische Berichte/Glass Science Technology* 64: 310–17.

Lierke, R. 1993a. "*Aliud torno teritur*—Rippenschalen und die Spuren einer unbekannten Glastechnologie: Heisses Glas auf der Töpferscheibe," *Antike Welt* 24: 218–34.

Lierke, R. 1993b. "It was the turning wheel and not the lathe: Moldpressing and mold-turning of hot glass in ancient glass vessel production," *Glastechnische Berichte/Glass Science Technology* 66: 321–29.

Lierke, R. 1995a. "Glass vessels made on a turning wheel in Roman times (survey)," *Annales de l'Association Internationale pour l'Histoire du Verre* 13: 55–62.

Lierke, R. 1995b. "Glass vessels made on a turning wheel: Cameo glass," *Annales de l'Association Internationale pour l'Histoire du Verre* 13: 63–76.

Lierke, R. 1998. "The ancient glass pottery process," *Annales de l'Association Internationale pour l'Histoire du Verre* 14: 198–202.

Lierke, R. 1999. *Antike Glastöpferei: Ein vergessenes Kapitel der Glasgeschichte*. Mainz: Philipp von Zabern.

Lierke, R. 2001. "Re-evaluating cage cups," *Journal of Glass Studies* 43: 174–77.

Lierke, R. 2004. "Late antique cage cups and their cutting or grinding marks," *Instrumentum* 19: 18–20.

Lierke, R., and M. R. Lindig 1997. "Recent investigations of early Roman cameo glass, Part 1: Cameo manufacturing technique and rotary scratches of ancient glass vessels," *Glastechnische Berichte/Glass Science Technology* 70: 189–97.

McCray, P., and W. D. Kingery (eds.) 1998. *The prehistory and history of glassmaking technology*. Ceramics and Civilizations 8. Westerville, OH: The American Ceramic Society.

Moorey, P. R. S. 1994. *Ancient Mesopotamian materials and industries*. Oxford: Clarendon Press.

Naumann-Steckner, F. 1991. "Depictions of glass in Roman wall paintings," in Newby and Painter 1991: 86–98.

Nenna, M.-D. (ed.) 2000. *La route du verre: Ateliers primaires et secondaires du second millénaire av. J.-C. au Moyen Age*. Travaux de la Maison d'Orient Méditerranéen 33. Lyon: Maison de l'Orient Méditerranéen-Jean Pouilloux,

Nenna, M.-D. 2003. "Les ateliers traditionels d'aujourd'hui: Des modèles pour l'archéologie?" in D. Foy (ed.), *Coeur de verre: Production et diffusion du verre antique*. CH-Gollion: Infolio editeurs, 52–59.

Nenna, M.-D., et al. 2000. "Ateliers primaires et secondaires en Egypte à l'époque gréco-romaine," in Nenna 2000: 97–112.

Newby, M., and K. Painter (eds.) 1991. *Roman glass: Two centuries of art and innovation*. Society of Antiquaries Occasional Paper 13. London: Society of Antiquaries.

Newton, R. 1980. "Recent views on ancient glass," *Glass Technology* 21: 174–78.

Newton, R., and S. Davison. 1989. *Conservation of glass*. London and Boston: Butterworths.

Nicholson, P. T. et al. 1997. "The Ulu Burun glass ingots, cylindrical vessels and Egyptian glass," *Journal of Egyptian Archaeology* 83: 143–53.

Oliver Jr., A. 1970. "Persian export glass," *Journal of Glass Studies* 12: 9–16.

Oppenheim, A. L. 1970. "Glasses in Mesopotamian sources," in Oppenheim et al. 1970: 4–101.

Oppenheim, A. L et al. 1970. *Glass and glassmaking in ancient Mesopotamia*. Corning, NY: The Corning Museum of Glass Press.

Picon, M., and M. Vichy. 2003. "D'Orient en Occident: L'origine du verre à l'époque romaine et durant le haut Moyen Age," in D. Foy and M.-D. Nenna (eds.), *Echanges et commerce du verre dans le monde antique*. Actes du colloque de l'Association française pour l'archéologie du verre, Aix-en-Provence and Marseille, 2001. Monografies Instrumentum 24. Montagnac: Monique Mergoil, 17–31.

Plantzos, D. 1997. "Crystals and lenses in the Graeco-Roman world," *American Journal of Archaeology* 101: 451–64.

Price, J. 1991. "Decorated mould-blown glass tablewares in the first century A.D.," in Newby and Painter 1991: 56–75.

Pulak, C. 2005. "Das Schiff von Uluburun und seine Ladung," in Yalçin et al. 2005: 53–102.

Reade, W., et al. 2003. "Innovation or continuity? Early first millennium BCE glass in the Near East: The cobalt blue glasses from Assyrian Nimrud," *Annales de l'Association Internationale pour l'Histoire du Verre* 16: 23–27.

Rehren, T. 2005. "Der Handel mit Glas in der Spätbronzezeit," in Yalcin et al. 2005: 533–39.

Rehren, T. et al. 1998. "Glass coloring works within a copper-centred industrial complex in Late Bronze Age Egypt," in McCray and Kingery 1998: 227–50.

Rehren, T. et al. 2003. "The primary production of glass at Hellenistic Rhodes," *Annales de l'Association Internationale pour l'Histoire du Verre* 16: 39–43.

Rotroff, S. I. 1982. *Hellenistic pottery: Athenian and imported moldmade bowls. The Athenian Agora*, Vol. 22. Princeton, NJ: American School of Classical Studies.

Sabrié, R., and M. Sabrié 1992. "Un thème décoratif des peintures murales romaines: Le vase de verre," *Revue archéologique Narbonnaise* 25: 207–22.

Saldern, A. von. 1959. "Glass finds at Gordion," *Journal of Glass Studies* 1: 22–49.

Saldern, A. von. 2004. *Antikes Glas*. Munich: Beck.

Schiering, W. 1991. *Die Werkstatt des Pheidias in Olympia*. Vol. 2, *Werkstattfunde*. Olympische Forschungen 18. Berlin: Walter de Gruyter.

Schiering, W. 1999. "Glas für das Gewand einer klassischen Kolossalstatue (Nike?) in Olympia," *Antike Welt* 30: 39–48.

Shortland, A. J. 2004. "Evaporites of the Wadi Natrun: Seasonal and annual variation and its implication for ancient exploitation," *Archaeometry* 46: 497–516.

Sines, G., and Y. A. Sakellarakis 1987. "Lenses in antiquity," *American Journal of Archaeology* 91: 191–96.

Smith, A. M. 1996. *Ptolemy's theory of visual perception: An English translation of the* Optics *with introduction and commentary*. Transactions of the American Philosophical Association 86.2. Philadelphia: American Philosophical Association.

Spaer, M. 2001. *Ancient glass in the Israel Museum: Beads and other small objects*. Jerusalem: The Israel Museum.

Stern, E. M. 1985. "Die Kapitelle der Nordhalle des Erechtheion," *Athenische Mitteilungen* 100: 405–26.

Stern, E. M. 1989. "Colored glass inlays in architectural ornament: Athens and Rhamnous," *American Journal of Archaeology* 93: 254.

Stern, E. M. 1991. "Glassworking before glassblowing," *Annales de l'Association Internationale pour l'Histoire du Verre* 12: 21–31.

Stern, E. M. 1995. *Roman mold-blown glass: The first through sixth centuries. (The Toledo Museum of Art)*. Rome: L'Erma di Bretschneider.

Stern, E. M. 1997. "Glass and rock crystal: A multifaceted relationship," *Journal of Roman Archaeology* 10: 192–206.

Stern, E. M. 1998. "Interaction between glassworkers and ceramists," in McCray and Kingery 1998: 183–204.

Stern, E. M. 1999a. "Ancient glass in Athenian temple treasures," *Journal of Glass Studies* 41: 19–50.

Stern, E. M. 1999b. "Roman glassblowing in a cultural context," *American Journal of Archaeology* 103: 441–84.

Stern, E. M. 2000. "Three notes on early Roman mold-blown glass," *Journal of Glass Studies* 42: 165–67.

Stern, E. M. 2001. *Roman, Byzantine, and early medieval glass*. Ostfildern: Hatje Cantz.

Stern, E. M. 2002a. "The ancient glassblower's tools," in Kordas 2002: 159–65.

Stern, E. M. 2002b. "Glass for the gods," in Kordas 2002: 353–65.

Stern, E. M. 2004. "The glass *banausoi* of Sidon and Rome," in Beretta 2004a: 77–120.

Stern, E. M. 2005. "A la recherche de la première canne à souffler," *Instrumentum* 21: 15–18.

Stern, E. M., and B. Schlick-Nolte 1994. *Early glass of the ancient world, 1600 B.C.–A.D. 50*. Ostfildern: Verlag Gerd Hatje.

Sternini, M. 1995. *La fenice di sabbia: Storia e tecnologia del vetro antico*. Bari: Edipuglia.

Strano, G. 2004. "Glass and heavenly spheres: Astronomic refraction in Ptolemy's *Optics*," in Beretta 2004a: 121–34.

Thirion-Merle, V., et al. 2003. "Un nouvel atelier primaire dans le Wadi Natrun (Egypte), et les compositions des verres produits dans cette région," *Bulletin de l'Association française pour l'archéologie du verre* 11: 21–24.

Tolaini, F. 2004. "*De tinctio omnium musivorum*: Technical recipes for glass in the so-called *Mappae clavicula*," in Beretta 2004a: 195–219.

Triantaphyllides, P. 1998. "New evidence of the glass manufacture in classical and Hellenistic Rhodes," *Annales de l'Association Internationale pour l'Histoire du Verre* 14: 30–34.

Triantaphyllides, P. 2000. *Rodiakê Ualourgia*, Vol. 1: *Ta en thermôi diamorphômena diaphanê aggeia poluteleias*. Athens: *Upourgeio Aigaiou: kb' ephoreia proïstorikôn kai klasikôn archaiotêtôn*.

Triantaphyllides, P. 2001. "Achaemenian glass production," *Annales de l'Association Internationale pour l'Histoire du Verre* 15: 13–18.

Verità, M. 1995. "Le analisi dei vetri," in Foy 1995b: 291–300.

Weinberg, G. D. 1959. "Glass manufacture in ancient Crete: A preliminary study," *Journal of Glass Studies* 1: 10–21.

Weinberg, G. D. 1969. "Glass manufacture in Hellenistic Rhodes," *Archaiologikon Deltion* 24: 143–51.

Weinberg, G. D. 1972. "Mold-blown beakers with mythological scenes," *Journal of Glass Studies* 14: 26–47.

Weinberg, G. D. (ed.) 1988. *Excavations at Jalame: Site of a glass factory in Late Roman Palestine*. Columbia: University of Missouri Press.

Weinberg, G. D. 1992. *Glass vessels in ancient Greece*. Athens: Ministry of Culture, Archaeological Receipts Fund.

Wight, K. 1988. "Mythological beakers: Questions of provenance and production," *Annales de l'Association Internationale pour l'Histoire du Verre* 11: 71–76.

Yalçin, Ü., C. Pulak, and R. Slotta (eds.) 2005. *Das Schiff von Uluburun: Welthandel vor 3000 Jahren*. Bochum: Deutsches Bergbau-Museum.

PART V

TECHNOLOGIES
OF MOVEMENT
AND TRANSPORT

# CHAPTER 22

# LAND TRANSPORT, PART 1: ROADS AND BRIDGES

## LORENZO QUILICI

## THE STUDY OF ROMAN ROADS AND BRIDGES

The roads that the civilization of Rome created throughout the ancient world represented a political event of universal significance. It is sufficient to note that these structures still today often constitute the basis for the modern road system, not just in Italy and the countries around the Mediterranean, but also throughout Europe and the Middle East. Only the invention of modern paving techniques and the construction of limited-access highways resulted in additions to the ancient system. The public roads alone totaled an impressive 120,000 km throughout the Empire. The construction of such a vast, well-organized network, and its maintenance over a period of 800 years across the vast and varied territory ruled by Rome, constituted one of the foundations of public order; hundreds of millions of travelers made use of it, along with draft animals and vehicles—carrying goods and projecting ideas and power. The road network assisted the fusion of institutions, races, and cultures of the most diverse origins into the fertile synthesis that was imperial Roman culture. The roads are also a symbol of the Roman emphasis on public order and utility, *moles necessariae* ("indispensable structures") in contrast to the Egyptian pyramids, for example: *regum pecuniae otiosa et stulta ostentatio* ("the useless and stupid display of wealth by the Pharaohs"; Pliny, *HN* 36.75; cf.

Frontinus, *Aq.* 1.16). Strabo (5.3.8) praises the road system as part of the infra-structure of Roman imperial life: "The Romans gave particular attention to areas the Greeks neglected: paved roads, aqueducts, and sewers capable of washing the filth of the city out into the Tiber. Furthermore, they have also paved the roads in the countryside, adding both cuts through hills and viaducts across valleys so that wagons can take on a shipload." Dionysius of Halicarnassus, another historian of eastern Mediterranean origin, echoes these sentiments (*Ant. Rom.* 3.67.5): "The extraordinary greatness of the Roman Empire manifests itself above all in three things: the aqueducts, the paved roads, and the construction of the drains."

# PRE-ROMAN ROADS

This does not mean, of course, that the concept of a well-defined, paved road was a Roman invention. Even in Italy and the west there were well-defined routes of travel long before the spread of Roman rule. Note the ease and rapidity with which Caesar moved his forces around Gaul during the conquest of that region, and the use of preexisting trails and routes during the conquest of Spain and North Africa. Although Egypt could rely on the Nile as a convenient route of travel, already in the Bronze Age paved roads connected cities, sanctuaries, and necropoleis. Eratosthenes could not have calculated the circumference of the earth with such remarkable accuracy if he had not been able to depend on the careful measurement of the route between Alexandria and Syene (Aswan; Cleomedes 10). The level and treeless plains of the Tigris and Euphrates river valley facilitated land travel and fostered the earliest development of wheeled vehicles, but the Babylonian kings also prepared special processional roads for religious and political functions. The Assyrian kings projected their power across a large territory by sending their troops out on routes that often represented significant feats of engineering (Forbes 1965: 133–37; Dorsey 1997; Beitzel 1992). The "King's Highway" that can still today be followed from Damascus to Aqaba originated in the Bronze Age, as did the "Royal Road" or "Great Trunk Road" that follows the coastline of the Levant, connecting Egypt with Mesopotamia (Beitzel 1992: 778–79). In Greco-Roman traditions, however, the Royal Road across the Persian Empire enjoyed the greatest reputation among the pre-Roman road systems (Quilici 1989b; Beitzel 1992: 781–82; Chevallier 1997: 25–29). Significantly, this road alone benefited from an organizational infrastructure similar to what the Romans later provided. Herodotus described it (5.52–53):

> The nature of the road is as follows. All along it are royal rest stops and excellent
> lodgings, and the entire road runs through inhabited and safe country. . . . In
> all there are 111 stages with as many rest stops on the road going up from Sardis to
> Susa. If the Royal Road has been measured properly in *parasangs*, and the
> *parasang* is equivalent to 30 *stadia*, as it certainly is, then from Sardis to the royal

palace called Memnon the distance of 450 *parasangs* makes 13,500 *stadia* (ca. 2,600 km). And for people travelling at a rate of 150 *stadia* each day, just 90 days will be needed for the route.

The road was not paved, however, and Herodotus and Xenophon (*An.* 1.5.7) note the need to cross rivers at fords or on ferry boats, and the possibility of vehicles getting stuck in mud.

An extensive road network united the Mycenaean citadels and territories of the Greek mainland during the Late Bronze Age, including viaducts and bridges (Hope-Simpson and Hagel 2006), but after the fall of the palace system the political and economic factors that had supported the land routes no longer existed. By the classical period, the dangers and hardships Theseus suffered travelling the 125 km by land from Troizen to Athens had become the stuff of heroic legend. The worst part of this route was not fixed until the reign of Hadrian: "Originally, they say, the road from Megara to Corinth was made for travel by unencumbered and agile pedestrians, but the emperor Hadrian made it wider, and it was even suitable for chariots to pass each other when they met." (Pausanias 1.44.6). Typically, Greek routes for land travel were paths designed for mounted or foot traffic rather than wheeled vehicles. The one exception were the special "sacred roads" that connected many sanctuaries with their host city or a port: Athens and Eleusis, Sparta and Amyclae, and Elis and Olympia, for example (Forbes 1965: 140–45).

Given the opinion current even in antiquity that the Roman road system was a particularly extensive and well-developed example of that technology, this chapter will focus on the Roman accomplishment. Furthermore, given the enormous scope of the system, I will focus on the roads and bridges of the Italian peninsula. The literary sources and archaeological remains are particularly rich for this part of the system, and a focus on Italy also allows us to trace the earliest stages of its development and spread.

# THE VIA APPIA AND THE BEGINNINGS OF ROMAN ROAD CONSTRUCTION

The Via Appia, built in 312 B.C., represented a completely new approach to the networking of the landscape, not only because of the technologies involved but also in large part because of the historic and political aspects involved in the realization of its construction. In fact, it represented the affirmation of a rational design—even if at great cost—through areas considered very large at that time, where its route was impeded by natural obstacles and the territories of foreign states (figure 22.1). The design of the Via Appia can be compared to that of modern Italian autostradas: the ancient road did not aim at connecting even the important cities along

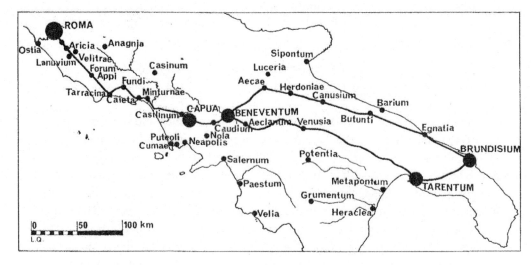

Figure 22.1. Route of the Via Appia from Rome to Brindisi. (L. Quilici.)

its path (such as Lanuvium and Velitrae), but they were accessed through branch roads. The road aimed as much as possible at the final, long-distance destination: Capua, in Appius Claudius Caecus' first realization (132 Roman miles, 196 km) (Castagnoli 1969: 78–96; Humm 2005: 133–44). For this reason, the route followed a series of perfectly straight lines, taking account only of narrow passages and passes enforced by the geomorphology of the territory traversed. There seems to have been little concern with any technical difficulties imposed by this approach, only to keep the route as short as possible. It is enough to mention the section from Rome to Terracina, a single straight line of almost 90 km, where the route crossed the Roman Campagna, the Alban Hills, and the vast area of the Pontine Marshes (Quilici 1990). The subsequent section was no less arduous, because of the presence of the mountains behind Terracina and Itri, the swamps and forests that surrounded Fondi, and the wide Garigliano and Volturno rivers (Quilici 1989a). The revolutionary character of this engineering undertaking is highlighted by the numerous challenges that were faced and surmounted: the topographic analysis of the territory to be traversed, the geological evaluation and surveys indispensable for the definition of the route, the requirement for enormous hydraulic projects for land reclamation within the region, the drainage and diversion of thousands of minor creeks, the impressive land excavations involved in opening trenches or cutting bedrock, the removal of excavated soil and the transport of materials for backfill and leveling, the completion of the support terracing for the road along both valley and mountainside, and the construction of bridges to cross large rivers.

With regard to the need for back-sights to verify the accuracy of survey over long distances, the completion of the straight line that runs between Rome and Terracina is technically significant. The back-sights were taken from the highest point along the route, at Colle Pardo near Ariccia, defining a straight line of 23 km toward Rome to the north, presumably with the temple of Diana on the Aventine as the target, and to the south a straight line of 61 km to Terracina, with the seaward cliff of Leano (near the Lucus Feroniae shrine) as the target, since its summit blocks the view of Terracina behind (Quilici 1990). These two sightlines differed in orientation by 5 degrees. Lewis (2001: 217–45) has reconstructed the instruments, procedures, and remarkable accuracy of Roman road surveying.

The creation of the Via Appia fostered the foundation of the colonies at Velitrae (Velletri) and Tarracina (Terracina) between 341 and 318 B.C. and the associated land reclamation works around those colonies, the Ufens River (Ufento) and the Ager Falernus in northern Campania (Quilici-Gigli 1983; Cancellieri 1990). Whether the reclamation and road works were contemporaneous or the road came later, it is notable how even at this early date the respective engineering projects could be coordinated. For a distance of almost 20 miles, from Tre Ponti to Amaseno, the substructures of the Via Appia served as one of the embankments of the transport and drainage canal fed by the Pontine Marshes. In the late first century B.C., Horace (*Sat.* 1.5.9–23; cf. Strabo 6.3.6) described a journey by passenger boat along this canal, which drained water from the flat plain toward the sea near Terracina (Quilici 1990: 55–57; see also chapter 12).

Appius Claudius' objective in laying out this route was military, focused on facilitating the rapid deployment of armies to the theater of operations in Campania, where the Second Samnite War was at its peak. This alternative was shorter than the tortuous itinerary of the ancient Via Latina inland along the Sacco and Liris valleys. The opening of the Via Appia, like that of all the roads that ultimately connected the city of Rome with the most distant borders of the empire, served as well as a conduit of Roman culture and Roman law, surmounting not only natural obstacles but also non-Roman ways of life. In consequence, these roads served as a technological metaphor for military triumph, and the magistrate who realized each project had the privilege of giving it his name. Triumphal arches were often placed at the beginning and end of a road, at the entrance to cities, and on the most grandiose bridges.

Originally, the Via Appia had only a gravel surface. Livy comments (9.29.6) that Appius Claudius "protected the road" (*viam munivit*), which implies something less than stone paving, and the *Elogium* to Appius in the Forum of Augustus simply uses the term *stravit* ("surfaced"; *CIL* 11.1827), which is ambiguous. Elsewhere, however, Livy (10.23.12) states that the first mile of the Via Appia, from the Porta Capena to the Temple of Mars, was paved "with dressed stone blocks" (*saxo quadrato*) in 296 B.C., and that in 293 B.C. the next 12 miles, from the Temple of Mars to Bovillae, were paved *silice*, "with basalt paving stone" (10.47.4). Livy also reports (38.28.3) that a century later the first mile was repaved *silice*, suggesting that the first paving material had been blocks of soft volcanic tuff.

We know in general the design and structure of the roadbed, as it still for the most part exists today as far as Capua. The paving, composed of polygonal basalt blocks, is consistently 4.1–4.2 m wide (14 Roman feet), a width that easily allowed two carriages to pass each other going in opposite directions (cf. Procopius, *Goth.* 1.14).

The pavement had a camber so that rainwater would flow to the curbs on either side. These were made of upright slabs and framed sidewalks made of packed gravel, which varied in width from 1.1 m to 3.0 m depending on the anticipated traffic. Upright blocks were built into the curb every 3 to 5 m, to prevent wheeled vehicles from riding up on the sidewalks and to assist travelers in mounting their pack animals. Milestones were also placed along the road, to record distances and the authorities responsible for paving or other improvements. The oldest known milestone on the Via Appia, found at mile LIII ("53," near Mesa) dates to 253/5 B.C. (*CIL* 10.6838).

The road was built by setting the curb stones, then excavating the earth between them until a firm base was reached. A layer of large diameter gravel was then laid in the cavity (essentially a long trench), and compacted to create the foundation for the structure (*rudus*). A layer of finer gravel was then added (*nucleus*), and the wedge-shaped bases of the polygonal basalt blocks that formed the pavement (*summum dorsum*) were firmly seated in this material. The partial renovation of the original paving of the Via Appia was recorded on milestones: those of Nerva between the Colli Albani and the Pontine Marshes, those of Trajan farther along by the 20-mile-long canal embankment (Di Vita-Evrad 1990), and one of Caracalla between Terracina and Formia (Quilici 2004: 541–42). It is particularly interesting that this last milestone specifies that the new basalt pavement replaced a worn-out limestone pavement (*CIL* 10.6854). This sequence has been documented archaelogically also for the stretch through the Pontine Marshes prior to Trajan and in the section beyond Fondi (Quilici 1990: 58–60; 2002: 139–40).

Even more interesting is archaeological evidence along the Pontine and Itri segments of a far more ancient phase of the road, where the road was surfaced only with gravel, in accordance with the literary sources. The first segment of the road consisted of an embankment with a double, stepped slope 6.6 m wide, reinforced by pilings in the marsh and contained on the sides by rectangular blocks, for a total width of 10.5 m (Quilici 1990: 55–60). In the segment by Itri there is a graveled foundation 9.5 m wide, in between terracing of polygonal blocks (Quilici 2002: 113, 124). These could be traces of the original road work.

The Via Appia, built as far as Capua by Appius Claudius when he was censor in 312 B.C., despite the elimination of the Samnites—to assist whose defeat it had been conceived—was extended to the Roman colony of Beneventum after its foundation in 268 B.C. following the Roman victory in the war against Pyrrhus. The road was then carried on to Venosa, a Latin colony since 291 B.C. After the final subjugation of Tarentum in 272 B.C. and the conversion of Brundisium (Brindisi) into a Latin colony around 240 B.C., the road was brought as far as the latter port, which subsequently took a leading role in the overseas conquests. The overall length of the road from Rome to Brundisium was 385 Roman miles, 569 km (Mazzarino 1969: 109–12; Quilici 1989a: 2:42–62).

No Roman road, perhaps no ancient road, had the same celebrity and importance as the Via Appia. It connected the most flourishing cities of central Italy with southern Italian ports that harbored vessels leaving for Greece, Egypt, and the Levant. It became, in fact, not only the most important road for military expeditions, but also a route of fundamental importance for commercial and cultural interchange. By communicating with the seaport of Puteoli (Pozzuoli), the closest protected anchorage to Rome, which lacked a proper harbor until A.D. 50, the Via Appia formed an important link with Africa. Because these regions were the most developed and prosperous in the Mediterranean, the network was always monitored with particular care by the authorities. As its land base, the road received special attention, and was termed "Queen of roads" (*Regina viarum*; Statius, *Sil.* 2.2.11), a paradigm for all the roads that connected Rome with the most remote regions of the known world.

For obvious reasons, the road was always maintained scrupulously until the very late Imperial age, and over time various improvements and restorations kept and enhanced its efficiency. Of particular note are the great terraces and retaining walls intended to stabilize the course of the road, and the bridges whose varied designs provide evidence of the commitment to the preservation of the the road's efficiency. In the countryside near Velletri, the Ponte di Mele is a primitive bridge, possibly dating back to the original construction of the road. It was partially cut into the bedrock and has a massive vault built of square blocks of tuff, with a span of 3.6 m (Quilici 1991a). The Ponte Alto bridge, in the last stretch of the road through the Pontine Marshes, was built of limestone during the first half of the second century B.C., 6 m wide with a span of 6.1 m (Lugli 1928: 58). The most spectacular roadwork is the viaduct at Ariccia, built at the end of the second century B.C. to carry the road over the steep valley slope at a low gradient. The structure (8.2–9.0 m wide at the top, 230 m long) consists of two massive walls up to 13 m high, built of blocks of volcanic tuff laid as headers and stretchers, that retain concrete fill. Four vaulted openings allowed the passage of transverse traffic and the flow of the water (Lilli 2002: 235–85).

An example of improvements and repairs can be seen in the mountain gorges near Itri, where the road is supported by impressive walls hundreds of meters long and up to 14 m tall, built in various techniques involving stone blocks and concrete that date from the fourth to the third century B.C. (Quilici 2002). Pullover areas, sometimes with services for travelers and animals, lightened the traffic along the difficult uphill stretches, such as the pass at Terracina and in the Aurunci Mountains (Lugli 1926: 181–209; Quilici 2004). Trajan built a marvelous series of bridges, in a refined style of elegant limestone blocks with bossing, along the canal in the Pontine Marshes. At Tre Ponti, in modern Fàiti, the Maggiore and Antico bridges, from 6.35 to 13 m wide, remain very solid and still support the intense flow of traffic; the third bridge has been destroyed (Quilici 1989a: 2:8–17). The complex is approximately 45 m long, the central part composed of two segmental arches with spans of 5.5–5.7 m, their height intentionally kept low to minimize the central peak; the central pier is only 1.2 m thick, involving techniques that can be seen well developed in bridges in the Veneto. Ponte Maggiore, which crosses the river Ufente, was built with a semicircular arch with a height of 10.5 m, to allow effective navigation beneath. The cutting across the face of Pisco Montano at Terracina, commonly attributed to Trajan, is a spectacular accomplishment. To avoid the steep ascent over the crags of Anxur, the limestone cliff face was cut back along the seashore, leaving a vertical cutting up to 36 m high, and allowing passage of the road around the obstacle just above sea level (Lugli 1926: 209–12). Large Roman numerals cut into the artificial cliff proudly record the progress of the excavation from top to bottom, at intervals of 10 Roman feet, finishing with CXX (120).

Other bridges neatly built in stone for Trajan are preserved just before Bene-vento (Quilici 1989a: 2:46–49). Concurrently with the magnificent series of stone bridges that Trajan built as he renovated the Via Appia, it is notable that bridges were constructed as well in a new technique, modeled on the brick arcades of aqueducts, and the bridge built over the Volturno River by Domitian 15 years before to connect the Via Appia with Cuma (see below). In order to impede erosion by the river, the foundations and piers were built completely of stone blocks, while the elevation was built of concrete, with a double course of bricks over the arches, which had spans of 14–15 m. There were also spectacular viaducts, such as those over the Cervaro and Carapelle Rivers, which kept the road level while crossing the river valleys; they are 320 m and 700 m long, respectively, with seventeen and ten central arches (Ashby and Gardner 1916; Quilici 1989a: 2:63–83; Mertens 1993). The design of the Hadrianic bridge-viaduct Ponte Rotto on the Via Appia over the Calore north of Eclano, is a further example of the evolution of the techniques of road and bridge construction during the Imperial age; it was almost 200 m long and up to 13–14 m high, with eight arches of which the central six had spans of 13.2–13.7 m (Quilici 1996b: 274–87).

# The Major Roman Roads in Italy

Just as the Via Appia represented the main artery for southern Italy, the Via Flaminia, built by the censor Gaius Flaminius between 220 and 219 B.C., served as the main artery for the northern part of the peninsula. With the purpose of colonizing the *ager Gallicus*, which included territories from Ancona to Rimini, he made this latter city the outpost for the conquest of the Po Valley (Ashby and Fell: 1921; Luni 1993; Messineo 1991; Bonomi 1993; Esch 1997: 59–90). The Via Aemilia, marked out around 175 B.C. by the consul M. Aemilius Lepidus, extended the road system to Bologna, which he had founded in 187 B.C. This urban center was destined to become the communications node for all northern Italy, and the road system for the territories at the head of the Adriatic Sea branched off from it. The Via Aemilia extended from Bologna to Aquileia, founded in 181 B.C. In 148 B.C. the consul Sp. Postumius marked out the Via Postumia from Aquileia to Genoa, passing through Verona and Cremona. In 132 B.C. the consul P. Popilius con-structed the Via Popilia from Rimini through Ravenna to Padova, improving a connection already marked out by the consul T. Annis in 153 B.C. (figure 22.2; De Feo 1997; Cera 2000; Postumia 2000; Quilici 2000; Annia 2004; Pellegrini 2004).

Figure 22.2. The roads of ancient Italy. (L. Quilici.)

The inextricable interrelationships among military activity, colonization, trade, and road building are clear in this region.

During the third and second centuries B.C., other roads penetrated deeply into the former Etruscan territories north of Rome. Along the seacoast, the Via Aurelia was built as far as the colony of Cosa, founded in 273 B.C., then on to Luni, founded in 177 B.C., and finally in 109 it was extended through the territories of Liguria to Genoa and Vado. Three other roads, the Viae Amerina, Clodia, and Cassia, penetrated the heartland of Etruria, already thoroughly urbanized in the sixth century B.C. on routes that date back to at least the same period. The Via Cassia was particularly important; it lead through Sutri to Volsinii (re-founded near Bolsena in 264 B.C.), then on to Chiusi and Arezzo, which gave access to the passes over the Apennines, and finally to Florence, founded in the mid-first century B.C. (Frederiksen and Ward Perkins 1957; Aurelia 1968; Degrassi 1982–1984, 1984–1985; Quilici 1989b; Esch 1997: 26–58; Talbert et al. 2000: 39–43).

In southern Italy, after the extension of Via Appia to Brindisi, the Via Popilia was built through to Reggio Calabria. Initially by T. Annius and finished by P. Popilius, both of whom were patrons of roads in the Po Valley (Burckhardt 1988: 41–46; Givigliano 1994: 287–318).

These roads, projected into the regions as the primary vehicle of civic life and economic progress, came to characterize the regions to such an extent that the name of the road could be used to indicate the territory itself: "are you departing to [the region served by] the Via Aurelia, or to Campania?" (*utrumque in Aureliam an in Campaniam abisti*; Fronto, *Ep.* 4.4.2, van den Hout ed.). The gloss on this passage (5.423.26) explains this phrase as "Aurelia is the region or the province." (*Aurelia terra est vel provincia*). In this way, referring to the road as synonymous of the places being crossed, the phrase *per Flaminiam* meant Picenum (*CIL* 6.1509), and still today the region Emilia takes its name from the ancient road (Cicero, *Fam.* 10.30.4; Martial 3.4). During the empire, the renovation and expansion of the road network took place on a grand scale. It is significant that already during the reign of Augustus, the inscription on his arch at Rimini contains the line "the numerous roads of Italy, sustained by his planning and authority" (*celeberrimeis Italiae vieis, consilio et auctoritate eius muniteis*; *CIL* 11.365). The emperor was in many ways synonymous with the means of land travel and transport, the network of roads that bound many parts of the empire together.

## DESIGN AND LAYOUT OF ROMAN ROADS

The Via Appia immediately became a model for the construction of new roads and the renovation of existing routes. The Via Latina, renovated soon after construction of the Via Appia, departed Rome with a series of amazing straight stretches, the first one 15 km long, and subsequently passed diagonally across the Alban Hills and entered the Sacco valley with decisive straight lines (Quilici 1990: 52–56; Caiazza 1995: 13–80). The straight-line configuration became the pattern, seen on stretches of the Via Aurelia 15 km and 30 km long through the flat land seaward of Cerveteri and Tarquinia (Aurelia 1968: 121–39). The 242-km route of the Via Aemilia from the Rubicon to Piacenza could even be considered a single straight line, and in the plains of the Cisalpine region there were many straight stretches along the Via Popilia, Via Annia, and Via Postumia (Bosio 1991; Calzolari 1992; Esch 1997: 26–58; Talbert et al. 2000: 39–42; Cera 2000). In hilly ground, at least, the straight stretch of road makes more sense as a pathway for fast-marching foot soldiers, or as a metaphor of domination and control, than as a cost-effective route for wheeled vehicles drawn by animals.

Despite their apparent simplicity, the longer straight stretches of road represent a triumph of accurate surveying, in that they usually imply an ability to calculate the direct line between two points out of sight of each other (Lewis 2001: 217–45). The Via Flaminia, as early as the third century B.C., is an excellent example of a road project that was planned and marked out rapidly over the very long distance of 213 miles (by the Augustan calculation; cf. *CIL* 11.6635): 314 km from the Tyrrhenian to the Adriatic Sea, through the territories of Veii, the Faliscans, Umbrians, and Picenes. The route was coordinated from south to north with a particular geological formation of the Apennine mountain chain that does not involve the typical parallel ridges that anywhere else make passage from sea to sea difficult. In Umbria the mountains bend like an arch, allowing easy communication to the north. The maximum height along the Via Flaminia, at the pass of Scheggia near Bevagna, is only 572 m above sea level, allowing descent to the Adriatic. An alternate route through Spoleto involves an ascent to the pass at Somma, at 869 m above sea level. The most difficult routes of passage were the valleys of Narni and Furlo, later made accessible by Augustus' bridge over the Nera, and Vespasian's tunnel (Grewe 1998: 129–35). The Roman road engineers clearly were able not only to evaluate the details of the landscape, but also to envision it on a very large scale and to choose the most effective routing.

What techniques were used to define these routes? We have already seen their model in the the Via Appia. The routing of such roads, or rather their potential plan and elevation, required a variety of skills in geometry and surveying. The Latin terms commonly used in the context of road construction are *viam innovare*, or *instituere*, *munire, sternere, struere*, which—depending on the context—might be interpreted as "to renew," or "lay out," "build," "pave," "construct," or "surface" a road, respectively. We can recognize the criteria for design and construction in the roads branching off from Rome and in the long straight stretches on well-documented roads such as the Via Salaria, Flaminia, Aemilia, and Postumia, or the road in the Valle d'Aosta. The axis of the straight stretches was marked directly on the ground, establishing on site where the road had to pass, including the intermediate destinations, but without excluding the possibility of corrections or improvements. The terrain to be crossed was evaluated: the nature of the soil and subsoil, its exposure, and the obstacles to be surmounted or avoided. The construction of the road required not only cuttings, bridges, viaducts, and tunnels, but also sewers, sinkholes, ditches, and drainage canals, along with structures designed to protect the roadbed from rainfall or ground water, falling rocks, and landslips, and—in higher elevations—from snow.

The mountain routes make particularly evident the effort of the Romans to overcome so many difficulties, and every element was studied to facilitate safe transit by man, beast, and vehicles. An amazing example is the Via Salaria in the high valleys of the Velino and Tronto. The road stays well above the river, which is very dangerous because of the floods, and passes the steep-walled gorge on a continuous shelf, partly excavated into the bedrock with cuttings up to 18 m high on the inside face, and supported on the outside by retaining walls 5–6 m high built of rectangular or polygonal blocks. The road itself varied in width from 4.5 to 6 m, with occasional stopping areas from 8 to 12 m wide. Some of these works date to the Republic, others to the empire, particularly the later first and early second century (Conta 1982: 337–402; Quilici 1993: 130–44). Also remarkable is the astonishing itinerary of the Via Flaminia through the valley of Burano, the descent from the pass over the Apennines to Metauro. The road enters the valley from the top with extraordinary rapidity and audacity; it descends almost headlong down the slopes then follows straight along the very tortuous gorge by means of imposing cliffside terraces, now flanking the river that laps against the lines of spectacular retaining walls, crossing the river time and again to cut off curves and shorten the distance, without economizing on bridges and cuttings, until its path exits the gorge of Furlo (Luni 1993; Gaggiotti 2004).

The difficult alpine passes have also preserved evidence of the amazing skill and determination of the Roman engineers. Augustus' road up the Valle d'Aosta, through the passes of the Small and the Great Saint Bernard, is emblematic: a road of extraordinary interest for the technical solutions employed, imposing itself on the conformation of the very tricky mountain slopes with viaducts hundreds of meters long, the foundations for their walls cut in the bedrock, and cuttings in the mountainsides up to 12 to 13 m high. The blocks extracted from the cuts were used in the supporting walls of the terraces on the valley side of the road, up to 16 m high, polygonal or regular stone blocks facing a concrete core. The walls were reinforced with buttresses and spur walls, placed at various heights to fit into the irregularities of the rocks, and blind arches set up over clefts and brooks. Spectacular bridges carried the road over gorges. The route was planned to keep above the potential flood level of the Dora and for the most part followed the left side of the valley, to have a favorable exposure, fundamental in an environment with weather characterized for most of the year by frost and snow. The slope was kept around 7 percent; 10 percent was the maximum. The width of the pavement was 4.4–4.75 m, and increased to more than 5 m in the most arduous passes, where it was flanked by areas that allowed stops or permitted vehicles to pass each other. The most difficult passes had ruts cut in the bedrock road surface to guide the wheels of the carriages, along with corrugations to provide traction to the animal hooves. The masterpiece of the road was the spectacular cut at Donaz, 222 m long and almost 13 m high, monumentalized by an arch and by a milestone carved in the rock (Mollo Mezzana 1992).

# CONSTRUCTION AND PAVING

Today, the Roman roads on most of the routes through Etruria, Latium, and Campania typically are paved with polygonal basalt blocks, which can be quarried in those regions. Elsewhere, considerations of practicality and economy enforced other sources, such as limestone in the Apennine Mountains. The Via Appia was paved with basalt as far as Capua, after which it was paved with limestone blocks (Pagano 1978; Carfora 2001; Zevi 2004: 875–77). Paved roads such as these reveal a constant width of 4.1–4.2 m (14 Roman feet), a canonical measure for the long-distance or high-volume roads, but often found as well on the secondary roads (figure 22.3). This standard dimension dominates road design from the first decades of the fourth century B.C. (Lugli 1957: 192–93). Even if the paved area of a road had the canonical width of 4.1 m, in particularly busy sections these dimensions could be expanded considerably. But the real, complete capacity of the road included also sidewalks for pedestrians, normally 3 m wide on each side, giving the road a total width of 10.2 m. While the road pavement was seldom reduced to less than 4.1 m, the sidewalks could even be decreased notably or even omitted.

Some paved roads, such as the Via Cassia as far as Volsinii, had a width of 3.8–3.9 m (13 Roman feet?). Although normally around 4.1–4.2 m in width, the paving of the Via Nomentana, Via Tiburtina, and Via Latina occasionally present the reduced dimensions of 3.8–3.9 m. The Via Valeria, in its original ascent of the hill of Arsoli, had a width of 3.6 m; this dimension seems to be related to a pre-Roman, Osco-Italic foot (of ca. 0.257 m?), 14 of which add up to the width of this paving. This foot could have remained in use during the middle Republic even after the diffusion of the Roman foot system, and it could even have been preserved fortuitously during renovation of the original paving (Quilici 1989b: 478–82; 1992: 26–30).

Livy's comments concerning the Via Appia in 293 B.C. (quoted above) suggest that the application of stone paving must have increased starting from the beginning of that century. The change may, however, have been gradual, since Livy also notes (41.27.5) that between 194 and 174 B.C., the censors let contracts "first of all for the roads within the city of Rome to be paved with basalt blocks, and those outside the city to be founded on gravel, and that they be given proper curbing, and that bridges should be constructed in many locations . . ." (*vias sternendas silice in Urbe, glarea extra Urbem, substruendas marginandasque primi omnium locaverunt, pontesque multis locis faciendos . . .*).

During the Augustan Age, when the literary and monumental sources celebrate the restoration of the great highways, other literary sources and inscriptions inform us as well about the commitment of private individuals to the paving or repair of local streets—such as Messalla Corvinus' road in the territory of Tusculum and the Via Mactorina between Velletri and the sea (Quilici 1992: 31). In this period the use of stone paving was general on both main and secondary road routes. Throughout the Roman suburbs, meaning all the region including Monti Tiburtini and Prenestini, Colli Albani, and Sabatini as far as the sea, all the roads, even those less important, were paved during the Imperial period (Quilici 1974b).

The infrastructure for the road system was, in general, that already outlined for the Via Appia. Nevertheless, when less firm ground had to be crossed, in particular sandy or flooded areas, the roadbeds were supported with more powerful fill and foundations, and by embankments with massive walls of cut stone or concrete. For example, through the flat land beyond the Milvian Bridge, the pavement of the Via

Figure 22.3. Paving of the Via Praenestina. (L. Quilici.)

Flaminia was laid over a foundation of building debris over 1 m thick and contained between walls of tuff blocks or concrete (Messineo 1991: 68, 72, 122) (figure 22.4). Because the Via Tiburtina, when passing the area of the Acque Albule, was subjected from time to time to the calcium carbonate deposits typical of those waters, it frequently had to be repaved. Excavation revealed four separate stone pavements over a height of 2.5 m, contained on the sides by deeply based walls 2.23 m wide, built of stone blocks or concrete.

## Via Ostiense

In order to understand better how this kind of technical intervention evolved over time, it will be useful to examine in detail some roads that went through such phases. Among the roads best documented by literary and archaeological sources is the Via Ostiense. After the restoration that followed the First Punic War, documented by milestone XI (*CIL* 6.31585), it was characterized by magnificent straight lines between the curves of Tiber and the hills to the east (Fischer-Hansen 1990: 35–38). In this epoch, the road was graveled, with a width of 6.1–6.9 m framed by blocks of volcanic tuff, and including magnificent engineering works such as the

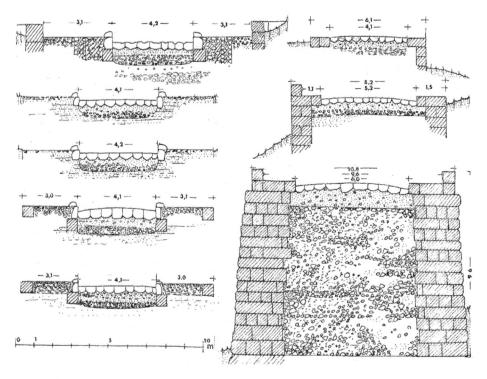

Figure 22.4. Section of the Via Flaminia between milestones VI and XXXII, from the Tomba dei Nasoni to the Muro del Peccato on the Treia. (L. Quilici.)

viaducts of Ponte Ladrone and Guardapasso in Acilia. The former, approximately 40 m long, with 12 arches 2.2–2.3 m in height, separated by powerful, buttressed piers of tuff blocks, crossed a small, steep-walled valley. The Guardapasso viaduct, 300 m long, with sides built of stone blocks pierced by vaulted drains, had arched buttress walls inside the foundation mound. The Via Ostiense may have been paved with stone during the Sullan period (early first century B.C.), when notable bridges were built. Moreover, the viaduct that carried the road through the boggy salt flats around Ostia can be dated to the second century B.C. This viaduct, 6.4 m wide, was framed by walls built of four courses of regular tuff blocks and reinforced with external buttresses. The interior fill consisted of a layer of crushed tuff 1.4 m thick, over a layer of river gravel 0.50 m thick, on a concrete base that was supported by oak pilings (Quilici 1996a).

## Via Salaria

The very old Via Salaria, which followed the left bank of the Tiber north of Rome, was originally surfaced with gravel, but it was paved with basalt presumably during the late Republican or Augustan period, at the canonical width of 4.1 m, supplemented by sidewalks flanked by drainage ditches. The gravel surface was kept even during the Imperial age on the portion of the route from Eretum past Rieti and as far as the pass of the Alto Velino in the Apennines. The width varied from 6.0 to 6.6 m between curbs built of one or more courses of limestone or travertine blocks, laid lengthwise, with an occasional header block keyed into the road's foundation. Although there may have been renovations, this configuration of the Via Salaria should date back to the period after the conquest of the Sabines by M'. Curius Dentatus in 290 B.C, with the concession to the region of *civitas sine suffragio* and then *optimo iure* in 268 B.C. During these years the road had to be radically renovated and made more efficient, since it was an important key to the new territorial arrangements. A precise date can be established for the Ponte Diavolo, which monumentalizes the entrance of the road into the territory of Trebula Mutuesca, just after the mid-second century B.C. The Via Salaria also underwent renovations during the late Republic, in the form of massive viaducts built after the earthquake of 76 B.C. at Rieti to ease the difficult approaches to the Ponte Sambuco. These ramps were about 64 m long and 5–7 m high, each perforated by a single arch with a span of only 3.7 m. Another viaduct, built of stone blocks with a series of arches with spans 5–6 m wide, gave access to the elevated city of Rieti (Quilici 1993, 1994).

## Via Domitiana

Laid out along the coast south of Sinuessa in A.D. 95 to connect the Via Appia with Puteoli (Pozzuoli), the Via Domitiana is a good example of a major road paved with stone from its first creation. The road was built over a short period of time, which is well documented by the surviving remains, and its construction was described carefully but with poetic drama by Statius (*Sil.* 4.3.40–55). Remarkably, this is the only technical description of road construction remaining to us from antiquity. The road is depicted as a new creation by an imperial patron, through marshes and vast forests and across large rivers such as the Volturnus. The description begins with the initial survey work, then the excavation for the foundations of the road, finally the construction of the roadbed itself. The associated tasks of quarrying, lumbering, and drainage are described as well, and—significantly—even the amount of time travelers saved by using the new road:

> The emperor Domitian, vexed at the slow journeys of his people and at the plains that lengthen a trip, banished the long windings and solidified the troublesome sand with a new construction. . . . Here the dejected traveler, carried on a single axle, once swayed back and forth on the swinging carriage pole, while the wicked earth sucked at the wheels, and the landlocked Latin people shuddered at the hazards of a sea voyage. . . . But now a journey that used to wear away a solid day is completed in scarcely two hours. . . .
>
> The first labor was to dig ditches and to cut out the borders of the road and to excavate the ground within to a great depth; next to fill in the emptied ditches with other materials and to prepare the interior for the high ridge of the road, so

that neither would the soil give way nor a treacherous foundation provide an unstable bed for the paving stones under the pressure of traffic; finally, to bind the road with blocks close-set on either side and with packed polygonal pavers. Oh, how many gangs are at work at the same time! This group cuts down forests and clears the mountains, another group smoothes stakes and fashions beams with iron tools; another binds the rocks and weaves together the work with lime and dusty pozzolana; still another group dries up the thirsty pools and draws the smaller streams far away by their labor.

The bridge over the Volturnus, also celebrated in Statius' poem (*Sil.* 4.3.67–100), was a boldly conceived structure with at least twelve arches, with elegant double voussoir courses of bricks facing a concrete core, and piers in mixed stone and brickwork (Crimaco 1991: 39). This bridge may represent the appearance of new engineering techniques and may have served as a model for the bridges engineers constructed for Trajan and Hadrian along the Via Appia.

## Gravel Roads

Despite the prominence of stone-paved roads in the archaeological record, roads surfaced with well-packed gravel, sometime with the addition of lime, were the most common type of local and even long-distance roads. There are archaeologically well-dated examples linked to the colonial foundations of the second half of the third and the beginning of the second century B.C. associated with the city/harbor pairs Caere/Pyrgi, Tarquinia/Gravisca, and Cosa/Heba. These routes vary in width from 10.2 to 13.6 m and were framed by curbs of stone blocks. The Tarquinia/Gravisca road was characterized by a line of blocks along its central axis, either to divide the road into lanes or to reinforce the marked camber. The Cosa/Heba road was characterized by a central path 3.9 m wide for vehicles, flanked by prominent sidewalks 4.4 and 5.3 m wide (Quilici 1989b: 460–61). It has been shown above that even major roads such as the Via Appia and Via Ostiense originally were not paved, or that stone paving was only laid on the first portion of the road, as on the Via Salaria. Even the other major roads that radiated from Rome were paved for varying distances, after which the surface became gravel. The Via Flaminia was not paved beyond Narni. The Via Aemilia, Via Popilia, Via Annia, Via Postumia, and even the Via Appia Traiana were gravel-surfaced for their entirety.

Roads did tend to be paved through cities and their immediate vicinity, where suburbs and cemeteries were concentrated. Roads might be paved when crossing a *vicus* (small village), in front of a *mansio* (rest house), or even in front of a particularly monumental villa or mausoleum, thanks to the euergetism of the owner. The Via Appia Traiana, for example, was paved through the cities it crossed, and on the bridges it was surfaced with small cobbles. The Via Popilia, normally graveled, was paved with trachite blocks from 4 km before Ravenna and for at least 2 km beyond it, 10 m and 9 m wide, respectively (Maccagnani 1994: 77–79). This pattern can also be seen on the Via Aemilia. An intermediate stage or economical alternative around minor population centers involved the construction of parallel wheel tracks, 0.10–0.30 m wide and 0.20–0.25 m thick, with deposits of stones from adjacent rivers (Ortalli 2000: 87–88; Quilici 2000: 127–30).

The foundation embankment that can still be traced for much of the Via Aemilia has been sectioned at several points and has provided evidence even for the initial road profile of 187 B.C. Originally, the road was laid out directly on the ground, normally with a width of 6 m, with lateral ditches for drainage: the ground between was excavated, and a foundation laid down of pebbles compacted with clay or sand, then raised 1–2 m above the original ground level with alternating layers of gravel, mud, and sand with lime. During the renovations of the late Republic, the foundation was rebuilt in more or less the same technique, but the width was enlarged from 6 to 7.5 m. The side ditches and drain of the clayey subsoil of crushed rock or brick were renovated in the Julio-Claudian period, or often rebuilt by means of lines of broken or intact amphoras in a disposition orthogonal to the street. In its manifestation during the Empire, the road surface, composed of layers of tamped gravel partly cemented with sand and lime, had a marked camber. The road and foundation embankment reached 2 to 4 m in height and a width on the top of 10–11 m, even 12 m during Late Antiquity (Marini-Calvani 1992; Ortalli 2000; Quilici 2000: 130–32).

The Via Aemilia represented the standard of the graveled roads of the Po Valley and the Veneto. Among those that we know best, the Via Sarsinate must be noted, which descends from the crest of the Apennines into the valley of Savio as far as Cesena, then continued through the flat plain toward Ravenna. The structure has been well documented around Sarsina. The simple layer of gravel laid down in the Republican period was replaced during the early Empire with a clayey embankment 4.2–4.8 m wide, built over an excavated foundation. The roadway was 3.4 m wide, with a slightly cambered roadbed made of well-seated flat cobbles, fixed with lime, gravel, sand, and grit. On the valley side there was a compacted earth sidewalk 0.8–1.4 m wide outlined by a cobblestone border, while the uphill side was flanked by a shallow trench 2 m wide that protected the road from water running down the slope (Ortalli 1992: 152–56).

Numerous graveled roads are known in the Veneto, on elevated foundation mounds and flanked by ditches. The Via Postumia, from Lagonzo north to Altino, had a base up to 32 m wide supporting a road from 6 to 10 m wide, and up to 7 m above ground level. The other road, called Arzeron of the Queen, north of Padova, has a base 30–36 m wide supporting a packed gravel road 18 m wide, up to 4 m above ground level. This foundation consists of clayey materials laid over gravel and brick ballast that guaranteed drainage. The practice of providing drainage fields composed of rocks or broken bricks beneath a clay road foundation is well documented in all of Padania and in Veneto. In particularly swampy areas, vertical and horizontal support posts were used in the sub-foundation, and planks or bundles of sticks. Near Adria, the Via Popilia was built on a high foundation mound of rocks, which was placed on a sub-foundation of concrete, laid in turn over thick oak pilings (Bosio 1991; Rosada 1992; Galliazzo 1994; Basso et al. 2004; Cerchiaro 2004).

# BRIDGES

No surviving bridges built of stone in Italy can be dated securely before the beginning of the second century B.C., a period of grandiose and innovative construction activity during which the use of the arch rapidly became commonplace and was used as well for bridging water courses. The first fundamental reference point appears to be the Pons Aemilius in Rome, which historical sources record as being built with a wooden superstructure on stone piers in 179 B.C. In 142 B.C. it received stone arches. In its final form the bridge was 135 m long, 8.9 wide, constructed of tuff blocks with six semicircular arches spanning 14.5–16.5 m (Galliazzo 1994: 18–20). It is likely that a structure on such a scale, over a major river, was the result of a very long period of experiment and practical experience. Whatever the background, by the first half of the second century B.C. bridges were being constructed on a large scale, completely of stone blocks held together with iron clamps, the voussoirs and extrados of the arches forming smooth curves (O'Connor 1993). By the second half of the century the stone-block facing was often backed by a concrete core. It is notable that these bridges rarely have wide spans, and the piers are thick in relation to the span of the arches in order to withstand their force.

The oldest bridges, dating back to the first half of the second century B.C., are those already mentioned along the Via Appia, near Velletri and on the Pontine Marshes, together with the Archi of S. Lidano. The latter bridge, 4.4 m wide and constructed of limestone blocks with iron clamps, incorporated three semicircular arches, the central one spanning 5.3 m, the side arches spanning 4.4 m. (Lilli 1996). Another early example is the small bridge under Ponte Nona on the Via Prenestina, 4.6 m wide with a span of 5.8 m, which must be earlier than the structure built on top of it around 100 B.C. (Galliazzo 1994: 40–44). From the beginning of the second century there were also spectacular viaducts, like those already mentioned on the Via Ostiense and, in the second half of the century, the large stone block structure on the Via Aurelia right after the Pons Aemilia that bypassed the bogs along the right bank of the Tiber. This viaduct was at least 65 m long and 5.9 m wide, rose more than 5 m above contemporary ground level, and was supported by 11 or 12 semicircular arches with 3 m spans and piers 2.35 m thick. These proportions resemble those of a contemporary arcade of the Aqua Marcia (Gatti 1940), reminding us of the necessary interchange among engineers of information regarding designs and materials. The spectacular viaduct on the Via Appia at Ariccia (mentioned above) can be compared with the Muro del Peccato on the Via Flaminia in the valley of Treia. This structure, 250–300 m long and up to 9.6 m high, climbing 45 m over its length, had two framing walls of tuff blocks laid as headers and stretchers and a fill of gravel and earth; the body of the structure tapers in width from 13 m at the base to 10.8 m at the level of the road (figure 22.4; Ashby and Fell 1921: 158–60; Quilici 1989b: 499–502).

Two nearly identical bridges on the Via Aurleia in S. Marinella, south of Civitavecchia, can be dated to just after the mid-second century B.C. They have powerful courses of bossed limestone voussoirs, originally with iron clamps, and an independent core of concrete; their widths are 7.2 m and 6.2 m, with spans of 4.4 m and 6.6 m, respectively (Favilla 1996). Another work of the same age is the Ponte della Catena in Cori (Galliazzo 1994: 81), which, like some contemporary city gates, has an arch composed of two superimposed voussoir courses. Once again, identical construction techniques can be seen in very different types of engineering projects.

A particularly impressive bridge from this period is the Ponte Milvio, which was built in 109 B.C. to carry the Via Flaminia over the Tiber north of Rome. It is nearly 150 m long and 7.2–7.7 m wide; in addition to the small arches of the access ramps, there are four major arches with spans of 18–18.5 m. An advanced characteristic is that the arches are segmental (slightly less than semicircles in form), allowing wider spans with respect to the rise in the structure. The piers, which are prow-shaped on the upstream side, carry small open arches meant to allow the passage of water during particularly high flood levels and thus relieve stress on the structure. The piers and outer courses of the arches are built of travertine blocks that bond into the tuff blocks forming the body of the structure (Delbrück 1907: 3–11; Galliazzo 1994: 32–36).

This technique of constructing arches with outside courses of voussoirs that alternately bond with the fabric behind them was particularly widespread in central Italy in the late second and early first centuries B.C.; examples include the viaduct of Ariccia, the bridges at Tor di Valle and Malafede of the Via Ostiense, the Nomentano and Mammolo bridges on the Via Nomentana and Via Tiburtina, and the Ponte di Nona on the Via Praenestina. This last bridge, 125 m long and 10.2 m wide, built of tuff blocks and concrete, is much like a viaduct that flattens the passage across a small valley. The seven vaults in the central portion rested on massive piers and spanned 6.2–7.1 m (Quilici 1974a: 363–81).

Many other bridges of this period were constructed in massive blocks of limestone, laid without mortar and reinforced with external buttresses, such as the Ponte del Diavolo on the Via Salaria (Quilici 1994). The Ponte del Diavolo in Manziana, a viaduct 90 m long with a single arch about 11 m high, was built of tuff blocks in the same technique (Galliazzo 1994: 58–59). The Ponte Manlio at Cagli on the Via Flaminia, was built of limestone with one arch spanning 10.8 m, after which the structure continues as a viaduct for over 100 m (Galliazzo 1994: 157–60).

The Ponte di S. Cono in Buccino, on the boundaries of Lucania, is a very elegant structure, although it is only 3.2 m wide and on a secondary route. The tall central arch, spanning 17.3 m, rests on bedrock, with a smaller relieving arch on one side, and prominent buttresses against the force of the water. The structure was built of travertine blocks with iron clamps, the voussoirs arranged in groups of headers and stretchers. It is interesting that, in contrast to most bridges, which were part of a large, imperial plan, numerous inscriptions relate that this bridge was constructed by the local municipality Volcei, and financed with public money and private contributions (Quilici 1996b).

A particularly bold bridge along this same design was the Ponte Salario on the Anio river, with a semicircular arch spanning 25 m, and travertine voussoirs on the facades that bond with tuff blocks and a concrete core. Inscriptions on the parapets record a reconstruction by Narses in the mid-sixth century, but the structure belongs to the impressive accomplishments of the late Republic (Quilici and Quilici-Gigli 1996: 103–12).

The age of Augustus was an extraordinary epoch for the realization of bridges, which sometimes appeared consistently along entire itineraries, for example along the Via Flaminia or the road up the Valle d'Aosta. The uniformity of the designs is valuable, since it constitutes a verifiable chronological reference for engineering techniques involved. On one side of the Apennines, the Augustan bridges of the Via Flaminia were constructed in the traditional materials of tuff or limestone blocks, with varying degrees of bonding, smooth or with rusticated surfaces, with a core of dry rubble or concrete, the arches smooth even along the extrados. Examples can be seen in the beautiful bridges on the Piccino river toward Gallese, or those of Calamone, Cardaro, S. Giovanni de Butris, and Fonnaia on the path after Narni toward Bevagna, or in the bridge Sanguinario in Spoleto (Quilici 1991b: 77; Maraldi 1996: 143–46; Galliazzo 1994: 179–80, 182).

The bridge of Narni is one of the most amazing works of ancient engineering: it was originally 180 m long, 8 m wide, and up to 33 m high, with four semicircular arches with spans of 19.6, 32.1, 17, and 16 m, framed by very strong shoulders and piers. It was built of limestone blocks around a core of concrete; the blocks have elegant bossing defined by cornices that highlight the architectural elements of the elevation, for example the external curves of the arches (figure 22.5). The span of 32.1 m is among the widest known for block-built structures in antiquity. Furthermore, one of the arches, different from the others, has a vault formed by five distinct courses of voussoirs, equidistant and covered by slabs, similar to a technique seen in the Augustan bridges of the Valle d'Aosta (Galliazzo 1994: 183–90).

Bridges such as this represent another, spectacular approach to bridge engineering: these structures are all seated directly on the bedrock, with well-decorated square piers built of local stone, buttresses where the river beds appeared more dangerous, and only one span. The voussoirs can have curved or polygonal extrados, and the most astonishing example, at Saint Martin, has a span of 32 m. This bridge and others, such as those at Bard, Châtillon, and Saint Vincent, have vaults built in parallel courses of voussoirs independent of each other, following a technique that is typical of this valley and which we find again only in the bridge at Narni and in other Augustan bridges in Provincia Narbonensis. This technique appears to be characteristic of a single school of engineering, but it appears again in bridges in Africa in the second century (Lucchese 2004). Other spectacular bridges of the Augustan period with large spans are those of Solestà and Cecco in Ascoli Piceno, with semicircular spans of 14.5 and 22.2 m and many structural analogies with the bridge of Narni (Pasquinucci 1975: 6–18). It is clear that there was communication among the engineers who designed major public works such as roads and bridges, but the degree of influence and the method of communication are still difficult to define.

Figure 22.5. Surviving arch of the bridge on the Via Flaminia at Narni. (L. Quilici.)

During the Augustan age, the classical structure of the bridge persists: large piers and arches with rounded extrados, following a design that remains normal through the reigns of Trajan and Hadrian, for example in the bridges of the Via Giulia Augusta (Massabò 1996; Bulgarelli 1996). After Augustus, the arch with polygonal extrados became widespread as well, for example in the Ponte dell'Aquoria below Tivoli (Galliazzo 1994: 64–65). This technique, in which the voussoirs and the wall around them interlock, reaches a greater degree of refinement in the Pons Antico on the Via Appia Pontina and the Ponte del Diavolo in Civitavecchia, both Trajanic in date (Aurelia 1968: 91–92), and climaxes with the Pons Aelia in Rome, whose arches span 18.4 m and hide their polygonal extrados in an elegant cornice (Galliazzo 1994: 13–17; Ioppolo 1996).

Successful new initiatives can be noted, particularly in the late Republican and Augustan periods, involving the construction of spectacular arches that span more than 30 m. We can document a notable school or tradition of bridge architecture in the limited geographical area of the Veneto, where a series of bridges dating from the late first century B.C. to the mid-second century A.D has particular structural characteristics: the arches are segmental, with notable spans and springing from less massive piers than usual. The ratio between the span of the arch and the thickness of the piers seems on average to be about 5:1 and ranges from around 4:1 to a maximum of 8:1. The flattening of the arches, calculated as the ratio of the height above the springers to the span between them, corresponds to values between 1:3 and 1:5. The motivation for this structural innovation must have been the desire to avoid, in flat landscapes, the tiring ascent over a bridge with one or more high arches. Contributing factors were the generally soft sedimentary ground that would have offered difficulties to erection of the typical massive piers and high, semicircular arches, along with the generally slow-moving streams. In general these bridges were constructed of dry limestone masonry with iron clamps as facing for a concrete core. Bridges built in this manner are found in Verona, Vicenza, Padova, Concordia, Ceggio, and Fiuminicetto along the Via Annia. The most famous is the mid-first century B.C. bridge on the Via Postumia at Verona, 91.4 m long, originally with five arches spanning 13–18 m; two subsequently were joined to make one span of 32 m. The foundations of these engineering masterpieces are interesting, placed as in so many other bridges in the Veneto on very unstable swampy ground. They were frequently founded on horizontal boards laid on piles, often bonded to each other with transverse beams and filled with stones (Cera 1996).

We have already noted that a real technical revolution started with the construction of bridges in mixed materials, beginning with Domitian's bridge over the Volturno, which inaugurated the use of arcades with brick arches. This technique, probably borrowed from the last big aqueduct systems built at Rome, allowed spectacular viaducts on series of arches to cross the widest valleys while providing a level roadbed, with great economy of cost for both materials and construction. The mastery of the use of concrete, particularly from the reign of Hadrian through to the Late Empire, allowed the application of local stones to the facing of concrete cores. The final product was bridges composed of ten arches with spans of 10–15 m (Galliazzo 1994: 63, 121–22; Bendi 1996; Fozzati and Capotti 1996; Luni 1996: 160–63; Quilici 1997: 126–31; Olivieri 1998: 47–50; Borghi 2000).

# ROAD AND BRIDGE ENGINEERING
## OUTSIDE ITALY

The engineering patterns of the roads and their infrastructure seen within ancient Italy can serve as a paradigm for what Roman engineers realized within the rest of the Empire (Galliazzo 1994; Chevallier 1997). In Italy we have traced the appearance of roads surfaced with paving, pebbles, and gravel; roads built on an elevated foundation and those laid in a cutting across a ridge; rock-cuttings, terraces, galleries, and drainage systems. Other themes were the norms for the selection of routes, the dimensions of roads, restoration or amelioration to maintain or improve circulation of traffic. While some generalization was possible, we have also traced variations resulting from differences in topography, geology, climate, previous or contemporary history, and economic and political factors (Chevallier 1997: 107–18, 155–67, 200–70; Talbert et al. 2000: 7–93). Along these roads no structure had more significance than the bridge, the design and construction of which symbolizes the technological capabilities and the political will of Roman culture. There were, however, local differences. For example, no masonry bridge was built across the middle or lower course of the Po River, despite the fact that sophisticated bridges, with piers of stone and wood trusses of extraordinary length, were built on rivers such as the Rhine (at Cologne; 420 m long, on 19 piers, spans up to 34.4 m), and the Danube (at Turnu-Severin, 1,135 m long, with 21 arches, spans of 32.6 m) (Galliazzo 1994: 271–73, 280–84, 320–24). Outside Italy, the Iberian peninsula possesses the largest number of well preserved Roman bridges in the ancient world (Alarcao 1988; Galliazzo 1994: 313–19, 325–68; Mendes Pinto 1998).

Out of the many routes that made up the Roman road system, three can be pointed out as well-known, diverse examples of the technology: the Via Domitia in Gaul, the Via Egnatia that crosses the Balkans, and the caravan road from Aleppo to the Euphrates.

## The Via Domitia

Laid out in 116 B.C. by Cn. Domitius Ahenobarbus, the Via Domitia went through Gallia Narbonense, from the Alpine pass of Susa to a pass in the Pyrenees, in support of Roman military activity in Spain. Further work was undertaken in 77 B.C. by Pompey, then later by Augustus and subsequent emperors. The main route was 284 km long— deviations developed from time to time in response to the changing importance of habitation centers along the route— and it quickly became one of the most important in the northwest Mediterranean region for communications and commerce. Although long, the route incorporated an extraordinary number of straight stretches, particularly from Beaucaire to the Pyrenees. In the many stretches where the original roadway survives, it consists of a fine-grained self-cementing surfacing 6–10 m wide on a substantial gravel bedding, laid in turn on a rubble foundation. The total thickness varied from 0.60 to 1.80 m. As usual, the road was paved with stone through urban centers and some smaller stops; well preserved stretches, consisting of oblong blocks laid on edge, can be seen at Ambrussum and Castelnau. The passes across the Alps and Pyrenees were carefully selected to allow passage also in the winter, the track being cut in the bedrock in some places. Numerous bridges of the Augustan period, built of stone blocks, can be seen along the road; among the most spectacular are those at Ambrussum, more than 200 m long with 11 arches, at Sommières, 190 m long with 17 arches, and at Saint-Thibery and Beziers, more than 100 m long with 9 arches. Here and elsewhere in the Gallic provinces the bridges usually date to the Julio-Claudian period and resemble those built during the same period in Italy; for example, those at Saint-Chamas, Bonnieux, and Vaison-la-Romaine (Laforgue 1985; Galliazzo 1994: 246–66; Talbert et al. 2000: 15–17, 25).

## The Via Egnatia

Crossing the whole Balkan peninsula—Illyria, Macedonia, and Thrace—the Via Egnatia connecting the ports of Dyrrhachium (Epidamnus) and Apollonia with Thessalonica, then proceeded on via Cypsela in the valley of the Hebrus to the ports on the Hellespont and to Byzantium. It was considered a continuation of the Via Appia, which terminated at Brundisium on the other side of the Adriatic, thus providing a single route from Rome to Anatolia and the Black Sea. As a result, the Via Egnatia became the most important land passage connecting East and West. The road was laid out in the mid-second century B.C. by Cn. Egnatius while he was proconsul of Macedonia, then improved above all by Nero, and next by Trajan in connection with the completion of the Appia Traiana, by the Severans, and by the Tetrarchs—all with operations against the Parthians in mind. Finally, with the foundation of Constantinople, it became the connector between the old and new imperial capitals.

In creating the road, Cn. Egnatius made use of routes already laid out by the Macedonian kings, but his road was structured on a unitary plan, according to the principles of Roman road construction already described for Italy, and on a much larger scale, reaching 1,030 km in length. The route took the road through regions that were varied in climate and often with a geomorphology not propitious for road construction. Despite the difficulties, the Via Egnatia traced a remarkably regular path, with straight stretches of significant length. The road was for the most part surfaced with gravel or pebbles, but paved with stone slabs in urban centers or areas of significant use. The typical width was 6.0–6.7 m, but paved sections were 4.0–4.3 m wide, with sidewalks on either side; this approach is particularly well preserved near Philippi (Hammond 1974; Talbert et al. 2000; Fasolo 2003).

## Roads in Syria

A particularly important route led from Antioch on the Orontes via Beroia (Aleppo), to the Euphrates. This is a road that passed through an environment very different from that of the roads previously described: across deserts, following age-old caravan routes (Beitzel 1992: 778–80). By the Roman period a roadway 4–7 m wide was paved with pebbles and flanked by sidewalks of beaten earth framed by dry-stone walls. Particularly striking are stretches paved with solid ashlar stone blocks across difficult rocky or swampy terrain; after 2,000 years of erosion, these roads resemble wide, low walls passing across a stony landscape. The construction of the carriage way (in general 6 m wide) involved blocks laid along the line of the road, framed by upright blocks along the margins. The foundation consisted of a layer of mortar directly on the stone, or on pilings. These roads, along with the associated watch towers, seem to date to the Severan period. In the territory of Aleppo, three bridges are recorded on the route toward Zeitunak via Nebi Ouri, all of the Severan period and about 100 m long with three arches (Cumont 1917: 19–23; Wagner 1985; Bauzou 1989).

Although most bulk cargoes were carried by sea during the Greco-Roman period, significant local and regional trade went by land, on roads of varying degrees of finish. Military traffic was always important, along with short- and long-distance pedestrian traffic. During the period of Roman domination, the circum-Mediterranean region enjoyed greater freedom of movement by land than would be seen again until the mid-nineteenth century. An honorific inscription of A.D. 362 found at Ankara sums up these accomplishments: "To Julianus Augustus, ruler of the whole world, who opened up the road through the barbarians, destroying all who opposed him, and who traveled in only one summer season from the British sea to the Tigris" (Cagiano De Azevedo 1939: 47).

# REFERENCES

Alarcao, J. 1988. *Roman Portugal.* 2 vols. Warminster: Aris and Philips.

Annia 2004. *La via Annia e le sue infrastrutture.* Treviso: Antiga Edizioni.

Appia 1990. *La via Appia. Decimo incontro di studio del Comitato per l'Archeologia Laziale.* Quaderni del Centro di studio per l'Archeologia etrusco-italica 18. Roma: Consiglio Nazionale delle Ricerche.

Ashby, T., and R. Gardner 1916. "The Via Traiana," *Papers of the British School in Rome* 8: 192–271.

Ashby, T., and R. Fell 1921. "The Via Flaminia," *Journal of Roman Studies* 11: 125–61.

Aurelia 1968. *La via Aurelia da Roma a Forum Aureli.* Quaderni dell'Istituto di Topografia antica 4. Rome: De Luca.

Basso, P. et al. 2004. "La via Annia nella Tenuta di Ca' Tron," in Annia 2004: 41–98.

Bauzou T. 1989. "Les routes romaines de Syrie, II," in J. –M. Dentzer, W. Orthmann, C. Augé (eds.), *Archéologie et histoire de la Syrie, II: La Syrie de la l'époque achéménide à l'avènement de l'Islam.* Saarbrücken: Saarbrücker Druck & Verlag, 205-21.

Beitzel, B. J. 1992. "Roads and highways (pre-Roman)," in D. N. Freedman (ed.), *Anchor Bible dictionary.* New York: Doubleday, 5:775–82.

Bendi, C. 1996. "Il ponte di Selbagnone presso Forlimpopoli," *ATTA* 5: 207–14.

Bonomi, P. L. 1993. "Nuove conoscenze sulle infrastrutture della via Flaminia in Umbria," *ATTA* 2: 155–66.

Bonora, M. G. 1992. "Tecnica stradale nella Regio XI: La via Regina," *ATTA* 1: 51–55.

Borghi, R. 2000. "Ponte del Romito sull'Arno," *Orizzonti* 1: 205–14.

Bosio, L. 1991. *Le strade romane della Venetia e dell'Histria.* Padova: Editoriale Programma.

Bulgarelli. F. 1996. "Ponti romani della Val Quazzola e del Finalese lungo la via Iulia Augusta," *ATTA* 5: 231–50.

Burckhardt, L. A. 1988. *Politische Strategien der Optimaten in der Späten Römischen Republik.* Stuttgart: Franz Steiner.

Cagiano De Azevedo, M. 1939. *Civiltà romana: Le strade.* Roma: Colombo.

Caiazza, D. 1995. *Archeologia e storia antica del mandamento di Pietramelara e del Montemaggiore.* Vol. 2. Rome: Banca Popolare di Ancona.

Calvani, M. M., R. Curina, and E. Lippolis (eds.) 2000. *"Aemilia": La cultura romana in Emilia Romagna dal III secolo a.C. all'età costantiniana.* Venice: Marsilio.

Calzolari, M. 1992. "La via Postumia da Cremona a Verona: Aspetti topografici," in *Itinera. Scritti in onore di Luciano Bosio.* Padova: Società Archeologica Veneta, 45–58.

Cancellieri, R. 1990. "Il territorio pontino e la via Appia," Appia 1990: 61–71.

Carfora, P. 2001. *"Ad Novas*: Una stazione della via Appia tra Calatia e Caudium," *ATTA* 10: 233–42.

Castagnoli, F. 1969. "Il tracciato della via Appia," *Capitolium* 44: 77–100.

Cera, G. 1996. "Peculiari esempi di architettura strutturale in alcuni ponti delle Venetia," *ATTA* 5:179–94.

Cera, G. 2000. *La via Postumia da Genova a Cremona. ATTA* Suppl.7. Rome: L'Erma di Bretschneider.

Cerchiaro, K. 2004. "La tecnica stradale della Decima Regio: Un contributo," in Annia 2004: 241–51.

Chevallier, R. 1997. *Les Voies Romaines.* Paris: Picard.

Conta, G. 1982. *Asculum.* Vol. 2. Pisa: Giardini Editori.

Crimaco, L. 1991. *Volturnum.* Rome: Edizioni QUASAR.

Cumont, F. V. M. 1917. *Études syriennes*, Paris: Geuthner.

De Feo, F. 1997. " La via Postumia," in *Geographia antiqua,* Vol. 6. Firenze: Giunti gruppo editoriale, 79–105.

Degrassi, N. 1982–1984. "Via Clodia e Via Cassia: Nomi e percorsi," *Rendiconti della Pontifica Accademia di Archeologia* 55–56: 155–74.

Degrassi, N. 1984–1985. "La Tabula Peutingeriana e l'Etruria settentrionale tirrenica," *Rendiconti della Pontifica Accademia di Archeologia* 57: 169–90.

Delbrück, R. 1907. *Hellenistische Bauten in Latium.* Vol. 1. Strassburg: Trubner.

Di Vita-Evrard, G. 1990. "Inscriptions routières de Nerva et de Trajan sur l'Appia pontine," in Appia 1990: 73–93.

Dorsey, D. A. 1997. "Roads," in E. M. Meyers (ed.), *Oxford encyclopedia of archaeology in the Near East.* Oxford: Oxford University Press, 4.431–34.

Esch, R. 1997. *Römische Strassen in ihrer Landschaft.* Mainz: von Zabern.

Fasolo, M. 2003. *La via Egnatia.* Roma: Istituto Grafico Editoriale Romano.

Favilla, M. C. 1996. "I ponti di Santa Marinella," *ATTA* 5: 127–42.

Fischer-Hansen, T. 1990. *Scavi di Ficana.* Vol. 1. Rome: Istituto Poligrafico e Zecca dello Stato.

Forbes, R. J. 1965. "Land transport and road building," in R. J. Forbes, *Studies in ancient technology,* 2nd ed. Vol. 2. Leiden: Brill, 131–92.

Fozzati, L., and L. Capotti 1996. "Nuove scoperte in Piemonte," *ATTA* 5: 213–21.

Frederiksen, M., and J. B. Ward Perkins 1957. "The ancient road system of the central and northern Ager Faliscus," *Papers of the British School in Rome* 25: 67–203.

Gaggiotti, M. 2004. "Le iscrizioni della galleria del Furlo," *ATTA* 14: 121–33.

Galliazzo, V. 1994. *I ponti romani,* 2 vols. Treviso: Canova.

Gatti, G. 1940. "Il viadotto della via Aurelia nel Trastevere," *Bullettino della Commissione Archeologica Comunale* 68: 129– 41.

Givigliano, G. P. 1994. "Percorsi e strade," in S. Settis (ed.), *Storia della Calabria antica: età italica and romana,* vol. 2. Reggio Calabria: Gangemi, 214–62.

Grewe, K. 1998. *Licht am Ende des Tunnels: Planung und Trassierung im antiken Tunnelbau.* Mainz: von Zabern.

Hammond, N. G. L. 1974. "The western part of the Via Egnatia," *Journal of Roman Studies* 64: 185–94.

Hope-Simpson, R., and D. K. Hagel 2006. *Mycenaean fortifications, highways, dams and canals.* Studies in Mediterranean Archaeology 133. Sävedalen: Paul Åströms Förlag.

Humm, M. 2005. *Appius Claudius Caecus: La république accomplie.* Rome: École française de Rome.

Ioppolo, G. 1996. "Ponte Elio: indagini e restauri 1994," *ATTA* 5: 85–102.

Laforgue, J. 1985. *Amènagement de la via Domitia en Languedoc-Roussillon.* Montpellier: École d'Architecture.

Lewis, M. J. T. 2001. *Surveying instruments of Greece and Rome*. Cambridge: Cambridge University Press.

Lilli, M. 1996. "Gli archi di S. Lidano in Campo Setino," *ATTA* 5: 45–52.

Lilli, M, 2002. *Ariccia: Carta archeologica*. Rome: L'Erma di Bretschneider.

Lucchese, L. 2004, "I ponti romani di Pont-Saint-Martin, Bard, Saint-Vincent, Châtillon, Aosta e Lèvèrogne," *ATTA* 13: 7–23.

Lugli, G. 1926. *Ager Pomptinus, Anxur-Tarracina*. Rome: Unione Accademica Nazionale.

Lugli, G. 1928. *Ager Pomptinus, Circeii*. Rome: Unione Accademica Nazionale.

Lugli, G. 1957. *La tecnica edilizia romana*. Rome: Bardi.

Luni, M. 1993. *La Flaminia nelle gole del Furlo e del Burano*. Urbino: Quattro Venti.

Luni, M. 1996. "I ponti scomparsi della via Flaminia nella vallata del Metauro," *ATTA* 5: 151–63.

Maccagnani, M. 1994. "La via Popilia-Annia," *ATTA* 3: 69–105.

Maraldi, L. 1996. "I ponti di San Giovanni de'Budris e del Diavolo sulla via Flaminia oltre Carsulae," *ATTA* 5: 143–50.

Marini-Calvani, M. 1992. "Strade romane dell'Emilia occidentale," *ATTA* 1: 187–92.

Massabò, B. 1996. "I ponti romani di Loano lungo la via Iulia Augusta," *ATTA* 5: 223–30.

Mazzarino, S. 1969. "L'Appia come prima via censoria," *Capitolium* 44: 101–20.

Mendes Pinto, P. 1998. *Pontes romanas de Portugal*. Lisboa: Associaçao Juventude e Património.

Mertens, J. 1993. "Les ponts de la via Traiana dans la traversèe du Tavoliere de Foggia," *ATTA* 2: 7–18.

Messineo, G. 1991. *La Via Flaminia*. Rome: Editrice QUASAR.

Mollo Mezzana, M. R. 1992. "La strada romana in valle d'Aosta: Procedimenti tecnici e costruttivi," *ATTA* 1: 57–72.

O'Connor, C. 1993. *Roman bridges*. Cambridge: Cambridge University Press.

Olivieri, E. 1998. "I ponti romani di Claterna," *ATTA* 7: 43–50.

Ortalli, J. 1992. "La cispadania orientale: Via Emilia e altre strade," *ATTA* 1: 147–60.

Ortalli, J. 1995. "Nuove fonti archeologiche per Ariminum," in A. Calbi and G. Susini, *Pro poplo Ariminese*. Epigrafia e Antichità 14. Faenza: Lega, 469–529.

Ortalli, J. 2000. "Le tecniche costruttive," in Calvani et al. 2000: 86–92.

Pagano, M. 1978. "Note su una località della via Appia fra Sinuessa e Capua: Il 'pons Campanus,'" *Rendiconti dell'Accademia di Archeologia, Lettere e Belle Arti di Napoli* 53: 227–34.

Pasquinucci, M. 1975. *Asculum*. Vol. 1. Pisa: Giardini Editori.

Pellegrini, G. 2004. "*Item ab Aquileia Bononiam*: Un itinerario di età romana tea la via Emilia ed il Po," *ATTA* 13: 43–63.

Postumia 2000. *Tesori della Postumia*. Milano: Electa.

Quilici, L. 1974a. *Collatia*. Rome: De Luca.

Quilici, L. 1974b. "La Campagna Romana come Suburbio di Roma antica," *Parola del Passato* 29: 410–38.

Quilici, L. 1989a. *La Via Appia*. 2 vols. Rome: Palombi.

Quilici, L. 1989b. "Le antiche vie dell'Etruria," in *Atti del Secondo Congresso Internazionale Etrusco, Firenze 1985*. Rome: Giorgio Bretschneider, 451–506.

Quilici, L. 1990. "Il rettifilo della Via Appia tra Roma e Terracina: La tecnica costruttiva," in Appia 1990: 41–60.

Quilici, L. 1991a. "Il Ponte di Mele sulla via Appia," *Archeologia Classica* 43: 317–27.

Quilici, L. 1991b. Le strade. Viabilità tra Roma e Lazio. Rome: Edizioni QUASAR.

Quilici, L. 1992. "Evoluzione della tecnica stradale nell'Italia centrale," *ATTA* 1: 19–32.

Quilici, L. 1993. "La via Salaria da Roma all'alto Velino: La tecnica struttiva dei manufatti stradali," *ATTA* 2: 85–154.

Quilici, L. 1994. "Ponte del Diavolo sulla Salaria al confine territoriale tra Cures e Tremula Mutuesca," *ATTA* 3: 119–30.

Quilici, L. 1996a. "I ponti della via Ostiense," *ATTA* 5: 51–79.

Quilici, L. 1996b. "Evoluzione tecnica nella costruzione dei ponti: Tre esempi tra età repubblicana e alto medioevo," *ATTA* 5: 267–92.

Quilici, L. 1997. "I Simbruina stagna di Nerone nell'alta valle dell'Aniene," in *Uomo, acqua e paesaggio. ATTA* suppl. 2. Rome: L'Erma di Bretschneider, 99–142.

Quilici, L 2000. "Le strade dell'Emilia antica," *Orizzonti* 1: 115–38.

Quilici, L 2002. "La valorizzazione della Via Appia al valico di Itri," *ATTA* 11: 107–46.

Quilici, L 2004. "Santuari, ville e mausolei sul percorso della Via Appia al valico degli Aurunci," *ATTA* 13: 441–543.

Quilici, L., and S. Quilici-Gigli 1996. "I ponti del basso corso dell'Aniene," *ATTA* 5: 103–25.

Quilici-Gigli, S. 1983. "Sistemi di cunicoli nel territorio tra Velletri e Cisterna," in *Archeologia Laziale*, vol. 5. Quaderni del Centro di Studio per l'Archeologia etrusco-italica 7. Rome: Consiglio Nazionale delle Ricerche, 112–23.

Quiri, P. 1992. "Scavi e restauri lungo la via Flaminia nel tratto marchigiano," in *La Via Flaminia nell'Ager Gallicus*. Urbino: Quattro Venti, 327–35.

Rosada, G. 1992. "Tecnica stradale e paesaggio nella decima regio," *ATTA* 1: 39–50.

Talbert, R. J. A. et al. (eds.) 2000. *Barrington atlas of the Greek and Roman world*. Princeton: Princeton University Press.

Wagner, J. 1985. *Die Römer an Euphrat und Tigris. Antike Welt* Suppl. 16. Feldmeilen: Raggi-Verlag.

Zevi, F. 2004. "Attività archeologica a Napoli e Caserta nel 2003," *Atti del Convegno di Studi sulla Magna Grecia, 43, Taranto-Cosenza 2003*. Taranto: Società Magna Grecia, 853–923.

# CHAPTER 23

# LAND TRANSPORT, PART 2: RIDING, HARNESSES, AND VEHICLES

## GEORGES RAEPSAET

## HISTORIOGRAPHY AND METHODOLOGY

Transportation constitutes a constant activity in human life: to move, drive, drag, pull, push, lift, and carry are necessities during all moments of living and producing the means of life. Since the invention of the rope or the pole that hunter-gatherers used to drag along their wild quarry, long before the classical period, innumerable forms of traction and portage have been developed, and all the forms of human and animal power have been summoned to drive them. The yoking of animals was mastered during the long Neolithic period, and since then a great variety of methods of draft have been put to the service of transport. This chapter will attempt to define comprehensively the technical framework and the principle configurations of transport across the Greco-Roman world. Like this one, many of the more recent studies concerned with the productive technologies of classical antiquity have demonstrated that these technologies were neither insignificant nor marginal but were part of an energy and economic dynamism whose importance must not be obscured or devalued (Greene 1990; 1994; Schneider 1992; Amouretti and Comet 1994; Raepsaet 2002).

The analysis of land transport in antiquity is difficult, however, because the direct sources of evidence are few and scattered, and because the topic has often been approached by historiographers in a tone of controversy and polemic. Until the 1970s the subject of transport was seldom treated in studies of economic history or the history of technology, judged as irrelevant or even indicative of the under-development of technology in the classical world. At that time the accepted opinion, resulting from the convergence of two theories—the one economic, the other technological—minimized and devalued the importance of land transport. A conceptual dichotomy in the history of the Western world was proposed by Le-Fèbvre des Noëttes (1931): the classical cultures were "blocked" by a defective system of harnessing animals, while those of the medieval period liberated themselves and brought progress through the use of the horse collar. This approach was taken up and passed on in the "primitivist" vision of ancient culture in Marxist thought, manifested in particular in the early 1960s by Moses Finley (1965) and post-Finleyan minimalists—whose arguments have been dissected and refuted by Greene (1990, 1994, 2000). In this primitivist vision, the mediocre development of transport technology was justified by the absence of commerce in a quasi-subsistence economy producing little surplus, by the concept of cities that consumed rather than produced, and by the marginalization of exchange to a few, high-value-added commodities. In the supposed absence of productive reinvestment, no technological progress was possible. The allegedly undeveloped socioeconomic structure of the classical cultures reduced land transport for the most part to relations between the rural landscape and the nearby market town, in a largely noncommercial pattern of exchange. Even in the twenty-first century, the orthodox primitivist view, particularly the equation of the classical cultures with technological stagnation and blockage and with a minimal and irrational economic system, still has its proponents. To give just one example, J. G. Landels, in the revised edition of his *Engineering in the Ancient World* (2000: 170) writes: "The shortness of this chapter by comparison with the preceding one reflects—crudely but quite accurately—the unimportance of land transport by comparison with sea transport in the classical world." Clearly an epistemological prejudice concerning this topic still exists. A quantitatively very different evaluation of the technological and economic productivity of the classical cultures within and across small and large regions appears in the works of Laurence (1999) and Mattingly and Salmon (2001) on the one hand, and of Fellmeth (2002) on the other.

To evaluate properly the technology of land transport in the classical world, one must start with a close examination of the evidence in its own right and in the context of its practical application, and an analysis of the technical fact, such as it is, as part of the global group of preindustrial mechanical systems (Sigaut 1985; Langdon 1986; Haudricourt 1987; Amouretti and Sigaut 1998; Raepsaet 2002; Comet 2003), and one must start too with a long historical perspective (Jankuhn et al. 1989).

A harnessing system is composed of forces and resistance, the elements of whose operation must be understood. A technological analysis of transport involving harnessed animals must therefore be the first step, and to create and validate this analysis, evidence must be drawn from every region and historical period. The history of technology cannot be subdivided into periods, as can battles or social institutions. Grinding grain, drawing water from a well, pressing oil, or working the soil constitute some of the activities and practical know-how which can be at once extremely individual in technical style and microcultural environment, and at the same time participate in spatial and functional frameworks of activity that extend well beyond that specific period (e.g., Astill and Langdon 1997). Contrary to the persistent received opinion, the history of transport cannot be divided into a "primitive period" prior to the shoulder collar and a "modern" period subsequent to its appearance. "Before" and "after" better fit the replacement of human, animal, wind, and water power with that derived from nonrenewable fossil fuels, a "revolution" that took place in the nineteenth century in certain parts of the Western world, but one for which at least a third of the human race is still waiting (figure 23.1).

To carry out this attempt at clarification, it is best to use multiple and overlapping sources and approaches. The relevant preserved textual sources are few in number, although an important technical literature on the subject existed in antiquity (Nicolet 1996; Meissner 1999). But apart from the writers on warfare, Vitruvius (Fleury 1993), and some agricultural authors, these sources have rarely survived (Meijer and Van Nijf 1992; Humphrey et al. 1998: 409–42). Epigraphical sources provide important information, in part through accounts of construction works (Burford 1960; 1969; Raepsaet 1984) or the epitaphs of traders and transport personnel (Raepsaet and Raepsaet-Charlier 1987–1988), in part through texts written or scratched on objects of daily use. Papyrus documents are particularly valuable (Leone 1988, 1992). We owe much to three of the traditional subcategories of archaeological data as well (e.g., Garbsch 1986; *Vierrädriger Wagen* 1987; Oexle 1992): artifacts in context (chariot burials, pieces of harness), iconography, and the diffusion patterns of commercial products. The interpretation of an image, of course, requires caution, and a map of distribution patterns depends on the accuracy of the quantification of the data.

Recourse has frequently been made to comparative ethnology, used not as anecdotal illustration, but as a structural framework for the investigation (e.g., Fenton et al. 1973; Sigaut 1985; 1987; Mingote Calderon 1996; Raepsaet 2002). The fundamental importance of the ethnology of contemporary cultures and of ethnohistory as a frame for all research on ancient technologies deserves emphasis, not only from the materialist and functionalist points of view, but through the new epistemological concepts and historical topics derived from them: archaeology and history of skills and knowledge transfer, concepts of innovation and technological choices, concepts of technical identity, technical behaviors such as socioeconomic productions, and experimental archaeology, which helps to explain the "chaînes opératoires" (systems of production, or production lines). Emphasis is now placed on technological choices, behaviors, and styles as social products, the cultural manifestations of technical facts. These very interesting lines of research are bound to the deeper, interdisciplinary inquiries carried out on the territory of traditional villages and founded on an important collection of documentation that permits

Figure 23.1. Horses or mules pulling a wagon. Bas-relief on funeral monument at Gorsium in Pannonia (*AE* 1972: 435). (Photograph by G. Raepsaet.)

significant new conclusions. Unfortunately, the absence of data for classical antiquity only rarely permits one to approach these new horizons with precision. Nevertheless, it is clear that a harness and a carriage can be studied as much as cultural facts as mechanical contrivances, and that the interaction of the two approaches can only enrich our understanding. Today the form and function of a traditional means of land transport still has importance for the economic life of many counties around the world (Hopfen 1970; *Techniques rurales* 1971). The research of Starkey (2002) concerning the development of animal traction, carried out under the aegis of the Department for International Development in the United Kingdom, provides a sharp reminder of this. The point of view defended by the agronomists and animal husbandry experts of the emerging nations also concerns us. These experts reject the idea that a simple, so-called primitive technology must necessarily be rejected and replaced by a Western, so-called modern technology. The cultural and social values bound up with tools and technological behaviors cannot be denied, and they can no longer be considered at the start as something to be discarded. Today, in the dynamic of the economic, social, and intellectual emancipation of the populations concerned, the optimization of traditional knowledge is regarded with more favor than its eradication. In the research of the ethnologists, agronomists, and agricultural economists at work in the Third World there are conceptual tools and methodological principles of great interest for the historian, along with an immense reservoir of comparative documentation. Finally, experimentation constitutes an equally interesting approach, sometimes a decisive one, for understanding the function of a harness. Nevertheless, this remains above all an interesting trial of a hypothesis, an excellent test bench, but nothing more. The attempt is nonetheless indispensable in the study of ancient technical operations, given the absence of equivalent ethnological data.

# Mechanics of Forces and Potential Energy

If mechanics can be defined as the science of force and movement, the application of a force on a mass in order to move it in a given direction, along with the numerous associated constraints, are at the heart of the problem posed by transport (Abeels 1995; Cotterell and Kamminga 1990). From the classical period through the nineteenth century, mechanics as applied to farming and to transport was largely empirical, intuitive, or habitual in its applications. Even if Archytas of Tarentum can be seen to make some efforts at theoretical analysis, and we can detect in the works of Archimedes and Vitruvius a conscious desire to link theoretical and practical advances (Fleury 1993; Argoud and Guillaumin 1998; Healy 1999; Whitehead and Blyth 2004), one must wait for the end of the eighteenth or the beginning of the nineteenth century for the birth of an "agricultural mechanics" as an important part of industrial mechanics. The works of Poncelet, Morin, Coulomb, Lecamus, and Gasparin (1863) are concerned as much with the capacities of the animal as with the draft of carriages, and they share a common desire to understand the action, to construct the theoretical basis, and to perfect it in order to increase the output. Even if mechanical sophistication, bound up notably with some fundamental changes in the sources of energy used, is a relatively recent phenomenon, the concepts of progress in mechanics, of choice, of innovation are always—along with the applications—of considerable importance with regard to the level of output or economy of effort. This fundamental mechanics is inscribed in slow and discontinuous rhythms, but it lacks neither interesting manifestations nor effectiveness (Cotterell and Kamminga 1990).

Certain obvious points concern us: every mass to be moved implies in reality some constraints or obstacles more or less difficult to overcome (Raepsaet 2002: 19–30). The importance of the coefficients of stationary or rolling friction, the effects of

Table 23.1. Comparison of capacity for dragged loads (so-called hook measures).

| Type of Animal | Maximum dragging traction in kilograms | |
| --- | --- | --- |
| | *2 hours of effort* | *4 hours of effort* |
| Heavy Horses | 260–290 | 240–270 |
| Light Horses | 180 | 160 |
| Mountain Cattle | 160–170 | 140–150 |
| Lowland Cattle | 140–150 | 120 |

slope, and their linked and interrelated effect on the effort required show that transport is a mechanical setup that must be mastered both in its separate parts and in its overall configuration. The same defined input of force can be sufficient at a given location but insufficient at another, or at the same location but on a slope. Likewise, the nature of the surface on which the haulage takes place, and of the contact between it and the weight, can modify all the assumptions concerning a method of transport. Easily accommodated on the smooth paving of a Roman road, a wagonload of the same weight becomes unmanageable on soft ground. In the same way, the sinuous line of a road can be directly linked to the need to diminish the effects of slope. To overcome inertia and the effects of rolling friction, it is always necessary to marshal a potential force superior to the combined forces of resistance. Between the load (resistance) and the motivating force there is a structure that intercepts, transmits, applies, and responds to the force exercised on the mass to move it; in the circumstances of harnessed transport, this is the draft harness.

Did the classical cultures have a concept of the mechanics of forces? It is all a question of theoretical knowledge as opposed to practical and empirical knowledge, and of the relation between the two, and—underlying it all—that of the capacity (sometimes contested) of the classical cultures to move from theory to application or to develop a theoretical analysis of applied technologies. Gille (1980) is one of the first to have highlighted the existence of a true technical culture in the classical world, composed of an accumulation of research, success, setbacks, methods, principles, and self-awareness. At Alexandria one can even speak of a school of practitioners of technical arts who in a real way gave birth to technology (Argoud and Guillaumin 1998; Lewis 2000).

Formerly, Chersiphron, Metagenes, Rhoecus, and Eupalinus appeared to be engineers rather than architects, men of the earth and practitioners rather than theoreticians. Archaeology shows that the architecture of archaic Greece clearly reveals a great empirical knowledge of the application of the mechanics of force, as well as the mechanisms for multiplying force (see chapter 9). The loss of ancient literature is often lamented, but technical literature suffered much more than philosophy, poetry, or rhetoric. The misunderstanding of this reality among contemporary historians may in great part be responsible for the stubborn misinterpretation of the very existence of technology in the classical world. A snippet from

Table 23.2. Comparison of the potential force and power of the principal portage and draft animals.

| Animal | Mean Weight | Approximate traction force in kg | Mean speed of work | Power Developed | |
|---|---|---|---|---|---|
| | | | | Kgm/s | Horsepower |
| Light Horse | 400–700 | 60–80 | 1m/sec | 75 | 1 |
| Steer | 500–900 | 60–80 | 0.6–0.85 | 56 | 0.75 |
| Buffalo | 400–900 | 50–80 | 0.8–0.9 | 55 | 0.75 |
| Cow | 400–600 | 50–60 | 0.7 | 35 | 0.45 |
| Mule (male) | 350–500 | 50–60 | 0.9–1.0 | 52 | 0.70 |
| Ass | 200–300 | 30–40 | 0.7 | 25 | 0.35 |

Vitruvius (De arch. 10.3.7–8) is a revelation not only of the interest an ancient technical writer could bring to bear on a problem of animal traction, but also of the wish to carry it to level of mechanical theory. The question concerns the balancing of weights:

> When very heavy loads are carried by groups of four or six porters, the burden is distributed evenly at the very center of the carrying poles, . . . so that each porter carries an equal portion on his shoulder. . . . Following the same principles, oxen draw an equal load when their yoke is fixed (to the draw pole) by binding straps at its midpoint. When the oxen are of unequal strength, however, and one by exerting more force causes difficulty for the other, the thong is repositioned so that one side of the yoke is longer and thus assists the weaker animal.

Humans and animals constitute the primary reservoir of energy utilized in the movement of loads by road, whether by portage or harnessed vehicle. This is always the case today in the undeveloped part of the world. We have at our disposal many comparative studies of the force and harnessed power of animals (Hopfen 1970: 12; Raepsaet 2002: 31–64; Cotterell and Kamminga 1990: 207). In general, one can assume that the tractive force of an animal is directly proportional to its weight and corresponds to approximately one-tenth of its weight. For horses, the proportion rises to 15 percent, and for short periods horses can exert a force close to half their weight, or more. Animal experts have observed, among other things, that small animals in general produce an output greater with respect to their size than large animals, principally because their angle of traction is lower. They also have greater energy and endurance, which compensates for their lesser weight. This is true for both small horses (of 400 kg and a height of 1.35–1.40 m at the withers, statistics close to those of the ancient horse) and bullocks (Hopfen 1970: 8–12). In all traditional societies bovine draft animals play an important role (Raepsaet 1998–2001). The ox, with the capacity to exert 300–400 watts of force for six hours, and the capability of a strong pair of oxen to exert maximum force on the order of 20–25 horsepower over 100 m, the ox constituted the principal motive force in economic activities involving heavy burdens (tables 23.1, 23.2).

Figure 23.2. Tondo of an Attic red-figure vase representing a mule with pack-saddle (After Raepsaet 2002: 70, fig. 5.)

In the hierarchy of economic applications, the ass family (asses and mules; Raepsaet 1998–2001, 2002) ranks immediately after the bovines, and, in some regions for a great number of applications they still constitute the main potential source of energy, the only source of energy to supplement that of humans. Even in the temperate parts of Europe in the mid-nineteenth century, there was discussion concerning the respective advantages and drawbacks of the horse, mule, and ass. The mule has three excellent advantages under harness, nearly equivalent to those of a light horse: more constant effort, lesser fragility, and a marked docility (figure 23.2). The skeletal structure of the asses allows use of the yoke instead of the collar, at a lesser cost in terms of both purchase and maintenance. While the price of a well-formed mule is nearly the same as that of a country horse, the ass is notably cheaper, which gives it an enormous role in hilly or dry landscapes. For hours it can carry its own weight, sometimes more. The ass's capacity for tractive force is no less. In France, some river barges were drawn by a pair of yoked asses even at the beginning of the twentieth century.

The strength of the horse has been celebrated frequently and for numerous reasons, but not necessarily in proportion to its real economic benefit (Raepsaet 1998–2001; 2002: 35–37). Both Eurocentric historiography and sympathetic appreciation of the animal have had a great effect. From the beginning of the tenth century A.D., the association of the horse with the shoulder collar optimized its potential energy, which was utilized in an ever increasing manner in northern and western Europe. The mean harnessed power of a small or medium-sized horse is

Table 23.3. Capacities for portage.

| | Load (kg) | Distance/Day (km) | Speed (kmph) | Total Carried/Day (kg) |
|---|---|---|---|---|
| London Docker | 90–150 | | | |
| Sedan-Chair Porter | 70 | | 2.5 | |
| Stevedore with Constant Load (19th c.) | 40 | 20 | 2.7 | 800 |
| Stevedore with One-Way Loads (19th c.) | 60 | 11 | | 660 |

approximately 40 to 80 kg m/sec for a task carried out over a day. At work, the mean effort is 40–50 kg m/sec. Gasparin (1863: 3, 88–97) gives as well 45 kg m/sec for a light horse (360 kg) on a good gravel road harnessed to a load of 1.5 tons, that is, a force greater than 10 percent of its weight at moderate effort. For an average African horse of 400–700 kg weight, Hopfen records a force of 60–80 kg m/sec and a power of 75 kg m/sec (which corresponds to 1 HP). The literature concerning the capacities of the horse is immense (Vigneron 1968; Hyland 1990), along with the research concerning the anatomy of the draft horse, particularly in the nineteenth century, and especially in relation with application of new breeds of "carriage horses" and heavy draft horses. This has little importance for us, because the horse was seldom put to use for its tractive force either in the classical world or anywhere else later on, with the exception of modern western Europe.

The capacities that animals offer with respect to carrying and dragging burdens were considerable and were well known from the Neolithic onward. There was often, however, a considerable discrepancy between the theoretical potential of the animal and its real capacity, as a result of zoological and technological knowledge, economic and social contexts, cultural traditions or the capacity for investment, and the state of veterinary medicine and the medical treatments the animals received.

# General Categories of Portage and Harnessed Transport

Contrary to the opinion expressed by Lefèbvre des Noëttes and often repeated since, the techniques and the related functional structures for locomotion and transport in the Greco-Roman world were not generally specific to the ancient world alone, but relevant as well to traditions present in Europe up to the nineteenth century and still active today in some parts of the world. In fact, the sources of energy available and consumed to move a weight—human, animal, and hydraulic—changed little

**Table 23.4. Performance of animals with packsaddle.**

|  | Load (kg) | Distance (km/day) | Speed (km/h) | Transport per day (kg/km) |
|---|---|---|---|---|
| Horse (walking) | 100–120 | 40 | 4 | 4,000–4,800 |
| Horse (at a trot) | 80 | 60 | 8 | 4,800 |
| European Mule | 150–180 | 20–24 | 3–5 | 3,600–3,900 |
| European Army Mule | 70–80 | 30–48 | — | 2,500–3,500 |
| British Army Ass | 80–100 | 24–30 | — | 2,400 |
| Dromedary |  |  |  |  |
|   Middle East, normal | 230 | 40 | — | 9,200 |
|   Middle East, short distance | 450 | — | — | — |
|   British Army, Egypt | 170 | — | — | — |
|   India | 300–320 | 32 | 3–4.5 | 8,300 |
|   Australia | 400 | — | — | — |
| Bactrian Camel, Middle East | 250 | 48 | — | 12,000 |

from the Neolithic period to the invention of the steam engine and, soon afterward, fossil fuels. This stability did not stand in the way of either a great diversity of vehicles and harnesses or multiple forms of progress, innovations, and adaptations to the needs encountered in each type of society or preindustrial environment.

Seen, however, from a global and structural point of view, packsaddle and portage are universal (Raepsaet 2002: 66–68), as is yoked traction by two bovines or asses, at least in the major and dominant modes of economic transport on land (table 23.3). In the restricted economies of mountainous regions, portage remains important even today. On certain steep and winding paths, only portage on the human back is feasible. Likewise, in many domestic and rural activities, in ports and in workshops, occasional or professional portage by humans is the best solution. Ethnography gives us an idea of the capacity. In equatorial Africa, 25 kg can be carried on the head over 25 km in one day. In the mountains, some Tibetan porters carry up to 100 kg on their backs, sometimes with the assistance of a staff or a carrying pole. A pair of porters can make use of a suspension pole, a litter, or a stretcher, as in the case of transporting game that has been killed. In the classical cultures there were professional porters, known as *saccarii* in Roman ports, for example, and various forms of the pack bag (*pera*), pouch (*mantica*), and other means of assisting carriage, all the way up to the comfortable sedan chair, or litter (*lectica*). Curiously, although sedan chairs were a common feature of Roman urban life, very few visual representations have survived.

Portage by animal, and, in its developed form, with the packsaddle (Raepsaet 2002: 68–72) was of fundamental importance for the transport of burdens that could be subdivided (table 23.4). In economies with brief transactions and a low volume of exchange, for example from a small rural estate to a nearby market town, the ass, mule, and to a lesser extent the horse transported between 100 and 200 kg of goods, according to the terrain and the climate. Columella (*Rust.* 6.37) terms the mule "better suited to the packsaddle" (figure 23.2). Dependence on the packsaddle is still common today in the mountains of Arcadia, in the Troodos Mountains of Cyprus, and elsewhere in the world. The miserable life of the badly treated ass is the subject of numerous jokes, traditional sayings, and fables. There were several variations on the packsaddle, from the soft double sac, the *mantica* with two pouches that is balanced on the shoulders or the back, to the complex frameworks of wood covered with cloth or fitted with straps (*sagma, stratum*). The packsaddle could even be adjusted for the transport of persons (*astraba*). The animal thus saddled is a porter led by a walking merchant, the typical means of transport in long convoys devoted to foodstuffs. The guild of the *utricularii*, for example, comes to mind, which in the Gallic provinces carried and distributed skins of wine and other foodstuffs by means of pack animals, undoubtedly mules (Deman 2002).

From the Neolithic to our day conveyance involving the harness and the yoke has been universal, along with its multiple applications in every sphere of activity involving tractive power: plowing, towing, milling, hauling, and carriage. The vehicle with a draw pole pulled by two horses is traditionally considered the standard form of harnessing in the Greco-Roman world (Lorimer 1903; Roring 1983; Crouwel 1992; Raepsaet 2002: 72–154). It is the means most prominent in the iconography, but the least obtrusive in the economic reality. In its military, ceremonial, or sport version, the small cart with two wheels (*biga*), low box, draw pole (*temo*), and double yoke (*iugum*) is well documented in the texts and iconography, but it represents poorly the everyday reality of land transport. The structural basis for the traction is the rigid joining of the draw pole and yoke; the latter is placed on the animals' backs and held in place by a girth strap or flexible band which exerts its pressure on the lower portion of the neck, in front (cf. Homer, *Il.* 24.268). It was the understanding of this system for the transmission of force that elicited the negative evaluation by Lefèbvre des Noëttes. On the basis of a restricted, poorly understood iconographical corpus he concluded that the girth strap strangled the horse and that the yoke damaged the withers, severely restricting its tractive power. A new reading of the ancient documents, accompanied by an important set of experimental data, permitted Spruytte (1977) to propose a new interpretation of the tractive power of equids in antiquity. According to him, the yoke rested on the curve of the back, behind the shoulders, and was attached to a girth strap that exerted force on the shoulder joints and not on the throat. When correctly understood, this harness could be classified as an "abbreviated breast harness" (bricole écourtée). The arrangement for exerting force is mechanically correct. Experiment showed that loads of a ton on a small four-wheeled wagon posed no problem for two horses, even on difficult terrain. Supplementary, "roped" horses (*funales*) could be added to a two-horse arrangement, outside the team yoked to the draw beam, to create the three- and four-horse teams that the Greek vase-painters were so fond of. There are some exceptional cases as well, of multiple pairs of horses harnessed along an extended

Figure 23.3. Mule cart with amphoras, detail of Theban Cabiric vase. (After Raepsaet 2002: 172, fig. 94.3.)

draw beam, but these are of lesser technological importance. The problem of the harnessing of horses with a yoke and breast strap, now well understood for the Greek and Roman world, appears in nearly identical form in the Near East and Egypt, where the very rich iconographical evidence presents war and parade chariots (Littauer 1968; Littauer and Crouwel 1979; Crouwel 1981; Rommelaere 1991).

The only basic harnessing system that had a true economic significance for the transport of merchandise was the yoking of steers or oxen, asses or mules. Varro (*Rust.* 1.20, 2.8) summarizes the situation: "Some use asses, others steers or mules" (*alii asellis, alii vaccis ac mulis utuntur*); "For all vehicles on the roads are drawn by mules yoked in pairs" (*hisce* [= *mulis*] *enim binis coniunctis omnia vehicula in viis ducuntur*). Concerning asses, Columella (*Rust.* 7.1.2) writes: "The ass pulls significant loads on a wagon" (*asellus . . . non minima pondera vehiculo trahat*). Here as well, the equipment consisted of a small two-wheeled cart, draw pole, and double yoke, but the box, often raised on props or axle-blocks (Greek: *hamaxopodes*; Raepsaet 1984), could take a variety of forms adapted to the varied needs of transport and cargo. In this case, the iconography is restricted, but ethnographic evidence is useful in supplementing our evidence, since the size of the ass family and bovines and their capacity for traction under the yoke is more or less a constant and has always been utilized in certain regions. The morphology and anatomy of the ass and of the mule are favorable to providing a good seat for the yoke. As for the ox, it carries the yoke on the horns or nape of the neck—the advantages of one or the other arrangement were discussed in the same terms by both Latin agronomists and those of the nineteenth century: "For the yoke fits better on the neck, and thus this manner of yoking finds the most approval. But in some areas there is the odd habit of tying the yoke to the horns" (*iugum melius aptum cervicibus indicat. Hoc enim genus iuncturae maxime probatum est. Nam illud, quod in quibusquam provinciis usurpatur, ut cornibus illigetur iugum*; Columella, *Rust.* 2.2; cf. Palladius, *Ag.* 2.3). The heavier the loads, the more there was a tendency to make use of oxen. The transport of large stones for construction was reserved for oxen, yoked in line or fanned out, both at the Pentelic quarries in 450 B.C. (Raepsaet 1984) and at the quarries of Carrara in 1920. At this level of load—blocks of eight or ten tons were

Figure 23.4. Yoked cattle in Portugal, ca. 1910. (Photograph by J. Malvaux.)

not rare—the problems of transport are concerned more with the solidity of the frame or wagon and with the terrain than with the available tractive power. Argument over the relative importance of the two-wheeled cart or the four-wheeled wagon is pointless. A situation of broken terrain, with a need for stability and braking capacity favors the wagon, but the cart had the advantages of lightness, maneuverability, and speed (figures 23.3–4).

In both the iconographic and textual evidence, the choice of vehicle appears linked to the means, needs, functions, and circumstances of transport: the *hamaxai* have two wheels in the narrow streets of Athens and the vineyards of Corinth (Raepsaet 1988), but four-wheeled wagons (*tetrakukloi*) were used to carry column and architrave blocks up to Epidaurus (Burford 1969) or down to Eleusis. The situation appears the same at Rome (Adam 1984: 44–53). On a fresco at Boscoreale, two-wheeled carts are shown at a construction site (Adam 1984: 216). But the winegrowers of Langres used a solid four-wheeled wagon (Molin 1987–1988). As for travelers, above all during the Roman imperial period, they had at their disposal carriages of various designs and arrangements, with either two or four wheels (figure 23.5).

We must examine in more detail the problems involved with heavy transport across the Isthmus of Corinth on the *diolkos*, a paved road by means of which, from archaic Greece through the Roman Empire, ships or their cargoes were hauled between the Saronic Gulf and the Gulf of Corinth. This road is a paradigmatic example that summarizes all the technical difficulties of heavy transport in antiquity and all the solutions brought to bear to solve them (Raepsaet 1993): the length of the route on land (6–7 km), slopes of up to 6 percent, the weight and volume of the loads to be transported (even the smallest ships weighed at least 10 tons, while a trireme surpassed 30 tons), haulage of the boats from the sea to dry land—always a

Figure 23.5. Ox-drawn wagon with large barrel, relief sculpture from tomb monument, second or third century A.D., Langres. (Photograph by G. Raepsaet.)

difficult task, even for boats with an abbreviated keel. The course of the road has been badly disturbed by the modern Corinth canal, but the traces preserved, the arrangements of the quay at the entrance to the Gulf of Corinth, and portions of the paving with ruts at Loutraki provide enough information to allow a tentative reconstruction of the transport procedures and the mechanical devices used.

The paved road, like the quay, was constructed with large facing blocks. Between 3.40 m and 5.60 m wide, the paving is marked with a complex pattern of ruts caused by wear, in particular in the area of a paved ramp that interrupts the course of the road 600 m from its west end. Both downhill and at the approach to this inclined plane, alongside the principal ruts, which are approximately 1.5 m apart, there are numerous traces that make clear important maneuvers by the carts involved. Grooves cut by the friction of cables are also visible, sometimes nearly cutting entirely through blocks in the structure. Analysis of the contour lines of the topography is the key element in the interpretation of the techniques of the rolling stock put to use. The first 800 m from the coastline along the Gulf of Corinth correspond to the zone of beach and marine sands, 12 m deep. The slope here is modest, around 1.5 percent. At the point just below where the ramp is located the slope increases to 2.5 percent for a few hundred meters, then to 3.5 percent above it, then very quickly to 6 percent before reaching the summit at a level area 4 km east of the Gulf of Corinth, at a height of 75–80 m above sea leval. The descent to Kalamaki was 2.5–3 km long. By taking account of the constants of topography, archaeological remains, and naval and mechanical technology, it can be seen that the pick-up of the boats hauled out on the quay was accomplished with strong vehicles, or with a line of wagons, or by means of multiple pairs of wheels without chassis, in each case pulled by oxen, doubtlessly more than 20. Along the first stretch of road where the slope was gentle, the ruts belong to the same type of trace left by traditional carts elsewhere in the ancient world. After the ramp, where the slope increases significantly, the profile of the ruts changes, and they become regular, smoothed, calibrated. This was a *hodopoiia*, a special road track, practically a "railway," executed with the greatest care in order to lower the coefficient of rolling friction to the

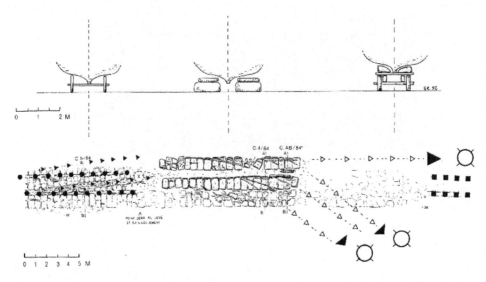

Figure 23.6. Reconstruction of transport carts and windlass location at the Diolkos. (After Raepsaet 1993: 254, fig. 11.)

lowest possible level and to tackle the effect of the increasing slope in the best conditions. In this way the negative effects of slippage and the possible problems of guidance were eliminated. The required effort for the heaviest cargoes remained considerable, however, up to 20,000–35,000 Newtons. The operation, in consequence, must be understood to have involved two phases: a classic haul-out, followed by a change in the lading through the transfer of the boat to another support by means of the ramp. For the most difficult portion of the route, a battery of capstans would have been necessary; an analysis of the wear lines in the blocks of the ramp and thus the directions of pulling, even allows location of their positions. A frame or support mounted on wheels calibrated to the dimensions of the grooves would have served for the means of transport (figures 23.6–7).

This complex originated without doubt in the sixth century B.C. In fact, the functioning of the *diolkos* is the product of a series of activities that had been relatively common since the beginning of the sixth century B.C., both in the removal and transport of monoliths in quarries and workshops and in activities associated with harbors. The analysis of this project highlights the exceptional quality of the interrelated chain of technologies put to work at Corinth. One notes all at once the scope of the installations, the precision of the track way, the knowledge of the effects of slope, the remarkable care expended on the *hodopoiia*, and the sagacity shown in the selection and interplay of the techniques and means of hauling. Did Sicilian wheat destined for Athens or amphoras of wine and oil from the Aegean on their way to Greek cities in the west all pass along the *diolkos*, or around the south end of the Peloponnese? The literary sources are silent on this subject, but a tax on its use, and the rental of infrastructure for economic and commercial activities, could have been advantageous for the city, along with the military application.

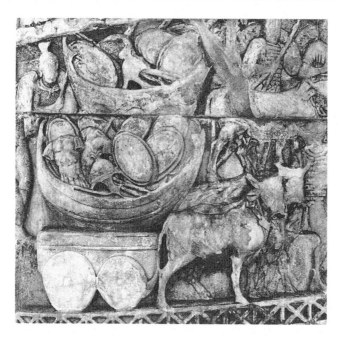

Figure 23.7. Military baggage on ox-drawn wagons, Column of Marcus Aurelius, ca. 180–193 A.D., Rome. (Photograph: Fototeca DAI Rome no. 55.1252.)

One of the oddities—and one of the most spectacular innovations—in the technology of transport during the Roman imperial period was the application of traction by means of a pair of shafts, or "single-headed" harnessing, in Italy and the northwest provinces (Raepsaet and Rommelaere 1995). This type of harness appeared in northern Italy and northern Gaul in the first century A.D. and revised the structure of harnessing by introducing draft with a single animal. The texts are silent on this subject, but the iconography is rich and shows a whole range of two-wheeled carts for traveling or mixed use drawn by an ass or a horse with the aid of a small yoke (also called *jouguet*, "little yoke" or "single yoke") placed on the neck (Raepsaet 1982; Molin 1987–1988). The use of this harness seems to have been restricted to the Celtic and German provinces. The technological value of the innovation has been contested, exclusively on the basis of iconographical evidence, by Lefèbvre des Noëttes for the same reasons as the alleged strangulation of the harnessed draft animal. The discussion has now been completely revised, following the discovery of a complete and well-preserved single yoke, along with portions of the harness, in a second-century Roman well in Bade-Wurtemberg (Raepsaet 2002: 266–67). These artifacts spawned an experimental research project led by the University of Brussels.

Draft by means of a single yoke is described by Pliny (*HN* 18.296) and Palladius (*Ag.* 7.2.2–4) with regard to the Gallic reaper (*vallus*), which the animal pushed from behind (Raepsaet 2002: 266–67). Among its other advantages, then, this harness could be used either for pulling or pushing, unlike the double yoke or

Figure 23.8. Wooden single yoke bar, molded copy and reproduction used in the Rochefort Experiment. Found in a second-century A.D. well at Pforzheim. (Photograph by G. Raepsaet.)

shoulder strap. The iconographical evidence, which had caused such perplexity among archaeologists and historians of technology (Vigneron 1968: 129–30), can now be clearly explained. The function of the single yoke is bound up, structurally and mechanically, with lateral "disks" that have the form of rounded swivel joints attached to the yoke. Leaning against the shoulder and designed to adjust closely to the morphology of the animal, these joints prevented the rubbing of the girth strap and transferred the support and push of the shoulders. This remarkable innovation relies on a knowledge of the anatomy of the draft animal, the structure of forces of traction and their transmission, as well as the balance of the harnessing technique. This harness, which bears some similarities with the "yoke saddles" of the Near East (Littauer 1968), is well adapted to the use of one animal for draft, particularly the ass or the mule. This arrangement has been tested on an ass pushing a reconstructed *vallus,* and it demonstrated remarkable efficiency in the task of harvesting grain on a slope and in difficult terrain (figures 23.8–9). The lateral "disks" are constantly in use during traction; they respond to all the movements of the shoulder and fore limbs, without hampering them, while transmitting their propulsive force. In summary, this *jouguet* with swivel joints represents an interesting compromise between high and low traction points and prefigures the medieval shoulder collar specifically designed for the horse.

The diversity of ancient cartage (Tarr 1969; Röring 1983; Treue 1986; *Rad und Wagen* 2004) reflects the variety of social contexts, economic needs, and geographical realities. Qualitative progress in the construction of these vehicles is not linear but is nevertheless perceptible during the Empire, above all in the evidence concerning the travel coach. In both the Greek and Roman world the transport coach is relatively

Figure 23.9. (Left) Experimentation with single-yoke harness at Rochefort (Belgium). (Right) Detail of single-yoke harness on mules, possibly at a milestone, Roman relief, Arlon (Belgium). (Photographs by G. Raepsaet.)

simple and adaptable (transformable and polyvalent) in comparison with the parade, war, or racing chariot. Official inscribed accounts at Eleusis (*IG* $2^2$ 1673), Epidaurus, and Didyma, however, show that wheelwrights on some occasions created heavy versions mounted on framework and disk wheels. The Roman Empire benefited from the contributions of Celtic technology (Schönfelder 2002), as the specialized Latin vocabulary tends to show. A rich terminology for land vehicles borrowed from Celtic—including *benna, carpentum, carruca, carrus, cisium, covinus, currus, petoritum, pilentum, plaustrum, sarracum,* and *triga*—is indicative of the growing functionality of Roman vehicles, above all for the movement of people. One must nevertheless point out that at one and the same time and in the same region, the lovely cart mounted on large 12-spoked wheels of the House of Menander at Pompeii could coexist with the rustic wagon of the Villa Regina farm at Boscoreale, which had solid wheels, an axle that turned with them, and a rudimentary box (Raepsaet 2002: 231). If the platform, box, and draw pole display carpentry skills, the construction of the wheel was generally a more specialized skill, and one that reveals regional traditions. Every design was present in the Greco-Roman world, from the primitive solid, one-piece disk wheel to the large 12-spoked wheel with a metal rim fastened at only one point. But there were also some common points, in that the wheel disk was always in the same plane—perpendicular to the surface on which it rolled. Rim offset and wheel camber did not appear in the west until the end of the medieval period. The design of the typical Greek wheel—the "cross-bar wheel"—is very original: four or six rim segments fixed on a central axle by means of perpendicular cross-bars (Raepsaet 1988), despite the fact that the Middle East had known the wheel with radial spokes for millennia and the Roman world of the Republic also rapidly developed this interesting technology. Another characteristic of ancient wheels is the thickness of the hub, and its projection. One must, however, avoid judging the quality of a wheel only on the basis of its degree of technical sophistication, size, or the number of spokes. It is also a question of competence, context, and profitability of the technological investment. Ethnographic evidence from southwestern France and northern Portugal includes transport carts with two disk wheels (either solid or with small cut-outs) that could carry more than a ton of cargo without difficulty.

The question of whether the two front wheels of a four-wheeled wagon were mounted so they could turn to one side or the other has now been solved. It is clear that from the Hallstatt period (Piggott 1983; *Vierrädrige Wagen* 1987), in the early first millennium B.C., the front wheels of a parade wagon were capable of pivoting beneath the box, thanks to a suspension working around a kingpin. Nevertheless, many representations of Roman wagons, if interpreted literally, show front wheels of a size that would have made such turns difficult, although not impossible. The size of the wheel made it impossible in many cases to execute a sharp turn, but the distance between the large-hub of the wheel and the platform of the wagon was sufficient to allow some pivoting of the front axle. Four-wheeled carts with a completely fixed front axle still exist in many parts of the world; they slip around the turn, carried by the team. There is no problem with maneuvering, but the wheels are worn out rapidly. Both the fixed and the turning axle coexisted, their contemporaneity more a question of quality of workmanship than of chronological evolution.

# Customs, Context, and Cost

Can we reconstruct the real situations and the practical applications of the transport of people and goods on land (Raepsaet 2002: 178–275)? From the rural estate to the construction site, from the harbor docks to traveling markets, land transport was omnipresent in antiquity, and multifarious. Neither marginal nor poorly developed, this technology was adapted to many aspects of the public and private economy, in domestic contexts and in commercial transactions, complementing the transport by sea, river, and canal. The vehicle drawn by animals was already part of the basic agricultural tool set on Hesiod's farm in Boeotia. By 600 B.C., long files of oxen yoked together in pairs carried boats over the *diolkos* at Corinth on trolleys, or enormous architectural members weighing many tons to construction sites at Didyma, Epidaurus, and Eleusis (figure 23.10).

The capability for transport is in practice more a capacity for organizing means of transport than of technological limitations. The small *hamaxai* of Athens carried everything: vegetables, wine amphoras, oil jars, three or four persons, a marriage party, or a funeral bier (Lorimer 1903). In Roman Apulia, caravans of asses with packsaddles formed long lines on their way to the sea (Varro, *Rust.* 2.6.5): "From Brundisium and the surrounding part of Apulia they transport oil or wine, likewise grain and anything else to the sea by means of asses with packsaddles" (*asellis*

Figure 23.10. Transport of marble on wagons, Carrara, ca. 1910. (After Raepsaet 2002: 110, fig. 40.)

*dossuariis*). Even if one misinterprets the ancient economy as having consisted only of food production on the estate and export from it, the problem of transport constituted a constant concern: manure on the farm, tree trunks in the forest, parts for mills or presses, cereals and fodder, various types of ceramic vessels, all carried for short or long distances on paved roads or winding paths. The ancient agronomists testify to this; for example, Varro (*Rust.* 1.16), for whom the choice of a farm is bound up with the necessity "to export our produce" (*fructus nostros exportare*), to which end it is advisable to have access to "roads and rivers" (*viae et fluvii*). Apart from the special cases of racing or ceremonial chariots, the movement of people often took place by the same means and methods as the transport of merchandise, and sometimes—as the iconography shows—the two were carried together.

In the Roman imperial world the sophistication, functionality, specialization, indeed the professionalism of transport and travel began to increase (Kolb 2000; Laurence 1999). Mounts and vehicles could be rented, with or without driver. In order to take care of the most varied needs of the state and of some private individuals, Roman culture developed some true traveling wagons and carts adapted to special circumstances, needs, or tastes, from the rather rustic *raeda* to the comfortable and expensive "sleeping wagon" (*carruca dormitoria*) on four wheels, from the light *cisium* to the covered *carpentum* on two.

Armies, of course, were important consumers of transport services. The Homeric chariot and the cavalry troop represent one aspect, but the logistics of supply and the transport of baggage are more important problems. The settled encampment in time of peace, the deployment of troops, and maneuvers in time of war all owe much to the efficiency of the means of transport. The examples are numerous: the hundreds of baggage carts that took part in Xenophon's march to the sea (*An.*

3.27), the convoys of thousands of mules that followed Alexander's army (Quintus Curtius 3.13.16; 8.7.4), the wagon train of 400 vehicles (*clitellae*) that proved insufficient to provision Capua in 212 B.C. (and were later heaped up as an improvised fortification) (Livy 25.36.7), or, finally, the hundreds of *carpenta* and *vehicula* taken as booty from the Gauls, Boiens, or Romans in various military actions during the second century B.C. The sculptured columns of Trajan and Marcus Aurelius in Rome provide a veritable compendium of the means of transport used by the Roman army (figure 23.7), including the movement of siege engines and siege towers or transport by ships on sea and river.

The notable development of means of transport during the Roman imperial period is bound up equally with the imperial message service, the *cursus publicus* (Kolb 2000; Stoffel 1994). Founded by Augustus, this express message service, at first carried out by horsemen, became a vast carriage service at the disposal of the State with an infrastructure of stations and fresh horses, and its own personnel, but it relied as well on requisitions. Various types of vehicles appear in the Theodosian Code (*De cursu publico angariis et parangariis* 5, 8), along with their load limits, from the *birota* rated at 200 pounds (66 kg) to the *raeda* rated at 1,000 pounds (330 kg) and the *angaria* rated at 1,500 pounds (492 kg). These statistics have often been considered, following the lead of Lefèbvre des Noëttes, as a decisive proof of the inefficiency of ancient harnessing technique. It has been shown above that heavy transport of ten tons or even more was, if not commonplace, at least perfectly feasible and had been accomplished already in archaic Greece. The figures in the Theodosian Code, then, present problems of interpretation, but they can in no way be considered a true indication of the technical limits of transport loads. Legislation concerned itself as well with the regulation of traffic in urban centers. The *lex Oppia*, passed during the period of the Punic Wars, forbade women from traveling in an animal-drawn vehicle within the walls of Rome (Livy 34.1.3). During the reign of Julius Caesar (*CIL* 1.593) privately owned wheeled vehicles were prohibited from entering Rome during daylight hours, and later on Claudius forbade travelers from entering towns in Italy "except on foot, in a sedan chair, or in a litter" (Suetonius, *Claud.* 25.2).

In addition to those who—on a casual or professional basis—rented out mounts or carriages, with or without a driver, at city gates, harbors, and highway rest stops, the personnel engaged in transport enjoyed an important role in both the private economy and in public services. They often organized themselves in professional associations that assumed an important part in large-scale commerce, in particular in the western provinces. The corporations of carriers by sea and river (*navicularii, nautae*) are well documented in the important cities and ports of Italy and the western provinces. The *nautae*, "entrepreneurs engaged in river transport," who specialized in a particular river basin, had to guarantee as well the transfer of goods by land between rivers, either personally or by subcontract. The complexity and the technical sophistication of long-distance transport justified the existence of a specialized group of workers and raises questions as to why fewer *collegia* (corporations)—apart from the *cisiarii* (cart drivers, *CIL* 11.2615)—are documented for land transport. Journeys by land were often shorter and perhaps easier to organize than those by water, so *negotiatores* (traders—well attested in epigraphical sources for a variety of products) must often have had to arrange their own means of transport, or have rented these services from the owners of teams, particularly farmers.

One must conjure up as well an image of the road system, which ought to be integrated in the statement of the issues involved in land transport (Laurence 1999; see also chapter 22). Contrary to a widespread misconception, the great Roman road network, although conceived in the spirit of strategic value and bound up with the needs stemming from the exercise of centralized authoritarian power, nevertheless constituted an important support for commercial transport. Besides, a paved road is not essential for movement on land, even with animal-drawn transport. Aside from traditional sources, archaeological and cartographical studies on the dispersion and diffusion of artifacts show that the process of commercial distribution, for example of *sigillata* wares (Raepsaet and Raepsaet-Charlier 1987–1988), makes use of all routes, from strategic armatures to local byways, and supplemented by rivers, which were not at all a marginal factor. With regard to the quality and quantity of the products purchased, there appears to have been no difference in purchasing power between sites on a river and those on a land route, despite the marked differences in cost among transport by road, river, or sea. One of the traditional props for the minimalist theory in matters of land transport is the comparatively very high cost of the latter. The figures given by Diocletian's Edict Concerning Maximum Prices show in effect that in every case of routes within the empire, transport by land was significantly more expensive than transport by river, and still more than that by sea. These statistics corroborate some anecdotal reports in literary texts (e.g., Cato, *Agr.* 22.3). This fact, which in the orthodox view would appear as a decisive argument against the importance of the role of land transport in the classical world, is in reality a widespread commonplace among preindustrial societies. In eighteenth-century England, for example, the relative cost of transport by sea, river, and land was on average a factor of 1, 4.7, and 22.6, respectively, figures close to those in the Roman Empire. Besides, the ancient system of commerce—in large part preindustrial in character—functioned by including the overhead costs of transport into the base cost of the merchandise. To speak of a handicap in the classical world is both anachronistic and epistemologically irrelevant.

Ancient land transport was based on human portage, the pack saddle, the light two-wheeled cart with draw pole and a pair of horses, asses, or mules, the heavy, four-wheeled wagon (or trolley with numerous wheels) drawn by oxen yoked together in pairs, sometimes several pairs in series, to which may be added the exceptional western Roman two-pole vehicle with a single draft animal. The Greek *hamaxa*, a small all-purpose cart with two crossbar wheels, existed alongside the heavy *tet-rakukloi* wagons, just as at Rome the small, fast *cisium* with spoked wheels complemented the imposing *carrucae*, veritable predecessors of the heavy mail coach. The Roman imperial culture was in the process of developing the means of transport by land, including an excellent control of the techniques for producing the spoked wheel, a functional range of service vehicles, integrating the interesting accomplishments of Celtic skill in cart construction. The *pax romana* favored a dynamic of development in which the quality of means of transport played an active role.

In general, in the Greco-Roman world transport in all its forms took part in all the surrounding economic systems, satisfying the demands made of it without any particular handicap. It relied on the traditional motive forces (human, animal, water, wind), which have the inconvenience of a lesser potential in comparison with modern fossil fuels, but the advantage of being indefinitely renewable. The principal ancient technique for harnessing is in every case bound up with the double or single yoke, the habitual method for bovines and asses. It is less well adapted to the morphology of horses, but their economic role was marginal. In any case, even with horses, experimentation has shown that, with a light load of a ton, or even more, the harness design does not pose any problems for traction. Structurally, with regard to the human and animal energy available and the principal draft harness used, the means of land transport in the classical world aligns itself well with the typical operation of transport in preindustrial societies. Its efficiency, however, reached a very exceptional peak during the Roman Empire, in terms of both public administration and private use. The technological innovation of the horse collar in certain parts of western Europe, associated with the economic growth of the beginning of the medieval period, finds an interesting prototype in the ancient Gallo-Roman single yoke. Some other qualitative jumps—with regard to the harness and the technology of animal draft: soft traces, whiffle-tree; with regard to the vehicle: the offset rim, wheel camber, suspension on longitudinal straps—mark the long stretch of history, but without causing any true general quantitative jump prior to the fundamental changes in the sources of energy that took place in the nineteenth century.

The social value of a technical component depends as much on the effectiveness and the coherence of the chain of technological links and on the economic environment as on its own specific mechanical quality. It constitutes one link in the means of production, dormant or active. The Greek and Roman cultures had at their disposal a technical capacity for land transport that was real and varied, even innovative, inscribing its own rhythms and inflections on the long-term patterns of preindustrial societies.

# REFERENCES

Abeels, P. 1995. "Les configurations de la traction aux brancards: Forces et effets," in Raepsaet and Rommelaere 1995: 13–29.

Adam, J.-P. 1984. *La construction romaine, matériaux et techniques.* Paris: Picard.

Amouretti, M.-C., and G. Comet 1994. *Hommes et techniques de l'Antiquité à la Renaissance.* Paris: Colin.

Amouretti, M.-C., and F. Sigaut (eds.) 1998. *Traditions agronomiques européennes: Elaboration et transmission depuis l'Antiquité*. Paris: CTHS.

Argoud, G., and J.-Y. Guillaumin (eds.) 1998. *Sciences exactes et sciences appliquées à Alexandrie*. Saint-Etienne: Publications de l'Université.

Astill, G., and J. Langdon (eds.) 1997. *Medieval farming and technology: The impact of agricultural change in northwest Europe*. Leiden: Brill.

Burford, A. 1960. "Heavy transport in ancient Greece," *Economic History Review* 13: 1–18.

Burford, A. 1969. *The Greek temple builders at Epidauros*. Liverpool: University Press.

Comet, G. (ed.) 2003. *L'outillage agricole médiéval et moderne et son histoire*. Toulouse: Presses universitaires du Mirail.

Cotterell, B., and J. Kamminga 1990. *Mechanics of pre-industrial technology*. Cambridge: Cambridge University Press.

Crouwel, J. H. 1981. *Chariots and other means of land transport in Bronze Age Greece*. Amsterdam: Allard Pierson.

Crouwel, J. H. 1992. *Chariots and other wheeled vehicles in Iron Age Greece*. Amsterdam: Allard Pierson.

Deman, A. 2002. "Avec les utriculaires sur les sentiers muletiers de la Gaule romaine," *Cahiers Glotz* 13: 233–46.

Fellmeth, U. 2002. *"Eine wohlhabende Stadt sei nahe...,"* *Die Standortfaktoren in der römischen Agrarökonomie im Zusammenhang mit den Verkehrs- und Raumordnungsstrukturen im römischen Italien*. St. Katharinen: Scripta Mercaturae Verlag.

Fenton, A. et al. (eds.) 1973. *Land transport in Europe*. Copenhagen: Nationalmuseet.

Finley, M. I. 1965. "Technical innovation and economic progress in the ancient world," *Economic History Review* 18: 29–45.

Fleury, P. 1993. *La mécanique de Vitruve*. Caen: Presses universitaires.

Garbsch, J. 1986. *Mann und Ross und Wagen*. München: Museum für Vor- und Frühgeschichte.

Gasparin Cte de. 1863. *Cours d'agriculture*. 3rd ed. Paris: Librairie agricole de la Maison rustique.

Gille, B. 1980. *Les mécaniciens grecs: La naissance de la technologie*. Paris: Seuil.

Greene, K. 1990. "Perspectives on Roman technology," *Oxford Journal of Archaeology* 9: 209–19.

Greene, K. 1994. "Technology and innovation in context: The Roman background to medieval and later developments," *Journal of Roman Archaeology* 7: 22–32.

Greene, K. 2000. "Technological innovation and economic progress in the ancient world: M. I. Finley re-considered," *Economic History Review* 53: 29–59.

Haudricourt, A.-G. 1987. *La technologie, science humaine*. Paris: Maison des Sciences de l'Homme.

Healey, J. F. 1999. *Pliny the Elder on science and technology*. Oxford: Oxford University Press.

Hopfen, H. J. 1970. *L'outillage agricole pour les régions arides et tropicales*. Roma: FAO.

Humphrey, J., J. P. Oleson, and A. Sherwood 1998. *Greek and Roman technology: A sourcebook*. London: Routledge.

Hyland, A. 1990. *Equus: The horse in the Roman world*. London: Batsford.

Jankuhn, H. et al. (eds.) 1989. *Untersuchungen zu Handel und Verkehr der vor- und frühgeschichtliche Zeit in Mittel-und Nordeuropa*. Vol. 5, *Der Verkehr*. Göttingen: Vandenhoeck and Ruprecht.

Kolb, A. 2000. *Transport und Nachrichtentransfer im Römischen Reich*. Berlin: Akademie Verlag.

Landels, J. G. 2000. *Engineering in the ancient world*. Rev. ed. Berkeley: University of California Press.

Langdon, J. 1986. *Horses, oxen and technological innovation: The use of draft animals in English farming, 1066–1500*. Cambridge: Cambridge University Press.

Laurence, R. 1999. *The roads of Roman Italy: Mobility and cultural change*. London: Routledge.

Lefèbvre des Noëttes, Ct. 1931. *L'attelage, le cheval de selle à travers les Ages*. Paris: Imprimerie nationale.

Leone, A. 1988. *Gli animali da trasporto nell'Egitto greco-romano e bizantino*. Roma: Editrice Pontifico.

Leone, A. 1992. *Gli animali da lavoro, da allevamento e gli hippoi nell'Egitto greco-romano e bizantino*. Roma: Edizioni Athena.

Lewis, M. 2000. "The Hellenistic period," in Ö. Wikander (ed.), *Handbook of ancient water technology*. Leiden: Brill, 631–48.

Littauer, M. A. 1968. "The function of the yoke saddle in ancient harnessing," *Antiquity* 42: 27–31.

Littauer, M. A., and J. Crouwel 1979. *Wheeled vehicles and ridden animals in the ancient Near East*. Leiden: Brill.

Lorimer, H. L. 1903. "The country cart in ancient Greece," *Journal of Hellenic Studies* 23: 132–51.

Mattingly, D., and J. Salmon (eds.) 2001. *Economies beyond agriculture in the classical world*. London: Routledge.

Meijer, F., and O. Van Nijf. 1992. *Trade, transport and society in the ancient world: A sourcebook*. London: Routledge.

Meissner, B. 1999. *Die technologische Fachliteratur der Antike*. Berlin: Akademie Verlag.

Mingote Calderon, J. L. 1996. *Tecnologia agricola medieval en Espana: Una relacion entre la etnologia y la arqueologia a traves de los aperos agricolas*. Madrid: Ministerio de agricultura.

Molin, M. 1987–1988. "La faiblesse de l'attelage antique ou la force des idées reçues en histoire ancienne," *Bulletin archéologique du Comité des travaux historiques* 23–24: 39–84.

Nicolet, C. (ed.) 1996. *Les littératures techniques dans l'Antiquité romaine*. Genève: Fondation Hardt.

Oexle, J. 1992. *Studien zu merowingerzeitlichem Pferdegeschirr am Beispiel der Trensen*. Mainz: von Zabern.

Piggott, S. 1983. *The earliest wheeled transport: From the Atlantic coast to the Caspian Sea*. Ithaca, NY: Cornell University Press.

*Rad und Wagen* 2004. *Rad und Wagen: Der Ursprung einer Innovation. Wagen im Vorderen Orient und Europa*. Mainz: von Zabern.

Raepsaet, G. 1982. "Attelages antiques dans le Nord de la Gaule: Les systèmes de traction par équidés," *Trierer Zeitschrift* 45: 215–73.

Raepsaet, G. 1984. "Transport de tambours de colonnes du Pentélique à Éleusis," *L'Antiquité Classique* 53: 234–261.

Raepsaet, G. 1988. "Charrettes en terre cuite de l'époque archaïque à Corinthe," *L'Antiquité Classique* 57: 56–88.

Raepsaet, G. 1993. "Le diolkos de l'Isthme à Corinthe: Son tracé, son fonctionnement," *Bulletin de Correspondence Hellenique* 117: 233–61.

Raepsaet, G. 1998–2001. *Der Neue Pauly. s.v.* Esel, 4: 130–135. *s.v.* Landtransport, 6: 1098–1106. *s.v.* Maultier, 7: 1043–1047. *s.v.* Pferd, 8: 692–703. *s.v.* Rind, 9: 1014–1020.

Raepsaet, G. 2002. *Attelages et techniques de transport dans le monde gréco-romain.* Bruxelles: Timperman.

Raepsaet, G., and M.-T. Raepsaet-Charlier 1987–1988. "Aspects de l'organisation du commerce de la céramique sigillée dans le Nord de la Gaule au IIe siècle de n. ère," *Münstersche Beiträge zur antiken Handelsgeschichte* 6: 1–29 and 7: 45–69.

Raepsaet, G., and C. Rommelaere (eds.) 1995. *Brancards et transport attelé entre Seine et Rhin de l'Antiquité au Moyen Âge.* Bruxelles-Treignes: ULB.

Rommelaere, C. 1991. *Les chevaux du Nouvel Empire égyptien.* Louvain-la-Neuve: UCL.

Röring, C. 1983. *Untersuchungen zu römischen Reisewagen.* Koblenz: Numismatischer Verlag.

Schönfelder, M. 2002. *Das spätkeltische Wagengrab von Boé (Dép. Lot-et-Garonne): Studien zu Wagen und Wagengräbern der jüngeren Latènezeit.* Mainz: Römisch-germanisches Zentralmuseum.

Schneider, H. 1992. *Einführung in die antike Technikgeschichte.* Darmstadt: WBG.

Sigaut, F. 1985. *L'évolution technique des agricultures européennes avant l'époque industrielle.* Paris: EHSS.

Sigaut, F. 1987. "Haudricourt et la technologie," in Haudricourt 1987: 9–32.

Spruytte, J. 1977. *Études expérimentales sur l'attelage: Contribution à l'histoire du cheval.* Paris: Crépin-Leblond.

Starkey, P. 2002. *Moyens de transport locaux pour le développement rural.* London: DFID.

Stoffel, P. 1994. *Über die Staatspost, die Ochsengespanne und die requirierten Ochsengespanne.* Bern: Lang.

Tarr, L. 1969. *The history of the carriage.* New York: Arco.

*Techniques rurales* 1971. *Techniques rurales en Afrique.* Vol. 13, *Manuel de culture avec traction animale.* Paris, Ministère des Affaires étrangères.

Treue, W. (ed.) 1986. *Achse, Rad und Wagen: Fünf Tausend Jahre Kultur- und Technikgeschichte.* Göttingen: Vandenhoeck and Ruprecht.

*Vierrädrige Wagen* 1987. *Vierrädrige Wagen der Hallstattzeit: Untersuchungen zu Geschichte und Technik.* Mainz: Ph. von Zabern.

Vigneron, P. 1968. *Le cheval dans l'Antiquité gréco-romaine.* Nancy: Université.

Whitehead, D., and P. H. Blyth 2004. *Athenaeus Mechanicus, On Machines.* Stuttgart: Steiner.

# CHAPTER 24

# SEA TRANSPORT, PART 1: SHIPS AND NAVIGATION

## SEÁN MCGRAIL

## SOURCES OF EVIDENCE

Nowhere in the world have technical discussions of shipbuilding or navigation come down to us from before late medieval times. Today, both technologies are primarily science based, but in the period under discussion—800 B.C. to A.D. 500—they were more of an art in that reliance was placed on personal experience and ability. During those centuries rafts, boats, and ships were built by eye and rules of thumb (McGrail 2003), while navigation—the art of determining a vessel's position on the open sea and taking her in safety from one place to another—was undertaken without instruments, using handed-on experience, local knowledge, and detailed observation of natural phenomena (McGrail 1996a). These ship-building and navigational skills were acquired by oral instruction and supervised "apprenticeships." We cannot, therefore, expect accounts of these techniques to have been compiled before ship design and navigation became science-based and printing became commonplace—that is, until the fifteenth century A.D.

## Textual Evidence

Nevertheless, some of the written works that have come down to us do provide clues to early shipbuilding and navigational techniques (see, for example, Humphrey et al. 1998: 442–84; Casson 1989). Furthermore, numerous two- and three-dimensional representations of boats and ships add to our knowledge, especially of masts, sails, and rigging (Basch 1987a). Excavated vessels, even if fragmentary, give us direct evidence of shipbuilding techniques, but archaeology throws little light on early navigation since, apart from the sounding lead and line, it was carried out without instruments. Contemporary ethnographic evidence offers some assistance.

Since the main aim of Homer, and of later classical authors such as Caesar, Strabo, and Pliny, was not to document shipbuilding or navigational techniques but to record events that had been handed down to them or that they themselves had observed, the nautical information found in their surviving works is mostly of a general nature and often inconsequential. Nevertheless, there are passages that alert us to some special characteristic of a contemporary form of water transport, leading to deductions about the capabilities of both ship and crew (Mark 2005).

## Iconographical Evidence

Representations of rafts and boats are the main source of evidence for the earliest stages of shipbuilding, prior to the Late Bronze Age. Moreover there are depictions of rafts and of boats made of hide, basketry, or logs, physical examples of which have not yet been excavated. Egyptian paintings and models are especially informative: they not only depict plank boats being built and boatmen with lead and line ready to check water depth (*pace* Oleson 2000) but also illustrate all forms of propulsion and steering. Furthermore, the survival, recovery, and recording of the Cheops ship of approximately 2600 B.C.—the earliest documented planked vessel—has provided some control on the interpretation of Egyptian iconography (figure 24.1). On the other hand, without extensive boat remains in the Aegean before the first millennium B.C., lack of effective controls has led to some imaginative interpretations of early boat depictions (McGrail 2004a: 120–22).

## Ethnographical Evidence

In India and other parts of the developing world, boats are still built using inherited tools and techniques, to a design handed on by the builder's predecessors. Such boats are built of wood and are propelled by muscle power or by the wind, characteristics that make it possible to use them to interpret clues to ancient technology found in excavated boat remains. There are problems in using cross-cultural analogies, but the more alike in technological, environmental, and economic terms the ancient and the recent cultures are, the greater the value of ethnographic boat

Figure 24.1. Cheops ship (ca. 2650 B.C.), Giza, Egypt. (Photograph by P. Johnstone.)

studies to the investigation of early nautical technologies and boat use. This is not to say that there is a one-to-one relationship between ancient technology and "living tradition." Ethnographic evidence may suggest a range of possible answers to questions arising from incomplete, fragmented, and distorted boat remains, but "only archaeology, in conjunction with the various natural sciences, can give the right answers" (Clark 1953: 357), bearing in mind that, in the present stage of knowledge, no answer may be possible at all.

## Archaeological Evidence

Egypt provides the world's earliest examples of excavated, planked vessels. Nevertheless, such excavated ships and boats do not instantly reveal their design principles, original form, sequence of construction, or propulsion and steering arrangements. They are incomplete (especially when wrecked rather than entombed): the sailing rig rarely survives, and individual timbers are distorted and displaced. Before a comprehensive account of such a vessel can be published, a lengthy multidisciplinary investigation has to be undertaken, leading, when sufficient evidence survives, to a theoretical reconstruction of the original vessel (or as near to that as it is now possible to get) in the form of a small-scale model or drawing, together with appropriate calculations (McGrail 2006). Occasionally this process leads to the building of a full-scale model (called a replica) of this reconstruction. This phase of post-excavation research (which is not only lengthy but also expensive) has not always been undertaken rigorously, sometimes leading to questionable results (Coates et al. 1995; Crumlin-Pedersen and McGrail 2006).

Until the late twentieth century, vessels were usually dated by the archaeological context from which they had been excavated, or from cargo or other finds associated with them. These indirect methods were sometimes insufficiently accurate, however, and in more recent times vessels have been dated directly by radiocarbon assay or by dendrochronology. A clearer understanding of technological changes within the early Mediterranean will only be possible when the more precise dates obtainable from tree ring analysis become available. Such investigations may also suggest the region where the parent trees of the ship's timber grew, and thus help in the search for origins.

Each early plank boat was unique, since until the end of our period they were conceived and built individually. Nevertheless, sufficient finds have now been excavated and published to show that groups of vessels can be identified, each member with its own individuality yet having several structural characteristics in common with other members of its group. These traditions are theoretical constructs that help our understanding; they may or may not be similar to the concepts of the people who built and sailed these vessels. Two such traditions recognized in our period are vessels with sewn-plank fastenings (figure 24.2) and vessels with locked mortise and tenon fastenings (figure 24.3). There are also "hybrid" boats that are mostly mortise and tenon fastened but with some sewn strakes (for an explanation of this and other nautical terms, see the glossary at the end of the chapter). Ships and boats of both traditions were built plank-first—that is, the planking was fastened together to form the shape of hull required; then the supporting framing was fastened to the planking. It may be that as the definition of individual building traditions in terms of structural features is refined, it will become practicable to recognize changes over time with precision and even to identify the region where the boat that constitutes an individual wreck had been built. Indeed, the long-term aim must be to narrow origins down to a particular shipyard identified by a personal touch given to several excavated wrecks by a particular master shipwright.

The identification of the timber species used in the hull, the dendrochronological examination of the timber, the home port of the ship's crew as deduced from their personal possessions, and the nature of the cargo and ballast carried have all been used to investigate a ship's origins. Cargo and ballast may be misleading, however, since both may be embarked late in the ship's life, far away from her supposed home port. On the other hand, the origin of the cargo may prove useful in determining what had been or was to be the vessel's route on the final voyage. Dendrochronological examination and species identification of hull timbers are the most promising ways to a ship's origins, followed by personal possessions, if these can be recognized as such.

Figure 24.2. Ma'agan Mikhael ship, reconstruction of sewn fastenings. (Photograph by: Y. Kahanov.)

Cargo found with a wreck can indicate that the original vessel was a merchant ship. If the reconstructed lines of the vessel show that she had a full transverse section and a length to breadth (L/B) ratio of the underwater hull of about 3:1, this function is confirmed. In the classical world a specialized warship had a L/B ratio of about 6:1 or 7:1; examples of the sixth or fifth century B.C. are likely to have had a ram and thus would have had a full complement of oarsmen. Apart from timbers inside the Athlit ram (Casson and Steffy 1991) no unambiguous warship remains have so far been identified. It has been argued (Morrison and Coates 1986: 128; Casson 1991: 82) that trireme warships needed no ballast and were built of such lightweight timber that they did not sink when damaged, but lay crippled on the surface until they could be towed away. If this was in fact the case, their remains are unlikely to be excavated.

A seagoing vessel has to have adequate freeboard and stability. Assessment of these and other qualities must be based on an authentic reconstruction of the original shape, structure, propulsion, and steering of an excavated vessel. An open boat of less than a certain size is unlikely to have been seagoing, but a decked vessel could have been. A rockered bottom, a "boat-shaped" underwater hull, and a sheerline rising toward the ends suggest a seagoing vessel; a box-shaped vessel, on the other hand, is likely to have been a river or harbor craft. It is important that such attributes and features are not worked into a reconstruction without good reason (Crumlin-Pedersen and McGrail 2006).

## Experimental Archaeology

Theoretical reconstructions of an ancient vessel, as well as the effectiveness or otherwise of deduced, noninstrumental methods of navigation, need to be tested at sea (Coates et al. 1995; McGrail 1993, 2004a: 7). Twentieth-century Micronesian

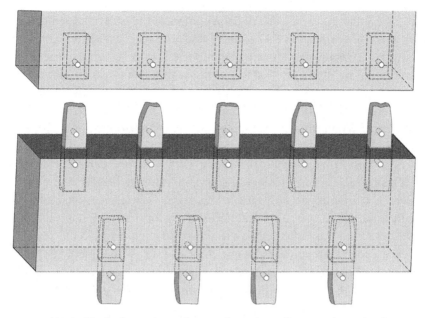

Figure 24.3. Typical locked mortise and tenon fastenings, diagram. (Drawing by S. Haad.)

methods of navigation have been successfully used under controlled conditions in the South Pacific (McGrail 2004a: 339–45). The findings of such trials are applicable to voyages undertaken after the initial discovery of islands during exploratory voyages. It would be much more difficult—probably impossible—to reenact an exploratory voyage on which the participants did not know what, if any, land lay ahead, other than the general direction of distant land from the flight line of migratory birds or the visible deflection of a swell by a faraway island. Nor would these first explorers have known with any certainty what environmental conditions lay ahead of them, except as projections of the weather and sea states recently experienced; this state of doubt would also be difficult to reenact.

Although experimental navigation has not yet been undertaken in the Mediterranean, it seems reasonable to expect that the theory and practice of noninstrumental navigation as they evolved in a South Pacific context are generally applicable to the Mediterranean. Indeed, they are probably valid worldwide, since the differences now noted between the navigational techniques used recently in Oceania, the China Seas, and the Indian Ocean are principally due to differences in latitude and other aspects of the maritime environment, rather than to fundamental differences in techniques (McGrail 2004a: 434). Moreover, there are passages in Homer's *Odyssey* from which it is clear that noninstrumental navigational methods used in the Early Iron Age Mediterranean fit the South Pacific model (McGrail 1996a; 2004a: 100–102; Mark 2005: 138–52).

Full-scale reconstructions of two notable Mediterranean vessels—both with mortise and tenon plank fastenings and nail-fastened framing—were designed, built and sailed during the 1980s (McGrail 2004a: 141–45; 151–52), each being an example of a particular approach to experimental boat archaeology. The first was a specific experiment, in which the documentation of the excavated remains of the Kyrenia wreck of around 300 B.C. (Steffy 1985; 1989; 1994: 45–59) was transformed (probably via a small-scale drawing or model) into a full-scale, seagoing ship (Katzev and Katzev 1986, 1987; Katzev 1989a, 1989b, 1990; Cariolou 1997).

In contrast, since there are no known remains of a trireme, the most extreme warship design of the sixth and fifth centuries B.C., the Trireme Project's aim was to reconstruct a representative example of an Athenian trireme of the fifth century B.C. It was hoped that this reconstruction would achieve historically documented measures of performance while complying with evidence derived from iconographic, historical, and archaeological sources illuminated by naval architectural principles (Coates and McGrail 1984: 11–12, 51–52; Coates et al. 1990; Shaw 1993; Morrison et al. 2000: 191–206). This full-scale reconstruction was subsequently commissioned into the Hellenic Navy as *Olympias* (figure 24.4).

There are many difficulties to be overcome by those who undertake either type of experiment (Coates et al. 1995; McGrail 1986, 1993, 2004b). Not the least of these are the addition of missing parts to the incomplete, dispersed, and distorted remains that are excavated, and the design of an appropriate propulsion and steering outfit. Both experiments have been evaluated (Westerdahl 1992; Tilley 1976, 1992, 1995, 2004; Basch 1987b; McGrail 1992). It is generally agreed that the Trireme Project has increased understanding of warship building and seafaring in the early eastern Mediterranean. This experiment was undertaken in a scholarly and scientific manner and progressed in phases, each being presented and/or published before moving on to the next phase. Planning began in 1982; an "advisory discussion" was held at the National Maritime Museum, Greenwich, in 1983; the proceedings, including an agreed design, were published in 1984, and the building of *Olympias* began in 1985. Reports on the planning, on the building, and on the several trial seasons were subsequently published (Morrison and Coates 1989; Coates et al. 1990; Shaw 1993). This openness to criticism generated confidence in the reconstructed ship, which, despite the choice of what was later deduced to be an inappropriate length of cubit as a module (Morrison et al. 2000: 245–46, 268), can now be seen to be as valid a reconstruction of a representative fifth-century B.C. trireme as can be expected with the evidence available (*contra*, Tilley 2004).

On the other hand, although the excavated evidence on which the Kyrenia ship reconstruction (*Kyrenia 2*) was specifically based has been well argued and presented by Steffy (1985; 1994: 45–59), a definitive report on the design, building, and use at sea of *Kyrenia 2* has yet to be published. The authenticity of this experiment cannot at present be confirmed, nor can its value to the study of a late-first-millennium B.C. Mediterranean cargo ship–building and use be determined. Doubts about the authenticity of reconstructions and the reliability and validity of experiments could be forestalled if experimenters were to publish their experimental philosophy and methodology and clearly state their chain of argument from evidence to reconstruction, before they committed to building a full-scale model. This should allow time for wide criticism so that, in time, an agreed "floating hypoth-

Figure 24.4. Reconstructed trireme *Olympias* under sail. (Photograph by P. Lipke, Trireme Trust.)

esis" could be built that would be archaeologically and historically valuable (McGrail 2004a: 5–6, 141–45, 151–52; 2006).

## Environmental Contexts

In order to understand the use of early water transport it is necessary to reconstruct the maritime environment in which it was operated: that is, former sea levels, coastlines, weather, currents, and tides. Over the past 3,000 years, however, the effects on Mediterranean seafaring of changes in sea level and climate have generally been insignificant (Murray 1987; McGrail 2004a: 89–95). In our period, the seasonal winds, local winds, land and sea breezes (prominent during a Mediterranean summer), and current flows are all thought to have been only slightly different from those of today. But tectonic movements, coastal erosion, silting, and soil erosion will have caused significant local changes. With this proviso, today's Mediterranean maps, charts, weather and tidal data may be applied to the late Iron Age.

Tidal ranges and streams can be influenced by sea level and coastline changes, but the Mediterranean's almost closed nature means that it is, and was, almost tideless: only in the straits of Gibraltar, Messina, and Euripus are there appreciable tidal flows, and only at the head of the Adriatic and in the Gulf of Gabes (Tunisia) do tidal ranges exceed one meter.

# Shipbuilding before 800 B.C.

## Egypt

Herodotus (2.5) described Egypt as "the gift of the River Nile," meaning that Egyptian civilization would not have existed without the fertile silt regularly carried northward by that great river. The Nile may also be said to be responsible for Egypt's nautical development, since it was the principle means of communication through the land, with no part of the valley more than 16 km from the river. Compared with the Mesopotamian rivers, the Nile had the advantage that it flowed north against the predominant northerly wind; thus sail could be used on boats heading southward against the river current, and was so used before 3100 B.C. (McGrail 2004a: 16, fig. 2.5; James 1983: 21–22). Excavated tomb paintings and models show that from the Early Dynastic Period (ca. 3100–2866 B.C.) onward reed bundle rafts were used on the Nile and in its wide-spreading delta channels. Such rafts have not been excavated, but there are several examples of excavated planked vessels from later periods.

In 1954, the Cheops ship was recovered from an underground chamber near the pyramid of Cheops (or Khufu) and dated to about 2650 B.C. (Lipke 1984; Haldane 1997b; Ward 2000: 45–60) (figure 24.1). As reassembled, the ship measures 43.4 x 5.9 x 1.8 m, with the ends rising to 6–7.5m. This impressive vessel was built plank-first, the cedar hull planks being positioned next to one another by projections from the plank's edges which enmeshed with indentations on adjacent planks, by treenails within the seams, and by unlocked mortise and tenon joints. Another version of that joint, in which the loose tenon was locked by treenails, was also known to Egyptian woodworkers, and was used in this vessel's superstructure but not in the hull. These fittings and features within plank seams not only relocated the planking during refits after dismantling for stitch renewal, but also resisted the tendency of adjacent planks to slide relative to one another when afloat, by carrying the shear stresses imposed on the hull.

The planks were fastened together by widely-spaced, individual lashings of halfa grass (*Demostachya bipinnata*), and the whole shell of planking fastened from sheer to sheer by transverse sewing, the sewing holes being worked within the thickness of the strakes so that stitches were not exposed externally, where they would be damaged when the ship was berthed. This Egyptian care for sewn fastenings is a feature of every later sewn-plank technology (McGrail and Kentley 1985; Mark 2005: 25–69). The planked hull was subsequently stabilized by crossbeams let into the top strake and by sixteen great floor timbers lashed to the planking. A central carling, lashed to the beams and supported by stanchions, reinforced the hull longitudinally.

Several other early Egyptian boats have been found on land. During the last decade of the twentieth century, a group of fourteen boat graves, provisionally dated to the period before 2600 B.C., were exposed at Abydos in the vicinity of second and first dynasty monuments. One vessel has been partly excavated (Ward 2003). The parallel-edged planks of these flat-bottomed boats were fastened together by lines of sewing over caulking, running transversely across the bottom and sides of the boat, as in the Cheops ship. Excavations between 1893 and 1895 around the pyramid of Sesostris (Senusret III) at Dahshur revealed six boats dated to around 1850 B.C. (de Morgan 1894–1903). The three planks forming the plank-keel of these boats were butted end to end and fastened together by wooden dovetail cramps set into the planks' inboard faces. The strakes were fastened together, edge to edge, by unlocked mortise and tenon joints and by widely spaced dovetail cramps; the ends of the fourth strakes, which do not run the full length of the hull, were lashed in position. Ward (Haldane 1996, 1997a) has suggested that the dovetail cramps are modern replacements for L- or V-shaped lashing holes within the planks' thickness. The boats have no framing but are reinforced by thirteen crossbeams lashed in position and held to the third strake by treenails.

The earliest known use of locked mortise and tenon fastenings in the Levant region is on a table from a Jericho tomb of the mid-second millennium B.C. (Wachsmann 1998: 241, figs. 10.28–29). Furthermore, Sleeswyk (1980) has shown that the Romans subsequently knew such joints as "Phoenician joints" (*coagmenta punicana*; Cato, *Ag.* 18.9). Mid-second-millennium B.C. wrecks off the Turkish coast at Uluburun and Cape Gelidonya, with their planking joined by locked mortise and tenon fastenings, have been identified from their cargo as Canaanite/ Syrian or Levantine (Bass 1991; 1997: 269; Pulak 1998: 214; Wachsmann 1998: 206–7), while Pulak (2003: 29) states that they were "built along the Syro-Palestinian coast or on Cyprus." The view that these vessels were built on the Levant coast has not gone unchallenged, and alternative origins in the Aegean have been suggested. Identifying a wreck's origin is difficult (McGrail 1991: 83–84; 2004a: 10), and a definitive answer may prove impossible. Nevertheless, the balance of evidence does seem to point toward an origin in the Levant or Cyprus region rather than in the Aegean. The locked mortise and tenon plank-fastenings in the Uluburun wreck (ca. 1305 B.C.) are the earliest known in a ship's hull. It is therefore conceivable that early Phoenician shipbuilders adopted Egyptian woodworking techniques and developed a locked joint that was watertight (Wachsmann 1998: 241). Such an innovation would have enhanced the Phoenician reputation for seafaring excellence (McGrail 2004a: 129). On their subsequent overseas trading voyages, the Phoenicians may well have introduced locked mortise and tenon hull plank fastenings to other Mediterranean lands (Basch 1981).

Early Egyptian seagoing ships are depicted with girdles at bow and stern, and with hogging hawsers (reinforcing cables) running from bow to stern. By the reign of Ramesses III (1198–1166 B.C.), however, hawsers and girdles are no longer depicted, suggesting that confidence had been increased in the structural integrity of the hull—this may have been due to the introduction of locked mortise and tenon fastenings subsequently seen in the mid-first millennium B.C. ship excavated at Matariya, near Heliopolis (Wachsmann 1998: 222).

If the conjecture that Phoenicians in the later second millennium inherited shipbuilding skills from the Egyptians is correct, the Phoenicians would, initially, have used sewn plank fastenings as well as mortise and tenon fastenings, and frames would have been lashed to that planking. No frames were excavated from the Uluburun or the Cape Gelidonya sites, and there were no frame fastenings visible on the small sections of planking recovered. It is unlikely, however, that such seagoing vessels were without framing, even though the sturdy tenons used in the Uluburun ship appear to have acted as internal frames. Furthermore, the small areas of planking surviving on both sites (the largest section of Uluburun planking measured 1.8 x 1.0 m) leave open the possibility that, toward bow and stern, the planking was also sewn. Such a blend of fastenings was not only an early Egyptian characteristic but was subsequently used on several of the first millennium B.C. excavated ships of the eastern and central Mediterranean (Mark 2005: 50–51, 60–69, 183–85).

A further conjecture is that in the third millennium B.C., before the Phoenicians became wide-ranging seafarers, Mediterranean hulls—of which we have simple representations (McGrail 2004a: 105–11) but no excavated examples—had lashed framing and sewn planking. Such a technological phase would be equivalent to what is thought to have been the earliest phase of plank-boatbuilding in northwest Europe and in southeast Asia (McGrail 2004a: 184–94; 297–98, 304–5).

## Propulsion and Steering

Oars were excavated with the Cheops ship, and paddles are depicted in tomb paintings and with models from the Old Kingdom (ca. 2600 B.C.) onward. There are also many illustrations of rowing in the sit-pull and stand-pull modes, oars being pivoted in grommets made fast to the vessel's sides. The earliest evidence for sail appears on a vase from Naqada of about 3100 B.C.: this is a single square sail on a pole mast stepped toward the bow (McGrail 2004a: fig. 2.5). Later depictions mostly show a square sail with a boom at its foot on a bipod mast stepped about one-third the waterline length from the bow, which, generally speaking, favors sailing with a wind in the stern sector. On the Nile, with a predominant northerly wind, sailing upstream with a following wind would have been the normal practice; at sea, however, a requirement to have the wind from astern could have been restrictive. By the mid-second millennium B.C. the pole mast stepped nearer amidships is almost exclusively depicted; it may have been possible to sail such vessels in other than following winds.

The standing rigging consisted of a forestay and a backstay, with auxiliary backstays that may have been moved abreast the mast to act as windward shrouds.

Sheets are sometimes illustrated; braces are shown running from both yardarms to the helmsman, and there is frequently a bowline from the sail's leading edge to the bows. Braces and bowline would have been used to trim the sail to a wind that was from forward of the stern sector. The use of a forked pole (a "tacking" spar) to bear out the sail's leading edge also indicates the ability to sail on a reach, with the wind on the beam. No block and tackles are depicted, so halyards and other running rigging were probably directly hauled and veered, possibly through greased holes in the mast. During the second millennium lifts were rigged to give yard and sail further support. The earliest depictions of sail in Mediterranean waters are ships with mast and rigging engraved on small Minoan stone seals of around 2000 B.C. (McGrail 2004a: fig. 4.16)

Vessels may be steered by paddle, steering oar, side rudder, or centerline rudder, and there are Old Kingdom (2686–2160 B.C.) depictions of each method. During the later third millennium, two side rudders were used, each pivoted on the vessel's quarter and against a vertical stanchion (Landström 1970: fig. 152): they were thus true rudders that were rotated around their own long axis. By the first millennium B.C., such paired side rudders had become standard fittings in the eastern Mediterranean. Egyptian depictions of a centerline rudder (which does not seem to have been used in the Mediterranean until late medieval times) became increasingly common by the end of the third millennium B.C. (McGrail 2004a: 34, fig. 2.18).

# Shipbuilding 800 B.C. to A.D. 500

Eastern Mediterranean shipbuilders and seamen of the early eighth century B.C. inherited much from their Egyptian and Phoenician predecessors: the rivers, coasts, and seas of the eastern and central Mediterranean, the Black Sea, and the Red Sea were well known, and the art of navigating without instruments, when out of sight of land, had been learned. All the basic types of water transport and all forms of propulsion and steering had been devised. Planked vessels were built in the plank-first sequence, the planks being aligned by treenails within the plank edges before being fastened together using two types of fastening—sewing and locked mortise and tenon. The vessel's framing was then lashed to the planking.

## Ships in Homer's Poems

The method for building a seagoing vessel in Homer's time is described in a passage in the *Odyssey* (5.259–87) that is both enigmatic and incomplete, doubtless because Homer was a poet and not a boatwright. Even if agreement could be reached on the precise meaning of key words in Homer's text, knowledge of ancient plank fastening techniques is needed to fill the gaps in his description. Furthermore, the building methods described have been interpreted as both those of a vessel fastened by locked mortise and tenon joints (Casson 1964; 1992) and those of a sewn-plank vessel (Mark 1991; 1996; 2005: 25–39). A third possibility, which could resolve this matter, is that Homer is describing the construction of a boat with both types of fastening, as in earlier Egyptian ships (see above), and as shown on the possibly Syrian ships (identified as such by the dress of crew and merchants) depicted in the mid-second millennium tomb of Kenamun at Egyptian Thebes (Wachsmann 1998: fig. 3.5).

## Early Use of Locked Mortise and Tenon Fastenings

The fragmentary remains of the Uluburun ship's planking, dated to about 1300 B.C., include the earliest known nautical use of locked mortise and tenon fastenings (Pulak 2003). Whether this planking was first positioned by treenails set into the plank edges, whether sewn fastenings were also used, and whether frames were lashed to the planking is not known due to the limited extent of the surviving planking. It is conceivable, however, that the Uluburun ship had sewn fastenings at her (nonsurviving) ends, similar to those depicted on the near-contemporary representations in Kenamun's tomb. Locked mortise and tenon fastenings (figure 24.3) are also thought to have fastened the planking of the wreck from Cape Gelidonya dated to around 1200 B.C (Bass 1991), and they were used in the seventh-century B.C. Mazarrón I wreck from Playa de la Isla, off southeast Spain (Negueruela et al. 1995). The frames of the latter ship were lashed to the planking. It is not yet clear whether she had sewn-plank fastenings in addition to locked mortise and tenon joints, as research is still in progress, but caulking in the seams appears to have been held in place by a light cord through sewing holes (Mark 2005: fig. 12). It seems possible that the combination of sewing with locked, watertight mortise and tenon fastenings was a second-millennium B.C. Phoenician development of established Egyptian practices, but this cannot yet be demonstrated. Locked mortise and tenon joints, like clenched nails, are positive fastenings on both sides of a seam, and do not need reinforcing by a second type of fastening. Moreover, when fitted tightly (in the ship's longitudinal direction) within their mortises, they have a significant resistance to shear forces (Coates 1996, 2001).

## Sewn Planking

A wide range of sewn-plank fastenings, dated from around 3000 B.C. to the present day, is known throughout the world (McGrail 1996b). Some of these consist of a series of individual stitches or lashings, as found in the Bronze Age Ferriby boats of the Humber estuary on the east coast of England (Wright 1990: 65, figs. 2.3, 3.10, 4.8), but the great majority involves continuous sewing. Boats with sewn planking are mentioned by Homer (*Il.* 2.133; *Od.* 5. 259–87) in the eighth century B.C., and by later authors ranging from the fifth century B.C. (Aeschylus, *Supp.* 134–35) to the fifth century A.D. (St. Jerome, *Ep*. 128.3): whether individual stitches or continuous sewing is unclear. These references are mainly within a Greek context.

No Mediterranean vessels with planking fastened by individual stitches or lashings have been excavated, but four Mediterranean vessels have continuous sewing wedged within the sewing holes. This sewing is along plank seams, not transversely across the hull as in earlier Egyptian vessels. It is found on the ships from Giglio, off the west coast of Italy (ca. 580 B.C.; Bound 1991); Bon Porté, off the south coast of France (540–510 B.C.; Basch 1976; Pomey 1981, 1985, 1997); Cala Sant Vicenç off the island of Mallorca (530–500; Kahanov and Pomey 2004: 14–15); and Place Jules-Verne 9, Marseilles (525–510 B.C.; Pomey 1995, 1996, 1999). Enough of the Place Jules-Verne Wreck's planking has survived to make it probable that she was entirely sewn, and the others may have been so as well.

There are also several wrecks with planking mainly fastened by locked mortise and tenon joints that also had wedged, sewn-plank fastenings in the lower hull, at bow and stern, or in repairs: Place Jules-Verne 7 and César 1, both of Marseilles and dated 525–510 B.C.; Gela 1, off southern Sicily of 500–480 B.C. (Kahanov and Pomey 2004: table 2; Pomey 1997; Freschi 1991); Grand Ribaud F off the south coast of France of 515–470 B.C. (Kahanov and Pomey 2004: 17–18); Gela 2 of 450–425 B.C.; and Ma'agan Mikhael off the Israeli coast of about 400 B.C. (Linder and Kahanov2003; Kahanov and Linder 2004). Except for Place Jules-Verne 7, César 1, Gela 2, and Ma'agan Mikhael, vessels in these two groups had their planking positioned by shear-resisting treenails within plank edges. Most of the ships with sewn planking had some form of caulking material associated with their stitching, and the stitches of Ma'agan Mikhael were wedged and sealed with a resin within their holes.

The frames of those ships solely fastened by sewing were widely spaced, at around 0.96 m; their undersurfaces were fashioned to fit over the stitching, and they were lashed to the planking. The floors and futtocks of the Place Jules-Verne Wreck were nailed (the earliest known use); the top timbers were lashed and treenailed; the frames of the César 1, Grand Ribaud F, and Gela 1 Wrecks were nailed. The Place Jules-Verne Wreck's nails, and the copper nails used in the Ma'agan Mikhael ship, were hook-clenched by turning the tip through 180 degrees, back into the inboard face of the frame. All these ships had a keel or plank-keel, and all had a full, transversely rounded hull except the Gela 2 and Ma'agan Mikhael Wrecks, which, like the Kyrenia ship of about 300 B.C., had wineglass-shaped cross-sections (Kahanov 2003: table 31; Kahanov and Pomey 2004: 18–19).

Ten sewn plank boats, dated from the late centuries B.C. to the eleventh century A.D., have been excavated from lakes and rivers in Croatia and the Po delta (Pomey 1981; Brusić and Domjan 1985; Beltrame 2000; Kahanov and Linder 2004: 66–76). The planking of these Adriatic vessels was fastened together by continuous sewing; nails were additionally used in two of the Po boats. Treenails within plank edges were noted on the Ljubljana boat of around 200 B.C., but not elsewhere; they may have been unnecessary in boats not intended to be seagoing. The stitches of the Nin/Zaton boats of Croatia, from the early centuries A.D., were wedged within sewing holes which were then blocked with resin and the outboard part of the stitch cut away—a technique used in the twentieth century in seagoing boats from the Lamu archipelago off east Africa so that stitching would not be damaged when a boat took the ground or was dragged across the foreshore (Prins 1965).

## Warships with Rams

The earliest depictions of warships with rams are found on Greek Geometric pottery of the ninth to eighth centuries B.C. (McGrail 2004a: fig. 4.24). Although there is some disagreement as to the purpose of these projections, they probably represent pointed rams intended to hole planking at or below the waterline. Blunt-ended rams are depicted during the sixth century (Casson and Linder 1991: fig. 5.4), and trident-headed rams appear about 400 B.C. A 600 kg bronze ram found on the foreshore at Athlit, south of Haifa, Israel, is of this latter type and is dated by its decorations to the first half of the second century B.C. (Murray 1991).

John Coates, naval architect of the *Olympias* project, considers that, since a warship's retardation when piercing a hole with a sharp ram would not have been excessive, the early, pointed rams could have been used by sewn-plank ships (personal communication). Blunt and finned rams, on the other hand, when not used to break the oars of the target ship, may have been used to thump the planking and start the seams: the effects of this on an attacking ship are disputed, but it is conceivable that she would have needed the stiffness and strength given by closely spaced mortise and tenon joints rather than sewn-plank fastenings (Steffy 1991).

## Propulsion and Steering

In Homer's time a single square sail on a mast stepped near amidships was probably the only sailing rig. From the late sixth century B.C. onward, occasional ships are depicted with a second square sail on a foremast (Casson 1996: fig. 97), or, from the first century A.D., as an *artemon* at the bow. A third sail on a mizzen is described in the mid-third century B.C. (Casson 1996: 240). Fore-and-aft sails are illustrated on small craft; a spritsail from the second century B.C. (Casson 1996: figs. 175–79), and a lateen from the second century A.D. (Casson 1996: fig. 181). Sails were probably made of linen, since Ezekiel, writing in the late-sixth century B.C., noted that sails of this material were used on Phoenician ships (27:7), and a second-century B.C. linen shroud fragment with an attached wooden brail ring, from the temple at Edfu, Egypt, has been identified as part of a sail (Black 1996).

Rigged with square mainsail and foresail, and in good sailing conditions, the closest to the wind that the experimental trireme *Olympias* could sail was with the wind one point or so forward of the beam, that is, some seven points (ca. 79°) off the wind (Roberts 2005). If this observation discounted the leeway of one point (ca. 11°) that was also noted, it may be concluded that an ancient Mediterranean ship similar to *Olympias* would probably have been able to make good a track across the wind and return on the reciprocal track. Ships were generally fitted with a side rudder on each quarter (Casson 1996: figs. 147–51). Sea trials of *Olympias* showed that the rudders induced such a disproportionate amount of drag that only one of the pair was generally used and that was partly immersed. It may be, however, that, a redesign of the trial rudders would have minimized this problem.

# TECHNOLOGICAL CHANGES—800 TO 300 B.C.

In the eastern Mediterranean we know of two ships before 800 B.C. (Uluburun and Cape Gelidonya Wrecks, with possible origins on the Levant coast) that were built in the plank-first sequence and had locked mortise and tenon plank fastenings, a woodworking technique that was earlier known in Egypt and in Phoenicia. The seventh-century B.C. Mazarrón 1 ship has this type of plank fastening and also lashed framing; both of these features may well have been characteristics of Phoenician-built ships of the first, and possibly second, millennium B.C. Whether these ships also had sewn plank fastenings (as did later vessels) is unknown, but such plank fastenings, with frames lashed to the planking, are likely to have been used from an early date throughout the Mediterranean. It also seems likely that seagoing, sewn-plank vessels of those times would have had treenails across seams, within the plank thickness. These would not only have helped in the positioning of adjacent strakes, initially and after periodic stitching renewal, but would also have minimized shearing stresses on the stitching when afloat, especially if the rays of the treenails were aligned with the plank seams (Coates 1985, 2001).

One interpretation of a passage of Homer, *Odyssey* 5.259–87, suggests that Greek ships of around 800 B.C. had sewn planking (Mark 2005); authors in later centuries appear to confirm that stitching was a characteristic of early Greek-built ships. An alternative hypothesis is that Homer's ships had both sewn and mortise and tenon fastenings. Four seagoing ships (the Giglio, Bon Porte, Cala San Vicenç and Place Jules-Verne 9 Wrecks—all of which could have been Greek-built), dated between 580 and 510 B.C., had sewn planking, as did a dozen or so boats of the late centuries B.C. to the eleventh century A.D. from Adriatic lakes and rivers. Furthermore, four seagoing vessels dated between 525 and 480 B.C. (Place Jules-Verne 7, Cesar 1, Grand Ribaud F, and Gela 1 Wrecks), Gela 2 Wreck of 450–425 B.C., and the Ma'agan Mikhael Wreck of around 400 B.C., all with nail-fastened framing, and planking mainly fastened by mortise and tenon joints, had sewn-plank fastenings at the ends, in the lower hull, or in repairs.

Leaving aside the somewhat isolated Adriatic boats, the sequential nature of these two groups suggests that, from about 525 B.C., Greek builders of seagoing ships changed from sewn-plank fastenings to (Phoenician?) locked mortise and

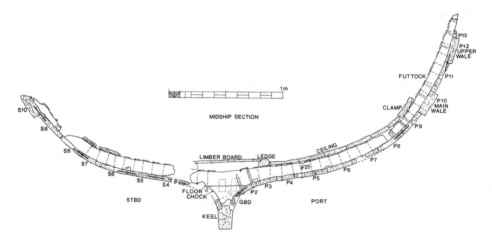

Figure 24.5. Transverse half-section of the Kyrenia ship showing structural details. (After Steffy 1994: fig. 3.31.)

tenon fastenings, supplemented by sewn fastenings in vulnerable parts of the hull. They also stopped using treenails across plank seams, decreased frame spacing (center to center) from 96–84 cm to 75–70 cm, and fastened frames to planking by hook-clenched nails rather than by lashings. The earliest evidence for hulls with a wineglass-shaped cross-section appears a century later, in the second half of the fifth century. Similarly, present evidence shows no ship's planking solely fastened by locked mortise and tenon joints until around 300 B.C.

## The Kyrenia Ship

This merchant ship of about 300 B.C. was excavated off the north coast of Cyprus in 1968/69 (Steffy 1985, 1989, 1994: 42–59; 1995). The remains were lifted and conserved, and are now on display in Kyrenia. The pine planking was fastened together with locked mortise and tenon joints; there was no sewing (although sewing holes were found in one reused ceiling plank) and there were no treenails in the seams. The framing, closely spaced at 25 cm, consisted of floor timbers (with chocks) spanning six to nine strakes each side, alternating with paired half-frames that did not quite reach the keel (figure 24.5). Side timbers were added in line with, but not fastened to, the floors and half-frames, and there were occasional top timbers. Copper nails, possibly driven through treenails, and clenched by hooking the point through 180 degrees back into the timber, were used to fasten framing elements to the planking. This framing pattern became characteristic of Mediterranean hulls until the changes that took place in the fourth to sixth centuries A.D. as a prelude to the shift from the plank-first to the frame-first sequence of building.

   Like the Gela 2 and Ma'agan Mikhael ships, the Kyrenia ship's underwater hull had a wineglass shape: that is, the lowest three or four strakes, seen in section, formed a reverse curve to the keel so that the garboards were nearer the vertical than in earlier ships, thereby enhancing the leeway-resisting properties of the underwater hull and keel. The rabbets worked along the length of the keel to take the garboard strakes, and the lead sheathing of the planking, were innovations.

# TECHNOLOGICAL CHANGES
## AFTER 300 B.C.

Tentative conclusions may be drawn from reports on a number of excavated merchant ships dated from the second century B.C. to the second century A.D., although the data from them can, in some cases, be challenged (McGrail 2004a: 158). These large ships had cargo capacities ranging up to 600 tons. They had double planking, keels with complex scarfs and of greater dimensions than earlier ones, and a greater than proportionate increase in tenon breadths: these features greatly added to hull strength and integrity. The fitting of prototype stringers and elongated mast-step timbers (effectively keelsons), and the fastening of some frames to the keel, further added to structural strength.

After the second century A.D., wrecks of such large vessels are rare, but six smaller vessels, from the fourth to the seventh century, show a shift in emphasis from plank fastenings toward increased reliance on framing, keelson, ceiling planking, and decking. The hull of the fourth century Yassi Ada wreck 2 (van Doorninck 1976) was, in many ways, conventional for her date: she was built plank-first, the planking was fastened by locked mortise and tenon joints, and the floors alternated with half-frames. The joints, however, were smaller than in earlier ships of comparable size, and tenons did not fill mortises, leaving gaps of 6–7 mm at each end and 17–18 mm at the sides; they were also more widely spaced, intervals being 320 mm in places (Steffy 1994: 79–80, fig. 4.1).

Five other ships, dated to the sixth and seventh centuries, show further signs of change. The Dor D Wreck off the coast of Israel (A.D. 550–650; Royal and Kahanov 2005), St. Gervais 2 Wreck of the coast of southern France (A.D. 600–625; Jezegou 1989), Yassi Ada Wreck 1 off the Turkish coast (seventh century; van Doorninck 1982), and Pantano Longarini Wreck from Sicily (seventh century; Throckmorton 1973) still retained some edge-fastened planking and therefore were probably built plank-first. Nevertheless, their mortise and tenon joints were mostly not locked, the tenons of those joints did not fill their mortises, and plank thicknesses decreased (Royal 2002).

Steffy (1994: 77–78, 83–85; 1995: 27) has suggested that these changes were the result of labor becoming more expensive due to the decline in slavery and to the growing importance of independent ship owners who preferred smaller, less costly ships. The classic style of shipbuilding, as seen in the Kyrenia Wreck, was skilled-labor-intensive, especially in the fashioning, fitting and fastening of the thousands of locked mortise and tenon joints needed in even a moderate-sized hull—so fine were woodworking skills that caulking was generally not needed. A reduction in the need for such joints resulted in fewer skilled shipwrights being employed and thus in reduced costs.

In retrospect, these changes can be seen as the beginning of a decline in building plank-first. Indeed, two fifth- to sixth-century A.D. ships from the Israeli coast, Dor 2001/1 and Tantura A, had no edge-fastened planking at all, and were built in the framing-first sequence (Kahanov 2001, 2003). There was caulking material within their seams, but mortise and tenon joints, sewing, and treenails were not found there. Furthermore, frames were nailed to the keel, and planking was butt-scarfed and nailed only at frame stations. These ships had been built in the following sequence: keel, posts, and elements of the framing were first set up and fastened together; then planking was fashioned and fastened to this framework; more framing and more planking followed. Although different in detail, this is similar to the building sequence used to build two ships and a seagoing boat of the Romano-Celtic tradition in second and third century A.D. northwest Europe (see below).

When using the plank-first sequence, each individual builder fashioned and fastened together planking so that a hull shape was achieved which rules of thumb and his experienced eye told him was appropriate to the role the ship was to undertake. In the framing-first sequence, on the other hand, it was the framework of posts, keel, and selected frames that determined hull shape. For anything bigger than a boat, that framework had to be designed. How that was done in the mid-first millennium A.D. is uncertain, but the method may have been similar to that subsequently used in Venetian shipyards from the fifteenth century (McGrail 2003: 128; 2004a: 164–65). In these later ships, the main dimensions were defined as proportions of a modular unit, which was usually either the keel length (Bellabarba 1993: 274) or the maximum beam (Steffy 1994: 93). The shape of the master frame (which was set up near amidships) was given by a traditional rule that specified the orthogonal coordinates of the required curve at four points (Ballabarba 1993: fig. 3). The shapes of the remaining designed frames were derived from the shape of the master frame using a wooden tablet (known as a *mezza luna*, "half moon") and a measuring stick. As the art and science of generating hull shapes developed and as understanding increased of the effects of shape changes on ship performance, improvements could readily be introduced into a design, and a successful design could be repeated.

This change to non-edge-fastened planking and the framing-first sequence of building was a fundamental technological shift. Subsequent to the fifth- to sixth-century Dor 2001/1 and Tantura A Wrecks, this technique is seen in the eighth-century Tantura F and the ninth-century Tantura B Wrecks (Kahanov 2003), and in the wreck from Serçe Limani off the Turkish coast dated to about A.D. 1025 (Steffy 1994: 85–91). Subsequently, ships of the Iberian-Atlantic tradition of the fifteenth century and later were built in this manner (Alves 2001).

# BOATS AND SHIPS OF NORTHWEST EUROPE

## Mediterranean-Style Vessels

A number of boats and ships of the first few centuries A.D. so far excavated in northwest Europe had been built in Mediterranean fashion, with planking fastened by locked mortise and tenon joints. Broad oak washstrakes had been fastened by such joints to the logboat base of a third/fourth century A.D. boat excavated in 1987 from Lough Lene, Co. Westmeath, some fifty miles northwest of Dublin (Ó hÉailidhe 1992). The remains of a ship dated to A.D. 290–300 were recovered from the County Hall site near the River Thames in London in 1910/11. Her fittings and features are almost entirely Roman, but dendrochronological examination has shown that she was built of oak from southeast England (Marsden 1994: 109–29). The elements of a steering oar blade and two boats (2A and 6), all from Zwammerdam in the Netherlands, and a boat from Vechten near Utrecht, had some mortise and tenon fastenings (de Weerd 1988; de Weerd and Haalëbos 1973). All these had been built locally, possibly by indigenous people under the supervision of Mediterranean shipwrights or influenced by observing their ships.

## Romano-Celtic Boats and Ships

During the late twentieth century, approximately 20 vessels dated from the first to fourth centuries A.D. were excavated at sites in an arc stretching from the Swiss lakes, along the River Rhine, to the Thames and the Severn, and on to Guernsey off the northwest coast of France. Most of these vessels are of elongated box shape and come from the Rhine region: they were probably river and canal barges (McGrail 2004a: 201–5). Seagoing vessels of this tradition, with plank-keels, raked posts, and a full, round hull but flat in the floor, have been excavated from three sites: the Thames in London in 1962 (Blackfriars 1 Wreck, ca. A.D. 150; Marsden 1994: 33–95); the main harbor of Guernsey in 1985 (St. Peter Port 1 Wreck, ca. A.D. 275; Rule and Monaghan 1993); and the northern shores of the Severn estuary, southeast Wales in 1993 (Barland's Farm Wreck, ca. A.D. 300; Nayling and McGrail 2004).

Several characteristics of these vessels echo Julius Caesar's first-century B.C. description of the ships of the Veneti, a Celtic seafaring people of southwest Brittany (*B Gall.* 3.13; cf. Strabo 4.4.1). It seems likely that the ships of the Veneti were forerunners of the excavated vessels we now know as members of the Romano-Celtic shipbuilding tradition: Celtic because they were excavated from sites which were formerly inhabited by Celtic-speaking people; Roman because all known finds are dated to the late Roman period. The latter term also acknowledges that some of the techniques used by the Celtic shipwrights originated in the Mediterranean. These vessels were built from oak timbers that had been sawn to shape—the main, probably the only significant, use of Roman technology. Some of the planking of two of the Rhine barges is fastened by locked mortise and tenon joints, another borrowing.

There are other features comparable with those found in contemporary Mediterranean vessels, but whether they were derived from Roman technology is unclear. Romano-Celtic planking was fastened to relatively massive frames by great iron nails (the size of Veneti frames and timbers was noted by Caesar), each one driven through a treenail inserted in the frame, and clenched by hooking the nail tip back into the inboard face of the framing timber (figure 24.6). This is comparable with the Mediterranean technique of fastening framing to planking using hooked copper nails (see above). Clenching a nail, by hooking the tip through two 90-degree bends and hammering it down on the inside surface of the strake or frame through which it had been driven, is first known in the Mediterranean on the Place Jules-Verne 7 vessel of 525–510 B.C. Arnold (1999: 42, fig. 7), however, has drawn attention to the north European use of turned and hooked iron nails in the second century B.C. *murus gallicus* and in Halstatt cart wheels before 500 B.C. Technological transfer could have taken place in either direction along the Rhone–Seine or the Po–Rhine routes that connected the North Sea and the Mediterranean.

There are differences between the two technologies: Celtic boat builders plugged nail holes with treenails before driving nails through them, and they used iron nails to fasten planking to frames rather than copper nails to fasten frames to planking. No elements of Celtic framing were joined together, whereas the Mediterranean tradition from the early sixth century B.C. involved scarfing futtocks to floors (see above); the form of the Celtic bow and stern posts, and the scarf joints between posts and plank-keel are unlike anything known elsewhere. Furthermore, the Celts stepped their masts about one-third of the underwater length of the boat from the bow, whereas Roman masts were nearer amidships.

The most innovative characteristic of the Celtic seagoing vessels of A.D. 175 to 300 was that they were built in the framing-first sequence: the flush-laid planking, caulked with macerated wood, was not fastened together, but each individual plank was fastened to the frames. This is comparable with the framing–first building sequence of the fifth- or sixth-century A.D. Dor 2001/1 and Tantura A ships from the Israeli coast (see above). On present evidence, Romano-Celtic use of the framing-first sequence is at least two hundred and may be four hundred years earlier than its first known use in the Mediterranean. Was this a case of technological transfer of what turned out to be a very significant innovation, or was it independent invention? A clue to the origins of this technique may lie in prehistoric times. Well before Caesar noted the Veneti ships, perhaps as early as the second millennium B.C., frame-first techniques must have been used in Celtic northwest Europe to build seagoing hide boats, skin over framework (McGrail 1990: 36–39).

In the medieval Mediterranean, the framing-first sequence of building ships became dominant except, perhaps, in smaller boatyards. After the fourth century A.D., however, the Romano-Celtic style of shipbuilding does not feature in the

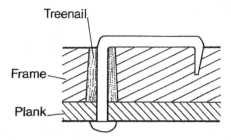

Figure 24.6. Method of fastening planking to framing in Romano-Celtic vessels. (After Nayling and McGrail 2004: fig. 7.3.)

archaeological record of northwest Europe, and the vast majority of early medieval finds are of the Nordic, clinker-built, tradition. It remains to be seen whether the framing-first technique lived on somewhere in northwest Europe through the migration period, a time of significant cultural change. The sixth or seventh century Port Berteau 2 Wreck, coastal and river boat, may be evidence for such survival. This boat, excavated from the River Charente on the west coast of France, had flush-laid planking which was not fastened together but treenailed to the frames (Rieth 2000; Rieth et al. 2001). Unlike the seagoing Romano-Celtic vessels, she had composite frames with futtocks fastened to floor timbers (Rieth et al. 2001: fig. 112). She may, therefore, have been built frame-first, in the strict sense of the term: that is, the entire framework may have been fashioned and fastened to keel and stems before any planking was positioned.

The framing-first or frame-first *caravella*, built by Portuguese shipbuilders in the early fifteenth century, were the predecessors of the ships in which Bartolomeu Dias, Vasco da Gama, Christopher Columbus, and Ferdinand Magellan explored the world. Whether this Atlantic version of frame-first building was inherited from the Mediterranean or from Celtic northwest Europe is the subject of continuing research.

# The Technological Achievements of the Classical World

Mediterranean shipbuilders and seamen of 800 B.C. to A.D. 500 consolidated and developed their inheritance from Egypt and the Levant coast: the warships and cargo ships of the fourth century B.C. and later were a technological advance on the ships of their predecessors. From the sixth century B.C. locked mortise and tenon fastenings began to replace sewn fastenings, at first in the Greek, then the Roman world. In the early centuries A.D. the use of this distinctive joint spread to northwest

Europe, even to Ireland outside the empire. It was probably also transmitted across the Indian Ocean around this time, since such fastenings have been excavated in northern Vietnam on a first-century B.C. plank-extended log boat from Dong Xa, and on planking reused as a coffin at Yen Bac in the second century A.D. (Bellwood et al. 2007). Locked mortise and tenon fastenings were also found in 1953 on an undated wreck excavated at Johore Lama in Malaya (McGrail 2004a: 302, 436).

In the first few centuries A.D., Mediterranean shipwrights abandoned plank fastenings and shifted to a framing-first sequence of shipbuilding, Whether or not these techniques had originated with northwest European shipwrights, this significant technological change seems to have been perfected within the medieval Mediterranean, and may have led to the worldwide seafaring achievements of the fifteenth- and sixteenth-century shipbuilders and mariners of the Iberian Atlantic coast. The social, political, and economic effects of these overseas voyages of exploration are still in evidence today.

# NAVIGATION BEFORE A.D. 500

In conditions of good visibility, all islands in the Mediterranean are visible from high ground on the European, African or Asian mainland, or from another island which is so visible, or from a boat when land earlier sighted is still in view (Henkel 1901: fig. 1), and most of these islands had been colonized by the end of Neolithic times. During the midsummer season, a boat under oars could have undertaken such voyages during daylight—even the longer passages to Cyprus, Malta, and the Balearic islands. In such conditions, when land, astern or ahead, is always in sight, the seaman uses pilotage techniques to note his position relative to a succession of recognizable landmarks. In other seasons, and in less than good weather, with land no longer visible, it seems likely that these early seafarers evolved simple navigational techniques such as estimating directions from the pole star, or, with less accuracy, from the sun at noon, or relative to the wind and swell.

The use of the sounding lead and line on a boat approaching the Nile delta is described by Herodotus (2.5), and many leads have been found in inshore waters, the earliest being from the Gela 1 Wreck of 500–480 B.C. (Oleson 2000). Lucan (8.177–81) tells us that, in his day, the zenith altitude of certain stars was estimated against the mast (presumably in harbor); such an estimate gave a measure of latitude relative to other harbors where similar estimates had been made (Taylor 1971: 47–48). A unique mechanism, excavated in 1900 from a first-century B.C. wreck off Antikythera, has bronze gear wheels which appear to have been capable of tracing out the relative movements of sun, moon, and certain stars (figure 29.1). Rather than a navigational instrument, this is now interpreted as an instructional aid, possibly for astrological calculations (de Sola Price 1974; Johnston 1997; see also chapter 29). It is not until the ninth century A.D. that we learn of instrumental aids to celestial navigation: an Arabian author, al-Khwarizmi, described a staff for measuring star altitudes at sea (Aleem 1980: 588; Fatimi 1996). The use of this proto-*kamal* may well have been based on the Greek angle-measuring device known as a *dioptra* (M. J. T. Lewis 2001).

Thus, apart from the sounding lead and line, no navigational instruments were used during our period. Today, seamen out of sight of land in several regions use noninstrumental navigational methods based on inherited traditions, personal experience and detailed observation of the maritime environment (McGrail 1998: 275–76; Morton 2001). Furthermore, Homer's *Odyssey* contains descriptions of open sea passages undertaken without instruments (3.188–95; 14.285–91). Although Odysseus had no chart, he would have had a mental map in his head on which he "plotted" the spatial relationships of the coastal lands and islands of the eastern Mediterranean (McGrail 1996a; Mark 2005: 138–52). For example, he used the Great Bear constellation (Ursa Major) to steer an easterly heading when leaving Calypso's island, and monitored the rising and setting of Orion, Arcturus and the Pleiades (Homer, *Od.* 5.298–304). Odysseus' use of this star compass suggests that he had a good working knowledge of astronomy (figure 24.7). Furthermore, he also used a wind compass (Homer, *Od.* 12.313, 350–51; 14.286, 337–38, 520). Eight elements of such a compass were depicted on the first-century B.C. Tower of the Winds in Athens (figure 29.3; McGrail 2004a: fig. 4.4). As in many maritime cultures, Odysseus' standard unit of distance was "a day's sail" (Homer, *Od.* 4.397), and the passage of time at night was marked by certain stars reaching their zenith (Taylor 1971: 48).

When on passage out of sight of land, Odysseus would have frequently used these environmentally based aids, together with his assessment of his boat's speed, to plot on his mental chart his estimated position relative to his home port or to his destination. When land was eventually sighted, after such a passage, Odysseus was able to identify the particular coastal landscape (for example: Pharos island, Homer, *Od.* 4.395–96, and the "wooded peak of windswept Neriton," *Od.* 9.23–24) and could then deduce the route to his intended destination.

From Homer onward, Greek and Roman writers recognized Phoenician seafaring abilities. Strabo (1.1.6) gave them precedence in navigation, and Pliny (*HN* 7.57) claimed that they were first to apply astronomical learning gained from the Chaldeans to navigation at sea. Phoenician seamen realized that the constellation Ursa Minor orbited the celestial North Pole in a tighter circle than did Ursa Major; they therefore used Ursa Minor to give them a more precise direction of north. The classical world came to call this useful, but not easily recognized, constellation *Phoinike* (Aubet 1993: 142).

In the fourth century B.C., written sailing directions (*periploi*) for coastal voyages began to be compiled from oral accounts (Dilke 1985). These were not just for the Mediterranean, but also for a passage from Atlantic Europe to Massilia (Marseilles; Murphy 1977: 7–9), passages along the coast of northwest Africa (Murphy 1977: 9–11; Oikonomides and Miller 1995), and from the Egyptian Red Sea harbor of Myos Hormos on one of two routes: either around the Horn of Africa and south to the Zanzibar region, or past the Persian Gulf and on to India and beyond. This last compilation, the *Periplus Maris Erythraei* (Casson 1989), written in Greek by an

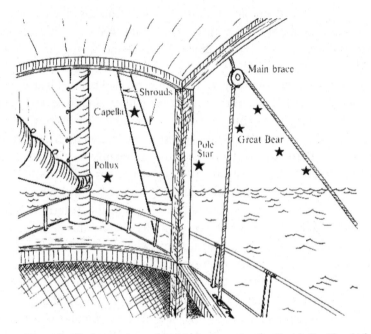

**Figure 24.7.** Diagram illustrating steering by the stars in the South Pacific. (After Lewis 1994: fig. 14; courtesy of University of Hawaii Press.)

Alexandrian merchant in about 50 A.D. (Reade 1996: 312), was a combination of what we nowadays would call sailing directions, a regional handbook, and a trading guide, useful both to pilots and merchants. Early Mediterranean seaman sailed these waters guided by oral versions of such *periploi*, and with the human eye and brain as their only navigational instruments.

After A.D. 500, Arab astronomers and seamen brought to the Mediterranean navigational ideas and techniques they had earlier learned from the Greeks. Thus were laid the mathematical foundations of the shift to navigation by instruments and charts that took place in the Mediterranean from the thirteenth century onward (Taylor 1971: 89–121).

# GLOSSARY OF NAUTICAL AND NAVIGATIONAL TERMS

*bilge*: region between sides and bottom of a vessel.
*bowline*: line used to keep the weather edge of a sail taut.
*brace*: line used to trim a yard.
*brail:* ropes used to bundle a sail rapidly.

*carling*: fore-and-aft timber at deck level.

*caulking*: material inserted between two timbers to make the junction watertight.

*cramp*: wooden fitting which draws together two timbers across a seam.

*floor*: transverse timber set against the planking and extending from turn of *bilge* to turn of bilge.

*fore-and-aft sail*: sail that is generally set in or near the fore-and-aft line of a vessel.

*frame*: transverse member made up of more than one timber.

*frame-first*: building sequence in which a framework of keel, posts, and *frames* is set up before planking is fashioned.

*framing-first*: building sequence in which keel, posts, and elements of the framing are set up before planking is fashioned.

*freeboard*: height of sides above the waterline.

*futtock*: pairs of timbers which, with a *floor*, constitute a *frame*.

*garboard*: *strake* next to the keel.

*grommet*: strands of rope layed up in the form of a ring.

*halyard*: line to hoist and lower yard and sail.

*kamal*: navigation instrument consisting of a wooden tablet at the end of a line that had knots tied in it at graduated intervals. Evolved in the Arab world in the ninth century A.D. and used to measure star altitudes (angle above horizon).

*keelson*: center-line timber on top of the *floors*, adding to longitudinal strength and stiffness.

*lateen sail*: triangular, fore-and-aft sail bent to a long yard.

*leeway*: the distance or angle a vessel is set down wind.

*lift*: line running from yardarm to mast.

*mast step*: fitting used to locate the heel of a mast.

*mizzen*: aftermost mast in a three-masted vessel

*pilotage*: techniques used to keep a vessel's reckoning when in sight of land.

*plank-first*: building sequence in which the planking is (partly) erected and fastened before framing is inserted.

*plank-keel*: a keel-like timber with a low cross section.

*rocker*: for-and-aft curvature of keel or bottom of vessel.

*settee*: quadrilateral *lateen* with a short leading edge.

*sheer(line)*: curve of the upper edge of the hull.

*sheet*: a rope that regulates the angle at which a sail is set to the wind.

*shroud*: line leading from masthead to the sides of a vessel to support the mast athwartships.

*sprit sail*: four-sided, fore-and-aft sail set on a sprit or spar, the lower end of which is made fast to the mast while its upper end supports the peak of the sail.

*square sail*: four-sided sail that is laced to a yard which lies square (i.e., at right angles) to the mast.

*stanchion*: an upright brace or support for a ship's deck.

*stay:* line leading from masthead forward and aft to support the mast.

*strake*: single plank or combination of planks that extends from one end of a vessel to the other.

*tidal range*: the difference between the height of high water and the next low water.

*timber*: any piece of wood used in boatbuilding.

*treenail*: wooden peg or dowel used to join two timbers.

*washstrake*: additional *strake* fitted to increase *freeboard*.

*yard:* spar suspended from a mast, and to which the head of a square sail is bent.

*zenith*: highest point of a heavenly body's trajectory.

# REFERENCES

Aleem, A. A. 1980. "On the history of Arab navigation," in M. Sears and D. Merriman (eds.), *Oceanography: The past*. New York: Springer Verlag, 582–95.

Alves, F. (ed.) 2001. *Proceedings of a symposium on archaeology of medieval and modern ships of Iberian-Atlantic tradition*. Trabalhos de Arqueologia 18. Lisbon: Instituto Português de Arqueologia.

Arnold, B. 1999. "Some remarks on Romano-Celtic boat construction and Bronze Age wood technology," *International Journal of Nautical Archaeology* 28: 34–44.

Aubet, M. E. 1993. *Phoenicians and the west*. Cambridge: Cambridge University Press.

Basch, L. 1976. "Le navire cousu de Bon-Porté," *Cahiers d'archéologie subaquatique* 5: 37–42.

Basch, L. 1981. "Carthage and Rome: Tenons and mortises," *Mariner's Mirror* 67: 245–50.

Basch, L. 1987a. *Le musée imaginaire de la marine antique*. Athens: Greek Institute for the Preservation of Nautical Tradition.

Basch, L. 1987b. "Review: J. Coates and S. McGrail (eds.), *Greek trireme of the 5th century BC*. Greenwich: National Maritime Museum, 1984; J. S. Morrison and J. Coates, *Athenian Trireme*. Cambridge: Cambridge University Press, 1986," *Mariner's Mirror* 73: 93–105.

Bass, G. F. 1991. "Evidence of trade from Bronze Age shipwrecks," in N.H. Gale (ed.), *Bronze Age trade in the Mediterranean*. Studies in Mediterranean Archaeology 90. Jonsered: Paul Åströms, 69–82.

Bass, G. F. 1997. "Mediterranean Sea," in Delgado 1997: 268–74.

Bellabarba, S. 1993. "Ancient methods of designing hulls," *Mariner's Mirror* 79: 274–92.

Bellwood, P., J. Cameron, N. Van Viet, and B. Van Liem 2007. "Ancient boats, boat timbers and locked mortise and tenon joints from Bronze-Iron Age northern Vietnam," *International Journal of Nautical Archaeology* 36: 2–20.

Beltrame, C. 2000. "*Sutiles naves* of Roman age," in J. Litwin (ed.), *Down the river to the sea*. Gdansk: Polish Maritime Museum, 91–96.

Beltrame, C. (ed.) 2003. *Boats, ships and shipyards: Proceedings of ISBSA 9 (Venice 2000)*. Oxford: Oxbow.

Black, E. 1996. "Where have all the sails gone?" *Tropis* 4: 103–12.

Bound, M. 1991. *Giglio Wreck. Enalia* Suppl. 1. Athens: Hellenic Institute of Marine Archaeology.

Brusić, Z., and M. Domjan 1985. "Liburnian boats: Their form and construction," in McGrail and Kentley 1985: 67–87.

Cariolou, G. A. 1997. "Kyrenia 2: The return from Cyprus to Greece of the replica of a Hellenic merchant ship," in S. Swiny, R. L. Hohlfelder, H. W. Swiny (eds.), *Res Maritimae: Proceedings of the 2nd International Symposium "Cities of the Sea," 1994.* Atlanta: Scholars Press, 83–97.

Casson, L. 1964. "Odysseus' boat," *American Journal of Philology* 85: 61–64.

Casson, L. 1989. *Periplus Maris Erythraei*. Princeton: Princeton University Press.

Casson, L. 1991. "Ram and naval tactics," in Casson and Steffy 1991: 76–82.

Casson, L. 1992. "Odysseus' boat," *International Journal of Nautical Archaeology* 21: 73–74.

Casson. L. 1996. *Ships and seamanship in the ancient world*. Rev. ed. Princeton: Princeton University Press.

Casson, L., and E. Linder 1991. "Evolution and shape of the ancient ram," in Casson and Steffy 1991: 67–71.

Casson, L., and J. R. Steffy (eds.) 1991. *Athlit Ram*. College Station. Texas A & M University Press.

Clark, J. G. D. 1953. "Archaeological theories and interpretation: Old World," in A. L. Kroeber (ed.), *Anthropology today*. Chicago: Chicago University Press, 342–60.

Coates, J. 1985. "Some structural models for sewn boats," in McGrail and Kentley 1985: 9–18.

Coates, J. 1996. "Appendix F," in J. S. Morrison, *Greek and Roman oared warships, 399–30 B.C.* Oxford: Oxbow, 347–48.

Coates, J. 2001. "Planking tenons in ancient Mediterranean ships built shell-first," *Tropis* 6: 153–70.

Coates, J., and S. McGrail (eds.) 1984. *Greek trireme of the 5th century BC*. Greenwich: National Maritime Museum.

Coates, J., S. McGrail, D. Brown, E. Gifford, G. Grainge, B. Greenhill, P. Marsden, B. Rankov, C. Tipping, and E. Wright 1995. "Experimental boat archaeology: Principles and methods," *International Journal of Nautical Archaeology* 24: 293–301.

Coates, J., S. K. Platis, and T. Shaw (eds.) 1990. *Trireme trials 1988*. Oxford: Oxbow Books.

Crumlin-Pedersen, O., and S. McGrail 2006. "Some principles for the reconstruction of ancient boat structures," *International Journal of Nautical Archaeology* 35: 53–57.

Delgado, J. P. (ed.) 1997. *Encyclopedia of underwater and maritime archaeology*. London: British Museum Press.

de Morgan, J. 1894–1903. *Fouilles à Dahchour*. 2 vols. Vienna: Adolphe Holzhausen.

de Sola Price, D. 1974. *Gears from the Greeks: The Antikythera Mechanism*. Transactions of the American Philosophical Society 64.7. Philadelphia: American Philosophical Society.

de Weerd, M. 1988. *Schepen voor Zwammerdam*. Amsterdam: de Weerd.

de Weerd, M., and J. K. Haalëbos 1973. "Schepen voor het opscheppen," *Spiegal Historiael* 8: 386–97.

Dilke, O. A. W. 1985. *Greek and Roman maps*. London: Thames and Hudson.

Fatimi, S. O. 1996. "History of the development of the *kamal*," in H. P. Ray and J.-F. Salles (eds.), *Tradition and archaeology: Early maritime contacts in the Indian Ocean*. New Delhi: Oxford Univesity Press, 283–92.

Freschi, A. 1991. "Note tecniche sul relitto Greco arcaico di Gela," *Atti* 4: 201–10.

Haldane, C. W. 1996. "Ancient Egyptian hull construction," *Tropis* 4: 235–44.

Haldane, C. W. 1997a. "Dahshur boats," in Delgado 1997: 122–23.

Haldane, C. W. 1997b. "Khufu ships," in Delgado 1997: 222–23.

Henkel, X. 1901. "Die sichtbarkeit im Mittelmeergerbiet," *Petermann's Geographische Mitteilungen.*

Humphrey, J. W., J. P. Oleson, and A. N. Sherwood 1998. *Greek and Roman technology: A sourcebook.* London: Routledge.

James, T. G. H. 1983. *Introduction to ancient Egypt.* London: British Museum.

Jézégou, M. P. 1989. "L'épave 2 de l'anse St Gervais à Fos-sur-mer," *Tropis* 1: 139–46.

Johnston, P. F. 1997. Antikythera Wreck," in Delgado 1997: 31–32.

Kahanov, Y. 2001. "Byzantine shipwreck (Tantura A) in the Tantura lagoon, Israel," *Tropis* 6: (1996): 265–71.

Kahanov, Y. 2003. "Dor D wreck, Tantura lagoon, Israel," in Beltrame 2003: 49–56.

Kahanov, Y., and E. Linder 2004. *Ma'agan Mikhael Ship,* vol. 2. Haifa: Israel Exploration Society.

Kahanov, Y., and P. Pomey 2004. "Greek sewn shipbuilding tradition and the Ma'agan Mikhael ship," *Mariner's Mirror* 90: 6–28.

Katzev, M. L. 1989a. "Kyrenia 2: Building a replica of an ancient merchantman," *Tropis* 1: 163–75.

Katzev, M. L. 1989b. "Voyage of Kyrenia 2," *Institute of Nautical Archaeology Newsletter* 16.1: 4–10.

Katzev, M. L. 1990. "Analysis of the experimental voyage of Kyrenia 2," *Tropis* 2: 245–55.

Katzev, M. L., and S. W. Katzev 1986. "Kyrenia 2," *Institute of Nautical Archaeology Newsletter* 13.3: 2–11.

Katzev, M. L., and S. W. Katzev 1987. *Kyrenia 2: An ancient ship sails again.* Piraeus: Hellenic Institute for the Preservation of Nautical Tradition.

Landström, B. 1970. *Ships of the Pharaohs.* London: Allen and Unwin.

Lewis, D. 1994. *We the navigators.* 2nd ed. Honolulu: University of Hawaii Press.

Lewis, M. J. T. 2001. *Surveying instruments of Greece and Rome.* Cambridge: Cambridge University Press.

Linder, E., and Y. Kahanov 2003. *The Ma'agan Mikhael ship: The recovery of a 2400-year-old merchantman: Final report,* vol. 1. Haifa: Israel Exploration Society.

Lipke, P. 1984. *Royal ship of Cheops.* National Maritime Museum, Greenwich, Archaeological Series 9. British Archaeological Reports, Intl. Series S225. Oxford: BAR.

Mark, S. E. 1991. "*Odyssey* (5.234–53) and Homeric ship construction," *American Journal of Archaeology* 95: 441–45.

Mark, S. E. 1996. "*Odyssey* (5.234–53) and Homeric ship construction: A clarification," *International Journal of Nautical Archaeology* 25: 46–48.

Mark, S. E. 2005. *Homeric seafaring.* College Station: Texas A & M University Press.

Marsden, P. 1994. *Ships of the Port of London,* vol. 1. London: English Heritage.

McGrail, S. 1986. "Experimental boat archaeology—Some methodological considerations," in O. Crumlin-Pedersen (ed), *Sailing into the past.* Roskilde: Viking Ship Museum, 8–17.

McGrail, S. 1990. "Boats and boatmanship in the southern North Sea and Channel Region," in S. McGrail (ed.), *Celts, Frisians and Saxons.* CBA Research Report 71. York: Council for British Archaeology, 32–48.

McGrail, S. 1991. "Bronze Age seafaring in the Mediterranean: A view from N.W Europe," in N. H. Gale (ed.), *Bronze Age trade in the Mediterranean.* Jonsered: Paul Åströms, 83–91.

McGrail, S. 1992. "Replicas, reconstructions and floating hypotheses," *International Journal of Nautical Archaeology* 21: 353–55.

McGrail, S. 1993. "Experimental archaeology and the trireme," in Shaw 1993: 4–10.

McGrail, S. 1996a. "Navigational techniques in Homer's *Odyssey*," *Tropis* 4: 311–20.

McGrail, S. 1996b. "Study of boats with stitched planking," in H. Ray and J.-F. Salles (eds.), *Tradition and archaeology: Early maritime contacts in the Indian Ocean*. New Delhi: Manohar.

McGrail, S. 1998. *Ancient boats in north-west Europe*. 2nd ed. London: Longman.

McGrail, S. 2003. "How were boats designed before the late-Medieval period?" in Beltrame 2003: 124–31.

McGrail, S. 2004a. *Boats of the world*. 2nd ed. Oxford: Oxford University Press.

McGrail, S. 2004b. "North-west European seagoing boats before AD 400," in P. Clark (ed.), *Dover Bronze Age Boat in context*. Oxford: Oxbow Books, 52–66.

McGrail, S.2006. "Experimental boat archaeology: Has it a future?" in L. Blue, F. Hocker, A. Englert, (eds.), *Connected by the sea: Proceedings of ISBSA 10, 2003*. Oxford: Oxbow: 8–15

McGrail, S., and E. Kentley (eds.) 1985. *Sewn plank boats*. British Archaeological Reports, Intl. Series S276. Oxford: BAR.

Morton, J. 2001. *Role of the physical environment in ancient Greek seafaring*. Leiden: Brill.

Morrison J. S., and J. Coates 1986. *Athenian trireme*. Cambridge: Cambridge University Press.

Morrison, J. S., and J. Coates (eds.) 1989. *An Athenian trireme reconstructed*. British Archaeological Reports, Intl. Series S486. Oxford: BAR.

Morrison, J. S., J. Coates, and N. B. Rankov 2000. *Athenian trireme*, 2nd ed. Cambridge: Cambridge University Press.

Murphy, J. P. (ed.) 1977. *Rufus Festus Avienus: Ora Maritima*. Chicago: Ares.

Murray, W. M. 1987. "Do modern winds equal ancient winds?" *Mediterranean Historical Review* 22: 139–67.

Murray, W. M. 1991. "Provenance and date," in Casson and Steffy 1991: 51–66.

Nayling, N., and S. McGrail 2004. *Barland's Farm Romano-Celtic boat*. CBA Research Report 138. York: Council for British Archaeology.

Negueruela, I., M. Pinedo, M. Gómez, A. Miñano, I. Arellano, and J. S. Barba 1995. "Seventh-century BC Phoenician vessel discovered at Playa de la Isla, Mazarron, Spain," *International Journal of Nautical Archaeology* 24: 189–97.

Ó hEailidhe, P. 1992. "Monk's boat: A Roman period relic from L. Lene, Co. Westmeath," *International Journal of Nautical Archaeology* 21: 185–90.

Oikonomides, A. N., and M. C. J. Miller (eds.) 1995. *Hanno the Carthaginian, Periplus*. Chicago: Ares.

Oleson, J. P. 2000. "Ancient sounding weights: A contribution to the history of Mediterranean navigation," *Journal of Roman Archaeology* 13: 294–310.

Pomey, P. 1981. "L'épave de Bon Porté et les bateaux cousus de Mediterranée," *Mariner's Mirror* 67: 225–43.

Pomey, P. 1985. "Mediterranean sewn boats in antiquity," in McGrail and Kentley 1985: 35–48.

Pomey, P. 1995. "Les Épaves Grecques et Romaines de la Place Jules-Verne á Marseille," *Comptes Rendus de l'Académie des Inscriptions et Belles-Lettres* 1995: 459–84.

Pomey, P. 1996. "Un example d'évolution des techniques de construction navale antique: De l'assemblage par ligature à l'assemblage par tenons et mortaises," in D.Meeks and D. Garcia (eds.), *Techniques et économie antiques et médiévales*. Paris: Editions Errance, 195–203.

Pomey, P. 1997. "Bon Porté wreck," in Delgado 1997: 252–53.

Pomey, P. 1999. "Les épaves Grecques du 6e siècle av. J-C de la Place Jules-Verne à Marseilles," in P. Pomey and E. Rieth (eds.), "Construction navale maritime et fluvialé," *Archaeonautica* 14: 147–53.

Prins, A. H. J. 1965. *Sailing from Lamu*. Assen: Van Gorcum.

Pulak, C. 1998. "Uluburun shipwreck: An overview," *International Journal of Nautical Archaeology* 27: 188–224.

Pulak, C. 2003. "Mortise-and-tenon joints of Bronze Age seagoing ships," in Beltrame 2003: 28–34.

Reade, J. (ed.) 1996. *Indian Ocean in antiquity*. London: British Museum and Kegan Paul.

Rieth, É. 2000. "Medieval wreck from Port Berteau 2," in J. Liwin (ed.), *Down the river to the sea*. Gdansk: Polish Maritime Museum, 225–28.

Rieth, É., C. Carrierre-Dubois, and V. Serna (eds.) 2001. *L'épave de Port Berteau 2*. Paris: Maison des Sciences de l'Homme.

Roberts, O. T. P. 2005. "Windward sailing capability of ancient Greek ships," *Mariner's Mirror* 91: 106–7.

Royal, J. 2002. *Development and utilization of ship technology in the Roman world in late antiquity*. PhD diss., Texas A & M University.

Royal, J. G., and Y. Kahanov 2005. "New dating and contextual evidence for the fragmentary timber remains located in the Dor D site, Israel," *International Journal of Nautical Archaeology* 34: 308–13.

Rule, M., and J. Monaghan 1993. *Gallo-Roman trading vessel from Guernsey*. Guernsey Museum Monograph 5. St. Peter Port: Guernsey Museum Services.

Shaw, J. T. (ed.). 1993. *Trireme project*. Oxford: Oxbow.

Sleeswyk, A. W. 1980. "Phoenician joints, *coagmenta punicana*," *International Journal of Nautical Archaeology* 9: 243–44.

Steffy, J. R. 1985. "Kyrenia ship: An interim report on its hull construction," *American Journal of Archaeology* 89: 71–101.

Steffy, J. R. 1989. "Role of three-dimensional research in the Kyrenia ship reconstruction," *Tropis* 1: 249–62.

Steffy, J. R. 1991. "Ram and bow timbers: A structural interpretation," in Casson and Steffy 1991: 6–39.

Steffy, J. R. 1994. *Wooden shipbuilding and the interpretation of shipwrecks*. College Station: Texas A & M University Press.

Steffy, J. R. 1995. "Shipwreck archaeology: An essential medium for interpreting ancient ship construction," in V. Karageorghis and D. Michaelides (eds.), *Cyprus and the Sea*. Nicosia: University of Cyprus, 23–31.

Taylor, E. G. R. 1971. *Haven-finding art*. London: Hollis and Carter.

Throckmorton, P. J. 1973. "Roman wreck at Pantano Longarini," *International Journal of Nautical Archaeology* 2: 243–66.

Tilley, A. F. 1976. "Rowing the trireme," *Mariner's Mirror* 62: 357–59.

Tilley, A. F. 1992. "Three men to a room: A completely different trireme," *Antiquity* 66.252: 599–610.

Tilley, A. F. 1995. "Warships of the ancient Mediterranean," *Tropis* 3: 429–40.

Tilley, A. F. 2004. *Seafaring on the ancient Mediterranean*. British Archaeological Reports, Intl. Series S1268. Oxford: BAR.

van Doorninck, F. H. 1976. "Fourth century wreck at Yassi Ada," *International Journal of Nautical Archaeology* 5: 115–31.

van Doorninck, F. H. 1982. "Hull remains," in G. Bass and F. H. van Doorninck (eds.), *Yassi Ada*, vol. 1. College Station: Texas A & M University Press, 32–64.

Wachsmann, S. 1998. *Seagoing ships and seamanship in the Bronze Age Levant*. College Station: Texas A & M University Press.

Ward, C. A. 2000. *Sacred and secular: Ancient Egyptian ships and boats*. Archaeological Institute of America Monograph Series 5. Philadelphia: University of Pennsylvania Museum.

Ward, C. A. 2003. "Sewn planked boats from Early Dynastic Abydos, Egypt," in Beltrame 2003: 19–27.

Westerdahl, C. 1992. "Review: F. Welsh, *Building the Trireme*. London: Constable, 1988," *International Journal of Nautical Archaeology* 21: 84–85.

Wright, E. 1990. *Ferriby boats*. London: Routledge.

# CHAPTER 25

# SEA TRANSPORT, PART 2: HARBORS

## DAVID J. BLACKMAN

## THE HISTORY OF RESEARCH ON HARBORS

Interest in ancient harbors was aroused in the nineteenth century by the discovery of wall paintings and mosaics with maritime scenes, mainly in Herculaneum and Pompeii.* Although ship depictions attracted the most attention, several harbor scenes were also identified (Blackman 1982). Such scenes were also found on all manner of other media, including glass panels and engraved glass flasks of the Roman period, the latter depicting the sites of Baiae and Puteoli. Reliefs, mainly from sarcophagi, provided a larger field for depicting a complex scene, such as a ship entering harbor and another ship made fast to a mooring-stone to enable unloading to take place. The harbor on the famous Torlonia Relief of about A.D. 200 (figure 25.1) is usually identified with the Claudian harbor at Portus ("the Port") near Ostia, based on comparison of the lighthouse with representations of the Portus lighthouse on local mosaics. Many coins, almost all Roman, depicted harbors, some clearly identifiable from the inscription or from structural details (Blackman 1982: 80–85). There was, however, little systematic work on ancient harbors in general. There was

*Given the unavoidably large number of sites mentioned in this chapter, I have decided in most cases to omit citation in the text of bibliographical references concerning sites mentioned more than once. The documentation for these sites can be found in a gazetteer placed before the references for this chapter. Further discussion and bibliographical information for most of these sites can also be found in Blackman (1982).

Figure 25.1. Torlonia Relief, stylized representation of Portus, ca. 200 A.D. Rome. (Courtesy of Bridgeman Art Library.)

discussion about the topography of Rome, which had an important river port, of Ostia/Portus at the mouth of the River Tiber; of Syracuse; and of Piraeus, the port of inland Athens. Otherwise few studies of harbor sites were published.

Much valuable material—including plans and descriptions—resulted from the work of nineteenth-century hydrographers preparing the first Admiralty Charts of the Mediterranean. For them, the features of ports such as location, water supply, identification marks, and hazards were of prime importance. But their work did not receive from archaeologists the attention that it deserved. Early in the twentieth century, two developments led to a new interest in the remains of ancient harbors and submerged coastal sites. First, major programs of drainage work were being carried out, along with the excavation of canals and the dredging and modernization of harbors. Second, the phenomenon of sea-level change was being studied, particularly in Greece and Italy. The evidence for earth movements in the Bay of Naples aroused the interest of geologists such as Günther (1903a–b) and archaeologists such as Dubois (1902, 1907), who wrote a book on ancient Puteoli and studied the harbor construction methods described by Vitruvius (*De arch.* 5.12). The first major work on ancient harbors was written by Lehmann-Hartleben (1923) in the years around World War I. Its subtitle indicated his particular interest: *Contributions to the History of City Planning in Antiquity*. Given the period, much of this monumental work is inevitably a compilation based on ancient texts and modern publications rather than on his own personal observation, but it was very thorough and detailed and remains an essential source for study of the subject. One defect is that Lehmann-Hartleben too readily assumed that methods of harbor construction developed and progressed evenly, and that innovations were adopted universally. We can now see that this was not so, and that small coastal settlements may not have had the resources or the need to construct sophisticated, major harborworks at any time in antiquity. More recent studies have emphasized the importance of small ports, and of cabotage (short-range coastal shipping) (McCann and Oleson 2004: 207–10).

Lehmann-Hartleben's book did not provide any immediate major stimulus to harbor studies, certainly not in the field. The next major figure was Antoine Poidebard (1939, 1951), a Jesuit priest who worked at Tyre from 1934 to 1936 and Sidon from 1946 to 1950, although his pioneering work was not fully appreciated until the 1960s. Poidebard was the first to recognize the value of air photographs for studying sites submerged in shallow water. At Tyre, he carried out underwater survey and photography to check the air photographs and published with remarkable speed a full survey of the outer roadstead and the inner harbor. At Sidon, using similar methods, he traced a similar pattern in the remains, and found and explained a remarkable de-silting system. Military experience during World War II confirmed the value of air photographs, and experts had much new material to exploit. Thus Bradford brilliantly deduced the existence of a west harbor at the city of Rhodes, now silted up and previously unknown to archaeologists. Schmiedt exploited the Italian air photo archive for the study of coastal sites, revealing many submerged remains and other sites now buried inland. He also researched evidence for sea-level change (Schmiedt 1972). Air photographs continue to be a valuable resource, since so many sites have been threatened with destruction in the industrial and touristic development of the Mediterranean coastline.

For some ancient cities lying under modern towns, like Rhodes, Corcyra (Corfu), or Syracuse, it has been possible to piece together ancient topography gradually thanks to the work of local archaeological services, who scrutinize modern building developments and investigate ancient remains in deep levels before the new buildings are started. In an extreme example, in Naples the ancient harbor was discovered only during Metro construction in 2003. Nevertheless, many ancient sites have been damaged or built over without proper study or recording.

Fortunately this was not the case with the Claudian harbor at Portus, much of which now lies under the Fiumicino airport; nor with the shore of the Vieux Port of Massalia (Marseilles), where important remains of ancient quays and slipways, and of beached ships, have been carefully excavated since the 1990s, in preparation for the construction of underground car parks. At Pisa the river harbor was discovered during work for a new high-speed train line. Other harbors were surveyed in advance of the arrival of a major coast road, for example Phaselis in Lycia. Other major sites have been excavated as land sites, even when not under threat: the Roman harbor at Leptis Magna in Tripolitania, and the harbors of ancient Carthage. Special techniques have been developed for the difficult task of survey and excavation in shallow water, for example in the Bay of Naples. With the increasing threat of coastal development, the survey of ancient harbor sites is a major priority, and much less expensive than excavation. A number of sites have been investigated since the 1970s with visual survey and subsequently with the latest techniques of geophysical prospection. The potential of the latter was demonstrated between 1997 and 2004 by dramatic results in the area between the harbor on the River Tiber and the Trajanic harbor at Portus (Keay and Millett 2006).

Increased public interest in all aspects of marine archaeology, including harbors and discoveries on harbor sites, has led to a renewed interest in, for example, Vitruvius' description of the laying of concrete foundations under water, now the subject of a major research project (Oleson et al. 2004, 2006). Much new evidence has been found for sea level changes in historical times, notably from slipways and fish-tanks, to contribute to geomorphologists' studies of the extent of such changes and of the processes that affect them (movements of the land and changes in the level of the sea itself). Sometimes the archaeologist may be able to indicate a fairly precise date for a particular sea level, and in return the geomorphologist may be able to help with dating otherwise undatable structures. Dating of dead marine fauna also has great potential. This is a continuing debate and is largely dependent on close cooperation among varied scientific disciplines (Blackman 2005). Wide interdisciplinary cooperation, for example, with sedimentologists, has brought valuable results in the study of the paleoenvironment of ancient harbors, for example, at Marseilles, Citium, Tyre, and Carthage (Marriner and Morhange 2007).

Large-scale excavation under water has been undertaken at only a few sites, notably Cenchreai, Cosa, Amathus, and Caesarea in Palestine, and one could add more limited work at Apollonia, the port of Cyrene, at Thasos, Halieis, Samos, Aegina, and Paphos (see the gazetteer at the end of this chapter, Shaw 1972, Blackman 1982, and entries in Delgado 1998). Many of the main results are referred to below. Major excavations in progress as this chapter was being prepared, which cannot be fully incorporated here, are those in the Great Harbor at Alexandria. Herakleion, 30 km to the east in Aboukir Bay by the Canopic mouth of the Nile, is a remarkable example of a port with four basins, linked to a sanctuary, and may prove to have been the predecessor of Alexandria (see Gazetteer). It is now submerged to uneven depths by catastrophic faulting, soil liquefaction, and subsidence.

In the first years of the twenty-first century there have been several regional surveys of coastlines, notably the ANSER (Porti antichi del mar Tirreno) project, which has enabled the study of the relationship between neighboring ports and their hinterland and offshore islands, from Latium to southern Spain (Gallina Zevi and Turchetti 2004). We now know much more about, for example, river ports on the Guadalquivir (ancient Baetis) and the first harbor installations of the pre-Roman Iberian period (fifth–fourth century B.C.) from Alicante.

# HISTORICAL OVERVIEW OF
# HARBOR DEVELOPMENT

Documentation for most of the developments mentioned in this chapter can be found in Blackman 1982. In the Dark Age that followed the collapse of the Bronze Age kingdoms of the Aegean and Near East at the end of the second millennium B.C., the main long-distance maritime activity seems to have been carried out by the Phoenicians. They resumed the use of rock-cut harbors along the Levantine coast, such as Tyre and Sidon, which had probably already been developed in the Late Bronze Age; perhaps they were the original builders. It was certainly the Phoenicians who added the built structures such as quays and jetties at Sidon, the original harborworks at Athlit and Akko, and a jetty at Tabbat el-Hammam dating from the ninth century B.C. (Blackman 1982: 90–94; Frost 1971, 1973, 1995; Raban 1995).

Within a century, Greek trade with the Near East revived, and Greek traders participated in the development of harbor facilities in that region. A number of Greek cities followed the Phoenicians in establishing trading posts for maritime trade in the West; this trend was further stimulated from the late eighth century by the settling of colonies in many parts of the Mediterranean and Black Sea. Colonization created the need for improved harbor facilities, which, like other major public works, were made easier to finance by the introduction of coinage in the seventh century.

Many of the known early public works in Greek cities were the work of powerful tyrants who built up their city's trade and prosperity and had the necessary resources of finance and labor. The earliest harborworks in the Aegean that are firmly dated are those built by Polycrates, tyrant of Samos, in about 530 B.C. and described by Herodotus (3.60.3) as a major feat of engineering. Some remains of his massive breakwater may survive; by its size it clearly marked a new stage in harbor development, but it was not the first built harborwork in the Aegean. A quay and breakwater on Delos have been dated to the late eighth century; this dating is not certain, but the late eighth and seventh centuries provide a very likely context for the first large-scale attempts to improve the available natural harbors in the Aegean. A seventh-century B.C. date was previously suggested for a rubble breakwater at Eretria, over 600 m long, running out into depths of over 20 m, diverting a silt-bearing stream and ending at a natural reef; but a sixth-century date now seems more likely (Walker 2004: 100). Rubble breakwaters were also built in much later periods.

The indented coastline of the Aegean provided many good natural harbors (Morton 2001), so many cities needed to build no more than a shoreline quay or jetty against which even large merchant ships could berth. But some cities lay on exposed coasts and required a different solution. A feature of certain harbors on exposed coastlines in Greece and Sicily may show Phoenician influence: an artificial harbor basin (*cothon*) excavated landward of the coastline. This technique was particularly important along Phoenician trade routes on the North African coast. The basin sometimes made use of existing low-lying ground or a lagoon, perhaps joined to the sea by one or more channels. The prime example of such a harbor is that at Carthage, a Punic foundation. Although the date of the visible features is much later, there is no reason to doubt that the harbor originated with an excavated basin. Rock-cut basins are difficult to date, but there is similarly no reason to doubt that the harbor of Mahdia also had a Punic origin (Blackman 1982: 93–94; Tusa 2004).

The island settlement at Motya in western Sicily had such a basin, although apparently not until the sixth century. Here we know from historical sources that we are dealing with a Phoenician construction, although its identification as a harbor has been disputed. Phoenician harborworks have also been suggested at Tharros in Sardinia, preceding the Roman structures. The only harbor on the Greek mainland that may reasonably be called a *cothon* is the inner harbor at Lechaeum, the west harbor of Corinth. The dating is uncertain, but it may plausibly be ascribed to Periander, the great tyrant of Corinth (reigned ca. 627–587) who was famous for his contribution to naval developments and who instituted transit tolls on traffic through the Corinthian ports.

# ANCIENT TECHNICAL LITERATURE

Unfortunately, no ancient technical handbooks on harbor construction survive, although some author's names and even titles survive; for example, *Limenopoiïka* (*Harbor Construction*) written by the engineer Philon in the late third century B.C. By this date there were flourishing schools of engineering, notably at Alexandria and Rhodes. Vitruvius, writing in the first century B.C., was able to draw on a body of technical literature, and possibly on his own experience, for his one chapter on harbor construction (*De arch.* 5.12). Oleson (Oleson et al. 2004: 205–6) plausibly suggests that there may by then have been a number of subliterary harbor engineering manuals, and perhaps even specialist *collegia* for those building ancient Roman harbors. Although we have the names of many specialist laborers who worked in harbors, we do not have any references to *collegia*, nor do we have any reference to a harbor engineer during the classical period. Names of authors of works titled *Harbors* are known to us, and some would have been experts: for example, Timosthenes of Rhodes, a captain in the Ptolemaic fleet in the third century B.C. (Strabo 9.3.10). But from what little we know of these literary works, they seem to have been geographical rather than engineering handbooks, like the *Coastal Pilots* or *Periploi*, of which a number survive (Blackman 1982: 79–80; Casson 1989; Morton 2001: 180–81).

# TECHNOLOGICAL EVOLUTION

From the late sixth century B.C. onward, the main developments in harbor engineering may be attributed to the Greeks and then to the Romans. A continuing contribution by the Phoenicians is hard to estimate, but it may have been more significant than we can now detect. Some have suggested a continuing Phoenician tradition in naval architecture, which may have extended to harbor engineering. Others, including the author, have wondered whether Greek architects built the shipsheds at Carthage and earlier at Citium. So far we know little about Etruscan harbor installations (McCann 1977; Oleson 1977; Bruni 2003).

The Greeks built harborworks much like normal land structures, using blocks of ashlar masonry joined without mortar, but often with clamps, to form the quays; breakwaters were built of rubble, but sometimes the upper surface and inner side were faced with ashlar. In the Roman period, architectural developments on land, following the invention of structural concrete, led to developments in harbor construction—notably the invention of the hydraulic form of concrete with a volcanic ash additive (pozzolana from the Bay of Naples) that would set under water. Instead of merely using stone blocks, engineers were able to build free-standing structures in the sea: the foundations for moles and breakwaters, quays, lighthouses, and other shoreline structures such as *piscinae* or fish-tanks (Oleson et al. 2004, 2006). The invention has not yet been precisely dated: it probably resulted from an accidental discovery or deliberate experiments in the Bay of Naples, per-haps at Puteoli itself, in the late third or early second century B.C. There are also possible indications of experiments with lime mortar and wooden forms in the harbor of Hellenistic Alexandria in the mid-third century B.C. Vitruvius describes the material and the methods of its use (*De arch.* 2.6.1; 5.12).

At present, our earliest evidence of a major structure built with hydraulic concrete are five concrete *pilae* (large piers or blocks) built on or by an earlier breakwater in the harbor of Cosa, a Roman colony on the coast of Etruria; the date is disputed between the late second and the mid-first century B.C., but analysis of new samples indicates the later date (Oleson et al. 2004). This technology was famously used in the construction of Herod the Great's harbor at Caesarea in Palestine (ca. 22 B.C.); analysis of the concrete used there has shown that the crucial ingredient, pozzolana, was indeed imported from the Bay of Naples (Branton and Oleson 1992). The same is true of a Roman mole in the smaller harbor of Cher-sonesus on the north coast of Crete (Brandon et al. 2005).

One could imagine that at first a few teams of skilled engineers traveled the Mediterranean to apply their (no doubt expensive) expertise in various ports for rich benefactors; or they may have been sent on an imperial mission at Caesarea and possibly Paphos, where the harbor needed major repair after a serious earthquake in 15 B.C. (Hohlfelder 1996: 95). But techniques cannot have been kept secret for long; they must soon have become widely known and copied, and perhaps described in engineering manuals. In time it was also discovered that some local volcanic sands could be used instead of pozzolana from Naples. This is the subject of a major research project, the Roman Maritime Concrete Study (ROMACONS: Oleson et al. 2004, 2006), which is taking samples of hydraulic concrete from a wide range of sites across the Mediterranean in order to define its structural characteristics and to elucidate its production technology and the history of its use, along with wider questions of its transportation, the financing of projects and the composition of the specialist labor force. Relative cost advantages may be part of the explanation of the success of this technology and the resulting rapid advances in Roman harbor construction. The experimental reconstruction of a *pila* with Vitruvian-type concrete has cast light on methods of placing this concrete. Analysis of the samples shows that Roman hydraulic concrete used in maritime structures is surprisingly soft and porous, but nevertheless durable (Oleson et al. 2004, 2006)

Crucial for the use of concrete for building structures in the water was the design and construction of timber formwork to hold the concrete in place and protect it from the waves until it had set. The forms could then be left in place, or removed. Vitruvius describes several formwork designs (*De arch.* 5.12), but evidence has been found for a number of methods, in timber or ashlar enclosures. The timber forms often show a high quality of carpentry, as if they had been built by shipwrights; sometimes single-mission barges built with the same care as ships were used as forms and sunk by the addition of a load of hydraulic concrete at the construction site (figure 25.2; Brandon 1999). In the west mole at Portus a huge merchant ship was sunk containing the concrete foundation of the lighthouse (Suetonius, *Claud.* 20.3; Pliny, *HN* 16.201–2, 36.69–70), and some smaller ships were also found in the concrete parts of the mole. Study of remains at many ports besides Caesarea show that the construction procedures varied, but the quality of the pozzolana concrete was relatively uniform. At some sites the formwork has not survived, but can be deduced from the impressions left on the surface of the concrete structure (Oleson et al. 2006), for example, at Side (Knoblauch 1977: figs. 75–77). Sometimes the traces are horizontal holes across the structure, which held timber tie-beams, such as the two rows across the concrete mole at Thapsus in North Africa. Study of the holes in the Roman moles at Antium has shown the complex structure of the timber armature (Felici 1993, 2002).

The use of hydraulic concrete combined with their generally sophisticated engineering skills enabled Roman engineers to build harbors wherever it was desirable for political, military, or economic reasons, and on coasts where, unlike the Aegean, there were few or no natural harbors: Italy, North Africa, or the Levant, for example. The large, deep open roadsteads needed for modern tankers would have been shunned by ancient shipping, which needed cozy, well-protected refuges, with no great depth, and, in the Mediterranean, no need to allow for tidal ranges. But engineers now had a range of choices, and harbors did not always make use of hydraulic concrete (Hohlfelder 1985, 1996; Oleson 1988). The harbor of Cenchreae was built with methods showing little similarity to the Vitruvian procedures, and a variety of construction is seen even within the Claudian harbor at Portus. Grandiose projects like the harbor of Leptis Magna involved the extensive use of massive ashlar masonry for quay faces and upper surfaces.

One can trace a gradual increase in the size of harbors in the Mediterranean from the classical Greek through the Hellenistic to the Roman periods, not only the area available for berthing or anchorage, but also the scale of the facilities, quays, and dockyard buildings. There was also a greater regularity in plan. But there were always exceptions: limited, simple harbor facilities built with traditional methods will have sufficed at many smaller sites (for example, Aperlae in Lycia), even in the

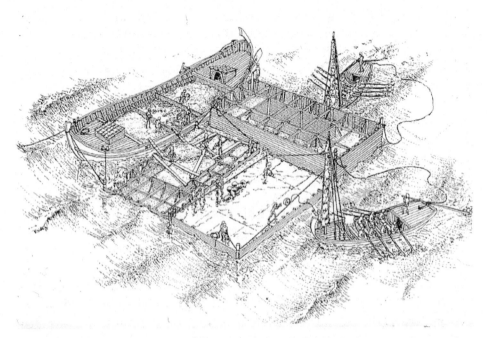

Figure 25.2. Single-use barge caissons being sunk over south breakwater at Caesarea in Palestine. (Reconstruction by C. Brandon, by permission.)

prosperous period of the early Roman Empire, and beaches remained a frequent alternative to harbor structures. Recent scholarship has emphasized the important role of cabotage throughout antiquity, and this kind of trade must have frequently made use of undeveloped harbors.

The developments in harbor technology are less clear in the Aegean area, where the Romans often took over existing ports, with the resulting problem that it is often difficult to distinguish pre-Roman facilities. This is true at Cenchreae or, to take a less well known example, the small site of Mavra Litharia, the port of Aegira west of Corinth, where the harbor facilities (built of hydraulic concrete below sea level and concrete with ashlar revetment above) seem to have been put out of action by a massive seismic uplift of about 4 m in the third century A.D. (Papageorgiou et al. 1993).

Evidence for late Roman harbors is sparse, except for Constantinople (Kingsley 2004: 131–59). Harbor construction by the sixth-century emperors Anastasius and Justinian is described by a contemporary writer, Procopius (*Aed.* 1.8.7–9, 11.18–20; 4.10.5–17; *Anec.* 8.7–8, 26.23), but his reference to the renovation of the harbor of Caesarea (*Panagyr. Anast.* 19) has found little confirmation in evidence from a thorough survey. A modest harbor such as Aperlae seems to have continued to operate, because it produced the lucrative *murex* or purple dye (Hohlfelder 2005). The only known works that probably date from this period are the last phase of the harbor of Anthedon in central Greece: two apparently hastily built moles and a quay, with rubble fill and hydraulic mortar in compartments divided and faced by rough courses of mainly reused blocks (Schläger et al. 1968). Because the courses were irregular, shallow slots were cut in their upper surface and filled with mortar to level off the top surface of the quay, methods very different from the sophisticated harbor engineering of the early Empire. Although the Anthedon harbor structures were probably a rapid construction by land engineers, intended to support the urgent land defense of central Greece against invasions from the north in the early sixth century, they have survived in good shape. A slipway, possibly a dry-dock, at Marea on the shore of Lake Mareotis in Egypt is the only known example from late Antiquity (Petruso and Gabel 1983).

# MOLES AND QUAYS

Moles and breakwaters were built to provide protection against both heavy seas and enemy attack. Their alignment, especially in relation to the prevailing winds and currents, and type of construction were important in fulfilling their main purpose, and also for dealing with the problem of siltation. The simplest breakwater was a natural line of reef or rocks, and some early harbors in the Levant, such as Sidon, made effective use of these, including wave traps to break the force of the waves. In the Greek world, construction of long, submerged embankments of rubble may go back at least to the seventh century (see above). At Cnidus in the fourth century, breakwaters of huge, roughly-cut blocks were built in 30 m of water.

The outer faces of such breakwaters naturally were sloped, both to stabilize the loose construction materials and to prevent undermining by wave action. The permeability of such structures, along with their alignment—where possible at an angle to the prevailing seas—helped to break the force of the waves. The height to which breakwaters were built above sea level cannot now always be determined. Some may have lost stones from their upper surface through storms or stone robbing in later periods, but many still look very solid, possibly having grown stronger with time through compaction of the rubble materials. It is now clear that some breakwaters have subsided under their own weight, through lack of a solid natural foundation or the destabilizing of the underlying levels by effects such as liquefaction—the mobilization of sediments by the sudden infusion of water, often as a result of earthquake. Evidence of subsidence can be seen in the very wide breakwater at Cosa, the north mole at Cenchreae, and probably the north breakwater of the commercial harbor at Cnidus and the south breakwater at Phaselis. The outer breakwater at Caesarea in Palestine seems to have sunk 5–6 m as a result of either the shift of a geological fault or the liquefaction of the sand beneath the harbor structures.

Some breakwaters did not support buildings and were intended to allow the waves simply to break over them, creating a current within the harbor that would help prevent silting. This seems to have been the original purpose of the Cosa breakwater. Such a strategy would work only in virtually tideless seas such as the Mediterranean, although tidal seas offered alternative methods of de-silting. Unless a breakwater had this special purpose, it could also be used to add to the berthing space available in the harbor. Thus the inner sides of moles were built up to serve as quays, and fortification walls were built along their outer sides, to include the harbors in the city fortifications (see below). There must often have been only a narrow quay space inside such walls, or none at all; but merchant ships could at least moor there in safety while waiting to unload at the shoreline quays or offload into lighters without ever berthing at a quay. Excavations on the "Mole of the Windmills" at Rhodes have shown that after Demetrius Poliorcetes landed on the unfortified breakwater during his unsuccessful siege of 305 B.C., the Rhodians built an impressive wall on it. By the second century B.C. its defensive role was less important, and a quay for commercial purposes was added along its inner side. In the period of the *pax Romana*, fewer moles around the Mediterranean bore fortification walls, leaving more space for loading areas and for buildings. Some Roman harbors such as Cenchreae and Leptis Magna had moles wide enough to carry quays, warehouses, temples, statues, fish-tanks, signal-towers, and a lighthouse. *Horrea* (grain warehouses) were a distinctive feature of Roman commercial harbors such as Portus. The later addition of a fortification wall at Leptis was a sign of renewed insecurity.

The new flexibility that hydraulic concrete gave to Roman engineers enabled them not only to build solid structures of concrete, or concrete faced with ashlar and brick, but also to experiment with arched structures, in particular detached piers joined by arches supporting a paved surface. This design seems to have been tried out experimentally for a short period during the first centuries B.C. and A.D. in Latium and Campania. The arched mole at Puteoli was 372 m long and 16 m wide, based on 15 piers of tufa blocks on concrete foundations. The arches were built of brick and limestone blocks with a fill of rubble and pozzolana. The line of piers is slightly curved, better to resist stormy seas from the south (Piromallo 2004: 273). The south mole of the naval harbor at nearby Misenum had two offset lines of piers. Some contemporary works of art, mainly paintings from the same region (e.g. Blackman 1982: fig. 5), illustrate similar structures, but we cannot be certain that the superstructures were not built of timber. The purpose of the design may have been to prevent silting up of the harbor basin by allowing currents of water to flow through it. Perhaps the currents proved too strong and the waves unmanageable during heavy seas and strong winds; but probably the main reason for the abandonment of the experiment was that the structures lacked longitudinal stability and collapsed. The mole at Puteoli, for example, had to be rebuilt in A.D. 139 (*CIL* 10.1640, 1641).

Another innovation, apparently of the Roman period, is the building of off-shore breakwaters. Pliny the Younger (*Ep.* 6.31) describes being summoned by Trajan to witness the building of a new harbor at Centumcellae (Civitavecchia), on the harborless coast north of Rome: an artificial island was being built in front of the harbor entrance, with enormous blocks brought out by boat and dropped, and piers added to the pile to make an arcaded facing or superstructure. In the second century A.D., a number of ports, such as Sabratha and Patras, were provided with long offshore breakwaters as their only protection; the aim seems to have been to prevent silting by allowing the coastal current to pass through unobstructed (Blackman 1982: 198).

Though the inner side of a mole was often used as a quay, the main quays were usually on the shore, backed by warehouses and all the facilities of a port. Quay construction methods, we may assume, developed roughly in parallel with those of moles: from rock-cut quays as at Sidon, to roughly faced and paved rubble, as in early Delos, to well-dressed ashlar revetments, and then, in the Roman period, to concrete structures, usually faced with ashlar or small stone blocks (*opus reticulatum*) or brick, or sometimes with timber. Rock-cut quays (such as those at Delos, Cnidus, and Mahdia) are very difficult to date except by general context.

A few solid Roman quays were faced with brick arches, and in some works of art quays seem to be depicted as supported on freestanding arches. The only remains that may belong to such a quay are those of the south quay at Puteoli, where two offset lines of piers may have been joined by arches; but the wall may in fact simply be the outer wall of a set of basins. Some quays and projecting jetties depicted in art do appear to be timber structures (wall paintings from Stabiae and the Temple of Isis at Pompeii, and the Palestrina mosaic from Praeneste: Blackman 1982: 83–85). Such structures have long been known from north of the Alps, from Roman Britain (e.g., the port of Roman London), Gaul, and the Rhineland (from river ports and embankments); now some evidence has been found from the Mediterranean coast—mainly from southern Gaul and northern Italy, but also in Alexandria from about 400 B.C. Survival of such remains may be the result of favorable conditions for the preservation of organic material, but it could also indicate local building traditions. Timber structures are known from the small port of Lattes in southern Gaul (Garcia et al. 2002: 67–70) and from the important regional port at Marseilles, the ancient Greek colony of Massalia. Much timber was used in the slipways of pre-Roman times (see below) and again in the quays of the first century A.D. One quay was built of pozzolana concrete in an open formwork of timber; the other involved a more elaborate timber structure: a rubble fill and a clay and cobbled surface was lined by a double row of pine piles, with horizontal planking between the piles consisting of reused timbers from at least nine boats (Hesnard 2004). Hesnard points out that Vitruvius may have been present at the siege of Massalia and suggests that the techniques used to build these quays illustrate Vitruvius' guidelines. However that may be, timber facing would have reduced the risk of damage to a quay from a ship coming alongside. Another timber structure at Massalia, a landing-stage at right angles to the shore, also contained reused ship timbers; it ran out 30 m into deeper water. The dramatic discovery of fifth-century A.D. ships in the Roman port of Olbia in Sardinia provides a vivid impression of how the ships were berthed—bow to shore in the typical "Mediterranean moor," probably between lines of timber piles (Kingsley 2004: 89–95).

Excavations in an ancient river port on the northwest edge of Pisa have revealed both a large number of ships wrecked by floods between the second century B.C. and late antiquity, and a number of timber structures along the river bank that gradually moved northward as a result of alluvial deposits. This site illustrates dramatically the problems faced by river ports. The earliest structure is a timber bank revetment, apparently of the late sixth century B.C., possibly our earliest evidence for Etruscan harborworks. A second timber revetment farther north, continued by a stone quay, may date from ca 400 B.C. Still farther north, a piece of timber first interpreted as part of a landing-stage may in fact be part of a gangway of the earliest of the shipwrecks so far discovered (Camilli 2004). In the Bay of Naples, a mole of concrete and timber has been discovered at Baiae. Some of these finds represent the use of various timber formwork techniques in quays and riverbanks; others confirm the generally accepted hypothesis of the existence of freestanding timber structures. A growing tendency toward regularity in the shape of harbor basins can be traced back to classical times, most probably since a relationship had to be established with the street plan of the city. Roman engineers were able to impose regularity even when it was not provided by the natural features.

Projecting jetties greatly increased the amount of quay space available within a harbor basin, which was otherwise restricted by natural contours until the great man-made harbors of the Roman period. Hellenistic Delos had an unusual length of quay for its period (1,700 m on a natural shoreline of 1,100 m), produced by projections and indentations. There were several small jetties in the main harbor of Piraeus. The north and south breakwaters at Sebastos, the Herodian harbor of Caesarea in Palestine, were 300 and 800 m long respectively, and probably occupied by quays along their entire interior length (figure 25.3; Josephus, *BJ* 1.411–13;). Trajan's hexagonal harbor basin at Portus had sides nearly 358 m long, almost entirely used as quay; the Claudian harbor basin had a combined quay length of about 1,350 m; Leptis Magna and Terracina both 1,200 m. At Alexandria, the latest estimate for the quay space in the first three inner basins, comprising only the eastern half of the Great Harbor and much increased by projecting jetties from the third century B.C. on, is about 3,000 m (figure 25.4; J. Cole, oral communication; this estimate may well rise as excavation progresses).

A few quays, like that at Leptis Magna, had two levels, but most had only one. The height of the quay surface above water level cannot have varied greatly from site to site. The archaeological remains of harbor structures are now at various heights with relation to sea level, but we have to allow for varied changes in relative sea level, both eustatic and isostatic in character, along with the subsidence of quays and moles, from the liquefaction of the sediments supporting them. As designed, quay surfaces not in exposed positions need not have been much more than 1 m above sea level, given the virtual lack of tidal change (Blackman 1982: 203). It has been argued that a depth of 2–3 m was necessary to float a ship close to a quay, and at Ephesus the harbor floor seems to have been 4 m below the waterline against a Roman quay; but preliminary conclusions from the ROMACONS project indicate that quays may have been built in much shallower water as well (Oleson et al. 2004: 221).

Figure 25.3. Reconstruction of Sebastos, the harbor of Caesarea in Palestine, early first century A.D. (Reconstruction by C. Brandon, by permission.)

Convenience suggests that a ship's deck should be level with the quay surface for unloading, as depicted on the Torlonia Relief (figure 25.1), but some ancient reliefs show the gangway at a steep angle (Basch 1987: fig. 1048; Casson 1996: fig. 174). Visual representations show that ancient merchant ships usually moored stem or stern to shore, although not necessarily perpendicular to the quay. In river harbors broadside mooring obviously would have been more common. Ships were made fast to pierced mooring-stones or bollards. Study of these features deserves more attention, for they may indicate ship sizes and mooring methods (Blackman 1988). A famous series are the pierced stone blocks set in the brick quay face of Trajan's harbor at Portus, probably originally totaling more than 100. Such mooring stones were built into the quays at the river port of Rome itself, as well as the quays of Terracina and Leptis Magna and the river harbor of Aquileia (Brusin 1934: 16–26). Although less common, they are found in pre-Roman, Greek harbors. At Teos they were wedge-shaped to take the lateral strain (Blackman 1973a: 115–17). Stone bollards were usually set vertically in the quay. Appian (*Pun.* 96) refers to cables in the commercial harbor at Carthage—presumably mooring cables that mariners could pick up on entering harbor.

The operation of berthing and unloading in a busy harbor was complex. The numbering of columns set back from the edge of the quays of the Trajanic harbor at Portus must have had the purpose of defining individual berths; the main purpose of the columns may have been to support a roof. Some ancient illustrations, almost entirely of the Roman period, give us a glimpse of harbor operations, particularly

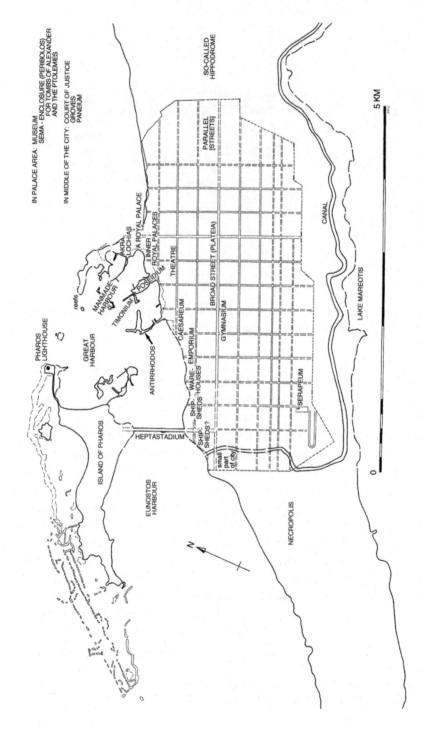

IN PALACE AREA: MUSEUM
SEMA - ENCLOSURE (PERIBOLOS)
FOR TOMBS OF ALEXANDER
AND THE PTOLEMIES

IN MIDDLE OF THE CITY: COURT OF JUSTICE
GROVES
PANEIUM

Figure 25.4. Alexandria: reconstructed plan of the port, with locations mentioned by Strabo. (Courtesy of J. McKenzie.)

unloading. Inscriptions, also mainly Roman in date, reflect the variety of the operations and skilled trades involved: crane operators, stevedores, sand-ballastmen, harbor-boatmen, lightermen, tugboatmen, divers, tally clerks, and so on (Casson 1996: 369–70). Elsewhere we have references to the operations of shipbuilding and repair, but, as has been said, no reference to harbor engineers: they must have counted simply as "engineers" (*mechanikoi*). All these were skilled trades that continued to be practiced throughout antiquity, and one wonders whether the Arab conquest made much difference to the composition of the skilled workforce in the lands they conquered.

Cranes were used on quaysides already in the classical Greek period, although the evidence is mainly epigraphic; various systems of pulley-blocks and tackle were also in use, which is not surprising given the importance of such devices for ships' rigging. For the Roman period there is somewhat more evidence for the use of cranes on both quays and building sites (Blackman 1982: 211, n. 103; cf. chapter 13). Vitruvius (*De arch.* 10.2.10) mentions a dockside crane on a rotating base that allowed more convenient pickup and deposit of the loads.

The water supply system was always an important facility for those working in the port and particularly for visiting mariners wishing to replenish supplies. At Leptis Magna, there was a barrel-vaulted water-cistern right on the quay at the southeast corner of the harbor; a watering point has been identified at Cosa; and remains of an aqueduct have been found at Portus, as would be expected. At Cenchreae and Forum Iulii (Fréjus) a well has been found beside the harbor, and at Antipolis an aqueduct and watering-point. At major fleet bases the need would have been particularly great: at Misenum a vast underground reservoir fed by an aqueduct was cut into the hill beside the harbor in the time of Augustus; it had a capacity of 12,600 cubic meters of water.

Behind the quays of larger harbors lay the warehouses, workshops, buildings for commercial transactions, bars, brothels, and hostels. At some Greek sites, such as Piraeus, the *emporion* was a well-defined area with its own boundary stones, aligned on the city grid, and the famous stoas. There and at Delos, Thasos, and Ephesus, for example, it is possible to identify the nature of some of the buildings as hostels (perhaps also brothels) or workshops. More evocative for Athens are our literary sources, such as Aristophanes (*Ach.* 545–54), for the sounds and smells of a port full of activity (Casson 1991: 97–112). Delos was an exceptional site, starting as a major sanctuary and becoming an important entrepôt and slave market, especially after 167 B.C. when the Romans declared it a free port. Cenchreae, at least for the Roman period, provides us with a vivid picture of harborside quays, warehouses, and a sanctuary of Isis. Archaeological evidence is more plentiful for all these features in the Roman period.

We obtain, mainly from epitaphs and other inscriptions, a clear impression of the large numbers of foreigners resident in ports, and the frequent grants of special legal status and the right to maintain their own cults. Ports were certainly the most cosmopolitan of ancient sites, and the place where the greatest variety of cults was found. For the Greeks the main focus was on divinities that ensured safe voyages, but a variety of foreign cults are well attested. At Alexandria there was a "foreigners' *emporion*," while Delos after 167 B.C., probably exceptionally, welcomed traders of every nation. In Roman times the foreign community was a standard feature of harbor towns. We know of many groups of foreign traders resident in places such as Ostia and Puteoli, and they must have contributed greatly to the wealth and to the rich maritime expertise of the harbor towns concerned. Dock laborers, however, were an unruly element (Rickman 1988).

# NAVAL HARBORS

From the early fifth century B.C. onward, one can see at most Greek coastal cities or their out-ports the development of a separate military harbor, or a section for warships within the harbor, provided with the greater security required for military installations (Baika 2006). At Piraeus, the out-port of Athens from the early fifth century, the two smaller harbors and part of the larger harbor were reserved for warships. The dockyard was probably a restricted area, walled off from the land-ward side, although the famous naval storehouse (Philon's Arsenal, built after 347/6 B.C.) could be visited by citizens to check public property. There is plenty of evidence in Athenian literature of the fifth and fourth centuries that the dockyard was a matter of great civic pride (e.g., Demosthenes 22.76, 23.207).

Other great ports such as Rhodes, Aegina, Thasos, Cnidus and, in the west, Carthage, also had separate military harbors. The harbor of Cnidus has not been investigated in detail, but the smaller, western harbor was known in antiquity as "the trireme harbor." A limited survey at Aegina has confirmed the north harbor as the military harbor, with remains of shipsheds. The separation of civil and military harbors should not, however, be exaggerated. It is logical to assume that there was one pool of skilled labor for specialist tasks in all port areas—rope- and sailmaking, caulking and repair of ships, shipbuilding, etc.—and that most of the population of the civil port would have also served as rowers in the warships of the Greek city states.

In their heyday, major naval powers such as Athens and Rhodes maintained naval bases at points on their own coasts, distant from the main naval base, to provide defense in depth. Athens maintained bases even beyond her borders. In many ways these are forerunners of the provincial fleet bases of the Roman Empire. In the classical and Hellenistic Greek periods, coastal cities and the out-ports of inland cities were normally fortified, and the actual harbor basin or basins was usually enclosed within the fortifications (Blackman 1982: 193–95). The city walls were extended along the harbor moles, to end in towers as at any normal city gate. Entrances were kept narrow enough to be covered by artillery mounted on the towers and for chains or booms to be used to close the entrance. Use of these devices is attested by historians describing sieges, and by authors of technical handbooks on siege techniques and countermeasures. Evidence for an entrance boom may be preserved at ancient Halieis, although the fittings may be for a land gate rather than a harbor entrance. Remains of towers and solid block buildings can still be identified at the entrance of many ancient harbors; in addition to housing artillery and the apparatus for hauling the entrance chains, they may also have served as lighthouses. At Thasos and Phalasarna, the course of the harbor walls incorporated towers. The improvements in artillery, which included ship-borne artillery, led to more heavy fortifications in general in the fourth century and later. There are some cases of harbor entrances being set back so that any enemy ship would be exposed to flanking fire from the shore if it tried to attack: Cantharus and Zea harbors in Piraeus and the "trireme harbor" at Cnidus are good examples. Controlled entrances were also a useful means of supervising commercial shipping; and research between 1996 and 2006 has revealed the fortified entrance from the Nile to the harbor basins at the sanctuary of Herakleion.

Ancient Greek geographers and coastal pilots refer to many cities as having a "closable harbor" (*kleistos limen*), which must refer to such arrangements (Lehmann-Hartleben 1923: 65–74, 122–61). A harbor that was closable would presumably normally have been enclosed within fortification walls as well. It is likely that military harbors would also have been walled off on the landward side. The same may have been true for major commercial harbors, where the authorities would have wanted to control the movement of people, particularly foreigners, and goods in and out of the city. In many cities the *emporion* was a clearly delimited area (Lehmann-Hartleben 1923: 105–21).

Significant for the history of ancient town planning is the growing evidence for the insertion of harbor installations into the city grid. We now know that the dockyard at Sicilian Naxos was aligned on the street grid and clearly formed part of the fifth-century B.C. city plan. At the new city of Rhodes (after 408 B.C.) the rectangular military harbor Mandraki, lined by shipsheds, also conformed to the city grid. It has even been suggested that the lines of the harbor influenced the original layout of the grid—a sensible arrangement since harbor installations had to take account of the line of the coast. In the fourth century B.C., Cnidus seems to have had two street grids, aligned on the two harbors—the military and the commercial. At Alexandria we know now from geophysical research that the *Heptastadion*, the famous causeway linking the island of Pharos to the mainland, was aligned on a main city street, and the main dockyard lay beside it (McKenzie 2003: 36–41; figure 25.4). The shipsheds in the Royal Harbor in the southeast corner of the Great Harbor were, however, on a different alignment.

In military harbors the most distinctive feature was the shipsheds, which must have taken up most of the available shoreline, leaving less space for quays than in commercial harbors (see below). The two smaller and exclusively military harbors of Piraeus were probably an extreme example. When the Athenian fleet went to sea,

Figure 25.5. Piraeus: Trireme harbor of Munichia in the fourth century B.C., reconstruction by John Coates. (After Morrison et al. 2000: 229, fig. 71; by permission of J. Coates.)

the triremes launched from the shipsheds of Munichia and Zea (figure 25.5) had to sail round to the *choma*, a jetty in the largest harbor, Cantharus, for official inspection, and it was probably there that most of the crew embarked. In Rhodes the military harbor may well have had shipsheds along most of its landward shoreline; it is plausible that most quay space was provided along the inner side of the mole that formed the eastern side of the harbor (Blackman et al. 1996). Archaeologists studying the military harbor of Thasos assume a similar arrangement there.

Military harbors needed considerable space for equipment, although not directly at the waterside. Oars and spars seem normally to have been stored in the shipsheds, and at Carthage there were storerooms for the gear above the shipsheds; elsewhere probably above or alongside the installations. The Athenian naval lists refer to a number of storage buildings in the dockyard area; the great naval storehouse (for sails and rigging) built by Philon in Piraeus was rediscovered in 1988–89. The naval harbors of the Roman period are not well known, even those of the Imperial period. In his magisterial survey, Reddé (1986: 145–319) stresses how little archaeological evidence we have for Roman naval installations, in striking contrast to their commercial harbors.

# ANCIENT SHIPSHEDS

By the early fifth century B.C., the constant struggle for naval superiority in the Aegean had led to the refinement of one of the most extreme warships of antiquity, the Greek trireme (Morrison et al. 2000). The successful employment of warships depended on having them regularly dried out, and since they could not operate in high waves, they were usually not taken out to sea after the end of the sailing season. The extreme qualities of the warships also made their light wooden construction vulnerable to the deteriorating forces of sun and rain. Furthermore, the aggressive shipworm (*Teredo navalis*) of the Mediterranean, against which commercial vessels could protect themselves by metal sheathing, inflicted serious damage on the warships. Thus, the delicacy of the construction and the large investment inherent in the ships made it necessary that they were carefully protected when not in use.

In order to protect warships effectively, it was necessary to haul them out of the water and provide them with cover against sun and rain. For this reason, permanent and purpose-built naval installations were constructed—*neosoikoi*, usually translated as "shipsheds." A single shipshed is basically a long and narrow roofed hall just large enough to house a ship. It is open toward the sea and has a sloping floor (slipway) with a gentle inclination from the water's edge up to the landward end. The slipways were sometimes rock-cut, sometimes built up with ramps of earth, plastered earth and rubble, or sand, most probably always clad with timber. The ship was moved into position outside the shipshed and then hauled, stern first, up the slipway until it was completely out of the water and under the roof. There it was braced and fastened, and could be kept in store until it was launched the next time. No remains of hauling-gear have yet been found at the top of slipways—a possible bollard in Munichia could be just for making the ship fast—so we must assume that the ships were manhandled up the slipways (as they were up the beach when away on a mission). The exception may be some very steep slipways such as those at Sounion.

Where a large number of ships had to be housed, several shipsheds were built next to each other in a continuous row, presenting a common front toward the sea. Good ventilation was necessary for the drying out and preservation of the ships, and to facilitate work in the sheds; this prompted the use of columns, pillars, or posts, rather than continuous walls, to support the roof. Only limited maintenance work could be done on the ships in these confined spaces, but we now know that this included painting, at least of the bow and stern where there was more space. Red pigment has been found in the Naxos shipsheds, effective as an anti-fouling paint, but dangerous for those applying it.

Some of the oldest shipsheds we know of were built on Samos around 530 B.C. No definite archaeological remains have been found there as yet, and we have only the testimony of Herodotus (3.39, 3.44–45) to confirm their existence. Herodotus

(2.159) also mentions having seen some kind of hauling installations (*holkoi*) built on the Red Sea shore during the reign of the Egyptian pharaoh Necho II (*c.* 600 B.C.), but it is not clear whether these were true shipsheds or not. The extant archaeological remains include shipsheds dated to the early fifth century B.C. at Corcyra, Abdera, and Aegina, and point to the leading role of the Greek *poleis* in the development of such facilities. It may be assumed that from this time onward every major Greek city that boasted its own fleet also had numerous shipsheds.

Athens had one of the largest fleets of the fifth and fourth centuries B.C., and consequently needed a corresponding number of shipsheds. The naval inventory lists prepared annually by the magistrates responsible for the dockyard in the fourth century B.C. (*IG* 2² 1604–1632) tell us of 372 shipsheds in the three harbors of Piraeus at Munichia, Zea, and Cantharus (today the main harbor). The majority of the sheds (196) lay in the military harbor of Zea. The series of shipsheds crowding the waterfront of Zea and Munichia constituted monumental constructions, outstanding among buildings in Athens for their sheer size (figure 25.5). Archaeological investigations, both on land and under water, were begun in 2001 on the Zea sheds, first excavated in 1885; these have revealed large areas of the ancient harbor installations, shipsheds, quays, fortifications, etc. Evidence indicating a relative rise in sea level here of about 2 m since antiquity probably explains why so much of the ancient harbor frontage has been preserved under water (http://www.zeaharbourproject.dk).

Besides Athens, other major naval powers had large-scale military harbor complexes with impressive numbers of shipsheds. Syracuse had 310 at the beginning of the fourth century B.C. (Diodorus 14.42.5); the military port of Carthage could accommodate 220 ships in the third/second century (Appian, *Pun.* 96); and finally Strabo (12.8.11) reports more than 200 shipsheds in the harbor of Cyzicus.

Medium-sized naval powers such as Rhodes, Samos, Massalia or Chios had naval bases with 50 to 100 shipsheds, while the norm seems to be bases for 10 to 50 warships, as in Aegina, Cos and Oeniadae, or Citium in Cyprus. Naxos in Sicily has a surprisingly small dockyard (figure 25.6). Finally, we also find single shipsheds or groups of two or three, usually rock-cut. They are mainly fortified and located on remote promontories strategically situated for the surveillance of maritime sea-lanes. Characteristic examples are the twin shipsheds at Sounion in Attica and the single fortified shipshed of Trypeti near Seteia in Crete (Baika 2003). Larger is the rock-cut complex of Oeniadae excavated in 1989 to 1995 (Kolonas 1989–1990). Besides Piraeus, major excavations have been carried out in the shipsheds of Carthage, Massalia, Citium and Naxos (Blackman 2003; Hurst 1977, 1979, 1994; Hesnard et al. 1999, 2001; Yon 2000; Blackman and Lentini 2003, forthcoming a, b). The shipshed complexes in major dockyards such as Carthage and Piraeus reflect more than mere utilitarian purposes. They attest a high level of technology and a massive expenditure of resources and effort, which raise practical questions about logistics and historical questions about political aspirations behind their creation.

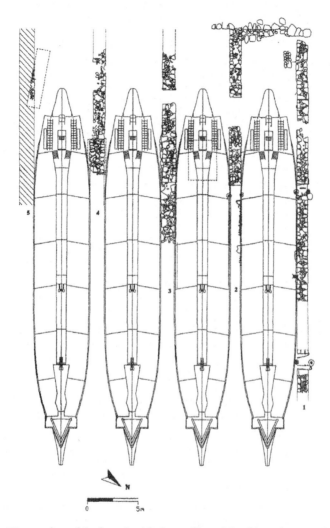

Figure 25.6.  Naxos: plan of dockyard, with the outline of the *Olympias* superimposed. (After Blackman and Lentini 2003: 407, fig. 23; courtesy of D. J. Blackman and M. C. Lentini.)

Examples of Greek and Phoenician shipsheds have been found all over the Mediterranean, from the Levantine coast (Raban 2003) to Massalia, and one of the most spectacular shipshed complexes was built in Carthage. At Massalia there appear to be remains of open slipways as well as roofed shipsheds. The use of shipsheds is testified throughout the Greek world in the classical and Hellenistic periods, and the need for them must have remained somewhat the same in the Roman period. Although Roman shipsheds are attested in literature and iconographic evidence, no definite archaeological evidence has yet been identified; possible examples are now being studied (Ciampoltrini and Rendini 2004; Blackman forthcoming; Rankov 2008; Cozza and Tucci 2006). Roman shipsheds were not necessarily confined to naval bases, and small groups may have been attached to major maritime villas.

Shipsheds are the only direct, concrete archaeological evidence that we possess for calculating the dimensions of ancient warships. Intended to house various types of oared vessels, a shipshed's dry length, clear width, and height (where it can be calculated with a certain precision) offer us the approximate outside measurements of the vessel that it once accommodated. The study of the hauling and launching operations on the inclined slipways, and the evaluation of the basic functioning of shipshed architecture, can help toward more precise understanding of the technology of the ships concerned, and of ancient maritime technology in general (cf. Blackman and Rankov forthcoming; Blackman and Lentini forthcoming b).

# HAULING-WAYS

Canal construction was a limited development in the classical Greek world (see chapter 12). Periander of Corinth tried to cut a canal across the Isthmus of Corinth in the sixth century B.C., to provide a shorter and safer route from the Aegean to the west, but was not successful; instead he built a stone runway across it (a *diolkos*, "haul-across"), over which warships and perhaps small merchant ships could be hauled (figure 23.6). This structure remained in use into the Roman period, and sections of it are still visible today. Thucydides (3.15.1) describes the Spartans constructing *holkoi* to carry ships across the isthmus in 428 B.C.; this sounds like hauling-gear or possibly wheeled cradles to transport the ships along the tracks still visible in the surface of the runway. The cradle could have been slipped under the hull at the submerged end of the runway, if it existed (but the ends are lost). Thucydides' references to the operation (e.g., 8.7) speak of carrying the ships across the isthmus, and do not use the word *diolkos*. There are possible remains of a crane near the west end of the *diolkos*, but this could have been for lifting cargo, not ships. It has been argued that the *diolkos* was mainly used for transporting cargo, and only occasionally ships (MacDonald 1986). Thucydides also describes the hauling of ships across the isthmus at Leucas (3.81.1, 4.8.2). A *diolkos* is mentioned at Alexandria, probably across the north end of the *Heptastadion*, but it has not been found (Fraser 1961). A *diolkos* may have connected the military and west harbors at Rhodes.

As mentioned above, Herodotus saw *holkoi* in Egypt, but it is not clear whether these were hauling-gear or hauling-ways. The fact that they were still visible in his time implies the latter. The *holkoi* at Delos seem to have been hauling-ways (Duchêne and Fraisse 2001: 158). Our evidence for horizontal hauling devices is limited to references in literature. Capstans, called *onoi* (donkeys) in Greek, were used by the Persians to draw tight the cables of their bridge across the Hellespont (Herodotus. 7.36), and by the Athenians in small boats to pull out the stakes of the palisade protecting the dockyard in the Great Harbor of Syracuse (Thucydides 7.25.6). No evidence for hauling-gear has been found in shipsheds. The earliest reference to ship-hauling gear is to the screw-windlass invented by Archimedes in the third century B.C. to launch a superfreighter built for Hieron II of Syracuse (reigned 269–215 B.C.; Athenaeus 5.207b; Casson 1996: 191–99; Baika 2002). It was subsequently discovered that the freighter could not enter existing harbors to deliver its cargo of grain, so Hieron gave the ship to the king of Egypt (Ptolemy III or IV). Perhaps the construction of enormous ships at Alexandria had forced the harbor technicians to develop special facilities to accommodate them. The "Forty-Banked" warship of Ptolemy IV (221–203 B.C.) was initially launched manhandled on a cradle, but later a Phoenician engineer conceived of the dry-dock method for docking it (Athenaeus 5.204c–d). In Latin literature we find references to *machinae* for hauling ships (Horace, *Carm.* 1.4.2; Livy 25.11.18, 39.50.3).

# LIGHTHOUSES

An important introduction of the early Hellenistic period was the lighthouse; the first known example was the Pharos of Alexandria, named after the island on which it was built. In antiquity lighthouses were used almost entirely as navigation marks indicating the position of harbors, and only rarely to warn against potential hazards to navigation (though harbor entrances could be dangerous, for example at Alexandria, Reddé 1979; Pensa 1999). Beacons, landmarks, and leading-marks were used earlier (Morton 2001: 210–14). The Colossus of Rhodes fulfilled a similar purpose: it almost certainly stood, not astride the entrance to the military harbor, as has often been suggested, but on its eastern side. Both the Pharos and the Colossus figured among the seven "Wonders of the Ancient World" (Brodersen 1992). The lighthouse at Portus stood near the entrance to the Claudian harbor, on the west mole (but not on a separate island, as was once thought). It was commonly depicted on mosaics, coins, reliefs, and lamps (figure 24.1; Reddé 1979). The lighthouse at Leptis Magna stood in a similar position, as did most others. A well-preserved lighthouse dating to the third quarter of the first century A.D. was found at Patara in 2003 (Yildirim and Gates 2007: 315). A few lighthouses, however, stood on commanding heights: for example on the top of the East Island at Apollonia, the port of Cyrene, and Roman lighthouses at Corunna in northwest Spain, and on two hilltops above the port of Dover and across the Straits at Boulogne.

# SHIPBUILDING YARDS

Shipsheds were not used for shipbuilding, since there was no space in them for more than limited repair or maintenance. We have long assumed the existence of impermanent structures, such as can be seen on beaches today, that have disappeared without trace. At Marseilles, a shipbuilding yard of just this sort, dating to the fifth and fourth centuries B.C., was found between 1992 and 1993, occupying at least 150 m of shoreline. Pieces of timber for shipbuilding lay on the beach, and basins had been cut in the sand for soaking timbers (Hesnard et al. 1999: 34–37; 2001: 173–74). Partially worked timbers and parts of boats waiting for reuse, together with carpenter's tools, have been found on the shore of the Roman port of Olbia in Sardinia (Kingsley 2004: 92). A *navale* for shipbuilders is attested at Ostia in an inscription of the late second century A.D. (*CIL* 14.376; Rankov 2008).

# SILTATION AND DREDGING

Siltation was a problem for harbor engineers in many parts of the Mediterranean, particularly at or near river mouths, which were otherwise ideal places for the harbors of cities with access to a deep hinterland (Blackman 1982: 199–202). Activities on shore nearby sometimes added to the problem, for example, the dumping of refuse from stoneworking activities into the harbor basin at Ephesus. One must remember that the depths of water to be maintained were smaller because of the lower draught of ships, and, in the Mediterranean, the small tide range, which was not an effective method of flushing harbor basins.

Basic dredging methods were developed in antiquity. Excavations at Naples have revealed dredging channels gouged across the sandy floor of the deepest levels of the harbor (late fourth century B.C.), and at Marseilles there is clear evidence of deep dredging in the first, third and probably fourth centuries A.D.; also the wrecks of three Roman dredgers were found abandoned on the beach or reused in foundations of a quay and landing-stage.

Much, however, depended on methods of preventing siltation, by the placing of breakwaters to deflect silt-bearing currents or to allow controlled currents through harbor basins (see above). This was easier to achieve if the harbor had two entrances. Flushing channels were already known in Phoenician Sidon, and underwater ashlar-lined channels are clearly visible in the north harbor of Mytilene; tunnels through moles have been reported elsewhere. At Paphos, there were two broad channels through the eastern breakwater, protected by an outer breakwater. Two long de-silting channels cut through the promontory at Cosa brought silt-free water into the harbor, but their primary purpose was to provide brackish water and a migration route for the adjacent fishery. A rock-cut de-silting channel has been identified at Phalasarna. At Seleucia Pieria, port of Antioch near the mouth of the Orontes, attempts were made to use the tide and then the river current, diverted through a canal, to flush the harbor basin. Roman engineers seem to have learned that some breakwaters only made matters worse by blocking coastal currents, so they started to build offshore breakwaters not connected to the shore, as at Centumcellae, and arched moles (see above).

# SEA LEVEL CHANGE

Changes in sea level greatly affect the functioning of harbors, and there is evidence that this possibility caused concern in antiquity. Actual relative sea level change at any particular site could be caused by sea level change or by earth movements; general appreciation of these factors grew during antiquity (Morton 2001: 13–29). The central Mediterranean is a geologically unstable area, with a line of plate tectonic boundaries. Evidence of human response in harbor rebuilding is so far limited, and deserves further study. At Rhodes the slipway ramps were raised, perhaps after the major earthquake of 227 B.C., and later uplift of the land may have caused the abandonment of the dockyard; the factor of relative sea level change is now taken into account in the study and interpretation of the shoreline features in Zea harbor. In some cases, as at Cenchreae, the submergence was too catastrophic for repair; the city of Helice was submerged by a tidal wave in the earthquake of 373 B.C. and disappeared. At other sites, such as Phalasarna in western Crete, the harbor was put out of action by massive uplift of more than 6 m. See Blackman 1973b, 2005.

# CONTEXT

Scholars have begun the complex task of setting ancient ports in their geographical, historical, economic, and cultural context (e.g., Horden and Purcell 2000; Cunliffe 2001; Rickman 2005 and associated bibliography). The questions are numerous and difficult to answer. How did ports relate with the city that they served, with their hinterland, and with other ports? How separate were the ports, both military and commercial, from the cities? How did some ports develop without apparent hinterland? The outstanding example of this is medieval Amalfi, but there are many ancient ports that seemed to have served rather for coastal traffic: cabotage needed a regular series of stopping points. Cities near river-mouths may have connected with river systems, canals, and lagoons—particularly in Spain, southern and Atlantic France, and the west coast of Italy, including Pisa and Rome (Pasquinucci and Weski 2004). The dramatic discovery of sunken boats in a silted-up river channel at Pisa has drawn most attention to the actual boats, but one may ask about the nature of the site where at least 20 boats were wrecked in antiquity.

# Select Bibliographical Gazetteer
# of Sites Mentioned

Aegina: Knoblauch 1969, 1972.

Alexandria: Jondet 1916; Fraser 1961; Goddio 1998; McKenzie 2003; Goddio and Bernand 2004; Goddio, Clauss et al. 2006; Empereur forthcoming; McKenzie 2006.

Apollonia: Flemming 1972: 95–126; Laronde 1996; Blackman and Rankov forthcoming; Sintès forthcoming.

Baiae: see Puteoli.

Caesarea in Palestine: Raban and Holum 1996; Hohlfelder 1996.

Carthage: Hurst 1979, 1994.

Cenchreae: Scranton, Shaw, and Ibrahim 1978; Hohlfelder 1985.

Citium: Karageorghis and Michaelides 1995; Yon 2000.

Cosa: McCann et al. 1987; Ciampoltrini and Rendini 2004.

Delos: Duchêne and Fraisse 2001.

Ephesus: Zabehlicky 1999.

Halieis: Jameson 1969, 1973.

Herakleion: Goddio 2007; Goddio et al. 2006.

Lecheum: Rothaus 1995.

Leptis Magna: Bartoccini 1958.

London: Milne 1985.

Massalia: Hesnard et al. 1999, 2001; Hesnard 2004.

Misenum: Maiuri 1958: 91–100; Döring 2003; Benini and Lanteri forthcoming.

Mytilene: Williams 2007.

Naples: Giampaola 2006; forthcoming.

Naxos: Blackman and Lentini 2003, forthcoming a; Lentini and Blackman forthcoming.

Ostia: see Portus.

Phalasarna: Hadjidaki 1988; Frost and Hadjidaki 1990.

Phaselis: Schäfer et al. 1981.

Piraeus: Garland 1987; Blackman and Rankov forthcoming.

Pisa: Bruni 2000, 2003; Camilli 2004.

Portus: Testaguzza 1970; Meiggs 1973; Keay et al. 2004; Rickman 2005; Keay and Millett 2006; Keay, Millet, and Strutt 2008.

Puteoli: Dubois 1907; Gianfrotta et al. 1993: 21–70; 2001 passim; 2002: 47–66; Döring 2003; Piromallo 2004; Miniero forthcoming.

Rhodes: Bradford 1957: 277–86; Brodersen 1992; Blackman et al. 1996.

Samos: Simossi 1991.

Seleucia Pieria: Chapot 1907; Lehmann-Hartleben 1923: 214–16; Poidebard and Lauffray 1951: 31–32.

Sidon: Poidebard and Lauffray 1951; Frost 1973.

Sounion: Goette 2000.

Thasos: Archontidou-Argyri et al. 1989; Blackman and Rankov forthcoming.

Tyre: Poidebard 1939; Frost 1971: 110–11.

# REFERENCES

Archontidou-Argyri, A., A. Simossi, and J.-Y. Empereur 1989. "The underwater excavation at the ancient port of Thasos, Greece," *International Journal of Nautical Archaeology* 18: 51–59.

Baika, K. 2002. "Dispositif du halage des hangars navals antiques: Étude ethno-archéologique," *Tropis* 7: 43–83.

Baika, K. 2003. "Operating on shipsheds and slipways: Evidence of underwater configuration of slipways from the neosoikos of 'Trypiti' (Crete)," in Beltrame 2003: 103–8.

Baika, K. 2006. "Early naval bases and military harbour infrastructure in the Mediterranean," in *The new view: Underwater archaeology and the historical picture*. Antiqua 40. Basel: Archäologie Schweiz, 176–92.

Bartoccini, R. 1958. *Il porto romano di Leptis Magna. Bollettino del Centro di Studi per la Storia dell'Architettura* Suppl. 13. Rome: Centro di Studi per la Storia dell'Architettura.

Basch, L. 1987. *Le musée imaginaire de la marine antique*. Athens: Hellenic Institute for the Preservation of the Nautical Tradition.

Beltrame, C. (ed.) 2003. *Boats, ships and shipyards: Ninth International Symposium on Boat and Ship Archaeology, Venice 2000, Proceedings*. Oxford: Oxbow.

Benini, A., and L. Lanteri forthcoming. "Il porto romano di *Misenum*: Nuove acquisizioni," in Blackman and Lentini forthcoming b.

Blackman, D. J. (ed.) 1973a. *Marine archaeology*. Colston Papers 23. London: Butterworths.

Blackman, D. J. 1973b. "Evidence of sea level change in ancient harbours and coastal installations," in Blackman 1973a: 115–39.

Blackman, D. J. 1982. "Ancient harbours in the Mediterranean," *International Journal of Nautical Archaeology* 11.2: 79–104; 11.3: 185–211.

Blackman, D. J. 1988. "Bollards and men," in I. Malkin and R. L. Hohlfelder (eds.), *Mediterranean cities: Historical perspectives: Mediterranean Historical Review 3.1*. London: Cass, 7–20.

Blackman, D. J. 1995. "Naval installations," in R. Gardiner (ed.), *The age of the galley*. London: Conway Maritime Press, 224–33.

Blackman, D. J. 2003. "Progress in the study of ancient shipsheds: A review," in Beltrame 2003: 81–90.

Blackman, D. J. 2005. "Archaeological evidence for sea level changes," *Zeitschrift für Geomorphologie*, n.s. Suppl. 137: 61–70.

Blackman, D. J. 2008. "Roman shipsheds," in Hohlfelder 2008: 23–36.

Blackman, D. J., P. Knoblauch, and A. Yiannikouri 1996. "Die Schiffshäuser am Mandrakihafen in Rhodos," *Archäologischer Anzeiger* 1996: 371–426.

Blackman, D. J., and M. C. Lentini 2003. "The shipsheds of Sicilian Naxos, researches 1998–2001: A preliminary report," *Annual of the British School at Athens* 98: 389–436.

Blackman, D. J., and M. C. Lentini forthcoming a. "Further research on the dockyard of Sicilian Naxos," *Tropis* 9.

Blackman, D. J., and M. C. Lentini forthcoming b. *Ricoveri per navi militari nei porti del Mediterraneo antico e medievale*. Workshop Ravello, 4–5 nov. 2005. Bari: Edipuglia.

Blackman, D. J., and N. B. Rankov (eds.) forthcoming. *Shipsheds of the ancient Mediterranean*.

Bradford, J. 1957. *Ancient landscapes*. London: Bell.

Brandon, C. 1999. "Pozzolana, lime, and single-mission barges (Area K)," in K. Holum, A. Raban, and J. Patrich (eds.), *Caesarea papers, 2. Journal of Roman Archaeology* Suppl. 35. Portsmouth, RI: JRA, 169–78.

Brandon, C., R. L. Hohlfelder, J. P. Oleson, and C. Stern 2005. "The Roman Maritime Concrete Study (ROMACONS): The harbour of Chersonisos in Crete and its Italian connection," *Méditerranée* 1.2: 25–29.

Branton, G., and J. P. Oleson 1992. "The technology of King Herod's harbour," in R. L. Vann (ed.), *Caesarea papers: Straton's Tower, Herod's Harbour, and Roman and Byzantine Caesarea. Journal of Roman Archaeology* Suppl. 5. Ann Arbor, MI: JRA, 49–67.

Brodersen, K. 1992. *Reiseführer zu den Sieben Weltwundern: Philon von Byzanz und andere antike Texte*. Frankfurt: Insel Verlag.

Bruni, S. 2000. *Le navi antiche di Pisa: Ad un anno dall'inizio delle ricerche*. Florence: Polistampa.

Bruni, S. 2003. *Il porto urbano di Pisa antica: La fase etrusca, il contesto e il relitto ellenistico*. Milan: Silvana.

Brusin, G. 1934. *Gli scavi di Aquileia*. Udine: "La Panarie."

Camilli, A. 2004. "Le strutture 'portuali' dello scavo di Pisa–San Rossore," in Gallina Zevi and Turchetti 2004: 67–86.

Casson, L. 1989. *Periplus Maris Erythraei*. Princeton: Princeton University Press.

Casson, L. 1991. *The ancient mariners*. 2nd ed. Princeton: Princeton University Press.

Casson. L. 1996. *Ships and seamanship in the ancient world*. Rev. ed. Princeton: Princeton University Press.

Chapot, V. 1907. *Séleucie de Piérie*. Mémoires de la Société nationale des antiquaires de France, 66: 1–78.

Ciampoltrini, G., and P. Rendini 2004. "Il sistema portuale dell'*ager Cosanus* e delle isole del Giglio e di Giannutri," in Gallina Zevi and Turchetti 2004: 127–50.

Cozza, L., and P. L. Tucci 2006. "*Navalia*," *Archeologia Classica* 57: 175–201.

Cunliffe, B. 2001. *Facing the ocean: The Atlantic and its peoples, 8000 BC–AD 1500*. Oxford: Oxford University Press.

Delgado, J. P. 1998. *Encyclopedia of underwater and maritime archaeology*. New Haven: Yale University Press.

Döring, M. 2003. "Römische Hafen- und Tunnelbauten der Phlegräschen Felder," in C. P. J. Öhlig (ed.), *Wasserhistorische Forschungen: Schwerpunkt Antike*. Siegburg: Deutsche Wasserhistorische Gesellschaft, 35–53.

Dubois, C. 1902. "Observations sur un passage de Vitruve (V.12)," *Mélanges de l'École française de Rome* 22: 439–67.

Dubois, C. 1907. *Pouzzoles antique (Histoire et Topographie)*. Bibliothèque des écoles françaises d'Athènes et de Rome 98. Paris: A. Fontemoing.

Duchêne, H., and P. Fraisse 2001. *Le Paysage portuaire de la Délos antique: Recherches sur les installations maritimes, commerciales et urbaines du littoral délien*. Exploration archéologique de Délos 39. Athens: École française d'Athènes.

Empereur, J.-Y. forthcoming. *Pharos I*, Études alexandrines, 9.

Felici, E. 1993. "Osservazioni sul Porto Neroniano di Anzio e sulla tecnica romana delle costruzioni portuali in calcestruzzo," in Gianfrotta et al. 1993: 71–104.

Felici, E. 2002. "Scoperte epigraphiche e topographiche sulla costruzione del porto neroniano di *Antium*," in Gianfrotta et al. 2002: 107–22.

Flemming, N. C. 1972. *Cities in the sea*. Garden City NY: Doubleday.

Fraser, P. M. 1961. "The *diolkos* of Alexandria," *Journal of Egyptian Archaeology* 47: 134–38.

Frost, H. 1971. "Recent observations on the submerged harbourworks at Tyre," *Bulletin du Musée de Beyrouth* 24: 103–11.

Frost, H. 1973. "The offshore island harbour at Sidon and other Phoenician sites in the light of new dating evidence," *International Journal of Nautical Archaeology* 2: 75–94.

Frost, H. 1995. "Harbours and proto-harbours, early Levantine engineering," in Karageorghis and Michaelides 1995: 1–21.

Frost F. J., and E. Hadjidaki 1990. "Excavations at the harbor of Phalasarna in Crete: The 1988 season." *Hesperia* 69: 513–27.

Gallina Zevi, A., and R. Turchetti 2004. *Le strutture dei porti e degli approdi antichi. Atti del II Seminario ANSER, Roma–Ostia Antica, 16–17.4. 2004*. Soveria Mannelli: Rubbettino.

Garcia, D., L. Vallet et al. 2002. *L'espace portuaire de Lattes antique*. Lattara 15. Lattes: Association pour le Développement de l'Archéologie en Languedoc-Roussillon.

Garland, R. 1987. *The Piraeus*. London: Duckworth.

Giampaola, D., et al. 2006. "La scoperta del porto di Neapolis: dalla ricostruzione topografica allo scavo e al recupero dei relitti," *Archaeologia Maritima Mediterranea* 2: 47–92.

Giampaola, D. forthcoming. "Il porto di Napoli," in Blackman and Lentini forthcoming b.

Gianfrotta, P. A., P. Pelagatti, E. Felici, and P. G. Monti 1993. *Archeologia Subacquea* 1. Università di Tuscia, Viterbo. Rome: Istituto Poligrafico e Zecca dello Stato.

Gianfrotta, P. A., P. Pelagatti, E. Felici, and P. G. Monti 2002. *Archeologia Subacquea* 3. Università di Tuscia, Viterbo. Rome: Istituto Poligrafico e Zecca dello Stato.

Gianfrotta, P. A., and F. Maniscalco 2001. *Forma Maris: Forum internazionale di Archeologia Subacquea, Pozzuoli 22–24 sett. 1998*. Naples: Massa.

Goddio, F. 1998. *Alexandria: The submerged royal quarters*. London: Periplus.

Goddio, F. 2007. *The Topography and Excavation of Heracleion-Tonis and East Canopus (1996–2006)*. Oxford: School of Archaeology.

Goddio, F., and A. Bernand 2004. *Sunken Egypt: Alexandria*. London: Periplus.

Goddio, F., M. Clauss et al. 2006 *Egypt's sunken treasures*. Munich/London: Prestel.

Goette, H. R. 2000. *Ho axiologos demos Sounion: Landeskundliche Studien in Sudost-Attika*. Rahden/Westf.: Leidorf.

Günther, R.T. 1903a. "The submerged Greek and Roman foreshore near Naples," *Archaeologia* 58.2: 499–560.

Günther, R. T. 1903b. "Earth movements in the Bay of Naples," *Geographical Journal* 22: 121–49, 269–89.

Hadjidaki, E. 1988. "Preliminary report of excavation at the harbor of Phalasarna in West Crete," *American Journal of Archaeology* 92: 463–79.

Hesnard, A. 2004. "Vitruve, *De architectura*, V, 12 et le port romain de Marseille," in Gallina and Zevi 2004: 175–204.

Hesnard, A., M. Moliner., F. Conche, and M. Bouiron. 1999. *Parcours de Villes. Marseille: 10 ans d'archéologie, 2600 ans d'histoire. Exposition du Musée d'Histoire de Marseille.* Aix-en-Provence: Edisud.

Hesnard, A., C. Maurel, and P. Bernardi 2001. "La topographie du port de Marseille, de la fondation de la cité à la fin du Moyen Âge," in *Marseille: trames et passages urbains de Gyptis au Roi René. Actes du colloque international d'archéologie, Marseille 3–5 nov. 1999.* Publications du Centre Camille Julian 7. Aix-en-Provence: Edisud, 159–202.

Hohlfelder, R. L. 1985. "The building of the Roman harbour at Kenchreai: Old technology in a new era," in A. Raban (ed.), *Harbour Archaeology.* British Archaeological Reports, Intl. Series S257. Oxford: BAR, 165–72.

Hohlfelder, R. L. 1996. "Caesarea's master harbor builders: Lessons learned, lessons applied?" in Raban and Holum 1996: 77–101.

Hohlfelder, R. L. 2005. "Swimming over time: Glimpses of the maritime life of Aperlae," in Pollini 2005: 187–210.

Hohlfelder, R. L. 2008. *The maritime world of ancient Rome.* Ann Arbor: University of Michigan Press.

Horden, P., and N. Purcell 2000. *The corrupting sea: A study of Mediterranean history.* Oxford: Oxford University Press.

Hurst, H. R. 1977. "Excavations at Carthage: Third interim report." *Antiquaries Journal* 57: 232–61.

Hurst, H. R. 1979. "Excavations at Carthage: Fourth interim report." *Antiquaries Journal* 59: 19–49.

Hurst, H. R. 1994. *Excavations of Carthage: The British Mission.* Vol. II.1, *The Circular Harbour, North Side.* London: The British Academy.

Jameson, M. H. 1969. "Excavations at Porto Cheli and vicinity, preliminary report, I: Halieis 1962–68," *Hesperia* 38: 311–42.

Jameson, M. H. 1973. "Halieis at Porto Cheli," in Blackman 1973a: 219–31.

Jondet, G. 1916. *Les ports submergés de l'ancienne Ile de Pharos.* Mémoires présentés à l'Institut Égyptien 9. Cairo: Institut Égyptien.

Karageorghis, V., and D. Michaelides 1995. *Cyprus and the sea.* Proceedings of the International Symposium, Nicosia. Nicosia: University of Cyprus/Cyprus Ports Authority.

Keay, S., M. Millett, and K. Strutt 2004. "*Portus Romae*: Recent survey work at the ports of Claudius and Trajan," in Gallina Zevi and Turchetti 2004: 221–32.

Keay, S., and M. Millett 2006. *Portus Romae.* Rome: British School of Archaeology.

Keay, S., M. Millett, and K. Strutt 2008. "Recent archaeological survey at Portus," in Hohlfelder 2008: 97–104.

Kingsley, S. A. (ed.) 2004. *Barbarian seas: Late Rome to Islam.* London: Periplus.

Knoblauch, P. 1969. "Neuere Untersuchungen an den Häfen von Ägina," *Bonner Jahrbücher* 169: 104–16.

Knoblauch, P. 1972. "Die Hafenanlagen der Stadt Ägina," *Archaiologikon Deltion* 27A: 50–85.

Knoblauch, P. 1977. *Die Hafenanlagen und die anschliessenden Seemauern von Side.* Ankara: Türk Tarih Kurumu Basimevi.

Kolonas, L. 1989–1990. "Anaskaphe Oiniadon," *Archaiognosia* 6: 153–58.

Laronde, A. 1996. "Apollonia de Cyrénaïque, archéologie et histoire," *Journal des Savants* 1996.1: 3–49.

Lehmann-Hartleben, K. 1923. *Die antiken Hafenlagen des Mittelmeeres: Beiträge zur Geschichte des Städtebaus im Altertum. Klio* Beiheft 14. Leipzig: Dieterich.

Lentini, M. C., and D. J. Blackman forthcoming. "Scavi recenti all'arsenale dell'antica Naxos," in Blackman and Lentini forthcoming b.

MacDonald, B. R. 1986. "The Diolkos," *Journal of Hellenic Studies* 106: 191–95.

Maiuri, A. 1958. *The Phlegraean Fields.* 3rd ed. Rome: Instituto Poligrafico dello Stato.

Marriner, N., and C. Morhange 2007. "Geoscience of ancient Mediterranean harbours," *Earth-Science Reviews* 80: 137–94.

McCann, A. M. 1977. "Underwater excavations at the Etruscan port of Populonia," *Journal of Field Archaeology* 4: 275–96.

McCann, A. M., et al. 1987. *The Roman port and fishery of Cosa.* Princeton: Princeton University Press.

McCann, A. M., and J. P. Oleson 2004. *Deep-water shipwrecks off Skerki Bank: The 1997 survey. Journal of Roman Archaeology* Suppl. 58. Portsmouth, RI: JRA.

McKenzie, J. 2003. "Glimpsing Alexandria from archaeological evidence," *Journal of Roman Archaeology* 16: 35–63.

McKenzie, J. 2006. *The Architecture of Alexandria and Egypt, 300 BC–AD 700.* New Haven: Yale University Press.

Meiggs, R. 1973. *Roman Ostia.* 2nd ed. Oxford: Oxford University Press.

Milne, G. 1985. *The Port of Roman London.* London: Batsford.

Miniero, P. forthcoming. "Baia sommersa e Portus Iulius: Il rilievo con strumentazione integrata multibeam," in Blackman and Lentini forthcoming b.

Morrison, J. S., J. F. Coates, and N. B. Rankov 2000. *The Athenian trireme: The history and reconstruction of an ancient Greek warship.* 2nd ed. Cambridge: Cambridge University Press.

Morton, J. 2001. *The role of the physical environment in ancient Greek seafaring. Mnemosyne* Suppl. 213. Leiden: Brill.

Oleson, J. P. 1977. "Underwater survey and excavation in the port of Pyrgi (Santa Severa), 1974," *Journal of Field Archaeology* 4: 297–308.

Oleson, J. P. 1988. "The technology of Roman harbours," *International Journal of Nautical Archaeology* 17: 147–58.

Oleson, J. P., C. Brandon, S. M. Cramer, R. Cucitore, E. Gotti, and R. L. Hohlfelder 2004. "The ROMACONS Project: A contribution to the historical and engineering analysis of hydraulic concrete in Roman maritime structures." *International Journal of Nautical Archaeology* 33.2: 199–229.

Oleson, J. P., C. Brandon, S. M. Cramer, R. Cucitore, E. Gotti, and R. L. Hohlfelder 2006. "Reproduction of a Roman maritime structure with Vitruvian hydraulic concrete," *Journal of Roman Archaeology* 19: 29–52.

Papageorgiou, S., M. Arnold, J. Laborel, and S. C. Stiros 1993. "Seismic uplift of the harbour of ancient Aigeira, Central Greece," *International Journal of Nautical Archaeology* 22: 275–81.

Pasquinucci, M., and T. Weski (eds.) 2004 *Close encounters: Sea- and riverborne trade, ports and hinterlands, ship construction and navigation in antiquity, the Middle Ages and in modern time.* British Archaeological Reports, Intl. Series S1283. Oxford: BAR.

Pensa, M. 1999. "Moli, fari e pescatori: La tradizione iconografica della città portuale in età romana," *Rivista di archeologia* 23: 94–130.

Petruso, K., and C. Gabel 1983. "Marea: A Byzantine port on Egypt's northwestern frontier," *Archaeology* 36.5: 62–63, 76–77.

Piromallo, M. 2004. "Puteoli, porto di Roma," in Gallina Zevi and Turchetti 2004: 267–78.

Poidebard, A. 1939. *Un grand port disparu: Tyr. Recherches aériennes et sous-marines, 1934–36.* Paris: Paul Geuthner.

Poidebard, A., and J. Lauffray. 1951. *Sidon: Aménagements antiques du port de Saida. Étude aérienne, au sol, et sous-marine, 1946–50.* Beirut: Ministère des Travaux publics.

Pollini, J. 2005. *Terra marique: Studies in art history and marine archaeology in honor of Anna Marguerite McCann.* Oxford: Oxbow.

Raban, A. 1995. "The heritage of ancient harbour engineering in Cyprus and the Levant," in Karageorghis and Michaelides 1995: 139–88.

Raban, A. 2003. "Ancient Slipways and Shipsheds on the Israeli Coast of the Mediterranean," In Beltrame 2003: 91–102.

Raban, A., and K. G. Holum 1996. *Caesarea Maritima: A retrospective after two millennia.* Leiden: Brill.

Rankov, N. B. 2008. "Roman shipsheds and Roman ships," in Hohlfelder 2008: 51–70.

Reddé, M. 1979. "La représentation des phares à l'époque romaine," *Mélanges de l'École française de Rome* 91: 845–72.

Reddé, M. 1986. *Mare Nostrum.* Bibliothèque des Écoles françaises d'Athènes et de Rome 260. Rome: École française de Rome.

Rickman, G. E. 1988. "The archaeology and history of Roman ports." *International Journal of Nautical Archaeology* 17: 257–67.

Rickman, G. E. 2005. "Portus Romae?" in Pollini 2005: 232–37.

Rothaus, R. 1995. "Lechaion, western port of Corinth: A preliminary archaeology and history," *Oxford Journal of Archaeology* 14: 293–306.

Schäfer, J., D. J. Blackman, and H. Schläger 1981. *Phaselis: Beiträge zur Topographie und Geschichte der Stadt und ihrer Häfen. Istanbuler Mitteilungen* Beiheft 24. Tübingen: Wasmuth.

Schläger, H., D. J. Blackman, and J. Schäfer 1968. "Der Hafen von Anthedon." *Archäologischer Anzeiger* 1968: 21–98; 1969: 229–31.

Schmiedt, G. 1972. *Il livello antico del mar Tirreno.* Florence: Olschki.

Scranton, R. L., J. W. Shaw, and L. Ibrahim 1978. *Kenchreai: Eastern port of Corinth, I: Topography and architecture.* Leiden: Brill.

Shaw, J. W. 1972. "Greek and Roman harbour works," in G. F. Bass (ed.), *A history of seafaring based on underwater archaeology.* London: Thames and Hudson, 87–112.

Simossi, A. 1991. "Underwater excavation research in the ancient harbour of Samos: September–October 1988," *International Journal of Nautical Archaeology* 20: 281–98.

Sintès, C. forthcoming. "Les *neoria* d'Apollonia," in Blackman and Lentini forthcoming b.

Testaguzza, O. 1970. *Portus.* Rome: Julia.

Tusa, S. 2004. "Il sistema portuale di Mozia: il Kothon," in L. Nigro, *Mozia X: rapporto preliminare della XXII canpagna di scavi.* Rome: Missione archeologica a Mozia, 445–64.

Walker, K. G. 2004. *Archaic Eretria.* London: Routledge.

Williams, H. 2007. "The harbours of ancient Lesbos," in P. Betancourt, M. C. Nelson, and H. Williams (eds.), *Krinoi kai limenes: Studies in honor of Joseph and Maria Shaw.* London: David Brown.

Yildirim, B., and M.-H. Gates 2007. "Archaeology in Turkey, 2004–2005," *American Journal of Archaeology* 111: 275–356.

Yon, M. 2000. "Les hangars du port chypro-phénicien de Kition," *Syria* 77: 95–116.

Zabehlicky, H. 1999. "Die Grabungen im Hafen von Ephesos 1987–1989," in H. Friesinger and F. Krinzinger (eds.), *100 Jahre österreichische Forschungen in Ephesos: Akten des Symposions, Wien 1995:* 479–84. Vienna: Academy of Sciences.

PART VI

# TECHNOLOGIES OF DEATH

CHAPTER 26

.......................................................................................................

# GREEK WARFARE AND FORTIFICATION

.......................................................................................................

## PHILIP DE SOUZA

### SOURCES OF INFORMATION

.......................................................................................................

The evidence for the study of ancient Greek warfare is not distributed evenly across all periods. Following the collapse of the Mycenaean civilization in the twelfth century B.C., there is a lengthy period in which artistic representations of armor and weapons, relatively common during the Late Bronze Age, become extremely scarce. The quantity and quality of archaeological finds also diminish rapidly after 1150 B.C., and at the same time the art of writing was lost to the Greeks. Written documents only begin to emerge from this Dark Age around the middle of the eighth century B.C. The descriptions of fighting in the Homeric poems, which were probably composed in Ionia between 750 and 700 B.C., may feature some equipment and practices recalled from earlier times, but for the most part they reflect a contemporary martial culture (Morris 1986; Snodgrass 1974; van Wees 1992: 5–23). Figurative art on painted pottery and other materials became widespread in the latter part of the eighth century B.C., and increasing technical and artistic refinements during the late seventh and early sixth centuries B.C. allowed artists and sculptors to depict warfare in a more realistic manner than at any time since the Late Bronze Age.

In the course of the eleventh, tenth, and ninth centuries B.C., iron was gradually adopted as a metal for making tools, ornaments, and, above all, weapons. Around this time the iron ore deposits of mainland Greece and the Aegean islands began to be worked, supplementing supplies from Asia Minor, Cyprus, and sources further away (Healy 1978: 62). It is sometimes assumed that iron was so far superior to bronze that it was pointless to continue using bronze if iron were available, but iron, unlike bronze, could not be cast by ancient metalworkers. It was also highly brittle, and the technique for improving its malleability by a process known as "carburization" involved a high level of wastage (chapter 4; Healy 1978: 225–36). So, while iron was quite swiftly adopted as the metal for swords and spears, bronze continued to be used in the Greek world for armor, especially helmets, and for some weapons, particularly those that could be cast, such as arrowheads; lead was also cast for slingshots (Snodgrass 1967: 36–40, 79–81, 84).

# HOPLITE WARFARE

Archaeological finds dating from about 720 B.C. onward show that Greek warriors were adopting new forms of defensive armor. These were the one-piece bronze helmet, which covered most of the face and head, the bronze cuirass, made in two or more pieces, which protected the torso, and bronze greaves, covering the legs from the ankle to the knee at the front, but only as far as the calves at the back. These accessories were used with a large round shield, nearly a meter in diameter, made of wood and usually faced with a thin sheet of bronze, and an iron headed spear, made of ash and typically 2.45 to 2.75 meters in length (Snodgrass 1967: 49–58; Connolly 1981: 51–63; Sekunda 2000: 9–17). Modern scholars generally refer to this combination of armor, shield, and spear as the "hoplite panoply." "Hoplite" is a modern rendering of the Greek word *hoplites*, a heavily armed soldier, which is derived from *hoplon*, meaning a tool or implement, but used in the plural *hopla* to refer to the equipment of a soldier. Weapons are tools in the technology of war.

To judge from artistic depictions and widespread archaeological finds, the most popular form of the helmet initially was the Corinthian, which enclosed the entire head, apart from narrow openings at the front for the eyes combined with a very narrow vertical breathing slit. Manufacturing such a helmet required great skill, as it had to be beaten out from a single sheet of bronze. Many variant designs were developed, however, which left more space for seeing and hearing, as well as reducing the overall weight. The convex hoplite shield (*aspis* in Greek) could also be extremely heavy. No complete shield has survived from antiquity, but reasonably accurate modern reconstructions have been prepared, based on partial remnants and artistic representations. These indicate that a typical wooden shield, with its bronze facing and bronze central arm-grip (*porpax*), could weigh as much as 7 kg. The convex shape and broad rim allowed the hoplite to bear some of the weight on his shoulder, but the *porpax* was an essential aid. In combination with a smaller handgrip (*antilabe*) attached to the inside of the rim, it enabled the hoplite to carry and maneuver this weight for an extended period (Connolly 1981: 51–54).

Figure 26.1. Hoplite warriors fighting, Corinthian vase-painting, ca. 600 B.C., Louvre Museum. (Photograph courtesy of Bridgeman Art Library.)

Modern scholarly accounts of how warriors actually fought using the hoplite panoply are heavily dependent on the interpretation of various artistic representations of battle, dating from the mid seventh to the fifth centuries B.C., in combination with written sources from the seventh, sixth, fifth, and fourth centuries B.C. (Connolly 1981: 29–63; Hanson 1991, 1995; van Wees 2000). Numerous vase paintings show warriors in combat with the essential items of hoplite equipment, namely the Corinthian helmet, the large, round shield with *porpax* and *antilabe*, and the long thrusting spear (figure 26.1). Artistic conventions encouraged the portrayal of warriors in "heroic nudity," so only one figure (on the ground) wears a cuirass, but they all wear bronze greaves. The sideways stance and overhead thrusting action with the spear seem to have constituted the usual combat style, judging from the painted pottery and bronze or lead figurines. Most scholars argue that hoplites marched and fought in a closely packed formation called a phalanx, which is described by Thucydides and Xenophon (Hanson 1989, 2000). Descriptions that are especially important because they were written by men with personal experience of similar battles are those of Thucydides on the Battle of Mantinea in 418 B.C. (5.70–75) and Xenophon on the Battle of Coronea in 394 B.C. (*Hell.* 4.3.17–23). Hoplites are sometimes depicted in Greek art wearing or using a double-edged sword with waisted sides (Greek *xiphos*), or a single-edged sword with a recurved blade that broadens out toward the tip (Greek *kopis* or *machaira*). Both were designed to be most effective in slashing or chopping actions.

By the beginning of the fifth century B.C., hoplites fought in armies numbering in the hundreds or thousands. They were grouped close together (how close is a matter of considerable debate) in phalanx formations, typically from four to eight men deep and hundreds of men long; a much greater depth of formation was

Figure 26.2. Sword fight between Greek hoplite and Persian warrior, Attic red-figure kylix by Triptolemos Painter, ca. 460 B.C. Edinburgh, National Museums of Scotland. (Photograph: Bridgeman Art Library.)

sometimes adopted at the expense of breadth. Often confrontations between two phalanxes, or groups of phalanxes if the armies comprised several allied contingents, were resolved without a close engagement, because one side withdrew, either before or soon after their opponents moved forward. If both sides were determined enough to advance and come to blows, then combat at close quarters could last for several hours, although there might be periods in which the front ranks drew apart somewhat to rest, gathering their strength and resolve for further clashes. Hoplites used their spears to stab at their opponents, relying mainly on their shields and armor to protect them from such attacks. Swords were secondary weapons, to be used if the spear was broken. This may be the situation depicted in the vase painting shown in figure 26.2, on which a Greek hoplite and a Persian archer are using swords of the *kopis* or *machaira* type. The hoplite's bronze helmet is Attic in style, with hinged cheek pieces and no noseguard. He wears greaves and a cuirass of stiffened linen. The Persian wears heavy clothing but no armor. The curved tips of his bow, his principal weapon, are just visible. The most successful hoplite forces were those that could keep up the pressure on their opponents without yielding. It may have been their dogged determination not to give ground, as much as their heavy armor and shields, that enabled Greek hoplites to defeat Persian armies at Marathon in 490 B.C. and Plataea in 479 B.C. (de Souza 2003: 25–39, 68–79). Eventually, one side would gain the upper hand, causing their opponents to waver, retreat, and flee, pursued by the victors, who then expected to inflict more casualties but suffer few themselves. Disintegration of the tight *phalanx* formation left the individual soldiers exposed. The extent of the slaughter depended largely on the duration of the pursuit, unless an enemy formation remained partially intact or regrouped and was able to confront the pursuers. Casualties were surprisingly low, perhaps because the majority of men in a phalanx did not actually come face to face with the enemy. The best modern estimate is an average of 5 percent losses for victors and 14 percent for the vanquished (Krentz 1985).

Scholars have long held that the introduction of the hoplite panoply necessarily implies the adoption of phalanx tactics in battle. The consensus has been that the new style of shield and armor were developed because in the late eighth century Greek warriors fought in a relatively static manner, standing so close to each other that they lacked the room to maneuver effectively, and they therefore needed greater protection (Hanson 1991: 63–84; 2000). The painted images referred to above, alongside references to massed ranks of fighters in the *Iliad* and Greek lyric poetry, have been used as evidence to support that assumption. More recently, however, a strong challenge has been mounted to this consensus (van Wees 2000; 2004: 45–60), proposing that the formations described in the *Iliad* and lyric poetry, and depicted on painted pottery, are not the same as the phalanxes that fought at Plataea, Mantinea, or Coronea. These early formations were looser, more fluid groupings of men, some of them heavily armed and armored hoplites, but others more lightly equipped with javelins and bows. Light-armed soldiers were an ever-present feature in Greek armies of the archaic, classical and Hellenistic periods, but ancient Greek artists and writers preferred to concentrate on the heavily-armed hoplites in their depictions of warfare. The pairs of spears that are regularly carried by hoplites depicted on seventh and sixth century painted pottery may be a javelin and a longer, thrusting spear, indicating considerable overlap in the use of weapons between heavy- and light-armed men. By the fifth century, however, hoplites seem only to carry one, the thrusting spear. Javelins have become the weapon of the non-hoplite soldiers, who are sometimes called peltasts, after the *pelte*, a lightweight, usually crescent-shaped wicker and leather shield favored by javelin throwers.

During the Peloponnesian War (431–404 B.C.), when troops from many different parts of the Greek world came into conflict with one another, the predominantly light-armed soldiers from northern, central and western Greece had considerable success against hoplites from Athens and Sparta. In 425 B.C., a small force of elite Spartan hoplites was trapped on the island of Sphacteria off the Peloponnesian coast and driven to surrender by lightly armed Athenians and their allies (de Souza 2002: 37–42). The historian Thucydides wrote that the other Greeks found this Spartan capitulation "the most amazing thing that occurred in the whole of the war" (4.40.1). This attitude of wonder reflects a major reason why less attention is paid to the non-hoplite soldiers in the ancient sources: their social status and military prestige were much lower than that of the wealthier, more heavily armed and armored infantrymen. As a result, images of the latter abound in ancient Greek art and are closely associated with the Homeric heroes (van Wees 2004: 61–85). In some cases the distinction was between master and slave, most especially among the Spartans, whose citizen hoplites were accompanied into battle by large numbers of helot attendants, as well as freeborn but subordinate allies from Laconia and the surrounding regions. The Spartans at Pylos were initially disdainful of the "spindles" shot and thrown at them on Sphacteria, but in the right circumstances missile troops could be more effective than hoplites. The lightly equipped troops are, however, far less visible archaeologically, since they wore little or no armor, carried shields made of highly perishable materials, and only the killing tip of their primary weapons was made of a durable material (Snodgrass 1967: 77–85).

The hoplite panoply seems to have been adopted in all parts of the Mediterranean where the Greeks settled, but its relative popularity and importance varied from place to place. There were far more hoplites among the Peloponnesians than among the Thessalians, for example. One explanation offered for this variation is that the hoplite style of warfare was ideally suited to the terrain of Southern Greece, where the numerous small poleis (city-states) had relatively limited areas of flat farmland to defend and therefore developed hoplite warfare as a means of settling their differences (Hanson 1995, 2000). It is also clear that hoplite warfare does not have to be associated with a particular form of government, whether it is democracy, oligarchy, or tyranny (d'Agostino 1990).

As hoplite warfare became common, so the typical hoplite seems to have become less of a bronze armored elite warrior and more of an ordinary soldier. Although artistic images of hoplites frequently feature a considerable amount of armor, in practice it seems that many hoplites wore little more than a tunic and a helmet. Most of the Greek hoplites who, with the aid of many light-armed men, defeated the Persians at Plataea in 479 B.C. probably wore bronze body armor and greaves, but cuirasses made of stiffened linen were already common in the fifth century B.C. Even these were abandoned as hoplites were increasingly required to fight against lightly armed troops in the late fifth and early fourth centuries, and began to shed their weighty, cumbersome armor in order to improve their mobility (van Wees 2004: 195–97). Cost was also a factor in determining how much of the panoply an individual might use. It has been argued that bronze cuirasses, being made of relatively thin metal, offered less protection than stiffened linen, but were more impressive and suggestive of the wearer's social and economic status, deliberately modeled on Homer's descriptions of bronze and even gold armor on the heroes who fought at Troy (van Wees 2004: 52–57). The citizen populations of the Greek poleis in the classical period comprised many who could not afford such status symbols, but nonetheless were needed to fight as hoplites in the numerous wars of the fifth and fourth centuries B.C. As long as they had a spear, a shield, and a helmet, they were well enough equipped. Conical felt caps (called *piloi*), worn underneath bronze helmets to provide a more comfortable and stable fit, provided the model for lighter, less restrictive helmets that became commonplace in the late fifth and early fourth centuries (Sekunda 2000: 58–59). Thus it is clear that the equipment and tactics of ancient Greek warfare were gradually evolving from around 700 B.C. onward, although none of the particular technical and tactical refinements can be considered very drastic until the military innovations that were introduced in Macedon around the middle of the fourth century B.C.

# THE MACEDONIAN WAR MACHINE

In the mid-fourth century B.C., after decades of dynastic conflict exacerbated by outside interference, the kingdom of Macedon was stabilized by a strong, innovative ruler, Philip II (359–338 B.C.). In order to achieve his imperialist ambitions he created a professional army, at the core of which was a new form of phalanx. In its fully developed form the Macedonian phalanx under Philip II and his son Alexander the Great consisted of large groups of men (1,500 was a standard number in the time of Alexander) each of whom was armed with a very long spear, or pike, called a *sarissa*. The length of these weapons varied considerably but typically was around 4 to 5 m. The shafts were made of hard wood; the Macedonians favored cornel wood. The *sarissa* had an iron head, much narrower than that of the hoplite spear, and a long pointed iron butt. It seems that sometimes the shaft came in two sections joined by an iron sleeve, so that it could be taken apart for transportation. The soldiers stood very close together (no more than about a meter apart), with the spearheads of the front five ranks projecting ahead of the formation in a fearsome "hedge" of sharp points. The men in the ten or more ranks behind held their weapons poised above the heads of those in front, forming a loose but effective screen to deflect missiles (Connolly 1981: 64–70; Sekunda 1984: 23–28).

Diodorus (16.3.2) claimed that the inspiration for this new tactical formation came from the description of densely packed phalanxes of warriors in the Homeric poems (*Il.* 13.128–35; 16.212–17; Lendon 2005: 121–24). Ancient sources also suggest that the young Philip learnt to appreciate the possibilities of densely packed formations of heavy infantry while an exile in Thebes (Justinus, *Epit.* 6.9.7; 7.5.1–3), where similar ideas had recently been put into practice. Whether or not Philip II was trying to imitate the fighting style of the Homeric infantry, it is clear that the *sarissa* enabled Macedonians to engage their enemies at a much greater distance than conventional hoplites. It was necessary to use both hands to wield the *sarissa*, so the large, heavy shields used by hoplites would have been too cumbersome for a Macedonian phalanx. Philip II's army may have used *peltai*, but the men in Alexander's phalanx, and those of the Successors who carved kingdoms out of Alexander's empire, carried small round shields with a diameter of about half a meter, often faced with bronze, silver, or gold. They were supported by a neck strap but also had the central armband and handgrip that are characteristic of the hoplite shield, allowing the shield to be maneuvered more effectively in close-quarter combat if the soldier lost or laid aside his *sarissa*.

It has already been noted that light-armed men with bows, slings, and especially javelins had been part of all ancient Greek armies throughout the archaic and classical periods. In the new-style Macedonian army such troops were integral parts of a carefully coordinated, combined-arms force. They provided crucial flanking cover to the slow, unwieldy phalanx, often in concert with light cavalry. The greatest innovation of all in the new-style Macedonian army was, however, the introduction of heavy cavalry as a striking force. The Greeks did not practice cavalry warfare before the classical period. Some of the wealthier hoplites had ridden to battle, but they fought on foot. The Greeks began to encounter large Near Eastern cavalry forces when the Persians conquered Ionia and invaded Greece. In the fifth century B.C., the larger poleis organized small troops of cavalrymen, but they rarely played a major role in battles. The stirrup was unknown to the ancient Greeks, they did not shoe their horses, and their saddles were little more than cloths. Horse riding was reserved for those who had both the time and the resources to develop equestrian skills, and it was only in plains of northern Greece, in regions like Thessaly and Macedonia that horsemen were plentiful (Ducrey 1986: 94–103).

Philip II equipped the aristocratic Macedonian cavalry (known as Companions) with a long spear called a *xyston*, shorter than the *sarissa* used by the Macedonian phalanx, but still much longer than traditional Greek or Persian cavalry weapons. It may have been modeled on the spears used by the nomadic peoples of the central Asian and east European steppes. The Companions wore bronze, Boeotian-style helmets with flared brims and cuirasses of small metal plates lined with linen and leather. The overall effect was to make the Companion cavalry into shock troops, whose charge could be effective against both cavalry and infantry formations (Connolly 1981: 71–74; Sekunda 1984: 14–23). A further development of cavalry warfare in the Hellenistic period was the use of very heavily armored mounted troops, usually called cataphracts (Greek *katakphraktoi*), by the Seleucid kings, descendants of Alexander's general Seleucus Nicator (305–281 B.C.). The cataphracts were usually Iranian horsemen who wore iron helmets and suits of armor made from iron scales, as did their horses, and fought with long swords and lances the Greeks called *kontoi* (Sekunda 1994: 21–22). With the growth of an independent Parthian kingdom in the third and second centuries B.C., recruitment of these cataphracts into the Seleucid armies declined, but the Parthian kings deployed them with great success against the Romans in the first century B.C. (Mielczarek 1993).

In the early Iron Age, before the introduction of the hoplite panoply, some Greek warriors may have ridden to a field of battle in chariots rather than on horses. There is no clear evidence that they actually fought from their chariots, just as the contemporary mounted warriors who rode to battle on horses do not seem to have fought as cavalry. But, whereas cavalry gradually became standard element of ancient Greek armies in the classical period, chariots did not, no doubt largely due to the unsuitability of most of the terrain on which ancient Greeks actually fought. It was only after the conquests of Alexander the Great opened up vast areas of Egypt and the Near East that chariots were adopted by the Successors as part of the huge armies with which they fought for control of the Near East. The favored type of chariot was the scythed war chariot, often used by the Achaemenid Persian kings in the fourth century B.C. This weapon was applied with great effect against inexperienced infantry formations (Xenophon, *Hell.* 4.1.17–18), but it was of very limited value against troops and commanders who were not terrified (Arrian, *Anab.* 3.13; Livy 37.40–41). The Seleucid monarchs frequently included four-horse or six-horse chariots in their field armies (Sekunda 1994: 26).

The most exotic aspect of the armies of the Hellenistic period, however, was the widespread use of elephants. The Greeks first encountered them when Alexander led his men into northern India. Although Alexander did not attempt to make tactical use of elephants he acquired as gifts, his successors deployed them by the hundreds. Maintaining their numbers was always a problem. Although the Seleucids attempted to breed them in Syria, they relied principally on eastern allies to supply them. The Ptolemaic kings of Egypt made use of smaller African elephants, as did the Carthaginians. The principal tactical application of elephants was against enemy cavalry, but it quickly became apparent that they could be as much of a liability as an asset. In spite of their training and the presence of *mahouts*, war elephants could easily become so frightened and enraged that they would charge into their own lines and cause havoc. As with scythed chariots, the tactical impact of elephants was considerably lessened as armies became used to them (Scullard 1974: 64–190; Connolly 1981: 74–75).

Almost all of the varied troop types that contributed to the success of the Macedonian and Hellenistic armies can be seen as adaptations of existing military technology. Organizational and socioeconomic differences are of considerable importance in our understanding of what made the Macedonian army so effective, and what enabled the Hellenistic monarchs to wage war on a much greater scale than had been the norm in the classical period. The underlying trend in the fourth century onward can be characterized as increasing participation in warfare among the lower socioeconomic classes, accompanied by what might be termed the "professionalization" of Greek warfare. In the late classical and Hellenistic periods professional, mercenary soldiers were used across the entire Greek world. Greek mercenaries had sold their services since the seventh century B.C., but it was after the Peloponnesian War that their numbers increased dramatically. Following the death of Alexander, many emigrants from Crete or mainland Greece were encouraged to settle in the new Successor kingdoms, receiving land in return for their military service (Cohen 1978; Ducrey 1986: 118–40).

State production and distribution of weapons and armor seems to have been an important element in Philip II's reforms. A bronze spear-butt stamped with *MAK* (for "Mac[edonian]") indicates that it was a state-issued item (Sekunda 1984: 28), and a late third century B.C. inscription from Amphipolis gives a schedule of fines for Macedonian soldiers who do not have their full set of weapons and armor. The fines are doubled for officers, whose equipment is expected to include a metal cuirass, rather than just a linen one (Connolly 1981: 77–80; Sage 1996: 171). Officers tended to be drawn from the wealthier, more aristocratic families, as had been the case in the classical period, but they also took their role as military leaders more seriously than their predecessors, who had prided themselves on their amateurism. Manuals and pamphlets on how to command and train military forces began to appear in the fourth century B.C., and the dedicated training of those engaged in warfare, which had been neglected by most Greeks outside of Sparta, became a standard polis activity (van Wees 2004: 87–95; Lendon 2005: 91–114).

The Greeks enjoyed a wide range of strenuous sports that helped prepare men for the grueling physical and psychological demands of ancient warfare. Military discipline, unit cohesion, and tactical coordination, however, were not skills that the average Greek citizen trained for. Spartans, who prided themselves on being trained soldiers, were the exception, along with some elite groups of hoplites modeled on the Spartans that were formed in Thebes and Argos. To man the Macedonian phalanx, in which independent action was virtually impossible, regular training as a unit was vital. Ancient written sources indicate that a program of military training known as the *ephebeia* was well established across the Greek world by the third century B.C. The main areas of instruction were close combat, archery, javelin throwing, and catapult firing. Trainees and mercenaries were often deployed on guard duty on the city walls and frontier fortifications that had become prominent features of the Greek landscape (Chaniotis 2005: 46–56).

# FORTIFICATIONS AND SIEGE WARFARE

Fortified settlements and strongholds had existed in the Greek world since the Bronze Age. Many of the Late Bronze Age Mycenaean citadels endured, their massive walls of polygonal masonry providing places like Athens, Corinth, and Miletus with a fortified acropolis. There was very little development of such sites through the Dark Age, except in a few cases where old Bronze Age walls were repaired or reused. In the archaic period, new fortifications were constructed, but mostly in different places and for different purposes than their Bronze Age predecessors. The emerging polis communities wanted protection for their entire urban area, rather than just a central place. Hence at Miletus the archaic-period fortifications enclosed a substantial area of land suitable for houses, rather than just the acropolis, as had been the case in the Bronze Age. By the end of the archaic period, the fortifications of the principal settlement on the northern Aegean island of Thasos had been extended from the small acropolis to enclose most of city, right down to coast. At Eretria on Euboea a similar extension of the acropolis defenses occurred. In the numerous overseas settlements that were established, especially in the western Mediterranean, larger areas were also enclosed, to protect the settlers from hostile neighbors or pirates. Walling off a peninsula was a preferred option, and was adopted at Smyrna in Ionia, Taras in Southern Italy, and Naxos in Sicily (Winter 1971: 290–94; Snodgrass 1986).

These defenses were little more than circuit walls five or six meters high, made of rubble or brick on a stone socle, that presented a barrier to attacking soldiers. Towers and bastions were rare, and gateways were often unprotected. Gradually, however, in the seventh and sixth centuries B.C., as they came into contact with Near Eastern peoples whose siege warfare techniques were well developed, the Greeks of Ionia learned how to strengthen their defenses. Miletus, which had strong walls and easy access to the sea, managed to resist both the Cimmerians and the Lydian kings (Herodotus 1.6; 1.15–27), but most of the Greeks of Ionia lacked the manpower to defend extensive walls over long periods, and many of their city areas had in any case spread beyond the circuit of their walls (Winter 1971: 294–302). When the Persians occupied Ionia in the second half of the sixth century B.C., they found that few cities had substantial walls, and even those that did, like Miletus, failed to keep Persians out. Nevertheless, the resistance that the Milesians put up at the end of the Ionian Revolt in 494 B.C. suggests that they had worked hard on improving their defenses; Herodotus (6.18) says the Persians needed to employ both siege engines and mines.

In mainland Greece there were fewer incentives to improve defensive fortifications. It is clear that by the late sixth century B.C. Athens had a circuit of city walls, because two passages refer to it in the immediate aftermath of the Persian sack of 480 B.C. (Thucydides 1.89.3, 93.2). The city had expanded so much by 480 B.C., however, that defending the walls was not considered a worthwhile act (Winter 1971: 62–64). In 478 B.C., following the expulsion of the Persians from the Greek mainland, the Athenians not only rebuilt but also extended their walls (Thucydides 1.93.2). According to Thucydides, Themistocles had a vision of Athens "attached to the sea" and projecting her power by means of a navy. A large fleet operating out of a strong harbor at Piraeus was essential to this vision, as it would enable the Athenians to defy both the armies of their Greek neighbors and those of the Persian king. The Athenians began to fortify the Piraeus peninsula in 493 B.C., at the instigation of Themistocles, but the project was unfinished in 480 B.C. The rivalry between the major poleis of Greece proved a greater incentive than the Persian threat for the construction of defensive fortifications (Winter 1971: 303–10). The Athenians built the Long Walls to link their city directly to the Piraeus. They were begun around 465 B.C. and completed in 446 B.C. The Northern Long Wall, roughly 6 km in length, ran from the southwestern quadrant of the city walls to the northeastern circuit of the Piraeus walls. A slightly shorter wall ran to the settlement at Phaleron, effectively closing off landward access to the whole of the Bay of Phaleron, but still leaving its shores exposed to potential invaders. In 446 B.C., a Middle Wall was constructed, parallel to the North Wall and only a short distance south of it, creating a narrow corridor between Piraeus and the city (Garland 1987: 14–26). The land within these walls was used for farming and residence during periods when the countryside around Athens was vulnerable to enemy raids. The Athenians provided similar fortifications for Megara, which also lay a short distance from its seaport of Nisaea around 460 B.C. These walls made it harder for Corinth to control her neighbor Megara, and in turn encouraged the Corinthians to build long walls linking their city to the harbor of Lechaeum, a few kilometers to the north (Rothaus 1995). The proliferation in city walls forced the Greeks to become more adept at sieges and assaults. In the fifth century B.C., the Athenians achieved a reputation for capturing cities and were credited with introducing the defensive tortoise and the battering ram to Greek warfare (Thucydides 1.102; Diodorus 12.28). These devices were already centuries old in the Near East, and it is clear that, in technical terms, defense seems to have had the upper hand over attack in the Greek world until the latter part of the fourth century B.C. Although the length of some ancient Greek defensive walls seems excessive, such as those encircling Messene in the Peloponnese, or the 6.5 km protecting the tiny city of Heracleia under Latmos in Anatolia, it is important to realize that they followed steep ridges wherever possible, making them hard to approach and especially difficult for any form of machines to be brought to bear on them (Winter 1971: 101–25).

The small city of Lato, situated on two slopes adjacent to the main ancient route between eastern and central Crete, is a fine example of how to make the most of both the natural setting and effective design in fortifications. Although Lato was an independent polis in the archaic and classical periods, the defenses that survive date from the mid-fourth to early second centuries B.C. A securely fortified urban center was essential during the Hellenistic period, when Lato was involved in the violent struggles for supremacy among the Cretan cities (Chaniotis 2005: 9–13). Lato's main entrance was a narrow gateway less than 2 m wide (figure 26.3), which led into a small, high-walled courtyard that could be closed off in the middle as well as at both ends. If an attacking force managed to get through this gateway complex, it had to turn sharply to the right and proceed up a steeply sloping main street, whose 90 steps were partly built and partly cut out of the rock. Here the attackers were faced by more strong fortifications. The walls of the houses on either side rise in a series of terraces constructed of thick polygonal masonry that acts like a second set of city walls, securing the houses and public buildings above and behind them. These walls are reinforced by several small tower rooms that help to protect their narrow entrances. On the right-hand (western) side, the rear walls are further protected by a rampart wall of irregular limestone blocks. It is likely that the flat roofs of compacted mud afforded good javelin, sling, or archery platforms. Because Lato was built on hills that lack natural springs, its inhabitants relied on cisterns to collect rainwater, which was not readily available to anyone attempting to invest the city. These relatively simple devices were designed to make Lato difficult to attack and easy to defend; there is no record of it ever having fallen to an assault. Another significant feature of Lato's position is that it is some 8 km inland but commands an excellent view over the Bay of Mirabello and the port of Lato pros Kamara (modern Aghios Nikolaos). This coastal settlement became the main urban center of the polis of Lato in the second century B.C. The physical movement of the population center reflects a profound shift in local attitudes. In the second century B.C., the people of Lato seem to have accorded greater importance to the access to seaborne commerce that their excellent harbor could provide than to the rugged defenses of their hilltop city (Picard 1992).

Figure 26.3. Remains of the fortified entrance courtyard at Lato, mid-fourth to early second centuries B.C. (Photograph by D. de Souza.)

In response to improved assault techniques, more sophisticated defensive elements became standard in fortifications. Gateways were strengthened by creating corridor approaches between protective towers. Walls across open land were given regular projecting towers and sally ports from which the defenders could counterattack. Stone superseded mudbrick and rubble as the preferred building material. Aesthetically pleasing polygonal and irregular masonry styles were largely replaced by regular ashlar blocks that were more resistant to battering (Winter 1971: 77–91). From the middle of the fourth century B.C., however, the pace of change quickened due to the emergence of professional armies under first the Macedonian kings Philip and Alexander and later the rulers of the Hellenistic Successor kingdoms. These monarchs had at their disposal the resources necessary to maintain and deploy effective siege trains, with experts who could construct and operate numerous powerful, stone-throwing torsion catapults and mobile siege towers with battering rams (Lawrence 1979: 39–66). They were skilled engineers as well, capable of supervising complex operations to undermine, batter, or drill walls to create breaches for assault. Ditches and moats were added in front of walls to make mining more challenging and to keep catapults back from the walls, but they could be quite easily overcome by filling and bridging (Winter 1982). At Syracuse in 213 B.C., Archimedes had the existing walls pierced at lower points to enable the missiles to be fired at attackers who were very close to the walls (Polybius 8.5.6; Livy 24.34.9), but such responses were rare. For the majority of Greek cities it was becoming too costly in men and money to defend long stretches of wall against the great concentrations of force available to the Hellenistic monarchs (McNicoll 1986).

The balance of power often lay with the attackers, provided they had sufficient resources of men and materials to see the job through (de Souza 2007b: 447–60).

A further aspect of many ancient Greek fortifications was their mutual visibility, which allowed signals to be passed between strong-points and enabled them to function as part of an integrated military system. The Athenians created such a defensive system as a direct consequence of their experiences during the Peloponnesian War, when the Spartans and their allies repeatedly invaded Attica and eventually occupied a fortified position of their own at Decelea, from which they raided the countryside, severely disrupting agriculture and bringing silver production in the Laurion region to a standstill. The Periclean strategy adopted at the outbreak of the Peloponnesian War relied on the strength of Athens' city walls and the Long Walls, but required the abandonment of much of the countryside of Attica. In the fourth century the aim was to keep enemy forces out of Attica altogether (Ober 1985). The fortress at Eleutherae (modern Gyphtokastro) guarded a major mountain pass into Attica from Boeotia (figure 26.4). By the late fourth century BC this stronghold was a formidable barrier to the progress of invading forces, allowing time to summon help from Athens via a series of watchtowers and relay stations (Winter 1971: 43–45; Ober 1985: 191–207). Similar sophisticated and wide-ranging defensive systems were developed elsewhere, like the chain of fortified settlements and forts, linked by watch and signal towers and covering all the approaches to Thebes south of Lake Copais (Fossey 1992).

# NAVAL WARFARE

Warfare at sea in the Bronze Age Mediterranean was a maritime version of land fighting, but the addition of a ram to the prows of oared ships, which occurred around 900 B.C., turned the ships themselves into weapons (cf. chapter 24). Gradually more oarsmen were added to make vessels faster (a major advantage in ramming) and raised decks were incorporated to act as fighting platforms when ships were in close proximity. The Phoenicians had added a second level of oarsmen by 700 B.C., and in the mid-sixth century B.C. warships incorporated a third level of oarsmen, rowing through an oar box or outrigger, perhaps again as the result of Phoenician innovation (figure 24.4). Three levels of oarsmen proved the maximum that could be accommodated by ancient oared warships, although an increase in the number of men pulling an individual oar permitted the construction of larger and more robust vessels (Casson 1996: 49–65, 77–123). The most common Greek warship type in the classical period was the "three," with one man per oar, usually in the form of the trireme, the standard vessel in the celebrated fleets of fifth-century Athens. The Rhodians preferred a sleeker version of the "three" called a *trihemiolia*, with two levels of oars operating through the outrigger (Morrison

Figure 26.4. Walls of the Athenian fortress at Eleutherae, ca. 450–late fourth century B.C. (Photograph by J. P. Oleson.)

1996: 319–21). The "four" (quadrireme) was similar in size to the trireme but had oars on just two levels, each pulled by two men. The "five" (quinquereme) usually had oars on three levels, with two men pulling the top two. This arrangement was favored by the Seleucid and Ptolemaic kingdoms, which could command large numbers of oarsmen and marines. A few very big warships were built in the late fourth and early third centuries B.C. They were powered by hundreds or even thousands of oarsmen, but these "polyremes" were of only limited use in sea battles, as they were slow and cumbersome. It may well be that they were designed to act as artillery platforms and assault ships in attacks on coastal cities and harbors, although their principal achievement was to enhance the prestige of individual monarchs (de Souza 2007a).

Naval warfare in the classical and Hellenistic periods usually involved ramming an enemy ship with the intention of holing it, or of grappling and then boarding. Many rams were broken off in combat, or taken from captured ships and displayed as trophies. So far, however, archaeologists have recovered only a single large bronze ram, at Athlit, on the coast of Israel. It weighs 462 kg, measures just over two meters long, and is blunt-ended with fins that would encourage splitting of the timbers of a ship's hull. It is clearly intended to penetrate to a short distance, presumably to reduce the risk of entanglement with its victim (Casson and Steffy 1991). The use of ramming without grappling or boarding as a fleet's primary tactic would have required relatively fast ships, which in turn implies well trained crews. The best mode of attack was from the rear or at an acute angle, which normally meant outmaneuvering an enemy ship in open water. The ship's captain and helmsman needed skill and judgment to time the attack. The ramming ship aimed to withdraw and attack another ship while its first victim flooded and sank, although the lack of heavy ballast in warships usually meant that when holed they would often just heel over, or continue to float with their decks awash. A variation on actual ramming was to use the stem post, the ram, and the projecting beams (Greek *epotides*) of the outrigger at a ship's prow to smash an enemy ship's oars and outrigger. Warship prows were designed to withstand the impact of ramming, and the mortise and tenon construction, along with heavy wales, allowed much of the shock to be transmitted along the length of the vessel. Less speed and maneuvering skill were needed to ram a vessel head on, or square on, but to do either risked serious damage to the ramming ship. Fleets whose captains were not confident in the speed and agility of their ships would prefer to ram prow to prow or obliquely, and then, as the opposing ships came together, the marines they carried would assault the enemy with arrows and javelins, often fired or thrown from a crouching position for better stability and then try to board their ship, a daunting challenge even in calm seas. One way to make it easier was to use grappling hooks to secure the enemy ship at close quarters. These devices, called *cheires siderai* (iron hands) by the Greeks, were routinely used when ships were operating in confined spaces such as straits or harbors (Casson 1996: 120–22).

Other types of missile weapons were also used to clear enemy soldiers and sailors from the decks of a ship. The earliest attested use of torsion catapults, hurling either bolts or stones, comes in the description of the naval battle at Salamis in 306 B.C., between the forces of Ptolemy I Soter and Demetrius Poliorcetes. Diodorus Siculus (20.49.4) says that the latter put stone-throwing catapults on his ships, along with arrow-shooting catapults on their prows. Since he had recently been assaulting the Cypriot city of Salamis, it is quite likely that these artillery weapons came from his siege train. They would have been most effective against the fighting personnel of an enemy ship and any artillery it may have had, when the warships were some distance from each other (de Souza, 2007b: 441–43). In a naval battle in 184 B.C., the exiled Carthaginian general Hannibal, commanding of the fleet of king Prusias of Bithynian fleet, used his catapults to hurl pots filled with poisonous snakes onto the decks of the warships of Eumenes II of Pergamon (Frontinus, *Strat.* 4.7.10–11).

The tactical, technical, and engineering achievements of the ancient Greeks in the sphere of warfare were impressive, but not outstanding. They did develop some distinctive and highly effective weapons, or weapons systems, particularly the hoplite and the Macedonian phalanxes, but neither of these was a radical departure from what had gone before, nor was either so innovative that it completely changed the nature of warfare. It could be argued that there was very little technological change in ancient Greek warfare from the eighth to the first century B.C. Armies still consisted of men who fought with spear, sword, bow, and sling, some on horseback but the majority on foot, as they had done in the preceding centuries, and as they would continue to do for many centuries to come. Greek achievements in fortifications and siege warfare were similarly modest. In the fourth and third centuries B.C., some very elaborate walls and defensive systems were constructed, but the introduction of siege towers and torsion catapults cannot be compared to the adoption of gunpowder-fired weapons in the fourteenth century, which forced wholesale changes in the engineering and architecture of defensive fortifications (Black 2002: 69–96). Even such a celebrated naval achievement as the trireme (possibly not a Greek invention anyway) was still just another rowed ship with a fighting a deck and a ram. Innovations like the mounting of torsion catapults and the increase in the size of the ships did not fundamentally change the way that naval warfare was conducted, as was the case when cannons were deployed on warships in the sixteenth century A.D. (de Souza 2001: 20–23, 97–118). While there can be no denying the lasting fame achieved by military leaders like Themistocles and Alexander, ancient Greek achievements in the techniques and tools of war between the eighth to the first century B.C. cannot be ranked as highly on a global scale as those in literature, architecture, philosophy, or science.

# REFERENCES

Black, J. 2002. *European warfare, 1494–1660*. London: Routledge.

Casson, L. 1996. *Ships and seamanship in the ancient world*. Rev. ed. Princeton: Princeton University Press.

Casson, L., and R. J. Steffy (eds.) 1991. *The Athlit Ram*. Texas A & M University Press.

Chaniotis, A. 2005. *War in the Hellenistic world: A social and cultural history*. Oxford: Blackwell.

Connolly, P. 1981. *Greece and Rome at war*. London: Macmillan Phoebus.

Cohen, G. M. 1978. *The Seleucid colonies: Studies in founding, administration and organisation. Historia* Einzelschriften 30. Wiesbaden: Steiner.

d'Agostino, B. 1990. "Military organisation and social structure in archaic Etruria," in O. Murray and S. Price (eds.), *The Greek city from Homer to Alexander*. Oxford: Oxford University Press, 59–84.

de Souza, P. 2001. *Seafaring and civilization: Maritime perspectives on world history*. London: Profile Books.

de Souza, P. 2002. *The Peloponnesian War, 431–404 B.C.* Oxford: Osprey Publishing.

de Souza, P. 2003. *The Greek and Persian Wars, 499–386 B.C.* Oxford: Osprey Publishing.

de Souza, P. 2007a. "Naval forces," in P. Sabin, H. van Wees, and M. Whitby (eds.), *The Cambridge history of Greek and Roman warfare*, vol. 1. Cambridge: Cambridge University Press, 357–67

de Souza, P. 2007b. "Naval battles and siege warfare," in P. Sabin, H. van Wees, and M. Whitby (eds.), *The Cambridge history of Greek and Roman warfare*, vol. 1. Cambridge: Cambridge University Press, 434–60.

Ducrey, P. 1986. *Warfare in ancient Greece*. New York: Schocken Books.

Fossey, J. M. 1992. "The development of some defensive networks in Eastern Central Greece during the classical period," in S. van de Maele and J. M. Fossey (eds.), *Fortificationes antiquae*. Amsterdam: Gieben.

Garland, R. 1987. *The Piraeus*. London: Duckworth.

Hanson, V. D. 1989. *The Western way of war: Infantry battle in classical Greece*. Oxford: Oxford University Press.

Hanson, V. D. (ed.) 1991. *Hoplites: The classical Greek battle experience*. London: Routledge.

Hanson, V. D. 1995. *The other Greeks: The family farm and the agrarian roots of Western civilization*. New York: Free Press.

Hanson, V. D. 2000. "Hoplite battle as ancient Greek warfare: When, where and why?" in H. van Wees (ed.), *War and violence in ancient Greece*. London: Duckworth, 201–32.

Healy, J. F. 1978. *Mining and metallurgy in the Greek and Roman world*. London: Thames and Hudson.

Krentz, P. 1985. "Casualties in hoplite battles." *Greek, Roman and Byzantine Studies* 26: 13–20.

Lawrence, A. W. 1979. *Greek aims in fortification*. Oxford: Oxford University Press.

Lendon, J. E. 2005. *Soldiers and ghosts: A history of battle in classical antiquity*. New Haven: Yale University Press.

McNicoll, A. 1986. "Developments in techniques of siegecraft and fortification in the Greek World ca. 400–100 B. C.," in P. Leriche and H. Tréziny (eds.), *La fortification dans l'histoire du monde grec*. Paris: CNRS, 305–13.

Mielczarek, M. 1993. *Cataphracti and Clibanarii: Studies in the heavy armoured cavalry of the ancient world*. Łódź: Oficyna Naukowa.

Morris, I. 1986. "The use and abuse of Homer," *Classical Antiquity* 5: 81–138.

Morisson, J. S. 1996. *Greek and Roman oared warships*. Oxford: Oxbow Books.

Ober, J. 1985. *Fortress Attica: Defense of the Athenian land frontier, 404–322 B.C. Mnemosyne* Suppl. 84. Leiden: Brill.

Picard, O. 1992. "Lato," in J. W. Myers, E. E. Myers, and G. Cadogan (eds.), *The aerial atlas of ancient Crete*. University of California Press, 154–59.

Rothaus, R. 1995. "Lechaion, western port of Corinth: A preliminary archaeology and history." *Oxford Journal of Archaeology* 14: 293–306.

Sage, M. M. 1996. *Warfare in ancient Greece. A sourcebook*. London: Routledge.

Scullard, H. H. 1974. *The elephant in the Greek and Roman world*. London: Thames and Hudson.

Sekunda, N. 1984. *The army of Alexander the Great*. Oxford: Osprey Publishing.

Sekunda, N. 1994. *Seleucid and Ptolemaic reformed armies, 168–145 B.C. Vol. 1: The Seleucid army under Antiochus IV Epiphanes*. Stockport: Montvert Publications.

Sekunda, N. 2000. *Greek Hoplite, 480–323 B.C.* Oxford: Osprey Publishing.

Snodgrass, A. M. 1967. *Arms and armour of the Greeks*. London: Thames and Hudson.

Snodgrass, A. M. 1974. "An historical Homeric Society?" *Journal of Hellenic Studies* 94: 114–25.

Snodgrass, A. M. 1986. "The historical significance of fortification in archaic Greece," in P. Leriche and H. Tréziny (eds.), *La fortification dans l'histoire du monde grec*. Paris: CNRS, 125–31.

van Wees, H. 1992. *Status warriors: War, violence and society in Homer and history*. Amsterdam: Gieben.

van Wees, H. (ed.) 2000. *War and violence in ancient Greece*. London: Duckworth.

van Wees, H. 2004. *Greek warfare: Myths and realities*. London: Duckworth.

Winter, F. E. 1971. *Greek fortifications*. Toronto: University of Toronto Press.

Winter, F. E. 1982. "A summary of recent work on Greek fortifications in Greece and Asia Minor," in P. Leriche and H. Tréziny (eds.), *La Fortification dans l'histoire du monde grec*. Paris: CNRS, 23–29.

## CHAPTER 27

# ROMAN WARFARE AND FORTIFICATION

## GWYN DAVIES

### WARFARE AND THE ROMANS

A message relayed to the Roman people by Romulus after his translation to the heavens, stands as an unambiguous endorsement of Roman military prowess. "Tell the Romans that it is the gods' will that my Rome shall be the capital of the world; therefore let them cultivate the arts of war and let them know and teach their children that no human force can resist Roman arms" (Livy 1.16.7). For Livy, the equation of Roman greatness with martial accomplishment was a truism that stood as a simple and unassailable explanation for the rise of the city to its pinnacle of imperial dominion. As the gods themselves had mandated, Roman success, the well-being of the state and its continuing expansion, were inextricably linked with the maintenance of military supremacy.

This glorification of war and its elevation as the primary causal factor in the construction of Roman hegemony was not just the view of a leading propagandist of the new Augustan age. Instead, a belief in the efficacy of warfare as both a tool of state policy and a worthy undertaking in its own right permeated Roman society. For the elite, political reputations were consolidated (or established in the first place) by demonstrable military achievements, and service in the army formed an important component of the successful *cursus honorum*. Further down the social scale, the status of ordinary soldiers was reflected in their receipt of a respectable income enhanced by occasional donatives and (for the imperial period at least) the prospect of significant "retirement" benefits at discharge. Additionally, the steady transformation of the army into a professional standing force (substantially completed by the start of the first century A.D.) meant that the state enjoyed access to trained personnel sufficiently versatile to assist the process of civil governance over a broad spectrum. In such a climate, the virtues of training, discipline, and competence were increasingly viewed as essential prerequisites for the army, both on campaign and in the performance of its domestic duties. As a result, it is not surprising to note that for the late Roman historian Vegetius "we see no other explanation of the conquest of the world by the Roman people than their drill-at-arms, camp discipline, and military expertise" (*Mil.* 1.1).

A considerable body of scholarship has been devoted to explaining the basis of Roman military power and to elucidating the technical aspects of its development and utilization, and it is not necessary to recapitulate these discussions here. Rather, this chapter will focus on the role of technology (and the complementary dimension of engineering competence) in improving the operational capabilities of the Roman state, allowing for the projection of power on a systematic and sustained basis. To this end, we will trace the organizational and weapon system developments that enabled Roman armies to engage their enemies with confidence in the field, alongside the evolution of fortification schemes that enabled economies of force essential to imperial security.

# The Army in the Field: Organization, Weapons, and Tactics

It is not unrealistic to claim that the Roman army was the most proficient military force of the ancient world. The successes that it enjoyed over several centuries of campaigning against a diversity of enemies in often difficult terrain and harsh environmental conditions oblige us to acknowledge the resilience of both individual soldiers and the system that sustained them in the field. This is particularly true when we recall that the general trajectory of battlefield superiority was not seriously checked even by such calamitous reverses as Cannae, Carrhae, Kalkriese (Teutoberg Forest), and Edessa that involved the complete loss of entire armies and even the capture (in the last instance) of the emperor himself (Valerian). This resilience stemmed in part from the inherent flexibility of the Roman army and its capacity to adapt to new challenges, whether in terms of the adoption of revised formations and weapon systems or the wholesale reorientation of its strategic posture to confront changing threats along the frontiers. As tempting as it might seem to ascribe a monolithic character to the Roman army and its institutions—a habit fostered by unhelpful modern references to the existence of a "Roman military machine"—it is increasingly apparent that an essential factor in the long-lived success of the Roman state was the capacity of its armed forces to evolve in the face of new threats.

# ARMY STRUCTURE AND ORGANIZATION

The centrality of the citizen army to the early Republic is made clear by the measures that formed part of the reforms generally attributed to Servius Tullius but whose introduction probably spanned a much wider period of time. A key component here was the division of society into different voting blocs based on gradations of wealth, and both Livy (1.43) and Dionysius of Halicarnassus (*Ant. Rom.* 4.19) make an explicit connection between the citizen's capacity to arm himself for battle and his place in the new social framework. Although considerable doubt has been cast on this particular equation of wealth, fighting potential, and political representation (Cornell 1995: 186–90), it is clear that the original impetus behind some of these constitutional measures lay in the more efficient mobilization of the state's military resources.

The expansion of the Roman state allowed for the steady increase in the size of the military forces at its disposal, and by the time of the First Punic War it was not unusual to have armies up to 40,000 strong operating at the end of lengthy lines of communication. This capacity to campaign at long range was instrumental for the projection of Roman power. During the Second Punic War, large-scale enterprises were sustained simultaneously in Spain, Italy, and Greece, a remarkable multi-front effort that testifies to Roman logistical and organizational capabilities. These demonstrations of Rome's developing strategic reach were also reinforced on the tactical level by the posture adopted for pitched battles. The Roman legion as described by Polybius (6.19–24) was composed of 30 maniples of paired centuries with a mix of heavy and light infantry. Each of the two front line formations (in the standard three lines of battle) had ten maniples each made up of about 120 heavy infantry and 40 skirmishers, while the rearmost line of battle had ten smaller maniples of 60 heavy infantry and 40 skirmishers. These lines were drawn up on the battlefield in open order, that is, each maniple was separated from its neighbors by a gap equivalent in width to the frontage of another maniple. The gaps in the line of battle were covered by the troops of the next line to the rear. The difference in manipular strength is explicable by the different tactical roles that each of these formations was intended to fulfill. The two front line formations were intended to engage the enemy forces directly, and if all went well the third line was not called into action. However, if matters proved less than successful for the troops of the first two lines, then the open order enabled these units to disengage and to fall back through the gaps and seek cover to reorganize behind the solid screen of the third line. Although the heavy infantry component of the maniples of the third line amounted to only half the strength of those of the other formations, these troops were exclusively comprised of veteran soldiers who might be relied upon to keep steady even in the face of a pressing enemy attack. The advantage of this system lay in its flexibility. A Roman army could in this way maintain a strong front line, with the luxury of a secure backstop provision at a reasonable economy of force. Furthermore, the provision of gaps in the formation allowed for the forward (and backward) movement of units without disrupting the entire battle line. Of course, crucial to the success of such maneuvers was the exercise of competent command and control and a high degree of unit discipline and training, allowing these re-deployments to be effected swiftly and efficiently. As a result of the reforms carried out by Marius at the end of the second century B.C., the professionalism of the army was dramatically enhanced as the legionary ranks were opened to the landless poor whose only qualification was the possession of Roman citizenship (Keppie 1984: 61–63). This measure, linked to the introduction of much better pay, meant that the army for the first time became an attractive career choice, and more citizens served longer terms in the ranks, allowing for continuity in useful military skills.

By the late Republic, this manipular system had undergone further revision, and the cohort now became the key tactical unit on the battlefield. The cohort comprised three of the old maniples (one being drawn from each of the three lines of battle) but with the crucial difference that the skirmishers formerly attached to each maniple were now transformed into heavy infantry as well. The cohort was divided into six centuries of 80 men each, giving it a field strength on paper of 480 men (the standard establishment by the early imperial period). Each legion comprised ten of these cohorts. Sometime in the first century A.D. (possibly as early as the reign of the practical soldier-emperor Tiberius), the first cohort of the legion was nearly doubled in size to improve overall striking power, giving each legion a combat strength of about 5,200 heavy infantry, supported by a small body of cavalry (Hyginus, *de Mun. Cast.* 3; Goldsworthy 1996: 14–15; Keppie 1984: 174–76).

This absorption of the skirmishers converted the legion into an exclusively heavy infantry formation and raised the pressing need to recruit additional forces that could fulfill other specialist combat roles. Although allied states had traditionally supplied a disproportionate element of cavalry strength to the Roman army, it was now necessary to expand (and regularize) this contribution. Accordingly, during the Principate of Augustus, the old *ad hoc* methods of securing allied troops for short-term campaigns were replaced by the systematic recruitment of these forces into permanent units of *auxilia*. These auxiliary forces, organized into cohorts of infantry or mixed infantry and cavalry, as well as pure *alae* (wings) of horsemen, played an essential role in the garrisoning of the provinces and added a useful dimension to Roman battlefield capability.

# Weapons and Equipment

The Roman army was not shy in changing its tactical dispositions to better confront its enemies, and it was equally prepared to adapt its armaments to the same end. This was particularly true when the Romans encountered equipage that had proved successful in the hands of their opponents, and several weapon types were acquired through this process of borrowing. Beyond this talent for improvisation, the Roman state also developed an impressive capacity for the large-scale manufacture of military equipment, complemented by a complex network of suppliers and producers who furnished the troops with most of their material requirements, from pack animals to pottery (Bishop and Coulston 2006: 233–52). A brief discussion of the basic panoply of the Roman soldier (figure 27.1) will introduce the technology of death employed on the battlefield.

Given the emphasis that the Romans placed on the aggressive use of force and the importance of seeking decisive battle at the earliest opportunity, it is appropriate to begin with a description of offensive rather than defensive equipment. As a general point, it is worth noting from the outset that our evidence derives from a combination of literary, representational, and archaeological sources, and that assumptions made as to the developmental sequence of any given type of equipment—or even its universal adoption—remain speculative.

## Spear and Sword

The personal weapon most closely associated with the Roman legionary soldier is the *pilum* or throwing spear. This javelin, with its characteristic long iron shank terminating in a pyramidal head, was a close-range shock weapon that was thrown at the enemy immediately before the physical collision of the confronting ranks. The intention was that a barrage of *pila* would serve to disrupt an opponent's front line. This result would have been achieved by the specific design of the weapon that allowed the 'bodkin' head of the javelin to punch through an enemy's shield, while the narrow iron shank up to 55 cm long (Bishop and Coulston 2006: 52), offered the possibility of striking the soldier sheltering behind. Even if the opposing soldier was not disabled by a direct hit on his body, the effect of the *pilum* crashing through the shield would have reduced much of its protective value by making the wielding of the shield much more cumbersome. As a result, the enemy may have dropped his shield altogether, making him much more vulnerable to sword thrusts when the lines of battle eventually collided. In effect, the use of the *pilum* made up for the relative paucity of missile troops in the Roman army, giving its heavy infantry a capability of engaging the enemy beyond the thrusting range of opposing spearmen or the stabbing/slashing arc of swordsmen. Training in the discharge of these *pila* was an important element in the daily weapons drill of the Roman

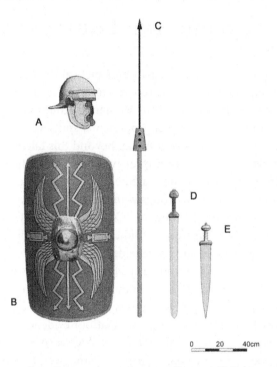

Figure 27.1. Elements of the Roman panoply: a: an "imperial" helmet of the first century A.D.; b: a first-century A.D. legionary shield; c: a late Republican *pilum*; d: a second-century A.D. *spatha*; e: a first-century A.D. *gladius Hispaniensis*. (Drawn by R. Carmenate; copyright G. Davies)

legionary, and Vegetius informs us (*Mil.* 1.14) that overweight javelins were employed in practice in order that the standard weapons could be hurled with greater effect in combat.

The antecedents of the *pilum* remain disputed, and although the earliest archaeologically recovered examples date from the last years of the third century B.C., it is uncertain whether the weapon was an adaptation of some foreign prototype or was an original Roman innovation. It seems, however, that the other main offensive weapon of the Roman infantryman, the sword, was introduced as a result of direct contact with foreign influences. The Roman identification of the weapon as the *gladius Hispaniensis* suggests that its point of origin lay in Spain and that the Romans became acquainted with the type as a result of their nearly continuous military involvement with the Celtiberians from the Second Punic War through the second century B.C. The essential characteristic of this sword was its dual purpose as a cut and thrust weapon, equally adept in a stabbing or slashing action (although Vegetius was adamant that military training emphasized the former over the latter as a more efficient killing stroke; *Mil.* 1.12). The earliest example of a recognizable sword of this type comes from Šmihel in Slovenia, from a context that has been dated to around 175 B.C. These weapons start off as slightly waisted blades approximately 65 cm in length, with long tapering points (Connolly 1998: 130), although by the early imperial period the edges of the blade had become straighter and the point shorter, giving a reduced sword length of 50 cm. The parallel-edged, still shorter "Pompeian" variant, seemingly introduced during the mid first century A.D., represents the final evolution of this form of multipurpose short sword, the use of which seems to have continued (from iconographic evidence) down to the end of the second century (Bishop and Coulston 2006: 154–57). Although some short swords of a notably different type appear to have persisted in use during the third century, the majority of troops at that time seem to have been equipped with the *spatha*, a longer bladed and narrower weapon originally issued to the cavalry (where a longer reach was essential for down-swinging strokes directed against infantry from horseback). The *spathae* that have survived in the archaeological record are less uniform in character than the short swords, with blade lengths varying considerably from 62 cm to 91 cm, although most group around approximately 70 cm (Bishop and Coulston 2006: 82, 130; Connolly 1998: 260). Presumably this degree of variation reflected the wider range of users that these blades were meant to accommodate. The change to a longer sword type suggests that the dynamics of close-order combat had also undergone revision. The emphasis on a short, upward stabbing action aimed at gutting an opponent immediately after the attacker had collided with him shield first, must have been replaced by a different style of contest. By stressing the continuing importance of using the point and not the edge of the sword, Vegetius may be implying that the *spatha* was employed in stabbing down over the shield top or sideways around the shield, the aim still being to inflict the enemy with a deep puncture wound rather than a slashing cut. It is equally possible, however, and perhaps more probable, that the adoption of the *spatha* is evidence for the dramatic transition to an open melee type of combat in which longer edged blades provided a more versatile repertoire prioritizing the cut over the thrust. Whichever explanation is preferred, it is worth noting that the *spatha* was not a finely balanced weapon, as its center of gravity was located low down the blade and the light pommel offered little in the way of counterweight (James 2004: 141). This characteristic made precision handling more difficult, possibly indicating the redundancy of the finer techniques of weapons drill and thus the abandonment of the regimented close-order fighting techniques of the past.

## Missiles

Although the *pilum* and the sword may have formed the primary offensive weapons of the Roman heavy infantry, the troops had recourse to other types of equipment from time to time. Prior to the reforms of the late Republic, the veteran soldiers who made up the third line of battle employed a heavy thrusting spear in lieu of a javelin, a weapon well suited to the task of repelling the onslaught of a successful foe who had broken through the first two Roman lines. In the later

Empire, we can note the appearance of a wide range of new types of thrown missiles, as replacements for the *pilum* (the rarity of which Vegetius notes with regret, *Mil.*1.20). These comprised a diverse set of light javelins and weighted darts or *flechettes* (*plumbata*), five of the latter being slotted into the back of the shield, to be "thrown at the first assault" according to Vegetius (*Mil.* 2.15). Reconstructions derived from examples of *plumbata* found at Wroxeter proved effective up to a range of 60 m (Eagle 1989).

Furthermore, legionaries as well as specialist units of *auxilia* also made use of other forms of missile weaponry. Since slings, bows, and catapults not only offered the potential to strike at an enemy from a distance but also delivered their projectiles with much greater kinetic force, it is not surprising that troops regularly underwent training in the use of such weapons. The large number of ovoid lead slingshot recovered from Perugia, many examples of which are impressed with propaganda messages attributable to both sets of combatants in the siege of 41–40 B.C. (Keppie 1984: 123–25), demonstrates how rapidly a significant quantity of these projectiles could be manufactured in the field. Archery equipment, arrows, and related materials are also excavated on a regular basis, suggesting the widespread use of composite bows in the Roman army. These bows were made of wood, laminated with horn on the inside and glued tendon on the outside to resist compressive pressure and add tensile strength whenever the weapons were drawn and released (Coulston 1985: 245–59). Unfortunately, no complete example of a Roman bow has survived, and our knowledge of the exact performance of these weapons must remain speculative.

## Artillery

One very important branch of missile forces was artillery, first manufactured on a significant scale in the Syracusan workshops of Dionysius I (ca. 399 B.C.; Diodorus Siculus 14.41.3–42.1), although the Ptolemies sponsored research as well (Philo of Byzantium, *Bel.* 50.3). These early weapons, essentially large bow-armed bolt-firers, were much improved by the invention of torsion-powered engines, seemingly by the corps of engineers and craftsmen employed by Philip II of Macedon (Marsden 1969). Such machines allowed an assailant to deliver heavier missiles with greater accuracy at a much longer range than could be offered by conventional bows or slings. Although Livy (6.9) makes anachronistic references to the use of artillery in Roman contexts as early as the first years of the fourth century, it is implausible that the Roman state had access to the appropriate technology until much before the First Punic War (264–241 B.C.). Thereafter, however, the Romans enthusiastically adopted these engines, although mainly employing them in static roles, either as emplaced weapons (on a city circuit or onboard ships) or as siege batteries. In doing so, they were following established tradition, as, notwithstanding their rare appearances on the ancient battlefield, artillery pieces remained too unwieldy with too slow a rate of fire to be anything more than fixed-base weapons. By the time of the First Dacian War, however, Roman technical proficiency had not only given rise to the "most powerful arrow-shooting engines ever produced in the ancient world" (Marsden 1969: 190), but had also endowed their artillery with a new and lethal mobile dimension.

Making its first appearance on the sculpted reliefs of Trajan's Column (scenes XL, XLIX, LXVI) is the cart-mounted *carroballista*. The sinew coils of the spring mechanism that provided this weapon's torsion power were protected by iron casings set further apart than in earlier *catapultae*. This not only provided a better degree of weatherproofing in the field, but also allowed the artillerymen to sight their weapon more efficiently. Further important advantages also accrued from the new all-iron frame: the catapult arm could be retracted further, allowing the bolt to be discharged with approximately 25 percent more power, and the compact design, with its standardized metal components, was not only easier to fabricate, but was also much lighter than its wooden-framed and metal-plated predecessors (Marsden 1971: 227–32). It is not surprising, therefore, that the relative mobility and efficacy of the *carroballista* made it a useful adjunct to field operations, lending plausibility to Vegetius' claim (*Mil.* 2.25) that 55 of these machines comprised the traditional complement of the legion. Of course, bolt-firers were not the only artillery employed by the army, as stone projectors of various calibers were also deployed in some numbers. The projectiles delivered by these latter engines varied from 0.5 kg grapefruit-sized shot to the large 25 kg missiles delivered by the siege artillery before Jerusalem in A.D. 70 (Josephus, *BJ* 5.270). These weapons could either be variants on the arrow-firing types or single-armed hurling devices (commonly identified as *onagri* during the later empire), ten of which were allocated to each legion according to Vegetius (*Mil.* 2.25). Large stone projectors of this nature were unsuitable for open battlefield conditions and could only be used effectively from prepared positions.

## Shields

The material discussed so far has been largely offensive in nature, but, of course, the Roman army also relied upon a wide range of defensive equipment to lend protection to its men. One element of the panoply of the Roman soldier forms a bridge linking both the means of attack and defense, namely the infantry shield. Although the curved, rectangular shield (often described in modern literature as a *scutum*, notwithstanding that this was the generic term employed for most Roman shields) may be familiar from its frequent depiction in contemporary reliefs, it is clear that the range of shield forms actually deployed was quite extensive. One important point to stress regarding the large infantry shield (whether it was of the rectangular, oval or even hexagonal type), was that this piece of equipment formed more than a passive shelter for the individual soldier. The aggressive use of the heavy infantry shield was an integral part of Roman weapons drill, with the soldier being encouraged to thrust his shield against his opponent's body as the battle lines collided, making use of the momentum of the charge to gain maximum advantage.

We are fortunate that a small number of surviving shields (particularly one from the Egyptian Fayum and others from Dura-Europos in Syria) allows us to reconstruct the manner in which these items were assembled. The strength of the Roman infantry shield derived from its laminated character, with three layers of light wooden strips being glued together with the central layer of the laminate laid crosswise between the horizontal strips of the front and back layers. The wooden strips were thicker at the center than at the edges (Bishop and Coulston 2006: 61), giving added strength at the central boss and greater flexibility at the sides, making the shield less liable to fracture at the moment of impact. A leather or felt cover encased the wooden core, held together by rawhide or (later in the first century) bronze stitching, and the face of the shield could be painted to display the device of the unit in question. A reevaluation of the Dura material suggests that there was no supplementary linen cover and that the paint or gesso for the shield decoration was applied directly to the leather casing (James 2004: 162–63). The back of the shield had a light wooden frame glued on over the leather which incorporated a central rib that provided a handgrip at the aperture left for this purpose in the middle of the board. A protruding metal boss both served to protect the hand of the wielder and to provide extra force during the clash of arms.

## Helmets and Body Armor

More exclusively protective in nature than the shield are two other classes of equipment: the helmet and body armor. Roman helmets owed much of their original inspiration to Celtic designs. The classic "Montefortino" helmet of the Republican period, an elongated bronze bowl with riveted or hinged cheekpieces, a distinctive crest fitting, and a shallow disc neck guard, was derived from north Italian types introduced by the Gallic invaders of the peninsula (Bishop and Coulston 2006: 65). The mainstream replacement of this helmet, the late Republican "Coolus" or "jockey cap" type, a more ergonomic, flattened (usually) iron bowl with larger cheekpieces and a ribbed, downward flaring neck guard, was also adapted from indigenous models encountered during the expansion into Celtic Europe beyond the Alps (Connolly 1998: 230). Although the Montefortino style was retained by the Praetorians long after its abandonment by frontline forces, its Coolus replacement was also phased out during the first century in favor of the "Imperial" helmet. This latest variant had better neck protection (eventually extending coverage to include the upper shoulders), built-in brow and ear guards and transversal reinforcing strips forming a crosspiece across the bowl top. Internal padding or a separate lining cap (as identified from the Dura assemblage, James 2004: 109) provided further shock absorption and, perhaps more importantly, improved comfort for the user. By the fourth century A.D., the one-piece helmet and neck guard seems to have been replaced by a simpler casque, often including an integrated nasal guard, comprised of (at least) two parts, with the join along the bowl crest being protected by a raised ridge. The cheekpieces and neck guards were now detachable or were replaced altogether by a *camail* suspended from the base of the helmet, prefiguring the form of a medieval *basinet*.

The earliest body armor employed by the Roman soldier was the mail shirt worn over an undergarment that combined a fair degree of protection with flexibility of movement. Mail shirts, however, were both expensive to manufacture (although relatively easy to repair) and heavy to wear, a drawback sometimes remedied by the substitution of a skirt of cured leather strips worn in conjunction with a short mail tunic rather than the full, hip-length shirt. Officers of sufficient means might have preferred a Greek-style bronze cuirass (often of the muscled variety) instead of mail, while the poorer citizen recruits might have had to make do with little more than a simple bronze pectoral plate of doubtful value. Although the date for its introduction remains uncertain, another possible option in lieu of mail was the use of scale armor, comprising thin bronze platelets wired together in an overlapping pattern and sewn onto a fabric undergarment. This so-called *lorica squamata* was easier to manufacture than pure mail and was less heavy to wear, but these advantages may have been discounted by the reduction in movement allowed by the more rigid sewn strips and a probable diminution in the protection offered, particularly against the impact of missiles (Bishop and Coulston 2006: 64).

The introduction of segmental plate armor (usually termed *lorica segmentata*) during the early first century provided heavy infantry with a new and effective form of body protection. Two complete sets of this armor, recovered from a second-century A.D. context at Corbridge, have allowed us to reconstruct the manner in which these articulating plates were intended to operate. The soldier's torso and back were protected by a set of overlapping horizontal iron strips or half-hoops linked to leather strapping by a series of hooks and buckles. The shoulders and upper arms were encased within a further set of vertically arranged iron plates that were hinged together and hooked onto the girdle plates of the chest and back. The whole ensemble combined the advantages of relative freedom of movement with the capacity to dissipate impact shock over a wider area than mail shirts could provide. The complex series of fasteners, straps, and buckles that gave the armor its articulating character, however, also proved its point of weakness, at least insofar as durability was concerned. The copper alloy elements of these fittings were not only relatively fragile, but were also subject to corrosion, particularly when in direct contact with the iron plates (Bishop and Coulston 2006: 98). The evidence we have for broken fastenings and for the replacement of hinges with rivets on some of the plates, suggests the degree to which unit *fabricae* were kept busy with the repair and maintenance of this equipment.

Although it was formerly believed that the use of segmental armor came to an end sometime in the third century, it now seems clear that the use of articulating plate in heavy infantry contexts continued into the fifth century. It is also worth pointing out that the adoption of heavy cavalry, from modest beginnings in the second century to more widespread deployment from the third century onward, also meant that some mounted units were provided with significant armored protection. The use of such *cataphractarii* or *clibanarii*, a concept originally borrowed from the Persian enemy, was more common in the East than the West, and we have our best evidence for the equipage of such troops from Dura-Europos. The site not only preserves graffiti depicting armored cavalry, but also produced at least four sets of equine "barding" covers, or armored coats, two of which were recovered almost intact. These examples of barding demonstrate that the Romans employed two large sheets of double-thickness linen which acted as backing for sewn rows of scale armor (both copper alloy and iron scales were employed) that were attached to one another by a wide leather strip that ran along the horse's spine (James 2004: 113–14). Presumably these covers were also supplemented by some form of neck guards and chamfrons (protective headpieces), as have been identified at other late Roman sites. The cavalryman was also encased in scale armor, possibly with some form of supplementary thigh guard, and his primary weapon appears to have been the long, heavy two-handed lance known as the *contus* (Dixon and Southern 1992: 49–50), a shock weapon that would have served equally well against other heavy horsemen and heavy infantry.

# Siegework Construction

The preceding discussion has allowed us to explore how Roman tactics and equipment may have been adapted to retain a technical edge on the battlefield, and it is now necessary to turn to the related issue of the engineering competence that also set the Roman army apart from most of its contemporaries. A convenient demonstration of these skills can be obtained by looking at Roman approaches to siege warfare.

As siege engines and related technical aids are considered elsewhere in this book (chapter 13), attention will be focused here on fixed structures built by the army to assist in the task of reducing stubbornly defended targets. These include works of circumvallation, assault ramps, siege mounds, mines, and other miscellaneous engineering projects that were intended to facilitate operational progress (Davies 2006). Diodorus Siculus (13.2.1) informs us that the Romans learned their siegecraft from the Greeks, but by being "pupils who always outstripped their masters . . . [they] had then forced the cities of their teachers to do their bidding." Certainly, the Hellenistic world had proved a rich testing ground for the emerging science of poliorcetics, but the determination, skill, and imagination with which Roman commanders waged *festungskrieg* make them the primary exponents of the art.

A regular part of the Roman training regimen concerned the rapid raising of earth-and-timber fortifications. Although the primary purpose of such exercises was to enable rapid preparation of temporary camps for protection in hostile territory (Welfare and Swan 1995), the process also built up familiarity with field engineering techniques in general. This was to serve the Roman army well on those occasions when siege operations were commenced in the course of an ongoing campaign when the troops at hand were required to undertake the requisite field-works without recourse to any specialist corps. Indeed, the Roman armies that produced the most sophisticated and extensive siege works were usually those that had been in the field for several years and whose personnel had developed a high degree of proficiency by repeated demands to reduce strongholds in their paths. Caesar's Gallic campaign and the suppression of the First Jewish Revolt by Vespasian and Titus are cases in point.

For sheer scale of endeavor it is impossible to ignore the works Caesar built before Alesia in 52 B.C., where the double encirclement, stretching for a combined distance of 35 km, was designed to hem in Vercingetorix and his 80,000 men while simultaneously defending the besieging force against the huge relief army massing beyond their lines. Although Caesar was hard-pressed at times, the elaborate measures that he put in hand for the protection of his army behind their lines of contravallation (facing the external threat) and circumvallation (facing the besieged) ensured that he had sufficient time to transfer reserves to threatened sectors before they were overwhelmed. The key to Caesar's success was the provision of impressive obstacle fields that fronted the most threatened sectors, backed up with a wide turf rampart amply provided with towers for the accommodation of light artillery. Modern excavation has revealed that these works may not have had the monolithic character that Caesar's own account imputes to them (*BG* 7.74), but they remain a testament to his ingenuity and the industry of his troops. In the most vulnerable section on the plain to the west of Alesia, the contravallation comprised a rampart nearly 6 m wide with towers set at 15 m intervals fronted by a ditch up to 3.2 m wide and 1.4 m deep. This ditch, however, was only the last element of the obstacle field. In front of it was a *glacis* up to 16 m wide with evidence for two bedding trenches for *cippi* (the ancient equivalent of barbed wire, comprising interleaved sharpened branches) and five rows of *stimuli* (logs set with iron spikes buried in prepared pits). Two ditches lay to the east of the *glacis*, the inner, a V-profiled feature of a consistent 2.7 m width and up to 1.5 m depth and the outer, up to 6.5m wide and 1.5m deep, which for some of its length was flooded with water diverted from a nearby stream. In other sectors the defensive configuration may not have been so elaborate, but nonetheless could include such features as *lilia* (man-traps with sharpened stakes at the base) or ground liberally studded with caltrops in lieu of some of these other obstacles.

Schemes of circumvallation were only one component of the siege repertoire deployed by Roman field engineers. More direct approaches might demand the investment of time, energy and expertise in the raising of either assault ramps or siege mounds. The former structures were designed to parallel the height of defensive walls in order to facilitate the passage of storming parties and to mount engines capable of effecting a breach, while the latter were intended to parallel or overtop the defenses so that emplaced artillery might sweep the ramparts clear of defenders and allow escalades or sapping operations to be mounted. The most sophisticated ramps built by the Romans (that can be termed "Avaricum-style" structures after the Gallic stronghold assaulted by Caesar) served to combine both functions. The most famous (and substantially intact) assault ramp is that at Masada (figure 27.2), a funnel-shaped structure 225 m long, between 50 and 200 m wide at the base, with a vertical rise of about 75 m. This latter dimension is a little misleading in the sense that the Roman engineers took advantage of an existing natural outcrop so that the actual built feature is only 25–30 m thick. Although this remains to be proven by excavation, it seems likely that the work crews of the Tenth Legion first cut a series of horizontal steps at regular intervals along each flank of the bedrock spur. Then a timber box-revetment (using local desert species, as the surviving elements demonstrate) was installed on each of these platforms and filled with rammed earth and rubble. The ramp core could then have been deposited between the stacked boxes of the two retaining revetments.

The ramp has a more or less uniform gradient of 17 degrees but an original slope of 20 degrees is likely, allowing for 1,900 years of weathering. This relatively steep profile did not prevent the attackers from deploying a heavy iron-clad tower and large ram at the summit, engines that presumably were winched up the ramp in short increments along a prepared track, on each occasion having chocks rammed in place to prevent slippage. Although much has been made of the use of Jewish corvée labor at the siege, there is no basis to suppose that they had anything to do with the process of raising this assault ramp. The Tenth Legion, long habituated to such endeavors after three years of campaigning, was more than capable of constructing such a work without assistance and in relatively short order. Indeed, there is no reason to extend any estimate for the time taken to complete this difficult technical operation (including the time taken to construct an unnecessarily comprehensive circumvallation) beyond five months, if it took that long (Roth 1995).

Although the use of circumvallation and assault ramps became a rarity in the later empire, there are still ample demonstrations of the technical proficiency of Roman soldier-engineers. During the late-third-century A.D. siege of Cremna, for example, the Roman commander built two lines of containment, well-sited artillery platforms, and an enormous siege mound to allow his assault parties to approach the enemy wall (see Mitchell et al. 1995; Davies 2000). At Boulogne, Constantius Chlorus' men denied the use of the harbor to the defenders by sinking piles into the seabed, despite the problems caused by the ebb and flow of the tide and the presence of a hostile flotilla (*Pan. Lat.* 6.6.2). Finally, in the course of his Persian campaign, the emperor Julian threw up a siege mound at Maiozamalcha while simultaneously extending mines beneath the enemy circuit, one of which at least, was intended as a mine of attack, to allow his troops surreptitious entry into the city rather than simply undermining the walls (*Zosimus* 3.22.4).

Figure 27.2. Roman assault ramp at Masada, A.D. 73. (Photograph by G. Davies.)

# ROMAN FORTIFICATIONS

Although the Roman army was often on the attack and made use of complex siege technology, it was also highly skilled in the preparation of defensive fortifications. The standard Roman "playing-card" fort of the first and second centuries A.D., an elongated rectangle with rounded corners and a limited number of internally projecting angle and interval towers, was laid out with only limited provision for point defense (Gregory 1986, 1996b). It is often claimed that this procedure conformed to the Roman preference for meeting an enemy in the field rather than awaiting an attack from the security of a prepared position, but it may also reflect the realities of the early empire, when Rome's enemies generally lacked the capacity to mount a serious threat to even modestly fortified positions. This second explanation is supported by the fact that certain forts sited in more remote and more vulnerable locations were often provided with a reinforced set of defenses, usually comprising multiple ditches that extended the obstacle field on their most vulnerable flanks. Thus, instead of the conventional two ditch configuration, Whitley Castle in Northumberland has seven ditches covering the approaches to its weakest point on the southwest. Birrens in southwest Scotland has six ditches on its north side, and Ardoch, in the wild country beyond the Antonine Wall, has five to its east. The intention in all cases was to disrupt the momentum of any attack and to subject the assailant to more effective missile fire as men bunched together while they sought to negotiate the obstacle field.

Greater care was lavished on overtly defensive measures during the third century, with new constructions often combining an irregular plan (to take maximum tactical advantage of the terrain) with the provision of many more towers either partially or fully projecting beyond the wall circuit (Johnson 1983; Lander 1984; Gregory 1996a, 1996b). The impetus for this latter measure was clearly driven by the need to provide enfilading fire along the line of the fort wall (a recognition that an enemy might now be in a position to threaten the same much more directly), and to provide firing platforms for artillery that would enable defenders to engage attackers at a considerable range. Such towers were usually provided with wide embrasures to allow catapults a greater traversing arc or were constructed with a solid concrete-rubble core that would have absorbed the recoil shock generated by heavy *onagri* (notwithstanding Ammianus' caution against emplacing these engines on stone-built structures, 32.4.5). The so-called Saxon Shore forts of southern Britain demonstrate many of these innovations: Pevensey has large, solid U-shaped towers boldly projecting outward, and Cardiff has five-sided solid bastions as interval towers fully bonded into the fort wall, hollow towers at the gateways, and an earth rampart *terreplein* reinforcing the inner face of the fort wall.

Elsewhere in the empire we see a similar pattern of evolution, with increasing emphasis being given to defensive capability over time. For example, on the eastern frontier we can see a process whereby the relatively small number of forts suggested as having second-century origins, such as Umm el-Quttein and the putative first phase at Qasr el-Azraq (Kennedy 2004), mostly of rectangular plan with no towers, are replaced by a much more extensive network of *castella* usually of fourth-century date, with enhanced defensive capabilities (Gregory 1996b; Parker 2000). Atypically, the Trajanic fort at Humayma (ancient Havarra) had a rectangular plan with projecting square towers (Oleson et al. 2003). The later *castella* range from the small garrison posts styled as *quadriburgia* to full-scale legionary fortresses—even if the late legion was a much different creature than its early empire predecessor (Tomlin 2000). Although there are variations in form from site to site, the *quadriburgium* at Yotvata (dated by inscription to A.D. 296/299) can be seen as typical. This is a broadly square enclosure, measuring about 40 m x 40 m, with four square angle towers that project about 3 m beyond the 2.5 m wide circuit wall that is built of stone to a height of nearly 2 m with mud-bricks above (up to seven courses still survive *in situ*). A simple entrance was built in the center of the east wall, and a narrow postern gate is set directly adjacent to the southwest angle tower. The care taken over these features suggests the new importance ascribed to providing even a small garrison post like this with a formidable defensive capability. This is even more apparent at the late legionary sites of el-Lejjun and Udruh in southern Jordan. These 4.7-hectare fortresses, with numerous U-shaped interval towers projecting about 11 m beyond the thick stone-faced and rubble mortared walls, and four massive semicircular fan-shaped corner towers with internal spiral staircases (see Kennedy 2004; Parker 2006), were as defensible as any crusader castle.

We can see a similar pattern of increasing concern with practical protective devices in the construction of urban fortifications. Walled cities were nothing new in Roman contexts: the defenses provided for veteran colonies such as Aosta or Turin, or for the new Augustan showpieces such as Autun or Fréjus, were often imposing and extensive, incorporating high circuit walls with ample interval towers (figure 27.3) and particularly fine multiple gateways (Johnson 1983: 17–18). We should not, however, forget that in the ancient world an impressive enceinte was considered to lend *dignitas* to a city and the construction of elaborate urban fortifications often had more to do with issues of status display rather than any pressing concern with security (Gros 1992). A dramatic change in attitude can be seen for the western provinces of the empire in the second half of the third century when, in the wake of the breakdown of central authority, most open cities in Gaul, Spain, and the Germanies underwent a rapid program of fortification as the population lost confidence in the illusive claim of an impermeable frontier. These new urban defenses were often limited in terms of the area enclosed by the walls (frequently following advantageous ground as at Angers or Senlis, or incorporating existing structures to provide an ersatz fortress, as with the amphitheater at Amiens or the forum at Bavai; see Johnson 1983: chap. 5) and the impression gained from the amount of *spolia* included within the fabric of these walls is of hasty demolitions put in hand to furnish the requisite building materials without delay (figure 27.4). But despite the speed with which many of these urban fortifications were raised, there can be little doubt that they were provided with sophisticated defensive attributes, particularly in terms of powerful towers with multiple embrasures suitable for mounting several light catapults with wide fields of fire. In many ways, Aurelian's new defenses of Rome itself provided the role model (Todd 1978). This decade-long building scheme (ca. A.D. 272–282) resulted in the creation of an 18 km circuit for the city, employing favorable terrain wherever possible, with eighteen major gates and several additional posterns. The wall, about 4 m thick and surviving up to 20 m in height, must have involved extensive clearance and demolition, although several existing structures along its line were pressed into service where feasible. Thus, the southern arcades of the *Amphitheatrum Castrense* were bricked up and its curving profile became the new wall line and the 27 m tall pyramid-tomb of Gaius Cestius was too monumental a structure to be removed, so the wall was simply butted up against it.

Aurelian's great achievement at Rome is overshadowed only by the tremendous complex that we know as the Theodosian Land Walls of Constantinople, which formed the most powerful urban fortifications of antiquity. Here, a 20 m wide moat formed the first line of defense, the water being retained by a series of dams. A low outwork and patrol track provided direct oversight of the moat and was backed by a *proteichisma* studded with towers. The final element was the inner wall, a stone and coursed-brick construction, 5 m wide and 12 m high, that was strengthened by 96 towers 20 m in height, offset from the towers on the second wall in order that the fire of their many engines might not be masked. This remarkable ensemble of works served the New Rome well: even during the final siege of 1453, it was human error and an open postern that brought about the fall of the city, rather than any failure of the thousand-year-old defenses.

There can be little doubt that the centrality of the army to social and political life serves to distinguish the Romans from their contemporary neighbors. With the

Figure 27.3. Urban defenses of Augustan Autun. (Photograph by G. Davies.)

possible exception of Macedonia in the reign of Philip II, no other state of the classical world laid such an emphasis on the role of the army either in the performance of its traditional security mission or in the management of the fabric of empire. Army units transcended their direct combat functions by assisting civilian administrators in a plethora of duties, ranging from the provision of specialist engineering and construction assistance, to the assignment of soldiers to mundane clerical and support positions on the staffs of provincial governors. The Vindolanda tablets suggest something of the scale of this commitment, with one strength report (*Tab. Vindol.* 1.154) revealing that over 60 percent of the fort garrison was out-posted on detached duty even though the north British frontier must still have been regarded as an active operational theater (Bowman 1994).

To a degree, this participation in the civilian realm served to offset the burden of maintaining the army in its provincial deployments, but nonetheless, the cost to the state remained substantial. Even though the early imperial field strength of some 30 legions (supplemented by auxiliaries in equal numbers) represented a remarkable economy of force, supplying the dispersed network of garrisons in the frontier zones with the necessary resources involved sustained investment. The distribution of wages to the troops caused a significant outflow of bullion from the core to the periphery, only partially offset by the exploitation of new precious metal sources. In fact, it is likely that many coin issues were struck for the purpose of paying troops (see chapter 30, part 2). This transfer of resources had the side effect of stimulating local spending in the areas where the soldiers were based. Even retired soldiers continued to be useful to the state. Although veteran settlements continued to serve a limited security role and to act as nodes of acculturation in under-urbanized

Figure 27.4. City wall at Side incorporating *spolia*, possibly third century A.D. (Photograph by G. Davies.)

areas, less formal arrangements could also be beneficial. When discharged soldiers reentered civilian life, perhaps moving into the *vici* that had grown up outside their old bases or returning to their home villages, a transfer of valuable skills and fresh capital also followed. This gave the former soldier enhanced status among his neighbors and also made future recruitment easier, as the benefits of service were made apparent to all.

In order to fulfill their heavenly mandate to be the rulers of the world, the Romans diligently applied themselves to the arts of war. Their successful mastery of battlefield techniques and their adoption, where appropriate, of equipment and technologies first introduced by their opponents allowed Roman armies to sustain the state over several hundreds of years of challenge and change. For reasons of length, this chapter has focused on the experiences and perspectives of the heavy infantry citizen soldiers, the definitive image of Roman power. As a result, little could be said about the vital role of *auxilia* and their organization and equipage, Roman naval capabilities, the various complex frontier systems, and the centralized production of state-organized *fabricae* manufacturing equipment during the later Empire. Nevertheless, enough has been said to confirm the complexity and sophistication of this technology and its role in establishing and maintaining the Roman imperial system.

# REFERENCES

Bishop, M. C., and J. C. N. Coulston 2006. *Roman military equipment.* 2nd ed. Oxford: Oxbow.

Bowman, A. K. 1994. *Life and letters on the Roman frontier: Vindolanda and its people.* London: Routledge.

Brewer, R. J. (ed.) 2000. *Roman fortresses and their legions.* London: The Society of Antiquaries.

Connolly, P. 1998. *Greece and Rome at war.* 2nd ed. London: Greenhill.

Cornell, T. J. 1995. *The beginnings of Rome.* London: Routledge.

Coulston, J. C. N. 1985. "Roman archery equipment," in M. C. Bishop (ed.), *The production and distribution of Roman military equipment: Proceedings of the Second Roman Military Equipment Research Seminar.* British Archaeological Reports, Intl Series S275. Oxford: BAR, 220–336.

Davies, G. 2000. "Cremna in Pisidia: A re-appraisal of the siege works," *Anatolian Studies* 50: 151–58.

Davies, G. 2006. *Roman siege works.* Stroud: Tempus.

Dixon, K. R., and P. Southern 1992. *The Roman cavalry.* London: Batsford.

Eagle, J. 1989. "Testing *plumbatae*," in C. van Driel-Murray (ed.), *Proceedings of the Fifth Military Equipment Conference.* British Archaeological Reports, Intl. Series S476. Oxford: BAR, 247–53.

Goldsworthy, A.K. 1996. *The Roman army at war, 100 BC–AD 200.* Oxford: Clarendon.

Gregory, S. 1986. "Not 'Why not Playing Cards?' but 'Why Playing Cards in the First Place," in P. Freeman and D. Kennedy, *The Defence of the Roman and Byzantine East.* 2 vols. British Archaeological Reports, Intl. Series S297. Oxford: BAR, 1: 169–75.

Gregory, S. 1996a. *Roman military architecture on the eastern frontier, A.D. 200–600.* 3 vols. Amsterdam: Hakkert.

Gregory, S. 1996b. "Was There an Eastern Origin for the Design of Late Roman fortifications? Some Problems for Research on Forts of Rome's Eastern Frontier," in D. Kennedy (ed.), *The Roman Army in the East.* Journal of Roman Archaeology, Suppl. 18. Ann Arbor: JRA, 169–210.

Gros, P. 1992. "*Moenia*: Aspects défensifs et aspects représentatifs des fortifications," in S. van de Maele and J. M. Fossey (eds.), *Fortificationes antiquae.* McGill University Monographs in Classical Archaeology and History 12. Amsterdam: Gieben, 211–25.

James, S. 2004. *The excavations at Dura-Europos, 1928–1937. Final Report VII: The arms and armour and other military equipment.* London: The British Museum Press.

Johnson, S. 1983. *Late Roman fortifications.* London: Batsford.

Kennedy, D. 2004. *The Roman army in Jordan.* 2nd ed. London: CBRL.

Keppie, L. 1984. *The making of the Roman army.* London: Batsford.

Lander, J. 1984. *Roman stone fortifications: Variations and change from the first century AD to the fourth.* British Archaeological Reports, Intl. Series S206. Oxford: BAR.

Marsden, E. W. 1969. *Greek and Roman artillery: Historical development.* Oxford: Clarendon Press.

Marsden, E. W. 1971. *Greek and Roman artillery: Technical treatises*. Oxford: Clarendon Press.

Mitchell, S., S. Cormack, R. Fursdon, E. Owens, and J. Öztürk 1995. *Cremna in Pisidia: An ancient city in peace and war*. London: Duckworth and The Classical Press of Wales.

Oleson, J. P., G. S. Baker, E. De Bruijn, R. M. Foote, J. Logan, M. B. Reeves, and A. N. Sherwood 2003. "Preliminary report of the al-Humayma Excavation Project, 2000, 2002," *Annual of the Department of Antiquities of Jordan* 47: 37–64.

Parker, S. T. 2000. "Roman legionary fortresses in the East," in Brewer 2000: 121–38.

Parker, S. T. 2006. *The Roman Frontier in Central Jordan: Final Report on the Limes Arabicus Project, 1980–1989*. Princeton: Princeton University Press.

Roth, J. 1995. "The length of the siege of Masada," *Scripta Classica Israelica* 14: 87–110.

Todd, M. 1978. *The walls of Rome*. Totowa, NJ: Rowman and Littlefield.

Tomlin, R. S. O. 2000. "The legions in the late Empire," in Brewer 2000: 159–78.

Welfare, H., and V. Swan 1995. *Roman camps in England: The field archaeology*. London: HMSO.

# PART VII

# TECHNOLOGIES OF THE MIND

# CHAPTER 28

# INFORMATION TECHNOLOGIES: WRITING, BOOK PRODUCTION, AND THE ROLE OF LITERACY

WILLY CLARYSSE

KATELIJN VANDORPE

## THE ARRIVAL OF WRITING

Today, virtually all humans are affected directly daily by technologies of writing, so it is difficult for us to imagine a completely oral society. "We live in a world of visible words" (Small 1997: 3). The invention of writing was a huge step in the development of civilization, because it extended human memory from the brain of single individuals to an external storage medium. Writing provided an artificial memory that could be consulted at any time; seeing replaced hearing as a means of communication and as the means of storing communication (Havelock 1986: 100). Instead of experts who could remember the things of the past, the new experts were able to "decode" the written symbols. In an oral society, versified language played a

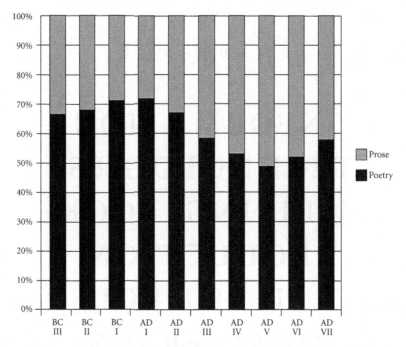

Figure 28.1. Percentage relationship between Greek and Latin texts in prose and poetry found in Egypt, third century B.C. to seventh century A.D.

much larger role because memorization largely depended on the use of rhythm, as Plato realized (*Tht.* 267a).

The earliest Greek literature was written in verse, and this is surely a remnant of the oral society. Identification of the Muses as the "daughters of memory" is linked with the functional use of poetry and music as "storage of cultural information for re-use, the instrument for the establishment of a cultural tradition" (Havelock 1986: 55–56). Greek prose literature starts only in the later fifth century B.C. and takes over from verse in such fields as philosophy, history, and epideictic oratory. The ongoing shift from verse to prose continues even in the later period, as is shown by papyrus documentation from Egypt (figure 28.1). Notwithstanding the continuing popularity of Homer in the school curriculum, prose texts climb from 30 percent of literary papyri in Hellenistic Egypt, to nearly 50 percent in early Byzantine Egypt (for actual totals rather than percentages, see LDAB). In Christian literature, church hymns and psalms take over from lyric and tragic poetry.

Sumerian cuneiform (Green 1981: 345–72) and Egyptian hieroglyphic writing (Dreyer 1998, with corrections by Kahl 2003) both developed at the end of the fourth millennium B.C., no doubt as devices to meet the administrative requirements of an increasingly complex society. It is no accident that the oldest texts are written for the purpose of bookkeeping, both in Sumer and in Egypt: writing came about through economic necessity, not for religious or cultural purposes. Cuneiform writing was developed to record transactions at the temple complex in Uruk, a city with perhaps 50,000 inhabitants, enormous for that period. It was the only way to collect and preserve information on such a large scale. Tokens and seals, which can be considered precursors of writing, were no longer sufficient.

The long-term evolution of writing tended toward an ever closer adaptation of script to sound. Some symbols did remain (most prominently digits, which are in fact multilingual symbols even today), but every new script rendered more closely the spoken word. Consonantal writing perhaps started as early as the Middle Kingdom in the so-called proto-Sinaitic scripts (Daniels and Bright 1996), which wrote Semitic languages with signs derived from Egyptian hieroglyphs. In Ugarit, cuneiform writing was used as the basis for two alphabets around 1200 B.C.; one of them already has the order aleph, bet, gimel (A, B, C). Writing systems based on a consonantal skeleton marking only the long vowels were adapted for several West-Semitic languages (Aramaic, Phoenician); such a system still functions quite well in modern Arabic.

The Greek alphabet was adopted and adapted from the North-Semitic (Phoenician) script. Both the time (first part of the eighth century B.C.?) (Jeffery 1990: 12–21; Powell 1991: 18–20; Harris 1996: 58–59) and place (the southern part of the Aegean, perhaps Rhodes, Cyprus, Crete, or Euboea, or a Greek trade post on the coast of North Syria, such as el-Mina; Jeffery 1990: 5–12; Powell 1991: 12–18; Woodard 1997) are still under discussion. There can be no doubt that Greek literacy started under the impulse of the Near East. Herodotus' well-known statement (5.58) that the Phoenicians brought the alphabet, is confirmed by the names of the letters (acrophonic *a-leph, b-et*, and so forth have a meaning in Semitic, but not in Greek), the order of the alphabet, the shapes of the letters, and the term *phoinikeia* (*grammata*) used in early Greek inscriptions. From the start, the Greek alphabet differed from its model in its use of five signs to denote the vowels. Vowel notation may first have been used within Phoenician for foreign names and then have become generalized in Greek.

The adoption of the Greek alphabet in Italy in the late eighth century B.C. is better documented. The alphabet of the Greek colony Cumae was taken over by the neighboring Etruscans and then quickly by the other peoples of the peninsula. There are about 120 Etruscan texts surviving from seventh-century B.C. Italy, compared with only 10 Latin texts (Cornell 1991: 8). Etruria was not far behind Greece, and the rest of Italy was not more than a generation behind them. Since the Romans came into contact with a local alphabet of the Greeks who lived in the West, the Latin alphabet differs from the classical Greek alphabet in a few details, such as the value of the symbols *X* (*ks* instead of *kh*) and *H* (*h* instead of the vowel eta) and the absence of a symbol for the sound *ps* at the end of the alphabet. In addition, Latin abandoned some letters that it did not need (such as theta and phi) and at a later stage created new ones (Lassère 2005: 34–35).

The earliest texts written in Greek date from the end of the eighth century B.C. They are written on pottery (as on the Dipylon vase) or stone; other materials (such as wax tablets) have not been preserved. The direction of writing was from right to left, as in their Semitic models. The oldest Latin texts, such as the heavily debated Fibula of Praeneste and the Duenos vases, were also written from right to left (Lassère 2005: 34, 81). In seventh-century B.C. Greece, the second line was often written from left to right and the next lines alternated. This *boustrophedon* script, named after the turning of the ox (Greek *bous*) in plowing, was popular in the archaic period and is also attested in some early Latin inscriptions. By the early fifth century B.C. our left to right direction—better suited to the right-handed majority, since the written letters remain visible and ink is not smeared by the hand—was already firmly established, although exceptions are found until the end of the century (Jeffery 1990).

Many of the earliest texts are "speaking objects" (Bodel 2001: 19), often metrical: "I am the cup of Nestor," "[So-and-so] dedicated me." The preserved texts written before 700 B.C. include a price inscription (Dipylon vase), an erotic spell (Nestor's cup), and a dedication (Mantiklos bronze), all three in hexameter form. There are also marks of ownership (personal names) and a maker's name. From the first half of the seventh century B.C., abecedaria (sample alphabets for instruction), funerary inscriptions, and curses are also found. The surveys found in Powell (1991: 119–81) and Thomas (1992: 52–61) are based on the standard work of Jeffery (1990). The city-states start to make use of written laws and lists of officials after 650 B.C. This marks the beginning of public inscriptions, which will become one of the hallmarks of Greco-Roman society. They were first written on wooden boards (Stroud 1979), later on slabs of marble or stones especially prepared for writing, and often set up in a temple precinct. The coloring of the letters in alternating red and blue and the *stoichedon* style, in which the letters are aligned both horizontally and vertically as in a wordsearch puzzle, a style popular in sixth- and fifth-century B.C. Greece, contributed to their monumentality and visibility rather than to their legibility.

Written law, however, did not supersede oral law: it added monumental weight and perhaps religious authority to some special laws that were meant to be read aloud by officials. Oral law continued, and sometimes laws were put in verse so that they could be learned by heart (Camassa 1988). The Cretan scribe Spensithius (called *poinikastas*, referring to the Phoenician origin of the script) was at the same time a *mnemon* (remembrancer; *SEG* 27.631 = Jeffery and Morpurgo-Davies 1970: 118–54; Detienne 1988: 67–70; Ruzé 1988: 83–85). Written law and oral tradition are not exclusive, but interact: archaic writing was in the service of the spoken word.

The diversity of local alphabets in the archaic and classical periods suggests that writing spread quickly, before all the problems of adaptation to Greek had been confronted (Harris 1996: 61). After Athens abandoned its own alphabet in 403 B.C., this diversity made place for a growing unity. From the Hellenistic period onward, Greek writing is remarkably uniform across the circum-Mediterranean world from Afghanistan to southern Italy. The Latin script became diversified again in late antiquity, when monastic scriptoria developed different styles in the provinces.

# WRITING MATERIALS

The variety of writing materials in antiquity may be illustrated by the last dispositions of Augustus: these were written on two (wooden) notebooks (*codices*) and copied onto three papyrus rolls (*volumina*) by the Vestal Virgins. The part recording his personal accomplishments (*res gestae*) was then displayed on bronze tablets in front of Augustus' mausoleum in Rome and on stone monuments in the provinces of the Greek East (Suetonius, *Aug.* 101.1, 4; Ridley 2003). The choice of writing materials was dictated by their availability and by the purpose they were meant to serve: standard materials, usually more perishable, for archival purposes and books, durable surfaces for public display.

Several perishable materials were available (cf. Bouquiaux-Simon et al. 2004). In ancient Egypt, the papyrus plant (Lewis 1974) played the same role as bamboo in the Far East. It was used for ropes, baskets, sandals, roof coverings, small boats, and furniture. The stem could even be eaten, giving the Egyptians the epithet "papyrus eaters" (*papyrophagoi*; Scholion Aeschylus, *Supp.* 761). But above all papyrus was used as a writing material. In Egypt it was cheap (Skeat 1995: 87–90) and remained the most common writing material for all kinds of texts until the arrival of paper around A.D. 900. Elsewhere it had to be imported and was therefore relatively expensive, which made other writing materials more competitive. Nevertheless, papyrus was, in both Greece and Rome, the most common writing surface for longer texts, especially literary works.

Animal skin is attested as a writing material from an early period in Greece and in the Near East (*diphtherai*; Herodotus 5.58). Finds from Dura-Europos at the Euphrates and Afghanistan (ancient Bactria) show that it was in common use in the East in the Hellenistic period. Parchment, a form of untanned leather, is traditionally linked with the royal court of the Attalids at Pergamon in Asia Minor, whence it gets its name (through Latin *charta Pergamena* and French *parchemin*). Parchment is more durable than papyrus but far more expensive to produce. In Egypt it is not found before the early second century A.D., and the oldest example is a Latin text (LDAB 4472). From the fourth century A.D. onward, parchment takes over from papyrus for luxury books in the Mediterranean, but not for ordinary documents. This only happens after the Arabs conquered Egypt (A.D. 650) and overseas import of papyrus became more expensive and difficult.

For everyday documents and archival purposes, thick wooden tablets (Greek *deltoi*; Latin *tabulae, tabellae*), often coated with wax and written on with a *stilus* (figure 28.2), were also commonly used in the Greco-Roman world. The example illustrated is one of five wax tablets forming the schoolbook of Aurelius Antonius, a young boy in Egypt who copied several times a Greek saying of the Athenian orator Isocrates: "For some people honor their friends only when they are present, other people also love them when they are far away." The beech tablet is deepened on both sides and coated with black wax (beeswax mixed with carbon). The Romans in particular preferred to write legal documents of a private and public nature on

Figure 28.2. Wax tablet from schoolbook of Aurelius Antonius, Egypt, fourth century A.D. (Papyrological Institute Leiden inv. V.20 = LDAB 2530.) (Photograph by permission of Papyrological Institute Leiden.)

tablets (Meyer 2004; Marichal 1992a; Lassère 2005: 456–57). Such tablets, usually bundled into booklets of two, three or multiple tablets (diptychs, triptychs, or polyptychs), were, for instance, filed in Rome's state archives and in the Campanian business archives (see below). Roman Britain produced another type of writing material: thin leaf tablets of wood, written on with ink and sometimes bundled into multileaved notebooks, have been excavated at the fort of Vindolanda immediately south of Hadrian's wall (Bowman and Thomas 1983: 32–45; 2003). It is easy to underestimate the importance of wooden tablets in Roman daily life, since only a small fraction of them have survived (Eck 1998).

Ostraka (potsherds) were a cheap alternative as a writing material, giving their name to the Athenian exile procedure called ostracism (Forsdyke 2005). Thousands of ostraka, mainly private letters, accounts, and tax receipts, have been discovered in Greco-Roman Egypt (e.g., Cuvigny 2000), but other regions, such as Bu Njem in modern Libya, have produced numerous examples as well (Marichal 1992b; Lassère 2005: 457–58). Lead was used for magical purposes, but also for letters and even for a record of horses of the Athenian cavalry (Kroll 1977).

More durable surfaces were preferred for public notices. Wooden boards, often whitened (Greek *leukomata*, Latin *alba*), were used extensively for temporary public notices in the Greek and Roman world, while stone and bronze (the latter especially in the Roman world) were meant for long term publicity and as symbolic memorials of important decisions. Only exceptionally were wooden boards used for permanent publication, as, for instance, in archaic Greece for the laws of Draco and Solon (Stroud 1979). Writing was not only used for the dissemination of public documents, but legends or other inscriptions could also accompany and clarify all kinds of objects and monuments, such as tombs, statues, public buildings, milestones, altars, vases (Immerwahr 1990), and even paintings, reliefs, and mosaics (Corbier 1995).

In Greece, "local variations in natural resources and political systems produced very different epigraphic profiles in different cities and regions" (Bodel 2001: 11–12). The importance of inscriptions in classical Athens, for instance, was closely linked to its democratic institutions and was enhanced by the ready supply of marble. An explosion of epigraphic activity in the Roman world is attested from the reign of Augustus onward, when strong, white marble from the Apuan Alps north of Pisa was shipped to Rome; "whether or not Augustus purposefully set out to reshape the epigraphic landscape, the example he set at the capital for acceptable forms of public display established a pattern and a set of standards that quickly spread throughout Italy and the western provinces" (Bodel 2001: 7). The Roman epigraphic habit during the first and second centuries seems to be typical of urbanized and militarized areas where individuals wanted to assert their status in a complex and changing society (Woolf 1998).

# Roll and Codex

Bookrolls were made of papyrus, rarely of parchment (Bouquiaux-Simon et al. 2004). For the production of papyrus sheets, the triangular stem of *Cyperus papyrus L.* was peeled and the stem was cut in thin slices, which were put side by side on a wooden board; a second row was placed over the first at 90 degrees. Some 20 or 40 such double thickness sheets (*kollemata*) formed a roll (see Pliny, *HN* 13.68–72, 74, 77, 81, 89). The dimensions of the sheets varied, but 30 cm was a normal height for a roll (figure 28.3). On the inside surface (recto) the papyrus fibers ran horizontally, along with the length of the roll, and the sheet-joins were vertical; on the outside (verso) both the papyrus fibers and the sheet-joins ran vertically. The sheet-joins (*kolleseis*) are usually 15–20 cm apart. In order to protect the roll, an extra leaf called *protokollon* (literally "first sheet") was provided. The difference between recto and verso is visible not only through the sheet-joins, however; the recto is also more polished, because writing always starts on that side. The verso, originally on the outside of the roll, was only used after the original text on the inside surface was no longer needed.

Since the Old Kingdom, Egyptian papyrus rolls (*tomoi* in Greek, *volumina* in Latin) were written, or rather painted with a brush, in successive columns (*selides* in Greek, *paginae* in Latin) side by side from top to bottom of a scroll oriented sideways. Since the Greeks wrote from left to right they just turned the rolls 180 degrees so that the reed pen (*kalamos*) still went "downhill" over the sheet joins, but they continued to write in columns (figure 28.4). Only in the Byzantine period

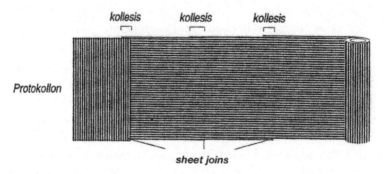

Figure 28.3. Diagram of the construction of a papyrus roll.

are some rolls written *transversa charta*, in a single column from top to bottom oriented the long way, as in medieval rolls (*rotuli*) in the West.

A standard roll of 20 sheets, measuring 320–360 cm (Skeat 1982), could contain only a limited amount of text, for instance, one play of Euripides. Multiple lengths were frequent, especially doubles, with some reaching up to 15 and 20 m (Johnson 2004: 143–52). Since very long rolls were cumbersome to manipulate, the scholars of the Alexandrian Museum cut up longer texts, such as Homer, into sections of approximately the same length, which we still call "books." Later authors spontaneously divided their works into similar "books," adapting themselves to the constraints of the medium. Bookrolls are attested from about 3000 B.C., and they

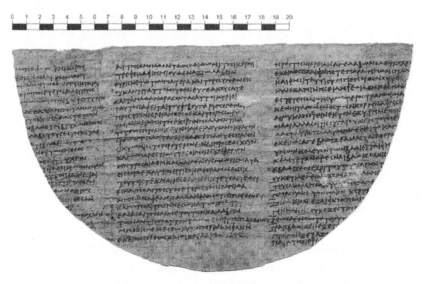

Figure 28.4. Late-third-century B.C. papyrus from Egypt containing fragment of Menander, *Sikyonios*, copied by a professional scribe. It was later used as secondhand paper in mummy cartonnage. Papyrus Sorbonne inv. 2272b = LDAB 2738. (Photograph by J. Gascou, by permission.)

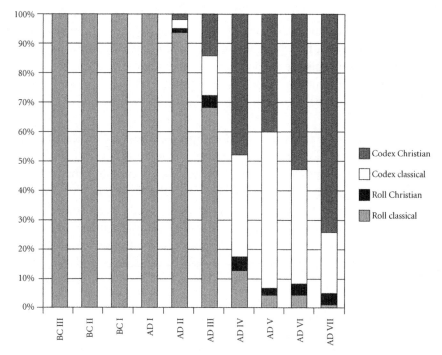

Figure 28.5.  Percentage relationship of codex and roll in Greek and Latin books found in Egypt, third century B.C. to the seventh century A.D.

were still used in the sixth century A.D. for administrative purposes as well as for literature. In order to facilitate the unrolling, a stick called a "navel" (Greek *omphalos*, Latin *umbilicus*) could be attached to the roll.

From the second century A.D. onward a new means of uniting longer texts became common: the book consisting of pages that are turned over rather than unrolled. The origin of the modern book, the *codex*, is the wooden notebook already known to the Assyrians. In Rome, a new type of notebook made from parchment (*membranae*) but modeled on the *codex* design, spread to literary texts. The new format had distinct advantages: both sides of the pages were now used from the start, saving space, and the book was easier to handle, transport, and consult. It took several centuries before the codex definitely superseded the roll. Clearly the habits of the Christians played a decisive part in this change: whereas in the second and third centuries most classical authors were still copied on rolls, Christian texts, especially the New Testament, were codices from the start. The Bible may have been considered a form of a handbook rather than a literary work, or the use of the codex may reflect some opposition to the Torah (still written on rolls today), or perhaps the conservative reflex just did not affect this new kind of book (figure 28.5). The scaled (percentage) graph illustrates the disappearance of the roll in the fourth century for Greek and Latin texts found in Egypt, and the absence of rolls for Christian literature.

The codex also allowed for easier and more precise referencing within a work. In the early fourth century A.D., Eusebius of Caesarea divided the gospels into short numbered paragraphs, which he used for concordances between parallel passages. Numbered columns are already found in the Herculaneum rolls, but pagination is much more common in codices. In any case, before the printing press was invented each book remained an individual copy, and pagination could not be used for reference.

It took some time before the new book form completely distanced itself from the scroll: the pages of the oldest papyrus codices were simply cut from rolls and were not yet divided into quires. Single-quire codices of more than 100 pages (25 folded sheets), however, are quite common in the third and fourth centuries (Turner 1977: 58). When the book is open, narrow columns, two and even three to the page, give the same panoramic view as a roll. The titles of a work in a bookroll came at the end, since it was up to the next reader to roll the book back to the beginning, and this habit continued for some time in the codex format as well.

## BOOK PRODUCTION AND BOOK TRADE

To us, ancient books seem notoriously unfriendly to the reader. Words were not separated, there were no capital letters and hardly any punctuation to mark a new beginning, no paragraphs or indents. Each column was an unbroken block of letters. Until the third century B.C., even poetry was written in continuous lines, as in the papyrus of the *Persae* of Timotheus (LDAB 4123). This *scriptio continua* is in fact a step backward from the Semitic alphabets, which distinguished words with spaces or dots, as do some of early Greek inscriptions and many Latin inscriptions. Changes of speaker in a dialogue were marked with a *paragraphos*-stroke at the beginning of the line, but the reader had to guess at the names of the speakers. Aesthetic motives apparently took priority over practical considerations, as the literary script imitated inscriptions. Accents and punctuation were gradually added, but sparingly, and word division was only introduced with minuscule writing in the ninth century A.D. Although reading Greek or Latin was, of course, far easier for native speakers than it is for us, the deficient layout certainly slowed down the reading of long or complicated texts. It also made word searches almost impossible. In fact, many texts were written down primarily to be read aloud by a reader or as mnemonic aids for a well-known text, whether it was the *Iliad* or the Bible. In documentary papyri, retrieving texts and adding figures is often facilitated by the layout.

The beginning of the book trade goes back to the late fifth century B.C. (Bouquiaux-Simon et al. 2004). Socrates tells us how the works of Anaxagoras could be bought at the marketplace for one drachma (Xenophon, *Ap.* 26d), Xenophon gives a description of ships full of books (*bibloi gegrammenai*) run aground in the Black Sea, wrecked and plundered by the Thracians (*An.* 7.5.14), and Aristophanes mocks the new habit of "reading books for the sake of instruction" (*Ran.* 1114). Since no copyright existed, anybody could copy and sell any work, nor was there any quality control outside the private copies made directly from the original (for instance in the philosophical schools).

This situation changed thanks partly to the founding of the famous library of Alexandria and the philological work in the Museum. Whereas in the third century B.C. copies of Homer are widely divergent, with verses added and omitted at random, the later texts become standardized; even the uniform verse numbering is the same as in modern editions. The new science of philology, based on careful copying of authoritative models, was taken over by the Christians, whose bibles present very few deviations from the norm. Of course, not all editions were perfect, and there was a great distinction between school books and the deluxe copies of the rich. In Rome, commercial reproduction by well-organized publishing firms could put a new book on the market in hundreds of copies in a few days time. Purchasers sometimes checked several copies in order to obtain a correct text. Martial (1.117) gives us an entertaining description of a bookshop in Rome: "Next to the Forum is a bookshop, where both doors are plastered with advertisements. These display the titles of the books in stock, and you need only cast a glance at the list. Go in and ask for my book. The owner—his name is Atrectus—will be extremely pleased to get a fine copy of Martial out of his first or second shelf and let you have it for five denarii."

# LIBRARIES

The oldest collections of books are attributed to the tyrants Polycrates of Samos and Pisistratus of Athens—the latter is even said to have opened his library to the public. Euripides also owned a private library. Aristotle's library, partly captured by Sulla, was the first to be systematically arranged (Casson 2001: 17–30). It was a model for the great libraries of Alexandria and Rome and had an enormous influence on the development of scholarship. Unlike Plato, who preferred oral discussion to the bookish accumulation of knowledge, Aristotle's encyclopedic type of scholarship was only possible with the help of an extensive collection of books. In the Hellenistic period large, semipublic libraries were sponsored by the eastern Mediterranean kings, most famously that in Alexandria, which for the first time attempted at being complete and formed the basis of Alexandrian scholarship (Casson 2001: 31–47; Bagnall 2006, with a warning against overestimation of its size). Here the best manuscripts were compared and the first commentaries and critical editions of texts were made. Roman nobles owned extensive libraries, of which only that of L. Calpurnius Piso, the father-in-law of Caesar, has partially survived in Herculaneum (1,800 charred scrolls). It was housed in a small room with shelves around the walls and a reading table in the middle. But in Rome and in the provinces many libraries were available to the public (28 in Rome alone at the time of Constantine; *Curiosum*, Appendix). Most libraries were designed for reading on the premises, but in some borrowing was possible (Casson 2001: 107–8, 161). Literary culture had indeed become one of the hallmarks of Greco-Roman civilization; its retreat within the walls of palaces and monasteries contributed to the new civilization of late antiquity.

With the barbarian invasions in the fifth century, literacy retreated in the western empire, while at the same time the wealth of inscriptions dried up in the cities of the east, and even in Egypt the number of papyri temporarily dwindled. But simultaneously literacy was on the rise, since natives started writing their own languages in a Greek alphabet (Coptic and Gothic) or with renewed vigor (Syriac). In religious matters, books suddenly became of prime importance. Whereas the pagan rites and myths were handed on by word of mouth and only very partially written down, the new religions, Christianity, Manichaeism, and later Islam, were "religions of the book," in which God communicated with this world through sacred scriptures. Christ himself, although he never seems to have written anything down, is represented in the apse of the churches with a codex Bible in his hands. Bible texts were copied for magic, read aloud in the church, learned by heart, and endlessly commented on by theologians. Believers split along religious lines (gnostics, Arians, orthodox, monophysites) according to the books they read or the interpretations they gave to them. This religious divide became one of the main problems of the early Byzantine Empire.

# Record-keeping

A discussion of record-keeping in antiquity may focus on various points of interest (compare Brosius 2003 and Nicolet 1994). Public and temple records are usually kept in or near buildings of officials or institutions in charge of them; even public records may be kept under the custody of gods. The writing material determined the arrangement of the records (wooden tablets were stored and labeled in a different way from papyrus rolls) and the construction of the archive rooms (Mesopotamian clay tablets had to be stored in rooms with the proper humidity to avoid crumbling). The classification systems used by the Greeks and Romans were gradually refined as the public archives increased in number, became more complex, and had to cope with falsifications and fraud. Roman Egypt developed an efficient system of archiving public and even private records. The availability of public records is an elementary part of modern archiving, but it is not always attested for ancient archives. Records on stone or bronze were not only meant for publishing or publicizing, but were also authoritative. For us they often form the only traces of the original records.

Our knowledge of techniques of record-making and record-keeping in the Greco-Roman world is scanty. Whereas the remains of several archival depositories have survived from the ancient Near East and the Minoan and Mycenaean world, the practice of archiving in Greece and Rome is only known when recorded on stone or bronze, or when referred to in literary works. Occasional building remains (such as the Athenian Metroon and the Roman Tabularium) or seals attached to archival records and baked by fire (e.g., in the Selinunte temple, Zoppi 1996, and in a Delian house, Boussac 1996) witness Greco-Roman record-keeping. Apart from some find spots such as Vindolanda in Roman Britain, Greco-Roman Egypt is the main exception. Here large groups of state and temple records have been uncovered in ancient dumps or through the antiquities market (Vandorpe 2009), but in general even Egypt has produced only a few archival establishments with their holdings. Some carbonized papyrus rolls were discovered in the ruins of the Roman record-office (*bibliotheke*) in Thmouis, the capital of the Mendesian *nome*, set on fire by furious taxpayers (Kambitsis 1985).

Notwithstanding the scarcity of archival records, the importance of Greek record-keeping may be clearly seen from the terms *arche* (magistracy) and *archeion* (office of the chief magistrates where public records could be kept), which have become internationally accepted archival terms in the Western world. This should not surprise us, since the polis "gave rise to a novel type of political life and government that could not fail to have a decisive bearing on archival organization and service" (Posner 1972: 91). Whereas the earlier palace civilizations mainly filed simple administrative records, the Greek democratic institutions and offices gave rise to numerous decrees, laws, and so forth, which were to be classified in the magistrates' or state archives. Record-keeping became even more complex when Greek cities made registration (*anagraphe*) and validation of private transactions obligatory, so that not only public but also private records had to be kept.

Very soon the Greeks realized the importance of written records for democracy: Aristotle regarded official archives as indispensable for his model state (*Politica* 6.1321B.34) and Euripides (*Supplices* 430–38) contrasts tyranny and democracy by comparing the availability of written laws: "Where the tyrant is, there are no common laws, but one man rules, in whose keeping and in his alone the law resides; so is equality no more. But when the laws are written down, the weak and the wealthy have equal justice and it is open to the weaker to use the same language to the prosperous when he is reviled by him, and the weaker prevails over the stronger if he has justice on his side."

Heavily debated is the Metroon or state archive of Athens (Posner 1972; Pritchett 1996: 14–36). When the enlarged Boule or Council became the supreme board by the reforms of Clisthenes in 509/8 B.C., its archive became the most important one, and its records were probably housed in a new building on the agora known as the Old Bouleuterion. This building was at the same time the meeting place for the newly organized board and the record office of documents needed by the board (Shear 1995; for a radical revision of the archaeological evidence, see Miller 1995). The alternative suggestion that the fifth-century B.C. Council relied on memory and oral communication, and that stone inscriptions served in some way as an official archive (Thomas 1989 and 1992) has been called into doubt (Sickinger 1994a; Pritchett 1996; Shear 1995: 186). Near the end of the fifth century a New Bouleuterion was constructed nearby. The old Council chamber was replaced by the Metroon, the sanctuary of the Mother of the Gods, which sheltered the growing number of records under the goddess's custody (Munn 2006: 330–32). The Metroon, often referred to as the "public archive" (*demosion*), played an important role in the storage of public documents (Georgoudi 1988). On a more optimistic view, it was a kind of central archive, where the Athenians gradually entered ancient public records and systematically filed new ones (Shear 1995). In the period when the Metroon was erected, a committee of "establishers of the laws" (*nomothetai*) was elected, who could undoubtedly find their working material in the new building (Munn 2006: 331).

The state archive holdings in the Metroon could be consulted not only by Council members, but also by litigants and other interested parties, for instance for research purposes (Posner 1972: 113; Sickinger 2004). The layout of the original building is unclear, as it was overbuilt by a Hellenistic Metroon in the second century B.C. (Miller 1995: 142; Shear 1995: 158). Here the archives probably occupied two of the four rooms.

The original records in Greek cities were written on perishable materials: wooden tablets, papyrus rolls (Sickinger 1994a: 295; Shear 1995: 186, 188), or even parchment in cities of Asia Minor when a security copy was needed. Wooden tablets were probably useful for records that had to be consulted regularly or had to be supplemented. It is unclear how the records were arranged. As suggested by Posner (1972: 112), wooden tablets may have been stored in jars. The enormous jar of the Metroon in which Diogenes the Cynic took up residence may have been such a storage jar. Records on papyrus may have been kept in niches comparable to those in contemporary library buildings. Undoubtedly, the date and the category to which a document belonged played a crucial role in the classification; catalogues are nowhere mentioned, but public slaves probably served as finding aids (Sickinger 2004: 103–4).

Alongside oral dissemination of decrees and laws "essential to democracy" (Thomas 1989: 61–68; 1992), state records could be published, although this did not happen systematically. Proposals and decisions might be temporarily displayed in public on wooden boards, for instance fixed on the base of the statues of the eponymous heroes in the agora (Thomas 1989: 62). Possibly these wooden boards were afterward entered in the archival depository so that they functioned twice: "exposées pour quelques jours à la vue de tous, afin de s'acquitter de leur mission informative, elles gagneraient ensuite leur dépôt" (Georgoudi 1988: 236). From the end of the sixth century B.C. onward, state documents that were considered important might be published on stone, serving a more permanent purpose (Sickinger

1994a: 2004). Some types of documents were even entrusted to bronze (Sickinger 2004: 100). The inscriptions were set up in the vicinity of places where the inscribed documents had particular relevance. Some inscriptions contained less detailed information than the original records (Sickinger 1994a). Nevertheless, the stone copies were for the Greeks as valid and authoritative as the originals; they could be consulted or quoted instead of the archival records. The Greeks did not know the "modern concept of a single, authoritative version of a particular document" (Sickinger 1994b: 277), although they clearly distinguished between the original decrees (*psephismata auta*) and their copy (*antigraphon*) (Shear 1995: 187). The symbolic value often attributed to inscriptions does not rule out their practical value (Sickinger 2002: 154–55).

In the Hellenistic period, a selection of inscribed public documents could constitute an archive on its own, as the texts were "picked out by the community (or responsible authority) to create and broadcast a particular theme and message." In an "inscriptional archive," like that displayed on the *anta* of the temple of Athena Polias, the people of Priene decided, after a period of hostilities, to bring together and publicize those records that established its entitlement to rights obtained in the past (Sherwin-White 1985: 74–80).

The Greek temples were also important centers of record-keeping. Like state institutions, they used wooden tablets or papyrus for their records and published part of them on stone. Their inscribed inventories, as for instance at the temple of Apollo at Delos, informed the city council and the gods about precious temple objects, but were at the same time symbols showing the wealth of a temple (Linders 1988; Thomas 1992: 86–87). The mobile archives of the *naopoioi*, responsible for the rebuilding of Apollo's temple at Delphi in the fourth century B.C., deserve special mention; their records were stored in wooden cases, which were carried by paid porters, from the seat of the officials to the workshop and vice versa, on the days when contracts and accounts were to be verified (Georgoudi 1988: 235–36).

The Athenian Metroon had counterparts in Rome in the Aerarium and Tabularium. The Aerarium, housed in the temple of Saturn at the foot of the Capitoline Hill, was foremost the repository of the state treasury. It was established in the early Republic and was for a long time run by the young and inexperienced quaestors, the consuls' financial assistants, until eventually, under Nero, more experienced prefects were put in charge (Millar 1964; Corbier 1974). Understandably, financial records pertaining to the treasury were kept at the Aerarium as well. At a later stage, nonfinancial documents such as copies of laws (*leges*) and senatorial decrees (*senatus consulta*) were also deposited in there. In 78 B.C., after a fire on the Capitoline Hill, a new archives building, the Tabularium, was constructed as an annex to Saturn's temple, presumably to store the increasing number of records. It was an impressive monument with a protected staircase leading traffic from the Forum to the Capitoline Hill. In what remains, no rooms really suitable for record-keeping were found; perhaps these were located on the second floor, which has not survived (Culham 1989: 101–2).

The Aerarium and annex-Tabularium cannot be considered a central archive in Republican times (compare the radical view of Culham 1989). The record-keeping of senatorial decrees (*senatus consulta*) may clarify this point (Talbert 1984 and Coudry 1994, who also discuss the *acta senatus*, records of the proceedings in the senate). Senatorial decrees were copied for a first time in the records (Greek: *deltoi*) of the consuls, undoubtedly kept by these magistrates as part of their private journals (*commentarii*) and taken home with them after their term of office. These could be consulted as long as the consuls lived and are considered to have played a key role in keeping a record of senatorial decrees, "un système complexe où les catégories du public et du privé se distinguent mal" (Coudry 1994).

But senatorial decrees became valid only after deposition (*delatio*) in the Aera-rium, "une formalité juridique . . . une opération marginale" (Coudry 1994: 94). The reason for deposition may be the belief that a document became effective only after it had been filed under the guardianship of a god, in this case Saturn (Culham 1989). Whatever the motive, a second copy was kept in the quaestorial records of the Aerarium (Greek: *deltoi demosioi tamieutikoi*), in the form of diptychs (two tablets hinged together, producing four pages). Both consular and quaestorial records were classified by year (named after the consuls or quaestors in charge) and within a year, by month; the records of each month were subsequently numbered. The diptychs were referred to by this number and by the page of the little book. Undoubtedly, these tablets took up much more space than papyrus documents. The approximately 12,500 characters of the senatorial decree recording the judicial proceedings against Piso under Tiberius discovered on bronzes (see below), were copied by the emperor's quaestor on fourteen tablets (*tabulae*), probably written on both sides and undoubtedly bundled into one booklet (Eck et al. 1996).

Probably no public access was provided to these essential state records of the Aerarium; only persons holding a magistracy could consult them. In addition, the record-keeping in the late Republic Aerarium stood in bad repute: records were not easily accessible and some were even falsified or destroyed (Culham 1989; Coudry 1994: 67, 71; Moreau 1994). Mark Antony, for instance, apparently deposited sen-atorial decrees that had never been voted (Cicero, *Phil.* 5.12). As they served for only a short term, the inexperienced quaestors had to rely on their subordinates, public servants (*apparitores*) who became the "real magistrates" (Plutarch, *Cat. Min.* 16.3). Cicero (*Leg.* 2.46) complained about the poor service: "We have no custody of the laws and therefore they are whatever the *apparitores* want them to be; we have to ask the copies from them, but we have no memory confided to the public records." As a quaestor, Cato the Younger tried to improve the situation.

The public archive of the Aerarium was slow in developing, partly because there were good alternatives for consulting, for instance, the Senate decrees (Posner 1972; Culham 1989; Coudry 1994). Apart from the consular records mentioned above, the plebeians started early in the Republic to deposit in the temple of Ceres both their own laws (*plebiscita*) and their own copies of Senate decrees which "were wont to be suppressed or falsified" (Livy 3.55.13). This archival depository was abolished by Augustus in 11 B.C. Finally, private record-keeping was well developed: Romans entered their transactions in their daybooks (*adversaria*) and at the end of the month made a summary in the register of receipts and expenditures (*tabulae* or *codex accepti et expensi*) (Thilo 1980). Rich households stored their records in a separate room called a *tablinum*; among these, privately purchased copies of public documents could be kept (Williamson 1987: 164).

Even though the Republican Aerarium did not function as a central archive, there was "un archivage très complet des documents issus du Sénat . . . , constatation qui va à l'encontre de l'idée courante selon laquelle la République aurait souffert d'une sorte de sous-administration" (Coudry 1994), but the role of the men of status in this system should not be underrated, as they were present as witnesses at all stages of the process of record-making (Williamson 1995) and had easy access to the public records.

Augustus tried to make the public archive of the Aerarium more efficient by redefining the tasks of the quaestors; probably in view of these reforms, the archive in the temple of Ceres was abolished (Coudry 1994: 67, 74). Subsequently, the public records at the Aerarium were no longer neglected. The records (*tabulae*), books (*libri*), and accounts (*rationes*) probably had to be written down (*scribere*) and classified (*ordinare*), and the responsible magistrates had to swear that there was no falsification or fraud (Coudry 1994: 75). As the Senate's powers diminished, an imperial archive developed composed of a private archive (*sacrarium, secretarium*), an accounts section of the imperial household (*tabularium castrense*), an imperial tabularium, and the chanceries called *ab epistulis, a libellis*, and *a memoria*.

How were public records given publicity in Rome? As the rate of literacy was relatively low, proclamation was important: heralds read laws and important decrees aloud in public meetings. In addition, some information, such as the praetor's annual edict and lists of prices, was temporarily posted in a visible place on whitened wooden boards (*alba*) (Eck 1998). Finally, important statutes, international treaties, and decrees could be published in bronze in Rome or even in provincial cities. After Cn. Calpurnius Piso, accused of the murder by poison of Germanicus and of other serious political offences, was condemned, the Senate ordered its resolution to be displayed on bronze in Rome in whatever place seemed best to Tiberius and likewise "in the most frequented city of each province and in the most frequented place in that city," and "in the winter quarters of each legion where the standards are kept." The Spanish province Baetica produced at least six bronze copies of this senatorial resolution (Eck et al. 1996; Griffin 1997; Damon and Takács 1999).

Like the Greek copies on stone, these bronze copies were authoritative, and legal copies could be made from them, like military diplomas that had been verified from the bronzes in Rome. The choice of the "eternal" bronze for permanent display was due to the absence of stone suitable for engraving in Rome's early days. Even when marble became common during the Empire, Romans stuck to their old traditions (Williamson 1987: 179); they had always linked bronze tablets to the notion of inviolability. Bronze tablets are part of a divine context: these "objects for or belonging to and therefore protected by the gods" are sacrosanct (Williamson 1987). In the western provinces, the habit of posting decisions on bronze was taken over, whereas the Greek cities in the East remained faithful to the medium with which they were familiar and displayed them on stone.

The most famous bronze collection was displayed on the Capitoline Hill, Rome's ritual center in front of Jupiter's temple. The bronze versions are sometimes considered an archive constituted cumulatively and accessible to every Roman citizen. State documents, however, were not systematically entrusted to bronze. In addition, the bronze copies were hard to read, even for literate individuals, because of both the juridical jargon and the cramped lettering. Therefore, the bronze tablets should not be considered as an archival collection meant to be consulted. They rather serve another purpose: "they ceremonially reinforce Roman greatness," already embodied on the Capitoline Hill (Williamson 1987). In contrast, display on stone is attested, for instance, for priestly records: the yearly *acta* (minutes of the proceedings) of the Arval Brethren, were, over a period of more than 250 years, inscribed on marble tablets at their headquarters in the grove of the Dea Dia shrine near Rome (Scheid 1990, 1994; Bodel 2001: 20).

For Roman provincial record-keeping we may turn to Roman Egypt (Cockle 1984; Burkhalter 1990), where the Romans built on an existing system of public record-keeping. This Roman province had "an extremely detailed system of archiving public and private documents, which seems to have been used to the full" (Cockle 1984), organized from the lowest administrative levels up to the central services in Alexandria and able to cope with falsification and fraud.

The public papyrus records, such as tax returns and census lists generated by the village scribes, were transferred, through the intermediary level of the toparchy, to the *nome* capital, where the officials in charge (the *strategos* and royal scribe) deposited them into the central "record office of public documents" (*bibliotheke demosion logon*). The archive keepers, often former gymnasiarchs, were responsible for their conservation and classification; they were not allowed to alter, add or delete anything in the texts. They gathered related documents, ordered them chronologically or alphabetically (for first-letter alphabetical order, see Verhoogt 1998: 215) and pasted them together into rolls (*tomoi sunkollesimoi*; the pasting of papyrus documents is already attested for official texts in Hellenistic Egypt, Clarysse 2003). These rolls were provided with a general title referring to the document type, such as "declaration by house." These rolls were subsequently classified into sections referring to the *nome strategos* in charge, the document type, the year, and the village. The records could be consulted on a regular basis by, for instance, the assistants of the provincial governor or of the *nome strategos*, or by litigants. Record offices in the *nome* capitals kept copies, as the original documents were sent to the *Patrika* record office in Alexandria.

A second *bibliotheke* in the *nome metropolis*, which split off from the public record office just mentioned in A.D. 72, was the "record office of landed property" (*bibliotheke ton enkteseon*). Here private persons registered their holdings in order to have their rights as owners or creditors guaranteed officially. Only declarations of property addressed to this record office, no title deeds, were kept in this *bibliotheke*; on the basis of these, the archive keepers drew up survey sheets (*dia-*

*stromata*) recording the owners with their properties. The holders of property within the *nome* were entered, in alphabetical order, by their place of origin; each owner took up one or more papyrus sheets (*kollema[ta]*) of a roll on which their holdings were classified by village and by category. The rolls as well as the papyrus sheets were referred to by numbers.

Further record offices are attested in Alexandria under the supervision of the *archidikastes*, the chief justice or "master of rolls." The *Patrika*, named after an Alexandrian quarter, housed the original public documents from all over Egypt. In addition, private documents were centrally registered in the capital: after entering the register of the *katalogeion*, they were deposited in the *bibliotheke* of the Nanaion, the temple of Isis Nanaia. After the creation of the temple of the divine Hadrian (Hadrianeion), the original documents were kept and protected in this new deposit registry, and duplicates could be consulted in the Nanaion.

Record-keeping techniques are also attested for some private archives, which are, as a rule, less complex than their public counterparts. Business archives of third-century B.C. Egypt have a registration system for letters showing that the documents were systematically arranged according to date and contents (Vandorpe 2009). Egypt was not alone in developing record keeping. A house on Delos that sheltered a large number of sealed papyrus records when it was destroyed by fire in 69 B.C., produced thousands of baked seals that allow the basic classification system to be reconstructed. The businessman entered documents by category and by client (Boussac 1996). Some Campanian archives of sealed waxed tablets furnish evidence for Italy (Andreau 1999: 71–79; Marichal 1992a; Meyer 2004). The first-century A.D. archive of the Sulpicii, a firm of financiers from Puteoli, for instance, consists of waxed tablets bound together in booklets (diptychs or triptychs). A summary is sometimes added either on one of the unwaxed outside tablets or on the spines of the booklets, or even on both (Camodeca 1999: 31–36).

# LITERACY

A person is illiterate who "cannot with understanding both read and write a short simple statement on his everyday life" (UNESCO 1977: 12). In antiquity, as now, elementary forms of reading (Greek *anagignoskein* = to recognize the letters) may well have been more widespread than the art of writing (Greek *graphein* = to scratch), and many writers were able just to scratch their name and not much more (for such a "signature literate," see figure 28.6). Statistics of ancient literacy rates can therefore be misleading.

Because of the difficulty of the Bronze Age cuneiform and hieroglyphic writing systems, each with hundreds of signs, partly phonetic and partly symbolic (ideo-

Figure 28.6. *Libellus* of the Decian persecution (A.D. 250), illustrating the difference between the hand of a professional scribe and the clumsy signature of one of the members of the commission. John Rylands Library inv. 112a and b = V. Martin et. al. (eds.), *Catalogue of the Greek and Latin Papyri in the John Rylands Library, Manchester,* Vol 2, *Documents of the Ptolemaic and Roman Periods* (Manchester: Manchester University Press, 1915), nos. 112 b and c. (Reproduced courtesy of the University Librarian and Director, the John Rylands University Library, The University of Manchester.)

grams and determinatives), writing and reading was mastered only by a small professional class of scribes, a typical feature of the cultures of this period. The introduction of the alphabet made it far easier to master the arts of reading and writing and no doubt resulted in a far higher literacy rate, although it is hardly possible to work out percentages. According to Harris (1989) only a minority of adult males (less than 10% in classical Greece, maximum 30% in imperial Rome) could read and write; mass literacy was thus never achieved in classical times. This does not, however, preclude the possibility that writing could penetrate deeply into the lives of ordinary people: Egyptian peasants who could neither read nor write carefully kept the potsherds with Greek tax receipts as proof that their salt tax or dyke tax was paid.

Even if only 10 percent of the male population could write in the Greco-Roman world, this was ten times more than in the Ancient Near East, where literacy was in fact limited to a small class of specialists. In Greece, writing was used from the start for private notices, graffiti, and everyday messages between individuals. When the community took hold of the new technology, it was applied for codifying laws and became a powerful political instrument. In Athens, the political implications were already used to the full at the end of the sixth century, when leading politicians could be banned for ten years by a negative naming or vote made on potsherds, known as ostracism (Forsdyke 2005). Thousands of such ostraka have been found (Martin 1989), but they constitute only a small percentage of what was written. Even if not every person was literate, this system implies a high degree of basic literacy among the male citizen population. Illiteracy carried no stigma, but being able to read and write was both practical in dealings with the government and a sign of prestige (Hopkins 1991). Although literates were still a minority, the Roman Empire later was bound together by writing, from an administrative, economic, and cultural point of view.

The spread of literacy became possible when education was no longer private and oriented toward physical development, music, and poetry, but became collective and based also on the teaching of letters. The "teacher of letters" (*grammatistes*) gradually became a "teacher" (*didaskalos*). Herodotus (6.27.2) refers to a school in Chios in 494 B.C. in which 119 children were killed by a collapsing roof. In Hellenistic Miletus and Teos, schools for freeborn boys and even girls were sponsored by a wealthy citizen, and clearly the children of citizens were expected to attend daily courses (*SIG* 2.577–78; cf. *SEG* 30 [1980] no. 1535.24–28, for Xanthus in Lycia) (Marrou 1965: 78–93, 218–42). The Ptolemies subsidized Greek education by exempting schoolteachers from the salt tax, and the ratio of teachers to male children of the whole population (including Egyptians) is as high as 1:165. This statistic confirms Marrou's optimistic view of widespread diffusion of Greek education in the Egyptian countryside, against Harris' more pessimistic view (Clarysse and Thompson 2006: 125–33). In Hellenistic and Roman Egypt, girls of the upper strata of society also received some degree of education, and even women teachers are not unknown (Cribiore 2001: 74–101). Literacy did not diminish in the early Byzantine period, as is shown by the numerous school texts (Cribiore 1996). Although the monastic movement prided itself on simplicity and even illiteracy, Pachomius' monastic rules explicitly stipulate that illiterate persons should be taught to read, in order to learn the sacred scriptures by heart.

Orality and literacy are indeed not opposites, but orality continued to hold a strong position throughout antiquity. Thus Plato's dialogues, masterpieces of written literature, explicitly proclaim the primacy of living discussion over the static written word. The dialogue genre is not only used for philosophical discussions, but even for biography and history, as in Thucydides' dialogue of the Melians. At school, Homer and Demosthenes were not only copied, but also learned by heart by generations of pupils; similarly the monks used the books in the monastic library to learn by heart the gospels and psalms: the written word is in the service of the spoken word. Ancient poets, orators, and even historians would give declamations of their works to a friendly audience before publishing it in written form, and oratory in general, like drama, could only be fully appreciated through performance.

# REFERENCES

Andreau, J. 1999. *Banking and business in the Roman world*. Cambridge: Cambridge University Press.

Bagnall, R. S. 2006. *Hellenistic and Roman Egypt: Sources and approaches*. Aldershot-Burlington: Ashgate.

Bodel, J. 2001. *Epigraphic evidence: Ancient history from inscriptions*. London: Routledge.

Bouquiaux-Simon, O., M.-H. Marganne, W. Clarysse, K. Vandorpe, and J.-C. Didderen 2004. *Les livres dans le monde gréco-romain*. Liège: Editions de l'Université de Liège.

Boussac, M.-F., 1996. "Étude statistique d'un dépôt d'archives à Délos," in M.-F. Boussac and A. Invernizzi (eds.), *Archives et sceaux du monde hellénistique. Bulletin de correspondance hellénique* Suppl. 29. Athènes: École française d'Athènes, 511–23.

Bowman, A. K., and J. D. Thomas 1983. *Vindolanda: The Latin writing-tablets*. London: Society for the Promotion of Roman Studies.

Bowman, A. K., and J. D. Thomas 2003. *The Vindolanda writing-tablets: Tabulae Vindolandenses II*. London: British Museum Press.

Brosius, M. (ed.) 2003. *Ancient archives and archival traditions: Concepts of record-keeping in the ancient world*. Oxford: Oxford University Press.

Burkhalter, F. 1990. "Archives locales et archives centrales en Égypte romaine," *Chiron* 20: 191–215.

Camassa, G. 1988. "Aux origines de la codification écrite des lois en Grèce," in Detienne 1988: 130–55.

Camodeca, G. 1999. *Tabulae Pompeianae Sulpiciorum (TPSulp.): Edizione critica dell'archivio puteolano dei Sulpicii*. 2 vols. Rome: Quasar.

Casson, L. 2001. *Libraries in the ancient world*. New Haven: Yale University Press.

Clarysse, W. 2003. "Tomoi Synkollesimoi," in Brosius 2003: 344–39.

Clarysse, W., and D. J. Thompson 2006. *Counting the people in Hellenistic Egypt*. 2 vols. Cambridge: Cambridge University Press.

Cockle, W. E. H. 1984. "State archives in Graeco-Roman Egypt from 30 B.C. to the reign of Septimius Severus," *Journal of Egyptian Archaeology* 70: 106–22.

Corbier, M. 1974. *L'aerarium Saturni et l'aerarium militare: Administration et prosopographie sénatoriale*. Collection de l'école française de Rome 24. Rome: École française de Rome.

Corbier, M. 1995. "L'écriture dans l'image," in Solin and Salomies 1995: 113–61.

Cornell, T. J. 1991. "The tyranny of evidence: A discussion of the possible uses of literacy in Etruria and Latium in the archaic age," in M. Beard, A. K. Bowman, and M. Corbier (eds.), *Literacy in the Roman world. Journal of Roman Archaeology* Suppl. 3. Ann Arbor: University of Michigan Press: 133–58.

Coudry, M. 1994. "Sénatus-consultes et acta senatus: rédaction, conservation et archivage des documents émanant du sénat, de l'époque de César à celle des Sévères," in Demougin 1994: 65–102.

Cribiore, R. 1996. *Writing, teachers, and students in Graeco-Roman Egypt*. Atlanta, GA: Scholars Press.

Cribiore, R. 2001. *Gymnastics of the mind. Greek education in Hellenistic and Roman Egypt.* Princeton: Princeton University Press.

Culham, P. 1989. "Archives and alternatives in Republican Rome," *Classical Philology* 84: 100–15.

Cuvigny, H. 2000. *Mons Claudianus: Ostraca graeca et latina. III. Les reçus pour avances à la "familia."* Cairo: Institut français d'archéologie orientale du Caire.

Damon, C., and A. S. Takács (eds.). 1999. "The Senatus Consultum de Cn. Pisone patre: Text, translation, discussion," *American Journal of Philology* 120: 1–162.

Daniels, P. T., and W. Bright 1996. *The world's writing systems.* Oxford: Oxford University Press.

Demougin, S. (ed.) 1994, *La mémoire perdue: À la recherche des archives oubliées, publiques et privées, de la Rome antique.* Série Histoire ancienne et médiévale 30. Paris: Publications de la Sorbonne.

Detienne, M. 1988. *Les savoirs de l'écriture en Grèce ancienne.* Lille: Presses Universitaires.

Dreyer, G. 1998. *Umm el-Qaab I: Das predynastische Königsgrab U-j und seine frühen Schriftzeugnisse.* Mainz: von Zabern.

Eck, W. 1998. "Inschriften auf Holz. Ein unterschätztes Phänomen der epigraphischen Kultur Roms," in P. Kneissl and V. Losemann (eds.). *Imperium Romanum: Studien zu Geschichte und Rezeption.* Stuttgart: Steiner, 203–17.

Eck, W., A. Caballos, and F. Fernández 1996. *Das Senatus Consultum de Cn. Pisone patre.* Munich: Beck.

Forsdyke, S. 2005. *Exile, ostracism, and democracy: The politics of expulsion in ancient Greece.* Princeton: Princeton University Press.

Georgoudi, S. 1988. "Manières d'archivage et archives de cités," in Detienne 1998: 221–47.

Green, M. W. 1981. "The construction and implementation of the cuneiform writing system," *Visible Language* 15: 345–72.

Griffin, M. 1997. "The Senate's story," *Journal of Roman Studies* 87: 249–63.

Harris, W. V. 1989. *Ancient literacy.* Cambridge, MA: Harvard University Press.

Harris, W. V. 1996. "Writing and literacy in the archaic Greek city," in Strubbe, Thybout, and Versnel 1996: 416–23.

Havelock, E. A. 1986. *The muse learns to write: Reflections on orality and literacy from antiquity to the present.* New Haven: Yale University Press.

Hopkins, K. 1991. "Conquest by book," in M. Beard, A. K. Bowman, and M. Corbier (eds.), *Literacy in the Roman world. Journal of Roman Archaeology* Suppl. 3. Ann Arbor, MI: University of Michigan Press, 133–58.

Jeffery, L. H. 1990. *The local scripts of archaic Greece.* Rev. by A. W. Johnston. Oxford: Clarendon Press.

Jeffery, L. H., and A. Morpurgo-Davies 1970. "*Poinikastas* and *poinikazein*," *Kadmos* 9: 118–54.

Johnson, W. A. 2004. *Bookrolls and scribes in Oxyrhynchus.* Toronto: University of Toronto Press.

Immerwahr, H. R. 1990. *Attic script: A survey.* Oxford: Clarendon.

Kahl, J. 2003. "Die frühen Schriftzeugnisse aus dem Grab U-j in Umm el-Qaab," *Chronique d'Égypte* 78: 112–35.

Kambitsis, S. 1985. *Le Papyrus Thmouis 1, colonnes 68–160.* Paris: Publications de la Sorbonne.

Kroll, J. H. 1977. "An archive of the Athenian cavalry," *Hesperia* 46: 83–140.

Lassère, J.-M. 2005. *Manuel d'épigraphie romaine.* Paris: Picard.

LDAB = *Leuven Database of Ancient Books.* Available on line: http://ldab.arts.kuleuven.be.

Lewis, N. 1974. *Papyrus in classical antiquity.* Oxford: Clarendon Press.

Linders, T. 1988. "The purpose of inventories," in D. Knoepfler (ed.), *Comptes et inventaires dans la cité grecque: Actes du colloque international d'épigraphie tenu à Neuchâtel du 23 au 26 septembre 1986 en l'honneur de Jacques Treheux.* Neuchâtel: Université de Neuchâtel. Faculté des lettres, 37–47.

Marichal, R. 1992a. "Les tablettes à écrire dans le monde romain," in E. Lalou, *Les tablettes à écrire de l'Antiquité à l'époque moderne.* Turnhout: Brepols.

Marichal, R. 1992b. *Les ostraca de Bu Njem.* Tripoli: Jamahira Arabe libyenne populaire socialiste.

Marrou, H.-I. 1965. *Histoire de l'éducation dans l'Antiquité*, rev. ed. Paris: Editions du Seuil.

Martin, A. 1989. "L'ostracisme athénien," *Revue des Études Grecques* 102: 124–45.

Meyer, E. A. 2004. *Legitimacy and law in the Roman world: Tabulae in Roman belief and practice.* Cambridge: Cambridge University Press.

Millar, F. 1964. "The Aerarium and its officials under the Empire," *Journal of Roman Studies* 54: 33–40.

Miller, S. G. 1995. "Old Metroon and old Bouleuterion in the classical agora of Athens," in M. H. Hansen, K. A. Raaflaub (eds.), *Studies in the ancient Greek polis.* Stuttgart: Steiner, 133–56.

Moreau, P. 1994. "La mémoire fragile: Falsification et destruction des documents publics au Ier s. av. J.-C," in Demougin 1994: 121–47.

Munn, M. H. 2006. *The Mother of the Gods, Athens, and the tyranny of Asia: A study of sovereignty in ancient religion.* Berkeley: University of California press.

Nicolet, C. 1994. "A la recherche des archives oubliées: Une contribution à l'histoire de la bureaucratie romaine," in Demougin 1994: v–xvii.

Posner, E. 1972. *Archives in the ancient world.* Cambridge, MA: Harvard University Press.

Powell, B. B. 1991. *Homer and the origin of the Greek alphabet.* Cambridge: Cambridge University Press.

Pritchett, W. K. 1996. *Greek archives, cults and topography.* Amsterdam: Gieben.

Ridley, R. T. 2003. *The emperor's retrospect: Augustus' Res gestae in epigraphy, historiography and commentary.* Leuven: Peeters.

Ruzé, F. 1988. "Aux débuts de l'écriture politique: Le pouvoir de l'écrit dans la cité," in Detienne 1988: 82–94.

Scheid, J. 1990. *Romulus et ses frères: Le collège des frères arvales, modèle du culte public dans la Rome des empereurs.* Bibliothèque des écoles françaises d'Athènes et de Rome 275. Rome: École française de Rome.

Scheid, J. 1994. "Les archives de la piété: Réflexions sur les livres sacerdotaux," in Demougin 1994: 173–85.

Shear, T. L. 1995. "Bouleuterion, Metroon, and the archives at Athens," in M. Hansen and K. Raaflaub (eds.), *Studies in the ancient Greek polis.* Stuttgart: Steiner: 157–90.

Sherwin-White, S. M. 1985. "Ancient archives: The Edict of Alexander to Priene, A reappraisal," *Journal of Hellenic Studies* 105: 69–89.

Sickinger, J. P. 1994a. "Inscriptions and archives in classical Athens," *Historia* 43: 286–96.

Sickinger, J. P. 1994b. "Review of R. Thomas, *Literacy and orality in ancient Greece.* Cambridge: Cambridge University Press, 1992," *Classical Philology* 89: 273–78.

Sickinger, J. P. 2002. "Literacy, orality, and legislative procedure in classical Athens," in I. Worthington and J. M. Foley (eds.), *Epea and grammata: Oral and written communication in ancient Greece. Mnemosyne* Suppl. 230. Leiden: Brill, 147–69.

Sickinger, J. P. 2004. "The Laws of Athens: Publication, preservation, consultation," in E. M. Harris, L. Rubinstein (eds.), *The law and the courts in ancient Greece*. London: Duckworth, 93–109.

Skeat, T. C. 1982. "The length of the standard papyrus roll and the cost-advantage of the codex," *Zeitschrift für Papyrologie und Epigraphik* 45: 169–76.

Skeat, T. C. 1995. "Was papyrus regarded as 'cheap' or 'expensive' in the ancient world?" *Aegyptus* 75: 75–93.

Small, J. P. 1997. *Wax tablets of the mind: Cognitive studies of memory and literacy in classical antiquity*. London: Routledge.

Solin, H., and O. Salomies (eds.) 1995. *Acta colloquii epigraphici latini*. Societas scientiarum Fennica. Commentationes humanarum litterarum 104. Helsinki: Academia scientiarum Fennica.

Stroud, R. S. 1979. *The Axones and Kurbeis of Drakon and Solon*. Berkeley: University of California Press.

Strubbe, J. H. M., R. A. Tybout, and H. S. Versnel (eds.) 1996. *Energeia: Studies on ancient history and epigraphy presented to H. W. Pleket*. Amsterdam: Gieben.

Talbert, R. J. A. 1984. *The Senate of imperial Rome*. Princeton: Princeton University Press.

Thilo, R. M. 1980. *Der Codex accepti et expensi im römischen Recht: Ein Beitrag zur Lehre von der Litteralobligation*. Göttingen: Muster-Schmidt.

Thomas, R. 1989. *Oral tradition and written record in classical Athens*. Cambridge: Cambridge University Press.

Thomas, R. 1992. *Literacy and orality in ancient Greece*. Cambridge: Cambridge University Press.

Turner, E. 1977. *The typology of the early codex*. Philadelphia: University of Pennsylvania Press.

UNESCO 1977. *Statistics of educational attainment and illiteracy, 1945–74*. Statistical Reports and Studies 22. Paris: UNESCO.

Vandorpe, K. 2009. "Archives and dossiers," pp. 216–55 in R. S. Bagnall (ed.), *Oxford handbook of papyrology*. New York: Oxford University Press.

Verhoogt, A. M. F. W. 1998. *Menches, Komogrammateus of Kerkeosiris: The doings and dealings of a village scribe in the late Ptolemaic period (120–110 B.C.)*. Leiden: Brill.

Williamson, C. 1987. "Monuments of bronze: Roman legal documents on bronze tablets," *Classical Antiquity* 6: 160–83.

Williamson, C. 1995. "The display of law and archival practice in Rome," in Solin and Salomies 1995, 239–51.

Woodard, R. D. 1997. *Greek writing from Knossos to Homer: A linguistic interpretation of the origin of the Greek alphabet and the continuity of ancient Greek literacy*. Oxford: Oxford University Press.

Woolf, G. 1998. "Monumental writing and the expansion of Roman society in the early Empire," *Journal of Roman Studies* 86: 22–39.

Zoppi, C. 1996. "Le cretule di Selinunte," in M.-F. Boussac and A. Invernizzi (eds.), *Archives et sceaux du monde hellénistique. Bulletin de correspondance hellénique* Suppl. 29. Athènes: École française d'Athènes, 327–40.

CHAPTER 29

......................................................................................

# TIMEKEEPING

......................................................................................

## ROBERT HANNAH

## TOWARD A SOCIOLOGY OF TIME

......................................................................................

For most of the thirty years that followed the publication of Sharon Gibbs' still fundamental *Greek and Roman Sundials* (1976), work on the early technology of timekeeping remained predominantly descriptive. Indeed, Turner commented in 1993 that the history of this technology could only just then start to rise above the level of description to questions of synthesis and interpretation (Turner 1993: ix–xi); this process has been slow. In related domains, such as the organization and division of time, or the representation of time, a shift had already been made from essential, but basic, data collection to studies of the philosophy, psychology, and sociology of time. This progress grew from a century of work on a social anthropology of time, starting with the research of scholars like Durkheim (1915) and Evans-Pritchard (1940). Nilsson (1920) to a degree represented a classicist's contribution to this new development, although his study tended still to be more descriptive than conceptually analytical. The period between the 1950s and the 1970s then witnessed a particularly rich maturation of this initial growth in what may be termed the study of "social time." Social anthropologists turned sociologists, such as Goody (1968) and Bourdieu (1990), increasingly problematized and theorized this notion of social time, in the process extending the scope of research from so-called primitive societies to their own western cultures. By the end of the twentieth century, Gell (1992) could successfully synthesize almost a hundred years of ethnographic and sociological work on time among modern societies.

But it was only from the mid-1980s that we have witnessed the proliferation of studies on the sociology of Greek and Roman time. Zerubavel (1985), with his investigation of the week in antiquity, was a pioneer. Since then, increasing numbers of researchers have displayed an interest in the social constructs of time as evinced by the literature, documentary texts, art and philosophy of the Greeks and Romans (e.g., Hannah 1986a, 1986b, 1989, 1993a, 1993b, 1997; Bettini 1991: Rüpke 1995; Dohrn-van Rossum 1996; Csapo and Miller 1998; Turetzky 1998; Darbo-Peschanski 2000; Rossiter and Suksi 2003). Yet the perceptions of time encapsulated in the mechanisms created to measure it generally escaped scholarly interest until early in the twenty-first century. Indicative of a shift in attitude has been the treatment given to the discovery of the most significant addition to Gibbs' corpus, the physical remains of the *horologium Augusti* in Rome. The excavator's detailed, if controversial, discussion of the scientific aspects of this sundial (Buchner 1982, 1993–1994; cf. Schütz 1990) was very soon accompanied by cultural readings of the monument (Wallace-Hadrill 1987; Beck 1994). Turner (1990) and Lippincott (1999) also showed the way, but because both are exhibition catalogues, they still necessarily depend on a taxonomy of time instruments and thereby maintain an artificial separation of these devices from their broader social contexts. The instruments of timekeeping are becoming less ends in themselves and more gateways into the ancient *mentalité* about time. This trend is worth pursuing, as it is the instruments themselves that are most likely to tell us what ordinary people thought on a daily basis about time.

# Natural Cycles of Time

The needs of the human body—for food, relief, sleep—provide the simplest marker of the passage of time. This is as true today as it was in the ancient world, however much we allow technology to order our days and so to control these basic demands. The story of how the Greeks and Romans learned to measure time can seem to be a history of the gradual distancing of people from nature, of their "denaturization" (Turner 1990: 20). The development of sundials and similar means of dividing the day and year into artificial segments can be paralleled by the development of calendars that achieve the same purpose and effects. Yet in both instances the abstraction from natural measures of time never creates a complete divorce. Underneath the complexities of built timepieces such as the Tower of the Winds in Hellenistic Athens or of temporal constructs such as the Julian calendar in late Republican Rome lie still visible vestiges of the natural cycles and phenomena from which they ultimately derived.

Underlying most of the ancient means of keeping time is the use of the celestial bodies—the sun, the moon, and the stars—either directly through observation or indirectly through calculated schemata based originally on observation, to enable people to track their lives and activities from day to day, month to month, year to year. Societies privileged the dawn and evening observations of celestial bodies, no doubt because these were the pivotal periods when people shifted from daytime activities to those of nighttime or vice versa (Goody 1968: 32). Even the political world could be subservient to this very simple, natural mechanism. The Assembly in classical Athens, for instance, began its regular meetings at sunrise (Aristophanes, *Ach.* 19–20), and the Roman Senate would usually meet after sunrise and cease business by sunset, to judge from the fact that decrees passed outside those times were deemed invalid (Aulus Gellius, *NA* 14.7.8).

The stars observed at sunrise and sunset provided a useful sequence of first and last visible risings and settings. Our earliest certain indications of the Greeks using this timekeeping method occur around 750–700 B.C., when Homer and Hesiod embedded such star lore in poems of quite different types, but with the same purpose: to indicate times of the year significant for agriculture or seafaring. Other seasonal indicators could also be used to triangulate the proper time for agricultural activity, such the migration of birds (Hannah 2005: 20–22). Hesiod mentions just ten observations of the risings, settings, or culmination of five stars or star groups. While this may seem a very small number of observations over a year, it has rightly been pointed out that Hesiod's economical set of data still provides a functional safety net of observations over the crucial parts of the agricultural year, from sowing to reaping (Reiche 1989). It has been argued that astronomical observations were used even earlier, in the Late Bronze Age, particularly in Crete, where it has been proposed that some buildings were oriented toward solar or stellar phenomena on the horizon (Henriksson and Blomberg 1996, 1997–1998; Blomberg and Henriksson 2003). But while the orientations seem convincing, in the absence of decipherable, contemporary documentary evidence it is difficult to see what purpose they served.

# PARAPEGMATA

Hesiod's data may have derived from a dedicated astronomical poem—an *Astronomica* was attributed to him—and it would be interesting to know how this compared with Egyptian and Babylonian texts, which are earlier, more extensive, and more systematized than what Hesiod gives us (Belmonte 2003; Parker 1974; Hunger and Pingree 1989). In the Near East, we have a sense of real star "calendars" into which events could be slotted. We have nothing of this sort in Greece until the fifth century B.C. This type of calendar—perhaps better called an almanac— appears in the form of an instrument called a *parapegma*. Its invention is connected with two Athenians, Meton and Euctemon, and some of the leading astronomers of the classical period were involved in its further refinement, notably Eudoxus and Callippus. Excerpts from these *parapegmata* were included in later literary compilations. In addition, fragmentary examples have been discovered in public urban contexts across the Mediterranean, most dating to the Hellenistic period (Lehoux

2000, 2007). Technologically, they are very simple instruments; surviving examples consist of sets of inscribed stone tablets, on which someone (it is odd that we do not know who) had to move a peg manually one day after another throughout the year, through a series of 365 holes. Alongside some of the holes were chiseled the star observations for the day (Hannah 2001b: 76–79, 2005: 59–61; Taub 2003: 20–27).

How the observations were made, and with what instrumentation beyond the naked eye, we do not know. Meton's teacher, a metic called Phaeinus, observed the solstices from Mount Lycabettus in Athens ([Theophrastus], *Sign.* 4), while Meton himself (fl. 432 B.C.) set up *stelai* and recorded the solstices (Aelian, *VH* 10.7). Meton also erected an instrument called a *heliotropion* on the Pnyx in Athens (scholiast on Aristophanes, *Av.* 997). The very name of this instrument suggests that it had something to do with the solar tropics of the solstices. Since astronomical observations were regularly oriented to the horizon at this time, the *heliotropion* is likely to have been a device aligned to an horizon rising or setting point, rather than a sundial casting the shadow of a noon sun, and perhaps it pinpointed the place of the solstices rather than assisted in discovering their time, which may already have been a "given" from Babylonian astronomy (Hannah 2005: 52–54; Bowen and Goldstein 1988). It is remarkable that the rising of the summer solstice sun, when seen from the Pnyx, occurs near the peak of Lycabettus, so natural topographical features might have assisted in the alignment of the *heliotropion*.

There is a good deal of evidence for the *parapegma* of Euctemon (fl. 432 B.C.), as it was one of the most popular star almanacs used in later times. The most extensive quotation appears in the collection of *parapegmata* attached to the first-century B.C. *Eisagoge* of Geminus. There, the observations from Euctemon's and others' *parapegmata* are arranged under the artificial signs of the zodiac (i.e., under solar months), recording that on the *n*th day of the sun's passage through a given zodiacal sign, this star or that rose or set at dawn or dusk, and occasionally coincided with certain weather conditions. This organization probably postdates Euctemon by a century or more, since artificial zodiacal signs of 30 degrees are not attested in Greek texts before the third century B.C., while he himself arguably arranged the observations simply according to the number of days between them (Bowen and Goldstein 1991; Hannah 2002). We can extract from this compilation the observations associated only with Euctemon, and so gain a "text" which reflects part, if not all, of the original. Overall, this text gives a greatly increased number of observations over Hesiod's—42 observations of 15 stars or star groups—together with notices of the solstices and equinoxes. Even the points in between, which are nowadays termed "quarter days," can be found, serving as markers for significant farming activity across the end of one season and the start of another (Hannah 2005: 59–70).

The accumulation of so many star observations was not dependant upon literacy, since oral societies also engaged in such activity. Nevertheless, writing probably enabled the Greeks to decontextualize these data and to place them in other quite abstract contexts, such as *parapegmata*, which in turn enabled them to discover more precise temporal relationships between these phenomena and the cycle of the sun, and indeed to understand that cycle much better (Hannah 2001a).

Others further up the chain of interpretation, so to speak, were helped by the *parapegmata* to organize their activities in time with the seasonal year. Columella (*Rust.* 9.14.12) refers explicitly to the star calendars of Meton and other astronomers being adapted to public (religious) festivals. A papyrus from Hibeh in Egypt (*P Hib.* 27), dating to about 300 B.C., preserves a festival calendar for the temple of Neith at Sais, which lists various religious festivals alongside astronomical and meteorological observations. The astronomical observations in this case were derived from the *parapegma* of Eudoxus, who worked a generation after Euctemon, and were structured within a scheme of 12 zodiacal months and then further worked into the native Egyptian calendar.

# THE ANTIKYTHERA MECHANISM

Although the development of the lunisolar calendars of the Greeks and of the subsequent Julian calendar of the Romans is extremely important in the history of timekeeping as a whole, it demonstrates little further technological dependency, except perhaps in the matter of correcting the leap-year error that was embedded with the initial adoption of the Julian calendar in Rome (Buxton and Hannah 2005). Further calendaric development is therefore not the subject of this study in any detail (see further Hannah 2005; Blackburn and Holford-Strevens 1999: 669–76, 712–16). Nonetheless, it is worth noting the invention in the fifth century B.C., in both Greece and Persia, of the 19-year "Metonic" cycle to help synchronize the otherwise incommensurate lunar and solar cycles, because this overarching cycle is incorporated into one of the most intriguing timekeeping instruments to have survived antiquity. This is the so-called Antikythera Mechanism, a highly sophisticated geared instrument recovered from a shipwreck off the coast of the Aegean island of Antikythera in 1900 and dating at the latest to the mid-first century B.C. (Price 1974; Zeeman 1986; Bromley 1986). This unique artifact has been the object of renewed critical study in the past twenty years or so, culminating in a physical reconstruction based on a mixture of autopsy of the badly corroded mechanism and educated conjecture (figure 29.1), and in a better understanding of the complex gearing (without the need, it may be noted, for a differential geared train, which had been previously assumed and yet was otherwise unique from antiquity). The instrument managed to correlate, in an ingenious system of geared wheels, the motions certainly of the sun and the moon, and arguably of the five planets known to antiquity, in epicyclic motion through the zodiac, all timed against the Egyptian calendar and a *parapegma* (Bromley 1990; Wright 2002, 2003a, 2003b, 2004, 2005a, 2005b, 2005c, 2005d, 2006a, 2006b). New reflectance imaging techniques and high-resolution X-ray tomography have begun to provide new information, indicating that the instrument could also be used to compute eclipses (Freeth et al. 2006).

Figure 29.1. Reconstruction of the Antikythera Mechanism by Michael Wright. (Photograph by M. Wright.)

There is evidence within the mechanism that it was a composite, cannibalizing parts of older devices, and thereby suggesting the existence of other similarly elaborate astronomical instruments (Wright 2006b). This device affords us a glimpse of the class of sophisticated instruments that replicated the motions of the celestial bodies and were so admired in antiquity, such as Archimedes' sphere (Cicero, *Rep.* 1.14.21–22).

We do not know for what purpose the Antikythera Mechanism was devised. It was originally identified as a "calendar computer" (Price 1974), and it has often subsequently been misinterpreted as a navigational aid, simply because it was recovered from a shipwreck. It is probably better termed a planetarium, which offered the facility to measure time in terms of both the Egyptian calendar on the front of the dial and of the Callippic lunisolar cycle of 76 years (four Metonic cycles less a day) on the back, a combined system used later by Ptolemy in the *Almagest*. Indeed, correlations with local civil, lunar calendars of the Greek world may also have been possible, particularly if those calendars were still aligned with the moon, as now seems proven (Wright 2005b; Buxton and Hannah 2005: 302). The *parapegma*—if that indeed is the appropriate term for the attached star-observation list—seems to be one of a kind, corresponding in its details to no single example known. Eclipse recording or forecasting are also likely functions, but to what specific end is not yet clear. Banal though it may now seem for so complex an instrument, horoscopal astrology has been suggested as one of its possible functions, since it would permit the rapid calculation of the positions of all the major planetary bodies essential to ancient astrology, positions which are recorded with a remarkable degree of accuracy in surviving tables from the imperial Roman period (Neugebauer 1941–1943: 209–50; cf. Neugebauer and Parker 1969: 225–35).

Certainly *parapegmata* were associated with forecasting, although of weather rather than other events. Astrometeorology had a long history throughout antiquity (Taub 2003: 15–69), and indeed it has been proposed that before the first century B.C. the Greeks were interested not so much in measuring time per se as in observing the orderly sequences of "omen events" such as star-rise and star-set, equinoxes and solstices, on which the sequences of agriculture and religion relied (Price 1975). This argument is attractive, but some caution is warranted: "omen-events" need careful definition, if we are not to do an injustice to the *parapegmata*, some of which (particularly the early Greek ones) expend much more space on pure fixed-star phase prediction than they do on the meteorological forecasts that might be read as a causal result of those star phases. The cultural context of astrometeorology in both the Near East and Greek worlds is now being given serious attention (Rochberg 2004; Taub 2001, 2003; Lehoux 2000, 2007).

# Sundials

The risings and settings of stars have a very long history as a timekeeping method, continuous from the Babylonian period to the Middle Ages. By the latter period, Christian monks were using the stars to signal the hours for prayer at night (McCluskey 1998). It is apparent from the remains of the *horologium Augusti*, where notice is preserved of the Etesian Winds, that the astrometeorological lore of the *parapegmata* not only persisted into the period of the Julian calendar, but also could be incorporated into sundial technology.

The shadow-casting *gnomon* may have found its way into Greece just before 500 B.C., when it is associated with the philosopher Anaximander (Diogenes Laertius 2.1). Herodotus (2.109) seems to refer to it later in the fifth century, saying that the Greeks gained knowledge of the *polos* and *gnomon* as well as the 12-part division of the day from the Babylonians (Lloyd 1988: 34–36). While there is nothing to suggest that it was used by ordinary people at that stage (Gibbs 1976: 6–7), nevertheless the use made by Greek comic playwrights from the late fifth century B.C. of the idea of reckoning the time for a meal by gauging the length of a person's shadow (Aristophanes, *Eccl.* 651–52; Athenaeus, 1.8b–c, 6.243a) demonstrates a familiarity with the principle underlying the *gnomon*. How sophisticated this human sundial was in reality is unclear. Although fixed shadow lengths throughout the year would lead to a variable time for the same meal, this may well have suited people's biological clocks, since the length of the day varied throughout the year, and meals would literally have been movable feasts. The moment it was decided that a fixed hour should serve for mealtimes, or for any other activity, a tension was created between people's physical needs and mechanical demands. This is the point behind the complaints against sundials as slave drivers retailed by Aulus Gellius (*NA* 3.3.4–5) and Alciphron (3.1) in the second century A.D., both of whom rely on a comic *topos* of at least three hundred years' vintage and so demonstrate the longevity of the issue.

At some stage, a type of sundial was developed that showed the passage of the shadow of the *gnomon* into each of the 12 zodiacal signs in the course of a year. A liberal reading of Vitruvius' attribution to Eudoxus of a type of sundial called the *arachne* (spider's web) (*De arch.* 9.8.1) has been seen as a reference to the zodiacal sundial and so has placed its invention in the fourth century B.C. (Ardaillon 1900: 257; Rehm 1913: 2418–19), but this interpretation is misguided. Although the *arachne* may well have derived its name from a weblike network of hour and season lines across its face (Gibbs 1976: 60–61), it is quite possible that the first dials to show the sun moving through the zodiac were much simpler, similar to a dial found on Chios dating perhaps to the second century B.C. (Hunt 1940–1945: 41–42). This is just a small, flat north–south meridian line, with the summer and winter solstices marked, together with the divisions between the zodiacal signs. If, on the other hand, the term *arachne* is correctly understood, and its association with Eudoxus reasonably founded, then it demonstrates the increased refinement of the divisions of the month and day that pertained by the fourth century B.C.

It is easy to imagine how helpful the basic meridian type of sundial would have been in marking out the passage of the seasons through the year, and even of dividing the year into smaller manageable chunks, the 12 zodiacal months. But how useful would it be on a day to day basis? Unfortunately, at the latitude of Athens in Greece (38° N), the shadow measured by even a human-sized *gnomon* changes only a little from day to day, too little to help in the distinction of one day from the next, the more so if the *gnomon* is even smaller in scale (the Chian dial may have had one only 72 cm in height). Such a sundial might be useful only over longer periods of several days or a month, if the events being timed by the dial are spaced well apart in the year. Still, the movement of the sun across the sky *in the course of the day* offered a better opportunity to organize events *within* the day, and we can see other sundials taking much more advantage of this feature.

The earliest surviving Greek sundial, dating to the third century B.C., comes from the small site of Delos, where 25 dials have been excavated. Another 35 have been unearthed in the town of Pompeii. Between them, the two sites demonstrate the popularity of the instrument from the Hellenistic period into the Roman Empire. The principal kinds of sundial available to the Greeks and Romans were the hemispherical, the cylindrical, the conical, and the planar. The hemispherical type of sundial was the most labor-intensive and difficult to construct, as it entailed carving out an even hemisphere of stone. But it was also the simplest to mark out, because it captured the celestial dome on a matching concave surface. Its *gnomon* hung out over the hollow hemisphere (figure 29.2). The conical type, with the related but much less common cylindrical form, was a variation on the hemispherical, representing a simpler, partial hollowing out of the stone block. At least

Figure 29.2. Spherical sundial, from Aphrodisias, Selçuk Archaeological Museum no. 375. (Photograph by R. Hannah.)

in the surviving archaeological record, it is easily the most popular type. This may occasion some surprise, given the apparent complexity of its theory and the greater difficulties in marking out the requisite interior lines, as these are now projected on to an awkwardly shaped curved surface, but it is likely that the conical was much easier to construct out of stone (the preferred material) than the hemispherical type, while its theoretical underpinning was kept to a minimum—and indeed probably not understood by many of the makers, to judge by their inaccuracies (Gibbs 1976: 17, 74–75). The ubiquity of such sundials in both the Greek and Roman worlds is well captured in a quip, attributed to the Roman emperor Trajan early in the second century A.D., that makes a real dial of the human face (*Anthologia Palatina* 11.418): "If you put your nose facing the sun and open your mouth wide, you'll show all the passersby the time of day."

The flat-plane type of sundial, which occurs in both horizontal and vertical forms (figure 29.3), is the easiest to construct but the most difficult to mark out. The difficulty arises from the projection of the hemispherical dome of the sky on to a completely flat surface. A shadow tracking the movement of the sun through the year is cast by a *gnomon* which is usually stuck perpendicularly into the flat surface of the sundial. Vitruvius (*De arch.* 9.7) provides an analemma for the dial's construction, which is now well understood despite the awkwardness of his text, and extendable to a variety of dial types (Drecker 1925: 3–4; Evans 1999: 247–51).

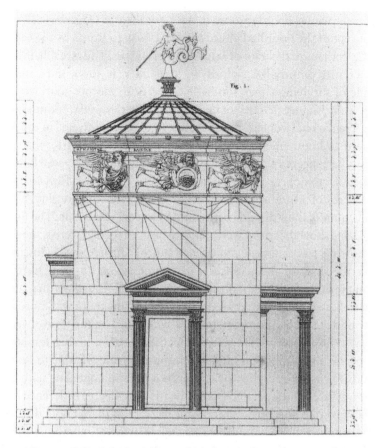

Figure 29.3. Tower of the Winds, Athens, elevation. (After J. Stuart and N. Revett, *The Antiquities of Athens* [London: Priestley and Weale, 1825], vol. 1, pl. 14, fig. 1.)

# HOURS

Sundials helped inculcate into society the concept of the seasonal, or unequal, hour. For most purposes in antiquity, such hours were the norm. From Egypt came the notion that each day or night could be divided into 12 hours from sunrise to sunset, and another 12 from sunset to sunrise (Parker 1974: 53; Quirke 2001: 42). Since daytime and nighttime change in length with the seasons, the length of each hour therefore changed also according to the season. Only at the spring and autumn equinoxes were the hours equal through the whole day. This gives us what is called the "equinoctial" hour, which we are used to because mechanical clocks and hourglasses have required them since their invention in the Middle Ages. But only astronomers tended to use them in antiquity, as can be seen in the Hibeh Papyrus (*P Hib.* 27) of about 300 B.C., where they are subdivided down to $\frac{1}{45}$th of an hour.

The shorter winter hour crops up in a joke in Plautus (*Pseud.* 1304), indicating that the concept of the hour had already made its way to Rome by the early second century B.C., perhaps in the train of actual Greek sundials. The rarer "half-hour" first appears in a fourth century B.C. comedy by Menander (fr. 1015), and is inscribed on just a couple of surviving Greek sundials (Gibbs 1976: 226 no. 3007, 239 no. 3020; 1979: 45, fig. 4). In his instructions for making sundials, Cetius Faventinus in the third century A.D. remarked (ironically to us moderns) that people were "in too much of a hurry to want to know more than what hour it is" (Pattenden 1979: 204, 207–8). Nonetheless, the concept of the half-hour was already sufficiently well known in the first century A.D. to appear in Christian apocalyptic literature (Rev. 8:1).

The accuracy of a sundial can be checked for its particular locality, because the solstice and equinox lines should correspond to a specific latitude. The lines on the dials from Delos show that most were made to be used there, whereas the dials from Pompeii show far less accuracy and do not suit its latitude well. This inaccuracy means that the days of the solstices and equinoxes in Pompeii were wrongly marked. On the other hand, the daily hour lines on Pompeian dials do match reality reasonably well, so it may be that among the Pompeians there was more emphasis on the time of day and on business *within each day* than on the time of year (Gibbs 1976: 90–92). Pliny's story (*HN* 7.214) of earlier Romans living for 99 years in ignorance of the inaccuracy of a sundial transported from Catania to Rome in 263 B.C. depends for its force on the dial's engraved lines not agreeing with the hours (*horas*) appropriate for Rome. Yet, ironically, the four-degree difference in latitude between the two cities affects the hours of the day far less than it does the days of the year: in the summer there would be a negligible error of 0.07 hours in the day, whereas the gnomon's shadow in Rome would never have fallen on the dial's summer solstice line, and would have fallen on the winter solstice line twice (Gibbs 1976: 96 n. 25). We do not know how the Romans discovered that the dial was inaccurate for them; the first water clock was not set up there until 159 B.C., so they do not seem to have relied on another type of instrument to tell them the correct time of day. On the other hand, perhaps it really was the time of year that was recognized as being inaccurately measured by the sundial, and the traditional translation of Pliny's *horas* as "hours," should be changed to the less common but alternate meaning "seasons" (as in Pliny, *HN* 9.107, 12.15, 17.132). In that case, he would be correctly representing the problem of the Sicilian sundial in Rome. If Roman comic playwrights in the early second century B.C. could raise a laugh at the notion of a town being "stuffed with sundials" that controlled ordinary life (Aulus Gellius, *NA* 3.3.5), then, even if the joke was a transplant from Greek New Comedy, it is possible that the presence in Rome itself of more and more sundials provided the observant with evidence that the Catania dial was unreliable.

Certainly we gain a distinct impression of a careful parceling out of the hours of the day among the Romans. In Rome, the *accensus* had the job of announcing when it was the third, sixth, and ninth hours of the day (Varro, *Ling.* 6.89; Pliny, *HN* 7.212), and a few sundials survive with these hours specifically marked out (Gibbs 1976: 300, no. 3080 for a list). In addition, the hour lines on dials were sometimes numbered. If this was done in Greek, the letters of the alphabet were used for numbers (see figure 29.2). A Greek epigram (*Anthologia Palatina* 10.43) puns neatly: "Six hours are sufficient for work. But the rest, when set out in letters, say 'Live!' to mortals." The first six hours of the day, to noon, were devoted to work, but the next four to leisure. This is a simple play on the letters for the hours 7, 8, 9, and 10, which were Z, H, Θ, and I read together, they formed the word "Live." The satirist Martial (4.8) provides sharper definition of the day: the first two hours were occupied by the *salutatio* between patron and clients; at the third hour the law courts opened; work throughout the city lasted till the end of the fifth hour, followed by a rest at the sixth, and a complete end to work at the seventh; the eighth hour was spent at the gymnasium; dinner came at the ninth; the tenth, the poet hopes, is when the emperor will read this latest book of epigrams! These hours may represent the norm, but variations certainly occurred. Retirement, not surprisingly, brought a more relaxed timetable for the rich, as Pliny the Younger (*Ep.* 3.1) demonstrates in his description of the typical day of the elderly but very fit Spurinna. Allowance could also be made for the variability of the seasons, with the time for bathing being shifted from the ninth hour in winter back to the eighth in summer.

## PORTABLE DIALS

As we have seen, already by the early second century B.C. the Romans found humor in the idea of a town being full of sundials, and indeed they were everywhere—in public squares, temples, town houses, and country villas. They were also used up and down the length and breadth of the Roman world, from Spain to Greece, and from Africa to Germany. Under the Empire they were even in people's hands, miniaturized and portable, the ancient equivalent of the modern pocket watch. The earliest portable sundial that we have is from Herculaneum. It is known as the "Ham Dial," because its distorted bronze plate looks just like a small leg of ham. A spike on one side threw a shadow onto a series of crisscrossing lines on the plate, from which one could read the hour of the day. Other portable dials are regularly circular in shape, or cylindrical, and some come with extra plates to suit different latitudes (Price 1969; Arnaldi and Schaldach 1997; Wright 2000). One small dial of perhaps mid-third century A.D. date consists of just two plates and a *gnomon* and yet permits the reading of the time of day anywhere between latitudes 30° and 60° N; 30 locations are specifically listed (Oxford, Museum for the History of Science, inv. no. 51358; Price 1969: 253–56; Schaldach 1998: 45–47; cf. figure 31.3).

These dials foreshadow the astrolabe, the portable timepiece *par excellence* of the Middle Ages. While no ancient astrolabe survives, the instrument was most likely a late Greek invention. It utilized stereographic projection to represent the celestial hemisphere two-dimensionally, a method of representation described by

Ptolemy in his *Planisphere* in the second century A.D. and perhaps known to Hipparchus in the second century B.C. The earliest treatise on the astrolabe, by Philoponus in the sixth century A.D., reflects an earlier one by Theon in the fourth century A.D. (Price 1957: 603–9; Neugebauer 1975: 868–79; Evans 1999: 253–54; Taub 2001: 920–21).

# WATER CLOCKS

The major timekeeping mechanism in the classical world, the water clock, initially did not rely on emulating the motions of celestial bodies; but even it eventually was adapted to do so. In origin this was not a clock in the strict sense, but a simple egg-timer type of mechanism, measuring the set times for certain activities by a fall or rise in water level. The earliest surviving water clock comes from Egypt and dates to about 1400 B.C., while the earliest mention of such an instrument there is from the late 16th century B.C. The Egyptians may well have borrowed the mechanism from the Babylonians (Turner 1990: 58, no. 49; Cotterell et al. 1986; Spalinger 1996). In the Greek world the term *klepsydra* (water thief) was borrowed from a device which worked like a large pipette (e.g., Aristotle, *Cael.* 294b.14–30; [Aristotle], *Pr.* 914b, Lewis 2000: 344, fig. 1), and it was applied to other containers, such as a bucketlike vase with a hole near the base for the outflow, which was used from the fifth century B.C. in Athens to time the speeches in the law courts ([Aristotle], *Ath. Pol.* 67; Aristophanes, *Ach.* 694, *Vesp.* 93). Indeed, the *klepsydra* became synonymous with the courts (Allen 1996: 158). A preserved example holds the equivalent of six minutes' worth of water (Young 1939). Something of the same aversion to being controlled by a time machine that we encountered with sundials is found also with the water clock (Plato, *Tht.* 172c–e), but while the necessity for brevity imposed by the *klepsydra* might have led to fallible judgments (Allen 1996: 159), it also ensured equality through standardization, a fundamental characteristic of the democracy.

Other utensils could be used as simple timers also, such as the ubiquitous clay oil lamp. This is occasionally described in Greek papyri from Egypt as containing specific amounts of oil. The contexts suggest that fixed periods of time are intended for the lamplight to burn during various magical rituals, notably in conjuring up and holding on to spirits (Betz 1986: 172–82, 336). Pliny (*HN* 33.96–97) also notes that work shifts for miners in Spain could be calculated by the exhaustion of their lamp oil.

The standardization of time through the *klepsydra* extended also to the definition of the legal day, which was divided into a certain quantity of water, which in turn was then further subdivided into various volumetric measures. This "day" itself was equated with the shortest days of the year, those of the Athenian month Poseideon in midwinter (Young 1939: 281). *Klepsydrai* of some kind were also used to measure out the length of night watches in the military world, but there a measure based on subdivisions of a standardized, winter day could not work for the longer days of the campaigning season, so attempts were made to ensure that the watches were equalized by adjusting the volume of water that the clocks held through coating the inner surface of the *klepsydra* with varying layers of wax (Aeneas Tacticus 22.24–25; Whitehead 2002: 158–60). The Romans continued to use *klepsydrai* in political, legal, and military contexts (e.g., Caesar, *B Gall.* 5.13; Pliny, *Ep.* 2.11.14).

Perhaps under the influence of these improvements in taking account of the variability of the day and night through the year, in the mid-fourth century an outflow water clock was built near the Heliaia in the agora in Athens, the social and political center of the city, with a capacity of 1,000 liters, large enough to operate uninterruptedly over the whole of a long summer's day (Camp 1986: 157–59). A very similar example has been found at the Amphiaraeum at Oropus (Turner 1990: 62–63, no. 65), where it may have timed rituals or performances at the nearby theater (cf. Aristotle, *Poet.* 1451a8). Others have been found around the Greek world (Dohrn-van Rossum 2003: 463).

From the Hellenistic period on, the inflow water clock was developed as an alternative to the outflow type (Lewis 2000: 363–66). A float, whether in the outflow tank or in the inflow, could be connected via gear wheels and even automated figures to some means of displaying the passage of time as water entered or exited the tank. This time display could be a simple cylinder marked with a scale of hour-lines, although the representation of the uneven seasonal hours presented difficulties. Alternatively, the passage of time could be tied explicitly to the motions of the celestial bodies through the incorporation of images of the zodiac or stereographic projections of the celestial sphere. Vitruvius describes sophisticated examples devised by Ctesibius in the third century B.C., including the anaphoric clock, which told the time via an automated representation of the sequential risings of the stars (*De arch.* 9.8.4–15; Lewis 2000: 366; Rowland and Howe 1999: 117, 290–91; Dohrn-van Rossum 1996: 26–27; Price 1957: 601–3). Physical remains of such complex machinery are rare. Fragments have been found of the star-plate of two such water clocks, both dating perhaps to the second century A.D., one from Salzburg, which was monumental in scale at a diameter of over one meter, and another much smaller one from Grand in Lorraine (Evans 1999: 251–53; Lewis 2000: 366–67).

In the Tower of the Winds in Athens (figure 29.3), built by Andronicus from Cyrrha (Müller 2001: 43–44), there are traces on the floor of channels for piping to some type of water clock that is no longer preserved. This 13 m high octagonal building, well known in antiquity to judge from its mention by both Varro (*Rust.* 3.5.17) and Vitruvius (*De arch.* 1.6.4–7), was a tour de force of timekeeping instruments. It incorporated not only a water clock inside but also nine sundials on its exterior walls and an annex. New research suggests an earlier date in the second century B.C. rather than the mid-first century B.C. On architectural grounds, eight of the external sundials, one on each outside wall, are accepted as an original element of the design, despite the absence of any mention of them by Vitruvius. This omission caused Delambre, their great elucidator, some concern and led to the suspicion that they may have been added afterward (Delambre 1817: 487–503). The influential reconstruction by Noble and Price of the interior water clock is now disputed (Noble and Price 1968; von Freeden 1983; Kienast 1993, 1997, 2005, and personal communication).

The fact that there is still something to be learned and understood in a monument that has been so familiar to western Europeans since its depiction in the eighteenth century is testament to the patchy state of our knowledge generally about ancient developments in the technology of timekeeping. So while future studies will undoubtedly continue the present trend to discuss the ancient artifacts from a sociological perspective, there is room still for the basic scientific, analytical description of those very same objects. Without that fundamental understanding, any further interpretation is simply speculation.

# REFERENCES

Allen, D. 1996. "A schedule of boundaries: An exploration, launched from the water-clock, of Athenian time," *Greece and Rome* 43: 157–68.

Ardaillon, E. 1900. "*Horologium,*" in *DarSag* 3: 256–64.

Arnaldi, M., and K. Schaldach 1997. "A Roman cylinder dial: Witness to a forgotten tradition," *Journal for the History of Astronomy* 28: 107–117.

Beck, R. 1994. "Cosmic models: Some uses of Hellenistic science in Roman religion," in T. D. Barnes (ed.), *The sciences in Greco-Roman society*. Apeiron 27. Edmonton: Academic Printing and Publication, 99–117.

Betz, H. D. (ed.) 1986. *The Greek magical papyri in translation, including the demotic spells.* Chicago: University of Chicago Press.

Belmonte, J. A. 2003. "The Ramesside star clocks and the ancient Egyptian constellations," in M. P. Blomberg, E. Blomberg, and G. Henriksson, (eds.), *Calendars, symbols, and orientations: Legacies of astronomy in culture.* Uppsala: Uppsala Astronomical Observatory, 57–65.

Bettini, M. 1991. *Anthropology and Roman culture: Kinship, time, images of the soul.* Baltimore: Johns Hopkins University Press.

Blackburn, B., and L. Holford-Strevens 1999. *The Oxford companion to the year: An exploration of calendar customs and time-reckoning.* Oxford: Oxford University Press.

Blomberg, M., and G. Henriksson 2003. "The Minoan peak sanctuary on Pyrgos and its context," in Blomberg, Blomberg, and Henriksson 2003, 127–34.

Bourdieu, P. 1990. *The logic of practice.* Trans. R. Nice. Cambridge: Polity Press.

Bowen, A. C., and B. R. Goldstein 1988. "Meton of Athens and astronomy in the late fifth century B.C," in E. Leichty, M. de J. Ellis, and P. Gerardi (eds.), *A scientific humanist: Studies in memory of Abraham Sachs.* Philadelphia: The University Museum, 39–81.

Bowen, A. C., and B. R. Goldstein 1991. "Hipparchus' treatment of early Greek astronomy: The case of Eudoxus and the length of daytime," *Proceedings of the American Philosophical Society* 135: 233–54.

Bromley, A. G. 1986. "Notes on the Antikythera Mechanism," *Centaurus* 29: 5–27.

Bromley, A. G. 1990. "Observations of the Antikythera Mechanism," *Antiquarian Horology* 18: 641–52.

Buchner, E. 1982. *Die Sonnenuhr des Augustus*. Mainz: von Zabern.

Buchner, E. 1993–1994. "Neues zur Sonnenuhr des Augustus," *Nürnberger Blätter zur Archäologie* 10: 77–84.

Buxton, B., and R. Hannah 2005. "OGIS 458, the Augustan calendar, and the succession," in C. Deroux (ed.), *Studies in Latin literature and Roman history*, vol. XII. Collection Latomus 287. Brussels: Latomus, 290–306.

Camp, J. M. 1986. *The Athenian agora: Excavations in the heart of classical Athens*. London: Thames and Hudson.

Cotterell, B., F. P. Dickson, and J. Kamminga 1986. "Ancient Egyptian water-clocks: A reappraisal," *Journal of Archaeological Science* 13: 31–50.

Csapo, E., and M. Miller 1998. "Democracy, empire, and art: Toward a politics of time and narrative," in D. Boedeker and K. A. Raaflaub (eds.), *Democracy, empire, and the arts in fifth-century Athens*. Cambridge, MA: Harvard University Press, 87–125.

Darbo-Peschanski, C. (ed.) 2000. *Constructions du temps dans le monde grec ancien*. Paris: CNRS Éditions.

Delambre, J. B. J. 1817. *Histoire de l'astronomie ancienne*. vol. 2. Paris: V. Courcier.

Dohrn-van Rossum, G. 1996. *History of the hour: Clocks and modern temporal orders*. Trans. T. Dunlap. Chicago: University of Chicago Press.

Dohrn-van Rossum, G. 2003. "Clocks," in H. Cancik and H. Schneider (eds.), *Brill's New Pauly*. Leiden: Brill, 3:458–64.

Drecker, J. 1925. *Die Theorie der Sonnenuhren*. Berlin: Vereinigung Wissenschaftlicher Verleger, Walter de Gruyter.

Durkheim, E. 1915. *The elementary forms of the religious life*. Trans. J. W. Swain. London: Allen and Unwin.

Evans, J. 1999. "The material culture of Greek astronomy," *Journal for the History of Astronomy* 30: 237–307.

Evans-Pritchard, E. 1940. *The Nuer: A description of the modes of livelihood and political institutions of a Nilotic people*. Oxford: Clarendon Press.

Freeth, T., Y. Bitsakis, X. Moussas, J. H. Seiradakis, A. Tselikas, E. Magkou, M. Zafeiropoulou, R. Hadland, D. Bate, A. Ramsey, M. Allen, A. Crawley, P. Hockley, T. Malzbender, D. Gelb, W. Ambrisco, and M. G. Edmunds 2006. "Decoding the ancient Greek astronomical calculator known as the Antikythera Mechanism," *Nature* 444 (30 November 2006): 587–91.

Gell, A. 1992. *The anthropology of time*. Oxford: Berg.

Gibbs, S. L. 1976. *Greek and Roman sundials*. New Haven: Yale University Press.

Gibbs, S. L. 1979. "The first scientific instruments," in K. Brecher and M. Feirtag (eds.), *Astronomy of the ancients*. Cambridge, MA: MIT Press, 39–59.

Goody, J. 1968. "Time: Social Organization," in D. L. Sills and R. K. Merton (eds.), *International encyclopedia of the social sciences*. New York: Macmillan, vol.16: 30–42.

Hannah, R. 1986a. "The Emperor's stars: The Conservatori portrait of Commodus," *American Journal of Archaeology* 90: 337–42.

Hannah, R. 1986b. "Et in Arcadia ego?—The finding of Telephos," *Antichthon* 20: 86–105.

Hannah, R. 1989. "... *praevolante nescio qua ingenti humana specie* ...: A reassessment of the Winged Genius on the base of the Antonine Column," *Papers of the British School in Rome* 57: 90–105.

Hannah, R. 1993a. "Alcumena's long night: Plautus, *Amphitruo* 273–76," *Latomus* 52: 65–74.

Hannah, R. 1993b. "The stars of Iopas and Palinurus," *American Journal of Philology* 114: 123–35.

Hannah, R. 1997. "The Temple of Mars Ultor and 12 May," *Römische Mitteilungen* 104: 374–86.

Hannah, R. 2001a. "From orality to literacy? The case of the Parapegma," in J. Watson (ed.), *Speaking volumes: Orality and literacy in the Greek and Roman world*. Leiden: Brill, 139–59.

Hannah, R. 2001b. "The moon, the sun and the stars: Counting the days and the years," in S. McCready (ed.), *The discovery of time*. London: MQ Publications, 56–99.

Hannah, R. 2002. "Euctemon's parapegma," in C. J. Tuplin and T. E. Rihll (eds.), *Science and mathematics in ancient Greek culture*. Oxford: Oxford University Press, 112–32.

Hannah, R. 2005. *Greek and Roman calendars: Constructions of time in the classical world*. London: Duckworth.

Henriksson, G., and M. Blomberg 1996. "Evidence for Minoan astronomical observations from the peak sanctuaries on Petsophas and Traostalos," *Opuscula Atheniensia* 21: 99–114.

Henriksson, G., and M. Blomberg 1997–1998. "Petsophas and the summer solstice," *Opuscula Atheniensia* 22–23: 147–51.

Hunger, H., and D. Pingree 1989. *MUL.APIN: An astronomical compendium in cuneiform*. Horn: Verlag Ferdinand Berger und Söhne.

Hunt, D. W. S. 1940–1945. "An archaeological survey of the classical antiquities of the island of Chios carried out between the months of March and July, 1938," *Annual of the British School in Athens* 41: 29–52.

Kienast, H. J. 1993. "Untersuchungen am Turm der Winde," *Archäologischer Anzeiger* 1993: 271–75.

Kienast, H. J. 1997. "The Tower of the Winds in Athens: Hellenistic or Roman?" in M. C. Hoff and S. I. Rotroff (eds.), *The Romanization of Athens: Proceedings of an international conference held at Lincoln, Nebraska (April 1996)*. Oxford: Oxbow, 53–65.

Kienast, H. J. 2005. "La Torre dei Venti di Atene," in E. Lo Sardo (ed.), *Eureka! Il Genio degli Antichi*. Naples: Electa, 245–51.

Lehoux, D. R. 2000. "Parapegmata; or, Astrology, weather, and calendars in the ancient world." PhD thesis, University of Toronto.

Lehoux, D. R. 2007. *Astronomy, weather, and calendars in the ancient world: Parapegmata and related texts in classical and Near-Eastern societies*. Cambridge: Cambridge University Press.

Lewis, M. 2000. "Theoretical hydraulics, automata, and water clocks," in Ö. Wikander (ed.), *Handbook of ancient water technology*. Leiden: Brill, 343–69.

Lippincott, K. 1999. *The story of time*. London: Merrell Holberton and National Maritime Museum.

Lloyd, A. B. 1988. *Herodotus Book II*. Vol. 3. Leiden: Brill.

McCluskey, S. 1998. *Astronomies and cultures in early medieval Europe*. Cambridge: Cambridge University Press.

Müller, W. 2001. "Andronikos (1)," in R. Vollkommer (ed.), *Künstlerlexikon der Antike*. Munich and Leipzig: K. G. Saur, 1.43–44.

Neugebauer, O. 1941–1943. "Egyptian planetary texts," *Transactions of the American Philosophical Society* 32: 209–50.

Neugebauer, O. 1975. *A history of ancient mathematical astronomy*. Berlin: Springer-Verlag.

Neugebauer, O., and R. A. Parker 1969. *Egyptian astronomical Texts*, vol. 3. Providence, RI: Brown University Press.

Nilsson, M. 1920. *Primitive time-reckoning: A study in the origins and first development of the art of counting time among primitive and early culture peoples.* Lund: Gleerup.

Noble, J. V., and D. J. de Solla Price 1968. "The water clock in the Tower of the Winds," *American Journal of Archaeology* 72: 345–55.

Parker, R. A. 1974. "Ancient Egyptian astronomy," in F. R. Hodson (ed.), *The place of astronomy in the ancient world.* London: The British Academy and Oxford University Press, 51–65.

Pattenden, P. 1979. "Sundials in Cetius Faventinus," *Classical Quarterly* 29: 203–12.

Price, D. J. de Solla 1957. "Precision instruments: To 1500," in C. Singer, E. J. Holmyard, A. R. Hall, and T. Williams (eds.), *A history of technology,* vol. 3. Oxford: Clarendon Press, 582–619.

Price, D. J. de Solla. 1969. "Portable sundials in antiquity, including an account of a new example from Aphrodisias," *Centaurus* 14: 242–66.

Price, D. J. de Solla. 1974. *Gears from the Greeks.* Transactions of the American Philosophical Society 64.7. Philadelphia: American Philosophical Society.

Price, D. J. de Solla. 1975. "Clockwork before the clock and timekeepers before timekeeping," in J. T. Fraser and N. Lawrence (eds.), *The study of time,* vol. 2. Berlin: Springer-Verlag, 367–80.

Quirke, S. 2001. *The cult of Ra: Sun-worship in ancient Egypt.* London: Thames and Hudson.

Rehm, A. 1913. "Horologium," in *RE* 8, 2416–33.

Reiche, H. A. T. 1989. "Fail-safe stellar dating: Forgotten phases," *Transactions of the American Philological Association* 119: 37–53.

Rochberg, F. 2004. *The heavenly writing: Divination, horoscopy, and astronomy in Mesopotamian culture.* Cambridge: Cambridge University Press.

Rossiter, J. J., and A. Suksi 2003. "The seasons: Greek and Roman perspectives." Special issue, *Mouseion* 47.3.

Rowland, I. D., and T. N. Howe (eds.) 1999. *Vitruvius: Ten Books on Architecture.* Cambridge: Cambridge University Press.

Rüpke, J. 1995. *Kalender und Öffentlichkeit: Die Geschichte der Repräsentation und religiösen Qualifikation von Zeit in Rom.* Berlin: Walter de Gruyter.

Schaldach, K. 1998. *Römische Sonnenuhren: Eine Einführung in die antike Gnomonik.* Frankfurt am Main: Verlag Harri Deutsch.

Schütz, M. 1990. "Zur Sonnenuhr des Augustus auf dem Marsfeld," *Gymnasium* 97: 432–57.

Spalinger, A. 1996. "Some times," *Revue d'Égyptologie* 47: 67–77.

Taub, L. 2001. "Destini della scienza greca: eredità e longevità degli strumenti scientifici," in S. Settis (ed.), *I Greci: Storia, Cultura, Arte, Società.* 4 vols. Turin: Einaudi, 3: 889–930.

Taub, L. 2003. *Ancient meteorology.* London: Routledge.

Turetzky, P. 1998. *Time.* London: Routledge.

Turner, A. J. 1990. *Time.* The Hague: Tijd voor Tijd Foundation.

Turner, A. J. 1993. *Of time and measurement: Studies in the history of horology and fine technology.* Aldershot: Variorum.

von Freeden, J. 1983. *OIKIA KYPPHΣTOY: Studien zum sogenannten Turm der Winde in Athen.* Rome: Giorgio Bretschneider.

Wallace-Hadrill, A. 1987. "Time for Augustus: Ovid, Augustus and the *Fasti,*" in M. Whitby and P. Hardie (eds.), *Homo viator: Classical essays for John Bramble.* Bristol: Bristol Classical Press, 221–30.

Whitehead, D. 2002. *Aineias the Tactician: How to Survive Under Siege.* 2nd ed. London: Bristol Classical Press.

Wright, M. T. 2000. "Greek and Roman portable sundials: An ancient essay in approximation," *Archive for History of Exact Sciences* 55:177–87.

Wright, M. T. 2002. "A planetarium display for the Antikythera Mechanism," *The Horological Journal* 144: 169–73, 193.

Wright, M. T. 2003a. "Epicyclic gearing and the Antikythera Mechanism, Part 1," *Antiquarian Horology* 27: 270–79.

Wright, M. T. 2003b. "In the steps of the master mechanic," in *He archaia Hellada kai ho Sunchronos Kosmos*. Patras: University of Patras, 86–97.

Wright, M. T. 2004. "The scholar, the mechanic and the Antikythera Mechanism: Complementary approaches to the study of an instrument," *Bulletin of the Scientific Instrument Society* 80: 4–11.

Wright, M. T. 2005a. "The Antikythera Mechanism: A new gearing scheme," *Bulletin of the Scientific Instrument Society* 85: 2–7.

Wright, M. T. 2005b. "Counting months and years: The upper back dial of the Antikythera Mechanism," *Bulletin of the Scientific Instrument Society* 87: 8–13.

Wright, M. T. 2005c. "Epicyclic gearing and the Antikythera Mechanism, Part 2," *Antiquarian Horology* 29: 51–63.

Wright, M. T. 2005d. "Il meccanismo di Anticitera: L'antica tradizione dei meccanismi ad ingranaggio," in E. Lo Sardo (ed.), *Eureka! Il Genio deglio Antichi*. Naples: Electa, 240–44.

Wright, M. T. 2006a. "The Antikythera Mechanism and the early history of the moon-phase display," *Antiquarian Horology* 29: 319–29.

Wright, M. T. 2006b. "Understanding the Antikythera Mechanism," in *2nd International Conference on Ancient Greek Technology*. Athens: Technical Chamber of Greece, 49–60.

Young, S. 1939. "An Athenian clepsydra," *Hesperia* 8: 272–84.

Zeeman, E. C. 1986. "Gears from the Greeks," *Proceedings of the Royal Institution of Great Britain* 58: 137–56.

Zerubavel, E. 1985. *The seven day circle: The history and meaning of the week*. New York: Free Press.

# CHAPTER 30

# TECHNOLOGIES OF CALCULATION

## PART 1: WEIGHTS AND MEASURES (CHARLOTTE WIKANDER)

The various systems of units used for weights and for measures both of volume and of space in the classical world are bewilderingly diverse. The only phenomenon that seems comparable is the measurement of time, particularly the many ways of organizing solar and lunar calendars (chapter 29). Obviously, all humans needed to measure weight, volume, space, and time from a very early period of social and technological development, explaining the variety of approaches—which survived in large part until the appearance of the metric system in the late eighteenth century. As with monthly and yearly calendars, weights and measures for the archaic and classical periods in Greece also present strictly local systems, some of which, however, through growing trade, could be used over larger areas as a complement to local measurements. This spread of influence happened mainly with the Aeginetan and, above all, Athenian standards.

The establishment of the new Hellenistic monarchies on the ruins of the Persian empire during the last decades of the fourth century B.C. does not seem to have changed the situation to any great degree. Both the Seleucid and Ptolemaic kingdoms to a large extent kept to traditional measuring standards, a mixture of local traditions and Persian customs, instead of trying to impose any consistent systems, even the widely accepted Athenian system. For example, in spite of the strongly centralized economic administration, the Persian dry-measure *artabe*, about 55 liters, was used in

Ptolemaic Egypt, but with widely different volumes ranging from 36 to 42 liters depending on time, place, and type of goods (Rostovtseff 1941: 1296–1300).

The situation gradually changed after Rome's subjugation of the Eastern Mediterranean: with the Mediterranean as an arena for trade *within* the Roman Empire, local systems were gradually adapted in order to accommodate exchange between regions, as well as customs regulations. These adaptations, however, were slow and for the most part took place only in the first century A.D. A pertinent example is the stone tablet of Leptis Magna in Libya, which, still in the second century A.D., gives standard comparative measures of Punic, Roman, and Ptolemaic length (Ioppolo 1967).

In view of this diversity, the presentation below will be divided into various categories of measurements (volumes: dry or wet, etc.) over a wide geographical and chronological span, illustrated by some tables with short comments—this, hopefully, to avoid total confusion to the reader. The tables will reflect the figures normally given in modern works, but may occasionally deviate from, for example, archaeological finds from different locations.

# Metrology

The collective category "metrology" was established as a field of investigation in the nineteenth century, as part of the German academic trend of enforcing positivistic order on the earlier chaos of research concerning classical antiquity. The first attempt at synthesis was published in 1838 (Böckh 1838) but was superseded in 1864 by Hultsch's *Griechische und römische Metrologie* (revised and enlarged edition, 1882). By then, Hultsch had also established a base for further research with his *Metrologicorum Scriptorum Reliquiae* (1864–1866), a collection of all known ancient texts dealing with metrology. Hultsch has in many instances remained a standard reference, the first serious attempt to systematize our knowledge of ancient measurement systems. Viedebantt provided the next major contribution, *Forschungen zur Metrologie des Altertums* (1917), then followed up and subdivided the field with his *Antike Gewichtsnormen und Münzfusse* (1923); he also wrote the *RE* article "Metrologie."

Once these fundamental bases for further research were established, then augmented by such works as Berriman 1953 and Richardson 2003, the metrological field tended to divide into different subsections, although with some cross-referencing. The most important of these subfields were weights (frequently coupled with numismatics), volume measurements (frequently coupled with amphora studies), and the study of Roman land measurement. The most obvious example of crossover into another field is the separation of the study of weight systems, which became strongly connected to numismatics, since the ancient coinage systems were based on metal weight.

Great help has been brought to the entire field in the twentieth century by a few important publications of archaeological finds, mainly standard tokens of weight and standard measures of volumes. Most notable is the work of Lang (1964) concerning the weights, measures, and tokens found in the Athenian agora, more recently complemented by Hitzl (1996) on the weights from Olympia. This volume also contains a report on the state of research concerning weights and coin values. Apart from amphora studies, the only significant contextual evidence for weights and measures from excavations other than those at Athens and Olympia is the material from Olynthus (Robinson 1941).

Since the ancient volumes and measures presented were normally based on a duodecimal system, they may puzzle the modern reader when translated into modern decimal, metric terminology. The modern situation, however, retains a certain amount of chaos in the measurement of distance, weight, and volume. Great Britain and the United States, for example, still make use of miles, yards, and inches, along with pounds and ounces, while the international oil market continues to measure crude oil in "barrels" (159 liters) whether or not the producing or consuming country uses the metric system for other purposes. Even in Europe length measurements based on parts of the human body (e.g., the cubit) were widely used through the mid-nineteenth century. There is thus nothing particularly abnormal in the ancient diversity.

## Dry Measures

In the various Greek city-states, measures for dry and liquid contents were strictly separated (see Table 30.1). The *medimnos* was the largest measurement, used generally although with different volumes in the different cities. The Attic standard, however, was widely used, for example in Syracuse. The *medimnos* was a large measurement, normally above 50 liters (although at Aegina and Sparta it was even more), and thus for normal use had to be subdivided into four smaller units: the *hekteis, hemihekton, choinix,* and *kotyle.* This smallest measurement, the *kotyle* (varying from 0.273 to 0.379 l.), was also used as a normal drinking cup.

The *medimnos* has attracted a great deal of interest from scholars of ancient history, since (according to Plutarch, *Sol.* 23.3) this was the basis of Solon's division of the political rights of the Athenian population during his archonship of 594/3 B.C. The highest class was defined by production, the *pentakosiomedimnoi,* those who had fields producing a minimum of 500 *medimnoi* of grain (ca. 25,000 liters, which for modern conditions would be a very low yield).

Excavations in Athens have yielded several examples from the fifth and fourth centuries B.C. of what has been plausibly identified as examples of standard measurements for dry goods, enabling traders and customers to check the correctness of volumes bought and sold. In the Athenian agora, many fragments of such cylindrical ceramic vessels, in some cases given the painted designation *DEM* (*demosion,* "of the people") were found in the immediate vicinity of the Tholos, the building where the five official magistrates overseeing the agora trade, the *agoranomoi,* had their office (Lang 1964). The conscientious official control of weights and measures

### Table 30.1. Dry measures

| Greek (Athenian) | | |
| --- | --- | --- |
| 1 kotyle | | 0.274 l |
| 2 kotylai | dikotylon/xestes | 0.547 l |
| 3 kotylai | trikotylon | 0.821 l |
| 4 kotylai | choinix | 1.094 l |
| 16 kotylai | hemihekton | 4.378 l |
| 32 kotylai | hekteus | 8.768 l |
| 192 kotylai | medimnos | 52.536 l |
| Roman | | |
| 1 cochlear | | 0.011 l |
| 4 cochlearia | cyathus | 0.046 l |
| 6 cochlearia | acetabulum | 0.068 l |
| 12 cochlearia | quartarius | 0.136 l |
| 24 cochlearia | hemina | 0.273 l |
| 48 cochlearia | sextarius | 0.546 l |
| 8 sextarii | semodius | 4.366 l |
| 16 sextarii | modius | 8.732 l |
| 48 sextarii | quadrantal/amphora | 26.196 l |

is further illustrated by the fact that the *agoranomoi* had the assistance of a college of five *Metronomoi*, specialized in the overseeing of official measurements. Similar magistrates were also employed in the Piraeus harbor and at Eleusis.

The basic Roman dry measure was the *modius* (shovel), originally and primarily used for grain. It held about 8.7 liters, and could be divided into various smaller measures (*sextarii, heminae, quartarii, acetabula*). Several physical examples of measuring containers for a *modius* have been preserved in the archaeological record, mainly from Roman Britain. They were open containers on low feet, made of wood or metal. The *modius* was the common measure of grain (wheat as well as barley) for all purposes: sowing, distribution of grain to the urban *plebs* of Rome, measuring rations for agricultural slaves (cf. Cato, *Ag.* 56; Columella, *Rust.* 2.12).

## Liquid Measures

The largest volume measure of fluids (primarily used for oil and wine) in the Greek world was the *metretes*, also named *amphoreus*, after the most common ceramic container (see Table 30.2). The Attic *metretes* measured 39.4 liters, and was divided into four smaller units (*chous, oxybathon, kotyle,* and *kyathos*). Both *kotyle* and *kyathos* were also names for drinking vessels, as the *chous* was for pouring. As usual,

## Table 30.2. Liquid measures

*Greek (Athenian)*

| | | |
|---|---|---|
| 1/6 *kotyle* | *kyathos* | 0.045 l |
| 1/4 *kotyle* | *oxybaphon* | 0.07 l |
| 1 *kotyle* | | 0.27 l |
| 12 *kotylai* | *chous* | 3.28 l |
| 144 *kotylai* | *metretes/amphoreus* | 39.4 l |

*Roman*

| | | |
|---|---|---|
| 1 *cochlear* | | 0.011 l |
| 4 *cochlearia* | *cyathus* | 0.046 l |
| 6 *cochlearia* | *acetabulum* | 0.068 l |
| 12 *cochlearia* | *quartarius* | 0.136 l |
| 24 *cochlearia* | *hemina* | 0.273 l |
| 48 *cochlearia* | *sextarius* | 0.546 l |
| 6 *sextarii* | *congius* | 3.275 l |
| 24 *sextarii* | *urna* | 13.09 l |
| 48 *sextarii* | *quadrantal/amphora* | 26.196 l |
| 960 *sextarii* | *culleus* | 524.00 l |

Aeginetan and Spartan measurements had their own standards, the Aeginetan substantially larger than the Athenian, 54.6 liters, while the Spartan equivalent was smaller, about 29 liters.

The Romans also used the vase shape *amphora*, a large container, as a measure. Its volume was based on the weight of wine, 80 *librae* (*libra* of ca. 327.5 g) giving a standard theoretical capacity of 26.2 liters. The amphora had seven subdivisions, the *urna, congius, sextarius, hemina, quartarius, acetabulum, cyathus*, and *cochlear*. Until the advanced second century A.D., however, the local volumes contained in actual amphoras could vary significantly (Peacock and Williams 1986: 51–53). With growing international trade, measures tended toward greater standardization from the reign of Nero (A.D. 54–68) on. At both Pompeii and Minturnae, stone tables with hollowed-out standards for measuring of fluids have been found (Mau 1908: 88–89).

# Weights

The weights used at the local markets or for long-distance trade in the Greek world (see Table 30.3) are very tangible archaeological objects, often of distinctive dimensions. They were fashioned of lead, bronze, or stone. For special purposes (in medicine or for precious metals) smaller weights were used, but they have left no

### Table 30.3. Weight standards

| Greek | Aeginetan | Attic |
|---|---|---|
| obolos | 1.04 g | 0.73 g |
| 6 oboloi = 1 drachme | 6.24 g | 4.37 g |
| 100 drachmai = 1 mina/mna | 623.7 g | 436.6 g |
| 60 minai = 1 talent | 37.42 kg | 26.2 kg |
| **Roman** | | |
| 1/144 uncia | siliqua | 0.19 g |
| 1/48 uncia | obolus | 0.57 g |
| 1/24 uncia | scripulum | 1.14 g |
| 1/12 uncia | dimidia sextula | 2.27 g |
| 1/8 uncia | drachma | 3.41 g |
| 1/6 uncia | sextula | 4.55 g |
| 1/4 uncia | sicilicus | 6.82 g |
| 1/3 uncia | binae sextulae | 9.1 g |
| 1/2 uncia | semuncia | 13.64 g |
| 1 uncia | | 27.29 g |
| 1.5 unciae | sescuncia | 40.93 g |
| 2 unciae | sextans | 54.58 g |
| 3 unciae | quadrans | 81.86 g |
| 4 unciae | triens | 109.15 g |
| 5 unciae | quincunx | 136.44 g |
| 6 unciae | semis | 163.73 g |
| 7 unciae | septunx | 191.02 g |
| 8 unciae | bes | 218.3 g |
| 9 unciae | dodrans | 245.59 g |
| 10 unciae | dextans | 272.88 g |
| 11 unciae | deunx | 300.16 g |
| 12 unciae | libra/pondus | 327.45 g |

archaeological record. Stone weights were sometimes marked with a pair of female breasts, while the mold-made metal weights could be square, rectangular, or triangular (Kisch 1965, O'Brien 1981–1984).

The close connection between the coinage system and daily weighing activities is reflected in the names for denominations of coins. The smallest weight was the *obol*—probably derived from the word *obeloi*, thin metal spits in bunches used by the early seventh century B.C. as a pre-stage of the weight and coinage systems combined (Orion, *Etymologikon* s.v. *obolos*), which was also the name of the small bronze coins in everyday use for shopping in classical Athens. Six obols more or less made a *drachme*, giving an Attic drachma of 4.37 g in weight. The *mina* or *mna* could vary from 70 to 150 drachmas. A common unit was the *stater*, with the weight of two minai. The *talent*, weighing 60 minai, was so large that it was rarely used outside state or official business. The standardization of weights and measures in Athens is regularly credited to Solon in the early sixth century B.C., following the influential passage of Aristotle (*Ath. Pol.* 10). Several complications are caused by the fact that "market weights" and standard coin weights usually were not quite the same, despite the use of the same names—the market weights being slightly heavier.

The two sites so far important as find-spots of weights are the agora in Athens (Lang 1964: 2–38) and the sanctuary at Olympia (Hitzl 1996). Olympia in particular has yielded sufficient archaeological material to allow precise analysis of the original weights, thus eliminating many earlier points of speculation. The Olympia excavations have clearly established the existence of an Aeginetan weight/coin system different from the Athenian, a supposition earlier based mainly on passages in Aristotle (*Ath. Pol.* 10) and Pollux (*Onomastikon* 9.76, 86–87; late second century A.D.), and subsequently hotly disputed.

The tolerance for aberration of precise weight was apparently quite wide: both Lang and Hitzl record a range of variation of approximately 20 percent in weight. This is surely not surprising, given the difficulties of fashioning cut-stone and cast-metal weights to a precise weight. The scales on which the weights were used were beam-balances, the oldest with equal-length arms, known from literature of the fifth century. The arms held bowls, into which the weights and the substance to be weighed could be placed. At least from the Hellenistic period, scales with unequal arms were in use, allowing the measurement of greater weights without the need for equivalent counterweights but requiring carefully calibrated yards (Lazzarini 1948).

The Aeginetan and the Athenian drachmas were exchanged at the rate of 70 to 100, but they were both used at the same time in the classical period at Olympia (Hitzl 1996: 53–54). One mina weighed 110 Attic drachmas, but only 77 Aeginetan drachmas. Hitzl's latest group, however, shows a combination: a standard mina of 110 drachmas (480.26 gr.). This standard was imposed on the Athenian subjects of the Delian league in the late decades of the fifth century, and seems to have prevailed also at Olympia.

While the growing Roman empire gradually imposed a standardized system of weights from the second century B.C. onward, local standards survived for a surprisingly long period in both Italy and the eastern Mediterranean. The original Roman/Italic basis for weight standard was the *libra* or *pondus*, the pound, which provided the unit both for early coinage (*aes signatum, aes grave*) and for market weight (*as*). While the coin and metal weights coincided, the actual standard weight varied substantially during the Republic, just as in Greece. There are, however, indications that the Roman pound was related and adjusted to the Greek system: thus, the Roman pound of 327.45 g was exactly the equivalent of three quarters of a Greek market *mina*.

The *libra* was the standard unit; there was no nomenclature for heavier weights, although archaeological evidence shows stone and metal weights of 2, 3, 4, and 5 pounds to be fairly usual; the 5-pound measure seems to have been particularly common. The libra itself had several subdivisions, notably the *semis, uncia, triens, quadrans*, and *sextans*.

## Measures of Length and Area

As in most premodern societies, in Greece and Rome length measurements were based on the human body (see Table 30.4). The basic measurements were taken from the arm (from the elbow to the tips of the fingers—*pechys, cubitus*, ell; ca. 46 cm), the foot (*pous, pes*, two-thirds of an ell; —ca. 30 cm), and the distance across the outstretched arms (*orgyia*, fathom; ca. 6 feet— or 1.8 m). For measuring longer distances, the foot was multiplied by five (*bema diplooun, passus*; 1.48 m), or by 5,000 to yield the mile (*milia passuum*; 1.48 km), the normal measurement for road distances in the Roman empire. One should, however, beware of regarding these measurements as very precise, since they vary significantly between localities and across time (Hecht 1979; Wikander 1993). In Greece, particularly in athletic contexts, we also encounter the *stadion* (600 feet, ca. 177–85 m, depending on local standards). The *stadion* for races at Olympia was exceptionally long, 192.3 m.

From an early stage in the sixth century B.C., we encounter in Greece the system of defining field surfaces as units of "plough-land," that is, the area which it was possible to plough during a working day, from sunup to sundown. Clearly this is an imprecise unit, since topography, type of soil, and the condition of the draft animals can affect the result. Nevertheless, the same method for measuring land is reflected in the Roman measurement *iugerum* (from *iugum*, yoke). The *iugerum*, however, which was the normal private and state unit for agricultural properties during the Republic, was well defined: a rectangle measuring 120 x 240 Roman feet (35.52 x 71.04 m, 2,523 sq m). It was subdivided according to a duodecimal system into *actus, unciae*, and *scripula*, suitable for smaller cultivation, such as kitchen gardens.

Roman engineers used collapsible brass measuring rulers, which gave the measure of a foot of 29.6 cm, subdivided into sixteen *digiti* (fingers), or twelve *unciae*. In order to measure long distances, particularly roads, a wheeled *hodometer* was used (Lewis 2001: 134–39). The engineer and architect Vitruvius described this machine around 25 B.C. (see chapter 31). It consisted of two wheels connected to a series of cogwheels, one vertical and one horizontal, which, counting the revolving of the wheels, dropped a small ball into a container for each mile passed. This corresponded to the system of the milestones (*miliaria*), spread along the roads of the Empire, giving the distances from Rome on the main military roads, and from the nearest town or city to the next urban center. Such milestones, giving also details of repairs, have been found in great numbers throughout the empire, their standard interval (where that can be determined) being 1,481.5 meters, around 1,000 *passus* or 5,000 *pedes*.

For measuring areas and distances the Roman *mensores* (measurers) used an instrument called the *groma*, which made it possible to plot straight lines and

**Table 30.4. Measures of length and area**

| Greek length | | | Roman length | | |
| --- | --- | --- | --- | --- | --- |
| 1/16 foot | *daktylos* | 1.7–2.2 cm | 1/16 foot | *digitus* | 1.85 cm |
| 1/8 foot | *kondylos* | 3.4–4.4 cm | 1/12 foot | *uncia* | 2.47 cm |
| 1/4 foot | *palaiste* | 6.8–8.8 cm | | | |
| 1 foot | *pus* | 27–35 cm (Athenian 32.5 cm) | 1 foot | *pes* | 29.6 cm |
| 1.5 feet | *pechys* | 40–53 cm | 1.5 feet | *cubitus* | 44.4 cm |
| 5 feet | *bema diplooun* | 1.35–1.75 m | 5 feet | *passus* | 1.48 m |
| 6 feet | *orgyia* | 1.62–2.10 m | 2 *passus* | *pertica* | 2.96 m |
| 10 feet | *akaina* | 2.70–3.50 m | 24 *passus* | *actus* | 35.56 m |
| 100 feet | *plethron* | 27–35 m | 125 *passus* | *stadium* | 185.2 m |
| 600 feet | *stadion* | 177–213 m | 1000 *passus* | Roman mile | 1,481.5 m |

| Greek area | | | Roman area | | |
| --- | --- | --- | --- | --- | --- |
| 1 sq foot | | 0.73–1.23 sq m | 1 sq foot | *pes quadratus* | 0.088 sq m |
| 10 × 10 feet | *akaina* | 7.3–12.3 sq m (Ptolemaic Egypt) | 100 sq feet | *scripulum* | 8.76 sq m |
| 100 × 100 feet | *plethron* | ca. 700–1,200 sq m | 2,400 sq feet | *uncia* | 210.28 sq m |
| | *medimnon* | ca. 2,700 sq m (Cyrenaica) | 6 *unciae* = *actus quadratus* | 120 × 120 feet | 1,262.00 sq m |
| 100 × 100 ells | *aroura* | 27.56 sq m (Ptolemaic Egypt) | 12 *unciae* = *iugerum* | 240 × 120 feet | 2,523.34 sq m |
| | | | 2 iugera | *heredium* | 5,046.68 sq m |
| | | | 200 iugera | *centuria* | 50.47 ha |
| | | | 800 iugera | *saltus* | 201.87 ha |

90-degree angles off established lines (Lewis 2001: 120–33). The use of this device is described by Heron of Alexandria (*Dioptra* 33), and it is illustrated on funeral reliefs; one example survived at Pompeii (Schiøler 1994: Brodersen 1995: 202). It was based on a vertical rod of man-height, with an offset crown to which a plumb line was attached to mark the survey point on the ground. A cross with four equal arms perpendicular to each other was mounted on the crown in such a way that it could turn. A plumb line was attached to the end of each arm, serving as crosshairs for sighting. Once the central plumb bob was in position, the horizontal cross arms could be adjusted to allow sighting on physical landmarks or the compass points, and the marking of straight lines or perpendiculars by men with range rods. Sighting from these lines across not too large distances, milestones or boundary markers for fields could be erected; the use of back-sightings to confirm the lines allowed remarkable accuracy with a simple device (Lewis 2001).

The systems of weighing and measuring in the classical world may seem bewildering in their diversity; nevertheless, they are usually quite logical and useful within their time and place, and they fostered significant accomplishments in agriculture, engineering, architecture, and commerce. The carefully calculated weight standards behind Athenian coinage in the fifth century B.C. and behind the coinage of Alexander in the fourth helped promote trade and prosperity in both periods (see part 2 of this chapter). The production of stone columns and architectural members in a graduated series of standard dimensions was an important contribution to the extraordinary productivity of the Roman imperial building program (chapter 10). The roads and colonial land allocations measured off by Roman surveyors opened up enormous areas of Europe and North Africa to settlement and commerce. Like literacy, numeracy, and timekeeping (chapters 28 and 29), the measurement of weight, length, and area constituted an important subsidiary technology facilitating the many other technical accomplishments of the classical world.

# REFERENCES

Berriman, A. E. 1953. *Historical metrology: A new analysis of the archaeological and the historical evidence relating to weights and measures.* London: Dutton.

Böckh A. 1838. *Metrologische Untersuchungen über Gewichte, Münzfüsse und Masse der Alterthums in ihrem Zusammenhange,* Berlin: Veit.

Brodersen, K. 1995. *Terra cognita: Studien zur römischen Raumerfassung.* Spudasmata 59. Hildesheim: Olms.

Hecht, K. 1979. "Zum römischen Fuss," *Abhandlungen der Braunschweigischen Wissenschaftlichen Gesellschaft* 30:1–34.

Hitzl, K. 1996. *Die Gewichte griechischer Zeit aus Olympia.* Olympische Forschungen 25. Berlin: de Gruyter.

Hultsch, F. 1864–1866. *Metrologicorum Scriptorum Reliquiae.* 2 vols. Leipzig: Teubner.

Hultsch, F. 1882. *Griechische und römische Metrologie.* 2nd ed. Berlin: Weidmann.

Ioppolo, G. 1967. "La tavola delle unità di misura nel mercato augusteo di Leptis Magna," *Quaderni di Archeologia Libia* 5: 89–98.

Kisch, B. 1965. *Scales and weights: A historical outline.* New Haven: Yale University Press.

Lang, M. 1964. *Excavations in the Athenian agora.* Vol. 10, *Weights, measures and tokens.* Princeton: The American School of Classical Studies at Athens.

Lazzarini, M. 1948. "Le bilance romane del Museo Nazionale e dell'Antiquarium Comunale di Roma," *Rendiconti della Classe di Scienze Morali, Storiche e Filologiche dell' Accademia dei Lincei* Ser. 8.3: 221–54.

Lewis, M. J. T. 2001. *Surveying instruments of Greece and Rome*. Cambridge: Cambridge University Press.

Mau, A. 1908. *Pompeji in Leben und Kunst*. Leipzig: Wilhelm Engelmann.

O'Brien, D. 1981–1984. *Theories of weight in the ancient world*. 2 vols. Leiden: Brill.

Peacock, D. P. S., and D. F. Williams 1986. *Amphorae and the Roman economy: An introductory guide*. London: Longman.

Richardson, W. F. 2003. *Numbering and measuring in the classical world*. 2nd ed. Bristol: Bristol Classical Press.

Robinson, M. 1941. *Metal and minor miscellaneous finds: An original contribution to Greek life*. Olynthus 10. Baltimore: Johns Hopkins University Press.

Rostovtzeff, M. 1941. *The social and economic history of the Hellenistic world*. 3 vols. Oxford: Oxford University Press.

Schiøler, T. 1994. "The Pompeji-Groma in new light," *Analecta Romana* 22: 45–60.

Viedebantt, O. 1917. *Forschungen zur Metrologie des Altertums*. Leipzig: Teubner.

Viedebantt, O. 1923. *Antike Gewichtsnormen und Münzfüsse*. Berlin: Weidmann.

Wikander, Ö. 1993. "Terracotta modules, Oscan feet and tile standards," in E. Rystedt, C. Wikander, and Ö. Wikander (eds.), *Deliciae fictiles: Proceedings of the First International Conference on Central Italic Architectural Terracottas at the Swedish Institute in Rome, 10–12 December, 1990*. Acta Instituti Romani Regni Sueciae 50. Stockholm: Åströms Förlag, 67–70.

# Part 2: Coinage
# (Andrew Meadows)

## The Technology of Coinage

Coinage is a technology in its own right. It is also the result of specific processes that represented, at least in the early stages, major technological advances. Within the context of this handbook, it is appropriate to stress the role of coinage as a facilitating technology. Without it, for example, many of the major engineering activities described in the other chapters of this book could never have left the realm of the theoretical. It was also responsible for major paradigmatic shifts in other areas of ancient behavior and thought. These are three bold claims; each must be addressed in turn.

In some form or another, money (by which we mean a substance that can be used as a store of wealth, an expression of value, or a medium of exchange) has existed almost as far back as the human documentary record extends, at least as far as the third millennium B.C. Coinage is a specific subset of money that might be defined as a piece of metal used as money which conforms to standards and bears a design (Howgego 1995: 1). As recently as the 1970s, the beginning of coinage appeared as a radical technological jump in economic history, but more recent scholarship has tended to situate coinage within a continuum of the development of monetary instruments. On the one hand, there has been a movement to play up the extent to which the Greek world had, before the arrival of coinage, adopted the Near Eastern practice of using both silver and gold bullion as a monetary medium (see especially Kroll 1998, 2001). At the same time, analysis of the Near Eastern archaeological record has suggested two ways in which coinage was foreshadowed by the use of silver ingots. There is fairly widespread evidence for the production of so-called chocolate-bar ingots, which were cast in a preportioned form, apparently to facilitate their subdivision for use in specific transactions (Thompson 2003). There is also growing evidence from as early as the twelfth to eleventh centuries B.C., both from literary and documentary texts and in finds of silver and *bullae*, for the practice of sealing determined amounts of silver, probably in linen bags, to provide easily usable quantities of guaranteed weight and fineness (Thompson 2003). Thus, in all three ways in which it is a distinctive monetary form—metallic composition, production to a fixed weight, and stamping with a design—it appears that coinage was a development from an existing Near Eastern tradition rather than a fundamentally new technology.

Nonetheless, coinage did bring with it technological advance. Research has suggested, for example in the case of the early electrum coinage, that the regularization of the production of gold stimulated the systematic use of gold refining. "It would seem that here was a technology awaiting a problem, a problem which was finally posed by the introduction of coinage, that is pieces of precious metal where the weight and purity were guaranteed" (Ramage and Craddock 2000: 212). The authors of this passage were puzzled that while the technological ability to refine gold by removing from it naturally occurring silver had long existed, there is no evidence for its systematic exploitation until the invention of electrum coinage. They push this hypothesis further to suggest that "everywhere, except possibly in India, the introduction of a gold coinage seems to have provided a stimulus for gold-refining" (Ramage and Craddock 2000: 12). This observation provides us with an important example of the way in which coinage as a concept drove the full development or application of a new technology from infancy to maturity.

Gold coinage, however, remained a marginal part of the economy for much of the ancient Greek and Roman world. Silver was the mainstay of the monetary market. Metal analysis that has been carried out on pre-coin monetary silver (Stos-Gale 2001) suggests that the metal was in general of high quality (97% pure or better). The earliest coinages matched these levels. Archaic Greek coinage, at many of the mints at which it was produced, generally achieved silver fineness of 98 percent or better (Gale et al. 1980). Nonetheless, debasement was always an option, and it was deployed at times as a financial stratagem but was rarely used in a "deceptive" sense. An interesting example is provided by a series of Roman coins of the early second century B.C. known to modern scholars as *quadrigati* (from their distinctive reverse types showing a four-horse chariot). These coins appear to have been produced routinely at about 72 to 93 percent fineness (Walker 1980: 58–61). At the same time, however, the Roman mint was producing the clearly separate *de-*

Figure 30.1. Brass sestertius of the emperor Titus (A.D. 79–81), with a design commemorating the completion of the Flavian amphitheater in A.D. 81. British Museum, BMCRE Titus 190. (By permission of the Trustees of the British Museum.)

*narius* coinage at full fineness. It seems that the easily recognizable debased *quadrigati* had a function separate from that of the *denarii*, and they were not intended to pass for full-fineness coins. When debasement of the coinage did began to occur more systematically, notably under the Roman Empire, it seems that this occurred as part of a considered and closely monitored strategy. Analysis of the imperial silver coinage of the Severan dynasty, for example, has suggested that a silver fineness of 46 percent was established empire-wide and observed not just at the mint of Rome, but also at the provincial mints in Syria and Tyre (Gitler and Ponting 2003). Such debasement continued into the third century and became a central element in the Roman state's attempts to increase the money supply when faced with increasing demands for expenditure.

The advent of coinage thus led to an important monetary development in the form of fiduciary financial instruments, although there were, in fact, much earlier precedents. Late in the fifth century B.C., coinage began to be produced in copper-based alloys. The value of these coins was, in general, notionally linked to their metal content. Bigger and heavier coins were worth more, but this higher value was not directly proportional to the extra amounts of metal in most cases. Manipulation of the alloys used to produce such fiduciary, lower-value coins, was at its most sophisticated following the reform of the coinage by Augustus (37 B.C.–A.D. 14). Under Augustus, two new high-value base coins were introduced, the *sestertius* (previously a silver denomination) and the *dupondius* (e.g., figure 30.1). Unlike the lower value *as*, which was a bronze coin, these higher denominations were produced in brass. The yellowish color of this alloy (*orichalcum*) seems to have had golden associations (see chapter 4; figure 4.5), which were played upon by the minting authorities to create confidence in higher-value base metal coin (Burnett 1987: 54). Later in the Roman imperial period, there is evidence for similar manipulation of expectation in the phenomenon of deliberate surface enrichment of low-fineness silver coins in an attempt to make them look more silver than they really were; Butcher and Ponting (1998: 310) discuss the "devious nature of ancient moneyers."

## Coinage as a New Technology

Coinage was hand produced, and as such it represented no great technological advance. The engraving of the dies used to strike the coins was a skill inherited from and shared with the producers of sealstones, which had a long history before the arrival of coinage and which continues even now. The application of the engraved dies to the coin blank—the obverse die below, embedded in the "anvil," the reverse die above—and the striking of the upper die with a hammer was not a sophisticated process either. Striking the coin represents nothing more than an adaptation of the application of seals to clay. Again the process is foreshadowed and paralleled by the stamping of such items as documents, bricks, or amphora handles. Nor is there anything even in the scale of use of coin dies, at least in the first three centuries of coin production, that represents a decisive shift from previous practice. Although the evidence may not be plentiful, we must imagine that the seals of important officials within the great empires of the Near East were a common sight on official documents, and widely recognized.

The technological advances that coinage brought through its mass-produced nature were rather advances of application, and we may divide them essentially into two categories: those intended by the original issuers, and those that resulted spontaneously from use.

Although, as has been noted above, several important facets of coinage as a monetary instrument were present in preexisting monetary traditions and objects, two key elements were not. First, coinage was, in the form that it was produced, ready-stamped with a seal that guaranteed it and gave it value within the context of the society that recognized the device. Second, it was produced at a series of fixed weights in a denominational system that provided for its use in making fixed payments at certain, different levels of value without any further treatment, such as cutting. These two elements combined to create a monetary form that was ideally suited to the making of large-scale identical payments in a way that had never been possible before, other than in kind. Indeed, it has been argued that the need to make such payments was always the motivating factor for the production of coinage in the ancient world (Crawford 1970). The technology embodied in coinage in this sense became the facilitator of a whole series of activities that had been unthinkable or impossible without coinage and forms the subject of this chapter's final section. Such developments, however, were not necessarily foreseen, desired, or intended by the issuers of coin.

There is another sense in which the design on the coinage presented new possibilities. For although personal seals and sealings had undoubtedly been and remained a common occurrence within administrative circles, the designs that

Figure 30.2. Silver tetradrachm of Alexander the Great (336–323 B.C.). British Museum, BMC 5c. (By permission of the Trustees of the British Museum.)

appeared on coins were different in two fundamental respects. First, by the fifth century B.C. and onward through the Hellenistic period down to the appearance of Roman coinage in late third and second centuries B.C., the designs on the coins had transcended the personal to become symbolic of the state that guaranteed the coinage. Even when personal badges did appear as coin designs, this was a function of the individual's role within the state apparatus, whether as servant of the state or embodiment of it. Second, after coinage had entered the mainstream of economic behavior, and once lower denominations suitable for small-scale transactions had become common, in the Hellenistic period and under the Roman Empire, the designs on coins penetrated to levels of society on a far wider basis than did the seal designs of the elites. In a world with no other form of mass medium, there was a golden opportunity to be seized here. Alexander the Great was the first to do so. The mechanism seems childishly simple to a modern eye. As Alexander moved his way eastward with his army and began to establish himself at the head of what had been the Persian Empire, he established mints to produce the coinage that the maintenance of his prodigious conquest required. Unlike his Persian predecessors, who had adopted no consistent monetary form, Alexander ensured that each of his mints produced coinage in exactly the same form in pure gold and silver (figure 30.2). By the time of his death, almost thirty different production centers were producing virtually identical coins, from Macedonia in the west to Babylon in the east (Price 1991: 72). To many of those inhabiting the vast realm that had become, within a very short space of time, Alexander's kingdom, coinage, and the messages it conveyed about Alexander's divine origins, royal status, and military prowess, would have been the single obvious sign of the new regime. Within a few years there could have been virtually no one within this kingdom who had not been exposed to the ideological ensemble of the coin designs. This was the birth of mass communication.

A similar approach was taken by some of the Hellenistic monarchies, but the phenomenon would not occur again on such a scale until the reforms of the third century A.D. that unified coin design across the Roman Empire. An interesting

Figure 30.3. Electrum stater signed by Phanes, perhaps minted at Ephesus, ca. 600 BC. British Museum, *BMC* 1. (By permission of the Trustees of the British Museum.)

early development of this potential occurred in Republican Rome during the later second and first centuries B.C., when the coin designs chosen by the monetary magistrates became for a while the vehicle for the development of family histories and the memorializing of ancestral tradition, as part of the political interplay of the major Roman *gentes* (Meadows and Williams 2001).

## Coinage as Facilitator of Technologies

As has already been noted, coinage was well adapted from the outset to perform a particular function, and it is often inferred from this suitability that that this function was one of the prime drivers behind coinage's invention, its uptake in the Greek world, and its eventual success as a monetary medium in the Greco-Roman world and beyond. That function is the making of broadly acceptable mass payments.

For the earliest coinages, the nature of the issuing and controlling body is unclear. The oldest Greek coin inscription informs us that the design on the coin is the badge of an individual named Phanes (figure 30.3). It is thus not impossible that early coins were produced by wealthy individuals. Throughout the classical Greek and Roman periods, however, virtually all coinage may reasonably be assumed to have been guaranteed and issued by the state (although the source of the bullion may at times have been private). Coinage will have entered circulation by being paid out by the state in return for services, labor, and produce. As such, coinage becomes indicative of an approach to public activity on a fundamentally different model than that of the royal and temple states of the Near East. Coinage did not emerge as a major part of the economy in Egypt, Mesopotamia, and Iran before the fourth century B.C. It was not produced in these areas much before the arrival of Alexander the Great. As a state payment device, coinage is the evidence for a state that functions by purchasing what it needs rather than commanding it. The precise relationship between the development of the Greek city and the concept of citizenship on the one hand, and the appearance of coinage on the other, remains unclear. There may be an element of cause and effect operating in both directions between the two; but it is certainly the case that coinage spread

Figure 30.4. Silver denarius issued by Mark Antony as *triumvir*, 32–31 B.C. British Museum, *BMCRR East* 189. (By permission of the Trustees of the British Museum.)

swiftly throughout the Greek world in the latter half of the sixth century B.C., the point at which many Greek states seem to have been coalescing as political units, drawing up law-codes, and wrestling with constitutional questions such as the nature of tyranny.

It is certainly true to say that key elements of the Greek and Roman states that we now consider definitive are scarcely imaginable without coinage. A prime case is that of the radical democracy at Athens. By the late fifth century B.C., a number of the integral institutions, such as the law-courts, the rotating council, and the assembly of all citizens, offered cash payments to facilitate participation on the part of the populace at large. Coinage was the oil that greased the wheels of this political apparatus. It was also at Athens and at this period that it became possible to maintain a paid, standing military force. The real implications of this development become most evident under the Roman Empire when, by the early third century A.D., there may been as many as a third of a million men earning more than 500 *denarii* per year (Alston 1994). At times the military nature of coin issues is explicit in their design, as in the case of the massive silver issues of Mark Antony in the 30s B.C. These coins are often described as "legionary denarii," since they were marked with the numbers of the legions for which they were destined to serve as pay (figure 30.4). The impact of such a development goes far beyond the military, of course. The soldiers themselves were engaged in areas that we would today regard as civil engineering, such as the building of roads and bridges. But other workers, too, from the fifth century B.C. onward, were paid for their services: masons, architects, doctors, lawyers, prostitutes, artists, actors, and musicians (Loomis 1998) (see figure 30.1). Coinage made it possible not only for the state to patronize these activities on a broad scale, but also for private individuals to pay for services.

The existence of a large body of citizens effectively divorced from the land by their full-time military, technical or artistic employment, and thus outside the basic subsistence farming structure of ancient society, created a cash-based market for the basic goods required to survive. The role of coinage in this new cash-based economy is clearly stated by ancient political philosophers such as Plato and Aristotle (*Pol.* 1.9):

It came to be agreed between men that for exchange purposes they would give and receive some sort of commodity, which was easy to handle and also useful for life, such as iron and silver and any other such substance. In the beginning value was decided by size and weight. Subsequently, stamps were placed upon it so as to remove the need for measurement: for the stamp was a mark of value. Once money had come into being to serve the needs of necessary exchange, the other form of moneymaking quickly came into being: trade. In the beginning this was perhaps fairly simple, but then became with practice more complex, as men learned where and how exchange might yield the greatest profit. This is why it appears that moneymaking principally involves coinage, and that the chief re-quirement for such moneymaking is the ability to see where the most money will come from, for that is where wealth and money are made. Indeed, it is often held that wealth is a large quantity of coin, because that is what moneymaking and trade is all about.

Coinage for Aristotle was clearly a technology that allowed exchange to function more smoothly within an advanced society, and also facilitated the accumulation of wealth. So far had it become embedded within everyday experience in the major cities of the late fifth century B.C., that it was impossible even for Plato, who gravely mistrusted the accumulation of wealth that it facilitated, to envisage a city without it (e.g., *Leg.* 5.742a–b). This is all the more remarkable when we consider that even in Plato and Aristotle's day, coinage was still being produced predom-inantly in denominations unsuitable for the fulfillment of small-scale transactions. Most Greek city states in the archaic and classical periods produced only silver coinage, and only at denominations of the value of about a week's pay. It was only in the Hellenistic and Roman periods that smaller silver and bronze denominations became the norm.

But by this point no one could stop coinage from performing precisely the function that Plato feared. By allowing individuals to take up paid employment and free themselves from the land, coinage created not just individuals able to devote themselves to professional activity and thus advance the technologies of their societies, but also a class with the leisure to participate in the enjoyment of the fruits of their labor. The Romans and Greeks who enjoyed the lavish bath com-plexes that adorned their cities, congregated around the splendid *nymphaea,* and traveled the fine new roads could do so because they had money. Coinage had given them that freedom and, for this reason above all others, was the most potent of all ancient technological advances.

# REFERENCES

Alston, R. 1994. "Roman military pay from Caesar to Diocletian," *Journal of Roman Studies* 84: 113–23.

Balmuth, M. (ed.) 2001. *Hacksilber to coinage: New insights into the monetary history of the Near East and Greece.* New York: The American Numismatic Society.

Burnett, A. M. 1987. *Coinage in the Roman world*. London: Seaby.

Butcher, K., and M. Ponting 1998. "Atomic absorption spectrometry and Roman silver coins," in W. A. Oddy and M. Cowell (eds.), *Metallurgy in numismatics, IV*. Royal Numismatic Society Special Publication 30. London: Royal Numismatic Society, 308–34.

Crawford, M. H. 1970. "Money and exchange in the Roman world," *Journal of Roman Studies* 60: 40–48.

Gale, N. H., W. Gentner, and G. A. Wagner 1980. "Mineralogical and geographical silver sources of archaic Greek coinage," in Metcalf and Oddy 1980, 3–49.

Gitler, H., and M. Ponting 2003. *The silver coinage of Septimius Severus and his family (193–211 AD: A study of the chemical composition of the Roman and Eastern issues)*. Milan: Ennere.

Howgego, C. J. 1995. *Ancient history from coins*. London: Routledge.

Kroll, J. 1998. "Silver in Solon's laws," in R. Ashton and S. Hurter (eds.), *Studies in Greek numismatics in memory of Martin Jessop Price*. London: Spink, 225–32.

Kroll, J. 2001. "Observations on monetary instruments in pre-coinage Greece," in Balmuth 2001, 77–91.

Loomis, W. T. 1998. *Wages, welfare costs and inflation in classical Athens*. Ann Arbor: University of Michigan Press.

Meadows, A. R., and J. H. C. Williams 2001. "Moneta and the monuments: Coinage and politics in republican Rome," *Journal of Roman Studies* 91: 27–49.

Metcalf, D. M., and W. A. Oddy (eds.) 1980. *Metallurgy in numismatics, I*. Royal Numismatic Society Special Publication 13. London: Royal Numismatic Society.

Price, M. J. 1991. *Coinage in the name of Alexander the Great and Philip Arrhidaeus*. London: British Museum Press.

Ramage, A., and P. Craddock 2000. *King Croesus' gold: Excavations at Sardis and the history of gold refining*. London: The British Museum Press.

Stos-Gale, Z. A. 2001. "The impact of the natural sciences on studies of Hacksilber and early silver coinage," in Balmuth 2001, 53–76.

Thompson, C.M. 2003. "Sealed silver in Iron Age Cisjordan and the 'invention' of coinage," *Oxford Journal of Archaeology* 22: 67–107.

Walker, D. R., 1980. "The silver contents of the Roman Republican coinage," in Metcalf and Oddy 1980, 55–72

# PART 3: PRACTICAL MATHEMATICS (KARIN TYBJERG)

Practical mathematics is related to technology in several ways. It is both a technology in its own right for administrating and facilitating daily life, economic transactions, and administration, and a tool for other technologies, such as land measuring, construction, warfare, and hydraulics. Practical math is not simply a matter of applying mathematics to practical ends; the relationship between mathematics and technology is two-directional, and practical methods are reflected back into theoretical mathematics. The evidence shows that mathematics played a central role in political and administrative control, that professional practitioners used mathematics to solve problems as well as to create an identity for themselves, and that the relationship between practical and theoretical mathematics is complex and dynamic. There is, however, one caveat: the source material on practical and particularly everyday mathematics is limited, varied, and frequently indirect. Often the methods and techniques for practical calculations and geometrical constructions have been lost, and only the results are preserved: accounts, measurements, loans, and records of inheritance and tax. Little is known about the relationship between what was taught and what was used, and the information transfer was predominantly oral, leaving little conclusive material.

## Mathematics as a Technology

In Aristophanes' *Wasps* (656; quoted from Rihll 1999: 45), a quick calculation is introduced with the remark "Reckon up, not with counters, but just on your hands, the amount of tribute." This comment illustrates two points about the use of mathematics in classical Athens: that finger reckoning was second best to a more sophisticated method of counters, and that mathematical calculations were performed and checked in public. It also indicates that, since numeracy played an important role in public life, a history of numeracy should be taken as seriously as the much-researched problem of literacy in the Greek world (see Netz 2002 on the role of numeracy and counters in classical Greek culture).

The earliest formal notation for numbers is known as the acrophonic system, and its symbols derive from the first letter in the word for each number (5 is Π for *penta*, 10 is Δ for *deka* and so on); the unit is simply I. This system developed in close conjunction with finance and trade and includes symbols for monetary units such as obols. While there are no literary sources for this notation, it is common on official inscriptions from Athens and other Greek communities. It is also found on stones probably used as counting boards and abaci, such as the famous Salamis tablet (of disputed date, but possibly late fourth century B.C.), whose markings can be interpreted as obol and drachma fractions (*IG* II$^2$ 2777; see Pullan 1970: 23–25; Heath 1921: 49–51) (figure 30.5). There is no evidence on how these boards were used, but it may be surmised that pebbles were arranged and manipulated on lines representing different numbers of units. This could be the method of counters alluded to by Aristophanes.

The importance of mathematical techniques in public life is clear from numerous inscriptions of records, lists, and accounts. They show, for instance, the tributes paid by other cities to Athens with amounts, subtotals, and totals, lists of loans to the state or temples, and inventories and accounts of construction work. The mathematical practices of accounting and recording thus had both a practical and a symbolic role. Not only did they allow officials to administrate resources; the public display of accounts also served the symbolic purpose of displaying power

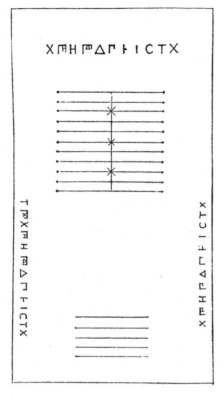

Figure 30.5. Greek calculation tablet, probably for use with pebbles. Salamis, uncertain date. (After E. Guillaume in *DarSag* 1.1, 1877: 2.)

and organization as well as transparency and objectivity. Practical mathematical techniques were used to produce "accountable" knowledge and acted as a guarantee for objectivity in social and political transactions as well as in commerce and finance (Cuomo 2001: 13–16).

From the third century B.C. on, alphabetic notation took over as standard. Numbers were named consecutively after the letters of the alphabet, in which the first nine represent 1–9, the next nine 10–90, and the last nine 100–900. In consequence, this notation was integrated with written culture and was used in high level Greek geometry, as well as for inscriptions and administrative documents.

Mathematical techniques played a central role in the complex bureaucracy of Ptolemaic and Roman Egypt, which monitored land holdings and land use. A large number of papyri and tablets deal with land surveys and provide detailed information on owners, location, dimensions, and crops. Typically, for Egyptian and later Greek mathematics, the numbers are listed in so-called unit-fractions—that is, the reciprocal values half, third, fourth, fifth, and so on. Values are then expressed as whole numbers plus decreasing fractions. The calculations performed in these surveys were approximations and often contained mistakes. Areas of quadrilateral fields were, for example, usually estimated by multiplying the averages of the two pairs of opposite sides. This gives advantage to the tax-man as the area is always overestimated, except in the case of a perfectly rectangular field.

Very similar arithmetical and geometrical techniques are found in Babylonian, Islamic, and medieval European sources, indicating a long-lived tradition of professional mathematics. Throughout this tradition we find not only simple approximation techniques, but also solutions to complex problems, which are totally unrealistic despite being set in practical contexts such as land measurement or horse-trading (see Høyrup 1990 on "sub-scientific" mathematical traditions). These problems demonstrate a theoretical outgrowth from practical techniques and solutions. Clear traces of this development are found in more theoretical authors, such as Diophantus, who presented the same arithmetical problems but without the horse-trading, and in Hero of Alexandria, who placed problems of land measurement in an Archimedean context. The boundaries between practical and theoretical mathematics were not watertight.

In general, the Roman world featured a grand administrative system of mathematically trained officials in both army and government. Roman magistrates were obliged to submit accounts after their period in office to a central archive, and precise accounts were also kept at lower levels. Some of the most precise and thorough accounts known from the Roman world stem from the pay-sheets of a couple of first-century A.D. soldiers (Ste. Croix 1956: 39–40). Training was systematized, and there is evidence from the Roman world for basic mathematical education that supported recording, accounting, and measuring, along with tables for conversion of measures and units (Cuomo 2001; Fowler 1999: 268–76).

The Roman numeral system was—like the Greek acrophonic system—closely linked to trade and calculation on the abacus, as the counters on the abacus are easily noted down, with each counter matching a symbol (Taisbak 1965). The abacus works by representing numbers by counters on lines with values 1, 5, 10, and 50; the number 15 was thus represented on the abacus by one counter on 10 and one on 5, and in Roman numerals by X for 10 and V for 5 (on the abacus, see Heath 1921, Pullan 1970). Figure 30.6 illustrates a reproduction of an abacus found at Pompeii; the counters in the upper rank are worth 5, while those below are worth 1. From left to right the columns represent 1,000,000, 100,000, 10,000, 1,000, 100, 10, 1, $\frac{1}{12}$ (*uncia*, ounce), and fractions of an *uncia*.

Both measurement and finance in the Roman world operated with a system of twelfths—the so-called *uncia* fractions ($\frac{1}{12}$, $\frac{2}{12}$, etc.). Surveyors, for example, divided their unit, the *iugerum*, into twelve parts, and the foot was divided into twelve *unciae pedis*; incidentally, this use of the word *uncia* gives rise to the English *inch*. In *Ars Poetica* (325–330), Horace describes schoolboys at work: "Tell us Albinus' son: if you subtract *uncia* ($\frac{1}{12}$) from *quincunx* ($\frac{5}{12}$), what is left? Come on, out with it!" "*Triens* ($\frac{1}{3}$)." "Good; you'll be able to look after your property" (quoted from Richardson 2004: 21–22).

A striking example of how mathematics could be used to demonstrate orderly government is found in Frontinus' account of the water-supply system for Rome, *De aquaeductu urbis Romae*. Frontinus estimates the amount of water entering the

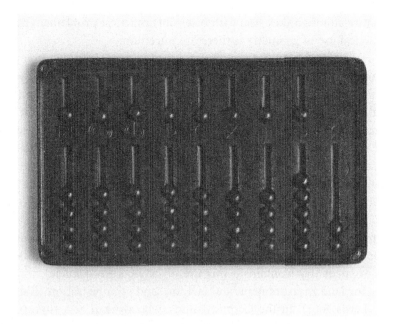

Figure 30.6. Modern reproduction of Roman abacus with sliding counters. Science Museum, London. (Courtesy of Science Museum/Science & Society Picture Library.)

water system for the city and, to account for these resources, he asks whether the intake matches the discharge to official supply structures. He found a considerable loss and sought to stop fraudulent diversion by standardizing pipe sizes. In this way, mathematics was used to secure a fair distribution of resources and—not unlike Horace's schoolboy—Frontinus demonstrates his competence at looking after the property of the state through a display of calculations with *uncia* fractions (cf. chapters 2 and 11).

Practical mathematics was thus not only essential in daily interactions of trade and commerce, but also highly significant in the administration of complex societies. Mathematics was an instrument for recording and control, quantification of power, and collective accountability.

## Mathematics in Technology

It is often claimed that mathematics and technology were unconnected in antiquity and that this separation barred progress. On closer scrutiny, however, many connections become apparent, and it is clear that mathematics was used in a variety of technologies, including land measurement, construction, hydraulics, town planning, astrology, and military engineering. Techniques for measuring and estimating areas and volumes were related to geometrical theory. The preserved treatises that employ geometry in technological problems provide, however, mainly a theoretical superstructure although they deal with ostensibly practical problems. The real extent of practical use of geometry is therefore uncertain.

The origin of geometry was said—for example, by Herodotus (2.109), Plato (*Phdr.* 274c), and Strabo (17.3)—to be in measuring land, and the term *geometria* had the dual significations of both land measurement and geometry. At the more theoretical end of the spectrum stands Hero of Alexandria with his *Metrica*, on calculating and dividing areas and volumes. This treatise offers a systematic treatment of geometrical objects and contains both methods of calculation and geometrical proofs. Although the work goes far beyond practical use with its consideration of polygons and sections of complex curves, it maintains a practical perspective. The section on dividing areas is explicitly related to land measurement, and three-dimensional objects are described as architectural elements.

That practical and theoretical work cannot easily be distinguished is also made clear in the *Corpus Agrimensorum Romanorum*, a large collection of Latin works on land measurement that contains a mixture of extracts from Euclid, treatises on techniques for land measurement, and laws on land administration (Blume et al. 1848–1852; Lewis 2001). In the *Corpus*, Balbus, who worked as a surveyor in the Roman Army under Domitian or Trajan, writes about his practical tasks, but also produces a taxonomy of geometrical objects and concepts. Practical experience is thus inserted in geometrical discourse when the curved, irregular lines of the landscape are listed with the straight and circular lines of geometry. In this way Balbus offers fellow surveyors a geometrical framework for their practical techniques and thus elevates the status of the mathematical expertise of surveyors. Columella takes almost the opposite approach in his treatise on farm management for gentlemen, *De re rustica* (A.D. 60–65), since he includes some practical geometrical techniques to demonstrate that he knows how it is done but specifically states that he leaves this sort of calculation to the surveyor (*mensor;* 5.1.3). He offers simple rules for calculating the areas of fields shaped like various geometrical objects—triangles, rectangles, and circles—among them the simple rule for quadrilaterals used in Roman Egypt (*Rust.* 5.1.4–2.10).

A similar range of techniques and geometrical superstructure is found in many other technical disciplines. Little is known of architectural geometry, but an Egyptian papyrus of Euclid refers to geometrical objects as architectural elements, such as stones or columns. The text thus appears to have been used in the training or study of architects, although the Euclidean geometry probably constituted no more than an educated background. The Roman architect Vitruvius points out in his handbook *De architectura* (ca. 25 B.C.) that geometry and arithmetic are needed by the architect to calculate cost, make measurements, lay out buildings, and solve problems of symmetry (*De arch.* 1.1.4). Vitruvius, however, lists mathematics among many other disciplines and thus demonstrates the learning of architects rather than explaining what happens on the building site; he uses mathematics to upgrade his technical expertise. At the same time, mathematics does appear to have been used for large building projects. In a fifth-century B.C. tunnel construction for water-supply—the Eupalinus tunnel—numbers are found engraved along the sides of the tunnel wall, probably measuring the distance into the mountain (Kienast 1995; cf. chapter 12). A more theoretical account of tunnel construction is found in Hero's instructions for triangulating across a mountain, so that the teams digging a tunnel from either end will meet in the middle. An inscription from the Roman colony of Saldae shows that this was a real concern. Two teams of workers had failed to meet in the middle because each veered from the straight line, that is, from proper geometrical control (*CIL* 8.2728; chapter 12).

Military machines were also subjected to mathematical treatment. In the third century B.C., Philo of Byzantium wrote on catapult construction and offered advice based not only on experience but also on geometrical proof. He relates the problem of scaling well-functioning catapults up or down to the famous geometrical problem of doubling the volume of a unit cube. He solves the problem with a moving ruler and thus combines mechanics and geometry in two ways: a geometrical problem is *set* in a practical context and *proved* by an instrument. In his *Poliorcetica* (*Siegecraft*), Philo also applies geometry to the problem of constructing fortifications. He recommends building walls in a zigzag shape of regular triangles, leaving the fortification less vulnerable to sieges by providing a more comprehensive range of fire from the walls. Although these models are more complex than strictly practicable, archaeological ruins of fortifications suggest that the principle was indeed applied. The importance of mathematics and in particular measurement to the military engineer is further illustrated by the oft-repeated admonition to measure the height of the walls of a fortification to ensure that the siege machines are sufficiently large (Polybius 9.19; Hero, *Dioptra* 190.14–19).

Geometrical techniques and proofs for measuring heights, areas, and volumes are thus employed in a number of technical disciplines. The role of the geometrical techniques is not just practical; they also serve to emphasize the special expertise of practitioners and raise the status of their disciplines. Although practical mathematics was often looked down upon—most notably by Plato (e.g. *Resp.* 7.525b–526b)—practical efficacy held status in its own right. Hero of Alexandria shows that practical methods provide a natural extension of geometrical methods for dealing with irregular areas and volumes (Tybjerg 2004) and Balbus inscribes irregular lines in a Euclidean context, but both proudly point to the practical prowess of their methods. The combination of geometry and technology may have been behind the complex tunnel buildings in antiquity, but certainly bolstered professional standing and status of many technical experts.

# REFERENCES

Blume, F., K. Lachmann, and A. Rudorff 1848–1852. *Die Schriften der römischen Feldmesser.* 2 vols. Berlin: G. Reimer.
Cuomo, S. 2001. *Ancient mathematics.* London: Routledge.

Fowler, D. 1999. *The mathematics of Plato's Academy: A new reconstruction*. 2nd ed. Oxford: Oxford University Press.

Heath, T. L. 1921. *A history of Greek mathematics*. 2 vols. Oxford: Clarendon Press.

Høyrup, J. 1990. "Sub-scientific mathematics: Observations on a pre-modern phenomenon," *History of Science* 28: 63–86.

Kienast, H. J. 1995. *Die Wasserleitung des Eupalinos auf Samos*. Bonn: Habelt.

Lewis, M. J. T. 2001. *Surveying instruments of Greece and Rome*. Cambridge: Cambridge University Press.

Netz, R. 2002. "Counter culture: Towards a history of Greek numeracy," *History of Science* 40: 321–51.

Pullan, J. M. 1970. *The history of the abacus*. 2nd ed. London: Hutchinson.

Richardson, W. F. 2004. *Numbering and measuring in the classical world*. 2nd ed. Bristol: Bristol Phoenix Press.

Rihll, T. E. 1999. *Greek science. Greece and Rome* New Surveys in the Classics 29. Oxford: Oxford University Press.

Ste. Croix, G. E. M. de 1956. "Greek and Roman accounting," in A. Littleton and B. Yamey (eds.), *Studies in the history of accounting*. London: Sweet and Maxwell.

Taisbak, C. M. 1965. "Roman numerals and the abacus," *Classica et medievalia* 26: 147–60.

Tybjerg, K. 2004. "Hero of Alexandria's geometry of mechanics," *Apeiron* 37: 29–56.

CHAPTER 31

........................................................................................

# GADGETS AND SCIENTIFIC INSTRUMENTS

........................................................................................

## ÖRJAN WIKANDER

THE category of "gadgets" includes a large number of devices (*automata*) and machines described by Greek inventors and engineers. These more or less complex devices, which constitute an important source of information on the theoretical as well as practical mechanical standard of the classical world, have been the subject of remarkably little detailed study. They have often been—and occasionally still are—dismissed as worthless toys or "marvels," intended to evoke religious awe among the superstitious public. For some time, however, a more serious judgment of the automata has prevailed, describing them as object lessons in mechanical and pneumatic principles, rather than as tricks intended to inspire wonder (e.g., Price 1962; Drachmann 1963; Bedini 1964). In addition to these ancient automata, this chapter will treat some practical applications of the physical principles they illustrated, for example water clocks, astronomical instruments, and hodometers.

# BACKGROUND

The so-called five simple machines were known and discussed by Greek engineers and scientists from at least the late third century B.C. onward, perhaps beginning with Philo of Byzantium. The early-fourth-century mathematical commentator Pappus describes them (*Collectio* 8.52):

> There are five powers [machines] by the use of which a given weight is moved by a given force.... But it has been shown by Hero and Philo that the above-mentioned powers [machines] are reducible to a single principle, even though they differ considerably from another in form. Their names are the following: wheel and axle, lever, compound pulley, wedge, and, moreover, the so-called endless screw.

The "single principle" referred to is, of course, that what you lose in distance, you gain in power. The five simple machines are fundamental for most mechanical devices. The wheel and axle, the lever, and the wedge were known by the Early Bronze Age, the pulley by the eighth or seventh century B.C., while the screw is not attested with certainty until the mid-third century B.C. Although four of the simple machines were known before the age of Alexander the Great, in general the knowledge of mechanical or pneumatic devices remained almost nonexistent before that time. The development of the screw and gearwheel, allowing the precise application of force in a circular motion, were essential to this development.

In consequence, it is not surprising that the phenomenon of automata is so strongly associated with the Hellenistic period, when their necessary prerequisites were finally at hand and the Museum at Alexandria was a hive of inventive activity. Given the lack of a mechanical and cultural context, there is good reason to feel dubious about the few gadgets alleged to be earlier than the third century B.C. Athenaeus (4.174c), for example, ascribes a complex clock to Plato: "But it is said that Plato provided a small notion of its [the water-organ's] construction by having made a clock for use at night that was similar to a water-organ, although it was a very large water-clock." There are numerous technical objections to the flying bird of Archytas, as described by Aulus Gellius (*NA* 10.12.9–10):

> By a certain theoretical knowledge and mechanical education, Archytas made a wooden model of a dove that was able to fly. It was obviously balanced by weights and driven forward by a current of air enclosed and concealed in it. Concerning such an absurd story, I would like to quote Favorinus' own words: "Archytas of Tarentum who, among other things, was an engineer, made a wooden, flying dove. When it alighted, it did not take flight again."

These two stories show interesting parallels. Both gadgets are attributed to very well known philosophers active in the first half of the fourth century B.C., and both descriptions come from sources about five centuries later: Gellius and his informant Favorinus wrote in the second century A.D., Athenaeus about A.D. 200. Gellius seems to doubt his own story, and Athenaeus—otherwise a notorious name-dropper—cannot refer to anything more specific than "it is said" (*legetai*). Diels (1915) attempted a reconstruction of Plato's alarm clock, but both the clock and the bird may well be as mythical as the robots allegedly constructed by Hephaestus (Homer, *Il.* 18.369–79) and Daedalus (Aristotle, *De an.* 1.3.406b).

# The Technological Boom of the Third Century B.C.

The basis for Hellenistic science was laid by Aristotle and his pupils in the Lyceum in the period from about 336 to 323 B.C., then further elaborated by his followers at the Lyceum and the scientists at the Museum of Alexandria. A fair picture of the state of mechanical research immediately before the explosion of technological accomplishments during the reigns of Ptolemy II Philadelphus and Ptolemy III Euergetes (283–221 B.C.) can be found in the *Mechanika* (*Mechanical Problems*) traditionally attributed to Aristotle, but presumably written by one of his pupils in the 280s B.C. The treatise is devoted mostly to the lever, wheel, wedge, and pulley, and the practical applications discussed show clearly the low level of mechanical knowledge at the time. But a dynamic development of both theoretical and practical mechanics was soon to begin. One particularly important discovery was the possibilities offered by air, water pressure, and steam resulting from studies concerning vacuum executed by Strato of Lampsacus, leader of the Lyceum from 287 to 269 B.C. This knowledge is partly preserved in the introduction to Heron's *Pneumatica*.

No less important was the invention of various devices for changing the speed or direction of a linear or rotating motion: the gear, the cam, and the screw. Only relatively recently has the fundamental development of ancient gearwheels been understood (see, particularly, Foley et al. 1982; Lewis 1997: 37–57). A number of uncertain points remain but, for the time being, our knowledge of the earliest history of the cogwheel or gearwheel may be summarized as follows. About 300 B.C., power was transmitted by the use of chains passing over pentagonal prisms, in the repeating catapult designed by Dionysius of Alexandria (Philo of Byzantium, *Bel.* 73–76). If the prisms had been provided with notches on each side in order to engage the chain better, the construction would not have been very dissimilar from a true cogwheel. In the 270s B.C., Ctesibius' water clock included a rack and pinion and perhaps gearwheels (Vitruvius, *De arch.* 9.8.5). By about 260 B.C. there is indirect but credible evidence for the worm gear, and shortly afterward for ordinary cogwheels engaging in parallel or at right angles, in descriptions of the hodometer and the planetarium of Archimedes (Vitruvius, *De arch.* 10.9.1–4; Cicero, *Rep.* 1.14.21–22).

As in the case of the water-mill, much scholarly energy has been devoted to questioning, not the existence, but the actual importance of the cam in antiquity.

Figure 31.1. Reconstruction of gears and cam on Nysa's vehicle. (Lewis 1997: fig. 25; courtesy of Dr. Michael J. T. Lewis, University of Hull.)

Today, however, there is little doubt that cams on the shaft of water-powered wheels played an important part in some ancient Roman industries (see chapters 6 and 13), and this device has been traced in the ancient descriptions of at least four Hellenistic automata (Lewis 1997: 84–88, figs. 25–28). The earliest certain example is the arm of a puppet carpenter moving a hammer up and down in the automatic theater of Philo of Byzantium, from the 230s B.C. (preserved in Heron, *Automatopoiika* 24; Schmidt 1899: 422–27, fig. 103). Lewis argues persuasively for two even earlier examples: the flute player of Apollonius of Perge around 240 B.C. (preserved only in a reworked Arabic version by Banu Musa) and the 4 m high, seated statue of Nysa carried in a procession of Ptolemy II Philadelphus in the 270s B.C. (figure 31.1). Athenaeus (5.198f) quotes an almost contemporary account by Callixeinus of Rhodes: "This stood up automatically without anyone putting his hands to it, and after pouring a libation of milk from a golden bowl sat down again."

According to ancient sources, the history of the screw started with Archimedes, who allegedly invented the water-screw during his stay as a youth in Egypt, perhaps in the 260s (Diodorus Siculus 1.34.2, 5.37.3; Strabo 3.2.9; Athenaeus 5.208f; Drachmann 1958). Through a misunderstanding of Diodorus' text (Kiechle 1967: 14, notes 1–2), some scholars maintain that Archimedes found the screw already in use in the Nile at his arrival. Nor is the attempt of Dalley convincing (in Dalley and Oleson 2003: 7–17) to envisage water-screws in Sennacherib's palace gardens in Nineveh four hundred years earlier. Obviously the water-screw was from the very beginning intended for practical use, but so were most applications of the screw, particularly the screw-presses discussed by Heron and Pliny (Heron, *Mechanika* 3.15, 19–21; Pliny, *HN* 18.317; Drachmann 1932: 50–85). Small metal bolts intended for joining pieces together remain scarce in antiquity; they are mostly to be found in small luxury objects, parade helmets, and medical instruments (Mutz 1969; Klumbach 1973; Gaitzsch 1983; Deppert-Lippitz 1995). The endless screw played an important part in the worm gear used by automata. The tapering wood-screw did not exist in the classical world.

The crank, finally, remains subject to controversy. No certain literary or archaeological evidence proves its existence in antiquity, even though some scholars argue for the invention of the crank by Archimedes (Drachmann 1973; Sleeswyk 1981a). Certainly it seems remarkable that a civilization familiar with the rotating hand-mill would not have applied the same principle to the crank, whose handle rotates in more or less the same way. In any case, none of the known ancient automata or other gadgets requires the crank to function.

# AUTOMATA

The adjective *automatos*, meaning "self-acting" or "spontaneous," can be found as early as Homer's description of the wheeled tripod robots of Hephaestus (*Il.* 18.376). Today, the word is the technical term for various mechanical gadgets, in particular those described by Philo of Byzantium and Heron of Alexandria. The power of the automata derives from forces such as hanging weights, revolving wheels, or the pressure of heated air, and in exceptional cases even the force of wind or steam pressure (Heron, *Pneumatika* 1.43, 2.6, 2.11; see chapter 6). Again, it is doubtful whether these gadgets could correctly be described as "toys," and it is a myth that they could to any appreciable extent have functioned as marvels stimulating religious awe. Landels (2000: 202–3) points out that, of 75 devices in Heron's *Pneumatika*, only five can justifiably be labeled "temple miracles": for example, burning incense on an altar is extinguished automatically by a libation (Heron, *Pneumatika* 1.12); holy water runs from a vending machine when a five-drachma coin is inserted (1.21); temple doors open when a fire is lit on the altar outside (1.38).

There is reason to doubt that even these rather few "miracles" were, in fact, realized in order to awake awe among the public. Five drachmas is an extremely high price for a dose of holy water, and the mechanism for opening the temple doors in the last example is so complex that it is very questionable whether it would function in practice. Nonreligious "miracles" are far more common, such as figurines of various animals drinking water (e.g., Heron, *Pneumatika* 1.29–31, 2.36–37) or of singing birds (e.g., 1.15–16, 2.4–5, 2.32). Even many of these may, in fact, be mere armchair inventions. Few, if any, of the gadgets could have been of any practical use. Possible exceptions are automatically replenished oil lamps (1.22–24) and lamps whose wick was pushed forward as the oil burned, by means of a rack engaging a cogwheel coupled to a float (1.34).

Many automata were certainly intended to cause astonishment, but, as has been pointed out by various scholars, the ultimate intent of these miracles was

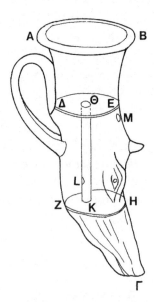

Figure 31.2. Magic drinking horn designed by Heron of Alexandria, *Pneumatika* 1.18. (Ö. Wikander, after Schmidt 1899: fig. 19.)

doubtless to illustrate physical and mechanical principles. There are many examples showing the function of communicating vessels and siphons, the powers of air-pressure and vacuum, the use of floats and gears, and so on. If the goal was educational, why was there so much emphasis on the manifestation of marvels? We are not in a position to say, but part of the answer may be connected with the social situation of the Alexandrian inventors. They were almost entirely dependent on the good will of the Ptolemaic rulers who sponsored the Museum and every scientist associated with it. The royal court (rather than the general public) probably was the most appreciate and lucrative audience for the entertainment and amusement offered by these *miracula*, long afterward collected in the works of Heron.

Several gadgets concerned with the pouring of wine or other beverages would have provided suitable entertainment at royal banquets. For example, one jug delivers the same amount of liquid every time one pours from it (Heron, *Pneumatika* 2.1). Another one pours various liquids separately from the same mouth (1.22). Yet another magic device (1.18) pours water, wine, or both (figure 31.2):

> Some drinking-horns (*rhyta*) are so designed that, when first wine and then water is poured into them, pure water flows out from them at one occasion, a mixture [of wine and water] at another, and pure wine at yet another. This is arranged in this way. A drinking-horn α β γ has two partitions δ ε and ζ η. Through both of them is led a pipe θ κ soldered together with the partitions and pierced with the little hole λ, which is placed slightly above the partition ζ η. But below the partition δ ε, there should be a vent μ in the hollow of the drinking-horn. Under these conditions, if one intercepts the outlet γ and pours in the wine, it will proceed through the hole λ to the space δ ε ζ η. For the air in that will depart through the vent μ. When we cover the vent μ with the finger, it will keep the wine in the part

δ ε ζ η. Now, when we pour water into the part α β ε δ of the drinking-horn, while covering the vent μ, the water will flow pure. But if we release the vent μ while the water is still above, a mixture will flow. When the water has flowed out, then the pure wine will flow. It is also possible, by [covering and] releasing the vent μ several times, to vary the outflows. But it is better first to pour water into the space δ ε ζ η and then pour wine, when the vent is covered. For it will follow at one occasion that pure wine will flow out, but, when the vent is released again, a mixture, and, when the vent is covered again, pure wine will flow. And this will happen as many times as we want.

# WATER-CLOCKS AND ASTRONOMICAL INSTRUMENTS

The inflow water-clock attributed to Ctesibius (ca. 280 B.C.) is the first device certainly including a true cogwheel: "The water flowing in at a regular volume through that opening raises an inverted bowl, which is called the 'cork' or 'drum' by the craftsmen. A bar and revolving drum are attached to this apparatus and both are fitted with regularly spaced teeth which, when meshing with one another, make measured rotations and movements" (Vitruvius, *De arch.* 9.8.5; Drachmann 1976). Archimedes further elaborated Ctesibius' water-clock, substituting a right-angle gear for Ctesibius' rack and cogwheel (Hill 1976; Sleeswyk 1990: 28–34; Lewis 1997: 37–41). Together, they became the point of departure for the construction of water-clocks during the Greco-Roman period and well into the medieval period (chapter 29).

From the very beginning, the construction of inflow water-clocks was closely related to that of astronomic instruments such as astrolabes, which later enjoyed popularity in the Islamic world and, in the fourteenth century, became the inspiration for the mechanical astronomical clocks of western Europe (Price 1974: 54–55; King and Millburn 1978). It is consequently quite appropriate that Archimedes, apart from his clock, was famous for his exquisite planetarium. In fact, this complex device, which was brought to Rome after the capture of Syracuse in 212 B.C., was described with admiration by four authors writing in Latin over four centuries: Cicero (ca. 54–51 B.C.; *Rep.* 1.14.21–22; *Tusc.* 1.63), Ovid (A.D. 2–18; *Fast.* 6.263–83), Lactantius (early fourth century A.D.; *Div. inst.* 2.5.18), and Claudian (ca. A.D. 400; *Carmina minora* 51 [68]). The most detailed description is given in Cicero's *De re publica* (whose dramatic date is 129 B.C.). The speaker is L. Furius Philus, consul in 136 B.C. and one of the leading statesmen of his time.

> I remember that C. Sulpicius Gallus—as you know, a most learned man—when he happened to visit M. Marcellus, who had been consul together with him, asked him to bring forward the celestial globe which Marcellus' grandfather had removed from the capture of the rich and beautiful Syracuse, even though he

had taken nothing else to his home from the immense booty captured. Although I had heard this globe mentioned frequently because of Archimedes' fame, I was not particularly impressed by its appearance; for the other globe that the same Archimedes had made and the same Marcellus had placed in the temple of Virtus was more beautiful and more widely known. But when Gallus had begun to explain the function of this device in an authoritative way, I realized that there had been greater genius in that famous Sicilian than it seemed possible for a human being to possess. For Gallus told us that the other solid and massive globe was an old invention, first constructed by Thales of Miletus. . . .

But this kind of globe, he said, which showed the motions of the sun and the moon and of those five stars which are called "wandering" and, so to speak, "strolling about" [i.e., the planets], contained more than could be accommodated in the solid globe. The invention of Archimedes was admirable inasmuch as he had contrived that one single turning device could represent uneven and varying movements with totally different rates of speed. When Gallus set this globe in motion, it so happened that the moon remained as many revolutions behind the sun in that bronze device as the number of days it was behind in the sky; accordingly, the same eclipse of the sun happened on the globe [as in the sun], and the moon came to the limit constituted by the shadow of the earth, when the sun from the region . . . [lacuna]

Although neither this description nor any of the others presents a clear picture of the function of this device, it clearly was capable of illustrating the interrelationships of numerous heavenly bodies. Even though there is no explicit mention of gears in Archimedes' "globe," we must presume that cogwheels transmitted the motion to its various different parts. In Hellenistic gadgets motion was more often transmitted by pulleys or plain friction wheels (the entire "automatic theater" of Hero worked in this way [Schmidt 1899: 334–453]), but with these methods it would have been impossible to reach the precision necessary for the functions described.

It is tempting to envisage Archimedes' "globe" as something reminiscent of a nineteenth-century orrery or planetarium, that is, a three-dimensional model of a pre-Copernican solar system in which the turning of a crank gave a clear illustration of the relative movements of the planets, moon, and sun around the earth. In all probability, however, it looked more like the well-known Antikythera Mechanism, discovered in a Roman shipwreck south of the Peloponnesus in 1900, but scientifically published only in 1974 (Price 1974: 5–51; with significant corrections by Bromley 1986, Wright 2002, 2006; see also chapter 29). This instrument was originally enclosed in a rectangular wood-and-metal box, 30 cm long, 15 cm wide and 7.5 cm high (figure 29.1). Although the details of the mechanism and its precise function are still under investigation, it may have included as many as 31 parallel cogwheels of bronze with between 15 and about 225 cogs each, by means of which complex astronomical calculations could be carried out. The results could be read on three dial plates on the front and back faces of the instrument. On the dials, solar years could be compared with lunar years and synodic months, and it was possible to predict solar and lunar eclipses, to read the rising and setting of various constellations, and perhaps other functions.

Although the myth survives in modern scholarship, Price and the scholars following him emphasize that this device had nothing whatsoever to do with the navigation of the ship on which it was found. It is an instrument whose scientific and technical complexity far surpasses what would seem reasonable for practical purposes. It is rather a precious luxury article, comparable with the Greek bronze statues conveyed, presumably to Rome, on the same ship. From astronomical arguments, Price suggested that the instrument was constructed around 87 B.C., a date that accords well with the probable date of the wreck, approximately 80 B.C. This is also a period when members of the Roman elite showed great interest in technical devices of this kind. Cicero also mentions (*Nat. D.* 2.34.88) a similar orrery constructed by the philosopher Posidonius, "which at each revolution presents the same result in the sun and the moon and in the five wandering stars [the planets] that takes place in heaven every day and night." Cicero was well acquainted with the device, as he knew Posidonius personally from his studies in Rhodes in 78 B.C. It is very unlikely, however, that the mechanism discovered at Antikythera is identical with Posidonius' planetarium.

Price saw a direct connection between devices like the Antikythera Mechanism and the Islamic astrolabes known from about AD 1000 (al-Biruni) onward, a hypothesis confirmed only nine years after the publication of his book by the discovery of four fragments of a Byzantine, brass sundial-calendar (Field and Wright 1985a and 1985b). It has been dated to the early sixth century A.D. and may be seen as the missing link between the devices of the classical world and those of early Islamic science (figure 31.3). The device made use of internal gears to provide a display of the god for each day of the week and the phases of the moon. The face plate carries coordinates for 16 towns and provinces around the Mediterranean; when the gnomon was set to the appropriate location and the indicator on the suspension set to the corresponding declination, the shadow would fall on the appropriate hour. As the sundial-calendar is in many ways almost identical with al-Biruni's astrolabe, it shows beyond doubt that that the astrolabe was not an Islamic innovation but, in fact, a late development from Hellenistic precursors.

In antiquity, the word *astrolabium* was used for two different devices, the *astrolabium planisphaerium* (related to the devices already described) and the "ring-astrolabium" invented by Hipparchus in the second century B.C. and described in detail by Ptolemy (*Alm.* 5.1; Kauffmann 1896). It consisted of several connected metal rings, one corresponding the ecliptic, another the colure of the solstices. The rings were divided into degrees and marked with astronomical symbols; by turning them, various astronomical calculations could be made. We get a clear picture of this device from an astronomical instrument discovered at Philippi in 1965 (Gounares 1978). It consists of two rotating rings connected with a third, larger one, with a diameter of 7.25 cm. Inscriptions make it possible to adjust the instrument according to months and geographic position (Vienne, Rome, Rhodes, Alexandria). The Philippi device, which has been dated to the fourth century A.D., could be seen as something between a true astrolabe and a portable sundial, about 15 of which have been found throughout the Roman Empire (Price 1969; Buchner 1971).

Figure 31.3. Reconstruction of a Byzantine portable sundial-calendar with settings for 16 locations, ca. A.D. 400–600. Science Museum, London, inv. 1985-222. (Courtesy Science & Society Picture Library.)

# HODOMETERS

Hodometers, mechanical instruments for measuring travel distances both on land and at sea, are described in detail by both Vitruvius (*De arch.* 10.9.1–4, 5–7) and Heron (*Dioptra* 34 and 38) and may have served a more important role than is often assumed. Many attempts have been made to reconstruct these complex machines (e.g., Drachmann 1963: 157–68). This discussion will concentrate on the land hodometer of Vitruvius.

> Let the wheels of the carriage have a diameter of four feet, so that, if a wheel has a marked point and starts moving forward from this point, rotating on the surface of the road, it will have completed a distance of precisely 12½ feet, when it arrives at the point from which it began its revolution. Then let a drum (*tympanum*) with one single tooth projecting from the circumference be fastened to the inner side of the wheel-hub. Moreover, in the wagon-body a box should be securely fastened with a drum rotating vertically and fixed to an axle. On the outside of this drum four hundred small teeth (cogs) shall be placed at equal distances, which mesh with the teeth of the lower drum. Moreover, at the side of the upper drum shall be fixed another little tooth projecting beyond the (other)

teeth. But above, there should be placed a horizontal drum, toothed in the same way and enclosed in another box, whose teeth mesh with the little tooth, which had been fixed to the side of the second drum. In this (third) drum, as many holes should be made as the number of miles that can be covered with the carriage in a day's journey. . . . In all these holes small round stones should be placed, and in the case of this drum . . . there shall be one opening with a small channel through which the stones placed in this drum, when they have arrived at this place, can fall one by one into the wagon-body and a bronze vessel placed below. Thus, when the wheel moves forward, it carries with it the lowest drum, and as the little tooth on this drum at each revolution drives the teeth in the upper [drum] forward, the result will be that, when the lowest [drum] has revolved 400 times, the upper drum revolves once; and the little tooth that is fixed to its side moves one tooth of the horizontal drum. Thus, as the upper [drum] will revolve once compared to 400 revolutions of the lowest drum, it will record a distance of five thousand feet, that is, one thousand paces. Consequently, the number of stones that fall will announce by their sound the passing of a single mile. But the number of stones collected from the bottom will show, by their sum, the number of miles for the day's journey.

Vitruvius' description is detailed, but not entirely clear. It is no surprise that Leonardo da Vinci was fascinated by it and tried to recreate the machine at his drawing-board (Sleeswyk 1981b: 159–62). Two fundamentally different solutions to the problem are preserved by his hand, but both differ decisively from Vitruvius' text, and later scholars have resigned themselves to the insolubility of the problem. Even Drachmann (1963: 156–59, fig. 61) considered the hodometer an armchair design impossible to construct in practice. In the late 1970s, however, Sleeswyk contrived a solution based in its entirety on Vitruvius' description, although he resorts to less conventional solutions to some details for which Vitruvius supplies no information. He has demonstrated the viability of his reconstruction by building a quarter-size scale model. In his drawn reconstructions (figure 31.4), the number of cogs has been drastically reduced for the sake of clarity, but the principle remains the same (Sleeswyk 1979, 1990: 23–28; Lendle 1990).

Sleeswyk's solution seems convincing, but his historical analysis is even more exciting, when he asks to whom Vitruvius referred when attributing the machine to "our predecessors" (*rationem . . . a maioribus traditam*). His argument starts from a small but revealing detail: the use of falling balls or stones—not uncommon in the Islamic world, but known in the classical world from one more case only, the water-clock attributed to Archimedes. The attribution is not absolutely certain, but it can be supported by a variety of arguments—for example, the very motive for the invention of the hodometer. What could be the purpose of providing a carriage with so complex (and certainly expensive) machine, when the main Roman roads were supplied with milestones at intervals of one Roman mile (1.48 km)? Sleeswyk argues convincingly that in fact it was the Romans who needed the hodometer, when they began to put out milestones in the 250s B.C. Perhaps some Roman official solicited a solution to the need for laying out roads over long distances and calculating quickly the requirements for materials and labor (Lewis 2001: 134–39).

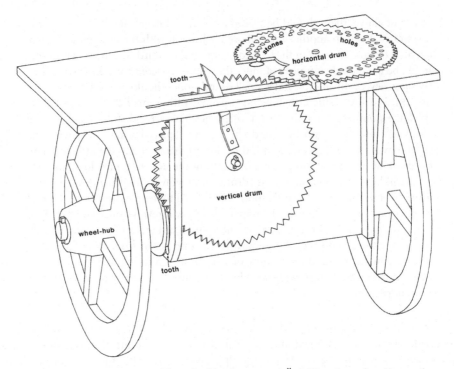

Figure 31.4. Reconstruction of Vitruvius' hodometer. ( Ö. Wikander, after Sleeswyk 1990: fig. 5.)

At this time, Archimedes was a man in his thirties, already respected for his scientific gifts and active at the court of Hieron II of Syracuse, one of Rome's close allies during the First Punic War. Sleeswyk's theory remains hypothetical, but plausible. Among Archimedes' earliest works is *Dimension of the Circle*, in which he fixed the value of pi between 3 10/70 and 3 10/71 (ca. 3.1418, within about 0.2 percent of the real figure), a study in accordance with approximately simultaneous work on the hodometer, a practical application whose function is dependent on a tolerably accurate value of pi.

## GADGETS IN THE ROMAN EMPIRE

The technology of the Roman Empire is mainly associated with large, low-technology machines based on Hellenistic inventions, for example the *saqiya* gear drive, the water-mill, and olive-presses. But various types of evidence prove that the knowledge of automata and other gadgets was passed on, too. Even though the majority of Heron's automata presumably belong to the third century B.C., it is worthy of note that he found it meaningful to write about them as late as the second half of the first century A.D. Astrolabes and planetaria survived. The series of literary testimonia concerning the planetarium of Archimedes over the four centuries from Cicero to Claudian shows the importance attached to the device. The same is true of portable sundials, the astrolabe from Philippi, and water-clocks, which indicate the technical skills that survived throughout the Roman Empire. We even have examples of the use of gadgets in Roman ceremonies and processions. The Nysa statue shown in Ptolemy Philadelphus' procession has its counterpart in an automated image of Julius Caesar's corpse, made of wax, displayed at his funeral: "The image was turned round by a mechanism in all directions, and all over the body and the face the twenty-three wounds could be seen that had so brutally been inflicted on him" (Appian, *B.Civ.* 2.20.147). When Herodes Atticus arranged the Panathenaic festival at Athens (ca. A.D. 139), the ship carrying the new peplos of Athena in the procession "was not propelled by draft animals, but slid forward by machinery hidden below" (Philostratus, *VS* 550).

The most natural place to look for imitations of the court miracles of the early Ptolemies is, of course, the Roman imperial court. It is hardly mere coincidence that some of the Roman gadgets mentioned in historical sources concern the emperor Nero and the contemporary satirical figure Trimalchio. Petronius (*Sat.* 54.4) speaks about walls in the *triclinium* of Trimalchio, which might split open to let in "some automata," perhaps referring to a practical joke actually realized at one of Nero's parties. In the Golden House of Nero, there was, among other technical refinements, a central "circular banquet hall, which revolved incessantly, day and night, like the heavens" (Suet., *Ner.* 31.2). Excavations in a central octagonal hall probably identical with the banquet hall reveal that this mysterious rotation may have been effected by water power (Prückner and Stortz 1974: 338–39). The reference to the revolution of the heavens may indicate that it was, in fact, not the banquet hall that turned, but rather a shell inside the vaulted roof. A similar construction was described almost a century earlier in an elaborate dining room at Varro's villa in Casinum (*Rust.* 3.5,17). A later passage in Pappus (*Collectio* 8.2) proves the survival of this type of construction into the fourth century; it mentions "sphere-makers, who construct models of the heavens based on the even and circular motion of water" (Oleson 1984: 65).

The pieces of evidence preserved are few, but considering the impressive, high-technology development demonstrated by the Antikythera mechanism, which has survived by the purest of accidents, it would be unwise to underestimate the accomplishments of imperial Rome in this area. Nevertheless, the direct technology transfer that took place from the Roman Empire to medieval western Europe as far as water-mills and similar machines are concerned, had apparently no counterparts in high technology. Here, the very limited knowledge actually transferred to the European Middle Ages apparently took the way through Byzantium and the Islamic world.

# REFERENCES

Bedini, S. 1964. "The role of automata in the history of technology," *Technology and Culture* 5: 24–41.

Bromley, A. G. 1986. "Notes on the Antikythera Mechanism," *Centaurus* 29: 5–27.

Buchner, E. 1971. "Antike Reiseuhren," *Chiron* 1: 457–82.

Dalley, S., and J. P. Oleson 2003. "Sennacherib, Archimedes, and the water screw," *Technology and Culture* 44: 1–26.

Deppert-Lippitz, B. 1995. *Die Schraube zwischen Macht und Pracht: Das Gewinde in der Antike.* Sigmaringen: Jan Thorbecke.

Diels, H. 1915. "Über Platons Nachtuhr," *Sitzungsberichte der Preussischen Akademie der Wissenschaften* 2: 824–30.

Drachmann, A. G. 1932. *Ancient oil mills and presses.* Det Kgl. Danske Videnskabernes Selskab. Archaeologisk-kunsthistoriske Meddelelser 1.1. Copenhagen: Levin and Munksgaard.

Drachmann, A. G. 1958. "The screw of Archimedes," in *Actes du VIIIe Congrès international d'Histoire des Sciences*, Vol. 3. Milan, 940–43.

Drachmann, A. G. 1963. *The mechanical technology of Greek and Roman antiquity: A study of the literary sources.* Copenhagen: Munksgaard.

Drachmann, A. G. 1973. "The crank in Graeco-Roman Antiquity," in T. Mikulás and R. Young (eds.), *Changing perspectives in the history of science.* London: Heinemann, 33–51.

Drachmann, A. G. 1976. "Ktesibios's waterclock and Heron's adjustable siphon," *Centaurus* 20: 1–10.

Field, J. V., and M. T. Wright 1985a. *Early gearing: Geared mechanisms in the ancient and mediaeval world.* London: Science Museum.

Field, J. V., and M. T. Wright 1985b. "Gears from the Byzantines," *Annals of Science* 42: 87–138.

Foley, V., W. Soedel, J. Turner, and B. Wilhoite 1982. "The origin of gearing," *History of Technology* 7: 101–29.

Gaitzsch, W. 1983. "Die 'römische' Schraube aus dem Kastell von Niederbieber," *Bonner Jahrbücher* 183: 595–602.

Gounares, G. 1978. "Chalkino phoreto heliako horologio apo tous Philippous," *Archaiologike Ephemeris* 1978: 181–91.

Hill, D.R. 1976. *On the construction of water-clocks: Kitab Arshimidas fi'amal al-binkamat.* London: Turner and Devereaux.

Kauffmann, G. 1896. "Astrolabium," *RE* 2, cols. 1798–1802.

Kiechle, F. 1967. "Zur Verwendung der Schraube in der Antike," *Technikgeschichte* 34: 14–22.

King, H. C., with J. R. Millburn 1978. *Geared to the stars: The evolution of planetariums, orreries, and astronomical clocks.* Toronto: University of Toronto Press.

Klumbach, H. (ed.) 1973. *Spätrömische Gardehelme.* Münchner Beiträge zur Vor- und Frühgeschichte 15. Munich: Beck.

Landels, J. G. 2000. *Engineering in the ancient world.* Rev. ed. London: Constable.

Lendle, O. 1990. "Vitruvs Meilenzähler (*De Arch.* 10.9.1–4)," in W. Goerler and S. Koster (eds.), *Pratum Saraviense: Festgabe für Peter Steinmetz.* Stuttgart: F. Steiner, 75–88.

Lewis, M. J. T. 1997. *Millstone and hammer: The origins of water power.* Hull: University of Hull Press.

Lewis, M. J. T. 2001. *Surveying instruments of Greece and Rome.* Cambridge: Cambridge University Press.

Mutz, A. 1969. "Römische Bronzegewinde," *Technikgeschichte* 36:161–67.

Oleson, J. P. 1984. *Greek and Roman mechanical water-lifting devices: The history of a technology.* Toronto: University of Toronto Press.

Price, D. J. de Solla. 1962. "Automata and the origins of mechanism and mechanistic philosophy," *Technology and Culture* 5: 9–23.

Price, D. J. de Solla. 1969. "Portable sundials in antiquity, including an account of a new example from Aphrodesias," *Centaurus* 14: 242–66.

Price, D. J. de Solla. 1974. *Gears from the Greeks: The Antikythera Mechanism—A calendar computer from ca. 80 B.C.* Transactions of the American Philosophical Society 64.7. Philadelphia: American Philosophical Society.

Prückner, H., and S. Stortz 1974. "Beobachtungen im Oktagon des Domus Aurea," *Römische Mitteilungen* 81: 323–39.

Schmidt, W. 1899. *Heronis Alexandrini Opera quae supersunt omnia.* Vol. 1, *Pneumatica et Automata.* Leipzig: Teubner.

Sleeswyk, A. W. 1979. "Vitruvius' waywiser," *Archives Internationales d'Histoire des Sciences* 29:11–22.

Sleeswyk, A. W. 1981a. "Hand-cranking in Egyptian antiquity," *History of Technology* 6: 23–37.

Sleeswyk, A. W. 1981b. "Vitruvius' odometer," *Scientific American* 245.4: 158–71.

Sleeswyk, A. W. 1990. "Archimedes' odometer and waterclock," in *Ancient technology, Finnish Institute at Athens, symposium held 30.3–4.4. 1987.* Tekniikan museon julkaisuja 5. Helsinki: Tekniikan museon. 23–37.

Wright, M. T. 2002. "A planetarium display for the Antikythera Mechanism," *Horological Journal* 144: 169–73.

Wright, M. T. 2006. "The Antikythera Mechanism and the early history of the moon-phase display," *Antiquarian Horology* 29.3: 319–29.

.....................................................................

# CHAPTER 32

# INVENTORS, INVENTION, AND ATTITUDES TOWARD TECHNOLOGY AND INNOVATION

.....................................................................

## KEVIN GREENE

THIS chapter has three parts. The first section looks at a selection of comments about invention in ancient sources; the second considers the nature of some ancient inventors; and the third surveys examples of Greek and Roman technology that reveal stability or change.

# ATTITUDES TO INVENTION AND INNOVATION IN GREEK AND ROMAN WRITERS

## Optimism, Pessimism, and Human Ingenuity

> What marvelous, stupendous accomplishments human effort has achieved in the fields of construction and textile production! How far it has progressed in agriculture and navigation! What accomplishments of imagination and application in the production of all kinds of vessels, various types of statues and paintings.... With what sharp minds humans grasp the paths and arrangement of the heavenly bodies! How great the knowledge of this world humans have filled themselves with! Who could describe it? (St. Augustine, *de Civ. D.* 22.24)

In the context of the western Empire in the early fifth century A.D., St. Augustine's assessment of the accumulated worldly achievements of Greek and Roman civilization is probably tempered by consciousness of its fragility, but credit for both useful and entertaining inventions is firmly attributed to the human intellect. This theme runs through many classical works, despite expressions of regret about decline from a better past or criticisms of utilitarian knowledge and labor. Hesiod's gloomy perception of a "fifth race" anticipated further destruction: "For now is the iron race, when humans never will cease from labor and sorrow by day and from suffering at night, since the gods will give only grievous concerns.... And Zeus will destroy this race of mortals too" (Hesiod, *Op.* 107–78). Plato associated a lack of iron with a lost life of simplicity when the gods provided humans with all they needed for material comfort—clothing, houses, and pottery (Plato, *Leg.* 3.677a–679b).

While many writers made obvious points about necessity prompting invention, a more interesting theme is that of humans gaining inspiration from nature. Lucretius credited humans with the ability to experiment: "Nature herself was the mother who first brought forth the model of sowing and the beginning of grafting: berries and acorns, having fallen from the trees, sent out swarms of sprouts on the ground beneath in proper season.... Then they tried one method after another to cultivate their dear little plot..." (Lucretius 5.1361–69).

Vitruvius' knowledge of Hellenistic technical treatises gave him a perception of the development of things that "were more easily done with machines [*machinae*] and their revolutions, some others with instruments [*organa*]" and how their authors had gradually improved "by their learning all those things that they believed useful for research, for the arts, and for established traditions" (*De arch.* 10.1.4–6). Nevertheless, nature remained the inspiration for human ingenuity: "Now all machinery has been modeled on Nature and set up with the revolution of the universe as instructor and teacher.... So when our ancestors noticed that this was the case, they took their models from Nature and imitating her, led on by divine help, they developed the amenities of life" (Vitruvius, *De arch.* 10.1.1–4).

## Contemporary Perceptions of Machines

The special character of devices powered by water rather than by human or animal labor, such as mills or water-wheels, impressed Greek and Roman writers over many centuries, from Antipater to Procopius (Humphrey et al. 1998: 31–34). A *noria* (water-lifting wheel powered by paddles) caught the imagination of one Latin poet: "It pours out and scoops up water, discharging on high the stream it carries, and it drinks up a river only to disgorge it. A marvelous achievement! It carries water and is carried along by water. In this fashion a stream is pushed up by a stream, and a new device scoops up the old-fashioned fluid" (*Anth. Lat.* 284).

A careful observer could deduce how a watermill or *noria* worked, whereas many Hellenistic automata produced magical effects from invisible mechanisms. Just as in eighteenth-century Europe, automata expressed the ambiguity of mechanical devices that mimicked nature (Dugan and Dugan 2000: 40–42) and led to speculation about robots and flying model birds (Humphrey et al. 1998: 61–62): "Craftsmen prepare a device whose first principle they conceal, so that only the wonder of the machine is apparent, the cause hidden" ([Aristotle], *Pr.* Preface, 848a.20–38).

Pappus reiterated a fundamental classification of machines in the fourth century A.D.: "There are five machines by the use of which a given weight is moved by a given force, and we will undertake to give the forms, the applications, and the names of these machines. . . . The names are as follows: wheel and axle, lever, system of pulleys, wedge, and, finally, the so-called endless screw" (Pappus, *Coll.* 8.52). Pappus also repeated Hero's specifications for the education of mechanicians, and defined their areas of operation: "conjurers" (*manganarioi*) or mechanicians (*mechanikoi*) who move weights; constructors of siege machines (*organopoioi*); machine-builders (*mechanopoioi*), especially for water-lifting; gadget-designers (*thaumasiourgoi*) who make automata, clocks, and so forth; and sphere-makers, who construct models of the heavens. It is interesting to note the persistence of an association between conjuring and mechanical ability (Pappus, *Coll.* 8.1–2; Humphrey et al. 1998: 47–48).

There was widespread awareness of the strategic importance of fostering theoretical and practical knowledge of technology in the Hellenistic world. Philo of Byzantium observed that royal patronage in Alexandria encompassed both forms of knowledge, for craftsmen were "heavily subsidized because they had ambitious kings who fostered craftsmanship. Not everything can be accomplished by the theoretical methods of pure mechanics, but much is to be found by experiment" (*Bel.* 50.3). Long before the famous engagement of Archimedes in the defense of Syracuse in 212 B.C., Dionysius I (ca. 430–367 B.C.) had assembled a "think tank" to generate military hardware—although Traina (1994: 68–69) considers modification or development of the catapult to have been more likely than actual invention. The focused work groups, high salaries, and performance bonuses all sound surprisingly modern. Diodorus Siculus (14.41.3–4, 42.1) recounts that

> Dionysius, therefore, immediately assembled technicians, commanding them to come from the cities he ruled, and luring them from Italy and Greece—and even from Carthaginian territory—with high wages. For he intended to manufacture weapons in great numbers and projectiles of every sort, and in addition

tetraremes and quinqueremes—no quinqueremes yet having been constructed at that time. After assembling a great number of technicians, he divided them into work-groups according to each one's own talents. . . . In fact, the catapult was invented in Syracuse on this occasion, since the most able technicians were gathered together from all over into one place. The high wages stimulated their enthusiasm, along with the numerous prizes offered to those judged the best.

## Ingenuity and the Status of Work

One of the best-known traditions in Greek and Roman literature is the association of leisure with an honorable life—Finley's "primitive" representation of the ancient economy (1973) relies heavily on generalizing the view of the literary elite to the rest of society. Seneca (*Ep.* 90.10–13) distinguished between wisdom and ingenuity, and attributed invention to the latter:

> I differ from Posidonius, when he concludes that tools for the crafts were invented by wise men. . . . It was human ingenuity, not human wisdom, that invented those things. In this also I differ from him, that it was the wise who devised mines for iron and copper when the earth, scorched by forest fires, poured out metal from liquefied surface veins of ore. The sort of men who discovered these mines are the same sort who work them today. Nor does the question of whether the hammer or the tongs came first seem as subtle to me as it did to Posidonius. Both were invented by someone with a mind that was nimble and sharp, but not great or elevated—along with anything else that must be sought with a bent body and a mind focused on the ground.

Seneca's specific example echoes the general statement by Aristotle that "we term 'banausic' those crafts that make the condition of the body worse, and the workshops where wages are earned, for they leave the mind preoccupied and debased" (*Pol.* 8.2.1 [1337b]). This attitude was foreshadowed by Xenophon (*Oec.* 4.2–3). However, approval of physical activity was also expressed in Greek and Roman literature (Hesiod, *Op.* 303–11, St. Paul, *Thes.* 3: 6–10). Furthermore, the living associates of deceased individuals saw no shame in commemorating them with gravestones that named their crafts or trades, and even pictured some of them at work in sculpted scenes (Zimmer 1982). Agriculture was normally considered an honorable exception among forms of human work, and, in addition, agricultural labor enhanced physical fitness for war ([Aristotle], *Oec.* 1.2.2–3). Such exceptions smoothed the way for machines associated with irrigation and the processing of crops, and all devices connected with warfare.

## Inventions

Antibanausic judgments remind us that we are not dealing with the utilitarian values of nineteenth-century Europe: "As more and more arts were discovered, some pertaining to necessities and some to pastimes, the inventors of the latter were always considered wiser than the inventors of the former, because their knowledge was not oriented toward utility" (Aristotle, *Metaph.* 1.1.11–17 [981a–982a]). Finley (1965: 33–34) contrasted Pliny the Elder's passion for naming inventors of nonutilitarian arts and crafts with his inability to identify the inventors of new machines such as the screw-press. He also cited two stories (Humphrey et al. 1998: 595) in which inventors were penalized or rejected, rather than rewarded; he argued that these "technological fables"—one about unbreakable glass (involving Tiberius), the other about a device for lifting columns (involving Vespasian)—demonstrated a real antagonism toward innovation that underpinned a culture of stagnation. Like Plutarch's comments about Archimedes, however, such stories were told to illustrate the character of an individual rather than to express antipathy to inventions (Greene 2000: 46–50).

In the second century B.C., Polybius noted that Romans copied Greek shields: "For this too is one of their virtues, to adopt new customs and emulate what is better" (6.25.10–11). In the following century, Cicero offered unambiguous praise for the qualities of Romans, who "have constantly shown themselves more clever at invention than the Greeks, or have improved on what they received from the Greeks—at least in those fields they judged worthy of their effort" (*Tusc.* 1.1.2). However, by the first century A.D. Pliny the Elder was complaining that Roman achievements had been accompanied by ignorance of Greek knowledge (*HN* 14.2–4):

> The research of the men of long ago was so much more productive or their industry so much more fortunate when, a thousand years ago at the very beginnings of literacy, Hesiod began to publish his instructions to farmers and numerous others followed his line of research. For this reason our task is greater, since now we have to investigate not only what was found out later, but also the discoveries made by the pioneers.

Pliny's near-contemporary Frontinus appears to confirm fears of complacency, for in a discussion of engineering works and catapults he observed, "I see no further scope for the applied arts" (*Str.* 3, Preface). This view, however, is belied by the anonymous fourth-century A.D. writer who set out designs for many devices to assist the late Roman army, including an ox-powered paddle-wheel warship using "animal power, enhanced by the resources of the human intellect"—specifically, 90-degree gears familiar from mechanical mills, and wheels with projecting vanes of the kind used for lifting water from rivers (*De rebus bellicis* 17.1–3).

# GREEK AND ROMAN INVENTORS

> But as for those benefits to humans that lay hidden in the earth—bronze, iron, silver, and gold—who else before me could claim to have found them first? . . . Learn the whole matter in a brief phrase: all arts possessed by mortals come from Prometheus. (Aeschylus, *PV* 442–506)

## Identifying Inventors in the Ancient World

Many fundamental crafts or inventions were associated with gods—for example, weaving (Athena), agriculture (Demeter), fire (Prometheus/Hephaestus), or wine (Dionysus). Only in recent centuries have inventions been ascribed to named individuals with any regularity, for the good reason that no clear concept of intellectual property rights backed by law existed before the fifteenth century A.D. (May 2002). Most modern classicists and archaeologists, when challenged to name Greek or Roman technical inventors or inventions, rarely get further than Archimedes and his water-screw or Heron and his steam-driven rotating sphere. Rather than indicating that invention was rare, this may indicate that we are looking for the wrong thing. In a preindustrial society, we should perhaps focus on processes by which technological innovations might be diffused and implemented, whether or not they were inventions *sensu strictu*.

How many of the names associated with technical inventions in ancient sources may be relied upon? Archimedes' water-screw raises most of the difficulties associated with this question (Dalley and Oleson 2003). The plentiful archaeological evidence and pictorial representations of water-screws in use dates from the first century A.D. at the earliest. Literary evidence begins in the second half of the third century B.C., however, and Vitruvius provided practical instructions for building one in the first century B.C. (without naming Archimedes). Diodorus Siculus (mid-first century B.C.) refers to the "so-called Egyptian screw, which Archimedes the Syracusan invented, called the screw on account of its design," but the Greek verb *eurisko* could mean "found" or "observed" as well as "discovered." The matter is complicated by Dalley's claim that this device had already been invented in Mesopotamia in the seventh century B.C., was introduced to Egypt when it fell under Assyrian control, and was observed there by Archimedes in the third century B.C. Thus, we have ambiguous vocabulary and contested origins for one of the most frequently cited technological inventions of the ancient world.

Pliny the Elder compiled comprehensive lists of origins in his *Natural History* (7.191–209), considering discoveries to be part of the subject of human nature. A short extract (*HN* 7.195–97) illustrates both his all-embracing approach and his inability to resolve differences between authorities:

> Tiles were invented by Cinyra, son of Agriopa, as well as mining for copper, both in the island of Cyprus, and also the tongs, hammer, crowbar and anvil; wells by Danaus who came from Egypt to Greece to the region that used to be called Dry Argos; stone quarrying by Cadmus at Thebes, or according to Theophrastus, in Phoenicia; walls were introduced by Thrason, towers by the Cyclopes according to Aristotle but according to Theophrastus by the Tirynthians; woven fabrics by the Egyptians, dyeing woolen stuffs by the Lydians at Sardis, the use of the spindle in the manufacture of woolen by Closter son of Arachne, linen and nets by Arachne, the fuller's craft by Nicias of Megara, the shoemaker's by Tychius of Boeotia.

On the other hand, people with technical skills *were* brought together with the purpose of producing useful devices, notably at the Museum at Alexandria in Egypt and at Syracuse in Sicily, where royal houses were "interested as much in broadcasting the prestige and imagery of technological success, the tangible evidence of human triumph over the forces of nature, as in the practical results" (Dalley and Oleson 2003: 25). Individuals such as Ctesibius, Philon, and Archimedes, whose names became associated with specific inventions, were at the very least responsible for memorable *innovations*, whether or not the devices that they brought into practical use were their own inventions.

## Archimedes (287–212/11 B.C.)

Archimedes' reputation is largely based not on technical inventions but on mathematical skills and a scientific discovery. His popular renown relies upon the flash of brilliance (*Eureka!*) involved in relating the level of bathwater to the measurement of specific gravity and on an antiheroic (but culturally symbolic) death while attempting to complete some calculations during the fall of Syracuse to the Romans. Toomer (1996) saw Archimedes as "the greatest mathematician of antiquity" and credited him with the invention of hydrostatics, but he made much less of his role as technical inventor: "Popular history knew him as the inventor of marvelous machines used against the Romans at the siege of Syracuse, and of devices such as the screw for raising water." The idea that science is somehow debased by practical application was attributed to Archimedes several centuries after his death but is often held to encapsulate the attitude of the entire ancient world:

> He possessed so high a spirit, so profound a soul, and such treasures of scientific knowledge that, though these inventions had obtained for him the renown of more than human sagacity, he yet would not deign to leave behind him any written work on such subjects, but, regarding as ignoble and sordid the business of mechanics and every sort of art which is directed to use and profit, he placed his whole ambition in those speculations in whose beauty and subtlety there is no admixture of the common needs of life. (Plutarch, *Marc.* 17.3–4)

Wilson has argued that Plutarch's point was to show how unusual Archimedes was in *not* putting technological knowledge to practical uses (2002: 4). Astronomy and mathematics were entirely respectable pursuits, while defending a city or raising royal revenues clearly placed mechanics in a worthy military and official context.

The most familiar device to which Archimedes' name is attached today is the water-screw, a cylinder with a close-fitting internal spiral that lifted water when the cylinder was rotated, but the association with Archimedes is not beyond all doubt (above). The water-screw is a good example of the kind of device associated with the Museum at Alexandria that involved scientific or mathematical principles but could be applied to the productivity of irrigated farmland on which the prosperity of Egypt depended. Furthermore, the relationship between Archimedes and Hieron II of Syracuse—who is also famous for creating a ship of unparalleled size

(Athenaeus, *Deip.* 5.206e–209b)—inevitably draws attention to the relationship between hydrostatics and shipbuilding (Pomey and Tchernia 2005). The renown of Archimedes' astronomical spheres (Cicero, *Rep.* 1.14.21–22) implies command of precision engineering as well as large machines. Lewis credits Archimedes with the invention of the hodometer, another very practical application of science to the needs of the state, for it could be used in contexts such as the marking of distances on the new Roman highways that were being extended through Italy (2000b: 632). Thus, if the superficial impression gained from Plutarch is set aside, Archimedes appears similar to other Hellenistic inventors.

## Ctesibius (fl. 270 B.C.)

The reputation of Ctesibius (Drachmann 1948: 1–41) is not based on surviving writings, but on authorship of treatises on machines that were quoted extensively by Philon, Vitruvius, and Heron. Such works give a clear impression that "the art of the ancient *mechanikos* apparently combined enquiries into the theory and design of devices with meticulous concern over details of their manufacture and operation" (Knorr 1996). As with Archimedes and the water-screw, it will never be possible to claim definitive priority for ancient inventors and the devices that are attributed to them, but Ctesibius is generally credited with inventing the force-pump, a keyboard-operated organ in which a constant flow of air was assured by water pressure, and with adding accuracy to the water-clock by ensuring a regular flow of water. His writings about artillery (known largely from Philon) probably put existing developments into a systematic form, since the innovation of using torsion springs on catapults has been attributed to unnamed engineers working for Philip II around 340 B.C.

Along with the Archimedean water-screw, the force-pump—known to Vitruvius (10.6–7) as *machina ctesibica*—is one of the very few ancient inventions to be named after an individual in antiquity. The water-clock and organ were not basic inventions, but refinements to existing devices involving the creation of an even flow of water or air. The twin-chambered pump, in which valves and pistons opened and closed alternately, also generated a continuous flow of water. The pneumatic devices associated with Ctesibius fit well into the range of activities that would have interested a Hellenistic ruler and the concerns of the Museum of Alexandria: water lifting, time keeping, and warfare. Vitruvius commented that in addition to the force-pump, Ctesibian devices included "many others of varied design driven by water pressure. Pneumatic pressure can be seen to provide effects which imitate nature, such as singing of blackbirds and mechanical acrobats, and little figures which drink and move, and other things that delight the senses by pleasing the eye and catching the ear (*De arch.* 10.7.1–4). The symposium and the entertainment of guests was an important state activity, while automata associated with temple rituals had another clearly utilitarian function in managing belief (Schürmann 1991).

## Philon of Byzantium (fl. 200 B.C.)

The name of Philon of Byzantium is not linked to any inventions, and much of his surviving work is concerned with artillery and siege works (Drachmann 1948: 41–74). His use of Ctesibius (and the subsequent use of both by Heron) contributed to the preservation and transmission of a body of knowledge that allowed Hill to speak of "a Greek school of mechanical engineering, stemming from Ctesibius (300–270 B.C.) and continuing through Philo and Hero, probably into Byzantium, whence it passed into Sasanid Persia" (1979: 21).

## Vitruvius (fl. 35/25 B.C.)

Knowledge of the achievements of the "Greek school of mechanical engineering" was made available in Latin in book 10 of Vitruvius' *De architectura* just as the Roman Empire began to be created under Augustus. Vitruvius is most closely associated with architecture (Howe and Rowland 1999), but his book on mechanics is particularly interesting to technological historians. Indeed, many of the devices attributed to Greek inventors—such as the hydraulic organ—proliferated in Roman times (Fleury 1993: 198–204). Vitruvius is frequently described in rather patronizing terms, as if Greek science had already given way to Roman pragmatism, despite his prolific citation of Greek philosophers, scientists and mathematicians. Vitruvius and Heron are particularly important because their works survive so much better than those of Ctesibius or Philon, while containing much material inherited from them. The cultural context is also particularly interesting, since Vitruvius is the first "Roman" writer on engineering, whereas the other major figures from Archimedes to Heron wrote in Greek and were connected, more or less directly, to the theoretical and applied mathematics and mechanics of the Museum of Alexandria. Few general writers associate Vitruvius with any topic *other* than architecture, and most fail to comment on his significance as a historian of science and philosophy who "appreciated that in its general and most humane form, architecture included everything which touches on the physical and intellectual life of man and his surroundings" (Tomlinson and Vallance 1996).

Like Archimedes, Vitruvius throws doubt on the supposed conflict between theory and practice in the ancient world, "often employing the theories of the most antibanausic Greek thinkers to elucidate his very practical subject.... For a man with interests practical and theoretical in equal measure, understanding the nature of nature was central to all" (Tomlinson and Vallance 1996). Perhaps because of the widespread belief that *techne* was contrary to nature, Vitruvius related the movement of machinery to that of the universe in a rather pious manner that contrasts with his practical description of the optimization of human power by means of machines such as catapults or oil presses (*De arch.* 10. 1. 1–4).

## Heron of Alexandria (fl. A.D. 62)

In addition to maintaining extensive knowledge of mathematics and science as a "Greek" writer operating in the early Roman Empire, Heron of Alexandria wrote about the same technical subjects as Ctesibius and Philon: artillery, surveying, mechanics, pneumatics, and so forth. Drachmann (1948: 74–99) considered his technical work to be working notes rather than a finished treatise (1948: 159). His popular reputation as an "inventor" rests largely on items that appear to anticipate important medieval and later developments. His description of a Ctesibian water-organ includes a pump powered by a windmill and trip-hammers, but most attention has been given to the aeolipile, a primitive reaction turbine persistently and incorrectly described as "an early form of steam engine" (e.g., Wilkinson 2000: 147). The aeolipile is one of many devices that use hydraulic or pneumatic power assisted by heating, and it was designed to demonstrate a scientific principle, not to serve as a power source (Keyser 1992). Despite wise words from Drachmann (1963: 260), it has carried a great historiographical burden as a symbol of the ancient world's inability to exploit technology:

> You can hear people contend, on the strength of such play-things, that the ancient Greeks could have invented the steam engine, if only they did not have the slaves, which made such an invention superfluous. But slave labor was not cheap, and the presence of slaves did not prevent the invention of the watermill, which could be constructed by the means in hand. The construction of the steam engine had to wait until it was possible to make iron pipes and put them together with screws.

# Stability, Continuous Development, and Change in Greek and Roman Technology

## Stability

It is important to stress that many areas of Greek and Roman technology remained remarkably static. No fundamental changes took place in techniques of forging or casting metal objects, whether made from individual metals or alloys, although brass came into regular use by the Roman period (Craddock 1990; see also chapter 4). Most changes were increases in scale: producing a life-size bronze statue for a Greek temple clearly demanded more people and better workshop organization than casting prehistoric bronze axes (Mattusch 1996; see also chapter 16). Likewise, the scale of demand for precious and base metals in the Roman Empire exceeded anything known previously, and the extraction of metals from mines provided an opportunity for the diffusion of many Hellenistic inventions for water-lifting and for using reciprocating machinery for crushing ores (Lewis 1997; Wilson 2002). Thus, a static manufacturing technology can coexist with innovations in extraction and processing.

Methods used in forming ceramics by hand or on a potter's wheel all existed long before archaic Greek times and persisted through the Roman Empire; finished vessels could be fired in simple bonfires or permanent kilns (Peacock 1982; see also chapter 19). Surface treatments included vitreous glazes, glossy slips, and painted decoration, but changes were the result of aesthetic or economic factors rather than technology. Potters making the relief-molded bowls that became popular in Hellenistic times were able to adopt the kinds of molds employed in casting their metal prototypes; they were already accustomed to molding other ceramic products, notably figurines, and often worked closely with metalworkers (Merker 2003). Most changes in the production, distribution, and consumption of pottery result from cultural or economic factors rather than technology. The diffusion of Greek and Roman cuisine demanded new serving and preparation vessels (Bats 1996), while classical architecture required the dissemination of knowledge about making specialized ceramic bricks, roof tiles and water pipes.

## Continuous Development

Continuous development occurred in one fundamentally important aspect of Greek and Roman civilization: warfare (chapters 26 and 27). Logistic and organizational innovations were demanded by changing scales of operation—conflict between city-states, war with Persia, Alexander's eastern conquests—culminating in the mature Roman Empire, which required permanent garrisons, frontier defenses and a professional standing army. Technical changes in equipment included the "invention" of mechanical catapults by Dionysius I's "think tank" in 399 B.C. Torsion springs improved Hellenistic artillery devices a little later, and remained the essential form of propulsion throughout the Roman imperial period. Archaeological study of surviving remains has revealed continual modification and improvement of this mechanism, as well as proliferation of its use (Marsden 1969; Baatz 1994). A heavier device for throwing large stones—the onager—was brought into extensive use by the third century A.D., presumably because devices suited to defensive rather than offensive warfare were required in the face of growing threats from "barbarians" beyond the frontiers.

Siege warfare became particularly important in later classical and Hellenistic Greece, and vivid accounts reveal valuable details. In terms of attacking a defended city, Demetrius I of Macedonia (336–283 B.C.), known as *Poliorketes*—"Besieger of Cities"—used large constructions and technical devices in a prolonged but ultimately unsuccessful siege of Rhodes. Defensive strategies are associated with Archimedes (287–212/11 B.C.), who turned scientific knowledge into technological inventions to counter the siege of Syracuse by Roman attackers. With the exception of episodes of warfare with their eastern neighbors, the Roman imperial army rarely had occasion either to besiege walled cities, or to defend their own cities from attackers equipped with machinery; the principal threats came from invading Germanic and other peoples who lacked technical resources. Physical barriers such as Hadrian's Wall (defending northern Britain, second century A.D.) or the Anastasian Wall (protecting Constantinople's western approaches, fifth century A.D.) gained defense in depth as city walls became increasingly elaborate, reinforced by multiple ditches and projecting towers to maximize the effectiveness of defense by long-range mechanical artillery and shorter-range archery. Similar fortifications and mechanical artillery devices continued in later Roman and Byzantine times; indeed, a nameless fourth-century writer proposed a number of technical and organizational innovations that were of sufficient interest in subsequent centuries for copies of the text and illustrations of *De rebus bellicis* to survive (Thompson 1952; Hassall 1979).

The personal equipment of soldiers underwent considerable change and development from classical Greek to Roman times, notably in the quantity of protective armor or chain mail available to ordinary soldiers. Plentiful weaponry and armor required extensive iron production and workshops for the manufacture and repair of equipment; clearly, a professional standing army provided the best context for infrastructure of this kind. Nevertheless, many items that became standard features of Roman armor and equipment had originally been adopted from enemies (Bishop and Coulston 1993: 194–95).

At sea, Greek naval power relied on the trireme galley with a projecting prow for ramming other ships; it was probably adopted from Carthage or Egypt. Competition between navies led to larger galleys with more oars and rowers—such as quinqueremes—better suited to boarding than to high-speed ramming. Triremes remained the staple of Roman naval power, as there were no longer any competing navies in the Mediterranean to stimulate greater size or further development. Away from the Mediterranean, Roman imperial military ships had to cope with large rivers such as the Rhine, and seas characterized by tides and large waves. Archaeological finds have revealed a mixture of Mediterranean-style galleys and more robust local vessels built in a different tradition using overlapping planks and nails, possibly related to the Venetic ships that had given Caesar so much trouble in the first century B.C. (Greene 1986:17–34).

Roman imperial buildings, such as the Coliseum (late first century A.D.), the Baths of Caracalla (ca. 200 A.D.) or the Basilica of Maxentius (ca. 300 A.D.), bear little resemblance to anything Greek predating the first century B.C. Their forms are related to the concerns and activities of the Roman state and its relationship with its citizens. Every component: bricks, arches, vaulting, concrete, surface decoration with exotic stone—can be traced back in one way or another to Greek architectural and ornamental features ultimately adopted from Mesopotamia and Egypt. What is new is a *kind* of building where internal space is supremely important (DeLaine 2002; chapter 10)—but is a vaulted bathing establishment or an imperial reception hall an invention? Hydraulic concrete is frequently cited as a Roman invention, but the term "discovery" seems more appropriate. Rather than being developed intentionally, it resulted from observing the properties of mortar in areas of Italy where volcanic sand was readily available. The chemical reaction between volcanic sand and mortar that allowed it to set underwater led to export of this sand for creating harbors or waterproofing aqueducts; this is a clear example of innovation leading to technology-in-use (Oleson and Branton 1992; Oleson et al. 2005, 2006).

Some classical Greek and Hellenistic inventions were directly linked to developments in science, notably instruments associated with astronomy and medicine (see chapters 29 and 31). Scientific analysis of harmony may have had an impact on a further class of objects for which little physical or documentary evidence survives: musical instruments (Landels 1998). There are direct links between practical application and abstract scientific knowledge in the water-organ associated with Ctesibius. Representations of lyres indicate changes in size, number of strings, and mechanisms for tuning that may have had a scientific basis.

A particularly interesting example of continuous development is coinage (Chapter 30, part 2). These small discs of metal were invented around 600 B.C., and, following the example of Lydia, provided Greek city-states with a convenient method of discharging obligations in pieces of bullion of guaranteed purity (Carradice and Price 1988). Their exchangeability, however, allowed a diversification of economic activities that broke tight social links with known and trusted partners, and provided new means of wealth storage and transfer over long distances. Smaller denominations were gradually introduced in base metals, and systematically reorganized in the early Roman Empire into something resembling modern ideas of token currency (Greene 1986: 45–52). Once coins had become a regular part of commercial exchanges, continual adjustments were necessary to maintain the correct weight ratios between gold, silver, and base denominations, requiring careful production of consistent alloys in different mints. In terms of technologies that change the way that people engage with the everyday world through material objects, coins were a major Greek invention, while the formalization of denominations by Augustus was a significant innovation that diffused to become technology-in-use from Britain to Egypt.

## Stepwise Change

Glass is the best example of significant technological change in an industrial product in classical times, and it illustrates the care with which terms need to be used to distinguish between invention and innovation (cf. chapter 21). The raw material had been discovered or invented in Mesopotamia and/or Egypt by 3000 B.C., probably as a by-product of heating minerals and chemicals for other purposes, and innovated as a means of adding a decorative coating to clay or faience. Hollow vessels made entirely from glass were an invention, but their production required no innovation since the raw material already existed, and early vessels were formed on a clay core, which—in contrast to that of glass-coated objects—was then removed. However, a dramatic change occurred in the first century B.C. when the discovery that a drop of molten glass on the end of a hollow rod could be expanded into a bubble led to the invention of hollow blown glass vessels (Israeli 1991). Since an extensive glass industry already existed, putting a new technique into use and creating a new range of hollow vessels was an innovation, which led to further technical innovations such as decorating vessels in relief by blowing them into a mold. In addition there was a considerable proliferation of decorative effects (for example that the inclusion of gold leaf), as well as diversification of production into mirrors, window panes, and mosaic cubes for wall decorations.

Our understanding of the adoption of blowing and the subsequent proliferation of forms relies on the excavation of workshops and studies of vessels in museum collections (Weinberg 1988; Whitehouse 1997, 2001). Perhaps the most interesting effect of changes in production technology was that blowing transformed glass vessels from luxuries to mass-produced everyday items (Fleming 1999). After the brief period of invention and innovation between about 50 B.C. and A.D. 50, it provides an example of Edgerton's concept of technology-in-use (1999: 112) and draws its significance from the fact that glass vessels came to be used by a wider social range of people. Glass was produced in increasing quantities and in a larger number of forms in the following centuries as production diffused to many parts of the Roman Empire.

The codex, in which separate leaves are bound along one edge between stiff covers, rarely appears in popular lists of Roman inventions, but it had displaced the scroll by the late Roman period and has remained the standard form of book ever since (Roberts and Skeat 1983; chapter 28). The earliest examples were small notebooks of parchment leaves modeled on collections of wooden writing tablets bound together in sets. A codex could accommodate much longer texts than a scroll, and it was better suited to parchment, which (although expensive) was more durable than Egyptian papyrus. It is not hard to see the functional convenience of the codex in a Roman imperial context, for the codex facilitated the use of reference works, law codes, and biblical texts. The codex would have assisted one of the most significant innovations of the Roman Empire: the diffusion of literacy from the Mediterranean basin to Europe and North Africa, which allowed technical knowledge to be transferred in written form in the wake of military engineers and provincial administrators.

There are less dramatic examples of technologies where a stepwise change occurred. In everyday commerce, the adjustable steelyard was an improvement on conventional balances because a single small counterweight could be moved to balance much larger objects. It could have been invented anywhere that an understanding of levers existed, and the principal was explained in the anonymous early mechanical treatise attributed to Aristotle (*Pr.* 20.853b–854a, 1.849b–850a; Humphrey et al. 1998: 50–51). It became common in Roman times, and many have been found at Pompeii, in its suggested region of invention (di Pasquale 1999). In terms of *instrumentum domesticum*, individual property could be protected more effectively when doors could be secured by locks with unique keys; the modern form of lock with a rotating key, however, is not found before the Roman period. This mechanism was sufficiently different from the Greek slotted key, which lifted a peg securing a bolt, to be classed as an invention—as can the idea of a padlock, independent of a door, which was in common use in Pompeii by A.D. 79 (Manning

1986: 90–97). The water-clock (*clepsydra*), which had been in use for many centuries, was refined (reportedly by Ctesibius) to ensure an even flow, and the hydraulic technology involved allowed entertaining "side effects" such as moving figures to be added (chapters 29 and 31). Likewise, mathematical understanding of angles allowed the sundial to be made more accurate from the third century B.C. Numerous examples were in everyday use in Pompeii (Gibbs 1976) (figure 29.2), and it could be made in a portable form (Field 1990) (figure 13.3) or scaled up to the Augustan Solarium in Rome ("die größte Uhr aller Zeiten"; Buchner 1982: 7).

It is a commonplace that farming was the most significant industry of the ancient world, and many technological developments are closely related to the processing of its products (chapter 14). Research has shown the innovative character of animal husbandry as well (chapter 8). Weaving was particularly extensive, and Wild has observed several developments in loom technology within the Roman imperial period that appear to be associated with the production of increasingly complex patterns (chapter 18). In particular, there was a change from a vertical to a horizontal loom (Wild 1987). Processing crops involved mills and presses for extracting juice from grapes or extracting oil from olives. The fitting of a counterweight to the lever of a press by means of a screw (rather than pulling it down with ropes) may be connected with Heron of Alexandria's description of a thread-cutting device (Humphrey et al. 1998: 55). The invention of direct screw presses, which did not require a lever, might have resulted from observing screwed counterweights, or could have been scaled up from traction instruments used by doctors setting broken bones. The water-powered mill used for grinding corn certainly was an invention, whether driven by a horizontal wheel that turns a millstone either directly, or indirectly by a vertical wheel whose drive is transmitted to the stone through 90 degrees by gears that allow the stone to rotate at a different speed to the waterwheel (chapter 6). All of the components described by Vitruvius in the late first century A.D. existed previously: rotary millstones, 90-degree angle gears, and large water wheels (Lewis 1997). The water-mill could not have been created until all of the individual elements had been developed; this process conforms to Usher's (1955) "cumulative synthesis" model of invention involving perception of a problem (substituting water power for human or animal labor), insight (awareness of a range of water wheels and gears), and critical revision (getting the materials, components, and operating speeds right). Compare also Schiffer's definition of "invention cascades" associated with "complex technological systems" (chapter 33). Specialist scientists/engineers associated with centers such as Alexandria would be well placed to make inventions of this kind, since they knew about the needs of their sponsors, understood mechanical principles, and explored the working of hydraulic machinery in devices such as water-clocks with displays and side effects— including wheels with gears, turned by water, as described by Philon of Byzantium (Lewis 2000a: 354). The expansion of the Roman Empire, and its enormous consumption of wine, oil, and grain, provided a context for the wide diffusion of pressing and milling technologies (Amouretti and Brun 1993; Mattingly 1996).

This discussion has demonstrated that each technological item may have gone through a different trajectory of discovery, invention, innovation, diffusion, and use. This process emphasizes the need for considerable care with vocabulary, and it complicates any attempt to examine *processes* of invention and innovation, for we only ever see the *results* in technical treatises or archaeological discoveries. There is a certain consistency about the best known inventors. Archimedes was primarily interested in mathematics, but many areas of his research had practical implications. Understanding of levers, weights, and hydrostatics, combined with the practical skills and concepts necessary for building astronomical spheres, provided ample knowledge for the construction of siege equipment or water-lifting devices. Hellenistic monarchs had every reason to support abstract philosophical and scientific pursuits, since intellectual knowledge could be turned to useful purposes: government, taxation, courtly entertainment, temple rituals, warfare, architecture, bulk transport, water supply, and irrigation. Whatever misgivings about banausic activities may have existed, there was clearly a need for knowledge about inventions to be transmitted in written form, and for new compilations to be assembled as political and economic circumstances changed. Descriptions and illustrations of the working of machines commonly dismissed as toys allowed basic principles to be grasped by engineers who lacked the scientific background of Archimedes or Heron (Lewis 2000a). Thus, while neither Vitruvius nor Heron can be classed as "inventors," they demonstrate the existence of an audience for treatises on technical subjects, which persisted into the late imperial and Byzantine period (Pappus, Pseudo-Heron). Without systems for creating and sharing such information, inventions could not have become innovations to be diffused into technology-in-use.

Vitruvius, Ptolemy, Galen, and Heron all consolidated centuries of scientific knowledge into systematic treatises at around the time that Pliny the Elder attempted to gather together as much knowledge as possible into his encyclopedic *Natural History*. This process did not end in the Roman period, of course; the survival of much of what we possess results from similar demands for systematic knowledge in the contexts of Byzantium, Persia, Islam, and Renaissance Italy, where rulers were faced with the same problems of government, defense, transport, food supply, ritual, or entertainment. There are no grounds in the technical writers whose work we know for making essentialist generalizations that contrast a Greek scientific spirit with a Roman talent for practical application.

Nothing survives of subliterary texts about such craft skills as making pumps out of blocks of wood rather than bronze, or the practical advantages of glass windows, of wooden barrels, or of codices. The only developments in the provinces to reach Pliny's ears were related to agriculture; the *vallus* and the wheeled plough presumably impressed him as an estate owner. In contrast, he had little to say about concrete vaulting or the expansion of glass production; only a garbled tale about "unbreakable" glass suggests awareness of recent innovations (Greene 2000: 46–47).

Archaeological finds provide a physical image of a Greek and Roman world in which technology was disseminated and implemented according to the scale of political units, with an apogee in the Roman Empire (Greene 1992, 1994). Multiple estate ownership by rich families would have encouraged such processes, and the same social class provided army officers and government officials who gained detailed knowledge of a number of provinces during their careers. Regional "schools" of mosaic designers, or standardized services of tablewares made in multiple production centers, reflect the dissemination of knowledge between craft workers, whether through molds, pattern books or wooden templates. Many Roman industries incorporated name-stamps into their products (e.g., tiles, pottery, bronze and glass vessels) which demonstrate that branch workshops could be opened and workers transferred between them (Harris 1993). The most interesting questions about Greek and Roman invention and innovation are not about priority or originality, but about the contexts in which such processes took place.

# REFERENCES

Amouretti, M.-C., and J.-P. Brun (eds.) 1993. *La production du vin et de l'huile en Méditerranée. Bulletin de Correspondance Hellenique* Suppl. 26. Athens: École Française.

Baatz, D. 1994. *Bauten und Katapulte des römischen Heeres*. Stuttgart: Franz Steiner.

Bats, M. (ed.) 1996. *Les céramiques communes de Campanie et de Narbonnaise (Ie av. J-C–IIe ap. J-C): La vaisselle de cuisine et de table*. Naples: Centre Jean Bérard.

Bishop, M. C., and J. Coulston 1993. *Roman military equipment from the Punic wars to the fall of Rome*. London: Batsford.

Buchner, E. 1982. *Die Sonnenuhr des Augustus: Nachdruck aus RM 1976 und 1980 und Nachwort über die Ausgrabung 1980/81*. Mainz: von Zabern.

Carradice, I., and M. J. Price 1988. *Coinage in the Greek world*. London: Seaby.

Craddock, P. T. (ed.) 1990. *2000 years of zinc and brass*. British Museum Occasional Paper 50. London: British Museum

Dalley, S., and J. P. Oleson 2003. "Sennacherib, Archimedes, and the water screw: The context of invention in the ancient world," *Technology and Culture*: 1–26.

DeLaine, J. 2002. "The Temple of Hadrian at Cyzicus and Roman attitudes to exceptional construction," *Papers of the British School at Rome* 70: 205–30.

di Pasquale, G. 1999. "Weighing instruments," in A. Ciarallo and E. de Carolis (eds.), *Pompeii: Life in a Roman town*. Milan: Electa, 283–85.

Drachmann, A. G. 1948. *Ktesibios, Philon and Heron: A study in ancient pneumatics*. Copenhagen: Munksgaard.

Drachmann, A. G. 1963. *The mechanical technology of Greek and Roman antiquity: A study of the literary sources*. Copenhagen: Munksgaard.

Dugan, S., and D. Dugan 2000. *The day the world took off: The roots of the Industrial Revolution*. London: Channel 4 Books.

Edgerton, D. 1999. "From innovation to use: Ten eclectic theses on the historiography of technology," *History and Technology* 16.2: 111–36.

Field, J. V. 1990. "Some Roman and Byzantine portable sundials and the London sundial-calendar," *History of Technology* 12: 103–35.

Finley, M. I. 1965. "Technical innovation and economic progress in the ancient world," *Economic History Review* 18: 29–45.

Finley, M. I. 1973. *The ancient economy.* London: Chatto and Windus.

Fleming, S. J. 1999. *Roman glass: Reflections on cultural change.* Philadelphia: University of Pennsylvania Museum.

Fleury, P. 1993. *La mécanique de Vitruve.* Caen: Centre d'Études et de Recherche sur l'Antiquité, Université de Caen.

Gibbs, S. L. 1976. *Greek and Roman sundials.* New Haven: Yale University Press.

Greene, K. 1986. *The archaeology of the Roman economy.* Berkeley: University of California Press.

Greene, K. 1992. "How was technology transferred in the Roman empire?" in M. Wood and F. Queiroga (eds.), *Current research on the Romanization of the western provinces.* British Archaeological Reports, Intl. Series S575. Oxford: BAR, 101–5.

Greene, K. 1994. "Technology and innovation in context: the Roman background to mediaeval and later developments," *Journal of Roman Archaeology* 7: 22–33.

Greene, K. 2000. "Technological innovation and economic progress in the ancient world: M. I. Finley reconsidered," *Economic History Review* 53: 29–59.

Harris, W. V. (ed.) 1993. *The inscribed economy: Production and distribution in the Roman Empire in the light of instrumentum domesticum. Journal of Roman Archaeology* Suppl. 6. Ann Arbor, MI: JRA.

Hassall, M. (ed.) 1979. *Aspects of the De rebus bellicis: Papers presented to E. A. Thompson.* British Archaeological Reports, Intl. Series S63. Oxford: BAR.

Hill, D. R. 1979. *The book of ingenious devices.* Dordrecht: Reidel.

Howe, T., and I. D. Rowland (eds.) 1999. *Vitruvius: Ten books on architecture. A new English translation with commentary and illustrations.* Cambridge: Cambridge University Press.

Humphrey, J. W., J. P. Oleson, and A. N. Sherwood (eds.) 1998. *Greek and Roman technology: A sourcebook.* London: Routledge.

Israeli, Y 1991. "The invention of blowing," in M. Newby and K. Painter (eds.), *Roman glass: Two centuries of art and invention.* London: Society of Antiquaries: 46–55.

Keyser, P. 1992. "A new look at Heron's 'steam engine.'" *Archive for the History of Exact Sciences* 44: 107–24.

Knorr, W. R. 1996. "Mechanics," *OCD*, 943–44.

Landels, J. G. 1998. *Music in ancient Greece and Rome.* London: Routledge.

Lewis, M. J. T. 1997. *Millstone and hammer: The origins of water power.* Hull: Hull University Press.

Lewis, M. J. T. 2000a. "Theoretical hydraulics, automata, and water clocks," in Ö. Wikander (ed.), *Handbook of ancient water technology.* Leiden: Brill: 343–69.

Lewis, M. J. T. 2000b. "The Hellenistic period," in Ö. Wikander (ed.), *Handbook of ancient water technology.* Leiden: Brill: 631–48.

Manning, W. H. 1986. *Catalogue of the Romano-British iron tools, fittings and weapons in the British Museum.* London: British Museum.

Marsden, E. W. 1969. *Greek and Roman artillery: Historical development.* Oxford: Clarendon.

Mattingly, D. J. 1996. "Olive presses in Roman Africa: Technical evolution or stagnation?" in M. Khanoussi, P. Ruggeri, and C. Vismara (eds.), *Africa romana: Atti dell'XI convegno di studio Cartagine, 1994.* Sassari: Universita degli Studi, 577–95.

Mattusch, C. C. 1996. *Classical bronzes: The art and craft of Greek and Roman statuary.* Ithaca, NY: Cornell University Press.

May, C. 2002. "Antecedents to intellectual property: The European pre-history of the 'ownership' of knowledge," *History of Technology* 24: 1–20.

Merker, G. S. 2003. "Corinthian terracotta figurines: The development of an industry," in C. K. Williams and N. Bookidis (eds.), *Corinth: The centenary, 1896–1996*. Princeton: American School of Classical Studies at Athens, 233–45.

Oleson, J. P. 2004. "*Well-pumps for dummies*: Was there a Roman tradition of popular sub-literary engineering manuals?" in F. Minonzio (ed.), *Problemi di macchinismo in ambito romano*. Archaeologia dell'Italia Settentrionale 8. Como: Comune di Como, 65–86.

Oleson, J. P., and G. Branton 1992. "The technology of King Herod's harbour," in R. L. Vann (ed.), *Caesarea papers: Straton's Tower, Herod's Harbour, and Roman and Byzantine Caesarea. Journal of Roman Archaeology* Suppl. 5. Ann Arbor, MI: JRA, 49–67.

Oleson, J. P., C. Brandon, S. M. Cramer, R. Cucitore, E. Gotti, R. L. Hohlfelder 2005. "The ROMACONS Project: A contribution to the historical and engineering analysis of hydraulic concrete in Roman maritime structures," *International Journal of Nautical Archaeology* 33: 199–229.

Oleson, J. P., L. Bottalico, C. Brandon, R. Cucitore, E. Gotti, R. L. Hohlfelder 2006. "Reproducing a Roman maritime structure with Vitruvian pozzolanic concrete," *Journal of Roman Archaeology* 19: 29–52.

Peacock, D. P. S. 1982. *Pottery in the Roman world: An ethnoarchaeological approach*. London: Longman.

Pomey, P., and A. Tchernia 2005. "Archimede e la Syrakosia," in E. lo Sardo (ed.), *Eurika! Il genio degli antichi*. Naples: Electra, 228–32.

Roberts, C. H., and T. C. Skeat 1983. *The birth of the codex*. London: British Academy/ Oxford University Press.

Schürmann, A. 1991. *Griechische Mechanik und antike Gesellschaft: Studien zur staatlichen Förderung einer technischen Wissenschaft*. Stuttgart: Franz Steiner.

Thompson, E. A. 1952. *A Roman inventor and reformer: Being a new text of the treatise De rebus bellicis*. Oxford: Clarendon Press.

Tomlinson, R., and J. Vallance 1996. "Vitruvius (Pol(l)io)," *OCD*, 1609–10.

Toomer, G. J. 1996. "Archimedes," *OCD*, 146–47.

Traina, G. 1994. *La tecnica in Grecia e a Roma*. Roma: Laterza.

Usher, A. P. 1929. *A history of mechanical inventions*. Cambridge, MA: Harvard University Press.

Usher, A. P. 1955. "Technical change and capital formation," in Universities National Bureau Committee for Economic Growth, *Capital formation and economic growth*. Princeton: Princeton University Press, 423–550.

Weinberg, G. D. 1988. *Excavations at Jalame: Site of a glass factory in late Roman Palestine*. Columbia: University of Missouri Press.

Whitehouse, D. 1997. *Roman glass in the Corning Museum of Glass, I*. Corning: Corning Museum of Glass.

Whitehouse, D. 2001. *Roman glass in the Corning Museum of Glass, II*. Corning: Corning Museum of Glass.

Wild, J.-P. 1987. "The Roman horizontal loom," *American Journal of Archaeology* 91: 459–72.

Wilkinson, P. 2000. *What the Romans did for us*. London: Boxtree.

Wilson, A. 2002. "Machines, power and the ancient economy," *Journal of Roman Studies* 92: 1–32.

Zimmer, G. 1982. *Antike Werkstattbilder*. Berlin: Gebr. Mann.

# PART VIII

# ETHNOARCHAEOLOGY AND MODEL-BUILDING

# CHAPTER 33

# EXPANDING ETHNOARCHAEOLOGY: HISTORICAL EVIDENCE AND MODEL-BUILDING IN THE STUDY OF TECHNOLOGICAL CHANGE

MICHAEL B. SCHIFFER

## EXPANDING ETHNOARCHAEOLOGY

Although ethnographic information has long been incorporated into inferences about past human behavior, not until the last third of the twentieth century did archaeologists undertake their own sustained and systematic observations in on-going societies (e.g., Binford 1978; Donnan and Clewlow 1974; Gould 1978, 1980; Longacre and Skibo 1994; Skibo 1992; Yellen 1977). This research activity is some-times called "living archaeology," although "ethnoarchaeology" now seems to be the preferred designation. This chapter suggests that an expanded ethnoarchaeology that exploits evidence from the historical records of both ancient and modern societies can become an important research strategy to obtain, refine, and evaluate general models and heuristics for investigating technological change. This proposal is grounded in the tenets of behavioral archaeology, a research program that privileges the study of people–artifact relationships in all times and all places (Reid et al. 1975; LaMotta and Schiffer 2001; Schiffer 1992, 1995a; Skibo et al. 1995; Zedeño 2000).

Ethnoarchaeology is usually regarded as the study, by archaeologists, of "traditional," non-Western societies, such as Australian Aborigines or Mayan Indians (for a synthesis of ethnoarchaeology, see David and Kramer 2001). Yet since the late 1970s ethnoarchaeological investigations have also taken place in Western industrial societies (e.g., Buchli and Lucas 2001; Gould and Schiffer 1981; Graves-Brown 2000; Rathje 1979; Rathje and Murphy 1992; Schiffer 1976, 1978). In the latter studies, ethnoarchaeology has come to resemble, in the artifacts examined, both historical archaeology and modern material-culture studies. Indeed, societies today are so interconnected by global commerce and travel that it is almost impossible to distinguish between ethnoarchaeology, historical archaeology, and modern material-culture studies on the basis of where and when the objects under investigation were made.

I suggest that ethnoarchaeology is set apart from other disciplines that study similar artifacts because its practitioners often ask *general* questions about the materiality of human behavior, including phenomena such as refuse-disposal practices, social boundary maintenance, and ritual technologies. Indeed, ethnoarchaeological research frequently leads to the provision of general principles—models, law-like statements, and theories—useful in constructing inferences and for explaining diversity and change in human behavior.

Ethnoarchaeologists are in an advantageous position to formulate general principles because researchers study the artifacts themselves and also draw on strong evidence describing the participation of those very same artifacts in activities. The latter evidence usually comes from the investigator's own observations, as in the study of a living society—any living society—or from accounts of people who once took part in activities no longer being practiced (i.e., oral history). If ethnoarchaeology is the study of general relationships between activities and artifacts *when strong evidence is available on both*, then in an expanded ethnoarchaeology researchers can make use of evidence from the historical record as well. After all, historical accounts may contain useful descriptions of both artifacts and the activities in which they took part.

Thus, I propose that ethnoarchaeology be regarded as a wide-ranging research strategy that includes the establishment of general principles through the study of strong evidence on both activities and artifacts. It matters not whether the evidence derives from the investigator's own fieldwork in a living society or from digging in the documents of dead ones. Thus, classical archaeologists, who rely on historical and archaeological materials, can—among other pursuits—conduct ethnoarchaeological research that aims to furnish and evaluate general principles. In the remainder of this chapter, I illustrate the vision of an expanded ethnoarchaeology by presenting models and heuristics derived from research on electrical technologies of the eighteenth and nineteenth centuries.

# EARLY ELECTRICAL TECHNOLOGIES AS A MODEL FOR EXPANDED ETHNOARCHAEOLOGY

Source material for studying early electrical technologies is copious. Accounts of the constituent artifacts, along with descriptions of activities such as manufacture and use, can be found in textbooks, monographs, journal articles, letters, instruction manuals, diaries, newspapers, magazines, and so on. Moreover, many of the artifacts themselves survive in private collections and in museums of technology throughout the West. Of course the historical record exhibits frustrating gaps, but the sheer amount of information available, even for the eighteenth century, is at times overwhelming. In the course of asking historical questions while seeking to write narratives about how our modern electrical world came to be, I have sometimes also asked general questions about technological change and exploited the rich historical record seeking answers. The result has been the provision of models and heuristics that might be useful in studying technological change in many social contexts.

## BEHAVIORAL FOUNDATIONS

The key framework that informs many behavioral models of technological change is the life history of artifacts and technologies. Long implicit in studies of chipped-stone technology (Bleed 2001), the life-history framework was made explicit and generalized during the 1970s in studies on inference and on the formation processes of the archaeological record (Schiffer 1972, 1975, 1976; Sullivan 1978). More recently, it has served in research on diverse topics including subsistence (Gumerman 1997) and territory formation (Zedeño 1997). This framework reminds us that every artifact, structure, and technological system had a life history that may have included processes such as procurement of raw materials, manufacture, use, reuse, and deposition. Life histories can be modeled in countless ways, depending on the investigator's research interests and the technology under investigation.

The most fine-grained life-history models are termed "behavioral chains"; they involve the sequence of specific activities in which an artifact participated during its entire existence. By focusing on the constituent activities of a behavioral chain, the investigator can isolate specific person–person, person–artifact, and artifact–artifact interactions. Behavioral chains are essential, for example, in building models to explain the design of artifacts (e.g., Schiffer and Skibo 1997; Skibo and Schiffer 2001).

Researchers can also employ a life-history model that describes three basic processes in the development of a *type* of artifact or technology: invention, commercialization (manufacture or replication), and adoption (LaMotta and Schiffer 2001; Schiffer 1995a). Keeping such processes distinct at the research-design stage is important because, for example, one cannot explain the occurrence of inventive activities by using models that account for the adoption of new technologies, and vice versa. Clearly, explanations of technological change require a plethora of *process-specific* models and theories (Schiffer 1995a; Schiffer et al. 2001).

Because behavioral theories and models attend assiduously to the materiality of human life, they often make reference to the behavioral capabilities of artifacts that facilitate specific interactions in specific activities. These behavioral capabilities are termed *performance characteristics* and enable symbolic and utilitarian functions (on performance characteristics, see Schiffer and Miller 1999: 16–20). Thus, in functioning as a cooking pot, a ceramic container has to possess, among other performance characteristics, adequate resistance to thermal shock. Likewise, a crucifix must have a certain form in order to be recognizable as a symbol of Christian beliefs.

The crucifix example suggests that performance characteristics also include behavioral capabilities dependent on human senses: tactile, olfactory, gustatory, auditory, and visual. Sensory performance characteristics, which contribute importantly to symbolic and aesthetic interactions, include a silk shirt's ability to feel "silken" when touching someone's skin, a clarinet's capacity to emit clarinetlike sounds when played, and a halibut's ability to smell like "fresh fish." During the conduct of most activities, diverse performance characteristics of the constituent artifacts—sensory and nonsensory—come into play and facilitate the activity's forward motion. The section Differential Adoption, below, further expands the fundamental notion of performance characteristic.

I now turn to three examples of an "expanded ethnoarchaeology": technological differentiation, differential adoption, and the cascade model of invention processes. Readers interested in the details of these studies and the written materials employed as evidence can turn to the original works cited in these discussions. For a survey of archaeological studies of technology, see Millar 2007.

# TECHNOLOGICAL DIFFERENTIATION

New technologies such as glassworking, aqueduct construction, and ceramic production often begin their life histories as a small number of forms definable on the basis of utilitarian and/or symbolic functions. Thus, the first pottery in any area often consisted of just a few jars with limited food-preparation functions; centuries later, vessels were manufactured in dozens of shapes and sizes that took part in diverse activities, from marriage ceremonies to brewing alcoholic beverages. Technologies that endure and proliferate possess an adaptability that permits people, in a changing social context, to create new forms to serve new utilitarian and symbolic functions. The increase in the varieties of a technology is a recurrent pattern discernible in countless archaeological sequences; the process responsible for this pattern is termed "technological differentiation."

In a study of twentieth-century home electronics, I called attention to technological differentiation, noting that the process is usually accompanied by functional specialization in the new forms (Schiffer 1992: 107–8). However, because the aim of that study was to deconstruct the notion of "technological revolution," no models of technological differentiation were built. Rather, the task of model building was taken up in a later study of eighteenth-century electrical technology (Schiffer 2002; Schiffer et al. 2003).

Electrical technology became distinguishable early in the eighteenth century with the appearance of a small number of esoteric devices—including Leyden jars (the first capacitors) and frictional generators—that natural philosophers employed to explore surprising phenomena, such as electricity's ability to produce light and sparks. From this modest beginning, people over the course of decades invented hundreds of specialized electrical artifacts that carried out utilitarian and symbolic functions in activities as varied as healing, giving public lectures, and experimenting with gases. Dozens of these inventions were replicated by philosophical instrument-makers and adopted by consumers.

To gain a behavioral understanding of technological differentiation, I constructed a framework based on the transfer of technologies among "techno-communities." A techno-community (or, simply, "community") is a group of people whose members—often drawn from different social, political, and ethnic groups—carry out particular activities employing particular technologies. Thus, electrophysicists used certain electrical devices for conducting cutting-edge physics experiments, whereas electrotherapists in their healing activities employed, in addition to generators and Leyden jars, some rather different sorts of electrical things. As a technology is transferred from one community to another, the recipient community's members invent new functional types whose performance characteristics are more suitable for participating in their own activities. For illustrative purposes, the following discussion makes reference to the technology transfer from electrophysicists to electrotherapists.

It is convenient to model technology transfer as a six-phase process, which begins with *information transfer*. In this phase people who are potential nuclei of new recipient communities learn about the technology in various ways, such as by word of mouth, through print media, and by examining the hardware itself. Thus, magazine articles and lectures about electrophysicists' experiments reached a wide public, including people who envisioned the use of electricity for ameliorating various afflictions. Obviously, inferring from the archaeological and historical records the precise modes of information transfer can be difficult, if not impossible. This is not, however, a fatal limitation because we know that, often, only a fraction of the individuals who learn about a new technology actually go on to modify or acquire it. The latter, who make up the recipient community, are the focus of the model.

The next phase, *experimentation*, usually begins when a few people try out the new technology, learning how well it performs in their activities. These early efforts often reveal that the technology shows some promise but its weighting of performance characteristics is unsuitable for the new activity. For example, it was found that the cumbersome instruments of early physics were not convenient for use in electromedicine.

In the *redesign* phase, people invent specialized types of the technology, which embody a more appropriate weighting of performance characteristics. Thus, electrotherapists designed compact and portable generators along with specialized conductors that could be used to apply electricity to afflicted areas of the human body, including feet, teeth, and eyes.

*Replication* involves manufacture of the redesigned technology and its distribution to purchasers and users. Thus, instrument makers manufactured and sold many devices that had been redesigned specifically for electromedical activities. During *acquisition* (also called consumption or adoption), people obtain examples of the new technology and thereby become members of the recipient techno-community. Apothecaries, surgeons, and physicians, among many others, comprised the community of electrotherapists. During the final phase, *use*, the acquired technology's use-related performance characteristics came into play as it interacted with healers, assistants, and patients.

The technology-transfer framework was formulated in tandem with my efforts to explain, in historical terms, the differentiation of eighteenth-century electrical technology. The rich historical record made it possible to fashion the six-phase model, whose application, in turn, enabled the crafting of a narrative that accounted for the differentiation of that very same technology in the hands of more than half a dozen techno-communities. Whether the technology-transfer model can be applied with profit to other cases of technological differentiation, such as the proliferation of worked-bone tools and ornaments during the Upper Paleolithic, glass in Rome, and lasers in the twentieth century, remains to be learned through future research.

At the very least, this framework invites the archaeologist to ask a great many questions about a differentiated technology. Research to answer these questions can lead to diverse inferences about, for example, the activities in which the technology's new varieties participated, contextual factors (social and environmental) that contributed to changes in activities, the functions of the technology in those activities, the performance characteristics of the new varieties that promoted their adoption over alternative technologies that might have served the same functions, and the social composition of the associated techno-communities. By synthesizing these inferences, the archaeologist can fashion a narrative to explain technological differentiation, one that contextualizes the new technologies in relation to changing social and environmental factors.

# DIFFERENTIAL ADOPTION

A common problem in the study of technological change is that of explaining patterns of adoption of a new technology that becomes available in the marketplace. Usually, new technologies are not adopted uniformly; that is, some but not all individuals, social units, or communities acquire and use the new technology. Thus, an understanding of adoption processes requires one to frame the problem as *differential* adoption, and invites us to seek explanations for both adoption and nonadoption decisions among potential adopters (i.e., those familiar with the technology). In the course of investigating the differential adoption of electrically-lit lighthouses during the late nineteenth century (Schiffer 2005a), I was able to refine the performance matrix, a heuristic tool that had been employed in previous studies of adoption processes (e.g., Schiffer and Skibo 1987; Schiffer 1995b, 2000). The performance matrix is particularly applicable to cases in which a new technology is competing with existing technologies for application in ongoing activities. If a new technology lacks competition, the study of adoption requires other models and heuristics, such as Hayden's (1998) "aggrandizer" model.

A behavioral analysis of adoption is founded on the premise that potential adopters consider the known and anticipated performance characteristics of the competing technologies. In a deliberative process that may not be explicit, potential adopters assign varying weights to specific performance characteristics in response to contextual factors—political, social, religious, demographic, and economic, for example. These weightings determine whether the technology is adopted. Because these diverse contextual factors differ among potential adopters, their weightings of performance characteristics also differ; the result is differential adoption. As I will show, patterns in the performance matrix enable the archaeologist to ascertain which performance characteristics were weighted in given adoption decisions. The researcher can then offer hypotheses about the specific contextual factors that affected the adoption decisions of individuals or groups. An investigation of electrically-lit lighthouses of the late nineteenth century will illustrate this research process.

Generator-powered electric lights, employing carbon arcs, were first installed in a lighthouse in 1859, in England. During the following decades, when many hundreds of new lighthouses were being built worldwide, the electric light was adopted only infrequently. Indeed, at the end of the century, the use of electric-arc illumination in lighthouses peaked at around 30. The adoption decisions are intriguing: France and England together installed nearly 20 electric lights, most other nations acquired none, and a few—including the United States—adopted just one or two. Electric arc lights had to compete against lamps that burned some kind of hydrocarbon (e.g., lard oil, rapeseed oil, or kerosene).

Adoption decisions were made by lighthouse boards, which were governmental or quasi-governmental organizations. They built new lighthouses, maintained old ones, and in a few nations, especially England, France, and the United States, supported experimental programs that assessed new illuminants and other light-house technologies. These experiments were often documented in published reports, which furnished information on the performance characteristics of oil and electric illuminants to potential adopters—and to this researcher. Moreover, contextual information was available from abundant primary and secondary sources. Thus, this case provided an ideal opportunity to refine the performance matrix as a tool for exploring differentiation adoption.

The performance matrix is a table for comparing, side by side, the performance characteristics of two or more competing technologies in *relevant life-history activities*. For each performance characteristic, the investigator indicates with plus and minus signs which technology did (+) or did not (−) achieve minimally adequate performance. Performance matrices can also be built with numerical values or presence/absence notations. To reveal any patterns in the performance matrix, the investigator shuffles the rows to create clusters of plusses and minuses within an activity category.

Because decisions of the boards affected most life-history activities of light-house illuminants, their members presumably took into account a wide range of performance characteristics. Thus, in table 33.1, performance characteristics are aggregated by major life-history activities: (1) acquisition and installation of components, (2) functions during use, and (3) operation, regular maintenance, and repair. In constructing this matrix it was necessary to employ an expansive conception of performance characteristics so as to implicate the entire range of contextual factors that might have influenced adoption decisions. Indeed, the entries in table 33.1 run the gamut of behavioral capabilities, such as costs of acquiring components, ease of administration, and the ability to convey particular meanings. This broad conception of performance characteristics, along with plus-and-minus entries, allows the archaeologist to incorporate into the analysis seemingly incommensurable factors, qualitative and quantitative. As a result, one can deal explicitly with the diverse contextual factors that likely influenced the weightings of performance characteristics and affected adoption decisions.

As long as the researcher includes all potentially relevant performance characteristics (from the standpoint of the individual or social unit making the adoption decision), the performance matrix serves as a *causally neutral* tool of analysis. Naturally, the reconstruction of performance characteristics in the context of the classical cultures will rely more on archaeological and ethnographic evidence than on the rich contemporary documentation available for nineteenth-century lighthouses. In principle, patterns appearing as clusters of plusses and minuses should indicate which performance characteristics were heavily weighted by past decision-makers and which were not.

The performance matrix of lighthouse illuminants exhibits several patterns. The dominant pattern is that the electric light competed poorly in acquisition, installation, operation, maintenance, and repair activities. This pattern suggests that the vast majority of maritime nations, those that adopted no electric lights, had assigned heavy weight to utilitarian and financial factors. By not adopting electric

### Table 33.1. A performance matrix for lighthouse illumination, ca. 1860–99 (adapted from Schiffer 2005a, Table 1).

| Acquisition of the Components, and Installation of the System | Electric | Oil |
|---|---|---|
| Ability to acquire system components commercially | + | + |
| System can be installed in lighthouses in any location | – | + |
| System can be easily installed in existing lighthouse structures | – | + |
| Affordability of a system's "first costs" | – | + |
| Existing expertise adequate for designing and installing the system | – | + |

| Functions During Use | Electric | Oil |
|---|---|---|
| Yields the whitest, brightest, most penetrating light | + | – |
| Can produce sufficiently steady light | + | + |
| Long outages are avoidable | + | + |
| Does not cast confusing shadows | – | + |
| Can avoid blinding mariners | – | + |
| Ability to symbolize special concern for the safety of ships and sailors | + | – |
| Can symbolize a nation's wealth and political power | + | – |
| Can symbolize modernity | + | – |
| Able to symbolize scientific/technological prowess | + | – |

| Operation, Regular Maintenance, and Repairs | Electric | Oil |
|---|---|---|
| Operable with traditional staff of keepers | – | + |
| Operable without complete backup systems | – | + |
| Ease of repairing breakdowns | – | + |
| Affordability of operating expenses | – | + |
| Ease of administration | – | + |

lights, these nations avoided readily predicted expenses and hassles. On the other hand, a lesser pattern in use-related functions indicates that the electric light was an adequate illuminant, especially in haze and light fog, and it especially excelled in symbolic capabilities because its light was distinctive in color and brightness. This lesser pattern helps one to formulate explanations as to why two nations, England

and France, adopted a handful of electric lights and why several others acquired one or two. It would appear that lighthouse boards in adopting nations had assigned, for political purposes, a heavy weight to symbolic capabilities, which outweighed the electric light's many utilitarian and financial performance deficiencies. To make a long story short, I concluded that adoptions were promoted by technological rivalries between long-time adversaries England and France as well as by the interests of a few other nations in advertising to all mariners a commitment to modernity through their mastery of a cutting-edge electrical technology.

The lighthouse case suggests that an archaeologist, using patterns in a performance matrix as a foundation, can construct a contextualized narrative that accounts, with reference to local factors, for instances of adoption and nonadoption of a new technology. Although the performance matrix had been employed previously in studies of technological change, even in a prehistoric case (Schiffer and Skibo 1987), the lighthouse project led to its significant refinement as a tool of analysis. Indeed, the lighthouse study sharply defined the role of the performance matrix as a causally neutral tool suitable for investigating differential adoption.

# INVENTION CASCADES

Many technologies, like lighthouse illuminants, canal-aqueduct systems, and domestic cooking utensils, consist of a set of artifacts that must interact appropriately with people and themselves, especially during activities of manufacture and use. How these relatively harmonious relationships come to be is the subject of the "cascade model" of invention processes (Schiffer 2005b). The cascade model assists in understanding the spurts of inventive activity that accompany development of a "complex technological system" (CTS); it does not, however, explain why the development of a CTS is initiated or pursued. The archaeologist enjoys wide latitude in defining a CTS, for it need consist only of a set of interacting artifacts. As such, CTSs can be expected to develop in virtually every human society, including technologies that range from the bow and arrow to the nuclear-powered submarine.

The cascade model was inspired by historian Thomas Hughes' (1983) model of "reverse salients." According to Hughes, during the development of a complex socio-technical system, such as an electric power network, certain components lag and present critical problems—generators of insufficient capacity to meet demand and power poles vulnerable to lightning strikes, for example. If the system is to become functional, then such problems must be solved—at first through invention. This key insight was the starting point for building the cascade model, which is a behavioral elaboration and generalization of Hughes' model.

The cascade model took shape as I confronted the bewildering array of inventions needed to create a functional electromagnetic telegraph system during the mid-nineteenth century (Schiffer 2005b). Especially intriguing were the numerous and diverse inventions offered to solve particular performance problems, many of which failed to be widely replicated and adopted. In a nutshell, the cascade model posits that, during a CTS's development, emergent performance problems—recognized by people as shortcomings in that technology's constituent interactions—stimulate sequential spurts of inventive activity. As adopted inventions solve one problem, people encounter new and often unanticipated performance problems, which stimulate more inventive spurts, and so on. The result is a series of "invention cascades." The distinctive feature of this model, which promotes its generality, is the premise that processes in a CTS's life history are the immediate contexts in which performance problems emerge and provoke invention cascades. Life-history processes, then, are the appropriate analytic units for investigating invention processes in CTSs.

Any CTS has a life history consisting of a minimal set of processes: creating a prototype, replication or manufacture, use, and maintenance. These processes do not comprise a unilinear sequence, for some may occur in parallel and others can recur. And, depending on the specific CTS, it may be necessary to delineate many more processes. Thus, to accommodate the telegraph's many invention cascades, I specified as analytic units additional processes that may apply only to CTSs in capitalist-industrial societies, including technological display, demonstrating practicality to potential financiers, and marketing and sales. Although life-history processes can be elaborated *ad infinitum*, the key premise remains invariant: life history processes, however enumerated, are the proximate contexts of invention cascades.

If the development of a CTS is to proceed, people must judge that its component artifacts have reached acceptable values of important performance characteristics. The failure of a component to perform adequately its major symbolic and/or utilitarian functions usually calls forth a spurt of inventive activity. Although most of the resultant inventions do not solve the performance problem, one or a few might, and these may be replicated and adopted. As development continues, other performance shortcomings are often encountered, which stimulate additional inventive spurts. The result is an invention cascade. The development of the electromagnetic telegraph, for example, involved cascades of inventions for telegraph senders, receiver-printers, poles, insulators, lightning protectors, underwater cables, and so forth.

The cascade model invites archaeologists to rewrite the story of any CTS by seeking evidence that its development proceeded in fits and starts, marked by invention cascades and the likely proliferation of unsuccessful components. In this way, the archaeologist may be able to account for previously ignored variability, such as unusual or unique artifacts that do not fit into established classifications. The search for traces of invention cascades can be guided by an appreciation for the performance requirements of the developing CTS, which dictates that the archaeologist understand how the system would have worked. To acquire such knowledge, one can exploit modern engineering literature and expertise, conduct experiments, and draw on ethnographic, archaeological, and historical information.

Using life-history processes as analytical units, the archaeologist can then seek evidence for the successful and unsuccessful components that arose during the CTS's development.

As Arnold (2007) demonstrates, the cascade model is also a potent antidote to diffusionist explanations of technological change. In fact, acquiring the "idea" for a specific CTS is usually the easiest part of the process. As one early experimenter pointed out, the idea of the electromagnetic telegraph was "obvious" (Barlow 1825: 105). Indeed, many people familiar with electrical technology in many nations tried to construct electromagnetic telegraphs. They soon learned that it was far from obvious how to design an entire suite of components that had to function together effectively in a telegraph system. Thus, each development team—for example, Morse and Vail in the United States, or Wheatstone and Cook in England—had to contrive specific components, usually by trial and error, with failures far outnumbering successes. In view of this process, in which the inventors' expertise and skill grew along with the proliferation of components, it would be facile to attribute multiple developments of the telegraph in several western nations to the diffusion of the telegraph idea. At best, the idea of a particular CTS is a starting point for a sometimes lengthy and costly development process that often makes use of local human and material resources (Arnold 2007).

Lacking familiarity with classical archaeology, I cannot presume to prescribe how a researcher might conduct ethnoarchaeological studies that exploit historical (and archaeological) evidence, such as those I carried out on electrical technologies of the eighteenth and nineteenth centuries. However, I would be dumbfounded if the surviving evidence of technologies in classical societies did not offer archaeologists a significant opportunity to generate and refine models of technological change. In the classical world, complex technological systems were developed, some technologies became highly differentiated, and technologies were no doubt differentially adopted. At the very least, classical archaeologists can assess whether the general models, concepts, and heuristics presented here have any utility for understanding specific cases of technological change.

It might appear that the expanded ethnoarchaeology advocated here is merely historical research. In a superficial sense that is true: the ethnoarchaeologist, like the historian, obtains evidence from the written record. By the same sort of argument one might also claim that traditional ethnoarchaeology is ethnography, since its practitioners also obtain information through studies of living people. I suggest, however, that the narrow focus on data gathering and sources of evidence is misplaced. What distinguishes traditional ethnoarchaeology from ethnography is the distinctive set of *general* questions that archaeologists bring to the field: a concern with people–artifact relationships of every kind, from processes of stone-tool manufacture to disposal practices for ritual technologies (e.g., Walker 1995). Likewise, what distinguishes an expanded ethnoarchaeology from history is the asking of *general* questions and an unapologetic concern with artifacts and processes of technological change. Working with historical materials as a historian, the researcher fashions explanatory narratives; working as an ethnoarchaeologist, that same researcher can build and evaluate models, theories, and heuristics of potentially widespread applicability.

# REFERENCES

Arnold, J. E. 2007. "Credit where credit is due: The Chumash ocean-going plank canoe," *American Antiquity* 72: 196–209.

Barlow, P. 1825. "On the laws of electro-magnetic action, as depending on the length and dimensions of the conducting wire, and on the question, whether electrical phenomena are due to the transmission of a simple or compound fluid," *The Edinburgh Philosophical Journal* 12: 105–14.

Binford, L. R. 1978. *Nunamiut ethnoarchaeology*. New York: Academic Press.

Bleed, P. 2001. "Trees or chains, links or branches: Conceptual alternatives for consideration of stone tool production and other sequential activities," *Journal of Archaeological Method and Theory* 8: 101–27.

Buchli, V., and G. Lucas (eds.) 2001. *Archaeologies of the contemporary past*. London: Routledge.

David, N., and C. Kramer 2001. *Ethnoarchaeology in action*. Cambridge: Cambridge University Press.

Donnan, C. B., and C. W. Clewlow, Jr. (eds.) 1974. *Ethnoarchaeology*. Los Angeles: UCLA Institute of Archaeology.

Gould, R. A. (ed.) 1978. *Explorations in ethnoarchaeology*. Albuquerque: University of New Mexico Press.

Gould, R. A. 1980. *Living archaeology*. Cambridge: Cambridge University Press.

Gould, R. A., and M. B. Schiffer (eds.) 1981. *Modern material culture studies: The archaeology of us*. New York: Academic Press.

Graves-Brown, P. (ed.) 2000. *Matter, materiality and modern culture*. London: Routledge.

Gumerman, G. 1997. "Food and complex societies," *Journal of Archaeological Method and Theory* 2: 105–39.

Hayden, B. 1998. "Practical and prestige technologies: The evolution of material systems," *Journal of Archaeological Method and Theory* 5: 1–55.

Hughes, T. P. 1983. *Networks of power: Electrification in Western societies, 1880–1930*. Baltimore: Johns Hopkins University Press.

LaMotta, V. M., and M. B. Schiffer 2001. "Behavioral archaeology: Towards a new synthesis," in I. Hodder (ed.), *Archaeological theory today*. Cambridge: Polity Press, 14–64.

Longacre, W. A., and J. M. Skibo (eds.) 1994. *Kalinga ethnoarchaeology: Expanding archaeological method and theory*. Washington, D.C.: Smithsonian Institution Press.

Millar, H. M. –L. 2007. *Archaeological approaches to technology*. London: Academic Press.

Rathje, W. L. 1979. "Modern material culture studies," *Advances in Archaeological Method and Theory* 2: 1–37.

Rathje, W. L., and C. Murphy 1992. *Rubbish! The archaeology of garbage*. New York: Harper Collins.

Reid, J. J., M. B. Schiffer, and W. L. Rathje 1975. "Behavioral archaeology: Four strategies," *American Anthropologist* 77: 864–69.

Schiffer, M. B. 1972. "Archaeological context and systemic context," *American Antiquity* 37: 156–65.

Schiffer, M. B. 1975. "Behavioral chain analysis: Activities, organization, and the use of space," in "Chapters in the prehistory of eastern Arizona, IV," special issue, *Fieldiana: Anthropology* 65: 103–19.

Schiffer, M. B. 1976. *Behavioral archeology*. New York: Academic Press.

Schiffer, M. B. 1978. "Methodological issues in ethnoarchaeology," in R. A. Gould (ed.), *Explorations in ethnoarchaeology*. Albuquerque: University of New Mexico Press, 229–47.

Schiffer, M. B. 1992. *Technological perspectives on behavioral change*. Tucson: University of Arizona Press.

Schiffer, M. B. (ed.) 1995a. *Behavioral archaeology: First principles*. Salt Lake City: University of Utah Press.

Schiffer, M. B. 1995b. "Social theory and history in behavioral archaeology," in J. M. Skibo, W. H. Walker, and A. E. Nielsen (eds.), *Expanding archaeology*. Salt Lake City: University of Utah Press, 22–35.

Schiffer, M. B. 2000. "Indigenous theories, scientific theories and product histories," in P. Graves-Brown (ed.), *Matter, materiality and modern culture*. London: Routledge, 72–96.

Schiffer, M. B. 2002. "Studying technological differentiation: The case of 18th-century electrical technology," *American Anthropologist* 104: 1148–61.

Schiffer, M. B. 2005a. "The electric lighthouse in the nineteenth century: Aid to navigation and political technology," *Technology and Culture* 45: 275–305.

Schiffer, M. B. 2005b. "The devil is in the details: The cascade model of invention processes," *American Antiquity* 70: 485–502.

Schiffer, M. B., K. L. Hollenback, and C. L. Bell 2003. *Draw the LIGHTNING Down: Benjamin Franklin and electrical technology in the Age of Enlightenment*. Berkeley: University of California Press.

Schiffer, M. B., and A. R. Miller 1999. *The material life of human beings: Artifacts, behavior, and communication*. London: Routledge.

Schiffer, M. B., and J. M. Skibo 1987. "Theory and experiment in the study of technological change," *Current Anthropology* 28: 595–622.

Schiffer, M. B., and J. M. Skibo 1997. "The explanation of artifact variability," *American Antiquity* 62: 27–50.

Schiffer, M. B., J. M. Skibo, J. Griffitts, K. Hollenback, and W. A. Longacre 2001. "Behavioral archaeology and the study of technology," *American Antiquity* 66: 729–38.

Skibo, J. M. 1992. *Pottery function: A use-alteration perspective*. New York: Plenum.

Skibo, J. M., and M. B. Schiffer 2001. "Understanding artifact variability and change: A behavioral framework," in M. B. Schiffer (ed.), *Anthropological perspectives on technology*. Albuquerque: University of New Mexico Press, 139–49.

Skibo, J. M., W. H. Walker, and A. E. Nielsen (eds.) 1995. *Expanding archaeology*. Salt Lake City: University of Utah Press.

Sullivan, A. P. 1978. "The Structure of archaeological inference: A critical examination of logic and procedure," *Advances in Archaeological Method and Theory* 1: 183–222.

Walker, W. H. 1995. "Ceremonial trash?" in J. M. Skibo, W. H. Walker, and A. E. Nielsen (eds.), *Expanding archaeology*. Salt Lake City: University of Utah Press, 67–79.

Yellen, J. 1977. *Archaeological approaches to the present: models for reconstructing the past*. New York: Academic Press.

Zedeño, M. N. 1997. "Landscapes, land use, and the history of territory formation: An example from the Puebloan Southwest," *Journal of Archaeological Method and Theory* 4: 67–103.

Zedeño, M. N. 2000 "On what people make of places: A behavioral cartography," In Michael B. Schiffer (ed,) *Social theory in archaeology*. Salt Lake City: University of Utah Press, 97–111.

# Index

Note: page numbers followed by *f* and *t* indicate figures and tables.

CPSIA information can be obtained
at www.ICGtesting.com
Printed in the USA
BVOW09s2235101117
499840BV00005B/18/P